WOMEN COMPOSERS

Music Through the Ages

WOMEN COMPOSERS

Music Through the Ages

EDITED BY
SYLVIA GLICKMAN
AND
MARTHA FURMAN SCHLEIFER

Volume 7

Composers Born 1800–1899
Vocal Music

New Haven, Conn. • Detroit • New York • San Diego • San Francisco
Cleveland • Waterville, Maine • London • Munich

For more information, contact
G.K. Hall & Co.
An Imprint of Gale
27500 Drake Road
Farmington Hills, MI 48331-3535

Music engraving by Philip Thomas.

Performance parts for works in these volumes are available from:

Hildegard Publishing Company
P.O. Box 332
Bryn Mawr, PA 19010
(610) 667-8634

http://www.hildegard.com

All Hildegard music is now distributed world-wide by The Theodore Presser Company, (610) 525-3636.

Library of Congress catalog number 95-24552

LIBRARY OF CONGRESS CATALOGING-IN-PUBLICATION DATA
Women composers : music through the ages / edited by Sylvia Glickman and Martha Furman Schleifer.
1 score.
". . . annotated, modern performance scores from the ninth through the twentieth centuries also contain . . . explanatory essays . . ."

Contents: v. 1 Composers born before 1599
v. 2 Composers born 1600–1699
v. 3 Composers born 1700–1799 — Keyboard Music
v. 4 Composers born 1700–1799 — Vocal and Choral
v. 5 Composers born 1700–1799 — Large and Small Instrumental Ensembles
v. 6 Composers born 1800–1899 — Keyboard Music
Includes bibliographical references and index.
ISBN 0-8161-0926-5 (v. 1 : alk. paper)
ISBN 0-8161-0563-4 (v. 2 : alk. paper)
ISBN 0-7838-1612-X (v. 3 : alk. paper)
ISBN 0-7838-1613-8 (v. 4 : alk. paper)
ISBN 0-7838-1614-6 (v. 5 : alk. paper)
ISBN 0-7838-8192-4 (v. 6 : alk. paper)

1. Music. 2. Women composers' music. 3. Women composers—Biography.
I. Glickman, Sylvia. II. Schleifer, Martha Furman.
M2.W88 1995 95-24552
CIP

ISBN 0-7838-8194-04 (alk. paper)

Printed in the United States of America

1 2 3 4 5 6 7 8 9 10

Contents of Volume 7

Composers Born 1800–1899
Vocal Music

Series Introduction

Women Composers: Music Through the Ages

Women's contribution to the arts and humanities has been the subject of an explosion of interest in recent years. Historically, there has been a deep-rooted prejudice against women composers. Those who created music in the earliest eras were either women in convents, aristocrats, or members of professional musical families. In the seventeenth century performer/composers (primarily singers) began to emerge, joining the groups that preceded them. The Italian *ospedali,* actually orphanages and hostels for the indigent, offered music instruction to their resident children as a way of helping them toward later employment. However, few examples of compositions by women educated there exist, as the emphasis was on musical performance. During the eighteenth century women appeared in public concerts and salons as soloists and composers. Many wrote music in appropriate small forms, but the unusual women ventured further and produced operas, orchestral and choral works. In the nineteenth century the new public, secular conservatories (an outgrowth of the *ospedali)* provided educational opportunities for women, although it was not until the end of the century that they were allowed into music theory or composition classes. A dramatic shift in musical activity from the private to the public sphere took place in the early twentieth century. Accepted into the labor force, women play in orchestras, appear professionally in public, and with all restrictions in conservatories lifted, now are exhibiting a burst of creative musical activity that demands acceptance by society.

Ignoring the creative output of women has denied them ongoing support for centuries. Nevertheless, imaginative, memorable music survived because it was worthy of preservation and we are now in the process of rediscovering it. *Women Composers: Music Through the Ages* is a new, valuable resource for the modern scholar, performer, teacher, student, and the general public. Until recently this music was scattered, often inaccessible, underexplored and therefore infrequently performed. This series remedies these circumstances and reveals hidden riches. International in scope, the twelve volumes contain annotated, modern performance scores from the ninth through the twentieth centuries and explanatory essays that add personal background and give historical perspective to not only the music but to the composers' lives as well.

Women Composers: Music Through the Ages is organized in strict chronological order. Volume 1 includes composers born before 1599. Volume 2 includes those born between 1600 and 1699. The eighteenth-century volumes (3, 4, 5), nineteenth-century volumes (6, 7, 8), and twentieth-century volumes (9, 10, 11, 12) are divided by genre (e.g., music for instrument[s], voice[s], and music for mixed combinations). The fourth twentieth-century volume (12) is devoted to experimental music. This series makes no attempt to be comprehensive; it includes music that exemplifies the exceptional woman composer. The traditional separation between male and female creators, indeed, the omission of the work of women in music history books, was a tacit implication of inequality of product. These volumes will prove otherwise.

The music, prepared from original materials and edited by experts, carefully differentiates between the original and the performance editions. Marks in brackets are editorial. All music is newly engraved to ensure clarity and ease of use for classroom and performance. Performance parts for included scores are available through the Hildegard Publishing Company.

We want to express our gratitude to all the contributors for their expertise and their efforts in helping to create this unique series.

Our warmest thanks go to our families and to our husbands, Dr. Harvey Glickman and Dr. Charles R. Schleifer, for their caring support which helped make this series a reality.

Sylvia Glickman
Martha Furman Schleifer

Introduction to Volume 7

The forty composers included in Volume 7 of *Women Composers: Music Through the Ages: Vocal Music* were born between 1800 and 1899. Some are also represented in the series Volume 6 (Keyboard Music) and Volume 8 (Large and Small Instrumental Ensembles). These works, for solo voice and piano, for voice and instruments, and scenes from three operas, are by women from nine countries: twelve from the United States (Bauer, Beach, Freer, Hier, Jessye, M.R. Lang, Moore, Price, Rogers, Salter, Strickland and Urner); nine from France (L. Boulanger, N. Boulanger, Grandval, Heritte-Viardot, Malibran, Puget, Viardot, Vieu and White); six from England (Allitsen, Carmichael, Clarke, del Riego, Lehmann and Prescott); six from Germany (Bronsart, Hensel, Kinkel, J. Lang, Schumann and Teichmüller); three from the Netherlands (Cramer, Dijk and Rennes), and one each from Austria (Mahler), Canada (Harrison), Italy (Giuranna) and Ireland (Maddison).

Those who were of musical families include the sisters Lili and Nadia Boulanger; sisters Maria Malibran (de Beriot) and Pauline Viardot, and Pauline's daughter Louise Heritte-Viardot; Eleanor Everest Freer, Barbara Giuranna, Fanny Hensel (Mendelssohn), Josephine Lang, Margaret Ruthven Lang, Liza Lehmann, Alma Mahler, Loïsa Puget, Clara Kathleen Rogers, Mary Turner Salter, and Clara Schumann. Previously unpublished music in the volume includes Lili Boulanger's choral music, the opera scenes of Barbara Giuranna, and the songs of Catherine Urner. Two African-American composers are included: Eva A. Jessye and Florence Price.

This volume contains examples of music in the many styles also practiced by their male contemporaries: the simple French *romance* (Malibran, Puget, Vieu); the German *lied* (Bronsart, Hensel, Josephine Lang, Schumann, Teichmüller); music from the Second New England School (Rogers); and music espousing Romanticism (Beach) and post-Romanticism (Cramer). There is impressionistic music (Bauer, the Boulangers, M.R. Lang, Maddison); models of the American Art Song (Bauer, Price, Urner), dialect songs (Hier, Strickland); religious and patriotic songs (Allitsen, Dijk), opera (Giuranna, Grandval, Moore), and musical comedy (Lehmann). Some of these songs became best sellers because famous singers of the nineteenth and twentieth centuries promoted them in performance.

The editors would like to thank the following who have kindly given permission for use of materials in this volume: Theodore Presser Company for the score to *Rendezvous* by Beach; Fondation Internationale Nadia et Lili Boulanger and Editions Durand for music by the Boulangers; Bayerische Staatsbibliothek for *Verwandlung* by Bronsart; The British Library for access to music by Carmichael; Oxford University Press for the songs by Clarke; the family of Giuranna for access to her music; Staatsbibliothek Preussischer Kulturbesitz in Berlin, Universitäts und Landesbibliothek Bonn, Universitätsbibliothek Leipzig, Music Division of the British Library (London), Württembergische Landesbibliothek Stuttgart, Boston Public Library, University of Nebraska Lincoln, and the University of Alaska Fairbanks for access to music by Kinkel; Music Library at the University of Michigan for Puget; Hildegard Publishing Company for music by Schumann; Harwood Academic Publishers (Switzerland) for Urner; Warner/Chappell Music, Ltd. London and Casa Ricordi-BMG for music by White.

All music titles and composer names appear on the music as in the original manuscript or first edition. Composers are identified in the articles with these names unless their reputations were established with their maiden or married names. Selected lists of works are in chronological order when possible; otherwise they appear in alphabetical order.

Special thanks to Sam Dennison for his expertise as indexer for this series, and to Philip Thomas for music engraving.

Sylvia Glickman
Martha Furman Schleifer

Fanny Mendelssohn Hensel

(1805–1847)

SEAN M. WALLACE

Fanny Mendelssohn Hensel (1805–1847) (see vol. 6), the older sister of Felix Mendelssohn-Bartholdy, was born into a prominent and wealthy Berlin family and was heir to a distinguished musical tradition. Her grandfather was Moses Mendelssohn, the important eighteenth-century Jewish philosopher, and her father, Abraham, was an influential banker. Hensel's musical education was similar to that of her brother Felix, including instruction in piano, voice, theory, and composition. Hensel's talents as a pianist were recognized very early, and as she grew, many acknowledged her musical gifts to be equal to that of Felix. Her father, however, while encouraging Felix's work, dissuaded her from pursuing a professional career either as a performer or composer. Later, Felix echoed his father's sentiments when he became head of the family. Preserved from the family's correspondence is her father's admonition, so characteristic of the time's attitude, that the pursuit of a professional career should never become the foundation of her life. In 1820, he wrote "Music will perhaps for him [Felix] become a profession, while for you it will always be only an ornament and never become the fundamental bass line of your existence and conduct . . . Remain in this conviction and behavior for they are feminine, and only the feminine is becoming to women."[1] And in 1828: "You must mold and shape yourself more earnestly and more diligently for your true profession, for the only profession of a young woman [*is*], a housewife."[2]

In 1829, she married Wilhelm Hensel, the Prussian court painter and an amateur poet. Their only child, Sebastian, was born the next year. In the early 1830s, following the tradition of her mother, Hensel found a medium for her musical expression by establishing a musical salon, for which she wrote most of her compositions and where she performed and conducted. Her salon and the Sunday afternoon performances *(Sonntagsmusik)* soon became a central part of Berlin's musical and social life and was attended by many of the great musicians, artists, actors, and writers of the day. Visitors to the Mendelssohn household included Carl Maria von Weber (1786–1836), Niccolò Paganini (1782–1840), Charles Gounod (1818–1893), Franz Liszt (1811–1886), Clara Schumann (1819–1896), Robert Schumann (1810–1856), E. T. A. Hoffman (1776–1822), Georg Wilhelm Hegel (1770–1831), and Heinrich Heine (1797–1856). In 1846, at the encouragement of her husband and close friends, and with rival publishing houses vying for her work, Hensel accepted an offer to publish some of her compositions, in opposition to the wishes of Felix and her father. But throughout their lives, Felix and Fanny had maintained a very close relationship, serving each other as friend, confidant, and musical critic, and Felix eventually gave his blessing to Hensel's publishing activities. While conducting a rehearsal for her salon, she suffered a stroke and died unexpectedly in 1847, at the age of forty-one.

During the past twenty years, as female composers have begun to receive the attention they and their music deserve, the name of Fanny Mendelssohn Hensel has become associated first with keyboard music and secondly with lieder. But she also made significant contributions to the choral genres of her time. In total, she composed three cantatas, one oratorio, three larger choral works with piano, and thirty a cappella part-songs.

Hensel's first choral piece, among her earliest compositions, is a chorus entitled *Es blühen Auen in der Wüste*, composed in 1821 when she was fifteen. It is scored for SATB chorus and SAT soli and was written as a closing chorus for the soprano aria *Ob Deiner Wunderzeichen stauen die Einbewohner ferner Zonen*. Hensel composed small choral pieces only intermittently between 1821 and 1846, concentrating instead primarily on lieder and piano pieces. However, in 1846, during the last full year of her life, she was inspired by the genre and composed eighteen of her thirty part-songs between February and September; eleven of these were performed at a salon (*Sonntagsmusik*) during that year. Six part-songs, including *Im Herbste*, were published early the next year by Bote & Bock of Berlin under the title *Gartenlieder*, op. 3.

On May 14, 1847, the day of Hensel's death, the *Gartenlieder* received a favorable review in *Neue Zeitschrift für Musik*. The reviewer commented that all six pieces were "bathed in a tender and poetic atmosphere, particularly, No. 1, *Hörst du nicht die Bäume rauschen* of Eichendorff, and No. 3, *Im Herbste* by Uhland. The reviewer also cited the middle section of *Im Herbste*, as "being remarkable well-turned."[3] The *Gartenlieder* became one of Hensel's most popular pieces. They received performances in Dresden under the direction of Robert Schumann with his Verein für Musik, and in Bonn with the Musikalische Liebhabergesellschaft under the direction of Johanna Kinkel (see this volume). [The *Gartenlieder* appeared in two English publications in the second half of the nineteenth century—Ewer & Co. in their part-songs series *Orpheus* sometime before 1867, and Novello in 1878 as a part of the *Novello's Part-Song Book* series. Bote & Bock also reissued the *Gartenlieder* sometime after 1871.]

There are three primary sources of *Im Herbste*: the autograph manuscript (MA Ms. 49), dated June 14 [1846]; the autograph choral parts (MA Ms. 67 and 68); and the first printed edition (Bote & Bock, 1847). The manuscripts are located in the Mendelssohn-Archiv at the Staatsbibliothek Preussischer Kulturbesitz, in Berlin. All of the modern editions currently available are based either on the first printed edition or on the autograph score. The present edition is based primarily on the 1847 edition; it is the first to consider all three sources.

Of the eleven part-songs for which there are extant choral parts, *Im Herbste* has the greatest number: four soprano, three alto, two tenor, and two bass, located in two separate manuscripts. There is some internal evidence which suggests that these parts were used for two different performances, but if they were used for a single performance, Hensel's choir could have numbered between eleven, (assuming one singer per choral part) and twenty-two (assuming two singers per choral part). Other evidence supports a choir of between ten and twenty members. Hensel apparently was not averse to having her part-songs performed by a quartet of voices. She composed an unknown number of part-songs (now lost) on the family's extended trip to Italy in 1839–1840. Her diary records an informal performance of these by a quartet with Hensel singing soprano.

The autograph scores of all of the *Gartenlieder* show numerous revisions, presumably made during or after the performances. Most of the revisions are small, e.g., dynamics, text, and individual note changes, but some are substantial. Even more changes were made before a fair copy was prepared for the publishers, for the Bote & Bock edition shows significant differences from the autograph score and parts not indicated by the revisions. In the case of *Im Herbste* these differences are significant enough (especially mm. 27–33), to warrant the inclusion in the present edition of an alternate ending based only on the autograph score and parts.

The text of *Im Herbste* is by Uhland, and although Hensel entitled this piece *Frühlingstraum* in the autograph parts, the title *Im Herbste* has been chosen here because it is the title under which the piece appeared in the *Gartenlieder* and it is the title under which the author originally published the poem in 1815.

In the present edition, the key signature has been modernized, slurs added, and small inconsistencies in punctuation and spelling have been changed without notice. All other editorial markings appear in brackets.

Notes

1. Sebastian Hensel, *Die Familie Mendelssohn 1729–1847, nach Briefen und Tagebüchern*, 5th ed., 2 vols. (Berlin: B. Behr, 1886), I: 97.

2. Peter Sutermeister, ed., *Felix Mendelssohn Bartholdy: Eine Reise durch Deutschland, Italien und die Schweiz* (Zurich: Neihans, 1958; reprint, Tübingen: Heliopolis, 1998), 283.

3. Dr. Emmanuel Klitsch, "Menhrstimmige Gesänge," review of *Gartenlieder*, op. 3 by Fanny Hensel *Neue Zeitschrift für Musik* 26 (May 14, 1847): 169; quoted in Françoise Tillard, *Fanny Mendelssohn*, trans. Camile Naish (Portland, Ore.: Amadeus, 1996), 331.

Selected List of Works

Choral Works with Orchestra

Festpiel "Die Hochzeit kommt" (1829), ed. Marilee Vana. SSATBB soli, SATB chorus, orchestra. Text by Wilhelm Hensel. Kassel: Furore, 1998.

Hiob (1831), ed. Conrad Misch. Alto solo, SATB chorus, orchestra. Kassel: Furore, 1992.

Lobgesang (1831), ed. Conrad Misch. SA soli, SATB chorus, orchestra. Kassel: Furore, 1992.

Oratorium nach Bildern der Bibel [a.k.a., *Musik für die Toten der Cholera-Epidemie 1831*] (1831), ed. Elka Mascha Blankenburg. SATB soli, SSAATTBB chorus, orchestra. Kassel: Furore, 1994.

Works with Piano

Dem Unendlichen (1832) [fragment]. TTBB chorus, piano. Text by Friedrich Klopstock. Unpublished.

Der Seele Ruhe ist es, Gott! (1820). (Precedes soprano aria), SATB chorale, flute, piano. Unpublished.

Einleitung zu lebenden Bildern (1841) [fragment]. SATB chorus, narrator, piano. Unpublished.

Es blühen Auen in der Wüste (1821). (Follows soprano aria), SATB chorus, SAT soli, piano. Unpublished.

Scene From Faust (1843), ed. Suzanne Summerville. SSSAA soli, SSAA chorus, piano. Text by Johann Wolfgang von Goethe. Kassel: Furore, 1998.

Zum Fest der heiligen Caecilia "Beati immasculati" (1833), ed. Willi Gundlach. SATB soli, SATB chorus, piano. Kassel: Furore, 1999.

Unaccompanied Works

Abendreihn (Between 1829 and 1846). TTBB chorus. Text by Wilhelm Müller. Unpublished.

Am Grabe (1826). SATB chorus. Text by Johann Heinrich Voss. Unpublished.

Ariel [a.k.a., *Gab die liebende Natur*] (1846). SATB chorus. Text by Johann Wolfgang von Goethe. In *Fanny Mendelssohn Hensel: Choral Music*, vol. 1. Bryn Mawr, PA: Hildegard Publishing Company, 1997.

Auf [a.k.a., *Frisch um der Blume Farbenring*] (1846). SATB chorus. Text probably by Wilhelm Hensel. Unpublished.

Dein Drohen selbst, O Gott des Heils ist furchtbar doch gerecht (1820) [chorale harmonization]. SATB chorus. Unpublished.

Feldlied (auch im Garten zu singen) [a.k.a., *Ein Gesang im Grünen schallet*] (1826). SATB soli, SATB chorus. Text by Johann Heinrich Voss. Unpublished.

Der Fischer (Between 1829 and 1846). TTBB chorus. Text by Johann Wolfgang von Goethe. Unpublished.

Gartenlieder, op. 3, nos.1-6. SATB chorus. Berlin: Bote & Bock, 1847, reprint after 1871; nos. 2-6 only in *Orpheus*. London: Ewer & Co., before 1867; In *Novello's Part-Song Book.* London: Novello, 1878; ed. Elka Mascha Blankenburg. Kassel: Furore, 1988 [based on autograph manuscript only]; Kassel: Furore, 1997 [based on first printed score]; nos. 3, 5, and 6 only. Ed. Gordon Paine. Corvallis, Ore: Earthsongs, 1993.

1. *Hörst du nicht die Bäume rauschen* [a.k.a., *Lockung*] (1846). Text by Joseph von Eichendorff. In *Fanny Hensel-Mendelssohn: Weltliche a-cappella-Chöre* von 1846, vol. 1. Kassel: Furore, 1988; In *Chorbuch Romantik: Weltliche Chormusik für gemischte Stimmen a cappella (Ausgewählte Sätze).* Wolfenbüttel: Möseler, 1990; In *Fanny Mendelssohn Hensel: Choral Music*, vol. 4. Bryn Mawr, PA: Hildegard Publishing Company, 1997.
2. *Schöne Fremde* (1846). Text by Joseph von Eichendorff. In *Fanny Hensel-Mendelssohn: Weltliche a-capella-Chöre* von 1846, vol. 4. Kassel; Furore, 1988; Wiesbaden: Breitkopf & Härtel, 1990 [octavo]; In *Fanny Mendelssohn Hensel: Choral Music*, vol. 1. Bryn Mawr, PA: Hildegard Publishing Company, 1997.
3. *Im Herbste* [a.k.a., *Seid gegrüsst*; a.k.a., *Frühlingstraum*] (1846). Text by Ludwig Uhland. In *Fanny Hensel-Mendelssohn: Weltliche a-capella-Chöre* von 1846, vol. 2. Kassel: Furore, 1988; In *Fanny Mendelssohn Hensel: Choral Music*, vol. 4. Bryn Mawr, PA: Hildegard Publishing Company, 1997.
4. *Morgengruss* [a.k.a., *Komm*, a.k.a., *Schnell fliehen der Schatten der Nacht*] (1846). Text by Wilhelm Hensel. In *The Alpine Glee Singer.* Ed. William Bradbury. New York: Mark H. Newman, 1850; In *Fanny Hensel-Mendelssohn: Weltliche a-capella-Chöre* von 1846, vol. 3. Kassel: Furore, 1988; Wiesbaden: Breitkopf & Härtel, 1988 [octavo]; in *Fanny Mendelssohn Hensel: Choral Music*, vol. 2. Bryn Mawr, PA: Hildegard Publishing Company, 1997.
5. *Abendlich schon rauscht der Wald* [a.k.a., *Abschied,* a.k.a. *Abendlich*] (1846). Text by Joseph von Eichendorff. In *Fanny Hensel-Mendelssohn: Weltliche a-cappella-Chöre* von 1846, vol. 1. Kassel: Furore, 1988; In *Chorbuch Romantik: Weltiliche Chormusik für gemischte Stimmen a cappella (Ausgewählte Sätze).* Wolfenbüttel: Möseler, 1990; In *Fanny Mendelssohn Hensel: Choral Music,* vol. 3. Bryn Mawr, PA: Hildegard Publishing Company, 1997.
6. *Im Wald* (1846). Text by Emanuel Geibel. In *Fanny Hensel-Mendelssohn: Weltliche a-capella-Chö*re von 1846, vol. 1. Kassel: Furore, 1988; In *Fanny Mendelssohn Hensel. Choral Music*, vol. 5. Bryn Mawr, PA: Hildegard Publishing Company, 1997.

Die Kapelle (Between 1829 and 1846). TTBB chorus. Text by Ludwig Uhland. Unpublished.

Lass dich nur nicht nichts dauern [a.k.a., *Pilgerspruch*] (1823). SATB soli, SATB chorus. Text by Paul Fleming. Unpublished.

Lass dich nur nicht nichts dauern [different version] (1825). SATB chorus. Text by Paul Fleming. Unpublished.

Lust'ge Vogel (1846). SATB chorus. Text by Joseph von Eichendorff. In *Fanny Mendelssohn Hensel: Choral Music*, vol. 3. Bryn Mawr, PA: Hildegard Publishing Company, 1997.

Morgengruss [a.k.a., *Um heller Blumen Farbenring*] (1846). SATB chorus. Text by Wilhelm Hensel. In *Fanny Mendelssohn Hensel: Choral Music*, vol. 5. Bryn Mawr, PA: Hildegard Publishing Company, 1997.

Morgenwanderung [a.k.a., *Wer recht in Freuden wandern will*] (1846). SATB chorus. Text by Emanuel Geibel. In *Fanny Mendelssohn Hensel: Choral Music*, vol. 1. Bryn Mawr, PA: Hildegard Publishing Company, 1997.

Nacht ruht auf den fremden Wegen (1846). SATB chorus. Text by Heinrich Heine. Unpublished.

Nachtreigen (1829). SSAATTBB chorus. Text by Wilhelm Hensel. Stuttgart: Carus, 1995.

O Herbst, in linden Tagen (1846). SATB chorus. Text by Joseph von Eichendorff. In *Fanny Mendelssohn Hensel: Choral Music*, vol. 3. Bryn Mawr, PA: Hildegard Publishing Company, 1997; In *Chorbuch Romantik: Weltliche Chormusik für gemischte Stimmen a cappella (Ausgewählte Sätze)*. Wolfenbüttel: Möseler, 1990.

Des Schäfer's Sonntagslied (Between 1829 and 1846). Tenor soli, TTBB chorus. Text by Ludwig Uhland. Unpublished.

Schilflied [a.k.a., *Drüben geht die Sonne scheiden*] (1846). SATB chorus. Text by Nikolaus Lenau. In *Fanny Mendelssohn Hensel: Choral Music*, vol. 1. Bryn Mawr, PA: Hildegard Publishing Company, 1997; In *Chorbuch Romantik: Weltliche Chormusik für gemischte Stimmen a cappella (Ausgewählte Sätze)*. Wolfenbüttel: Möseler, 1990.

Schon kehren die Vögel wieder ein (1846). SATB chorus. Text by Joseph von Eichendorff. In *Fanny Mendelssohn Hensel: Choral Music*, vol. 3. Bryn Mawr, PA: Hildegard Publishing Company, 1997.

Die Schwalbe (Between 1829 and 1846). TTBB chorus. Text by Wilhelm Müller. Unpublished.

Schweigend sinkt die Nacht (1846). SATB soli, SATB chorus. Text by Wilhelm Hensel. In *Fanny Mendelssohn Hensel: Choral Music*, vol. 2. Bryn Mawr, PA: Hildegard Publishing Company, 1997.

Schweigt der Menschen laute Lust [a.k.a., *Abend*] (1846). SATB chorus. Text by Joseph von Eichendorff. In *Fanny Mendelssohn Hensel: Choral Music*, vol. 3. Bryn Mawr, PA: Hildegard Publishing Company, 1997; In *Chorbuch Romantik: Weltliche Chormusik für gemischte Stimmen a cappella (Ausgewählte Sätze)*. Wolfenbüttel: Möseler, 1990.

Unter des Laubdachs Hut (1841). SATB chorus. Text by William Shakespeare (translated into German by August Wilhelm Schlegel). Wiesbaden: Breitkopf & Härtel, 1989.

Waldeinsam [a.k.a., *Wie hoffnungsgrün ist rings die Welt*] (1846). SATB chorus. Text by Wilhelm Hensel. In *Fanny Mendelssohn Hensel: Choral Music*, vol. 2. Bryn Mawr, PA: Hildegard Publishing Company, 1997.

Im Herbste

Seid gegrüsst mit Frülingswonne,	Be welcomed with the joy of Spring,
blauer Himmel, goldne Sonne.	Blue heaven, golden sun.
Drüben auch aus Gartenhallen,	Yonder from the garden's halls,
hör'ich frohe Saiten schallen.	I hear joyful music playing.
Ahnest du o Seele, wieder	Do you, o soul, await again?
sanfte, süsse Frülingslieder?	The soft, sweet songs of Spring?
Sieh umher die falben Bäume!	See all around us Fall's colorful trees!
Ach, es waren holde Träume.	Alas, they were only lovely dreams.

Im Herbste
from Gartenlieder

Ludwig Uhland

Fanny Mendelssohn Hensel
Op. 3 No. 3
Sean M. Wallace, editor

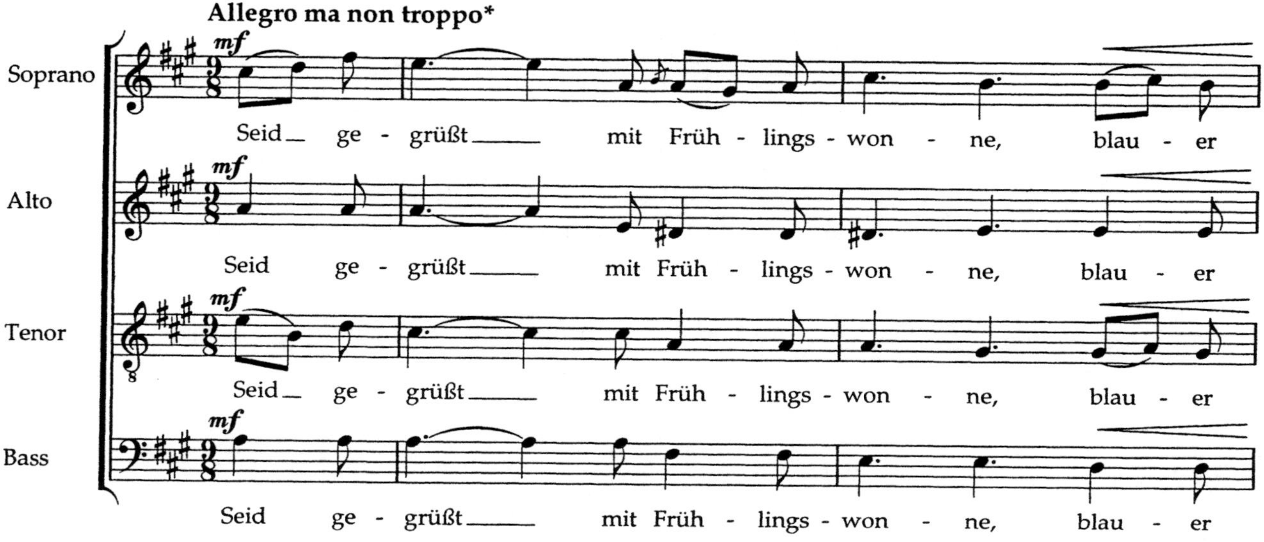

*In the autograph score and choral parts, the tempo marking is *Allegro gracioso* and the opening dynamic marking is ***p***

*This alto line appears in the autograph score and choral parts.

15
du, o See - le wie - der, sanf - te, sü - ße Früh - lings -
du, o See - le wie - der, sanf - te, sü - ße Früh - lings -
du, o See - le wie - der, sanf - te, sü - ße Früh - lings -
du, See - le wie - der, sanf - te, sü - ße Früh - lings -

18
lie - der? Sieh um - her, die fal - ben Bäu - me! sieh um -
lie - der? Sieh um - her,
lie - der? Sieh um - her,
lie - der? Sieh um - her,

21
cresc.
her, die fal - ben Bäu - me, ah - nest du, o See - le
sieh um - her, ah - nest du, o See - le
sieh um - her, ah - nest du, o See - le
sieh um - her, ah - nest du, o

24
[f]
dim.
wie - der, sanf - te, sü - ße Früh - lings - lie - der?
wie - der, sanf - te, sü - - ße Lie - der?
wie - der, sanf - te, sü - ße Früh - lings - lie - der?
See - le, sü - - ße Lie - der?
27
[See alternate ending]
p
pp
Sieh um - her die fal - ben Bäu - me, Ach, es
31
[mf]
wa - ren hol - de Träu - me, ach, es wa - ren hol - de

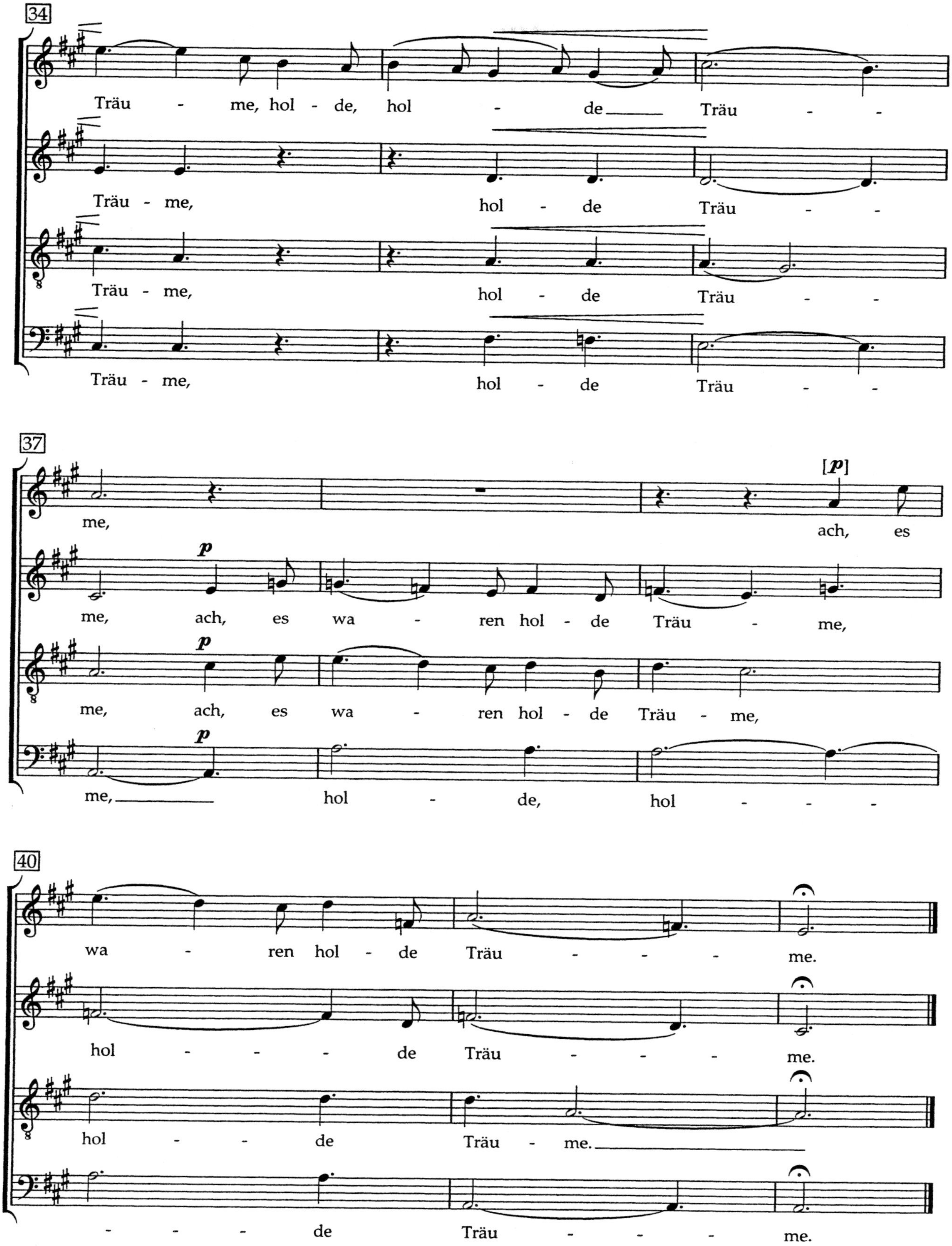

34
Träu - me, hol - de, hol - de Träu - -
Träu - me, hol - de Träu - -
Träu - me, hol - de Träu - -
Träu - me, hol - de Träu - -
37
[p]
me, ach, es
p
me, ach, es wa - ren hol - de Träu - me,
p
me, ach, es wa - ren hol - de Träu - me,
p
me, hol - de, hol - - -
40
wa - ren hol - de Träu - - - me.
hol - - - de Träu - - - me.
hol - - de Träu - me.
- - - de Träu - - - me.

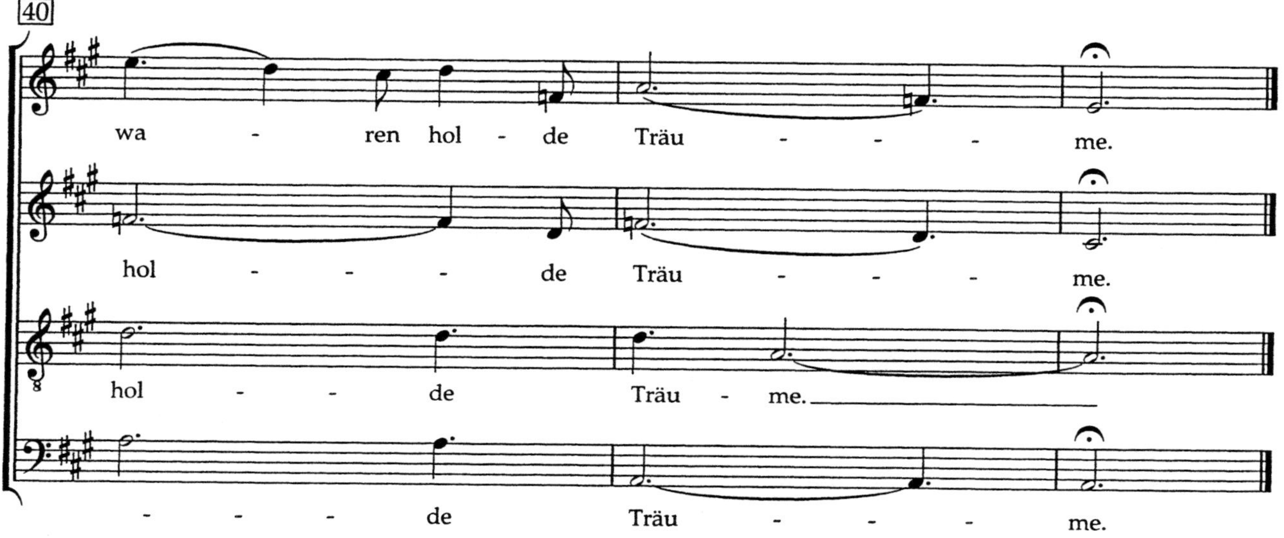

Im Herbste
from Gartenlieder
Alternate Ending, mm. 27–42
(Based on the autograph score and choral parts*)

Fanny Mendelssohn Hensel
Op. 3 No. 3

*See Introduction.

33
wa - ren hol - de Träu - me, wa - ren hol - de
wa - ren hol - de Trä - me, hol - de
wa - ren hol - de Trä - me, hol - de
wa - ren hol - de Trä - me, hol - de
36
Träu - - me,
[p]
Träu - - me, ach, es wa - ren hol - de
[p]
Träu - - me, ach, es wa - ren hol - de
[p]
Träu - - me, hol - de,
39
[p]
ach, es wa - ren hol - de Träu - me.
Träu - me, es wa - ren hol - de Träu - me.
Träu - me, hol - de Träu - me.
hol - - - - de Träu - me.

Fanny Mendelssohn Hensel

(1805–1847)

RUTH OCHS

Over one hundred and fifty years have passed since the death (born in Hamburg, November 14, 1805; died in Berlin on May 14, 1847) of one of the most prolific female composers of lieder in the nineteenth century, and we are still discovering the beauty of Fanny Hensel's musical contribution. Because her activities as a composer were restricted to the private family sphere, most of her works employ smaller forms such as lieder and short piano pieces.

Hensel's 250 solo lieder constitute the largest portion of her output and were composed during the period of 1819–1847. Only twenty-two songs were published during her lifetime. Her family posthumously published eleven more, and by late 1850 thirty-three of her solo songs were in print.[1] Beginning in the 1980s many of the others began to appear, accompanied by the release of several recordings. In 1994 Hans-Günter Klein published a catalogue of all of Hensel's manuscripts now housed in the Mendelssohn-Archiv at the Staatsbibliothek zu Berlin, Preussischer Kulturbesitz. Annette Mauer's thematic catalogue of Hensel's solo lieder, published in 1997, adds new insights and focus on their chronology, the texts, and stylistic development. (For more extensive biographical information on Fanny Hensel, see preceding article and Camilla Cai, "Fanny Hensel" in *Women Composers: Music Through the Ages*, Volume 6.)

Hensel's songs were composed primarily for her own use and enjoyment, and sometimes to honor certain occasions or dates. With the exception of the few publications in the 1820s and 1830s, she did not conceive of her work as deserving public attention until the 1840s. By 1846 she was able to overcome the longstanding misgivings of her father and her brother, Felix Mendelssohn, and prepared seven opus numbers for publication.

From 1831 until her death, Hensel assumed the music directorship of the semi-public *Sonntagsmusiken* hosted at the Mendelssohn residence on Leipziger Strasse 3 in Berlin. (Begun in the 1820s by her parents as a performing venue for their talented children, the *Sonntagsmusiken* were discontinued at the end of the decade when Felix started traveling; Hensel started them again in 1831.) Through the mid–1830s Hensel's younger sister, Rebekka, sang many of the lieder at these events; later she relied on singer friends. Alongside the works of Bach, Beethoven, Mozart, and her brother Felix, she presented her own solo lieder, her multi-voice works, the dramatic scene *Hero und Leander* (1831), one of her three cantatas from the year 1831 (presumably *Hiob* [1831]), the Overture (1832), the piano trio (1847), and other of her compositions.[2] It is possible that Hensel never heard all of her songs as finished works. In 1836 in a letter to her friend Carl Klingemann she expressed her discouragement at not having a "public" for her songs in Berlin.

> . . . I enclose two pianoforte-pieces which I have written since I came home from Düsseldorf. I leave it to you to say whether they are worth presenting to my unknown young friend, but I must add that it is a pleasure to me to find a public for my little pieces in London, for here I have none at all. Once a year, perhaps, someone will copy a piece of mine, or ask me to play something special—certainly not oftener; and now that Rebekka has left off singing, my songs lie unheeded and unknown. If nobody ever offers an opinion, or takes the slightest interest in one's productions, one loses in time not only all pleasure in them, but all power of judging of their value. Felix, who is alone a sufficient public for me, is so seldom here that he cannot help me much, and thus I am thrown back entirely on myself.[3]

Hensel's first composition foreshadowed the importance that song composition would occupy until the end of her life. Entitled *Lied zum Geburtstag des Vaters am 11ten Dezember 1819*, this song was composed for the celebration of her father's birthday. The text is presumed to have originated from within the Mendelssohn family circle. Maurer states that 163 songs, about two-thirds of the total, came from Hensel's pen between December 1819 and June 1829.[4] After her marriage to Wilhelm Hensel in October 1829 and the birth of their son, Sebastian, in June 1830, when she had assumed what her father called her "real calling, the only calling of a young woman—I mean the state of a housewife," she continued to compose songs.[5] However, her yearly output decreased.

The decline may be attributed to several facts. Many of her first songs were student exercises, accounting for their larger total. Also, in the early 1830s she began to redirect her creative energies to other genres. During 1831, for example, she produced three cantatas for voices with orchestra, and by the mid-1830s she was composing multi-voiced songs. While she necessarily spent time also pursuing her family tasks, her commitment to her work had become that of a mature composer. Her last lied, *Bergeslust*, a setting of a Joseph Eichendorff poem, is dated May 13, 1847, the day before she died.

The profile of Hensel's stylistic development can be traced in her lied oeuvre. The earliest compositions of the 1820s reflect the style of the Second Berlin Lieder School, of which Carl Friedrich Zelter (1758–1832) her teacher, was a significant representative. The aesthetics of this style dictated that the music should not interfere with the structure and comprehension of the poem, resulting in mainly strophic settings. Johann Wolfgang von Goethe (1749–1832), a close friend of Zelter's, in fact preferred that composer's settings of his poetry to the work of more prominent contemporaries such as Franz Schubert (1797–1828). In 1820 Goethe wrote to Zelter: "The purest and most exalted painting in music is that which you accomplish; the important thing is to put the listener into the mood that the poem establishes."[6]

Hensel's earliest settings show the influence of Zelter, her teacher from 1819–1826. In settings from the 1820s the vocal line is syllabic and melodically spans an easily singable range. The piano accompaniment, subordinate to the voice, characteristically doubles the vocal melody, providing a simple, chordal harmonization of the melody, or adds rhythmic energy to the total texture with arpeggio figures in the right hand. Although sometimes appearing simplistic, Hensel's settings are filled with expression and musical interest. By the end of the decade, when she was no longer guided exclusively by Zelter, her own inspiration took charge. Her lied composition moved away from the purely strophic, and the keyboard accompaniment and vocal range expanded. The piano took on a more independent role, functioning within the texture as a separate voice and contributing more harmonic diversity than in the earlier works.

The six songs published within Felix Mendelssohn's opp. 8 and 9, which appeared in 1827 and 1830 respectively, reveal the movement away from Zelter. Hensel's *Verlust* (Loss) is a remarkable example of her development by the late 1820s. Published in 1830 as Felix Mendelssohn's op. 9, no. 10, it is similar to Zelter's strophic style, while also vividly portraying the protagonist's pain from a broken heart. The idea of loss is poignantly conveyed through the piano's first and final chords. The first is a six-four chord built on the dominant, creating an unsettled mood; the lied ends on a root position dominant that remains unresolved. Hensel's authorship, although not made public, was inscribed in the lied text. She altered the gender of the protagonist by changing the gender of the personal pronouns.[7] By the end of the 1820s she had found her compositional voice.

By the mid-1830s, her lieder had achieved distinction, containing features that remained part of her mature style. Expanded in length with modified strophic forms, their piano parts often functioned as equal partners, exploring a variety of texture, rhythm, dynamic range, and harmonic mood. She used a hybrid song-form with some internal repetition, which offered a perceptible overall order, while leaving ample room for the composer's invention. *Zauberkreis* is an example of the musical contrast Hensel was able to construct around a modified-strophic skeleton.

Hensel wrote several through-composed songs, including *Nachtwanderer* (ca. 1843), a setting of a Joseph von Eichendorff text. The character of the music carefully follows the mood of the text. The poem and music climax and conclude on "mein Singen hier, ist wie ein Rufen, ein Rufen nur aus Träumen" (My singing is a call only from my dreams). This text, as Beatrix Borchard has suggested, is a fitting epitaph for Hensel's career as a composer.[8]

Hensel's selection of poetry displays noticeable trends throughout her career. Prior to 1829, she frequently set the work of family, friends, and other members of the Mendelssohn circle. After 1829 she concentrated on well-known poets such as Johann Wolfgang von Goethe, Heinrich Heine, Friedrich Klopstock, Ludwig Hölty, and Johann Voss, with the single exception of texts by her husband.

Hensel's shift in taste around 1829 has been described as a reaction to the expressed jealousy of Wilhelm Hensel, who was concerned that she set more poems by Gustav Droysen and other friends.[9] As she matured as a composer she had become more conscious of the quality of the poetry she chose. Goethe was her lifelong preference; she set forty of his poems. The leading German literary figure of the time, he was a significant figure for both the Mendelssohns; he was one of the "authorities" consulted to judge Felix's artistic potential. When Felix—not Fanny—visited the poet in Weimar in 1821, he brought along several of his sister's lieder, which were performed and praised by the poet. Fanny did meet Goethe in 1823. She set seven poems by Heinrich Heine between 1834 and 1836, and in the 1840s she turned to Eichendorff and Nikolaus Lenau for her solo and multi-voiced songs.[10] Eight of the poets Hensel set were women, including her sister-in-law, Luise Hensel, and Marianne von Willemer, the mistress of Goethe.

A major consideration for anyone concerned with the unpublished manuscripts of Hensel is the state of the final draft of each work. Of her 250 lieder Hensel prepared only a small portion for publication herself. The six lieder published in Felix Mendelssohn's opp. 8 and 9 appeared under his name. In 1846, when she overcame the misgivings of her brother and published under her own name, Hensel selected and polished (i.e., added more dynamics and expressive markings) the songs which she considered her best and probably her most saleable.[11] Had her life not been cut short she doubtless would have composed and published more. While the manuscripts do represent the musical and aesthetic essence of each work, posthumous publication, of necessity, may not finalize or fully clarify Hensel's intention. On the other hand, the manuscripts reveal that a performer would need to assume responsibility in shaping a song expressively for a given venue. In most instances where Hensel was performing at the piano, she would have determined the dynamics, tempos, or other revisions that may not have been put down on the page. The four songs prepared for this volume therefore do not contain her final revisions.

The autograph sources for each of the lieder in this volume are found in the manuscript collections of the Mendelssohn-Archiv, Staatsbibliothek zu Berlin, Preussischer Kulturbesitz. Other manuscripts reside in the Bodleian Library, Oxford, England, the Goethe-Museum and the Heinrich-Heine Institut, both in Düsseldorf, Germany, with a small number still in private hands.[12] Most of her lieder are preserved in chronological albums or bound *Konvolut* collections. Few sketches or notes survive. Some works exist in multiple copies; aside from those she made for herself, she bound her songs into special albums for presentation copies for family or friends. These were often additionally decorated with pencil sketches done by her husband.[13]

Mendelssohn-Archiv Ms. 128 is an instance of how her lieder were influenced by her personal life. For their tenth wedding anniversary in 1839 Fanny gave Wilhelm Hensel an album (MA Ms. 128) into which she copied seventy-six of her vocal works composed from 1820 to 1839, inscribing it: "Auswahl aus meinen Bücher" (Selections from my books). *In der stillen Mitternacht* and *Wenn der Frühling kommt* are in this album. Hensel selected her best lieder for it and each was significant as a remembrance of the specific occasion for which it was created.

Ist es möglich dates from 1825 and is an example of Hensel's use of a strophic form closely related to the poem, the style she practiced as a student of Zelter.[14] She set only the first of its six strophes, although she may have intended to add the remaining five later. The accompaniment, clearly subordinate to the voice, serves mainly as a harmonic foundation; the bass line, with stepwise motion and frequent chromatic passing tones, is a counterpoint to the melody. The repeated eighth-note rhythm in the right hand supplies background excitement. The lied has a narrow harmonic range and strays no further from C-major than its relative minor.

Taken from Johann Gottfried Herder's translation of *El Cid* (*Der Cid: Nach spanischen Romanzen*), *In der stillen Mitternacht* is one of Hensel's few duets for accompanied male and female voices. The vocal writing is intended for trained or semi-trained voices. The piano part here is flexible, beginning by accompanying and supporting the voices, and subtly varying its pattern starting in measure 22. In measure 34 the piano is alone, suddenly soft and in the treble register, extending the suspense of Chimene's demand, "Who are you, speak!" After Chimene has rejected Rodrigo and their dialogue ends, the piano postlude powerfully returns to the opening music. The quiet, uncertain rhythm of Rodrigo's approach is transformed into the spurned, sad steps of his departure.

Hensel's first settings of Heine's poetry predate Schubert's. She set only two of the three strophes of "Ach, die Augen sind es wieder," and she changed and softened the imagery of a phrase in "Warum sind denn die Rosen so blass?". Hensel knew Heinrich Heine in Berlin in the 1820s. Although her dislike of his personality is documented, she valued his poetry: "Even if one has felt contempt for him ten times in a row, the eleventh time he forces one to recognize that he's a poet, a true poet! Words sing for him, and nature speaks to him as she only speaks to poets."[15] She and her husband and son met Heine while on vacation at the French resort, Boulogne, in the summer of 1835. This encounter presumably was the inspiration for Hensel's *Wenn der Frühling kommt*; its earliest manuscript source is signed "Boulogne 24sten Aug. 35." Heine's poetry has been noted for its ironic and cynical metaphors, and while there are many instances when Hensel literally realized a poem, she did not do so here. As the song was composed while the Hensels were on vacation, it may have been conceived as a commemoration. Given the unfaithful rendering of the poem (Heine never saw the setting) it was probably meant for her intimate family circle.

Wenn der Frühling kommt is an exceptional example of Hensel altering the original poem text: she substituted new words for the final two lines of the poem and repeated lines to reshape the meaning and overall structure of the original.[16] The form might be described as a hybrid of modified-strophic and through-composed designs. This setting represents a strong re-reading of Heinrich Heine's text. The final two lines "Wie sehr das Zeug auch gefällt, / So macht's doch noch lang keine Welt" (However pleasant such stuff may be, /It doesn't by any means create a whole world) are revised to read "sind allen nur tändelnder Scherz,/und mein Welt ist dein liebendes Herz" (All are only trifling pleasantry,/And my world is your loving heart. (See pg. 33 for the complete poem.) Heine's cynical conclusions became a positive, personal statement of love.

Hensel was only temporarily inspired by Friedrich Rückert's metaphoric poem *Zauberkreis*. The only manuscript for the lied is a working copy with crossed-out notes and revisions, containing no dynamics or tempo markings. She did not complete writing out the third and fourth strophes. The lied is composed in a modified strophic form, with contrasting music for the second and fourth strophes. The piano part is an example of musical painting. The warbling and singing of the nightingale and the idea of circularity are composed into the repeated sextuplet figures, and ascending arpeggios in the right hand. This music embodies a distinct image of the poem's meaning, and is quite different from her settings of the 1820s.

Although it is probable that Hensel knew of the lieder of Schubert and Robert Schumann (1810–1856), there is no noticeable influence of these composers on her output. However, several scholars have described certain parallels between Hensel's songs and those of her brother,[17] concluding that she is an important representative of a Third Berlin Lieder School, together with Felix Mendelssohn and other Zelter students.[18] As her lieder in this volume reveal, this is an accurate description of Hensel's place in the history of the German lied.[19]

Acknowledgments

The four lieder edited for this volume are published with the kind permission of Dr. Hans-Günter Klein and the Mendelssohn-Archiv at the Staatsbibliothek Preussischer Kulturbesitz in Berlin. I would like to gratefully acknowledge the insight and support of Dr. Susan

Jackson, Dr. Ulrich Leisinger, and Dr. Michael Tusa while I was preparing this article and editions, and I thank Dr. Suzanne Summerville for her help in compiling my discography. My contact with the faculty of the Harvard Music Department and the Harvard Music Library equipped me to follow through on the project, and in particular, the resources of Harvard's Isham Memorial Music Library were of great assistance. The funding and support of the German Fulbright-Kommission and the Germanistic Society of America enabled me to pursue research on Fanny Hensel in Berlin, Germany.

Notes

1. See the list of published editions following this article.

2. Annette Maurer, "Fanny Hensel Mendelssohn: Biographie," 4 and "'Sein Verdienst um die Kunstzustände unserer Vaterstadt': Fanny Hensel's Sonntagmusiken," 12, both in *Viva Voce* 42 (May 1997).

3. Sebastian Hensel, *The Mendelssohn Family,* vol. 2, trans. Carl Klingemann (New York: Harper & Brothers, 1882), 31.

4. Annette Maurer, "Biographische Einflusse auf das Liedschaffen Fanny Hensels," *Fanny Hensel, geb. Mendelssohn Bartholdy: Das Werk*, ed. Martina Helmig (Munich: Edition Text und Kritik, 1997), 36. Maurer provides a table as an overview of Hensel's song output by year.

5. Translated and quoted by Marcia Citron "Felix Mendelssohn's Influence on Fanny Mendelssohn Hensel as a Professional Composer," *Current Musicology* 37/38 (1984): 10. Abraham Mendelssohn's statement was made in a letter written to Fanny on her twenty-third birthday.

6. Quoted in Jack Stein, *Poetry and Music in the German Lied from Gluck to Hugo Wolf* (Cambridge: Harvard University Press, 1971), 41–42.

7. Heine's text reads: "Nur Eine kennt meinen Schmerz:/Sie hat selbst zerrissen/Zerrissen mir das Herz" and Hensel's reads: "Nur Einer kennt meinen Schmerz:/Er hat selbst zerrissen." This gender switch is also discussed by Jürgen Thym, "Crosscurrents in Song: Five Distinctive Voices" in *German Lieder in the Nineteenth Century* (New York: Schirmer 1996), 164.

8. Beatrix Borchard, "'Mein Singen ist ein Rufen nur aus Träumen' Berlin, Leipziger Strasse Nr. 3," *Fanny Hensel, geb. Mendelssohn,* 9-22.

9. Maurer, "Biographische Einflusse," 33–37.

10. Ibid., 195-205. Maurer supplies a chronological index of Hensel's song titles and poets.

11. See Maurer, "Überlegungen zur Edition der Werke Fanny Hensels" in *Fanny Hensel geb. Mendelssohn Bartholdy* (Stuttgart: Metzlersche Verlagbuchhandlung, 1999), 182–94, for a detailed discussion of the considerations involved with modern publication of Hensel's music.

12. See Annette Maurer, *Thematisches Verzeichnis der Klavierbegleiteten Sololieder Fanny Hensel* (Kassel: Furore, 1997), 13–27.

13. See Klein's facsimile of *Traum* (Wiesbaden: Ludwig Reichert Verlag, 1997) or Maurer's *Thematisches Verzeichnis* for reproductions of some of these collaborative efforts.

14. See Editorial Procedures for more details on the manuscript source of each lied.

15. Françoise Tillard, *Fanny Hensel* (Portland, Oregon: Amadeus Press, 1996), 137. This was taken and translated from Sebastian Hensel, *Die Familie Mendelssohn, 1729–1847, nach Briefen und Tagebüchern* (Berlin: B. Behr's Buchhandlung, 1879), 1:210.

16. The published version in Heine's *Buch der Lieder* (Hamburg: Hoffman und Campe, 1827) is titled *Wahrhaftig* and reads:

Wahrhaftig (Truthfully)

Wenn der Frühling kommt mit dem Sonnenschein,
Dann knospen und blühen die Blümlein auf;
Wenn der Mond beginnt seinen Strahlenlauf,
Dann schwimmen die Sternlein hintendrein;
Wenn der Sänger zwei susse Äuglein sieht,
Dann quellen ihm Lieder aus tiefem Gemüt.
Doch Lieder und Sterne und Blümelein,
Und Äuglein und Mondglanz und Sonnenschein,
Wie sehr das Zeug auch gefällt,
So macht's doch noch lang keine Welt.

Translation of final two lines:
However pleasant such stuff may be,
It doesn't by any means create a whole world.

See page 33 for Hensel's complete version.

17. Gisela Muller, "'Leichen—' oder 'Blüthenduft'?: Heine-Vertonungen Fanny Hensels und Felix Mendelssohn Bartholdys im Vergleich," *Fanny Hensel geb. Mendelssohn*, 42. A comparison of the siblings' settings of the Goethe/Marianne von Willemer poem

Suleika ("Ach um deine feuchten Schwingen") reveals a similar approach to the form of the song.

18. Jürgen Thym, "Crosscurrents in Song: Five Distinctive Voices," *German Lieder in the Nineteenth Century*, ed. Rufus Hallmark (New York: Schirmer Books, 1996), 166.

19. Annette Maurer's two-volume set of selected Hensel lieder, *Hensel: Ausgewählte Lieder fur Singstimme und Klavier* (Wiesbaden: Breitkopf & Härtel, 1993 and 1994) offers the best opportunity to survey her output. The date of composition and information on the surviving sources is provided for each song in the Revisionsbericht at the end of each volume.

List of Works

Lieder

The following list of solo lieder is adapted from Annette Maurer's *Thematisches Verzeichnis der klavierbegleiteten Sololieder Fanny Hensels* (Kassel: Furore, 1997, Appendix 2)—which should be consulted for further information on the manuscript sources, poet, text source, etc. of each lied. The date Hensel indicated on the manuscript copy follows the title (in italics) and/or incipit (in quotation marks). Where a lied was left untitled by Hensel the text incipit has been adopted as its title and placed in italics. Multiple songs with the same title are followed by incipits in quotation marks. When the exact date is uncertain, Maurer's estimated date of composition has been adopted. This is followed by the publication status and edition information.

1819

Lied zum Geburtstag des Vaters am 11ten Dezember 1819 (December 11, 1819). Poet unknown. Unpublished.

1820

Lied des Schäfers (March 4, 1820). Text by Johann Ludwig Casper. Unpublished.

Romance de Claudine (March 22, 1820). Text by Jean-Pierre Claris de Florian. Unpublished.

Chanson des bergères (April 5, 1820). Text by Florian. Unpublished.

Romance de Galatée (April 8, 1820). Text by Florian. Unpublished.

Romance de Célestine (April 17, 1820). Text by Florian. Unpublished.

Isidore, "Vous, qui loin d'une amante" (April 26, 1820). Text by Florian. Fairbanks: Arts Venture, 1995.

Die Schönheit nicht, o Mädchen (April 29, 1820). Text by Johann Gottfried von Herder. Unpublished.

Némorin, "Arbre charmant, qui me rappelle" (May 10, 1820). Text by Florian. Fairbanks: Arts Venture, 1995.

Zoraide, "Rosier, rosier jadis charmant" (May 16, 1820). Text by Florian. Unpublished.

C'en est fait, je succombe, o fortune inhumaine! (May 27, 1820). Text by Florian. Unpublished.

Annette (June 3, 1820). Text by Florian. Unpublished.

Sérénade de Cortez (not dated, probably June 1820). Text by Florian. Fairbanks: Arts Venture, 1995.

Unique objet de ma tendresse (June 17, 1820). Text by Florian. Unpublished.

Wenn ich ihn nur habe (not dated, probably June–July 1820). Text by Novalis. Unpublished.

Erster Verlust (first setting) (July 1820). Text by Johann Wolfgang von Goethe. Unpublished.

Füllest wieder Busch und Tal (summer 1820). Text by Goethe. Unpublished.

Ave Maria (not dated, probably between July and September 1820). Text by Walter Scott. London: Samuel Leigh, 1832 with text in English.

L'Amitié, "Tout chaque jour dans la nature" (September 27, 1820). Poet unknown. Unpublished.

Schwarz ihre Brauen, weiss ihre Brust (October 6, 1820). Text by Franz Grillparzer. Unpublished.

C'est une larme qui sert d'accent à la douleur (November 29, 1820). Poet unknown. Unpublished.

So musst' ich von dir scheiden (December 13, 1820). Text by Scott. Unpublished.

1821

Némorin, "Du soleil qui te suit" (March 3, 1821). Text by Florian. Unpublished.

Le rocher des deux amants (March 9, 1821). Text by Florian. Unpublished.

Das stille Flehn um Gottes reichsten Segen (not dated, probably March 1821). Poet unknown. Unpublished.

La fuite inutile (March 21, 1821). Poet unknown. Unpublished.

Au bord d'une fontaine (not dated, possibly early 1821). Text by Jean Bertaut. Unpublished.

Nähe des Geliebten (first setting) (May 11, 1821). Text by Goethe. Unpublished.

Frühlingserinnerung (May 25, 1821). Text by Fanny Casper, née Robert. Unpublished.

1822

Fischers Klage (March 1822). Text by J. L. Casper. Unpublished.

Die Nonne (May 1822). Text by Ludwig Uhland. Berlin: Schlesinger, 1830.

Lauf der Welt (not dated, possibly May–June 1822). Text by Uhland. Unpublished.

Lebewohl (June 1822). Text by Wilhelm Hensel. Unpublished.

Du hast, mein Gott, durch deinen Willen (not dated, probably summer 1822). Text by Marianne Saaling. Unpublished.

Der Fischer (not dated, probably summer 1822). Text by Goethe. Unpublished.

Sehnsucht nach Italien, "Kennst du das Land" (August 17, 1822). Text by Goethe. Düsseldorf: Edition Donna, 1991.

Der Blumenstrauss (not dated, probably August–October 1822). Text by Uhland. Unpublished.

Mon coeur soupire dès l'aurore (October 14, 1822). Poet unknown. Unpublished.

Im Herbste, "Seid gegrüsst mit Frühlingswonne" (November 9, 1822). Text by Uhland. Unpublished.

Die Linde (November 28, 1822). Text by Luise Hensel. Unpublished.

Die Sommerrosen blühen (December 1822). Text by L. Hensel. Unpublished.

Schlaflied (December 1822). Text by Ludwig Tieck. Unpublished.

Das Ruhetal, "Wenn im letzten Abendstrahl" (before February 1822). Text by Uhland. Unpublished.

1823

Die liebe Farbe (January 1823). Text by Wilhelm Müller. Fairbanks: Arts Venture, 1995.

Des Müllers Blumen (January 14, 1823). Text by Müller. Fairbanks: Arts Venture, 1995.

Der Neugierige (January 20, 1823). Text by Müller. Fairbanks: Arts Venture, 1995.

Das Ständchen (January 22, 1823). Text by Uhland. Unpublished.

Gebet in der Christnacht (February 1, 1823). Text by Müller. Unpublished.

Wiegenlied, "Schlummre sanft, du holder Knabe" (March 1823). Text by Schick. Unpublished.

Die furchtsame Träne (April 16, 1823). Text by Schick. Unpublished.

Erinnerung (May 2, 1823). Text by Grillparzer. Unpublished.

Der Abendstern (May 18, 1823). Text by Johann Nepomuk Graf von Mailáth. Van Nuys, Calif.: Alfred, 1995.

Lied der Fee (May 30, 1823). Text by F. Casper, née Robert. Unpublished.

Die sanften Tage (June 15, 1823). Text by Uhland. Unpublished.

Der Sänger (June 18, 1823). Text by Novalis. Unpublished.

Die Schwalbe (June 20, 1823). Text by Friederike Robert. Karlsruhe: Gottlieb Braun, 1824.

Schäfers Sonntagslied (June 29, 1823). Text by Uhland. Unpublished.

Einsamkeit (July 12, 1823). Text by Müller. Unpublished.

Abendreihn (August 1, 1823). Text by Müller. Unpublished.

Seefahrers Abschied (August 1, 1823). Text by Müller. Unpublished.

Die Kapelle (September 6, 1823). Text by Uhland. Unpublished.

Am Morgen nach einem Sturm (September 15, 1823). Text by Grillparzer. Unpublished.

Frühe Sorge (September 20, 1823). Text by Tieck. Unpublished.

Wanderlied, "Frei wie der Wind" (September 22, 1823). Text by Friederike Robert. Unpublished.

Die Spinnerin (September 30, 1823). Text by Tieck. London: Elkin, 1959.

Die Liebende (October 1823). Text by Tieck. Unpublished.

Wonne der Einsamkeit (October 12, 1823). Text by Tieck. Unpublished.

Erster Verlust (second setting) (October 17, 1823). Text by Goethe. Unpublished.

Ferne, "O alte Heimat süss!" (October 29, 1823). Text by Tieck. Leipzig: Breitkopf & Härtel, 1850.

Vereinigung (November 22, 1823). Text by Müller. Unpublished.

Canzonetta (December 11, 1823). Text by Giovanni Pindemonte. Unpublished.

An die Entfernte (December 13, 1823). Text by Goethe. Unpublished.

Ohne sie (December 26, 1823). Text by Gerstenberg(k). Unpublished.

Mein Herz das ist begraben (December 31, 1823). Text by Gerstenberg(k). Unpublished.

Die glückliche Fischerin (1823 or ca. 1825). Text by Müller. Unpublished, partial facsimile in *Mendelssohn and His World.* Princeton: Princeton University, 1991, 255.

1824

Wo kommst du her? (January 2, 1824). Text by Gerstenberg(k). Unpublished.

Auf der Wanderung (January 17, 1824). Text by Tieck. Van Nuys, Calif.: Alfred, 1995.

Klage (January 24, 1824). Text by Tieck. Unpublished.

Abschied (March 24, 1824). Text by Tieck. Unpublished.

Sehnsucht, "Ach, aus dieses Tales Gründen" (April 3, 1827). Text by Friedrich Schiller. Unpublished.

Frage (April 6, 1824). Text by Tieck. Unpublished.

Herbstlied, "Feldeinwärts flog ein Vögelein" (April 10, 1824). Text by Tieck. Unpublished.

Frühlingsnähe (April 17, 1824). Text by Friederike Robert. Unpublished.

An einen Liebenden im Frühling (April 24, 1824). Text by Tieck. Unpublished.

Mailied (April 28, 1824). Text by Goethe. Van Nuys, Calif.: Alfred, 1995.

Jägers Abendlied (May 13, 1824). Text by Goethe. Unpublished.

Glück (June 10, 1824). Text by Tieck. Unpublished.

Leben, "Wechselnd gehn des Baches Wogen" (June 24, 1824). Text by Tieck. Unpublished.

Das Heimweh (July 19, 1824). Text by Friederike Robert. Berlin: Schlesinger, 1827.

Eilig ziehn in weiter Ferne (August 2, 1824). Text by Sophie Dellevie (pseud. Leontine Romainville). Unpublished.

Nacht, "Im Windsgeräusch, in stiller Nacht" (September 12, 1824). Text by Tieck. Unpublished.

Leiden (September 16, 1824). Text by Johann Peter Eckermann. Unpublished.

Verlor'nes Glück (September 24, 1824). Text by Eckermann. Unpublished.

Sonnenuntergang (October 21, 1824). Text by Eckermann. Unpublished.

Am stillen Hain, im Abendschein (November 5, 1824). Poet unknown. Unpublished.

1825

Sehnsucht, "Zeit meiner Kindheit, Land süsser Träume" (January 3, 1825). Text by Eckermann. Unpublished.

Verloren (January 19, 1825). Text by Eckermann. Unpublished.

Der Einsamwandelnde (January 29, 1825). Text by Eckermann. Unpublished.

Wandrers Nachtlied "Der du von dem Himmel bist" (first setting) (March 23, 1825). Text by Goethe. Unpublished.

An Suleika (April 25, 1825). Text by Goethe. Unpublished.

Suleika und Hatem (Duet) (April 28, 1825). Text by Goethe. Berlin: Schlesinger, 1827.

Suleika, "Ach um deine Feuchten Schwingen" (first setting) (May 5, 1825). Text by Marianne von Willemer. Unpublished.

Deinem Blick mich zu bequemen (June 3, 1825). Text by Goethe. Unpublished.

Sonett aus dem 13. Jahrhundert (June 10, 1825). Text by Herder. Unpublished.

Das holde Tal (incomplete) (June 16, 1825). Text by Goethe. Unpublished.

Mond (June 29, 1825). Text by Ludwig Heinrich Christoph Hölty. Fairbanks: Arts Venture, 1997.

Ecco quel fiero istante (June 29, 1825). Text by Metastasio. Unpublished.

Ist es möglich, Stern der Sterne (June 13, 1825). Text by Goethe. New York: G. K. Hall, 2001.

Italien (Zwischen Gaeta und Capua), "Schöner und schöner schmückt sich der Plan" (August 24, 1825). Text by Grillparzer. Berlin: Schlesinger, 1827.

Dir zu eröffnen mein Herz (September 5, 1825). Text by Goethe. Unpublished.

Numi clementi, se puri (not dated, probably September 1825). Poet unknown. Unpublished.

Herbstlied, "Wie rauschen die Bäume so winterlich schon" (October 17, 1825). Text by Tieck. Unpublished.

Harfners Lied, "Wer sich der Einsamkeit ergibt" (November 5, 1825). Text by Goethe. Wiesbaden: Breitkopf & Härtel, 1993.

Erinnerungen in die Heimat (November 8, 1825). Text by Marianne Saaling. Unpublished.

Die Schläferin (not dated, but between November 8, 1825 and February 8, 1826). Text by Johann Heinrich Voss. Unpublished.

1826

Der Rosenkranz (March 3, 1826). Text by Voss. Leipzig: Breitkopf & Härtel, 1850.

Der Eichwald brauset (not dated, probably early 1826). Text by Schiller. Wiesbaden: Breitkopf & Härtel, 1994.

Am Grabe (May 6, 1826). Text by Voss. Unpublished.

Sie liebt, mich liebt die Auserwählte (May 17, 1826). Text by Voss. Unpublished.

Abendlandschaft (June 10, 1826). Text by Friedrich von Matthisson. Unpublished.

Erwachen, "Ei, da sind die Schwalben wieder" (June 19, 1826). Text by Friedrich Voigts. Unpublished.

Waldlied (July 3, 1826). Text by Voigts. Unpublished.

Mignon (July 12, 1826). Text by Goethe. Düsseldorf: Edition Donna, 1991; Mainz: Schott, 1992.

Geheimnis (*Unverstanden*), "Im dunkelgrünen Walde" (July 12, 1826). Text by Voigts. Unpublished.

Die Äolsharfe auf dem Schlosse zu Baden (July 15, 1826). Text by Friederike Robert. Bonn: J. M. Dunst, ca. 1840 as *Schloss Leibeneck.*

Der Sprosser (July 24, 1826). Text by (pseud.) Selt. Unpublished.

An einem Herbstabende (August 23, 1826). Text by G. Schulze. Unpublished.

Der Frühlingsabend (not dated, probably between late August and October, 1826). Text by Voss. Unpublished.

Marias Klage (November 14, 1826). Text by Voss. Unpublished.

Nähe des Geliebten (second setting) (November 18, 1826). Text by Goethe. Van Nuys, Calif.: Alfred, 1995.

Sehnsucht, "Ist es Mitleid, Filomela" (November 23, 1826). Text by Voss. Van Nuys, Calif.: Alfred, 1995.

Neujahrslied (December 22, 1826). Text by Voss. Unpublished.

1827

Sehnsucht, "Süsse Kehle des Hain" (January 24, 1827). Text by Hölty. Fairbanks: Arts Venture, 1997.

Maigesang (February 4, 1827). Text by Hölty. Fairbanks: Arts Venture, 1997.

Seufzer (February 14, 1827). Text by Hölty. Fairbanks: Arts Venture, 1997.

Die Ersehnte (February 26, 1827). Text by Hölty. Leipzig: Breitkopf & Härtel, 1850.

Kein Blick der Hoffnung (March 4, 1827). Text by Hölty. Wiesbaden: Breitkopf & Härtel, 1994.

An den Mond (March 16, 1827). Text by Hölty. Fairbanks: Arts Venture, 1997.

Die Schiffende (March 27, 1827). Text by Hölty. Berlin: Schlesinger, 1836; Wiesbaden: Breitkopf & Härtel, 1994.

An die Ruh (March 30, 1827). Text by Hölty. Fairbanks: Arts Venture, 1997.

Sehnsucht, "Würde mein heisser Seelenwunsch Erfüllung" (May 2, 1827). Text by Hölty. Fairbanks: Arts Venture, 1997.

Am Flusse (May 27, 1827). Text by Goethe. Unpublished.

Sehnsucht, "Du jungfräulicher Geist" (July 4, 1827). Text by Voss. Unpublished.

Umsonst (July 24, 1827). Text by Voss. Unpublished.

Was will die einsame Träne (August 5, 1827). Text by Heine. Unpublished.

Der Maiabend (August 30, 1827). Text by Voss. Leipzig: Breitkopf & Härtel, 1850.

Die Sommernacht (September 12, 1827). Text by Friedrich Gottlieb Klopstock. Van Nuys, Calif.: Alfred, 1995.

Suleika, "Wie! mit innigstem Behagen" (October 4, 1827). Text by Marianne von Willemer/Goethe. Unpublished.

Achmed an Irza (*Im Garten*) (November 16, 1827). Text by Stieglitz. Unpublished.

Am leuchtenden Sommermorgen (December 14, 1827). Text by Heine. Unpublished.

Verlust, "Und wüssten's die Blumen, die kleinen" (December 28, 1827). Text by Heine. Berlin: Schlesinger, 1827.

1828

Wenn ich mir in stiller Seele (January 19, 1828). Text by Goethe. Unpublished.

Sehnsucht, "Ich weiss ein Tal" (February, 17, 1828). Text by Friedrich Adolf Märker. Unpublished.

Abendluft (Mid-June 1828). Text by Hölty. Fairbanks: Arts Venture, 1997.

Sehnsucht, "Fern und ferner schallt der Reigen" (June 24, 1828). Text by Johann Gustav Droysen. Berlin: Schlesinger, 1830.

Allnächtlich im Träume (July 21, 1828). Text by Heine. Unpublished.

Heut' in dieser Nacht (August 5, 1828). Text by Droysen. Unpublished.

Die frühen Gräber (October 9, 1828). Text by Klopstock. Leipzig: Breitkopf & Härtel, 1850; Wiesbaden: Breitkopf & Härtel, 1994.

Über die Berge steigt schon die Sonne (November 20, 1828). Text by Heine. Unpublished.

Nacht liegt auf den fremden Wegen (November 20, 1828). Text by Goethe. Unpublished.

Aglaë, "Was ich allein behalten" (December 30, 1828). Text by Goethe. Unpublished.

1829

Gram (January 6, 1829). Text by Droysen. Unpublished.

Selmar und Selma (March 4, 1829). Text by Klopstock. Unpublished.

Durch zartes Mailaub blinkt die Abendröte (March 26, 1829). Text by Klopstock. Unpublished.

Liederkreis. An Felix Während seiner ersten Abwesenheit in England (May 25–June 2, 1829). Text by Droysen. Fairbanks: Arts Venture, 1995.

Lebewohl, Grüner Frühling, süsse Mailuft, Nun ist's nicht öd in meiner Brust, O sprich, wo blieb dein heitrer Sinn?, Hochland, Wiedersehen Schlafe, schlaf! (September 21, 1829). Text by W. Hensel. Unpublished.

Zu deines Lagers Füssen tret' ich im Sehnsuchttraum (October 1829). Text by W. Hensel. Unpublished.

1830

Wie dunkel die Nacht, wie dunkel mein Sinn (January 19, 1830). Poet unknown. Unpublished.

Genesungsfeier. An Rebecca (April 10, 1830). Text by W. Hensel. Unpublished.

Minnelied des Grafen Peter von Provence (November 16, 1830). Text by Tieck. Unpublished.

Frühlingslied (November 19, 1830). Text by W. Hensel. Unpublished.

Der Schnee, der ist geschmolzen (not dated, probably 1830–1831). Poet unknown. Unpublished.

1831

Nacht, "Die Sonne ist gesunken" (October 1, 1831). Text by Friederike Robert. Unpublished.

O wie beseligend gehen und kommen die Stunden (December 21, 1831). Unpublished.

1832

Wiegenlied, "Wenn die Vögel mit Gesange" (September 14, 1832). Poet unknown. Unpublished.

1833

Gegenwart, "Alles kündet dich an!" (August 1, 1833). Text by Goethe. Wiesbaden: Breitkopf & Härtel, 1994.

In die Ferne (August 29, 1833). Text by Hölty. Düsseldorf: Edition Donna, 1991.

1834

Drei Lieder nach Heine (March 16, 1834). Text by M. Alexander. Fairbanks: Arts Venture, 1995.
Once o'er my dark and troubled life
I wander through the wood and weep
What means the lonely tear

Der Pilgrim vor St. Just (Carl V) (Pentecost 1834). Text by August Graf von Platen. Unpublished.

Wo sich gatten jene Schatten (May 29, 1834). Text by Platen. Unpublished.

Ich ging lustig durch den grünen Wald (not dated, probably 1834–1835). Poet unknown. Unpublished.

1835

An Cidli (incomplete) (May 22, 1835). Text by Klopstock. Unpublished.

Über allen Gipfeln ist Ruh (August 22, 1835). Text by Goethe. Wiesbaden: Breitkopf & Härtel, 1993.

Wenn der Frühling kommt mit dem Sonnenschein (August 24, 1835). Text by Heine. New York: G. K. Hall, 2001.

1836

Wie dich die warme Luft umscherzt (February 26, 1836). Text by Platen. Unpublished.

Gleich Merlin (March 13, 1836). Text by Heine. Van Nuys, Calif.: Alfred, 1995.

Neue Liebe, neues Leben (May 3, 1836). Text by Goethe. Mainz: Schott, 1992.

Das Meeresleuchten (November 21, 1836). Poet unknown. Unpublished.

Suleika, "Ach, um deine feuchten Schwingen" (second setting) (December 4, 1836). Text by von Willemer. Wiesbaden: Breitkopf & Härtel, 1993.

There by none of beauty's daughters (December 29, 1836). Text by Byron. Fairbanks: Arts Venture, 1996.

1837

Warum sind denn die Rosen so blass? (January 26, 1837). Text by Heine. Berlin: Bote & Bock, 1846; Wiesbaden: Breitkopf & Härtel, 1994.

Altes Lied (May 26, 1837). Text by Brentano. Fairbanks: Arts Venture; 1995.

Farewell! (June 1, 1837) Text by Byron. Fairbanks: Arts Venture, 1994.

Wanderlied, "Von den Bergen zu den Hügeln" (not dated, probably between early June and Mid-August 1837). Text by Goethe. Berlin: Bote & Bock, 1846; Wiesbaden: Breitkopf & Härtel, 1994.

Bright be the place of thy soul (not dated, probably summer 1837). Text by Byron. Fairbanks: Arts Venture, 1994.

Ach, die Augen sind es wieder (December 20, 1837). Text by Heine. Wiesbaden: Breitkopf & Härtel, 1993.

1838

Fichtenbaum und Palme (March 30, 1838). Text by Heine. Wiesbaden: Breitkopf & Härtel, 1993.

Die Mainacht (June 24, 1838). Text by Hölty. Leipzig: Breitkopf & Härtel, 1850; Wiesbaden: Breitkopf & Härtel, 1994.

Ich wandelte unter den Bäumen (August 7, 1838). Text by Heine. Van Nuys, Calif.: Alfred, 1995.

Das Meer erglänzte weit hinaus (September 6, 1838). Text by Heine. Van Nuys, Calif.: Alfred, 1995.

1839

Sehnsucht, "Was zieht mir das Herz so" (February 2, 1839). Text by Goethe. Düsseldorf: Edition Donna, 1991.

Du bist die Ruh (May 4, 1839). Text by Friedrich Rückert. Berlin: Bote & Bock, 1847.

1840

Cavatina, "Deh torna a me" (March 13, 1840). Text by Ludovico Ariosto. Unpublished.

Hausgarten (1840). Text by Goethe. Unpublished.

1841

Nach Süden (not dated, probably April–May 1841). Poet unknown. Leipzig: Breitkopf & Härtel, 1850; Wiesbaden: Breitkopf & Härtel, 1994.

Von dir, mein Lieb, ich scheiden muss (not dated, probably April–May 1841). Text by Burns, trans. Kaufman. Van Nuys, Calif.: Alfred, 1995.

Gondellied (June 4, 1841). Text by Emanuel Geibel. Berlin: Bote & Bock, 1846.

Anklänge. Drei Lieder (June 7, 1841). Text by Joseph Freiherr von Eichendorff. Düsseldorf: Edition Donna 1991; Wiesbaden: Breitkopf & Härtel, 1993.

Traurige Wege (July 28, 1841). Text by Nikolaus Lenau. Düsseldorf: Edition Donna 1991; Wiesbaden: Breitkopf & Härtel, 1993.

Auf dem See (von Como) (August 11, 1841). Text by Goethe. Düsseldorf: Edition Donna, 1991.

Totenklage (August 14, 1841). Text by Kerner. Van Nuys, Calif.: Alfred, 1995.

1843

An Frau Theresa Wartel (May 15, 1843). Text by Fanny or Wilhelm Hensel. Unpublished.

Nachtwanderer (not dated, probably 1843 or earlier). Text by Eichendorff. Berlin: Bote & Bock, 1847; Wiesbaden: Breitkopf & Härtel, 1994.

Dämmrung senkte sich von oben (August 28, 1843). Text by Goethe. Wiesbaden: Breitkopf & Härtel, 1993.

Zauberkreis (not dated, probably 1843–44). Text by Rückert. New York: G.K. Hall, 2003.

Mutter, o sing mich zur Ruh (not dated, probably between October 28, 1843 and May 1, 1844). Text by Felicia Hemans. Unpublished.

1844

Die Stille (January 5, 1844). Text by Eichendorff. Unpublished.

Liebe in der Fremde (January 6, 1844). Text by Eichendorff. Düsseldorf: Edition Donna, 1991.

Im Herbst, "Der Wald wird falb" (January 27, 1844). Text by Eichendorff. Wiesbaden: Breitkopf & Härtel, 1993.

Traum, "Ihr fernen Heimathöhen" (October 18, 1844). Text by Eichendorff. Wiesbaden: Ludwig Reichert, 1997 (facsimile).

1846

Das Veilchen, "Ach, Veilchen, armes Veilchen" (January 23, 1846). Poet unknown. Van Nuys, Calif.: Alfred, 1995.

Im Herbste, "Auf des Gartens Mauerzinne" (January 23, 1846). Text by Geibel. Leipzig: Breitkopf & Härtel, 1850; Wiesbaden: Breitkopf & Härtel, 1994.

Es rauscht das rote Laub (March 21, 1846). Text by Geibel. Van Nuys, Calif.: Alfred, 1995.

Erwache, Knab', erwache nun (June 16, 1846). Text by W. Hensel. Unpublished.

Dein ist mein Herz (July 11, 1846). Text by Lenau. Berlin: Bote & Bock, 1846.

Bitte (August 7, 1846). Text by Lenau. Berlin: Bote & Bock, 1847.

Stimme der Glocken (August 28, 1846). Text by Lenau. Van Nuys, Calif.: Alfred, 1995.

Abendbild, "Friedlicher Abend senkt sich aufs Gefilde" (September 2, 1846). Text by Lenau. Leipzig: Breitkopf & Härtel, 1850; Wiesbaden: Breitkopf & Härtel, 1994.

Erwin, "Ihr verblühet, süsse Rosen" (October 4, 1846). Text by Goethe. Berlin: Bote & Bock, 1847.

Ich kann wohl manchmal singen (October 5, 1846). Text by Eichendorff. Wiesbaden: Breitkopf & Härtel, 1993.

Nacht ist wie ein stilles Meer (October 22, 1846). Text by Eichendorff. Wiesbaden: Breitkopf & Härtel, 1993.

Abendbild, "Stille wirds im Walde" (November 21, 1846). Text by Lenau. Unpublished.

Beharre (November 27, 1846). Text by Helmina von Chézy. Van Nuys, Calif.: Alfred, 1995.

Kommen und Scheiden (December 27, 1846). Text by Lenau. Van Nuys, Calif.: Alfred, 1995.

1847

Bergeslust (May 13, 1847). Text by Eichendorff. Berlin: private publication, 1847; Leipzig: Breitkopf & Härtel, 1850; Wiesbaden: Breitkopf & Härtel, 1994.

Lieder without Dates

Maurer's estimation is given in brackets (see Maurer, *Thematisches Verzeichnis*, 205).

Wonne der Wehmut (Maundy Thursday, no year, (1828–1830?)). Text by Goethe. Unpublished.

Schwanenlied (1835–1838?). Text by Heine. Berlin: Bote & Bock, 1846.

Maienlied (after 1840). Text by Eichendorff. Berlin: Bote & Bock, 1846.

Morgenständchen (after 1840). Text by Eichendorff. Berlin: Bote & Bock, 1846; Wiesbaden: Breitkopf & Härtel, 1994.

Frühling (after 1840). Text by Eichendorff. Berlin: Bote & Bock, 1847; Wiesbaden: Breitkopf & Härtel, 1994.

Vorwurf, "Du klagst, dass bange Wehmut dich beschleicht" (1841 or 1846?). Text by Lenau. Leipzig: Breitkopf & Härtel, 1850; Wiesbaden: Breitkopf & Härtel, 1994.

Wandrers Nachtlied, "Der du von dem Himmel bist" (second setting) (October 28, no year, after 1840?). Text by Goethe. Wiesbaden: Breitkopf & Härtel, 1993.

Published Editions of Lieder

Editions Published during Hensel's Lifetime

Music supplement to *Rheinblüthen*. Karlsruhe: Verlag von Gottlieb Braun, [1824]. This song was published anonymously as a facsimile copy of the autograph.
Die Schwalbe. Text by Friederike Robert.

Felix Mendelssohn Bartholdy's *Zwölf Gesange*, op. 8. Berlin: Schlesinger, 1827. Nos. 2, 3 and 12 by Fanny Hensel; her authorship was not indicated in the original publication.

2. *Das Heimweh*. Text by Friederike Robert
3. *Italien*. Text by Franz Grillparzer
12. *Suleika und Hatem*. Text by Johann Wolfgang von Goethe. Duet for tenor and soprano with piano accompaniment

Felix Mendelssohn Bartholdy's *Zwölf Lieder*, op. 9. Berlin: Schlesinger, 1830. Nos. 7, 10 and 12 by Fanny Hensel; her authorship was not indicated in the publication.

7. *Sehnsucht*, "Fern und ferner schallt der Reigen." Text by Johann Gustav Droysen
10. *Verlust*, "Und wüssten die Blumen, die kleinen." Text by Heinrich Heine
12. *Die Nonne*. Text by Ludwig Uhland

In *The Harmonicon* 10. London: Published for the Proprietors by Samuel Leigh, 1832.
Ave Maria. Text by Walter Scott.

In *Album: Neue Original-Compositionen für Gesang und Piano*. Berlin: Schlesinger, 1836.
Die Schiffende, "Sie wankt dahin." Text by Ludwig Hölty.

In *Rhein-Sagen und Lieder*, vol. 1. Bonn: J. M. Dunst, ca. 1840. The song is titled in all its autograph sources as *Die Äolsharfe auf dem Schlosse zu Baden*.
Schloss Liebeneck, "O schöne Zeit, wo Schloss und Zinne." Text by F. Robert.

Sechs Lieder für eine Stimme mit Begleitung des Pianoforte von Fanny Hensel geb. Mendelssohn Bartholdy 1stes Heft, op. 1. Berlin: Bote & Bock, 1846. Reprinted 1985.

1. *Schwanenlied*, "Es fällt ein Stern herunter." Text by Heine
2. *Wanderlied*, "Von den Bergen zu den Hügeln." Text by Goethe
3. *Warum sind denn die Rosen so blass?* Text by Heine
4. *Maienlied*, "Läuten kaum die Maienglocken." Text by Joseph Eichendorff
5. *Morgenständchen*, "In den Wipfeln frische Lüfte." Text by Eichendorff
6. *Gondellied*. Text by Emanuel Geibel

Sechs Lieder für eine Stimme mit Begleitung des Pianoforte componiert und ihrer Schwester, Frau R. Jejeune Dirichlet zugeeignet von Fanny Hensel geb. Mendelssohn Bartholdy. 2tes Heft, op. 7. Berlin and Breslau: Bote & Bock, 1847. Reprinted 1985.

1. *Nachtwanderer*. Text by Eichendorff
2. *Erwin*. Text by Goethe
3. *Frühling*, "Übern Garten, durch die Lüfte." Text by Eichendorff
4. *Du bist die Ruh*. Text by Friedrich Rückert
5. *Bitte*. Text by Nikolaus Lenau
6. *Dein ist mein Herz*. Text by Lenau

Posthumous Publications Prepared by Her Family

Bergeslust, "O Lust, vom Berg zu schauen." Text by Eichendorff. Privately published posthumously in facsimile, 1847. The family titled the publication *Das letzte Lied von Fanny Hensel geb. Mendelssohn-Bartholdy*.

Sechs Lieder mit Begleitung des Pianoforte componiert von Fanny Cäcilia Hensel geb. Mendelssohn Bartholdy, op. 9 der nachgelassenen Werke. Leipzig: Breitkopf & Härtel, 1850.

1. *Die Ersehnte*, "Brächte dich meinem Arm der erste Frühling." Text by Hölty
2. *Ferne*, "O alte Heimat süss!" Text by Tieck
3. *Der Rosenkranz*, "An des Beetes Umbuschung." Text by Voss
4. *Die frühen Gräber*, "Willkommen, o silberner Mond." Text by Klopstock
5. *Der Maiabend*, "Umweht von Maiduft." Text by Voss
6. *Die Mainacht*,"Wenn der silberne Mond." Text by Hölty

Fünf Lieder mit Begleitung des Pianoforte componiert von Fanny Cäcilia Hensel geb. Mendelssohn Bartholdy, op. 10. Leipzig: Breitkopf & Härtel, 1850.

1. *Nach Süden*, "Von allen Zweigen schwingen."
2. *Vorwurf*, "Du klagst, dass bange Wehmut dich beschleicht." Text by Lenau
3. *Abendbild*, "Friedlicher Abend senkt sich aufs Gefilde." Text by Lenau
4. *Im Herbste*, "Auf des Gartens Mauerzinne." Text by Geibel
5. *Bergeslust*, "O Lust, vom Berg zu schauen." Text by Eichendorff

Modern Editions

Ave Maria, ed. and arr. by Jack Werner. London: J. Curwen & Songs Ltd., 1934.

Classical Discoveries no. 5, ed. Jack Werner. English translation by Robert Elkin. London: Elkin, 1959.
The Spinning Girl. [*Die Spinnerin*.]

One Hundred Years of Eichendorff Songs, ed. Jürgen Thym. Madison, Wis., 1983, 13–15. *Nachtwanderer* (op. 7, no. 1). Text by Eichendorff.

Historical Anthology of Music by Women, ed. James R. Briscoe. Bloomington, Ind., 1987, 115–18, with introduction by Marcia Citron. Reprinted from Berlin: Bote und Bock, 1846.
Schwanenlied (op. 1, no. 1). Text by Heine.

Ausgewählte Lieder für Singstimme und Klavier, ed. Aloysia Assenbaum. Düsseldorf: Edition Donna, 1991 (in transposition for mid-range).
Sehnsucht nach Italien, "Kennst du das Land." Text by Goethe
In die Ferne. Text by Hölty
Sehnsucht, " Was zieht mir das Herz so." Text by Goethe
Anklänge: Drei Lieder. Text by Eichendorff
Traurige Wege. Text by Lenau
Auf dem See. Text by Goethe
Liebe in der Fremde. Text by Eichendorff

In *Frauen komponieren: 25 Lieder für eine Singstimme und Klavier*, ed. Eva Rieger and Käte Walter. Mainz: Schott, 1992.
Mignon, "Nur wer die Sehnsucht kennt." Text by Goethe
Die Ersehnte (op. 9, number 1). Text by Hölty
Neue Liebe, neues Leben. Text by Goethe

*Hensel: Ausgewählte Lieder für Singstimme und Klavie*r, vol. 2, ed. Annette Maurer. Wiesbaden: Breitkopf & Härtel, 1993.
Traurige Wege. Text by Lenau
Harfners Lied. Text by Goethe
Dämmrung senkte sich von oben. Text by Goethe
Über allen Gipfeln ist Ruh. Text by Goethe
Wandrers Nachtlied, "Der du von dem Himmel bist." Text by Goethe
An Suleika. Text by Goethe
Suleika, "Ach, um deine feuchten Schwingen" (second setting). Text by Marianne von Willemer
Ach, die Augen sind es wieder. Text by Heine
Fichtenbaum und Palme. Text by Heine
Nacht ist wie ein stilles Meer. Text by Eichendorff
Ich kann wohl manchmal singen. Text by Eichendorff
Im Herbst, "Der Wald wird falb." Text by Eichendorff
Anklänge: Drei Lieder. Text by Eichendorff

Hensel: Ausgewählte Lieder für Singstimme und Klavier, vol. 1, ed. Annette Maurer. Wiesbaden: Breitkopf & Härtel, 1994.
Wanderlied (op. 1, no. 2).Text by Goethe.
Warum sind denn die Rosen so blass? (op. 1, no. 3).Text by Heine
Morgenständchen (op. 1, no. 5).Text by Eichendorff
Nachtwanderer (op. 7, no. 1). Text by Eichendorff
Frühling (op. 7, no. 3). Text by Eichendorff
Die frühen Gräber (op. 9, no. 4). Text by Klopstock

Die Mainacht (op. 9, no. 6). Text by Hölty
Nach Süden (op. 10, no. 1). Poet unknown
Vorwurf (op. 10, no. 2). Text by Lenau
Abendbild, "Friedlicher Abend senkt sich aufs Gefilde" (op. 10, no. 3). Text by Lenau
Im Herbste (op. 10, no. 4). Text by Geibel
Bergeslust (op. 10, no. 5). Text by Eichendorff
Die Schiffende. Text by Hölty
Kein Blick der Hoffnung. Text by Hölty
Der Eichwald brauset. Text by Schiller
Gegenwart, "Alles kündet dich an!" Text by Goethe

Three Songs by Fanny Hensel for Voice and Piano, ed. Suzanne Summerville. Text by Lord Byron. Fairbanks: Arts Venture, 1994.

1. *Bright be the place of thy Soul*
2. *There be none of Beauty's daughters*
3. *Farewell!*

Sixteen Songs: Fanny Mendelssohn Bartholdy, ed. John Glenn Paton. Van Nuys, Calif.: Alfred Publishing, 1995.
Der Abendstern. Text by Mailáth
Auf der Wanderung. Text by Tieck
Mailied, "Wie herrlich leuchtet mir die Natur!" Text by Goethe
Nähe des Geliebten. Text by Goethe
Sehnsucht, "Ist es Mitleid, Filomela." Text by Voss
Die Sommernacht. Text by Klopstock
Gleich Merlin, "Gleich Merlin, dem eitlen Weisen." Text by Heine
Ich wandelte unter den Bäumen. Text by Heine
Das Meer erglänzte weit hinaus. Text by Heine
Von Dir, mein Lieb, ich scheiden muss. Text by Burns
Totenklage. Text by Kerner
Das Veilchen. Poet unknown
Es rauscht das rote Laub. Text by Geibel
Stimme der Glocken. Text by Lenau
Beharre. Text by von Chézy
Kommen und Scheiden. Text by Lenau

Altes Lied. The Spinstress' Song—a poem by Clemens Brentano for high voice and piano by Fanny Hensel, ed. Suzanne Summerville. Fairbanks: Arts Venture, 1995.
"Es sang vor langen Jahren."

Liederkreis: An Felix während seiner ersten Abswesenheit in England 1829 by Fanny Hensel, ed. Suzanne Summerville. Fairbanks: Arts Venture, 1995.

1. *Lebewohl*, "Stören möcht' ich deinen Schlaf nicht"
2. *Grüner Frühling, süsse Mailuft*
3. *Nun ist's nicht öd in meiner Brust*
4. *O sprich, wo blieb dein heitrer Sinn?*
5. *Hochland*, "Im Hochland, Bruder, da schweifs du umher"
6. *Wiedersehen*,"Wir trugen unverdrossen"

Three Poems by Heinrich Heine in the Translations of Mary Alexander by Fanny Hensel (Drei Lieder nach Heine von Mary Alexander), ed. Suzanne Summerville. Fairbanks: Arts Venture, 1995.

1. *Once o'er my dark and troubled Life*
2. *I wander through the Wood and Weep*
3. *What means the lonely Tear*

Three Poems from Wilhelm Müller's "Die schöne Müllerin" by Fanny Hensel, ed. Suzanne Summerville. Fairbanks: Arts Venture, 1995.
Des Müllers Blumen, "Am Bach viel kleine Blumen stehn"
Der Neurgierige, "Ich frage keine Blume"
Die liebe Farbe, "In Grün will ich mich kleiden"

Three Songs on Texts by Jean Pierre Claris de Florian by Fanny Hensel, ed. Suzanne Summerville. Fairbanks: Arts Venture, 1995.
Némorin, "Arbre charmant, qui me rappelle"
Isidore, "Vous, qui loin d'une amante"
Sérénade de Cortez, "Dérobe ta lumière"

Eight Songs for Voice and Piano by Fanny Hensel, ed. Suzanne Summerville. Texts by Hölty. Fairbanks: Arts Venture, 1997.
Abendluft, "Wehet mir Kühlung, ihr Lüfte"
An den Mond, "Was schauest du so hell und klar"
An die Ruhe, "Tochter Edens, o Ruh"
Maigesang, "Röter färbt sich der Himmel"
Mond, "Dein Silber schien durch Eichengrün"
Sehnsucht, "Süsse Kehle des Hains"
Sehnsucht, "Würde mein heisser Seelenwunsch Erfüllung"
Seufzer, "Die Nachtigall singt überall"

"Traum": Lied auf einen Text von Joseph von Eichendorff für Singstimme und Klavier, F-dur, 1844. Wiesbaden: Ludwig Reichert Verlag, 1997. Published in facsimile with an introduction by Hans Günter Klein.

Bibliography

Borchard, Beatrix. "'Mein Singen ist ein Rufen nur aus Träumen' Berlin, Leipziger Strasse Nr. 3." In *Fanny Hensel, geb. Mendelssohn: Das Werk*, ed. Martina Helmig, 9-22. Munich: Edition Text und Kritik, 1997.

_____, and Monika Schwarz-Danuser, ed. *Fanny Hensel Geb. Mendelssohn Bartholdy: Komponieren Zwischen Geselligkeitsideal und romantischer Musikästhetik*. Stuttgart: J. B. Metzler, 1999.

Bowers, Jane, and Judith Tick. *Women Making Music*. Urbana, Ill.: University of Illinois Press, 1986.

Citron, Marcia J. "Fanny Mendelssohn (-Bartholdy) [Hensel]." In *The Norton/Grove Dictionary of Women Composers*, ed. Julie Anne Sadie and Rhian Samuel. New York: W. W. Norton, 1994.

_____. "Felix Mendelssohn's Influence on Fanny Mendelssohn Hensel as a Professional Composer." *Current Musicology* 37/38 (1984): 9–17.

_____. "The Lieder of Fanny Mendelssohn Hensel." *Musical Quarterly* 69 (1983): 570–94.

_____, ed. *The Letters of Fanny Hensel to Felix Mendelssohn.* Stuyvesant, NY: Pendragon Press, 1987.

Das verborgene Band: Felix Mendelssohn Bartholdy und seine Schwester Fanny Hensel. Ausstellung der Musikabteilung der Staatsbibliothek zu Berlin. Wiesbaden: L. Reichert, 1997.

De la Motte, Diether. "Einfall als Bereicherung der Musiksprache in Liedern von Fanny Hensel." In *Fanny Hensel, geb. Mendelssohn Bartholdy: Das Werk*, ed. Martina Helmig, 58-67. Munich: Edition Text und Kritik, 1997.

_____. "Liebeserklärung für Fanny," *Viva Voce* 47 (May 1997): 5-7.

Elvers, Rudolph. "Verzeichnis der Musik-Autographen von Fanny Hensel im Mendelssohn-Archiv zu Berlin." In *Mendelssohn Studien 1*, ed. Cecile Lowenthal Hensel. Berlin: Duncker und Humblot, 1972.

_____. "Weitere Quellen zu den Werken von Fanny Hensel." In *Mendelssohn Studien 2*, ed. Cecile Lowenthal Hensel. Berlin: Duncker und Humblot, 1975.

Gabler, Barbara. "Tradieren und Edieren aus Verlagssicht." In *Fanny Hensel geb. Mendelssohn Bartholdy: Komponieren zwischen Geselligkeitsideal und romantischer Musikästhetik*, ed. Beatrix Borchard and Monika Schwarz-Danuser, 176–81. Stuttgart: J. B. Metzler, 1999.

Gorrell, Lorraine. *The Nineteenth-Century German Lied.* Portland, Ore.: Amadeus Press, 1993.

Hellwig-Unruh, Renate. "'Ein Dilettant ist schon ein schreckliches Geschöpf, ein weiblicher Autor ein noch schrecklicheres . . .': Sechs Briefe von Fanny Hensel an Franz Hauser (1794–1870)." In *Mendelssohn Studien 10*. Berlin: Duncker und Humblot, 1997.

_____. "'. . . so bin ich mit meiner Musik ziemlich allein': Die Komponistin und Musikerin Fanny Hensel, geb. Mendelssohn." In *Stadtbild und Frauenleben: Berlin im Spiegel von 16 Frauenporträts*, ed. Henrike Jülsbergen. Berlin: Berlinische Lebensbilder, 1997.

_____. *Thematisch-chronologisches Verzeichnis der Kompositionen von Fanny Hensel, geb. Mendelssohn (1805–1847).* Lottstetten, Adliswil/Zürich: Edition Kunzelmann, 2001.

Helmig, Martina, ed. *Fanny Hensel, geb. Mendelssohn Bartholdy: Das Werk.* Munich: Edition Text und Kritik, 1997.

Hensel, Fanny. *The Letters of Fanny Hensel to Felix Mendelssohn*, ed. and trans. Marcia J. Citron. Stuyvesant, NY: Pendragon Press, 1987.

_____. *Italienisches Tagebuch*, ed. Eva Weissweiler. Frankfurt am Main: Societäts-Verlag, 1982.

_____, and Felix Mendelssohn. *"Die Musik will gar nicht rutchen ohne Dich": Briefwechsel 1821 bis 1846*, ed. Eva Weissweiler. Berlin: Propyläen, 1997.

Hensel, Sebastian. *Die Familie Mendelssohn, 1729–1847, Nach Briefen und Tagebüchern.* 3 vols. Berlin: B. Behr's Buchhandlung, 1879. Reprint 1995, Frankfurt: Insel Verlag.

_____. *The Mendelssohn Family (1729–1847) from Letters and Journals*. 2 vols. Trans. Carl Klingemann. New York: Harper & Brothers, 1881.

Huber, Annegret. "Schillers Gedicht 'Des Mädchens Klage' in den Vertönungen von Fanny Hensel und Felix Mendelssohn Bartholdy," *Viva Voce* 42 (May 1997): 8–13.

Klein, Hans-Günter. "Autographe und Abschriften von Werken Fanny Hensels im Mendelssohn-Archiv zu Berlin: Verzeichnis der Abschriften und der Neuerwerbungen 1976–1990." In *Mendelssohn Studien 7. Berlin: Duncker und Humblot, 1990.*

_____. "A Present to a Person Unknown: Fanny Hensel's Fair Copy of Her Song Traum." Introduction to *Fanny Hensel geb. Mendelssohn Bartholdy, Traum: Lied auf einen Text von Joseph von Eichendorff für Singstimme und Klavier, F-dur, 1844, Faksimile des Autographs*. Wiesbaden: Ludwig Reichert Verlag, 1997.

_____. *Die Kompositionen Fanny Hensels in Autographen und Abschriften aus dem Besitz der Staatsbibliothek zu Berlin.* Tutzing: H. Schneider, 1995.

Lambour, Christian. "Quellen zur Biographie von Fanny Hensel, geb. Mendelssohn Bartholdy." In *Mendelssohn Studien 6. Berlin: Duncker und Humblot, 1986.*

_____. "Quellen zur Biographie von Fanny Hensel, geb. Mendelssohn Bartholdy." In *Mendelssohn Studien 7*, 171–78. Berlin: Duncker und Humblot, 1990.

Maurer, Annette. "Biographische Einflüsse auf das Liedschaffen Fanny Hensels." In *Fanny Hensel, geb. Mendelssohn Bartholdy: Das Werk*, ed. Martina Helmig. Munich: Edition Text and Kritik, 1997.

_____. *Thematisches Verzeichnis der klavierbegleiteten Sololieder Fanny Hensels.* Kassel: Furore, 1997.

_____. "Überlegungen zur Edition der Werke Fanny Hensels." In *Fanny Hensel geb. Mendelssohn Bartholdy: Komponieren zwischen Geselligkeitsideal und romantischer Musikästhetik*, ed. Beatrix Borchard and Monika Schwarz-Danuser. Stuttgart: J. B. Metzler, 1999.

_____. "Vorwort." *Hensel: Ausgewählte Lieder für Singstimme und Klavier*, Band I. Wiesbaden: Breitkopf & Härtel, 1994.

_____, and Annegret Huber. "Fanny Mendelssohn Bartholdys Lied *Die Schwalbe* als Musikbeilage des Almanachs *Rheinblüthen.*" In *Fanny Hensel, geb. Mendelssohn Bartholdy: # Das Werk*, ed. Martina Helmig. Munich: Edition Text und Kritik, 1997.

Mörchen, Roland. "Weit Mehr als eine 'Sonntagsmusikerin': Vor 150 Jahren starb die Komponistin Fanny Hensel." *Das Orchester* 6 (1997): 21-23.

Müller, Gisela. "'Leichen—' oder 'Blütheduft'? Heine-Vertonungen Fanny Hensels und Felix Mendelssohn Bartholdys im Vergleich." In *Fanny Hensel, geb. Mendelssohn Bartholdy:Das Werk*, ed. Martina Helmig. Munich: # Edition Text und Kritik, 1997.

Reich, Nancy. "The Power of Class: Fanny Hensel." In *Mendelssohn and his World*, ed. R. Larry Todd. Princeton: Princeton University Press, 1991.

Sirota, Victoria Ressmeyer. *The Life and Works of Fanny Mendelssohn Hensel.* Ph.D. dissertation, Boston University, 1981.

Tillard, Françoise. *Fanny Mendelssohn.* Paris: Éditions Belfond, 1992. English translation by Camille Naish. Portland, Ore.: Amadeus Press, 1996.

Thym, Jürgen. "Crosscurrents in Song: Five Distinctive Voices." In *German Lieder In the Nineteenth Century*, ed. Rufus Hallmark. New York: Schirmer, 1996.

Walker, Nancy. "Parallels between Fanny Mendelssohn Hensel and Clara Wieck Schumann: Their Lives and Their Songs." *The NATS Journal* 50 (March/April 1994): 9–13.

Weissweiler, Eva, ed. *Fanny und Felix Mendelssohn: Briefwechsel 1821 bis 1846.* Berlin: Propyläen, 1997.

_____, ed. *Hensel, Fanny: Italienisches Tagebuch.* Frankfurt am Main: Societäts-Verlag, 1982.

Werner, Jack. "Felix and Fanny Mendelssohn." *Music and Letters* 28 (1947): 303-37.

Whalen, Meg Freeman. "Fanny Mendelssohn Hensel's Sunday Musicales." *Journal of the Conductor's Guild* 14 (winter–spring 1994): 8–18.

Discography

Fanny Hensel Rediscovered. Susan Larson, soprano, Virginia Eskin, piano, Liederkreis Ensemble. Northeastern Records NR 213 (LP), 1984.
Bergeslust (op. 10, no. 5)
Bitte (op. 7, no. 5)
Dein ist mein Herz (op. 7, no. 6)
Die frühen Gräber (op. 9, no. 4)
Die Mainacht (op. 9, no. 6)
Ferne. "O alte Heimat süss!" (op. 9, no. 2)
Frühling "Übern Garten, durch die Lüfte" (op. 7, no. 3)

Also contains *Gartenlieder*, op. 3, nos. 1, 3, and 4

In *Lieder by Women Composers from the Classical Period to Modern Times, Vol. 1: From Maria Walpurgis to Clara Schumann.* Yoshie Tanaka, mezzo-soprano, Wolfgang Holzmair, baritone, Rosario Marciano, piano. MHS 512350, 1989.
Die Nonne (Felix Mendelssohn Bartholdy's op. 9, no. 12)
Duett (Suleika und Hatem) (FMB's op. 8, no. 12)
Das Heimweh (FMB's op. 8, no. 2)
Sehnsucht. "Fern und ferner schallt der Reigen." (FMB's op. 9, no. 7)
Verlust (FMB's op. 9, no. 10)

In *Felix Mendelssohn Bartholdy: Lieder*. Barbara Bonney, soprano; Geoffrey Parsons, piano. Teldec 2292-44946-2, 1992. (Works published as Felix Mendelssohn Bartholdy's op. 9)
Die Nonne (FMB's op. 9, no. 12)
Sehnsucht (FMB's op. 9, no. 7)
Verlust (FMB's op. 9, no.10)

In *The Women Composers: Clara Schumann, Fanny Mendelssohn, Alma Mahler.* Claude Verhaeghe, soprano; Jean Micault, piano. AAOC-93292, 1994.
Bitte (op. 7, no. 5)
Dein ist mein Herz (op. 7, no. 6)
Du bist die Ruh (op. 7, no. 4)
Gondellied (op. 1, no. 6)

Nachtwanderer (op. 7, no. 1)
Schwanenlied (op. 1, no. 1)
Wanderlied (op. 1, no. 2)
Warum sind denn die Rosen so blass? (op. 1, no. 3)

Fanny Hensel-Mendelssohn: Ausgewählte Lieder. Barbara Schlick, soprano; Aloysia Assenbaum, hammerflügel. Cavalli Records CCD 302, 1997.
Abendbild. "Friedlicher Abend senkt sich aufs Gefilde"
Abendbild. "Stille wird's im Walde"
Auf dem See (von Como)
Bergeslust
Bitte
Das Veilchen
Dein ist mein Herz
Du bist die Ruh
Erwache Knab'
Erwin
Erwins Lied. "Ich kann wohl manchmal singen"
Im Herbste
In die Ferne
Liebe in der Fremde
Mignon. "Nur wer die Sehnsucht kennt"
Nach Süden
Nacht ist wie ein stilles Meer
Nachtwanderer
Schwanenlied
Sehnsucht nach Italien
Sehnsucht. "Was zieht mir das Herz so?"
Stimme der Glocken
Traurige Wege
Vorwurf
Warum sind denn die Rosen so blass?

Fanny Hensel-Mendelssohn: Lieder. Lan Rao, soprano; Micaela Gelius, piano. Arte Nova 74321 56342 2, 1997.
Ach, die Augen sind es wieder
An Suleika
Bergeslust (op. 10, no. 5)
Dämmrung senkte sich von oben
Der Eichwald brauset
Die Ersehnte (op. 9, no. 1)
Die Mainacht (op. 9, no. 6)
Die Schiffende
Du bist die Ruh (op. 7, no. 4)
Erwin (op. 7, no. 2)
Fichtenbaum und Palme
Frühling, "Übern Garten durch die Lüfte" (op. 7, no. 3)
Gegenwart
Gondellied (op. 1, no. 6)
Harfners Lied
Im Herbst, "Der Wald wird falb"
Im Herbste (op. 10, no. 4)
Maienlied (op. 1, no. 4)
Mignon
Nach Süden (op. 10, no.1)
Nachtwanderer (op. 7, no. 1)
Neue Liebe, neues Leben
Schwanenlied (op. 1, no. 1)
Suleika, "Ach! um deinen feuchten Schwingen"
Über allen Gipfeln ist Ruh
Vorwurf (op. 10, no. 2)
Warum sind denn die Rosen so blass? (op. 1, no. 3)

Fanny Hensel Mendelssohn (1805–1847). Michaela Krämer, Kerstin Heesche-Wagner, Monika Kleinhenz, soprano; Gerhild Romberger, Michaela Günther, Ilga Bülte, alto; Volker Wierz, tenor; Gerrit Miehlke, bass; Ulrich Urban, piano; Kammerchor der Universität Dortmund, Willi Gundlach, conductor. Thorofon CTH 2398, 1998.
An Suleika
Dämmrung senkte sich von oben
Gegenwart
Harfners Lied
Liederkreis: An Felix während seiner ersten Abwesenheit in England 1829
Über allen Gipfeln ist Ruh
Wandrers Nachtlied "Der du von dem Himmel bist."

Also contains *Zum Fest der heiligen Cäcilia, Szene aus "Faust II,"* Three duets on Goethe texts, four Chorlieder, and *"Schlafe du, schlafe du süss."*

Fanny Mendelssohn: Lieder & Trio. Donna Brown, soprano; Françoise Tillard, and the Trio Brentano. Opus 11 OPS 10–012, 1998.
Abendbild "Stille wirds im Walde"
Ach! die Augen sind es wieder
Bergeslust (op. 10, no. 5)
Ferne (op. 9, no. 2)
Gondellied (op. 1, no. 6)
Harfners Lied
Ich wandelte unter den Bäumen
Im Herbste (op. 10, no. 4)
Italien (FMB's op. 8, no. 3)
Kommen und Scheiden
Nach Süden (op. 10, no. 1)
Sehnsucht (FMB's op. 9, no. 7)
Warum sind denn die Rosen so blass? (op. 1, no. 3)

Also contains *Trio,* op. 11, *Lied für Klavier* in Es-Dur.

Felix Mendelssohn: Songs and Duets. Sophie Daneman, soprano, Eugene Asti, piano. Hyperion 66906, 1998.
Die Nonne (FMB's op. 9, no. 12)
Verlust (FMB's op. 9, no. 10)

Keine von der Erden Schönen/There be none of Beauty's daughter. Adelheid Vogel, soprano; Suzanne Summerville, mezzo-soprano; Martin Petzold, tenor; Jochen Kupfer, baritone; Ulrich Urban, Pianist; Children's Choir of the MDR Radio Leipzig, Gunter Berger, conductor. Querstand VKJR 9803, 1999.
Altes Lied—The Spinstress' Song
Drei Lieder aus "Die schöne Müllerin"
Des Müllers Blumen
Der Neugierige
Die liebe Farbe
Drei Lieder nach Heine von Mary Alexander/Three Poems by Heinrich Heine in the Translations of Mary Alexander
Once o'er my dark and troubled Life
I wander through the Wood and Weep
What means the lonely Tear
Drei Lieder nach Texten von J.P. Claris de Florian
Némorin. "Arbre charmant, qui me rappelle"
Vous, qui loin d'une amante
Sérénade de Cortez
Drei Lieder nach Texten von Lord Byron
Bright be the place of the Soul
There be none of Beauty's daughters
Farewell!
Liederkreis: An Felix während seiner ersten Abwesenheit in England 1829
Wenn der Frühling kommt. Also contains three duets on texts of J. W. von Goethe, three duets on texts of Heinrich Heine, *Szene aus Goethe's Faust*

Fanny Mendelssohn: Lieder. Susan Gritton, soprano; Eugene Asti, piano. Hyperion CDA67110, 2000.
Abendbild, "Friedlicher Abend senkt sich aufs Gefilde" (op. 10, no. 3)
Bergeslust (op. 10, no. 5)
Bitte (op. 7, no. 5)
Dämmrung senkte sich von oben
Dein ist mein Herz (op. 7, no. 6)
Der Maiabend (op. 9, no. 5)
Der Rosenkranz (op. 9, no. 3)
Die Ersehnte (op. 9, no. 1)
Die frühen Gräber (op. 9, no. 4)
Die Mainacht (op. 9, no. 6)
Die Schiffende
Du bist die Ruh (op. 7, no. 4)
Erwin (op. 7, no. 2)
Ferne (op. 9, no. 2)
Frühling "Übern Garten, durch die Lüfte" (op. 7, no. 3)
Gondellied (op. 1, no. 6)
Ich wandelte unter den Bäumen
Im Herbste (op. 10, no. 4)
Italien, "Schöner und schöner schmückt sich von oben." (FMB's op. 8, no. 3)
Maienlied (op.1, no. 4)
Morgenständchen, "In den Wipfeln frische Lüfte" (op. 1, no. 5)
Nach Süden (op. 10, no. 1)
Nachtwanderer (op. 7, no. 1)
Schwanenlied (op. 1, no. 1)
Suleika, "Ach! um deinen feuchten Schwingen"
Traum
Vorwurf (op. 10, no. 2)
Wanderlied, "Von den Bergen zu den Hügeln." (op. 1, no. 2)
Warum sind denn die Rosen so blass? (op. 1, no. 3)

The Art of Mendelssohnian Song: Lieder by Fanny Hensel (1805–1847) & Felix Mendelssohn Bartholdy (1809–1847). Francine van der Heijden, soprano; Ursula Dutschler, fortepiano. Claves Records CD 50-9901, 2000.
Ave Maria
Cavatina. "Deh torna a me, mio sol rimena."
Liederkreis: An Felix während seiner ersten Abwesenheit in England 1829
Nachtwanderer (op. 7, no. 1)
Schwanenlied (op. 1, no. 1)
Three Songs on texts of Byron
Bright be the place of thy soul
There be none of Beauty's daughters
Farewell

Songs of Love, Nature and Romance [Felix Mendelssohn and Fanny Hensel] Carolin Masur, mezzo-soprano; Camelia Sima, piano. Klavier Records 11097, 2000.
An Suleika
Dämmrung senkte sich sich von oben
Harfners Lied
Wanderlied, "Von den Bergen zu den Hügeln" (op. 1, no. 2)
Wandrers Nachtlied I "Der du von dem Himmel bist"
Wandrers Nachtlied II "Übern allen Gipfeln ist Ruh"

Editorial Procedures

As described above, the manuscript versions of the following lieder do not represent the level of completeness at which Hensel would have published her work. In preparing these editions my primary goal was to preserve what Hensel had written down and to supplement only where absolutely necessary. Dynamic markings have not been added and only in a few instances have tempo markings been suggested.

When more than one draft of a lied survives, the musical text of this edition primarily follows the latest draft of the work (these are contained in Ms. 128). Earlier sources were consulted and in some instances incorporated in this edition. These occasions are noted in the commentary.

The lied texts have been written in modern German, and apostrophes that did not appear in Hensel's manuscript have been added without comment. Changes in punctuation have been noted. The text translation follows the word order as closely as possible, but not consistently, as I also aimed to depict the poem's general meaning. Many phrases are open to multiple interpretations. The word substitutions Hensel made to the original text have been noted.

The musical notation follows modern practice. Fanny Hensel often did not write out accidentals in all registers, or in both the piano and voice. Such accidentals have been added without mention. Sometimes it is unclear whether an accidental is intended to apply to an entire measure or just a single vertical sonority. In these instances the logical harmonic solution has been adopted and noted.

Editorial Comments

Ist es möglich

Staatsbibliothek zu Berlin—Preussischer Kulturbesitz, Mendelssohn-Archiv.
MA Ms. 35, p. 23, dated July 13, 1825 (holograph fair copy).

m. 5 D-natural on beat three is editorial. The punctuation for the first sentence of Goethe's poem is an exclamation point; Hensel omitted the punctuation in the manuscript, a neutral period has been added.

m. 11 Hensel changed the punctuation to an exclamation point. Goethe's text had a period.

m. 18 The accidental for Bb is not marked in the piano part.

In der stillen Mitternacht

Staatsbibliothek zu Berlin—Preussischer Kulturbesitz, Mendelssohn-Archiv.
MA Ms. 42, 36–43 dated February 26, 1835 (holograph working copy).
MA Ms. 128, 72–77 dated February 26, 1835 (holograph fair copy).

This edition is based on the fair copy, Ms. 128. Ms. 42, a working copy, contains many crossed out measures and revisions. Slight differences in accompaniment figuration exist. Ms. 42 was consulted for clarification, as noted below.

m. 17 Herder's text reads "Schmerz", which Hensel changed to "Gram".

m. 28 Herder's text reads "zu" in place of "um".

m. 29 Ms. 42 reads *p* on beat four in the soprano.

m. 31 Ms. 42 reads *p* on beat four in the soprano.

mm. 36-38 It is not clear if the slur in the piano extends to m. 38, but it probably should be performed as if it were to match the vocal phrasing.

m. 41 F-sharp on beat one in the piano RH may be a quarter-note in Ms. 128

m. 43 D-natural in LH from Ms. 42.

m. 79 *A tempo* is editorial.

Wenn der Frühling kommt

Staatsbibliothek zu Berlin—Preussischer Kulturbesitz, Mendelssohn-Archiv.
MA Ms. 42, 52-55 (holograph working copy).
MA Ms. 128, 82-85 (holograph fair copy).
Both manuscripts are dated Boulogne (France), August 24, 1835.

m. 3 Heine's text is "dann knospen" changed by Hensel to "so knospen".

m. 5 The RH's first chord is from Ms. 42. This is consistent with how the figure has been used elsewhere in the piece. It is shown as rolled in Ms. 128.

m. 7 Heine's text "dann schwimmen" appears in Ms. 42; Hensel changed it to "so schwimmen" in Ms. 128.

m. 9 A-natural on the last sixteenth-note of the measure is not marked in the piano part in either manuscript, but has been added editorially to match the vocal line and the secondary dominant function of the harmony.

m. 10 In Ms. 42 the chords on the sixth and seventh sixteenth-notes in the LH read from the bottom F-sharp-A-E (rather than F-sharp B-E).

m. 12 "dann", rather than "so" appears in Ms. 42.

m. 13 Editorial G-sharp has been added on the sixth eighth-note beat to match the harmonic function.

m. 23 Ms. 128 reads "Frühling kommt, mit dem Sonnenschein" while Ms. 42 does not have the interceding comma and reads "Frühling kommt mit dem Sonnenschein"; the song text here is without the comma.

m. 26 Heine's "dann quellen" changed by Hensel to "so quellen".

m. 29–32 The piano accompaniment is voiced differently in Ms. 42.

m. 33ff. Hensel rewrote the final two lines of Heine's poem replacing "Wie sehr das Zeug auch gefällt,/So macht's doch noch lang keine Welt" with "Sind allen nur tändelnder Scherz,/Und meine Welt ist dein liebendes Herz."

m. 37 The vocal slur in this measure has been taken from Ms. 42.

m. 39 Beaming in the vocal line follows Ms. 42, p. 55.

m. 42 Editorial A-natural on the last sixteenth-note (see m. 9 above).

m. 44 Editorial A-natural.

Zauberkreis

Staatsbibliothek zu Berlin—Preussischer Kulturbesitz, Mendelssohn-Archiv.
MA Ms. 86, 47-49 (working copy).

This lied is not dated, but is bound in a *Konvolut* with other compositions dating from 1843–44 (see Maurer, *Thematisches Verzeichnis,* 14, 15).

Slurs over the two-note appoggiatura figures that often occur at the end of the phrase and final syllable of each line of text are not consistently marked in the manuscript. The missing slurs have been added. The manuscript contains musical shorthand, which has been editorially expanded. Hensel partially wrote out the text for the repeat: only the first line of the poem's third strophe and the last line of its last strophe appear in the manuscript. She did recognize the syllabic symmetry between strophes 1–2 and 3–4, and the full text has been added by the editor.

m. 2 A repeat sign is not indicated in the manuscript suggesting the repeat is *da capo* back to m. 1. At the first ending (m. 30) the piano accompaniment is very similar to m. 1, suggesting that the repeat might have been intended to return to m. 2, where it is indicated in this edition. See Hensel's setting of *Suleika* (Fanny Hensel *Ausgewählte Lieder*, vol. 2) for a similar example.

m. 10 It is unclear whether the R.H. seventh eighth-note triplet is A^2 or C^3, probably C^3.

m. 12 This measure in the manuscript contains only three beats. The original rhythm read: dotted-quarter note followed by three eighth-notes.

m. 21 The G-natural, rather than G-sharp in the voice on beat four is an editorial addition; while it matches the harmony, it is uncertain what Hensel would have intended.

m. 24 In the manuscript a fermata appears in the vocal line both in m. 24 over the E-flat^2 and over the vocal rest in m. 25. The first fermata has been removed. The E-flat^2 was originally A^2, which Hensel crossed out.

m. 25 There is no indication of *a tempo* at any point after either the *poco ritenuto* in m. 15 or the *accelerando* in m. 21 leaving Hensel's intentions unclear. This leaves some performance flexibility; the *a tempo* at m. 25 is an editorial suggestion. Mm. 16 through 21 might be executed more slowly and the *accelerando* from mm. 21-25 could return to the original tempo starting with the anacrusis to m. 26.

***Ist es möglich* ***

Ist es möglich, Stern der Sterne,	Can it be, star of stars,
Drück' ich wieder dich ans Herz!	I press you again to my heart!
Ach! was ist die Nacht der Ferne	Ach! What an abyss, what pain,
Für ein Abgrund, für ein Schmerz.	is the night of separation!
Ja du bist es! meiner Freuden	Yes it is you, sweet,
Süsser, lieber Widerpart;	dear counterpart of my pleasure;
Eingedenk vergangner Leiden	Mindful of past grieving
Schaudr' ich vor der Gegenwart.	I shudder in the present.

* This first strophe (of six) of the poem entitled *Wiederfinden* (*Reunited*) is part of Goethe's *West-östlicher Divan* (Stuttgart: Cottaische Verlag, 1819).

In der stillen Mitternacht* from *Der Cid: Nach spanischen Romanzen*

Rodrigo:	
In der stillen Mitternacht, Wo nur Schmerz und Liebe wacht, Nah' ich mich hier, Weinende Chimene— Trockne deine Träne!— Zu dir	In the quiet midnight, Where only sorrow and love wake, I am approaching, Weeping Chimene— Dry your tears!— you.
Chimene:	
In der dunkeln Mitternacht, Wo mein tiefster Gram erwacht, Wer nahet mir?	In the dark midnight, Where my deepest sorrow awakes, Who is approaching?
Rodrigo:	
Vielleicht belauscht uns hier Ein uns feindselig Ohr. Eröffne mir—	Maybe there is, listening to us here, A hidden, hostile ear. Reveal yourself to me—
Chimene:	
Dem Ungenannten, Dem Unbekannten Eröffnet sich zu Mitternacht Kein Tor. **	To the unnamed, The unknown, No gate [fool] will open itself in the middle of the night
Enthülle dich; Wer bist du, sprich!	Reveal yourself; Who are you, speak!
Rodrigo:	
Verwaisete Chimene, Du kennest mich.	Orphaned Chimene, You do know me.
Chimene:	
Rodrigo, ja ich kenne dich; Du Stifter meiner Tränen, Der meinem Stamm sein edles Haupt, Der meinen Vater mir geraubt.	Rodrigo, yes I recognize you; You, cause of my tears, The one who robbed my people of its noble head, The one who robbed me of my father.
Rodrigo:	
Die Ehre tat's, nicht ich. Die Liebe will's versöhnen.	Honor did it, not I. Love wishes to reconcile it.
Chimene:	
Entferne dich! unheilbar ist mein Schmerz.	Go away, my pain cannot be healed.
Rodrigo:	
So schenk', o schenke mir dein Herz; Ich will es heilen.	So give, o give me your heart, I want to heal it.
Chimene:	
Wie? zwischen dir und meinem Vater, dir und ihm, mein Herz zu teilen?	How, between you and my father, You and him, divide my heart?

Rodrigo: Unendlich ist der Liebe Macht.	Endless is the power of love.
Chimene: Rodrigo, gute Nacht!	Rodrigo, good night!

*The text first appeared in 1805 (Tübingen: Cotta).
**The use of "Tor" in German has two meanings as "gate" or "fool".

Wenn der Frühling kommt

Wenn der Frühling kommt mit dem Sonnenschein, So knospen und blühen die Blümlein auf, Wenn der Mond beginnt seinen Strahlenlauf, So schwimmen die Sternlein hintendrein. Wenn der Sänger zwei süsse Äuglein sieht, Dann quellen ihm Lieder aus tiefem Gemüt. Doch Lieder und Sterne und Blümelein, Und Äuglein und Mondglanz und Sonnenschein, Sind allen nur tändelnder Scherz, Und meine Welt ist dein liebendes Herz.	When Spring arrives with its sunshine So bud and bloom the little flowers, When the moon begins its radiant path So the tiny little stars swim behind it. When the singer beholds two sweet little eyes, Then songs swell out of the depths of his heart. But, songs and stars and little flowers And eyes and moonlight and sunshine, All are only trifling pleasantry, And my world is your loving heart.

Zauberkreis *

Was steht denn auf den hundert Blättern Der Rose all? Was sagt denn tausendfaches Schmettern Der Nachtigall? Auf allen Blättern steht, was stehet Auf einem Blatt; Aus jedem Lied weht, was gewehet Im ersten hat: Dass Schönheit in sich selbst beschrieben Hat einen Kreis, Und keinen andern auch das Lieben Zu finden weiss. Drum kreist um sich mit hundert Blättern Die Rose all, Und um sie tausendfaches Schmettern Der Nachtigall.	What is written on the hundred petals Of the rose? What say then the thousand-fold warbles Of the nightingale? Upon all petals is written, what is written Upon one petal; Out of every song sounds, that which had resounded In the first: That beauty has made in itself A circle, And even Love Can find no other. Therefore the rose surrounds itself With a hundred petals, And around it the thousand-fold warbles Of the nightingale.

* This poem first appeared in 1822 in *Östlichen Rosen*, and in subsequent collections of Rückert's poetry.

Translations by Ruth A. Ochs

Ist es Möglich

Johann Wolfgang von Goethe

Fanny Mendelssohn Hensel
Ruth Ochs, editor

12
bist es mei-ner Freu - den sü-ßer, lie - ber Wi - der - part,

16
ein - ge-denk ver - gang - ner Lei - den, ein - ge-denk ver -
*

19
gang - ner Lei - den, schaudr' ich vor der Ge - gen - wart.

*This note F in the manuscript

In der stillen Mitternacht

from Der Cid: Nach Spanischen Romanzen

Johann Gottfried Herder

Fanny Mendelssohn Hensel

Ruth Ochs, editor

12
p
In der dun - keln Mit - ter -
p
trock - ne _ dei - ne Trä - ne, nah' ich mich hier zu dir,
16
cresc.
f
p
nacht, wo mein tief - ster Schmerz er - wacht, wer na-het mir?
p
in der
cresc.
f
p
20
in der dun - keln Mit - ter - nacht.
f
dun - keln Mit - ter - nacht. Viel-leicht be-lauscht uns hier ein uns feind - se-lig

24
p
cresc.
Dem Un - ge-nann-ten, dem Un - be-
Ohr, er-öff - ne mir–, er-öff - ne mir–,
28
f
dim.
kann-ten er-öff-net sich um Mit - ter - nacht kein Tor, ent-hül - le
p
er-öff - ne mir–,
32
f
dich, wer bist du, sprich!
cresc.
er-öff - ne mir–,
cresc.
f
pp

36
f
p
Rod -
Ver - wai - se - te Chi - me - ne, du ken - nest
40
vivace
ri - go, ja ich ken - ne dich, du Stif - ter mei - ner Trä -
mich.
f
43
cresc.
nen, der mei - nem Stamm sein ed - les Haupt, der mei - nen Va - ter mir ge -

46
dim.
raubt, der mei - nen Va - ter, mei - nen
f
dim.
49
p
Va - ter mir ge - raubt.
p
Die Eh - re tat's, nicht
52
ent -
cresc.
p
ich, die Lie - be will's ver - söh - nen,

55
fer - ne dich, un - heil - - - - - bar
58
ist mein Schmerz, un - heil - bar ist mein
so schen - ke mir, o schen - ke mir dein
61
Schmerz, un - heil - bar ist mein Schmerz.
Herz, o schen - ke, schen - ke mir dein Herz. Ich will es

64
f
Wie zwi-schen dir und mei - nem Va - ter, mein Herz zu tei-len, zwi-schen
hei - len, ich will es
67
dir und ihm, zwi-schen dir und mei - nem
hei - len, schenk', o schen - ke mir dein Herz, schenk', o
70
f
Va - ter, zwi-schen dir und mei - nem Va - ter mein
f
schen - ke mir dein Herz, Ich will, ich

73
dim.
Herz zu tei - len,
dim.
will es hei - len,
p
un - end - lich
p
76
pp
ritard.
[a tempo]
Rod - ri - go, gu - te Nacht!
ist der Lie - be Macht!
pp
80

Wenn der Frühling kommt

Heinrich Heine

Fanny Mendelssohn Hensel
Ruth Ochs, editor

Allegro di molto

Alto

Piano

Wenn der Früh - ling kommt_ mit dem Son - nen_

3

schein, so knos - pen und_ blü - hen_ die_ Blüm - lein_

5

auf, wenn der Mond_ be - ginnt_ sei-nen Strah - len -

7
lauf, so schwim - men die Stern - lein hin - ten -
9
drein. Wenn der Früh-ling kommt, mit dem Son-nen-schein, wenn der Mond be-ginnt sei-nen
11
Strah - len - lauf, so knos-pen und blü - hen die Blüm - lein
14
auf. Wenn der Sän - ger zwei - sü - ße Äug - lein

16
sieht, dann quel - len ihm Lei - der aus tie - fem Ge - müt. Wenn der
19
Sän - ger zwei sü - ße Äug - lein sieht, so quel - len ihm Lie - der aus
22
tie - fem Ge - müt. Wenn der Früh-ling kommt mit dem Son-nen-schein, wenn der
24
Mond be-ginnt sei-nen Strah-len-lauf, wenn der Sän - ger zwei sü - ße

26
Äug - lein sieht, so quel - len ihm Lie - der aus tie - fem Ge - müt.
29
Doch Lie - der und Ster - ne und Blü - me - lein und Äug - lein und
32
Mond-glanz und Son - nen - schein, sind al - len nur tän - deln - der
35
Scherz, und mei - ne Welt ist dein lie - ben - des Herz,

38
mei - ne Welt ist dein lie - ben-des,
41
lie - ben - des Herz, dein lie - ben - des
44
Herz, dein lie - - - - -
46
- - - - ben - des Herz.

Zauberkreis

Friedrich Rückert

Fanny Mendelssohn Hensel
Ruth Ochs, editor

10
[♮]
[♮]
Blät - tern der Ro - se all? Was sagt denn tau - send - fa - ches
schrie - ben hat ei - nen Kreis, und kei - nen an - dern auch das

13
poco riten.
Schmet - tern der Nach - ti - gall, der Nach - ti - gall? Auf al - len
Lie - ben zu fin - den weiß, zu fin - den weiß. Drum kreist um

16
[a tempo]
Blät - tern steht, was ste - het auf ei - nem Blatt, aus je - dem
sich mit hun - dert Blät - tern die Ro - se all, und um sie

19
accel.
cresc.
Lied weht, was ge - we - het im er - sten hat, auf al - len
tau - send - fa-ches Scmet - tern der Nach - ti - gall, drum kreist um
cresc.
6

22
f
Blät - tern steht, was ste - het auf ei - nem Blatt,
sich mit hun - dert Blät - tern die Ro - se all,
6
Ped.

25
[a tempo]
aus je - dem Lied weht, was ge - we - het im
und um sie tau - send - fa - ches Schmet - tern der

29
1.
2.
ers - ten hat,
Nach - ti -
gall,
und um sie
6
6

31
tau - send-fa-ches Schmet - tern der Nach - ti -
6

34
gall.
6

Maria Felicia Malibran

(1808–1836)

JAMÉE ARD

Maria Felicia García Malibran was born on March 24, 1808, the second child of singer, teacher, and composer Manuel Vicente del Popolo García (1775–1832) and his wife, singer María Joaquina Sitchès. Arriving in Paris barely a year before his debut in February 1808, they were nearly destitute despite his earlier triumphs in Naples as the colleague and collaborator of Gioacchino Rossini (1792–1868). García was an immediate success in Paris and he soon became the "leader of the troupe" at the Théâtre Italien.[1] The brilliant life of daughter Maria Felicia García Malibran (hereafter called Malibran) began blazing its path when she was very young and would, in its short span, take her to the major stages of London, New York, Paris, Naples, Milan, Bologna, and Rome. Her older brother, Manuel Patricio García (1805–1906), became a famed vocal pedagogue and her younger sister, Pauline (later Pauline García-Viardot; see this volume), was a composer, Ivan Turgenev's muse, and the inspiration for many composers of vocal works in the nineteenth century. Malibran was the archetypal prima donna during her own era and for decades beyond.

Malibran learned to read music before words and made her acting debut at the age of five in Ferdinando Paër's (1771–1839) *Agnese* at Naples Teatro Fiorentini, where she precociously prompted the prima donna who had forgotten her music.[2] At this time Malibran could speak four languages and was studying solfeggio and piano with Auguste Panseron (1795–1859) and Louis Hérold (1791–1833), both winners of the Prix de Rome. When the family returned to Paris, Malibran studied primarily with her father, although the relationship was fraught with bitterness and, at times, physical violence. According to Joaquina García, Malibran achieved her vocal skills through sheer will as her natural voice was limited in range and she often sang with such poor intonation that it was thought she was tone deaf.[3] However, at age fifteen Malibran sang the contralto role in Rossini's *Penalver Cantata* before the members of her father's prestigious musical circle in Paris, displaying not only her musical talents but a vivacious stage presence which was as much her trademark as her vocal abilities.

In 1825 Malibran joined her family on a trip to the United States. García brought the first Italian opera company to the United States, a troupe that performed Rossini's *Il barbiere di Siviglia*, *Tancredi*, and *Otello*, as well as García's own *L'Amate Astuto*. In all the productions, Malibran was the leading female singer and was soon touted by both press and audiences in New York City.

On March 14, 1825 (shortly before her eighteenth birthday), while still in the United States, Malibran married François Eugène Malibran (b. 1781), a union that allowed her to escape the tempestuous relationship with her father. François Eugène Malibran, the son of a French father and a Spanish mother, had come to New York from Paris to run an import-export company, shipping his brother's produce from Cuba to the United States and Europe. García agreed to accept the marriage only after François Eugène Malibran agreed to pay him $50,000 for the loss of a daughter and prima donna.[4]

Malibran began to live the life of a society wife. By the end of 1826, however, the unstable economic climate forced her husband to default on large loans, propelling Malibran back to the stage where she garnered some of the highest fees ever paid a performer in America.[5] Despite her growing renown and offers for concerts in Philadelphia and Baltimore, economic pressures from her husband's burgeoning debts forced Malibran to return to Paris where she commanded even higher fees.

Six weeks after her arrival in Paris, Malibran received an offer from Rossini to perform with the Paris Opéra. After a competing offer from the other Paris company, the Théâtre Italien, she made her debut on April 8, 1828, at the Italien in a production of *Semiramide*. Merely twenty years old, Malibran had the opera world of Paris at her feet, clamoring for her audacious acting and supple voice.

In the summer of 1829 Malibran returned to London for her first appearance in four years in a brilliant season that included performances of arias and duets by Rossini. She composed the embellishments and cadenzas for the arias; they were published later that year by Ignaz Moscheles (1794–1870) as *Gems à la Malibran*.

Malibran fell in love with Charles de Bériot (1802–1870), a violinist and another European musical celebrity, while she was performing at the chateau of the Princess de Chimay in Belgium in

1829. She turned to Louis Viardot, the future husband of her younger sister, Pauline, to help extricate herself from her failed marriage to Eugène. Because the French courts refused to dissolve those contracts made in the United States, and the courts in the United States refused to rule on a union made before a French consul,[6] she attempted to create a new divorce law. In the summer of 1831, still married to Eugène Malibran, she became pregnant by de Bériot. However, she maintained her performing schedule until January 1832 when she retired to await the birth of her first child, a girl who died shortly after birth. Vowing not to sing in Paris again until she was "Madame de Bériot," Malibran and de Bériot left for Brussels and Italy, where she made her debut at the Teatro Valle in Rome as Desdemona in Rossini's *Otello*. While there she learned of the death of her father on June 9, 1832. Despite the turmoil of their relationship, Malibran wrote "if my father had not been so severe with me I would not have done anything well. I was lazy and stubborn – a real gypsy."[7]

During her stay in Italy Malibran became pregnant with her second child by de Bériot, forcing her to cancel the contract for her debut at La Scala. Returning to Brussels, she gave birth to a son, Charles Wilfred de Bériot. In April of 1833 Malibran, de Bériot, and Charles moved to London and while in England, Malibran regularly appeared at the English music festivals in such cities as Gloucester, Chester, and Birmingham. Wherever she appeared, Malibran performed her own songs, accompanying herself on the piano, harp or guitar. Her own compositions were often published in the cities where she performed. When the season closed in London in October of 1833, Malibran and Charles left for Naples. Her performance there in *Norma* by Vincenzo Bellini (1801–1835) so moved Hans Christian Andersen, who was in the audience, that he immortalized her in his book *The Improvisatore*.

After a wait of seven years, on March 29, 1836, Malibran finally became Mme de Bériot. In July, during the London opera season, Malibran, who was then three months pregnant, joined a hunting party and while riding was thrown and dragged by her horse. Despite the pleas of her friends, she performed at the opera that evening. During the next three months, she continued to make public appearances rather than care for the injuries whose effects had escalated into extreme headaches and personality changes. On Friday, September 23, 1836, at the age of twenty-eight, she died from her wounds. The city elders of Manchester refused Charles de Bériot's numerous requests to return Malibran's remains to Belgium for burial. This conflict was a subject of international debate until her mother went to Manchester in December 1836 and had her daughter's body exhumed in secret and transported back to Belgium where it was interred in the cemetery at Laeken. The mausoleum erected in her honor contains a statue by Guillaume Geefs of Malibran as Norma.[8]

Composition was a natural outlet for members of the prodigiously creative García family; both sisters and the father were prolific composers. A study of Malibran's songs is a labyrinth of titles and publishers. It was a common practice during her time to sell a song for publication in Paris and then sell the same song, perhaps in a different translation, to another publisher in Germany, London or Naples.

Most of Malibran's compositions are *romances*, a genre that was very popular and common in early nineteenth-century France. The vocal lines are limited in range, unadorned, and naive. With subordinate accompaniment, the texture is sparse.

Published posthumously, the song *Il Silfo*, included here, is a through-composed arietta on a text by the Marquis Bocella. Although its accompaniment is simple and consists mainly of arpeggiated chords, the vocal line has daring flashes of *fioratura* and lies in a high *tessitura*, indicating that this piece was for an accomplished singer and not for the amateurs that flocked to the *romances*. Harmonically, *Il Silfo* moves boldly from the dominant of its opening F major to A-flat major before returning to the original key. With its singular sophistication, *Il Silfo* illustrates a compositional style Malibran might have developed further had it not been for her untimely death.

Notes

1. François-Joseph Fétis, *Biographie universelle des musiciens et bibliographie générale de la musique,* vol. 3. (Paris: Librarie de Firmin Didot et Cie., 1875–1883), 404.

2. April Fitzlyon, *Maria Malibran, Diva of the Romantic Age.* London: Souvenir Press 1987, 3.

3. Ibid., 4.

4. Henry Malherbe, *La Passion de la Malibran* (Paris: A. Michel, 1937), 247.

5. Howard Bushnell, *Maria Malibran* (University Park: Pennsylvania State University, ca. 1979), 35.

6. Maria de las Mercedes Merlin, *Memoirs and Letters of Maria Malibran,* vol. 1 (London: H. Colburn, 1844), 152.

7. Anna Eugénie Schoen-René, *America's Music Inheritance* (New York: G. P. Putnam Sons), 114.

8. Bellini's Druid Princess became significant to both the daughters of Manuel García in life as well as death. "Norma" was said to be the last word of Pauline Viardot-Garcia on her deathbed.

List of Works

Addio a Nice. Text by Metastasio. Los Angeles: The Malibran Society, n.d.

Les Adieux d'un brave. Text by Mr. Zacharie. Paris: Chez Garcia, ca. 1820.

Album lyrique. Paris: Troupenas, 1831; New York: Da Capo Press, 1984.
1. *Le Réveil d'un beau jour*. Text by Ambroise Bétourné
2. *La Voix qui dit: je t'aime*. Text by Sylvain Blott
3. *Le Village*. Text by Mr. Zacharie fils
4. *La Tarantelle*. Text by Ambroise Bétourné
5. *Les Refrains*. Text by Ambroise Bétourné
6. *Rataplan*. No author listed
7. *La Bayadère*. Text by Ambroise Bétourné
8. *La Résignation*. Text by Ambroise Bétourné
9. *Le Ménestrel*. Text by Alex Duponchel
10. *Row, Boys!* [English and French text, no author listed]
11. *Le Ratelier*. Duet. No author listed
12. *Le Rendez-vous*. Duet. Text by Ambroise Bétourné
13. *Belle, Viens à moi*. Duet. Text by Marceline Desbordes-Valmore
14. *Le Lutin*. Duet. No author listed

An die Nachtigallen. See *La Voix qui dit: Je t'aime* in *Album Lyrique*.

Belle, Viens à moi. French words by Marceline Desbordes Valmore. Los Angeles: The Malibran Society, n.d.

Dernières Pensées. Milan: B. Girard, 1837.
1. *Il mattino*. Poet unknown

Dernières pensées. Paris: Troupenas, 1839.
1. *La Fiancée du brigand*. Text by Ambroise Bétourné
2. *Le Message*. Text by Émile Deschamps
3. *Prière à la Madone*. Text by le Marquis de Louvois
4. *Hymne des matelots*. No author given
5. *Les Noces d'un marin*. Text by Ambroise Bétourné
6. *Au bord de la mer*. Text Émile Deschamps
7. *Adieu à Laure*. Text trans. Émile Deschamps
8. *Addio a Nice*. Text by Pietro Metastase
9. *Le Montagnard*. Text by Ambroise Bétourné
10. *Les Brigands*. Text by F. Géraldi
11. *La Morte*. Text by Antonio Benelli

The Drummer. See *Rataplan* in *Album Lyrique*.

L'Écossais. Text by A. Bétourné. Paris: G. Brandus, Dufour et Cie., (1855?); Los Angeles: The Malibran Society, n.d.

En soupirant. London: Mori & Lavenu, (1830?).

Entends-tu les gondoles? London: S. Chappell, 1860. See *Belle, Viens à moi* in *Album Lyrique*.

La Fête du village. Text by Mr. Zacharie. Paris: Chez Garcia, ca. 1820.

Heart-Wounding Cares. See *Le Retour de la Tyrolienne*.

L'Indifférence. London: Mori & Lavenu, (1830?).

J'étais sur la rive fleurie. London: Mori & Lavenu, (1830?).

Lève-toi jeune enfant. See *Le Réveil d'un beau jour* in *Album Lyrique*.

Le Message. Text by M. Émile Deschamps. Los Angeles: The Malibran Society, n.d.

La Morte (Le Moribund). Text by Benelli, trans.into French by Émile Deschamps. Los Angeles: The Malibran Society, n.d.

Le Prisonnier. Text by Pierre-Jean Béranger. Paris: Pacini, n.d.

Le Retour de la Tyrolienne. Text by Mr. Loraux de Ronsière. Paris: Chez Cosmar et Krause, (1820?); Los Angeles: The Malibran Society, n.d. *

Rouse Thee Up, Shepherd Boy! See *Le Réveil d'un Beau Jour* in *Album Lyrique*.

Le Sommeil. Text by Mr. Zacharie fils. New York: Debois & Stodart, n.d.; Los Angeles: The Malibran Society, n.d.

Spread Thy Wings and Away! See *Le Message* in *Dernières pensées*.

Ständchen. See *Belle, Viens à moi* in *Album lyrique*.

Strike, Strike the Lute. See *Le Retour de la Tyrolienne*.

Schwing dich auf, Hirtenknab. See *Le Réveil d'un beau jour* in *Album Lyrique*.

Songs and Duets of Garcia, Malibran and Viardot. New York: Alfred Publishing, Co., Inc., 1997.
1. *Il Mattino*. Author of text unknown
2. *La Voix qui dit: je t'aime*. Text by Sylvain Blot
3. *Le Prisonnier*. Text by Pierre-Jean Béranger

There is No Home Like My Own. London: D'Almaine & Co., (1840?). See *Le Reveil d'un beau jour* from *Album Lyrique*.

'Tis the Gondolas' Sound. See *Belle, Viens à moi* in *Album lyrique*.

The Tyrolese Girl. See *Le Retour de la Tyrolienne*.

The Tyrolese Maiden's Song. See *Le Retour de la Tyrolienne*.

Tyroliennes and *Barcarolles*. Paris: Troupenas, 1828.

Variazioni di bravura. Milan and Turin: Lucca, n.d.

Der Wassergeist. See *Notre Grande Mère*.

Zapfenstreich. See *Rataplan* in *Album Lyrique*.

* Published as *Heart Wounding Cares*, London: Birchall & Co., 1825. Also published in 1829 as a ballad by F. T. Latour in London. An additional version entitled *Strike, Strike the Lute* was sung by Madame Elizia Vestris in the musical farce *Sublime and Beautiful*. Published as *The Tyrolese Maiden's Song* in *The Musical Bijou for 1837* (pages 42–45) without the refrain. (See *Le Retour de la Tyrolienne* published by The Malibran Society, 2508 Medlow Avenue, Los Angeles, California.)

Bibliography

Association des Amis d'Ivan Tourgueniev, Pauline Viardot et Maria Malibran. *Cahiers Ivan Tourgueniev, Pauline Viardot et Maria Malibran*. Paris: UNESCO, 1977– .

Berlioz, Hector. "Revue critique: Dernières pensées musicales de Marie Félicité Garcia de Bériot," *Revue et gazette musicale* 2 (July 1837): 228–99.

Bernardi, G.G. "La Malibran a Venezia," *Musica d'Oggi* (August-September 1936): 269–75.

Bushnell, Howard. *Maria Malibran: a Biography of the Singer*. University Park: Pennsylvania State University Press, ca. 1979.

Castil-Blaze [Françoise Henri Joseph Blaze], "Revue du monde musical; Mme Malibran–Fin," *Revue de Paris* 34 (1836): 63-69, 139-45.

Cottinet, Edmond. "Maria Malibran & Alfred de Musset," *Les Lettres et les Arts* 4 (1889): 91–100.

Curtis, John. "A Century of Grand Opera in Philadelphia," *The Pennsylvania Magazine of History and Biography* 44 (1920): 122–57.

Desternes, Suzanne, and Henriette Chandet. *La Malibran et Pauline Viardot*. Paris: Fayard, 1969.

Engel, Carl. "Again Lafayette and Maria-Felicia Malibran," *The Chesterian*, January-February (1925): 105–10.

Fétis, François. *Biographie universelle des musiciens et bibliographie générale de la musique*. Paris: Librairie de Firmin Didot et Cie., 1875–1883.

Fischer-Dieskau, Dietrich. *Wenn Musik der Liebe Nahrung ist*. Stuttgart: Deutsch Verlags–Abstalt, 1990.

Fitzlyon, April. *Maria Malibran, Diva of the Romantic Age*. London: Souvenir Press , 1987.

_____. *The Price of Genius*. London: John Calder, 1964.

Flamant, Albert. *Une étoile en 1830, La Malibran*. Paris: P. Lafitte, ca.1928.

Gara, Eugenio. "Maria Felicita Malibran," *La Scala* (December 15, 1951): 39–44; (January 15, 1952): 29–35.

Héritte-Viardot, Louise. *Memories and Adventures*. Translated by E. S. Bucheim. London: Mills & Boon, Ltd., 1913.

Heron–Allen, Edward. "A Contribution toward an Accurate Biography of Charles Auguste de Bériot and Maria Felicia Malibran–Garcia." London: J. W. Wakeham, 1894.

Julien, Adolphe. "Maria Malibran," *L'Art*, vol. 2, series 3 (1902): 305–16.

Lafayette, Marie Joseph Paul Yves Roch Gilbert Du Motier. "Six Unpublished Letters from Lafayette to Maria Malibran," *The Chesterian* (March-April 1926): 147–50.

Levien, John. *Six Sovereigns of Song*. London: Novello & Co., 1948.

Malherbe, Henry. *La Passion de la Malibran*. Paris: A. Michel, 1937.

Merlin, Maria de las Mercedes. *Memoirs and Letters of Maria Malibran*. London: H. Colburn, 1840.

Monaldi, Gino. "Giudetta Pasta e Maria Malibran," *Nuova Antologia* (July–August 1903): 100–106.

Nathan, Isaac. *Memoirs of Madame Malibran-de Bériot*. London: J. Thomas, 1836.

Paliotti, Vittorio. *Maria Malibran, casta diva scandalosa*. Naples: F. Pagano, ca. 1992.

Pontmartin, Armand. "The Bath of Madame Malibran," *Overland Monthly* (August 1892): 214–18.

Pougin, Arthur. *Marie Malibran*. London: Eveleigh Nash, 1911.

Prod'homme, Jacques G. "Lafayette and Maria–Felicia Malibran," *The Chesterian* (September 1919): 17–20.

Teneo, Martial. "La Malibran après des documents inédits," *Sammelbände der Internationalen Musik-Gesellschaft* 7 (1905–1906): 437–82.

Discography

Adkins Chiti, Patricia, mezzo-soprano, and Gian Paolo Chiti, pianist. Kicco K00793 0 (1995). *Morirò* and *Chanson de L'Infante*.

Adkins Chiti, Patricia, mezzo-soprano, and Gian Paolo Chiti, pianist. Kicco K6370 4 (1985). *Parad!* and *Le Courrier*.

Adkins Chiti, Patricia, mezzo-soprano, and Gian Paolo Chiti, pianist. European Network Production (1992).

Adkins Chiti, Patricia, mezzo-soprano, and Gian Paolo Chiti, pianist. RAI TRE (1996).

From a Woman's Perspective. Katherine Eberle, mezzo-soprano, and Robin Guy, pianist. Vienna Modern Masters (1993). *Les Brigands* and *La Morte*.

Il Silfo

Oh pietoso il Silfo accogio Bella dama del castello. Od il Silfo poverello, Sulla soglia spirerò M'apri, ah m'apri.	Oh beautiful lady of the castle Receive the tender sylph.* Otherwise the poor sylph Will pass away on the threshold. Open me, ah, open me.
E già notte freddo il vento Che sarà se mi ricusi. E già notte, i fiori sono chiusi E nessuno m'accoglieva Apri, apri, ah m'apri.	It is already night, The wind will be cold if you refuse me. It is already night, the flowers are closed And nobody received me. Open me, ah, open me.
Hai di me forse spavento? Sono gentile ho l'ali d'oro. Di profumi io sono tesoro Sono più lieve del sospiro. M'apri, m'apri ah m'apri.	Are you afraid of me? I am kind, I have golden wings. I am a perfume's treasure I am lighter than breath. Open me, ah, ah open me.

* A sylph in German mythology is a somewhat devilish being that lives in the air. They are said to inflict illness on humans and animals.

Translation by Silvia Fubini

Il Silfo

M. Le Marquis Bocella

Maria Malibran de Beriot

Jamée Ard, editor

Andante (♩ = 76)

p

6

p

Oh pie -

11

to - so il Sil - fo ac co - gli Bel - la da - ma

16

del cas - tel - - - lo Od il Sil - fo po - ve -

21
rel - - lo sul - la so - glia spi - re - rò
26
m'a - - - - - - pri Ah
31
m'a - - - - - - pri m'a - -
36
- - pri ah m'a - pri m'a - pri

41
m'a-pri
E già not - te, e fred - do il ven - to
46
che sa-rà, se mi ri - cu - si
E già
51
not - te, i fior son chiu - si i fior son chiu - si
56
E nes-sun m'ac-co - glie - va a-pri
p
cresc.

61
a-pri
ah
m'a - - - - - pri
66
hai di me for - se spa ven - to son gen -
[p]
71
til ho l'a - li d'o - - ro Di pro - fu - mi io
76
son te - so - ro son più lie - ve del sos -

81
pir
m'a - pri m'a - pri m'a -
86
pri
ah
m'a - pri
91
m'a - pri m'a - pri m'a - - pri
95
ah
m'a - pri
f
f
f
f

Loïsa Puget
(1810–1889)

Sondra Wieland Howe

Loïsa Puget (Louise Françoise), French composer and singer, was born in Paris on February 11, 1810. She studied with her mother, a singer, and with the French composer Adolphe Adam (1803–1856). She wrote over three hundred *romances* that appeared in editions in French, German, and English; most on texts written by Gustave Lemoine (1802–1885), an actor and author whom she married in 1842. The *romances* were also published in piano arrangements. Puget died on November 27, 1889, in Pau in the Basses-Pyrénées. Although there is very little available information on her life, many of her compositions have survived.[1] (Many of Puget's songs are now located in the Women Composers Collection at the University of Michigan.)

Puget's *romances* have simple, attractive melodies and humble, sentimental texts. She published these in illustrated volumes annually between 1830 and 1854. A successful concert and salon singer in Paris from 1832 to 1842, Puget sang her songs in the salons on the rue Saint-Denis, in pensions for young women, and in convents.[2]

In addition to *romances*, Puget wrote two operettas. *Le mauvais oeil*, an *opéra comique* in one act, libretto by Eugène Scribe and Gustave Lemoine, was performed at the Théâtre Royal de L'Opéra Comique on October 1, 1836. *La veilleuse, ou les nuits de milady*, an operetta in one act, text by Gustave Lemoine, was performed at the Théâtre du Gymnase in Paris on September 27, 1869. Puget knew the stars of the Paris Opéra and the Opéra Comique; they may have sung her *romances* in concert in addition to performing in her operettas. Puget also wrote several solo piano works including *Mystère de Paris*, a set of quadrilles for four hands.[3]

Puget's music received conflicting comments in the mid-nineteenth century. François Fétis (1864) wrote, "The romances of Mademoiselle Puget have a tenderness, a little ordinary as a matter of fact, but of an agreeable turn; her popular songs have a liveliness and gaiety."[4] Pietro Scudo (1806–1864) in 1856 commented on the ten-year success of Puget, and her many *romances* depicting the life of middle-class people. He aligned her with the group of French composers that included Daniel-François Auber (1782–1871) and Adolphe Adam (1803–1856).

> It is not only the passion or imagination that shines in the work of Mademoiselle Puget. That which distinguishes her talent is a pleasant sensibility restrained by good sense, of frankness, and much of that malicious gaiety which has created vaudeville. . . . By the style of her easy flowing melodies and good rhythms, by the fluency and correctness of her accompaniments, by the liveliness and gaiety of her spirit, Mademoiselle Loïsa Puget belongs to that family of pleasant composers of whom M. Auber is the glorious leader, and which counts M. Adam among its most famous notabilities.[5]

Puget could effectively describe the ordinary events of common people. Scudo continued:

> She set to music the little events of the life of the middle class, the restraint of desires, contentment of the heart in a humble condition, peace, innocence, love of work and a resignation towards Providence, who watches over the poor child and gives food to young birds.[6]

Frits Noske wrote in 1954 that Charles Gounod found the salons a disgusting phenomenon and made disparaging comments about the *romances* of Puget.

> The *Romance Puget, L'Album musical* has, in a word, reached its highest level of brutalizing influence. It pleases me little, as you may imagine. Although such epidemics are insufficient to kill art, they still destroy too many ears that might perhaps be destined to hear "the good voice." How unfortunate that one cannot prevent weeds from growing.[7]

Puget received further unfavorable comments when Noske compared her *romances* to Schubert's songs: "After you have feasted on this bountiful and satisfying music [Schubert song], try if you can fall back on the twittering of Mlle. Puget; it is impossible."[8] However, Puget's *romances* must be understood in her time period.

The eighteenth-century *romance* is a lyrical, strophic poem of love, set to music with simplicity of expression and simple accompaniment. By 1800 the *romance* was a very popular genre with historical, pastoral, or sentimental texts, and had become a specialty of the composers Antoine Romagnési (1781–1850) and Pauline Duchambge (ca. 1778–1858; see vols. 4 and 5). In addition to Duchambge, other women composers of *romances* in the late eighteenth and early nineteenth centuries included Mademoiselle Florine Dezède (no dates available), Mademoiselle Lucile Grétry (1772–1790), and Amélie Julie Candeille (1767–1834; see vols. 4 and 5). Hortense de Beauharnais (1783–1837), wife of Louis Bonaparte, King of Holland, composed *romances* and also encouraged artists, poets, and musicians in her Paris salon. It was her idea to include illustrations for songs in published albums.[9]

From 1830 to 1848, during the reign of Louis Philippe, *romances* remained fashionable. They were commercially valuable for both composers and publishers. Albums appeared at the end of each year, sometimes serving as bonuses for subscribers to musical journals. Most editions had illustrations, often by well-known artists. By the middle of the nineteenth century, the *romance* had given way to the *mélodie*, which was a more dramatic form in which French song writers used complex harmonies and set more elaborate texts.[10]

An analysis of three *romances* from *Douze romances* (Twelve Romances) will show how Puget's pleasant melodies and careful setting of Lemoine's texts effectively described the concerns of the French middle class in the early nineteenth century. The collection was published in Paris (1840?) by the firm of J. Meissonnier (1783–1857) on 22 rue Dauphine.[11] Established in Paris in 1812 as a publisher of light music, in 1839 the firm joined the company of Jacques Léopold Heugel (1815–1883). Heugel, still in existence today, was then known for its illustrated albums of popular songs. Puget published with both the Meissonnier and Heugel firms, as well as with Schott and Schlesinger in Berlin.[12]

The volume of *Douze romances* is dedicated to Her Majesty, Marie Amélie de Bourbon, Queen of France. The texts by Puget's husband, Gustave Lemoine, are illustrated with sketches by Mrs. Deveria Grenier and Jules David. Each song is dedicated to a different person.

The *romances* begin with opening refrains, followed by several *couplets* (verses). The piano parts offer introductions and interludes, and accompany the vocal lines with *ostinati*, solid and broken chords, sometimes doubling the melody. The musical style is usually simple with stepwise or triadic melodies. There are interpretive markings and some ornamentation; the soloist may add further ornaments in the passages marked *ad libitum*.

The romances display the wide variety of subjects typical of this genre. Some songs are sad and religious. *Matines* (Matins) depicts people praying in a garden. In *Plus de mère!* (No More Mother!) an orphan is crying and begging outside a church. In *L'Aigle* (The Eagle) an eagle takes a child away while the mother sleeps, but the child is returned when the mother prays to Mary. The love and joys of the young are portrayed in *Belle pour lui!* (Beautiful for Him!), *Jeune fille, à quinze ans* (Young Girl of Fifteen), *Et moi, toi!* (And Me, You!), and the marriage proposal of *La chanson du charbonnier* (The Song of the Coalman). Other songs recall the past: *Souviens-toi!* (Do you Remember?) and the lonely fisherman in *Le pêcheur Breton* (The Fisherman of Breton). Some songs tell of foreign lands: *La bayadère* (The Indian Dancing Girl), *Nanna la Créole* (Nanna the Creole), and *La Retraite* (The Retreat).

Belle pour lui! included here, is dedicated to Madame la Csse. De Sparre. A young girl named Marie tells how she wants to please her boyfriend by being very beautiful for him tonight. The illustration in the original publication shows a girl in a long dress, putting a flower in her hair. The lively piano introduction sets a happy mood with the bolero rhythm of an eighth note followed by two sixteenth notes in $\frac{3}{4}$ meter. The song, in C major, opens with an unresolved D7 chord (V/V), moves to an F minor chord (iv), and returns to the tonic, C major. The vocal refrain is a simple stepwise melody. The word "belle" (pretty or beautiful) is elaborated with sixteenth notes. At measures 14–16 the words "lui plaire aujourd'hui" (to please him today) are emphasized with a trill, as the harmony modulates briefly to E minor (vi). This passage is marked *ad libitum*, freeing the singer to add more ornamentation or to stretch the rhythm. The refrain has a simple chordal accompaniment, with tonic and dominant chords over a tonic pedal. The interlude is a repeat of the introductory material.

The vocal range of the three verses spans an eleventh, with many sixteenth notes and grace notes. Small leaps in the melody (mm. 40–46) culminate in an ascending leap of an octave (m. 47) for "Marie est Reine" (Marie is Queen). Each verse begins in G major over a tonic pedal and a broken chord accompaniment. The second half of the verse is in C major with some secondary dominant chords; the verse ends on the dominant before the song returns to the refrain.

The second work, *La chanson du charbonnier ou Blanc et noir* (The Song of the Coalman or White and Black), dedicated to a Monsieur Chaudesaigues, is a humorous song about a coalman who wants to marry Suzanne, the daughter of his neighbor, a miller. The miller emphatically says "non" many times. He makes insulting remarks about the coalman and contrasts his dirty, black appearance with the white color of his daughter's skin. (Perhaps he is discriminating against the social class of the coalman, thinking that the occupation of selling black coal is beneath that of a miller selling white flour.) The coalman is persistent as he persuades the miller that charcoal is essential for the miller's ovens. He praises the miller for being a good father and offers him a cask of good wine. The miller suddenly changes his mind and says the coalman is a handsome man whom he wants in his family. A deal has been made. The illustration shows the coalman and miller seated at a table, with Suzanne standing behind her father and smiling at her lover.

The song opens with a lively piano introduction in A minor and $\frac{6}{8}$ meter, reminiscent of a tarantella. The coalman begins the refrain with a descending stepwise melody, repeating an octave leap before the miller answers with the same melody. The octave leaps compare a sack of flour with a sack of charcoal and the miller sings a long string of "nons." An interlude based on the introductory material follows. This section is in A minor with i, iv and V unbroken triads.

The beginning of each verse changes mood with a simple melody that outlines a C chord, followed by stepwise motion. The verse modulates to E minor as the conversation becomes more animated and ends in A minor before returning to the refrain.

Jeune fille, à quinze ans (A Young Girl of Fifteen), dedicated to Madame J. Colon-Leplus, tells the story of a pretty young girl who thinks she will always be young in a world of gentle springs and days of festivals. The writer of the text reminds her she will not always be young. The illustration shows a young girl holding flowers.

Broken chords accompany the piano introduction melody in the right hand. The refrain begins with the same melody describing the young girl who sings like a lark and enjoys the gentle spring. The first half of the refrain is harmonically static with broken tonic and dominant chords over a tonic (C major) pedal. In the second half of the refrain, the author cynically comments that the poor young girl naively believes life will always be festive. Here the melody includes leaps and ornaments ending with an optional descending passage, followed by some chromatic chords. The interlude recapitulates the simple introductory material.

The melody for the verses is more elaborate, containing sixteenth notes, trills, and a final chromatic passage. The verse is in E minor, the refrain in C major. The final refrain has some text changes and the melody is more complex.

Notes

1. Judy S. Tsou, "Puget, Loïsa," in *The Norton/Grove Dictionary of Women Composers,* ed. Julie Anne Sadie and Rhian Samuel (New York and London: W. W. Norton, 1995), 378–79; and "Puget, Loïsa," in *The New Grove Dictionary of Music and Musicians*, ed. Stanley Sadie (London: Macmillan, 1980).

2. Pietro Scudo, "Esquisse d'une histoire de la romance," *Critique et littérature musicales,* 3rd ed. (Paris: Librarie de L. Hachette et Cie, 1856), 349.

3. Tsou, "Puget, Loïsa," *Norton/Grove Dictionary*.

4. "Puget, Loïsa," in *Biographie universelle de musiciens*, ed. François Fétis, vol. 7 (Paris: Firmin Didot Frères, 1964), 137. Les romances de mademoiselle Puget ont de la tendresse, un peu bourgeoise à la vérité, mais d'un tour agréable; ses chansonnettes ont de l'entrain et de la gaieté.

5. Scudo, "Esquisse," 350–51. Ce n'est donc pas la passion ni la fantaisie qui brillent dans l'oeuvre de mademoiselle Puget. Ce qui caractérise son talent, c'est une sensibilité douce tempérée de bon sens, de la rondeur et beaucoup de cette gaieté maligne qui a créé le vaudeville. . . . Par le genre de ses mélodies faciles et bien rhythmées, par la facilité et la correction de ses accompagnements, par l'entrain et la gaieté de son esprit, mademoiselle Loïsa Puget appartient à cette famille de compositeurs aimables dont M. Auber est le glorieux chef, et qui compte M. Adam parmi ses plus illustres notabilités.

6. Ibid., 349. Elle se mit à chanter les petits épisodes de la vie bourgeoise, la modération des désirs, le contentement du coeur dans une humble condition, la paix, l'innocence, l'amour du travail et la résignation à la Providence, qui veille sur l'enfant du pauvre et donne la pâture aux petits des oiseaux.

7. Frits Noske, *French Song from Berlioz to Duparc,* trans. Rita Benton (New York: Dover Publications Inc., 1970), 171.

8. Ibid., 34.

9. Scudo, "Equisse," 338-40.

10. Noske, *French Song,* 1-5, 7-8.

11. Transcription of the songs has been made from microfilm of *Douze romances* (1840?), from the Women Composers Collection (WCC 1139) at the University of Michigan.

12. Robert S. Nichols, in *The New Grove Dictionary of Music and Musicians*, ed. Stanley Sadie (London: Macmillan, 1980).

Selected List of Works

Song Collections

(Located in the Women's Music Collection, University of Michigan.)

Album. Text by Gustave Lemoine. Paris: J. Meissonnier, 1838.

Album lyrique composé de douze romances & chansonnettes. Text by Gustave Lemoine. Paris: J. Messonnier, (184–?).

Anthology of Songs. (Reprint of ten songs by Pauline Duchambge, Loïsa Puget, Pauline Viardot, Jane Vieu.) Introduction by Susan C. Cook and Judy S. Tsou. New York: Da Capo Press, 1988.

Collection des romances. Text by Gustave Lemoine. Paris: J. Meissonnier, (1840?).

Douze mélodies ou chansonnettes, par Melle. Loïsa Puget. Text by Gustave Lemoine. Paris: J. Meissonnier, (184–?).

Douze romances. Text by Gustave Lemoine. Paris: J. Meissonnier, (1840?).

Douze romances: pour une voix avec accompagnement de pianoforte. Text by Gustave Lemoine. Berlin: Schlesinger, (1840?).

Six nouvelles romances de Loïsa Puget. Text by Gustave Lemoine. Paris: A. Meissonnier, Heugel et Cie., (184–?)

Album de Melle. L. Puget. Text by Gustave Lemoine. Paris: J. Meissonier, 1840, 1842.

Album. Text by Gustave Lemoine. Paris: Heugel et Cie., 1844.

Album 1847 par L. Puget et Étienne Arnaud. Texts by Mrs. Gustave Lemoine, E. Baroteau, and Eugène de Lonlay. Paris: A. Meissonier et Heugel, 1847.

Opera

(Located in the Library of Congress.)

Le mauvais oeil. Opéra comique in one act. Text by Eugène Scribe and Gustave Lemoine. Paris: J. Meissonier, (1836?).

La veilleuse, ou Les nuits de mylady. Operetta in one act. Text by Gustave Lemoine. Paris: Heugel et Cie., (1869?).

Bibliography

Cook, Susan C., and Judy S. Tsou. Introduction to *Anthology of Songs* by Pauline Duchambge, Loïsa Puget, Pauline Viardot, Jane Vieu. New York: Da Capo Press, 1988.

Nichols, Robert S. "Heugel." In *The New Grove Dictionary of Music and Musicians,* edited by Stanley Sadie. London: Macmillan, 1980.

Noske, Frits. *French Song from Berlioz to Duparc.* Translated by Rita Benton. New York: Dover Publications Inc., 1970.

"Puget, Loïsa." In *Biographie universelle de musiciens,* vol. 7. Edited by François Fétis. Paris: Firmin Didot Frères, 1964.

"Puget, Loïsa." In *Dictionnaire de la musique.* Edited by Marc Honegger, 870. Paris: Bordas, 1970.

"Puget, Loïse." In *International Encyclopedia of Women Composers*, vol. 1. Edited by Aaron I. Cohen. New York and London: Books and Music, 1987.

"Puget, Loïsa." In *The New Grove Dictionary of Music and Musicians.* Edited by Stanley Sadie. London: Macmillan, 1980.

Scudo, P. "Esquisse d'une histoire de la romance." *Critique et littérature musicales*, 3rd ed. Paris: L. Hachette et Cie., 1856.

Tsou, Judy S. "Puget, Loïsa." In *The Norton/Grove Dictionary of Women Composers.* Edited by Julie Anne Sadie and Rhian Samuel. New York and London: W. W. Norton, 1995.

Belle pour lui!

[Refrain]
Oui, pour lui je veux être belle,
Bien belle, très belle;
Je veux, à ses désirs fidèle,
Lui plaire, aujourd'hui.
Oui, ce soir, je veux être belle,
Bien belle, très belle,
Je veux à ses désirs fidèle,
Être belle pour lui!

1. O Marie, si jolie,
Me dit-il, en me quittant,
Ta figure, blanche et pure,
Se passe d'ornement;
Veux tu savoir comment je t'aime?
Point de bijoux, de diamant!
Rien qu'une fleur, pour diadême!
Marie est Reine, en se montrant.
Et pour lui . . .

[Refrain]
Yes, for him I want to be pretty,
Quite pretty, very pretty;
I want to be true to his longings,
To please him today.
Yes, tonight I want to be pretty,
Quite pretty, very pretty;
I want to be true to his longings,
To be beautiful for him!

1. O Marie, so lovely,
He tells me when leaving me,
Your face, white and pure,
Without any ornament.
Do you know how much I love you?
Without jewels, without a diamond!
Nothing but a flower, for a diadem!
Marie is Queen on display.
And for him . . .

2. Ma toilette est parfaite,
Car j'ai mis, selon ses voeux,
Pour parure, pour coëffure [*sic*],
Sa fleur dans mes cheveux.
En me voyant ainsi parée,
Saura-t-il deviner mon coeur?
Saura-t-il lire la pensée,
Qui fait, ce soir, tout mon bonheur!
Oui, pour lui . . .

3. Mais silence! Je m'avance
Et déjà j'entre au salon;
Admirée, entourée,
L'on veut savoir mon nom.
La foule accourt, toute ravie,
Mais c'est lui seul que je verrai;
Chacun dira: qu'elle est jolie!
Mais c'est lui seul que j'entendrai.
Oui, pour lui . . .

2. My toilette is perfect,
For I have worn, according to his wishes,
For an ornament, for a head dress,
His flower in my hair.
When he sees me so adorned,
Will he know how to guess my heart?
Will he know how to read my thought,
Which makes me happy tonight!
Yes, for him . . .

3. But silence! I move forward
And already I enter the salon;
Admired, surrounded,
People want to know my name.
The crowd hastens, all delighted,
But it is him alone whom I will see;
Each one will say: she is pretty!
But it is him alone whom I will hear.
Yes, for him . . .

La chanson du charbonnier ou Blanc et noir

[Refrain]
(Le charbonnier)
Blanc farinier, donnez moi votre fille;
Donnez la moi, je la trouve gentille,
Et nous ferons et nous ferons,
Et nous ferons une bonne maison.

(Le farinier)
Noir charbonnier, tu n'auras pas ma fille,
Je marierais, la drôle de famille!
Sac de farine, sac de farine
Sac de farine avec sac de charbon,
Non non non non non non
Non non non non non non,
Non, non, tu n'auras pas Suzon,
Non non non non non non
Non non non non non non,
Non, non tu n'auras pas Suzon.

1. (Le farinier)
Mon ami, tu n'as donc jamais vu ta mine!
Car ma fille et toi, c'est la nuit et le jour.
Suzon a le teint plus blanc que ma farine,
Et le tien, mon cher est plus noir que mon four!
Ton seul aspect effarouche l'amour,
Oui, ton aspect effarouche l'amour.
Blanc farinier . . .

[Refrain]
(The Coalman)
White miller, give me your daughter;
Give her to me, I find her pretty,
And we will make, and we will make,
And we will make a good home.

(The Miller)
Black Coalman, you will not have my daughter.
If I let her marry, I will be the joke of the family!
Sack of flour, sack of flour,
Sack of flour with a sack of coal,
No no no no no no
No no no no no no,
No, no, you will not have Suzanne,
No no no no no no
No no no no no no,
No, no you will not have Suzanne.

1. (The Miller)
My friend, you have not seen your appearance!
For my daughter and you, it is night and day.
Suzanne has a color whiter than my flour,
And yours, my dear, is blacker than my oven!
Even your look scares away love,
Yes, your look scares away love.
White Miller . . .

2. (Le charbonnier)
Il faut me voir, le Dimanche, mon compère,
Quand j'ai barbe faite et veste de velours;
Et puis, la beauté, c'est chose passagère!
Moi, j'ai du charbon, cela se vend toujours.
(Parlé) Ah! Ah!
Car il en faut pour allumer vos fours,
Il vous en faut, pour allumer vos fours.
Blanc farinier . . .

2. (The Coalman)
One must see me, on Sundays, my old fellow,
When I have shaved and have a jacket of velvet;
And then, beauty, it is a fleeting thing!
Me, I have charcoal, it sells always.
(Spoken) Ah! Ah!
Because you need it to light your ovens,
It is needed, to light your ovens.
White Miller . . .

3. (Le charbonnier)
Mon voisin, je sais que vous êtes bon père;
Quitter votre fille, est pour vous un chagrin;
Mais j'ai des écus, pour arranger l'affaire
Et puis, dans ma cave un tonneau de bon vin.
(Parlé fort) Hein?
(Fort) Pour vous aider à noyer le chagrin,
(Plus fort) Pour nous aider à noyer le chagrin.

3. (The Coalman)
My neighbor, I know you are a good father;
For you it is a grief to leave your daughter;
But I have the money to arrange the affair
And then, in my cellar a cask of good wine.
(Spoken loudly) Eh?
(Loud) To help you drown your sorrow,
(Louder) To help us drown our sorrow.

[Refrain]
(Le farinier — vivement)
Noir charbonnier, soyez de la famile;
Marché conclu, je vous donne ma fille;
Vous me plaisez, vous me plaisez,
Vous me plaisez, vous lui plairez, un jour;
Car vous avez un charmant caractère
Et de très près quand on vous considère,
Vous êtes beau, vous êtes beau,
Vous êtes beau, mon cher, comme le jour!
Et de
Plus et de plus, vous êtes fait au tour,
Enfin vous êtes un amour!
Oui mon cher,
Oui mon cher, vous êtes fait au tour!
Vous êtes un petit amour!

[Refrain]
(The Miller — lively)
Black Coalman, be in our family;
The deal is concluded, I give you my daughter;
You please me, you please me,
You please me, you will please her one day.
For you have a charming character
And moreover when one looks at you,
You are handsome, you are handsome,
You are handsome, my dear, as the day!
And
Moreover, you have made a deal,
At last you are a love!
Yes my dear,
Yes my dear, you have made a deal!
You are a little love!

Jeune fille, à quinze ans

[Refrain]
Jeune fille, à quinze ans,
Chante comme l'alouette;
Jeune fille, à quinze ans,
Croit toujours au doux printems [*sic*];
Car alors la pauvrette
Ne rêve que jours de fête,
Car alors la pauvrette
Croit avoir toujours quinze ans.

[Refrain]
A young girl, of fifteen,
Sings like a lark;
A young girl, of fifteen,
Always believes in a gentle spring;
For then the poor girl
Only dreams of festival days,
For then the poor girl
Thinks she'll always be fifteen.

1. La voyez-vous bondir
Dans le jardin de son père!
Les baisers d'une mère,
Voilà tout son avenir.
[Refrain]

1. See her leaping
In her Father's garden!
The kisses of a Mother,
That is her only future.
[Refrain]

2. En mirant ses attraits,
Si fraiche et si joliette,
Elle dit, la coquette!
Je ne vieillirai jamais!
[Refrain]

3. Elle voit, dans son cours,
L'eau ravir sa marguerite,
Sans penser que, plus vite,
Le tems [*sic*] ravit ses beaux jours.
[Last refrain]
Jeune fille, à quinze ans,
Croit toujours être jeunette
Jeune fille, à quinze ans,
Croit toujours au doux printems;
Car alors la coquette
Ne rêve que jours de fête;
Mais hélas! la pauvrette
N'aura pas toujours quinze ans.

2. In showing her charms,
So fresh and so pretty,
She says, the coquette!
I will never grow old!
[Refrain]

3. She sees, in her path,
The water carries off her daisy,
Without thinking that, very quickly,
Time carries away these beautiful days.
[Last refrain]
A young girl, of fifteen,
Believes she'll always be young
A young girl, of fifteen,
Always believes in a gentle spring;
For then a coquette
Only dreams of festival days.
But alas! The poor girl
Will not always be fifteen.

Translations by Sondra Wieland Howe

Belle pour lui!

17
ce soir, je veux ê - tre bel - le, bien bel - le, très bel - le, je
p
21
veux à ses de-sirs fi - dè - le, ê - tre bel - le pour lui!
25
2 1
29
[Fine]

33
doux et gracieux
1. O Ma-rie - e, si jo-li - e, me dit-il, en me quit-tant,
Ped.
37
ta fi-gu - re, blanche et pu - re, se pas-se d'or - ne-ment; veux tu sa -
41
voir com-ment je t'ai - me? point de bi - joux, de di-a - mant! ri-en qu'une
45
fleur; pour di-a - dê - me! Ma-rie est Reine, en se mon - trant. Et
rall. ad lib.
dim.
D.S. [al Fine]
D.S. [al Fine]

La chanson du charbonnier ou Blanc et noir

Gustave Lemoine

Loïsa Puget
Sondra Wieland Howe, editor

17
nier, tu n'au-ras pas ma fil - le, je ma-rie - rais, la drô - le de fa - mil - le! Sac de fa -
rf
rf
p
21
ri - ne, sac de fa ri - ne, sac de fa - rine a - vec sac de char - bon, non non non non non
rf
rf
rf
25
non non non non non non non, non, non, tu n'au - ras pas su - zon, non non non non non
29
Très fort
non non non non non non non, non, non tu n'au - ras pas su - zon.
ff

33
37
[Fine]
1er Couplet
41
(Le farinier)
1. Mon a - mi, tu n'as donc ja-mais vu ta mi - ne!
45
Car ma fille e toi, c'est la nuit et le jour.

49
Su - zon a le teint plus blanc que ma fa - ri - ne,
53
et le tien, mon cher est plus noir que mon four!
ff
57
rf
Ton seul as - pect ef - fa - rou - che l'a -
60
rf
mour, oui, ton as - pect ef - fa - rou - che l'a - mour
D.S.
[al Fine]
(Le charbonnier)
Blanc fa - ri -
D.S.
[al Fine]
f
rf
p

Jeune fille, à quinze ans

Gustave Lemoine

Loïsa Puget
Sondra Wieland Howe, editor

21
ad lib.
f
lors la pau - vret - te croit a - voir tou - jours quinze
suivez
24
ans
29
1er Couplet
La voy -
33
tr
ez - vous bon - dir dans le jar - din de son pè - re! les bai -

37
rall.
ad lib.
a tempo
D.S.
sers d'u - ne mè - re, voi - là tout son a - ve - nir. Jeu - ne
D.S.
suivez

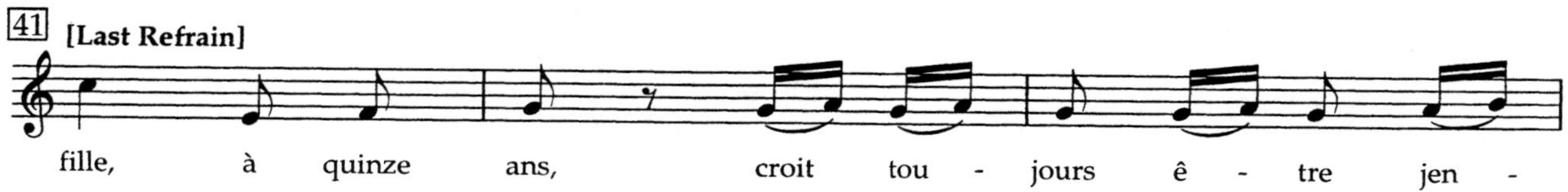
41
[Last Refrain]
fille, à quinze ans, croit tou - jours ê - tre jen -

44
net - te jeu - ne fille, à quinze ans, croit tou -

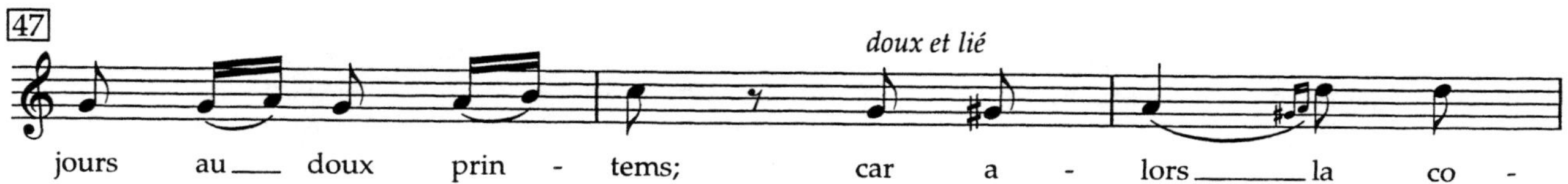
47
doux et lié
jours au doux prin - tems; car a - lors la co -

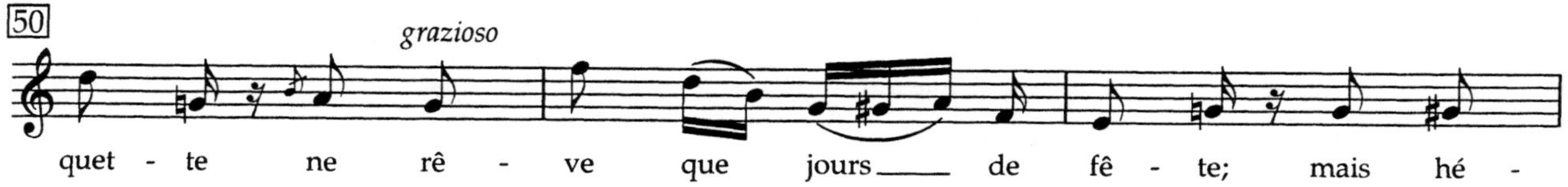
50
grazioso
quet - te ne rê - ve que jours de fê - te; mais hé -

53
ad lib.
f
las! la pau - vret - te n'au - ra pas tou - jours quinze ans.

Johanna Kinkel
(1810–1858)

SUZANNE SUMMERVILLE

"So richly blessed with talents,
though not a genius in any single one."[1]

Johanna Mockel Mathieux Kinkel, (hereafter called Kinkel) German composer, pianist, choral conductor, poet, journalist, novelist, music educator, and historian, was born Johanna Mockel in Bonn on July 8, 1810. At the time of her birth her father, Peter Joseph Mockel,[2] was a teacher at the French Lycée [3] that shortly afterwards was renamed the Royal Bonn Gymnasium. Her mother, Maria Johanna Lahm, was described in Johanna's memoirs as a pious woman who kept strictly to the Catholic ritual.[4]

Kinkel's musical talents were apparent at a very early age, though the Mockels seemed unable to understand her needs or to guide her studies. As an adult she wrote to a friend:

> To be allowed to stay at home, to make music or to read, was what I wanted to do. But I was required to spend all my leisure hours with my family and we had no common interests. That was unfortunate, because we really loved each other.[5]

After the death of her brother, Kinkle became the pampered child of both her parents and grandparents. This, however, did not keep the Mockels from insisting that the only acceptable female role was that of a wife and mother, or from submitting the young girl to the exhaustive religious activities that resulted in her lifelong aversion to the formal practice of Catholicism.[6]

Kinkel was allowed piano lessons, but the systematic musical education she desired was withheld. Franz Anton Ries (1755–1846),[7] her first instructor, had been Beethoven's childhood violin teacher. With Ries' support, she began a career as coach, accompanist, and choral director while still in her teens.

Bonn's musical ambience during the time of Kinkel's childhood and adolescence did not compare with the intellectual climate, particularly in philosophy and political science, provided by the University of Bonn. The presentation of musical events in this small university town was split among groups of mostly amateur performers. There was no dominant musical personality in the city until Kinkel emerged to fill that void. Her group of amateur singers met weekly in various homes and performed small ensemble pieces and portions of operas by Wolfgang Amadeus Mozart (1756– 1791), Carl Maria von Weber (1786–1826), Ludwig van Beethoven (1770–1827), Johann Lepomuk Hummel (1778–1837), Daniel François Esprit Auber (1782–1871), and Ries himself.[8]

On September 13, 1832, at the age of twenty-two, Kinkel married Cologne book and music merchant, Johann Paul Mathieux. She had hoped that marriage would free her from the religious pressures imposed by her parents and that she would be able to find ways to expand her musical studies. This was not the case. The relationship was an abusive one and her husband's marital expectations left her even less time for her musical career.[9]

Joseph Joesten (b. 1850) described the event that ended her troubled marriage after fewer than six months:

> Contemporaries described Johanna as being a poor housewife. She disliked setting foot in the kitchen, preferring to play the piano all day long. One day her young husband came home and, in a fit of anger, threw her music out of the window. She stood up coldly and walked to her parents' home in Bonn. The marriage was over.[10]

Kinkel fell into a prolonged period of depression, during which time she was unable to teach or to compose.[11] The divorce proceedings lasted seven years; she continued to use the name Mathieux until her second marriage.

In 1836, the period of paralyzing depression ended and Kinkel again expressed a desire to further her musical studies. She felt that she needed to leave Bonn. With the assistance of Dorothea Schlegel (1764–1839)[12] Kinkel met Felix Mendelssohn (1809–1847) in Frankfurt when he was there to direct the *Cäcilienverein* (St. Cecilia Society). She played compositions by Bach and Beethoven for him and asked for his judgment of her talent and for suggestions for further study. Mendelssohn strongly encouraged her to pursue a musical career, and remained a supporter of her work throughout his life.[13]

Kinkel followed his advice and moved to the capital, Berlin, in November of that year where she studied counterpoint and fugue with Karl Böhmer (1799–18?)[14] and piano with Wilhelm Taubert (1811–1891).[15] She may also have had lessons with Hubert Ries (1802–1886), the son of her teacher in Bonn.[16]

To finance her studies, Kinkel gave private piano lessons. Among her students were the three daughters of Bettine von Arnim (1785–1859) (see vol. 4). For a time she lived in the von Arnim home at Unter den Linden 26. In a letter dated January 31, 1837, Kinkel wrote of her life as a member of Bettine von Arnim's inner circle:

> With my current patroness Bettine von Arnim, I feel myself very lucky. Her daughters are extremely musical. The oldest (Maximiliane or Maxe) is happiest playing piano and the second (Armgard) possesses a phenomenal soprano voice that has no limits in the high ranges. The third daughter (Gisela) is the most talented of all. In this household, I seem to myself totally stupid, like a Basilio in a group of Figaros and Don Alfonsos. [17]

Kinkel's high level of musicianship and pianistic abilities must have been readily evident, if one is to believe the acclaim she received from numerous sources.[18] The opinions of Carl Schurz (1829–1906) and Bettine von Arnim are but two examples: "She had a truly thorough musical education and she played the piano masterfully. I have seldom heard Beethoven and Chopin compositions played more perfectly"[19] and, "You, surely, will make your way in Berlin. You are no everyday artist."[20]

Her talents as a singer were more controversial, however. She loved to sing to her own accompaniment in front of small audiences. Adolf Strodtmann (1829–1879) described her lack of vocal talent:

> Johanna's voice was large, but it seemed rough, sharp, and hoarse to those who listen only to the music and not to her soul. . . . She fought with this unpleasant voice to express her feelings, and often — strangely enough — brought thoughtful, intelligent listeners to tears. From an artistic point of view, she sang very beautifully. She could express herself vocally from the highest tragedy to the most tender of expressions and back again to the comic. One forgot that her medium, the voice, was really pretty bad. [21]

Carl Schurz wrote simply, "She understood the art of singing without having a voice." [22]

Kinkel took part in the activities of Bettine's literary circle, *Lindenblatt* (leaf of the lime tree), and performed in Fanny Hensel's *Sonntagsmusik* (Sunday Musicals). She wrote of her admiration for Hensel's talents as composer, pianist and, especially, conductor. [23]

Kinkel's life in the von Arnim household was not an easy one; she soon acknowledged that Bettine was "eine weiblicher Napoleon im Kleinen" (a female Napoleon in miniature).[24] Her mother wrote, "I was right when I said that your association with the brilliantly gifted Frau von Arnim would not make you any smarter." [25] In late May 1837, Kinkel moved to a small garden house in Kupfergarten 5. Von Arnim accepted her departure and continued to invite her to happenings in her home.

Because of her still pending divorce proceedings, Kinkel returned to her parents' home in Bonn in 1839. The "excruciating torment of the endless process" and the often cruel narrow-mindedness of the Bonn citizenry brought back her depression and thoughts of suicide.[26] When the divorce was finally granted on May 23, 1840, she became involved again as a conductor, performer, and composer with various chamber music and vocal ensembles in her home city.

As a music student, performer, and composer in Berlin, Kinkel had obtained access to the most famous houses and salons of the day, becoming acquainted with the finest poets and the newest movements in contemporary composition. While in Bonn, she became the guiding force in presenting the works of Felix Mendelssohn and Frederick Chopin. The city's first performance of Mozart's *Requiem* took place under her auspices. She founded a series of morning concerts in her apartment where several of her new compositions, including a setting of Heine's ballad *Don Ramiro*, op. 13, were premiered.[27] "Since I have returned, everyone is absolutely crazy to have musical gatherings; there is almost more singing than talking," was how she herself described these years.[28]

During this period in her life, she composed her only explicitly religious work, *Hymnus in Coena Domini,* for full chorus (SATB) and string orchestra. Eck, in Cologne, published it as op. 14 in 1840.

Kinkel's new *Gesangverein* (singing society) took part in several important concerts for charity. The program presented on a concert for the poor in December 1839 included Giovanni Battista Pergolesi's *Stabat Mater* and the "Furies" scene from Christoph Willibald Gluck's (1714–1787) *Orfeo ed Euridice*. She played a sonata by Beethoven, a fugue by Bach, and a capriccio by Mendelssohn. In early 1840, she directed another charity concert in support of Bonn's orphanage that was held in the *Kasinosaal* (Casino Hall). Other benefit concerts soon followed for Bonn's Women's Society and the Elisabethschule, a new school for girls.[29]

Her second marriage to Gottfried Kinkel (1815–1882) increased her responsibilities as breadwinner. Five years younger than Johanna and a very handsome man when they met, Gottfried was a *Privatdozent* (adjunct faculty member) and *Hilfsprediger* (substitute preacher) in Bonn and engaged to a Protestant minister's daughter. Joanna was a Catholic divorcée, emancipated, and consequently, considered an immoral woman. It was only after she had converted to Protestantism and Gottfried had broken his engagement that they could be married. Considerable damage was done to both their reputations by the gossip among members of Bonn's upper middle class.[30]

The Kinkels moved into an apartment in the Poppelsdorfer Palace owned by Bonn University. Rehearsals of her *Gesangverein* were held in the Botanical Lecture Hall of the palace. Royalty from Holstein, Meiningen, and Prussia, as well as traveling singers, composers, and virtuoso instrumentalists including Heinrich Marschner (1795–1861), Louis Spohr (1784–1859), and Franz Liszt (1811–1886) were among the members of her audiences. Gluck's

Iphigenie in Aulis, and Weber's *Oberon* were performed on March 9, 1845, and Spohr's opéras *Jessonda* and *Faust* were part of the group's repertoire. They presented Marschner's opera *Hans Heiling* at the Bonn City Hall on December 5, 1845, and Spohr's *Pietro von Albano* during the following months. Johanna Kinkel's *Gesangverein* also presented various choral works by George Frideric Handel (1685–1759) and took part in the Bonn Beethoven Festival in 1845. They sang Handel's *Israel in Egypt* at the last major concert before the group disbanded in 1848. Kinkel had prepared Spohr's opera *Der Berggeist*, but there was no performance due to the worsening political situation. Her work was called the *Brennpunkt* (highpoint) of Bonn's social and artistic life. Her *Gesangverein* although forgotten today, was one of the first choral organizations in nineteenth-century Germany to be conducted by a woman.[31]

As busy as she was with teaching, writing, composing, and directing during the early years after her second marriage, Kinkel remained an active member of the *Maikäferbund* (Maybug Society), a literary group she had helped Gottfried Kinkel to organize soon after her return to Bonn from Berlin. She championed the poetry of its young members and set a number of their texts to music.[32] Kinkel also aided Gottfried with the publication of a journal, *Der Maikäfer — eine Zeitschrift für Nichtphilister* (The Maybug — A Newspaper for Non-philistines) that published work by the group's members.

In 1848–1849, a time of revolutionary upheaval in Germany, Johanna Kinkel's literary and musical circles collapsed. Gottfried, always a strong activist, founded a radical democratic society and became editor of its newspaper, the *Neue Bonner Zeitung*. Kinkel wrote numerous articles for the journal and supported her husband in his leftist endeavors by assuming the editorship when he was away. During this period she composed several songs that portrayed the revolutionary ideas then encircling Germany's staid aristocracy. Because of her political engagement, many parents withdrew their children from her piano studio.[33]

Gottfried was chosen by the democratic electorate to represent Bonn in the National Assembly that was convened in Berlin in 1848. When he was arrested and condemned to death for his political activities, Kinkel solicited the help of Bettine von Arnim and others and successfully had his death sentence overturned and changed to life imprisonment. Carl Schurz, then a revolutionary student and later a well-known German-American statesman, helped Gottfried escape from Spandau prison in November 1850.[34] He fled to London where Kinkel and their four children joined him in January 1851.

Kinkel's pedagogical works were published during the several years of political turmoil that followed the Revolution of 1848. They included *Anleitung zum Singen: Übungen und Liedchen für Kinder von 3-7 Jahren, mit Begleitung des Klaviers* (Instructions for Teaching Singing to Young Children from 3 to 7 Years), *Acht Briefe an eine Freundin über Klavierunterricht* (Eight Letters to a Friend about Playing the Piano) (1852), and *Songs for Little Children* (English words adapted to Madame Kinkel's German "Kindergesangschule") (1852). Both *Anleitung zum Singen* and *Acht Briefe* were addressed specifically to mothers who wanted their own children instructed in music at home.[35]

Ann Willison Lemke's article, "Die revolutionäre Musik der Bonnerin Johanna Kinkel" (The Revolutionary Music of the Bonner Johanna Kinkel) details the startling length to which Kinkel went to spread her democratic ideals. A radical poem about a child's father standing guard duty with a bayonet in his hand and holding a flag in the revolutionary colors of black, red and gold as a background found its way into the *Anleitung zum Singen*. It was used as the text in song number 10 (*von der Bürgerwache)*, an exercise that clarifies the differences between intervals of the 6th and 7th.[36]

Kinkel fully supported her husband in his political pursuits in their adopted country. The Kinkels became the center of London's expatriate German community, entertaining many guests, although their means were meager. Gottfried taught part time at Hyde Park College and lectured on German art history at the University of London. Kinkel, who spoke English well, gave piano lessons and taught singing to small children. She also directed a choir and wrote music, librettos, poetry, and a two-volume novel entitled *Hans Ibeles in London: Ein Familienbild aus dem Flüchtlingsleben* (Hans Ibeles in London: Pictures of a Family's Life in Exile).[37] In a letter to Willibald Beyschlag dated November 20, 1857, Kinkel wrote of a new interest:

> Before the beginning of the season, I had more time than before to spend on my studies in music history. I am working in the British Museum where the books I need are. . . . I have an invitation to give lectures in music history and it seems that [I] will be able to do them. That pleases me very much, not only because it pays better than giving lessons, but also because I have discovered my ability to do them and in my later years I will have a completely new occupation.[38]

She presented lectures on the music of Beethoven and Mozart. Her scholarly paper, "Frederic Chopin as Composer,"[39] and another on the works of Felix Mendelssohn, published after her death, originate from this period.[40]

In 1857, Kinkel's health began to fail and her heart condition became serious. On an overcast November day, Kinkel's body was discovered in the garden of her home. She had either fallen or had jumped to her death from the third floor window of her bedroom. No one had observed her death and there were varying opinions over the cause of the fatal accident. Reasons for the return of her depression, perhaps the worsening heart ailment or a suspicion that Gottfried had been unfaithful, were discussed in family letters in the context of her novel *Hans Ibeles in London*. That she had gone to her window to fetch a breath of fresh air and had suffered a heart seizure and then had collapsed over the low balcony could not be ruled out.[41]

Kinkel was not forgotten in her native country while she resided in English exile. She lived in the memory of the German intellectuals as an eccentric revolutionary and as a musician with a broad cultural background. Ferdinand Freiligrath (1818–1876),[42] who had been a member of the *Maikäferbund*, wrote a beautiful poem at the time of her tragic death. He mourned her "as one of those unhappy exiles who were greater and more patriotic than most of those remaining in their Fatherland," wrote of her courage, her music, and ended with these words:

> She has merited the soil of England as her grave, the soil on which Milton, the poet, and rebel, on which Cromwell and Sidney walked. Her name will be honored wherever the free shall breathe.[43]

Kinkel was buried in the cemetery in Woking. The words *Freiheit, Liebe, und Dichtung* (Freedom, Love, and Poetry) were inscribed on her tombstone.

In her article "Die Stille Opposition: Heine-Vertonung von Frauen,"[44] Eva Weissweiler wrote of the limitations of society and opportunity that caused so many nineteenth-century women composers to choose the piano-lied as their most usual form. The lied's "at home" performance suitability, coupled with the fact that it was relatively easy to write and inexpensive to publish, made the genre a popular one. A miniature, the piano-lied fit neatly into the generally accepted belief that women were less creative than men.

Nature and love were the most common topics in poetry favored by a majority of nineteenth-century women composers. Texts describing the "enjoyment of alcohol" or patriotically extolling *Der Vaterland* (The Fatherland), both masculine subjects, were seldom chosen. Johanna Kinkel, however, was one woman who often broke the barriers of subject matter. Besides composing a drinking song, she wrote on both "Fatherland" and "Revolution." Her list of works includes a substantial number of compositions utilizing Gottfried's political texts and, on several occasions, she set her own radical sentiments in songs and theatrical presentations.

Kinkel wrote almost one hundred songs that she prepared for publication. Her smaller *Liederspiele* (song plays) and operetta-like theatricals were intended only for amateur performances.

Kinkel's groupings of six solo songs or three duets follow the cyclical form used by Felix Mendelssohn, Louis Spohr, and other German composers of the period. She was well-versed in the development of the Second Berlin School, as well as in her own Rhineland heritage. There is, however, little to show that she was influenced by the two great masters of nineteenth-century song, Franz Schubert (1797–1828) and Robert Schumann (1810–1856).

In her article "Über die modernen Liederkomponisten" (About Modern Song Composers) published in *Der Maikäfer*, Kinkel wrote:

> Franz Schubert, who wrote but a few large compositions, poured the whole of his rich soulfulness into lied, mostly in the extended form of the through-composed song. He gained the singular reputation of being the foremost lyric composer in Germany. . . . No one can compare to him in ardor and depth of feeling, richness of fantasy, originality and beauty of rhythm as well as melody. It is a shame that Schubert set his beautiful airs far too often to the worst of poetry.[45]

Schumann songs were not mentioned. In fact, in all of her writings on music and composers, his name is never featured.[46]

Under the tutelage of her piano teacher Franz Anton Ries, Kinkel created her first large composition at the age of twenty. *Die Vogelkantate* (The Bird's Cantata),[47] for which she wrote both text and music, was performed in Bonn during Carnival by and for a circle of Ries' students and friends. In this charmingly funny work for solo voices and piano, *Nachtigall* (Nightingale), soprano, *Elster* (Magpie), soprano, *Papagai* (Parrot), mezzo-soprano, and *Rabe* (Raven), baritone, are invited by *Kuckuck* (Cuckoo), mezzo-soprano, to prepare a serenade to be sung for *Adler* (Eagle, representing the King) in celebration of his name day. The rehearsal was planned for Cuckoo's house. Cuckoo is awaiting the arrival of the other birds when the scene opens. They are late and Cuckoo, in his opening recitative, becomes increasingly agitated at their tardiness (see example 1, mm. 1–27).[48] (Examples 1–6 from *Die Vogelkantate* are in note 48, pp 88-92.) When the others finally arrive, the rehearsal begins. At first, there is complete unity, but soon the group effort becomes strained. Nightingale proposes to sing a bravura aria (see example 2, mm. 82–97). Magpie and Raven then quickly thrust themselves forward to sing a duet accompanied by the other three birds. The group's unity completely breaks down when Cuckoo says that he will be the conductor. "I will conduct," sings the Cuckoo. "Wie? Was? Herr Cuckoo, what in the world are you thinking about?" sing all the others and offer themselves one by one to be the ensemble's leader (see example 3, mm.114–124/25). The outrage is quelled. "In Cuckoo's name, be quiet! Anyone who wants to can be the conductor. Begin the chorus: Music alone is important!" trumpets Cuckoo (see example 4, mm. 178-85). Two voices rise a half step too high and the others accuse both for this harmonic impropriety (see example 5, mm. 201-2). Again Cuckoo interferes for the good of the group and together they praise the Goddess of Harmony for charming each heart and for bringing happiness to one and all (see example 6, mm. 239–58).

The comic cantata, often in the form of a rehearsal with arguments among participants, was typical of the Rheinish Carnival tradition during the first half of the nineteenth century.[49] But the idea of using birds to portray the protagonists was Kinkel's own.

Sarcasm and humor are ever present here. Eva Weissweiler pointed out in *Komponistinnen aus 500 Jahren* how successful Kinkel was in her only half joking depiction of Raven as the symbol of *Unmusikalität* (unmusicality); Magpie as a representation of the number of female singers who only after a period of squabbling and clamoring are ready to become part of an ensemble; and Nightingale, known to every choral director, as the "want-to-be-primadonna."[50]

Although the piano accompaniment is relatively easy, the singers are called upon for true virtuoso singing. Nightingale should be a real coloratura soprano with a high C. Dressed in costume, the singers portraying the various species were amusingly caricatured on the cover of the published version.

Performances of *Die Vogelkantate* in Bonn and later in Berlin brought Kinkel her first successes as a composer. Published by Trautwein in 1838, it became her op. 1. The music critic Ludwig Rellstab, writing in *Iris im Gebiet der Tonkunst*, compared its humor to that of Mozart's musical jokes.[51]

Another critic, G. W. Fink, wrote about *Die Vogelkantate* in the Leipzig *Allgemeine musikalische Zeitung* on May 1, 1839. He called it "droll" and spoke of its many performances and even quoted Kinkel's own evaluation of it, "I wrote the cantata and my own critique of it can be said in three words, '*Sie ist allerliebst!*'" (It is the sweetest thing!). Fink thought that the overall success of the work depended upon the charm of the text and he especially praised the funny headgear the birds had to wear.[52]

Die Vogelkantate was performed again years later during Kinkel's exile in London. The presentations in her new circle were so successful that an English firm offered to republish it. That was not contractually possible, so Kinkel wrote a new comic work and was even prepared to bring it out at her own expense. This *Katzenkantate* or *Mäusekantate* (Cat's Cantata or Mouse Cantata) featured children singing fugues as they portrayed cats and mice.[53]

Early in her career, Kinkel's Rheinland humor gave her the reputation of a musical clown. Her comic operas *Zum Geburtstag des Herrn von Savigny — Themis und Savigny oder die Olympier in Berlin* (For the Birthday of Herr Savigny — Themis and Savigny or the Olympians in Berlin), *43 Verrückte Komödien — Der Wettstreit der schottischen Minstrels* (43 Crazy Comedies — The Contest of the Scottish Minstrels), *Vaudeville für den Hochzeitstag der Professors von Henning* (Vaudeville for the Wedding Day of Professor von Henning), and an operetta with the title *Die Landpartie* (The Picnic) were written and performed during her stay in Berlin (1836–1839).

In 1838 and 1840, the publishing houses Kistner (Leipzig) and Trautwein (Berlin) brought out her opp. 6, 7, 8, and 10. These were groupings of six songs each. Op. 9, a single song composed to Adelbert von Chamisso's poem *Schloss Boncourt,* appeared in 1839. Opp. 11 and 12, each of three duets for soprano and alto voices on texts by Heine, Goethe, and C. Wolfgang Müller, the Düsseldorf poet and follower of Heine, appeared in 1839 and 1840.

Robert Schumann and members of his Leipzig circle became aware of Kinkel's work when op. 6 appeared. A critique in *Die neue Zeitschrift für Musik* written by Schumann's coworker Oswald Lorenz praised her work but did not refrain from describing it as feminine in his review.[54]

On July 14, 1838, Kinkel wrote to her good friend Angela Oppenhoff: [55]

> My second set of songs has now come out and I have another request from my publishers for the fall. After the publication of the first set, a group of young song composers in Leipzig who had read Rellstab's critique, feigned innocence and pretended to have recognized immediately that the songs had been written by a women composer. Among other things, they used the words *sanfte* (soft, gentle, mild, meek, placid) and *zarte* (tender, soft, pale, placid) in a droll manner and joked about one of the *Mondscheinlieder* (one of the songs about the shining moon). They then changed horses in midstream and one of the club members (not the critic) wrote me a very flattering letter, mentioning nothing more than my name and the list of songs, and asked me to send one of my compositions to be included in a new insert to a music journal. This was for me a choice opportunity to pay back his use of *zarte* and *sanfte*. I replied with a simpering letter and sent with it a copy of my wildest drinking song for men's chorus for which I had written the text as well. I would love to see the face of my unknown correspondent when he gets that letter.[56]

Kinkel's drinking song, *Trinklied,* appeared in the third edition of the *Beiträgen* (Supplements) to the *Neue Zeitschrift für Musik* in 1838. A song by Pauline García Viardot (1821–1910) (see this volume) was reviewed in the same article. Schumann's description of the publication with his critique of the two composers' works may be found in the appendix to his *Gesammelte Schriften über Musik und Musiker*: "Two female names, so we hear, that in recent times have brought a great deal of the musical world's attention upon themselves, are included in the *Beiträgen*. . . ." Changing the subject from Pauline García Viardot's contribution to that of Kinkel, Schumann continued:

> Very different from the richly talented artist's composition is the other, a drinking song, and even more interesting, a drinking song in G minor. The dark and almost wild choice of keys does not seem necessary from the content of the poem to me, but if that is the choice of the composer. . . . Perhaps it is a sign of the times and comes out of the poetry school that we know from the works of Rahel [57] and Bettina. Anyone who would like to learn more about the composer, her musical, thoroughly feminine nature, may study her volume of songs that recently came out. They are worth the appreciation they have found everywhere.[58]

During the same year that Schumann wrote about Kinkel's compositions in his journal, G. W. Fink, editor and critic of the *Allegemeine musikalische Zeitung,* discussed her op. 7 in the issue that appeared on August 8:

> . . . charming songs that have already received much acclaim. There is not a single one in the group that isn't a breath of fresh air. . . . See for yourself, buy them and sing them. . . . The eighth opus has just been published, and the composer is not a man, but a woman.[59]

Kinkel set texts by some of the greatest German nineteenth-century poets of song. Her list of renowned poets includes Johann Wolfgang von Goethe (1749–1832), Heinrich Heine (1797–1856), Emanuel Geibel (1815–1884), and Adelbert von Chamisso (1781–1838). The less well known are August Kopish (1799–1853), Sebastian Longard, Alexander Kaufmann (1817–1893), C. Wolfgang Müller, and Nikolaus Becker (1809–1845). There is a single poem by Platen and one religious text from the seventh century (*Hymnus in Coena Domini*). In Kinkel's list of works there is nothing taken from the Bible and not a single literary work by another woman writer is included. A large proportion of her compositions are based on her own writings or on those of her husband.

With few exceptions, her solo songs are for low voice, either alto or baritone. Even her book of scales and solfeggio with piano accompaniment (*Tonleitern und Solfeggien,* op. 22) is for alto.

Kinkel's first group of published songs, op. 6, was composed to poems by Geibel, Heine, Kopisch, Goethe, and one of her own. In a letter dated December 10, 1837, to Angela Oppenhoff, Kinkel wrote that she felt only two of the songs familiar to her, *Die Zigeuner* and *Der Mond kommt still,* were acceptable for publication. Everything else was too immature, she thought, and so she included newer compositions in the group sent to Kistner. Perhaps only half in jest, Kinkel closed, "Mit zagendem Herzen sehe ich der Rezension entgegen. Wenn Rellstab mich nur nicht frisst!" (With a panting heart I await the critique. If only Rellstab doesn't eat me alive!)[60]

The sentiments in *Verlornes Glück* (Lost Happiness, op. 6, no. 5), included here, are autobiographical and are almost certainly based on the emotions she felt during the first of several periods of depression in her life that led to her possible suicide in London in 1858. This small song of only sixteen measures imparts in its three stanzas the helplessness of one who cannot be helped. The vocal range is only a minor seventh. A single chord in the piano introduces the G minor mode and the voice begins in a rather listless conversational tone. In measures 5-6 there are hints of the positive moments of hope in B-flat major. Nevertheless, even in measure 9, with the strong intent of the melody line to soar to a high G (heut'), the voice is not allowed to go beyond E-flat and the piano accompaniment transcends the vocal line. By adding a C-sharp to form a seventh in measure 10, the dissonance on the word "Loss" (fate) is crushing. The song ends with a five-measure postlude and closes in G minor.

Heine's text, " Ich will meine Seele tauchen" (in *Six Songs*, op. 10, no. 2) speaks of an expression of love that is only memory and imagination. It is whispered, he imagines, by the lily, the symbol of purification. There is a trembling and quivering in the poem "like the kiss from his beloved's mouth that once she gave to him in a wonderfully sweet moment." Kinkel's setting of this lovely text was highly praised by Ludwig Rellstab in his review in *Iris im Gebiet der Tonkunst* in 1839: "The second song, based on one of the most charming of Heine's poems is also in the musical setting one of the most successful songs we know from this composer." Rellstab goes on to discuss the difficulty of the accompaniment:

> Could the accompaniment, which really isn't easy to play if one makes the accents and still plays sweetly as the whole is supposed to be done, be made easier and still be as meaningful? Is it really necessary to be so complex or could it be more natural and perhaps be even more beautiful? These are questions that do not have theoretical answers, only practical ones, if someone could do an accompaniment in the discussed manner. However, as the present one is very lovely and the difficulty possible to overcome – the problem lies in the double stops of three or four tones. . . . The whole song is very beautiful, what more would anyone want? . . . "The whole collection will surely gain the enthusiastic applause of the public.[61]

The key changes are both subtle and sudden. The first example of this is the replacement of G-sharp (piano, top voice) with a G-natural (m. 13) which propels the song from its beginning in F to the dominant key of C major. Between measures 8–14 the key of A minor is established by the use of the German augmented sixth in measure12. In the following C major section (mm. 14–18) the A-flat augmented chord in measure18, while not functional in any of the foregoing keys, moves to the key of A-flat major in measures 12–23 — the mediant key to the parallel minor. The song ends in the expected key of F major.

Ich will meine Seele tauchen could hardly be more stepwise in its melodic setting. Kinkel extended the sustained vocal line across the word "tauchen" (to plunge, dip, submerge) (mm. 3–4) against the motion of the accompaniment's constant sixteenth notes and rest patterns. The piano, as the agent of mood, brings Kinkel's style closer to that of Schumann rather than that of Mendelssohn.

Abschied, Kinkel's title for a song based on Heine's poem *Schöne Wiege meiner Leiden,* is the only composition by Kinkel currently known to have been published in an arrangement for voice with guitar accompaniment. It was issued together with Jacques Offenbach's *O bleib bei mir* by the publishing house M. Schloss in Cologne. The original version for low voice and piano is found in *Six Songs*, op. 19, no. 5.

Ritters Abschied from *Zwei Volks Lieder für Männerchor*, based on an eighteenth-century student song, *Weh, dass wir scheiden müssen,* was unquestionably Kinkel's most popular and often performed composition. It is the one that traveled to the United States and was sung by men's choruses on the east coast well into the early twentieth century.[62]

Kinkel's song *Auf wohlauf, ihr Candioten* (*Six Songs*, op. 18, no. 3) published in Berlin by Schlesinger, (1843) is based on her husband's 1841 poem, *Schlachtgesang der Kandioten.* It concerns the Greek War of Independence (1821–1829) that freed the region known today as Greece from the Turkish rule in place since the fall of Constantinople in 1453. The word *Candioten* or *Kandioten* — comrade or perhaps warrior comrade — is not found in either current or nineteenth-century German dictionaries. Kinkel's setting of the poem's twelve stanzas has several punctuation discrepancies from Gottfried's original. Its bright key of G major and its triumphantly martial rhythms are magnetic.[63]

Goethe's poem *Nachtgesang* is a late creation and falls into the same period (Middle and Old Age, 1800–1832) as his masterpiece Faust. It is somewhat difficult to include this poem of a single speaker (*ich* or I) in the category of a duet for women's voices. Kinkel, however, who would have been familiar with many of Goethe's great poems, chose to set it together with two poems by the Düsseldorf poet and *Maikäferbund* member, C. Wolfgang Müller, as her op. 12, no. 3. The three duets, published by Trautwein in 1840, were dedicated to Fräuleins Adele and Emily Thormann.

Nachtgesang opens with a four measure piano introduction in the key of A minor, after which the voices enter in thirds with some passing decorations in the soprano melody. Section A, the poem's first verse, closes in A major. The alto begins the second verse alone, section B (m. 13), in the key of G major. After several quick modulations, the soprano enters with a pickup to measure 21 in the dominant. Both the alto and the soprano accent the importance of the words "Die ewigen Gefühle" (The eternal affections or feelings) with the largest intervals in the composition, 6ths from G to E and B to G. The alto solo returns in measure 28, again alone, as if to underscore the line "trennst Du mich nur zu sehr" (You wrest me — tear me away).

Perhaps the most unexpected thing about the duet is the final cadence in A minor after an apparent return to A major (m. 42). Surely, this is textually caused. Measures 11–12 and mm. 42–43 are the same, but A minor changes to A major and then returns to A minor. The positive A major "Schlafe, was willst du mehr?" (Sleep, what more could you wish?) is weakened by the repetition of "Schlafe! Schlafe!" (Sleep! Sleep!) in the closing phrase's repeated pondering of the question.

In closing, a quote from Paul Kaufmann, whose relatives in the previous generation took part in the activities Kinkel created in their native city of Bonn: "A woman of her attributes does not disappear with physical death. The magic of her towering personality lives on forever."[64]

Notes

1. "So reich mit Talenten begabt und doch in keinem Fach Genie." Although Emanuel Geibel (1815–1884) had been a student at the University of Bonn, he did not meet Kinkel until Bettine von Arnim (1785–1859) introduced them in Berlin during the winter of 1837. Bettina Brand, "Johanna Kinkel: Biographische Notiz," in *Komponistinnen in Berlin* (Berlin: Musikfrauen e.V. Berlin, 1987), 79–81.

2. J. F. Schulte, *Johanna Kinkel: Nach ihren Briefen und Errinerungs-Blättern*. Münster: Heinrich Schöningh, 1908, 4–6, and Else Thalheimer, "Johanna Kinkel als Musikerin." Dr. phil. diss., University of Bonn, 1922, foreword, 1–2.

3. Bonn was under the control of France from 1792–1815.

4. Schulte, *Johanna Kinkel*, 4.

5. Ibid., 6, note 4. A quote from Marie Goslich, ed. "Briefe von Johanna Kinkel an Familie von Henning," in *Preussische Jahrbücher*, Bd. 97 (1899): 192.

6. Ibid., 7–8.

7. Franz Anton Ries, known as the "older" Ries, was first concertmaster and later music director for the Kurfürst Max Franz of Cologne.

8. Thalheimer, "Johanna Kinkel als Musikerin," 10-11.

9. Schulte, *Johanna Kinkel*, 9.

10. Ibid., 10-11, note 4. A quote from Joseph Joesten, "Musikalisches Leben in Bonn," in *Bonner Zeitung* (December 17, 1898): 25.

11. Eva Weissweiler, *Komponistinnen aus 500 Jahre* (Frankfurt am Main: Fischer, 1981), 221-22. Medical records in the University of Bonn's archives include the following report written by the physician who saw her during the spring and summer 1833: "Frau Johanna Mathieux's (born Mockel) divorce from her first husband was in every way legitimate. . . . She suffered from shattered nerves with a consuming fever induced by the cruelty and torment that she had to endure almost without halt from her husband. . . ."

12. Dorothea Schlegel was Felix's Mendelssohn's aunt on his mother's side.

13. Thalheimer, "Johanna Kinkel als Musikerin," 2 and VII, note 3. Weissweiler, *Komponistinnen*, 223 and 236, note 78, states that there is a letter extant in the Archives in Bonn written by Felix's sister, Rebekka (Rebecka) Dirichlet, to Johanna. Rebekka offers to write letters of introduction for her and says, "You may have letters for many circles. . . . because Felix was such an admirer of your compositions, all of your music, doors and gates will be open to you." (. . . kann aber für sehr viele Kreise Briefe erhalten, und das einfache Factum, dass Felix ein grosser Bewunderer Ihrer Kompositionen, Ihrer ganzen Musik war, öffnet Ihnen Tür und Tör.) However, Paul Kaufmann in "Johanna Kinkel: Neue Beiträge zu ihrem Lebensbild," in *Preussische Jarhbücher* (1930): 7, said that this letter was written in 1850 by Rebekka's husband, Lejeune Dirichlet. His offer to write letters of introduction because Felix had been such a lifelong enthusiast pertained to Johanna's move to London and not to her earlier stay in Berlin. See also K. Feilchenfeldt, "Karl August Varnhagen von Ense: Sieben Briefe an Rebecka [Rebekka] Dirichlet," in *Mendelssohn-Studien*, Bd. 3 (1979): 51–79.

14. Karl Hermann Böhmer, born in the Haag, was a chamber musician and violinist in the Royal Orchestra in Berlin. He taught composition and was a critic of instrumental music for the *Neuen Berliner mus. Zeitung.*

15. Karl Gottfried Wilhelm Taubert was a composer and conductor of the Royal Orchestra in Berlin.

16. Hubert Ries was a violinist, chamber musician, composer, and concertmaster of the Royal Berlin Orchestra. He became the conductor of the Philharmonic Society, a position he held until after 1860.

17. Kaufmann, "Johanna Kinkel: Neue Beiträge zu Lebensbild," 7–8. Reprinted by Bettina Brand in "Johanna Kinkel," in *Komponistinnen in Berlin*, 79.

18. Thalheimer, "Johanna Kinkel als Musikerin," 16–18. Besides those of Carl Schurz and Bettine von Arnim quoted here, Thalheimer notes other similar opinions of Johanna's piano playing talents by Leopold Kaufmann, Willibald Beyschlag (both members of the *Maikäferbund*), and Adolf Strodtmann. Credits for these critiques are included in *Anmerkungen zum Kapitel II*, X. She suggests that there are parallels between Johanna's early career as a gifted pianist and the description of the professional life of the young pianist in her novel *Musikalische Orthodoxie*.

19. Ibid., 18. A quote from Carl Schurz, *Lebenserinnerungen*, 2. Bde. (1906).

20. Ibid. A quote from Gottfried Kinkel, Jr. "Aus Johanna Kinkels Memorien," in *Der Zeitgeist, "Beiblatt zum Berliner Tageblatt,"* Nr. 39–47 (1886).

21. Ibid. Thalheimer's source was Adolf Strodtmann in *Gottfried Kinkel: Wahrheit ohne Dichtung*, 2. Bde. (1850).

22. Ibid. A quote from Carl Schurz, *Lebenserinnerung*, 2. Bde. (1905).

23. Ibid.

24. Brand, "Johanna Kinkel," 79.

25. Ibid., 79-80.

26. Weissweiler, *Komponistinnen*, 226, Discussed from descriptions in Gottfried Kinkel's *Selbstbiographie*, (1931), 224.

27. Ibid., 226, 228, and note 86, based on personal recollections of Berta Augusti in *Erinngerungsblätter aus dem Leben einer deutschen Frau*, Cologne and Leipzig, 1887, 129.

28. Thalheimer, "Johanna Kinkel als Musikerin," 12–13.

30. Weissweiler, *Komponistinnen*, 229–31.

31. Thalheimer, "Johanna Kinkel als Musikerin," 16.

32. Ibid. The *Maikäferbund* included in its membership Willibald Beyschlag, Karl Simrock, Ferdinand Freiligrath, Jacob Burkhardt, Alexander Kaufmann, and C. Wolfgang Müller.

33. Weissweiler, *Komponistinnen*, 231–32. An extensive description of Kinkel's political and journalistic activities may be found in Weissweiler's radio script, "Wie ein Kampfgenossen — Zur politischen und künstleroschen Emanzipation der rheinischen Komponistin Johanna Kinkel," written for Samstagabend im WDR III, February 23, 1980.

34. See Carl Schurz, *Die Befreiung Gottfried Kinkels aus dem Zuchthaus in Spandau* (Munich: Schumacher-Gabler), 1992.

35. Winifred Glass and Hans Rosenwald, ed. and trans., *Piano Playing Letters to a Friend* (Chicago: Publishers Development Company, 1943), 17.

36. Ann Willison Lemke, "Die Revolutionäre Musik der Bonnerin Johanna Kinkel," in *Kontrapunkt Kalender* (Kassel: Furore, 1999), 122–23 and 128–29 and the *Anleitung zum Singen: Übungen und Liedchen für Kinder von 3–6 Jahren mit Begleitung des Klaviers*, op. 20 (Mainz: Schott, 1849),16.

37. See H. Schiller, ed., "Briefe an Cotta," Bd. 3. *Vom Vormärz bis Bismark 1833–1863* (Stuttgart and Berlin: n.p., 1934) and Ruth-Ellen Boetcher Joeres, "The Triumph of the Woman: Johanna Kinkel's *Hans Ebeles in London* (1860)," in *Euphorion: Zeitschift für Literaturgeschichte*, vol. 70 (Heidelberg: n.p. 1976), 187-97.

38. Schulte, *Johanna Kinkel*, 110–11 and Eva Rieger, "'Ich schmachte, schmachte nach Geist' (Briefe 1838–1857)," in *Frau und Musik* (Kassel: Furore, 1990), 92–93.

39. "Friedrich Chopin als Komponist" was discussed in *Deutsche Revue*, Jg. 27, Bd. I (January/March 1902) and the *Bonner Zeitung* (February15/May 15, 1903). See also Weissweiler, *Komponistinnen*, 237, note 83.

40. Adelheid von Asten-Kinkel's article "Johanna Kinkel über Mendelssohn" appeared in *Deutsche Revue*, Jg. 28, Bd. I (1903).

41. Schulte, *Johanna Kinkel*, 112–35. What might have caused Kinkel to jump or to fall from her window and the reactions of Gottfried Kinkel, her children, and her friends to her death are extensively discussed.

42. Ferdinand Freiligrath's poem for Kinkel was entitled *Nach Johanna Kinkel Begräbnis, 20 Nov. 1858*. (Her death occurred on November 15 and she was buried five days later.) The poem is quoted in ibid., 120–22.

43. Glass and Rosenwald, *Piano Playing Letters*, 11.

44. Weissweiler, "Die Stille Opposition: Heine-Vertonungen von Frauen — Am Beispiel von Johanna Kinkel und Clara Schumann," in *Komponistinnen in Berlin*, 96–103.

45. Brand, "Johanna Kinkel," 88, quoted from a 1984 reprint, 22ff.

46. Thalheimer, "Johanna Kinkel als Musikerin," 54.

47. *Die Vogelkantate: Musikalischer Scherz*, op. 1 (Berlin: Trautheim, 1838). Music examples that follow are taken from this work.

48. Examples 1-6 from *Die Vogelkantate*.

Ex. 1
Allegretto
Kuckkuck
recit.
Hier sitz' ich ar-mer Kuck-kuck ver - steckt in mei-nem Ne-ste, und
6
war-te auf die Vö-gel die heut sind mei-ne Gä-ste. Wir müs-sen Pro-be hal-ten wohl auf das Al-ler-be-ste, da - mit wir zu des Kö-nigs, des
11
Ad-lers, Na-mens-fe-ste mit Zwit-schern und mit Sin - gen mit Zwit-schern und mit Sin - gen ein fro-hes Ständ-chen brin-gen.
17
Wo mö-gen sie nur blei-ben!
23
Die Zeit mir zu ver - trei-ben, will ich den Ast hier auf und ab spa - zie - ren, und un-ter-dess ein biß-chen sol-feg - gi - ren

Ex. 2

82
Nachtigall
solo
Ich will ei-ne gros - se Bra-vour = A-rie sin - gen; da sol-len Tril-ler und Rou-la den er - klin - gen, da sol-len
87
Tril - ler und Rou - la - den, ja, ja, Rou - la - den
91
tr
klin - gen.
ad lib
ti ti ti ti tia tia tia tia
trrrrrrrrrrrrrrrrrrrrrrrrrrrrrrrrrrrrrrrrrrrrrrrrrrrrrit,
Elster u. Kuk
piep, piep,
Pap
Auch ein Du - et - to
Rabe
Auch ein Du - et - to
Ex. 3
114
Allegro molto
Chor
pp
Wie? was? wie? was? wie? was? wie?
f
wie? was? wie?
pp
cresc.

121
Nachtigall, Elster, Pap
was? Herr Kuck-kuck, was fällt Ih - nen ein? Herr Kuck-kuck, was fällt Ih - nen ein?
Kuckkuck
ff
Zum Kuck-kuck!
Rabe
was? Herr Kuck-kuck, was fällt Ih - nen ein? Herr Kuck-kuck, was fällt Ih - nen ein?
Ex. 4
178
Kuckkuck
recit.
In's Kuck-kucks Na-men seyd doch still, mag di - ri - gi - ren wer da will; stimmt an den
182
Chor: Die Mu - sik le - be hoch! Je - doch pau - sirt vor - her sechs Tak - te noch.
Ex. 5
201
[ff]
Leid, und je - de Freu - de wird ver - schönt.
[ff]
Leid, und je - de Freu - de wird ver - schönt.
cresc.
[ff]
Leid, und je - de Freu - de wird ver - schönt.
ff

Ex. 6

239
Wir hö - ren.
Wir hö - ren.
Wir hö - ren.
recit.
Ich bit - te die Vö - gel um ein ge - neig - tes Ohr.
Wir hö - ren.
242
Kuckkuck
Sin - get doch vor Al - lem erst den Chor, dann könnt Ihr nach vol - len - de - tem Ge - sang mit Lust und
245
Nachtigall u. Elster
Es le - be hoch die Göt - tin Har - mo -
Kuckkuck u. Papagai
Lieb' auch en - den eur' Ge - zank. Es le - be hoch die Göt - tin Har - mo -
Rabe
Es le - be hoch die Göt - tin Har - mo -

248
nie die je - des Herz ent - zückt, es le - be hoch die Göt - tin Har - mo -
nie die je - des Herz ent - zückt, es le - be hoch die Har - mo -
nie die je - des Herz ent - zückt, es le - be hoch die Har - mo -
252
nie die je - des Herz ent - zückt, das sich ihr weiht. Sie
nie die je - des Herz ent - zückt, Sie
nie die je - des Herz ent - zückt, Sie
p
255
trö - stet uns in je - dem Leid, und je - de Freu - de wird ver - schönt durch
trö - stet uns in je - dem Leid, und je - de Freu - de wird ver - schönt durch
trö - stet uns in je - dem Leid, und je - de Freu - de wird ver - schönt durch
cresc.

49. Thalheimer, "Johanna Kinkel als Musikerin," 45, based on a study of Carnival music in Cologne during the nineteenth century by Dr. E. Langsam.

50. Weissweiler, *Komponistinnen*, 221.

51. Thalheimer, "Johanna Kinkel als Musikerin," 49. This and other critiques of Kinkel's compositions by Ludwig Rellstab are found in *Iris im Gebiet der Tonkunst*, no. 9 (1838), and nos. 2 and 3 (1839).

52. Ibid., 50.

53. Ibid., 51–52. In a letter to Auguste Heinrich dated February 1, 1855, Kinkel wrote: "My *Bird's Cantata* was performed this past summer and the next day I had an inquiry from a publisher about the possibility of publishing it. Unfortunately, this was not possible."

Kinkel's *Mouse Cantata* figured in another letter to Augusta Heinrich dated 1854. Thalheimer says that the score disappeared and there was no opportunity to compare it to her *Bird's Cantata*.

54. Weissweiler, *Komponistinnen*, 224 and information taken from Kaufmann, "Johanna Kinkel." Copies of several pages of this publication are to be found in Brand's "Johanna Kinkel," 79–81. (Bettina Brand photocopied several pages from original publications, but omitted the original page numbers.)

55. Angela Oppenhoff (1814–1881), one of Kinkel's closest friends, was born in Bonn, the daughter of a family of civil servants. In their letters they used the diminutive nicknames "Engelchen" and "Hänuchen" as forms of address and closing.

56. From a letter reprinted in Eva Rieger, ed., *Frau und Musik* (Kassel: Furore, 1990), 87.

57. Rahel Varnhagen von Ense, née Levin (1771–1833) was the wife of Karl August Varnhagen von Ense, dipomat and writer and a frequent visitor to the Mendelssohn househhold. Rahel herself was the focal point of a leading Berlin literary salon organized in the 1790s.

58. Schumann was quoted in Kaufmann, "Johanna Kinkel," 33.

59. Thalheimer, "Johanna Kinkel als Musikerin," 64.

60. Kaufmann, "Johanna Kinkel," 25.

61. Rellstab's critique in *Iris im Gebiet der Tonkunst*, No. 23/1839 is reprinted in Brand, "Johanna Kinkel," 89.

62. See introductory notes to *Weh, dasz wir scheiden müssen* in *Neues Deutsches Liederbuch.* Deutsche Abteilung der Staats-Universität von Wisconsin, ed. B. Q. Morgan, Max Grienschand, and A. R. Hohlfeld (Boston: D. C. Heath, 1931), 139: "The favorite song of the great German-American Carl Schurz and his friend Gottfried Kinkel. The melody comes from Kinkel's wife. The song has become beloved in American circles as well. It can be found, as an example, as *Soldier's Farewell* in the collection "College Songs" (Boston: Oliver Ditson, 1887 and later)."

The versions used in this entry are no. 1 in *Zwei Volks Lieder für Männerchor* (Leipzig and New York: J. Schuberth, 1872) and *Soldier's Farewell*, L. C. Elson, trans., in *The Boylston Club Collection* (Boston: Oliver Ditson, 1875), 109.

63. Resource for the text: *Gedichte von Gottfried Kinkel* (Stuttgart und Augsburg: J. G. Cotta'scher Verlag, 1857).

64. Kaufmann, "Johanna Kinkel," 3. *Eine Frau wie sie kann auch als Tote nicht sterben. Der Zauber ihrer überragenden Persönligkeit wirkt fort.*

Selected List of Works

(The first seventeen opus numbers were published under the name Johanna Mathieux.)

Songs with Opus Numbers

Six Songs, op. 6. Leipzig: Kistner, n.d. [published 1838].

1. *Sehnsucht nach Griechenland Herz.* Text by Emanuel Geibel
2. *Wasser und Wein.* Text by August Kopisch (solo lied with choral sections)
3. *Die Geister haben's Vernommen.* Text by Heinrich Heine
4. *An Luna.* Text by Johann Wolfgang von Goethe
5. *Verlornes Glück.* Text by Johanna Mathieux. Sitze hier an lieber Stelle
6. *Die Sprache der Sterne.* Text by Heinrich Heine. Es stehen unbeweglich die Sterne

Six Songs, op. 7. Berlin: Trautwein, 1838.

1. *Nachtlied.* Text by Emanuel Geibel
2. *Wunsch.* Text by August Kopisch
3. *Vorüberfahrt.* Text by J. Mathieux
4. *Die Lorelei.* Text by Heinrich Heine
5. *An den Mond.* Text by Johann Wolfgang von Goethe
6. *Die Zigeuner.* Text by Emanuel Geibel

Wunsch, no. 2 and *An den Mond,* no. 5, in *Frauen komponieren, 25 Songs for Voice and Piano,* ed. Eva Rieger and Käte Walter. Mainz: Schott Edition 7810, 1992.

Six Poems by Geibel, op. 8. Berlin: Trautwein, [published 1838].

1. *Der spanische Zitherknabe*
2. *Die Rheinsage*
3. *Das Gondellied*
4. *Die Abendfeier*
5. *Trennung*
6. *Abreise*

Das Schloss Boncourt, op. 9. Text by Adelbert von Chamisso. Berlin: Trautwein, 1838 and Fairbanks: ArtsVenture, 2001.

Six Songs, op. 10. Berlin: Trautwein, 1839.
1. *Nachgefühl*. Text by Johann Wolfgang von Goethe
2. *Ich will meine Seele tauchen in den Kelch der Liebe hinein*. Text by Heinrich Heine
3. *So wahr die Sonne scheinet*. Text by Friedrich Rückert
4. *Wiegenlied*. Text by Johanna Mathieux
5. *Traumdeutung*. Text by Johann Wolfgang von Goethe
6. *Der Müllerin Nachbar*. Text by Adelbert von Chamisso

Don Ramiro, op. 13. Text by Heinrich Heine. Ballad for alto or baritone. Cologne and Amsterdam: Eck and Leipzig: Hofmeister, n.d.

Six Songs, op. 15. For alto or baritone and piano. Cologne and Amsterdam: Eck, n.d. [ready for publication in 1841]. Second edition, Leipzig: Hofmeister, n.d.
1. *Römische Nacht*. Text by Gottfried Kinkel
2. *Du nah'st*. No poet listed
3. *Wiegenlied*. No poet listed
4. lost
5. lost
6. *Allegretto*. No poet listed

Römische Nacht, op. 15, no. 1, in *Frauen komponieren, 25 Songs for Voice and Piano*, ed. Eva Rieger and Käte Walter. Mainz: Schott Edition 7810, 1992.

Six Songs, op. 16. Leipzig: Hofmeister, n.d. [listed for publication in December 1841].
1. lost
2. lost
3. lost
4. *Gegenwart*. Text by Johann Wolfgang von Goethe
5. *Rheinfahrt*. Text by Sebastian Longard
6. *Klage*. Text by Sebastian Longard

Six Songs, op. 17 (medium voice and piano). Berlin and Breslau: Bote & Bock, n.d. [published between 1844 and 1851].
1. *Blaue Augen*. Text anon.
2. *Schwarze Augen*. Text by Sebastian Longard
3. *Abendruhe*. Text anon.
4. *Die Stimme der Geliebten*. Text by Platen
5. *In der Bucht*. Text by Alexander Kaufmann
6. *Welt, o Welt! Wie liegst du so weit!* Text anon.

Six Songs, op. 18. Berlin: Schlesinger, n.d. [published 1843].
1. *Stürmisch wandern*
2. *Am Ufer*. Text by J.G.
3. *Auf wohlauf ihr Candioten*. Text by Gottfried Kinkel
4. *Seelige Nacht*. Text anon.
5. lost
6. lost

Six Songs, op. 19. For alto or baritone and piano. Cologne: Schloss, n.d. and 2nd. ed. Berlin: Ries & Erler, n.d. [published between 1844 and 1851].
1. *Die Mandoline*. Text by W. Seibt
2. lost
3. lost
4. lost
5. *Abschied*. Text by Heinrich Heine
6. lost

Abschied, op. 19, no. 5. Text by Heinrich Heine. Arranged for guitar and voice. Cologne: Schloss, n.d. (published together with J. Offenbach's *O, Bleib bei Mir!*) and Fairbanks: ArtsVenture, 2001.

Six Songs, op. 21. Texts by Gottfried Kinkel. For low voice and piano. Mainz: Schott, n.d. [published between 1841 and 1851].
1. lost
2. lost
3. lost
4. *Das Provençaliche Lied*. Text from *Die Assassinen*.
5. *Abendlied*. Text from *Nach der Schlacht*.
6. *Des Lohnsmanns Abschied*. Text is folk song from *Friedrich Barbarossa in Busa*

(There are several versions and publications of song no. 6 including a version for TTBB.)

Lieder, vol. I, ed. Linda Siegel. Texts by Goethe and Geibel. Bryn Mawr, PA: Hildegard Publishing Company, 2000.
1. *Sehnsucht nach Griechenland*, op. 6, no. 1 (1837). Text by Geibel
2. *Nachtlied*, op. 7, no. 1 (1837). Text by Geibel
3. *Die Zigeuner*, op. 7, no. 6 (1837). Text by Geibel
4. *Der Spanische Zitherknabe*, op. 8, no. 1 (1838). Text by Geibel
5. *Rheinsage*, op. 8, no. 2 (1838). Text by Geibel
6. *Gondellied*, op. 8, no. 3 (1838). Text by Geibel
7. *Abendfeier*, op. 8, no. 4 (1838). Text by Geibel
8. *Trennung*, op. 8, no. 5 (1838). Text by Geibel.
9. *Abreise*, op. 8, no. 6 (1838). Text by Geibel
10. *Wolle Keiner Mich Fragen*, op. 18, no. 5 (1843). Text by Geibel
11. *An Luna*, op. 6, no. 4 (1837). Text by Goethe
12. *An den Mond*, op. 7, no. 5 (1837). Text by Goethe
13. *Nachgefühl*, op. 10, no. 1 (ca. 1839). Text by Goethe
14. *Traumdeutung*, op. 10, no. 5 (ca. 1839). Text by Goethe
15. *Lust und Qual*, op. 15, no. 5 (ca. 1841). Text by Goethe
16. *Gegenwart*, op. 16, no. 4 (ca. 1841). Text by Goethe

Music for Two or More Voices

Duets for Women's Voices

Three Duets for Women's Voices, op. 11. Text by Heinrich Heine. Berlin: Trautwein, 1839.
1. *Das Lied der Nachtigal*
2. *Die Geisterinsel*
3. *Der Seejungfers Gesang* (Heine's poem *Wasserfahrt*)

Three Duets for Women's Voices, op. 12. Berlin: Trautwein, 1840.
1. *Die Fischerkinder.* Text by C. Wolfgang Müller
2. *Der Sommerabend.* Text by C. Wolfgang Müller
3. *Nachtgesang.* Text by Johann Wolfgang von Goethe

Quartets for Male Voices

Trinklied. Text by Johanna Mathieux, published in the musical supplement of Robert Schumann's *Neue Zeitschrift für Musik,* Bd. 9, *Zur musikalischen Beilage* Heft 111, 1838.

Cantatas

Die Vogelkantate: ein Musikalischer Scherz. (1830), op. 1. Berlin: Trautwein, 1838, and Gerhard Rahm, ed. Stuttgart: Carus CV12.402, 1966.

Hymnus in Coena Domini, op. 14. Text from the seventh century for soli, chorus, and string orchestra. Cologne: Eck, 1840, and Christa Roelke, ed. Cologne: Tonger 2276, 1994.

Jubilaeum des Grossvaters (1849). Unpublished.

Music for Children

"Aus meiner Kindheit:" *Katzenkantate* (also called *Mäusekantate*). Missing.

The Baker and the Mice (n.d.). Unpublished.

Songs for Little Children. English words adapted to Madame Kinkel's German "Kindergesangschule." London: n.p., 1852.

Opera, Operetta, and Theater Pieces for Amateur Performers

Die Assassinen (1843). Text by Gottfried Kinkel. *Liederspiel* in four acts. Unpublished.

Die Fürstin von Paphos. n.d. Unpublished.

Humoristische Satyre (1842). Text by Gottfried Kinkel. Unpublished.

Die Landpartie (before 1840). Text by the composer. Comic opera. Unpublished.

Das Malztier oder Die Stadt-Bönnischen Gespenster (1840). Comedy in the Bonn dialect with songs and arias based on well-known opera melodies. Unpublished.

Otto der Schütz [1842]. Text by Gottfried Kinkel. *Liederspiel* in one act. (A copy of this ms. is in the Württemberg State Library, Stuttgart). Unpublished. (See vol. 8.)

Vaudeville für den Hochzeitstag des Professors von Henning (1837). Unpublished.

Verrückte Komödien aus Berlin — Der Wettstreit der schottischen Minstrels (1838). Unpublished.

Zum Geburtstag des Herrn von Savigny — Themis und Savigny oder Die Olympier in Berlin (1837). Unpublished.

Bibliography

Tales, Novels, Comedies and Other Miscellaneous Works

Kinkel, Gottfried and Johanna. *Erzählungen*, Zweite unveränderte Auflage, Stuttgart und Tübingen: J. O. Cotta'scher Verlag, 1851.

Kinkel, Gottfried, Johanna Mockel, and A. Simons. *Die Heilung des Weltschmerz(l)e(r)s*, Comedy in Three Acts, 1838–1840.

Kinkel, Johanna. *Bilder aus Cölln's Vorzeit* (ode).
_____. *Aus dem Tagebuch eines Componisten: Skizze von Johanna Kinkel.*

_____. *Dä Hond on dat Eechhorn, ä Verzellsche für Blahge.* Bonn, n.p., 1849.

_____. *Der Letzte Salzbock.* Political drama in five acts. N.p., 1842/1843.

_____. *Der Musikant: Eine rheinische Bürgergeschichte.* N.p., n.d.

_____. *Des Fuderfass zu Trarbach.* A comedy performed at the Rheinischen Maskenfest on February 14, 1842. N.p.

_____. (Mockel) *Die Unerschütterlichkeit der weiblichen Treue.* A novel in letters by several authors. N.p., 1840.

_____. *Eine deutsche Frau in der Fremde.* N.p., n.d.

_____. "Erinnerungsblätter aus dem Jahre 1848," in *Deutsche Review*, April–June and July–September, 1894.

_____. "Erinnerungsblätter aus dem Sommer 1849," ed. Adelheid von Asten-Kinkel, (no journal name) Darmstadt: n.p., 1929.

_____. *Hans Ibeles in London; ein Familienbild aus dem Fluchtlingsleben.* Stuttgart: n.p., 1860.

_____. *Kruckhalfens Trautchen: Eine Dorfgeschichte.* N.p., n.d.

_____. "Lebenslauf eines Johannisfünkchens; aus dem Tagebuch eines Komponisten," in *Bibl. der Deutschen Klassiker: Die Roman- und Novellendichter der Neuzeit,* 2. Teil. Hildburghausen: n.p., 1864.

_____. Various Texts in "Der Maikäfer: Zeitschrift für Nichtphilister," edited together with Gottfried Kinkel (as Mockel until 1843, then Kinkel), Bonn, 1840 until 1846. Reprint in Veröffentlichungen des Stadtarchivs Bonn, 1982.

_____. *Musikalische Orthodoxie: Anachronistische Novelle für das Stifftungsfest 1846,* 1844 and a later version, Berlin: n.p., 1927.

_____. *2 Erzählungen: "Der Jubilarius"* and *"Blumentod". N.p., n.d.*

Writings on Music by Johanna Kinkel

Published

Kinkel, Johanna. *Acht Briefe an eine Freundin über Clavierunterricht.* Stuttgart and Tübingen: n.p., 1852.

_____. "Friedrich Chopin als Komponist." Ed., Adelheid von Asten-Kinkel. *Deutsche Revue* (1902).

_____. *Musik as Mode: Musiktheorie für Mädchen,* 1852. Reprint in Eva Rieger. *Frau und Musik.* Kassel: Furore, 1990.

_____. *Piano Playing Letters to a Friend.* Ed. and trans., Winifred Glass and Hans Rosenwald. Chicago: Publishers Development Company, 1943.

Secondary Sources

Allgemeine musikalische Zeitung. Leipzig. Jg. 40-43, 1838–1841 and Jg. 46, 1844.

Altman: *Kurzgefasstes Tonkünstler-Lexikon*; 14. Aufl. Regensburg: n.p., 1963.

Asten-Kinkel, Adelheid von., ed. "Johanna Kinkel in England." *Deutsche Revue,* Jg. 26 1901/1.

_____. "Johanna Kinkel über Mendelssohn." *Deutsche Revue.* Jg. 28 1903/1.

_____, ed. "Johanna Kinkels Glaubensbekenntnis." *Deutsche Revue,* October–December. Jg. 27 Bd. 4, 1902.

Blos, Anna. *Frauen der deutschen Revolution 1848.* Dresden: n.p., 1928.

Brand, Bettina. "Johanna Kinkel." *Komponistinnen in Berlin.* Berlin: Musikfrauen e.V., 1987.

Bröcker, Marianne. "Johanna Kinkels schriftstellerische und musikpädagogische Tätigkeit." In *Bonner Geschichtsblätter,* Bd. XXIX. Bonn, 1977.

Büttger, F., ed. *Frauen im Aufbruch. Frauenbriefe aus dem Vormärz und der Revolution von 1848.* Darmstadt/Neuwied: n.p., 1979.

Cohen, Aaron."Johanna Kinkel," in *International Encyclopedia of Women Composers,* vol. I, 2nd. ed. New York: Book and Music, 1987.

Drewitz, Ingeborg. *Bettine von Arnim: Romantik-Revolution-Utopie.* Düsseldorf, 1969.

Ewens, F. J. *Lexikon des Chorwesens,* 2. Aufl. Mönchengladbach, 1963.

Feilchenfeldt, K. "Karl August Varnhagen von Ense: Sieben Briefe an Rebecka [Rebekka] Dirichlet." *Mendelssohn-Studien,* Bd. 3. Berlin: Mendelssohn Gesellschaft, 1979.

Fellerer, K.G. *Rheinische Musiker,* 4. Köln: Folge, 1966.

Fink, G. W. "Sechs Lieder für eine Singstimme mit Begleitung des Pianoforte von J. Mathieux." *Allgemeine musikalische Zeitung,* Jg. 40, Nr. 32, 1838.

Ganz, Rudolph. "Johanna Mathieux." *History of the German Song between Schubert and Schumann,* Ph.D. diss. N.d.

Geiger, L., ed. "Briefe von Johanna Kinkel." *Frankfurter Zeitung,* August 3 and 4, 1900.

Goozé, Marjanne and Ann Willison Lemke. "The Political Music of Bettine von Arnim and Johanna Kinkel." *Women in German Year Book,* 1998.

Goslich, Marie, ed. "Briefe von Johanna Kinkel an Familie von Henning." *Preussische Jahrbücher,* Bd. 97, 1899.

Gruber, F. "Johanna Kinkel. Geist und Tat einer bedeutenden Frau: Sie starb vor hundert Jahren im Exil in London." *Druck und Papier.* Zentral Organ der Industriegewerkschaft Druck und Papier. 10. Jg., Nr. 24, 1958.

Gustedt, Silke. *Johanna Kinkel: Leben und Werk einer Komponistin im 19 Jahrhundert*. Zulassungsarbeit zum Staatsexamen, University of Hamburg, August 3, 1981.

Harzen-Müller, A.N. "Johanna Kinkel als Musikerin." *Musikalisches Wochenblatt* 41. Jg. Nr. 13, 1910.

Havlice, Patricia Pate. *Popular Song Index*. Munich, n.p., 1975.

Henseler, Theodor. A. "Das musikalische Bonn im 19. Jahrhundert." In *Bonner Geschichtsblätter*, Bd. XIII, Bonn, 1959.

Hesse, W. "Gottfried und Johanna Kinkel in Bonn." In *Bonner Archiv* V, Bonn, 1893.

_____. Joeres, Ruth-Ellen Boetcher. "The Triumph of the Woman: Johanna Kinkel's *Hans Ebeles in London*." In *Euphorion: Zeitschrift für Literaturgeschichte*, 6900 Heidelberg, vol. 7, 1976.

Hofmeister. *Handbuch der Musikalischen Literatur*, Bd. 9-12. Leipzig, 1887–1906.

Honneger/Massenkeil. *Das grosse Lexikon der Musik*. Bd. 4. Freiburg/Basel/Wien, 1981.

Joesten, J. "Musikalisches Leben in Bonn." In *Bonner Zeitung*, December 17, 1898.

_____. Gottfried Kinkel, sein Leben, Streben und Dichten für das deutsche Volk. Cologne, 1904.

_____. "Ungedruckte Kinkel-Briefe," in *Bonner Zeitung*, December 19–24, 1905.

Kaufmann, Paul. "Johanna Kinkel: Neue Beiträge zu ihrem Lebensbild." In *Schriftenreihe der Preussischen Jahrbücher*, Nr. 22, Berlin, 1931.

_____. "Noch einmal auf Johanna Kinkels Spuren." In *Sonderabdruck der Preussischen Jahrbücher*, 1932.

Kinkel, Gottfried, Jr., ed. "In Memoiren." In *Der Zeitgeist*, "Beiblatt zum *Berliner Tageblatt*," Nr. 39–47, 1886.

_____. "Drei Jahre aus dem Leben eines deutschen Dichterpaares." In *Zeitgeist*, Nr. 13-17, 1887.

Lemke, Ann Willison. "'Alles Schaffen ist wohl eine Wechselwirkung von Inspiration und Willen.' Johanna Kinkel als Komponistin." In *Annäherung IX–an sieben Komponistinnen: Mit Berichten, Interviews und Selbsdarstellungen*. Ed. Clara Mayer. Kassel: Furore, 1998.

_____. "Bettine's Song: The Musical Voice of Bettine von Arnim, née Brentano, (1785–1859)." Ph. D. diss., Indiana University, 1998.

_____. "Briefe einer Bettina-Verehrerin: Ein Beitrag zur frühen Rezeption von Goethe's Briefwechsel mit einem Kinde." In *Internationales Jahrbuch der Bettina-von-Arnim-Gesellschaft* 10, 1998.

_____. "Die revolutionäre Musik der Bonnerin Johanna Kinkel." In *Kontrapunkt Musikkalender 1999*. Kassel: Furore, 1999.

_____. "Johanna (née Mathieux; Mockel) Kinkel," in *New Grove Dictionary of Music and Musicians*. London: Macmillan, 2000.

Lenzen, H.L. "Johanna Kinkel." In *Die Frau*, 34 Jg., Nr. 3, 1926.

Leppla, R. ed. "Johanna und Gottfried Kinkel: Briefe an Katinka Zitz, 1849–1861." In *Bonner Geschichtsblätter* XII. Bonn, 1958.

Lewald, Fanny. *Zwölf Bilder nach dem Leben*. Berlin, 1888.

Lorenz, Oswald. "Rezensionen von Liedern v. J. Kinkel." In *Neue Zeitschrift für Musik*, Bd. 8, 1838. (Reprint, 1963)

_____. "Deutsche Liederkomponistinnen." In *Neue Zeitschrift für Musik*, Bd.12, 1840.

Marciano, Rosario, and Jorge Sanchez-Chiong. "Johanna (née Mathieux; Mockel) Kinkel." In *The Norton/Grove Dictionary of Women Composers*. New York: W. W. Norton, 1994.

Meysenbug, Malwida von. *Briefe an Johanna und Gottfried Kinkel (1849–1885)*, eds. Stefania Rossi and Yoko Kikuchi. Bonn: Ludwig Röhrscheid, 1982.

_____. *Memoiren einer Idealistin*. Stuttgart, Berlin, Leipzig, 1922.

Pahncke, K., ed. "Briefe von Johanna Kinkel an Willibald Beyschlag." In *Preussische Jahrbücher*, Bd.122, 1905.

Rellstab, Ludwig. Critiques of Kinkel's compositions in *Iris im Gebiet der Tonkunst*. Jg. 9, 1838; Nr. 2 and 31, Jg. 10, 1839; Nr. 1, Nr. 23 and Nr. 31, Jg. 12, 1841.

Rieger, Eva, ed. "'Ich schmachte, schmachte nach Geist' (Briefe 1838–1857)." In *Frau und Musik*. Kassel: Furore, 1990.

Rittershaus, A., ed. "Felix Mendelssohn und Johanna Kinkel." (Unpublished diaries and letters.) In *Neue Freie Presse*, Vienna, April 19, 1900.

_____. "An die Mutter und an Auguste Heinrich 1851–1857." In *Deutsche Revue*, 1901.

Schiller, H., ed. "Briefe an Cotta." In *Vom Vormärz bis Bismarck* 1833–1863, Bd. 3. Stuttgart and Berlin: n.p., 1934.

Schloenbach, A. *Erinnerung an Johanna Kinkel*. Deutsches Museum, 1859.

Schulte, J. F. *Johanna Kinkel: Nach ihren Briefen und Erinnerungs-Blättern: Zum 50. Todestage Johanna Kinkels.* Münster in Westf.: Verlag von Heinrich Schöningh, 1908.

Schumacher, Bettina. *Die Situation der komponierenden Frau im deutschen Biedermeier, dargestellt an den Beispielen von Fanny Hensel, Johanna Kinkel, Josephine Lang und Clara Schumann.* Wissenschaftl. Hausarbeit; Frankfurt am Main, 1983.

Schumann, Robert. Critique and a copy of *Trinklied* by J. Kinkel. In *Neue Zeitschrift für Musik*, Bd. 9, *Zur musikalischen Beilage* Heft 111, 1838.

Summerville, Suzanne. "Adelbert von Chamisso: The Poet of Marriage and the Frauenliebe und Leben." In National Association of Teachers of Singing *Bulletin*, January-February, 1984.

Snyder, Lawrence D. *German Poetry in Song: An Index of Lieder.* Berkeley, Calif.: Fallen Leaf Press, 1995.

Thalheimer, Else. "Johanna Kinkel als Musikerin." Ph.D. Diss., University of Bonn, 1922.

Tritten, Barbara. "Johanna Kinkel's Anleitung zum Singen." M. Music thesis, University of Alaska Fairbanks, 1992.

Weissweiler, Eva. "Die Stille Opposition: Heine-Vertonungen von Frauen — Am Beispiel von Johanna Kinkel und Clara Schumann." In *Komponistinnen in Berlin.* Berlin: Musik-Frauen eV., 1987.

_____. "Fanny Hensel, Josephine Lang, Johanna Kinkel: Komponistinnen um Schumann und Mendelssohn." In *Komponistinnen aus 500 Jahren. Eine Kultur-und Wirkungsgeschichte in Biographien und Werkbeispielen,* Frankfurt: Fischer, 1981.

Werner, J. *Maxe von Arnim 1818–1894.* Leipzig: n.p., 1937.

Verlornes Glück

Sitze hier an lieber Stelle;
wo ich einst nicht sass alleine;
Damals klang hier süsse Rede;
wo ich heut' mein Loss beweine.

Schön und hell nennt man die Erde,
voller Lust und voller Freuden;
Doch ist mir sie ewig dunkel,
weil ich soll ihr Schönstes meiden.

Von den vielen duft'gen Kräutern,
die in diesem Garten stehen,
wird kein einz'ges, mich heile;
Ich muss qualvoll untergehen.

I sit here in this cherished place;
where once I sat but not alone.
Then there were pleasant conversations;
where today I bemoan my fate.

Beautiful and bright one describes the earth,
full of happiness and full of joys;
But for me it is forever dark,
because I must forgo its loveliness.

Of the many fragrant herbs,
that grow in this garden,
not even one can cure me;
I must suffer to the end.

Translation by Suzanne Summerville

Ich will meine Seele tauchen

Ich will meine Seele tauchen
In den Kelch der Lilie hinein;
Die Lilie soll klingend hauchen
Ein Lied von der Liebsten mein.

Das Lied soll schauern und beben
Wie der Kuss von ihrem Mund',
Den sie mir einst gegeben
In wunderbar süsser Stund'.

I will plunge my soul
Into the lily's deep chalice;
The lily's breath shall whisper
A song from my beloved.

The song shall quiver and tremble
Like the kiss from her lips,
That once she gave to me
In a wonderfully sweet moment.

Translation by Suzanne Summerville

Abschied

1. Schöne Wiege meiner Leiden,
Schönes Grabmal meiner Ruh,
Schöne Stadt, wir müssen scheiden,
Lebe wohl! ruf' ich dir zu.

Lebe woh! du heil'ge Schwelle,
Wo da wandelt Liebchen traut;
Lebe wohl! du heil'ge Stelle,
Wo ich sie zuerst geschaut.

2. Hätt' ich dich doch nie gesehen,
Schöne Herzenskönigin!
Nimmer wär' es dann geschehen,
Dass ich jetzt so elend bin.

Nie wollt' ich dein Herze rühren,
Liebe hab' ich nie erfleht;
Nur ein stilles Leben führen
Wollt' ich, wo dein Odem weht.

3. Doch du drängst mich selbst von hinnen,
Bittre Worte spricht dein Mund;
Wahnsinn wühlt in meinen Sinnen,
Und das (mein) Herz ist krank und wund.

Und die Glieder matt und träge,
Schlepp' ich fort am Wanderstab,
Bis mein müdes Haupt ich lege
Ferne in ein kühles Grab.

1. Lovely cradle of my suffering,
Lovely sepulcher of my repose,
Lovely town, we now must part,
Farewell! I call to you.

Farewell! you holy portal,
Where my beloved wandered;
Farewell! you sacred place,
Where I first saw her.

2. Had I not ever seen you,
Beautiful queen of my heart!
It would have never happened,
That I would be as sad as I am now.

I never wanted to touch your heart,
I never implored you to love me;
To live a quiet life where your breath
Wafts in the air was all I ever wanted.

3. But you reject me,
Your lips speak bitter words;
Madness surges through my senses,
And my heart is sick and wounded.

My limbs are lifeless and inert,
Supported by my cane I must wander on,
Until I lay my tired head down
In a cool grave far away.

Translation by Wolfgang Westermann and Suzanne Summerville

Ritters Abschied

Weh, das wir scheiden müssen, Lass dich noch einmal küssen; Ich muss an Kaisers Seiten Ins falsche Welschland* reiten: Fahr wohl, fahr wohl, mein armes Lieb!	How can I bear to leave thee, One parting kiss I give thee; And then what e'er befalls me, I go where honor calls me: Farewell, farewell, my own true love!
Ich werd aus Maienauen Dich niemals wieder schauen, Der Feinde grimme Scharen Sind kommen angefahren: Fahr wohl, fahr wohl, mein armes Lieb!	Ne'er more may I behold thee Or to this heart enfold thee, With spear and pennon glancing I see the foe advancing: Farewell, farewell, my own true love!
Ich denk an dich mit Sehnen, Gedenk an mich mit Tränen; Wenn meine Augen brechen, Will ich zuletzt noch sprechen: Fahr wohl, fahr wohl, mein armes Lieb!	I think of thee with longing, Think thou, when tears are thronging; That with my last faint sighing, I'll whisper softly while dying: Farewell, farewell, my own true love!

* Welschland could be either Italy or France.

Translation by L.C. Elson in The Boylston Club Collection

Auf wohlauf, ihr Candioten

1. Auf wohlauf, ihr Candioten, schwinget hoch das Kreuzpanier, Funkeln lasst die weissen Felsen in des Blutes Purpurzier!	1. Stand up you warrior comrades, swing high the cross's banner, the white rocky crags dip into sparkling crimson blood!
Unser ist das Land, das mächtig aus dem Ozean sich hebt; Unser sei es, bis es mördrisch neu der Ocean begräbt!	Ours is the land, that heaves itself with strength; Ours it is, until it is buried anew in that ocean!
Unser ist des Kornes Fülle, unser ist des Weines Glut, Unser die metall'ne Ader die in ew'gen Bergen ruht.	Ours is the corn's abundance, ours is the glow of wine, Ours is the metallic vein that rests forever in the eternal mountains.
2. Auf, wohlauf, ihr Candioten, hoch das Kreuz und hoch den Speer! Und der Rosshuf des Osmanli stampfe nie den Boden mehr.	2. Stand up, you warrior comrades, hold high the cross and spear! let the hooves of Osman horses never again trample this ground.
Unser sind die hundert Städte hoch mit Ruhme sonst genannt; Ach es blieben wenig Dörfer hingemordet und verbrannt.	Ours are the hundred cities glorious as they were known; Oh, the remaining are small villages pillaged and burned down.

Unser sind die frischen Rosen rein aus Hellas Blut entstammt! Soll sie der Barbare rauben nur zu schnö der Lust entflammt?	Ours are the velvet roses pure from Hellas noble roots! May the Barbarian disgrace them imbued only with distainful lust?
3. Steig herauf, gerechter Minos, der des Orkus Waage hält, hilf du rechten Deinem Volke rechten mit der Christenwelt,	3. Oh, be seen righteous Minos, who is holding Orcus' scale, Do the right things for your people and the same for Christendom,
Die des Kreuzes freien Kriegern schon mit neuen Ketten dräut; Die verräth'rischen uns gerathen, unterwerfung uns gebeut.	While the cross of the free warriors threatened by confining chains; Which the treacherous have told us, for submission be the end.
Wehe aber, dreifach Wehe jedem, der des Volkes Schritt, hemmet auf dem Pfad der Freiheit, ihn zermalmt der Rache Tritt.	Woe, oh, three times woe to those, who stop the people's quest for freedom, they will be crushed by deep revenge.

Translation by Annegret Wilder and Suzanne Summerville

Nachtgesang

O gieb, vom weichen Pfühle, Träumned, ein halb Gehör! Bei meinem Saitenspiele. Schlafe! was willst Du mehr?	Lying on your soft pillow, Dreaming, lend half an ear! To the sounds of my strings. Sleep! what more could you wish?
Bei meinem Saitenspiele Segnet der Sterne Heer Die ewigen Gefühle; Schlafe! was willst Du mehr?	As I play upon these strings The starry host blesses The eternal affections; Sleep! what more could you wish?
Die ewigen Gefühle Heben mich, hoch und kehr, Aus irdischem Gewühle; Schlafe! was willst Du mehr?	The eternal affections Lift me aloft, soaring, Away from earthly troubles; Sleep, what more could you wish?
Vom irdischen Gewühle Trennst du mich nur zu sehr, Bannst mich in diese Kühle; Schlafe! was willst Du mehr?	From earthly troubles You tear me away, And hold me hostage in this cool place; Sleep! what more could you wish?
Bannst mich in diese Kühle; Giebst nur im Traum Gehör. Ach, auf dem weichen Pfühle Schlafe! was willst Du mehr?	In this cool place you imprison me; You listen only in your dreams. Ah, on your soft pillow Sleep! what more could you wish?

Translation by Suzanne Summerville

Verlornes Glück

J. Mathieux

J. Mathieux [Johanna Kinkel]
Op. 6, no. 5

Andante
Sit - ze hier an lie - ber Stel - le, wo ich einst nicht sass al -
Schön und hell nennt man die Er - de, vol-ler Lust und vol-ler
Von den vie - len duft' gen Kräu - tern, die in die - sem Gar-ten
5
lei - ne; da - mals klang hier süs - se Re - de, wo ich
Freu - den; doch ist mir sie e - wig dun - kel, weil ich
ste - hen, wird kein einz' - ges, ach, mich hei - len; ich muss
9
heut' mein Loss be - wei - ne.
soll ihr Schön - stes mei - den.
qual - voll un - ter - ge - hen.
13

Ich will meine Seele tauchen

Heinrich Heine

J. Mathieux [Johanna Kinkel]
Op. 10, no. 2

Andante con moto

Ich will mei - ne See - le tau - - - -

pp

[sim.]

4

chen in den Kelch der Li - lie hin - ein.

8

Die Li - lie soll klin - gend hau - - - -

12

chen ein Lied von der Lieb - sten mein.

16
Das Lied soll schau - ern und be - -
20
ben wie der Kuss von ih - rem Mund,
24
den sie mir einst ge - ge - -
28
ben in wun - der-bar süs - ser Stund.
32
rall.
Ped.

Abschied
Heinrich Heine
Johanna Kinkel
Op. 19, no. 5
Larghetto
Guitarre
Schö - ne_ Wie - ge mei - ner Lei - den, schö - nes
Hätt' ich_ dich doch nie___ ge - se - hen, schö - ne
Doch du_ drängst mich selbst___ von hin - nen, bitt - re
8
Grab - mal mei - ner Ruh, Schö - ne Stadt, wir müs - sen schei - den,
Her - zens - kö - ni - ginn! Nim - mer wär' es dann ge - sche - hen,
Wor - te spricht dein Mund; Wahn - sinn wühlt in mei - nen Sin - nen
15
Le - be wohl! ruf ich dir zu. Le - be wohl! du heil' - ge
dass ich jetzt so e - lend bin. Nie wollt' ich dein Her - ze
und das Herz ist krank und wund. Und die Glie - der matt und
22
Schwel - le, wo da wan - delt Lieb - chen traut; Le - be wohl! du
rüh - ren, Lie - be hab' ich nie er - fleht; nur ein stil - les
trä - ge schlepp' ich fort am Wan - der - stab; bis mein mü - des
29
molto rall.
heil' - ge Stel - le, wo ich sie zu - erst___ ge - schaut.
Le - ben füh - ren wollt' ich, wo dein O - dem weht.
Haupt ich le - ge fer - ne in ein küh - les Grab.

Ritters Abschied

Johanna Kinkel

Dieses Zeichen (') bedeutet Athem zu nehmen.

Auf wohlauf ihr Candioten

Gottfried Kinkel

Johanna Kinkel
Op. 18, no. 3

Tempo di marcia

f

Auf wohl-auf, ihr Can - di - o - ten, schwin - get hoch das
Auf wohl-auf, ihr Can - di - o - ten, hoch das Kreuz und
Steig her - auf, ge - rech - ter Mi - nos, der des Or - kus

f

trem.

4

Kreuz pa - nier, fun - keln lasst die weis - sen _ Fel sen
hoch den Speer! und der Ross - huf des _ Os - man - li
Waa - ge hält, hilf du rech - ten Dei - nem _ Vol - ke

7

mf

in des Blu - tes Pur - pur - zier. Un - ser ist das Land das
stam - pfe nie den Bo - den mehr. Un - ser sind die hun - dert
rech - ten mit der Chris - ten - welt, die des Kreu - zes frei - en

mf

10

mäch - tig aus dem O - ze - an _ sich _ hebt;
Städ - te hoch mit Ruh - me sonst ge - nannt;
Krie - gern schon mit neu - en Ket - ten _ dräut;

13
Un - ser sei es bis es mör - drisch neu der O - ce - an be -
Ach es blie - ben we - nig Dör - fer hin - ge - mor - det und ver -
Die ver-räth' - risch uns ge - ra - then, Un - ter - wer - fung uns ge -
sfz
f
sfz
16
f
gräbt. Un - ser ist des Kor - nes Fül - le,
brannt. Un - ser sind die fri - schen Ro - sen
beut. We - he a - ber, drei - fach We - he
f
19
un - ser ist des Wei - nes Glut, un - ser die me - tall' - ne
rein aus Hel - las Blut ent - stammt! Soll sie der Bar - ba - re
Je - dem, der des Vol - kes Schritt: hem - met auf dem Pfad der
sfz
22
A - der die in ew' - gen Ber - gen ruht.
rau - ben nur zu schnö - der Lust ent - flammt?
Frei - heit, ihn zer - malmt der Ra - che Tritt!

Nachtgesang

Johann Wolfgang von Goethe

Johanna Mathieux
Op. 12, no. 3

Adagio

Soprano I

Soprano II

Piano

mf

4

p

O gieb vom wei - chen Pfüh - le träu-mend ein halb Ge -

p

O gieb vom wei - chen Pfüh - le träu-mend ein halb Ge -

pp

Ped. *

8

hör. Bei mei - nem Sai - ten - spie - le schla - fe! was willst Du

mf

hör. Bei mei - nem Sai - ten - spie - le schla - fe! was willst Du

Ped. *

12
mehr?
mf
mehr? Bei mei - nem Sai - ten - spie - le seg - net der Ster - ne
mf
16
f
Heer die e - wi-gen ge - füh - le, schla - fe! was willst Du
p
20
f
Die e - wi-gen ge - füh - le he - ben mich hoch und
mehr?
f

24
hehr aus ir - di-schem Ge - wüh - le; schla - fe! was willst Du
28
mehr?
mf
Vom ir - di-schen Ge - wüh - le trennst Du mich nur zu
32
Bannst mich in die - se Küh - le; schla - fe! was willst Du
sehr, bannst mich in die - se Küh - le; schla - fe! was willst Du

36
mehr? bannst mich in die - se Küh - le, giebst nur im Traum Ge -
mehr? bannst mich in die - se Küh - le, giebst nur im Traum Ge -
pp
40
hör. Ach auf dem wei - chen Pfüh - le schla - fe! was willst Du
hör. Ach auf dem wei - chen Pfüh - le schla - fe! was willst Du
mf
44
mehr? Schla - fe! schla - fe! was willst Du mehr?
mehr? Schla - fe! schla - fe! was willst Du mehr?
pp smorz.

Josephine Lang
(1815–1880)

HARALD KREBS

Josephine Lang was born in Munich on March 14, 1815, into a family rich in musical background. Her father, Theobald Lang (1783–1839), was a violinist, and her mother, Regina Hitzelberger (1788–1827), a singer who was active on the operatic stage until her marriage. She then taught and performed at Court and in church. Lang's brother was a famous actor, occupying a prominent position at the Munich Court Theater.[1]

Lang herself took great pleasure in music even in the first years of her life. Her mother taught her piano and singing, and she began to show compositional talent at the age of five. As she grew older, she took piano lessons from numerous teachers, but found the lessons "excruciating," because the instruction was "disorganized and lacking in method."[2] At age eleven she began to study piano with Josephine Berlinghoff, who, in recognition of her talent, gave her lessons free of charge. She made significant progress, and soon began to teach piano herself. Her teaching income was a help to her impoverished family, but a severe burden on her weak constitution.[3] In spite of her busy schedule and poor health, her composing flourished. By the age of fifteen, she had written many songs of striking originality, including the sparkling *Fee'n-Reigen* (Fairy Dance), op. 3, no. 4, and the ecstatic Goethe setting, *Frühzeitiger Frühling* (Early Spring), op. 6, no. 3.

She was encouraged in her activities by her godfather, the painter Joseph Stieler, who had known Goethe and Beethoven, and who extended hospitality to the greatest artists of the day. Among the prominent guests at the Stielers was Felix Mendelssohn, who stayed there on his way to Italy in 1830 and during his return trip in 1831. On both occasions, Lang heard Mendelssohn play, and sang her own compositions for him (including the two songs mentioned above). Mendelssohn made a lasting impression on her, but no less deep was the impression that she made on him. On October 6, 1831 he wrote to his family:

> She . . . has the gift to compose songs and to sing them in a way the like of which I have never heard; it is the most perfect musical pleasure that I have ever been granted. When she sits down at the piano and begins a song, the tones sound different — all of the music moves back and forth so strangely, and in each note lies the deepest, finest feeling. When she sings the first note with her gentle voice, everyone becomes quiet and thoughtful, and everyone in his own way is moved through and through. If only you could hear that voice! [4]

Mendelssohn believed that Lang's parents were misusing her gifts; after an exhausting day of study and teaching she was frequently required to sing and play at social gatherings. Mendelssohn also found that she was deficient in knowledge of repertoire and in critical judgment. In 1831, he gave her twelve hours of theory lessons himself, and urged that she be sent to Berlin for further study with his sister Fanny and with Carl Zelter.[5] But her father could not bring himself to allow her to leave home. A few years later (in 1839), when a sojourn in Vienna for the purposes of further study had been arranged for her, he reacted similarly; seeing his obvious sorrow at her imminent departure, she canceled the trip. When her father died later that year, her opportunities to seek an education outside of Munich became even more severely restricted; she was now, more than ever, needed at home to contribute to the support of the family.

Aside from one pleasure trip to Salzburg in 1838 and numerous visits to Tegernsee, where the Stielers had a summer home (and where she composed many of her songs),[6] she left Munich only for the purpose of convalescence from especially severe illness, or in order to recover from emotional stresses. Given the paucity of her opportunities for travel, it is fortunate that her environment in Munich was so stimulating. She continued to meet prominent figures of the day, including musicians Peter Cornelius (1824–1874), Franz Lachner (1803–1890), Franz Liszt (1811–1886), Wilhelm Taubert (1811–1891), and Sigismond Thalberg (1812–1871). She became quite famous in Munich; Ferdinand Hiller writes that she was "the rage" (*Mode*) in the highest society.[7] New avenues for the enhancement of her musical education were opened to her when she was admitted to the choir of the Royal Chapel in 1835 and when she became a *Kammersängerin* (court singer) in 1840, positions that enabled her to become familiar with a great deal of sacred music.

Two of Lang's short trips led to significant developments in her career and personal life. In 1835, she was betrothed, following the wishes of her father, to a man whom she did not love. She fled to Augsburg, where she gathered the strength to break the engagement.[8] During this difficult time, she stayed with one of the most prominent families of Augsburg, the Hoesslins. In their home, she met the pianist and composer Stephen Heller, with whom, during this and later visits to Augsburg, she conversed about music, and for whom she performed her songs. Many years later, Heller wrote, "I still vividly remember several of her songs, especially one called 'Butterfly,' although I have not seen or heard them for over thirty years. She sang so charmingly and accompanied herself in a heavenly manner."[9] Lang's acquaintance with Heller led to an important publication and review of one of her songs. Heller introduced her to the music of Robert Schumann, which he revered.[10] When he informed Lang that he was corresponding with Schumann, she asked him to send Schumann some of her songs; after some delay, he did so. Schumann at first referred to the songs as "horrid."[11] Undaunted, Heller thereupon sent him a second shipment, with the suggestion that he publish one of the songs in the *Neue Zeitschrift für Musik*. This time, Schumann wrote, "I must have misjudged Lang; at least I don't understand how [her music] suddenly has so much that is tender and intimate."[12] Schumann published Lang's *Traumbild* (Dream Vision) in a supplement to his journal late in 1838.[13] He also reviewed the song, writing that "the song is a fine, extremely tender shoot, which we recommend to the attentive scrutiny of the reader. It appeals to us thoroughly in its intimacy, particularly where it modulates to C; the whole is very expressively declaimed."[14]

Another trip that led to a turning point in Lang's life took place after the death of her father in 1839. One of her royal supporters, the dowager Karoline Friederike Wilhelmine (1776–1841), second wife of King Maximilian I Joseph of Bavaria (1756–1825), became aware of her prostration after this event, and arranged for her to take a cure at Bad Kreuth in the Bavarian Alps in June 1840. There, she met Christian Reinhold Köstlin (1813–1856), who was also recuperating from a serious illness. Though trained as a lawyer, Köstlin was intensely interested in theater and music. He had wished to become an actor, attending the theater frequently during his student years, and had written several plays, hundreds of poems, and several novellas. He played the piano, and was very knowledgeable about music.[15] Heinrich Köstlin states that Lang and Köstlin met on July 1, 1840.[16] If this is true, they fell in love almost immediately, for one of Lang's manuscript booklets contains a sketch for a song entitled *Erstes Begegnen* (First Meeting), the text of which begins, "I feel as though I had known you for years, so at home do I feel with you." At the top of the sketch page, Lang wrote, "Pure and gracious like your soul will be your love." The German for "pure and gracious" is "rein und hold" — a pun on "Reinhold." The sketch, headed "Kreuth on the first of July, 1840, Wednesday 3:30, at the piano,"[17] appears to be the first of a series of approximately twenty-five collaborations between Köstlin and Lang that came into being during the period of their courtship. When Lang went to Tegernsee to visit the Stielers, Köstlin followed her, and the glorious, intoxicating days of romance and creativity continued. Among the Köstlin texts that Lang set in Tegernsee is *O sehntest du dich so nach mir* (If you longed for me), op. 14, no. 1. The upward-striving vocal line beautifully suggests longing and yearning.

The Tegernsee idyll ended with a shock: Köstlin, after declaring his love, abruptly departed on August 13, 1840. He soon wrote to Lang and explained his behavior; he was involved with, though not betrothed to another woman, and needed time to break this relationship.[18] Both Köstlin and Lang suffered much during this time of separation. Köstlin found solace in writing to Lang, as Lang did in continuing to set Köstlin's texts.[19] *Nach dem Abschied* (After the Farewell), op. 9 no. 3, a lovely, pensive song in F-sharp major (September 14, 1840), and the ecstatic *Ob ich manchmal dein gedenke?* ([You ask] if I sometimes think of you?), op. 27 no. 3 date from this period. The manuscript of the latter song is superscribed, "Composed 6 April 1841, 3:00 p.m. in eternal expectation."

The period of anxious waiting came to an end on April 16, 1841, when Köstlin wrote to Lang with a proposal of marriage, which she joyfully accepted. A few days later, she set his poem *Frühling ist gekommen* (Spring has come — her op. 27 no. 4) to music of Mendelssohnian exuberance and sprightliness, superscribing the manuscript with the words, "Composed 19 April, 1841, in the most joyful mood." Lang and Köstlin were married in Stuttgart on March 29, 1842, and settled in Tübingen, where Köstlin had just been offered a position at the university.

The marriage appears to have been a happy one.[20] Lang and Köstlin were acquainted with many prominent figures, including the poets Ludwig Uhland and Berthold Auerbach, and the composers Immanuel Faisst and Friedrich Silcher. In spite of her interaction with these composers Lang's move from Munich to Tübingen essentially isolated her from the musical world. Professional concerts, in particular, were scarce in Tübingen. Lang and Köstlin attempted to compensate for this lack by playing symphonies on the piano (four hands), and later by encouraging their six children to engage in musical activities.[21]

Initially, both Lang and Köstlin remained creatively active (although in Lang's case, much less so than before her marriage).[22] Reinhold's letters to Felix Mendelssohn reveal that he was writing plays and poetry.[23] Lang wrote only fourteen songs during the fourteen years of her marriage (plus a few fragments), most of them settings of Köstlin's poems. In 1844, she published some of these songs as her op. 12, including some works from the years prior to her marriage. She dedicated the set to "her friend Felix Mendelssohn." Mendelssohn indeed continued to act as a friend, putting in a good word for her with the publisher Friedrich Kistner in Leipzig, and checking her songs for errors.[24]

As time went on, Lang's domestic duties became increasingly arduous. Her own ill health, and the necessity of caring for her husband and children when they were ill, inevitably resulted in a decrease in her musical productivity.[25] Her second son Theobald suffered from a paralytic disease and required constant attention.

In the early 1850s, Reinhold Köstlin, too, became ill; because of a steadily worsening throat ailment (probably cancerous), his doctor ordered him not to speak, which forced him to relinquish his university duties.[26] During the years of his illness, Lang appears to have written no music at all; none of her song manuscripts are dated 1854, 1855, or 1856.

In September 1856, at the young age of 43, Reinhold Köstlin died. Lang was now forced to engage in musical activities in a more consistent way in order to support her six children. Teaching was one obvious method of earning income, and Lang soon became popular in Tübingen as an instructor of voice and piano; even the local nobility eventually numbered among her students. She was the only voice teacher in town and thus could have taken many students. Her ability to perform this work was, however, limited by her health, particularly by a weak throat.[27] She attempted to supplement her teaching income by publishing her songs — both unpublished earlier works as well as newly composed works.[28] One of the early songs that she revised for publication shortly after Köstlin's death is the Uhland setting *Frühlingsglaube*, op. 25, no. 1 (composed 1833, revised 1858). Marked "lively and fiery," the song reaches a powerful climax at the words "Nun muss sich alles wenden" (Now everything must change). One gains the impression of a very personal reaction to these words — of a fervent hope that the recent tragic loss might be succeeded by renewed joy.

In her endeavor to publish songs, Lang initially had to endure many rejections. Three years after Köstlin's death, she finally decided to seek the help of influential acquaintances, including Clara Schumann and Ferdinand Hiller. Clara Schumann had heard of Lang through Felix Mendelssohn, and although no meeting between the two women is documented, they were warmly interested in each other's activities.[29] Upon receipt of Lang's plea for help, Clara Schumann attempted to interest publishers in Lang's songs, and later suggested to Hiller that a benefit concert (at which she herself would play) should be organized on Lang's behalf.[30] The conductor and composer Ferdinand Hiller, whom Lang had met in Munich in 1832,[31] became a very active supporter; he not only put in a good word for her with publishers, but published a biographical essay about her in the year 1867, based on notes that she had sent him.[32] This essay aroused a great deal of interest in Lang's music, and also inspired a number of individuals, including Felix Mendelssohn's brother Paul, to come forward with offers of financial assistance.[33] Primarily as a result of Hiller's essay, Lang regained some prominence as a composer and became successful in having her songs accepted for publication. She wrote to Hiller that "a veritable magic must rest on my destiny since my life passed through your dear hands."[34] Lang dedicated some of her finest songs to both of her primary supporters. The collection dedicated to Clara Schumann (op. 26) contains a *Wiegenlied* (Lullaby), in which Lang sets a soothingly low-pitched vocal line against reiterated chimes in the high piano register. The group dedicated to Hiller, her op. 38 (39), begins with the charming song *Vorsatz* (Resolution), in which playfulness and deep emotion are strikingly blended — the former dominating in the lilting piano introduction, the latter in the lyrical middle section in the key of the flat submediant, which builds up to an impressive climax.

Lang remained in her home in Tübingen until her death, only occasionally undergoing, with great reluctance, prescribed rest cures at nearby resorts, or visiting her youngest son and his family in Friedrichshafen. Although she continued to have little opportunity to hear music, she remained interested in the music of the past and present, studying scores of Handel, Beethoven, and Ferdinand Hiller, and exploring opera scores with her son-in-law, the singer Johannes Schleich.[35]

Her final years were filled with tribulations. Her firstborn son Felix, after a promising beginning in a course of theological studies, gradually descended into mental illness, was committed to an asylum, and died there in a fire in 1867. Her second son Theobald died in 1873. Her two daughters Therese and Maria married in 1868 and 1870, respectively; although Lang was pleased with their choice of husbands, their departure from the household greatly increased her own workload and her loneliness.[36] Her third son Eugen became ill, returned home to be under her care, and died in 1880. She was frequently seriously ill herself; during one of her illnesses, she was deaf for ten days, and during another, blind for eight weeks.[37] These illnesses, of course, brought financial problems with them, frequently rendering her unable to teach for weeks at a time.

Surprisingly, Lang remained active as a composer throughout these trials. She usually composed during the walks that her doctor had prescribed, rarely having leisure to do so at other times.[38] Among her finest late songs are settings of several of the poems appended to Viktor von Scheffel's epic, *Der Trompeter von Säckingen*. Lang died of a heart attack on December 1, 1880.

Lang's songs more obviously constitute reactions to personal experience than those of many other nineteenth-century lieder composers. She did not, like Schumann or Wolf, seek out large bodies of the best poems of the century in order to plumb their meaning via musical settings. She seems rather to have searched for poems that were relevant to her personal situation; several such examples are cited above. Her oft-quoted remark that "her songs were her diary" is absolutely accurate.

Lang's musical style is more reminiscent of that of Felix Mendelssohn than of any other composer. Her harmony, like his, remains primarily diatonic, even in the second half of the century when chromaticism dominated the music of so many of her contemporaries. She employs dissonance, however, more prominently than Mendelssohn does. Some of the dissonance arises from unorthodox voice leading, for example, from parallel motion by seconds, as in measure 9 of *Auf der Alpe* (On the Alpine Meadow), op. 3, no. 2.

Like many nineteenth-century composers, Lang favors modulations to third-related keys; many of her songs move to the mediant or flat mediant (see, for example, *Ewige Nähe*, op. 8, no. 3, see page 140). Her melodies frequently span a wide range and include large leaps. Her accompaniment patterns, as varied in character as those of Schubert, are often quite difficult to play; see *Am Flusse* (By the River), op. 14, no. 2, evoking a rippling brook, or *Schmetterling* (Butterfly), op. 8, no. 1 (see page 132).[39] Some of her accompaniments interact contrapuntally with the vocal line, either by imitating it, or by weaving an independent melody around it; a fine example of the latter technique is the Byron setting *Erinnerung* (published posthumously), in which the beautiful melody of the piano introduction is joined by an independent and equally beautiful vocal line.

Lang's compositional procedure involved the preparation of a pencil sketch including the voice part and text, then the filling in of the piano part, followed either by inking over or rewriting the song. She tested her songs in performance, singing them herself as long as she was able, and later having her daughter Maria sing them.[40] Composition apparently came quite easily to her; she wrote to one of the poets whose works she set to music,

> I deserve neither praise nor thanks [for my songs], but rather I must thank you and your generous muse, who gave me this poem! The poem is in itself already a melody, so that I must confess that it formed itself into a song as I read it through, without any contribution from me! [Composition] is simply a flourishing weed which cannot be eradicated in me, even in the autumn of life, and which is so interwoven with my nature and existence that it belongs to my basic needs.[41]

Lang's *Drei Lieder* op. 8 were published by Tobias Haslinger in Vienna, in June 1838.[42] The songs are dedicated to Karoline Hoesslin, Lang's friend and patron in Augsburg. The first song of the set, *Schmetterling*, was, according to the autograph, originally entitled *Fanny an einen Schmetterling* (Fanny [Addressing] a Butterfly).[43] The author of the text is unknown.

The piano part is one of Lang's most evocative. Whimsical changes of various types suggest the unpredictability of the flight of a butterfly. These include sudden changes of direction and register: for example, the leap upward following the plunging diminished seventh chord, mm. 6-7, the lunge to a higher octave (m. 12), the change from a double-note/single-note to a single-note/double-note pattern in mm. 20-21, the change of rhythm in the final two measures of the song, and the replacement of triplet rhythm by duple eighth notes is very striking.[44] The vocal line is beautifully sculpted. Soaring above the piano part in gentle curves, the line is likely intended to represent "Fanny," the sorrowing maiden. It is only the vocal line that expresses the poignant sense of loss to which the final lines of text refer; the fluttering piano part, like the inconstant "butterfly," remains untouched by such emotion.

The song must not be performed too quickly; it must sound playful, not panic-stricken. The pianist must establish a sense of lightness from the outset. Staccato markings in the autograph in the left hand (mm. 1 and 3), albeit abandoned in the final version, suggest that Lang was thinking in terms of a *leggiero* approach. At measure 21, a light delivery in both voice and piano parts highlights the word "flatterst" (flutter). Again, the autograph suggests that Lang had such a delivery in mind; the original rhythm of the vocal line included rests (i.e., more "air"), and the left hand of the piano part was marked *staccato*.

The section comprising measures 41-68 is a varied repetition of measures 9-32. Lang avoids monotony by inserting a new melodic segment (mm. 57-60), by making small rhythmic changes (cf. the vocal line in mm. 49-53 and 17-21), and by adding the *ritardando* (m. 67). (It would not be wise to do a similar *ritardando* at the corresponding earlier point — mm. 31-32.)

The *ritardando* in the postlude (m. 79) should be minimal the first time through. The second time, a substantial slowing at that point, followed by an immediate return to the tempo, creates a charming effect.

The second song, *In die Ferne* (Into the Distance) is dated "Augsburg 22 September [18]37. Afternoon at 3:30." Robert Schumann thought highly of this song, writing to Stephen Heller, "Among the published songs, the second, 'Into the Distance,' seemed most remarkable to me; it is the best setting of this text that I have encountered."[45] In his response to Schumann, Heller provides more information about the song, stating that Lang wrote it in about forty to fifty minutes. He begged her to send it to Mannheim, where a competition for the best setting of this text was being held, but she "became embarrassed, and said that 'she could only be laughed at for competing.'"[46]

The song justifies Schumann's praise. The music expresses in various ways the yearning for faraway places to which the text refers. For example, the upward-striving vocal line reaches a high D (m. 13), an E (m. 21), then the high point, F (mm. 25 and 34). The latter registral climaxes are appropriately associated with the outcry "Ach," and with the crucial word "Ferne" (distance), respectively. The harmony also contributes to the representation of yearning by the placement of a chromatic progression over a pedal tone (mm. 29-31); the "centrifugal" chromaticism suggests yearning for "Ferne," while the pedal tone implies the reality — the inability to travel to faraway places.[47]

The tempo must not be too slow; the song must not "plod." Performers should search out the harmonies toward which the individual phrases flow and create a sense of striving toward them. For example, the descending bass line of measures 1-2 must move toward the temporary goal of the diminished seventh chord in measure 3.

Even more numerous than in *Schmetterling* are the changes among the three stanzas of this strophic setting. For instance, Lang alters the rhythm of two quarter notes at measure 9 to the rhythm "eighth note, eighth rest, quarter note" at measures 50 and 91. This change is motivated by the text; the added rests set off the exclamations "Ach!" and "O!" The half note and quarter rest in measure 12 are fused into a dotted half in measure 53; again, the text inspired this change, for at measure 12 there is a comma, whereas in m. 53 there is none. In the corresponding measure 94, Lang employs a dotted half note in spite of the presence of a comma in the text. The effect that she seems to desire is one of urgency, of forward motion without an intervening breath into the following exclamation, "O." Performers could enhance this urgency by rushing slightly into measure 95. In measure 14, Lang uses quarter notes, but in the corresponding measure 55, an added eighth rest sets off the crucial words "die Liebe." In measure 99, which corresponds to measures 17 and 58, Lang adds an eighth rest after the second beat; the resulting breathless effect is appropriate for the textual reference to the swift passing of life. Such small details can make a world of difference in a setting, and in a performance.[48]

Performers may contribute to the differentiation of the three stanzas by progressively intensifying the sensation of yearning. One means to this end is increasing the *stringendo* at each iteration (m. 29, none; m. 70, some; m.111, more.)

On the autograph of the third song of op. 8, *Ewige Nähe* (Eternal Nearness), Lang writes that it was composed on January 6, [18]38, "on a beautiful winter evening." The text is by Agnes von Calatin, Lang's closest friend in the 1830's (she refers to her on the autograph as "my dear angel"). The text begins with the word "Heller" (brighter). When this word reappears later in the text, Lang places an accent on its first syllable (m. 19). The prominence of the word "Heller" in the text and the musical setting suggests that a pun on the name of Stephen Heller might be intended.[49] If so, Heller must be the object of the love to which the text refers; either Lang or Calatin may have been romantically interested in Heller.[50]

Ewige Nähe is not a strophic song, so the issue of changes between stanzas does not arise. Performers should nevertheless be aware of small differences between corresponding sections of music. For example, the singer should breathe after measure 2, for the rules of punctuation require a comma here.[51] In the corresponding measure 6, however, there is no comma, and there should be no breath before the high G.

As the contrasting section in the flat mediant key begins at measure 9, the singer must change the vocal color (as Lang's *dolce* marking suggests). The pianist must not overdo the dynamic accents in measures 9-16, which lie within a *pianissimo* dynamic. The rather quick downward leaps in the right hand throughout this section are challenging.[52]

The *a tempo* marking at the return of the opening material in measure 17 suggests that Lang had a subtle *ritenuto* in mind in measure 16. Notice the slur in the voice part between measures 16-17; it is unusual for a slur to bridge two phrases and sections, but correct performance of the slur, with a breath during the following eighth rest, gives a fine effect. The accent in measure 19 should not consist merely of a louder dynamic, but also of a prominent consonant "h," and even a momentary lingering. At the minor variant of the opening material at measure 21, another subtle color change in the voice part is necessary — a darkening of the tone quality, as well as a softer dynamic level (implied by the *p* in the piano part). In measures 24-25, performers should emphasize the turning point in the text; the description up to measure 24 of the darkness that would result from the separation from the beloved is followed by the firm rejection of this possibility in measure 25 and the remainder of the text. A holding back in measure 24, followed by a return to the tempo and a risolute delivery in measures 25-28 would be appropriate.[53] Attention to the rests in the vocal line in measures 25, 27, and 29 will lend a suitably impassioned quality to the section.

The singer should conceptualize the vocal line of measures 25-33 as a gradual rise through the E-flat of measure 26 and the F in measure 31 toward a triumphant and climactic high G in measure 33. The pianist should not treat the final two chords of the song as an afterthought; they reinforce the affirmative mood of the final lines of text, and their uppermost pitches summarize the rise to the final climax by reiterating the high F and G of measures 31 and 33, respectively.

Acknowledgments

Sharon Krebs has collaborated with me in the researching and performing of the music of Lang since 1994. She located and transcribed many of the letters cited in this article. The Social Sciences and Humanities Research Council of Canada generously provided funding for this research. I am grateful to the staff at the Bodleian Library, the Deutsche Staatsbibliothek, the Deutsches Literaturarchiv, the Historisches Archiv der Stadt Köln, the Sächsische Landesbibliothek, the Schumann-Haus in Zwickau, and the Württembergische Landesbibliothek for giving me access to manuscript materials.

Notes

1. For a detailed discussion of Lang's family background, see Roberta C. Werner, "The Songs of Josephine Caroline Lang: The Expression of a Life," (Ph.D. diss., University of Minnesota, 1992), vol. 1, 1-25. In the biographical portion of the present article, I have included as much material as possible that is not mentioned by Werner, and have consulted nineteenth-century biographical accounts and primary sources rather than simply referring to Werner's work. The most significant nineteenth-century biographies of Lang are those of Ferdinand Hiller ("Josephine Lang, die Lieder-Componistin," *Aus dem Tonleben unserer Zeit* [Leipzig: H. Mendelssohn, 1868], vol. 2, 116-36) and of her son, Heinrich Adolf Köstlin ("Josefine Lang: Lebensabriss," *Sammlung musikalischer Vorträge* [Leipzig: Breitkopf und Härtel, 1881], 51-103; and "Köstlin, Josephine Caroline," *Allgemeine Deutsche Biographie* [Berlin: Duncker & Humbolt, n.d.], vol. 51, 345-50).

2. See Hiller, "Josephine Lang, die Lieder-Componistin," 120, and Köstlin, "Köstlin, Josephine Caroline," 346.

3. Her health was always weak; one of the friends of her youth remembers her as being "pale and transparent." Charlotte Hagn to Josephine Lang, Berlin, August 28, 1844. Köstlin papers, A: Köstlin Familie 46090/216, Deutsches Literaturarchiv, Marbach. Translations in this article are my own.

4. Paul and Carl Mendelssohn-Bartholdy, eds., *Felix Mendelssohn, Briefe aus den Jahren 1830 bis 1847*, 2nd ed. (Leipzig: Hermann Mendelssohn, 1870), 214.

5. The length of Lang's study with Mendelssohn is given in Stephen Heller to Robert Schumann, Augsburg, August 17, 1836, *Stephen Heller, Briefe an Robert Schumann*, ed. Ursula Kersten, Europäische Hochschulschriften, series 36, vol. 37 (Frankfurt: Peter Lang, 1988), 59.

6. Many of Lang's autographs are headed by detailed information as to date, time, and circumstances of composition.

7. Hiller, "Josephine Lang," 126.

8. Köstlin, "Lebensabriss," 65.

9. Stephen Heller to Ferdinand Hiller, Paris, June 5, 1867, Reinhold Sietz, *Aus Ferdinand Hillers Briefwechsel*, Beiträge zur Rheinischen Musikgeschichte (Cologne: Arno Volk Verlag, 1958–70), vol. 28, 100.

10. Heller to Schumann, Augsburg, August 31, 1837, *Stephen Heller, Briefe an Robert Schumann*, 102.

11. Heller cites this remark in Heller to Schumann, Augsburg, September 4, 1837, ibid., 105.

12. Schumann to Heller, Leipzig, August 18, 1838. A transcription of this letter is housed at the Schumann-Haus in Zwickau. All of the original letters from Schumann to Heller were destroyed in a fire in Heller's home.

13. The Schumann family papers housed at the Sächsische Landesbibliothek in Dresden contain an autograph of Lang's "Traumbild" with emendations in Schumann's hand (Schumann 148). The final page, which contains most of the emendations, is reproduced in Wolfgang Boetticher, ed., *Briefe und Gedichte aus dem Album Robert und Clara Schumanns* (Leipzig: VEB Deutscher Verlag für Musik, 1979), 341. For detailed discussion of this autograph, see Harald Krebs, "Josephine Lang and the Schumanns," *Selected Proceedings of the Conference on 19th-Century Music, Bristol 1998* (Aldershot, Eng.: Ashgate [forthcoming]).

14. The review is reprinted in *Gesammelte Schriften über Musik und Musiker von Robert Schumann*, 5th ed. Ed. Martin Kreisig (Leipzig: Breitkopf and Härtel, 1914), vol. 2, 334.

15. This information about Köstlin is gathered from a number of letters and autobiographical documents. For information about his illness in 1841, see Köstlin to Mendelssohn, Tübingen, February 9, 1841, Ms. M.D. Mendelssohn d. 39 no. 68 (Green Book 13), Bodleian Library, Oxford. He expressed his determination to become an actor in a letter to "Herrn Vicar Wagner" (first name unknown), place and date unknown, acc. Darmst. 1912.47, Deutsche Staatsbibliothek Preussischer Kulturbesitz, Berlin. His frequent attendance of dramatic productions is evident from an undated diary excerpt (Köstlin papers, Z2692, Deutsches Literaturarchiv, Marbach); since the excerpt contains a transcription of a letter dated 1832, it likely originated in that year. In the same document, Köstlin mentions the works for piano that he was playing at the time (including Beethoven sonata movements). His critical involvement with music is evident from the essay "Agnese Schebest. Eine dramaturgische Skizze mit besonderer Beziehung auf das Gastspiel der Künstlerin auf dem Stuttgarter Theater im November 1837," Köstlin papers, Z2683, Deutsches Literaturarchiv, Marbach. Among other things, the article contains Köstlin's opinions about the need for a truly German opera (pp. 4-6).

16. Köstlin, "Lebensabriss," 68-69.

17. Mus. fol. 53u, p. 17v, Württembergische Landesbibliothek, Stuttgart.

18. For Köstlin's account of these events, see Köstlin to Mendelssohn, Tübingen, December 8, 1841, Ms. M. D. Mendelssohn d. 40 no. 214 (Green Book 14), Bodleian Library, Oxford. The woman in question was the talented singer and actress Agnese Schebest.

19. Lang did not wish to write to Köstlin until his situation had clarified; see Köstlin, "Lebensabriss," 72.

20. For vivid descriptions of the couple's family life in the early years of their marriage, see Köstlin to Mendelssohn, Tübingen, February 3, 1843, Ms. M. D. Mendelssohn d. 43 no. 63 (Green Book 17), Bodleian Library, Oxford; Lang to Mendelssohn, Tübingen, June 10, 1844, Ms. M. D. Mendelssohn d. 45 no. 294 (Green Book 19); and Köstlin to Mendelssohn, Tübingen July 26, 1844, Ms. M. D. Mendelssohn d. 46 no. 32 (Green Book 20).

21. For a reference to the young couple's music-making, see Köstlin to Mendelssohn, Tübingen, January 3, 1844, Ms. M. D. Mendelssohn d. 45 no. 9 (Green Book 19), Bodleian Library, Oxford. I shall continue to refer to Lang by her maiden name, for her later songs were published under this name. The publisher Friedrich Kistner mentions in a letter to Mendelssohn that Lang had submitted songs to him under the name "Köstlin, née Lang," and states the opinion that just "Lang" looked better on title pages; see Kistner to Mendelssohn, Leipzig, July 26, 1844, Ms. M. D. Mendelssohn d. 46 no. 33 (Green Book 20). Perhaps Kistner persuaded her to continue to use her maiden name.

22. Köstlin to Mendelssohn, "You will be displeased when I confess that my wife has composed but little during the past ten months." Tübingen, October 2, 1842, Ms. M. D. Mendelssohn d. 43 no. 130 (Green Book 17), Bodleian Library, Oxford.

23. Köstlin asked Mendelssohn several times to bring his plays to the attention of his friends in theatrical circles, which Mendelssohn graciously promised to do when the opportunity presented itself (see Mendelssohn to Köstlin, Leipzig, February 12, 1843, MA Nachl. 7, 85, 6, Deutsche Staatsbibliothek Preussischer Kulturbesitz, Berlin). Many of Köstlin's literary manuscripts are preserved at the Deutsches Literaturarchiv, Marbach.

24. Lang to Mendelssohn, Tübingen, June 10, 1844, Ms. M. D.

Mendelssohn d. 45 no. 294 (Green Book 19), Bodleian Library, Oxford.

25. Virtually all of Köstlin's letters to Mendelssohn written during their marriage mention that Lang was ill.

26. Lang to Moriz Rapp, Tübingen, June 9, 1854, Köstlin papers, Rapp 86107, Deutsches Literaturarchiv, Marbach.

27. Lang to Clara Schumann, Rothenbach, August 16, 1859, Mus. Nachl. K. Schumann 5, 216, Deutsche Staatsbibliothek Preussischer Kulturbesitz, Berlin: "With respect to my weakened speaking and singing organ and my reduced strength in general, I am truly not well. I am always battling fatigue and am forced to make many sacrifices to my health! It especially prevents me from constant work, and from gaining an income through lessons, of which I could give so many here, and a wide field over and above my powers is available to me. But my health, my throat above all — permits me to give at most two to three hours per day — along with housekeeping, this is the most [that I can manage]! In addition, music takes a lot out of me inwardly as well as outwardly."

28. A third source of income that Lang explored was the publication of her husband's unfinished law treatises. The story of her ultimately unsuccessful negotiations with a friend of her husband's with respect to completing and publishing these works can be gleaned from seven letters from Friedrich Walther of Munich to Josephine Lang, the first dated September 17, 1856, the last April 14, 1857, (Köstlin papers, A: Köstlin Familie 46061/1-7, Deutsches Literaturarchiv, Marbach). Two of Köstlin's legal works did appear in 1858 and 1859 (*Abhandlungen aus dem Strafrechte von C. Reinhold Köstlin*, ed. Theodor Gessler (Tübingen: Laupp, 1858); *Geschichte des deutschen Strafrechts im Umriss*, ed. Theodor Gessler (Tübingen: Laupp, 1859)).

29. For Clara Schumann's brief account of Mendelssohn's words about Lang, see *Clara Schumann: 'Das Band der ewigen Liebe,' Briefwechsel mit Emilie und Elise List*, ed. Eugen Wendler (Stuttgart and Weimar: Verlag J. B. Metzler, 1996), 100. Heinrich Köstlin writes that the two women were "close friends" from 1852 onward ("Lebensabriss," 86-87). The friendship must have been a *Brieffreundschaft*; Richard Fellinger (son of Dr. Richard and Maria Fellinger) states that the two women were already corresponding during Robert Schumann's lifetime, and cites two letters from Clara Schumann to Josephine Lang (Richard Fellinger, "Ein jung gebliebenes hundertjähriges Tübinger Haus", unpublished typescript [Deutsches Literaturarchiv, Marbach], 9). I have as yet located no correspondence between the two composers aside from the letter cited in note 27.

30. For Clara Schumann's efforts to find publishers for Lang, see Clara Schumann to Johannes Brahms, Wildbad, August 6, 1859, *Clara Schumann, Johannes Brahms: Briefe aus den Jahren 1853–1896*, ed. Berthold Litzmann (Leipzig: Breitkopf und Härtel, 1927), vol. 1, 272. The benefit concert is mentioned in Clara Schumann to Ferdinand Hiller, Baden-Baden, August 17, 1867, Sietz, *Aus Ferdinand Hillers Briefwechsel*, vol. 2, 100.

31. Köstlin, "Lebensabriss," 61.

32. Hiller asked for the notes in 1861; Lang refers to this request in Lang to Hiller, Tübingen, September 20, 1861, (Hiller papers, no. 30, p. 737, Historisches Archiv der Stadt Köln). She was unfortunately unable to find time to prepare the notes until 1867; see Lang to Hiller, Tübingen, March 23, 1867, Hiller papers, no. 36, p. 185. Hiller first published the essay in the *Kölnische Zeitung*, May 29, 1867, p. 3. He later reprinted it in the collection of essays entitled *Aus dem Tonleben unserer Zeit* (see note 1).

33. Lang refers with intense gratitude to monetary gifts from several individuals in Lang to Hiller, Tübingen, June 18 and July 4, 1867, (Hiller papers no. 36, pp. 520 and 616), and April 27, 1868 (no. 37, p. 378). To the letter of June 18, she attaches a copy of the letter from Paul Mendelssohn that accompanied his gift.

34. Lang to Hiller, Tübingen, July 4, 1867; Hiller papers, no. 36, p. 615, Historisches Archiv der Stadt Köln.

35. Lang complains of the paucity of professional concerts in Tübingen, but also mentions a *Verein* that performed oratorios and chamber music in Lang to Hiller, Tübingen, October 22, 1859, Hiller papers, no. 28, p. 709, Historisches Archiv der Stadt Köln. She mentions her studies of scores of Beethoven and Handel in Lang to Hiller, Tübingen, April 14, 1867, (Hiller papers no. 36, p. 299), and Lang to Hiller, Tübingen, December 5, 1866, (no. 36, p. 24), respectively. Her interest in Hiller's own works is mentioned in numerous letters, including the one just cited (p. 24). The reference to readings of opera scores with Johannes Schleich is found in Lang to Hiller, Tübingen, February 27, 1870, Hiller papers, no. 39, p. 126.

36. Therese married the aforementioned singer Johannes Schleich and moved to Berlin. Maria married Dr. Richard Fellinger and also moved to Berlin. There, the Fellingers became friends with Clara Schumann and her daughters. They later moved to Vienna where they became close friends of Johannes Brahms; for a detailed documentation of this friendship, see Richard Fellinger, *Klänge um Brahms: Erinnerungen von Richard Fellinger*, ed. Imogen Fellinger (Mürzzuschlag: Österreichische Johannes Brahms-Gesellschaft, 1997). For Lang's reaction to these marriages, see Lang to Hiller, Tübingen, December 9, 1867, Hiller papers, no. 36, p. 1183, and February 27, 1870, Hiller papers, no. 39, p. 129.

37. Lang to Hiller, Tübingen, April 19, 1860, Hiller papers, no. 29, p. 365, and December 5, 1866, Hiller papers, no. 36, p. 18.

38. Lang to Hiller, Tübingen, December 5, 1866, Hiller papers, no. 36, p. 23.

39. Franz Hauser, director of the conservatory in Munich, playfully criticized the excessive difficulty of her accompaniments; see Hauser to Lang, Munich, July 7, 1847, (Mus. ep. Hauser 6, Deutsche Staatsbibliothek Preussischer Kulturbesitz, Berlin).

40. Lang to Hiller, Tübingen, February 27, 1870, Hiller papers, no. 39, p. 132.

41. Lang to Eduard Eyth (no date, but probably early in 1861, as the settings of Eyth's poems originated at that time), A: Eyth 28801, Deutsches Literaturarchiv, Marbach.

42. The third song was not composed until January 1838, and in a letter to Stephen Heller in August 1838, Robert Schumann refers to the songs as having appeared in print (Schumann to Heller, Leipzig, August 18, 1838; transcription at Schumann-Haus in Zwickau).

43. In the autograph, a sketch of a butterfly in ink appears beside the title. Lang's manuscript booklets contain numerous ink drawings, including portraits of her friends.

44. The latter two changes are not present in the autograph; they seem to have been added later.

45. Schumann to Heller, Leipzig, August 18, 1838; transcription at Schumann-Haus in Zwickau.

46. Heller to Schumann, Augsburg, August 22, 1838, *Stephen Heller*, 131.

47. The song may well be an expression of Lang's feelings around 1837!

48. Lang worked on such details between the time of the autographs and the published versions. In measures 33, 74, and 115, for instance, she originally wrote three quarter notes. The revision to "eighth note, eighth rest, dotted quarter, eighth note" is much more poignant; it sets off the word "Ach," and provides more urgency toward the word "Ferne" on the following downbeat — in other words, expresses the "drive toward the distance" to which the text refers.

49. Both Lang and Calatin were fond of such puns. Lang's pun on the name "Reinhold" is mentioned above. In one of her manuscript booklets, Lang noted that Agnes had constructed a riddle that punned on the same name; Württembergische Landesbibliothek, Mus. fol. 53w, p. 30v.

50. Eva Weissweiler claims that Lang was engaged to Heller, in *Komponistinnen aus 500 Jahren: eine Kultur- und Wirkungsgeschichte in Biographie und Werkbeispielen* (Frankfurt: Fischer Taschenbuch Verlag, 1988), 212. There is no documentary evidence of such an engagement. Heller's letters to Schumann make clear that he was in love with another woman when he met Lang in Augsburg; see Heller to Schumann, Augsburg, August 31, 1837, *Stephen Heller*, 86, 122. If there was any romantic link between Heller and Lang, it would appear to have been one-sided.

51. The comma is missing in the first edition of the song, but it is present in the autograph.

52. The first edition gives a *decrescendo* hairpin in the piano part in measure 12. I have altered it to an accent mark. It is likely that Lang intended the chords in the low register to be accented in the same way throughout this section.

53. It is interesting to note that in the autograph Lang began the *stringendo* at measure 25, that is, precisely at the textual turning point.

List of Works

This list of Josephine Lang's compositions is a work in progress; further research will no doubt result in additions and emendations. For updated information, see the database of Josephine Lang's manuscripts (prepared by Harald and Sharon Krebs) at www.wlb-stuttgart.de/%7Ewww/referate/musik/lang.html#daten

Abbreviations:
BH — Breitkopf und Härtel's publication of forty selected songs (Leipzig, 1882)
DCP — Da Capo Press reprint of BH, with twelve additional songs (*Selected Songs*, 1982)
BSB — Bayerische Staatsbibliothek, Munich
SBPK — Deutsche Staatsbibliothek Preussischer Kulturbesitz, Berlin
WLB — Württembergische Landesbibliothek, Stuttgart

Published Works with Opus Number

Lang's opus numbers are in disarray. Her first seven publications appeared without opus number; Lang supplied opus numbers in a list of works prepared in 1867. After op. 15, some numbers are used twice, some not at all. The opus numbers given here are taken from the list prepared by Josephine Lang's son Heinrich Adolf Köstlin as an appendix to his biography of the composer ("Lebensabriss," 1881). Köstlin gives two numbers for several works; the first number is taken from the respective title pages, and the second number (in square brackets) is Köstlin's correction.

When Lang uses the same title for more than one song, I have supplied a portion of the first line of text in parentheses. Dates of composition are taken exclusively from Lang's autographs, many of which are dated. Dates of composition given in Heinrich Adolph Köstlin's list frequently conflict with those found on the autographs, and are therefore not included in this list. The autographs sometimes give a date of composition and a date of notation; I have included the former date only. The sources of publication dates are Adolf Hofmeister's *Jahresverzeichnisse* and *Monatshefte*, and O. E. Deutsch's *Musik Verlags Nummern–Eine Auswahl von 40 datierten Listen 1710–1900* (Berlin: Verlag Merseburger, 1961). The first names of some of the obscure poets whose works Lang set are unknown at this point. Readers are referred to the website of the Württembergische Landesbibliothek for the most current information.

Acht deutsche Lieder, [op. 1]. Munich: Falter und Sohn, 1831.

1. *An die Entfernte.* Text by Johann Wolfgang von Goethe
2. *An den Frühling.* Text by Friedrich Schiller
3. *Liebessehnen.* Text by Ludwig I, King of Bavaria
4. *Am Tag, wo freudiges Entzücken*
5. *Wie lieb du mir im Herzen bist.* Text by Jean Paul (?)
6. *Hexenlied.* Text by Ludwig Hölty
7. *Abschied vom Herbst.* Text by Ludwig I, King of Bavaria
8. *Das Wunderblümchen.* Text by Theodor Körner

Published exemplars of these songs not yet located. The following are probably autographs of songs from op. 1, located at the WLB: no. 1—Mus. fol. 53a, p. 3v; no. 2—Mus. fol. 56b, p. 27v; no. 3—Mus. fol. 54a, p. 6r; no. 4—Mus. fol. 53a, p. 2r; no. 6—Mus. fol. 53a, p. 5r; no. 7—Mus. fol. 54a, p. 5r; no. 8—Mus. fol. 54d, p. 14r.

Sechs deutsche Lieder, [op. 2]. Munich: Falter und Sohn, 1834.

1. *Lied zur Geburtstagsfeier der viel geliebten königlichen Mutter Karoline*
2. *Seligkeit.* Text by Ludwig Hölty
3. *Lied* ("In der Hand die Himmelsgabe")
4. *Lied* ("Leichte Lüfte, linde, süsse")
5. *Lied* ("An dem Ufer sitz' ich da"). Text by Pückler
6. *Die Abendglocke auf dem Berge*

Original publication available at SBPK and as a photocopy at WLB.

Vier deutsche Lieder, [op. 3]. Munich: Falter und Sohn, 1834.

1. *Der Wanderer.* Text by Gottwalt (Johann Georg Seegemund)
2. *Auf der Alpe zu singen.* Text by August Graf von Platen
3. *Liebesgrüsse.* Text by Leopold Feldmann
4. *Fee'n-Reigen.* Text by Friedrich von Matthisson

Original publication not yet located. No. 2 is found in a miscellaneous collection at SBPK (N. Mus. O. 2814). No. 4 is printed in BH and DCP. The following are probably autographs of the remaining songs from op. 3, located at the WLB: no. 1—Mus. fol. 54c, p. 3r and pp. 4r-4v; no. 3—Mus. fol. 53i, pp. 28-30.

Vier deutsche Lieder, [op. 4.] Munich and Bern: Joseph Aibl, before 1844.

1. *Schlummerlied.* Text by Johann Georg Jacobi
2. *Veilchen.* Text by Johann Georg Jacobi
3. *Ständchen* ("Aufgewacht, aufgewacht"). Text by Wilhelm von Marsano
4. *Sehnsucht.* Text by August Graf von Platen

Original publication available at BSB, WLB, and as a photocopy at SBPK. Nos. 2 and 4 reprinted in BH and DCP.

Vier deutsche Lieder, [op. 5]. Munich: Falter und Sohn, 1834.

1. *Nähe des Geliebten.* Text by Johann Wolfgang von Goethe
2. *Lied* ("Auf dem frischen Rasensitze"). Text by Johann Georg Jacobi
3. *Glückliche Fahrt.* Text by Johann Wolfgang von Goethe
4. *Geistertanz.* Text by Friedrich von Matthisson

Original publication available at BSB, and as a photocopy at WLB. No. 1 reprinted in BH and DCP.

Vier deutsche Lieder, [op. 6]. Munich: F. A. Schäffer.

1. *An* ___. Text by Wilhelm Müller
2. *Lied* ("Liebe findet schnell die Worte"). Text by Gottwalt (Johann Georg Seegemund)
3. *Frühzeitiger Frühling.* Text by Johann Wolfgang von Goethe
4. *Geisternähe.* Text by Friedrich von Matthisson

Original publication available at BSB and as a photocopy at WLB. No. 3 is reprinted in BH and DCP.

Sechs Gesänge, op. 7. Munich: Joseph Aibl, 1838.

1. *Spinnerlied.* Text by Johann Georg Jacobi
2. *Die freien Sänger.* Text by Friedrich Förster
3. *Frühlings Ruhe* (1833). Text by Ludwig Uhland
4. *Im Herbst.* Text by Justinus Kerner. Also published as op. 11, no. 6
5. *Das Asyl.* Text by Ludwig I, King of Bavaria
6. *Mein Plätzchen.* Text by Widmann(?)

Original publication available at BSB and WLB.

Drei Lieder, op. 8. Vienna: Tobias Haslinger, 1838.

1. *Schmetterling* ("Frühlingsbote! Schmetterling!")
2. *In die Ferne* (1837). Text by Hermann Klätke
3. *Ewige Nähe* (1838). Text by Agnes von Calatin

Original publication available at WLB and SBPK.

Sechs Lieder, op. 9. Leipzig: Friedrich Kistner, 1841.

1. *Lebet wohl, geliebte Bäume* (1834). Text by Johann Wolfgang von Goethe
2. *Frühlingsgedränge.* Text by Nikolaus Lenau
3. *Nach dem Abschied* (1840). Text by C. Reinhold [Köstlin]
4. *Am Morgen* (1840). Text by C. Reinhold [Köstlin]
5. *Lied* ("Freund ach, und Liebling"—1838). Text by Johann Aloys Blumauer
6. *Komm Liebchen.* Text by Johann Georg Jacobi

Original publication available at WLB and SBPK.

Sechs Lieder, op. 10. Leipzig: Friedrich Kistner, 1841.

1. *Gedenkst du mein?* (1841). Text by C. Reinhold [Köstlin]
2. *Mignons Klage* (1835). Text by Johann Wolfgang von Goethe

3. *Die Schwalben* (1835). Text by Christoph August Tiedge
4. *Im Frühling* (1839). Text by W. Wackernagel
5. *Scheideblick* (1840). Text by Nikolaus Lenau
6. *Abschied* ("Ich liebte dich"—1837). Text by Ernst Schulze

Original publication available at WLB, BSB, and SBPK. No. 5 reprinted in DCP.

Sechs deutsche Lieder, op. 11. Leipzig: Friedrich Kistner, 1845.
1. *Antwort* (1832). Text by Ludwig Uhland
2. *Ruhetal* (1833). Text by Ludwig Uhland
3. *Frühlings-Ahnung* (1832). Text by Ludwig Uhland
4. *Abschied* ("Als wir schieden"—1835). Text by Justinus Kerner
5. *Sängers Trost* (1834). Text by Justinus Kerner
6. *Im Herbst*. Text by Justinus Kerner. Also published as op. 7, no. 4

Original publication available at SBPK and WLB.

Sechs Lieder, op. 12. Texts by C. Reinhold [Köstlin]. Leipzig: Friedrich Kistner, 1845.
1. *Am Wasserfall* (1841)
2. *Nachts* (1841)
3. *Abermals am See* (1841)
4. *O wärst du da* (1841)
5. *Der Herbst*
6. *Die wandernde Wolke* (1843)

Original publication available at SBPK and WLB. Nos. 4 and 6 reprinted in DCP.

Sechs Lieder, op. 13. Mainz, Antwerpen, and Brussels: B. Schott und Söhne, 1847.
1. *Abschied*. Text by C. Reinhold [Köstlin]
2. *Der Wanderer an die Quellen* (1837). Text by Heinrich Wenzel
3. *Aus der Ferne*
4. *Schmetterling* ("Der Schmetterling ist in die Rose verliebt"—1838). Text by Heinrich Heine
5. *An die Entfernte* (1839). Text by Nikolaus Lenau
6. *Namenlos* (1838). Text by Apollonius von Maltitz

Original publication available at WLB, BSB, and SBPK. Nos. 1 and 5 reprinted in BH and DCP.

Sechs deutsche Lieder, op. 14. Texts by C. Reinhold [Köstlin]. Leipzig: Breitkopf und Härtel, 1848.
1. *O sehntest du dich so nach mir* (1840)
2. *Am Flusse* (1841)
3. *Gedenke mein!* (1840)
4. *An den See* (1840)
5. *Vögelein* (1842)
6. *Auf dem See in tausend Sterne* (1841)

Original publication available at WLB and BSB. Nos. 1-4 and 6 reprinted in BH and DCP.

Sechs deutsche Lieder, op. 15. Leipzig: Breitkopf und Härtel, 1848.
1. *Nur den Abschied schnell genommen* (1838)
2. *Lied* ("Mag da draussen"). Text by Heinrich Heine (first stanza) and E. Meier (second and third stanzas)
3. *Ferne*. Text by J. G. Droysen
4. *Lied* ("Lüftchen ihr plaudert"). Text by Lord Byron
5. *Der Winter ist ein böser Gast*. Text by Leopold Feldmann
6. *Sehnen* (1836). Text by Jos[ephine] Stieler (?)

Original publication available at WLB, BSB, and SBPK. Nos. 1-3 and 5 reprinted in BH and DCP.

Josephine Lang did not publish works under the opus numbers 16 to 19.

Am Bache, op. 20 (1857). Text by C. Reinhold [Köstlin]. Published in a supplement to the Berlin music journal *Echo*, vol. 12, 1859. Original publication available at WLB.

Josephine Lang did not publish a work under the opus number 21.

Auf der Reise, op. 22 (1837). Stuttgart: Eduard Ebner, 1855. Text by Ludwig Bechstein. Original publication available at WLB and BSB.

Drei Lieder, op. 23. Stuttgart: Eduard Ebner, 1859.
1. *In Welschland* (1849). Text by C. Reinhold [Köstlin]
2. *Wenn du wärst mein eigen* (1840). Text by Ida Gräfin von Hahn-Hahn
3. *Der Himmel mit all' seinen Sonnen* (1837)

Original publication available at BSB and WLB.

Josephine Lang did not publish a work under the opus number 24.

Sechs Lieder, op. 25. Leipzig: Friedrich Kistner, 1860.
1. *Frühlings-Glaube* (1833; revised 1858). Text by Ludwig Uhland
2. *Winterseufzer* (1838). Text by Nikolaus Lenau
3. *Barcarole* (1839)
4. *Lied* ("Immer sich rein"—1834). Text by Schober (?)
5. *Die Wolken*. Text by Felix Köstlin (?)
6. *Das Paradies*. Text by Friedrich Rückert

Original publication available at WLB and SBPK. No. 4 reprinted in DCP.

Sechs Lieder, op. 26. Leipzig: Friedrich Kistner, 1860.
1. *Wiegenlied* (1859). Text after Hoffmann von Fallersleben
2. *Bei Nacht und Nebel* (1847). Text by C. Reinhold [Köstlin]
3. *Du denkst an mich so selten* (1838). Text by August Graf von Platen
4. *Frühes Sterben* (1838). Text by Friedrich Mayer
5. *Zusammen*. Text by C. Reinhold [Köstlin]
6. *Schilflied* (1838). Text by Nikolaus Lenau

Original publication available at WLB and SBPK.

Sechs deutsche Lieder, op. 27. Texts by C. Reinhold [Köstlin]. Stuttgart: Eduard Ebner, 1872.
1. *Traumleben* (1841)
2. *An einer Quelle* (1853)
3. *Ob ich manchmal Dein gedenke?* (1841)
4. *Frühling ist gekommen* (1841)
5. *Lebt wohl, ihr Berge*
6. *Zu Tod möcht' ich mich lieben*

Original publication available at WLB and BSB. Nos. 3, 4, and 6 reprinted in DCP.

Zwei Lieder, op. 28. Vienna: Tobias Haslinger, 1861.
1. *Traumbild* (1834). Text by Heinrich Heine
2. *Herz, mein Herz*. Text by J[osephine] Stieler (?)

Original publication available at WLB and SBPK. No. 1 reprinted in DCP.

Lieder des Leid's, op. 29. Texts by Albert Zeller. Bonn: Simrock, 1862.
1. *Leb' wohl, leb' wohl, du schöne Welt* (1861)
2. *Den Pfad, den du so oft gezogen* (1861)
3. *Gib dich dahin in Gottes Sinn*

Original publication available at WLB and BSB. No. 1 reprinted in DCP.

Zwei Lieder, op. 30. Texts by Ottilie Wildermuth. Stuttgart: Eduard Ebner, 1864.
1. *Glockenblume*
2. *Wiegenlied in stürmischer Zeit*

Original publication available at WLB.

Opp. 31-32 are piano pieces. Two pieces were published as op. 31; the work that Köstlin lists as op. 31 is *Elegie auf den Tod Ludwig Uhland's* (Stuttgart: G. A. Zumsteeg, 1863), and the work that he calls op. 31[32] is a *Festmarsch*, dedicated to Emma Müller (Stuttgart: Eduard Ebner, 1866). Op. 32 [33] is a pair of Character Pieces (*Nachtgesang* and *Romanze*), dedicated to Caroline von Bergmaier (Stuttgart: G. A. Zumsteeg, 1864).

Disteln und Dornen, op. 33 [34]. Hamburg: G. W. Niemeyer, 1865 (Heft 1) and 1869 (Heft 2).
1. *Du gleichst dem klaren blauen See*. Text by Felix Kunde Also published as op. 40 no. 1
2. *Wann sehen wir uns wieder?* Text by Felix Kunde
3. *Sprache der Liebe* (1839). Text by Kilzer
4. *Sie liebt mich* (1840). Text by Johann Wolfgang von Goethe
5. *Herzens Reise*. Text by Niklas Müller
6. *Wenn zwei von einander scheiden* (1864). Text by Heinrich Heine

Original publication available at WLB. Nos. 1, 4, and 6 reprinted in BH and DCP.

Zwei Lieder, op. 34 [35]. Stuttgart: Eduard Ebner, 1865.
1. *Im reinsten Gold* (1864). Text by Felix Kunde
2. *Die Blumen sind alle verblüht* (1860). Text by Felix Kunde

Original publication available at WLB and SBPK.

Drei Lieder, op. 34 [36]. Leipzig: Schlesinger, 1872.
1. *Mein Stern*. Text by Koch
2. *Vöglein im Wald* (1835)
3. *Blumentrauer*. Text by Niklas Müller

Original publication available at WLB.

[op. 35 [37]] is a pair of songs without words for piano, dedicated to Franziska Ammermüller (published in Halbergers Klavier Salon in 1860 and 1861).

Drei Lieder, op. 36 [38]. Leipzig and Winterthur: J. Rieter-Biedermann, 1867.
1. *Es sang vor langen Jahren* (1863). Text by Clemens Brentano
2. *Rausche, rausche, froher Bach* (1863). Text by Friedrich Oser
3. *Seid mir gegrüsst* (1863). Text by Helen of Orleans

Original publication available at WLB and SBPK.

Josephine Lang did not publish a work under opus number 37.

Sechs Lieder, op. 38 [39]. Leipzig and Winterthur, J. Rieter-Biedermann, 1867.
1. *Vorsatz* (1864). Text by Robert Prutz
2. *Der Liebe Bann* (1862). Text by Niklas Müller
3. *Schon wieder bin ich fortgerissen* (1839). Text by Heinrich Heine
4. *Seit die Liebste mir entfernt* (1851). Text by Heinrich Heine
5. *Wie lieb du mir im Herzen bist!* (1839). (Text by Jean Paul?)
6. *Seelied* (1861). Text by C. Reinhold [Köstlin]

Original publication available at WLB and SBPK.

Josephine Lang did not publish a work under the opus number 39.

Sechs deutsche Lieder, op. 40. Stuttgart: Theodor Stürmer, 1867.
1. *Sonnenblick* (1864). Text by Albert Träger.
2. *Mailied* (1833). Text by Johann Wolfgang von Goethe
3. *Im Wasser wogt die Lilie* (1865). Text by August Graf von Platen
4. *Lied* ("Wehe so willst"). Text by August Graf von Platen
5. *Und wüssten's die Blumen* (1864). Text by Heinrich Heine
6. *Ständchen* ("Wach auf du schöne"—1865). Text by Julius von Rodenberg

Original publication available at WLB. No. 5 reprinted in DCP. Lang originally published "Du gleichst dem klaren blauen See" as op. 40, no. 1. She had, however, already published this song as op. 33

[34] no. 1. When Stürmer discovered the error, he requested a replacement ("Sonnenblick") and required that Lang pay for re-publication (see Lang to Hiller, 5 December, 1866). Both versions of op. 40 are available at WLB. (H. A. Köstlin lists yet another song — "Lied", text by Robert Prutz—as op. 40 no. 1!)

Ich möchte heim!, op. 41 (1867). Text by Carl Gerok. Leipzig and Winterthur: J. Rieter-Biedermann, 1867.
Original publication available at WLB and SBPK.

Op. 42 is a *Wedding March*, dedicated to Prince Wilhelm of Württemberg and his wife. Stuttgart: Eduard Ebner, 1878.

Fünf Gesänge, op. 43. Stuttgart: Eduard Ebner, 1879.
1. *Hochzeitsgesang*. Text by Matthias Claudius.
2. *Das Ständchen*. Text by Ludwig Uhland
3. *Sommerfahrt*. Text by Carl Gerok
4. *Scheiden* (1878). Text by C. Reinhold [Köstlin]
5. *Nur keinen Abschied*. Text by Albert Zeller

Original publication available at WLB.

Op. 44 is a song without words for piano, entitled *Gruss in die Ferne*, dedicated to Baroness Emilie von Samson. Stuttgart: Eduard Ebner, 1879.

Fünf Lieder aus dem Trompeter von Säckingen, op. 45. Texts by Josef Viktor von Scheffel. Weimar: T. F. A. Kühn, 1879.
1. *Lied des jungen Werner: Es hat nicht sollen sein*
2. *Lied des jungen Werner: Am Ufer blies ich* (1869)
3. *Einen festen Sitz hab' ich veracht't*
4. *Als ich zum erstenmal dich sah* (1869)
5. *Lied des Katers "Hiddigeigei"*

Original publication available at BSB. Nos. 2 and 5 reprinted in DCP.

Op. 46 is a piano piece entitled *Danse infernale* (1878). Dedicated to Baron Oscar von Samson Himmelstierna. Weimar: T. F. A. Kühn, 1879.

Josephine Lang did not publish a work under the opus number 47.

Op. 48-50 are works for piano — *Deutscher Siegesmarsch*, *Zwei Mazurken*, and an Impromptu entitled *In der Dämmerung*, all published posthumously by A. Michaelis, Leipzig (1888).

Published Works without Opus Number

Abschied vom See (1839). Text by Leopold Lechner. Munich: Falter und Sohn and Jos. Aibl. Also published in Leopold Lechner's *Die Landparthie. Poetische Beschreibung des Würmsees und seiner Umgebung*. Munich: Deschler'sche Schriften, 1840. Both publications available at BSB.

An die Träne (1838). Munich: Falter und Sohn and Jos. Aibl. Reprinted in BH and DCP.

Arie ("All' mein Leben" — 1868). Text by Thomas Aquinas. Leipzig: Breitkopf und Härtel, 1882. Reprinted in DCP.

Auf ein zerbrochnes Herz von Carneol (1839). Text by Lord Byron. Leipzig: Breitkopf und Härtel, 1882. Reprinted in DCP.

Blick' nach Oben (1870). Text by Julius Hammer. Leipzig: Breitkopf und Härtel, 1882. Reprinted in DCP.

Dem Königs-Sohn (1870). Text by Max von Schenkendorf. Leipzig: Breitkopf und Härtel, 1882. Reprinted in DCP.

Die Augen der Blinden. Text based on the Bible (Isaiah 29, 18). Leipzig: Breitkopf und Härtel, 1882. Reprinted in DCP.

Dort hoch auf jenem Berge (1869). Text after Clemens Brentano. Leipzig: Breitkopf und Härtel, 1882. Reprinted in DCP.

Drei Klavierstücke (*Arabeske*, *Der trauernde Humor: Menuett*, *Heimweh*). Published Frankfurt, E. H. Schuncke. Available at WLB.

Erinnerung (1839). Text by Lord Byron. Leipzig: Breitkopf und Härtel, 1882. Reprinted in DCP.

Es ist noch eine Ruhe vorhanden. Leipzig: Breitkopf und Härtel, 1882. Reprinted in DCP.

Fischerlied (1839). Text by Leopold Lechner. Published in Lechner's *Die Landparthie. Poetische Beschreibung des Würmsees und seiner Umgebung*. Munich: Deschler'sche Schriften, 1840. Original publication available at BSB.

Getäuscht hat mich ein Schimmer (1864). Text by Agnes von Calatin. Leipzig: Breitkopf und Härtel, 1882. Reprinted in DCP.

Gott, sei mir Sünder gnädig. Leipzig: Breitkopf und Härtel, 1882. Reprinted in DCP.

Heimat (1835). Leipzig: Breitkopf und Härtel, 1882. Reprinted in DCP.

Herbst-Gefühl. Text by Carl Gerok. Leipzig: Breitkopf und Härtel, 1882. Reprinted in DCP.

Ich gab dem Schicksal dich zurück (1868). Text by Carl Stieler. Leipzig: Breitkopf und Härtel, 1882. Reprinted in DCP.

Ich liebe dich und will dich ewig lieben. Text by Fr. von Weling. Leipzig: Breitkopf und Härtel, 1882. Reprinted in DCP.

Im Abendstrahl (1864). Text by Carl Stieler. Leipzig: Breitkopf und Härtel, 1882. Reprinted in DCP.

Ostern. Text by Karl Heinrich von Bogatzky. Quedlinburg: Chr. Friedrich Vieweg's Buchhandlung, 1882.

Perle und Lied (1864). Text by Carl Egon Ebert. Leipzig: Breitkopf und Härtel, 1882. Reprinted in DCP.

Seebild (1868). Text by Carl Stieler. Leipzig: Breitkopf und Härtel, 1882. Reprinted in DCP.

Wein' aus deine Freude (1868). Text by J.C.K. [Josephine Caroline Köstlin?]. Leipzig: Breitkopf und Härtel, 1882. Reprinted in DCP.

Wie glänzt so hell dein Auge (1866). Text by Agnes von Calatin. Leipzig: Breitkopf und Härtel, 1882. Reprinted in DCP.

Wie, wenn die Sonn' aufgeht (1861). Text from a prayer-book by Tiede and Sturm. Leipzig: Breitkopf und Härtel, 1882. Reprinted in DCP.

Unpublished Works

Information taken from the manuscript collection at the Württembergische Landesbibliothek, Stuttgart. Fragments are not included in this list.

Songs for Solo Voice and Piano

Abschied ("Strahle mit Wonne")

Ach, ich denke, ach, ich senke. Text by C. Reinhold [Köstlin] (1840).

Alpenreise. Text by Mallikman.

Am Grabe. Text by J. S. [Josephine Stieler?].

Am Morgen (1840). Text by C. Reinhold [Köstlin]. A different setting of this text is published as op. 9 no. 4.

An ___ (Ich denke dein)

An die Leyer (1832). Text by Gellinger.

An einer Quelle (two settings, 1840 and 1853). Text by C. Reinhold [Köstlin] (a third setting of this text is published as op. 27 no. 2).

An Sie. Text by Carl von Lilien.

Arietta italiana (1834)

Auf dem Felsen (1861). Text by Eduard Eyth.

Aus Byron's Corsar. Text by Lord Byron.

Aus der Pilgerfahrt. Text by Therese von Niemeyer.

Aus einem Gebetbuch (1864). Text from a prayer-book by Tiede and Sturm.

Aus Tiedge's Urania, Vierter Gesang: Unsterblichkeit (1837). Text by Christoph August Tiedge.

Blumengruss (1843). Text by C. Reinhold [Köstlin].

Cäcilia. Text by Martins.

Da liegst du endlich still vor mir. Text by C. Reinhold [Köstlin].

Das blaue Aug' (1869). Text by Medikus.

Das ist die wehmutvollste Zeit (1868; revised 1870). Text by M. K. [Maria Köstlin?].

Das Schifflein. Text by Ludwig Uhland (two settings).

Das Veilchen im Tale (1834). Text by Friedrich Kind.

Das wäre Liebe? (1836). Text by Ludwig Uhland (?).

Das Wandern. Text by Wilhelm Müller.

Deine blauen Augen (1838). Text by Heinrich Heine.

Den 6ten Januar 1814 (1835). Text by Ernst Schulze.

Der braven Kinder Schullied (1879)

Der kleine Fritz an seine jungen Freunde. Text by Karl Müchler.

Der lieben Mutter (zur guten Nacht)

Der Liebenden Vergesslichen zum Geburtstage

Der Nebel weicht. Text by Felix Müller.

Der schwere Abend (1839—voice part only). Text by Nikolaus Lenau.

Der Traum (1839). Text by Koch.

Der treue Hirte. Text by Albert Zeller.

Des Mädchens Klage. Text by Friedrich Schiller (two incomplete settings).

Die alte Geschicht: Gallinnens Schwanengesang. Text by Josephine Lang (?).

Die Flamme (1834). Text by Leopold Feldmann.

Die Freunde sie ziehen zum Thor hinaus. Text by Josephine Lang (?).

Die Grabschrift (1838). Text by Apollonius von Maltitz.

Die holden Wünsche blühen (1838). Text by Heinrich Heine.

Die Liebende schreibt (1834). Text by Johann Wolfgang von Goethe.

Die sanften Tage. Text by Ludwig Uhland.

Die scheidende Braut (1869). Text by Josephine Lang.

Die Wacht am Rhein (1841). Text by Max Schneckenburger.

Die Waldglocken (1862). Text by Eduard Eyth.

Du bist ja niemals fern von mir (1838). Text by Graf von Giech.

Du bist mir lieb (1879). Text by Julius von der Traun.

Duetto (Her Therese!). Text by Josephine Lang (?).

Dunkel rauscht des Stromes Quelle. Text by Aloys Schreiber.

Durch die ganze Schöpfung bebet. Text by Martins.

Ein Knödel find't ja schon das andere

Ein Lebewohl (1863). (Same music also used for *Gruss der Engel an ein geätztes bezauberndes Stimmband: Eine dramatische Hymne für Tenor nach 'Lohengrin'*).

Einziger Trost (1868). Text by Ottilie Stieler.

Erinnerung (1837)

Erinnerung an die Heimat (1835). Text by Pünder.

Es sang vor langen Jahren (1863). Text by Clemens Brentano. A different setting of this text was published as op. 36[38] no. 1.

Frühlings-Gesang

Gebrochen ist der Sturm (1867). Text by Albert Zeller.

Gestern und heute (1833). Text by Fernanda Pappell.

Geständnis (1841). Text by Franz Danzi.

Geständnis der Liebe (1836). After a Russian text.

Hätt' ich tausend Arme. Text by Wilhelm Müller.

Herr! Der du rufst dem Morgenrot (1867). Text by Friedrich Oser.

Ich denke dein, im heiligen Abendschimmer (1838)

Ich denke dein wenn durch den Hain. Text by Friedrich von Matthisson.

Ich frage keine Blume. Text by Wilhelm Müller.

Ich hab' dich geliebet (1838). Text by Heinrich Heine.

Ich hab' im Kreise der Lieben

Ich hab' in guten Stunden (1863). Text by Christian Gellert.

Ich möchte dir wohl gerne sagen. Text by Jean Paul (?). This song may be op. 1, no. 5. A different setting of the same text is published as op. 38 [39], no. 5.

Ich möchte weinen. Text by E. Betzfanger.

Ihr Blümlein alle. Text by Wilhelm Müller.

Im Herbste. Text by Ludwig Uhland.

Ins Blaue (1833). Text by Fernanda Pappell.

In's Stammbuch—Wenn du an deine Freunde denkest

In's Stammbuch—Wenn ich einst im stillen Grabe (1834)

In's Stammbuch der kleinen Maria Jäger (1848)

Jägerlied. Text by Theodor Körner.

Junger Liebe Rosen Schimmer. Text by Ludwig I, King of Bavaria.

Klag' deine Not dem lieben Gott (1866). Text by Albert Zeller.

Kommt a Vogerl geflogen. Text from a German folk song.

Leise sinkt der Abend nieder (1844). Text by C. Reinhold [Köstlin].

Letzter Trost (1834). Text by Justinus Kerner.

Lieb Kind (1834). Text by Johann Wolfgang von Goethe.

Liebes-Duett. Text by Targino (?).

Lied ("Hans, Hans, hat a schön's").

Lied ("Kein Lämpchen scheint durch's Fenster").

Lied ("Lieb ist schön wie Morgenröte"). Text by Louise Brachmann.

Lied ("Mag der Wind im Segel beben"—1834). Text by August Graf von Platen.

Lied ("Sah ein Knab ein Röslein stehn"). Text by Johann Wolfgang von Goethe.

Lied ("Seit die Liebste mir entfernt"—1835). Text by Heinrich Heine. A different setting of the same text is published as op. 38 [39], no. 4.

Lied ("Und wenn die Mutta sagt").

Lied ("Wenn der Sterne gold'ner Schimmer"— 1835).

Lied ("Wo weilt die Seele"). Text by Johann Gaudenz von Salis-Seewis.

Lied vor der Schlacht. Text by Theodor Körner.

Lied zu singen bei einer Wasserfahrt (1830). Text by Johann Gaudenz von Salis-Seewis.

Mädle ruck ruck ruck. Text from a German folk song.

Mailied. Text by Ludwig Hölty.

Mein Vaterland. Text by Theodor Körner.

Meine Lieblingsblümchen (1853). Text by Rosa Bürkle.

Meine Wünsche. Text by Johann Wilhelm Ludwig Gleim.

Morgengruss. Text by Wilhelm Müller.

Mutterlieb' sorget, Mutterlieb' wacht (1879). Text by Therese von Niemeyer.

Namenloses (1838). Text by Apollonius von Maltitz.

Nichts über Ruh (1839). Text by Agnes von Calatin.

Nimmer auf der Mauer (voice part only).

Noch einmal fühl' ich jugendliches Leben.

O flieg' Gedanke hin zu ihr.

Ob sie meiner noch gedenkt! (1836). Text by Johann Nepomuk Vogl.

Ruhe. Text by Ignaz Hub.

Scheidegruss der teuren Freundin zur Abreise im Sommer 1877 (1877). Text by Josephine Lang.

Scheiden. Text by C. Reinhold [Köstlin]. A different setting of this text is published as op. 43 no. 4.

Schlummerlied an mein Herz (1869). Text by Sophie Landmann.

Schlummerliedchen (1871). Text by Josephine Lang.

Schuhmacher Lied.

Seh' ich sie am Bache sitzen. Text by Wilhelm Müller.

Sehnsucht. Text by Johann Gottfried Herder.

Sehnsucht nach der Heimat (1837).

Seliger Glaube (1868). Text by Ottilie Stieler.

Serenade eines Eifersüchtigen (1834).

Ständchen aus der Ferne. Text by Theodor Hell.

Stummsein der Liebe (1834). Text by Justinus Kerner.

Süsse, liebliche Vertraute. Text by Louise Brachmann.

Trinklied vor der Schlacht. Text by Theodor Körner.

Über Wildemann, ein Bergstädtchen am Harz (1835). Text by Ernst Schulze.

Und noch von dir kein Wort (1840). Text by C. Reinhold [Köstlin].

Veilchen. Text by Christian Adolph Overbeck.

Verfehlte Werbung. Text after Johann Heinrich Voss.

Verschmähte Liebe. Text by Joseph Zuccarini.

Verständnis. Text by Weinberg.

Viel Grüsse, schöne frische (1863). Text by Anastasius Grün.

Waldvöglein (1867). Text by Friedrich Oser.

Wehmut. Text by Eleonore von Kersdorf.

Wenn der Abendstern die Rosen. Text by Helmine von Chezy.

Wer es wüsste, wer es dächte (1840). Text by C. Reinhold [Köstlin].

Wer wird nun deine Freiheit schützen? Text by Georg Maria (two settings).

Wie bettel arm ein Herz doch bliebe (1867). Text by Ernst Scherenberg.

Wie ich bin verwichen. Text by A. Schritt.

Wie zieht ein Wanderer leicht dahin (1863). Text by Albert Zeller.

Wiegenlied an den kleinen Prinzen Ulrich (1880). Text by Therese von Niemeyer.

Willst du nach meiner Heimat fragen.

Wir sassen so traulich zusammen. Text by Wilhelm Müller.

Wo ein treues Herz in Liebe vergeht. Text by Wilhelm Müller.

Zur Erinnerung an 'Wh.' (1838). Text by Apollonius von Maltitz.

Zur Feier die wir heute froh begehn

Choral Works

Adelheids Hochzeitslied (female voices). Text by C. Reinhold [Köstlin].

Ave Maria (versions for SATB, female voices, and male voices).

Der Ungenannten (male voices). Text by Ludwig Uhland.

Deutsches Lied (1848; male voices). Text by C. Reinhold [Köstlin].

Deutsche Völker allesamt (male voices). Text by Müller von der Werra.

Fischer Chor (male voices). Text by Johann Gaudenz von Salis-Seewis.

Gebet: O sanctissima (SATB); also called *Schlacht-Gebet.* Text by Theodor Körner.

Herbstlied (male voices). Text by Johann Gaudenz von Salis-Seewis.

Kyrie (SATB), two settings.

Ständchen (three female voices). Text by Robert Reinick.

Trinklied im Mai (male voices; also SATB and soloist). Text by Ludwig Hölty.

Piano Pieces

Numerous waltzes

Numerous Songs without Words

Chamber music

Elegie in G, violin and piano.

Minuet and Trio in C major, string quartet.

Sonata for Violin and Piano in Eb major, first movement, incomplete (1838).

Bibliography

Citron, Marcia. "Women and the Lied, 1775–1850." In *Women Making Music*, ed. Jane Bowers and Judith Tick. Chicago: University of Illinois Press, 1986.

Dürr, Albrecht. "*Meine Lieder sind mein Tagebuch. . . .*" In *Annäherung X — an sieben Komponistinnen*, ed. Clara Mayer. Kassel: Furore Verlag, 1999.

Dürr, Walther. "Musikanalytische Beobachtungen." In *Annäherung X — an sieben Komponistinnen*, ed. Clara Mayer. Kassel: Furore Verlag, 1999.

Friedrichs, Elsbeth. "Josephine Lang." *Neue Musik-Zeitung* 36/10 (February 1905): 220-22.

Hagn, Charlotte to Josephine Lang, Berlin, August 28, 1844. Köstlin papers. Deutsches Literatur-Archiv, Marbach.

Hauser, Franz. Letters to Josephine Lang. Deutsche Staatsbibliothek Preussischer Kulturbesitz, Berlin.

Hiller, Ferdinand. "Josephine Lang, die Lieder-Komponistin." *Aus dem Tonleben unserer Zeit*, vol. 2. Leipzig: H. Mendelssohn (1868), 116-36.

———. Papers. Letters and diaries. Historisches Archiv der Stadt Köln.

Kersten, Ursula. *Stephen Heller, Briefe an Robert Schumann.* Europäische Hochschulschriften, series 36, vol. 37. Frankfurt: Peter Lang, 1988.

Köstlin, Heinrich A. "Josefine Lang: Lebensabriss." *Sammlung musikalischer Vorträge.* Leipzig: Breitkopf und Härtel (1881).

———. "Köstlin, Josephine Caroline." *Allgemeine Deutsche Biographie*. Berlin: Duncker & Humblot [n.d.], vol. 51.

Köstlin, Reinhold. Papers. Diary excerpts and letters. Deutsches Literatur-Archiv, Marbach.

Krebs, Harald. "Josephine Lang and the Schumanns," *Selected Proceedings of the Conference on 19th-Century Music, Bristol 1998*. Aldershot, Eng.: Ashgate, (forthcoming).

Kreisig, Martin, ed. *Gesammelte Schriften über Musik und Musiken von Robert Schumann*, 5th ed. vol. 2. Leipzig: Breitkopf and Härtel, 1914.

Lang, Josephine. Letter to Clara Schumann. Deutsche Staatsbibliothek Preussischer Kulturbesitz, Berlin.

———. Letters to Eduard Eyth. Köstlin papers. Deutsches Literatur-Archiv, Marbach.

Mendelssohn-Bartholdy, Felix. Papers. Bodleian Library, Oxford.

Mendelssohn-Bartholdy, Paul and Carl, eds. *Felix Mendelssohn, Briefe aus den Jahren 1830 bis 1847*. 2nd ed. Leipzig: Hermann Mendelssohn, 1870.

Peacock Jezic, Diane. "Josephine Lang: The Public Sphere." *Women Composers: The Lost Tradition Found*. New York: The Feminist Press at the City University of New York, 1988.

Rosenwald, Hermann. "Das deutsche Lied zwischen Schubert und Schumann." Ph.D. diss., University of Heidelberg, 1929.

Schumann, Robert to Stephen Heller, Leipzig, August 18, 1838. Transcription, Schumann-Haus, Zwickau.

Sietz, Reinhard, ed. *Aus Ferdinand Hillers Briefwechsel*. Cologne: Arno Volk Verlag (1958), vol. 1 and vol. 3.

Tick, Judith. Introduction to *Josephine Lang: Selected Songs*. New York: Da Capo Press, 1982.

Walther, Friedrich. Letters to Josephine Lang. Köstlin papers. Deutsches Literatur-Archiv, Marbach.

Weissweiler, Eva. *Komponistinnen aus 500 Jahren: eine Kultur- und Wirkungsgeschichte in Biographie und Werkbeispielen*. Frankfurt: Fischer Taschenbuch Verlag, 1988.

Werner, Roberta C. "Songs of Josephine Lang: The Expression of a Life." 3 vols. Ph.D. diss., University of Minnesota, 1992.

Discography

(WoO, "Werk ohne Opus," indicates work without opus number)

Josephine Lang. Dana McKay, soprano; Thérèse Lindquist, piano. SBPK Deutsche Schallplatten DS 1016-2 (1995). *Seelied*, op. 38, no. 6; *Erinnerung*, WoO; *Mag da draussen Schnee sich türmen*, op. 15, no. 2; *Das Paradies*, op. 25, no .6 *Seit die Liebste mir entfernt*, op. 38, no. 4; *Der Liebe Bann*, op. 38, no. 2; *Im Wasser wogt die Lilie*, op. 40, no. 3; *Wie lieb du mir im Herzen bist*, op. 38, no. 5; *Herbst-Gefühl*, WoO; *Immer sich rein*, op. 25, no. 4; *Scheideblick*, op. 10, no. 5; *Im Abendstrahl*, WoO; *Wie glänzt so hell dein Auge*, WoO; *Am Bache*, op. 20; *O sehntest du dich so nach mir*, op. 14, no. 1; *Nur den Abschied schnell genommen*, op. 15, no. 1; *Der Winter*, op. 15, no. 5; *Wiegenlied in stürmischer Zeit*, op. 30, no. 2; *Schon wieder bin ich fortgerissen*, op. 38, no. 3; *An die Träne*, WoO; *Vorsatz*, op. 38, no. 1; *Sehnen*, op. 15, no. 6; *Zu Tod möcht' ich mich lieben*, op. 27, no. 6.

Josephine Lang, Johanna Kinkel: Ausgewählte Lieder. Claudia Taha, soprano; Heidi Kommerell, piano. Bayer Records BR 100 248 (1995). *Erinnerung*, WoO; *Nur den Abschied schnell genommen*, op. 15, no. 1; *An den See*, op. 14, no. 4; *Am Flusse*, op. 14, no. 2; *Frühzeitiger Frühling*, op. 6, no. 3; *In weite Ferne*, op. 15, no. 3; *Auf dem See in tausend Sterne*, op. 14, no. 6; *Blick nach oben*, WoO; *Im Frühling*, op. 10, no. 4; *Mignons Klage*, op. 10, no. 2; *Die Schwalben*, op. 10, no. 3; *Sehnsucht*, op. 4, no. 4; *O sehntest du dich so nach mir*, op. 14, no. 1; *Sie liebt mich*, op. 33, no. 4.

Lieder of Clara Schumann, Fanny Mendelssohn, Josephine Lang, and Pauline Viardot-García. Katherine Ciesinski, mezzo-soprano; John Ostendorf, bass-baritone; Rudolph Palmer, piano. Leonarda LPI 107 (1981). *Der Winter ist ein böser Gast*, op. 15, no. 5; *Frühzeitiger Frühling*, op. 6, no. 3; *Wie glänzt so hell dein Auge*, WoO; *Wie, wenn die Sonn' aufgeht*, WoO; *O sehntest du dich so nach mir*, op. 14, no. 1.

Lullabies for Samantha. Sharon Krebs, soprano; Harald Krebs, piano. Independent release (1997). *Wiegenlied*, op. 26, no. 1.

Münchner Komponistinnen der Klassik und Romantik. Christel Krömer, soprano; Jutta Vornehm, piano. Musica Bavarica MB 902. Reissued on CD as MB 75121 (1997). *Immer sich rein kindlich erfreu'n*, op. 25, no.4; *Frühzeitiger Frühling*, op. 6, no. 3 (incorrectly listed as WoO); *Leb'wohl, leb' wohl, du schöne Welt*, op. 29, no. 1; *Abschied*, op. 13, no. 1; *Zu Tod möcht' ich mich lieben*, op. 27, no. 6; *Der Himmel mit all seinen Sonnen*, op. 23, no. 3; *Ob ich manchmal dein gedenke*, op. 27, no. 3; *Im Abendstrahl*, WoO; *Nur den Abschied schnell genommen*, op. 15, no. 1.

Von Goethe inspiriert. Lieder von Komponistinnen des 18. und 19. Jahrhunderts. Elisabeth Scholl, soprano; Burkhard

Schaeffer, piano. Salto Records International SAL 7007 (1999). *Frühzeitiger Frühling*, op. 6, no. 3; *Glückliche Fahrt*, op. 5, no. 3; *Mignons Klage*, op. 10, no. 2; *Lebet wohl, geliebte Bäume*, op. 9, no. 1; *Ich denke dein*, op. 5, no. 1.

Women Composers: The Lost Tradition Found (companion cassettes to the volume of that name). Katherine Ciesinski, mezzo-soprano; John Ostendorf, bass-baritone; Rudolph Palmer, piano. Leonarda LPI 3-4 (1988). *Der Winter ist ein böser Gast*, op. 15, no. 5; *Frühzeitiger Frühling*, op. 6, no. 3; *Wie glänzt so hell dein Auge*, WoO.

Women's Voices: Five Centuries of Song. Neva Pilgrim, soprano; Steven Heyman, piano. Leonarda LE 338 (1996). *Frühzeitiger Frühling*, op. 6, no. 3.

Editorial Procedures

The Haslinger edition of op. 8, the only one extant, forms the basis for the edition below. The only autographs that I have discovered are found in two different manuscript booklets in the collection housed at the Württembergische Landesbibliothek in Stuttgart, the autograph of no. 1 in Mus. fol. 53f, pp. 7r-9r, those of nos. 2 and 3 in Mus. fol. 53q, pp. 10-11 and 18-20, respectively. (It was Lang's usual procedure to collect songs composed at different times into small sets for publication purposes.) Although I took details of these autographs into consideration in my performance suggestions, they cannot be taken into account in preparing an edition; it is evident that they are early versions. Whereas all of these autographs are quite similar to the published versions in terms of notes and rhythms, that of the first song is in a higher key, and all of the autographs are much less detailed than the published scores in terms of dynamics, suggesting that there must have existed final versions which Lang sent to Haslinger. I have not yet located these later autographs; many of Lang's *Stichvorlagen* were returned to her, and are now housed at the Württembergische Landesbibliothek, but the *Stichvorlagen* of op. 8 are not among them.

The Haslinger edition of op. 8 appears to be quite "clean"; the only obvious error is the omission of a flat before the vocal D in measure 13 of *Ewige Nähe*. Editions of Lang's other early songs (by the Munich publishers Aibl and Falter) contain many more errors.

***Schmetterling*, op. 8, no. 1**

Frühlingsbote! Schmetterling! Sanft wie Zephirs lindes Wehen, schmeichelnd wie der Liebe Flehen flatterst du mit leichtem Sinn durch die Blumenwelt dahin!	Harbinger of spring! Butterfly! Soft as the gentle breath of Zephyr, flattering as the pleading of love you flutter with a light heart through the world of flowers!
Frühlingsbote! Schmetterling! Mit des Schmeichelns süssem Kosen gaukelst du um junge Rosen, wendest dann mit Männersinn dich zu andern Blumen hin!	Harbinger of spring! Butterfly! With the sweet caress of flattery you flit about the young roses, then you turn, in the manner of a man, toward other flowers!
Frühlingsbote! Schmetterling! Ist dein ganzes Leben Scherz, fesselt nichts dein kleines Herz, o so nenne nicht die Triebe deiner Flatterseele Liebe!	Harbinger of spring! Butterfly! If your whole life is a jest, if nothing can bind your little heart, oh then do not call the urges of your fluttering soul "love!"
Frühlingsbote! Schmetterling! Bunter Wechsel scheint dein Ziel, aber grausam ist dies Spiel. Ach! ein Schmetterling wie du nahm mir tändelnd meine Ruh'!	Harbinger of spring! Butterfly! Colorful change seems to be your aim in life, But this game is cruel. Alas, a butterfly like you carelessly deprived me of all my peace!

(Poet unknown)

In die Ferne, op. 8, no. 2

Siehst du am Abend die Wolken zieh'n,
siehst du die Spitzen der Berge glüh'n,
mit ewigem Schnee die Gipfel umglänzt,
mit grünen Wäldern die Täler umgrenzt[?]
Ach! in die Ferne sehnt sich mein Herz!

Ach! in den Wäldern so ewig grün
kann still und heimlich die Liebe glühn.
Der Morgen sieht sie, der Abendschein,
und Lieb' ist mit Liebe so selig allein.
Ach! in die Ferne sehnt sich mein Herz!

O könnt' ich ziehen im Morgenrot,
o, hauchte Abend mir Liebestod[!]
Es schwindet das Leben, du weisst es kaum,
o ew'ge Liebe, o ewiger Traum!
Ach! in die Ferne sehnt sich mein Herz!

Do you see the clouds passing at evening,
do you see the tops of the mountains glowing,
the peaks shining with eternal snow,
and the valleys bounded by green forests[?]
Oh! my heart longs for faraway places!

Oh! in the eternally green forests
love may glow silently and secretly.
Morning sees it and the evening glow sees it,
and the lover is rapturously alone with the beloved.
Oh! my heart longs for faraway places!

Oh, could I but pass away in the morning light,
oh, if evening could bring me love's death[!]
Life is passing away, you barely notice it,
oh eternal love, oh eternal dream!
Oh! my heart longs for faraway places!

(Klätke)

Ewige Nahe, op. 8, no. 3

Heller ward mein inn'res Leben,
schöner seit ich dich erkannt,
seit ein gleiches hohes Streben
Herz mit Herz so eng verband.

Meine Lieder, wie mein Fühlen,
Alles hab' ich dir geweiht.
Nichts konnt' meine Liebe kühlen,
keine Trennung und kein Leid!

Und doch soll ich dir entsagen,
dir mein heller Lebensstern,
soll die tiefe Nacht ertragen,
dass du mir auf ewig fern!

Nein, ach nein, so darf's nicht werden,
nein, es darf kein Abschied sein[.]
Ob getrennt, ob nah auf Erden!
hier im Herzen bleibst du mein!

My inner life became more radiant,
more beautiful since I met you,
since the same exalted striving
so closely united our hearts.

My songs, like my feelings,
everything I have dedicated to you.
Nothing could cool my love,
neither separation nor pain!

And yet I am to give you up,
you my radiant star of life,
I am to endure the dark night
of eternal separation from you!

No, oh no, it must not be so,
no, there must be no parting[.]
Even if you are separated from me on earth!
in my heart you shall remain my own!

(Agnes von Calatin)

Schmetterling

Poet unknown

Josephine Lang, Op. 8, no. 1
Harald Krebs, editor

26
dimin.
Blu - - men Blu - men Welt da - hin!
Flat - - ter - see - le Lie - - - - be!
p
dimin.
33
cresc.
f
p
40
Früh - lings - bo - te! Schmet - ter - ling! Mit des
Früh - lings - bo - te! Schmet - ter - ling! Bun - ter
46
Schmei - chelns süs - sem Ko - sen, gau - kelst du um jun - ge Ro - sen[,]
Wech - sel scheint dein Ziel, a - ber grau - sam ist dies Spiel

53
wen - dest dann mit Män - ner - sinn dich zu an - dern Blu - men
Ach! ein Schmet - ter - ling wie du nahm mir tän - delnd mei - ne
60
p
hin, dich zu an - - dern an - dern Blu -
Ruh, nahm mir tän - delnd tän - delnd mei -
67
ritard.
- - men hin!
- - ne Ruh!
cresc.
f
74
tr
p
ritard.
80
a tempo
8va
loco
p
pp

In die Ferne

Klätke

Josephine Lang, Op. 8, no. 2
Harald Krebs, editor

Allegro moderato [♩ = 96]
p
f
8
pp
molto legato
p
Siehst du am A - bend die Wol - ken ziehn, siehst du die
14
dol.
cresc.
Spit - zen der Ber - ge glühn, mit e - wi - gem Schnee die Gi - pfel um -
20
dim.
p
pp
glänzt, mit grü - nen - den Wäl - dern die Thä - ler um - grënzt? Ach! in die Fer - ne

27
sehnt sich mein Herz, ach! in die Fer - ne sehnt sich mein Herz,
33
ach, in die Fer - ne sehnt sich mein Herz, sehnt
f
[>]
cresc.
39
p
sich mein Herz!
dimin.
46
Ach! in den Wäl-dern so e - wig
pp

53
dol.
grün kann still und heim-lich die Lie - be glühn. Der Mor - gen
dol.
p
p
p
59
sieht sie, der A - bend - schein, und Lieb ist mit Lie - be so se - lig al -
cresc.
f
65
p
string.
lein. Ach! in die Fer - ne sehnt sich mein Herz, ach, in die
p
pp
legato
71
Fer - ne sehnt sich mein Herz, ach, in die Fer - ne sehnt sich mein
p

77
dimin.
Herz, sehnt sich mein Herz!
p
cresc.
84
dol.
decresc.
p
pp
91
O könnt' ich zie - hen im Mor - gen - roth, o, hauch - te A - bend mir
p
97
cresc.
Lie - bes - tod[!] Es schwin - det das Le - ben, du weisst es kaum,
cresc.
f

103
f
o ew' - ge Lie - be, o e - wi - ger Traum! Ach! in die Fer - ne sehnt sich mein
fz
cresc.
pp
fz
110
string.
Herz, ach, in die Fer - ne sehnt sich mein Herz, ach! in die
116
Fer - ne sehnt sich mein Herz, sehnt sich mein
123
Herz!
pp
fz
dim.

Ewige Nähe
Agnes von Calatin
Josephine Lang, Op. 8, no. 3
Harald Krebs, editor
Andante con moto [♩ = 96]
Hel - ler ward mein inn - res Le - ben, schö - ner seit ich
dich er - kannt, seit ein glei - ches ho - hes Stre - ben
cresc.
Herz mit Herz so eng ver-band. Mei - ne Lie - der,
dol.
pp
wie mein Füh - len, Al - les hab' ich dir ge-weiht,
cresc.
pp
p

13
Nichts konnt' mei - ne Lie - be küh - len[,] kei - ne Tren - nung
cresc.
16
[poco rit.]
a tempo
und kein Leid! Und doch soll ich dir ent - sa - gen[,]
cresc.
19
sf
dir, mein hel - ler Le - bens-stern, soll die tie - fe
f
p
22
[ritenuto]
Nacht er - tra - gen, dass du mir auf e - wig fern!

[a tempo, risoluto]
25
cresc.
f
fz
p
stringendo
Nein, ach nein[,] so darf's nicht wer - den, nein, ach nein es darf kein
cresc.
f
28
fz
Ab - schied sein, ob ge - trennt, ob nah auf Er - den!
p
cresc.
31
ffz
ritard.
ritard.
ff
hier im Her - zen bleibst du mein[,] hier im Her - zen
ffz
f
p
fz
cresc.
35
p
ritard.
a tempo
bleibst du mein!
p
fz
f
[col] 8

Clara Schumann
(1819–1896)

NANCY B. REICH

Clara Wieck Schumann (see vol. 6 for more extensive biography) is remembered primarily as a concert pianist and the wife of composer Robert Schumann (1810–1856); it is often forgotten that she was also a composer of considerable distinction. Her piano works were held in esteem by Robert Schumann, Felix Mendelssohn (1809–1847), Frédéric Chopin (1810–1849), and Johannes Brahms (1833–1897), among others; most were published, reviewed, reprinted, and performed throughout the nineteenth century. Her songs were not as well known but with the publication of two modern editions[1] and an increasing number of song performances in the concert hall and on compact disk, her lieder, richly rewarding for both singer and audience, are entering the repertoire.

That Clara Wieck Schumann was a gifted song composer should not come as a surprise. Her musical education, carefully structured by Friedrich Wieck (1785–1873), her father-teacher-manager, included voice lessons along with theory, harmony, orchestration, counterpoint and fugue, violin and score reading with the leading teachers in Leipzig, Dresden, and Berlin. At fourteen, Clara was sent to Dresden to study with Johann Aloys Miksch (1765–1845), a renowned voice teacher of his day. Wieck believed that every pianist should understand the art of singing; in his introduction to *Clavier und Gesang*, he wrote: "A piano teacher endowed with both intelligence and heart . . . must understand the art of singing" and further declared that a knowledge of singing and the shaping of beautiful tones is "the foundation of the loveliest possible touch on the piano."[2] Indeed, in his late years, he devoted himself entirely to teaching voice and incorporated theory and general musicianship into his lessons in vocal technique much as he had with his piano teaching.[3]

From her earliest years, Clara composed lieder that were performed at her concerts along with the piano solos, orchestral overtures, guitar duets, and other musical works so popular with audiences of the 1830s and '40s. Her first published song, *Walzer*, appeared when she was fifteen.

Clara Schumann rarely sang her own songs in public; she preferred to accompany. Most of the songs mentioned in her girlhood diary and documented on her early concert programs are lost. Autographs and/or prints of only twenty-five songs remain.[4] Of these, all but two were composed after her marriage, between 1840–1853, and almost all were written for her husband as Christmas or birthday presents.

Eighteen songs by Clara Wieck Schumann were published during her lifetime; another seven did not appear in print until 1992 although they were preserved in archives and known to scholars. It is known that in her youth Schumann composed a number of songs; the search continues and previously undiscovered compositions may well see publication in the near future. She set texts by Heinrich Heine, Justinus Kerner, Johann Peter Lyser, Friedrich Rückert, Emanuel Geibel, Robert Burns (in translation), her friend Friederike Serre, and the Austrian poet, Hermann Rollett. As far as is known, the last song she composed was a setting of Goethe's *Das Veilchen* composed in July 1853.

The young Clara Wieck was acquainted with the lieder of her contemporaries: Franz Schubert's (1797–1828) *Die Forelle* was on the program when the nine-year old Clara played in her first concert in the Leipzig Gewandhaus; other songs on her girlhood concert programs included Schubert's *Gretchen am Spinnrade*, and *Erlkönig* (of which she owned an autograph). The lieder of Felix Mendelssohn and his sister Fanny Hensel (see this volume) were performed in her concerts. Robert Schumann's lieder were, of course, an intimate part of her life; she gave them their first hearings, singing and playing them at home for her husband and for close friends including Mendelssohn. She presented them in public throughout her life.

Clara Schumann was always somewhat ambivalent, even apologetic, about her creative efforts.[5] That she was married to a great song composer certainly accounted for some of her lack of confidence; these feelings were undoubtedly intensified by societal disapproval of women who aspired to be composers.

When, in March 1840, a few months before their marriage, Robert Schumann begged her to write something for his journal: "Clärchen, don't you have something for my [*Neue Zeitschrift für Musik*] supplement? . . . Do you perhaps think that just because I am composing so much, you can be idle. Just compose a song!

Once you begin, you cannot leave it. It is far too seductive,"[6] she demurred, replying:

> I just cannot compose, I too am quite unhappy about it, but it really doesn't go. I haven't any talent for it. Don't think it is laziness. And now, you want me to do a complete song — I couldn't do that *at all*; to compose a song, to understand a text thoroughly, one needs genius for that . . . [7]

And yet, despite all her protests, she continued to compose throughout her years of marriage and wrote to friends of the joy and fulfillment brought by creative work.[8]

After the death of her husband, however, Clara Schumann composed very little. She edited and supervised the *Collected Works of Robert Schumann* (1879–1887),[9] composed some works for special occasions,[10] made piano arrangements and transcriptions of songs and other works of her husband and his friends,[11] wrote out her daily improvisations,[12] but composed no more songs herself.

There has been much speculation about why Clara Schumann ceased to compose after 1856. Practical reasons unquestionably played a part in this decision: the widow and mother of seven children, she went to work as a concert pianist to support the family; constant touring and the arrangements for her concerts left little time or inclination for creative work. The loss of her husband and his encouragement may also have contributed to her decision.

The songs of Clara Schumann were written for concert performance and require the same level of artistry as the lieder of her male colleagues. During her lifetime, Clara Schumann's songs were performed by some of the greatest singers of the nineteenth century in the great halls of Europe. *Am Strande* was premiered by Sophie Schloss, Leipzig's leading vocalist, at the concert in which Felix Mendelssohn conducted the premiere of Robert Schumann's "Spring" Symphony.

Appropriately enough, Clara Schumann's first song publication after her marriage, *Zwölf Gedichte aus Rückerts Liebesfrühling* (Twelve Songs from Rückert's Liebesfrühling) op. 37/12, was by husband and wife. It contained his op. 37 and her op. 12. Three songs were Clara's: *Er ist gekommen, Liebst du um Schönheit,* and *Warum willst du and're fragen,* but published without her name so that reviewers were never certain which of the two was the composer.[13] This joint work has attracted much attention about performance issues as well as issues of gender.[14]

Her second group of published songs, op. 13, composed between 1840 and 1843, includes two great favorites: *Ich stand in dunklen Traümen* (*Ihr Bildnis* in the first version), programmed frequently throughout the nineteenth century, and *Die stille Lotosblume,* regarded by many as a quintessentially romantic song, resonating with images of the lotus flower, the sea, moon, and swan and closing with an unanswered question. The texts of op. 23, six songs composed in June 1853, are set to poems from Hermann Rollett's novel, *Jucunde*. Spirited evocations of forest, field, flowers, and birds, these lieder are stamped with a joyfulness rare in Clara Schumann's work.

The seven songs unpublished during the composer's lifetime are powerful, dramatic, even tragic, and have great emotional affect; the romantic themes of yearning, unrest, melancholy, foreboding, separation, death, and mystery are all explored. In their harmonies, their intensity, and their sensitivity to the text, her songs are remarkable. Some, like *Volkslied, Die gute Nacht, Sie liebten sich beide,* and *Oh weh* employ sparse accompaniments to express the poets' thoughts.

Lorelei and Goethe's *Das Veilchen* are works that can now proudly take their place among the more familiar settings of these poems. In *Lorelei*[15] the repetitive triplets create an atmosphere of intensity and fear that builds to a terrifying climax (reminiscent of Schubert's *Erlkönig*); in the virtuoso piano part, we hear the master hand of the concert pianist. *Am Strande*, one of the three songs created in 1840, and *Er ist gekommen*, from op. 37/12, have equally brilliant piano accompaniments.

Autographs of sixteen songs by Clara Schumann are in Robert-Schumann-Haus, Zwickau [RSH]. A collection of twenty-three song autographs is in a music notebook in the Staatsbibliothek zu Berlin Preussischer Kulturbesitz, Musikabteilung mit Mendelssohn Archiv Mus. Ms. Autogr. C. Schumann 5 [SBPK/5]. On the title page of the notebook, Robert Schumann listed sixteen songs composed by Clara between 1840 and 1846 in the order in which they were composed. The six songs of op. 23 and *Das Veilchen*, all composed in 1853, are listed on the next page, probably by Marie Schumann, the eldest Schumann daughter. The composer herself wrote out each song giving the date of composition and the author of the text.

The three songs given here, unpublished until 1992,[16] represent the diverse song styles of Clara Wieck Schumann. The text of *Volkslied* by Heinrich Heine (1797–1856) is the second of a trio of poems titled "Tragödie," published in 1829. This edition was used by Clara Schumann. A footnote signed "H.H." identified the second of the two poems as follows: "This second song [lyric] is a Rhenish folksong; only the first and third poems were my own)." *Volkslied*, the one song which Clara and Robert Schumann both set for solo voice and piano, provides a useful (though admittedly meager) basis for comparison. Robert Schumann's version,[17] a simpler, folklike setting (1841) published in 1847, expresses sorrow and unhappiness. Clara Schumann's setting of *Volkslied,* which remained unpublished until 1992, is dramatic and haunting. The postlude carries the themes of tragedy and death to the hopeless end. *Volkslied* was another of three songs (the others were *Ich stand in dunklen Träumen*, op. 13, no. 1, and *Am Strande*) given by Clara to Robert as a Christmas gift in 1840. Sources used for *Volkslied* are the autographs in RSH, 5984-A1 and SBPK/5, No. 3.

Die gute Nacht is from *Liebesfrühling* (The Springtime of Love), a cycle of poems by Friedrich Rückert (1788–1866) written in 1821, the year of his marriage. After receiving three songs at Christmas 1840, Robert Schumann urged his wife to set some of the poems from *Liebesfrühling*. *Die gute Nacht*, written for op. 37/12 but not chosen for publication, did not appear in print until 1992. Sources for *Die gute Nacht* are RSH, 5985-A1 and SBPK/5, No. 6.

Lorelei, the poem by Heinrich Heine, is known to every German school child and in its folklike setting by Friedrich Silcher

(1789–1860) is sung around the world. First published in 1824, it rapidly became a favorite for composers and has been set by many, including Liszt. Clara Schumann's version is among the most compelling settings of this poem. Sources for this edition are RSH, 5987-A1 and SBPK/5, No. 12.

Notes

1. *Clara Schumann: Sämtliche Lieder*, ed. Joachim Draheim and Brigitte Höft, 2 vols. (Wiesbaden: Breitkopf & Härtel, 1990, 1992) and *Clara Schumann: Seven Songs*, ed. Kristin Norderval (Bryn Mawr, PA: Hildegard Publishing Company, 1993).

2. *Piano and Song; (Didactic and Polemical)* by Friedrich Wieck, trans. Henry Pleasants (Stuyvesant, NY: Pendragon Press, 1988), 10.

3. See Amy Fay's description of her visit to Wieck in Dresden in *Music-Study in Germany* (Chicago: McClurg, 1880; reprint, New York: Dover, 1965), 166.

4. Draheim and Höft include two additional songs, originally attributed to Friedrich Wieck, that they believe were composed by the young Clara Wieck. See *Clara Schumann: Sämtliche Lieder*, "Vorwort," 5.

5. Her autographs were invariably presented to her husband with such inscriptions as "composed and dedicated to her ardently beloved Robert with the *deepest modesty* from his Clara . . ." (inscribed on cover page of autographs of *Am Strande*, *Volkslied*, and *Ihr Bildnis*, in Robert-Schumann-Haus, A1-5984). In their *Marriage Diary* (December 14–20, 1840), she wrote about the same songs, saying, "They are actually of little value, merely a feeble effort."

6. Berthold Litzmann, ed., *Clara Schumann: ein Künstlerleben nach Tagebüchern und Briefen.* 3 vols. (Leipzig: Breitkopf & Härtel, 1902, 1905, 1908), 1:411.

7. Ibid., 412.

8. Ibid. vol. 2:139-40 and 274.

9. *Robert Schumann's Werke*, ed. Clara Schumann (Leipzig: Breitkopf & Härtel), 1879–1887. An additional volume, edited by Johannes Brahms, appeared in 1893.

10. The *Romanze* (B minor), inscribed to Brahms and dated "Christmas 1856," and the *Marsch* in E-flat written for the golden wedding anniversary of friends in 1879.

11. The piano transcriptions of Robert Schumann lieder published in 1873 and the arrangement for piano two hands of Robert Schumann's op. 56 and op. 58 published in 1896. Unpublished arrangements include arrangements for solo piano of 2 movements of Brahms *Serenade*, op. 11, the entire Brahms *Serenade*, op. 16, and the *Andantino Cantabile*, op. 17/2 for Piano 4 hands by William Sterndale Bennett.

12. See Valerie Goertzen, ed., "Preludes," in "Clara Schumann," *Women Composers: Music Through the Ages*, ed. Sylvia Glickman and Martha Schleifer, vol. 6 (New York: G. K. Hall, 1999), 44-104. (reprinted and expanded by Hildegard Publishing Company, 2001).

13. A similar situation existed when some of Fanny Mendelssohn Hensel's lieder were published with those of her brother without attribution.

14. See Melinda Boyd, "Gendered Voices: The Liebesfrühling Lieder of Robert and Clara Schumann," in *19th Century Music 23* (Fall 1999), 145-62 and Rufus Hallmark, "The Rückert Lieder of Robert and Clara Schumann," in *19th Century Music* 14 (Summer 1990): 3-30.

15. The version of *Lorelei* presented here is from *Clara Schumann: Seven Songs*, ed. Kristin Norderval (Bryn Mawr, PA: Hildegard Publishing Company, 1993). In the Norderval publication the title is spelled *Loreley* as in the folk version; in the autograph of Schumann's song it is spelled *Loreleÿ;* the poet spelled it *Lorelei.*

16. First published in Draheim and Höft, vol. 2 (1992); published a year later, with English translations, in Norderval.

17. The second song of his trilogy, *Tragödie* (op. 64, no. 3b), is known by its first line, "Es fiel ein Reif in der Frühlingsnacht."

Selected List of Works

Published and unpublished songs by Clara Schumann are arranged in chronological order. Starred compositions have no opus number. Titles are from first editions.

**Der Abendstern* (early 1830s). Text: unknown. Wiesbaden: Breitkopf & Härtel, 1992.

**Walzer* (1833) Text by J.P. Lyser. Leipzig: Schaarschmidt, 1833.

**Am Strand* [*sic*] (1840) Text by Robert Burns. Trans. Wilhelm Gerhard. *Neue Zeitschrift für Musik*, July 1841 supplement.

**Volkslied* (1840). Text by Heinrich Heine. Wiesbaden: Breitkopf & Härtel, 1992.

Zwölf Gedichte aus F. Rückert's Liebesfrühling für Gesang und Pianoforte von Robert und Clara Schumann, op. 37/12 (1841). Texts by Friedrich Rückert. Leipzig: Breitkopf & Härtel, 1841.

Er ist gekommen, op. 12, no. 2
Liebst du um Schönheit, op. 12, no. 4
Warum willst du and're fragen, op. 12, no. 11

* *Die gute Nacht*, (1841). Text by Friedrich Rückert. Wiesbaden: Breitkopf & Härtel, 1992.

Sechs Lieder, op. 13. Leipzig: Breitkopf & Härtel, 1844.

1. *Ich stand in dunklen Träumen*, op. 13, no. 1 (1840). Text by Heinrich Heine
2. *Sie liebten sich beide*, op. 13, no. 2 (1842). Text by Heine
3. *Liebeszauber*, op. 13, no. 3 (1842). Text by Emanuel Geibel
4. *Der Mond kommt still gegangen*, op. 13, no. 4 (1843). Text by Geibel
5. *Ich hab' in deinem Auge*, op. 13, no. 5 (1843). Text by Friedrich Rückert
6. *Die stille Lotosblume*, op. 13, no. 6 (1843). Text by Geibel

**Lorelei* (1843). Text by Heinrich Heine. Wiesbaden: Breitkopf & Härtel, 1992.

**Oh weh des Scheidens* (1843). Text by Friedrich Rückert. Wiesbaden: Breitkopf & Härtel, 1992.

**O Thou My Star* (1846). Text by Friederike Serre. Translation by Leopold Wray of *Mein Stern*. London: Wessell, 1848.

**Mein Stern* (1846). Text by Friederike Serre. Wiesbaden: Breitkopf & Härtel, 1992.

**Beim Abschied* (1846). Text by Friederike Serre. Wiesbaden: Breitkopf & Härtel, 1992.

Sechs Lieder aus Jucunde von Hermann Rollett, op. 23 (1853). Texts by Hermann Rollett. Leipzig: Breitkopf & Härtel, 1856.
Was weinst du, Blümlein, op. 23, no. 1
An einem lichten Morgen, op. 23, no. 2
Geheimes Flüstern, op. 23, no. 3
Auf einem grünen Hügel, op. 23, no. 4
Das ist ein Tag, op. 23, no. 5
O Lust, o Lust, op. 23, no. 6

**Das Veilchen* (1853). Text by J. W. von Goethe. Wiesbaden: Breitkopf & Härtel, 1992.

Problematical Attribution

Der Wanderer (1831?). Text by Justinus Kerner. Wiesbaden: Breitkopf & Härtel, 1992.

Der Wanderer in der Sägemühle (1831?). Text by Justinus Kerner. Wiesbaden: Breitkopf & Härtel, 1992.

Selected Modern Publications

Clara Schumann: Sämtliche Lieder. 2 vols. Ed. Joachim Draheim and Brigitte Höft. Wiesbaden: Breitkopf & Härtel, 1990, 1992.

Clara Schumann: Seven Songs. Ed. Kristin Norderval. Bryn Mawr, PA: Hildegard Publishing Company, 1993.

Bibliography

Boyd, Melinda. "Gendered Voices: The Liebesfrühling Lieder of Robert and Clara Schumann." In *19th Century Music* 23 (Fall 1999): 145-62.

Chissell, Joan. *Clara Schumann: A Dedicated Spirit*. London: Hamish Hamilton, 1983.

Citron, Marcia. "Women and the Lied." In *Women Making Music: The Western Art Tradition, 1150-1950*, eds. Jane Bowers and Judith Tick. Urbana: University of Illinois Press, 1986, 224-248.

Fay, Amy. *Music-Study in Germany*. Chicago: McClurg, 1880. Reprint, New York: Dover, 1965.

Gorrell, Lorraine. *The Nineteenth-Century German Lied*. Portland, OR: Amadeus Press, 1993.

Hallmark, Rufus. "The Rückert Lieder of Robert and Clara Schumann." In *19th Century Music*, 14 (Summer 1990): 3-30.

Litzmann, Berthold, ed. *Clara Schumann: Ein Künstlerleben nach Tagebüchern und Briefen*. 3 vols. Leipzig: Breitkopf & Härtel, 1902, 1905, 1908. English translation (abridged) by Grace E. Hadow as: *Clara Schumann: An Artist's Life; Based on Material Found in Diaries and Letters*. 2 vols. London: Macmillan, 1913.

May, Florence. *The Girlhood of Clara Schumann (Clara Wieck and Her Time)*. London: Edward Arnold, 1912.

Nauhaus, Gerd, ed. *The Marriage Diaries of Robert and Clara Schumann; From their Wedding Day through the Russia Trip*. Translated by Peter Ostwald. Boston: Northeastern University Press, 1993.

Reich, Nancy B. *Clara Schumann: The Artist and The Woman*. Ithaca, NY: Cornell University Press, 1985. Revised edition, 2001.

_____. "Schumann, Clara." In the *New Grove Dictionary of Women Composers*, edited by Julie Anne Sadie and Rhian Samuel. London: Macmillan, 1994, 411-416.

_____. "European Composers and Musicians, 1800–1890." In *Women and Music: A History*, edited by Karin Pendle. Bloomington: Indiana University Press, 1991. Second edition, 2001.

Reich, Nancy B. "Schumann, Clara." In *The New Grove Dictionary of Music and Musicians*. Second edition. London: Macmillan, 2001. vol. 22: 754-58.

Schumann, Robert. *Tagebücher*. vol. I (1827–1838), ed. Georg Eismann. Leipzig: Deutscher Verlag für Musik, 1971, 1987. Vol. II (1836–1854), ed. Gerd Nauhaus. Leipzig: Deutscher Verlag für Musik, 1987. Vol. III *Haushaltbücher* (1837–1856), ed. Gerd Nauhaus. Leipzig: Deutscher Verlag für Musik, 1982.

Stein, Deborah, and Robert Spillman. *Poetry into Song. Performance and Analysis of Lieder*. New York: Oxford University Press, 1996.

Weissweiler, Eva, ed. *Clara und Robert Schumann Briefwechsel. Kritische Gesamtausgabe 1832–1838*. 2 vols. Basel: Roter Stern, 1984, 1987; English translation by Hildegard Fritsch and Ronald L. Crawford as *The Complete Correspondence of Clara and Robert Schumann*. 2 vols. New York: Peter Lang, 1994, 1996.

Wieck, Friedrich. *Piano and Song (Didactic and Polemical); The Collected Writings of Clara Schumann's Father and Only Teacher*. Trans., ed., and ann., Henry Pleasants. Stuyvesant, NY: Pendragon, 1988.

Selected Discography

The recordings selected are those that include a broad or complete selection of the songs of Clara Schumann.

Clara Wieck-Schumann. Sämtliche Lieder. Isabel Lippitz, soprano and Deborah Richards, piano. Bayer Records, BR 100 206 (1992). Twenty-five Clara Schumann songs.

Completely Clara; Lieder by Clara Schumann. Korliss Uecker, soprano and Joanne Polk, piano. Arabesque Z6624 (1992). Nineteen Clara Schumann songs.

Songs by Clara Schumann, Poldowski, Amy Beach. Lauralyn Kolb, soprano; Don McMahon, piano. Albany Records, Troy 109 (1994). Op. 13, *Sechs Lieder*; op. 23, *Sechs Lieder aus Jucunde*.

Clara Schumann, Fanny Hensel, Alma Mahler: Lieder. Christina Högman, soprano, Roland Pöntinen, piano. BIS CD 738 (1995). *Am Strand*; *Sie liebten sich beide*, op. 13, no. 2; *Beim Abschied*; *Er ist gekommen*, op. 12, no. 2; *Liebst du um Schönheit*, op. 12, no. 4; *Warum willst du and're fragen*, op. 12, no. 11; *Die guteNacht; Lorelei*; *Geheimes Flüstern*, op. 23, no. 3; *O Lust, o Lust*, op. 23, no. 6.

Das Herz des Dichters. Lieder von Robert und Clara Schumann. Bo Skovhus, baritone, Helmut Deutsch, piano. SK 63272 (1996). *Liebeszauber*, op. 13, no. 3; *Der Mond kommt still gegangen*, op. 13, no. 4; *Die stille Lotosblume*, op. 13, no. 6; *Liebst du um Schönheit*, op. 12, no. 4; *Warum willst du and're fragen*, op. 12, no. 11; *Ich hab' in deinem Auge*, op. 13, no. 5; *Die gute Nacht*; *Ich stand in dunklen Träumen*, op. 13, no. 1; *Sie liebten sich beide*, op. 13, no. 2; *Volkslied*; *Lorelei*.

Clara Schumann Lieder. Lan Rao, soprano, Micaela Gelius, piano. Arte Nova Classics 74321 43308 2 (1996). Twenty-seven Clara Schumann songs including two listed above as "problematical."

The Songs of Clara Schumann. Susan Gritton, soprano, Stephan Loges, baritone, Eugene Asti, piano. Hyperion Records CDA 67249 (2002). Twenty-seven songs.

Volkslied

Es fiel ein Reif in der Frühlingsnacht, Er fiel auf die zarten Blaublümelein, Sie sind verwelket, verdorret.	A frost fell in the spring night, It fell on the tender forget-me-nots, They faded, they withered.
Ein Jüngling hatte ein Mädchen lieb, Sie flohen heimlich von Hause fort. Es wusst' weder Vater noch Mutter.	A youth loved a maiden, Secretly they fled from home. And neither father nor mother knew.
Sie sind gewandert hin und her, Sie haben gehabt weder Glück noch Stern, Sie sind gestorben, verdorben.	They wandered here and there, The fates were against them, They were ruined, they perished.

Die gute Nacht

Die gute Nacht, Die ich dir sage, Freund, hörest du!	The good night, Which I bid you, Friend, do hear me!
Ein Engel, Der die Botschaft trage, Geht ab und zu.	An angel, Who brings the tidings, Approaches and departs.
Er bringt sie dir Und hat mir wieder Den Gruss gebracht:	He brings them to you And has brought me Greetings in return:
Dir sagen auch Des Freundes Lieder Jetzt gute Nacht.	And to you also The songs of your friend Are saying good night.

Lorelei

Ich weiss nicht, was soll es bedeuten, Dass ich so traurig bin; Ein Märchen aus alten Zeiten, Das kommt mir nicht aus dem Sinn.	I know not what it means, And why I am so sad; A tale from olden times, Will not leave my mind.
Die Luft ist kühl und es dunkelt, Und ruhig fliesst der Rhein; Der Gipfel des Berges funkelt Im Abendsonnenschein.	The air is cool and dusk is falling, And the Rhine flows peacefully; The mountain peak sparkles In the sunlight of evening.
Die schönste Jungfrau sitzet Dort oben wunderbar, Ihr gold'nes Geschmeide blitzet, Sie kämmt ihr gold'nes Haar.	The most beautiful maiden is sitting Up above wondrously, Her golden jewels gleam, She is combing her golden hair.
Sie kämmt es mit gold'nem Kamme Und singt ein Lied dabei; Das hat eine wundersame, Gewaltige Melodei.	She combs it with a golden comb And sings a song all the while; That has a wondrous, powerful melody.
Den Schiffer im kleinen Schiffe Ergreift es mit wildem Weh; Er schaut nicht die Felsenriffe, Er schaut nur hinauf in die Höh'.	The sailor in his little boat Is seized with its wild distress; He does not see the rocky cliffs, He looks only upwards.
Ich glaube die Wellen verschlingen Am Ende Schiffer und Kahn; Und das hat mit ihrem Singen Die Lorelei getan.	In the end I believe the waves swallowed sailor and boat; And this with her singing The Lorelei has done.

Volkslied

Heinrich Heine

Clara Schumann
Kristin Norderval, editor

Adagio — Schwermütig *p*

Es fiel ein Reif in der Früh-lings-

5 nacht, — er fiel auf die zar-ten Blau-blü-me - lein: Sie sind ver-wel-ket, ver-

9 dor - ret. Ein Jüng - ling hat-te ein Mäd - chen lieb; sie

12 floh - en heim-lich von Hau - se fort, ——— es wußt' we-der Va - ter noch

p *cresc.* *mf* *f* *dim.*

15
Mut-ter.
p
Sie
p
19
sind ge-wan-dert hin und her,
sie ha-ben ge-habt we-der Glück noch Stern
23
morendo
sie sind ge-stor-ben,
ver-dor - ben.
ben legato
p
p
28

Die gute Nacht

Friedrich Rückert

Clara Schumann
Kristin Norderval, editor

32
hat mir wie - der den Gruß ge - bracht:
37
rit.
a tempo
pp
mf
Dir sa - gen auch des Freun - des Lie - der
cresc.
pp
43
p
pp
jetzt gu - te Nacht.
pp
49
p
3

Lorelei

Heinrich Heine

Clara Schumann
Kristin Norderval, editor

Schnell
Ich weiß nicht, was soll es be-deu - ten daß ich___ so trau - rig
p
4
bin;
p
Ped.
8
Ein Mär - chen aus al - ten Zei - ten, das
Ped.
11
2
kommt mir nicht aus dem Sinn.
p
Die Luft ist kühl ___und es
p

14
dun - kelt, und ru - hig fließt der Rhein; Der
17
p
Glip - fel des Ber - ges fun - kelt im A - bend-son - nen -
p
20
schein.
p
24
p
Die schön - ste Jung - frau sit - zet dort
p

27
o - ben wun - der - bar; Ihr gold' - nes Ge-schmei - de
p
30
blit - zet, sie kämmt ihr gold' - nes Haar. Sie
mf
mf
33
kämmt es mit gold'- nem Kam - me und singt ein Lied da -
36
bei;
sf
Ped.

40
Das hat ei - ne wun - der - sa - me ge -
43
wal - ti - ge Me - lo - dei.
Den Schif - fer im klei - nen
46
Schif - fe er - greift es mit wil - dem Weh;
49
er schaut nicht die Fel - sen -

52
f
rit.
p
rif - fe, er schaut nur hin-auf in die Höh'. Ich
p
55
glau - be die Wel - len ver - schlin - gen am En - de Schif - fer und
58
poco - - a - poco - - cresc.
f
Kahn; und das hat mit ih - rem Sin - gen die
poco - - a - poco - - cresc.
Ped.
Ped.
61
Lo - re - ley ge - tan, und
Ped.
Ped.
Ped.

63
2
das hat mit ih - rem Sin - gen die
65
Lo - - - re - lei ge -
67
tan.
sf
f
sf
sf
sf
70
sf
sf
f
sf

Pauline García Viardot
(1821–1910)

Jamée Ard

Pauline García Viardot was born in Paris, France, July 18, 1821, into one of the most illustrious musical families of the nineteenth century. Her father, Manuel del Popolo Vicente García (1775–1832), was a remarkable, charismatic man whose family originated in Seville, Spain, where he studied singing with Antonio Ripa (1720–1795) and Juan Almarcha (n.d.).[1] In 1807, García, his wife, the singer María Joaquina Sitchès, and their young son, Manuel, (later the inventor of the laryngoscope and a renowned vocal pedagogue), moved to Paris. Shortly after their arrival in France a second child, Maria (later Maria Malibran; see this volume) was born.

Manuel García enjoyed an eclectic career while in Paris, singing, composing (over forty operas and operettas and many songs), and teaching voice. In 1811 the family moved to Naples.[2] While there, García collaborated with Gioacchino Rossini (1792–1868), creating the roles of Norfolk in the composer's *Elisabetta regina d'Inghilterra* (Naples, 1815) and Almaviva in *Il barbiere di Siviglia* (Rome, 1816).

García returned to Paris in 1816, where he sang regularly with the Théâtre Italien, produced his own operas, and continued to teach. When he was forty-six Manuel García's third child, Michelle Ferdinande Pauline García, was born. When she was four, the family traveled to the United States. They were now an opera company powered by Manuel García. Joined by singers Domenico Crivelli *fils* (1793–1851), Carlo Angrisani (ca. 1760–?), and Francisco Barbieri (1823–1894), the company gave seventy-nine performances at New York's Park and Bowery theaters.[3] Before the tour was finished, Maria (1808–1836; see this volume), Pauline's sister (and the troupe's prima donna) severed herself from the family by marrying the French businessman Eugène Malibran against their wishes.

The formal musical education of Pauline García (hereafter called Viardot) began at the age of eight in 1829 when the family returned to Paris. She studied composition with Anton (Antoine) Reicha (1770–1836), the teacher of Hector Berlioz (1803–1869) and Franz Liszt (1811–1886). By this time her abundant musical gifts were so apparent that her sister, Maria, then at the height of her own fame, said that Viardot would "eclipse us all."[4] Viardot studied piano with Liszt and thought of herself then primarily as a pianist. (She was so adept at the keyboard that Berlioz enlisted her help with the piano reduction of his opera *Les Troyens*.[5]) However, after singing an aria for her mother at the age of fifteen, she was ordered to "close the piano"[6] and to focus her studies on singing.

The basis of her vocal technique was the García method, remembered from the hours spent in her father's studio and passed on to her by her mother. (Viardot was, by then, without the guidance of both her father, who had died in 1832, and her sister, who died from injuries sustained in a riding accident in 1836.) She made her debuts in 1839 in Rossini's *Otello* at Her Majesty's Theatre in London, and in Paris at the Théâtre Italien, where she had been contracted to sing by Louis Viardot (1800–1883), the director of the theater. One year after her Paris debut, she married him, a man twenty-one years her senior. Their home soon became a center for musical, literary, and political luminaries such as French painters Eugène Delacroix (1790–1863) and Ary Scheffer (1795–1858), and writer George Sand (Armandine Lucile Aurore, née Dupin); who immortalized the singer in her novel *Consuelo*.

Viardot's active singing career spanned approximately twenty-four years. She sang the *bel canto* repertoire embraced by her sister and soon added works composed for her. She premiered roles in *Le prophète* (1849) by Giocomo Meyerbeer (1791–1864), *Sapho* (1851) by Charles Gounod (1818–1893), *Il trovatore* (1855) by Guiseppe Verdi (1813–1901), *Alto Rhapsody* (1870) by Johannes Brahms (1833–1893), and *Samson et Delila* (1874) by Camille Saint-Saëns (1835–1921). Théophile Gautier, in his poem "Contralto," described her voice as "homme et femme à la fois . . . Hermaphrodite de la voix!" (man and woman at the same time . . . Hermaphrodite of the voice!)[7]. [Other accounts indicate that although hers was a flawed voice of unusual timbre, her performances were extraordinary combinations of vocal intensity and dramatic profundity.] H. F. Chorley, critic for London's *Athenaeum*, commented on her portrayal in Vincenzo Bellini's (1801–1835) *La Sonnambula* by saying that there was none "whose sleep was said to have been so dead as Mme Viardot's."[8]

Heinrich Heine said she was:

> terribly ugly but with a kind of ugliness which is noble, I should almost like to say beautiful . . . Indeed, the García recalls less the civilized beauty and tame gracefulness of our European homelands than she does the terrifying magnificence of some exotic and wild country . . . At times, when she opens wide her large mouth with its blinding white teeth and smiles her cruel, sweet smile, which at once charms and frightens us, we begin to feel as if the most monstrous vegetation and species of beasts from India and Africa are about to appear before us.[9]

Although physically unusual she was said to have an alluring personal charisma. Her magnetism sparked a lifelong liaison with Ivan Turgenev (1818–1883) who lived either with or near the Viardot family for most of his life, and depicted their relationship in his novel *A Month in the Country*. Viardot had met the writer when she traveled to Russia in 1843 to perform and hired him to teach her Russian, her sixth language. In addition to Turgenev, she also received confessions of love from Berlioz, Gounod, and Ary Scheffer, who dedicated a painting of Dante's *Inferno* to her, hoping to encourage her to break off the romance with Turgenev.[10]

After retiring from the stage in 1863, Viardot and her husband and four children (Louise Héritte-Viardot, 1841–1918 [see this volume]; Claudie, 1852–1914; Marianne, 1854–?; Paul, 1857–1941) moved to Baden-Baden, Germany where she turned her energies to teaching and composing. Turgenev joined them in 1864, building a villa on the same grounds. Viardot sponsored weekly salons where her students performed music that she and her contemporaries composed including her three operettas with libretti by Turgenev.

The outbreak of the Franco-Prussian War in 1870 and the reign of the Second Empire in France forced the Viardots to flee, penniless, to England. Returning to Paris in 1871 they resumed their involvement in the musical circles that now boasted Gabriel Fauré (1845–1924), Jules Massenet (1842–1912), and Saint-Saëns. In 1883 both Louis Viardot and Ivan Turgenev died. During the ensuing twenty-seven years, Viardot continued to teach and compose until she died on May 18, 1910, speaking the word "Norma," the name of the opera character she had sung seventy years earlier.[11] She is buried in Montmartre.

Viardot's life as a composer was complemented and bolstered by her work as a performer. She regularly collaborated with many of the important composers of the nineteenth century not only as a prima donna but also as a creative equal. (Berlioz referred to *Les Troyens* as "our opera" when speaking of it with Viardot.[12]) Others, including Brahms, Fryderyk Chopin (1810–1849), Fauré, César Franck (1822–1890), Saint-Saëns, Robert Schumann (1810–1856), and Piotr Ilyich Tchaikovsky (1840–1893), dedicated scores to her. She was encouraged to compose by her two confidants, Sand and Turgenev, who arranged for publication of her songs by the Russian publisher A. Johansen at his own expense. Viardot, however, continued to doubt her skills as composer, remarking to Sand that she hoped she would not disgrace her friend's poetry by setting it to music.[13]

While there are no extant manuscripts of Viardot's works; many were published during her lifetime. The earliest publication, *Album de Mme Viardot*, dates from 1843. The first documented performance of the song *L'Hirondelle et la Prisonnière* was in 1841.[14] Most of her songs were published after 1860, when she retired from the stage and moved to Baden-Baden. In all, Viardot composed more than one hundred songs, four operettas, one opera, some works for piano, a few chamber pieces and some vocal transcriptions.

Stylistically, Viardot's songs form a bridge between the *romance*, a simple, lyrical, strophic song that was widely popular in early nineteenth-century France, and the *mélodie*, the French counterpart of the German lied. Some of her earliest arrangements are vocal transcriptions of the works of other composers including the mazurkas of Chopin. Chopin, introduced to Viardot by George Sand, knew and approved of the transcriptions and even accompanied a performance of them at a recital in 1848.[15] These are connected stylistically to the *romance* with their simple display of melody, uncomplicated harmonies, and transparent texture. Whether these characteristics resulted from Viardot being a novice composer or from the necessity to conform to another's work is difficult to determine.

Although Viardot's later works also display the straight-forward approach of the *romance*, they often transcend this style and include passages of intricate piano writing attributable to her exceptional keyboard skills, and elaborate vocal cadenzas reminiscent of the *bel canto* repertoire she was familiar with as a performer. These piano accompaniments are more sophisticated than those in the earlier *romance*, but they never quite attain the independence or evocative qualities of accompaniments in the *mélodie*. Only occasionally do the later songs use the pre-symbolist poetry found in the *mélodie*. Favoring the poems of centuries past, Viardot's songs are dramatic and virtuosic, painting the musical atmosphere with the broad strokes of Bizet rather than the impressionism of Debussy.

Viardot's songs are set to texts ranging from innocence to high drama, colored with sweeping lyricism and striking declamation. One of her most frequent collaborators was Louis Pomey, a little-known actor, possibly related to Turgenev.[16]

Poet Alfred de Musset (1810–1857) was quite smitten with both of Manuel García's daughters, and dedicated numerous poems to them. He suffered immensely at the death of Maria but joyfully declared that "La Malibran est revenue au monde . . ." (Malibran has returned to the world) after hearing Viardot's debut.[17] She returned his adoration by dedicating one of her songs (*Madrid*) to him and by setting one of his texts (*Les filles de Cadix*) to music.

In strophic form, *Les filles de Cadix* uses only two of the original three verses, set with the requisite Spanish flair, teasing, and flirtation. In case these qualities elude the singer, Viardot reminds them with the marking "avec coquetterie" in measure 36. The vocal line contains brief coloratura flourishes, which help to depict the atmosphere of Cadix and its bullfight. The accompaniment is simple and chordal, utilizing repetition of a dance-like rhythmic motive. The song is straightforward and harmonically uncomplicated. It opens in F major as the narrator describes the bullfight, the three youths, and their dance of the bolero.

Nixe Binsefuss, published under the name Pauline Viardot-García, utilizes somewhat more sophisticated musical language. It is a through-composed song in a loose ABA[1] form. The A section opens in G minor and remains in that key until the sprite's spirited exclamations coincide with a modulation to D major (m. 39). The accompaniment is varied and contains independent thematic material, unlike that of *Les filles de Cadix*. A skipping, rhythmic theme depicts the water sprite. The B section (m. 54) is in G major. Legato, arpeggiated gestures serve as underpinning for a description of the "little maid" and her sweetheart. At measure 74 the original A material, slightly varied, returns in the original key of G minor. The four-measure coda (m. 107) reprises material from section B in G major. This difficult song is probably beyond the grasp of the amateur singer, with wide ascending leaps that resemble yodeling depicting the outbursts of the sprite. Viardot's predominant strength as a composer, the ability to vividly capture a nationalistic flavor and atmosphere, are evident in the two songs included here.

Notes

1. John Mewburn Levien, Six *Sovereigns of Song* (London: Novello & Co Ltd., 1948), 39.

2. F.-J. Fétis, *Biographie universelle des musiciens et bibliographie générale de la musique* (Paris: Librairie de Firmin Didot et Cie., 1878), 404.

3. Theodore Baker (revised by Nicolas Slonimsky), *Baker's Biographical Dictionary of Musicians* (New York: Schirmer, 1992), 600.

4. April Fitzlyon, *The Price of Genius* (London: John Calder, 1964), 25.

5. D. Kern Holoman, *Berlioz* (Cambridge, Mass.: Harvard University Press, 1989), 231.

6. Fitzlyon, *The Price of Genius*, 37.

7. "Contralto" by Théophile Gautier was published by Gascon ca. 1900.

8. Henry F. Chorley, *Thirty Years' Musical Remembrances* (New York and London: Alfred A. Knopf, 1926), 234.

9. Leonard Schapiro, *Turgenev: His Life and Times* (New York: Random House, 1978), 42.

10. John Russell, "Inspired by the Troubadours," *The New York Times*, October 11, 1996, C30: 1.

11. Nicole Barry, *Pauline Viardot: L'égérie de George Sand et de Tourgeniev* (Paris: Flammarion, 1990), 409.

12. Fitzlyon, *The Price of Genius*, 361.

13. Thérèse Marix-Spire, "Vicissitudes d'un Opéra Comique," *Romantic Review*, 35 (1944), 130.

14. Barry, *Pauline Viardot*, 72.

15. Fitzlyon, *The Price of Genius*, 229.

16. Alexandre Zviguilsky, "Un frère français de Tourgueniev: Louis Pomey," *Cahiers Ivan Tourgueniev, Pauline Viardot et Maria Malibran* 7 (1983), 139.

17. Yvette Sieffert-Rigaud, "Pauline Viardot: Femme et Artiste," *Romantisme* 17 (1987): 19.

Selected List of Works

Songs

L'Affligée. Text by Louis Pomey. Paris: E. Gérard & Cie, [188–?].

Aimez-moi. Text by Louis Pomey, after a fifteenth-century poem. Paris: H. Heugel, 1886.

Les Attraits. Author of text unknown (eighteenth-century poem). Paris: Enoch Frères & Costallat, 1893.

Au Jardin de mon père. Text by [unknown]. Paris: E. Fromont, 1900.

Aurore. Text by Afanasij Feth. Translated into French by Louis Pomey. Paris: E. Gérard, 1866.

Bonjour mon coeur. Text by Ronsard. Paris: Enoch et Cie., 1895.

Chanson de la faucille. Text by Koltsoff. Translated into French by Louis Pomey. Paris: Gérard, 1866.

Chanson de la pluie. Text by Ivan Turgenev. Paris: Enoch et Cie., 1900.

Chanson de l'infante. Fifteenth-century poem. Translated into French by Louis Pomey. Paris: H. Heugel, 1886.

La Chanson villageoise. Text by Louis Pomey. Paris: Gérard, 1881.

Chant du soir. Text by Afanasij Feth. Translated into by French Louis Pomey. Paris: Gérard, 1866.

La Chevelure. Text by Löys. Paris: G. Miran, 1905.

Elle passe. Text by Pauline Viardot. Paris: G. Miran, 1886.

En Douleur et tristesse. Text based on fifteenth-century poem. Paris: G. Miran, 1905.

Évocation. Text by Aleksandr Pushkin. Translated into French by Louis Pomey. Paris: Gérard, 1866.

Fleur desséchée. Text by Aleksandr Pushkin. Translated into French by Louis Pomey. Paris: Gérard, 1866.

Fünf Gedichte. St. Petersburg: A. Johansen, 1874.
1. *Der Nachtwandler*. Text by R. Pohl
2. *Finnischeslied*. Text by W. Goethe
3. *Der Jüngling und das Mädchen*. Text by Aleksandr Pushkin
4. *Die Soldatenbraut*. Text by Eduard Mörike
5. *Im April*. Text by E. Geibel

Géorgienne. Text by Aleksandr Pushkin. Translated into French by Louis Pomey. Paris: Gérard, 1866.

Grands oiseaux blancs. Text by Louis Pomey. Paris: Enoch, 1893.

In der Frühe. Text by Eduard Mörike. Leipzig & Weimar: Robert Seitz, n.d.

Indécision. Text by Louis Pomey. Paris: Gérard, 1881.

Lamento. Text by Théophile Gautier. Paris: Enoch Frères & Costallat, [188–?].

Liberté. Text by Stéphan Bordèse. Paris: G. Miran, 1905.

Mélodies. Paris: G. Miran, 1904.
1. *Le Toréador*. Text by Victor Hugo
2. *Peronelle*. Fifteenth-century poem
3. *Poursuite*. Tuscan poem
4. *Sara la baigneuse*. Text by Victor Hugo
5. *Le Vase brisé*. Text by Sully Prudhomme
6. *Le Savetier et le Financier*. Text by LaFontaine

La Mésange. Text by Ivan Turgenev. Paris: Gérard, 1866.

Nixe Binsefuss. Text by Eduard Mörike. Leipzig & Weimar: Robert Seitz, [1860?].

Parme. Text by Sully Prudhomme. Paris: Enoch, 1893.

Les Ombres de minuit. Text by Afanasij Feth. Translated into French by Louis Pomey. Paris: Gérard, 1866.

L'Orage. Text by Aleksandr Pushkin. Translated into French by Louis Pomey. Paris: Gérard, 1866.

Reproches! Text by Louis Pomey. Paris: Gérard, 1881.

Ressemblance! Text by Sully-Prudhomme. Paris: Durand & Schoenewerke, 1889.

Rossignol, rossignolet. Text by Joseph Boulmier. Paris: Enoch & Costallet, 1893.

Scène d'Hermione. Text by Racine. Paris: H.Heugel, 1887.

Sérénade Florentine. Text by Louis Pomey. Paris: E. Gerard, [188–?].

Six Mélodies. Paris: Au Ménestrel, 1884.
1. *Sylvie*. Text by Boileau
2. *Berceuse*. Text by Auguste de Chatillon
3. *Sérénade*. Text by Théophile Gautier
4. *L'Enigme*. Text by R. Pohl
5. *Le Miroir*. Text by Louis Pomey
6. *Insommie*. Text by [unknown]

Six Mélodies. Paris: Au Ménestrel, 1888.
1. *A la fontaine*. Text by Eugène Hubert
2. *Belle Yoli*. Text by Roger de Beauuvoir
3. *Ici-bas tous les Lilacs meurent*. Text by Sully Prudhomme
4. *Sérénade à Rosine*. Text by Louis Pomey
5. *Madrid*. Text by Alfred de Musset
6. *Les Filles de Cadiz*. Text by Alfred de Musset

Six Mélodies et une Havanaise variée à 2 Voix. Paris: H. Heugel, 1880.
1. *La Main*. Text by Henri Charles Read
2. *Dernier Aveu*. Text by Théophile Gautier
3. *J'en mourrai*. Text by Victor Wilder
4. *Hai Luli!* Text by Xavier de Maistre
5. *Gentilles Hirondelles*. Text by Victor Wilder
6. *Chanson mélancholique*. Text by d'Armand Silvestre
7. *Havanaise variée*. Text by Louis Pomey

Twelve Lieder. Bryn Mawr, PA: Hildegard Publishing Company, 1994.
1. *Das Blümlein*. Text by Aleksandr Pushkin
2. *Auf Grusien's Hügeln*. Text by Aleksandr Pushkin
3. *Ruhige heilige Nacht*. Text by Afanasij Feth
4. *Mittternächtige Bilder*. Text by Afanasij Feth
5. *Flüstern, anthemscheues Lauschen*. Text by Afanasij Feth
6. *Die Beschwörung*. Text by Aleksandr Pushkin
7. *Die Meise*. Text by Ivan Turgenev
8. *Zwei Rosen*. Text by Afanasij Feth
9. *Des Nachts*. Text by Aleksandr Pushkin
10. *Der Gefangene*. Text by Aleksandr Pushkin
11. *Das Vöglein*. Text by Aleksandr Pushkin
12. *Die Sterne*. Text by Afanasij Feth

Trois jours de Vendange. Text by A. Daudet. Paris: Enoch, 1893.

Transcriptions for Voice

Canzonetta de Concert (La nuit monte). String Quartet no. 17, op. 3, no. 5. Second Movement by Joseph Haydn. Transcribed for voice by Pauline Viardot. Text by Louis Pomey. Paris: Heugel et cie., [1845?].

Les Cavaliers. Hungarian Dance #1 and #7 by Johannes Brahms. Transcribed for voice by Pauline Viardot. Text by Louis Pomey. New York: Da Capo, 1988.

Tes Yeux. Waltz (D. 969 no. 9) by Franz Schubert. Transcribed for voice by Pauline Viardot. Text by Louis Pomey. Paris: J. Hamelle, [1890?].

12 Mazurkas. Frederic Chopin. Transcribed for voice by Pauline Viardot. Text by Louis Pomey. Jerome Rose, editor. New York: International Music Company, 1988.

1. *Seize Ans*
2. *Aime-moi*
3. *Plainte d'Amour*
4. *Coquette*
5. *L'Oiselet*
6. *Séparation*
7. *La Fête*
8. *Faible Coeur!*
9. *La jeune Fille*
10. *Berceuse*
11. *La Danse*
12. *La Beauté*

Opera/Operetta

Trop de Femmes (1867). Text by Ivan Turgenev. Unpublished.

L'Orge (1868). Text by Ivan Turgenev. Unpublished.

Le Dernier Sorcier (*Der Letzte Zauberer*) (1869). Text by Ivan Turgenev. Unpublished.

Le Conte de Fées (1879). Unpublished.

Cendrillon. Paris: Miran, [1904?].

Piano Music

2 Airs de Ballet. Paris: G. Miran, [1906?].

Chamber and Ensemble Music

Chœur Bohémien (SSA chorus and soli). Paris: Enoch & Cie, [188–?].

Chœur des Elfes (SSA chorus and soli). Paris: Enoch & Cie, [1890?].

Six Morceaux pour Violon et Piano. Bryn Mawr, PA: Hildegard Publishing Company, 1993.

Sonatine pour Piano et Violon. Bryn Mawr, PA: Hildegard Publishing Company, 1993.

Les trois belles demoiselles (for three voices). Paris: H. Heugel, [188–?].

Pedagogical Studies

Une Heure Étude. (First and Second series). Paris: Heugel et Fils, [1880?].

Bibliography

Association des Amis d'Ivan Tourgueniev, Pauline Viardot et Maria Malibran. Cahiers Ivan Tourgueniev, Pauline Viaradot et Maria Malibran. Paris: UNESCO, 1977– .

Baker, Theodore, trans. "Pauline Viardot Garcia to Julius Rietz: Letters of Friendship." *Musical Quarterly* 1 (July 1915): 350-80; v. 2: 526-59.

Barry, Nicole. *Pauline Viardot: L'égérie de George Sand et de Tourgueniev*. Paris: Flammarion, 1990.

Berlioz, Hector. *À Travers Chant*. Paris: Calmann Lévy, 1872.

Bowers, Jane, and Judith Tick. *Women Making Music: The Western Art Tradition, 1150–1950*. Urbana and Chicago: University of Illinois Press, 1986.

Chorley, Henry F. *Thirty Years' Musical Remembrance*. New York and London: Alfred A. Knopf, 1926.

Christiansen, Rupert. *Prima Donna: A History*. London: Bodley Head, 1984.

Cofer, Angela Faith. "Pauline Viardot-García: The Influence of the Performer on Nineteenth-Century Opera." D.M.A. dissertation, University of Cincinnati, 1988.

Desternes, Suzanne and Henriette Chandet. *La Malibran et Pauline Viardot*. Paris: Fayard, 1969.

Dulong, Gustav. *Pauline Viardot: tragédienne lyrique*. Paris: Association des Amis d'Ivan Tourgueniev, Pauline Viardot et Maria Malibran, 1987.

Fischer-Dieskau, Dietrich. *Wenn Musick der Liebe Nahrung ist*. Stuttgart: Deutsch Verlags-Abstalt, 1990.

Fitzlyon, April. *The Price of Genius.* London: John Calder, 1964.

Héritte-Viardot, Louise. *Memories and Adventures.* Translated by E.S. Buchheim. London: Mills & Boon, Ltd. 1913.

Kaplan, Arthur. "Saint-Saëns et Pauline." *San Francisco Opera Magazine* 6 (Fall 1983): 45, 60-68.

Lehrman, Edgar H. *Turgenev's Letters: A Selection.* New York: Alfred A. Knopf, 1961.

Marek, George, and Maria Gordon-Smith. "Pauline Viardot and Frédéric Chopin." *About the House* 5 (December 1978): 28-31.

Marix-Spire, Thérèse. "Gounod and His First Interpreter, Pauline Viardot." *Musical Quarterly* 31 (April 1945) 2: 193-211, 3: 299-317.

_____. "Vicissitudes d'un Opéra Comique La Mare au Diable de George Sand et Pauline Viardot." *Romantic Review* 35 (1944): 125-46.

_____, ed. *Lettres inédites de George Sand et de Pauline Viardot, 1839–1849.* Paris: Nouvelles Editions latines, 1959.

Sand, George. "Le Théâtre-Italien et Mlle Pauline García." *Revue des deux mondes* 4 (February 15, 1840): 580-90.

Sieffert-Rigaud, Yvette. "Pauline Viardot: Femme et Artiste." *Romantisme* 17 (1987): 17-32.

Stewart, Sylvie H. "The Vocal Compositions of Pauline Viardot-García." M.M.A. thesis, Yale University, 1985.

Torrigi-Heiroth, L. *Mme Pauline Viardot-García: sa biographie, ses compositions, son enseignement.* Geneva: W. Kündig and Sons, 1901.

Turgenev, Ivan. *Lettres à Madame Viardot.* Edited by E. Halperine-Kaminsky. Paris: Bibliothèque Charpentier, 1907.

Viardot, Pierette Jeanne. "Les Jeudis de Pauline Viardot." *Revue Internationale de Musique Français* 8 (June 1982): 87-104.

Waddington, Patrick. "Dickens, Pauline Viardot, Turgenev: A Study in Mutual Admiration." *New Zealand Slavonic Journal* 1 (1974): 55, 69.

_____. "Henry Chorley, Pauline Viardot & Turgenev: A Musical and Literary Friendship." *Musical Quarterly* 67 (April 1981): 165-92.

_____. "Pauline Viardot-García as Berlioz's Counselor and Physician." *Musical Quarterly* 59 (July 1973): 382-98.

_____. "Turgenev and Pauline Viardot: An Unofficial Marriage." *Canadian Slavonic Papers* 26 (March 1984): 42-64.

Zekulin, Nicholas G. *The Story of an Operetta: Le Dernier Sorcier by Pauline Viardot and Ivan Turgenev.* Munich: Verlag O. Sagner, 1989.

Discography

Chant d'Amour. Cecilia Bartoli, mezzo-soprano, Myung-Whun Chung, piano, Decca Record Company (452 667 2), April, 1996.

Pauline Viardot-García Songs. Karin Ott, soprano, Christoph Keller, piano, CPO Digital Recording (999 044 2), November 1987, June 1988.

Lieder. John Ostendorf, bass-baritone, Katherine Ciesinski, mezzo-soprano, Rudolph Palmer, piano, Leonarda (LPI 107), January and February 1981.

Women's Work. Mertine Johns, mezzo-soprano, R. Rundle, M. May, piano, E. Steinbeck, cello. Gemini Hall Records (Stereo RAP-1010), 1975.

Les Filles de Cadix

Nous venions de voir le taureau,
Trois garçons, trois fillettes.
Sur la pelouse il faisait beau
Et nous dansions un boléro
Au son des castagnettes.
"Dites-moi, voisin
Si j'ai bonne mine?
Et si ma basquine
Va bien ce matin?
Vous me trouvez la taille fine?"
Ah! ah! Les filles de Cadix,
Ah! ah! aiment assez cela.
Vous me trouvez la taille fine?
Ah! ah! Les filles de Cadix, etc.

Et nous dansions un boléro.
Un soir, c'était Dimanche,
Vers nous s'en vint un hidalgo,
Tout cousu d'or, plume au chapeau,
Et le poing sur la hanche.
"Si tu veux de moi,
Brune au doux sourire,
Tu n'as qu'à le dire,
Cet or est à toi."
"Passez votre chemin, beau sire."
Ah! ah! Les filles de Cadix,
Ah! ah! n'entendent pas cela.
Passez votre chemin, beau sire.
Ah! ah! Les filles de Cadix, etc.

We'd just seen the bullfight,
three boys, three girls.
It was fine on the green
and so we danced a bolero
to the sound of castenets.
"Tell me, neighbor,
if I look good?
And if my skirt
becomes me this morning?
Is my waist slim?"
Ah! ah! The daughters of Cadiz,
Ah! ah! are very fond of that.
Is my waist slim?
Ah! ah! The daughters of Cadiz, etc.

And we were dancing a bolero.
One evening, it was a Sunday,
a Hidalgo came up to us,
all dressed in gold, a feather in his hat,
and with fist on hip.
"If you fancy me,
dark-haired girl with the gentle smile,
you only have to say so,
this gold is yours."
"Go your way, handsome sir."
Ah! ah! The daughters of Cadiz,
Ah! ah! don't listen to that.
Go your way, handsome sir.
Ah! ah! The daughters of Cadiz, etc.

Nixe Binsefuss

Des Wassermanns sein Töchterlein
tanzt auf dem Eis in Vollmondschein,
sie tanzet ohne Furcht und Scheu,
wohl an des Fischers Haus vorbei.

"Ich bin die Nixe Binsefuss,
und meine Fisch wohl hüten muss,
meine Fisch' die sind im Kasten
sie haben kalte Fasten,
von Böhmerglas mein Kasten ist,
da zähl' ich sie zu jeder Frist.

Gelt, Fischermatz? Gelt, alter Tropf?
dir will der Winter nicht in Kopf?
Komm mir mit deinen Netzen!
Die will ich schön zerfetzen!

Dein Mägdlein zwar ist fromm und gut,
ihr Schatz ein braves Jägerblut.

Drum häng ich ihr zum Hochzeitstrauss,
ein schilfen Kränzlein vor das Haus,
und einen Hect, von Silber schwer,
er kommt von König Artus her,

ein Zerglein-Goldschmieds-Meister-Stück,
wer's hat, dem bringt es eitel Glück:
er lässt sich schuppen Jahr für Jahr,
da sind's fünfhundert Gröschlein baar.

Ade, mein Kind! Ade für heut',
der Morgen hahn im Dorfe schreit."

The water elf's daughter is dancing
on the ice in the full moonlight,
she dances boldly without fear,
passing by the fisherman's house.

"I am the Maiden Reedfoot,
and must care well for my fish,
my fish are in a tank
and are having a cold Lent,
my tank is made of Bohemian glass,
so that at every opportunity I can count them.

Hey, Fisherbrat? Hey old rascal?
Can't you get it in your head that it's winter?
Come near me with your nets!
And I'll shred them to pieces!

Surely your little maid is gentle and good,
her sweetheart is a brave hunter.

As a wedding bouquet,
I'll hang a wreath of reeds on the door,
and a pike made of heavy silver,
that comes from King Arthur,

a masterpiece by a dwarf goldsmith,
brings its owner nothing but luck:
year after year it sheds its scales,
worth five hundred groschen.

Farewell, my child! Farewell for today,
the rooster is crowing in the village."

Translations by Jamée Ard

Les filles de Cadix

Alfred de Musset

Pauline Viardot

25
tes. "Di - tes - moi, voi -
che. "Si tu veux de
31
p avec coquetterie
sin, Si j'ai bon - ne mi - ne? Di-tes-moi, voi -
moi, Brune au doux sou - ri - re, Si tu veux de
37
sin, Si j'ai bon - ne mi - ne Et si ma bas-qui - ne Va bien ce ma -
moi, Brune au doux sou - ri - re, Tu n'as qu'à le di - re, Cet or est à
43
tin? Vous
toi." "Pas -

49
me trou-vez la tail - le fi - ne, Vous me trou-vez la tail - le
sez vo - tre che - min, beau si - re, Pas - sez vo - tre che - min, beau
55
fi - ne, Ah! ah! Les fil-les de Ca - dix, Ah!
si - re, Ah! ah! Les fil-les de Ca - dix, Ah!
f
p
f
Ped.
61
ah! ai-ment as-sez ce - la. Vous me trou-vez la tail - le
ah! n'en-ten-dent pas ce - la. Pas - sez vo - tre che-min, beau
p
mf
p
Ped.
67
fi - ne, Vous me trou-vez la tail - le fi - ne, Ah!
si - re, Pas - sez vo - tre che - min, beau si - re, Ah!
p
p
p
Ped.

73
ah! Les fil-les de Ca-dix, Ah! ah! ai-ment as-sez ce-
ah! Les fil-les de Ca-dix, Ah! ah! n'en-ten-dent pas ce-
p
Ped. * Ped. * Ped. *
79
la 1re fois p
ten. la 2de avec toute la voix
animé
la. Ah! ah! ah! ah! Les fil-les de Ca-dix, ai-ment as-sez ce-la."
la. Ah! ah! ah! ah! Les fil-les de Ca-dix, n'en-ten-dent pas ce-la."
ad lib.
suivez
p
84
1.
f
Et
D.C.
91
2.
ff
sf
sf

Nixe Binsefuss

Ed. Mörike

Pauline Viardot

5
Des Was-ser-manns sein Töch - ter-lein
9
tanzt auf dem Eis im Voll - mond - schein,
13
sie tan-zet oh-ne Furcht und Scheu, wohl an des Fi-schers Haus vor -

17
bei. "Ich bin die Ni xe Bin - se - fuss, und mei - ne Fisch' wohl hü - ten
21
muss, mei - ne Fisch' die sind im Kas - ten, sie ha - ben kal - te
25
Fas - ten, von Böhm - er - glas mein Kas - ten ist, da zähl' ich sie zu je - der
29
Frist, da zähl' ich sie zu je - der Frist, da zähl'
cresc.

33
ich sie zu je-der Frist.
tr
f
37
Gelt, Fi-scher-matz? gelt, al-ter Tropf?
p
41
dir will der Win-ter nicht in Kopf? Gelt, al-ter Tropf,
p
p
45
dir will der Win - ter nicht in Kopf? Komm mir mit dei-nen

49
Net - zen! Die will ich schön zer - fet - zen!
f
dim.
53
pp
Ped.
57
Dein Mägd-lein zwar ist fromm und gut, ihr Schatz ein brav-es
p
61
Jä - ger-blut, ihr Schatz ein brav-es

65
Jä - ger-blut. Dein Mägd-lein zwar ist fromm und gut, Dein Mägd - lein
69
rit.
zwar ist fromm und gut, ihr Schatz, ihr Schatz ein brav-es
p
p
73
Tempo I
Jä - ger - blut.
p
p
77
f
Drum häng' ich ihr zum Hoch-zeit -
cresc.
f

81
p
f
strauss, ein schil-fen Kränz-lein vor das Haus, und ei-nen Hecht, von
p
sf
Ped.
85
f
Sil - ber schwer, er kommt von Kö - nig Ar - tus her,
f
sf
89
ein Zwerg-lein-Gold-schmieds-Meis-ter - Stück, wer's
f
p
Ped.
92
hat, dem bringt es ei-tel Glück: er lässt sich schup-pen Jahr für Jahr, da
Ped.

96
sind's fünf-hun-dert Grösch-lein baar, er lässt sich schup - pen Jahr für
Ped. Ped. Ped. Ped.
99
Jahr, da sind's fünf - hun - dert Grösch-lein
f
cresc.
tr
103
baar. A -
p
cresc.
f
107
ad libitum
a tempo
pp
de, mein Kind! A - de für heut', der Mor-gen-hahn im Dor-fe schreit."
p
Ped. Ped. Ped. Ped.

Hermina Maria Amersfoordt-Dijk

(1821–1892)

HELEN H. METZELAAR

Hermina Maria Dijk was born in Amsterdam on June 26, 1821. Her father, Barend Dijk Jr. (1792–1870), worked in the family medicinal herb business in Amsterdam. Her mother, Unica Wilhelmina Maria Cock (1795–1849), hailed from eastern Holland and belonged to the Dutch branch of an old learned family from Bremen, Germany. Hermina, nicknamed Mina, was the third of ten children, three of whom died in infancy. For many years her father, an avid music lover, was secretary of the music department of the Felix Meritis Society, a well-known organization that promoted the ideals of the Enlightenment and was open to well-to-do Amsterdam burghers (men only). As secretary, Barend Dijk's main task was to organize about twenty concerts per season held in the Society's relatively small oval concert hall, designed by Jacob Otten Husly in 1788, considered one of the best in Europe.

Extant handwritten programs reveal that by the age of eight Dijk was appearing at Felix Meritis as a prodigy pianist.[1] In 1830 she accompanied the Dutch violinist Johannes Bernardus van Bree in a medley by Ignaz Moscheles and Charles Philippe Lafont. Henri Viotta, in 1881, noted that as a child Dijk studied with Lafont and Van Bree, who was the conductor of the Felix Meritis orchestra from 1830 until his death in 1857.[2] Dijk's talent must have been considerable as she is recorded as performing in 1831 for King William I and his family. Her concerts followed a set formula, characteristic of the time: the first piece was always an orchestral work, often an overture or a single symphonic movement. It was followed by one or two pieces by the soloist, then the first half ended with another orchestral piece, often a single symphonic movement. This formula was repeated after intermission, so that the soloist made appearances both before and after the intermission.

The works Dijk performed were typical of the Biedermeier period: variations and fantasies based on popular songs or opera melodies. She also began composing at an early age. A program from 1838 lists her performing a movement from the *Piano Concerto in B minor* by Johann Nepomuk Hummel, and her own variations on the song *Ma Normandie*.

Her last recorded appearance, in the Felix Meritis hall was on February 7, 1840. She may have stopped performing in order to take care of her sickly mother, or she may have bowed to the social norm at the time which frowned upon public performances by a young lady of her standing. It appears that after her mother died in 1849 she was able to devote more time to composing. Viotta writes that she studied composition with Johan George Bertelman (1782–1854), author of various music treatises and a specialist in orchestration and the development of orchestral instruments. This study may have been in the early 1850s.[3]

On February 26, 1852, Dijk married Jacob Paulus Amersfoordt (1817–1885), an intellectual with a double degree in law and literature. Both he and his first wife, who died in childbirth in 1850, had participated in Felix Meritis concerts as vocalists. Dijk's betrothal inspired her to compose the cantata *Floris V*, which was performed to celebrate the banns of their marriage. Unfortunately, while the author of the text for *Floris V,* J. A. Alberdingk Thijm, took care to have his poem published, her cantata remained in manuscript form and is now lost.[4]

The Amersfoordts' honeymoon took them to Paris, where they attended numerous concerts and operas. In a lengthy article for the French magazine *Journal le Souvenir*, her husband described his impressions of Parisian cultural life. Amersfoordt-Dijk's sweetly romantic song, *Le Souvenir,* dates from this period. In addition,while in Paris she took a few composition lessons from Antoine Elwart (1808–1877), a French theorist and composer. When back in Amsterdam, Amersfoordt-Dijk composed a piano sonata, which, according to Viotta, Franz Liszt (1811–1886) praised when he was in Rotterdam in 1854.[5] Amersfoordt-Dijk soon turned to writing large-scale orchestral works, a highly unusual activity for a Dutch woman composer at this time. Her first Overture, op. 19, was discovered in a little known music collection belonging to the Concertgebouw Ltd. It was performed in 1854 at a special Felix Meritis concert devoted to Dutch music. Her second overture was premiered in Felix Meritis the following year.

Because she was wealthy enough to not have to earn a living as a musician, Amersfoordt-Dijk was considered a dilettante. Although the term "dilettante" originally denoted a person from the upper classes active in the arts, it gradually acquired a negative connotation. As performance standards improved in the later nineteenth century, the separation between professional musicians and dilettantes became more pronounced. Increasingly, Dutch music periodicals carried articles berating poor performances by dilettantes; the term dilettante acquired two quite separate connotations, one a negative qualification, the other indicative of class.

Reviews of Amersfoordt-Dijk's music always noted that she was a dilettante, reflecting her class origin. Her orchestral works, however, made her a unique figure.

> The task which the Dilettante has set herself, as well as the manner in which she has accomplished this, prove to be a sound endeavor which earns the greatest praise; we did not find new or bold thoughts or audacious flight in this Overture, and the orchestration, as far as the brass goes, seems to us to be a bit too rich here and there, but the main movement is flowingly and meritoriously written.[6]

Although dilettante composers abounded in the nineteenth century, their realm of writing was generally limited to small-scale works. When at the age of twenty-one Catharina van Rees (1831–1915) published a *Grande Valse* for piano, one critic remarked,

> that women compose is very sweet, and that they dedicate something to a girlfriend, why not, but when publishing what they have written, the beauties should be careful not to set their foot publicly as a composer in the world of art before experts have honestly assured her that her work is important enough to appear in print.[7]

In 1855 Amersfoordt-Dijk's husband bought some 500 acres in the Haarlemmermeer polder, newly reclaimed land not far from Amsterdam. While most landowners leased out their barren, muddy polder properties to poor tenant farmers, Jacob was determined to personally run his homestead, with the aim of creating a huge model farm based on the latest scientific principles. Their extensive farming estate soon included nine homes for workers and their families, plus a wide array of barns and sheds for livestock, dairy farming, and the storage of grains and fruits. In a speech given at Felix Meritis, Jacob outlined various prerequisites for new landowners, including his views on an ideal wife.

> In case a landowner wants to practice husbandry [farming] himself, he should own [*sic*] a wife who does not oppose his wishes and who does not consider it beneath herself to keep an eye on the milking and the garden or the chicken coop, who doesn't long to stay in the city the whole winter and endlessly visit balls, comedies and concerts . . . Happy is he who has found a wife who has enough sense to find satisfaction on one's own property, and who, through the gifts of her spirit, knows how to make the monotonous life in winter evenings agreeable; who helps him, the farmer, when his sick farmhands need medication, [provides] guidance for their children, and addresses and fosters orderliness in their wives.[8]

Pioneering life in the muddy polder was not easy, but by all accounts Amersfoordt-Dijk matched her husband's energy and expectations. She looked after the farmhands and their families, took charge of the butter and cheese-making for both home and market production, conducted a sewing club for the needy twice a week, and did the bookkeeping. Impoverished farmers were often stricken with contagious diseases, and when a cholera epidemic struck many hundreds in 1866, Amersfoordt-Dijk superintended a sizeable makeshift hospital on their estate, slowly nursing her patients back to health. Because her husband was soon appointed to a number of official positions, including mayor of the municipality, she also bore responsibilities as the wife of a prominent community leader.

Occasionally husband and wife took time off to travel abroad, sometimes combining visits to international agricultural expositions with cultural outings. In 1864 Amersfoordt-Dijk and her husband returned to Paris, where she contacted her former teacher, Antoine Elwart. Her husband noted in his travel journal that Elwart listened to both her piano sonatas and to "our duet *L'hymne au printemps*," perhaps meaning that he had contributed the text to this duet.[9]

Although in the first years of their marriage, this husband and wife team still had time to produce a historical play (he the script, she the music), by the 1860s their model farm began to attract an endless stream of international visitors interested in contemporary agricultural techniques. Surviving visitor registers include guests such as Kaiser Maximilian of Mexico, the King of Bavaria, ex-president of the United States Ulysses Grant, and Queen Sophia of Holland. Amersfoordt-Dijk soon combined her talents in composing, performing, and improvising with her role as hostess. When Emperor Pedro of Brazil and his minister of agriculture visited in 1877, his wife, the Empress, was entertained by Amersfoordt-Dijk. A local newspaper article, written by her husband, relates: "At the request of Her Majesty, Mrs. Amersfoordt sat at the piano and rendered a *Religioso* from her first sonata and a piece called *Capriccio*, also her own composition (both unpublished)."[10] After the Emperor had finished touring the farmstead, he insisted on hearing her perform: "Thus it took place, the Emperor attentively listening to the witty leaps of the elegant music . . ." [11] When he asked for more,

> Mrs. Amersfoordt began to improvise, something, as she later explained, she thought would be pleasing to the character of the man whom she had learned to know today. The room became silent; one pretty motif followed another . . . In the twenty-five years that Mr. Amersfoordt had owned his wife, he had never heard more expression, more eloquence in her playing.[12]

It was probably during the long winter evenings that Amersfoordt-Dijk worked on her greatest accomplishment, the full-length oratorio *Gottes Allgegenwart*, op. 40. It was first performed on January 25, 1872, conducted by Gustav Heinze in the well-known Park Hall in Amsterdam. This oratorio later received two more full performances, in 's-Hertogenbosch in 1876, and in Utrecht the following year. A lengthy review of the Amsterdam performance opened with:

> About a month ago we called general attention to a highly remarkable occasion, which was of great importance to the musical life in our capital because of its rarity . . . A woman, already greeted as one of the most beautiful manifestations of dilettantism, appeared with an extensive work . . .[13]

Although generally positive, some commentators were critical of the first part of *Gottes Allgegenwart* for its lack of drama. The critic of the *Algemeen Handelsblad* also expressed surprise that the climax in part one, an aria expressing God's supremacy, was sung by a soprano instead of a bass. Here we see an example of nineteenth-century ideas on typecasting according to gender: texts on God's supremacy were to be sung by low, powerful male voices.[14]

Other critics generally avoided gender comments about this oratorio, the first large-scale work to be written by a Dutch woman composer. In spite of being written by a woman, it was not praised for its virile numbers, nor for its typically feminine handling. However it was never suggested that women were incapable of writing large-scale works. An article in the *Utrechtsch Provinciaal en Stedelijk Dagblad* suggests that women's emancipation was on its way:

> In our days, which are less narrow-minded and more tolerant, letting talent express itself from whatever side it appears, women dare to take a try at the more penetrating study of composition, in order to claim a part of the terrain in which her spirit and emotions feel so at home . . . If, during a woman's development, heart and spirit are not allowed to express themselves together, both will become lame, but where permitted to reveal themselves, supported by the sympathy of the non-prejudiced, there they bring much good, much beauty, and show the budding of the sublime and the great.[15]

The above author also noted that women were inclined to write religious works because of their natural religious propensity.

Aside from the publication of two songs in 1876, Amersfoordt-Dijk published little else and was soon forgotten. When her husband died in 1885, their farm was sold and she moved back to Amsterdam. Her death in 1892 received scant attention, with one Amsterdam newspaper remarking that only older people would be able to remember this pianist and composer.

Many factors contribute to her isolation in Dutch music history. By all accounts, Amersfoordt-Dijk seems to have been a hard-working, self-effacing woman, a woman who faithfully worked for her husband. Although he was supportive of her creative endeavors, Amersfoordt-Dijk's musical development was secondary to her work on her husband's model farm, which certainly limited her music production. Moreover, Dutch musical life was centered in cities, so that living out on the farm helped sideline her from the mainstream. A third factor is that women composers were still rare exceptions; Amersfoordt-Dijk could not gain support from other women colleagues. Her status as a dilettante meant that she was not considered a professional musician, in spite of her thorough training. Moreover, much of her music remained in manuscript form and was performed for local events only. Because it was never published, much has unfortunately been lost to posterity.

Amersfoordt-Dijk's earliest extant song, *Le Souvenir*, reveals a propensity for French music, rare among Dutch composers of the time, who largely wrote Germanic works. She undoubtably was influenced by her brief study with Antoine Elwart in Paris. Another influence may have been her first teacher, Johannes van Bree, who was also drawn to French genres.

Her next extant work is the *Overture* no. 1, op. 19. This independent genre was quite popular in Europe during the first half of the nineteenth century. Hers is similar to those of other Dutch overtures: pleasantly conventional in mood, orchestration, and structure. The estimated length of this work in sonata form, some twelve minutes, is also average for overtures of this period. Stylistically, op. 19 shows influences of Beethoven and his contemporaries. It is well orchestrated, clearly not the work of a beginner. The second theme, a chorale, is especially effective, and contrasts well with the first theme.

Although not many of her compositions have survived, we may conclude from the titles of missing scores that Amersfoordt-Dijk soon turned towards German genres. In 1876 two well-crafted, appealing lieder appeared in print. The melancholic *Das Fischermädchen*, through-composed with regular eight-measure phrases, has an ongoing sixteenth-note accompaniment in $\frac{6}{8}$ time. The second song, *Liebesgruss*, also through-composed, is filled with longing for a loved one. *Loflied*, her last extant work, is a simple, unaccompanied four-part song, written to celebrate that the Haarlemmermeer polder had been drained/created twenty-five years ago. It was published in 1877 in a local newspaper as a free supplement, a special large foldout decorated with an elaborate garland.[16]

Included here is a quartet from her largest work, the oratorio *Gottes Allgegenwart*, op. 40, based on religious poems compiled and edited by the composer herself. At least three authors contributed to the libretto. The title page names two German poets "and others," with Henri Viotta specifying her husband as the main contributor of the texts for the second half.[17] Essentially a biblical narrative, *Gottes Allgegenwart* has no named characters. The first half, although largely a *Te Deum Laudamus*, also includes several arias and choruses from the viewpoint of a sinner fearful of a wrathful, angry God. Part two has a greater overall development of tension and resolution. It opens with a sense of urgency, a male chorus calling for war. The unnamed antagonist ridicules and denies God, forcing his people to obey him. A tenor soloist responds, warning him that God is almighty. After praising the powers of love, the chorus warns that God is more powerful than love and that both love and nature are subservient to God.

The choral numbers show great variety, ranging from strictly homophonic, anthem-like numbers to an *a capella* metrical hymn, to a closing large-scale fugal work. Much care is taken to ensure that variation and dramatic opportunities are well exploited. Both chorus and orchestra utilize pictorial representation. Using a key architecture built on D major, minor keys are saved for dramatic moments and distant keys to intensify moods. One of the last numbers, a short *a capella Credo* (*Wir glauben all' an Gott allein* [We all believe only in God]) written in the Protestant syllabic psalm tradition of two-in-a-measure, is in the key of G-flat major, which at the time was regarded as a secretive key. In order to preclude an endless succession of separate items, many numbers are linked, most often through a simple dominant, to form either pairs or groups of three. The first three numbers form a unit, as do numbers 20, 21, and 22, followed by the last three numbers (23, 24, and 25). These larger units anchor the opening and closing in the musical arch of this oratorio.

The published vocal-piano reduction (1871) opens with the complete text in three languages: German, English and Dutch. However, only the German and English texts have been printed under the music itself, probably an indication that the composer did not prefer the Dutch translation. Number 11, in the piano-vocal reduction, is included here. Tempo indications were added by the choral conductor Hendrik de Vries (1857– 1929), former owner of the score. For this number de Vries added *Andante Cantabile*, and a metronome marking of sixty to the quarter note. This quartet functions as a quiet aftermath to the previous, lengthy number in which God's almighty power was first questioned, and then affirmed. It opens with a quietly beautiful *a capella* sixteen-measure melody in E-flat major: "Wir zagen nicht, Gott is die Liebe" (We tremble not, God is so gracious). When the accompaniment enters in measure 17, the writing becomes imitative. Triplets in the accompaniment are set against eighth notes in the vocal parts. A highpoint is reached in measure 28, with C major illustrating dawn's glorious light. Distant keys are used in the ensuing developmental section, leading to C-flat major through G-flat major in measure 53. Solidly constructed and of high quality, this oratorio deserves contemporary performances.

Notes

1. Gemeentearchief Amsterdam, FM 59/339.

2. Henri Viotta et al., *Lexicon der Toonkunst,* vol. 1 (Amsterdam: P. N. van Kampen & Zoon, 1881): 74-5.

3. Eduard Reeser, *Een eeuw Nederlands muziek 1815–1915* (Amsterdam: Querido, 1950); rev. ed. (Amsterdam: Querido, 1986): 46.

4. Jozef A. Alberdingk Thÿm, *Het Voorgeborchte en andere gedichten* (Amsterdam: C. L. van Langenhuysen, 1853): 31-42.

5. Henri Viotta et al., *Lexicon*: 75.

6. *Caecilia* 13 (1856): 53.

7. *Caecilia* 9 (1852): 137.

8. Jacob Paulus Amersfoordt, *Het Haarlemmermeer,* (Haarlem: A. C. Kruseman, 1857): 50.

9. Jacob Paulus Amersfoordt, "Aanteekeningen . . ." two manuscript travelogues in the Gemeentearchief Haarlemmermeer, 9377.5 Amer; 236-7.

10. *Weekblad van Haarlemmermeer* (July 27, 1877).

11. Ibid.

12. Ibid.

13. *Algemeen Handelsblad* (January 30, 1872): supplement.

14. Ibid.

15. This journalist is representative of a number of early Dutch male authors, who publicly supported women's emancipation, a phenomenon only recently acknowledged. See F. Dieteren, "De vrouwenkwestie in de negentiende eeuw" in *De Negentiende Eeuw* 18 (1994): 98-103.

16. *Weeklad van Haarlemmermeer* (June 29, 1877).

17. Henri Viotta et al., *Lexicon: 75.*

Selected List of Works

Extant Works

Songs for Voice and Piano

Le Souvenir (1852). Text by Jacob Paulus Amersfoordt. Paris: Journal Le Souvenir et N. Paté, 1852.

Das Fischermädchen. Text by Ernest Eckstein. Dutch translation probably by H. M. Amersfoordt-Dijk. Amsterdam: *Album van oorspronkelijke Compositiën van Nederlandsche Toondichters,* 1876. (Pages 11-16 in the *Album*, this song is number 4, part of a serial production.)

Liebesgruss. Text by Robert Hamerling. Dutch translation probably by H. M. Amersfoordt-Dijk. Amsterdam: *Album van oorspronkelijke Compositiën van Nederlandsche Toondichters,* 1876. (Pages 32-35 in the *Album*, this song is number 11.)

Choral Works

Gottes Allgegenwart, op. 40. Oratorio for soloists, chorus, organ, orchestra. German text by Johann Andreas Cramer, Johann Wilhelm Ludwig Gleim and 'others'. Includes English and Dutch translations. Piano-vocal score: Amsterdam: J. H. & G. van Heteren, 1871. (Full score unpublished.)

Loflied (July 1, 1877). SATB. Text by J. P. Amersfoordt. Haarlemmermeer: *Weekblad van Haarlemmermeer* (weekly newspaper), June 29, 1877.

Orchestra

Overture no.1, op. 19 (1854). Unpublished.

Lost Compositions

Dates listed are performance dates; composition dates unknown.

Voice and Piano

Sterbeklänge. Text by Ludwig Uhland. (1858).

Piano

Variations on *Ma Normandie* (1838).

Variations on a theme from the opera *Norma* by Vincenzo Bellini (1838).

Waltz for piano (1839).

Sonata (1854).

Sonata (1864).

Capriccio (1877).

Choral

Psalm 22 for SATB and piano. Text by Jan Pieter Heije. (1849).

Floris V, cantata. Text by Jozef Alberdingk Thijm. (1851).

Choral numbers for the play *Willem Bardes*. Text by Jacob Paulus Amersfoordt. (1858).

Anbetung, cantata for soloists, chorus and orchestra. Text by Johann Andreas Cramer. (1860).

L'hymne au printemps, duet, vocal? (1864).

Instrumental

Duet for violin and piano (1850).

Ouverture no. 2 (1855).

Violin Concertino (1859).

Bibliography

Alberdingk Thÿm, Jozef A. *Het Voorgeborchte en andere gedichten*. Amsterdam: C. L. van Langenhuysen, 1853.

Amersfoordt, Jacob Paulus. "Aanteekeningen . . . ." Two manuscript travelogues in the Gemeentearchief Haarlemmermeer, 937.5 Amer.

______. *Het Haarlemmermeer*. Haarlem: A. C. Kruseman, 1857.

______. *Willem Bardes, tooneelspel*. Amsterdam: J. H. & G. van Heteren, 1858.

Dieteren, F. "De vrouwenkwestie in de negentiende eeuw." In *De Negentiende Eeuw* 18 (1994): 98-103.

Elson, Arthur. *Woman's Work in Music*. 1904. Reprint, Portland, Maine: Longwood Press, 1976.

Ferchault, Guy. "Elwart, Antoin." In *Die Musik in Geschichte und Gegenwart* 3. Kassel: Bärenreiter-Verlag, 1949-79.

Grégoir, Édouard Georges Jacques. *Biographies des artistes-musiciens néerlandais des XVIIIe et XIXe siècles et des artistes étrangers résidant ou ayant résidé en Néerlande à la même époque*. Antwerp: L. de la Montagne, 1864; Bruxelles: Schott, 1864; The Hague: Belinfante, 1864.

Metzelaar, Helen H. "Amersfoordt-Dijk, Hermina Maria." In *Die Musik in Geschichte und Gegenwart*. Personenteil 1. Kassel: Baienreiter. 1994.

______. *From Private to Public Spheres: Exploring Women's Role in Dutch Musical Life from c. 1700 to c. 1880 and Three Case Studies*. Utrecht: Koninklijke Vereniging voor Nederlandse Muziekgeschiedenis, 1999.

Molhuysen, R. C., and J. J. Blok, eds. "Amersfoordt, Jacobus Paulus." In *Nieuw Nederlandsch Biografisch Woordenboek*,Vol. 1. Leiden: A. W. Sijthoff, 1911.

[no author]. "Kunstnieuws." *Provinciale Noordbrabantsche en 's-Hertogenbossche Courant*. December 2, 1876.

Reeser, Eduard. *Een eeuw Nederlandse muziek 1815–1915*. Amsterdam: Querido 1950. Rev. ed. Amsterdam: Querido, 1986.

Viotta, Henri et al. *Lexicon der Toonkunst*. Vol. 1. Amsterdam: P. N. van Kampen & Zoon, 1883.

No. 11 Quartet from *Gottes Allgegenwart*, op. 40:

Wir zagen nicht! Gott ist die Liebe!
Sein Vaterauge fehlt uns nicht!
Und wär's um uns auch noch so trübe,
So ward's um uns noch wieder Licht!
Gott is die Lieb', wir zagen nicht!
Er hat noch keinmal uns verlassen,
Er läszt uns nicht in dieser Noth,
Er kommt, er kann sein Kind nicht lassen,
Wir sehen schon sein Morgenroth!
Er läszt uns nicht in dieser Noth!

We tremble not! God is so gracious!,
His fatherhand* clears up the skies!
Though darkness fills the heavens so spacious,
The morning's dawn doth glorious rise!
Merciful God, we tremble not!
God's children never were forsaken,
Nor shall we now his care forego,
He comes, our trust remains unshaken,
We see his morning brightly glow!
No, we shall ne'er his care forego!

* fatherhand: God's hand

No. 11, Quartet
from Gottes Allgegenwart, Op. 40

Hermina Maria Amersfoordt-Dijk

10
za - gen nicht, Gott ist die Lie - be, Gott ist die Lie - be, Gott ist die Lie - be, sein
za - gen nicht, Gott ist die Lie - be, Gott ist die Lie - be, Gott ist die Lie - be, sein
za - gen nicht, Gott ist die Lie - be, Gott ist die Lie - be, Gott ist die Lie - be, sein
za - gen nicht, Gott ist die Lie - be, Gott ist die Lie - be, Gott ist die Lie - be, sein
15
Va - ter au - ge fehlt uns nicht,
Va - ter au - ge fehlt uns nicht, und
Va - ter au - ge fehlt uns nicht, und wär's um uns auch noch so trü - be,
Va - ter au - ge fehlt uns nicht,

19
wär's — um uns auch noch so trü - be,
und wär's — um uns auch noch so
22
und wär's — um uns auch noch so trü - be, so
so
so
trü - be,
so

25
ward's um uns, so ward's um uns, so ward's um uns doch wie - der Licht! Gott ist die
ward's um uns, so ward's um uns, so ward's um uns doch wie - der Licht! Gott ist die
ward's um uns, so ward's um uns, so ward's um uns doch wie - der Licht! Gott ist die
ward's um uns, so ward's um uns, so ward's um uns doch wie - der Licht! Gott ist die
30
Lieb' wir za - gen nicht, wir
Lieb' wir za - gen nicht, Gott ist die Lieb', wir
Lieb' wir za - gen nicht, Gott ist die Lieb', wir
Lieb' wir za - gen nicht, Gott ist die Lieb', wir

36
mf
za - gen nicht,
Er
mf
za - gen nicht, Er hat - noch kein - mal uns ver - las - sen,
mf
za - gen nicht,
Er
mf
za - gen nicht, Er hat - noch kein - mal uns ver - las - sen,
39
p
hat - nog kein - mal uns ver - las - sen, Er läszt uns nicht in
p
Er läszt uns nicht in
p
hat - nog kein - mal uns ver - las - sen, Er läszt uns nicht in
p
Er läszt uns nicht in

42
die - ser Noth, Er kommt, er kann sein Kind nicht las-sen, wir se - hen schon sein
die - ser Noth, Er kommt, er kann sein Kind nicht las-sen, wir se - hen schon sein
die - ser Noth, Er kommt, er kann sein Kind nicht las-sen, wir se - hen schon sein
die - ser Noth, Er kommt, er kann sein Kind nicht las-sen, wir se - hen schon sein
46
cres - - - - - - - - cen - -
Mor - gen-roth. Er kommt, er kann sein Kind nicht las - sen wir se - hen schon sein
Mor - gen-roth. Er kommt, er kann sein Kind — nicht las - sen wir se - hen schon sein
Mor - gen-roth. Er kommt, er kann sein Kind nicht las - sen wir se - hen schon sein
Mor - gen-roth. Er kommt, er kann sein Kind — nicht las - sen wir se - hen schon sein

50
do
f
Mor - gen-roth, wir se - hen schon sein Mor - gen - roth,
do
f
Mor - gen-roth, Mor - - - gen - roth,
do
f
Mor - gen - roth, wir se - hen schon sein Mor - gen - roth,
do
f
Mor - gen-roth, Mor - - - gen - roth,
p
Ped.
54
p
Gott ist die Lie - be,
p
Gott ist die
p
Gott ist die Lie - be,
p
Ped.
Ped.

57
fehlt uns nicht,
Lie - be, sein Au - ge fehlt _ uns _ nicht,
sein Va - ter _ au - ge, sein Au - ge fehlt uns
sein Va - ter au - ge, sein Au - ge fehlt _ uns _
p
60
sein Va-ter - au - ge fehlt uns nicht, Er kann sein
sein Va-ter - au - ge fehlt uns nicht, Er kann sein
nicht, sein Va-ter - au - ge fehlt uns nicht, Er kann sein
nicht, sein Va-ter - au - ge fehlt uns nicht, Er kann sein

66
f
mf
Kind nicht las - sen, Er läszt uns nicht in die - ser Noth, Er kommt,
Kind nicht las - sen, Er läszt uns nicht in die - ser Noth, Er kommt,
Kind nicht las - sen, Er läszt uns nicht in die - ser Noth, Er kommt,
Kind nicht las - sen, Er läszt uns nicht in die - ser Noth, Er kommt,
71
Er kommt, wir se-hen schon sein Mor - gen - roth!
Er kommt, wir se-hen schon sein Mor - gen - roth!
Er kommt, wir se-hen schon sein Mor - gen - roth!
Er kommt, wir se-hen schon sein Mor - gen - roth!
p

Marie Grandval

(1830–1907)

LYDIA LEDEEN

Marie Félicie Clémence de Reiset, later to become the Vicomtesse de Grandval, was born in Saint-Rémy-des-Monts at the Château de la Cour-du-Bois (Sarthe) in 1830. By the age of six, she decided that she wanted to be a composer and indeed, she dedicated her life to music. By the time she was twelve, she was studying composition with Friederich Freiherr von Flotow (1813–1883), a family friend and composer of the opera, *Martha*. Unfortunately Flotow left France (ca. 1848) before she could acquire a background in all aspects of composition. Yet she was able to continue composing (a septet among other works) under the watchful eye of her diplomat-father, himself a pianist-composer. About the same time, Marie started to study piano with Chopin and came to the realization that she had to make a choice between developing a career either as a pianist or as a composer. Thus, shortly after her marriage, as the new Vicomtesse de Grandval, she became a pupil of Camille Saint-Saëns (1835–1921) staying for several years until she felt ready to work independently. Grandval successfully composed in many genres: *mélodies* (as the solo song was called in France after 1840), chamber music, symphonies, cantatas, lyric dramas, operas.[1]

Between 1859 and 1892, Grandval wrote thirteen dramatic works, from her one-act operetta, *Le Sou de Lise* in 1859 to her grand opera *Mazeppa* in 1892.[2] Although *Sainte-Agnès* (1881) and *La Fille de Jaïre* (1881) are sacred dramas and *Jeanne d'Arc* (1861), *La Forêt* (1875), and *La Fiancée de Futhiof* (1891) are not true operas, writing these lyric-dramatic works allowed Grandval the opportunity to work out musical-dramatic scenes for voice and orchestra. Her stage works came to life with the writing and production of *Le Sou de Lise*,[3] followed by *Les Fiancés de Rosa,* a comic opera written in 1863. *La Contessa Eva* (1864), a one-act comic opera, was followed by yet another comic opera, *La Pénitente* (1868), performed that same year at the Opéra-Comique in Paris.[4] *Piccolino* (1869), Grandval's three-act Italian opera, received wide acclaim.[5] Her lyric poem, *La Forêt* (1875), is operatic in conception and although not staged as a drama, 300 performers participated in its production.[6]

Sixteen years passed before Grandval's next dramatic work, *Atala* (1891), was written and performed. It was followed one year later by her last dramatic work, *Mazeppa* (1892). The culmination of her operatic works, *Mazeppa* was by far the most distinguished of her music dramas.

A grand opera in five acts and six tableaux, based on a libretto of Charles Grandmougin and Georges Hartman, *Mazeppa* had its première under the direction of M. T. Gravière, conducted by Ch. Haring in the Grand-Théâtre of Bordeaux on April 24, 1892. From all accounts, both critics and audiences thought the opera a great success. According to one account:

> the opera was well received and thus a genuine success, particularly the lovely berceuse sung by Matréna in the first act; in the second act, her duet with Iskra, and the 'eventful' scene in Poltava with the triumphal march, the chorus of young girls and the final episode, a great dramatic effect; in the third act, the symphonic prélude and the grand passionate duet between Matréna and Mazeppa; and especially, in the fourth act, the very colorful dances and the final curse.[7]

Prior to the official première of *Mazeppa* Grandval held a private performance for special guests in the Salle Pleyel in Paris. The Parisian critic H. Barbedette of the journal *Le Ménestral* was there and wrote:

> It is very difficult to give a perfunctory account of a work as important as *Mazeppa,* of which Mme de Grandval gave the first private performance to her numerous guests in the Salle Pleyel.
>
> What one can note first of all is the incontestable success of the composer and her musicians. Mme de Grandval played the piano accompaniment in a brilliant manner. What struck us in *Mazeppa* is the sincerity of the work. Mme de Grandval knew how to remain personal without adapting the exaggerations of the modern school, and without keeping the dated aspects of the old traditions, ill-suited to modern taste. On the other hand, the rules of harmony are observed,

> and the melodies stand out with regularity, perfect symmetry, and great intensity. Another noteworthy observation is that the work is clear, concise, and is never tiring.[8]

Mazeppa is a real figure in history. We meet Ivan Stepanovich Mazeppa in the poetry of Victor Hugo and Lord Byron, and in a drama by Pushkin. We also meet him in Tchaikovsky's three-act opera based on a libretto that he wrote with Burenin after the Pushkin drama. An even earlier setting of *Mazeppa* was made in 1858 by Boris Viettinghoff-Scheell (1829–1901), a noble dilettante. Other versions of *Mazeppa* exist, not as operas but as a *ballade*, an *étude*, a tone poem for piano and a symphonic poem for orchestra. In his symphonic poem, Liszt describes the insurrection and death of Mazeppa (1708), a Polish nobleman who became a Cossack leader in the Ukraine and sided with King Charles XII of Sweden against the Russian Czar Peter I in an attempt to win Ukranian independence from Russia. As a young page in the court of King Casimir in Poland, Mazeppa is said to have had an affair with the wife of an older courtier, who had Mazeppa seized, stripped naked, then tied to a wild horse which was then driven into the Ukraine. After a long violent ride that almost cost him his life, he was rescued by the Cossacks and eventually became their *hetman* (leader).[9]

Grandval's *Mazeppa*[10] opens with a fiery orchestral *prélude* depicting the end of the wild ride. (Act II, Scenes 4 and 5 with a piano reduction of the orchestral score are included here.) Inspired by Victor Hugo's poem, we find the following quote noted on the piano/vocal score of the orchestra prelude: ". . . Il court, il vole, il tombe/Et se relève roi!"(he runs, he flees, he falls, and he gets up a king). We meet Mazeppa as he regains consciousness. (The other main characters are Matréna [daughter of Kotchoubey; she falls in love with Mazeppa], Iskra [he loves Matréna], Kotchoubey [leader of the Ukranians], and the Archimandrite [delegate of the Patriarch of Constantinople]). There are choruses of officers, soldiers, warriors, nobles, bourgeoisie, Ukranian peasants and Swedes, and a chorus of young girls. The orchestra is large, in keeping with the sweep of grand opera. The chorus, playing an important dramatic role, comments, narrates, argues and praises the action of the moment. The humming chorus sets the forlorn mood of emptiness while the contrasting *a capella* chorus (both in Act I) sings of the sunrise and joy of the coming day. A chorus, of tenors and basses, sings a hymn of glory to their leader (Kotchoubey). As the story unfolds, Kotchoubey convinces Mazeppa that he was sent from heaven to be their leader and Iskra questions the choice of a stranger to lead them in their fight for independence. A divided chorus responds, one group agreeing with Iskra, the other affirming Mazeppa as the new leader. The entire ensemble presents a brilliant conclusion to Act I affirming the choice of Mazeppa as their new leader and reaffirming their will to fight to the death for independence. In Scene 3 of Act II Mazeppa is again reaffirmed as leader, but with each affirmation Mazeppa's arrogance manifests itself more forcefully and in the scene where Mazeppa is told by Iskra to spare Kotchoubey from death, Mazeppa's anger flares as he responds with the words, "how dare you . . . I am the one who decides . . ."

In Scene 4 of Act II Matréna is falling in love and declares she must go where destiny takes her (m. 78), underlined by an orchestral "love" theme that keeps returning. This method of breaking down an emotion by giving it to the orchestra is characteristic of Grandval. She also makes the orchestra the chief narrator of the unfolding tragedy. Matréna's aria is followed by a haunting and memorable *berceuse* as she reflects "When my mother cared for me in times gone by" (m. 79). Even Grandval's short phrases, motivic bits, and cadences have memorable melodic contours. There are few large skips and none of the jagged, instrumental writing for voices found in composers who think instrumentally rather than vocally. An effective Grandvalian device is to have the voice begin in a monotone, reiterating the same pitch, while the melody is delineated in the orchestra.

Iskra sings of the warriors who will triumph in the coming battle, and "after the battle the same good fortune will smile on both of us." Iskra assumes that his love for Matréna is reciprocated. But when she tells him in no uncertain terms "I will never be yours" (m. 83), Iskra tells Matréna that sooner or later she will change her mind. In the passionate aria that follows he names her attributes — her tenderness, her enchanting voice, her warm friendship, etc. Voicing these feelings gives him hope for their love. In the ensuing narration, Iskra lies to Matréna telling her that Mazeppa is dead; Matréna with a calm certainty tells Iskra that he is mistaken (m. 87). She indicates to Iskra that she does love him but like a brother, unlike her feelings for Mazeppa. This revelation inflames his jealousy and in the following duet Iskra proclaims that he will take revenge and [Iskra's] justice will triumph. He convinces Matréna that Mazeppa is indeed dead. The orchestra ceases playing as Matréna tries to grasp the fact, "il est mort." Iskra realizes the depth of her feelings when she passionately sings the words "even in death I will love him" (m. 94). In the distance the warriors (TB) are toasting Mazeppa (m. 96). Matréna hears this and becomes more and more animated as she realizes that Mazeppa lives. "I will die of joy," she sings, the orchestra *tacet*. The orchestra was also *tacet* when Matréna thought Mazeppa was dead. Grandval felt that these deepest emotions should be delineated by the voice alone with no intrusions by the orchestra. Iskra in a fury curses Matréna and Mazeppa and vows revenge. On the words, "It is he who returns triumphant," the meter switches to triple time and except for one measure in duple meter, it remains in triple meter for six measures (three phrases) and with great emotion the full orchestra and chorus acclaim, "Glory to Mazeppa" (m. 101) bringing the first tableau to a brilliant conclusion.

Scene 5 of the second tableau takes us to the Place de Poltava. The brilliant, powerful scene opens to the sounds of a joyous march, the crowd (SATB) singing once more to the glory of Mazeppa (m. 103), now that the enemy has been defeated. An orchestral "cortège" (twenty-five measures), leads into the final part in which Grandval lets out all stops in the orchestra. Although the only complete score available is piano-vocal, the orchestral score of the *Divertissement* has been located,[11] attesting to Grandval's reputation as an orchestral colorist.

The *Divertissement* in Act IV acts as a colorful contrast with its variety of dances and instrumental sonorities. The full score of the ballet glitters, effectively utilizing the usual pairing of winds, brass and complement strings, and enhanced by the piccolo, four horns, trumpets, four trombones, two harps, a large battery of percussion, four bassoons, alto saxophone, and a sax-tuba.[12] Three of the five acts of the opera end with ensemble finales (Acts I, II, IV). Act V is the shortest, the music recalling the setting and some of the music of Act I.

Grandval transcribed the *Mazurka* from the fourth act *Divertissement* for two pianos and also for piano 4-hands. Both versions were published by Choudens Fils in 1894, and dedicated to the opera singer / concert pianist, Pauline Viardot (see this volume).

Mazeppa and Grandval's earlier operas, with the exception of *Le bouclier de diamant*, have been performed in France and Germany.[13] Those works performed in Paris were never performed at the Paris Opéra whose administrators were, until the 1890's, unwilling to mount new works by French composers. However, with a growing sense of nationalistic feeling among the French, the "Concerts de l'Opéra" (November 17, 1895–April 4, 1897) premièred more works of the "jeune école" than any other organization of the time.[14] The name Clémence de Grandval (one of the pseudonyms used by the Vicomtesse) is listed with Jules Massenet (1842–1912), Gabriele Fauré (1845–1924), Paul Dukas (1865–1935), and Saint-Saëns.[15] Programmed at the "Concerts de l'Opéra" of February 9, 1896, and February 16, 1896, along with excerpts from the operas of Jean-Philippe Rameau (1683–1764) and Christoph Willibad Gluck, (1714–1787) was Grandval's triumphal chorus from *Mazeppa*.[16]

Among the thirty-one living French composers heard at the "Concerts de l'Opéra," more than a third were at least fifty years old, Grandval was sixty-five years old in 1895. Olin comments that "many of these composers have been excluded from the inner circle of official musical power"[17] and notes the many sarcastic jokes about seventy-year-old composers who now performed as part of the "jeune école." Grandval and *Mazeppa* have certainly waited long enough.[18]

Notes

1. F. J. Fétis, *Biographie universelle des musiciens et bibliographie générale de la musique*, Supplément et Complément published under the direction of Arthur Pougin, Tome premier. (Paris: Librairie de Firmin Didot et Cie., 1881), and *Review Gazette Musicale*, no. 26 (1850): 229. "Elle a abordé successivement tous les genres, faisant preuve dans chacun d'eux si non d'un talent véritable."

2. Actually fourteen if the three-act opera, *Le bouclier de diamant*, her only unperformed opera, is counted. (The score has not been located to date.)

3. *Le Sou de Lise* was written under the pseudonym Caroline Blangey.

4. Plot summaries and brief commentaries on the music of five operas by Grandval (*La Pénitente, Le Sou de Lise, Mazeppa, Piccolino* and *Les Fiancées de Rosa)* can be found in the *Dictionnaire des Opéras*, vol. 2, by Félix Clément and Pierre Larousse, revised by Arthur Pougin (Paris, n.p., 1905).

5. This opera was written under the pseudonym Clémence Valgrand.

6. *La Chronique Musicale*, Tome VIII, no. 44, 83-84.

7. *Le Dictionnaire des Opéras*, 2: 723-24. The original French reads as follows:

"Mme de Grandval a écrit une partition qui a été fort bien accueillie et dont le succès a été réel. On en a particulièrement signalé au premier acte une jolie berceuse chantée par Matréna; au second, son duo avec Iskra, et la scène vivante et mouvementée de la place de Poltava avec la marche triomphale, le chœur des jeunes filles et l'épisode final, d'un grand effet dramatique; au troisième, le prélude symphonique et le grand duo passionné de Matréna et de Mazeppa; et surtout, au quatrième, des danses très pittoresques et le finale de la malédiction" (724).

8. Hippolyte Buffenoir, *La Vicomtesse de Grandval* (Paris, 1894). The original French is located in the article "Marie Grandval: Vicomtesse-Composer," by Lydia Ledeen, in the journal ARS MUSICA (Denver) (spring 1994): 25.

9. Edward Downes, *The New York Philharmonic Guide to the Symphony* (New York: Walker and Company, 1976), 505.

10. *Mazeppa*, Opéra en Cinq Actes et Six Tableaux, Ch. Grandmougin et Georges Hartmann, Musique de C. de Grandval (Paris: Choudens Fils, 1892).

11. The full score of the *Divertissement* can be found in the Music Division of the Boston Public Library.

12. A valved brass instrument of great power built by Adolphe Sax of Paris in 1852. It was circular in form and came in seven sizes. Sibyl Marcuse, *Musical Instruments. A Comprehensive Dictionary* (New York: W.W. Norton, 1975), 461.

13. For plot summaries and brief commentaries on the music of the following works see *Le Dictionnaire des Opéras*, vol. 2.

14. Elinor Olin, "The Concerts de l'Opéra 1895–97: New Music at the Monument Garnier," *19th Century Music*, vol. 16, no. 3 (spring 1993): 253.

15. Ibid., 261.

16. Ibid., 265.

17. Ibid., 260.

18. For an overview of Grandval's background and compositions, see Ledeen, "Marie Grandval: Vicomtesse-Composer," 19-30.

Selected List of Works

Vocal Melodies and Chansons

Album de 7 mélodies. Paris: Durand, 1942.
1. *Barcarolle*. Text by Camille Distel
2. *La Cloche*. Text by Camille Distel
3. *Consolatrix* (no poet listed)
4. *Chant d'hiver*. Text by Camille Distel. (Paris: E. Fromont, 1898)
5. *La Fleur*. Text by Camille Distel
6. *Le Grillon*. Text by A. Lamartine. (Paris: Durand, 1941)
7. *Promenade*. Text by Camille Distel

A l'Absente. Text by François Coppée. Paris: E. Fromont, 1893.

Au bord de l'eau. Text by Sully Prudhomme. Paris: G. Hartmann, 1886.

L'Attente. Text by Mme Desbordes-Valmore. Paris: Durand et fils, 1922.

Avril. Text by Rémy Belleau. Paris: De Baudon, n.d.

Berceuse. Text by Mme La Baronne Reiset. Paris: H. Lemoine, 1891.

Le bohémien. Text by Michel Carré. Paris: Heugel et Cie., 1886.

Chanson. Text by Alfred de Musset. Paris: Ménestral, 1897.

Chanson d'autrefois. Duet or one voice and piano. Text by Sully Prudhomme. Paris: G. Hartmann, 1890.

Chanson de Barberine. Text by Alfred de Musset. Paris: H. Lemoine, 1890.

Chanson de la Coquille. Text by Z. Astruc. Paris: G. Hartmann, 1876.

Chanson d'hiver. Text by Paul Delair. Paris: E. Fromont, 1898.

Chanson laponne. Text by Armand Silvestre. Paris: E. Fromont, 1893.

Chant du reître. Text by Ch. Grandmougin. Paris: G. Hartmann, 1887.

Les Clochettes. Text by Mme La Baronne Reiset. Paris: Ménestral, 1897.

Defi. Text by Fernand Gregh. Paris: E. Fromont, 1901.

La Délaissée. Text by J. Du Boys. Paris: 1893.

Dieu seul peut tout savoir. Text by Paul Nibelle. Paris: Ménestral, 1899.

L'Éternité. Melody for tenor. Text by Paul Collin. Paris: G. Hartmann, 1883.

L'étoile du soir. Text by Mme La Baronne Reiset. Paris: H. Lemoine, n.d.

La Fiancée de Frithiof. Text by Ch. Grandmougin. Paris: Heugel et Cie., 1891.

La fileuse. Text by Mme La Baronne Reiset. Paris: H. Lemoine, 1891.

Heures. Four voices with piano. Paris: n.d.

Hymne à la terre. Text by Paul Collin. MS Autograph, n.d.

La Jeune Fille et le Lys. Text by Paul Nibelle. Paris: Ménestral, 1899.

Juana. Possibly text by Mme La Baronne Reiset. Paris: H. Lemoine, n.d.

Menuet. Text by Fernand Gregh. Paris: E. Fromont, 1901.

Mignonne. Text by Ronsard. Paris: Ménestral, 1897.

Le Myosotis. Text by Paul de La Baume. Paris: H. Lemoine, 1890.

Ne le dis pas. Text by Paul Nibelle. Paris: Ménestral, 1899.

Ne grandis pas. Text by Paul Nibelle. Paris: H. Lemoine, 1891.

Les Papillons. Text by Théophile Gautier. Paris: E. Fromont, 1893.

Pâquerette. Text by Clovis Michaux. Paris: Durand, 1922.

Parfums des Tilleuls. Text by Paul Delair. Paris: E. Fromont, 1898.

Rappelle-toi. Duet. Text by Alfred de Musset. Paris: Ménestral, 1897.

Recueil. Text by Sully Prudhomme. Paris: Hartmann, n.d.

Le Rendez-vous. Text by Mme La Baronne Reiset. Paris: H.

Lemoine, 1891.

Rosette. Villanelle. Text by Desportes. Paris: Heugel et Cie., 1894.

Sacrifice. Text by Sully Prudhomme (in *Album du Gaulois*). Paris: Prime, 1885.

Si j'étais Dieu. Duet. Text by Sully Prudhomme. Paris: E. Fromont, 1898.

Si tu m'aimais. Text by Charles Reynaud. Paris: Ménestral, 1897.

Six Poésies de Sully Prudhomme. Paris: G. Hartmann, 1884.
1. *Au bord de l'eau*
2. *Le Vase Brisé*
3. *L'hirondelle*
4. *Prière*
5. *Soupir*
6. *Le Galop* (récit dramatique)

Solitude. Text by Fernand Gregh. Paris: E. Fromont, 1898.

Stalactites. Text by Sully Prudhomme. Paris: E. Fromont and G. Hartmann, n.d.

Trilby. Text by Paul Nibelle. London: n.p., 1860.

Operas/Operettas

Le bouclier de diamant. Opéra fantastique. Text by Adenis et Hartmann. Unpublished.

La Comtesse Eva (1864?). Opéra comique. Text by Michel Carré. Unpublished.

Les fiances de Rosa. Opéra comique under the pseudonyme Clémence Valgrand. Text by A. Choler. Paris: Choudens, 1863.

Mazeppa. Opéra. Text by C. Grandmougin and Georges Hartmann. Paris: Choudens et fils, 1892.

La pénitente. Opéra comique. Text by H. Meilhac and W. Busnach. Paris: A. Leduc, 1868.

Piccolino. Opéra Italien. Italian text by A. De Lauzières. French translation by D. Tagliafico. Paris: Heugel et Cie., 1869.

Le Sou de Lise. Opérette under the pseudonyme Caroline Blangy. Text by A. Choler. Paris: Choudens, 1859.

Lyric and Dramatic Scenes

Atala. Lyric poem. Chorus and piano. Text by Louis Gallet. Paris: G. Hartmann, 1888.

Le Bal. Sung waltz for one or two voices. [poet?] Paris: Heugel et Cie., 1898.

Fleur du Matin. Two female voices, chorus, and piano; also for piano. Text by E. Guinand. Paris: E. Fromont, 1894.

Hébé. Lyrical Scene for soprano and piano. Text by Paul Collin. Paris: A. Quinzard, 1892.

Jeanne d'Arc. Scene for contralto or baritone with piano and organ. Text by Casimir Delavigne. Paris: Heugel et Cie., 1861.

La forêt. Lyrical poem; solos, chorus, and orchestra. Paris: G. Hartmann, (188?).

Les lucioles. Rêverie for mezzo-soprano, with violin, piano, and organ. Text by Ernest Legouvé. Paris: Heugel et Cie., 1866.

Marche, chœur triomphale: Gloire à toi (*Mazeppa*). Mixed chorus and piano.

Regrets. Lyric scene for mezzo-soprano. Paris: Heugel et Cie., 1866.

La ronde des songes. Scene fantastique for solo, chorus, and orchestra. Words by Paul Collin. Paris: G. Hartmann, 1880.

Rose et Violette. Duo for two sopranos. Text by Galoppe d'Unguaire. Paris: Ménestral, 1899.

Villanelle. Solo, chorus, piano, flute. Text by Pousserat. Paris: Richault, 1877.

Sacred Music

Agnus Dei. Soprano and tenor with piano. Paris: Durand, 1925.

Ave verum. Paris: Durand, n.d.

Benedictus. Three voices or mixed chorus, organ and piano. Paris: Durand, n.d.

Gratias. Two voices, piano and organ. Paris: Durand, n.d.

Guide us, Father. Trio for soprano, alto, tenor with organ accompaniment in Schirmer's collection of part-songs and choruses for mixed voices, nos. 5229 and 5230.

Kyrie. Soprano and alto or female chorus. Paris: Durand, 1962.

Kyrie. Soprano and alto with organ accompaniment. Paris: Durand, Schoenewerk et Cie., 1925.

La fille de Jaïre. Oratorio/Religieuse scene for solo, chorus SATB, and orchestra. Text by Paul Collin. Paris: G. Hartmann, 1881.

Messe. Three voices. Paris: P. Pégiel, ca. 1867.

Messe, no. 2. Solo, chorus, and orchestra. Paris: P. Pégiel, n.d.

Messe brève. Two Masses for female voice and organ.
1. Soprano, organ or harmonium: Paris: A. Durand et fils, n.d.
2. Two sopranos: Paris: W. Cengens Couvreur, 1867

Noël. Voice with piano and oboe. Text by Sully Prudhomme. Paris: E. Fromont, 1902.

Offertoire. Voices and instruments. (See "Offertoire" under *Instrumental Music*.)

O Salutaris. For one or two voices with organ: soprano or soprano and contralto/two sopranos. Text by Durand. Paris: P. Pégiel, n.d.

Pater Noster. Soprano with piano and organ. Paris: Heugel et Cie., 1863.

Quartet — Qui est homo . . . Soprano, contralto, tenor, and baritone solo with piano and organ. Paris: Durand Schoenewerk et Cie., n.d.

Sainte Agnès. Sacred drama in two parts by Louis Gallet, ca. 1876. Paris: G. Hartmann, 1881. Paris: Heugel et Cie., 1892.

Stabat Mater. Cantata for four voices, soloists, and chorus with piano and organ. Contains *Marche à Calvary*, *Juxta Crucem* (air), *Pro peccatis* (chorus), and *l'Inflammatus* (quartet). Paris: Durand, Schoenewerk et Cie., 1872.

Two choruses from *Stabat Mater*. Edited by Horatio Parker. New York: G. Schirmer, n.d.

Power Eternal, Judge and Father! Quartet for soprano and alto with mixed chorus and organ accompaniment.

Tarry with Me O My Savior. Three voices. Text by Ditson.

Instrumental Music

Amazones. Lyrical symphony.

Andante con moto. Cello and piano. Paris: Costallat, 1885. Paris: Richault, 1883. (See *Trois pièces pour violoncello et piano*)

Andante et intermezzo. Piano, violin, and cello. Paris: Bruneau, 1889.

Chanson suisse. Cello and piano. Paris: Heugel et fils, 1882.

Chant serbe. Cello and piano. Paris: Richault, 1883. (See *Trois pièces pour violoncelle et piano)*

Concertino. Violin and orchestra. Paris: G. Hartmann, 1874.

Concerto, op. 7 (for oboe). Also arranged for oboe and piano. Paris: Heugel et Cie.

Deux pièces. Violin and piano or orchestra. Paris: G. Hartmann, 1882.
1. *Andantino expressivo*
2. *Bohémienne*

Deux pièces. Oboe, cello, and piano. Paris: Richault, 1884.
1. *Gavotte*
2. *Romance*

Deux pièces. Oboe with orchestra or piano. Paris: G. Hartmann, 1877.
1. *Lamento*
2. *Scherzo*

Deux pièces. B^b clarinet and piano. Paris: Richault, 1885.
1. *Invocation*
2. *Air slave*

Deux pièces. Double bass and piano. Paris: G. Hartmann, 1877.
1. *Lamento*
2. *Scherzo*

Deux pièces. Cello and piano. Paris: Heugel et Cie., 1882.
1. *Romance*
2. *Gavotte*

Divertissement hongrois. Orchestra. (ca. 1890)

Esquisses Symphoniques. Paris: G. Hartmann, 1874.

Gavotte. Piano and orchestra. Paris: A. Chaimboud, 1889.

Gavotte. Cello, piano, and double bass. Paris: Costallat, n.d.

Grand Trio, No. 2. Piano, violin, cello. Paris: Heugel et Cie., 1853. Bryn Mawr, PA: Hildegard Publishing Company, 1994.

Marche des Rapins. Piano (Piccolino). Paris: Heugel et Cie., 1869.

Mazurka du ballet. Two pianos, also for four-hands (from *Mazeppa*). Paris: Choudens, 1894.

Menuet. Paris: E. Fromont, n.d.

Musette. Violin and also for violin and piano or orchestra. Paris: G. Hartmann, 1873.

Nocturnes, op. 5 and op. 6 (for piano). Paris: H. Lemoine, n.d.

Offertoire. Violin, cello, harp and piano or one voice, cello, and piano or organ.

Overture for Orchestre Symphonique. Unpublished.

Prélude et variations. Violin and piano or orchestra. Paris: G. Hartmann, 1882.

Quatre Morceaux. Tenor oboe or clarinet with piano. Paris: Hartmann, 1885.

Romance. Cello, double bass and piano.

Ronde de nuit. Orchestra and for two pianos and four-hands. Also arranged for four-hands. Paris: Richault et Cie., 1879.

Sérénade. Cello and piano. Paris: Costallat, 1885. (See *Trois pièces pour violoncelle et piano*).

Sonate, op. 8 (for violin and piano). Paris: H. Lemoine, ca. 1860.

Suite de cinq morceaux. Flute and piano. Paris: H. Lemoine, 1877.

Suite. Piano and flute. Paris: Richault, 1876.
- I/II Prélude et Scherzo
- III Menuet
- IV Romance
- V Final

Trio de salon. Oboe, bassoon, and piano. Paris: H. Lemoine.

Trio No. 1. Violin, piano, and cello. MS Autograph, n.d.

Trois pièces. Cello and piano. Paris: Richault, 1883.
1. *Andante con moto*
2. *Sérénade*
3. *Chant serbe*

Valse mélancolique. Flute and harp. Paris: Heugel, 1891.

Bibliography

Biographie universelle des musiciens et bibliographie générale de la musique, ed. F. J. Fétis, Supplément et Complément published under the direction of Arthur Pougin, Tome premier, Paris: Librarie de Firmin Didot et Cie., 1881.

La Chronique Musicale, Tome 111, no. 18, March 15, 1874.

Le Dictionnaire des Opéras, vol. 2 by Félix Clément and Pierre Larousse, revised by Arthur Pougin. Paris, 1905.

Dictionary-Catalogue of Operas and Operettas which have been performed on the public stage. Compiled by John Towers. Morgantown, W. Va.: Acme Publishing Co., 1910.

Downes, Edward. *The New York Philharmonic Guide to the Symphony*. New York: Walker and Company, 1976.

Encyclopédie de la musique et dictionnaire du conservatoire. Paris: Albert Lavignac, 1914.

Ledeen, Lydia. "Marie Grandval: Vicomtesse-Composer." In ARS MUSICA (Denver) (Spring 1994).

Marcuse, Sibyl. *Musical Instruments. A Comprehensive Dictionary*. New York: W. W. Norton, 1975.

Olin, Elinor. "The Concerts de l'Opéra 1895–97: New Music at the Monument Garnier." In *19th Century Music*, vol. 16, no. 3 (Spring 1993): 253.

Review Gazette Musicale, no. 26. Paris: 1850.

Scene 4

Matréna	
Il ne soupçonne rien . . . sa bonté souveraine N'a pas su deviner rêves sont les miens! Malgré moi, je m'en vais où le destin m'entraîne. Mazeppa c'est à toi qu'à jamais j'appartiens! Quand jadis, ma mère attentive, Berçait mon enfance craintive, Elle disait: (pur souvenir!) "Je suis là..dors en paix, sans peur de la nuit sombre, Ton père s'approche dans l'ombre. Le grand guerrier va revenir!" Mon enfance a fui comme un rêve .. Une autre voix en moi s'élève, Qui me parle de l'avenir! C'est l'amour qui me berce et plane sur ma vie, Et chante à mon âme ravie: Le grand guerrier — va revenir! Ah! avec surprise, reconnaissant Iskra qui l'observe Iskra! près de moi . . .	He suspects nothing . . . his majesty doesn't understand that his dreams are mine! Despite of myself, I must go where destiny leads me. Mazeppa, I belong to you forever! When my mother cared for me in times gone by, she would sing a lullabye soothing my childhood fears, She would say (a pure memory) "I am here . . . sleep peacefully, without fear of the dark night, Your father is near in the shadow. The great warrior will come back! My childhood flew by like a dream. Another voice rises in me, Who speaks to me of the future! It is love that rocks me and soars over my life, and sings to my ravished soul: The great warrior returns! Ah! surprised, Matréna notices Iskra! who observes him Iskra! near me . . .
Iskra	
Les guerriers, nos frères, ayant triomphé des destins contraires, Victorieux enfin, vont être de retour! Je les ai devancés, et ton beau cri d'amour Me rend mon espoir et mon rêve! Après les grands périls et les jours hasardeux, la terrible guerre s'achève, Et le même bonheur nous sourit à tous deux!	The warriors, our brothers, having triumphed over adversity, finally victorious, will be coming home! I have anticipated them and your beautiful cry of love [love call] Again gives me hope and my dream! After great perils and hazardous days, the terrible war is finished, And the same happiness (luck) smiles on both of us!
Matréna	
De quel boheur veux-tu parler?	Of what happiness do you speak?
Iskra	
Ma fiancée, mon amour En ton âme est-il chose effacée?	My fiancée, my love, in your soul Is my love a thing erased?
Matréna	
Je ne serai jamais ta femme!	I will never be your wife!

<u>Iskra</u>
Qu'as-tu dit? Quel trouble as-tu jeté
dans mon coeur interdit?
Ne te souviens-tu plus de ces
heures bénies, Où nous mêlions
nos jeux d'enfant?
Où, plus tard, tes yeux clairs
aux douceurs infinies
Berçaient mon espoir triumphant!

What do you say? What trouble have
you cast in my forbidden heart?
No longer do you remember all these
blessed hours, Where together we played
our childhood games?
Where, later, your clear eyes of
infinite sweetness
Soothed my triumphant hope!

<u>Matréna</u>
Je me souviens, Iskra!
Je t'aimais comme un frère,
Je t'aime encore ainsi!

I remember, Iskra!
I loved you like a brother,
I still love you thus!

<u>Iskra</u>
Tu m'aimes! mot trompeur!
Et moi, je veux croire au contraire,
Qu'un autre amour a pris ma place
dans ton coeur!

You love me! deceiving word!
And me, I would believe the contrary,
That another love takes my place
in your heart!

<u>Matréna</u>
Insensé!

Mad!

<u>Iskra</u>
Tu m'aimais quand pleine de tendresse,
Ta douce main pressait ma main!
Quand ta chaude amitié,
ta voix enchanteresse,
Me faisaient espérer un radieux hymne!

You loved me when filled full of tenderness,
Your sweet hand was pressing my hand!
When your warm friendship,
your enchanting voice,
Let me hope with a radiant joy!

<u>Matréna</u>
Tu te trompes!
Je suis pareille un lac paisible,
Que ne ride aucun souffle en
un beau soir d'été!
Tu prends pour un coeur insensible,
Un coeur plein de sérénité!

You are mistaken!
I am like a peaceful lake
that no ripples whisper on
a beautiful summer evening!
You mistake a sensitive heart for a
heart that has no feeling!

<u>Iskra</u>
C'est me donner la mort que
m'arracher mon rêve
Et renier un coeur aimant!
Un autre à mes baisers t'enlève!
Un autre a reçu ton serment!

You are condemming me to death by
snatching away my dreams and denying
My loving heart!
Another is taking you away from my kisses!
Another received your oath!

<u>Matréna</u>
N'irrite pas mon âme indulgente
et calmée.
Dis-moi plutôt comment,
au sortir des combats,
Te voila seul, ici, loin de l'armée?
Comment les autres chefs
ne t'accompagnent pas?

Don't anger my forgiving and
calm soul.
Tell me rather how,
upon leaving combat
You remain alone, here, far from the army?
How is it the other leaders
don't accompany you?

Iskra	
Je viens annoncer à ton père, Que malgré la victoire et les destins prospères, S'est accompli là-bas un sombre évènement! Mazeppa notre chef . . .	I come to tell your father, that in spite of victory and a prosperous future, It is done by a dark event! Mazeppa our leader . . .
Matréna	
Mazeppa! quel tourment Fais-tu naître soudain en Mon âme oppressée?	Mazeppa! what torment have you suddenly created in My oppressed soul?
Iskra	
Il est mort!	He is dead!
Matréna	
Il est mort! Il est mort!	He is dead! He is dead!
Iskra	
Je lis dans ta pensée Et le voile s'est déchiré! Ah! tu trahis toute ton âme!	I read your thoughts And the veil has torn itself away! Ah! you betray your entire soul!
Matréna	
Il est mort!	He is dead!
Iskra	
Ta douleur proclame Ta passion perfide et ton amour navré!	Your sorrow proclaims Your perfidious passion and your heatbroken love!
Matréna	
Eh bien! Oui, je l'aimais! Qu'importe? Tu ne comptes pour rien dans mes tristes amours! Oui, mon âme pour toi, doit être une âme morte! Et lui, même expiré, je l'aimerais toujours, toujours! Adieu! Adieu!	Well! Yes, I love him! What's the difference? You count for nothing in my sad loves! Yes, my soul for you must be a dead soul! And him, even dead I will love him always, always! Farewell! Farewell!
Iskra	
Son âme entière est enchainée A celui qu'elle s'est donnée Mais la justice aura son tour Je saurai venger mon amour!	Her entire soul is bound to him that she gave herself to But justice will have his turn I will avenge my love!
La Foule	
Vive! Vive! Vive Mazeppa!	Long live Mazeppa!

Matréna Vive Mazeppa! puis-je croire A ces cris joyeux? Mazeppa n'est pas mort! On acclame sa gloire!	Long Live Mazeppa! Do I believe these are cries of joy? Mazeppa is not dead! They acclaim his glory!
Iskra O rage!	Oh rage!
La Foule Vive!	Long life!
Matréna Vivant! il est vivant! Je vois s'ouvrir les cieux!	Living! he is living! I see the heavens open!
Iskra Enfin! j'ai su t'arracher tes aveux!	Finally! I have extracted your confession!
Matréna Je vais aujourd'hui mourir de joie!	Today I am going to die of joy!
Iskra Malheur à toi! Malheur à lui! C'est lui qui revient triomphant.	Curse you! Curse him! It is he who returns triumphant.
Matréna Le guerrier que j'adore et dont venait ma peine!	The warrior that I adore and for whom I grieved!
Iskra Lui que ton coeur adore, Malheur à lui!	He who your heart adores, Curse him!
Matréna Celui dont la valeur défend — Le peuple opprimé	He whose worth defends the oppressed people
Iskra En vain ton amour le défend — Malheur à toi	In vain your love defends him — Curse you!
Matréna De l'Ukraine!	The Ukraine!
Iskra Malheur à lui!	Curse him!
Acclamations des Peuples (Chœur) Gloire! Gloire à Mazeppa! Victoire! Victoire! Gloire! Victoire!	Acclamations of the People (Chorus) Glory! Glory to Mazeppa! Victory! Victory! Glory! Victory!

Scene 5

La Foule

Gloire! Gloire à toi, Mazeppa!
la Pologne est soumise!
Gloire à toi! Gloire!
Ta vaillance enfin réalise
Un voeu trop longtemps étouffé!
trop longtemps étouffé! Gloire à toi,
défenseur d'une cause sacrée,
Notre patrie est délivrée,
Et la justice a triomphé!
Ton audace guidait nos armes,
L'Ukraine aujourd'hui sans entraves,
Eclate en transports glorieux!
Gloire! Gloire à toi! Gloire à toi!
Gloire! Gloire à toi! Gloire!
Gloire à toi, Mazeppa!
Salut au guerrier triomphant!
Honneur à son nom tout puissant!
Exaltons sa gloire! Victoire!
Gloire à Mazeppa! Gloire! Gloire!
Victoire! Gloire à Mazeppa!

Glory! Glory to you, Mazeppa!
Poland is subdued!
Glory to you! Glory!
Your bravery is finally realized
A wish too long stifled!
too long stifled! Glory to you,
defender of a sacred cause,
Our country is liberated,
And justice triumphs!
Your daring guided our armies,
to the Ukraine today without obstacles,
Exploding in glorious rapture!
Glory! Glory to you! Glory to you!
Glory! Glory to you! Glory!
Glory to you, Mazeppa!
Greet the triumphant warrior!
Honor to his all powerful name!
Let us exalt his glory!
Glory to Mazeppa! Glory! Glory!
Victory! Glory to Mazeppa!

Mazeppa

Salut, salut, ô peuple bien aimé.
O nouvelle patrie
O terre hospitalière, Je reviens
Je reviens par vous acclamé!
Mon nom naguère obscur,
surgit dans la lumière,
Mais j'ai bien plus eneore de
bonheur que d'orgueil!
O rude nation que je sers et
que j'aime, Car la superbe Ukraine
injustement en deuil,
Méritait dès longtemps
méritait la victoire suprême!

Greetings! o well loved people,
O new fatherland
O hospitable earth, I return
I return to your acclaim!
My formerly obscure name,
springs up in the light,
But I had well more
happiness than pride!
O difficult nation that I serve and
that I love, Because the superb Ukraine
unjustly mourns,
Worthy from times gone by
merited supreme victory!

Jeune Filles

O chef, il nous est doux
Aujourd'hui de bénir-
Le grand héros qui nous délivre!
Celui par qui vient de revivre notre avenir!
Sois loué par nos voix sincères, Toi,
Qui nous as rendu la victoire et la paix!
Toi, par qui les jours noir d'opprobre
Et de misère
Sont évanouis pour jamais!

O leader, for us it is sweet
to bless today
The great heros who deliver us!
He who comes to revive our future!
Be praised by our sincere voices, You,
Who bring us victory and peace!
You, through your dark days of shame
and of misery
Vanished forever!

Mazeppa

Fille de Kotchoubey, ta parole troublante,
Révèle ton âme brûlante,
Et me remue au fond du coeur!

Daughter of Kotchoubey, your troubling words,
Reveal your burning soul,
And move me to the bottom of my heart!

Au milieu des périls je te voyais sans trêve.	In the midst of these perils I see you without pause.
<u>Matréna</u> Ah! ce n'était donc pas un rêve! Il m'aime!	 Ah! this would not thus be a dream! He loves me!
<u>Mazeppa</u> Et tes regards profonds,	 And your deep looks
<u>Matréna</u> Je le sens,	 I sense it,
<u>Mazeppa</u> charmants comme un beau rêve, M'ont aidé,	 charming, like a beautiful dream, come to help me,
<u>Matréna</u> ma torture s'achève, je n'ai plus que	 my torture is finished I no longer have
<u>Mazeppa</u> tu le sais, A revenir vainqueur!	 You know, To return conqueror!
<u>Matréna</u> ma joie au coeur! Il m'aime!	 such joy in my heart! He loves me!
<u>Mazeppa</u> vainqueur! O rêve . . . rêve charmant!	 conqueror! O dream . . . lovely dream!
<u>Mazeppa</u> Mais, ce n'est pas en roi que je viens de la guerre, C'est en soldat hereux favorisé du ciel, Je serais aujourd'hui ce que j'étais naguère, sans l'invincible appui de l'arbître éternel!	 But, it is not as king that I come to fight, It is as a happy favored soldier of heaven, I would be today as I was unknown, without the unconquerable support of the eternal referee!
<u>L'Archimandrite</u> Gloire à Dieu, qui permit, par un heureux mystère, Que ton nom tout à coup devint si radieux! Oui, c'est toi Mazeppa, qu'il a choisi sur terre, Pour accomplir ici la volonté des cieux!	 Glory to God, who permits through a happy mystery That your name suddenly became so radiant! Yes, it is you Mazeppa, that he chose on earth To accomplish here heaven's will!
<u>Chœur</u> Gloire à Dieu! Oui, c'est toi, Mazeppa, qu'il a choisi sur terre, Pour accomplir ici la volonté de toi!	 Glory to God! Yes, it is you, Mazeppa, that he chose on earth To accomplish here his will!

Translation by Lydia Ledeen

Mazeppa
Act II, Scene 4

Charles Grandmougin

Marie Grandval
Lydia Ledeen, editor

13
M.
tiens!
dim.
17
p doux et simple
Quand ja-dis, ma mére at-ten-ti - ve, Ber-çait mon en - fan-ce crain-ti - ve,
21
El-le di-sait: (par sou-ve - nir!)
25
p trè doux
"Je suis là dors en paix, sans peur de la nuit som - bre,
p

29
M.
Ton pè - re s'ap - pro - che dans l'om - bre
Le grand guer -
32
cresc.
p
rier va re-ve-nir!"
p
mf
p
36
p
Mon en-fance a fui comme un rê - ve
Une au - tre voix en moi s'é-lè - ve,
p
40
Qui me par - le de l'ave - nir!

44
M.
p très doux
C'est l'a-mour qui me ber - ce el pla-ne sur ma vi - e,
p
48
M.
Et chante à-mon à - me ra-vi - e:
"Le grand guer -
51
cresc.
p
rier va re-ve-nir!"
cresc.
ah!
p
pp
55
M.
Allegro
(avec surprise, reconnaisant Iskra qui l'observe)
f
Is-kra!
pp
ff

59
Allegro moderato
M.
près de moi...
p
62
Allegro maestoso
Iskra
I.
p
Les guer - riers, nos
marquez le chant
64
frè - res, A - yant tri - om - phé des des -
66
Allegro
cresc.
f
tins con-trair - es, Vic-to - ri-eux en - fin, vont ê - tre de-re -
cresc.
f

70
Moderato molto
I.
tour! Je les ai de-van-cés, et ton beau cri d'a - mour Me
pp
73
cresc.
rend mon es-poír et mon rê - ve! A - près les grands pér-ils et les
cresc.
75
p
jours ha-sar-deux, La ter-ri-ble guer - re s'a-chè - ve, Et le
p
79
M.
(avec surprise)
p
De quel bon -
mê - me bon-heur nous sou - rit à tous deux!
p
fp

82
M.
heur ___ veux-tu par - ler?
(avec tendresse)
cresc.
I.
Ma fi-an-cé - e, Mon a-mour en ton
fp
86
(résolve)
Je ne se-rai ja-mais ta fem - me!
f
âme est-il chose ef-fa-cé - e? Qu'as-tu
fp
suivez
90
dit?
fp
92
f
dim.
Quel trou - ble as-tu je - té dans mon coeur in - ter - dit?
f

95
Andante con moto
très doux
I.
Ne te sou - viens-tu plus de ces heu - res bé -
p doux
99
ni - es, Où nous mê-lions nos jeux d'en - fant?
expressif
103
p
Où, plus tard, tes yeux clairs aux dou - ceurs in - fi -
3
pp
107
M.
p
Je me sou - viens, Is -
cresc. f
ni - es Ber-çaient mon es - poir tri-om - phant!
cresc.
f
p

112
poco cresc.
M.
kra! je t'ai-mais comme un frè - re, Je t'aime en-cor ain -
pp
poco cresc.
117
Animez
M.
si!
(avec forcer)
I.
Tu m'ai - mes! mot trom-peur! Et moi, je veux
Animez
121
cresc.
I.
croire au con-trai - re, Qu'un autre a-mour a pris ma pla - ce dans tou
cresc.
p
suivez
125
M.
f
In - sen - sé!
Tempo I°
I.
f
coeur!
p
Tu m'ai-mais
Tempo I°
f
pp

128
I.
quand, plei-ne de ten - dres - se,
Ta dou-ce main pres-sait ma
132
Animez
cresc.
main!
Quand ta chaude a - mi - tié,
ta voix en-chan-te -
cresc.
136
f
res - se,
Me fai - saient es - pé - rer
un ra-di-eux hy -
139
f
men!
dim.

141
Moderato quasi andantino
(calme) p
M.
Tu te trom - pes! Je suis pa - reille au lac pai -
I.
Moderato quasi andantino
p
pp lié
144
si - - ble, Que ne ri - de au eun souf - fle en
146
un beau soir d'é - té! Tu
148
prends pour un coeur in - sen - si - - - ble, Un
pp

150
M.
coeur plein de sé-ré-ni-té! Tu
pp
152
prends pour un coeur in-sen-si-ble, Un
154
coeur plein de sé-ré-ni-
p rit.
p suivez
156
Tempo
Allegro
té!
I.
f
C'est me don-ner la Mort!

159
I.
que m'ar - ra - cher mon rê - ve Et re - ni - er un coeur ai -
p
161
mf
mant!
Un au - tre à mes bai -
f
163
f
sers t'en - lè - ve!
Un au - tre a re - cu ton ser -
p
f
p suivez
166
ment!
Allegro agitato
f

169
Andante con moto
M.
p
N'ir-ri-te pas mon âme in-dul-gente et cal-mé-e
p
f
172
Récit.
(avec inquiétude)
cresc.
f
Dis-moi plu-tôt com-ment, au sort-ir des com-bats, Te voi-là seul, i-
Allegro moderato molto
f
174
Allegro
p
ci, loin de l'ar-mé-e? Com-ment les au-tres chefs ne t'ac-com-pagn-ent pas?
I.
p
Je
Allegro
p
pp
177
poco cresc.
viens an-non-cer à ton pè-re, Que mal-gré la vic-toire et les des-tins pros-pè-res,
poco cresc.

181
I.
(en hésitant)
S'est ac-com-pli là - bas un sombre é - vè-ne - ment! Ma-zep -
p
184
M.
(avec effrei)
f
Ma-zep-pa!
(avec angoisse)
mf
quel tour -
I.
pa no - tre chef
cresc.
mf
187
M.
ment Fais-tu naî - tre sou-dain en mon âme op-pres - sé - e?
f
Animez
(avec désespoir)
190
M.
f
Il est mort! Il est mort!
(sombre)
I.
Il est mort!
p (e'animent)
Je tis dans ta pen -
Animez
suivez

193
cresc.
I.
sé - e Et le voi - le s'est dé - chi - ré!
p cresc.
196
f (déclamé)
Ah! tu tra-his tou - te ton â - me!
f
199
f (avec désespoir)
M.
Il est mort!
I.
Ta dou-leur pro -
f
202
ff
cla - - me, Ta pas - si - on per - fide et ton a - mour na -
ff
suivez

205
Tempo animato
(éclatant)
Allegro agitato
M.
Eh bien!
I.
vré!
Tempo animato
Allegro agitato
mf con fuoco
207
M.
Oui, je l'ai-mais! Qu'im - por - te?
210
M.
Tu ne com - ptes pour rien dans mes tris - tes a - mours!
213
M.
Oui, mon â - me pour toi, doit être uce â - me

216
M.
(avec passion)
mor - te! Et lui, mê - me ex - pi -
cresc.
219
M.
dim.
ré, je l'ai - me - rai tou - jours, tou -
dim.
222
M.
jours! A - dieu! A -
225
M.
dieu!
(avec douleur)
I.
Son â - me en - tière est en - chai - né -

229
M.
Oui! je l'ai - mais!
I.
- - - e, A ce-lui qu'el - le s'est don-né -
p
233
M.
Tris - tes a - mours! A - dieu! A -
I.
- - - - - - e, Mais la jus - ti - ce au - ra son tour
f
236
M.
dieu! Je l'ai - me - rai tou - jours!
I.
Je sau - rai ven - ger mon a - mour!
ff

239
Allegro
M.
Oui, tou - jours!
I.
mon a - mour!
Allegro
ff Trompettes au dehors
243
Ténors LA FOULE ff
(au dehors)
Vi - ve! Vi - ve!
Basses ff
Vi - ve! Vi - ve!
247
Matréna
p (dans le plus grand trouble)
Vi - ve Ma - zep -
Vi - ve Ma - zep - pa!
Vi - ve Ma - zep - pa!
pp

250
M.
cresc.
pa! puis - je croi - re A ces cris joy -
poco cresc.
252
(e'animant plus en plus)
eux? Ma - zep - pa n'est pas
mf cresc.
Vi - ve
mf cresc.
Vi - ve
mf
254
mort! On ac - cla - me sa
f
Vi - ve Ma - zep - pa!
f
Vi - ve Ma - zep - pa!
f
f

256
ff
M.
gloi - - - - - re!
I.
ff
O ra - - - - - ge!
Vi - - - - - - - ve!
Vi - - - - - - - ve!
7
Allegro maestoso
258
(éperdue)
Vi-vant! il est vi - vant! Je vois s'ouv - rir les
ff
marquez le chant
3
261
Allegro non troppo
cieux!
f (avec rage)
En-fin! j'ai su t'ar-ra-cher tes a -
Allegro non troppo
3

264
M.
Lui! vi-vant! je vais au-jourd hui Mou-rir de joi - e!
I.
veux!
suivez
267
Allegro maestoso rit.
(avec ivresse)
Ah! C'est
(avec fureur)
Mal-heur à toi! Mal-heur à lui! C'est
Allegro maestoso rit.
269
lui qui re - vient tri - om - phant!
lui qui re - vient tri - om - phant!
vibrato

272
M.
Le guer-rier que j'a-do - re, et dont ve-nait ma
I.
Lui que ton coeur a-do - re, Mal-heur à
275
M.
p
pei - ne! Ce - lui dont la va-leur dé-fend
I.
f
lui! En vain ton a - mour le dé-fend
278
(largement)
M.
Le peuple op-pri-mé de l'Uk - rai -
ff
I.
Mal-heur à toi! Mal - heur à
ff

281
Allegro animato
M.
ne!
I.
lui!
Sop. ff (acclamations du peuple, au dehors)
Gloi - re! Gloire à Ma - zep - pa!
Contr. ff
Gloi - re! Gloire à Ma - zep - pa!
Ténors ff
Gloi - re! Gloire à Ma - zep - pa!
Basses ff
Gloi - re! Gloire à Ma - zep - pa!
Allegro animato

283
Vic - toi - re!
Vic - toi - re!
Vic - toi - re!
Vic - toi - re!
Vic - toi - re!
Vic - toi - re!
Vic - toi - re!
Vic - toi - re!
RIDEAU
285
fff
Gloi - re!
Vic - toi - re!
Gloi - re!
Vic - toi - re!
Gloi - re!
Vic - toi - re!
Gloi - re!
Vic - toi - re!
fff

Mazeppa
Act II, Scene 5

Charles Grandmougin

Marie Grandval
Lydia Ledeen, editor

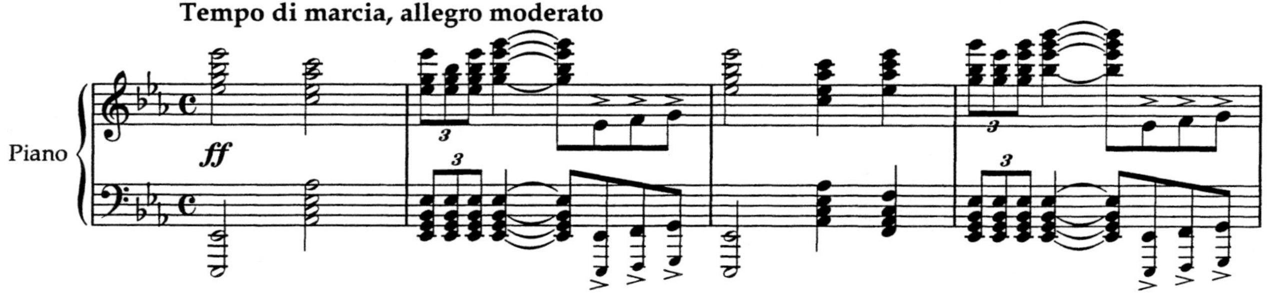

13
Gloi - re à toi, Ma - zep - pa! la Po-logne est sou -
Gloi - re à toi, Ma - zep - pa! la Po-logne est sou -
Gloi - re à toi, Ma - zep - pa! la Po-logne est sou -
Gloi - re à toi, Ma - zep - pa! la Po-logne est sou -
16
mi - - - se! Gloi - re à toi!
mi - - - se! Gloi - re à toi!
mi - - - se! Gloi - re à toi!
mi - - - se! Gloi - re à toi!

*♪ in first print

26
temps é - touf - fé!
temps é - touf - fé!
temps é - touf - fé!
temps é - touf - fé!
28
p
Gloire à toi, dé-fen - seur d' u - ne cau - se sa -
p
Gloire à toi, dé-fen - seur d' u - ne cau - se sa -
p
Gloi - re!
p
Gloi - re!

31
cresc.
cré - e, No - tre pa - tri - e est dé - li -
cré - e, No - tre pa - tri - e est dé - li -
Gloi - re à toi! No - tre pa -
Gloi - re à toi! No - tre pa -
34
mf
f
vré - e, Et la jus - ti - ce a tri - om - phé! Ton au -
vré - e, Et la jus - ti - ce a tri - om - phé! Ton au -
tri - e est dé - li - vré - e,
tri - e est dé - li - vré - e, Ton au -

37
da - ce gui-dait nos ar - mes, L'U - kraine au-jourd' hui sans en-
da - ce gui-dait nos ar - mes, L'U - kraine au-jourd' hui sans en-
f
Ton au - da - ce gui-dait nos ar - mes, L'U -
da - ce gui-dait nos ar - mes, L'U - kraine au-jourd' hui sans en-
3
3
40
ff
tra - - - ves, E - cla - te en trans -
tra - - - ves, E - cla - te en trans -
krai - - - ne E - cla - te en trans -
tra - - - ves, E - cla - te en trans -

43
ports glo - - ri - eux!
ports glo - - ri - eux!
ports glo - - ri - eux!
ports glo - - ri - eux!
45
mf
Gloi - re!
f
gloire à toi!
fff
gloi - re à
Gloi - re! gloire à toi! gloi - re à
Gloi - re! gloire à toi! gloi - re à
Gloi - re! gloire à toi! gloi - re à
[mf]
8vb

48
toi!
toi!
toi!
toi!
sost.
mf
51
CORTÈGE
poco rit.
dim.
sost.
54
58
cresc.
f

* ♩ in first print

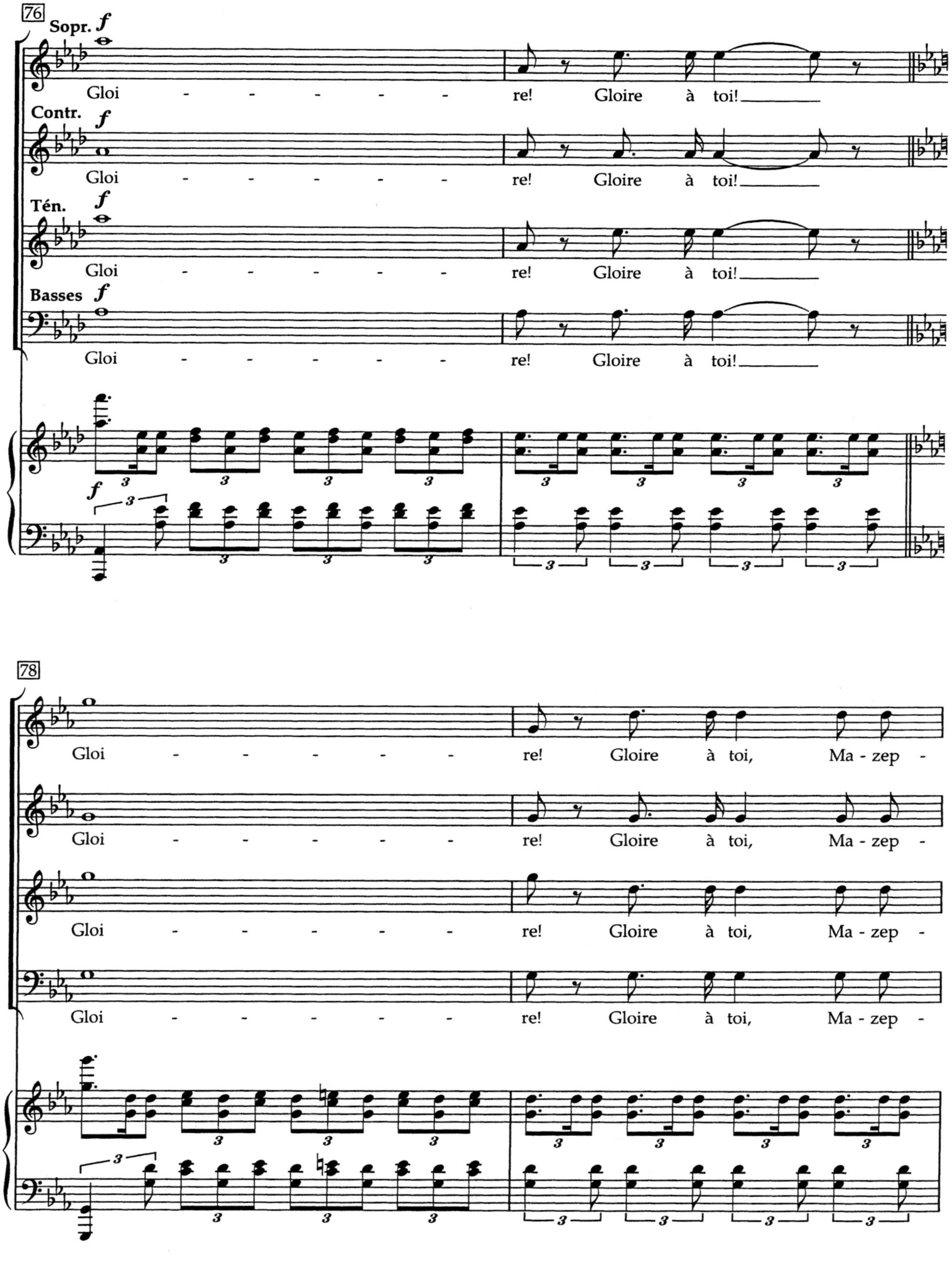

76

Sopr. *f*

Gloi - - - - - - re! Gloire à toi!

Contr. *f*

Gloi - - - - - - re! Gloire à toi!

Tén. *f*

Gloi - - - - - - re! Gloire à toi!

Basses *f*

Gloi - - - - - - re! Gloire à toi!

f

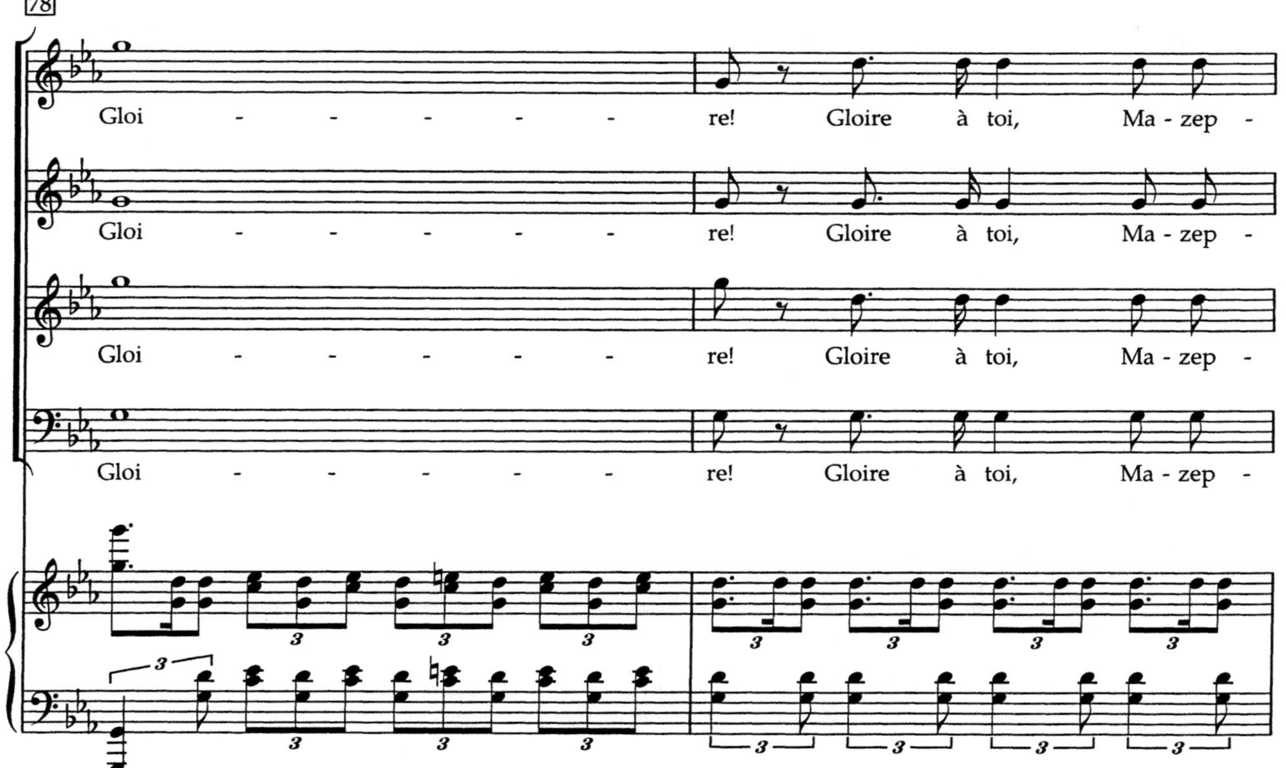

80
rit.
ff
Andante con moto
pa! Sa - lut au guer - rier tri - om - phant!
pa! Sa - lut au guer - rier tri - om - phant!
pa! Sa - lut au guer - rier tri - om - phant!
pa! Sa - lut au guer - rier tri - om - phant!
Andante con moto
rit.
ff Cloches
83
Hon-neur à son nom tout puis-sant!
Hon-neur à son nom tout puis-sant!
Hon-neur à son nom tout puis-sant!
Hon-neur à son nom tout puis-sant!

87
Ex - al - tons sa gloi - - - -
Ex - al - tons sa gloi - - - -
Ex - al - tons sa gloi - - - -
Ex - al - tons sa gloi - - - -
90
fff
rit.
re! Vic - toi - - - - - - - - -
re! Vic - toi - - - - - - - - -
re! Vic - toi - - - - - - - - -
re! Vic - toi - - - - - - - - -
fff
rit.

93
Allegro moderato
re!
re!
re!
re!
Allegro moderato
ff
95
Animez
Gloire à Ma - zep - pa!
Gloire à Ma - zep - pa!
Gloire à Ma - zep - pa!
Gloire à Ma - zep - pa!
Animez

97
Gloi - re!
Vic -
Gloi - re!
Vic -
Gloi - re!
Gloi - re!
Gloi - re!
Vic -
Gloi - re!
Gloi - re!
Gloi - re!
Vic -
100
toi - re!
toi - re!
toi - re!
toi - re!

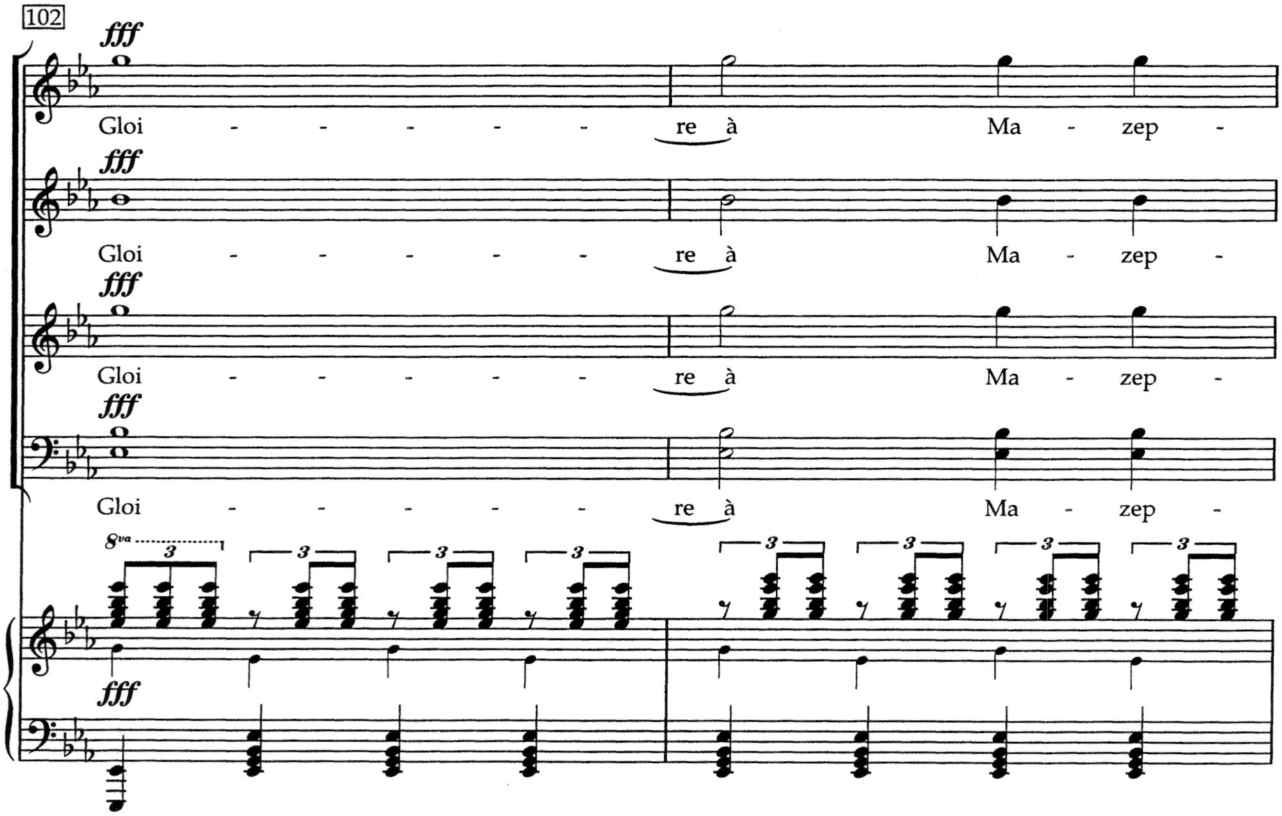

102

fff
Gloi - - - - - - re à Ma - zep -

fff
Gloi - - - - - - re à Ma - zep -

fff
Gloi - - - - - - re à Ma - zep -

fff
Gloi - - - - - - re à Ma - zep -

8va

fff

Ingeborg von Bronsart
(1840–1913)

JAMES DEAVILLE

Ingeborg [Lena] Bronsart von Schellendorf [known as Ingeborg von Bronsart], née Star(c)k,[1] was born in St. Petersburg on August 12 or 24, 1840, and died in Munich, June 17, 1913. Originally a virtuoso pianist, she became perhaps the most noted woman composer in Germany during the second half of the nineteenth century. This is evidenced by the substantial publication and performance history of her music (above all her operas), her prominent position in late nineteenth-century biographical anthologies devoted to women composers and musicians, and her significant involvement in the music for the Women's Exhibit at the Columbian Exposition in Chicago in 1893.

Although born in Russia and eventually a resident of Germany, she remained proud of her Swedish ancestry. Her father, Otto Wilhelm Star(c)k, was born in Stockholm and settled in St. Petersburg in the late 1830s.[2] Various authorized biographical sketches of Bronsart indicate her father was a member of the Russian merchant's guild. However, in a confidential letter to biographer La Mara (Marie Lipsius),[3] Bronsart notes that she had suppressed her father's noble birth to the Count Björnstema, one of the most distinguished men of Sweden, because he was actually Court Saddler in St. Petersburg, owner of a saddle factory, and thus an industrialist. She requested that La Mara instead indicate that she was from a "respected Swedish *Bürger* family," out of consideration for her German relatives (i.e., her husband Hans von Bronsart's noble and prominent family — his father was a Prussian general). Her mother Margarethe Elisabeth was the daughter of a Swedish captain named Ockermann, who had settled and married in Finland.

The earliest musical influences upon Bronsart were her mother's violin playing, her father's flute playing, and the Swedish folk songs sung by her governess. When her sister Olivia (who was nine years older) began piano lessons, Bronsart insisted on receiving them as well, and within half a year surpassed her sister.[4] By the age of eight, she showed creative talent by composing simple melodies and short dances. At the age of ten she came under the tutelage of the amateur musician Nicolas von Martinoff, who was well placed within St. Peterburg's musical circles and introduced his young pupil to the opera there. She changed teachers at age eleven to the noted pianist and composer Constantin Decker, under whose instruction she advanced so rapidly that by the following year she was able to stage a concert that featured her piano performance and a work of her own (orchestrated by Decker).

A concert with orchestra became an annual tradition for the developing musician, who also performed in her family's weekly salons and enjoyed favor with some of the leading artistic and political personalities of St. Petersburg. (Her lifelong friendship with Anton Rubinstein [1829–1894] dates back to this period.) By the age of thirteen she had composed three *études*, a tarantella, and a nocturne (published in 1855), and within a few years she turned to larger forms of composition for piano.

Documents are unusually silent about her two years of study with Adolf Henselt (1814–1889) in St. Petersburg (1855–1857). Indeed, the major sources for information about Bronsart's early years are not letters, which are all but nonexistent from the years before her residence in Weimar, but rather biographical sketches of Bronsart's early life that purport to be based on personal communications from her.[5] Later in life she would fondly recall her studies with Henselt, who undoubtedly advanced her pianism to such a high degree that, as the result of his urging, she could leave Russia to test her abilities in the broader world.

Bronsart moved to Weimar in early 1858 to continue her training with Franz Liszt (1811–1886). Biographer Elise Polko states that her desire to study in Weimar came from a tête-à-tête about Liszt with Hans von Bronsart, who had given a concert in St. Petersburg.[6] Although Hans did play in that city and Bronsart may well have heard him, the story appears to be apocryphal, since it is not confirmed in any other source.

It is clear from letters by Franz Liszt (1811–1886) and others that during her short period of residence in Weimar, he came to esteem her as both pianist and composer. He wrote to Louis Köhler, "I have grown much attached to Fräulein Stark, as hers is a particularly gifted artistic nature. The same will happen to you, when you hear her remarkable sonata."[7]

Liszt was accustomed to saying of her, "she plays like a volcano."[8] One of their first encounters in Weimar was the source of what would become the most famous anecdote from her life. Liszt retold the story in the same letter to Köhler: "Moreover, Ingeborg composes all sorts of fugues, toccatas, etc. I recently remarked to her that she actually does not at all look like it. Her fitting response was 'I am quite glad I do not have a fugal face.'" [9] She later recounted the most important aspect of Liszt's instruction: "His direction protected me from artistic one-sidedness, and the example of his wonderful artistic nature taught me to seek for and assimilate the beautiful in music everywhere, regardless of the tendency of its creator."[10]

Composing in smaller lyric forms for piano prior to coming to Weimar, once there she not only wrote fugues (including one on the musical letters from the names of Maria and Martha von Sabinin),[11] but composed sets of variations, toccatas, and a sonata. Still, until the mid-1860s, she did not write for any performance medium other than her own instrument, some of that music for use on her concert tours. This early mastery of larger, complicated forms for piano nevertheless presaged her later activity as composer of operas.

In the winter of 1858 she embarked upon a successful, decade-long career as a traveling virtuoso, while maintaining Weimar as "home base" for at least the next two years.[12] During that winter, she played at court in Weimar, performed in the Leipzig Gewandhaus, in Dresden, and in Paris. It was in Paris that she not only came to know Rossini and Auber, but also Richard Wagner, whose *Mein Leben* calls her a "vision of elegance" during her concert visit in the late spring of 1860.[13] She also gave concerts in such cities as St. Petersburg, Danzig and Löwenberg, but ill health restricted the extent of her tours.[14] During her later travels, she was often accompanied by the conductor/pianist — and fellow Liszt pupil — Hans Bronsart von Schellendorf (1830–1913), whom she married on September 14, 1861. In correspondence between Hans von Bronsart and Liszt from 1860, it is clear that as her fiancé, he had initially felt the need for a secret marriage because of her family.[15] Furthermore, as a Liszt letter notes, there was rivalry within the circle of young Liszt pupils in Weimar for her hand, especially between Bronsart and Eduard Lassen.[16] The marriage produced two children: Clara (1864–ca. 1929) and Fritz (1868–1918).[17]

When not on the road, she supported Hans in his various conducting engagements, usually as soloist, either in concerti or solo piano pieces. He first conducted the Euterpe concerts in Leipzig from 1860 until 1862, as a New-German alternative to the conservative Gewandhaus.[18] For the Euterpe series, Bronsart played (among others) Liszt's arrangement of Weber's *Polonaise brillante* for piano and orchestra, Chopin's *Piano Concerto in E minor*, op. 11, Liszt's *Tarantella di bravura* on *La Muette de Portici* (for piano solo), and Bach's *Concerto in the Italian Style*. During the Leipzig years they also performed in Löwenberg. They then spent a winter in Dresden, where they presented their own series of subscription orchestral and chamber-music concerts. The final stage of this "Wanderleben" (wandering life) was a two-year engagement (1864–1866) for Hans as Hans von Bülow's (1830–1894) successor in Berlin as conductor of the concerts of the *Gesellschaft der Musikfreunde*. It was in that series in Berlin that Bronsart created a sensation with a performance of Schubert's *Wanderer Fantasy* in Liszt's arrangement, and where she played with success in the Thursday soirées of Queen Augusta and the salon of Princess Friedrich Karl von Preussen (1830–1894).[19]

During this period after her marriage to Hans, she composed only three works: a piano concerto in the progressive new-German style of Liszt, a setting of *Die Loreley* [*sic*] (her first song), and the opera *Die Göttin von Sais oder Linas und Liane*, on a text by the Prussian Queen Augusta von Sachsen-Weimar's lector named Meyer. She worked on the opera during the Berlin years (the libretto was published in 1866) and the work as a whole received its first and only performance (accompanied by piano) in the Crown Prince Friedrich Wilhelm's palace in 1867. By all accounts, the libretto was too weak for a three-act opera. Because the score is no longer in existence, it is impossible to assess the music; however, considering that Bronsart does not significantly refer to it in her later autobiographical writings and failed to do anything more with the work, she appears to have distanced herself from the composition.

Bronsart was required to forsake her career as a pianist as a result of her husband's appointment as Intendant at the court theater in Hannover, beginning in 1867.[20] She did play in the weekly matinées in their own salon in Hannover and continued to perform in public for benefits and charitable causes. She shared the stage on three occasions (and played four-hand piano music) with her mentor Liszt at concerts in 1875 and 1876 for the benefit of the Bach monument in Eisenach and to help finance the Bayreuth Festival, and at the 1877 festival of the Allgemeine Deutsche Musikverein in Hannover.

The Franco-Prussian War of 1870–1871 brought an interruption to the routine of the Bronsarts in Hannover, for despite a hand injury, patriot Hans volunteered for military service.[21] The separation evoked a flood of correspondence,[22] and the war brought forth patriotic feelings in the composer as well, resulting in her first published collection of songs, *Drei Lieder*; her first choral work, *Hurrah Germania!* for male chorus; and her most famous piece for piano *Kaiser Wilhelm March*; all from 1871. The march had the distinction of being performed at the festivities in the Berlin opera house after the return of the troops in 1871,[23] and then again in 1893 at the Columbian Exposition.[24] *Frisch auf, zum letzten Kampf und Streit!* from the *Drei Lieder* is discussed below.

After these "war" publications, other works, especially song collections, followed in quick and regular succession. In a way, the loss of the performing career may have been a boon to her creative career, for Bronsart was then able to focus on composition. Her first major work from Hannover was the musical setting of Goethe's one-act *Singspiel* entitled *Jery und Bätely*. She composed it during 1871 and 1872, and it was premiered in Weimar on April 26, 1873. It was by far her most successful work: the press was very favorable; it received performances in well over ten German cities;[25] and it was published in vocal and full score fairly soon after the premiere (1876). The work had particularly memorable performances in Leipzig in 1883 as part of a Goethe cycle and in Berlin in 1884 at the Court Opera.[26] In reviewing the Baden-Baden performance of 1874, Richard Pohl identified features that undoubtedly contributed to the work's popularity: fresh, noble and pleasing melodic invention, skillful work, fine and effective instrumentation, and a dramatically climactic progression from simpler forms to the broad finale.[27] *Jery und Bätely* also succeeded because, as a *Singspiel*, it did not represent an infringement of the "gender-genre gap," whereby women were regarded as being incapable of working in larger forms. Her success with this work may to a certain extent have worked against the wider acceptance of her later serious opera, *Hiarne*.

The premiere of *Jery und Bätely* was unfortunately tainted by a major family dispute that is not mentioned in any of the secondary literature. Envious of his wife's success, Hans threatened Bronsart with divorce if she did not desist from her artistic activity. The two existing letters from this time (April of 1873), both by the composer, reveal a tortured woman who was trying to balance domestic activities and career, but who also felt that she needed her freedom:

> If I am supposed to forget that which happened between us, then you have to do the same, and give me *now* the same freedom as I had *at that time* and no longer insult me with any mistrust . . . Moreover I know that I do not neglect my duties as housewife and mother, and can account for my industry in the eyes of God and humanity.[28]

> If it was your intention to tarnish and poison all happy memories of Weimar, you have succeeded in your goal. Were one to draw conclusions from your disdainful comments about my musical talents, it would have to be that no spark of talent resides in me, since from the start you could consider every success I have solely a travesty of several acquaintances who wish me well. It is striking to me that Frau Viardot, who with her world-renowned name has a much larger circle of followers than I do, has not found here such a general and enthusiastic reception with her little opera than I have with my unassuming Singspiel.[29]

According to the epistolary evidence, there must have been a fairly quick resolution to the crisis. The stigma of the time against divorce undoubtedly encouraged the couple to cover up any sign of marital difficulties in the official renderings of their lives that they and colleagues committed to print, which explains the silence of the secondary sources.

In the next years she wrote smaller works for piano and for violin and cello with piano accompaniment,[30] and, especially between 1878 and 1882, a number of song collections. Although they are frequently united by the poetry, none of the collections have unifying features that would warrant the designation of song cycle. Among the "classical" poets, she seems to have had a preference for Goethe and Heine. Later poets who captured her attention included Friedrich von Bodenstedt (five collections, two under his pseudonym Mirza Schaffy), Ernst von Wildenbruch (one collection), Peter Cornelius (one collection), and Paul Heyse (several individual songs). It is no coincidence that, with the exception of Cornelius, the poets were personal friends of the family, which in the case of Wildenbruch is documented by an interesting correspondence between composer and poet (see pages 250-251). The musical settings of the poetry were quite varied, depending on the text, but most could be characterised by what reviewers of the day noted as a mixture of nobility with warm-bloodedness and engagement.[31] Worthy of special note are the op. 17 songs to low-German children's poetry by Klaus Groth, which reveal a simple, folk style of composition.

In 1876, Bronsart and Hans traveled to Bayreuth to attend the premiere of Wagner's *Ring des Nibelungen*. Curiously, the best published source about their visit is the memoir of Eduard Hanslick, Wagner's nemesis, who seems to have found a kindred spirit in Bronsart, at least in her alleged distaste for the opera.[32] He saw her there in the company of Friedrich von Bodenstedt, and all three agreed that the festival was four days of martyrdom. Regarding Bronsart, Hanslick made the following observation: "[She enjoys] today a respectable circle of admirers for her own compositions."[33]

In 1887, the family (Hans, Ingeborg, and daughter Clara) moved to Weimar, where Hans had been appointed *Generalintendant*. The position in the city and on the stage of their venerated master clearly attracted the Bronsarts and during this period, they tried to keep the Liszt tradition alive in Weimar.[34] At least one of Liszt's pupils, Kapellmeister Eduard Lassen, was still active in Weimar at the time.

Most of Bronsart's energies during the early 1890s were devoted to preparing her serious opera *Hiarne* for its premiere and securing further performances. She was particularly proud of the work, which had a long gestation period. Hans claimed that he had begun work on a libretto to an opera *Hiarne* in 1857,[35] under the influence of *Tannhäuser*. Although Hans never composed his libretto, friend Bodenstedt approved of the project, thoroughly reworking the libretto that Bronsart gradually set to music between the years 1870 and 1890.

Hiarne was favorably received at its premiere at the Court Opera in Berlin on February 14, 1891. It was also performed with success in Hannover, Gotha, Hamburg, Weimar (seven times over two seasons), and in Dessau. However, it never became established in the permanent repertory of any of these stages.[36] Bronsart regarded it as her "greatest and best work,"[37] and in bringing *Hiarne* to the German stage, clearly saw herself as a pioneer among women composers, able to succeed in writing a large-scale work. Still, in response to *Hiarne* she wrote with pride in 1910: ". . . I am the *first* and up to now, *the only* dramatic woman composer of Germany, and I am also *the first woman* who has had a *major opera* (Hiarne) produced on stage."[38]

Even critics inclined favorably to Bronsart's opera demonstrated the familiar bias against women as composers of larger works. For example, Georg Davidsohn noted in the *Berliner Börsen-Courier* that "the entire work does not betray the hand of a woman."[39] During the Weimar period, Bronsart was involved in the preparations for music for the Women's Exhibit at the Columbian Exposition in Chicago in 1893,[40] at which she was represented by the *Kaiser Wilhelm March*. The march was performed at the opening on May 1, 1893, under the baton of Theodore Thomas, conducting members from the Chicago Orchestra (predecessor of the Chicago Symphony Orchestra). Actually, Bronsart, always on the search for performance opportunities, appears to have originally motivated a certain Herr Wermuth, the Reichs-Kommissar for the German delegation in Chicago, to request a performance of *Hiarne* for the Exposition, drawing upon the card of the strong support of "Her Royal Highness the Princess Carl [*sic*] Friedrich von Preussen."[41] Bronsart herself wrote to Thomas about *Hiarne*, noting how the failure to perform the work would offend the Princess and would represent a waste of the money invested in sending the parts, and how he should support a fellow German.[42] The letter did not induce Thomas to perform the opera, but he did program the march again at a Pops Concert in Chicago on August 8, 1893.

Hans retired from service in Weimar in 1895, and the family left the city in 1896. The next years were spent traveling and it was not until 1901 that they finally settled down in Munich. At that time, Bronsart composed what she called a "one-act music drama," *Die Sühne* (The Reconciliation), which was produced in Dessau in 1909. She wrote the text herself (after Theodor Körner), and composed the music in a Wagnerian style. It was staged only once, and she never was able to find a publisher for the full score (it did appear in piano-vocal score). The last years of her life were largely taken up with trying to find publishers for her large body of unpublished material and to arrange performances of her operas. She realized how her compositions were not current in style, for in a letter to La Mara, she noted that she would have difficulty finding a publisher for her simple but deeply felt songs in that "modern age."[43] An elaborate celebration of her fifty-year activity as performer in April 1903 represented a high point in her final years. For that occasion, Breitkopf und Härtel published several of Bronsart's songs. She died in Munich on June 17, 1913, only five months before her husband of over fifty years.

Bronsart's compositional output embraces the major genres of the time, except for the symphony and oratorio. Regardless of genre, her music displays vocally derived melodies, traditional forms and mildly chromatic harmonies; it is generally characterized by technical mastery. For the piano music and some of the songs, Liszt served as the model, whereas Wagner's works exerted an influence upon her last two operas although she herself vehemently denied any indebtedness to Wagner's musical style. Her more successful works, including the opera *Jery und Bätely* and the *Zwölf Kinderreime*, op. 17, incorporate elements derived from folk music. The other operas suffer from poor librettos. The sensitive declamation of Bronsart's vocal music anticipates the style of Richard Strauss' songs and operas. Unfortunately, much of the early piano music and, according to a letter from 1902, more than thirty songs were never published.[44]

The six songs selected for publication here represent a variety of Bronsart's styles and are from several periods. As already noted, Bronsart turned to song composition at about the same time she began working on opera, which represents a shift from the piano composition of her virtuoso years toward vocal-based creation. In general, the songs reveal a composer rooted in the compositional traditions of Liszt, although her oeuvre also feature works in a simpler folk song style. Her choice of texts, as reflected in the selection here, ranges from the classic poetry of Goethe to the sentimental style of the late nineteenth century (Wildenbruch, Heyse), although the latter far outweigh the former in her total song production.

The song *Frisch auf, zum letzten Kampf und Streit!* from the *Drei Lieder* of 1871 sets an aggressively nationalistic text that reflects popular sentiment in Germany toward the Franco-Prussian War. The march-like melody over diatonic chords and the dotted rhythms in the four-measure piano introduction set the martial tone of this song in B-flat major. Temporary excursions to B-flat minor and G minor are the only harmonic relief within the first stanza, which above all is striking through its pointed rhythms. The next two stanzas represent a slightly modified version of the first. As the last two stanzas of the poem proceed through battlefield imagery to an apotheosis, the music becomes more dramatic. Although based on thematic material from the first three stanzas, the final two build to a climax through dynamics, tempo and harmonic tension. Particularly interesting is the movement toward the Neapolitan of the dominant (G-flat major) just before the final cadence. The variety and nuances of this music certainly elevate *Frisch auf* above the military music of the period. The song reveals Bronsart's talent for the martial style, which would later serve her well in the popular *Kaiser Wilhelm March*. It also reflects an aspect of her emotional life at the time that is easily passed over today, namely the patriotic feelings evoked by the Franco-Prussian War.

Appearance both as a regular song publication (the second of the *Fünf Lieder* of 1878) and as a musical supplement to a widely read music journal (the *Neue Musik-Zeitung*) ensured that the Goethe setting *Blumengruss* would become Bronsart's most widely disseminated song composition. A model of simplicity, the music for the six verses recalls standard Goethe settings of the early nineteenth century (i.e., Carl Friedrich Zelter), rather than her mentor Liszt's frequently dramatic and extended treatments of the poet's texts. The largely stepwise motion of the voice, the almost undisturbed diatonic harmony, and the gentle rhythmic flow in $\frac{6}{8}$ meter all contribute to the folk-style feeling of *Blumengruss*. Even in a song of just 15 measures Bronsart is able to introduce several affective crescendi/decrescendi and ritardandi.

Bronsart's unpublished letters to Wildenbruch make it clear that her setting of his poetry, entitled *Fünf Gedichte*, op. 16 (1882), originally consisted of three songs: *Ständchen, Zwei Sträusse*, and *Der Blumenstrauss*. She added the newly composed song *Letzte Bitte* in the summer, about which she wrote the following to the poet:

> The poem "Letzte Bitte," which is so dear to me, also musically fills my spirit. However, I fear that it will be difficult for me to reproduce it in the way that I perceive the beauty of the poem. Still, I do not give up the hope that I will one day succeed at it.[45]

Wildenbruch responded with comments that provide fascinating insights into the poet's desires for the musical setting of his work. He clearly wished to influence composer Bronsart:

> I am very happy that the "Letzte Bitte" also engaged your musical fantasy. I think that this song would have to be extremely effective, if its lamenting tone is captured. Would it not be best set for alto? I am thinking here of Marianne Brandt, who desires to sing this song once.[46]

On September 26, 1882, she sent Wildenbruch a complete copy of the songs (dedicated to him), which had appeared in print a few days earlier.[47] In the finished song, she appears to have been able to satisfy him on both accounts: she captured the poem's lamenting tone, and set it for a low voice. She accomplished the former through a metrically free C minor recitative-like section that frames the whole and expresses the pessimistic mood of the departing lover. To underscore the lamenting quality, Bronsart begins the song with a striking gesture, an unprepared dissonant suspension on the dominant of the main key. The resolution is delayed by two beats, heightening the poignancy. Throughout the framing sections, the music contains irregular phrases, dissonances not resolving according to tradition, and changing meters, as if the expressive content outweighs musical logic. The two-part middle section (AA^1), although presenting more sentimental imagery with expressive melodic lines, underlines a strong sense of stability despite its freely roaming keys (beginning and ending in C major) and agitated left-hand figuration. This song represents Bronsart's most advanced musical style, which would give way in later years to renewed simplicity.

Published in 1882, her *Zwölf Kinderreime*, op. 17 are in complete contrast to the Wildenbruch songs. The low-German texts were by Klaus (Claus) Groth (1819–1899), from his 1858 collection *Vör de Görn* (called *Vaer de Gaern* in the title of Bronsart's publication). The twelve folk poems set by Bronsart are simple and straightforward, dealing with such childhood subjects as animals and naughty children. Bronsart has adapted a folksong style in her equally simple musical settings, which frequently engage in descriptive melodies and accompaniments (a turn figure to designate the hedge sparrow, a repeated-note accompaniment for ducks, etc.). The first song of the collection, *Ik weet en Leed, wat Niemand weet*, exemplifies the folk song style, with its regular four-measure phrases, almost completely diatonic harmonies and simple vocal melody. The song is charming in its naïveté. Bronsart nevertheless is able to introduce some irregularity through an inserted measure of $\frac{3}{4}$ in what could be considered the second stanza, which itself is metrically irregular. The original publication of the songs featured ten wood engravings by Ludwig Richter, adding to the interest of the collection.

According to an unpublished letter by Bronsart to La Mara dated December 2, 1902, the *Drei Lieder* published by Breitkopf & Härtel in 1902 were actually older songs for which she had just found a publisher.[48] In the absence of autographs or references in the letters, it is impossible to determine when the songs were written, although they do reveal stylistic affinities with the songs from the 1880s. The third in the collection, a setting of Heinrich Heine's *Ich stand in dunkeln Träumen*, merits closer study because of its unusual form. While it is unified through an arpeggiated figure in the accompaniment and begins and ends with a similar four measures, the song can nonetheless be considered through-composed, by virtue of its progressive tonality (from F minor through G major, A-flat major, and F minor to A-flat major at the end), its non-repetition of melodic material, and its metrical progression from triple to duple time. This freer approach to form is motivated by the text, with its progression from despair over the loss of a beloved to a fondly remembered vision of her face, back to the grief of the present, and ending with the uncertainty of whether the lover really lost her. The frequent surges of dynamics and changes of tempo support this flood of emotion, as does the fluid harmony. Bronsart weakens the sense of stable key by the use of inverted chords at key moments and ongoing chromaticism in the harmony. Some of the dissonances are striking, such as the clash in measure 10 between stacked fourths D-G-C in the left hand of the piano and the arpeggiated A minor triad in the right hand (supporting the voice's A-E-A motion), which underscores the text word "mysteriously." In *Ich stand in dunkeln Träumen*, Bronsart has created a miniature dramatic scene, which shows how effectively the composer could link music and word for expressive purposes.

Although the autograph of the unpublished song on the poem *Verwandlung* by Paul Heyse is not dated, the Bayerische Staatsbibliothek has indicated it was composed in 1910, which would make it one of Bronsart's last works. Only thirty-two measures in length, the song falls into a type of ABA^1B^1 structure. The opening A section in E minor (with some tendency toward G major) contrasts with a B section in D-flat major that is rhythmically more active in the accompaniment. Both A and B are shortened when they return at the end, the former in E minor, the latter in E major. Largely diatonic, the piece does progress through a variety of keys, and the two pivotal distantly related keys (E minor, D-flat major). Like the Heine setting discussed above, musical choices seem to be governed by the text: the two stand in an intimate relationship with each other. For example, it is not coincidental that the highest point in the vocal line is reached at the word "heaven" at the end of the song. Also, the opening lines about turning windmill sails and the blowing wind occasion a gentle yet constantly moving accompaniment. In keeping with the romantic sentiments and imagery of the text, Bronsart has marked frequent modifications of dynamics and tempi, which tend to give the sonority a surging quality. Her style here again reflects a composer indebted to Lisztian traditions of song composition, which may have been progressive in the first years of her creative activity, but positioned her with the conservatives in her first decade of the twentieth century.

Notes

1. Her maiden name is spelled "Starck" in some sources, "Stark" in others, which is why this text presents it as "Star(c)k," except in citations, where the spellings of the sources are retained.

2. Unpublished letter from Ingeborg von Bronsart to La Mara [Marie Lipsius], March 5, 1878; Weimar, Stiftung Weimarer Klassik, Goethe- und Schiller-Archiv, Liszt-Nachlass, La

Mara-Nachlass, 59/389, U9, 1.

3. Unpublished letter from Ingeborg von Bronsart to La Mara, May 25, 1881; Leipzig, Stadtgeschichtliches Museum, La Mara-Nachlass, Rp. 5, Biographisches, 1.

4. La Mara, "Ingeborg von Bronsart," in *Die Frauen im Tonleben der Gegenwart* (*Musikalische Studienköpfe*, vol. 5), 3rd ed. (Leipzig: Breitkopf und Härtel, 1902), 40.

5. Ibid., 37-53; Alfred Michaelis, "Ingeborg von Bronsart," in *Frauen als schaffende Tonkünstler: Ein biographisches Lexikon* (Leipzig: A. Michaelis, 1888): 8-9; Anna Morsch, "Ingeborg von Bronsart," *Gesangspädagogische Blätter* 4 (1910): 100-102.

6. Elise Polko, "Ingeborg von Bronsart: Biographisches Skizzenblatt," *Neue Musik-Zeitung* 9 (1888): 142.

7. "Als eine ganz ausserordentlich begabte Künstlernatur, habe ich Fräulein Stark sehr lieb gewonnen. Dasselbe wird Ihnen passiren, wenn Sie ihre merkwürdige Sonate hören." Letter of Liszt to Louis Köhler, from Weimar, dated September 3, 1859; *Franz Liszt's Briefe*, ed. La Mara, vol. 1 (Leipzig: Breitkopf und Härtel, 1893), 330.

8. "Elle joue comme un volcan." Otto Neitzel, "Ingeborg von Bronsart," undated, unidentified published biographical sketch. In an undated letter to La Mara, probably from late 1901, she recalls Liszt as saying, "elle joue comme un petit voleau" (Leipzig, Stadtgeschichtliches Museum, La Mara-Nachlass Rp. 5, Biographisches, 2).

9. "Obendrein componirt Ingeborg allerlei Fugen, Toccatas etc. Ich bemerkte ihr neulich dass sie eigentlich gar nicht darnach aussähe. 'Es ist mir auch ganz recht, keine Fugenmiene zu besitzen,' war ihre treffende Antwort." Letter from Liszt to Köhler, from Weimar, dated September 3, 1859; *Franz Liszt's Briefe*, 330.

10. "Seine Leitung hat mich vor künstlerischer Einseitigkeit bewahrt, und das Beispiel dieser wunderbaren Künstlernatur lehrte mich, das Schöne in der Musik überall zu suchen und in mich aufzunehmen, gleichviel welcher Richtung ihr Schöpfer angehörte." La Mara, "Ingeborg von Bronsart," 44.

11. See the footnote commentary of La Mara to Liszt's letter to Ingeborg Starck, from Weimar and dated November 2, 1859; *Franz Liszt's Briefe*, 338.

12. Polko, "Ingeborg von Bronsart," 142, identifies two study periods in Weimar, separated by a brief virtuoso tour, but there is no corroborating evidence that her return to Weimar was anything but a brief respite during her larger activity as traveling virtuoso.

13. Richard Wagner, *My Life*, trans. Andrew Gray, ed. Mary Whittall (Cambridge, England: Cambridge University Press, 1983), 613. Wagner also notes the presence of another Liszt pupil from Weimar, Aline Hund, who played with Ingeborg.

14. In an unpublished letter to Liszt from Hannover, dated April 17, 1878, husband Hans makes note of her poor health due to nervous asthma (Weimar, Stiftung Weimarer Klassik, Goethe- und Schiller-Archiv, Liszt-Nachlass, 59/9, no. 16, 3).

15. In a letter from January 25, 1860, Liszt advised him against the secret marriage (*Franz Liszt in seinen Briefen*, ed. Hans Rudolf Jung [Berlin: Henschelverlag, 1987], 179-80). Several days later, Liszt chastised Bronsart for "wanting to save Inga from the persecution of her parents," when the young man clearly did not know the family (letter from January 30, 1860; Weimar, Stiftung Weimarer Klassik, Goethe- und Schiller-Archiv, Liszt-Nachlass, 59/58, no. 31, 1-2). Bronsart's family supported the marriage, although under the stipulation that he first find a permanent position. See his letter to Ingeborg, dating from September 10, 1859; Thüringisches Hauptstaatsarchiv Weimar, Nachlass Hans Bronsart von Schellendorf, #95.

16. Letter of Franz Liszt to Agnes Street-Klindworth, from Weimar, dated August 20, 1859; *Franz Liszt and Agnes Street-Klindworth: A Correspondence*, 1854–1886, ed. Pauline Pocknell (Hillsdale, NY: Pendragon Press, 2000), pp. 164-166.

17. Clara studied piano, but had to give up performance due to an unidentified nervous disorder, the treatment of which was the source of much concern in her parents' later years. In fact, the great majority of the over forty letters from Ingeborg to Hans preserved in the Thüringisches Hauptstaatsarchiv in Weimar (call number 128) originated during trips to various specialists and spas for Clara's diagnosis and treatment.

18. Regarding the Euterpe "experiment" of the New Germans, see Deaville, "The New-German School and the *Euterpe* Concerts, 1860–1862: A Trojan Horse in Leipzig," in *Festschrift Christoph-Hellmut Mahling zum 65. Geburtstag,* in Mainzer Studien zur Musikwissenschaft, vol. 37 (Tutzing: Hans Schneider, 1997), 253-70.

19. La Mara, "Ingeborg von Bronsart," 47.

20. At that time, wives of Prussian officers and civil servants were not allowed to appear on stage. See ibid., 49.

21. His family was noted for its military service: as indicated in *Neue Deutsche Biographie*, his father Heinrich (1803–1874) was a Prussian general, as was his brother Paul (1832–1891), who also served as Prussian Minister of War from 1883 until 1889. See Walter Bussmann, "Bronsart v. Schellendorf," in *Neue Deutsche Biographie*, vol. 2 (Berlin: Duncker & Humblot, 1955), 636-37.

22. The Bronsart-Nachlass of the Thüringisches Hauptlandesarchiv in Weimar preserves over fifty letters and eighteen postcards from Hans to Ingeborg from 1870–1871.

23. An anonymous Berlin correspondent for the *Allgemeine Musikalische Zeitung* took a rather negative position on the work, calling it "rather mediocre" and suggesting that it was on the programme because her father-in-law was a Prussian general. "Berichte, Nachrichten und Bemerkungen," *Allgemeine Musikalische Zeitung*, vol. 6, no. 3 (July 26, 1871), col. 478.

24. In a letter to La Mara, she notes with satisfaction how her march was used to open the women's exhibit, and how for that distinction she received "the medal with certificate" (unpublished letter from February 19, 1903; Leipzig, Stadtgeschichtliches Museum, La Mara-Nachlass, Rp. 5, Biographisches, 2, 5).

25. The work was staged in Weimar, Karlsruhe, Baden-Baden, Schwerin, Kassel, Wiesbaden, Braunschweig, Hannover, Königsberg, Mannheim, Berlin, Leipzig, Bremen, and Munich.

26. On the occasion of the Berlin performance, Minister von Maybach organized a banquet in the composer's honor, at which she played the piano and Ernst von Wildenbruch delivered a poem of tribute. See Wilhelm Asmus, "Ingeborg von Bronsart," *Neue Zeitschrift für Musik*, vol. 65, no. 17 (April 27, 1898), 194-95.

27. Cited in La Mara, "Ingeborg von Bronsart," 51.

28. "Wenn ich vergessen soll, was zwischen uns vorgefallen, so musst Du dasselbe thun, und mir *jetzt* dieselbe Freiheit lassen wie ich sie *sonst* hatte, und mich mit keinem Misstrauen mehr beleidigen . . . Dass ich meine Pflichten als Hausfrau u. Mutter darüber nicht vernachlässige, weiss ich, u. kann vor Gott u. Menschen meinen Fleiss verantworten." It is unfortunate that none of Hans' letters to Ingeborg from this period seem to have survived. Unpublished letter from Ingeborg to Hans von Bronsart, dated Weimar, April 23, 1873; Thüringisches Hauptlandesarchiv Weimar, Nachlass Hans von Bronsart, no. 128, 4-5.

29. "Wenn es Deine Absicht war mir alle freundlichen Erinnerungen an Weimar zu trüben u. zu vergiften, so hast Du Deinen Zweck erreicht. Von Deinen verächtlichen Aeusserungen über meine musikalischen Begabungen zu schliessen, wohnt kein Funke von Begabung in mir, da Du von vornherein jeden Erfolg dessen ich mich zu erfreuen haben könnte, lediglich u. allein für ein Machwerk einiger mir wohlwollenden Bekannten hältst. Merkwürdig ist es mir, dass Frau Viardot die bei ihrem weltbekannten Namen eine viel grössere Anzahl von Anhängern hat als ich, hier mit ihrer kleinen Oper einen so allgemeinen u. lebhaften Beifall nicht gefunden wie ich mit meinem anspruchslosen Singspiel." Unpublished letter from Ingeborg to Hans von Bronsart, dated Weimar, April 28, 1873; Thüringisches Hauptlandesarchiv Weimar, Nachlass Hans von Bronsart no. 128, 1-2.

30. The problem women encountered when they undertook instrumental compositions becomes apparent from an anonymous review of the Nocturne, Elegie, and Romanze for violoncello, published in the *Allgemeine Musikalische Zeitung* of 1879. The critic noted how he was willing to close one eye when regarding such products of a "charming woman who was enthusiastic for art." "Anzeigen und Beurtheilungen. Für Violoncell und Clavier," *Allgemeine Musikalische Zeitung*, vol. 14, no. 46 (November 12, 1879), col. 730.

31. Ibid.

32. Eduard Hanslick, *Aus meinem Leben*, 2nd ed., vol. 2 (Berlin: Allgemeiner Verein für deutsche Litteratur, 1894), 179-80.

33. "Heute [erfreut sie] mit ihren eigenen Kompositionen einen ansehnlichen Kreis von Verehrern." Ibid., 179.

34. In 1888, Hans had become Chair of the Allgemeine Deutsche Musikverein, an organization with important ties to Liszt and Weimar: founded by Liszt and associates in Weimar in 1861, the ADMV represented his cause well into the twentieth century (and Liszt served as its honorary President for over a decade). As Chair of the organization (until 1898), Hans remained true to Lisztian principles.

35. Unpublished letter of Ingeborg von Bronsart to La Mara, from Munich, dated February 19, 1903; Leipzig, Stadtgeschichtliches Museum, La Mara-Nachlass, Rp. 5, Biographisches, 2, 7. By late 1859, Liszt had seen and tentatively approved the libretto: see his letter to Hans von Bronsart, from Weimar, dated December 2, 1859, in which Liszt provides detailed comments on the libretto (*Franz Liszt in seinen Briefen*, 177-78).

36. She herself was unable to explain the reason why the work could not maintain itself on the stage, although she seemed persuaded that her failure to find a publisher contributed to it. Perhaps as a result of insecurities, the score was in a constant state of revision, with changes to instrumentation and cuts amounting to one-half hour. In the hopes of finding a publisher and generally keeping the work in the public's eye, Ingeborg requested in 1903 that La Mara's article for her fiftieth artist's jubilee "write about *Hiarne* with friendly interest" (letter from February 19, 1903, 6).

37. Ibid.

38. ". . . Ich bin die *erste* und bis jetzt *die einzige* dramatische Componistin Deutschlands und . . . ich bin auch *die erste Frau*, von der eine *grosse Oper* (Hiarne) auf die Bühne gebracht worden ist." Unpublished letter from Ingeborg von Bronsart to La Mara, from Munich, dated April 25, 1910; Weimar, Stiftung Weimarer Klassik, Goethe- und Schiller-Archiv, Liszt-Nachlass, La Mara-Nachlass, 59/389, U9, 6, 4.

39. Review in *Berliner Börsen-Courier* from February 15, 1891. "Das ganze Werk verräth nicht die Hand der Frau."

40. A detailed account of the music by women composers at the exposition is provided by Ann Feldman in "Being Heard: Women Composers and Patrons at the 1893 World's Columbian Exposition," *Notes*, vol. 47, no. 1 (September, 1990), 7-20.

41. Ibid., 13-14.

42. Ibid., 16. This letter is undated, and is preserved among the Theodore Thomas Letters at the Newberry Library of Chicago.

43. Unpublished letter from Ingeborg von Bronsart to La Mara, from Munich, dated January 15, 1905; Leipzig, Stadtgeschichtliches Museum, La Mara-Nachlass, Rp. 5, Pianistinnen, 12, 8.

44. Unpublished letter from Ingeborg von Bronsart to La Mara, from Munich, dated December 2, 1902; Weimar, Stiftung Weimarer Klassik, Goethe- und Schiller-Archiv, Liszt-Nachlass, La Mara-Nachlass, 59/389, U9, 3, 2.

45. "Auch das Gedicht 'Letzte Bitte' — das mir so theuer ist — schwebt mir musikalisch im Geiste vor, doch fürchte ich, dass es für mich schwer sein wird es so wiederzugeben wie ich die Schönheit des Gedichtes empfinde — doch gebe ich die Hoffnung nicht auf, dass es mir dennoch einstens gelingen wird." Unpublished letter from Ingeborg von Bronsart to Ernst von Wildenbruch, from St. Andreasberg (am Harz), dated June 19, 1882; Weimar, Stiftung Weimarer Klassik, Goethe- und Schiller-Archiv, Wildenbruch-Nachlass, 94/160, 1, no. 2, 2-3.

46. "Dass auch die 'letzte Bitte' Ihre musikalische Phantasie beschäftigte, freut mich sehr; ich denke, dass dieses Lied, wenn der klangende Laut desselben getroffen wird gesungen äusserst wirksam sein müsste. Ob dasselbe nicht am Besten für Alt zu setzen wäre? Ich denke dabei an Marianne Brandt, die sich danach sehnt, dies Lied einmal zu singen." Copy of an unpublished letter from Ernst von Wildenbruch to Ingeborg von Bronsart, from Berlin, dated June 21, 1882; Weimar, Stiftung Weimarer Klassik, Goethe- und Schiller-Archiv, Wildenbruch-Nachlass, 94/298, 1, no. 1, 1-2.

47. Unpublished letter from Ingeborg von Bronsart to Ernst von Wildenbruch, from Hannover, dated September 26, 1882; Weimar, Stiftung Weimarer Klassik, Goethe- und Schiller-Archiv, Wildenbruch-Nachlass, 94/160, 1, no. 5, 1.

48. Unpublished letter from Ingeborg von Bronsart to La Mara, from Munich, dated December 2, 1902; Weimar, Stiftung Weimarer Klassik, Goethe- und Schiller-Archiv, Liszt-Nachlass, La Mara, 59/389, U9, 3, 2.

List of Works

Opera

Die Göttin von Sais oder Linas und Liane. Idyllic opera in 3 acts, text by Meyer. Premiere: Berlin, Kronprinzliches Palais, 1867. Libretto: Berlin, 1867.

Jery und Bätely. Singspiel in 1 act, text by Goethe. Premiere: Weimar, Court Theater, April 26, 1873. Full and vocal scores: Leipzig: Kahnt, 1876.

Hiarne. Opera in 3 acts, text by Hans von Bronsart and Friedrich Bodenstedt. Premiere: Berlin, Court Theater, February 14, 1891. Libretto: Weimar, 1896. Score never published.

Die Sühne. Music drama in 1 act, text by composer, based on Theodor Körner. Premiere: Dessau, Court Theater, April 12, 1909. Vocal score: Berlin: Harmonie, 1909.

Vocal Music

(all songs for voice and piano unless otherwise indicated)

Die Loreley [*sic*]. Text by Heine. Mainz: Schott, 1865.

Und ob der holde Tag vergangen (1870). Text by Sturm. Unpublished.

Drei Lieder. Mainz: Schott, 1871.
1. *Frisch auf zum letzten Kampf*. Text by Zeise
2. *Den Trauernden*. Text by Dunker
3. *Eil' hin mein Ross*. Text by Neubauer

Hurrah Germania! Chorus for male choir. Text by Freiligrath. Hannover: Pinkvoss, 1871.

Drei Lieder. Hannover: Nagel, 1872.
1. *Abendlied*. Text by Roquette
2. *Weisst du noch?* Text by Roquette
3. *Ich hab' im Traume geweinet*. Text by Heine

Kennst du die rothe Rose? Chorus for soloist, male choir, mixed choir. Berlin: Sulzer, 1873.

Fünf Lieder. Oldenburg: Schulze, 1878.
1. *Nachtgesang*. Text by Goethe
2. *Blumengruss*. Text by Goethe
3. *Ich liebe dich*. Text by Rückert
4. *Lass tief in dir mich lesen*. Text by Platen
5. *Du hast mit süssem Liedesklang*

Sechs Lieder des Mirza Schaffy, op. 8. Text by Friedrich Bodenstedt. Leipzig: Kahnt, 1879.
1. *Zuléikha*
2. *Im Garten klagt die Nachtigall*
3. *Wenn der Frühling auf die Berge steigt*
4. *Gelb rollt mir zu Füssen*
5. *Die helle Sonne leuchtet*
6. *Ich fühle deinen Odem*

"Hafisa": Drei Lieder des Mirza Schaffy, op. 9. Text by Friedrich Bodenstedt. Leipzig: Kahnt, 1879.
1. *Wenn zum Tanz die jungen Schönen*
2. *Neig', schöne Knospe, dich zu mir*
3. *O, wie mir schweren Dranges*

Sechs Gedichte, op. 10. Text by Friedrich Bodenstedt. Leipzig: Kahnt, 1879.
1. *Mir träumte einst ein schöner Traum*
2. *Abschied vom Kaukasus*
3. *Wie lächeln die Augen*
4. *Nachtigall, o Nachtigall*
5. *Das Vöglein*
6. *Sing', mit Sonnenaufgang singe*

Fünf Weihnachtslieder, op. 11. Text by Otto Jacobi. Oldenburg: Schulze, 1880.
1. *Es strahlt am Himmelsrande*
2. *Die Weisen brachten Gaben dir*
3. *Die Nacht ist aufgegangen*
4. *Ich sehe Lichter ohne Zahl*
5. *O neige deine Flügel*

Fünf Gedichte, op. 12. Text by Friedrich Bodenstedt. Oldenburg: Schulze, 1880.
1. *Mein Lebenslauf*
2. *Ständchen*
3. *Einst wollt' ich einen Kranz dir winden*
4. *Hier unter Rebenranken*
5. *In meinem Lebensringe*

Fünf Gedichte, op. 16. Text von Ernst von Wildenbruch. Breslau: Hainauer, 1882.
1. *Abendlied*
2. *Ständchen*
3. *Zwei Sträusse*
4. *Der Blumenstrauss*
5. *Letzte Bitte*

Zwölf Kinderreime, op. 17. Text by Klaus Groth. Leipzig: Georg Wigand, 1882.
1. *Ik weet en Leed, wat Niemand wee*
2. *Gnegelputt*
3. *En Vagel*
4. *Beim Baden*
5. *Hanz Danz*
6. *Puthöneken*
7. *Nachtleed*
8. *Matten Has'*
9. *Aantenleed*
10. *Zaunkönig*
11. *Bispill*
12. *Slapleed*

Sechs Gedichte, op. 20. Text by Lermontov. Leipzig: Kahnt, 1891.
1. *Liebesglück*
2. *Der Kosakin Wiegenlied*
3. *Das gelbe Blatt*
4. *Der Stern*
5. *Dein blaues Auge*
6. *Gebet*

Drei Gedichte, op. 22. Text by Peter Cornelius. Leipzig: Kahnt, 1891.
1. *Könnt' ich die schönsten Sträusse winden*
2. *Du meiner Seele schönster Traum*
3. *Ich möcht' ein Lied dir weihen*

Drei Lieder, op. 23. Berlin: Bote und Bock, 1892.
1. *Nähe des Geliebten.* Text by Goethe
2. *An die Entfernte.* Text by Lenau
3. *Aufschub der Trauer.* Text by Platen

Im Lenz (1898). Text by Paul Heyse. Unpublished.

Rappelle-toi!, op. 24. Text by Alfred de Musset. Leipzig: Breitkopf und Härtel, 1902.

Drei Lieder, op. 25. Leipzig: Breitkopf und Härtel, 1902.
1. *Sang wohl, sang das Vöglein.* Text by Friedrich Bodenstedt
2. *Heidenröslein.* Text by Goethe
3. *Ich stand in dunkeln Träumen.* Text by Heine

Abschied, op. 26. Text by Felix Dahn. Leipzig: Breitkopf und Härtel, 1902.

Osterlied, op. 27. Chorus for mixed choir. Text by Platen. Leipzig: Schuberth, 1903.

Lieder (ca. 1903). Text by Friedrich Bodenstedt. Unpublished.

Verwandlung (1910). Text by Paul Heyse. Unpublished.

Orchestral and Chamber Music

Piano Concerto in F minor (by 1863). Unpublished.

Kaiser Wilhelm March for orchestra. Berlin: Bote und Bock, 1872.

Romanze in A minor for violin and piano. Berlin: Sulzer, 1873.

Notturno in A minor, op. 13, for violoncello and piano. Leipzig: Breitkopf und Härtel, 1879.

Elegie in C major, op. 14, for violoncello and piano. Leipzig: Breitkopf und Härtel, 1879.

Romanze in B-flat major, op. 15, for violoncello and piano. Leipzig: Breitkopf und Härtel, 1879.

Phantasie, op. 21, for violin and piano. Leipzig: Kahnt, 1891.

Piano Music

Trois études. St. Petersburg: Bernard, 1855.

Nocturne. St. Petersburg: Bernard, 1855.

Tarantella. St. Petersburg: Bernard, 1855.

Fuge über die Namen Maria und Martha (von Sabinin) (by 1859). Unpublished.

Fugues (by 1859). Unpublished.

Variationen über Themen von Bach (by 1859). Unpublished.

Variations (by 1859). Unpublished.

Toccatas (by 1859). Unpublished.

Sonata (by 1859). Unpublished.

Kaiser Wilhelm March. Berlin: Bote und Bock, 1871.

Vier Clavierstücke. Mainz: Schott, 1874.
1. *Valse-Caprice in A major*
2. *Impromptu in F-sharp major*
3. *Wiegenlied in F-sharp major*
4. *Wiegenlied in A major*

Phantasie in G-sharp minor, op. 18. Leipzig: Breitkopf und Härtel, 1891.

Bibliography

Asmus, Wilhelm. "Ingeborg von Bronsart," *Neue Zeitschrift für Musik* 65 (1898): 193-95.

Bussmann, Walter. "Bronsart v. Schellendorf." In *Neue Deutsche Biographie*. Vol. 2. Berlin: Duncker & Humblot, 1955.

Crusen, Georg. "Ingeborg von Bronsart's *Hiarne* im Königlichen Theater zu Hannover," *Neue Zeitschrift für Musik* 59 (1892): 85-86.

Deaville, James. "Ingeborg von Bronsart." In *The New Grove Dictionary of Women Composers*. London: Macmillan, 1994. *Norton/Grove Dictionary of Women Composers*. New York: Norton, 1995.

Feldman, Ann. "Being Heard: Women Composers and Patrons at the 1893 World's Columbian Exposition," *Notes* 47 (1990): 7-20.

Jung, Hans Rudolf. "Bronsart v. Schellendorf." In *Die Musik in Geschichte und Gegenwart* 15 (supp.): cols. 1112-1113. Kassel: Bärenreiter, 1973.

La Mara [=Marie Lipsius]. "Ingeborg von Bronsart." In *Die Frauen im Tonleben der Gegenwart* (*Musikalische Studienköpfe*, vol. 5), 3rd ed. Leipzig: Breitkopf und Härtel, 1902.

Mendel, Herrmann. "Ingeborg von Bronsart." In *Musikalisches Conversations-Lexicon*. Vol. 2. Berlin: R. Oppenheim, 1872.

Michaelis, Alfred. "Ingeborg von Bronsart." In *Frauen als schaffende Tonkünstler: Ein biographisches Lexikon*. Leipzig: A. Michaelis, 1888.

Morsch, Anna. "Ingeborg von Bronsart," *Gesangspädagogische Blätter* 4 (1910): 100-102.

Neitzel, Otto. "Ingeborg von Bronsart," undated, unidentified published biographical sketch.

Pohl, Richard. "Die 14. Tonkünstler-Versammlung des Allgemeinen Deutschen Musikvereins," *Neue Zeitschrift für Musik* 44 (1877): 233-34.

Polko, Elise. "Ingeborg von Bronsart: Biographisches Skizzenblatt," *Neue Musik-Zeitung* 9 (1888): 142-43.

Simon, Paul. "Hiarne," *Neue Zeitschrift für Musik* 57 (1890): 553-55.

Simon, Paul. "Die erste Aufführung der Oper Hiarne von Frau Ingeborg von Bronsart im Königl. Opernhause zu Berlin," *Neue Zeitschrift für Musik* 58 (1891): 87.

Spanuth, August. "*Die Sühne*," *Signale* 67 (1909): 550-52.

Weissweiler, Eva. *Komponistinnen aus 500 Jahren: Eine Kultur- und Wirkungsgeschichte in Biografien und Werkbeispielen*. Frankfurt am Main: Fischer, 1981.

Discography

Vier Clavierstücke. Recording of No. 1, *Valse-Caprice in A major*, on Turnabout TV 34685 (1979), *Piano Works by Women Composers*, Rosario Marciano, piano.

Jery und Bätely. Recording of *Endlich, endlich darf ich hoffen* and *Liebe! Liebe! hast du uns verbunden*, on Gemini Hall Records RAP 1010 (1975), *Woman's Work: Works by Famous Women Composers*, Berenice Branson, soprano, and Michael May, piano.

Editorial Comments

This edition represents a re-engraving of the first editions of all songs except the last, which is the first publication of the song fromthe autograph preserved in the Abteilung für Handschriften und seltene Drucke of the Bayerische Staatsbibliothek (*Verwandlung* is reproduced with their kind permission). The absence of autographs for the five published songs means that those first editions, which appeared during the composer's lifetime, must be taken as definitive, especially in the absence of contradictory indications in Bronsart's correspondence. The edition reproduces the primary sources in all details, including performance indications and pedaling. Obvious minor printing errors are corrected and missing accidentals added without further commentary, while editorial additions are indicated within square brackets. The first editions or (in the case of *Verwandlung*) the autograph are the sole sources for the occasional fingerings in the piano part.

Frisch auf, zum letzten Kampf und Streit!

Frisch auf zum letzten Kampf und Streit Ihr Männer alt' und Knaben, Frankreich will Deutschlands Herrlichkeit Vernichten und begraben.	Courage for the final battle and struggle, You old men and boys, France desires to destroy And bury Germany's splendor.
Rasch nehmt die Büchsen von der Wand, Die scharfen Schwerter nehmt zur Hand, Frankreich will Deutschlands Herrlichkeit Vernichten und begraben!	Quickly take your rifles from the wall, Take your sharp swords in your hand, France desires to destroy And bury Germany's splendor.
Nicht gilt's allein dem deutschen Rhein, Das Höchste gilt's erraffen. Ganz Deutschland strahlt in Waffenschein, Das Volk in Wehr und Waffen.	It is not only the German Rhine, It is about capturing the highest, All of Germany radiates the shine of weapons, The people fully armed.
Es blitzt in jeder Hand das Schwert, Wir kämpfen treu für Haus und Heerd. Ganz Deutschland strahlt in Waffenschein, Das Volk in Wehr und Waffen!	The sword flashes in every hand, We fight faithfully for hearth and home, All of Germany radiates the shine of weapons, The people fully armed.
Nicht unsrer Brust glüht Zorn und Hass, Es gilt die Gluth zu kühlen, Den Spartern gleich am Felsenpass Der stolzen Thermopylen.	In our breasts glow anger and hate, It is a matter of cooling the passion Of the Spartans right at the mountain pass Of the proud Thermopylaeans.
Und naht sich der Franzosen Heer, Den Persern gleich, wie Sand am Meer, Wir schützen treu ohn' Unterlass Die deutschen Thermopylen!	And if the French army approached, As innumerable as the Persians, We will faithfully and unceasingly Protect the German Thermopyles!
Frisch in den Kampf, die Trommeln rührt, Und Herz und Arm erhoben, Der greise Heldenkaiser führt Uns stolz in's Schlachtentoben.	On to the battle, the drums beaten, And heart and arm lifted, The old hero-emperor leads Us proudly into the tumult of battle.

Wir folgen seinem Wink der Hand Zum Kampf für Gott und Vaterland. Frisch in den Kampf, die Trommeln rührt, Und Herz und Arm erhoben!	We follow the wave of his hand Into the battle for God and the fatherland. On to the battle, the drums beaten, And heart and arm lifted!
Und wer da fällt im Kampf als Held Für uns're heil'ge Sache, An dessen Wahlplatz steht und hält Die deutsche Ehre Wache.	And he who heroically falls in battle For our holy cause, Stands in his place of choice And German honor stands guard.
O Vaterland, nimm unser Blut, Wir kämpfen für das höchste Gut, Du Gott, hoch über'm Sternenzelt, Schirm' Deutschlands heil'ge Sache, Schirm' Deutschlands heil'ge Sache!	O Fatherland, take our blood, We fight for the highest good, God, high over heaven's vault, Protect Germany's holy cause, Protect Germany's holy cause!

Blumengruss

Der Strauss, den ich gepflücket, Grüsse dich viel tausend mal! Ich habe mich oft gebücket, Ach, wohl ein tausend mal, Und ihn an's Herz gedrücket Wie hunderttausend mal!	The wreath that I picked Greets you a thousand times! I have often bent over Ah, indeed, a thousand times, And pressed it to my heart As if one hundred thousand times.

Letzte Bitte

Wenn du mich einstmals verlassen wird, Künd' es nicht vorher mir an, Plötzlich thu's, so ist es gescheh'n, Plötzlich sterbe ich dann.	If you were once to leave me, Don't tell it to me in advance, Do it quickly, then it has happened, I will then quickly die.
Wenn dann mein Bildniss dir wiederkehrt, Das du vor Zeiten geliebt, Wenn es wie ein verdorrtes Blatt Dir vom Baum der Erinnerung stiebt,	When you see again my picture, Which you loved at one time, When like a dried out leaf It flies about you from the tree of memory,
Hebe, ach hebe dann nicht den Fuss, Stosse es nicht von dir fort, Leise rauschend ertönen wird's, Leise rauschend ertönen wird's, Wie ein verklungenes Wort, Wie ein verklungenes Wort.	Do not lift your foot, Do not kick it away from you, It will sound, softly rustling, It will sound, softly rustling, Like a word that died away, Like a word that died away.
Thätest du's ach, du thätest nicht recht, Nimmer verdient' ich's um dich Wenden würd' ich mich tief, tief ins Grab, Weinen, weinen bitterlich, weinen, weinen bitterlich.	If you do so, you wouldn't do right, I never deserved it from you, I would turn deep, deep in my grave and bitterly cry, cry, and bitterly cry, cry.

Ik weet en Leed, wat Niemand weet

[1] Ik weet en Leed, wat Niemand weet,
Dat lehr ik vun Klaus Groth:
Ik schull min Hanna den Strump opbinn,
Un kreeg er, un kreeg er bi den Foot, ja, ja,
Un kreeg er bi den Foot.

[2] Ich weiss ein Lied, was Niemand weiss,
Das lernt ich von Klaus Groth:
Ich sollt' meiner Hanna den Strumpf aufbinden
Und fasste sie, und fasste sie am Fuss, ja, ja,
Und fasste sie am Fuss.

[3] I know a song that no one knows,
I learned it from Claus Groth:
I am supposed to help Hanne put on her stockings
And touched her, touched her on the foot.
Yes, yes, and touched her on the foot.

Ich stand in dunkeln Träumen

Ich stand in dunkeln Träumen
Und starrte ihr Bildnis an,
Und das geliebte Antlitz
Heimlich zu leben begann.

Um ihre Lippen zog sich
Ein Lächeln wunderbar,
Und wie von Wehmutstränen
Erglänzte ihr Augenpaar.

Auch meine Tränen flossen
Mir von den Wangen herab
Und ach, ich kann es night glauben,
Dass ich dich verloren hab'!

I was darkly dreaming
And stared at her picture,
And the beloved face
Mysteriously began to live.

There formed around her lips
A wonderful smile,
And her pair of eyes sparkled
As from tears of longing.

My tears also flowed
Down my cheeks,
And ah, I cannot believe it,
That I have lost you.

Verwandlung

Mühlen träg die Flügel drehn,
Über die Stoppeln schleicht der Wind,
Dunkle Hütten im Grunde stehn,
Kleine Fenster trüb und blind.

Sieh, da kommt ein Sonnenschein,
Stiehlt sich durchs Gewölk heran:
Mühlen, Feld und Fensterlein
Fangen flugs zu lachen an.

Liebes Herz, so bist du ganz,
Blöd und blind viel Tag und Nacht,
Bis ein leiser Liebesglanz
Dir die Welt zum Himmel macht.

Mills slowly turn their wheels,
The wind lazes over the stubble,
Dark cottages stand in the forest,
Small windows, opaque and unseeing.

Look, there comes a ray of sunshine,
Which sneaks up through the clouds:
Mills, field, and little window
At once begin to laugh.

Dear heart, thus you are wholly,
Stupid and blind many a day and night,
Until a soft gleam of love
Makes the world your heaven.

Translations by James Deaville

Frisch auf, zum letzten Kampf und Streit!

Heinrich Zeise

Ingeborg von Bronsart
James Deaville, editor

Allegro moderato

f

Frisch auf zum letz - ten Kampf und Streit ihr Män - ner alt' und Kna - ben, Frank - reich will Deutsch - lands Herr - lich - keit ver - nich - ten und be - gra - ben.

rit. *f* **[a tempo]**

Rasch nehmt die Büch - sen von der Wand, die

cresc. *marc.*

20
poco rit.
[a tempo]
schar - fen Schwer - ter nehmt zur Hand. Frank - reich will Deutsch-lands Herr - lich -
24
keit ver - nich - ten und be - gra - ben! Nicht
29
gilt's al - lein dem deut - schen Rhein, das Höch-ste gilt's er - raf - fen, ganz Deutsch-land
uns - rer Brust glüht Zorn und Hass, es gilt die Gluth zu küh - len, den Spar - tern
34
strahlt in Waf-fen - schein, das Volk in Wehr und Waf - fen.
gleich am Fel-sen - pass der stol - zen Ther - mo - py - len.

39
rit.
f
[a tempo]
Es blitzt in je-der Hand das Schwert, wir
Und naht sich der Fran-zo-sen Heer, den
cresc.
f
44
poco rit.
[a tempo]
f
käm-pfen treu für Haus und Heerd. Ganz Deutsch-land strahlt in Waf-fen-schein,
Per-sern gleich, wie Sand am Meer, wir schüt-zen treu ohn' Un-ter-lass
f
49
1.
2.
das Volk in Wehr und Waf-fen! In
die deut-schen Ther-mo-py-len!
3
f
f
55
f
poco rit.:
più p
Frisch in den Kampf, die Trom-meln rührt, und Herz und Arm er-ho-ben, der
più p

60
il tempo
più f
rit.
f
dim.
[a tempo]
p
grei - se Hel-den - kai - ser führt uns stolz in's Schlach-ten - to-ben. Wir fol - gen sei-nem
più f
f
p
65
poco più f
rit.
ten.
a tempo, risoluto
f
Wink der Hand zum Kampf für Gott und Va-ter-land. Frisch in den Kampf, die Trom-meln
ten.
poco più f
ten.
f
70
allargando
f
[a tempo]
rührt, und Herz und Arm er - ho - ben!
f
f
76
un poco rit.: il tempo
f
più p
Und wer da fällt im Kampf als Held für uns're heil' - ge Sa - che, an
più p

81
più f
rit.
f
dim. p
[a tempo]
des - sen Wahl-platz steht und hält die deut-sche Eh - re Wa-che. O Va - ter-land nimm
86
poco più f
rit.
ten.
a tempo
mf
un - ser Blut, wir käm-pfen für das höch-ste Gut, Du Gott, hoch ü-ber'm Ster-nen -
91
f
zelt, schirm' Deutsch-lands heil'-ge Sa - che, schirm'
marc.
96
rit.
[a tempo]
Deutsch-lands heil' - ge Sa - che!

Blumengruss

Johann Wolfgang von Goethe

Ingeborg von Bronsart
James Deaville, editor

Allegretto espressivo

[*mp*]

Der Strauss, den ich _ ge - pflü - cket,

mp

5

grü - sse dich viel tau - send mal! Ich ha - be mich oft _ ge -

8

poco rit. *cresc.* **Più lento** **Tempo I**

bü - cket, ach, wohl ein tau - send mal, und ihn an's Herz _ ge -

cresc.

12

poco rit. **Più lento** *f* *ten.* **Tempo I**

drü - cket wie hun - dert - tau - send mal!

ten.

f *ten.* *mp* *p*

Letzte Bitte

Ernst von Wildenbruch

Ingeborg von Bronsart
James Deaville, editor

Andante molto rit. [a tempo]

Wenn du mich einst-mals ver-las-sen wirst,—

mf dim. mp più f mp Ped. ❊ Ped. ❊

4

più p mf f meno f rit.

künd' es nicht vor-her mir an, plötz-lich thu's, so ist es ge-

espr. mp più f f Ped. ❊ Ped. ❊

8

rit. a tempo rit.

più p dim. p

scheh'n, plötz-lich ster-be ich dann.

espr. mf più p dim. mp p mp espr. dim. ten. Ped. Ped. ❊ Ped. ❊ Ped. ❊

13
a tempo
Wenn dann mein Bild - niss dir wie - der - kehrt,
espr.
mp
Ped.
Ped.
Ped.
Ped.

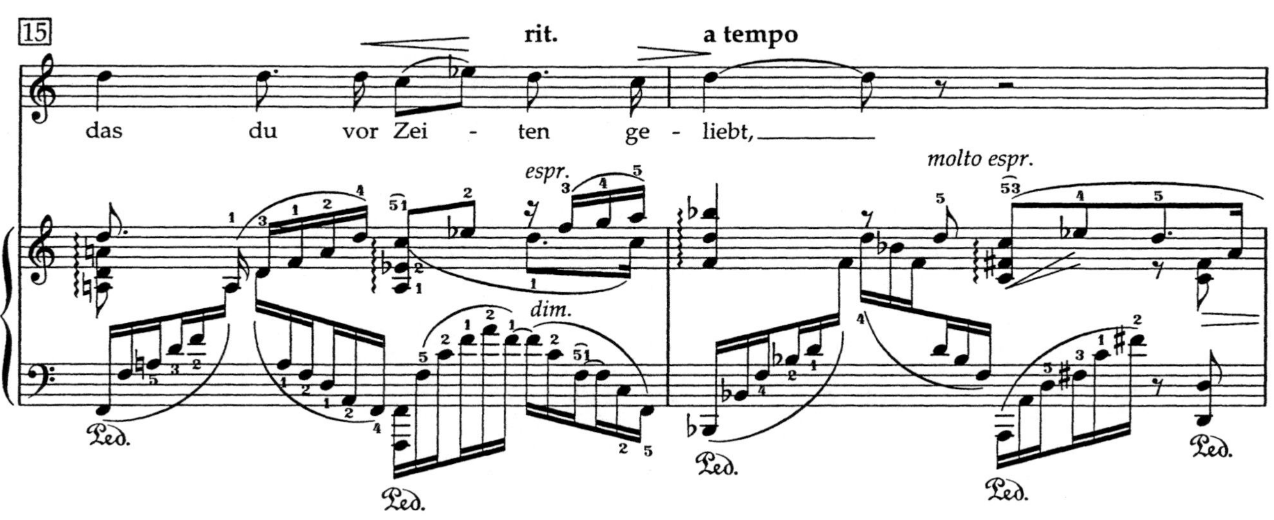
15
rit.
a tempo
das du vor Zei - ten ge - liebt,
espr.
dim.
molto espr.
Ped.
Ped.
Ped.
Ped.
Ped.

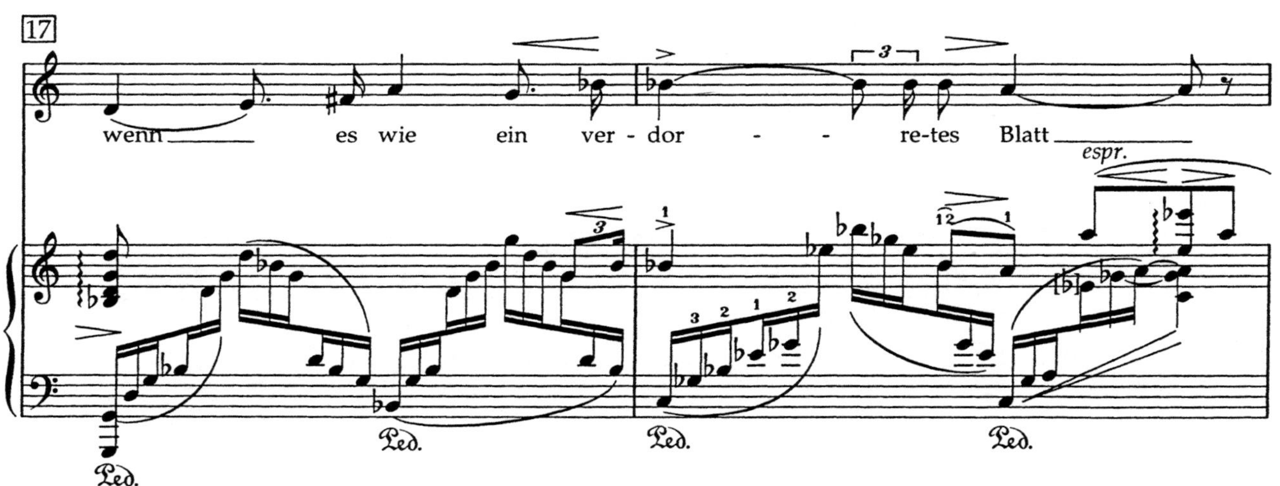
17
wenn es wie ein ver - dor - - re-tes Blatt
espr.
Ped.
Ped.
Ped.
Ped.

19
molto rit.
più p
dim.
a tempo
dir vom Baum der Er-in-ner-ung stiebt,
espr.
cresc.
più p
dim. molto
con espressione
pp
poco più f
21
rit.
più f
p
pp
espr.
23
Un poco più moderato il tempo
mp
più p
he-be, ach he-be dann nicht den Fuss, sto-sse es nicht von dir fort,
mp
più p
25
Meno moderato (il tempo come prima)
poco rit.
lei - se rau - schend er - tö - - - nen wird's,
espr.
p dolciss.

27
a tempo
rit.
lei - se rau - schend er - tö - - - nen wird's,
molto espr.
cresc.
dim.
29
a tempo
wie ein ver - klun - ge - nes Wort,
p
pp
31
meno p
wie ein ver - klun - ge - nes Wort.
p
dim.
pp
33
molto rit.
dim.
ppp
mf
mp
[Ped.]

35
[a tempo]
Thä - test du's ach, du thä - test nicht recht, nim-mer ver-dient' ich's um
38
dich wen - den würd' ich mich tief, tief im
41
Grab, wei-nen, wei-nen bit - ter-lich,
44
a tempo
rit. molto
a tempo
rit.
wei - nen, wei-nen bit - ter-lich.
ben tenuto

Ik weet en Leed, wat Niemand weet

Claus Groth

Ingeborg von Bronsart
James Deaville, editor

Ich stand in dunkeln Träumen

Heinrich Heine

Ingeborg von Bronsart

James Deaville, editor

13
riten.
più p
pp
16
L'istesso tempo
p
Um ih - re Lip - pen zog sich ein
19
rit.
a tempo
poco più f
Lä - cheln wun - der - bar, und wie von Weh - muts-
poco più f
22
mf
rit.
trä - nen er - glänz - te ihr Au - gen-

25
Poco più lento
rit.
a tempo
paar.
Auch mei - ne Trä - nen
flos - sen
molto espr.
28
cresc.
poco accel.
mir von den Wan - gen her - ab
und
ach, ich kann es nicht glau-ben,
und
espr.
cresc.
dim.
rit. molto
31
cresc.
ten.
mp
ach,
ich kann es nicht glau - ben,
dass
ich dich ver -
cresc.
33
rit.
dim.
ten.
a tempo
rit.
lo - ren hab'!
ten.
dim.
dim.
ten.
pp

Verwandlung

Paul Heyse

Ingeborg von Bronsart
James Deaville, editor

9
rit.
trüb und blind.
ten.
p
poco più f
rit. e dim.
p
ten.
Ped.
Ped.
Ped.
Ped.

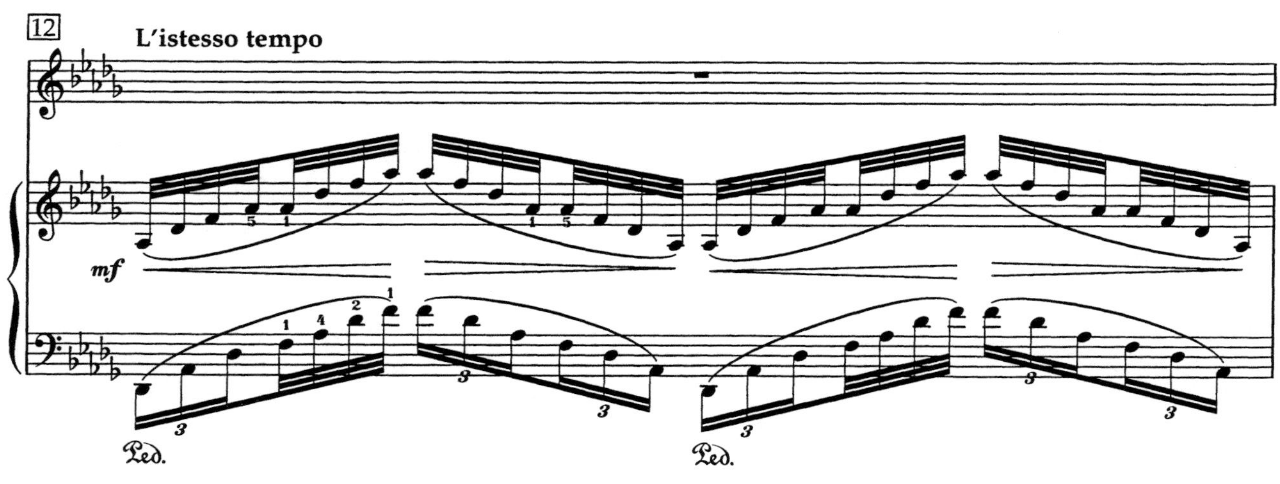
12
L'istesso tempo
mf
Ped.
Ped.

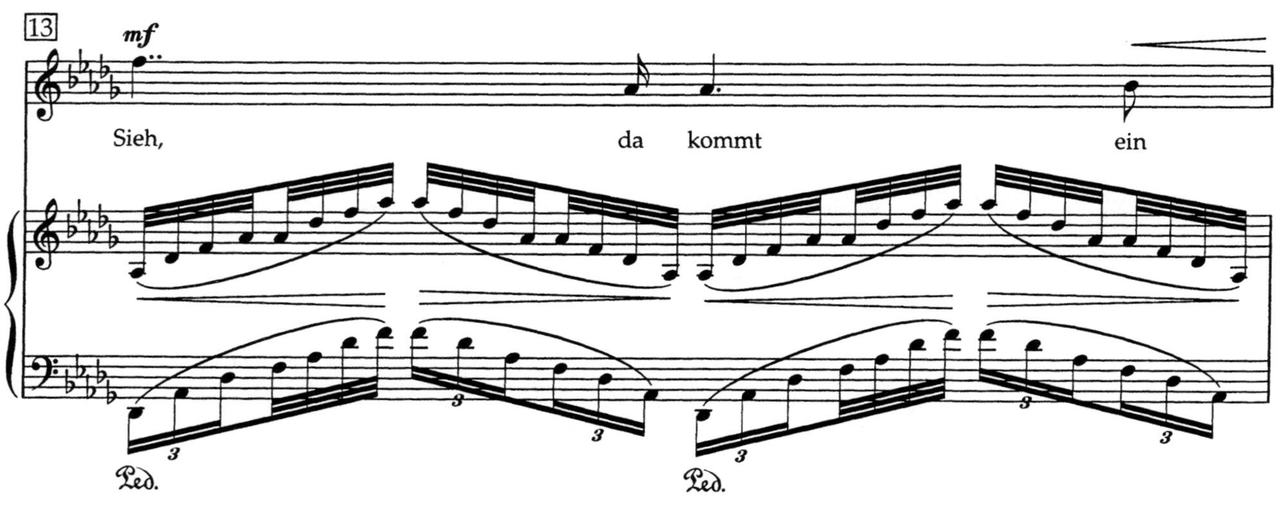
13
mf
Sieh, da kommt ein
Ped.
Ped.

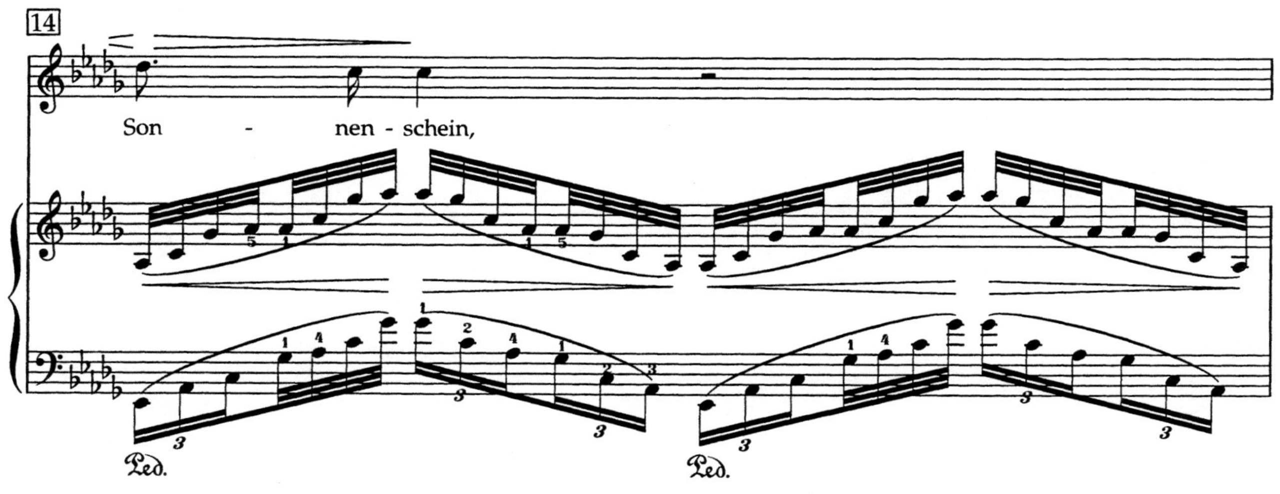
14
Son - nen - schein,
Ped.
Ped.

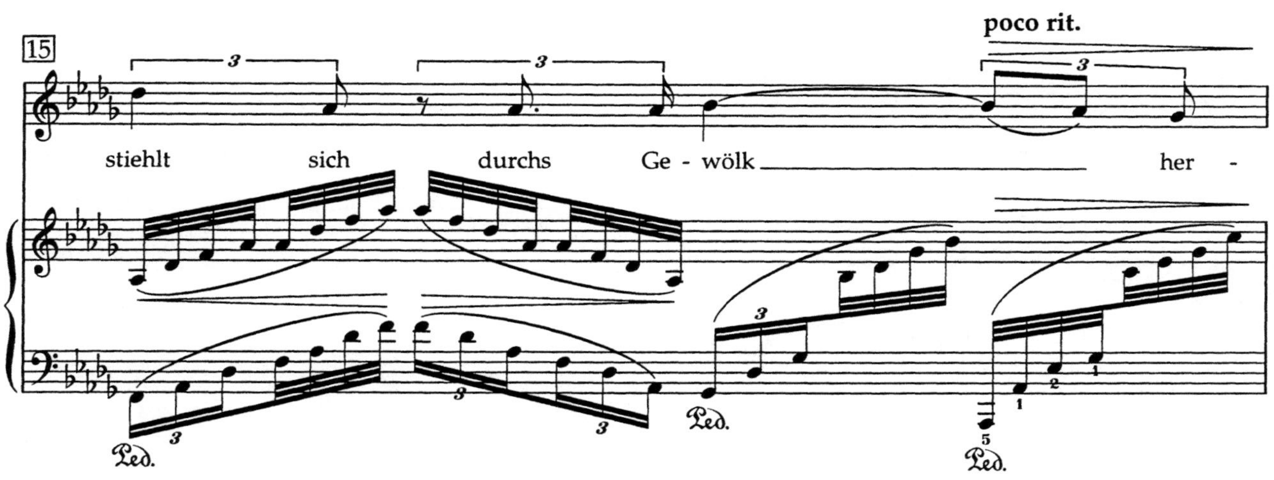
15
poco rit.
stiehlt sich durchs Ge - wölk her -
Ped.
Ped.
Ped.

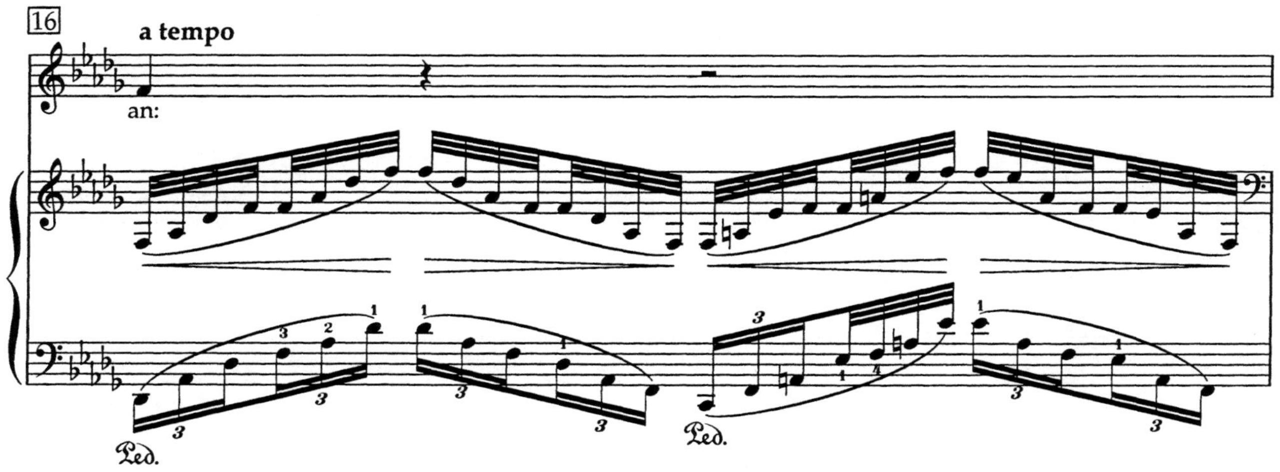
16
a tempo
an:
Ped.
Ped.

17
Müh - - - len, Feld und
Ped.
Ped.

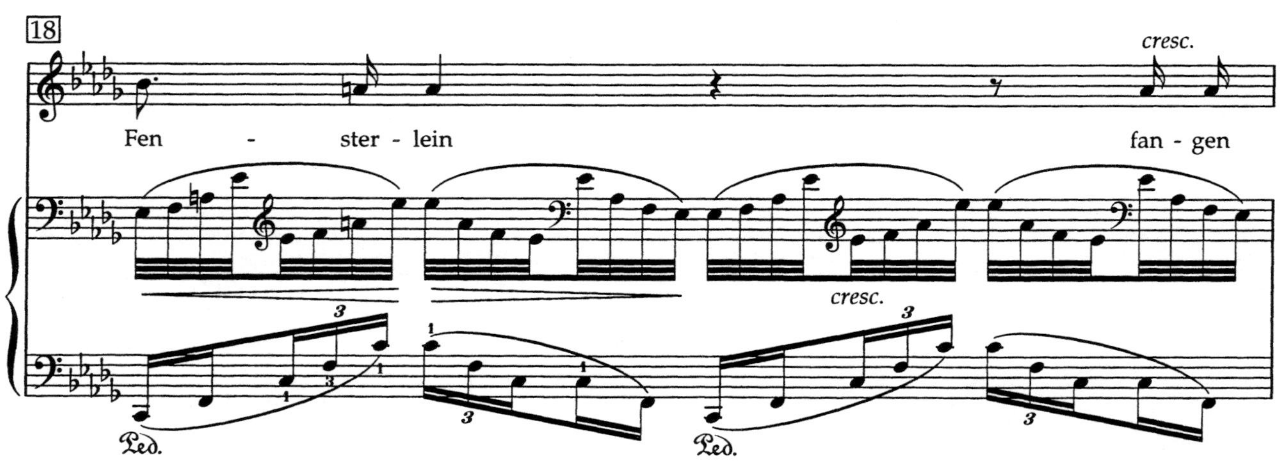
18
cresc.
Fen - ster - lein fan - gen
cresc.
Ped.
Ped.

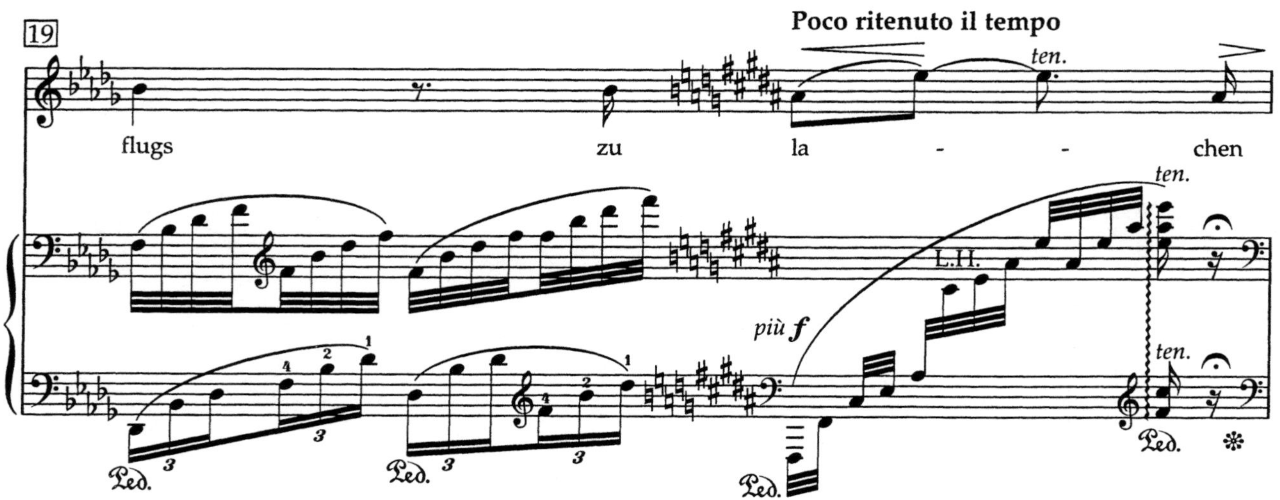
19
Poco ritenuto il tempo
ten.
flugs zu la - - chen
ten.
L.H.
più f
ten.
Ped.
Ped.
Ped.
Ped.

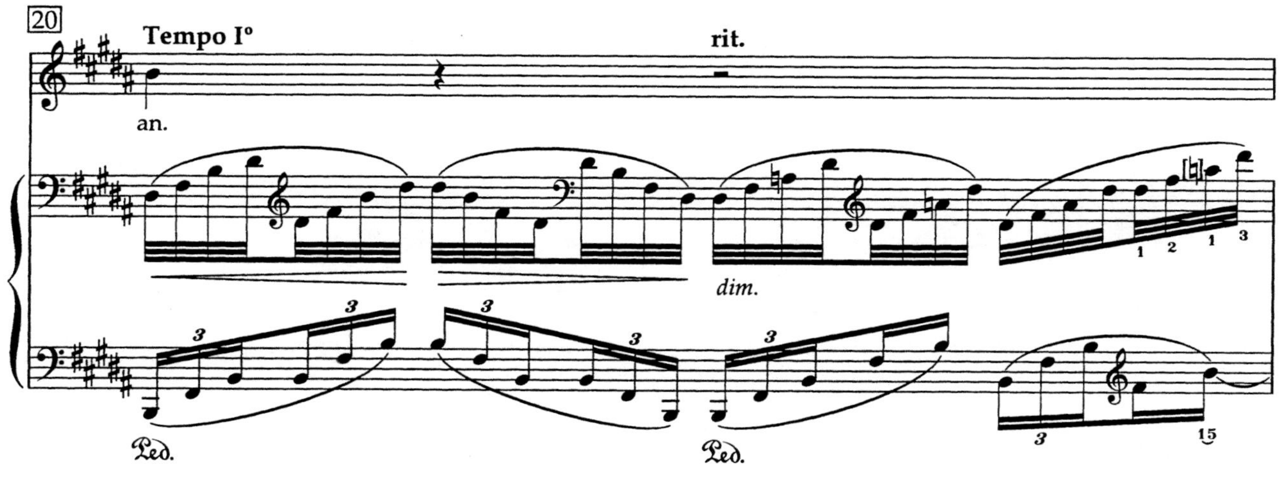
20
Tempo I°
rit.
an.
dim.
Ped.
Ped.

21
Un poco più lento
mp
Lie - bes Herz, so bist Du ganz,
ten.
p
mf
mp
Ped. Ped.
Ped.
Ped.

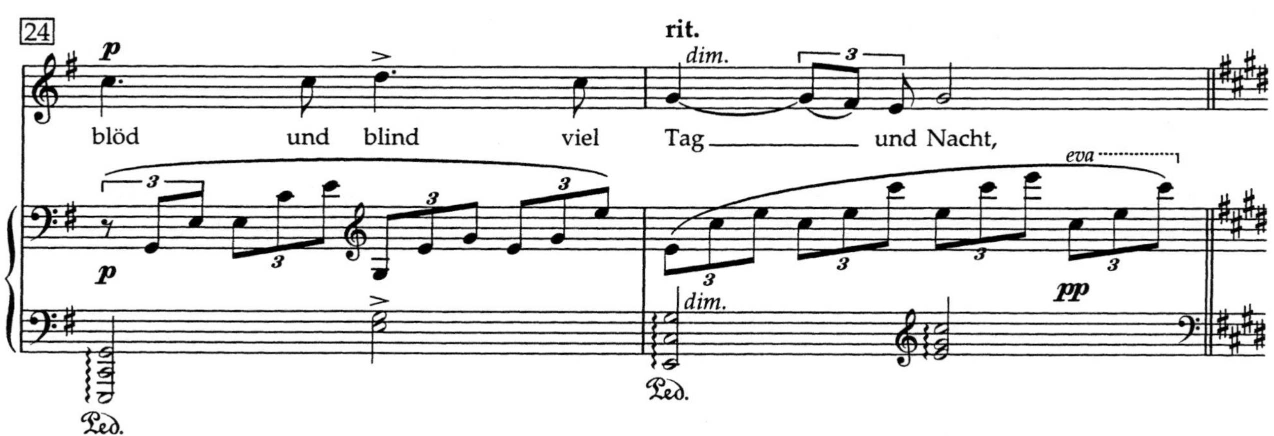
24
p
rit.
dim.
blöd und blind viel Tag und Nacht,
eva
p
dim.
pp
Ped.
Ped.

26
Con più di moto
bis ein lei - ser Lie - - - - bes-
mf
28
rit.
a tempo
cresc.
glanz
Dir die Welt zum
più f
30
f
ten.
Him - - - - - - - - - mel
8va
31
poco rit.
macht.
mf
mp
L.H.
mf

Louise Héritte-Viardot

(1841–1918)

JAMÉE ARD AND MARTHA FURMAN SCHLEIFER

Louise Héritte-Viardot was the first child of mezzo-soprano Pauline Viardot (see this volume) and Louis Viardot (1800–1883), author, opera impresario and art connoisseur. She was born on December 14, 1841, in Paris, the second year of the marriage that joined these two illustrious figures of Parisian musical and intellectual circles. Her sisters, Claudie (Chamerot) (1852–1914) and Marianne (Duvernoy) (1854– ?), were born ten and twelve years later; her brother Paul was born in 1857 (d. 1941) and became a renowned violinist.

Pauline Viardot, only twenty years old when Héritte-Viardot was born, was deeply engrossed in her international singing career. The child was often left in the care of her maternal grandmother, nannies or friends of the Viardots when her mother traveled abroad for performances.[1] This situation caused Héritte-Viardot's relationship with her parents to be strained. From the age of six to thirteen she attended a boarding school in Paris. Héritte-Viardot wrote that she was taught solfeggio by a Spanish friend of her grandmother, Torre Morrell (n.d.), and theory by Barbereau (n.d).[2] On her own she studied string quartets and read Berlioz' "Traité d'instrumentation".

Weekly soirées at the Viardot home hosted many of the most influential and creative people in early nineteenth-century Parisian society including musicians Hector Berlioz (1803–1869), Fryderyk Chopin (1810–1849), Charles Gounod (1818–1893), Henri Vieuxtemps (1820–1881), Camille Saint-Saëns (1835–1921); painters Ary Scheffer (1795–1858) and Henri Martin (1810–1883); and writers George Sand (pseudonym for Armandine Lucile Aurore Dudevant (1804–1876)), and Charles Dickens (1812– 1870).

Despite her lack of formal training Héritte-Viardot submitted her cantata *Das Bacchusfest* to the Prix de la ville de Paris where she was one of two finalists. (The other was *Tasso* by Benjamin Godard [1849–1895]). She relates in her memoirs that she was later told the jury decided not to award her the grand prize because "We can't possibly give the prize to this work. I [a juror] know the writing. It's by a woman, and it would be a disgrace to us if we awarded the prize to a woman."[3]

In 1862, Héritte-Viardot married M. Ernest Héritte, an employee of the diplomatic service twenty years her senior. They initially made their home in Berne, Switzerland. M. Ernest's next assignment was in Capetown, South Africa; their son was born shortly before the move. While there, Héritte-Viardot led an eclectic life of hunting, training and riding horses, and formed an amateur choral society.

Héritte-Viardot left her husband in 1865 and returned to her parents, now living in Baden-Baden, where their home continued to be the meeting place of composers, authors, performers and artists. There she met Anton Rubinstein (1829–1894) who recommended her to the Grand Duchess Helena of Russia, founder of the Saint Petersburg Conservatoire (Russia). (Rubinstein had been the director there from 1862–1867). During Héritte-Viardot's tenure the faculty at the Conservatoire included Henryk Wieniawski (1835–1880), Carl Czerny (1791–1857), Leopold Auer (1845–1930), and Karl Davidoff (1838–1889). St. Petersburg Grand Duchess Helena asked Héritte-Viardot to continue her mother Pauline's tradition of organizing weekly concerts in the palace. Héritte-Viardot's first concert was the presentation of *Acis and Galatea* by Georg Friedrich Händel (1685–1759).[4] While in Russia, Louise developed her interest in color relationships to keys and days of the week. The colors listed in italics in the following chart were definite in her mind.

Major	Minor
C, *white*	C, *brown*
D, terracotta	D, nut brown
E, *deep blue*	E *grey*
E-flat flat, *sky blue*	
F, bright violet	F, shining *black*
G, *red*	G, *yellow*
A, grass green	A, pearl grey
A-flat, *deep velvety green*	
B-flat, copper	
B, gold	B, color of an Havannah cigar
D-flat, a lovely *garnet*	C-sharp, and F-sharp are very *dark* or quite *black*[5]

"Now I must mention something so strange that it sounds almost ridiculous. The keys signify the days of the week to me. c major is Sunday, a major is quite certainly Monday, f major is Tuesday, d major is Wednesday, g major is Thursday, d minor is Friday, b major is Saturday."[6]

Héritte-Viardot befriended the composer Alexander Nikolaevich Serov (1820–1871)[7] whose widow, Valentina Semenova Bergmann Serov (1846–1927), later convinced her to pursue a career singing Russian opera. Relinquishing her post at the Conservatoire, Héritte-Viardot made her debut at the Imperial Opera in Serov's *Rogneda* on five day's notice.

Forced to stop singing as a result of severe bronchitis, Héritte-Viardot left Russia in 1871 and went to the Geneva Academy becoming one of the first women to study there. She took courses in physiology, anatomy, zoology, and literature, and then traveled through Dresden, Paris, Carlsbad, Finland and Stockholm, where she remained from 1872–1875. Héritte-Viardot also visited Italy for the first time during this period. In order to earn money she presented chamber concerts, coached opera singers, and conducted a performance of her cantata, *Das Bacchusfest*, written years earlier for the competition in Paris. Héritte-Viardot became ill again in Sweden and "For a long time I was very depressed, till one fine day a desire to compose overcame me and I was saved. I could earn my living by teaching, and compose to satisfy the cravings of my soul."[8]

Upon her return to Paris she met Eduard Lassen (1830–1904), the court music director in Weimar from 1858–1895. He arranged a performance of her opera *Lindoro* in Weimar and while she was there she spent a great deal of time with Franz Liszt (1811–1886). He had planned to conduct her cantata *The Cloud of Fire* (text by Victor Hugo) at the Tonkünstlerverein festival, but he died before the performance could take place. "This and the affair of the *Prix de la Ville de Paris . . . were the severest disappointments in my* musical career, and I learnt by bitter experience that luck is just as necessary for getting on as talent."[9]

In a subsequent railroad accident in the late 1880s Héritte-Viardot injured her arm, preventing her from playing the piano or giving lessons. "I was not idle during my enforced rest, for I composed a great deal — trios, quartets, plays without words, and a number of songs. I have composed over 300 works, and I suppose they will all be published in good time, though I care very little about it."[10]

She spent some time in Frankfurt teaching singing at the Hoch Conservatoire. "My greatest pleasure was my friendship with Clara Schumann [1819–1896, see this volume], who had known me since birth, [and] with Brahms, when he came to see her. . . ."[11] Héritte-Viardot next moved to Berlin where she founded an operatic school that she ran for two years before returning to Paris. From 1891–1904, she taught in London and finally settled in Heidelberg in 1904 where she remained until her death on January 17, 1918.

The song *Sérénade* was published in 1876 by Heugel. Its formal simplicity "ABAB" outlines the four stanzas of text. The accompaniment has moments of complexity and dense texture but generally remains subservient to the straightforward vocal line, which lies in a moderate range. Very much in keeping with the *romances* written in France in the early nineteenth century, word painting and textual illumination is subtle, and vocal lines are pleasing for voice and ear. Harmonically, the piece is uncomplicated. The "A" sections are in A major, and A minor is touched upon in the second and fourth stanzas.

Notes

1. Louise had spent so much time as an infant with George Sand that she called her "Maman." See April Fitzlyon, *The Price of Genius* (New York: Appleton-Century, 1964), 132.

2. Louise Héritte-Viardot, *Memories and Adventures* (New York: Da Capo Press, 1978), 32-34. See also, Fitzlyon, *The Price of Genius*, 326, who characterizes Louise's musical education as "superficial."

3. Ibid., 108.

4. Ibid., 147.

5. Ibid., 215.

6. Ibid., 216.

7. Alexander Serov, the father of the famous painter, was a composer and critic, whose writings both literary and musical were modeled on those of Richard Wagner.

8. Viardot, *Memories*, 230.

9. Ibid., 242.

10. Ibid., 249.

11. Ibid.

Selected List of Works

Vocal

Drei Lieder. Germany: Kahn, n.d.
Arme kleine Liebe
Tag und Nacht
Unter'm Machendelbaum

Listen a Minute. London: Boosey, n.d.

Lullaby. New York: Leonard, n.d.

Nineteenth-Century French Art Songs. Bryn Mawr, PA: Hildegard Publishing Company, 2001. Songs by various composers, includes *Sérénade*.

Praises (for voice, piano, violin or cello). London: Ditson, n.d.

Sechs lieder. Unpublished.

Sérénade. Paris: Heugel, n.d.

Seven Lieder. Text by Anna Ritter. Bryn Mawr, PA: Hildegard Publishing Company, 1998.

1. *In verschwiegener Nacht*
2. *Mein Falke*
3. *Erlösung*
4. *Schlimme Zeichen*
5. *Ich glaub', lieber Schatz*
6. *Wen die Sterne scheinen*
7. *Sehnsucht*

Shower of Blossoms. London: Ditson, n.d.

Spinning Song. London: Ditson, n.d.

Vers le sud. Paris: Heugel, n.d.

Operas

Lindoro (1879). Text by E. Dohm. Unpublished.

Cantatas

Die Bajadere. Unpublished.

Das Bacchussfest (1880?). Unpublished.

Cain. Unpublished.

The Cloud of Fire. (Text by Victor Hugo). Unpublished.

Wonne des Himmels. Germany: C. F. Kahnt, n.d.

Piano

Sonata (2 pianos). Unpublished.

In Gondola. London: Novell & Company, n.d.

Sérénade. Paris: Heugel, n.d.

Chamber Music

Piano Quartet, op.9 (*Im Sommer*). Bryn Mawr, PA: Hildegard Publishing Company, 1995.

Sonata, op. 40 (violin and piano). Leipzig: Hofmeister, 1909.

Spanisches Quartette, op. 11. Leipzig: Peters, 1883; Bryn Mawr, PA: Hildegard Publishing Company, 1997.

Unpublished Chamber Music

Four string quartets

Third piano quartet

Two piano trios

Bibliography

Ard, Jamée and April Fitzlyon. "Viardot [née Garcia], (Michelle Ferdinande) Pauline." In *The New Grove Dictionary of Women Composers*. London: The Macmillan Press Limited, 1994.

Association des Amis d'Ivan Tourgueniev. Pauline Viardot et Maria Malibran. *Cahiers Ivan Tourgueniev, Pauline Viardot et Maria Malibran*. Paris: UNESCO, 1977– .

Baker's Biographical Dictionary. Eighth Edition. New York: Schirmer Books, 1992.

Barry, Nichole. *Pauline Viardot: L'Egérie de George Sand et de Tourgueniev*, Paris: Flammarion, 1990.

Cohen, Aaron. *International Encyclopedia of Women Composers*, 2nd edition. New York: Books & Music, Inc., 1987.

Dictionnaire des musicians français. Paris: Seghers, 1961.

Fétis, F. *Biographie universelle des musicians et bibliographie génerale de la musique*, second edition. Paris: Firm in Didot Frères, 1866-1870. Reprint., Brussels: Culture et Civilisation, 1972.

Fischer-Dieskau, Dietrich. *Wenn Musik der Liebe Nahrung ist*. Stuttgart: Deutsch Verlags- Abstalt, 1990.

Fitzlyon, April. *The Price of Genius: a Biography of Pauline Viardot*. London: John Calder, 1964.

Héritte de la Tour, Louis. *Memoires de Louise Héritte-Viardot:une famille de grands musicians: notes et souvenirs anecdotiques sur Garcia, Pauline Viardot, La Malibran, Louise Héritte-Viardot et leur entourage/par Louise Héritte de la Tour.* Paris: Stock, 1923.

Héritte-Viardot, Louise. *Memories and Adventures*, trans. by E. S. Bucheim. N.c.: Mills & Boon, 1913; New York: Da Capo Press, 1978.

Jezic, Diane Peacock. *Women Composers: The Lost Tradition Found*. New York: The Feminist Press, 1988.

Marix-Spire, Thérèse, ed. *Lettres inédites de George Sand et de Pauline Viardot, 1839–1849.* Paris, 1959.

Polk, Joanne. "Distaff Dynasties." In *The Musical Woman: An International Perspective.* Vol. 3. New York: Greenwood Press, 1984. Stern, S. *Women Composers: A Handbook.* Metuchen, NJ: Scarecrow Press, 1978.

Towers, J., comp. *Dictionary-Catalogue of Opera and Operetta.* Morgantown, WV: Acme, 1910. Reprint, New York; Da Capo Press, 1967.

Viardot, P.J. "Les Jeudis de Pauline Viardot." *Revue internationale de musique française*, vii (1982): 87-104.

Woman Composers: A Biographical Handbook of Womens Work in Music. New York: Chandler-Ebel, 1913.

Zaimont, Judith Lang, ed. *The Musical Woman*, vol. 1. Westport, CT: Greenwood Press, 1984.

Discography

"Serenade" from *Spanisches Quartette*, op. 11. Gemini Hall 1010, University of Oregon. Phonodisc DMds A922.

Women's Work: Works by Famous Women Composers. Berenice Branson, soprano; Mertine Johns, mezzo-soprano; Michael May, piano. Gemini Hall Records, RAP 1010, 1975.

Women Composers: the Lost Tradition Found (accompanies book by same title). New York: Leonarda, LPI 3-4.

Sérénade

Tout est riant dans la nature, Déjà les lilas sont en fleurs Et pour achever leur parure Fraîche aurore a versé ses pleurs.	All of nature is smiling, Already the lilacs are in bloom And to achieve their luster New dawn sheds tears.
Les colombes sous la ramée Soupirent leurs chants amoureux; Je suis seul, les ramiers sont deux, Je suis seul et les vois heureux, Et je rêve à ma bien aimée.	The doves under the green boughs Sigh their amorous songs; I am alone, the doves are together, I am alone and see how happy they are, And I dream of my beloved.
Du ciel brillant les fleurs charmantes Parfument les sentier divins; Feux Tremblants, vos flammes errantes nous font rêver sur nos chemins.	In the glittering sky the luscious flowers Perfume the sacred footpath; Flickering Fire, your rambling flames Make us dream on our travels.
Astrés dont la voûte est semée, D'un rayon pur charmez les cieux, Mais qu'ils sont pâles tous vos feux, Près des yeux de ma bien aimée.	Stars from the vault are strewn In an inviolate beam that graces the sky, But all your fires are pale, Next to the eyes of my beloved.

Translation by Jamée Ard

Sérénade

J. Bertrand **Louise Héritte-Viardot**

Allegretto
p
f
Tout est ri - ant dans la na - tu - - -
re, Dé - jà les li - las sont en fleurs
Et pour a - che - ver leur pa - ru - - - - re Fraîche au - ro - re a - ver -

20
riten.
a tempo
sé ses pleurs.
f
25
p
Les co - lom - bes sous la ra -
dim.
p
28
mé - e Sou - pi - rent leurs chants a - mou - reux;
31
f
p
Je suis seul, les ra - miers sont deux, Je suis seul et
f
p
cresc.

34
ff
les vois heu - reux,
Et
je rève à ma bien ai -
ff
37
a tempo
mée, à ma bien ai - mé - - - - - e.
cresc.
suivez
f
41
Du ciel bril -
dim.
p
p
46
lant les fleurs char-man - - - - tes
Par-fu - ment les sen-tiers di -

51
vins;
Feux Tremblants, vos flam - mes er - ran - - -
p
56
rit.
a tempo
tes nous font rè-ver sur nos che-mins.
f
61
p
As - trés
dim.
p
65
dont la voûte est se - mé - e, D'un ray - on pur char - mez les

68
f
p
cieux,
Mais qu'ils sont pà - les
tous vos feux,
f
p
71
ff
Qu'ils sont pà - les
tous vos feux,
Près
des
cresc.
ff
74
a tempo
yeux de ma bien ai - mée, de ma bien ai - mé - - - - - e
suivez
f
78
dim.
pp

Oliveria Prescott
(1842– 1919)

JOHN R. GARDNER AND TAMARA BELDOM

Oliveria Louisa Prescott did not devote herself to music until she was thirty years old. Born in London on September 3, 1842, she was the last and longest serving amanuensis of composer Sir George Macfarren (1813–1887) and adhered to all his teachings, considered reactionary by his contemporaries. Prescott was an industrious composer, however her works seldom found their way into concerts for the general public, and most of them remained unpublished. As a lecturer she was imaginative and sometimes deliberately controversial. She lived in London until she was fifty-four, then moved to Chilworth, near Guildford, Surrey, where she died on September 9, 1919.

Prescott studied privately with Lindsay Sloper (1826–1887) for several years before entering the Royal Academy of Music in 1872. Her compositions quickly became eagerly anticipated features of the student concerts, and were regularly performed at the concerts of the Musical Artists Society, of which she was an early and long serving elected committee member. Extant programs of the student concerts include her songs *How Canst Thou Calmly Slumber?* and *The Steadfast Lover*, performed February 27, 1873. At the concert on June 3, 1874, her setting of *Psalm 13* for soprano solo, chorus, and orchestra was performed despite the fact that the parts had only been crudely lithographed and were barely readable. The work had such a favorable reception that it was repeated on July 25. On July 21, 1874, she won an Academy bronze medal, the only prize awarded for harmony in that year, and in 1875 she won the Charles Lucas gold medal for composition; composer Arthur Sullivan, her elder by only a few months, was one of the examiners.

Prescott's teachers at the Academy were Frederick Jewson for piano, and Frederick Folkes and Francis Ralph for violin. However, it was Sir George Macfarren (1813–1887), who became principal of the Academy on the death of Sterndale Bennett (1816–1875), who was the greatest influence on Prescott. Macfarren had resigned from the Academy in 1847 because he was criticized for teaching Alfred Day's old-fashioned theories of harmony; he rejoined the staff in 1851. When he became completely blind in 1860 Prescott became his secretary, first during her student days, and continuing until his death on October 31, 1887. Macfarren's biographer, Henry Charles Banister, wrote "Oliveria Prescott assisted her revered professor with an affection only equalled by its efficiency until his death allowed his able amanuensis to lay down her pen."[1] As his assistant she gained a valuable insight into the methods used by the most respected British composer of the mid-Victorian years.

In 1879 Prescott left the Academy and became the teacher of harmony at the Church of England High School for Girls, Baker Street, London, where she remained until 1893. From mid-1881 to mid-1883 she contributed weekly articles to the *Musical World* (London)[2], and in June 1883 her collected articles were published as a book entitled *Form and Design in Music*. A second book, *About Music*, dedicated to the memory of Macfarren, was prefaced by a quotation from the Book of Job: "I was eyes to the blind."

She continued to compose, lecture, and write during the following years. Her anthem, *The Righteous Live for Ever More*, published in 1877, was added to the repertoire of St. Paul's Cathedral, London. The *Andante* from her unpublished *Symphony in B-flat* was performed at the Covent Garden Promenade concert in London on September 23, 1880. In September 1890 her part-song, *Lord Ullin's Daughter,* was performed several times with orchestral accompaniment at the Women's College, Sydney, Australia, and on December 1 of that year her programmatic orchestral suite *In Woodlands* was performed at the Bristol Monday Pops.

Prescott was acknowledged as the leader of the movement to gain higher musical education for women. When on February 6, 1885, Cambridge University recommended that women be admitted to their musical examinations, Prescott was appointed to supervise their musical correspondence courses at Newnham College, the women's college. However, her own view as to why women had not equalled men in the field of musical composition was that:

> they had no fighting power . . . There is an amount of fight neccessary for a man to make his way as a composer, but for a woman to be a fighter goes dangerously near taking away her womanly qualities; and then what becomes of her power of writing womanly music?[3]

Her statement implies that she believed music written by women should ideally be of a feminine quality.

During her lifetime she also tolerated the "royalty ballad" system saying that a neglected song was like "Sleeping Beauty" waiting for a singer to wake it from sleep.[4]

Prescott regularly attended lectures of the Musical Association in London and reported on them for various periodicals. Some of her topics included "Musical form" (February 4, 1885), "A phase of realism in music" (June 8, 1889), and "From ballad tune to sonata form" (May 3, 1895).

She was also an enthusiastic member of the Incorporated Society of Musicians. At one of their earliest meetings, on January 4, 1889, at the Archaeological Museum, Cambridge, her unpublished *String Quartet in A* was performed. Her *Concert Finale for Piano Duet* [5] was performed on January 3, 1894, at the Grand Hotel, Scarborough, and again at the Bradford School of Music on June 9.

Many of Prescott's early compositions were orchestral, and unusually ambitious for a woman in the 1870s. She also wrote a substantial amount of chamber music although towards the end of her life she became disillusioned at the lack of success of her own compositions. (The fate of her unpublished manuscripts is unknown.)

She brought a marked diversity to the part-song, her favorite type of composition, represented here by *A Border Ballad*. The title refers to the English/Scottish border region where warfare and bloodshed prevailed. Ballads have depicted this troubled zone for centuries.

A Border Ballad begins with all four voices singing a unison melody constructed in stepwise movement. The song breaks into four parts in measure 4 and moves to the relative minor (m. 9). Prescott sets the second verse (m. 18) almost exactly the same way; a change occuring in measure 28 leads to the final section, extended from five to thirteen bars. *A Border Ballad* was published in the April 1882 edition of *Musical Times* (London).

Notes

1. Banister's book contains letters written by Macfarren to Prescott and her account of their method of work. See Henry Charles Banister, *George Alexander Macfarren, his life, works and influence* (London: G. Bell & Sons, 1891).

2. *Musical World* (London), various issues. Prescott contributions include "Musical Form" (February 9, 1884), "Music and Accoustics" (June 14, 1884), "Vocal Art" (February 14, 1885), "Musical Style and how to cultivate it" (March 20, 1886), "Discord , dire sister" (August 10, 1889), and "Brothers and sisters" (January 25, 1890).

3. *Musical World* (London), October 14, 1882.

4. Under the "royalty ballad" system a music publisher paid a fee to the singer (as well as to the composer) for singing a song in public. The English contralto Charlotte Dolby added to her income by inaugurating the practice, though she brought the system into disrepute.

5. *Concert Finale for Piano Duet* was an arrangement of the last movement of her unpublished *Concerto in A for Piano and Orchestra*. She played it with her brother Edgar on June 7, 1884, at a concert at 135 New Bond Street, London.

Selected List of Works

Songs

Ask Me No More (with cello obbligato). Text by Alfred Tennyson. London: Stanley Lucas & Weber, 1874.

Cheerio (*A whistling song*). Text by Stephen Phillips. London: Weekes & Co., 1915.

How Canst Thou Calmly Slumber? (1872). Text anonymous. Unpublished.

The Steadfast Lover (1872). Text anonymous. Unpublished.

Four-part Songs

The Douglas Raid. Text by James Stewart. London: Novello & Co., 1883.

The Huntsman. Text by James Stewart. London: Hutchens & Romer, 1883.

Lord Ullin's Daughter. Text by Thomas Campbell. London: Novello & Co., 1889. (Orchestral parts available for hire).

The Righteous Live for Ever More. Text from *Wisd. of Sol.* 5:15-16. London: Stanley Lucas & Weber, 1877.

Choral Music

Psalm 13 (1873). Soprano, chorus and orchestra. Unpublished.

Chamber Music

Concert Finale for Piano Duet (arrangement of last movement of *Concerto in A for Piano and Orchestra*). London: Stanley Lucas, Weber & Co., 1878.

String Quartet in A minor (1878). Unpublished.

String Quartet in B-flat. (1878). Unpublished.

String Quartet in C minor. (1892) Unpublished.

Orchestral Music

Tithonus Overture (1876). Unpublished.

Symphony in B-flat (1877). Unpublished.

Alkestis Symphony (1878). Unpublished.

Concerto in A for Piano and Orchestra (1877). Unpublished.

In Woodlands (orchestral suite) (1890). Unpublished.

Operetta

Carrigraphuga or The Castle of the Fairies. Text by Stephen Phillips. London: Weekes & Co., 1914.

Bibliography

Banister, Henry Charles. *George Alexander Macfarren, His Life, Works and Influence*. London: G. Bell & Sons, 1891.

Prescott, Oliveria Louisa. *Form or Design in Music*. London: Aschenberg & Co., 1883.

_____. *About Music and What it is Made Of.* London: Methuen & Co., 1904.

Ritter, Fanny Raymond. *Woman as a Musician*. London: William Reeves, 1877.

A Border Ballad

F. W. Bourdillon

Oliveria Prescott

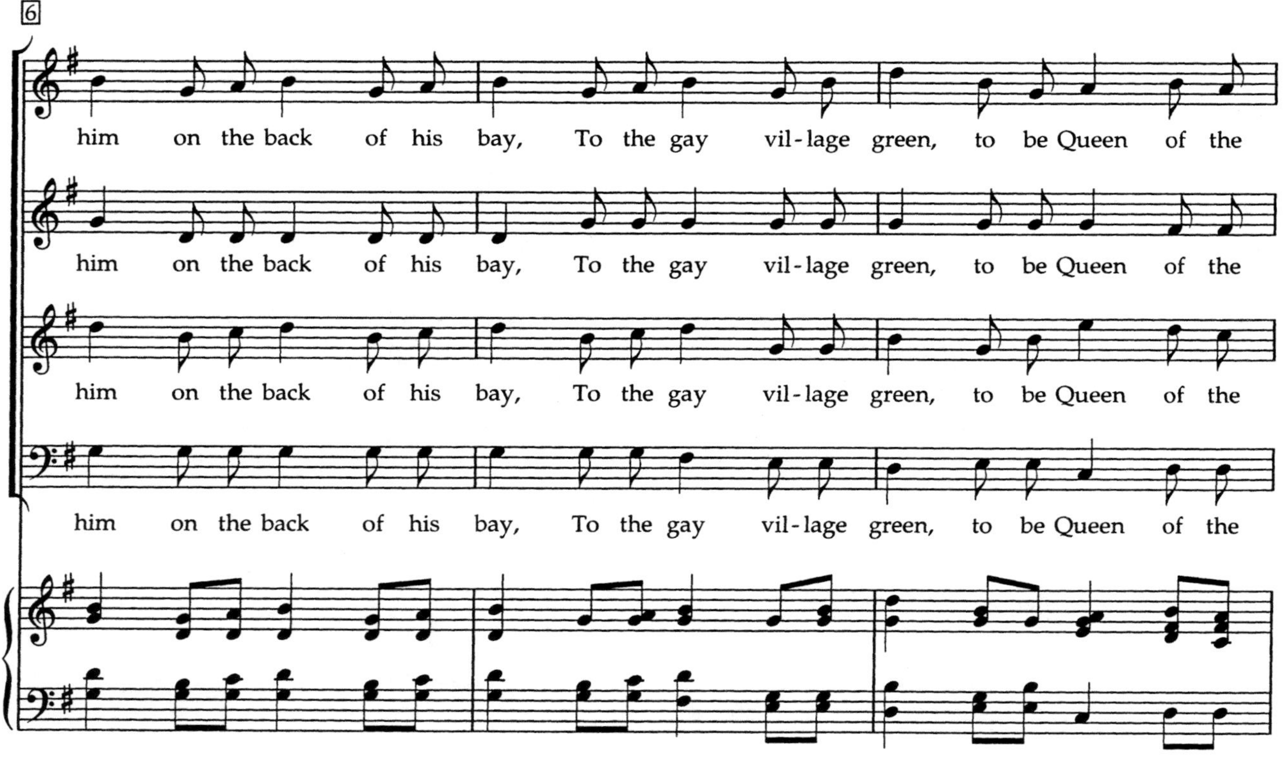
6
him on the back of his bay, To the gay vil-lage green, to be Queen of the
him on the back of his bay, To the gay vil-lage green, to be Queen of the
him on the back of his bay, To the gay vil-lage green, to be Queen of the
him on the back of his bay, To the gay vil-lage green, to be Queen of the

9
p legato
May. It was o - ver the val - leys and hills_ far from sight, By glen_ and by
p legato
May. It was o - ver the val - leys and hills far from sight, By glen and by
p legato
May. It was o - ver the val - leys and hills far from sight, By glen and by
p legato
May. It was o - ver the val - leys and hills_ far from sight, By glen_ and by
p legato

12
cresc.
tor - rent at deep_ dead of night, That his fierce___ ri - val car-ried me
tor - rent at deep dead of night, That his fierce ri - val car-ried me
tor - rent at deep dead of night, That his fierce ri - val car-ried me
tor - rent at deep_ dead of night, That his fierce___ ri - val car-ried me
15
f
help - less a-way, And_ swore he would wed_ me with break - ing of day.
help - less a-way, And swore he would wed me with break - ing of day.
help - less a-way, And swore he would wed me with break - ing of day.
help - less a-way, And swore he would wed me with break - ing of day.

18
mf
It was o - ver the moun - tains my love fol-lowed me, From the rage of his
mf
It was o - ver the moun - tains my love fol-lowed me, From the rage of his
mf
It was o - ver the moun - tains my love fol-lowed me, From the rage of his
mf
It was o - ver the moun - tains my love fol-lowed me, From the rage of his
mf

21
p
ri - val his true love to free; And there in the grey dawn his foe - man he
p
ri - val his true love to free; And there in the grey dawn his foe - man he
p
ri - val his true love to free; And there in the grey dawn his foe - man he
p
ri - val his true love to free; And there in the grey dawn his foe - man he
p

24
cresc.
p legato, sotto voce
found, And when the day broke there was blood on the ground. It is o - ver the
cresc.
p legato, sotto voce
found, And when the day broke there was blood on the ground. It is o - ver the
cresc.
p legato, sotto voce
found, And when the day broke there was blood on the ground. It is o - ver the
cresc.
p legato, sotto voce
found, And when the day broke there was blood on the ground. It is o - ver the
cresc.
p legato, sotto voce
27
moun - tains a - way to the sea, It is o - ver the o - cean my true love must
moun - tains a - way to the sea, It is o - ver the o - cean my true love must
moun - tains a - way to the sea, It is o - ver the o - cean my true love must
moun - tains a - way to the sea, It is o - ver the o - cean my true love must

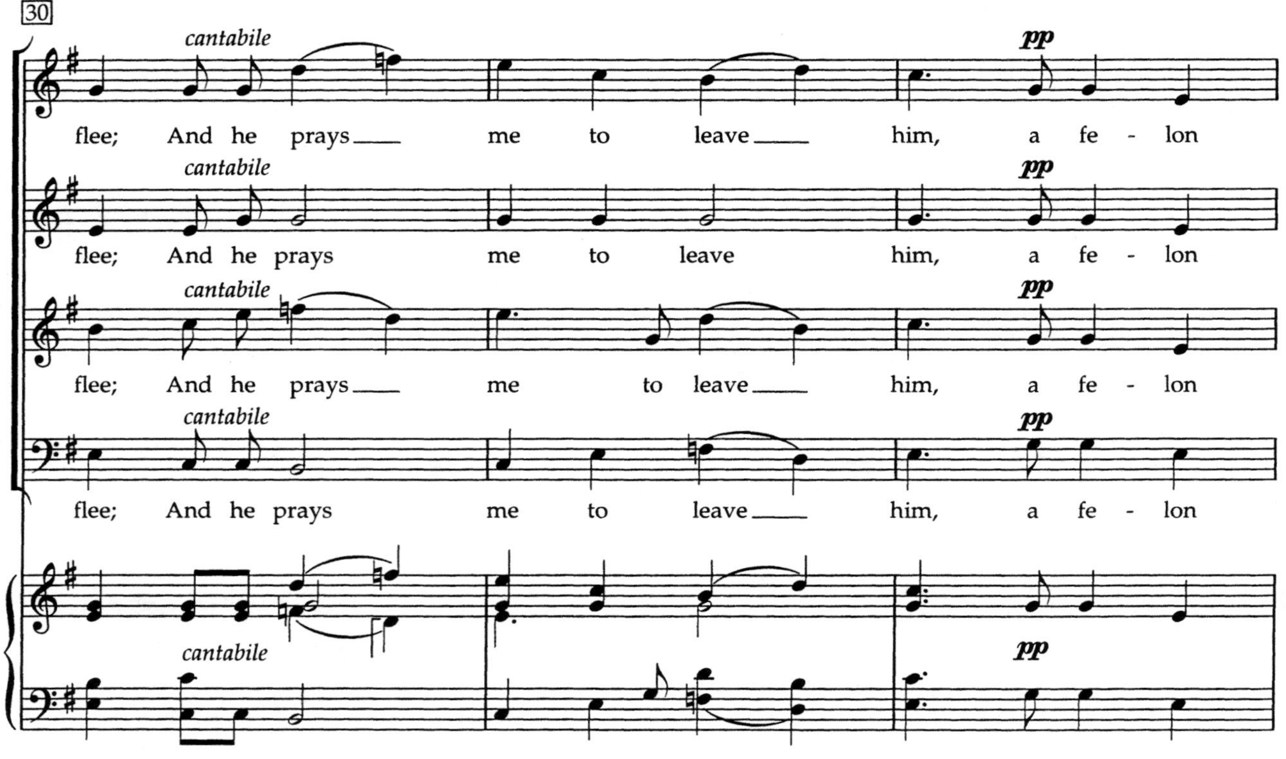
30
cantabile
pp
flee; And he prays me to leave him, a fe - lon
flee; And he prays me to leave him, a fe - lon
flee; And he prays me to leave him, a fe - lon
flee; And he prays me to leave him, a fe - lon

33
f
out - cast; But if e'er I for - sake
out - cast; But if e'er I for - sake
out - cast; But if e'er I for - sake
out - cast; But if e'er I for - sake

36
— him, if e'er — I for - sake — him, if e'er — I for -
— him, if e'er I for - sake — him, if e'er — I for -
— him, if e'er — I for - sake — him, if e'er — I for -
— him, if e'er — I for - sake — him, if e'er — I for -

39
marc.
rit.
sake — him, for - sake him, that day be my last.
sake — him, for - sake him, that day be my last.
sake him, for - sake — him, that day be my last.
sake him, for - sake — him, that day be my last.

Clara Kathleen Rogers

(1844–1931)

JUDITH RADELL AND DELIGHT MALITSKY

The British-born soprano Clara Doria came to Boston during the 1872–1873 opera season and remained to become a major influence on the musical life of that culturally important city. In private life she was Clara Kathleen Barnett Rogers, a woman whose professional and social activities brought her into contact with some of the most important literary and musical figures of the time, including Henry Wadsworth Longfellow, Amy Lowell, Arthur Foote (1853–1937), Benjamin J. Lang (1837–1909), Margaret Ruthven Lang (1867–1972), and Edward MacDowell (1860–1908). Born on January 14, 1844, in Cheltenham, England, Clara Kathleen was the daughter of the opera composer, John Barnett (1802–1890).[1] She received her earliest musical training from her parents and continued her education at the Leipzig Conservatory from 1857 to 1860. After a period of study with Antonio San Giovanni in Milan, she made her operatic debut in Turin as Isabella in Giacomo Meyerbeer's (1791–1864) *Roberto il Diavolo* (1831), and went on to sing major roles with Italian opera companies between 1863 and 1867. Clara spent four years as a concert singer in England before joining the Parepa-Rosa Opera Company on their American tour. After settling in Boston she sang professionally at Trinity Church and performed frequently at the Harvard Symphony Concerts. Following her marriage in 1878 to the prominent attorney Henry Munroe Rogers, Clara gave up public performing but continued to teach and compose. She published her first book on vocal technique, *The Philosophy of Singing,*[2] in 1893, and she joined the faculty of the New England Conservatory in 1902. During the following twenty-one years, she published four more books on singing and a three-volume autobiography. (Further biographical information is contained in volume 6.)

In the 1880s, Rogers decided to publish some of her songs. She had begun composing early in life; the skill evident in her youthful writing suggests the possibility that she had received some training, perhaps from her father. Since she had been denied a place in the composition classes at the Leipzig Conservatory because of her gender, she felt most confident writing in the smaller forms: "(Lacking formal training,) I have had to content myself with writing music in the simpler forms (she cites her sonatas as exceptions). . . ."[3]

Between 1882 and 1906 Rogers published fifty-seven songs, a *Romanza* and two scherzi for piano, and a *Sonata for Violin and Piano.*[4] Many of her songs were reprinted by her publisher, Arthur P. Schmidt, in collections or in albums of her own compositions.

The songs represent an extraordinary body of work in their variety and in the unfailing ability of the composer to be an advocate for the poet. Rogers's first set, op. 10, was published in 1882. In January 1883 a review appeared in the *Musical Herald,* praising the songs as "poetic and generally beautiful," but adding that "fewer changes of key, and, at times, less variable modulation would improve the set."[5] The *Musical Herald*'s standards were high; only composers of good quality such as Arthur Foote, John Knowles Paine (1839–1906), and Antonín Dvořák (1841–1904), received favorable reviews. That Rogers's songs were given serious consideration shows how highly she was regarded by the Boston musical community.

The appraisal contained in the review reveals stylistic elements that characterize Rogers's compositions from her earliest to her latest works. She often used abrupt modulations, usually up or down a second or a third. The *Herald's* reviewer notes that the modulation from F major to A major in *The Clover Blossoms* is "very effective." However, he is less enthusiastic about the same key relationship in *At Break of Day*: "The connection between the tonic and mediant notes is strongly insisted on; and the song swerves between C and E major without much . . . intervening modulation."[6] In her late songs, such as *A Woman's Last Word* and *Adieu,* the juxtaposition of distantly related chords often challenges the tonal center. The harmonic language of Rogers's mature works is decidedly late Romantic.

Other elements of her style also developed throughout her oeuvre. Her earliest songs, six each in op. 10 and in op. 20, have simple accompaniments and fairly simple melodies. The vocal melody is frequently dependent upon a characteristic rhythm, and the accompaniment often merely supports the melody. The character of her accompaniments begins to change in op. 22, with the piano part becoming truly independent in the sets of Browning songs. Similarly, throughout her oeuvre the vocal melody becomes less ballad-like and more independent of the meter of the poem. (An obvious exception is the set of *Six Folk Songs*, op. 34.)

In 1886, the *Musical Herald* praised Arthur Foote and George Chadwick (1854–1931) for "bringing (the American song) past the English ballad style, nearer to the German *lied*."[7] Clara Rogers's early songs reflect both the influence of her father's British theater songs and the influence of the lieder she had sung in Leipzig. By 1893, the German influence had become the more prominent. In her finest songs, *Two Songs with Words by Dante Gabriel Rossetti* op. 33 and *Overhead the Treetops Meet* op. 36, Rogers combines German, English and French elements to form a sophisticated and personal style.

Perhaps the most important characteristic of Rogers's vocal writing is her fidelity to the text. Clara Rogers set a wide variety of poetry. Her settings of verses by relatively unknown poets are notable for the seriousness with which they treat the words. She was particularly interested in the poets associated with the Pre-Raphaelite Brotherhood, and she set texts by Rossetti and Philip Bourke Marston with special sympathy. She met some of these writers through her brother-in-law, Robert Francillon:

> One of the most notable *salons* to which we were escorted by my sister and brother-in-law, was that of the renowned critic and playwright, Dr. Westland Marston, whose "Sunday evenings" at his house in Northumberland Terrace, Regents Park, were frequented by such brilliant literary lights as Rossetti, Swinburne . . . , Robert Browning, William Morris, and that ilk . . . Philip Bourke Marston, Dr. Marston's blind son, a somewhat pathetic figure, was a true poet . . . .[8]

Her greatest songs were inspired by the poetry of Robert Browning and Dante Gabriel Rossetti. Although she considered setting their poems a great challenge, the ability of these poets to transcend the meter, as well as their sympathetic philosophies, inspired Rogers to write some of her most artistic music.[9]

Clara Rogers's extraordinary ability to set a text stemmed from the principles that governed her singing and teaching. She set out those principles in *The Philosophy of Singing*, positing emotion as the inspiration for sound: ". . . where the poet is true to his own emotion, and the musician (composer) true alike to the poet's emotion and his own, the singer . . . cannot help following suit by a true expression in turn."[10] She advocated a natural, relaxed use of the body, which she termed "the soul's instrument of expression."[11] As principles of vocal technique, she suggested the "perfect tone-attack," the "perfect 'legato,'" the "'messa di voce,' or swelling and decreasing on a single note," the "distinct pronunciation of the vowels," and the "perfect articulation of the consonants."[12] Her own fine technique and musicianship were noted in reviews:

> Miss Doria sang the beautiful Aria of Sextus in *La Clemenza di Tito*, in a clear, sweet, even voice, with a finished elegance of execution, and a sincere and chaste, not cold, expression, which wins the heart more truly than the affected and exaggerated Italian Opera sort of "passion."[13]

Rogers's commitment to expression drove her vocal composition: "I have found in song writing a keen interest and satisfaction by seeking to reproduce the mood of the poet with subtle touches of emotion suggested in the poem...."[14] Moreover, in editing her compositions she was careful in her expressive and technical instructions to the performer. Rogers precisely notated swells, accents and the *messa di voce* in the vocal part and often in the accompaniment as well. Copies of music held at the New England Conservatory's Spaulding Library contain such pencilled markings in a hand that appears to be Rogers's; it is quite likely that she added further nuances to the scores of her pupils.

As singer, writer and composer, Clara Rogers was respected by her musical and literary colleagues. Edward MacDowell dedicated his op. 47 songs to her in 1893. After reading *The Philosophy of Singing*, Teresa Carreño (see vol. 6) sent Clara an effusive letter of praise, initiating a lifelong friendship between the musicians.[15] Rogers contributed actively to the musical and intellectual life of her community until her death in 1931. The songs included in this volume were written in the last two decades of the nineteenth century and are representative of the composer's style, harmonic language, and ability to "reproduce the mood of the poet."

Aubade, op. 16, is the first of two songs with violin obligato written by Rogers between 1880 and 1890. The obligato song, with its roots in German music, appears to have been a popular form in Boston in the late nineteenth century.[16] In her exploration of this genre, Clara Rogers joined colleagues such as Arthur Foote and Charles Martin Loeffler (1861–1935), a distinguished violinist who was her frequent chamber music partner. Rogers's skill as a composer is apparent in the treatment of vocal, violin, and piano parts, which are of equal importance and often have their own characteristic material. *Aubade* was first published in 1885 and appeared in A.P. Schmidt's catalog as a single piece and in collections.

Rogers describes her lyrics as "from the French of Victor Hugo." Originally entitled *Autre Chanson* (Another Song), the poem is the twenty-third of Hugo's *Les Chants du crépuscule* (Songs of Twilight).[17] She lists no translator; it is possible that the adaptation is her own. The free translation allows her to set the song in an AABA[1] form, rather than merely following the form of the poem. Hugo's poem contains a refrain (stanzas 2, 4, and 6), which may be roughly translated as, "O my charming one, / Listen to / The lover who sings / And weeps as well." In Rogers's adaptation, there is no such refrain, and the reference to "weeping" is delayed until nearly the end of the song. She uses Hugo's first and third stanzas for her first two A sections. As a text for her B section she uses a very free translation of the fifth stanza of the original poem. A literal translation of the second and third lines of this stanza might be, "God who through you has completed me, has made my love for your soul . . ." The translator renders this poetically: "Apart we miss our nature's goal, / Why strive to cheat our destinies? / Was not my love made for thy soul . . . ?" The final section is based on the refrain combined with a more general expression of the poem's theme.

Come Not When I Am Dead was first published by A.P.

Schmidt in 1887 as the fourth of *Five Songs*, op. 24, and it received a second printing in *A Collection of Songs with Accompaniment for Pianoforte* (1903). The form of the song is ABCDEC[1], with the C sections serving as a refrain to unify the work (mm. 20-33 and 53-69). The mood is somber, and Rogers's pronounced use of diminished seventh chords gives the work an unsettled quality. The opening phrase is emphatically declamatory, ending with a melodic sigh on the word "grave." In measures 11 and 12, Rogers alters Alfred Tennyson's original "trample round my fallen head" (line 3 of the poem) to "trample on my fallen head."[18] She makes effective use of word-painting here, in the falling E minor scale, and in the piano's imitation of the "plover's cry" in measures 24 and 25. The E section, measures 42-52, is almost a recitative. A chromatic vocal line accompanied by broken chords creates a ghostly, wind-like effect in the song's refrain. Roger's near-perfect setting of Tennyson's words makes this song a small masterpiece.

Apparitions was published in 1893 as the third number of op. 27, Rogers's first set of songs, based on poems by Robert and Elizabeth Barrett Browning. In setting Robert Browning's poem, which is actually the proem to his *Two Poets of Croisic*, Rogers makes slight changes in punctuation, but is faithful to the mood shifts of the text.[19] *Apparitions* is strophic, with the last verse expanded and followed by a codetta. Each verse begins in C minor and ends in C major. The return to C minor each time is accomplished by the piano part, which is characterized, during most of the song, by a restless figure comprised of an eighth note followed by two sixteenths. The sense of tension is heightened by Rogers's use of the tritone, both melodically and in diminished and half-diminished seventh chords. This tension breaks abruptly in the middle of the last stanza, measures 46-47, where Rogers returns to C major, giving the piano a triumphant triplet accompaniment based on the voice's motive in measure 14. When the voice restates this motive in measure 50, the piano extends it to sequential statements in A major, D major, B major and E major before the voice's final phrase. The same triumphant motive accompanies the song's concluding phrase.

Acknowledgments

Autographs for Clara Rogers's songs may be found in the Arthur P. Schmidt Collection, Library of Congress, and in the Collection of Clara Barnett Rogers and Henry Munroe Rogers, Courtesy of the Harvard Theatre Collection, the Houghton Library, Harvard University. The authors thank John Newsome of the Music Division of the Library of Congress and Fredric W. Wilson, Curator of the Harvard Theatre Collection, for their assistance. Good collections of first editions may be found in the Allen A. Brown Collection of the Boston Public Library, and at Spaulding Library of the New England Conservatory of Music. We wish to acknowledge Diane Ota, Curator of Music at the Boston Public Library and Jean Morrow, Director of Libraries at the New England Conservatory, for their help with our research.

Notes

1. While Clara Rogers appears to have given her birth year as 1844, Clara Barnett's registration form from the *Conservatorium der Musik zu Leipzig* shows a birth date of January 14, 1845. The Barnett documents are held in the Hochschulbibliothek, Bereich Archiv, Hochschule für Musik und Theater, Leipzig.

2. Clara Kathleen Rogers, *The Philosophy of Singing* (New York: Harper and Brothers Publishers, 1893).

3. Clara Kathleen Rogers, *The Story of Two Lives* (Norwood, Mass.: Privately printed, Plimpton Press, 1932), 80-81.

4. A list of "Compositions by Mrs. Clara K. Rogers" in the Arthur P. Schmidt Collection, Library of Congress, shows fifty-eight songs and an *Album of Fourteen Songs*. There are three songs that belong to more than one opus number: *The Year's at the Spring*, *I Have a More Than Friend*, and *Ah, Love, But a Day*. Missing from the list are the songs, *She Is Not Fair*, op. 24, no. 5, and *Nothing*, op. 10, no. 6. The *Album of Fourteen Songs* is comprised of songs already on the list.

5. "Review of New Music," *Musical Herald* 4 (January 1883), 24.

6. Ibid., 4, 24.

7. Ibid., 7 (January 1886), 32.

8. Rogers, *The Story*, 92.

9. ". . . the verses of Gabriel Rossetti and of the unlyrical Robert Browning (make) special appeal to me by drawing on all one's musical ingenuity for adequate expression!" Rogers, *The Story*, 81.

10. Rogers, *The Philosophy*, 18.

11. Ibid., 33.

12. Ibid., 96.

13. John S. Dwight, "First Symphony Concert," review of concert performance, in *Dwight's Journal of Music* 33 (November 15, 1873), 126.

14. Rogers, *The Story*, 81.

15. Teresa Carreño to Rogers, February 27, 1897. Collection of Clara Barnett Rogers and Henry Munroe Rogers, Courtesy of the Harvard Theatre Collection, the Houghton Library, Harvard University.

16. For a discussion of this topic, see Elizabeth Ann Sears, *The Art Song in Boston, 1880–1914* (Ann Arbor: University Microfilms, Inc., 1993).

17. Victor Hugo, "Les Chants du crépuscule," in *Poëmes choisis*, ed. Yves-Gérard le Dantec (Paris: Éditions de Cluny, 1948), 1.

18. Alfred Tennyson, "Come Not When I Am Dead," in *Victorian Poetry*, ed. E. K. Brown and J. O. Bailey (New York: The Roland Press, 1962).

19. Robert Browning, "Two Poets of Croisic," in *Robert Browning: The Poems*, ed. John Pettigrew/Thomas J. Collins (New Haven and London: Yale University Press, 1981), 2.

Selected List of Works

(see vol. 6 for list of piano and chamber works)

Solo Songs

Autographs for the unpublished songs are held in the Rogers Collection of the Harvard Theatre Collection. Since they are undated, they have been placed after the published songs, in the order in which they appear in the collection. Clara Rogers did not always cite a poet for her published songs. In those cases, we have not listed an attribution for the text.

Six Songs, op. 10. Boston: Arthur P. Schmidt and Co., 1882.
1. *She Never Told Her Love.* Text by William Shakespeare
2. *The Clover Blossoms.* Text by Oscar Leighton
3. *The Year's at the Spring.* Text by Robert Browning
4. *At Break of Day*
5. *The Rose and the Lily.* Text by Heinrich Heine
6. *Nothing.* Text by Alice Cary

Six Songs, op. 20. Boston: Arthur P. Schmidt and Co., 1884.
1. *A Match.* Text by Algernon Charles Swinburne
2. *Confession*
3. *Mona.* Text by Alice Cary
4. *Rhapsody.* Text by J. Berry Bensel
5. *What Does the Little One See Down There?*
6. *Spring*

Three Songs, op. 22. Boston: Arthur P. Schmidt and Co., 1885.
1. *Look Out, O Love.* Text by Lewis Morris
2. *Those Eyes.* Text by Ben Jonson
3. *The Heath This Night Must Be My Bed.* Text by Sir Walter Scott

Five Songs, op. 24. Boston: Arthur P. Schmidt and Co., 1887.
1. *She Was More Fair Than Beauty.* Text by Julia R. Anagnos
2. *The Sweetest Dream.* Text by Philip Bourke Marston
3. *Love Lies A-Dying.* Text by Philip Bourke Marston
4. *Come Not When I Am Dead.* Text by Alfred Tennyson
5. *She Is Not Fair.* Text by Hartley Coleridge

Six Songs, op. 26. Boston: Arthur P. Schmidt and Co., 1888.
1. *Invitation.* Text by J. Ashcroft Noble
2. *Fair, O Fair.* Text by Henry Phelps Perkins
3. *I Dare Not Ask.* Text by Robert Herrick
4. *The Answer.* Text by Celia Thaxter
5. *Oh My Garden Full of Roses.* Text by Philip Bourke Marston
6. *A Love Song.* Text by Sidney Wadman

Browning Songs (First Series), op. 27. Boston: Arthur P. Schmidt and Co., 1893.
1. *Out of My Own Great Woe.* Text by Elizabeth Barrett Browning (from Heinrich Heine)
2. *Summum Bonum.* Text by Robert Browning
3. *Apparitions.* Text by Robert Browning
4. *Ah, Love, But a Day.* Text by Robert Browning
5. *I Have a More Than Friend.* Text by Elizabeth Barrett Browning
6. *The Year's at the Spring.* Text by Robert Browning

Three Songs, op. 28. Boston: Arthur P. Schmidt and Co., 1890.
1. *I Have a More Than Friend.* Text by Elizabeth Barrett Browning
2. *Ah, Love, But a Day.* Text by Robert Browning
3. *Under a Cherry Tree.* Text by William James Linton

Two Songs, op. 30. Boston: Arthur P. Schmidt and Co., 1893.
1. *Night and Sleep*
2. *Too Young for Love.* Text by Oliver Wendell Holmes

Before the Blossom. Text by Robert Underwood Johnson. Boston: Arthur P. Schmidt and Co., 1896.

My Dark to Light. Text by Newman Hall. Boston: Arthur P. Schmidt and Co., 1896.

Reverie. Text by Charles J. Sprague. Boston: Arthur P. Schmidt and Co., 1896.

The Voice That Sang Alone. Text by Clellan Waldo Fisher. Boston: Arthur P. Schmidt and Co., 1896.

Browning Songs (Second Series), originally op. 32. Text by Robert Browning. Boston: Arthur P. Schmidt and Co., 1900.
1. *My Star*
2. *Appearances*
3. *A Woman's Last Word*
4. *Good to Forgive*
5. *One Way of Love*
6. *Love*

Two Songs with Words by Dante Gabriel Rossetti, op. 33. Text by Dante Gabriel Rossetti. Boston: Arthur P. Schmidt and Co., 1900.
1. *Sudden Light*
2. *Adieu*

Six Folk Songs of Different Nationalities, op. 34. Boston: Arthur P. Schmidt and Co., 1900.
1. *For Love is Blind.* Text by Helen [*sic*] Mackay Hutchinson
2. *My Heart is Sair*. Text by Thomas Faed
3. *The Stars Are with the Voyager*. Text by Thomas Hood
4. *An Irish Love Song*. Text by Robert Underwood Johnson
5. *Jenny Kissed Me*. Text by Leigh Hunt
6. *When One Has a Sweetheart.* Text translated by Charles J. Sprague

A Little Love Song, op. 35. Text by Clarence Urmy. Boston: Arthur P. Schmidt and Co., 1901.

Overhead the Treetops Meet (from "Pippa Passes"), op. 36. Text by Robert Browning. Boston: Arthur P. Schmidt and Co., 1903.

If We But Knew. Text by Clarence Hawkes. Boston: Arthur P. Schmidt and Co., 1906.

The Wanderer. Text by Austin Dobson. Unpublished.

Perche. Text by Alardo Alearchi. Unpublished.

My Little Pretty One. Text from the old English. Unpublished.

Not As I Will. Text by Helen Hunt Jackson. Unpublished.

Andantino. Unpublished.

He Loved Two Women. Unpublished.

The Violet. Text by Johann Wolfgang van Goethe. Translated by George Birdseye. Unpublished.

Vignettes in Rhyme. Text by Austin Dobson. Unpublished.

Frühlingslied. Text by Emanuel von Geibel. Unpublished.

An den Mond. Unpublished.

Hush, My Baby's Asleep. Text by Annie G. Murray. Unpublished.

The Three Lovers. Unpublished.

Cossack Song. Unpublished.

Folk Songs. Unpublished.
1. *Go Away Death*. Text by Alfred Austin
2. *Thou Art to Me*. Text by Arthur Macy
3. *Triolet*. Text by George Macdonald

Miyoko San. Text by Mary McNeil Fenollosa. Unpublished.

The Lass wi' the Bonny Blue Een. Text by Robert Burns. Unpublished.

The Golden Ring. Unpublished.

Roumanian Folk Song. Text by Hélène Vacaresco. Unpublished.

Come My Darling. Text from the French, Twelfth century. Unpublished.

Romaic Love Song. Text by W. Guernsey. Unpublished.

Songs with Violin Obbligato

Aubade, op. 16. Text from the French of Victor Hugo. Boston: Arthur P. Schmidt and Co., 1885.

Kiss Mine Eyelids, Lovely Morn, op. 17. Text by Oliver Wendell Holmes. Boston: Arthur P. Schmidt and Co., 1890.

Four-part Songs

Three Four-part Songs. Unpublished.
Ich tret in deiner Garten
O My Luve's Like a Red, Red Rose. Text by Robert Burns
At End. Text by Louise Chandler Moulton

Hat einer ein Schaetzerl. Unpublished.

Autumn Song. Text by Ellen Mackay Hutchinson. Unpublished.

Bibliography

Ammer, Christine. *Unsung*. Westport, Conn.: Greenwood Press, 1980.

Barnett, John. Diaries. Collection of Clara Barnett Rogers and Henry Munroe Rogers, Courtesy of the Harvard Theatre Collection, the Houghton Library, Harvard University.

Block, Adrienne Fried, "Arthur P. Schmidt, Music Publisher and Champion of Women Composers." In *The Musical Woman*, vol. 2 edited by Judith Lang Zaimont. Westport, Conn.: Greenwood Press, 1987.

Browning, Robert. "Two Poets of Croisic." In *Robert Browning: The*

Poems, edited by John Pettigrew, supplemented and completed by Thomas J. Collins. New Haven and London: Yale University Press, 1981.

Cook, Susan C., and Judy S. Tsou. *Cecilia Reclaimed*. Urbana and Chicago: University of Illinois Press, 1994.

Dwight's Journal of Music. 41 vols. 1853–1881.

Ebel, Otto. *Women Composers: A Biographical Handbook of Woman's Work in Music*. Brooklyn: Chandler-Ebel Music Co., 1902.

Elson, Louis C. *The History of American Music*. New York: Macmillan Publishing Company, 1925. Reprint: Lenox Hill Publishing and Distributing Company (Burt Franklin), 1971.

Glickman, Sylvia, ed. *American Women Composers: Piano Music from 1865–1915*. Bryn Mawr, PA: Hildegard Publishing Company, 1990.

Harvard University Library. *The Rogers Memorial Room: An Account of the Nature, Origin, and Significance of the Memorabilia Presented to Harvard College in 1930 by Clara Kathleen and Henry Munroe Rogers*. Boston: The Cosmos Press, Inc., 1935.

Hugo, Victor. "Les Chants du crépuscule." In *Poëmes choisis*, edited Yves-Gérard le Dantec. Paris: Éditions de Cluny, 1948.

Lowell, Amy. Letters. The Houghton Library, Harvard University.

Knight, Ellen. *Charles Martin Loeffler: A Life Apart in American Music*. Urbana and Chicago: University of Illinois Press, 1993.

MacDowell, Edward A. *Songs*, op. 40, 47, 56, 58, 60. Introduction by H. Wiley Hitchcock. New York: Da Capo Press, 1972.

Musical Herald. 14 vols. 1880–1893.

Rogers, Clara Kathleen. *Clearcut Speech in Song*. Boston: Oliver Ditson Co., 1927.

____. *English Diction in Song and Speech (Part II)*. Norwood, Mass.: Plimpton Press, 1912.

____. *English Diction Part I: The Voice in Speech*. Boston: Oliver Ditson Co., 1915.

____. Holograph manuscripts. Arthur P. Schmidt Collection, Library of Congress.

____. *Journal-Letters from the Orient*. Norwood, Mass.: Privately printed, Plimpton Press, 1934.

____. Letters to Amy Lowell. The Houghton Library, Harvard University.

____. Letters to Arthur P. Schmidt. Arthur P. Schmidt Collection, Library of Congress.

____. *Memories of a Musical Career*. Boston: Little, Brown and Co., 1919.

____. Musical manuscripts. Collection of Clara Barnett Rogers and Henry Munroe Rogers, Courtesy of the Harvard Theatre Collection, the Houghton Library, Harvard University.

____. *My Voice and I*. Chicago: A. C. McClurg and Co., 1910.

____. *The Philosophy of Singing*. New York: Harper and Brothers Publishers, 1893.

____. Scrapbooks of letters, journals. Collection of Clara Barnett Rogers and Henry Munroe Rogers, Courtesy of the Harvard Theatre Collection, the Houghton Library, Harvard University.

____. *The Story of Two Lives*. Norwood, Mass.: Plimpton Press, 1932.

____. *Your Voice and You*. Boston: Oliver Ditson Co., 1925.

Sears, Elizabeth Ann. *The Art Song in Boston, 1880–1914*. Ann Arbor: University Microfilms, Inc., 1993.

Tennyson, Alfred. "Come Not When I Am Dead." In *Victorian Poetry*, eds. E. K. Brown and J. O. Bailey. New York: The Roland Press, 1962.

Discography

Women at an Exposition. Susanne Mentzer, mezzo-soprano; Sunny Joy Langton, soprano; Elaine Skorodin, violin; Kimberly Schmidt, piano. Koch International Classics 3-7240-2H1 (1993). *Ah, Love, But a Day*, op. 27, no. 4; *Out of My Own Great Woe*, op. 27, no. 1.

Editorial Comments

Aubade

Rogers's commitment to the craft of composition is revealed through examination of her extensive revision process. The holograph of *Aubade* in the A.P. Schmidt Collection of the Library of Congress contains revisions that yield a score roughly similar to an interesting set of copies held in the Library Archives of the New England Conservatory of Music, Boston. These marked copies, which may be corrected proofs, are found in a folder that also contains signed title pages of *A Collection of Favorite Songs with Accompaniment of the Pianoforte and Another Instrument*, an album published by Schmidt ca. 1885. On each of the four copies is a different set of corrections in Rogers's hand. The title page of the collection is undated; however, since the collection itself was reissued after 1890 with a much richer table of contents, it is possible to identify this version of the *Favorite Songs* as a fairly early collection. The corrected copies in the folder may have been used by Rogers as alternative drafts for the final version of the work, as it appeared in a Schmidt album of Rogers's works, *A Collection of Songs with Accompaniment for Pianoforte* (1903).

The violin parts of the Schmidt Collection's autograph and of the early printing of *Aubade* are more active than that of the final version. The ending seems to have been especially troublesome for Rogers, and the vocal part in the holograph, if taken literally, would have produced more beats than could be contained in measure 65. The holograph also begins with an indication for cut time. The copies at the New England Conservatory eliminate the cut time and smooth out the rhythm of measure 65 but they retain the active violin part of the holograph. Between holograph and printed copy, Rogers revised dynamics or accents in measures 3, 5, 10, 15, 16, 17, 23, 26, 30, 57, 58, 61, 64, 66, and 67. Note revisions took place in measures 25 and 26. Rogers altered a note duration in measure 30, added the fermata in measure 50, added violin slurs in measures 45 and 46, and placed a pedal indication in measure 67.

The corrections on the four copies at the New England Conservatory represent revisions of greater significance. First, the composer revised sections in which the activity of the violin part or the thickness of the piano texture might overpower the vocal line. Second, she made the vocal line more singable at the song's conclusion. The ending was transformed so that the soprano no longer sings the words "art thou" on e^2 and g^2, but reaches the high notes with the more vocal syllable "ah." Third, she extended the range of the violin part to show the lower register in measures 45 and 46, and to conclude the song on b^2. Fourth, she wrote alternative vocal notes so that the song became appropriate for mezzo-soprano. Finally, the composer made decisions concerning metronome markings, expression markings, and tempo changes. A list of specific revisions Clara Rogers made to the proofs at the New England Conservatory in preparing the version in the 1903 *Collection* appears below.

1. Added metronome marking.
2. *Molto legato* was added in measure 6.
3. The composer added vocal nuances to measures 7-9, 11, 12, 16, 20, 21, 24, 25, 28, 29, 39, 40, 47, 48, 50, 53, 54, 63 and 64. A nuance was added to the violin part in measure 17.
4. A violin part based on the opening motive was eliminated in measures 7-9 and 20-22.
5. The composer revised chord doublings, bass pitches and slurs for the piano part in measures 7-9 and 20-22; the new part is generally thinner in texture.
6. She revised the piano and violin parts for measures 11-12 and 24-25, adding piano accents in measures 11-12, giving the piano fuller chords and reducing the importance of the violin part.
7. *Sforzandi* were added to piano left-hand first notes, in measures 13, 14 and 27; an accent was added to the first piano beat in measure 15.
8. Rogers added vocal articulations in measures 13 and 26.
9. A *rallentando* was added to measures 15, 28 and 32; an *a tempo* was added to measures 16, 29, 33 and 56.
10. Rogers revised the vocal part in measure 24 from its original dotted-eighth-sixteenth pattern on beat 2.
11. The composer changed the instruction *con calore* to *appassionato* in measure 39; *appassionato* was also added to the violin entrance at measure 41.
12. In measures 45-46, the earlier version's violin part was an octave higher; its *ritard* was originally in measure 46 rather than measure 45.
13. Rogers added an alternative vocal e-flat^2 to the half-note in measure 50; she added the note g^1 to the piano's right-hand chord.
14. The composer revised the dynamics in measures 53-56. The earlier vocal part had no dynamic marking until measure 54, which showed a *pianissimo* on the word "where," rather than a *decrescendo*. There was no dynamic marking in measure 55 in the earlier version.
15. Rogers added an alternative lower part in measures 62-65.
16. In measure 65, the composer revised both vocal and violin parts. The violin originally had a quarter note e^2, and a quarter note g^2 tied so that it lasted until the final measure. The vocal part originally had a suspended half note e^2 ("where"); this was tied to the first of two eighth notes, followed by a g^2 on the second eighth. The fourth beat of measure 65 was a quarter note g^2 on the word "art," and measure 66 kept the g^2 on the word "thou."
17. Rogers added fingering to the left-hand piano part in measures 68-69.

In preparing this edition of *Aubade*, the editors have used the final version of the work, in the 1903 *Collection*, as the primary source. A copy of the work is held in the Allen A. Brown Collection of the Boston Public Library. The holograph copy in the Arthur P. Schmidt Collection, Library of Congress, was also consulted in preparing the edition. In addition, the copies of the early printing in *A Collection of Favorite Songs with Accompaniment of the Pianoforte and Another Instrument*, held in Spaulding Library of the New England Conservatory, were consulted for comparison purposes.

In editing *Aubade* we have retained all the expression markings of the final edition, changing only the placement of the vocal nuances in measures 7, 8, 11, 12, 25, 47, and 48, since Rogers emphasized the upper eighth note in most of her drafted revisions. These altered nuances have been placed in parentheses. We have added an *a tempo* in parentheses in measure 47 to follow the *ritard* in measures 45-46, and we have regularized the *ritard* in m. 53 among the parts. We have kept Rogers's rare piano fingerings, and have added editorial fingering for both piano and violin. All violin bowing is editorial and most frequently divides Roger's measure-long slurs in half. In all the songs, we have retained Rogers's division of words.

Come Not When I Am Dead

No autograph for *Come Not When I Am Dead* is known to exist. Sources for the present edition are a copy of the original edition, held by Spaulding Library of the New England Conservatory, and a copy of the song as it appears in the 1903 *Collection* held in the Allen A. Brown Collection of the Boston Public Library. The two Schmidt editions differ in several respects; however, it is not clear that the differences represent revisions or improvements made between the earlier and later printings. The second printing contains an obviously incorrect alto C-sharp and a rhythmic error in measure 7 of the piano part. The metronome marking is missing, and the instruction *un poco più mosso* is absent in measures 20 and 34. The second printing contains thicker or differently voiced piano chords in measures 11 and 50, and lacks the original's dynamics, nuances or accents in measures 16, 40, 52, 55, and 56. It is possible that the second printing reproduces an old, uncorrected version of the work. Rogers was usually meticulous in her revisions, as the revised copies of *Aubade* attest. Further evidence of her attention to detail is the condition of the holographs in the Arthur P. Schmidt collection at the Library of Congress, which contain many revisions. However, during the second half of 1903, she was on leave from the New England Conservatory, traveling first to California, and then to the Orient with her husband and Phoebe Hearst. She may not have had the opportunity to correct proofs of this work before the 1903 *Collection* was published. The editors of the present edition have chosen to use the richer version presented in the original edition as our source. We have retained the dynamics and articulations of the first edition without change. Piano fingerings have been added editorially.

Apparitions

In revising *Apparitions*, Rogers seems to have worked on problems connected to the major-minor juxtaposition and the final, triumphant major section until the work's publication. It is interesting to note that a draft of the work, held in the Collection of Clara Barnett Rogers and Henry Munroe Rogers in Harvard University's Theatre Collection, breaks off in measure 46, before the final section. In the holograph held by the Arthur P. Schmidt Collection, Library of Congress, Rogers has added mode-changing accidentals in pencil or red pencil in measures 10, 11, 12, 13, and 14. Further corrections in the holograph concern the addition of dynamic or expression marks in measures 5, 7, 8, 10, 17, 18, 20, 24, 40, 41, 42, 43, and 51. The piano bass interval on the first beat of measure 20 has been changed by Rogers from a sixth to a fifth. In measure 58, the C-CC octave on the first beat is the result of a revision. Rogers pasted the corrected piano interlude, measures 34-38, over her original version; the revisions to this section appear to have introduced the hand-crossing.

In editing *Apparitions* we have used the first edition, held by Spaulding Library of the New England Conservatory and by the Allen A. Brown Collection of the Boston Public Library, and the autograph in the Arthur P. Schmidt Collection of the Library of Congress as primary sources. The draft for the work in the Rogers Collection at Harvard University was also consulted. We have made few changes to the first edition. A breath mark in measure 57, present in the holograph, has been added in parentheses, and the dynamic markings in measures 59 and 61 have been returned, in parentheses, to the position in which they were placed in the holograph. Piano fingerings are editorial. All other instructions and suggestions are as they appear in the original edition.

Aubade

Victor Hugo **Clara Kathleen Rogers**

Judith Radell and Delight Malitsky, editors

12
[rall.]
wakes the rose, A - wak - en al - so thee? A - wak - en al - so
rall.
sf
Ped.
16
a tempo
thee?
mf
dim.
p
a tempo
dim.
20
All look for thee, Love, Light and Song; Light in the sky, deep red a -
Ped.

23
bove, Song in the lark of pin - ions strong And in thy heart true
Ped.
27
[rall.]
[a tempo]
love And in thy heart true love.
mf
dim.
rall.
a tempo
dim.
Ped.
sf
31
[rall.]
a tempo
A - part we miss our na-ture's
p
rall.
a tempo
p

35
[rit.]
appassionato
goal, Why strive to cheat our des - ti - nies?
Was not my love made
rit.
40
for thy soul,
appassionato
Thy beau-ty for mine eyes?
sf
44
rit.
[a tempo]
p
No long-er sleep
IV
espressivo
rit.
[a tempo]

48
Oh list-en now! I wait and weep, I wait and weep But where art
52
rit.
thou? But where art
[rit.]
56
[a tempo]
thou?
dim.
[a tempo]

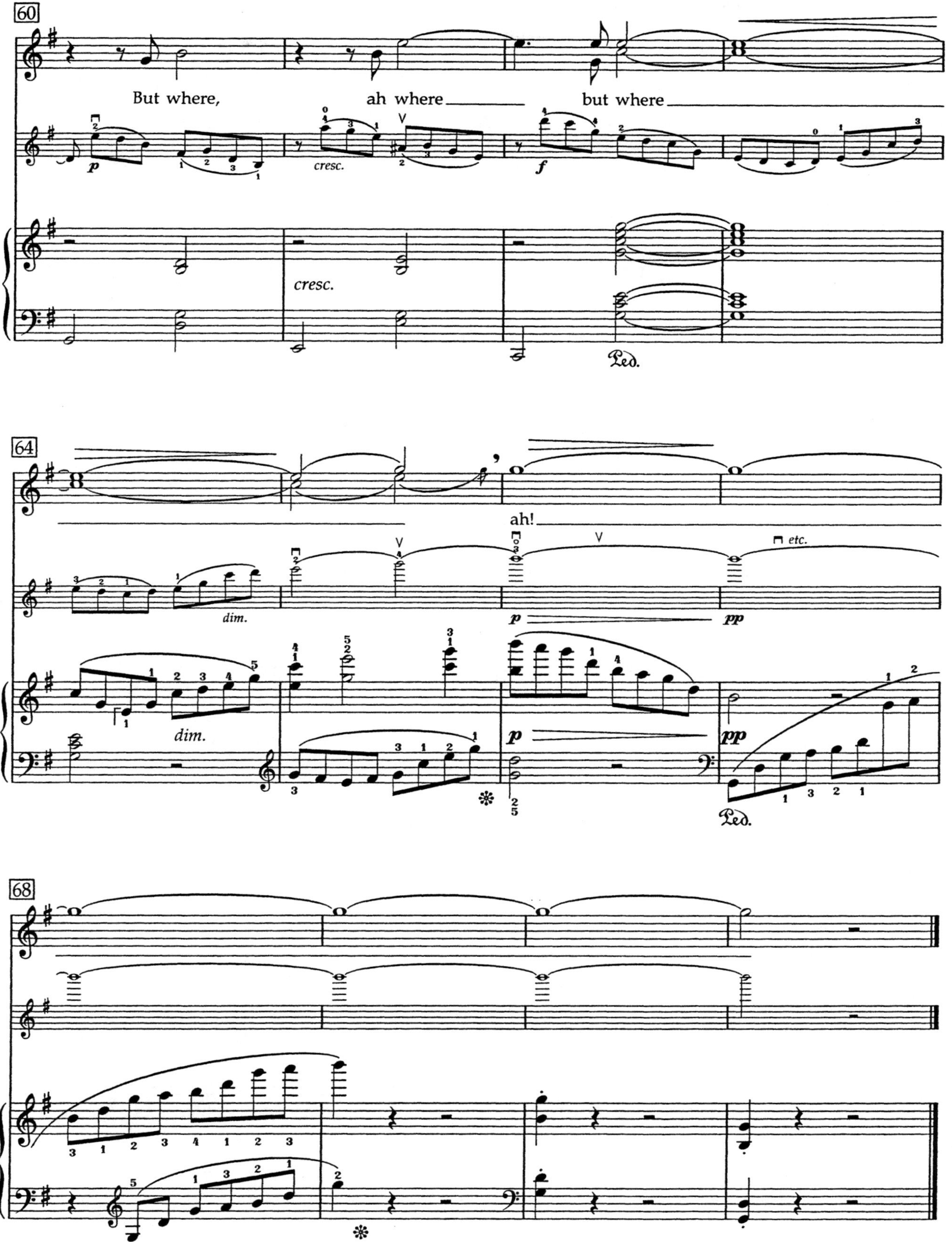
60
But where,
ah where
but where
cresc.
cresc.
Ped.
64
ah!
etc.
dim.
dim.
Ped.
68

Come Not When I Am Dead

Alfred Tennyson

Clara Kathleen Rogers

Judith Radell and Delight Malitsky, editors

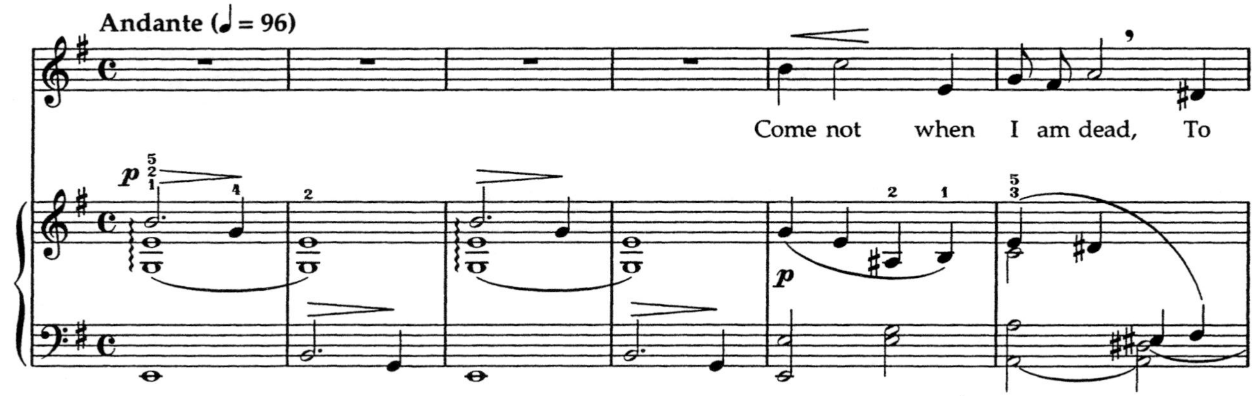

16
Un poco più mosso
p
— thou would'st not save.
There
21
let the wind sweep
and the plov - er
24
cry;
But thou, but thou, go
f
28
by.
rit.

Un poco più mosso
34
p espr.
Child, if it were thine er - ror or thy crime I care no long - er
p dolce
39
be - ing all un - blest:
Solenne
Wed whom thou
mf
44
wilt, but I am sick of time And I des - ire to rest,
p
50
p
And I des - ire to rest.
p
Pass
p
p
sf

54
on, weak heart, and leave me where I
56
lie,
dim.
Ped.
58
rit.
p
a tempo
Go by, go by, go by.
p
63
p
p

Apparitions

Robert Browning

Clara Kathleen Rogers
Judith Radell and Delight Malitsky, editors

13
cross: Vi - o - lets were born!
3
16
vio - lets were born!
p
R.H.
19
22
Sky what a scowl of cloud
ten.

25
Till near and far
ten.
28
sf
Ray on ray spilt the shroud:
31
f
Splend - id a star!
cresc.
allarg.
splend-id a star!
f
cresc.
f
sf
35
[R.H.

39
World
how it walled a - bout
ten.
ten.
42
p
Life
with dis-grace,
ten.
ten.
dim.
45
espr.
Till God's own
mp
Ped.
48
smile came out,
That was thy

51
face!
cresc.
54
That
57
was thy face.
61
dim.

Frances Allitsen

(1848–1912)

SOPHIE FULLER

Born Mary Bumpus on December 30, 1848, Frances Allitsen was one of seven children of the well-known London bookseller John Bumpus and his wife Emma Louisa. Allitsen's earliest ambition was to become a writer, but even as a small child she was improvising both music and words for ballads.[1] Her parents disapproved of her desire to embrace a public life by becoming a composer, and it was not until the early 1880s, when she was in her thirties, that Allitsen became a student at the Guildhall School of Music in London. By this time she had already appeared as a singer with the Kilburn Musical Association under the name Frances Allitsen, the pseudonym by which she was known throughout her career. Her music — songs, piano pieces, and orchestral works — was frequently heard and well reviewed at Guildhall student concerts. By 1882 she was a Corporation Exhibitioner at the school and in 1884 her orchestral overture *Undine* won the Lady Mayoress's Prize.[2] Very few of these early works were published and no manuscripts appear to have survived.

After leaving the Guildhall sometime in the mid-1880s, Allitsen began gradually to build a career as a popular songwriter, also earning money by teaching singing. Her first success in composition came with *An Old English Love Song* (text from John Dowland's *Song Book*), which was frequently performed by the celebrated singers Herbert Thorndike and Charles Santley. A detailed record of Allitsen's negotiations with publishers in the period 1885–1896 has survived. It shows that Boosey (London) gave her a down payment of £5 for this song, with a further sum of £15 when sales reached 2,000 copies, which occurred in April 1895.[3] For other songs Allitsen was paid a royalty, usually three pence per copy. It is clear from the terms offered by her various publishers that her more complex music, such as *Unto the Heart*, a serenade with obbligato violin to words by Victor Hugo (1888), or a *Nocturne* for piano (1888), were seen as more of a financial risk than the more obviously popular songs and ballads.

In the late 1890s Allitsen became particularly well known for her religious and patriotic songs. An earlier *Song of Thanksgiving* (1891) to words by James Thomson had been widely performed and was followed by two highly successful psalm settings: *The Lord is My Light* (1897), sung by Clara Butt, and *Like as the Hart Desireth* (1898), sung by Ada Crossley. During the Boer War (1899–1902), Allitsen produced several stirring nationalistic ballads, including *England, My England* (1900) to words by William Ernest Henley and *The Boys Who Will Not Return* (1901) to words by J. A. Edgerton. Such subject matter, together with her powerful musical language and potentially ambiguous first name, led to a contemporary presumption that she was a male composer.[4] This misconception continued as late as 1966 when Sydney Northcote included her as "Francis Allitsen" in a list of the ten most popular Victorian songwriters in his book *Byrd to Britten: A Survey of English Song*.[5]

During the first decade of the twentieth century, Allitsen began publishing works in more expanded forms such as the song cycle *Moods and Tenses (Phases in a Love Drama)* (1905), and several large-scale dramatic works. The first of these was *Cleopatra*, a *scena* for contralto and orchestra to a text by Shakespeare, first performed by Clara Butt in 1903. It was followed by *For the Queen*, a cantata for baritone, mezzo-soprano, bass, chorus and orchestra to a text by Frank Hyde, premiered at the Crystal Palace in 1911. Neither of these works was particularly well received by contemporary critics. This may have added to the difficulty Allitsen faced in trying to obtain a performance of her most ambitious work, the opera *Bindra the Minstrel*, to her own libretto based on *Songs from the Book of Jaffir*.[6] A diary kept by Allitsen for three months in 1911 shows that there was a possibility, never realized, of a performance of the opera in Berlin. The brief diary entries also show that at this point in her life Allitsen was far from well and frequently despondent. Typical remarks include: "As usual — health delicate, people unkind, remiss and neglectful — professional anxieties and indecisions . . ." and ". . . suffered hideously from depression & ill health."[7] After contracting pleurisy in 1912, she died at home in London on October 1, 1912.

Allitsen was one of several female composers of popular songs working in England at the turn of the century, who built on the success of an earlier generation of songwriters. Unlike Allitsen, these women do not appear to have composed music in extended or instrumental genres. Unfortunately, because no manuscripts or letters by Allitsen seem to have survived, it is difficult to know whether she continued to write instrumental or orchestral works between the early student efforts heard at the Guildhall concerts and the dramatic works which appeared towards the end of her life. Certainly none were published. The music that survived, however, demonstrates that her musical language ranges more widely than the few well-known ballads still occasionally found in the repertoire might suggest.

Rich chromatic harmonies and driving rhythms generally characterize Allitsen's music. Those songs that are not religious or patriotic frequently are about the passions of love. She uses vivid word painting in both vocal line and piano accompaniment while employing formal structures that are often much more elaborate than those of her contemporaries. The desire to move beyond the traditional confines of the simple strophic song can also be seen in her fondness for adding another instrument, whether obbligato or *ad lib.* to the piano accompaniment. These accompaniments, with widely spaced chords and frequent modulations, were perhaps too difficult for the general song-buying public for whom they were intended.[8] A more restrained musical idiom is found in songs such as her collection of Heine settings, published by Robert Cocks in 1892 in its *Series of Artistic Songs*, or in the deliberately oriental open fourths and fifths of her *Four Songs from 'A Lute of Jade'* (1910).

Although her songs were usually published in a variety of keys and vocal ranges, Allitsen's preference for lower female voices can be clearly seen in her later dramatic works. *Cleopatra* is written for a contralto, while the heroines of *For the Queen* and *Bindra the Minstrel* are both mezzo-soprano roles.[9] Allitsen may simply have been writing for her own voice range (she was a mezzo-soprano) but she may also have been avoiding the operatic stereotype of the tragic soprano heroine. Both Narenta in *For the Queen* and Otomis in *Bindra the Minstrel* are strikingly active, heroic characters.

Allitsen's setting of Tennyson's famous lyric "Come not when I am dead" was first published as one of her *Six Songs*, issued by Ascherberg in 1889. The collection was well received, with one reviewer describing it as "very fresh and pleasing, with well-chosen words."[10] It continued to sell well enough to be reissued, with a renewed copyright, in 1897. The other songs in the collection, settings of John Hay, W. H. Mallock, Fanny Kemble, Marie Corelli, and another poem by Tennyson, are all typically rich and dramatic. The most impassioned setting, with an impulsive piano accompaniment under a powerful vocal line, is the turbulent *Prince Ivan's Song* to a poem from bestselling author Marie Corelli's first novel, *The Romance of Two Worlds* (1886). *Come Not When I Am Dead* differs from the other five songs in its poignant simplicity. Through-composed, it has an unassuming chordal piano accompaniment which becomes distinctly chorale-like for the *tranquillo ma con dolore* setting of Tennyson's second stanza. The vocal line contains some characteristic wide leaps, especially at the climactic end of the first stanza.

There's A Land is probably Allitsen's best-known song. A simple but typically bombastic setting of a poem by Marie Corelli's father, Charles Mackay, it was first published in 1896. It became popular a few years later when head mistress Agnes Sibly[11] added a particularly patriotic third verse for her girls to sing during the Boer War. Boosey (London) reissued the song with the extra verse added and Clara Butt performed it throughout England. There is no surviving manuscript for either of these two songs. Only a few minor editorial additions and corrections to the published versions were deemed necessary.

Notes

1. See Allitsen's reminiscences of her childhood as recounted in Percy Cross Standing, "Some Lady Composers: Miss Frances Allitsen," *Lady's Pictorial* 39 (June 2, 1900): 1020.

2. See Corporation of London Records Office, Guildhall School of Music and Drama Archives, Programmes, vol. 1 (1879–1885).

3. See Frances Allitsen, *Book for entering Musical and Literary agreements*, British Library Additional Manuscript 50071. This notebook also contains a brief diary for 1911.

4. See, for example, Harold Simpson, *A Century of Ballads 1810–1910: Their Composers and Singers* (London: Mills and Boon, 1910), 310.

5. Sydney Northcote, *Byrd to Britten: A Survey of English Song* (London: John Baker, 1966), 81.

6. The publication Allitsen probably used is *Songs from the Book of Jaffir* adapted from the Persian translation of Jamshid of Yeezdthe Guebr (London: Macmillan, 1900).

7. Allitsen, *Book for entering Musical and Literary agreements*, n.p.

8. See, for example, Simpson, *A Century of Ballads,* 308.

9. It should also be noted that of all her male roles, only the villain of *Bindra the Minstrel* is written for a tenor rather than a baritone or bass.

10. Anonymous review in a column entitled "New Song Albums," *Athenaeum* 3279 (August 30, 1890): 299.

11. She was "head of a ladies' school in the West of England," according to Simpson, *A Century of Ballads*, 309.

Selected List of Works

Selected Songs and Other Vocal Works

Stars of the Summer Night (ca. 1882). Text by Henry Wadsworth Longfellow. Unpublished.

A Moorish Serenade (ca. 1884). Text unknown. Violin obbligato. Unpublished.

My Lady Sleeps. Text by Henry Wadsworth Longfellow. London: Reid Bros, 1885.

O Hemlock Tree. Text by Henry Wadsworth Longfellow. London: Reid Bros, 1885.

After Long Years. Text by Frances Allitsen. London: Boosey, 1886.

Forget Thee! Text by John Moultrie. London: Boosey, 1886.

Give a Man a Horse He can Ride. Text by James Thomson. London: Hutching, 1886.

Love, We Must Part! Text by Frances Allitsen. London: Reid Bros, 1886.

One or Two. Text by Will Carleton. London: Chappell, 1886.

Over the Bridge. Text by James Thomson. London: Reid Bros, 1886.

Mary Hamilton. Text by Whyte Melville. London: Boosey, 1887.

An Old English Love Song. Text from Dowland's *Song Book.* London: Boosey, 1887.

When the Boys Come Home. Text by John Hay. London: Boosey, 1887.

Marjorie. Text by W. Eltringham Kendall. London: Ascherberg, 1888.

Unto Thy Heart. Text by Victor Hugo. With violin obbligato. London: Ascherberg, 1888.

My Bonny Curl. Text by Amélie Rives. London: Boosey, 1889.

There be None of Beauty's Daughters. Text by Lord Byron. London: Pitt and Hatzfeld, 1889.

Six Songs. London: Ascherberg, 1889.

1. *Not Quite Alone.* Text by John Hay
2. *Come Not When I Am Dead.* Text by Lord Tennyson
3. *Margaret.* Text by W. H. Mallock
4. *Thy Presence.* Text by Fanny Kemble
5. *Prince Ivan's Song.* Text by Marie Corelli
6. *Thy Voice is Heard Thro' Rolling Drums.* Text by Lord Tennyson

Afterward. Text by Ellis Walton. London: Phillips and Page, 1890.

Answered. Text by Ellis Walton. London: Mocatta & Co., 1890.

Love in Spring Time. Text by Lewis Morris. London: Boosey, 1890.

My Laddie. Text by Amélie Rives. London: Boosey, 1890.

The Stars of June. Text by Frederick E. Weatherly. London: Boosey, 1890.

Cavalry Song. Text by Edmund Clarence Stedman. London: Boosey, 1891.

A Song of Thanksgiving. Text by James Thomson. London: Boosey, 1891.

The Stars Are with the Voyager. Text by Thomas Hood. London: Phillips and Page, 1891.

Apart for Evermore. Text by Caris Brooke. London: R. Cocks, 1892.

Before We Part. Text by Ellis Walton. London: Boosey, 1892.

False or True. Text by Clifton Bingham. London: R. Cocks, 1892.

King and Slave. Text by Adelaide Proctor. London: R. Cocks, 1892.

A Song of the Four Seasons. Text by Austin Dobson. London: R. Cocks, 1892.

Warning. Text by Hermann Lingg. London: R. Cocks, 1892.

The Wayside Seat. Text by Ellis Walton. London: J. B. Cramer, 1892.

Album of Eight Songs. Text by Heinrich Heine. London: R. Cocks, 1892.

1. *A Pine-tree Standeth Lonely*
2. *Two Sapphires Those Dear Eyes*
3. *Diamonds Hast Thou and Pearls*
4. *King Duncan's Daughters*
5. *Since My Love Now Loves Me Not*
6. *Fathoms Deep May Drift the Snow*
7. *Oh, Death, it is the Cold, Cold Night*
8. *Katherine*

O Give Me All My Heart! Text by Ellis Watson. London: Phillips and Page, 1893.

In Time of Old. Text by Thomas Love Peacock. London: R. Cocks, 1894.

Wilt Thou Take me for Thy Slave. Text by Wilfred Scawen Blunt. London: R. Cocks, 1894.

Spring Contrasts. Text by William Ernest Henley. London: R. Cocks, 1894.
1. *The Spring, My Dear, is No Longer Spring*
2. *The Nightingale has a Lyre of Gold*

Be My Star. Text by Frederick Langbridge. London: Enoch, 1895.

Bygones. Text by Ellis Watson. London: Enoch, 1895.

The Lute Player. Text by William Watson. London: Willcocks, 1895.

L'intérieur for speaker and piano (1895?). Text by Maurice Maeterlinck. Unpublished.

The Colleen Rue. Text by Katherine Tynan. London: Chappell, 1896.

Dainty Clare. Text by Florence Hoare. London: Houghton, 1896.

Mabel's Song. Text by A. C. Swinburne. London: Boosey, 1896.

The Norseman's Song. Text by M. Ingle Ball. London: Houghton, 1896.

There's A Land. Text by Charles Mackay. London: Boosey, 1896.

The Old Clock on the Stairs. Text by Henry Wadsworth Longfellow. London: Boosey, 1896.

The Lord is My Light. Text Psalm 27. London: Boosey, 1897.

The Lover's Wish. Text by Victor Hugo. London: Houghton, 1897.

My Life and Thine. Text by Constance Sutcliffe. Violin *ad lib.* London: Chappell, 1897.

True Love. Text by Frances Allitsen. London: Strickland Bros, 1897.

When We Two Parted. Text by Lord Byron. London: Boosey, 1897.

In the Sunshine. Text by Augusta Webster. London: Chappell, 1898.

Like as the Hart Desireth. Text Psalm 43. Cello obbligato. London: Boosey, 1898.

Like Violets Pale. Text by James Thomson. London: Boosey, 1898.

Oh! For a Burst of Song. Text by Frances Ridley Havergal. London: Boosey, 1898.

Severed. Text by "Hal." London: Boosey, 1898.

Sunset and Dawn. Text by Frances Ridley Havergal. London: Boosey, 1898.

Two Songs. Text by Owen Meredith, Earl of Lytton. London: Metzler, 1898.
1. *Since We Parted*
2. *Absence*

On the River. Text by James Thomson. Duet. London: Chappell, 1899.

Break, Diviner Light! Text by Lord Tennyson. Duet. London: Boosey, 1899.

Lady! In this Night of June. Text by Alfred Austin. Cello obbligato. London: Metzler, 1899.

A Song of Farewell. Text by Sir Edwin Arnold. London: Chappell, 1899.

Three Songs. London: G. Schirmer, 1899.
1. *Whether We Die or We Live*. Text by George Meredith
2. *A Cavalier's Song*. Text by William Motherwell
3. *A Song of Dawn*. Text by Ellis Walton

England, My England! Text by William Ernest Henley. London: Boosey, 1900.

Sing Me to Rest. Text by Harold Whitaker. Violin *ad lib.* London: Boosey, 1900.

Heini of Steir, the Meistersinger (1900). Text by Victor Scheffel. Violin obbligato. Unpublished.

Sons of the City. Text by Bernard Malcolm Ramsay. London: Ascherberg, 1900.

Thanksgiving for Victory. Text by G. W. Choral song. London: Metzler, 1900.

The Boys Who Will Not Return. Text by J. A. Edgerton. London: Boosey, 1901.

I Know a Little Rose. Text by Bayard Taylor. London: G. Schirmer, 1901.

In Our Boat. Text by Dinah Maria Craik. Duet. London: G. Schirmer, 1901.

Two Christmas Songs. London: Boosey, 1901.
1. *The Star in the East*. Text by William Theodore Peters
2. *From Heart to Heart*. Text by Robert F. Murray

Glory to God on High. Text by Robert F. Murray. London: G. Schirmer, 1902.

Like a Garden after Rain. Text by Alfred Austin. London: Ricordi, 1902.

My Lady's Pleasure. Text by Edward Teschemacher. London: Jeffreys, 1902.

The Scottish Pipers. Text by Bernard Malcolm Ramsay. London: Chappell, 1902.

Two Songs. London: Metzler, 1902.
1. *Think on me Dear.* Text by Sir Edwin Arnold
2. *Always Together.* Text by William Theodore Peters

Hymn of Trust. Text by Oliver Wendell Holmes. Organ or harmonium *ad lib.* London: Enoch, 1903.

Love's Despair. Text by Diarmid O'Curhain. London: Boosey, 1903.

The Sovereignty of God. Text by Frances Ridley Havergal. Organ *ad lib.* London: Chappell, 1903.

Who Would Not Captive Be? Text by MacKenzie MacBride. London: Boosey, 1903.

Forgetfulness. Text by Fred Vigay. London: Metzler, 1904.

The Hidden Grief. Text by Thomas Ingoldsby. London: Metzler, 1904.

The Loyalty of Love. Text by Lord Lytton. London: Boosey, 1904.

Youth. Text by Edward Teschemacher "after the Swedish." London: Boosey, 1904.

The Wayfarer. Text by John Mansfield. London: Boosey, 1904.

A Song of Faithfulness. Text by Florence Hoare. London: Boosey, 1905.

Song of the Gun. Text by J. E. MacManns. London: Metzler, 1905.

Moods and Tenses (Phases in a Love Drama). London: Boosey, 1905.
1. *Rebellion.* Text by Amelia B. Edwards
2. *Love's Mandate.* Text anon
3. *As the Buds Look Up.* Text by William C. Scully
4. *Regret.* Text by Frank Hyde
5. *Doubts.* Text by Lord Lytton
6. *Resolve.* Text by Frank Hyde
7. *Rapture.* Text by Frank Hyde
8. *Love's Victory.* Text by Robert Bridges

Adoration. Text by Frances Ridley Havergal. Organ *ad lib.* London: Boosey, 1907.

Forward. Text by Edna Dean Proctor. London: Stainer & Bell, 1907.

A Lover's Song. Text by W. J. Lancaster. London: Chappell, 1907.

Two Short Songs. Text by William Theodore Peters. London: Stainer and Bell, 1907.
1. *Love and Grief — Nature and Art*
2. *The Mountain and the Star*

Lift Thy Heart. Text by Fred Bowles. Organ or harmonium *ad lib.* London: Chappell, 1908.

Eastern Serenade. Text by Dorothy Johnson. London: Chappell, 1908.

Praise Thou the Lord, O My Soul. Text Psalms 145 and 146. London: J. Church, 1908.

Soul's Dedication. Text by William Akerman. London: Chappell, 1908.

Two Songs. Text by C. Whitworth Wynne. Violin, cello or horn obbligato. London: J. Church, 1908.
1. *Nocturne*
2. *The Sou'Wester*

Tell Her, Sweet Thrush! Text by C. Whitworth Wynne. London: Weekes, 1909.

Three Love Letters. London: Chappell, 1909.
1. *A Letter.* Text by William Theodore Peters
2. *Sweet Sorrow.* Text by William Theodore Peters
3. *As Cooling Dew.* Text by Georgina Hubi-Newcombe

Four Songs from 'A Lute of Jade.' London: Weekes, 1910.
1. *The Waning Moon.* Text from *The Odes of Confucius*
2. *The Nightless Tryst.* Text from *The Odes of Confucius*
3. *High O'er The Hill.* Text by Wang Seng Ju
4. *A King of Liang.* Text by Kao-Shih

England, Queen of the Seas! Text by Charles Cayzer. London: Weekes, 1912.

Choral and Stage Works

Cleopatra. Text by Shakespeare and Thomas S. Collier. Scena. London: Boosey, 1904.

Magnificat ("A Hymn of the Woodlands"). Text by Arthur L. Salmon. Contralto or baritone solo with chorus. London: Boosey, 1909.

For the Queen. Text by Frank Hyde. Cantata for baritone, mezzo-soprano and bass soloists, chorus and orchestra. London: Boosey, 1911.

Bindra the Minstrel. Libretto adapted by Frances Allitsen from *Songs from the Book of Jaffir*. Opera. London: Weekes, 1912.

Works for Piano

Sonata in F minor (1881?). Unpublished.

Caprice (1882?). London: Boosey, 1886.

Danse humoresque. London: Boosey, 1888.

Nocturne. London: Augener, 1888.

Doushka (Polka-Mazurka). London: Joseph Williams, 1891.

Instrumental Works

Three Sketches for violin and piano (1884?). Unpublished.

Cradle Song for violin and piano. London: R. Cocks, 1893.

Lullaby for violin and piano. London: R. Cocks, 1893.

Preghiera for violin or cello and piano. London: Chappell, 1907.

Orchestral Works

Suite (1883?). Unpublished.

Overture "Slavonic" (1884?). Unpublished.

Overture "Undine" (1884?). Unpublished.

Funeral March. Unpublished.

Tarantella. Unpublished.

Bibliography

Allitsen, Frances. *Book for entering Musical and Literary agreements*. British Library Additional Manuscript 50071.

Fuller, Sophie. "Frances Allitsen." In *The Pandora Guide to Women Composers: Britain and the United States, 1629– present.* London: Pandora, 1994.

_____. "Women Composers During the British Musical Renaissance, 1880–1918." Ph.D. diss., King's College, London, 1998.

Northcote, Sydney. *Byrd to Britten: A Survey of English Song*. London: John Baker, 1966.

Simpson, Harold. *A Century of Ballads 1810–1910: Their Composers and Singers*. London: Mills and Boon, 1910.

Standing, Percy Cross. "Some Lady Composers: Miss Frances Allitsen." *Lady's Pictorial* 39 (June 2, 1900): 1020.

Discography

John McCormack sings Panis Angelicus. John McCormack, tenor (and various). Pearl GEMM 176E (1979). "The Lord is my Light."

Come Not When I Am Dead

Alfred, Lord Tennyson

Frances Allitsen
Sophie Fuller, editor

Andante sostenuto

[*p*]

7

mf molto espressivo

Come not, when I am dead, To drop thy

12

foo - lish tears up - on my grave! [*p*] To *cresc.* tram - ple round my

sf *p* *cresc.*

16

fal - len head, And [*f*] vex th'un - hap - py dust thou *sf* would'st not

[*f*] *sf*

20
p dolce
save. There let the wind sweep, and the plo-ver
pp
Ped. Ped. Ped. Ped. Ped.
24
ff
sf appassionato
sf
sf
dim.
tempo sostenuto
cry, But thou, but thou go by, go by.
ff molto marcato
sf
sf
mf
Ped. [*]
Ped.
29
p tranquillo ma con dolore
Child if it were thine
p tranquillo
35
[p]
er - ror or thy crime, I care no lon - ger be - ing all un - blest.
[p]

40
cresc.
[mf]
molto espressivo
Wed whom thou wilt, but I am sick of time, and I de -
cresc.
[mf]
legato
colla voce
44
sire to rest, to rest,
dim.
pp
49
mf sostenuto
appassionato
f
dim.
Pass on, weak heart, and leave me, where I lie. Go
mf sostenuto
appassionato
f
marcato
dim.
53
[p]
by, go by.
[p]
dim.
morendo
pp

There's A Land

Charles Mackay
Third verse by Agnes M. Sibly

Frances Allitsen
Sophie Fuller, editor

13
Show - 'ry! Flow - 'ry! Cheer - ful! Tear - ful! Eng-land, wave - guard - ed, and
marcato
16
green to the shore! West land! Best land! Thy land! My land!
rall.
cresc.
19
tempo
maestoso e marcato
Glo - ry be with her, and Peace ev - er-more.
maestoso
fanfare
cresc.
22
rall.
tempo
There's a
marcato

25
maestoso
land, a dear land, where our vig - our of soul Is fed by the tem - pests that
maestoso
28
blow from the Pole; Where a slave can - not breathe, or in - va - der pre - sume To
[Con] 8
31
ask for more earth than will co - ver his tomb. Sea land! Free land!
34
Fair - est! Rar - est! Home of brave men and the girls they a-dore!
marcato

* R.H.: A-flat in original; A natural suggested.

48
[p]
no - blest and best; Where the peo - ple love Peace, but, at
[p]
sf
sf
[Con] 8
sf
50
marcato
sound of the drum, A my - riad of sol - diers and
cresc.
marcato
52
[f]
[mf]
[f]
[mf]
he - roes be-come. Pur - est! Sur - est! Roy - al! Loy - al!
[f]
[mf]
[f]
[mf]
55
[f]
This year and all years we'll sing and we'll pray:—
[f] marcato

57
rall.
Glo - rious! Vic - to - rious! Thy Realm! My Realm!
[Con] 8
[tempo]
59
[ff] molto marcato
God bless our Em - pire both now and for aye,
[ff] molto marcato
61
rall.
God bless our Em - pire both now and for
63
Animato al fine
aye.
cresc. molto
fff
sf
[Con] 8

Mary Carmichael
(1851–1935)

JOHN R. GARDNER AND TAMARA BELDOM

Mary Grant Carmichael, an English composer and accompanist, was born in Birkenhead, Cheshire, in 1851. Her father was John Carmichael of Birkenhead and Corozal,[1] but registration papers which would have established Mary's exact date of birth and the occupation of her father have not been located. Carmichael studied with Heinrich Porges in Munich.[2] After returning to the United Kingdom she became a pupil at the Academy for the Higher Development of Piano Playing, a school founded in London by Oscar Beringer,[3] where her teachers were Beringer himself, Walter Bache, Franklin Taylor, Fritz Hartvigson and Ebeneezer Prout. She also took private composition lessons from Prout. At the July 1876 pupils' graduation concert at the Academy she played her own *Mazurka & Humoreske*.

One of Carmichael's earliest public appearances was at Langham Hall in London on May 5, 1877, when, with an older sister, she played her own recently published *Five Waltzes for Two Performers on a Pianoforte*. Her *Hymn to Diana* was performed at a Musical Artists Society concert in London on July 26, 1879.

Carmichael's debut as a recital accompanist took place on May 22, 1880, when she played for a vocal recital at Steinway Hall in London. This was followed by her appointment as accompanist to the newly founded Saint Cecilia Ladies Choir and Orchestra in 1880. (She may have been the first public professional female accompanist in Britain.) In 1884 she became one of the regular accompanists at the famous Monday and Saturday Popular concerts (known as Pop concerts) given at St. James Hall in London. At the Monday Pop concert on February 9, 1885, her Shakespearean duets *Who is Sylvia?* and *A Poor Soul Sat Sighing* were performed. These duets were also included in a recital at Princes Hall in London on May 14 that year.

The term accompanist as we understand it today was not used in Britain until the last quarter of the nineteenth century. Before this the ambiguous term "conductor" was used and applied to men. It was considered effeminate for a man to play the piano in the British Victorian home where music was regarded as part of the feminine domestic realm. Although women acted as amateur accompanists in the home and many were employed by solo singers and choral societies for private rehearsals, they risked the charge of encroaching into the domain of male professionalism if they appeared in public.

Carmichael spent her annual winter holidays in Florence, Italy, where her brother Montgomery served as British vice-consul in 1892.[4] It was in Florence that she met the tenor William Nicholl[5] and subsequently played a joint recital with him on January 13, 1886, which was praised by the local press. She returned to London for the Pop concert the following month at which her Shakespearean duet *It was a Lover and his Lass* was performed and on June 16, 1886, she and William Nicholl gave a London recital reviewed in *The Times* (London), June 18, 1886.

> Miss Mary Carmichael and Mr. William Nicholl gave an interesting and well attended recital at Princes Hall on Wednesday evening, when the programme consisted of numerous vocal and instrumental pieces. Miss Carmichael, who is a graceful and melodious composer, contributed several of her own works, the duet *It was a lover and his lass* [*sic*] being well sung. Even more successful were two of her tenor songs *The Milkmaid* and *Love's Wishes*, in which Mr. Nicholl displayed an agreeable voice and considerable musical intelligence.[6]

Carmichael was unanimously elected a lady associate of the Philharmonic Society, London, in November of 1887 the year in which her song cycle *Songs of the Stream* had its premiere at the Lyric Club. Her association with Nicholl continued throughout his life; the duo was invited to Balmoral, Scotland to perform for Queen Victoria on November 6, 1890. However, the last artist whom she regularly accompanied was probably the most celebrated, the English tenor Gervaise Elwes.[7]

Carmichael retired in April 1926. She spent her time reading and listening to the radio, which she particularly enjoyed when her own music was broadcast. Carmichael died at her home, 18 Steeles Road, Hampstead, London, on March 17, 1935, at the age of 84. An unnamed friend contributing to her obituary notice in *The Times*

(London) reported some of her last words: "How glad I am that my eldest sister, when I was eight years old, made me learn a little piece by Bach; she put me on the right road. There must be music in heaven."[8]

Carmichael's first published compositions were for the piano. These pieces were not too difficult for the average pianist, but were superior to average drawingroom works. She soon began to write songs, the most acceptable genre of music from a female composer, and therefore the most profitable. *The Milkmaid* was her most popular song, but her own favorites were her two-part songs. Carmichael's accompaniments are always varied, fresh, harmonically resourceful, and effective. Her technique of repeating certain detached words to suit her musical convenience or to extend the musical phrases worked well for her settings of sixteenth- and seventeenth-century verse, but seemed slightly out of place for her settings of later poetry.

Carmichael composed about seventy-five songs: twenty two-part songs, ten four-part songs, five albums of songs for children, a Mass and an operetta called *The Frozen Heart* (based on Hans Christian Andersen's story *The Snow Maiden*).

Her imaginative songs for children are short and simple settings of excellent poetry: *Sing Song* (Christina Rossetti), *A Child's Garden of Verses* (Robert Louis Stevenson), *Nature Songs for Children* (Lilian Bransby), and *Sunbeams* (Frederick Weatherley).

The song *Hey! Jolly Robin Hood!* combines elements of old English song and children's song. The vocal line of this strophic piece with words from "The Musical Dream" by Robert Jones is echoed by the right hand of the piano part. Notated in the treble clef, it is intended as a bass song, a common practice in Victorian vocal music. The chordal framework is simple, with suspensions and unresolved passing notes adding sophistication to the musical language. The introduction begins with a heraldic fanfare outlining a C major arpeggio that is then answered by a skipping phrase. In each verse the chords change on every word, establishing a fast harmonic pace. The pattern of one syllable to one note is broken only when a *melisma* is introduced on the word "love" in measures 15, 37 and 59, 83. Between the verses a rising heraldic figure develops into a horn call that suggests a hunting scene in the "green wood." The fourth departs from the first three in the second line when it moves straight to the dominant without traveling through the expected E minor. The third line is extended from six to eight measures and is totally in the triumphant tonic key of C major. The singer's final C functions as a tonic pedal under which the piano plays a melody which is immediately repeated a third lower, harmonized by a diminished chord. This short postlude ends with a plagal cadence.

Kitty Bawn is Carmichael's most popular work. It is the sixth song in her *Album of Six Songs*, with texts by A. P. Graves, an Irish writer who was her contemporary. The lyrics have elements of a traditional Irish love song: the time of day, the name of the beloved, and her qualities. However, Carmichael makes no attempt to provide pseudo-Irish music. The voice part includes several instances of unprepared dissonant minor-second intervals in eighth notes resolving to consonances in the accompanying quarter note chords. The words "I looked" (mm. 10-11) in the first verse and "the glance" (mm. 38-39) in the third verse are set in the style of a trumpet call. In the third verse the piano accompaniment becomes harmonically fuller, changing from a quarter note pattern to an eighth note pattern, in keeping with the more ardent nature of the words. The climax of the song occurs on the first beat of measure 41 where the word "glance" is set as eighth notes on an F rising to an upper A-flat. In this measure, too, Carmichael uses her favorite effect of repeating seemingly unimportant words. "The glance that she gave me" is set so that the word "gave" has its proper emphasis, then the phrase "she gave me" is repeated so that this time the emphasis is on the word "me" falling on the first beat of measure 42. This enables the song's final word "by" to appear on the weak third beat and to be sustained in to the final measure of the voice part.

Acknowledgments

The British Library, London, has copies of most of Carmichael's published works. I acknowledge with thanks the kindness of Stainer & Bell Ltd. for permission to use the song *Hey! Jolly Robin Hood!* Copies can be obtained from Stainer & Bell Ltd., Victoria House, 23 Gruneisen Road, London N3 1DZ, UK.

Notes

1. Corozal is on the northern border of Belize, Central America.

2. Heinrich Porges (1837–1900) was a music critic in Leipzig from 1863 to 1867. He then went to Munich where, in 1871, he became director of the Royal School of Music and founded his own choir in 1886.

3. Oscar Beringer (1844–1922) was an English pianist. His Academy opened in 1871 and closed in 1897.

4. Montgomery Carmichael (1857–1936) was British consul at Livorno, Italy from 1908 to 1922. He was an authority on Italian church art.

5. William Nicholl (1851–1902) left Scotland for India in his youth with his father. He came to London in 1883 and entered the Royal Academy of Music in 1884. He went to Florence to complete his vocal studies in July 1885, then returned to London.

6. *The Times* (London), June 18, 1886, p. 9.

7. Gervaise Elwes (1866–1921) was in the British diplomatic service before becoming a professional tenor in 1903. He was noted for his singing in *The Dream of Gerontius* by Edward Elgar (1857–1934).

8. M. E. G. of H. Obituary in *The Times* (London), March 2, 1935, p. 16.

Selected List of Works

Vocal

Songs

Hymn to Diana (1877). Text anonymous. Unpublished.

The Flower of the Vale. Text by Thomas Cox. London: Stanley Lucas & Weber Co., 1883.

Dawn Talks to Day. Text by William Morris. London: Stanley Lucas, Weber & Co., 1884.

The Old Oak Tree. Text by Thomas Cox. London: Weekes & Co., 1885.

Love's Wishes (1886). Text anonymous. Unpublished.

The Milkmaid. Text by Austin Dobson. London: Weekes & Co., 1886.

A June Song. Text by Louisa Sarah Bevington. London: Cramer & Co., 1886.

It's No'In Titles. Text by Robert Burns. London: J. & J. Hopkinson, 1887.

Songs of The Stream (Song Cycle). Texts by Wm Blake, M. Collins Robt. Herrick, Wm Shakespeare. N.c., n.p., 1887

Love Song. Text by Samuel Daniel. London: Metzler & Co., 1890.

Hey! Jolly Robin Hood! Text by Robert Jones. London: Weekes & Co., 1895.

Album of Six Songs by A. P. Graves. Text by Alfred Perceval Graves. London: Boosey & Co., 1890.

1. *Love's Wishes*
2. *The White Blossom's Off the Bog*
3. *The Limerick Lasses*
4. *Jack the Jolly Ploughboy*
5. *The Rose of Kenmare*
6. *Kitty Bawn*

Two-part Songs

Six Shakespearean Songs for two voices. Text by William Shakespeare. London: J.Curwen & Sons, 1885.

1. *Tell Me Where Is Fancy Bred*
2. *A Poor Soul Sat Sighing*
3. *Under the Greenwood Tree*
4. *Take, O Take Those Lips Away*
5. *When I Was a Tiny Little Boy*
6. *Who is Sylvia?*

At Daybreak. Text by May Gillington. London: J. & J. Hopkinson, 1889.

Under the Thorn Tree. Text by Edith Nesbitt. London: R. Cocks & Co., 1892.

Songs for Children

Sing Song. Text by Christina Rossetti. Twenty-seven settings (solos and part-songs). London: Augener & Co., 1884.

14 Nature Songs for Children. Text by Lilian Bransby. London: Augener & Co., 1907.

Four-part Songs

A Single Star in a Rose Sky. Text by William Davies. London: Weekes & Co., 1887.

Bibliography

Rieman Musik Lexicon, Erganzungsbad Personentiel, L-Z. Mainz: Schott & Co., 1975.

The Times (London). June 18, 1886.

The Times (London). Obituary. March 2, 1935.

Who Was Who 1929–1940. London: Adam & Charles Black Ltd., 1941.

Hey! Jolly Robin Hood!

Robert Jones **Mary Carmichael**

Con spirito

f

4

In Sher-wood lived stout Ro - bin _ Hood, An ar - cher great, none

8

great - er, His bow and shafts were sure and good, Yet Cu - pid's were much

12

mf p

bet - ter, Hey! _ jol - ly _ Ro - bin Hood! Love ___

17
cresc.
finds out_ me As_ well as_thee, To fol-low me, to fol-low me to the
cresc.
f
21
green - - wood.
25
mf
A no - ble thief was Ro - bin_Hood,
mf
8
29
Wise was_ he could de - ceive him, Yet Ma - ri - an in his bra - vest mood,

33
f
Could of his heart be - reave him:
mf
Hey! jol - ly Ro - bin Hood!
37
p
Love finds out me As well as thee, To
41
f
fol-low me, to fol-low me to the green - - wood.
45
An
8

49
mf
out - law was this Ro - bin Hood, His life free and un -
mf
52
ru - ly, Yet to fair Ma - rian bound he stood, And
55
f
love debt paid her du - ly:
f
mf
Hey! jol - ly Ro - bin Hood!
mf
59
p
Love finds out me As well as thee, To
p

63
f
fol-low me, to fol-low me to the green - - wood.
f
67
Now
f
8
71
mf
wend we home, stout Ro - bin Hood, Leave we the woods be - hind us, Love -
mf
75
poco rit.
f
pas - sions must not be with stood, Love ev' - ry where will find us
f

79
a tempo
f
Hey! jol - ly — Ro - bin Hood! Ho! jol - ly — Ro - bin Hood!
f
83
mf
Love — finds out me As — well as — thee, To
mf
87
fol - low me, to fol - low — me — to the green - - -
f
90
wood. —
f

Kitty Bawn

Alfred P. Graves

Mary Carmichael

Poco allegretto
p
Be - fore the first _ ray of
p
p
4
blush - ing _ day _ who should come by _ but _ Kit - ty _ Bawn? With her
7
poco cresc.
cheek like the rose _ on a bed of _ snows, And her bo - som be - neath like the
poco cresc.
10
mf
p
sail - ing _ swan. I look'd and look'd I
mf
p

13
f
look'd and look'd till my heart was gone.
16
p
With the foot of the fawn she crossed the lawn
p
19
mf
Half con - fi - ding and half in fear
p
Half in fear and
p
22
half con - fi-ding: And her eyes of blue they thrill'd me through

25
poco accel.
f
One bless-ed mi-nute; then like the deer A - way she dart - ed, and
f
28
left me here. Oh!
31
mf
Sun, you are late at your gold - en gate, For you've no-thing to show be -
mf
34
cresc.
neath the sky To com - pare to the lass who crossed the grass of the
cresc.

37
sham - rock field, ere the dew was dry, And the
39
poco rit.
cresc.
glance the glance And the
41
rit.
glance that she gave me, she gave me, as she went by
43

Maude Valérie White
(1855–1937)

SOPHIE FULLER

At the turn of the last century Maude Valérie White was known and critically acclaimed throughout Britain and abroad for her heartfelt and beautifully crafted songs. The variety of her songs, set to texts in many different languages, reflects her cosmopolitan childhood. Born near Dieppe on June 23, 1855, to English parents, she spent the first few years of her life in England, then lived with a governess in Germany for two years before being sent to school, first in Wolverhampton and then in Paris. After her father died in the late 1860s, White returned to England where she gradually became more immersed in music. By 1873 she had started writing songs and was soon taking private composition lessons with Oliver May. Determined to receive a thorough musical education, White eventually persuaded her mother, who disapproved of a professional training for her daughter, to allow her to study at the Royal Academy of Music, London. She entered the Academy in the autumn of 1876, the year in which her first songs appeared in print. Three years later she became the first woman to be awarded the coveted Mendelssohn scholarship for composition. In 1880 her songs began to reach a much wider public when they were taken up by the renowned baritone Charles Santley and performed at prestigious venues in London and elsewhere.

In 1881 White's mother died. White gave up her scholarship and spent nearly a year with relatives in Chile. A few months after her return to London, she moved into independent lodgings and began to establish herself as a professional musician, supplementing a small private income by publishing her songs, accompanying a variety of singers at public concerts and private soirées, and by teaching the piano to wealthy amateurs and their children. White and her music were soon frequently heard in London's concert halls and at society parties of music lovers and patrons such as May Gaskell, Lady Gladys de Grey, and Frankie Schuster.

In 1883, shortly before becoming, in her own words, "a *bona fide* professional,"[1] she took further composition lessons with Robert Fuchs in Vienna. Fuchs, like her other teachers, recognized White's talent and tried to persuade her to compose in genres other than the solo song. White attempted to write a concerto but, like so many women of the time, suffered a debilitating lack of confidence in her own capabilities. She not only found writing the concerto impossible but, far worse, soon felt "as if every scrap of music in me were dead."[2] Encouraged by a letter from her former teacher, Oliver May, which advised her not to be ashamed of embracing song writing as a vocation, White made the conscious decision not to attempt writing in larger genres — with happy results:

> No sooner did I feel that no one expected me to write sonatas or concertos than I began to compose again with the greatest ease. The relief of finding that I could still write was a real joy. Instead of feeling that mentally I was developing into the equivalent of something rather more stodgy than a half-boiled suet pudding, I began to feel like a gay and cheerful soufflé.[3]

For the rest of her life, White proudly remained a song-writer, pouring all her energy into creating a substantial body of work in this one genre. Only a very few instrumental works by her have survived, including some piano pieces, a ballet (*The Enchanted Heart*),[4] and an unfinished opera (*Smaranda*).[5]

White never married nor does she appear to have had any romantic or sexual relationships. However, she believed passionately in love, a central theme for many of her songs. She developed important friendships that supported her both professionally and emotionally. One of the many singers who became a close personal friend was Liza Lehmann (see this volume). In the early 1890s the two women both lived in Pinner near London and frequently gave each other advice and encouragement on their latest work. In 1896 White moved to the picturesque village of Broadway where she lived next door to the actor Mary Anderson who recalled of her friend that "for a long time her only furniture was a grand piano and a bathtub."[6] Broadway at that time had been colonized by painters, musicians and writers from London; White frequently involved this artistic community in concerts that she organized at the village inn, The Lygon Arms.

White's closest companion in the later part of her life was undoubtedly the writer Robert Hichens who left the following vivid description of his friend:

> She had very bad health, though she lived to a great age, but her spirit was unconquerable and her vitality was astounding. She was not merely gifted — she won the Mendelssohn scholarship at the [Royal] Academy of Music, and Santley introduced her first songs to the world when she was only a girl — but she was exceptionally clever, extraordinarily humorous and amusing, a linguist, an omnivorous reader, and one of the most entertaining talkers in London or anywhere else. She was also great-hearted, impulsive, enthusiastic, impetuous, and beneath it all deeply religious. . . . As a pianist she was brilliant: she played the music of Chopin quite exceptionally well. . . . At our first meeting she played to me for a couple of hours until I was almost dazed by her orchestral energy and the multifarious character of her powers.[7]

By the time of their first meeting, in about 1898, White was at the height of her fame as a songwriter. Her songs were sung at prestigious concerts throughout the country by all the best known singers of the day, including Clara Butt, Harry Plunket Greene and Robert Kennerley Rumford. White also organized annual concerts of her own, a risky but potentially profitable enterprise.

As well as being popular, her songs were also regarded highly by the musical establishment. The entry on her music in the first edition of Grove's *A Dictionary of Music and Musicians* (1899) described her songs as "graceful, melodious, well-written, and well-adapted to the voice" and welcomed "her careful attention to the metre and accents of the verse," singling out for praise her Herrick settings with their "pure, quaint, and measured music" as well as claiming of *My Soul is an Enchanted Boat* (1883) that "it is not too much to say that the song is one of the best in our language."[8]

White was an inveterate traveler and from the late 1880s spent much of her time traveling through Europe, Russia and North Africa. She was fascinated by the traditional music of the countries she visited; echoes of various folk musics found their way into her own work. In 1901 she settled in Sicily, although she continued to travel for much of the year, staying with friends in England and elsewhere in Europe. She was later based in Florence and, after the First World War, in Rome, but she appears to have spent the last few years of her life back in England. By the 1920s and '30s White's intensely emotional music had fallen somewhat out of fashion and while she continued to compose a series of increasingly inventive songs and to organize concerts, she also turned to translation work in order to make ends meet.[9] White died in London on November 2, 1937, at the age of 82, leaving everything to her beloved sister Emmie White and asking for her funeral "to be absolutely simple like that of a poor person."[10]

From an early stage in her career White was credited with raising the standard of British songwriting. In an 1887 article for a series on women composers in *The Englishwoman's Review*, André de Ternant wrote:

> If ever the time shall come to regenerate the once honoured English ballad, the name of Maude Valérie White will certainly be remembered as one of those who did their best to prepare the way.[11]

In January 1896 a writer for *The Musical Times* described her as "that foremost of English songwriters."[12] As a composer of Victorian song, one of the most denigrated and misunderstood of genres, White's reception has suffered immeasurably in the late twentieth century. Whereas late-nineteenth-century critics classified her songs as high-class art music, later writers dismiss her as a composer of "drawing-room ballads," a confused and confusing distinction, not usually founded on any detailed knowledge of the songs themselves. Simply in terms of her influence on later British songwriters, White was an important historical figure. Her friend Roger Quilter was undoubtedly indebted to her approach to songwriting, as were, to a lesser extent, composers such as Ralph Vaughan Williams and Edward Elgar.

In her memoirs White explained her method of composition by describing her first attempt at creating a song at the age of seventeen:

> I was sitting alone in the drawing-room when something compelled me to go to the piano and sing Byron's "Farewell, if ever fondest prayer." I knew the poem well, and improvised the music to the words without the slightest difficulty. It is the way I have composed the melody of almost every song I have ever written, naturally working up the accompaniment and adding many little details afterwards.[13]

Such an image plays down her scrupulous study of composition: at the Royal Academy of Music with George Macfarren and Frank Davenport; in Vienna with Robert Fuchs (a period when she spent four hours every day working at counterpoint); and later in her lessons in orchestration with Sydney Waddington and Herbert Bedford. Inspired by the passion and emotion that were so important to her and which she found mirrored in the poetry that she chose to set, White's songs were always carefully constructed. She paid close attention to word setting but usually avoided obvious word painting and preferred to work in strophic (or modified strophic) rather than through-composed forms. Her songs display a heartfelt lyricism expressed in delicately arching and drawn out melodies supported by subtle piano accompaniments that pick up on motifs from the long vocal lines that usually avoid expected cadence points. The accompaniments that White herself played were often considerably more difficult than those that were eventually published.[14]

But White was never afraid of simplicity; some of her songs use strikingly minimal vocal lines. *Be Near Me When My Light is Low* (1885), for example, the last of a group of four songs setting extracts from Tennyson's *In Memoriam A. H. H.*, opens with a chant-like setting of the first verse that is almost entirely on one note, a dominant pedal, over extremely slow moving piano chords.

White's arrangements of folk songs gathered during her European travels included *6 Volkslieder* (1893), Tuscan folk songs in translations by John Addington Symonds (1895), and numerous works using Sicilian folk music. Other musical experiences found their way less directly into her music, as can be heard in the echoes of Hungarian gypsy music in *Die Zigeuner* (1887) or in the lively rhythms of Spain and Latin America in *Serenata Española* (1883). She attempted to write down the Arab music that she heard when traveling in North Africa but found it frustratingly elusive. Nevertheless she apparently used her impressions when composing the incidental music (now lost) for Robert Hichens' play *The Law of the Sands*.

As is apparent even in a selected work list, the texts that White set cover a wide range, including Norwegian and Swedish lyrics, seventeenth-century English poems, contemporary French verse, and the classic lieder poetry of Heine. The details of her musical language varied according to her texts. For settings of Herrick or Suckling, for example, she used a deliberately old-fashioned and measured style whereas in her late French settings, in particular *Le Foyer* (1924) to words by Paul Verlaine, she created a decidedly impressionistic and sensual sound world.

White's song *To Mary* was the only song that she wrote while in deep mourning for her mother in the early 1880s in Chile. She set Shelley's plaintive poem to a typically elongated melody, accompanied by a delicate piano part continually echoing and in dialogue with the vocal line. In her memoirs, she described the song's creation:

> One evening, returning home from my ride, I saw a little star nestling in the curve of the new moon. It reminded me of Shelley's poem "To Mary," and I set it to music there and then. I hardly ever hear it sung without recalling that lovely evening under the shadow of the great Andes.[15]

So We'll Go No More A' Roving remains one of White's best known and most frequently performed songs. She chose to set Byron's short lyric, written to express his apprehension at the approach of middle age, after a drive to Sorrento during a visit to Italy in the early spring of 1887:

> I shall never forget that drive, that exquisite drive along the mountain road, that exquisite view across the dark blue bay that lay spread beneath its canopy of stars! . . . The soft wind blew the delicious smell of orange blossoms towards us - the delicious smell that conjures up visions of the South so magically and fills the lover of the south with such unspeakable nostalgia! It was after that drive that, some weeks later, shut up in a room in London, I wrote 'So we'll go no more a' roving.'[16]

This song provides a vivid example of White's avoidance of the straightforward cadence and also of her ability to build a haunting melody out of the simplest of materials, here the interval of a minor third. The passion she felt for her beloved Italy and the freedom that it offered her to go "a'roving" is elegantly expressed in the decorated vocal line, rich harmonies, dramatic crescendos, and rhythmic impulse of the persistent eighth-note, quarter-note, eighth-note accompanying figure.

Isaotta Blanzesmano, a setting of a poem by Gabriele d'Annunzio, was written in Italy in 1904 and first performed by Elsie Swinton in London the following year. The publisher Tito Ricordi described the song as like "un rêve d'opium."[17] There is a strangely static quality to the strophic setting as the voice floats over repeated improvisatory-style motifs in the piano accompaniment. White vividly conveys an atmosphere of languid sensuality, using a tonality firmly anchored in F minor but with frequent added notes and dissonances, such as the coloring of the voice's opening phrase with a persistent B natural.

Mon petit lin is the first of *Trois Chansons Tziganes* (1913), settings of three Russian poems from one of Leo Tolstoy's plays in French translation. The songs were inspired by a visit White made to the south of Russia in 1912 and by her lifelong fascination with gypsy music and culture. She uses the Phrygian mode for this short but effective *Song of the Flax*, creating an evocative and improvisatory vocal line over a deceptively simple piano accompaniment.

Notes

1. Maude Valérie White, *Friends and Memories* (London: Edward Arnold, 1914), 166 and 291.

2. Ibid., 264.

3. Ibid., 265.

4. *The Enchanted Heart* was written 1912–1913. A performance planned for the theater in the British Embassy at Rome in the spring of 1914 fell through and the dancer Adeline Genée's attempt to have the work performed in London the following year also failed. Henry Wood arranged to perform an orchestral suite arranged by White from her score at the 1915 Promenade Concerts, but, due to the war, all performances of new works for that season were cancelled. The manuscript is held in the Uncatalogued Manuscript Collection of the Royal Academy of Music.

5. White worked on *Smaranda* (to a libretto by Alma Strettell based on Romanian ballads collected by Mademoiselle Helene Vacaresco as *The Bard of the Dimbovitza)* between 1894–1895 and 1911. Surviving manuscripts held at the Royal Academy of Music (Uncatalogued Manuscripts Collection) show that she completed most of Act I, almost all of Act II but only part of Act III and the Epilogue either in piano or full score.

6. Mary Anderson de Navarro, *A Few More Memories* (London: Hutchinson, 1936), 59.

7. Robert Hichens, *Yesterday. The Autobiography of Robert Hichens* (London: Cassell, 1947), 167. Hichens (1864–1950) was best known for his novels *The Garden of Allah* (1904) and *The Green Carnation* (1894), a satire on his friends Oscar Wilde and Lord

Alfred Douglas. Hichens was gay and it has never been suggested that his close friendship with White was anything other than platonic.

8. Mrs. Edmond Wodehouse, "Maude Valérie White," in *A Dictionary of Music and Musicians*, ed. Sir George Grove (London: Macmillan, 1899), 451.

9. White's translations included Lili Froehlich-Bum, *Ingres: His Life and Art* (London: William Heinemann, 1926); Panait Istrati, *Uncle Anghel* (New York: A. A. Knopf, 1927), and Max Mell, *The Apostle Play,* published in *Seven Sacred Plays* (London: Methuen, 1934). In 1887 she had published a translation of the Swedish writer Axel Munthe's book on Italy, *Letters from a Mourning City.*

10. Maude Valérie White, Will (Witnessed May 15, 1932).

11. André de Ternant, "Short Sketches of Contemporary Women Composers: Maude Valérie White," *The Englishwoman's Review* (February 15, 1887): 59.

12. *The Musical Times* 37 (January 1896), 49.

13. White, *Friends and Memories*, 105.

14. See, for example, ibid., 175.

15. Ibid., 220.

16. Ibid., 327.

17. Maude Valérie White, *My Indian Summer* (London: Grayson and Grayson, 1932), 92.

Selected List of Works

Songs

Farewell, If Ever Fondest Prayer. Text by Lord Byron. London: Stanley Lucas, Weber & Co., 1874.

Assis sur la verte colline. Text anon. London: Duncan Davison, 1876.

Ave Maria. Paris: Choudens, 1876.

The Lassie I Love Best. Text by Robert Burns. London: Duncan Davison, 1876.

La Risposta. Text anon. London: Duncan Davison, 1876.

Thine Is My Love. Text anon. London: Chappell, 1876.

When Twilight Dews. Text by Thomas Moore. London: Chappell, 1876.

Espoir en Dieu. Text by Victor Hugo. Paris: Choudens, 1878.

Es war ein König in Thule. Text by Johann Wolfgang von Goethe. London, 1878.

Zwei Lieder von Heine. Text by Heinrich Heine. London: Stanley Lucas, Weber & Co., 1878.
1. *Liebe*
2. *Im wunderschönen Monat Mai*

Loving and True. Text by Maude Valérie White. London: Stanley Lucas, Weber & Co., 1879.

My Ain Kind Dearie O. Text by Robert Burns. London: Stanley Lucas, Weber & Co., 1879.

Two Songs. London: Stanley Lucas, Weber & Co., 1879.
1. *To Blossoms.* Text by Robert Herrick.
2. *Montrose's Love Song.* Text by The Marquis of Montrose.

Absent Yet Present. Text by Edward Bulwer-Lytton. London: Stanley Lucas, Weber & Co., 1880.

I Prithee Send Me Back My Heart. Text by John Suckling. London: Stanley Lucas, Weber & Co., 1880.

Das Meer hat seine Perlen. Text by Heinrich Heine. London: Stanley Lucas, Weber & Co., 1880.

To Daffodils. Text by Robert Herrick. London: Stanley Lucas, Weber & Co., 1880.

When Delia On the Plain Appears. Text by George Lyttelton. London: Stanley Lucas, Weber & Co., 1880.

Zwei Lieder. Text by Heinrich Heine. London: Stanley Lucas, Weber & Co., 1880.
1. *Ein Jüngling liebt ein Mädchen*
2. *Aus meinen Thränen spriessen*

Chantez, chantez jeune inspirée. Text by Victor Hugo. London: Stanley Lucas, Weber & Co., 1881.

Heureux qui peut aimer. Text by Victor Hugo. London: Stanley Lucas, Weber & Co., 1881.

A Spanish Love Song. Text anon. London: Boosey, 1881.

There's a Bower of Roses. Text by Thomas Moore. London: Boosey, 1881.

To Electra. Text by Robert Herrick. London, 1881.

To Music to Becalm His Fever. Text by Robert Herrick. London: Stanley Lucas, Weber & Co., 1881.

Ich fühle deinen Odem. Text by "Mirza Schaffy." London: Stanley Lucas, Weber & Co., 1882.

Ophelia's Song. Text by William Shakespeare. London: Boosey, 1882.

Sweetheart, Farewell. Text by Ruthven Jenkins. London: Boosey, 1882.

To Althea From Prison. Text by Richard Lovelace. London: Boosey, 1882.

To Mary. Text by Percy Bysshe Shelley. London: Boosey, 1882.

When Passions Trance. Text by Percy Bysshe Shelley. London: Ricordi, 1882.

Ye Cupids Droop Each Little Head. Text by Catullus. Translated by Byron. London: Chappell, 1882.

The Devout Lover. Text by Walter Herries Pollock. London: Ricordi, 1883.

Frithjof's Gesang. Text by Esaias Tegner. London: Stanley Lucas, Weber & Co., 1883.

Mary Morison. Text by Robert Burns. London: Chappell, 1883.

Le mie vole. Text by Francesco Rizzelli. London: Ricordi, 1883.

My Soul Is an Enchanted Boat. Text by Percy Bysshe Shelley. London: Chappell, 1883.

Semper Fidelis. Text by Marion Chappell. London: Chappell, 1883.

Serenata Española. Text anon. London: Ricordi, 1883.

The Summer Is Past and Over. Text by Jetty Vogel. London: Stanley Lucas, Weber & Co., 1883.

Chansonettes. Text by Walter Herries Pollock. London: Chappell, 1883.

1. *L'amour fait ici bas la vie*
2. *Un Fâcheux*

Ich habe gelebt und geliebt. Text by Johann Christoph Friedrich von Schiller. London: Chappell, 1884.

What I Do, and What I Dream. Text by Elizabeth Browning. London: Chappell, 1884.

Bonnie Leslie. Text by Robert Burns. London: Boosey, 1885.

Du bist die Ruh. Text by Friedrich Rückert. London: Stanley Lucas, Weber & Co., 1885.

Er ist gekommen. Text by Friedrich Rückert. London: Ricordi, 1885.

Forget Not Yet. Text by Sir Thomas Wyatt. London: Ricordi, 1885.

Go Lovely Rose! Text by Edmund Waller. London: Ricordi, 1885.

Home Thoughts From Abroad. Text by Robert Browning. London: Stanley Lucas, Weber & Co., 1885.

How Do I Love Thee? Text by Elizabeth Browning. London: Ricordi, 1885.

Liebe, Liebe, ach die Liebe. Text by Alexander Petöfi. London: Stanley Lucas, Weber & Co., 1885.

There Be None of Beauty's Daughters. Text by Lord Byron. London: Ricordi, 1885.

Four Songs from Tennyson's In Memoriam. Text by Lord Tennyson. London: Chappell, 1885.

1. *I Sometimes Hold It Half a Sin*
2. *'Tis Better To Have Loved and Lost*
3. *Love Is and Was My Lord and King*
4. *Be Near Me When My Light Is Low*

Maude Valérie White's Album of German Songs. London: Stanley Lucas, Weber & Co., 1885.

1. *Liebe*. Text by Heinrich Heine
2. *Im wunderschönen Monat Mai*. Text by Heinrich Heine
3. *Hör'ich das Liedchen klingen*. Text by Heinrich Heine
4. *Ein Jüngling liebt ein Mädchen*. Text by Heinrich Heine
5. *Aus meinen Thränen spriessen*. Text by Heinrich Heine
6. *Die Himmelsaugen*. Text by Heinrich Heine
7. *Es war ein König in Thule*. Text by Goethe
8. *Ich fühle deinen Odem*. Text by 'Mirza Schaffy'
9. *Tod und Leben*. Text by Karl Sieben
10. *Das Meer hat seine Perlen*. Text by Heinrich Heine
11. *Der Kindesengel*. Text by Julius Sturm
12. *Stille Thränen*. Text by Justinius Kerner
13. *Wenn dein Auge freundlich*. Text by Julius Sturm
14. *Frithjof's Gesang*. Text by Esaias Tegner
15. *Wird er wohl noch meiner Gedenken?* Text by Robert Burns
16. *Anfangs wollt'ich fast verzagen*. Text by Heinrich Heine

Du sternlein mein. Text anon. London: Stanley Lucas, Weber & Co., 1886.

A Finland Love Song. Text anon. London: Hutchings and Romer, 1886.

God Bless Thee, My Beloved. Text by Elizabeth Browning. London: Metzler, 1886.

O hur vidgas ej ditt bröst. Text anon. London: Stanley Lucas, Weber & Co., 1886.

O Were My Love Yon Lilac Fair. Text by Robert Burns. London: Stanley Lucas, Weber & Co., 1886.

Prayer for Mary. Text by Robert Burns. London: Stanley Lucas, Weber & Co., 1886.

To God. Text by Robert Herrick. London: Metzler, 1886.

Au bord de l'eau. Text by Armand Sully Prudhomme. London: Pitt and Hatzfeld, (1887?).

Hidden Love. Text by Bjørnstjerne Bjørnson. London: Ricordi, (1887?).

Hungarian Gypsy Song (*Die Ziegeuner*). Text by Alexander Petöfi. London: Ricordi, (1887?).

Ici-bas. Text by Armand Sully Prudhomme. London: Pitt and Hatzfeld, 1887.

It Is Na, Jean, Thy Bonnie Face. Text by Robert Burns. London: Stanley Lucas, Weber & Co., 1887.

Adieu Suzon. Text by Alfred de Musset. London: Pitt and Hatzfeld, 1888.

Come To Me in My Dreams. Text by Matthew Arnold. London: Chappell, 1888.

New Albums of Songs with German and English Words. Volume 1. London: Pitt and Hatzfeld, (1888?).

1. *Sie liebten sich beide*. Text by Heinrich Heine
2. *Mit Kosen und Lieben*. Text by Adelbert von Chamisso
3. *Wirthin und Betyar*. Text by Alexander Petöfi
4. *Det første mødes sødme*. Text by Bjørnstjerne Bjørnson
5. *Kind es wäre dein Verderben*. Text by Heinrich Heine
6. *Die Wolken*. Text by Alexander Petöfi
7. *Die Arme-sünderblum*. Text by Heinrich Heine
8. *Ich wollte meine lieder*. Text by Heinrich Heine
9. *Dass du mich lieb hast o mopschen*. Text by Heinrich Heine
10. *Der Sturm*. Text by Heinrich Heine

New Albums of Songs with German and English Words. Volume 2. London: Pitt and Hatzfeld, (1888?).

11. *Warme Lufte*. Text by Alexander Petöfi
12. *Weit über das Meer*. ('Over the ocean's breast') (translated B. F. Wyatt-Smith)
13. *To brune ojne*. Text by Hans Andersen
14. *Das treue Herz*. Text by Alex Petöfi
15. *Wer zum eistem male liebt*. Text by Heinrich Heine
16. *Sommer im Herzen*. Text by Heinrich Heine
17. *Ich habe gelebt und geliebt*. Text by Johann Christoph Friedrich von Schiller
18. *Sorrento*. Text by Carl Snoilsky
19. *Der Schnee ist glatt*. Text by Alexander Petöfi
20. *Goldne Brücken*. Text by Emmanuel Geibel

Prière. Text by Armand Sully Prudhomme. London: Pitt and Hatzfeld, 1888.

So We'll Go No More A' Roving. Text by Lord Byron. London: Chappell, 1888.

When June Is Past. Text by Thomas Carew. London: Stanley Lucas, Weber & Co., 1888.

A Widow Bird Sate Mourning. Text by Percy Bysshe Shelley. London: Pitt and Hatzfeld, 1888.

At Her Spinning Wheel. Text by W. H. Bellamy. London: W. Morley, (1889?).

The Bonny Curl. Amélie Rives. London: Chappell, 1889.

Ask Not. Text by Clifton Bingham. London: W. Morley, ca.1890.

A Farewell Song. Text by Maude Valérie White. London: Ricordi, ca. 1890.

Love Me, Sweet, With All Thou Art. Text by Elizabeth Browning. London: Boosey, 1890.

Soft Lesbian Airs. Text by J. F. Kelly. London: Chappell, 1890.

The Throstle. Text by Lord Tennyson. London: Chappell, 1890.

John Anderson, My Jo. Text by Robert Burns. London: Ricordi, (1891?).

To Corinna Singing. Text by Thomas Campion. London: Chappell, 1891.

Amour fidèle. Text by Armand Sully Prudhomme. London: Stanley Lucas, Weber & Co., 1892.

Infinite Love. Text by Dante Gabriel Rossetti. London: R. Cocks, 1892.

The Meeting. Text by Thomas Moore. London: Boosey, 1892.

My Nannie. Text by Robert Burns. London: Stanley Lucas, Weber & Co., 1892.

The Sunshine of My Heart. Text by Matilde Blind. London: Ashdown, 1892.

Victorious Charm. Text by Victor Hugo. London: Chappell, 1892.

Douleurs divines. Text by Emile Augier. London: R. Cocks, 1893.

Music's Strain. Text by Thomas Moore. London: W. Morley, 1893.

Si j'étais Dieu. Text by Armand Sully Prudhomme. London: R. Cocks, 1893.

Since I Am Hers. Text anon. London: Chappell, 1893.

Song and Music. Text by Dante Gabriel Rossetti. London: Chappell, 1893.

Ton nom. Text by Armand Sully Prudhomme. London: R. Cocks, 1893.

6 Volkslieder. London: R. Cocks, 1893.

Twelve Songs for Children. Texts by various authors. London: Boosey, 1893.

Crabbed Age and Youth. Text by William Shakespeare. London: Boosey, 1894.

A Greeting. Text by Friedrich Rückert. London: Boosey, 1894.

Did One But Know. Text by Christina Rossetti. London: Chappell, 1895.

For England's Sake. Text by Rennell Rodd. London: Stanley Lucas, Weber & Co., 1895.

Mary's Ghost. Text by Thomas Hood. London: R. Cocks, 1895.

A Protest. Text by Robert Bridges. London: Boosey, 1895.

Waiting. Text Tuscan folk song. London: Ricordi, 1895.

When Love Began. Text Tuscan folk song. London: R. Cocks, 1895.

Demain! Text by Armand Silvestre. London: Stanley Lucas, Weber & Co., 1896.

Ihre Stimme. Text by Friedrich Rückert. London: Lucas, 1896.

Die Sonne kommt. Text by Friedrich Rückert. London: Stanley Lucas, Weber & Co., 1896.

When The Old Land Goes Down To the War. Text by Gerald Massey. London: Boosey, 1896.

Marching Along. Text by Robert Browning. London: Chappell, 1897.

Stand To Your Horses! Text by G. J. Whyte Melville. London: Boosey, 1897.

The Story and the Poet. Text by Maude Valérie White. London: Ricordi, 1897.

Three Little Songs. London: Chappell, 1897.
1. *When the Swallows Homeward Fly*. Text folk song
2. *A Memory*. Text anon.
3. *Let Us Forget*. Text by M. Darmesteter

King Charles. Text by Robert Browning. London: Boosey, 1898.

La Meilleure Morale. Text anon. London: Chappell, 1898.

When You Return. Text by Arthur Philip Coxford. London: Boosey, 1898.

An Exile's Song. Text by M. Boyle. London: J. Church, 1899.

Little Boy Love. Text by Arthur Conan Doyle. London: Boosey, 1899.

A Mother's Song. Text anon. London: J. Church, 1899.

The Old Grey Fox. Text by Arthur Conan Doyle. London: Chappell, 1899.

The Spring Has Come. Text anon. London: Chappell, 1899.

Une [sic] Sueño. Text folk song. London: J. Church, 1899.

Why Was Cupid a Boy?. Text by William Blake. London: Metzler, 1899.

Five Songs. Text anon. traditional. London: Laudy and Co., 1899.
1. *Auf Wiederseh'n*
2. *Ein alter Traum*
3. *An den Geliebten*
4. *Wanderlied*
5. *Glück auf!*

Among the Roses. Text by Hoffman von Fallersleben. London: Chappell, 1900.

A Ballad of the Ranks. Text by Arthur Conan Doyle. London: Chappell, 1900.

Du fragst mich was ich sehen will. Text anon. London: Chappell, 1900.

A Lay of the Links. Text by Arthur Conan Doyle. London: Chappell, 1900.

Little Pictures of School Life. Text by Robert Hichens. For speaker and piano. London: Metzler, 1900.

Two Songs. Text by William Ernest Henley. London: Chappell, 1900.
1. *Last Year*
2. *The Fifes of June*

Es muss doch Frühling werden. Text by Emanuel Geibel. London: Chappell, 1901.

The Irish Colonel. Text by Arthur Conan Doyle. London: Chappell, 1901.

The Morning of Life. Text by Thomas Moore. London: Chappell, 1901.

Pourquoi. Text by Armand Silvestre. London: Chappell, 1901.

Das Taube Mütterlein. Text by Halm. Cincinnati: J. Church, 1901.

To a Little Child. Text anon. London: Chappell, 1901.

Voices of the Children. Text by William Blake. London: Boosey, 1901.

April's Lady. Text by Algernon Swinburne. London: Chappell, 1902.

God with Us. Text by William Ernest Henley. London: Chappell, 1902.

Slumber Song. Text by William Sharp. London: Chappell, 1902.

There Are Days That No-one Can Ever Forget. Text anon. London: Chappell, 1902.

Ere You Come. Text by Mary Cholmondeley. London: Metzler, 1903.

Land of the Almond Blossom. Text by William Sharp. London: Chappell, 1903.

A Song of the Sahara. Text by Robert Hichens. London: Ricordi, (1904?).

To His Beloved. Text by Thomas Bailey Aldrich. London: Chappell, 1904.

Two Songs of Innocence. Text by William Blake. London: Boosey, 1904.
1. *Sleep, Sleep, Beauty Bright*
2. *Little Lamb*

Love in the Desert. Text by Shams al-Din Muhammad Hafiz. London: Chappell, 1905.

Love Me To-day. Text by A. Mary F. Robinson. London: Chappell, 1905.

In Golden June. Text by Ian Malcolm. London: Chappell, 1906.

In the Summer Garden. Text by Adrian Ross. London: Chappell, 1906.

Isaotta Blanzesmano. Text by Gabriele d'Annunzio. London: Ricordi, 1906.

Petit Pied Rose. Text French traditional. London: Chappell, 1906.

Quand viendra le jour. Text by Marguerite de Navarre. London: Ricordi, 1906.

Under the Moon. Text by Lord Robert Houghton. London: Chappell, 1906.

When Songs Have Passed Away. Text by Ellis Walton. London: Chappell, 1907.

Lead Kindly Light. Text by John Henry Newman. London: Boosey, 1908.

The Sceptre of June. Text by William Ernest Henley. London: Lengnick, 1908.

Unexpected Joy. Text by Shams al-Din Muhammad Hafiz. London: Chappell, 1908.

Six Songs with German and English Words. London: Chappell, 1908.
1. *Ein Stern.* Text by Heinrich Heine
2. *Frühling und Liebe.* Text by Hoffmann von Fallersleben
3. *Divina Pruvidenza.* Text Sicilian Prayer
4. *Es muss doch Frühling nerden.* Text by Emanuel Geibel
5. *Des Kindes Abendgebet.* Text anon.
6. *Junge Liebe.* Text by Maude Valérie White

Trois Chansons Tziganes. Text by Leo Tolstoy. London: Boosey, 1913.
1. *Mon petit lin*
2. *Mes jeunes gars*
3. *A la pelouse*

Dreams. Text by Cecil Frances Alexander. London: Boosey, 1915.

Moonlight on the Valley. Text by W. A. London: Chappell, 1916.

Le Départ du Conscrit. Text by Maude Valérie White. London: Winthrop Rogers, 1917.

On the Fields of France. Text by N. McEachern. London: Winthrop Rogers, 1919.

To Lesbia. Text by Rennell Rodd. London: Chappell, 1924.

Two Songs. London: Chappell, 1924.
1. *Le foyer*. Text by Paul Verlaine
2. *La flûte invisible*. Text by Victor Hugo

Two Songs. Text anon. London: Chappell, 1924.
1. *Tortorella Sconsolata*
2. *L'Orticello*

Leavetaking. Text by William Watson. London: Stainer and Bell, 1927.

Addio, Lucia. Text traditional. London: Pitt and Hatzfeld, nd.

Kleines Frühlingslied. Text by Heinrich Heine. London: Ricordi, nd.

Puisqu'ici bas toute âme. Text by Victor Hugo. London: Ricordi, nd.

Choral and Other Vocal Works

Benedictus (1877). Four solo voices and chorus. Unpublished.

Agnus Dei (1879). Soloists, chorus, and orchestra. Unpublished.

Two Part-Songs for Men's Voices. Text anon. London: Stanley Lucas, Weber & Co., 1880.
1. *O Nanny Wilt Thou Go With Me?*
2. *The Stars Are With the Voyager*

Credo (1881). Soloists, chorus, and orchestra. Unpublished.

Prayer. Text by Santa Teresa de Jesus. SATB chorus. London, 1883.

Three Duets. Text anon. London: Stanley Lucas, Weber & Co., 1886.
1. *Was fliesst auf der wiese?*
2. *Dein blaues Auge*
3. *Du Sternlein mein*

Du bist wie eine Blume. Text by Heinrich Heine. Part-song for five voices. London: Stanley Lucas, Weber & Co., 1890.

Quand on est deux. Text by Alphonse de Lamartine. Duet. London: Ashdown, 1892.

Russian Love Song. Text by Mrs. Wyatt Smith. Part-song for five voices. London: Boosey, 1893.

Stage

Incidental music for *The Medicine Man* (play by Henry Duff Traill and Robert Hichens) (1898). Unpublished.

Incidental music for *The Law of the Sands* (play by Robert Hichens) (after 1902). Unpublished.

Smaranda (ca. 1894–1911). Opera, libretto by Alma Strettell. Unpublished.

The Enchanted Heart (1912–1913). Ballet. Unpublished.

Piano

Rondo scherzando. London, 1879.

Eight South American Airs for piano duet. London: Boosey, 1882.

Scherzetto. London: Stanley Lucas, Weber & Co., 1883.

Four Sketches. London, n.p., 1886.

Danse Fantastique. London: Ricordi, 1888.

Pensée Fugitive. London: Ricordi, 1888.

Pictures from Abroad. "A Set of Fourteen Pieces for the Pianoforte." London: E. Ashdown, 1892.

Barcarolle. London: Stanley Lucas, Weber & Co., 1893.

From the Ionian Sea (before 1907). Unpublished.

La Fanfaluca. London: Chappell, 1916.

Instrumental Music

Naissance d'amour for cello and piano. London: R. Cocks, 1893.

Serbian Dances (1916?) for orchestra. Unpublished.

Bibliography

Fuller, Sophie. "Maude Valérie White." In *The Pandora Guide to Women Composers: Britain and the United States, 1629–present*. London: Pandora, 1994.

____. "Women Composers During the British Musical Renaissance, 1880–1918." Ph.D. diss., King's College, London 1998.

Grove, Sir George, ed. *A Dictionary of Music and Musicians*. London: Macmillan, 1899.

White, Maude Valérie. *Friends and Memories*. London: Edward Arnold, 1914.

____. *My Indian Summer*. London: Grayson and Grayson, 1932.

____. Will (Witnessed May 15, 1932).

Discography

In Praise of Woman. Anthony Rolfe Johnson, tenor; Graham Johnson, piano. Hyperion CDA66709 (1994). *The Throstle*, *My Soul Is an Enchanted Boat*, *The Devout Lover*, *So We'll Go No More A' Roving*.

Favourite English Songs. Felicity Lott, soprano; Graham Johnson, piano. Chandos CHAN 8722 (1990). *So We'll Go No More A' Roving*.

An Anthology of English Song. Peter Jeffes, tenor; John Constable, piano. Gamut GAMD 506 (1991). *To Mary*.

Women at an Exposition. Suzanne Mentzer, mezzo-soprano; Sunny Joy Langton, soprano; Elaine Skorodin, violin; Kimberly Schmidt, piano. Koch International Classics 3-7240-2 H1 (1991). *Ici bas*.

Mélodies sur des poèmes de Victor Hugo. Felicity Lott, soprano; Graham Johnson, piano. Harmonia Mundi HMA 1901138 (1985). *Chantez, chantez, jeune inspirée*.

Gervase Elwes. Gervase Elwes, tenor and various others. Opal CD 9844 (1990). *So We'll Go No More A' Roving*.

Dame Nellie Melba. Nellie Melba and various. National Film and Sound Archive/Larrikin CDLRH221 (1988). *John Anderson, My Jo*.

Editorial Comments

No manuscripts appear to have survived for any of White's songs. Obvious mistakes in the published editions have been rectified but otherwise editorial intervention has been kept to a minimum. Some extra dynamic markings have been added to *To Mary* and *So We'll Go No More A' Roving* in order to aid performance. In general, pedaling has been clearly marked in the published editions of *Isaotta Blazesmano* and *Mon petit lin*, but a few obvious omissions have been rectified.

Isaotta Blanzesmano

Torna in fior di giovinezza Isaotta Blanzesmano; Dice: 'Tutto al mondo è vano, Ne l'amore ogni dolcezza'.	Lo, in the flower of youth returneth Isaotta Blanzesmano Sighing: 'All on earth is vanity, In love alone undying sweetness'.
Fanno l'ore compagnia Alla bionda Blanzesmano; Dicon: 'Tutto al mondo è vano, Ne l'amore ogni dolcezza'.	And th'attendant hours surround her Isaotta Blanzesmano; Sighing: 'All on earth is vanity, In love alone undying sweetness'.
S'apra come rosa in fiore Alla gioia il cuore umano, Poichè tutto al mondo è vano, Ne l'amore ogni dolcezza.	Ev'n as the rose unfolds her petals So the heart of all that's human Turns to love, since all else is vanity And in love alone undying sweetness.

Translated by Maude Valérie White

Mon petit lin

Oh mon lin, mon petit lin,
Vert et fin, oh mon lin.
J'ai semé, jeté la semence;
J'ai chanté, chanté l'air de danse;

J'ai dansé, dansé en cadence.
Jeté la semence.
Réussis, réussis,
Blanc et fin, oh mon lin.

Translated from the Russian by N. Minksky

Flax of mine, blessings be thine,
Rain or shine, flax of mine!
Who but I sang at thy sowing,
Danced and sang all to speed thy growing?

See, I dance and sing together,
To bring thee growing weather.
Goodly seed, God thee speed,
Rain or shine, flax of mine!

Translated by Paul England

To Mary

Percy Bysshe Shelley

Maude Valérie White
Sophie Fuller, editor

12
[f] appassionato
[f]
Sing - ing love to its lone mate
In the i - vy bower dis-
p
p
15
rall.
a tempo
rall.
con - - so - late,
[rall. colla voce]
18
[a tempo]
p con tenerezza
Ma - ry dear, come to me soon,
p
21
I am not well whilst thou art far;
As sun - set to the spher - ed

24
moon, As twi - light, as
27
espressivo
3
twi - light to the west - ern star, Thou be-lov - ed, be-lov - ed
30
rall.
a tempo
art to me. Oh
33
rall.
[a tempo]
Ma - ry dear, that you were here!
[colla voce]

So We'll Go No More A' Roving

Lord Byron

Maude Valérie White
Sophie Fuller, editor

[a tempo]
9
p carezzando
So we'll go no more a ro - ving So
p
11
late in - to the night,
13
Though the heart be ne'er as lov - ing And the
15
moon be still as bright,
cantabile

17
rall.
dolce
[a tempo]
Though the heart be ne'er as lov - ing And the moon be
20
still as bright, Though the
23
f
appassionato
heart be ne'er as lov - - ing And the moon be
f
26
rall.
rall.
still as bright.
p

29
Risoluto
f
For the sword out-wears the
sf
attacca
32
sf
sheath, And the soul wears out the breast, And the
f
sf
sf
35
ff
heart it-self must pause And love it-self have
p
rall.
espressivo
rall.
ff
p
38
Tempo primo
rest.
p

41
pp ma sempre affretando
Though the night was made for lov - ing, And the
pp
44
day re - turns too soon;
sempre cresc.
Yet we'll go no
sempre cresc.
47
ff
appassionato
more a ro-ving By the light of the moon.
ff
50
p
espressivo
dolce
Though the heart be ne'er as lov - ing, And the moon be
p

53
still
as bright.
56
p
And
the moon
be
p
59
still
as bright.
p
rall.
p
62
molto rall.
L.H.
pp

Isaotta Blanzesmano

Gabriele D'Annunzio

Maude Valérie White
Sophie Fuller, editor

Allegretto ma non troppo

languido

p

m.s.

Ped. * Ped. * Ped. *

5 Andantino

con tenerezza

Tor - na in fior di gio-vi-nez - za I - sa-ot - ta Blanz-zes-ma - no;

9

con tristezza

f **p** *dolce* Allegretto ma non troppo *languido*

Di - ce: Tut - to al mon-do e va - no, Ne l'a - mo - -

p *languido e delicato*

13

pp *ancora più dolce e più languido* poco rit. rall.

re, ne l'a - mo - re o - gni dol - cez - -

17
Allegro ma non troppo
za, Ne l'a - mo - re o - gni dol - cez - -
[p]
21
Andantino
[mf]
za
m.s.
Fan - no l'o - re com-pa -
25
animato
gni - a Al - la bion - da Blan - zes-man - no;
Di - con:
29
con amarezza
f
Allegretto ma non troppo
p dolce
languido
ancora più dolce e più languido
pp
"Tut - to al mon-do è va - no, Ne l'a - mo - re, ne l'a -
p languido e delicato

33
poco rit.
rall.
ravvivando
con passione
mo - re, o - gni dol - cez - - - za, Ne l'a -
37
mo - - - - - re o - gni dol - cez - -
appassionato
40
lunga pausa
Andantino
pp con la più grande tenerezza
za"
m.s.
lunga pausa
S'a - pra co-me ro - sa in
f
lunga pausa
pp
Ped.
45
f svegliando
fio - re Al - la gio - ia il cuo - re u - ma - no,
Poi - chè
f

49
con slancio e passione
rit.
dolce come sognando ma languido
tut - to al mon - do è va - no Ne l'a - mo - - - - -
p
p languido e delicato
p
52
pp sempre più dolce e più languido
morendo
rit.
re, ne l'a - mo - - - - re o - gni dol -
m.s.
pp
55
rall.
pp come sognando
morendo
colla più
pp grande dolcezza
cez - - - za, Ne l'a - mo - - - - re o - gni dol -
morendo
p languido
60
cez - - - za.
p

Mon petit lin

Leo Tolstoy
translated into French by N. Minsky

Maude Valérie White
Sophie Fuller, editor

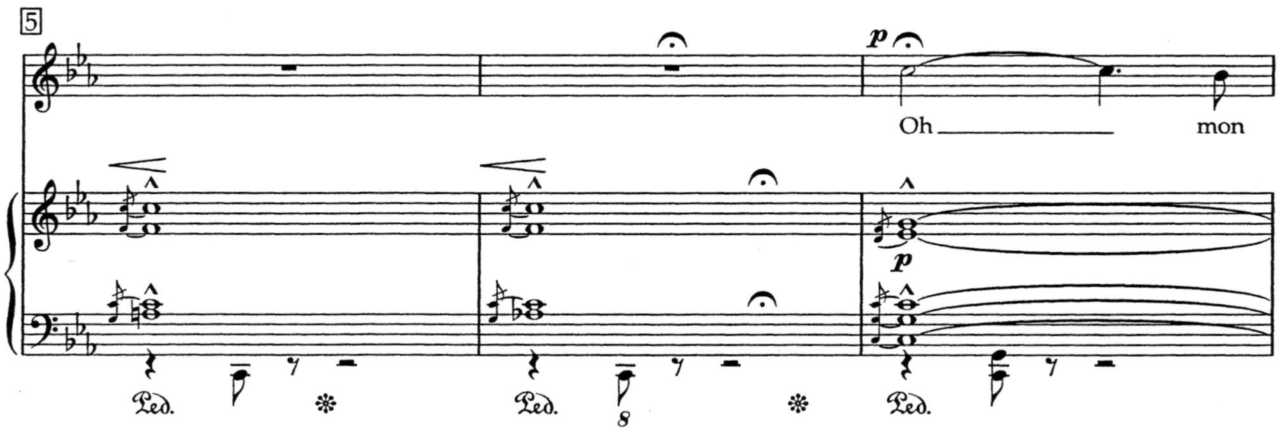

11
poco rit.
a tempo
Oh mon lin, mon pe - tit lin.
14
f
J'ai se-mé, je-té la se - men - - - - ce;
f giojoso
J'ai chan-té,
[Ped.]
[*]
17
tempo giusto
chan - té l'air de dan - se;
J'ai dan-sé,
dan - sé en ca-den - ce,
20
p
Je - té la se - men - ce.
Ped.

22
Un poco più lento
p
pp
ppp
Ré - us-sis,
ré - us-sis,
Blanc et fin,
[Ped.]
Ped.
Ped.
25
carezzando
mon pe-tit lin.
[Ped.]
28
pp
ppp
[Ped.]
31
morendo
Ped.

Mary Turner Salter
(1856–1938)

JOHN GRAZIANO

Mary Turner Salter was born in Peoria, Illinois, on March 15, 1856, where her parents had recently moved from Portland, Maine. The family soon moved to Oquiawka, a small town in western Illinois, near the Iowa border. Both parents were musical; Mary's father had a deep bass voice and her mother sang and played the piano. Mary's musical talents were developed by her mother, who gave her piano lessons. It appears that Mary's voice developed while she was still a child. According to her brief autobiography, she sang naturally. While still in her teens, she took voice lessons from Alfred Arthur, an Englishman who settled in Burlington, Iowa (about 10 miles from Oquiawka) as choir director of the Congregational Church there. She gave her first public performance in Burlington on December 15, 1870, just before her fifteenth birthday, when she sang the "Inflammatus" from Rossini's *Stabat Mater*.

After lessons with Gustav Schilling (1805–1895) in New York City she moved to Boston in 1873. Salter enrolled at the New England Conservatory and studied voice with John O'Neill (n.d.) and Lillian Nordica (1857–1914). While studying, she began to sing professionally, first at St. Paul's Episcopal Church, and then, at the urging of Erminie Rudersdorff,[1] in a touring company with contralto Annie Louise Cary, violinist Ole Bull, and conductor George Henschel. Rudersdorff was impressed with Mary's voice; in her autobiography, Salter writes she "was greatly interested in my voice and enthusiastic about my talent which she said amounted to genius."[2]

When Rudersdorff returned to New York City from Boston, Salter followed her. There her career blossomed; she succeeded American soprano Emma Thursby (1845–1931) as soloist at the Broadway Tabernacle, then sang at the Zion (Episcopal) Church, and at Trinity Church in New Haven. While pursuing her career, she also taught for two years at Wellesley College.

In 1881, Mary married Sumner Salter, a fellow musician, whose academic appointments brought them from city to city. After twelve years, she decided to stop singing: "I found myself in more or less conflict between professional and domestic interests in life at Syracuse, Buffalo, Atlanta, and finally New York, where I definitely retired from professional singing in 1893."[3]

Although she had never studied composition or continued with piano lessons after studying with her mother, Mary Salter had always composed tunes to relax. Once she stopped singing professionally, she began to develop an interest in composition. While in New York City, she wrote several anthems and songs. Many of the latter, such as *The Pine Tree*, *The Swan*, and *The Water-Lily* are nature songs, inspired by her observations while strolling in Central Park. After moving to Williamstown, Massachusetts in 1906, where her husband had become Organist and Director of Music at Williams College, her interest in composition grew. The greater part of her songs were written there. In her brief autobiography, Salter notes that her husband "attended to the suitable preparation for publication of everything I have written."[4]

In 1923, the Salters and their five children moved back to New York City after her husband's retirement from Williams College. She continued to compose occasionally and to attend symphony concerts and piano recitals. She notes, in her autobiography, that she cares less for opera, but "adores" Toscanini [Arturo (1867–1957)] and Rachmaninoff [Sergei (1873–1943)].[5] During the last five years of her life, her health deteriorated; she died in Orangeburg, New York on September 12, 1938.

The majority of Salter's songs were written during the first two decades of the twentieth century. A published poet, she used many of her own poems in her musical settings. She composed more than eighty songs, most of which were published by G. Schirmer and Oliver Ditson. Several were performed by well-known concert artists, including Ernestine Schumann-Heink (1861–1936).

The song cycle *Love's Epitome* was published in 1905. The five poems by Salter describe a life cycle in terms of love. Although they suggest that the narrator is a man, these songs are set for a female voice. The first song, *Since First I Met Thee*, describes the narrator's devotion to his love, even if she disdains him. He tells her that he "thrilled with joy" whenever he felt her presence near him. In the second song, *In The Garden*, he compares her to stately shimmering white lilies and tells her she is the sweetest, fairest, and best flower in the garden. *She Is Mine*, the third song of the cycle, celebrates the consummation of love. Salter's ecstatic poem compares love to radiant sunshine and to the silver moonbeam; it "illumes the darkest night." At the climax of the song, the narrator proclaims "She is mine, my dearest, my fairest, Mine for all eternity." The fourth song, *Dear Hand, Close Held In Mine*, is quiet and contemplative; the narrator relates the essence of his lover's touch, through their lives together, including death: "And more, when life is done, Thy touch will lead me on." The final song, *Requiem*, continues with this previous thought: "Ah! she is gone, my love, my little love, And now the rain falls on her where she lies." As the cycle concludes, however, the narrator internalizes his loss: "Still in my heart shall she be warm, And feel but the love-rain falling from my eyes."

Although she was self-taught, Salter's musical setting of *Love's Epitome* is unusually rewarding and imaginative. The songs are through-composed, with motivic and rhythmic repetitions serving as the connections within and between pieces. Salter's harmonic palette is clearly drawn from music of the late-nineteenth century. Her use of chromatic harmonic progressions demonstrate that, through her career as a singer, she absorbed much of the music of the 1870s and 1880s; for example, she is fond of that staple of late-nineteenth-century harmony, the flat-VI chord, and freely uses borrowed chords to lend color to key words or phrases in the poems.

At first glance, the songs in this cycle do not appear to have a strong harmonic connection. The first two songs, in E-flat and A-flat major, seem to have some harmonic relationship, possibly delineating a dominant-tonic relationship. The third song, in C major, can be viewed as the III of A-flat, or in the context of the next song, the dominant of F major. If A-flat is the tonic key of the cycle, then F major functions as the VI of that key. This possible analysis would be satisfactory if one could tie the keys of each of the songs in the cycle together with the final song. However, the last song is set in E minor/E major, which has little to do with A-flat major, unless it is viewed enharmonically as F-flat minor/major. But it is difficult to justify that analysis when the cycle ends without returning to the tonic key. Alternatively, one might analyze the cycle in E-flat major, with the second song functioning as the subdominant, and the third and fourth songs functioning as a move to the supertonic. If the final song had been set in E-flat minor/major, that solution would seem reasonable. But once again the final song defeats that premise, unless one wants to use the enharmonic argument as before. There is no compositional reason the final song could not have been set a half-step lower, in E-flat. The range of the vocal line is not as large as some of the other songs, and transposing it down one-half step would not have created any problems for the vocalist. Since this final song refers to the opening of the cycle, if it had been set in E-flat, there would have been harmonic and motivic closure.

Salter's settings are unusual in that they do not follow traditional formulas that one might expect in song literature. There is no strict ABA form, no strophic form, and almost no repetition of melodic lines within a song. Instead, Salter uses a novel device to delineate structure. Periods are constructed with rhythmic rhymes; new periods sometimes introduce new rhythms. In the third song, for example, the first period introduces a four-measure rhythmic phrase that is repeated with some variation. The next period presents a contrasting new four-measure rhythmic phrase, which is answered once again by a varied consequent phrase. In the third period Salter introduces yet another rhythmic phrase, which is truncated at the climax of the song. In the final period, Salter returns to her opening rhythm for the first four measures, but abandons it in the second part of the period for yet another new rhythm. In spite of her general avoidance of repetition, the song fulfills its promise due to the continuity of the accompaniment. The other songs display similar construction.

The first song, *Since First I Met Thee*, opens with a two-measure introduction that is not heard again, melodically or rhythmically, in the rest of the song. We will encounter it again later when, in retrospect, it will take on a deeper meaning. The first four lines of the poem are set irregularly. Periodic structure is not clear, since the downbeat in measure 3 is part of a melodic gesture and is not strongly emphasized. The vocal line, however, rhymes rhythmically, in two three-measure phrases. Harmonically the vocal line is supported by a strong arrival on the tonic in measure 6 and on the dominant in measure 9. In the second part of the song, Salter introduces a new two-measure rhythmic phrase; it is stated three times, in G-flat major (mm. 11-12), on a D dominant seventh/G major progression (mm. 13-14), and in a B-flat seventh/ E-flat/D diminished progression (mm. 15-16). A coda section, to the words "I loved thee" closes the song, but not without some tonal ambiguity on the last "thee," where the listener expects a resolution to the tonic E-flat, but hears instead an E-flat seventh chord, which implies a move to A-flat, the key of the next song. After a quick resolution, Salter ends in E-flat, although the harmonic "stage" has been set for song 2.

In the second song, *In The Garden*, after a four measure introduction, Salter introduces a new rhythmic pattern which moves in four-measure phrases. The first eight measures are in the tonic, A-flat major, while the next eight stop on the mediant, C minor, and the dominant. The beginning of the second section appears to be continuing the pattern established in measures 5 through 20. But at measure 25 Salter abruptly changes the accompaniment figure and indicates a slowing of the tempo. The text at this special moment is "Thy voice is the nightwind," and Salter will indirectly refer to it in the following song. The climax of the song begins at measure 29, as a new rhythmic motive is introduced. This seven-measure period, which disrupts the four-plus-four pattern heard up to now, also emphasizes the subdominant, D-flat major. A coda follows; the vocal line seems to indicate a four measure phrase, but the harmony of the accompaniment contradicts it by parsing the music into two three-measure phrases.

The third song, *She Is Mine*, is clearly meant to serve as the climax of the cycle. It is the only song with a fast tempo, *Allegro appassionato*, and is exuberant in its celebration of the power of love. The song opens with a four-measure introduction in A-flat major. The melody has been carried over from the previous song; it is from that special moment when the words "Thy voice is the nightwind" were sung. After a quick modulation, the song proper begins.

The fourth song, *Dear Hand, Close Held In Mine*, opens with a three measure introduction that once again has no connection to the remainder of the song. The vocal line alludes to the opening of Wagner's *Siegfried Idyll.* Whether this is a specific reference to the sentiment attached to Wagner's piece or has another private meaning is not known. Salter uses the rhythm established in the opening phrase in the same manner as we have seen previously. The song moves from F major to A major in the first four-measure phrase. The second four-measure phrase is in C-sharp major. The third phrase returns to A major and ends back on the tonic. At that point, the rhythmic motive fades away; it is followed by a coda-like period that moves primarily in half and dotted-half notes.

The final song, *Requiem* begins in E minor with a four-measure introduction. A descending line in the voice, which is reminiscent of the opening of the first song, is joined by the accompaniment. While the descending line continues in the accompaniment in two additional four-measure phrases, the voice part is delayed in the second group, and is not heard at all during the last. In this section Salter avoids the active harmonic language that permeated the earlier songs; here she moves from the tonic to the mediant and back to the tonic, ending on the dominant, B major, in the last of these phrases (m. 16). At the change of mode to E major, to the words "Still in my heart," Salter reintroduces the motive heard at the beginning of the cycle in the introduction to the first song. The association of this text to the introduction to the entire cycle can now be seen as a remembrance of a departed love, one who has been joined (in the third song) "for all eternity" to her life-mate. Similarly, the association of the two texts "Since first I met thee" and "Ah! she is gone" to the same music alludes to the life cycle, which is the central theme of the fourth song as well. Salter ends the cycle with a brief coda, reiterating the "Still in my heart" motive one last time.

Mary Turner Salter's songs, now almost entirely forgotten, clearly need to be investigated in more depth, particularly those that are written to her own poems. As the preceding analysis has demonstrated, though they are deceptively simple on the surface, the songs in this cycle are constructed with a great deal of subtlety, and are sustained not through melodic repetition, but through rhythmic motives and a particular sensitivity to word painting. Examination of Salter's other songs will allow us to discover whether these songs are indicative of her compositional techniques in general, or are unique in her oeuvre.

Notes

1. Erminie Rudersdorff (1822–1882) was a famous opera and oratorio soprano and a well-known teacher. Her most famous student was Emma Thursby. She emigrated to the United States in 1872 when she was recommended to Patrick Gilmore to sing in his Peace Festival in Boston. Her son by her second marriage was Richard Mansfield, famous British artist, actor, and composer.

2. [Anonymous], *In Memoriam: Mary Turner Salter* (n.p.: 1939), 3.

3. Ibid., 4.

4. Ibid., 5.

5. Ibid., 6.

List of Works

Two Songs. Text by Mary Turner Salter. Boston: Oliver Ditson Publishing Co., 1902.
1. *A Water Lily*
2. *Little Boy, Good-Night*

Fair White Flower. Poet unknown. Cincinnati: John Church Co., 1902.

Songs of the Garden. New York: G. Schirmer, Inc., 1904.
1. *Come to the Garden, Love*. Text by Katrina Trask
2. *The Pine-Tree*. Text by Mary Turner Salter
3. *A Proposal.* Text by Mary Turner Salter
4. *Autumn Song*. Text by Mary Turner Salter

Three Spring Songs, op. 4. Text by Mary Turner Salter. New York: G. Schirmer, Inc., 1904.
1. *March Wind*
2. *Song of April*
3. *The Time of May*

In Some Sad Hour. Text by Henry Elliot Harman. Boston: Oliver Ditson Publishing Co., 1904.

Serenity. Text by Mary Turner Salter. Boston: Oliver Ditson Publishing Co., 1904.

Sleep, Little Lady. Text by Mary Turner Salter. Boston: Oliver Ditson Publishing Co., 1904.

Love's Epitome. Text by Mary Turner Salter. New York: G. Schirmer, Inc., 1905.
1. *Since First I Met Thee*
2. *In the Garden*
3. *She is Mine*
4. *Dear Hand, Close Held to Mine*
5. *Requiem*

Contentment. Text by Mary Turner Salter. Boston: Oliver Ditson Publishing Co., 1905.

The Cry of Rachel. Text by Lizette Woodworth Reese. New York: G. Schirmer, Inc., 1905.

A Little While. Text by Mary Turner Salter. New York: G. Schirmer, Inc., 1905.

My Lady. Text by Mary Turner Salter. Boston: Oliver Ditson Publishing Co., 1905.

The Sky-Meadows. Text by Mary Turner Salter. New York: G. Schirmer, Inc., 1905.

The Swan. Text by Mary Turner Salter. New York: G. Schirmer, Inc., 1905.

A Toast. Text by Ernest Whitney. New York: G. Schirmer, Inc., 1905.

The Willow. Text by Mary Turner Salter. Boston: Oliver Ditson Publishing Co., 1905.

A Bunch of Posies. Text by Abbie Farwell Brown. New York: G. Schirmer, Inc., 1906.

1. *The Chrysanthemum*
2. *Morning-Glories*
3. *The Dandelion*
4. *The Naughty Tulip*

A Night in Naishapûr. Text by Nathan Haskell Dole. New York: G. Schirmer, Inc., 1906.

1. *Long, Long Ago*
2. *In the City the Mizgar*
3. *The Song*
4. *The Moon Has Long Since Wandered*
5. *If I Could Prove My Love*
6. *The Farewell*

Gethsemane. Text by J. B. S. Monsell. New York: G. Schirmer, Inc., 1906.

Mary's Manger Song: Sleep My Little Jesus. Poet unknown. New York: G. Schirmer, Inc., 1906.

O Lord of Life. Text by Mary Turner Salter. New York: G. Schirmer, Inc., 1906.

Songs of the Four Winds, op. 12. Text by Edwin Warren Guyol. New York: G. Schirmer, Inc., 1907.

1. *The East Wind*
2. *The West Wind*
3. *The North Wind*
4. *The South Wind*

Three German Songs. New York: G. Schirmer, Inc., 1907.

1. *Die Schmetterling*. Text by Heinrich Heine
2. *Die Stille Wasserrose*. Text by Emanuel Geibel
3. *Für Musik*. Text by Emanuel Geibel

Three Love Songs. New York: G. Schirmer, Inc., 1907.

1. *Her Love Song*. Text by Frank Dempster Sherman
2. *I Breathe Thy Name*. Text by Mary Turner Salter
3. *The Lamp of Love*. Text after Paracelsus

Japanese Cradle Song. Text by S. Naidu. New York: G. Schirmer, Inc., 1907.

Primavera. Text by Edwin Bjorkman. New York: G. Schirmer, Inc., 1907.

To a Moon Flower. Text by Mary Turner Salter. New York: G. Schirmer, Inc., 1907.

To Somnus. Text by Mary Turner Salter. New York: G. Schirmer, Inc., 1907.

Outdoor Sketches. New York: G. Schirmer, Inc., 1908

1. *The Elves*. Text by Louise Medbery
2. *Winter*. Text by Mary Turner Salter
3. *October*. Text by G. W. Pangborn
4. *The Tanager*. Text by L. McKinney
5. *Afterglow*. Text by T. Walsh
6. *The Kingdom of the Spring*. Text by I. E. Mackay

Lyrics from Sappho, op. 18. Text from Sappho. Translated by Bliss Carman. New York: G. Schirmer, Inc., 1909.

1. *Hesperus, Bringing Together*
2. *Well I Found You*
3. *There is a Medlar Tree*
4. *If Death Be Good*
5. *It Can Never Be Mine*
6. *I Grow Weary*
7. *Over the Roofs*
8. *So Falls the Hour of Twilight*

Four Songs. New York: G. Schirmer, Inc., 1910.

1. *The Call of Cupid*. Text by Mary Turner Salter
2. *Enchantment*. Text by J. G. Williams
3. *Last Night I Heard the Nightingale*. Text by E. L. Cox
4. *Remembrance*. Poet unknown

Good Night. Text by P. B. Shelley. Boston: Oliver Ditson Publishing Co., 1910.

Just for Today. Text by S. Wilberforce. New York: G. Schirmer, Inc., 1910.

Memories. Text by A. M. F. Robinson. Boston: Oliver Ditson Publishing Co., 1910.

A Rain Song. Text by R. Loveman. Boston: Oliver Ditson Publishing Co., 1910.

A Rose-Rhyme. Text by Alfred H. Hyatt. New York: G. Schirmer, Inc., 1910.

A Sky of Roses. Text by Alfred H. Hyatt. New York: G. Schirmer, Inc., 1910.

Unseen. Text by Mary Turner Salter. New York: G,. Schirmer, Inc., 1910.

From Old Japan. Text by Alfred H. Hyatt. Chicago: Clayton F. Summy, 1911.

1. *Three Maidens of Japan*
2. *Lady Moon*
3. *Little Miss Butterfly*
4. *By the Lotus Lake*
5. *To an Idol of Jade*
6. *Queen of the Mulberry Garden*

My Dear. Text by Alfred H. Hyatt. Boston: Arthur P. Schmidt and Co., 1912.

For Memory. Text by M. A. Robinson. New York: G. Schirmer, Inc., 1912.

The Lake. Text by Mary Turner Salter. New York: G. Schirmer, Inc., 1912.

I Lay My Sins on Jesus. Text by H. Bonar. Boston: Arthur P. Schmidt and Co., 1912.

Juliet's Song. Text by R. Loveman. New York: G. Schirmer, Inc., 1912.

O Rose That Lay Upon Her Breast. Text by F. H. Martens. New York: G. Schirmer, Inc., 1912.

The Salutation of the Dawn. Text from the Sanskrit. New York: G. Schirmer, Inc., 1912.

Song of Agamede. Text by A. Upson. Boston: Arthur P. Schmidt and Co., 1912.

The Sweet o' the Year. Text by Mary Turner Salter. Boston: Arthur P. Schmidt and Co., 1912.

There Is a Blessed Home. Text by H. W. Baker. Boston: Arthur P. Schmidt and Co., 1912.

To My Fair. Text by A. O'Shaughnessy. New York: G. Schirmer, Inc., 1912.

The Veery. Text by Mary Turner Salter. New York: G. Schirmer, Inc., 1912.

When Lovers Dance Upon the Green. Text by Alfred H. Hyatt. New York: G. Schirmer, Inc., 1912.

The Young Musician. Text by L. A. Garnett. Boston: Arthur P. Schmidt and Co., 1912.

An April Message. Text by Mary Turner Salter. Chicago: Clayton F. Summy, 1913.

Be Thou Ever Near. Text by W. Mitchell. Boston: Arthur P. Schmidt and Co., 1913.

Blossom-Time. Text by Mary Turner Salter. Boston: Oliver Ditson Publishing Co., 1913.

A Boy's Soliloquy. Text by Mary Turner Salter. Boston: Arthur P. Schmidt and Co., 1913.

By the Fire. Text by A. L. Phelps. Boston: Arthur P. Schmidt and Co., 1913.

In Saragossa (Serenade). Text by F. H. Martens. Boston: Arthur P. Schmidt and Co., 1913.

Love of an Hour. Text by F. H. Martens. Boston: Oliver Ditson Publishing Co., 1913.

One Day in Betty's Life. Text by J. S. Gates. Indianapolis: Bobbs-Merrill Co., 1913.

Requiem of the Sea. Poet unknown. Boston: Arthur P. Schmidt and Co., 1913.

A Rose and a Dream. Text by A. L. Hughes. Chicago: Clayton F. Summy, 1913.

She is a Winsome Wee Thing. Text by Robert Burns. Boston: Oliver Ditson Publishing Co., 1913.

They're Like a Cloud of Butterflies. Text by F. H. Martens. Boston: Arthur P. Schmidt and Co., 1913.

Tonight. Text by C. L. Moulton. Chicago: Clayton F. Summy, 1914.

Five Songs. New York: G. Schirmer, Inc., 1916.

1. *The Ideal*. Text by Mary Turner Salter
2. *A Singing Bird*. Text by A. L. Phelps
3. *The Resting Place*. Text by Mary Turner Salter
4. *A Fancy*. Text by Mary Turner Salter
5. *Life*. Text by Paul Laurence Dunbar

May-Time. Text by M. W. Mears. Boston: Oliver Ditson Publishing Co., 1916.

Since Thy Lips Pressed Mine. Text by J. P. Mills. New York: Huntzinger & Dilworth, 1916.

To the West Wind. Poet unknown. Boston: Oliver Ditson Publishing Co., 1916.

Valentine Song. Poet unknown. Boston: Oliver Ditson Publishing Co., 1916.

Wanderer's Night Song. Text by Johann Goethe. Boston: Oliver Ditson Publishing Co., 1916.

The Wind's Tales. Text by H. M. Hutchinson. Boston: Oliver Ditson Publishing Co., 1916.

Slumber Sea. Text by Jean Stansbury Holden. Cincinnati: John Church Co., 1919.

Ulysses. Text by Burton Braley. Cincinnati: John Church Co., 1919.

Vox Invicta. Text by Nina Salamon. Boston: Oliver Ditson Publishing Co., 1919.

Maid o' Mine. Text by Neva McFarland Wadham. Philadelphia: Theodore Presser, 1923.

Spring Wonder. Text by Cornelia M. J. Howe. New York: G. Schirmer, Inc., 1923.

The Lady April. Poet unknown. Publisher unknown, 1931.

Christmas Song. Poet unknown. Publisher unknown, 1936.

Bibliography

[Anonymous.] *The Songs of Mary Turner Salter.* New York: G. Schirmer, [1909?].

[Anonymous.] *In Memoriam: Mary Turner Salter.* N.p.: 1939.

Howard, John Tasker. *Our American Music: Three Hundred Years of It.* 3rd ed. New York: Thomas Y. Crowell, 1946.

The International Cyclopedia of Music And Musicians, ed. Oscar Thompson. New York: Dodd, Mead & Co, 1939.

Love's Epitome

I. Since First I Met Thee

Mary Turner Salter

Mary Turner Salter

11
first I heard thy voice en - chant - ing, And look'd with-in thine eyes soft
cresc.
cresc.
Ped.
14
accel.
f
p
glanc - ing, I thrill'd with joy when - e'er I
f
16
rit.
affettuoso
cresc.
felt thy pres-ence near me: I loved thee, I
p
cresc.
19
p
rall.
loved thee, I loved thee!
p
pp
Ped.

Love's Epitome
II. In The Garden

Mary Turner Salter

Mary Turner Salter

12
cresc.
white, Bring thoughts of thee, love,
15
espr.
grace - ful and fair, While eve - ning
col canto
18
shad - ows lie hid in the dark of thy hair
21
mf
rit.
Ros - es thy lips are, Hearts - ease thine eyes, Thy

25
Poco più lento
mf
voice is the night - wind, breath - ing soft
Ped.

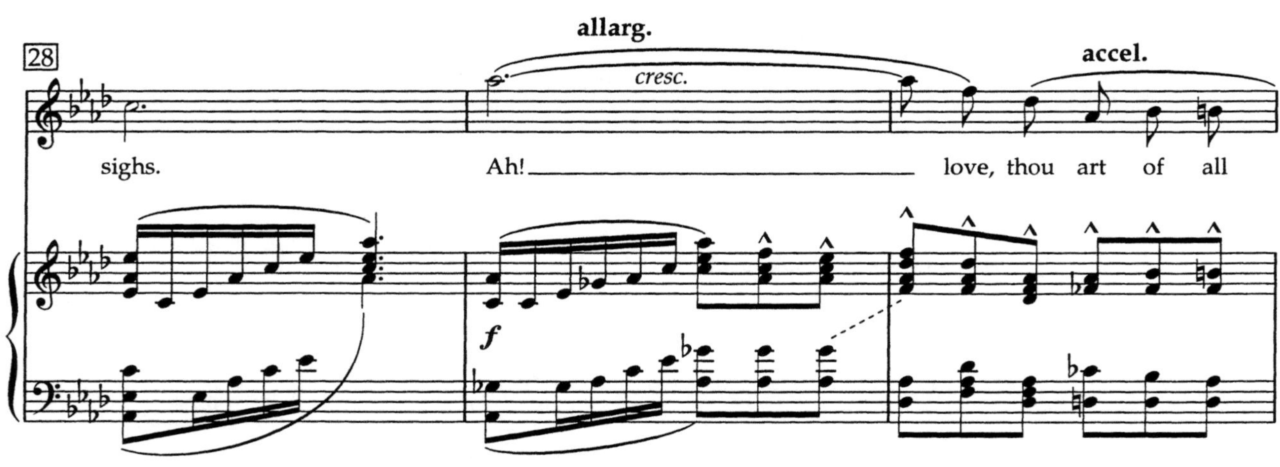
28
allarg.
cresc.
accel.
sighs. Ah! love, thou art of all
f

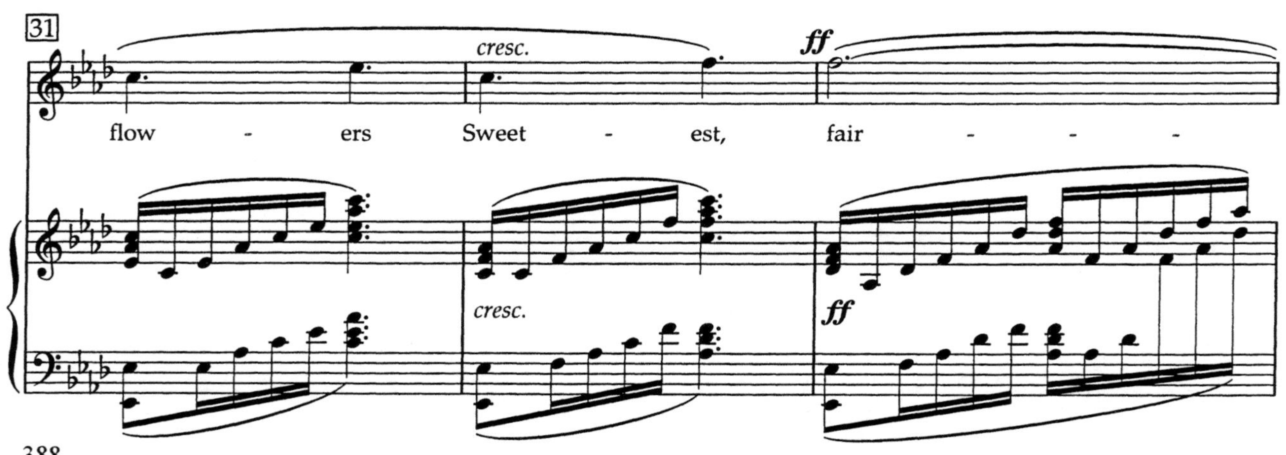
31
cresc.
ff
flow - ers Sweet - est, fair - - - -
cresc.
ff

34
rall.
Più lento
p
- est and best: Sleep on, my
sf
p

37
rall.
pp
flow'r! Sweet be thy
pp

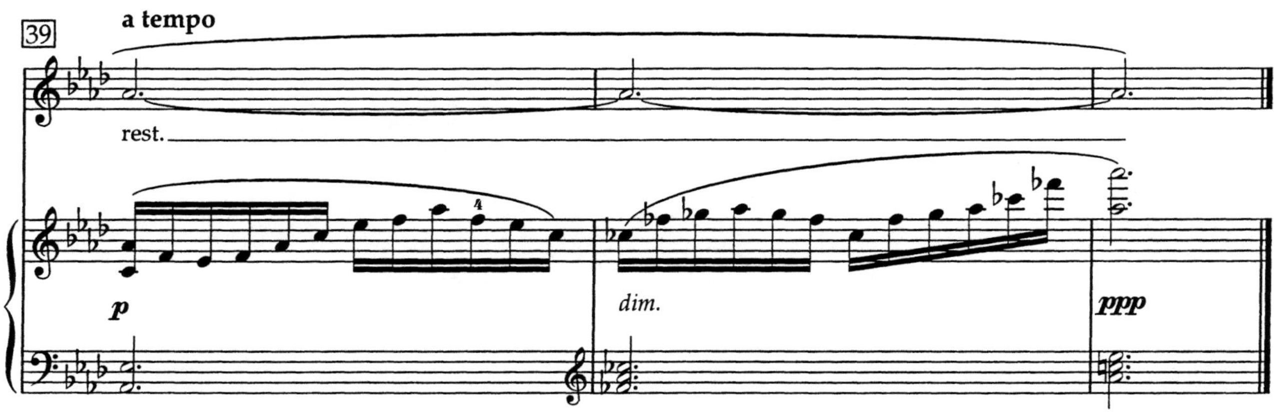
39
a tempo
rest.
p
dim.
ppp

Love's Epitome

III. She Is Mine

Mary Turner Salter **Mary Turner Salter**

10
con passione
world with ma - gic beau - ty, Sweeps o'er my heart with its sa - cred
f
12
mp
cresc.
fire. Love is like the ra - diant sun - shine,
mp
cresc.
15
f
Fill - ing all my day with light,
Ped.
17
con espr.
cresc.
Love is like the sil - ver moon - beam, Love il-lumes the dark - est
col canto
p
cresc.

20
allarg.
a tempo
night.
Ah! what joy, this dear pos - ses - sion!
Ped.
23
poco rit.
a tempo
Ne'er I dream'd that it could be;
25
accel.
She is mine, my fair - est, She is mine, my dear - est
cresc.
27
allarg.
rit.
Mine, for all e - ter - ni - ty,

30
a tempo
Life is full of sweet-est prom-ise,
Now my own has come to
f
Ped.
33
accel.
cresc.
me;
She is mine, my
35
allarg.
cresc.
dear-est, my fair-est,
Mine for all e-
cresc.
37
ff
a tempo
rit.
ter-ty!
ff
sf
sf sf sf
Ped.
Ped.

Love's Epitome

IV. Dear Hand, Close Held In Mine

Mary Turner Salter

Mary Turner Salter

14
espr.
— from thy soul to mine Of rest from wear - y
col canto
17
strife, And sweet con-tent in life. And more, when life is
21
done, Thy touch will lead me on. Dear
p
espr.
25
teneramente
hand, close held in mine
pp

Love's Epitome
V. Requiem

Mary Turner Salter

Mary Turner Salter

12
lies.
cresc.
dim.
16
Tranquillo
Still in my heart, in my heart shall she be
p
20
con molta espr.
warm, And feel but the love-rain fall-ing from my
24
eyes.
pp

Catharina van Rennes

(1858–1940)

HELEN H. METZELAAR

During her lifetime Catharina van Rennes, born in Utrecht on August 2, 1958, enjoyed considerable renown in the Netherlands as one of the best Dutch women music pedagogues. Highly esteemed for her excellent songs, Van Rennes is one of the few Dutch women to be included in international music encyclopedias, including *The New Grove Dictionary of Music and Musicians* and *Das Musik in Geschichte und Gegenwart.*

After studying voice, theory, and composition with Richard Hol (1825–1904) and completing her vocal studies with Johannes Messchaert (1857–1922), van Rennes graduated from the Toonkunst Muziekschool in Utrecht in 1883 with degrees in music teaching and piano, and in 1884 with degrees in singing and singing pedagogy. For a short time she appeared as a soprano soloist in various operas and oratorios, but in 1887 founded her own music school in Utrecht, teaching singing and the basics of music theory at various levels. In 1901 she moved into a home large enough to accommodate her school, which she called Bel Canto. The building housed a family enterprise, with her brother Jacob operating his music publishing business upstairs, and her sister teaching the youngest children.

Dissatisfaction with existing children's teaching repertory motivated van Rennes to write her own materials, with texts geared to various age levels. These songs soon became well loved, particularly because of their appeal to children's imagination. They loved attending her classes; instead of sitting still they were encouraged to clap and hop in various rhythms, while van Rennes improvised at her grand piano. She also encouraged the children to contribute their own poetry, which she set to music.

In 1898 the Dutch government asked her to compose an *aubade* for the coronation of Queen Wilhelmina of Orange-Nassau (1880–1962). For this spectacular event, van Rennes conducted an immense chorus of 1,800 children in the *Oranje-Nassau-Cantate,* op. 33, accompanied by a military band. (Another musician orchestrated her piano score, a common practice at the time.) Although van Rennes assumed that she had been commissioned to compose this cantata, she later discovered that she had been expected to write it without payment. In her extended correspondence on this subject, she pleaded that artists had a right to be paid for their work, much to the irritation of state officials.[1]

At regular intervals van Rennes would invite parents to sit in during her lessons. Soon she was organizing public afternoon concerts in various concert halls, taking her young pupils with her on the train. This led to her teaching in Hilversum, Amsterdam, and The Hague. With her reputation growing steadily, Queen Wilhelmina requested that she teach Princess Juliana (b. 1909), her daughter, in a small class at the palace in The Hague from 1916 to 1921. In addition to teaching children, van Rennes also organized and conducted a women's chorus, for which she wrote various cantatas, such as the *Kerstcantate* (Christmas Cantata) op. 9, *De schoonste feestdag* (The Finest Feast-day), op. 18, and *Avond Cantate* (Evening Cantata), op. 27.

Van Rennes was very interested in rhythmic gymnastics, a method linking musical expression to bodily movements, as developed by the Swiss music pedagogue Émile Jaques-Dalcroze (1865–1950). Carl Orff (1895–1982) and Rudolf Steiner (1861–1925) later promoted his concepts. In 1907 she went to study with Jaques-Dalcroze in Geneva. After gaining a *Diplôme d'honneur* in 1911, she opened several classes in the Netherlands based on his theories. However, in a rare interview she once revealed that what she really longed to do was to conduct. As a child she had often flourished a table knife, conducting imaginary symphonies in the kitchen: "Yes, that's the only reason that I sometimes feel bad about not having been born a boy. Even though I once conducted [Willem] Mengelberg's perfect orchestra [Concertgebouw Orchestra, HM], my dearest wish, that walk in life, is unfortunately not yet open to women."[2]

Occasionally, large-scale events organized by the women's emancipation movement afforded her conducting opportunities. At the Nationale Tentoonstelling van Vrouwenarbeid (National Exhibition of Women's Work) in 1898 she conducted a chorus singing her own works, including *De schoonste feestdag*, op. 18, *Drei Quartette für Frauenstimmen*, op. 24, and her four and five-voiced *a capella* arrangements of Renaissance songs. She also conducted a chorus of 380 women, girls and boys singing her own music at the opening ceremony of an international congress on women's right to vote, held in the Amsterdam Concertgebouw 1908. The chorus was accompanied by the 7th Military Regiment, which caused one critic to notice that "even dressed in their warrior's uniforms, they sat like obedient children."[3] This critic, clearly not taken with van Rennes' conducting, included a long tirade against her attire, a so-called "reform" dress that allowed her more freedom of movement.

In 1950 the eminent Dutch musicologist Eduard Reeser (b. 1908) published a work on nineteenth-century Dutch music, still standard today, in which he sought to define the Dutch style of composition. He concluded that van Rennes and her colleague, Hendrika van Tussenbroek[4] (1854–1935), had captured essential characteristics of Dutch music in their children's songs. He lauded them for their pioneering work and,

> if one would attempt to establish the characteristics of truly Dutch music, the simple melodies in both their work would be a better measure than most 'podium music' by their contemporaries. For example, that the *Zonnelied* by Cath. van Rennes had already seen ten editions by 1898 is proof of how much such a composition answered the needs of those who did not only want to passively enjoy music.[5]

From our perspective today we see that van Rennes belonged to a relatively small but new group of emancipated Dutch women eager to develop public careers. That women wrote music for children was easily accepted as it was considered simply an extension of rearing children, which was the domain of women. That van Rennes taught singing was accepted for the same reason. Both van Rennes and van Tussenbroek were highly productive throughout their lives, probably due to the fact that they remained single. In fact, a remarkably large number of highly productive Dutch women composers remained single, or if married, remained childless.[6]

All her life van Rennes inspired a love of music in both young and old. Together with van Tussenbroek she created a new genre for children that remained viable in the Netherlands until the 1960s. In 1927, after forty years of leadership at her singing school, van Rennes was knighted by the Order of Oranje-Nassau. She died in Amsterdam on November 23, 1940.

Van Rennes produced more than 150 songs and duets, including fifty solo songs for adults in the German romantic style, plus a number of cantatas. She also published a number of fairy tales, which she read to children, interspersing them with short musical illustrations at the piano, similar to Wilhelm Tappert's (1830–1907) *Erzählungen am Clavier*.

Interestingly, the status of children's music was at this time much higher than is currently the case. She composed two types of children's songs: those meant for children to sing, and those meant for children to listen to. Several song collections have two versions of the same song, one for children and one for adults. This second type is closely related to German *volkstümliche* (popular) songs. Song recitals by leading Dutch singers such as Tilly Koenen and Johannes Messchaert often ended with songs by van Rennes, whose style was greatly influenced by Brahms and Schumann. It should also be noted that in part her popularity with Dutch audiences was due to the usage of the Dutch language, a welcome change from recitals that were often entirely in foreign languages. Favorites included songs from the collection *Instantaneetjes*, op. 42.

The choral works in this volume, *Drei Quartette für Frauenstimmen*, op. 24, comprise a short trilogy dating from before 1892 and based on three poems by Emil Claar. Written in romantic style, these homophonic songs are well suited for amateurs. After their performance in 1905 in the Amsterdam Concertgebouw, a critic noted they "sounded so fresh and happy that the audience was carried away by them and wanted them repeated."[7] The first song, *Uralt!* in F major, only twenty measures long, has brief moments of imitation that enliven the texture. The repetition of "bischen" gains intimacy, progressing from "a little bit of May sun" to "a little bit of lip to lip."

The second song, *Ich schreite heim*, is the most moving and more Schumann-like than the other two. The opening, in A minor, begins quite innocently: "I walk home after the ball." The slowing down of the accompaniment from quarter notes to half notes in measures 3-6 creates a heaviness at the words, "[I] drag old sorrow with me, and there's no glow and no happiness." The ensuing step-by-step descent to the dominant sung in unison to illustrate "Ich schreite heim" (I'm walking home) is particularly effective. A rather sudden harmonic shift from A minor to C major is made in measures 13-14 to address the falling snow. The rising melodic sequence and a return to A minor lead to the closing sad words, a plea to the snowfall, first to literally cover the narrator's head and finally to cover her/his life and sadness.

The entire third song, *Ich reite hinaus in das Weite*, is based on a rollicking rhythmic motif, an excellent accompaniment to illustrate the dancing pace of a little horse, "riding outside into the wide open space." Just as in the first song, short imitative moments enliven the texture (mm. 21-22). Nature joins in the fun as sorrow and tears are completely forgotten. A joyful exclamation closes this sweet trilogy: "I reign over my passion."

Notes

1. Archive Catharina van Rennes, Haags Gemeentemuseum, The Hague.

2. *Nieuw Rotterdams Courant,* quoted in "Een componiste: Catharina van Rennes" in *Vrouwen op de bres: drie kunstenaressen rond 1900* [ed. M. Kyrtova-Klerk and others], (The Hague: Haags Gemeentemuseum, 1980), 22-26.

3. *Oprecht Haarlemsche Courant,* June 22, 1908.

4. Hendrika van Tussenbroek and van Rennes were not personal friends. However, both studied in Utrecht, taught extensively, and wrote children's music, often with a pedagogical slant, such as van Tussenbroek's *Wie geen R kan zeggen, die blijft thuis*, meant to teach children the correct pronounciation of "r" in Dutch.

5. Eduard Reeser, *Een eeuw Nederlands Muziek 1815–1915* (Amsterdam: Querido 1950; rev. ed., Amsterdam: Querido, 1986), 255-56. Reeser also warns that not all women composers seem to realize how important composing for children is and exhorts them not to neglect this genre.

6. Other music pedagogues include Maria Berdenis van Berlekom (1860–1922), Johanna Veth (1852–1932), and Cornélie van Zanten (1855–1946). Examples of composers include Gertrude van den Bergh, Hermina Amersfoordt-Dijk, Elisabeth Kuyper, Cornélie van Oosterzee, Anna Cramer, Dina Appeldoorn, Hanna Beekhuis, Henrietta Bosmans, Saar Bessem, Andrée Bonhomme, and many others.

7. Critic simply noted as "v M," *Algemeen Handelsblad,* November 3, 1905.

Selected List of Works

Solo Songs

Drie liederen, op. 8. The Hague: G. H. van Eck en Zoon, 1899.
1. *Zonnelied.* Text by Anna Fles
2. *Verraden.* Text by C. Honigh
3. *Nacht.* Text by W.L. Welter

Moederlied, op. 12. Text by B. ter Haar Bzn. Gent: Willems-Fonds, 1911.

Drie liederen, op. 14. Amsterdam: G. Alsbach en Co. n.d.
1. *Nacht.* Text by B. ter Haar Bzn. Translated by C. K. v.d. C.
2. *Twee bloemkens.* Text by Eldar. Translated by Hemann Köcher
3. *Annie.* Text by Dirk Troelstra. Translated by C. d. R.

Jubelliedje, op. 16. Text by Jacoba Mossel. Gent: Willems-Fonds, 1905.

Zwei Lieder für eine tiefe Stimme, op. 19. Amsterdam: De Algemeene Muziekhandel, Stumpff en Koning, n.d.
1. *Wenn dein ich denk!* Text by Georg von Dyherrn
2. *Ein Lebewohl.* Author unknown

Drie Hollandsche liederen, op. 20. Amsterdam: G. Alsbach en Co., n.d.
1. *Van 't wiegsken in 't graf.* Text by Antheunis
2. *Liedeken.* Text by Louis Couperus
3. *De liefste slaapt.* Text by J. N. van Hall, after Longfellow

Zonnetje, op. 22 (1905). Text by J. D. C. van Dokkum. Gent: Willems-Fonds, 1906.

Twee Hollandsche liederen, op. 26. Text by Elsa van Brabant. Leiden: Joh. M. Eggers, n.d.
1. *Als uw geluk een bloem was*
2. *Oud lieken*

Vaak als vergeefs naar ruste, op. 31. Text by W. E. Welter. Gent: Willems-Fonds, 1898.

Een kunststukje, op. 32. Text by J. P. Heye. Published in *Nederlandsche Muziekkalender,* 1898.

Op vleuglen van verlangen, op. 34. Text by Marie Boddaert. Gent: Willems-Fonds, 1898.

Herfstgeneurie, op. 35. Text by Willem Kloos. Utrecht: Jac. van Rennes. 1900.

Nacht, op. 36. Text by Marie Boddaert. Gent: Willems-Fonds, 1909.

De gefopte vogelaar, een lustig liedeken voor lichte stem, op. 37. Text by Freia [J. D. C. van Dokkum]. Utrecht: Jac. van Rennes, 1899.

Ach, nur ein Viertelstündchen, op. 39. Text by Ludwig von Hörmann. Utrecht: Jac. van Rennes. 1899.

Zwei ernste Lieder für eine tiefe Stimme, op. 43. Text by U. B. and Emil Claar. The Hague: Haagsche Boekhandel en Uitgevers Maatschappij, n.d.
1. *Schlichtes Lied*
2. *Leidesahnung*

Idylle, op. 48. Text by Hélène Duvivier. Gent: Willems-Fonds, 1904.

Brechtjebuur, een liedeken op snaakschen trant, op. 49. Text by J. D. C. van Dokkum. Utrecht: Jac. van Rennes, 1904.

Kleengedichtjes, op. 52. Text by Louise de Clercq. Utrecht: Jac. van Rennes, n.d.

Madonnakindje, op. 54. Text by Louise de Clercq. Utrecht: Jac. van Rennes, 1904.

Eenzaam moedertje, op. 56. Text by Dolores. Gent: Willems- Fonds, 1908.

Welkom aan moeder en kind, op. 60 (a). Text by J. D. C. van Dokkum. Published in *Het Nieuws van den Dag,* May 25, 1910.

Etsen op den notenbalk, three lieder for soprano, opus 65. Utrecht: Jac. van Rennes.
1. *Het geite-weitje.* Text by Jacqueline van der Waals
2. *Kindeke in Wei.* Text by W. F. Gouwe
3. *Verlangens blijdschap.* Text by A. Roland Holst

Et s'il revenait un jour . . ., op. 66. Text by Maurice Maeterlinck. Utrecht: Jac. van Rennes, n.d.

Waar het kindje slaapt, op. 74. Text by A. Roland Holst. Utrecht: Jac. van Rennes, n.d.

Drie Hollandsche liederen in den volkstoon, op. 76. Utrecht: Jac. van Rennes, 1928.
1. *Mijn land.* Author unknown
2. *Bij moeders pappot.* Text by A. E. Janssonius van Epen
3. *Met mijn liefken.* Text by M. Fokker-Kessler

Stedelied van Utrecbt, op. 77. Text by F. van der Elst-Boonzajer. Utrecht: Jac. van Rennes, 1929.

O, kopje op het kussen, op. 78. Text by Jo Loosjes-Gedeking. Published in *Astra-Magazine,* March 1930.

Drie ernstige liederen.
1. *Zoo stil . . . .* Text by van C. v. d. B.
2. *O, Nacht . . . .* Text by D. Buys
3. *Die mijns barten vrede zijt.* Text by Jacqueline van de Waals. Utrecht: J. A. H. Wagenaar, n.d.

Children's Songs

Voorjaarsbloernen, een bundeltje van 12 kinderliedjes, op. 1. Amsterdam: G. Alsbach en Co., n.d.

Moeders jaardag, op. 2. Text by Anna Fles. Amsterdam: Brix von Wahlberg, n.d.

Vaders verjaardag, een liedje voor vroolijke kinderen, op. 3. Text by C. E. Amsterdam: Brix von Wahlberg, n.d.

Jong Holland, op. 4. Text by Jacoba Mossel, Anna Fles, Molster. Utrecht: J. A. H. Wagenaar, 1885.

Meizoentjes, 12 kinderliederen, op. 11. Text by C. v. R., W. F. van Oostveen, Agatha Snellen, A. van Harpen-Kuyper, Anna Fles, C. Kappeyne v. d. Coppello. Strassburg, i. E.: Süddeutscher Musikver lag; Utrecht: Jac. van Rennes, n.d.

Windekelken, zes liedekes voor meisjesstemmen, op. 21. Text by Agatha Snellen, Anna van Harpen-Kuyper, C. Kappeyne v. d. Coppello, Louise de Clercq. Strassburg, i. E.: Süddeutscher Musikverlag; Utrecht: Jac. van Rennes, 1897.

Vlindervlucht, 12 kinderliederen, op. 23. Text by Viola, Agatha Snellen, Titia van der Tuuk, Jacoba, Anna van Harpen-Kuyper, Maleia, (from Berthe Vadier). Strassburg, i. E.: Süddeutscher Musikverlag; Utrecht: Jac. van Rennes, 1894.

Miniatuurtjes, zes liedekes, for girls' voices, op. 30. Text by Kate Greenaway. Strassburg, i. E.: Süddeutscher Musikverlag; Utrecht: J. van Rennes, 1897.

Instantaneetjes uit de kinderwereld, op. 38. Text by Freia [J. D. C. van Dokkum]. Utrecht: Jac. van Rennes, 1899.

Instantaneetjes uit de kinderwereld, op. 42. Text by Freia. Utrecht: Jac. van Rennes, 1900.

Rondedans voor onze kinderen, op. 44. Text by Catharina van Rennes (?). Utrecht: Jac. van Rennes, 1901.

Een Vaderlandsch lied van Michiel de Ruyter, voor kinderkoor, op. 46. Text by H. J. Schimmel. Brussel: Nationale Muziekdrukkerij, n.d.

Silhouetten, op. 51. Text by Freia. Utrecht: Jac. van Rennes. 1904.

Zon en Zang, op. 55. Text by W. F. Gouwe, C. M., J. D. C. van Dokkum, V. v. E. Strassburg, i. E.: Süddeutscher Musikverlag; Utrecht: Jac. van Rennes, 1907.

Speelsche wijsjes, zeven kinderliedjes, op. 62. Text by Anna Sutorius, J. M., C. v. d. B. Utrecht: J. van Rennes; Strassburg, i. E.: Süddeutscher Musikverlag. 1911.

Klingklang, klokke-bei, zes meiliedjes, op. 73. Text by D. Tomkins. (nr. 5 *Lentedroom.* Text by René de Clercq.) Utrecht: Jac. van Rennes, 1920.

Midden in de me i (de waterviolier). Text by David Tomkins. Published in *Eigen Haard* 52-14, April 3, 1926.

Als vlindertjes! Text by Jeanne Houtzagers. Published in *Eigen Haard,* April 1927.

Een dansje bij de harmonica. Text by J. D. C. van Dokkum. Published in *Droom en Daad* 5-9, September 1927.

Het erfprinsesje van Bibelabon. Text by Pol de Mont. Published in *Eigen Haard*, 1927.

'n Instantaneetje uit de kinderwereld 'Samen uit!' Text by J. D. C. van Dokkum. Published in *Astra Magazine*, May 1927.

Verjaarsgroet aan prinses Juliana op 30 april. Text by C. van Rennes. Utrecht: J. A. H. Wagenaar, 1934.

Duets

De boomen ruischen, tweezang. Text by Jacoba Mossel. Gent: Willems-Fonds, 1907.

Tweezang, duet for soprano and baritone or alto, op. 25. Text by A. F. Utrecht: Jac. van Rennes, n.d.

Singspiel for Children

Lentebloemen, kinderzangspel. Text by C. M. van Hille-Gaerthé. Rotterdam: Nijgh en van Ditmar's Uitgevers Maatschappij, ca. 1920.

Choral Ensembles

2 Terzette für 3 Frauenstimmen. Leipzig: Breitkopf und Härtel, 1896.
1. *De macht van 't kleine*, from op. 1. Author unknown
2. *Klaas Vaak*, from op. 4. Author unknown [in both German and Dutch]

4 Terzette für Frauenstimmen, a capella with piano ad libitum, op. 10. Text by Laurillard, Schliermacher, Ant. L. de Rop. Utrecht: J. A. H. Wagenaar, 1893.

Uralt, Ich reite hinaus in das Weite, Ich schreite Heim, Drei Quartette für Frauenstimmen mit klavierbegleitung, op. 24. Text by Emil Claar. Utrecht: Jac. van Rennes, n.d.

Ons Hollandsch lied, feestzang, for mixed chorus a capella with piano ad libitum, op. 41. Text by J. D. C. van Dokkum. Utrecht: Jac. van Rennes, 1900.

Cantatas

Kerstcantate, [for children's chorus with piano,] op. 9. Text by Jacoba Mossel. Utrecht: J. A. H. Wagenaar, n.d.

De schoonste feestdag, cantata for children's chorus soprano and piano, op. 18. Text by W. E. Randi. Utrecht: J. A. H. Wagenaar, n.d.

Avond-cantate, (een stemmingsbeeld) voor driestemmig vrouwenkoor en altsolo, op. 27. Text by I. H. Hooijer. Utrecht: Jac. van Rennes, n.d.

Oranje-Nassau Cantate voor meerstemmig kinderkoor, op. 33. Text by J. D. C. van Dokkum. Utrecht: Jac. van Rennes, 1898.

Oud-Hollands nieuwe tijd, cantata for women's and girls' voices, op. 33. Text by J. D. C. van Dokkum. Utrecht: Jac. van Rennes, 1908.

Van de zeven zonnestraaltjes, cantata for women's and girls' voices with piano, op. 50. Text by Ca. Ha. de Jong. Utrecht: Jac. van Rennes, 1905.

Bibliography

Annegarn, Alfons. "Rennes, Catharina van." In *Das Musik in Geschichte und Gegenwart*. Vol. 11. Kassel: Bärenreiter, 1989.

Brusse, J. "Catharina van Rennes." Four articles in *Nieuwe Rotterdamsche Courant, May 14, 17, 18, 19, 1910.*

Dokkum, J. D. C. van. *Catharina van Rennes*. In "Mannen en Vrouwen van Beteekenis." Baarn: Hollandia Drukkerij, 1917.

____, ed. *Feestgave voor Catharina van Rennes, 1887–1927.* Wageningen: Drukkerij "Vada," 1927.

Elst, Nancy van der. "Catharina van Rennes." In *Zes vrouwelijke componisten*, ed. Helen Metzelaar. Zutphen: Walburg Pers, 1991: 53-84.

____. "Catharina van Rennes als pedagoog en haar liedjes uit 't Rooie Boekje". In *Harmonie en perspectief*, ed. A. Annegarn and others. Deventer: Sub Rosa, 1988.

Metzelaar, Helen H. *From Private to Public Spheres: Exploring Women's Role in Dutch Musical Life from c. 1700 to c. 1880 and Three Case Studies.* Utrecht: Koninklijke Vereniging voor Nederlandse Muziekgeschiedenis, 1999.

____. "Rennes, Catharina van." In *The New Grove Dictionary of Music and Musicians*. Vol. 6. London: Macmillan, 2001.

Reeser, Eduard. *Een eeuw Nederlands Muziek 1815–1915.* Amsterdam: Querido 1950. Rev. ed., Amsterdam: Querido 1986.

Sanders, Maria Johanna Elisabeth. *Het Nederlandse kinderlied (van 1770–1940)*. Amsterdam: H. J. Paris, 1958.

[M. Kyrtova-Klerk and others, ed.] "Een componiste: Catharina van Rennes". In *Vrouwen op de bres: drie kunstenaressen rond 1900.* The Hague: Gemeentemuseum, 1980.

Discography

Catharina van Rennes 1858–1940. Mirasound Musica 441983 (1983).

Six Women Composers from the Netherlands. NM 92018. Includes *Drei Quartette für Frauenstimmen,* op. 24, by Catharina van Rennes.

Uralt!
by Emil Claar

So bischen Maiensonne,
So bischen eitel Gold,
Das von den Zweigen herab träuft,
Es bleibt doch wunderhold.

So bischen Lippe an Lippe,
So bischen Herz an Herz,
Es bleibt doch wunderwonnig
Und immer ein süsser Scherz.

Such a little bit of May sun,
Such a little bit of pure gold,
Dropping down from the twigs,
It's always very charming.

A little bit of lip to lip,
A little bit of heart to heart,
It's always very delicious
And always a sweet game.

Ich schreite heim
by Emil Claar

Ich schreite heim vom Ball, von Tanze,
Und schleppe zurück das alte Leid
Und nichts vom Glanze und nichts vom Glück.
Ich schreite heim.

Es schreien die Raben und fällt der stille Schnee,
Als wollt' er begraben die ganze Welt.
Mit deinem Falle, mit deinem Weben,
Du stiller Schnee bedeck mein Haupt,
Bedeck mein Leben, bedeck mein Weh.

I walk home from the ball, from the dance,
And drag old sorrow home with me
And there's no glow and no happiness.
I'm walking home.

The ravens are screaming, and the silent snow is falling,
As if it wanted to bury the whole world.
With your falling, with your weaving,
You silent snow, cover my head,
Cover my life, cover my sadness.

Ich reite hinaus in das Weite
by Emil Claar

Ich reite hinaus in das Weite,
Hinaus in die blühende Welt.
Hinein in den Wald,
In das breite blättrige grüne Gezelt.

Da schallt das Vogelgeschmetter
Dem Rösslein zu tanzendem Schritt,
Und alle Blüthen und Blätter
Rauschen und tanzen mit.

Es tanzet die flatternde Mähne,
Es tanzt mir das Herz in der Brust.
Vergessen ist Gram und Thräne,
Ich halte am Zügel die Lust.

I ride out into the wide open space,
Into the flowering world,
Into the forest,
Into the wide leafy green roof.

The loud chirping of the birds
Invites the little horse to a dancing pace,
And all the blossoms and leaves
Rustle and join the dance.

The waving manes dance,
My heart in my breast is dancing.
Sorrow and tears are forgotten,
I rein over my passion.

Translations by Helen H. Metzelaar

Uralt!

Emil Claar

Catharina van Rennes, Op. 24, No. 1

7
ten.
mf
bleibt doch wun - der - hold. So bis - chen Lip - pe an
bleibt doch wun - der - hold. So bis - chen Lip - pe an
bleibt doch wun - der - hold. So bis - chen Lip - pe an
bleibt doch wun - der - hold. So bis - chen, bis - chen Lip - pe an
10
cresc.
Lip - pe, so bis-chen Herz an Herz, es bleibt doch wun-der -
Lip - pe, so bis-chen Herz an Herz, es bleibt doch wun-der -
Lip - pe, so bis-chen Herz an Herz, es bleibt doch wun-der -
Lip - pe, so bis-chen, bis-chen Herz an Herz, es bleibt doch wun-der -
Ped.

14
mit Wärme
won - nig und im - mer ein sü - sser Scherz, es
espr.
won - nig und im - mer ein sü - sser Scherz, es bleibt doch
won - nig und im - mer ein sü - sser Scherz, es
won - nig und im - mer ein sü - sser Scherz, es
17
ten.
bleibt doch wun - der - won - nig und im - mer ein sü - sser Scherz!
bleibt doch wun - der - won - nig und sü - sser Scherz!
bleibt doch wun - der - won - nig und sü - sser Scherz!
bleibt doch wun - der - won - nig und sü - sser Scherz!

Ich schreite heim

Emil Claar

Catharina van Rennes, Op. 24, No. 2

7
p
sfz
Ich schrei - te heim. Es schrei-en die Ra - ben und
Ich schrei - te heim. Es schrei-en die Ra - ben und
Ich schrei - te heim. Es schrei-en die Ra - ben und
Ich schrei - te heim. Es schrei-en die Ra - ben und
11
riten.
fällt und fällt der stil - le Schnee, als wollt' er be-gra - ben die
ten.
fällt und fällt der Schnee, als wollt' er be-gra - ben die
fällt und fällt der stil - le Schnee, als wollt' er be-gra - ben die
fällt und fällt der stil - le Schnee, als wollt' er be-gra - ben die
ben legato
Ped.
2 Ped.

14
rall.
a tempo
p ben cantando
mf
gan - ze Welt. Mit dei - nem Fal - le, mit
p
gan - ze Welt. Dei - nem Fal - le,
p
gan - ze Welt. Dei - nem Fal - le,
p
gan - ze Welt. Dei - nem Fal - le,
rall.
a tempo
p
ben legato e dolce
18
dim.
dei - nem We - ben, du stil - ler, stil - ler,
mf
dei - nem We - ben, stil - ler, stil - ler,
mf
dei - nem We - ben, stil - ler, stil - ler,
mf
p
dei - nem We - ben, stil - ler, stil - ler,
p

22
p
Schnee be - deck mein Haupt, be - deck mein Le - ben, be -
Schnee be - deck mein Haupt, be - deck mein Le - ben, be -
Schnee be - deck mein Haupt, be - deck mein Le - ben, be -
Schnee be - deck mein Haupt, be - deck mein Le - ben, be -
Ped.
25
deck mein Weh!
deck mein Weh!
deck mein Weh!
deck mein Weh!
pp
Ped.

Ich reite hinaus in das Weite

Emil Claar **Catharina van Rennes, Op. 24, No. 3**

8
p und leicht
brei - te blätt - ri-ge grü - ne Ge - zelt! Da
p und leicht
brei - te blätt - ri-ge grü - ne Ge - zelt! Da
p und leicht
brei - te blätt - ri-ge grü - ne Ge - zelt! Da
p und leicht
brei - te blätt - ri-ge grü - ne Ge - zelt! Da
pp und leicht
12
schallt das Vo - gel-ge - schmet - ter dem Röss-lein zu tan -
schallt das Vo - gel-ge - schmet - ter dem Röss-lein zu tan -
schallt das Vo - gel-ge - schmet - ter dem Röss-lein zu tan -
schallt das Vo - gel-ge - schmet - ter dem Röss-lein zu tan - zen-dem,

16
- zen - dem Schritt, und al - le Blüth - en und Blät - ter
[·]
- zen - dem Schritt, und al - le Blüth - en und Blät - ter
[·]
- zen - dem Schritt, und al - le Blüth - en und Blät - ter,
[·]
tan - zen-dem, tan - zen-dem Schritt, und al - le Blüth - en und Blät - ter
20
rau - schen und tan - zen, rau - schen und tan - zen mit.
rau - schen und tan - zen, rau - schen und tan - zen, mit.
al - le rau - schen und tan - zen, rau - schen, tan - zen
rau - schen und tan - zen, tan - zen, rau-schen und tan - zen

23
Con animo
Es tan - zet die flat - tern-de Mäh - ne,
Es tan - zet die flat - tern-de Mäh - ne,
sfz
mit.
Es tan - zet die flat - tern-de Mäh - ne,
sfz
mit.
Es tan - zet die flat - tern-de Mäh - ne,
Con animo
27
cresc.
es tanzt mir das Herz in der Brust! Ver -
cresc.
es tan - zet, tan - zet das Herz in der Brust! Ver -
cresc.
es tan - zet, tan - zet das Herz in der Brust! Ver -
cresc.
es tan - zet das Herz in der Brust! Ver -
marc. e cresc.

31
ges - sen ist Gram und Thrä - ne, ich hal - te am Zü -
ges - sen ist Gram und Thrä - ne, ich hal - te am Zü -
ges - sen ist Gram und Thrä - ne, ich hal - te am Zü -
ges - sen ist Gram und Thrä - ne, ich hal - te am Zü -
35
- gel die Lust!
- gel die Lust!
- gel die Lust!
- gel die Lust!
L.H.
R.H.

Susan Frances Harrison

(1859–1935)

ELAINE KEILLOR

The only daughter of John Riley and Frances Drought, Susan (Susie) Frances (hereafter called Harrison) was born in Toronto, Canada, on February 24, 1859. Harrison, who appears to be the first Canadian woman to have completed an opera, received her music and literary education at private schools in Toronto and Montreal where one of her music teachers was Frederic Boscovitz (1836–1903). When the family moved to Montreal she studied English, French, Latin, and Greek, attended some classes at McGill University, and was an active member of the Montreal Ladies' Literary Association.

At the age of sixteen her writings and verse began to appear in various publications such as *Canada's Illustrated News, Stewart's Quarterly* (New Brunswick), *Belford's Magazine,* and *Rose-Belford Canadian Monthly.* For most of these Harrison used the pseudonym of "Medusa." Later her signature, S. Frances, was misread as "Seranus," the name she assumed most frequently for music and literary publications. Perhaps to conceal her work as that of a woman composer, she also used the pseudonym "King, Gilbert" or "G. R." for some vocal and piano compositions. It is likely that journalistic work by the pseudonym "Rambler" was also the product of her pen. (Beginning in the 1850s Canadian women used their own names as well as pseudonyms when publishing.)

In 1879 she married the organist and conductor John W. F. Harrison (1848–1935). He had studied music in London, Paris, and Naples and arrived in Montreal in 1872 to become the organist at St. George's Anglican Church. Soon after their marriage they moved to Ottawa where he became music director of the Ladies' College and organist at Christ Church Cathedral. This marriage produced two children, Frederick John Lang and Frances Maria.

While living in Ottawa, Harrison worked as a correspondent for the *Detroit Free Press.* In 1883 she wrote the words and arranged the music of the *Address of Welcome to Lord Lansdowne,* which was performed for Lord Lansdowne's arrival in Canada. During a two-year period (1882–1884) she completed a three-act opera set in France in 1718 called *Pipandor,* based on a libretto by Frederick Augustus Dixon. It was written "after the fashion of the Gilbert and Sullivan's operas" with a number of French-Canadian songs "re-arranged and adapted by Seranus to Dixon's patter songs and comic verse."[1] Although the musical score has not been located, the libretto of *Pipandor* was published in 1884. The frustration of the composer in not hearing it performed or seeing it published was expressed in her short story, *Crowded Out!* (from *Crowded Out! And Other Sketches* [1886])

> I have come to London to sell or to part with in some manner an opera, a comedy, a volume of verse, songs, sketches, stories. I compose as well as write. I am ambitious. . . If nobody will discover me I must discover myself. I must demand recognition. I must wrest attention. They are my due. . . . I have left a continent behind; I have crossed a great water. . . . Here is my opera. This is my *magnum opus,* very dear, very clear, very well preserved. For it is three years old. I scored it nearly altogether. . . . Tomorrow . . . I will take the opera to the theatres. I will see the managers. . . . They will never listen to me, though I play my most beautiful phrase for I am nobody.[2]

Despite her problems with the opera, Harrison appears to be the first Canadian woman to have completed a work in this genre. She made several unsuccessful trips to New York and London to seek publishers for her musical compositions and literary works.[3]

In the preface to her first book, *Crowded Out! And Other Sketches* (1886), ten stories and a novella set in various locales ranging from Europe to the Canadian Northwest, Seranus wrote:

> I present these "Sketches". . . to my Canadian public, hoping that the phases of colonial life they endeavour to portray will be recognized as not altogether unfamiliar. Some of them are true, others have been written through the medium of fancy.[4]

In the same year, when John Harrison was appointed organist at Jarvis Street Baptist Church, the family moved to Toronto. He later became music director at the Church of St. Simon-the-Apostle from 1888–1916, conducted the Whitby Choral Society, the Musical

Union of Toronto, and taught organ/piano at the Ontario Ladies' College.

In Toronto Harrison wrote for *The Mail* and *The Globe*. She was a contributor to *The Week* and for a time was its acting and literary editor. She edited and published the first anthology of Canadian poetry, *The Canadian Birthday Book with Poetical Selections for Every Day in the Year* (1887). It included English, French, and some Native verse in translation. Her own prose and poetry continued to be published in various American and English periodicals, including *Pall Mall Magazine* and *New England Magazine*. A frequent theme in her writing was the musical heritage of Quebec, and in the 1890s she often gave recital-lectures on "The Music of French Canada." The critic of the *Montreal Gazette* stated on May 8, 1896:

> The gifted lady who undertook the task of giving to her hearers the literary as well as the musical side of the folk-songs of New France . . . was equal to the task, and that she was successful was evinced by the warmth of the applause which greeted the rendering of the several numbers on the programme. . . . Mrs. Harrison is an accomplished pianist and the possessor of a sweet and sympathetic voice, admirably adapted for the delineation of the music which she essays. . . . Perhaps the prettiest number was a composition by Rousseau. . . which was very sweetly sung to a most effective piano accompaniment, and her playing of the "Nocturne et Dialogue." [5]

Harrison's later literary publications include two novels. *The Forest of Bourg-Marie,* completed in 1888 but not published until 1898, explored the tragic consequences of the contemporary conflict between American materialism and French-Canadian traditionalism and was highly praised by the New York *Nation* on March 2, 1899.[6] The publishing company Hodder and Stoughton paid her a hundred pounds for *Ringfield* (1914), the story of a Methodist minister who becomes infatuated with a French-Canadian actress. Her collection of poems *Pine, Rose and Fleur de lis* (1891) received high praise; five more collections of verse appeared in the twentieth century. However, much of her creative writing remained unpublished and unpreserved. One of these was a ballad version of the Canadian legend *Rose Latulippe*. This was made into a folk play by Edward Devlin and published in 1935. In turn it became the basis for three Canadian ballets with music: in 1935 by Maurice Blackburn (1914–1988), in 1966 by Harry Freedman (b. 1922), and in 1966 by Michael McLean (probably born 1952).

Harrison's musical activities during the remainder of her life were those of administrator and teacher as well as writer. She helped to improve musical activity in Ottawa by reviving the Ottawa Philharmonic Society and organizing concerts that included works by Johann Sebastian Bach (1685–1750). On April 17, 1902, a complete program "of original work by Seranus" including piano pieces, songs (as well as *When I Grow Old* with violin obbligato), selections from *Pipandor*, and literary readings, was presented at the Toronto Conservatory of Music.[7] For twenty years she served as principal of the Rosedale Branch of the Toronto Conservatory of Music. She edited *The Conservatory (Bi-)Monthly* (1902–1913) and was a frequent contributor to *The Conservatory Quarterly Review* (1918–1935). Harrison died in Toronto on May 5, 1935. The major collection of her musical compositions and most of her published books are located at the Music Division, National Library of Canada in Ottawa. Harrison's correspondence is housed in the Thomas Fisher Rare Book Room, University of Toronto Library; the W. D. Lighthall Papers, Rare Book Department, McGill University Library, Montreal, Quebec; and the Queen's University Archives, Kingston, Ontario.

Although many have been lost, most of her known musical compositions were published in the 1880s. Some have survived in undated manuscripts. Among these is the *Quartet on Ancient Irish Airs* for string quartet. It is the earliest known extant work other than religious anthems/motets/hymns, songs or piano pieces by a Canadian woman composer. Her last compositions were piano pieces published in 1887. The works of Harrison reveal the natural musical gifts of a composer who had limited knowledge of harmony and compositional techniques of the late nineteenth century. Because she was so fascinated with the melodies of the old French-Canadian, folk songs that she heard in Quebec, she frequently juxtaposed modal melodies and harmonies with touches of chromatic harmonic progression. Some of her writing for piano and voice demands virtuosic skills.

When I Grow Old, a song with words by Frederick Augustus Dixon, also the librettist for her opera *Pipandor*, shows Harrison's sensitivity to words and declamation. Characterized by irregular phrases, the C major, triple meter song opens with a five-measure piano introduction. Section A opens with two seven-measure phrases that utilize a descending scalar gesture in the vocal part. In measure 19 this gesture is heard in A major, F-sharp minor, and A minor before it returns to the tonic C major (m. 30) where the introductory piano material is now accompanied by the voice. Section A is repeated (mm. 36-66). In section B (m. 67) the meter changes to common time, the tempo increases, and the descending gesture is modified. This C major section leads to the climax of the song, starting at measure 81, where the descending scale gesture reappears, now in A major with an accompaniment intensified by use of triplet repeated chords and a marking of *con molto espressione*. A *rallentando* leads to the restatement of the introductory material, now acting as a coda.

Acknowledgments

I am grateful to the granddaughter of Susan Frances Harrison, Katharine Vickers, and to her grandnieces, Freya Godard and Nancy Godard, for personal information about the family, and copies of compositions that they had in their possession. Nancy Godard, Freya Godard, and Katharine Vickers have given permission for the selected compositions to be published.

Notes

1. Agnes Ethelwyn Wetherald, "Some Canadian Literary Women—I. Seranus," *The Week* 5 (March 22, 1888): 267.

2. Seranus, *Crowded Out! And Other Sketches* (Ottawa: Evening Journal, 1886), 5, 7.

3. Personal communication from Harrison's granddaughter, Katharine Vickers.

4. Seranus, ii.

5. *Montreal Gazette*, (May 8, 1896), n.p.

6. *The Forest of Bourg-Marie,* completed in 1888 but not published until 1898, explored the tragic consequences of the contemporary conflict between American materialism and French-Canadian traditionalism and was highly praised in "Book Reviews," *Nation* (New York), March 2, 1899.

7. Program dated April 17, 1902.

List of Works

Songs

The British Volunteers. Text by Susan Frances Harrison. Published under G. R. King. Toronto: King & Co.,1884.

My Own Ador'd Love. Text by Susan Frances Harrison. Published under Gilbert King. Toronto: King & Co., 1884.

Our Canada True to the Core. Text by Susan Frances Harrison. (Patriotic song and chorus.) Published under G. R. King. Toronto: King & Co., 1884.

God Bless Our Family Royal. Published under G. R. King, Toronto: Briggs, 1886. Not located.

The Old Musician's Song. Text by G. Weatherley. Published under name Seranus. London: Hutchings & Co., 1886.

The Angelus. Music by Seranus. Unpublished.

The Butterfly. Music by Seranus. Unpublished.

The Dream That Died. Music by Seranus. Unpublished.

England's England Yet. Music by Seranus. Unpublished.

Hymn: O Voice of the Beloved. Music by Seranus. Unpublished.

The Ladies of St. James. Music by Seranus. Unpublished.

An Old-fashioned Love Song. Text anonymous. Published under Seranus. London: Edwin Ashdown, n.d.

The Priest's Song. Music by Seranus. Unpublished.

The Prodigals. Music by Seranus. Unpublished.

Singer of Persephone. Unpublished.

Sisters Three. Text by Susan Frances Harrison. Unpublished.

Soldiers of Christ. Text from *Hymns Ancient and Modern*. (Sacred song tenor/soprano.) [Also arranged as Processional Hymn.] Music by Seranus. Unpublished.

Someone Like You. Unpublished.

Spring Song. Music by Seranus. Unpublished.

There is a Land of Pure Delight. Text from *Hymns Ancient and Modern*. (Sacred song, versions for soprano/tenor, contralto/baritone.) Music by Seranus. Unpublished.

When I Grow Old. Text by Frederick Augustus Dixon. Unpublished.

The Young Lady in White. Text by Seranus. Unpublished.

Piano Solo

Light as a Feather: Waltz (with vocal part *ad lib*). Published under Gilbert King, n.p.: W. F. Shaw, 1886.

Eldorado Valse for piano. Published under Gilbert King, Toronto: I. Suckling & Sons, 1886.

Trois Esquisses Canadiennes (Three Canadian Sketches), Toronto: Nordheimer, 1887.

No. 3. Chant du voyageur Reprint in *Piano Music II*, edited by Elaine Keillor. *Canadian Musical Heritage*, Volume 6. *Ottawa: Canadian Musical Heritage, 1986, 16-20.*

Danse polonaise for piano. Published under Gilbert King, Toronto: I. Suckling & Sons, 1888. Not located.

Chamber Music

Quartet on Ancient Irish Airs. Parts for string quartet. Unpublished.

Opera

Pipandor. Libretto by Frederick Augustus Dixon. 1882–1884. Not located.

Arrangement

Address of Welcome to Lord Lansdowne. Text by Susan Frances Harrison. 1883. Not located.

Published Compositions by Gilbert King

(copyright information only, medium unknown)

Marche canadienne (Canadian March), I. Suckling & Sons, 1888, copyright deposit No. 4628.

On the Wing, I. Suckling & Sons, 1888, copyright deposit No. 4629.

I Do Object To That, Anglo-Canadian Music Publishers' Association, 1894, copyright deposit No. 7681.

Published Books

Crowded Out! And Other Sketches. Ottawa: Evening Journal, 1886.

The Canadian Birthday Book. Toronto: Robinson, 1887.

Pine, Rose and Fleur de lis. Toronto: Hart, 1891.

The Forest of Bourg-Marie. London: Arnold, 1898; Toronto: Morang, 1899.

In Northern Skies and Other Poems. Toronto, 1912.

Ringfield. Toronto: Musson, 1914; London: Hodder & Stoughton, 1914.

Songs of Love and Labor. Toronto, 1925.

Later Poems and Villanelles. Toronto: Ryerson, 1928.

Four Ballads and a Play. Toronto, 1933.

Penelope, and Other Poems. Toronto, 1934.

Translations from German into English

Lautz, Henry J. *In Church. In der Kirche*. (Song) Words by M. Greif. English version by Mrs. J. W. F. Harrison. Winnipeg/ Toronto: Whaley Royce, [1910].

Selected Articles on Musical Topics

"Historical Sketch of Music in Canada." In *Canada: An Encyclopedia of the Country*, vol. 4, ed. J. C. Hopkins. Toronto: Linscott, 394.

"On French-Canadian Folksong." *Musical Canada* 2 (1908): 8-10.

"The Future of Musical Composition." *Conservatory Quarterly Review* 3 (1920): 6-8.

"To the Young Teacher." *Conservatory Quarterly Review* 3 (1921): 63-64.

"The New Criticism." *Conservatory Quarterly Review* 4 (1922): 31-33.

"A Few Words About Singing." *Conservatory Quarterly Review* 4 (1922): 90-92.

"On the Encouragement of Musical Composition." *Conservatory Quarterly Review* 5 (1922): 6-8.

"Some Aspects of Chamber Music." *Conservatory Quarterly Review* 5 (1923): 34-36.

"Music for the Masses." *Conservatory Quarterly Review* 6 (1923): 5-7.

"What is 'Classical Music'." *Conservatory Quarterly Review* 5 (1924): 74-76.

"Piano versus Violin." *Conservatory Quarterly Review* 7 (1924): 9-11.

"Brahms — in Advance." *Conservatory Quarterly Review* 8 (1926): 87-90.

"The Great Craftsman — J. S. Bach." *Conservatory Quarterly Review* 9 (1927): 85-90.

Bibliography

Aodh o Reill, Padraig mac. *Songs of Uladh*. Belfast: William Mullan, 1904.

Gerson, Carole. "Susan Frances Harrison." In *Canadian Writers Before 1890*. Vol. 99. Ed. W. H. New, *Dictionary of Literary Biography*. Detroit/London: Clark Layman Book, Gale Research Inc., 1990.

Jones, Gaynor. "Harrison, Susie Frances." In *The Norton/ Grove Dictionary of Women Composers*. Eds. Julie Anne Sadie and Rhian Samuel. New York/London: W. W. Norton, 1995.

Keillor, Elaine. "Harrison, Susie Frances." In *Encyclopedia of Music in Canada*, 2nd edition. Eds. Helmut Kallmann and Gilles Potvin. Toronto: University of Toronto Press, 1992.

———. *Piano Music II, Canadian Musical Heritage*. Vol. 6. Ottawa: Canadian Musical Heritage, 1986.

Krassen, Miles. *O'Neill's Music of Ireland: New & Revised*. New York: Oak Publications, 1976.

Laforte, Conrad. *Le Catalogue de la chanson folklorique française III: Chansons en forme de dialogue, Les Archives de folklore*. Vol. 21. Québec: Les Presses de l'Université Laval, 1982.

Wetherald, Agnes Ethelwyn. "Some Canadian Literary Women — I. Seranus," *The Week* 5 (March 22, 1888): 267-68.

Whitridge, Margaret. "The Distaff Side of the Confederation Group: Women's Contribution to Early Nationalist Canadian Literature," *Atlantis* 4 (autumn 1978): 30-39.

Willison, Marjory. "Mrs. J. W. F. Harrison — 'Seranus'," *The Canadian Bookman* 14 (July–August 1932): 80-81.

Discography

Piano Music by Torontonians 1834–1984. Elaine Keillor, piano. World WRC1-3315 (1984). *Chant du voyageur*.

By a Canadian Lady. Elaine Keillor, piano. Carleton Sound CSCD1006 (1999). *Dialogue*.

When I Grow Old

Frederick Augustus Dixon
S. F. Harrison "Seranus"
Elaine Keillor, editor
Andante
f
*
6
p not too slow
When I grow old, give me mem - 'ry of mu-sic's hours,
10
mf
p
Birds' song and scent of flo - wers, May I have sight to see
mf
p
15
f
What of earth's beau-ty rare My life's last days may share.
mf

*F's in manuscript

19
f
Fresh may my mem-'ry be,
Fresh may my mem-'ry be
f
23
of all dear forms and fa - ces
Bright days and well-lov'd pla - ces.
27
f
rit.
rall.
a tempo
My heart not dry and cold when I grow old,
When I grow
colla voce
p
semplice
32
p
old, When I grow old.
p
And may there come to
p

38
me Mu - sic of child-ren's voi - ces; No mirth old age re -
mf
42
p
joy - ces Like child - ren's glee. Their feet up-on the
p
47
stair, Their fig-ures 'round my chair,— And gath-er'd at my knee,
mf
f
52
And gath-er'd at my knee, With o-pen eyes of won - der,

56
f
And ro-sy lips a - sun - der,
Hear - ing old sto-ries told,
When I grow
f
61
p
old,
When I grow old,
When I grow old.
p
66
Più mosso
p
So on the mis - ty land,
p
69
pp
So on the mis - ty land,
Where hu - man know - ledge
pp

72
cea - ses, And faith a-lone in - crea - ses
75
pp
accel.
And life is shift - ing sand;
And all we have is
78
rall.
largamente
nought
And hope can-not be bought.
81
Con molto espressione
f
All hum - bly may I stand,
All hum - bly may I

84
stand, With lov - ing forms be - side me
f
cresc.
87
And lov - ing hands to guide me And wait with loo - sen'd
cresc.
90
rall.
a tempo
hold, When I grow old, When I grow
p
94
rall.
old, When I grow old.
f

Anna Teichmüller

(1861–1940)

SUZANNE SUMMERVILLE

"Enjoy your destiny, it is God's path for your soul."[1]

Anna Teichmüller, German composer, pianist, and teacher, was born in Göttingen on May 11, 1861. She was the daughter of Gustav Teichmüller (1832–1888), university lecturer in Dorpat and Professor of Philosophy and Religion in Göttingen and Basel, and his first wife, Anna von Cramer, the daughter of a wealthy Estonian landowner.[2] After the birth of a second daughter and the untimely death of Anna von Cramer in 1862, Gustav Teichmüller married his first wife's younger sister, Lina von Cramer. They had six children, including the three sisters to whom Anna Teichmüller dedicated her *Abendlied*, op. 21.[3]

Teichmüller began her musical training in Dorpat and continued her studies in Jena and Berlin. Although notes in her diary and letters to her family during her absence in Berlin tell of voice lessons with Sophie Plehn and of singing before small social gatherings, of renting a piano, and about recitals, concerts, and opera performances she attended, there is no specific information to show that she studied piano or attended formal composition classes.[4]

During her student years she became acquainted with two of the outstanding German literary figures of the late nineteenth and early twentieth centuries: Carl Hauptmann (1858–1921) and his brother, Gerhart Hauptmann (1862–1946), winner of the 1912 Nobel Prize for Drama. In 1900, Teichmüller moved to Schreiberhau,[5] a village in Prussian Silesia, now part of Poland. Gerhart Hauptmann had preceded her to Schreiberhau in 1891 where Carl and his family also lived. Teichmüller composed the majority of her compositions in Schreiberhau during the second half of her life.

In an article written in 1960 to commemorate the twentieth anniversary of Teichmüller's death, Ilse Reicke described Teichmüller, as "belonging to the *Kreis von Schreiberhau*," a circle of painters, poets and artists who lived in the small mountain village.[6] Thanks to the brothers Hauptmann, Schreiberhau became an important focal point of German intellectual life during the late nineteenth and early twentieth centuries.

It was both Carl Hauptmann's friendship and the pleasure that mountainous landscapes gave her that convinced Teichmüller to make her home in the village. Elisabeth Kuhnert, in her 1950 article, described Teichmüller's reason for choosing Schreiberhau in these words:

> Love, yes, and passion were not strange to her. Womanly sacrifice and the desire to live for others were constituent also, but she felt that her path led to the lonely mountain heights that would allow her to create that which was growing inside her.[7]

Although Teichmüller's family in Dorpat was wealthy and in her youth she had traveled extensively, her financial situation as an adult was much more constrained. Nevertheless, in Schreiberhau she managed to live alone and to entertain her many guests graciously. Her residence was the renovated side apartment of a simple country house close to the old blacksmith's shop, a pond, and the Carl Hauptmann home in the Middle–Schreiberhau valley surrounded by meadows and the mountains. A small library and several fine works of art complemented her large and comfortably appointed music room. It was there in the early morning hours that she preferred to "create the music that caused so many to take notice and even won over men who before had never given credence to a woman's genius in the realm of composition."[8]

Berlin audiences and music critics realized that "Die Schöpferin dieser Musik ist keine gewöhnliche Frau" (The creator of this music is no ordinary woman) and as she became better known, her compositions were programmed with those of Bach, Beethoven and Brahms. Berlin's powerful critics and members of the arts community worked together during the 1920s to obtain an annual state grant for her. They accomplished this and Teichmüller's last years were less difficult because of it.[9]

Teichmüller, who had been labeled Carl Hauptmann's "Liederbraut" (bride of song),[10] set a long list of his poems (see List of Works), including the cantata *Ostergesang* (Easter Song), op. 6. A performance of *Ostergesang* was given in Berlin's Cottbuser Oberkirche (an important church on Cottbus Square) with

Teichmüller in the audience. Kuhnert described the cantata's performance as having "beautified the service and uplifted the souls of the worshipers."[11] A choir from the Riesengebirge chose *Ostergesang* to perform as a last tribute to Silesia's poet laureate and Teichmüller's close friend, Carl Hauptmann.

Teichmüller, a Protestant, wrote her only mass, the *Missa Poetica*, to a text by the poet Ilse von Stach. Its first performance in Berlin's old Garnisonkirche (military garrison church) was highly praised by the city's most important critics. The creation and the premiere in one of Berlin's historical churches were high points in Teichmüller's artistic life. The most influential and important people in Berlin's musical elite had come together to make the performance possible. Elisabeth Kuhnert described the scene: "We see still the old Garrison Church before our eyes — 6,000 worshipers listening intently to the choruses, the soloists, and the powerful sounds of the organ and the orchestra."[12] A second performance of this now missing work took place some years later in a large Protestant church in Silesian Schweidnitz.

Ilse Reicke wrote that Teichmüller was "often talked about for the power and strength of her compositions, as well as for their profoundness."[13] Kuhnert praised her further by saying, "She was not only one of the finest composers of her time, but for today's generation that is finally beginning to discover women composers, Teichmüller is one of the first who is due a particular round of thanks."[14]

Toward the end of her life, Teichmüller's financial situation worsened and she had to move into a small upstairs apartment in the town's orphanage where she gave piano and singing lessons. She had long been a friend to children and in her list of compositions are several written especially for youthful performers. These include *Songs,* op. 17 ("To be sung by children" and dedicated to Ellen, Hansi, Olaf, Fränze, Edda, Wölfchen and Gerda), *Seven Small Piano Pieces,* op. 44, and the fairy tale musical *Der Froschkönig* (The Frog King or Prince).

In her last years she compiled and organized her father's correspondence and publications. This extensive collection is now extant in the library of the University of Basel where Gustav Teichmüller once taught.[15]

Teichmüller was a member of the Genossenschaft deutscher Tonsetzer (Society of German Composers) and the Reichsverband deutscher Tonkunstler und Musiklehrer (Society of German Musicians and Music Teachers). Her peaceful death occurred in Schreiberhau in 1940. She was buried in the Bergfriedhof (Mountain Cemetery) in Lower-Schreiberhau near the final resting place of Carl Hauptmann.[16]

In her article "Anna Teichmüller zum 100. Geburtstag," (Anna Teichmüller on her 100th Birthday), Magdalena Malorny remembered her last visit in 1940 with the seventy-nine year old composer and Teichmüller's parting reflection: "We want to shoulder our destiny, not drag it around."[17]

Paul Dubray (1883–1940), French artist and engraver,[18] visited Schreiberhau and wrote the following description of Teichmüller and her music. It was published in 1910 in the early women's magazine, *Frauen-Zukunft* (*Women-Future)*:

> Anna Teichmüller came from the Baltic provinces. She had listened to the gray wind that slowly gusts over the unending Russian steppe. Her songs have the magic of a melody that resounds in those distant, hilly crags. Her soul is meditative, heart-felt, and ardent, with a tender melancholia that is always mournfully sad like the warm sigh of an autumn evening. A pleasant music after the noise of today. There is nothing artificial about her compositional style, a conspicuous distancing from musical erudition. Not a single page is composed solely to overcome technical difficulties. Every song is an experience of the *anima* in its total unpretentiousness, and the listener believes each time from anew that he or she is listening to an old, seldom heard melody, one that rises out of the national soul.
>
> A strong personality and the feeling of homogeny greet us in the works of Anna Teichmüller. She presents herself in her works persuasively and as having a steadfast, imperturbable will. Seldom is work "production." With Anna Teichmüller, the word "craft" loses its meaning of "workmanlike" or "mechanical." One cannot praise highly enough each creative labor that desires nothing more than to dream its dream, years through, far from the crowds, full of pensive inner joy.
>
> The folk songs and the children's songs are especially full of sweetness and originality. They are meant for good children who live in a loving environment where the sun smiles down with tenderness upon a caring landscape. Where lilacs diffuse their aroma over the cradle. They are like the rustle of a row of stitching, a seam that softly escorts one to sleep; a caress that one barely senses, as in a land where the heavens are pearl gray, and where in the distance, doleful intonations of a tower bell sound in the slow winds that blow across an unending steppe.
>
> The songs she composed based on texts by Carl Hauptmann are for the most part folksongs too. They are full of the feel of autumn, full of the quiet melancholy of the unfortunate, like the earth bathed in a foggy mist, their tragic nature — heart-wrenching.[19]

Partly because Teichmüller set a text by Paul Verlaine[20] to music, Dubray felt impelled to close his article with a comparison between the solo violin's gently bowed double stops in her cantata *O Welt, du Wunder* (op. 26), and the following verse from Verlaine:

> Snow is falling in shredded linen flakes
> Through the slow setting of the blood red sun
> And the air feels like an autumnal sigh
> So soft is this monotone evening
> Wherein a languid landscape languishes.[21]

Kuhnert, in her article, described Teichmüller as not only one of the important music personages of her time, but she also stressed the fact that Teichmüller was a great admirer of the art of poetry, evidenced by her close friendship with Carl Hauptmann. Often in the morning Hauptmann would go to Teichmüller's home and ask her to criticize his work of the previous day. Her unfailing, strict opinion of Hauptmann's work was often decisive.[22]

Cornelia Bartsch found that Teichmüller's "melody and rhythm are carefully coordinated for the most part according to 'speech sound.'"[23] For these reasons, special attention is paid here to Teichmüller's setting of the texts in the examples that follow. *Windlied*, op. 1, no. 2 (1904), poetry by Carl Hauptmann, is marked *Allegretto* and with an indication that the accompaniment should swell and recede like an Aeolian harp ("Die Begleitung an und abschwellend wie eine Windharfe"), depicting the constancy of the blowing with repetitive left-hand strums on the beat followed by rolled chords in the right hand in measures 11-28. The song begins and ends in A minor, shifting between minor and major. The added quarter notes on the first beat of measures 22-24 underscore the musical demands of the blowing wind and the question "woher? wohin?" (whither? whence?). The postlude closes with overlapping strums, settling to closure with the right hand joining the left for the first time in measures 42-43.

Although their creative lives overlapped for many years, Teichmüller composed only one song based on the poetry of Rainer Maria Rilke (1875–1926). *Maria* was included as number four in her *Fünf Lieder*, op. 2 published by Helianthus in 1904. The poem is number VII in *Mir zur Feier: Gebete der Mädchen zur Maria* (A Celebration of Myself: Prayers of a Maiden to Maria) — a group of sixteen poems with a poetic introduction. Fourteen of the poems were written between May 5–7, 1898, when Rilke was in Florence, Italy. One poem, number III, was listed as written on July 22, 1898, in Berlin-Schmargendorf. *Maria — du weinst* was the only poem in the cycle undated and without a place of origin.

The piano accompaniment introduces the key of C minor in the bass and the voice of the girl states simply, "Maria! you are crying." The exclamation mark in the published music is not in Rilke's original text and "du weinst" (you are crying) is a statement underscored by a dissonant diminished seventh resolving to the dominant G major. The exchange between the girl and Maria, spoken over a sustained piano accompaniment decorated with downward falling figures, shows that their concern for each other should be quietly rendered. A crescendo in the accompaniment (measures 9-10) leads into a clashing dissonance of a B diminished-seventh chord placed over the G pedal as the voice sings "Und da möcht' ich weinen" (And therefore, or because of that, I wish to weep) in measure 11. Harsh dissonance continues in measure 13 with the G-flat in the A diminished-seventh chord clashing with the ongoing G-natural pedal in the bass. The vocal line rises here in triplets to express the pressing of her forehead against stones.

Instead of firmly returning to C minor in measure 17, the music moves to the subdominant F minor in measure 18. In measures 19-23, where the conversation concerns the possibility of a song being created as a legacy, the pianist duplicates the singer's melody for the only time in the composition. However, a legacy is not to be and the piano begins the transition back to C minor alone (mm. 24-25). The singer renders the poem's final statement, "Aber die Stunde stirbt ohne Vermächtnis" (But the hour dies without a legacy . . .) spoken over quiet chords before the piano closes with a three measure postlude, ending on an open fifth.

Wie leise scheue Kinder, op. 7, no. 2 (1906), poetry by Marianne Blaauw, is marked "Bewegt und Zart" (with gentle motion and tender) and set in B minor. Section A begins with a rocking motion that represents the "to and fro" of a lullaby. In measures 15-20, Teichmüller describes the heart's long and difficult search for love, "der Weg ist steil und der Weg is lang" (the path is steep and the path is long). In measure 22, the dotted half note patterns in the accompaniment return. Now they are decorated, beginning in the bass clef (mm. 22-23) and continuing in the treble clef with dotted eighth–sixteenth–eighth patterns. The poet's thoughts, depicting shy children are shown soaring to almost heavenly heights (compare mm. 7-9 and 24-27).

Klein Christel, op. 9, no. 7 (1907), a simple folksong setting, is a good example of Teichmüller's penchant for coordinating rhythm and melody to underscore words. Verses one and three are given altered note values in the accompaniment (mm. 1 and 17) to describe the small child and the adult Virgin Mary. Under the first strophe Teichmüller uses eighth notes and rests to portray "Little" Christel. Beneath the description of the adult Mary, she changes the note values in the accompaniment to two quarters and a half note.

The repetitions of Christel's question, "Darf Olaf aber zum Himmel eingeh'n?" (May Olaf enter into heaven?) underscore the importance of the request to the little girl. To emphasize that urgency, the third request, "darf Olaf" (may Olaf), measures 13-14, begins on two high Fs, the highest notes to that point in the song.

Acknowledgments

Many of Teichmüller's published songs and choral works are extant in the holdings of the Music Library, University of California, Santa Barbara, and in the Hauptmann Collection at the Staatsbibliothek zu Berlin, Haus 2 and in the Music Collection, Haus 1. Larry Snyder (CA) and Petra Stallbörger (Berlin) aided in the acquisition of those works. Dr. Cornelia Bartsch of Berlin was my source for Teichmüller's piano compositions, Ellen Röhner of the Gesellschaft für interregionalen Kulturaustausch, e.V. (Berlin) assisted with dates and newspaper articles, and Elisa Burchert (Görlitz) aided with the Hauptmann translations. Other colleagues who were helpful in the writing of this contribution to *Women Composers: Music Through the Ages* include Annegret Wilder; Dr. David Stech, University of Alaska Fairbanks; and Dr. Harald Krebs, University of Victoria, British Columbia.

In her article, *Anna Teichmüller zum 100. Geburtstag* (1961), the author Magdalena Malorny wrote that she was in possession of the manuscripts of three songs based on texts by Carl Hauptmann: *Der Fischerfrau Lied*, *Über silbernen Wellen*, and *Harfenlied*. However, it was not possible to find these or any other of Teichmüller's manuscripts.

Neither Dr. Cornelia Bartsch nor I were able to locate any of the late publications listed as published by the firm Röbke in Hirschberg or the Verlagsamt Deutsche Tonkünstler in Leipzig and Berlin. The current German composers' organization, Deutsche Tonkünstlerverband e.V., with offices in Munich, had no listings as of summer 1998. It is very possible that information on these compositions was lost during World War II.

Teichmüller's Dreililien publications are still under copyright. The majority may be ordered from: Richard Birnbach, Aubinger Strasse 9, D-82166 Gräfelfing-Lochham, Germany.

Notes

1. Elisabeth Kuhnert, "Anna Teichmüller zum Gedanken: Komponistin, Förderin schöner Künste und Freundin der Jugend," in *Heimatbrief für Schlezier und Sudetendeutsche*, Nr. 9, Jg. 2 (May 1950). A quote from Teichmüller's diary: "Habe Dein Schicksal lieb, denn es ist der Weg Gottes mit Deiner Seele."

2. Cornelia Bartsch, "Die Komponistin Anna Teichmüller — ein Rechercherbericht," in the catalogue for the exhibit *Die imposante Landschaft: Künstler und Künstlerkolonien im Riesengebirge im 20. Jahrhundert*, Ein deutsch-polnisches Ausstellungsprojekt. Gesellschaft für interregionalen Kulturaustauschft e.V. (1999), 91.

Author's note: Nicolas Slonimsky, in his article on Robert Teichmüller in *The International Cyclopedia of Music and Musicians*, 6th ed. (New York: Mead, 1952), 1873, listed Robert, the well-known professor of piano at the Hochschule für Musik in Leipzig, as Anna's brother. This was not the case. There was, however, a familial relationship between the several Teichmüllers in Braunschweig.

3. *Abendlied*, op. 21 (SSAA) (Text by Carl Hauptmann). Berlin: Dreililien, n.d. (Dedicated to her sisters Haloga, Sif and Erda.)

4. Bartsch, "Die Komponistin Anna Teichmüller," 91. Descriptions of her life in Berlin are taken from letters written by Teichmüller to her family and an entry in her diary dated November 28, 1887.

5. Schreiberhau, a village in Silesia's *Riesengebirge* region, is known as Szklarska Pořeba in Polish.

6. Ilse Reicke, "Anna Teichmüller: Zu ihrem 20. Todestag am 6. September," in *Riesengebirgsbote*, Nr. 9, Jg. 12, Ülzen (September 1960). "Anna Teichmueller gehörte in den 'Kreis von Schreiberhau,' der dank der Brüder Carl und Gerhart Hauptmann, in den beiden Jahrzehnten um die Jahrhundertwende den kleinen schlesischen Riesengebirgsort zu einem der geistigen Brennpunkte Deutschlands machte. In jenem Kreisen dem auch die Maler Hanns Fechner und Hermann Hendrich, der Naturwissenschaftler Wilhelm Bölsche, der Volksbildner und Poet Bruno Wille, der Volkswirtschaftler Werner Sombart, der Dichter Hermann Stehr angehöten, bedeutete Anna Teichmüller die Seele der Musik."

Besides the Hauptmann brothers and Teichmüller, other members of the group were the painters Hanns Fechner and Hermann Hendrich, natural scientist Wilhelm Bölsche, educator and poet Bruno Wille, political economist Werner Sombart, and poet Hermann Stehr.

7. Kuhnert, "Anna Teichmüller zum Gedenken: Komponistin." "Liebe, ja, und Leidenschaft waren ihr nicht fremd — auch nicht frauliche Aufopferung, das Lebenwollen für andere, doch sie fühlte, dass ihre Wege sie in Höhen führte, die einsam müssten, um das zu schaffen, was in ihr wuchs."

8. Ibid. "In diesem Räumen arbeitete Anna Teichmüller in stillen Morgenstunden am liebstem, schuf die Musik, deren Klang viele aufhorchen liess und auch Männer begeisterte, die von der Frauen Genius auf musikalischen Gebiet nicht viel hielten."

9. Ibid. "Die Schöpferin dieser Musik ist keine gewöhnliche Frau, so stellen nicht nur die begeisterten Zuhörer und Freunde fest, sondern auch die Kritiker, deren Stimmen zur Regierung der zwanziger Jahre dringen, die der zu dieser Zeit wirtschaftlich bedrängten Kunstlerin einen Jahressehrensold bewilligt."

10. Ilse Reicke, "Anna Teichmüller: Zu ihrem 20. Todestag am 6. September." "Anna Teichmüller, 'die Liederbraut' des Dichters vertonte eine grosse Reihe seiner Dichtungen."

11. Kuhnert, "Anna Teichmüller zum Gedenken." "den Gottesdienst verschönte und die Kirchen Besucher erhob."

12. Ibid. "Ein Höhepunkt in Anna Teichmüllers Leben bedeutete die Uraufführung ihrer Missa Poetica, deren Text von Ilse von Stach gedichtet worden war. Bedeutende Musikgrössen Berlins hatten sich zusammengefunden, um diese Uraufführung zur Wirklichkeit werden zu lassen. Wir sehen noch die alte Berliner Garnisonkirche vor uns — 6000 andächtig lauschende Menschen hören die Chöre, Soli, die mächtigen Klänge der Orgel und des Orchesters."

Author's note: Ilse Reicke wrote incorrectly in her 1960 article that the first performance was held in Berlin's *Gedächtniskirche*.

13. Reicke, "Anna Teichmüller." "Immer wieder wurde die Kraft und Grösse bei aller Innigkeit dieser Komponistin hervorgehoben."

14. Kuhnert, "Anna Teichmüller zum Gedenken." "In der heutigen Zeit, die endlich beginnt, den weiblichen Komponisten zu entdecken, gebührt Anna Teichmüller als einer der ersten ein besonderes Gedanken."

15. Bartsch, "Die Komponistin Anna Teichmüller," 101-2. Extant in the Teichmüller Collection in Basel are diaries and letters from Anna to her family telling of her travels in Germany in 1876

and 1883, from Paris in 1880, and other family correspondence dating to 1893.

16. Kuhnert, "Anna Teichmüller zum Gedenken."

17. Magdalena Malorny, "Anna Teichmüller zum 100. Geburtstag," in *Der Schlesier,* Jg. 13 (May 1961). "Wir wollen unser Schicksal tragen, nicht schleppen."

18. For a biography of Dubray, see Mathilde Antoinette Galvaing, *Jean Paul Dubray: Graveur* (Paris: n.p., 1940). Dubray's given name is variously listed as Paul or Jean-Paul.

19. Paul Dubray, "Anna Teichmüller" in *Frauen-Zukunft*, vol. 1\3 (Munich and Leipzig: Frauen-Verlag, 1910), 239-40. "Anna Teichmüller stammt aus den baltischen Provinzen. Sie hat dem grauen Winde gelauscht, der langsam über die Unendlichkeit der russischen Ebenen streicht. Ihre Lieder haben den Zauber einer Melodie, die fern in den Steppen verweht. Eine träumerische Seele, innig, mit der zärtlichen Schwermut oder sanftesten Zärtlichkeit, die immer schwermütig ist, wie warmer Duft an Herbstabenden. Eine wohltuende Musik nach dem Lärm von heute. Nichts Künstliches darin, ein sichtbares Fernhalten von aller musikalischen Gelehrsamkeit. Keine Seite ist geschrieben, um technische Schwerigkeiten zu bewältigen. Jedes Lied ist ein Erlebnis der Seele in seiner ganzen Schlichtheit, daher man immer von neuen meint, einem alten, seltenen Liede zuzuhören, das aus der Seele des Volkes aufsteigt.

Eine starke Persönlichkeit und das Gefühl grosser Einheitlichkeit begenet uns in dem Werke Anna Teichmüllers. Sie hat sich ihrem Werke ganz gegeben mit einem fausten aber unerschütterlichen Willen. Selten ist Arbeit Schaffen. Aber bei Anna Teichmüller verliert das Wort den Sinn des Handwerksmässigen. Nicht hoch genug kann man jene Kraft verehren, die nichts will als ihren Traum träumen, durch Jahre hindurch, fern der Menge, voll Freude etwas in sich zu sein.

Die Volkslieder und Kinderlieder haben ganz besondere Anmut und Ursprünlichkeit. Sie sind für gute Kinder in einem lieblichen Lande, wo die Sonne mit einer fast sinnlichen, sorglichen Zärtlichkeit niederlächelt. Wo Flieder seinen Duft über die Wiege bereitet. Sie sind wie ein Rauschen von Kleidersäumen, das sanft zum Schlummer leitet, wie Liebkosungen, die kaum berühren, wie ein Land, dessen Himmel perlgrau ist, und wo die fernen Stimmen von Glocken in dem langsamen Wind der unendlichen Ebene verwehen.

Auch die Lieder zu den Texten von Carl Hauptmann sind zum grossen Teil Volkslieder. Voll Herbststimmung, voll der leisen Schwermut der armen und in Nebel gebadeten Erde, — selten bis zur Erschütterung der Tragik.

Nicht deshalb, weil Anna Teichmüller einen Text von Verlaine vertonte, drängt sich mir der Vergleich auf. Aber für mich wecken in 'O Welt, du Wunder' (op. 26) die Violine mit ihren leise gestrichenen Terzen kein anderes Schwesterbild, als diese Verse Verlaines (Verlaine verse in French): 'La neige tombe à longs traits de charpie/A travers le couchant sanguinolent./Et l'air a l'air d'être un soupir d'automne/Tant il fait doux par ce soir monotone/Où — se dorlote un paysage lent. — —'"

20. Anna's settings of Paul Verlaine's *Clair de lune* and Dubray's *Berceuse* were published together in 1910 as op. 24, nos. 3 and 4.

21. See Verlaine poem in original French above in note 19. Translation from *Sagesse* III, IX, 1880.

22. Kuhnert, "Anna Teichmüller zum Gedenken." "Aber sie war nicht nur eine von Musikgrössen ihrer Zeit anerkannte Komponistin. . . . Sie war auch eine Verehrerin der Dichtkunst. Sie fand sich darin in der Freundschft mit Carl Hauptmann, dessen Beraterin sie häufig war. Schon am frühen Morgenstunden zur Arbeit zu verwenden — müsste sie seine Entwürfe zu neuen Arbeiten prüfen. Ihr unbeirrbares, strenges Urteil war ihm oft massgebend."

23. Bartsch, "Die Komponistin Anna Teichmüller," 98. ([Teichmüller's] "Melodie und Rhythmus orientieren sich im wesentlichen am 'Sprachklang.'")

List of Works

Voice and Piano

Fünf Gedichte von Carl Hauptmann, op. 1. Berlin: Verlag Helianthus, 1904.

1. *Der Tod*
2. *Windlied*
3. *Stillung*
4. *Sehnsucht*
5. *Erdgeboren*

Fünf Lieder, op. 2. Berlin: Verlag Helianthus, 1904.

1. *Die Reu'*. Text anon.
2. *Stiller Abend sinkt.* Text by Carl Hauptmann
3. *An der duftverlor'nen Grenze jener Berge.* Text by Nickolaus Lenau
4. *Maria! Du weinst.* Text by Rainer Maria Rilke
5. *Schwüle.* Text by Conrad Ferdinand Meyer

(Verlag Helianthus became Dreililien and works after 1905 appeared under the Dreililien name)

Sechs leichte Lieder, op. 3. Berlin: Dreililien, 1905.

1. *Vor der himmlischcn Thür.* Folk song
2. *Die Princessin.* Text by Björnstyerne Björnson
3. *Lärchenbaum, mein Lärchenbaum.* Folk song
4. *Frau Nachtigall, sagt ihr Kõnigin.* Text by Carl Hauptmann

5. *Blüthenschwere Mai.* Folk song
6. *Wiegenlied.* Text by Friedl Zacharias

Drei Lieder, op. 4. Berlin: Dreililien, 1905.
1. *Ici bas tous les lilas meurent.* Text by Sully Prudhomme
2. *Trois Princesses.* Folk song. Derrier' chez mon père
3. *Finnisches Volkslied*

Zwei Liebeslieder, op. 5. Berlin: Dreililien, 1905.
1. *Wo du nicht bist.* From the Indian of Bhartrihari by Leopold von Schroeder
2. *In meiner Träume Heimat.* Text by Carl Hauptmann

Drei Lieder, op. 7. Berlin: Dreililien, 1906.
1. *Erdenkeinleins Wiegenlied.* Text by Carl Hauptmann
2. *Wie leise scheue Kinder.* Text by Marianne Blaauw
3. *Unbegreiflich.* Text by Carl Hauptmann

Vier Lieder, op. 8. Berlin: Dreililien, 1906.
1. *Der Gefangene.* Folk song from Krain
2. *Im Dämmer der Nacht.* Text by Carl Hauptmann
3. *Wo kein Strahl des Lichts.* Text by N. Lenau
4. *Frühlingslied.* Text by Carl Hauptmann

Leichte Lieder, op. 9 (II Edition). Berlin: Dreililien, 1907.
1. *Auf früher Reise.* Text anon.
2. *Vöglein Du.* Folk song
3. *Flamme in Nächten.* Text by Carl Hauptmann
4. *Ach, es bebt der Blütenkeim.* Folksong
5. *Herbst.* Text by Carl Hauptmann
6. *Der Fischerfrau Lied.* Text by Carl Hauptmann
7. *Klein Christel.* Folk song

Mandschurisch, op. 10. Text by Grete Ziegler-Bock. Berlin: Dreililien, 1907.

Der Seelchenbaum, op. 11. Text by Ferdinand Avenarius. Berlin: Dreililien, 1907.

Vier Lieder, op. 12. Berlin: Dreililien, 1907.
1. *Frühlingswinde.* Text by Carl Hauptmann
2. *Klage mich nicht an.* Text by Gottfried Keller
3. *Reiterlied.* Folk song
4. *Am Wachtfeuer.* Text by Carl Hauptmann

Zwei Balladen, op 13. Berlin: Dreililien, 1907.
1. *Der Besuch des Eros.* Anacreon
2. *Die beiden Raben.* Scottish

Held Owain, op. 14. Text is a Scottish ballad. Berlin: Dreililien, 1907.

Fünf Lieder, op. 15. Berlin: Dreililien, 1907.
1. *Berghäuers Lichter.* Text by Carl Hauptmann
2. *Wie ein Sturmwind.* Text anon.
3. *Säerspruch.* Text by Conrad Ferdinand Meyer
4. *Abendgefühl.* Text by Christian Friedrich Hebbel
5. *Das ungestüme Mädchen.* Text by Kolzow

Weihnachtslied, op. 16. Berlin: Dreililien, 1907.

Lieder, op. 17. Berlin: Dreililien, 1907. (*Kindern gesungen*)
1. *Ringelreigen.* Text by Friedrich Zacharias
2. *Vöglein.* Folk song
3. *Zigeunerzauber*
   a. Niwaschi
   b. Wespe
4. *Elfenarbeit.* Text by Wolrad Eigenbrodt
5. *Gold'ne Äpfel.* Folk song
6. *Auf der roten Heide.* Text by Wolrad Eigenbrodt

Julnacht, op. 18. Text by F. Hugin. Berlin: Dreililien, 1907.

Fünf Lieder, op. 24. Berlin: Dreililien, 1910.
1. *Annel's Lied.* Text by Carl Hauptmann
2. *All' deine Anmut.* Text by Hans Reisiger
3. *Claire de Lune.* Text by Paul Verlaine
4. *Berceuse.* Text by Paul Dubray
5. *Schlaffen, Schlaffen.* Text by Christian Friedrich Hebbel

Drei Lieder, op. 25. Berlin: Dreililien, 1910.
1. *Nächtlicher Auslug.* Text by Carl Hauptmann
2. *Ein Berittener.* Text by Gottfried Keller
3. *Die einsame Nacht.* Text by Carl Hauptmann

Zwei Weichnachtslieder, op. 31. Berlin: Dreililien, 1914.
1. *Vor der Weihnachtsfeier.* Text by A. von Keller
2. *Weihnacht.* Text by Carl Hauptmann

Voices a capella

Abendlied, op. 21 (SSAA). Text by Carl Hauptmann. Berlin: Dreililien, n.d.

Voice(s) and Instruments

Ostergesang (*Atem aus Knospen*), op. 6. Text by Carl Hauptmann. Berlin: Dreililien, 1906. (Small Easter Cantata for Mixed Chorus and Soloists with Piano Accompaniment)

Benedictus, op. 20. Berlin: Dreililien, 1910. (Trio for Soprano, Alto and Baritone with Piano or Organ)

Waldnacht, op. 22. Berlin: Dreililien, 1910. (Voice with Cello and Piano)

Hymne an die Nacht, op. 23. Text by Carl Hauptmann. Berlin: Dreililien, 1910. (Soprano and Baritone with Cello and Piano)

O Welt, O Wunder, op. 26. Text by Carl Hauptmann. Berlin: Dreililien, 1910. (Trio for Soprano, Alto, and Bass with Violin and Piano)

Piano

Variationen über ein eigenes Thema, op. 37. Hirschberg: Röbke, n.d.

Die georgische Prinzessin, op. 43. Berlin and Leipzig: Verlagsamt Deutsche Tonkünstler, 1925.

Sieben kleine Klavierstücke in leichter Spielart, op. 44. Berlin and Leipzig: Verlagsamt Deutsche Tonkünstler, 1925.

1. *Mückentanz*
2. *Zum Einschlafen*
3. *Kleiner Walzer*
4. *Lied*
5. *Trauer*
6. *Ellen's Wiegenlied*
7. *Springinsfeld*

Compositions

(mentioned in the writings about Teichmüller, not located to date)

Der Froschkönig (*The Frog King* or *Prince*), a "Märchen-Singspiel" (Fairy Tale).

Harfenlied aus "mehere Duette nach Löns" (several duets after Löns listed in Reicke).

Über silbernen Wellen (mentioned by Magdalena Malorny).

A Suite for Piano and Violin.

Nal und Damajanti (opera).

Missa Poetica (mass). Text by Ilsa von Stach. (Berlin 1924?).

Bibliography

Bartsch. Cornelia. "Anna Teichmüller." In the catalog to *Die imposante Landschaft: Künstler und Künstlerkolonien im Riesengebirge im 20. Jahrhundert*, Ein deutsch-polnisches Ausstellungsprojekt. Gesellschaft für interregionalen Kulturaustauschft e.V., 1999.

Dubray, Paul. "Anna Teichmüller." In *Frauen-Zukunft*, vol. 1\3. Munich and Leipzig: Frauen-Verlag, 1910.

Frank, Paul. *Kurzgefasstes Tonkünstler-Lexikon*, 12 Aufl. Ed. Wilhelm Altmann, 1926.

Galvaing, Mathilde Antoinette. *Jean-Paul Dubray: Graveur*. Paris: n.p., (1940?).

Hauptmann, Carl. *Leben mit Freunden: Gesammelte Briefe*. Berlin-Grunewald: Horen Verlag, 1928.

Hauptmann, Gerhart. *Tagebücher 1897–1905*. Ed. Martin Machatzke. Berlin: Propylän, 1987.

Kuhnert, Elisabeth. "Anna Teichmüller zum Gedanken: Komponistin, Förderin schöner Künste und Freundin der Jugend." In *Heimatbrief für Schlesier und Sudetendeutsche*, Nr. 9, Jg. 2, May 1950.

Malorny, Magdalena. "Anna Teichmüller zum 100. Geburtstag." In *Der Schlesier*, Jg. 13, May 1961.

Meyers Konversations-Lexikon, VI. Leipzig: Leipzig-Bibliographisches-Institut, 1908.

Minden, Heinrich. *Carl Hauptmann und das Theater*. Kastellaun: A. Henn Verlag, 1976.

Müller, Erich H., ed. *Deutsches Musiker-Lexikon*. 1929.

Reicke, Ilse. "Anna Teichmüller: Zu ihrem 20. Todestag am 6. September." In *Riesengebirgesbote*, Nr. 9, Jg. 12. Ülzen, September, 1960.

Rilke, Rainer Maria. *Sämtliche Werke*, Dritter Band: *Jugendgedichte*. Wiesbaden: Insel-Verlag, 1959, 246 and 930.

Slonimsky, Nicolas, ed. "Robert Teichmüller." In *The International Cyclopedia of Music and Musicians*, 6th ed. rev., 1873. New York: Mead, 1952.

Exhibits, May–December 1999

Die imposante Landschaft: Künstler und Künstlerkolonien im Riesengebirge im 20. Jahrhundert, Ein deutsch-polnisches Ausstellungsprojekt. Gesellschaft für interregionalen Kulturaustauschft e.V. Openings: Kreismuseum Hirschberg/ Jelenia Gora, May 22; Breslau/Wroclaw, September 5; and Berlin, Künstlerhaus Bethanien, November 29. The Berlin opening included a recital of Teichmüller songs by mezzo-soprano Regine Gebhardt.

Discography

Anna Teichmüller als Komponistin. Suzanne Summerville, mezzo-soprano, Jamila Hla Shwe, piano, a CD prepared to accompany the exhibit: *Die imposante Landschaft: Künstler und Künstlerkolonien im Riesengebirge im 20. Jahrhundert*, May–December 1999. *Zwei Gedichte von Carl Hauptmann*: *Stiller Abend sinkt*, op. 2, no. 2 [1904], *In meiner Träume Heimat*, op. 5, no. 2 [1905] and *Ellen's Wiegenlied* aus *Sieben kleine Klavierstücke in leichter Spielart*, op. 44, no. 6 [1925].

Windlied, op. 1, no. 2 (1904)
Poetry by Carl Hauptmann

(Author's note: One expects that "the song" will be blown away, scattered, but the poem interposes "bin," meaning "I" and not "it" will be blown away or scattered overnight in the blowing wind.)

In den Wind, in den Wind sing' ich mein Lied, Frage nicht, frage nicht, wohin es zieht, Treiben Blüthen, treiben Liederseelen her, Frage nicht, frage nicht, woher, woher.	Into the wind, into the wind I sing my song, Don't ask, don't ask where the wind is blowing, Propelling blossoms, driving the songs' souls here and there, Don't ask, don't ask just where, just where.
Wer gäb' Antwort je, Wer gäb' Antwort, woher, wohin? Treibe selbst ein wehend Lied dahin. In den Wind, in den Wind, kaum erwacht, Bin verweht über Nacht.	Who could give an answer? Who could say, whence or whither? Cast yourself a wafting song thither. In the wind, in the wind, scarcely awake, (It or I) will be blown away, scattered over night.

Maria, op. 2, no. 4
Poetry by Rainer Maria Rilke

(Author's note: This poem is printed the way Rilke and Teichmüller would have seen it. There is no explanation why Teichmüller (or the copyist-engraver) used the ! on the music or why there are such discrepancies in punctuation and capitalization from Rilke to her published version. One can only surmise that she got the poem directly from him or from a mutual friend in Berlin, before it was finished and published.)

Maria du weinst, – ich weiss Und da möcht ich weinen zu deinem Preis. Mit der Stirne auf Steinen weinen . . .	Maria you are crying, - I know And therefore, I want to weep to your glory. With my forehead pressed against stones crying . . .
Deine Hände sind heiss; könnt ich dir Tasten darunterschieben, dann wäre dir doch ein Lied geblieben. Aber die Stunde stirbt ohne Vermächtnis . . .	Your hands are hot; could I but place a keyboard under them, then you would at least be left with a song. But the hour dies without a legacy. . .

***Wie leise scheue Kinder*, op. 7, no. 2**

Poem by Marianne Blaauw

Wie leise scheue Kinder, So geh'n meine einsamen Gedanken im Tiefen Herzen ein und aus.	Like quiet, shy children, My lonely thoughts travel in and out of my innermost heart.
Wie leise scheue Kinder, So suchen sie deine Liebe und der Weg is steil und der Weg ist lang.	Like quiet, shy children, They search for your love and their path is steep and long.
Wie leise scheue Kinder, So geh'n meine einsamen Gedanken im tiefen Herzen ein und aus.	Like quiet, shy children, My lonely thoughts travel in and out of my innermost heart.

Klein Christel, op. 9, no. 7

Folk Song

Klein Christel kam vor die Himmelspfort! Ihr öffnet Jungfrau Maria sofort. Jungfrau Maria rückt ihr die Bank: Sitz nieder klein Christel, und ruh' vom Gang!	Little Christel stood before heaven's portal! It was opened by the Virgin Mary without delay. The Virgin Mary gave her a stool: Have a seat, little Christel, and rest from your journey!
Ich bin nicht müde, Ich kann wohl steh'n. Darf Olaf aber zum Himmel eingeh'n? Darf Olaf, darf Olaf aber zum Himmel Eingeh'n?	I'm not tired, I can just as well stand. May Olaf enter into heaven? May Olaf, may Olaf enter into heaven?
Jungfrau Maria lächelt gelind: Setz dich nieder, ein Weilchen, geschwind. Es wehen die Lüfte im himmlischen Saal, Zwei Kindlein herzen und freu'n sich zumal.	The Virgin Mary smiles gently: Hurry and just sit yourself down for a while. Breezes blow through the heavenly hall, The children embrace each other and are happy.
Zwei Kindlein entweilen auf himmlischer Au, Hold selig lächelt die heiligste Frau.	The children hasten away to the heavenly mead, The most holy of women smiles graciously.

Windlied

Carl Hauptmann | **Anna Teichmüller**
Op. 1, no. 2

19
Ant - wort je, wer gäb' Ant - wort, wo - her, wo - hin? trei-be
f
cresc.
p
25
selbst ein we-hend Lied da - hin. In den
p
pp
31
Wind, in den Wind, kaum er - wacht bin ver - weht ü-ber
cresc.
p
37
Nacht.
p
pp

Maria

Rainer Maria Rilke

Anna Teichmüller
Op. 2, no. 4

Larghetto

Ma-ri - a! Du weinst

6

ich weiss.

cresc.

10

Und da möcht' ich wei-nen zu dei - nem Preis,

cresc.

dolce ma forte

13

rit.

mit der Stir-ne auf Stei - nen wei - nen

rit.

cresc.

decresc.

17
dolce
Dei - ne Hän - de sind heiss; könnt' ich dir Tas - ten da-run - ter
dolce
20
schie - ben, dann wä - re dir doch ein Lied ge - blie - ben.
24
riten.
A - ber die Stun - de stirbt
28
riten.
rit.
oh - ne Ver - mächt - niss.
sfz
cresc.
p
pp

Wie leise scheue Kinder

Marianne Blaauw

Anna Teichmüller
Op. 7, no. 2

14
su - chen sie dei - ne Lie - be und der Weg ist steil und der
cresc.
f
cresc.
17
Weg ist lang, und der Weg ist steil und der Weg ist lang.
cresc. sempre
f
f
dim.
2
21
Wie lei - se scheu - e Kin - der, so
p
24
geh'n mei-ne ein - sa-men Ge-dan - ken im tie-fen Her-zen ein und aus.
p
p
pp

Klein Christel

(Volkslied)

Anna Teichmüller
Op. 9, no. 7

Allegretto
Klein Chri - stel kam vor die Him - mels pfort! Ihr

3
öff - net Jung - frau Ma - ri - a so-fort. Jung - frau Ma - ri - a

6
rückt ihr die Bank: Sitz nie - der klein Chri - stel, und ruh' vom Gang! Ich

9
bin nicht mü - de, ich kann wohl - steh'n, darf O - laf a - ber zum
12
Him - mel ein-gehn? Darf O - laf, darf O - laf a - ber zum
15
Him - mel ein-geh'n? Jung - frau Ma - ri - a
pp
18
lä - chelt ge - lind: Setz dich nur nie - der, ein Weil - chen, ge-schwind. Es

21
we - hen die Lüf - te im himm - li-schen Saal, zwei Kind - lein her - zen und
24
freu'n sich zu - mal. Zwei Kind - lein ent - ei - len auf himm - li - scher Au, hold -
27
se - lig lä - chelt die hei - lig - ste Frau, hold - se - lig, hold -
30
se - lig lä - chelt die hei - lig-ste Frau.
pp

Liza Lehmann

(1862–1918)

SOPHIE FULLER

Liza Lehmann's family background was somewhat different from that of most middle- or upper-class British female composers of her generation, such as Ethel Smyth and Maude Valérie White (see this volume), who had to battle with their parents before being allowed to study for the music profession. On the contrary, Lehmann was encouraged to take up a career as a singer by her father, the painter Rudolph Lehmann, and her mother, the composer Amelia Lehmann (who published as "A. L."). She was born in London on July 11, 1862, and spent her earliest years in Italy. She studied singing with her mother, Alberto Randegger, and Jenny Lind, and made her professional debut as a lyric soprano at a Monday Popular Concert in 1885 in London at the age of twenty-three. She soon became very popular, and was in demand for performances at festivals, concert halls, and private musical parties throughout Britain. Her repertoire included her own songs, which began to appear in print in 1888, and old English songs by composers such as Thomas Arne or Henry Purcell, which she copied herself from scores in the British Museum.

In 1894, at the age of 32, Lehmann married Herbert Bedford, a partner in a London firm and an amateur composer. She retired from the public stage to concentrate on composing. Her private musical education had included composition lessons and she later wrote of her intense longing to compose, inspired by the achievements of other women of her generation: "I simply worshipped at the shrine of any woman who wrote music. Maude Valérie White, Marie Wurm, Chaminade — they seemed to me goddesses!"[1]

In 1896 she wrote the song cycle *In a Persian Garden* for four voices and piano. Her best known work, Lehmann deemed it her "first serious composition,"[2] was described by a critic at an early performance as "one of the most impressive works ever penned by a female composer."[3] Lehmann's text was the twelfth-century Persian poet Omar Khayyám's *Rubáiyát*, meditations on life, death and the "mysteries of existence," in the 1859 translation by Edward FitzGerald. The poem reflected the *fin-de-siècle* fascination with oriental mysticism, as well as contemplating the passing of time and inevitable fading of beauty. Lehmann's music was regarded by the critics as suitably exotic, and the work became extremely popular, frequently performed throughout Britain and the United States for many decades.

Lehmann followed the success of *In a Persian Garden* with extended vocal works such as her setting of Walter Scott's *Young Lochinvar* for baritone solo, chorus and orchestra, premiered at the Wakefield Festival in 1899, and her setting of Longfellow's *Endymion* for soprano and orchestra, published in the same year. She also produced further song cycles, including *In Memoriam* (1899), an intense and involved setting for tenor and piano of excerpts from Tennyson's long lament at the death of a friend. Her very different song cycle, *The Daisy-chain* (1900), setting poems by various authors for four solo voices and piano, which she described as "a garland of songs of childhood written in a light-hearted vein,"[4] became nearly as popular as *In a Persian Garden*.

The Daisy-chain and its sequel *More Daisies* (1902) signaled a move by Lehmann towards a simplified and lighter musical style and subject matter, as in works such as the fairy cantata *Once Upon a Time* (G. H. Jessop, 1903), or the much performed song *There Are Fairies at the Bottom of our Garden* (Rose Fyleman, 1917). Her texts for such works were often about childhood or aimed at children — a favorite theme of the Edwardian era. These works were frequently humorous and included her Lewis Carroll settings entitled *Nonsense Songs* (1908), for four voices and piano, subtitled *The Songs That Came Out Wrong from Alice in Wonderland* and her Hilaire Belloc settings *Four Cautionary Tales and a Moral* (1909), for two voices and piano. These works were in great demand from both the public and Lehmann's publishers. They provided a useful income when Bedford found himself in financial difficulties.

Lehmann began to write for the theater and in 1904 was the first woman to be commissioned to write the music for a musical comedy. *Sergeant Brue*, with a libretto by "Owen Hall" [pseudonym for James Davis (1853–1907)] and lyrics by J. Hickory Wood, was an undoubted success, playing in London for 290 performances between 1904 and 1905.[5] Lehmann was proud of her work in these more popular genres but also saddened by the comparative neglect of more "serious" works such as her *Four Shakespearian Part-Songs* (1911), the song *Magdalene at Michael's Gate* (Henry

Kingsley, 1913) and her opera *Everyman*, based on the fifteenth-century morality play and staged by the Beecham Opera Company in December 1915 on a double bill with Debussy's *L' Enfant Prodigue*.[6]

Lehmann's popularity continued throughout the early years of the twentieth century. In 1909 she made a highly successful tour of the United States, a visit which inspired the "North American Indian Song-Cycle" for four voices and piano, entitled *Prairie Pictures* (1911), to her own poems, and *Cowboy Ballads* (1912) for voice and piano to texts collected by J. A. Lomax. Although she no longer appeared as a singer, Lehmann frequently accompanied her own music in public and was also in demand as a singing teacher, taking on a post as a professor at the Guildhall School of Music in London. In 1913 she published a teaching manual, *Practical Hints for Students of Singing* (1913), followed by collections of *Useful Teaching Songs* (1914), and *Studies in Recitative* (1915). Her position as one of Britain's leading women composers was acknowledged when she was asked to serve as the first president of the Society of Women Musicians at its formation in 1911. In one of the speeches she made to the organization she stressed her conviction that "the Society of Women Musicians has 'come to stay' and to shed the beneficial influence of its sincere and noble aims on all who come into contact with it. It is a great movement, and one capable of immense expansion. . . ."[7]

In 1916 Lehmann's beloved son Rudolph, a senior gunner-cadet at the Royal Military Academy in Woolwich, died of pneumonia. Lehmann was devastated and never really recovered from this loss. She died on September 19, 1918, two weeks after finishing her posthumously published memoirs, *The Life of Liza Lehmann*.

Lehmann's success and popularity as a composer was considerable. Like many of her female contemporaries she concentrated on writing vocal music; the genres she embraced ranged from solo songs, duets and part-songs through song cycles and cantatas, to musicals and operas. As an acclaimed singer, Lehmann was able to promote her early songs herself. Although she later regretted the years she had spent on the public stage, wishing that she had been able to devote them to composition, her gradual exposure and experience as a composer was undoubtedly beneficial to her later career. One of her major achievements was to popularize the song cycle among British composers. Before *In a Persian Garden*, few works in this genre had been produced by composers working in Britain. Those that had appeared, such as the collaboration between Sullivan and Tennyson on *The Window, or The Songs of the Wrens* (1869) for single voice and piano, had not been particularly successful.

There were marked changes in the critical reception of Lehmann's work during her lifetime. In the late 1890s her works were regarded as musically advanced. The novelist George du Maurier, for example, is reported to have said of *In a Persian Garden*: "I confess it is too modern for me — I cannot follow it!"[8] At this early point in her composing career, Lehmann was championed by progressive critics such as Edwin Evans and generally regarded as a highbrow composer of art music. But before the end of the first decade of the twentieth century her music had fallen from favor with the critics, while finding an increasing popularity with the general public. By the time of her death Lehmann was generally regarded as a composer of lightweight songs, remembered for her charmingly humorous evocation of childhood in *There Are Fairies at the Bottom of our Garden* rather than for the far more sombre and complex philosophising of *In Memoriam*.

It is certainly true that Lehmann's musical styles varied considerably, but it is also clear that there was a general backlash in Britain against the work of women composers at the same time as Lehmann's music began to be downgraded by the critics. Her concentration on subjects that could be dismissed as feminine, such as songs about or for children, undoubtedly contributed to the change in critical opinion of her works, as did the general artistic move towards a modernist aesthetic, which was responsible for the downgrading of much Victorian and Edwardian music.

Whether in the disarmingly simple style of *Daddy's Sweetheart*, a song setting of what is to twenty-first-century minds a somewhat disturbing poem by Curtis Hardin-Burnley, or in the much more complex language of a large-scale work such as *In Memoriam*, there are certain distinguishing features in Lehmann's music, such as her fluent gift for creating compelling melodies. In an interview she gave in 1910, she remarked that

> . . . if one desires to be a composer, the melodies must come, and they must be melodies that have an individual and original interest. Without the facility to produce beautiful melodies it is foolish to strive to become a composer.[9]

Informed by her years as a singer, Lehmann's vocal lines are rewarding for the performer; her eloquent setting of the English language, frequently praised by contemporary critics, is remarkable. *In a Persian Garden* (1896) provides a clear example of the variety of her approaches to setting text, moving from a chromatic declamatory style to the tuneful lyricism of the popular tenor solo *Ah, Moon of my Delight*. It is interesting to note that Benjamin Britten, the composer credited with bringing a fresh fluency to the setting of English poetry, knew Lehmann's work well. Despite her somewhat haphazard compositional training, Lehmann always displays an assured technique; even her simplest songs are carefully crafted. Her large-scale, more complex works, such as *In Memoriam* (1899), demonstrate her vivid use of harmonic coloring and an inventive use of recurring themes and motifs. The piano accompaniments to her songs are always well judged and often strikingly atmospheric, as in the repeated chromatic accompaniment motif used in her setting of Shelly's "A Widow-Bird Sate Mourning" (1895). Unfortunately, very little of her orchestral or instrumental writing has survived.

Wiegenlied, one of Lehmann's earliest songs, was published in her collection *Eight German Songs* of 1888. A reviewer for *The Musical World* claimed that the volume was: "Decidedly worthy of a foremost place among the vocal music recently to hand."[10] It included several *volkslieder* and settings of poetry by poets such as Heinrich Heine, but *Wiegenlied* was given no author (either for the original German or the English translation), suggesting that the text may have been written by Lehmann herself. Three years later, when Lehmann sang the song at Princes' Hall it was described in *The Athenaeum* as "remarkably pleasing and tasteful."[11] *Wiegenlied*, with its use of expressive dissonance, shows that Lehmann was already developing an interesting approach to harmonic coloring. It also demonstrates the confident sense of vocal line that was to become a hallmark of her musical style.

Sweet Rhodoclea is the first song from the song cycle *Cameos* for tenor or baritone and piano, subtitled *Five Greek Love-Songs*. Dedicated to Consuelo, the Duchess of Manchester, it was published by Enoch in 1901. The texts include translations of anonymous Greek poetry and lyrics by Rufinus, Meleager, and Paul the Silentiary made by Jane Minot Sedgwick, and published in her collection *Songs from the Greek* in 1896. The cycle was premiered by Joseph O'Mara at the London Pops on February 15, 1902.[12] Lehmann intended the cycle to be extremely versatile, suggesting that the songs could be sung separately (with the piano interludes and introductions omitted), or as a shorter cycle of the first, third and fourth songs. The poems she chose to set represent different aspects of love and often convey the same sense of pensive philosophizing occurring in *In A Persian Garden*. In *Sweet Rhodoclea* the poet reminds his beloved that, like the garland of flowers that he has sent to her, she will fade and die. As in *In a Persian Garden*, this somewhat melancholy mood is reflected in the rich harmonic accompaniment to the tuneful melody, with the piano's treble line frequently echoing the line of the voice.

The Wren is the fourth of Lehmann's five *Bird Songs* for soprano and piano that were first performed in Edinburgh in 1907[13] and published in the same year. They soon became very popular, especially in performances by the singer Blanche Marchesi. The poems are by "A. S.," thought to be Alice Sayers, the Bedford family nurse.[14] The collection is in Lehmann's simpler style with straightforward, tuneful vocal lines and accompaniments that use uncomplicated harmonies and textures. *The Wren* also provides the vocalist with an opportunity for display in a cadenza-like passage, echoing the piano opening and producing a virtuosic imitation of bird song.

Evensong is a setting of a poem by Constance Morgan from her collection *The Song of a Tramp, and other poems* (1911). It was published in 1916 and dedicated to Lehmann's contemporary, the composer Florence Aylward (1862–1950). Short and atmospheric, *Evensong* is a straightforward strophic setting in C major using a simple but appealing melody for the voice and a repeated sixteenth-note pattern in the piano accompaniment. The vocal part requires considerable control, especially in the leaps to long, quiet notes in the upper register, but is, as with all Lehmann's work, always grateful for the singer.

Notes

1. Liza Lehmann, *The Life of Liza Lehmann* (London: T. Fisher Unwin, 1919), 23.

2. Lehmann, *The Life of Liza Lehmann*, 70.

3. *The Musical Times* 38 (January 1897): 20.

4. Lehmann, *The Life of Liza Lehmann*, 93. *The Daisy-chain* was dedicated "to my small son Rudolf."

5. See Kurt Ganzl, *The British Musical Theatre 1* 1865–1914 (London: Macmillan, 1986), 866-67.

6. J. P. Wearing, *The London Stage 1910–1919: A Calendar of Plays and Players*, vol. 1. (Metuchen, N. J.: Scarecrow Press, 1982), 606.

7. Lehmann, *The Life of Liza Lehmann*, 173.

8. Ibid., 61.

9. "To the Young Musician who would Compose: An Interview with Mme Liza Lehmann," *The Musical Standard* 33, no. 857 (1903): 371.

10. *The Musical World* 66 (May 26, 1888): 408.

11. *The Athenaeum*, no. 3325 (July 18,1891).

12. *The Monthly Musical Record* (March 1902): 73.

13. *The Musical Times* (December 1907): 813.

14. See Steuart Bedford, sleeve notes to *Liza Lehmann*, Collins Classics (The English Song Series 4) 15082 (1997), 6.

Selected List of Works

Songs, Duets, Part-songs, Collections, and Song Cycles

Das Mädchen spricht. Text by R. Prutz. London: Stanley Lucas, Weber & Co., 1888.

Eight German Songs. London: Chappell, 1888.

1. *Herber Abschied*. Text Volkslied
2. *Sonnenlicht, Sonnenschein*. Text Volkslied
3. *Gute Nacht*. Text by Betty Paoli
4. *Ach, was hilft ein blümelein*. Text Volkslied
5. *Wiegenlied*. Text anon.
6. *Lieb' Liebchen, Leg's Händchen*. Text by Heinrich Heine
7. *Deine Auge*. Text by Dilia Helena
8. *Der Wirthin Tichterlein*. Text by Johann Ludwig Uhland

My true Love hath my Heart. Text by Philip Sidney. London: Metzler, 1888.

Album of Twelve German Songs. London: Stanley Lucas, Weber & Co., 1889.

1. *Das Mädchen spricht*. Text by R. Prutz
2. *Die Nachtingall, als ich sie fragte*. Text by "Mirza-Schaffy" [pseudonym]
3. *Wenn ich an Dich gedenke*. Text by Emanuel Geibel
4. *Im Rosenbuch*. Text by Hoffmann von Fallersleben
5. *Das Kraut vergessenheit*. Text by Emanuel Geibel
6. *Wenn ich ein Vöglein wär*. Text Volkslied
7. *Hier unter Bebenranken*. Text by "Mirza-Schaffy"
8. *Kindlein's Abenlied*. Text Volkslied
9. *Wohin mit der Freud*. Text Volkhumliches Lied by R. Renick
10. *Mag auch heiss das scheiden brennen*. Text by Emanuel Geibel
11. *Da ich der Ost-wind bin*. Text by Friedrich Rückert
12. *Cita mors ruit*. Text by Emanuel Geibel

The Castilian Maid. Text by Thomas Moore. London: Boosey, 1890.

Printemps d'avril. Text by Thomas de Banville. London: Chappell, 1891.

Titania's Cradle. Text by William Shakespeare. London: Boosey, 1892.

The Exile. Text by Lady Lindsay. London: Boosey, 1893.

Mirage. Text by Henry Malesh. London: Enoch, 1894.

Album of Nine English Songs. London: Boosey, 1895.

1. *The Unearthly One*. Text anon.
2. *Sigh No More Ladies*. Text by William Shakespeare
3. *A Widow-Bird Sate Mourning*. Text by Percy Bysshe Shelley
4. *If Music Be the Food of Love*. Text by William Shakespeare
5. *She Is Not Fair to Outward View*. Text by Samuel Taylor Coleridge
6. *The Young Rose*. Text by Thomas Moore
7. *Music, When Soft Voices Die*. Text by Percy Bysshe Shelley
8. *Anne Boleyn's Lament*. Text by Anne Boleyn
9. *Blind Cupid*. Text by William Shakespeare

The Fountains Mingle with the River. Text by Percy Bysshe Shelley. London: Boosey, 1895.

To My Beloved. Text by Adelaide Procter. London: Metzler, 1895.

In a Persian Garden. Text from the Rubáiyát of Omar Khayám. Translated by Edward Fitzgerald. Song cycle for four voices and piano. London: Metzler, 1896.

To Dianeme. Text by Robert Herrick. London: Keith Prowse, 1897.

The Guardian Angel. Text by E. Nesbit. London: E. Ascherberg, 1898.

In Memoriam. Text by Alfred, Lord Tennyson. Song cycle for baritone or mezzo-soprano and piano. London: John Church, 1899.

The Daisy-chain. Four voices and piano. London: Boosey, 1900.

1. *Foreign Children*. Text by Robert Louis Stevenson
2. *Fairies*. Text anon.
3. *Keepsake Mill*. Text by Robert Louis Stevenson
4. *If No One Ever Marries Me*. Text by Laurence Alma Tadema
5. *Stars*. Text by Robert Louis Stevenson
6. *Seeing the World*. Text anon.
7. *The Ship that Sailed Into the Sun*. Text by W. B. Rands
8. *The Swing*. Text by Robert Louis Stevenson
9. *Mustard and Cress*. Text by Norman Gale
10. *The Moon*. Text by Robert Louis Stevenson
11. *Thank You Very Much Indeed*. Text by Norman Gale
12. *Blind Man's Buff*. Text anon.

Cameos. Tenor (or baritone) and piano. London: Enoch, 1901.

I. Text by Rufinus
II. Text by Meleager
III. Text by Paul the Silentiary
IV. Text anon.
V. Text anon.

Five French Songs. London: J. Church & Co., 1901.

1. *Paix du soir*. Text by Georges Boutelleau
2. *La Rose*. Text by Georges Boutelleau
3. *Le Colibri*. Text by Georges Boutelleau
4. *L'Oiseleur*. Text by Georges Boutelleau
5. *La Race*. Text by Frédéric Plessis

A Lake and a Fairy Boat. Duet. Text by Thomas Hood. London: Ascherberg, 1902.

Lead Kindly Light. Text by John Henry Newman. Soprano, chorus, and organ or piano. London: Novello, 1902.

More Daisies. Four voices and piano. London: Boosey, 1902.

1. *Up into the Cherry Tree*. Text by Robert Louis Stevenson
2. *A Moral*. Text by Robert Louis Stevenson
3. *For Good Luck*. Text by J. H. Ewing
4. *Goodnight and Good Morning*. Text by Lord Houghton

5. *Every Night my Prayers I say.* Text by Robert Louis Stevenson
6. *In Dreamland.* Text by Harriet Trowbridge
7. *The Cuckoo.* Text by W. B. Rands
8. *Marching Song.* Text by Robert Louis Stevenson
9. *My Shadow.* Text by Robert Louis Stevenson
10. *The Captain.* Text by Robert Louis Stevenson
11. *A Child's Prayer.* Text by M. Betham-Edwards
12. *Fairy Chimes.* Text by W. B. Rands

At Love's Beginning. Text by Thomas Campbell. Duet. London: Boosey, 1903.

Rose Song. Text by Flora Steel, from the Persian. London: Chappell, 1903.

Songs of Love and Spring. Text by Emanuel Geibel. Translated by A. P. Graves. [Songs for] Two voices and piano. London: Boosey, 1903.
1. *Sir Spring*
2. *When Young Love comes Knocking*
3. *In April Mood*
4. *Dawning Love*
5. *Disturb it not*
6. *Golden Bridges*
7. *A Dream of Violet*
8. *Star Fancies*
9. *Love's Emblems*
10. *My Secret*
11. *Love Enthroned*

If I Built a World for You. Text by Herbert Fordwych. London: Boosey, 1904.

In Lotos Land. Text by Tom Heffernan. London: Boosey, 1905.

The Life of a Rose. Text by Liza Lehmann. London: Boosey, 1905.
1. *Unfolding*
2. *June Rapture*
3. *The Bee*
4. *Lovers in the Lane*
5. *Summer Storm*
6. *Roseleaves*
7. *Rosa Resurget*

Bird Songs. Text by A. S. Soprano and piano. London: Boosey, 1907.
1. *The Woodpigeon*
2. *The Yellowhammer*
3. *The Starling*
4. *The Wren*
5. *The Owl*

The Little Blush Rose. Text by Liza Lehmann. London: Boosey, 1907.

Bleak Weather. Text by Ella Wheeler Wilcox. London: Boosey, 1908.

Mr. Coggs and other Songs for Children. Text by E. V. Lucas. London: Chappell, 1908.
1. *Mr Coggs*
2. *Pa's Bank*
3. *The Bird Stuffer*
4. *London Sparrows*
5. *The Barber*

Nonsense Songs. Text by Lewis Carroll. Four voices and piano. London: Chappell, 1908.
1. *How doth the Little Crocodile*
2. *Fury Said to a Mouse*
3. *You are Old, Father William*
4. *Speak Roughly to your Little Boy*
5. *Will you Walk a Little Faster?*
6. *Mockturtle Soup*
7. *The Queen of Hearts*
8. *They told Me You had been to Her*
9. *To Alice*

Two Seal Songs. Text by Rudyard Kipling. London: Chappell, 1908.

Breton Folk-Songs. Text by Frances M. Gostling. Four voices and piano. London: Chappell, 1909.
1. *Sir Fanch and the Fairy*
2. *I dreamt my love was singing*
3. *The Ruby Necklace*
4. *The Nightingale*
5. *No Candle was there and no Fire*
6. *The Spinning Wheel*
7. *L'Ankou*
8. *King Gralon's Daughter*
9. *St. Peter's Night*

Four Cautionary Songs and a Moral. Text by Hilaire Belloc. Two voices and piano. London: Chappell, 1909.
1. *Rebecca*
2. *Jim*
3. *Matilda*
4. *Henry King*
5. *Charles Augustus Fortescue*

Thoughts have Wings. Text by Frances M. Gostling. London: Chapell, 1909.

Abou Ben Adhem and the Angel. Text by Leigh Hunt. London: Chappell, 1910.

Clementina's Song. Text from a Polish folk song, from *The Princess*

Clementina. London: Chappell, 1910.

Five Little Love Songs. Text by Cora Fabbri. London: Chappell, 1910.
1. *There's a Bird Beneath your Window*
2. *Along the Sunny Lane*
3. *Just a Multitude of Curls*
4. *If I Were a Bird, I Would Sing All Day*
5. *Clasp Mine Closer, Little Dear White Hand*

In Sherwood Forest. Text by Basil Hood. Vocal intermezzo for women's voices. London: Chappell, 1910.

Daddy's Sweetheart. Text by Curtis Hardin-Burnley. London: Chappell, 1911.

Four Shakespearian Part-Songs. Text by William Shakespeare. SATB. London: Novello, 1911.
1. *I Know a Bank*
2. *When Icicles Hang*
3. *Tell Me, Where is Fancy Bred*
4. *Under the Greenwood Tree*

The Lake Isle of Innisfree. Text by W. B. Yeats. London: Boosey, 1911.

Prairie Pictures. Text by Liza Lehmann. "North American Indian Song-Cycle" for four voices and piano. London: Chappell, 1911.

Songs of a "Flapper." Text by Liza Lehmann. London: Chappell, 1911.
1. *In the Garden*
2. *This Beautiful World*
3. *My Sister Nell*
4. *The Ball*
5. *Goodnight Little Stars*

At the Gate. Text by Alfred, Lord Tennyson. London: Boosey, 1912.

Cowboy Ballads. Texts collected by J. A. Lomax. London: Chappell, 1912.
1. *The Rancher's Daughter*
2. *Night-herding Song*
3. *The Skew-ball Black*

How Sweet the Moonlight Sleep Upon this Bank. Text by William Shakespeare. Duet. London: Boosey, 1912.

The Well of Sorrow. Text from "The Bard of Dimbovitza" collected by Hélène Vacaresco. Contralto and piano. London: Boosey, 1912.
1. *Forsaken*
2. *The Broken Spindle*
3. *Beside the Maize-Field*

Wynken, Blynken and Nod. Text by Eugene Field. Three-part chorus, piano and *ad lib*. violin. London: Boosey, 1912.

Album of Five Tenor Songs. London: Chappell, 1913.
1. *Go Lovely Rose*. Text by Edmund Waller
2. *She Dwelt Among the Untrodden Ways*. Text by William Wordsworth
3. *When All the World is Young*. Text by Charles Kingsley
4. *Trysting Song*. Text by Liza Lehmann
5. *Mock Turtle Soup*. Text by Lewis Carroll

Hips and Haws. Text by Marguerite Radcylffe-Hall. London: Chappell, 1913.
1. *I Be Thinkin'*
2. *Country Courtship' Dusk in the Lane*
3. *Jealousy*
4. *Bells Across the Meadows*
5. *Tramping*

Magdalen at Michael's Gate. Text by Henry Kingsley. London: Chappell, 1913.

The Weathercock. Text by Henry Wadsworth Longfellow. London: Boosey, 1913.

Three Snow Songs. Text by Liza Lehmann. Voice and piano with organ and women's chorus. London: Chappell, 1914.
1. *Snowflakes*
2. *Robin Redbreast*
3. *Christmas Eve*

Parody Pie. Text by various authors. Four voices and piano. London: Chappell, 1914.

The Poet and the Nightingale. Text by James White. London: Chappell, 1914.

The Birth of the Flowers. Text by Madeline Lucette. Quartet for women's voices. London: Chappell, 1916.

Evensong. Text by Constance Morgan. London: Chappell, 1916.

There are Fairies at the Bottom of our Garden. Text by Rose Fyleman. London: Chappell, 1917.

Little Brown Brother's Baby Seed Song. Text by E. Nesbit. London: Chappell, 1918.

Whene'er a Snowflake Leaves the Sky. Text anon. London: J. B. Cramer, 1918.

When I Am Dead, My Dearest. Text by Christina Rossetti. London: Boosey, 1919.

If I Had But Two Little Wings. Text by Samuel Taylor Coleridge. London: J. B. Cramer, 1921.

Three Songs for Low Voice. London: G. Schirmer, 1922.
1. *Prospice*. Text by Robert Browning
2. *Dusk in the Valley*. Text by George Meredith
3. *Love, If You Knew the Light*. Text by Robert Browning

Vocal Works with Orchestra

(Published editions all in piano score. No full scores or orchestral parts appear to have survived.)

Young Lochinvar. Text by Walter Scott. Baritone solo, chorus and orchestra. London: Boosey, 1898.

Endymion. Text by Henry Wadsworth Longfellow. Soprano and orchestra. London: John Church, 1899.

Once Upon a Time. 'Retold' by G. H. Jessop. Narrator, two sopranos, two mezzo-sopranos/contraltos, tenor, chorus, orchestra, and piano. London: Boosey, 1903.

The Golden Threshold. Text by Sarojini Naidu. Soprano, contralto, tenor and baritone soloists, chorus, and orchestra. London: Boosey, 1906.

Leaves from Ossian. Translated by Macpherson. Soprano, contralto, tenor and baritone soloists, chorus, and orchestra. London: Chappell, 1909.

Recitations

The Happy Prince. Text by Oscar Wilde. Speaker and piano. London: Chappell, 1908.

The Selfish Giant. Text by Oscar Wilde. Speaker and piano. Unpublished. Composed 1911.

The High Tide — On the Coast of Lincolnshire, 1571. Text by Jean Ingelow. Speaker and piano. London: Elkin, 1912.

Behind the Nightlight. Texts "invented" by Joan Maude. Speaker and piano. London: Boosey, 1913.

Operatic and Theatrical Works

The Secrets of the Heart. Text by Austin Dobson. Soprano and contralto (or mezzo-soprano) and piano. London: J. Williams, 1895.

Good-Night, Babette! Text by Austin Dobson. Soprano, baritone, piano, violin, and cello. London: Boosey, 1898.

The Eternal Feminine. Text by Lilian Eldée. "A Musical Monologue." London: Chappell, 1902.

Incidental music for *The Twin Sister*. Text by Louis N. Parker, after Ludwig Fulda. Four-act comedy. Performed 1902.

Sergeant Brue. Lyrics by J. H. Wood. "A Musical Farce." London: Hopwood and Crew, 1904.

The Vicar of Wakefield. Libretto by Laurence Housman, after Oliver Goldsmith. Opera. London: Boosey, 1907.

Everyman. Text traditional. Opera. Performed 1915. Published privately.

Arrangements and Educational Works

Thomas Arne, *Polly Willis*. London: Chappell, 1890.

James Hook, *When First the East Begins to Dawn*. London: Boosey, 1891.

Francesco Bianchi, *Vieni, Dorina bella*. London: Chappell, 1893.

Caroline, Baroness Nairne, *The Hundred Pipers*. London: Chappell, 1903.

A.L., *Twelve Old Scotch Songs*. London: Boosey, 1912.

Practical Hints for Students of Singing. London: Enoch, 1913.

Useful Teaching Songs for All Voices. 5 volumes. London: Chappell, 1914.

Studies in Recitative. London: Chappell, 1915.

Lilies of the Valley. A medley of old English Songs arranged for girls' voices. London: Chappell, 1917.

Instrumental Works

Album of Ten Pianoforte Sketches. London: Chappell, 1892.

Romance. Piano. London: Chappell, 1892.

Romance. Violin and piano. London: Chappell, 1892.

Trois Valses de Sentiment. Piano. London: Chappell, 1892.

Romantic Suite. Violin and piano. London: Keith Prowse, 1903.

Cobweb Castle: Album of Six Sketches for the Pianoforte. London: Chappell, 1908.

Je pense à toi. Piano. London: Chappell, 1912.

Bibliography

Anon. "Mr and Mrs Herbert Bedford (Liza Lehmann)," *Strand Musical Magazine* 3 (January–June 1896): 158-59.

Anon. "To the Young Musician who would Compose: An Interview with Mme Liza Lehmann," *The Musical Standard* 33, no. 857 (1903): 373-75.

Bush, Geoffrey, ed. *Songs 1860–1900* in *Musica Brittanica* 60. London: The Musica Brittanica Trust and Stainer & Bell, 1989.

Evans, Edwin. "Modern British Composers: Liza Lehmann," *The Musical Standard* illustrated series 20 (October 17, 1903): 242-43.

Fuller, Sophie. "Liza Lehmann." In *The Pandora Guide to Women Composers: Britain and the United States, 1629–present.* London: Pandora, 1994.

____. "Women Composers during the British Musical Renaissance, 1880–1918." Ph.D. diss., King's College, London, 1998.

Lawrence, Arthur. "Women and Musical Composition: A Chat with Miss Liza Lehmann (Mrs. Herbert Bedford)," *The Young Woman* 8 (1899–1900): 414-16.

Lehmann, Liza. *The Life of Liza Lehmann.* London: T. Fisher Unwin, 1919.

Discography

In Memoriam: Songs by Liza Lehmann. Henry Wickham, baritone; Susie Allan, piano. Meridian CDE 84322 (1996). *In Memoriam*; *Cameos*; *The Selfish Giant*; *The Billet Doux.*

The English Song Series: Liza Lehmann. Janice Watson, soprano; Catherine Wyn-Rogers, mezzo-soprano; Toby Spence, tenor; Neal Davies, baritone; Steuart Bedford, piano. Collins 15082 (1997). *Bird Songs*; *Four Cautionary Tales and a Moral*; songs from *The Daisy Chain*; *Cherry Ripe*; *Magdalen at Michael's Gate*; *Evensong*; *Endymion*; *Music When Soft Voices Die*; *To a Little Red Spider*; *Dusk in the Valley*; *The Lily of a Day*; *When I Am Dead, My Dearest.*

In Praise of Woman. Anthony Rolfe Johnson, tenor; Graham Johnson, piano. Hyperion CDA66709 (1994). *A Widow Bird Sate Mourning*; *Ah, Moon of My Delight*; *The Lily of a Day*; *Thoughts Have Wings*; *Henry King*; *Charles Augustus Fortescue*.

Editorial Comments

The sources for all four songs by Lehmann are the printed editions. The only changes made have been to correct obvious misprints.

Wiegenlied

Gut' nacht holdes Kind, gieb Dich zur Ruh, schlafe geschwind die Aeuglein schleiss zu, Die Engelein wachen, sie sind nicht weit, Singen und lachen an Deiner Seit.	Goodnight little darling, peacefully rest, Slumber till morning lull'd on my breast. Angels are watching, Angels are near, Whispering softly have no fear.
Es freut sich herzlich ein gutes Kind, sie scheiden schmerzlich wo Böse sind, d'rum brav geschwin de geib Dich zur Ruh, Schutzgeist Dir binde die Aeuglein zu.	If baby smiles, they gladly stay, If baby weeps they fly away; Then sleep my darling do not cry Mother is singing a lullaby.

Translated by Sophie Fuller

Wiegenlied

Anonymous

Liza Lehmann
Sophie Fuller, editor

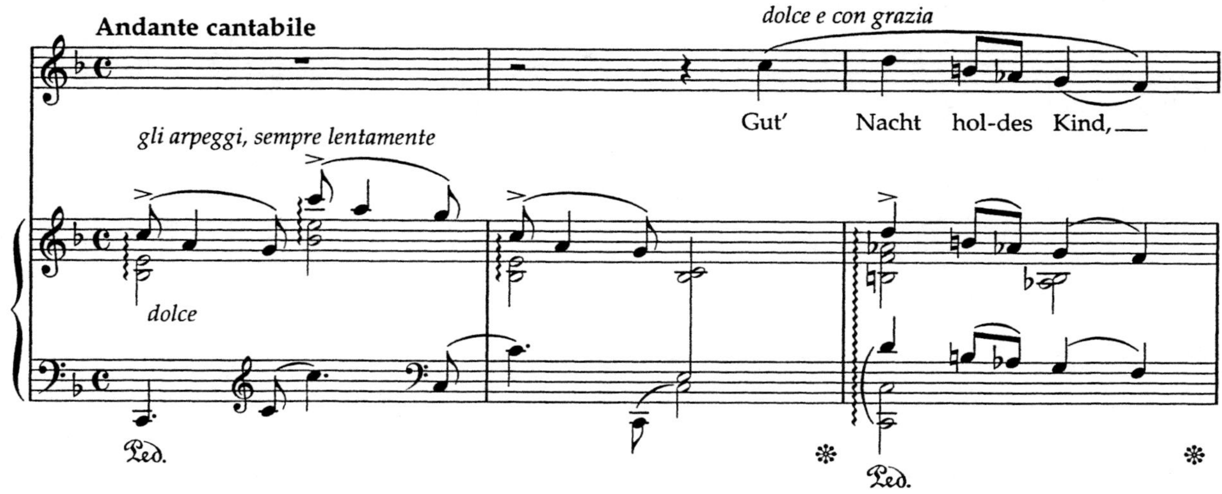

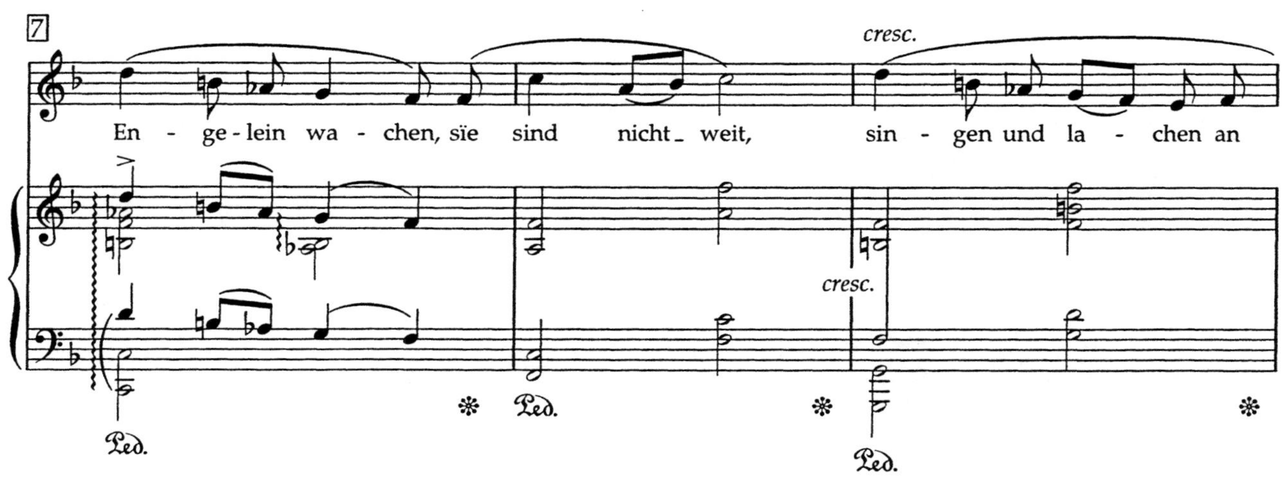

10
parlante
p
Dei - ner Seit. Es freut sich herz - lich ein gu - tes Kind, sie
[>]
13
poco rall.
a tempo
schei - den schmerz-lich wo Bö - se sind, d'rum brav ge-schwin de
16
gieb Dich zur Ruh, Schutz - geist Dir bin - de die Aeug - lein zu,
dolce
19
pp
die Aeug-lein zu.
arpeggiando lentamente

Sweet Rhodoclea

Rufinus
translated by Jane Minot Sedgwick

Liza Lehmann
Sophie Fuller, editor

11
And the ro - se's crim - son cup
With the night - dews brim - ming up;
13
Nar - cis - sus that the rain hath wet,
15
And the pur - ple vi - o - let.
L.H.
R.H.
p dolce
L.H.
18
più f
Then, with my gar - land on thy brow,
cresc.
For - get to hold thy

21
proud head high,
For tho', like it, thou bloom - est
8
23
now,
Like it,
Thou too shalt
L.H.
f
mp
Ped.
26
con portamento
fade
and
die.
R.H.
29
R.H.
L.H.
pp

The Wren

A.S.
[probably Alice Sayers]

Liza Lehmann
Sophie Fuller, editor

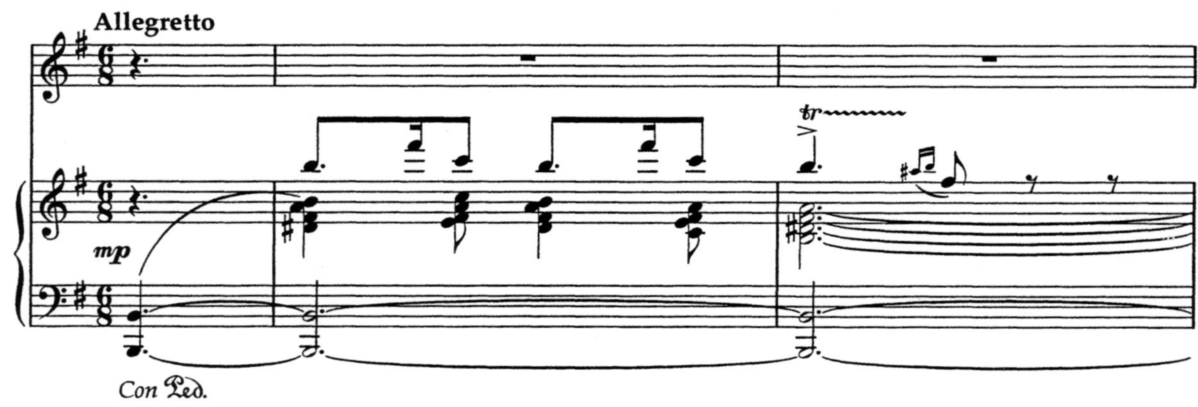

10
12
rall.
Moderato
p very simply
A wren just un - der my win - dow Has
p
[9]
8
15
sud - den - ly, sweet - ly sung; He woke me from my
L.H.
18
slum - bers With his sweet shrill

20
tongue. It was so ve - ry ear - ly, The
23
dew - drops were not dry, And pearl - y cloud - lets
L.H.
26
float - ed A - cross the ro - sy sky.
29
Allegretto
Più mosso ad lib.
Ah
tr

*Omit this passage if desired.

43
lit - tle wife sits all day, And
45
p
by her side he sings to her,
L.H.
47
pp
And
L.H.
49
(very simply and without rall.)
nev - er flies far a - way.
pp

Evensong

"Fold your white wings, dear Angels."

Constance Morgan

Liza Lehmann

Sophie Fuller, editor

13
mf
A - cross the lawn lie
mf
16
sha - dows, So still, so deep,
p
19
cresc.
Dear, lov - ing An - gels, pass not by, Hush me to
cresc.
22
rall.
sleep.
L.H.

25
Tempo I
pp
Night falls, and whis - p'ring goes the wind A - long the
28
sea;
cresc.
Fold your white wings, dear An - gels,
31
più cresc.
Fold them, dear An - gels,
pp
Fold them round
p dolce
pp
colla voce
35
me.
morendo
L.H.
ppp

Eleanor Everest Freer

(1864–1942)

SYLVIA M. EVERSOLE

Eleanor Everest was born in Philadelphia on May 14, 1864, to musical parents. Her father, Cornelius Everest, taught music theory at Girls' Normal School,[1] where he also conducted the orchestra and chorus. He was a gifted composer, arranger, and linguist; his book, *The Music Teacher*,[2] contains original vocal exercises, songs, hymns, and translations of well-known French, German, and Italian songs. Professor Everest also maintained a private studio for teaching voice where the famous baritone David Bispham (1857–1921) was among the many singers who came for lessons or coaching. Mrs. Everest, a mother and homemaker, was a singer of professional caliber who frequently entertained at special musicales in the homes of wealthy Philadelphia socialites. The Everests entertained many performing artists, both musical and literary, who came to the city on concert tours.

In this environment their daughter Eleanor and her younger brother were exposed to the discipline and perseverance demanded by the fine arts. Eleanor showed prodigious musical gifts, singing, playing the piano, and composing her own songs and piano pieces before she was of primary school age. Fearing that their daughter's unusual talents would be hampered by ordinary instruction, the Everests educated her at home. Offers to take her to Europe for vocal training were refused until she was nineteen (1883), when they accepted a scholarship that allowed her to study voice in Paris at the École Marchesi.[3]

Mathilde Marchesi (1821–1913) became Freer's voice teacher for the ensuing three years. She met singers then working with this much-sought-after vocal pedagogue: Emma Eames (1865–1952), Nellie Melba (1861–1931), and Emma Nevada (1859–1940), all of whom later established operatic careers. Freer also studied composition with Benjamin Godard (1849–1895), and was coached in art song by Charles Widor (1844–1937), Jules Massenet (1842–1916), and Herbert Bemberg (1859–1931). Her sight-reading abilities as both a singer and accompanist astonished Marchesi and the other faculty members. She studied French with Charles Marchand at the Paris Academy, becoming fluent in the language.

Despite her many musical gifts, Freer decided to become a teacher rather than pursue an operatic and concert career. She resolved to bring back to her own country the European "secrets" she was sent abroad to learn. Several other factors influenced her: European composers had written most of the vocal music heard in concerts and operas; it was sung in foreign languages. She was further resolved to seek American composers who could write operas and art songs in English.

Freer returned to Philadelphia in 1886 certified to teach the Marchesi method of vocal production. She began teaching voice privately, eventually seeing sixty students each week. She arranged recitals which she accompanied on the piano, and occasionally performed herself in private musicales in New York, Philadelphia and Boston. In 1889 Jeannette Thurber (1851–1946), founder, invited her to teach at the National Conservatory of Music of America in New York City. Everest traveled to New York twice weekly as a faculty member of the Conservatory (1889–1891) where she became friends with George Chadwick (1854–1931), Charles Martin Loeffler (1861–1935), and Ethelbert Nevin (1862–1901).

In the spring of 1891, she married Archibald Freer of Chicago, and ended her teaching career. A year later they moved to Leipzig, Germany, where Mr. Freer completed his medical education while his wife studied languages and literature, soon becoming fluent in German. A daughter, Eleanor, was born in 1894, and the family returned to Chicago so the child could have American schooling. Archibald Freer's family had long been in the upper echelons of Chicago society, and Eleanor Everest Freer was immediately welcomed into the social circle of wealthy women who organized and arranged cultural events in Chicago.[5] The Arts Club of Chicago and the famous Fortnightly Club later became opportune places for performances by Freer herself and, later, for performances of her own compositions.

She began studying composition with Bernhard Ziehn (1845–1912) in 1902. The musical creativity she had evidenced in her own light piano pieces as a teenager, and subsequently developed in Paris, returned; she produced solo piano works, choral pieces, and numerous songs under Ziehn's tutelage. Ziehn's harmonic theories[6] inspired Freer. She continued to experiment with his ideas following his death in 1912. By 1921 she had written sixty-nine songs, fourteen piano solos, eleven vocal ensembles, and four song cycles. The largest work written during this period was a setting of Elizabeth Barrett Browning's *Forty-four Sonnets from the Portuguese*. At the same time she translated ten Italian dramas into English.[7]

The death of Freer's five-year-old granddaughter in 1921 inspired her to write a chamber opera for children based on the legend of the Pied Piper of Hamelin. The creation of this work unleashed an avalanche of activity. Recalling her wish to encourage American composers to write operas with English libretti, Freer, with the support of her colleagues in the Arts Club of Chicago, organized the Opera in Our Language Foundation (OOLF). This group was dedicated to arranging performances of new operas by American composers and traditional operas sung in English translation. Two Chicago periodicals, *Music News* and *Musical Leader*, published numerous articles relating the pros and cons of this unprecedented venture.[8] Freer wrote many letters and editorials supporting opera in English. She appealed to musicians and composers throughout the United States to add to the growing number of works that slowly began to appear at her urging.

To commemorate the death of her old friend David Bispham in 1921, Freer established the David Bispham Memorial Fund, offering a memorial medal to be awarded to American composers whose operas were deemed worthy of performance by OOLF. In 1924 these two organizations merged to become the American Opera Society of Chicago (AOSC).[9] During the many controversies and problems surrounding the disciples of the "opera in English" movement, Freer continued to compose, and by the end of her life her total oeuvre included eleven chamber operas, 158 songs including those in five song cycles, nineteen piano solos, one duo-piano piece, and thirteen vocal ensembles. Her works were performed mostly in the Chicago area, frequently at benefit concerts for the philanthropic organizations the Freers supported. David Bispham's scrapbooks[10] show that he performed several Freer songs on his American tours, where he often championed works by American composers. Her colleagues in the Music Teachers' National Association, the Arts Club of Chicago, and the Fortnightly Club arranged staged or concert performances of Freer's chamber operas. Her fortunate social and economic position provided her with opportunities for private publication and performance of her works.

Freer's activity as a composer spanned the years 1902 to 1942, when many new musical forces were superceding previous concepts of theory and composition. Although her music shows a total isolation from the twentieth-century techniques of serialism, bi-tonality, and pan-diatonicism, her unexpected chord choices and rhythmic creativity are often interesting and fresh-sounding, particularly in the songs, where the text provides additional impetus for special harmonic coloring. It must be remembered that her initial composition studies with Ziehn took place a considerable length of time after her short period of work with Godard. There is no record of works produced while the French composer was her mentor. The earliest pieces for piano show a distinct relationship to the technical *études* of Moritz Moszkowski (1854–1925) and J. B. Cramer (1771–1858), with which Freer certainly became acquainted as a young piano student of her father. In the songs, one can find many of the same patterned accompaniment styles used by nineteenth-century French and German composers. In all cases, however, Freer's particular hallmark seems to be an emphasis on shifting tonalities. It is possible that Ziehn's practice of handling each note in each chord as a free-moving musical element rather than as a sound ordered by a tonal goal, was a new idea, supremely exciting to the conservatively trained composer. From this technical process emerges the ever-present changing tonalities and the absence of a strong tonic-dominant relationship that characterize many of Freer's works. Though not always successful, these procedures often bring to the Freer compositions a unique flavor that provokes the listener's interest and curiosity.

Freer's eleven chamber operas are written mainly in the *arioso* style, with few independent solo sections that might be identified as arias. The short length of these works suggests that any one of them may be paired with another of similar length on a single program. Their subjects include mythical or historical figures (in *Frithiof, Joan of Arc*), and adaptations of tales by American authors Henry Wadsworth Longfellow, Washington Irving, and Louisa May Alcott (in *Preciosa*, *Legend of Spain*, *Little Women*). Of special interest are the interpolations, in the later operas especially, of individual songs or choral pieces written much earlier during the period between Ziehn's death (1912) and the establishment of OOLF (1921).

The songs of Eleanor Everest Freer are arguably the best of her compositions. Two have been selected for inclusion here: *Sweet in Her Green Dell*, op. 17, no. 2 (1917), and *Summer Night*, op. 12, no. 6 (1907). As a singer and performer, Freer was fully aware of the importance of setting texts with regard for a singer's technical problems. These settings are predominantly syllabic, often with interesting rhythmic contrasts against a motivic accompaniment. In *Sweet in Her Green Dell* one encounters duplets and quadruplets in the voice part over the insistent triplet feeling of the compound $\frac{9}{8}$ meter. Although a published edition has not been found, Freer's note to a prospective publisher on her manuscript indicates that she thought of this song in the key of D major. The relative minor and its subdominant, however, occupy most of the piece, with D major appearing only in the last four measures, and its dominant chord the concluding sonority. *Summer Night* also presents an ambiguous tonality from its start; the seventh measure is reached before the piece comes to rest in B major. The key is fleeting — the text in subsequent measures seems to require a minor mode. Augmented sixth chords and enharmonic modulations keep the actual tonality a mystery, the theoretical practice that must have fascinated Freer, as a study of her works discloses.

Notes

1. Girls' Normal School of Philadelphia was a state-supported teacher-training institution, which required its graduates to teach only in the state of Pennsylvania.

2. Published by Lee and Walker in Philadelphia, 1867.

3. Information about Marchesi's school and her teaching can be found in Sara Hershey Eddy, "Madame Marchesi: Her Personality and Methods of Work," an interview in *Music Review* 12 (May–October 1897): 677-91.

4. Mathilde Marchesi, *Marchesi and Music* (London and New York: Harper and Row, 1897).

5. These well-known women included socialites Edith Rockefeller McCormick and Mrs. Potter Palmer.

6. Bernhard Ziehn, *Manual of Harmony, Theoretical and Practical*, vol. I (Milwaukee, Wis.: Wm. Kaun, 1897).

7. These are listed in Agnes Greene Foster, *Eleanor Everest Freer, Patriot, and Her Colleagues* (Chicago: Musical Art Pub. Co., 1927).

8. Otto Luening, *Odyssey of an American Composer* (New York: Charles Scribner's Sons, 1980), Chapter 10, gives many humorous details about this controversy.

9. A complete history of this organization is available in the Scrapbooks of the American Opera Society of Chicago, at the Newberry Library in Chicago.

10. David Bispham's scrapbooks can be found in the Music Division of the New York Public Library.

Selected List of Works

Voice and Piano

Six Songs to Nature, op. 10. Unpublished. (Manuscript at Library of Congress.)

1. *The World Beautiful.* Text by John Milton
2. *Before the Rain.* Text by Thomas Bailey Aldrich
3. *After the Rain.* Text by Aldrich
4. *The Harvest Moon.* Text by Henry Wadsworth Longfellow
5. *My Garden.* Text by Thomas Edward Brown
6. *To the Western Wind.* Text by Percy Bysshe Shelley

Songs from the Greek, op. 15. (Manuscripts at Library of Congress.)

1. *To Love, the Soft and Blooming Child.* Text by Anacreon. Translation by Thomas Moore
2. *Golden Eyes.* Text by Rufinus. Translation by Andrew Lang. New York: Church, Paxson, and Co., 1912
3. *Bridal Songs of Sappho.* Translations by Francis Palgrave, Tennyson, and others
4. *When Spring Adorns the Dewy Scene.* Text by Anacreon. Translation by Thomas Moore
5. *Of the Need of Drinking.* Text by Anacreon. Translation by Vincent Bourne. New York: Church, Paxson, and Co., 1912
6. *To A Painter.* Text by Anacreon. Translation by Thomas Moore

Three Songs, op. 20. Unpublished. (Manuscripts at Library of Congress).

1. *Ships That Pass in the Night.* Text by Hester Bancroft
2. *During Music.* Text by Arthur Symons
3. *Evening Song.* Text by Sidney Lanier

Forty-four Sonnets from the Portuguese, op. 22. Text by Elizabeth Browning. French version by Eleanor Everest Freer. Chicago: Music Library of Chicago Press, 1939. (Manuscripts and published edition at Library of Congress.)

Chamber Operas

Legend of the Piper, op. 28. Text by Josephine Preston Peabody. Boston: Summy-Birchard and Co., 1921.

A Christmas Tale, op. 35. English text by Barrett Clark, from the French of Maurice Bouchor. Milwaukee, Wis.: Wm. A. Kaun Music Co., Inc., 1928.

Joan of Arc, op. 38. Text by Eleanor Everest Freer. Milwaukee, Wis.: Wm. A. Kaun Music Co. Inc., 1929.

Keyboard

Nine Lyric Studies for Piano, op. 3 (1904). Milwaukee, Wis.: Wm. A. Kaun Music Co., Inc., 1907.

Four Modern Dances for Pianoforte, op. 31 (1926). Excerpts from the opera *The Chilkoot Maiden*. Milwaukee, Wis.: W. A. Kaun Music Co., Inc., 1926.

Bibliography

Davis, Ronald. *Opera in Chicago.* New York: Appleton-Century, 1966.

Eversole, Sylvia. "Eleanor Everest Freer: Her Life and Music." Ph.D. diss., City University of New York, 1992.

Foster, Agnes Greene. *Eleanor Everest Freer, Patriot, and Her Colleagues.* Chicago: Musical Art Publishing Co., 1927.

Freer, Eleanor Everest. *Recollections and Reflections of an American Composer*. N.p., n.d.

Luening, Otto. *The Odyssey of an American Composer.* New York: Charles Scribner's Sons, 1980.

Scrapbooks of the American Opera Society of Chicago. At the Newberry Library, Chicago.

Ziehn, Bernhard. *Manual of Harmony, Theoretical and Practical*, vol. 1. Milwaukee, Wis.: Wm. A. Kaun Music Co., Inc., 1907.

Sweet in Her Green Dell

George Darley

Eleanor Everest Freer
Op. 17, No. 2

Lento [♩. = 48-52]
Sweet in her green dell The flower of beau-ty slum - bers,
4
Lull'd by the first bree - zes sigh - ing through her hair;
7
Sleeps she, and hears not the mel-an-cho-ly num - bers
10
poco rall.
Breathed to my sad lute 'mid the lone - ly air.

13
[a tempo] [♩. = ♪.]
Down from the high cliffs the riv - u - let is teem - ing To
15
Wind toward the wil - low leaves that lure him from a - bove;
17
Oh, that in tears from my rock - y Pri - son stream - ing,
19
I too could glide To the flow - er of my love!
*

*original rhythm was: ♪ 𝅀 𝅘𝅥𝅯♪. 𝄾 𝅀 𝅘𝅥𝅯♪

21
Ah! where the wood-bines with slee - py arms have bound her,
23
Opes she her eye - lids to the dream of my lay,
25
List-'ning, like the dove, while the Foun - tains e - cho
27
round her
To her lost mates' call in the For - ests far a -

30
way. Come then, my bird, for the peace thou ev-er bear - est,
33
Still Hea-ven's mes-sen - ger of com-fort to me
36
Come! this fond bo-som, oh faith - ful-lest and fair - est,
38
Bleeds with its death wound, its wound of love for thee!

Summer Night

Alfred Tennyson

Eleanor Everest F
Op. 12, No. 6

7
[𝄐]
me.
Now droops the milk-white pea - cock like a
9
ghost, And like a ghost she glim-mers on to me.
11
f
Now lies the Earth all Da - na - ë to the stars,
f
13
And all thy heart lies o - pen un - to me.
Now slides the si - lent Me - teor
p
p

15
rall.
on, and leaves a shin-ing fur - row, as thy thoughts in me.
18
a tempo
Now folds the lil - y all her sweet-ness up, And slips in -
20
to the bos - om of the lake: So fold thy - self, my dear - est, thou,
22
a piacere
a tempo
rall.
and slip In - to my bos - om and be lost in me.
p colla voce
pp

Adela Maddison
(1866–1929)

SOPHIE FULLER

Adela Maddison was born Katharine Mary Adela Tindal on December 15, 1866, probably in Ireland, into a well-to-do family. Her father, Louis Symonds Tindal, was a Vice Admiral in the British Navy. Although the details of her musical education remain unknown, she was probably, like most young girls of her class, given private tuition. In 1883, at the age of 16, she married the lawyer Frederick Brunning Maddison, a director of Metzler, the publishing company that had published her earliest surviving works, a song and a piano piece, the previous year.

Maddison's early married life mirrored that of most upper-class women of the time. She gave birth to two children and spent much time traveling on the Continent and going to balls and society parties. Music, however, also played a central and increasingly important part in her busy life. She continued to compose and publish songs, including a collection of *Twelve Songs* that appeared in 1895. It was at about this time that Maddison and her husband first met Gabriel Fauré (1845–1924). They became close friends of the composer and were key figures in the promotion of his music in England. It is likely that Frederick Maddison was responsible for Fauré's 1896 contract with the publisher Metzler while Adela Maddison translated several of his songs and other vocal works for performance and publication in England. On at least two occasions her songs were programmed together with his at public concerts in London. Fauré may have given her composition lessons — in 1898 she was described in the French newspaper *Le Figaro* as "a remarkable pupil of Fauré."[1] He had a very high opinion of her work, writing to a mutual acquaintance:

> Has she never let you hear the five or six most recent songs from Paris and London? They are quite remarkable! but difficult to figure out and take in at first acquaintance. She is extraordinarily gifted and I would like her to be encouraged as much as she deserves.[2]

Toward the end of 1898, Maddison moved to Paris without her husband or children, opening a boarding house, which also became a venue for musical performances. With very little documentation surviving from this period of her life, it is hard to interpret this somewhat startling change in her circumstances. Fauré's biographers Robert Orledge and Jean-Michel Nectoux assume that she was having an affair with Fauré.[3] However, this interpretation overlooks evidence which shows that she was living with her husband again some years later,[4] as well as ignoring the possibility that the move was simply a result of her own ambition. At this time upper-class couples in England often led remarkably separate lives. In the first decade of the twentieth century, for example, the composer Poldowski (pseudonym of Irene Wieniawska (1879–1932) left her English husband Sir Aubrey Dean Paul for several extended periods of study in Paris. However, the fact that Maddison appears to have needed to earn money by taking in lodgers does suggest that her husband may no longer have been supporting her. Even when husband and wife were briefly together again, there are indications that they had undergone considerable financial loss. At the outbreak of World War I (by which time Frederick Maddison was dead), Maddison was certainly extremely short of money. It is worth noting, in a curious case of life imitating art, that the feminist writer Mona Caird's *The Daughters of Danaus* was published in 1894, four years before Maddison went to Paris. This novel, well-known in its day, tells the story of a female composer who leaves her husband and children behind in England to go and study composition in Paris, where she is supported and encouraged by (but does not have a sexual relationship with) a great French composer.[5]

Whatever Maddison's reasons for settling in Paris at the end of the nineteenth century, she certainly found herself at the center of a thriving and supportive musical world where she mixed with other musicians such as Georges Enesco (1881–1955), Ricardo Viñes (1875–1943), Frederick Delius (1862–1934), Maurice Ravel (1875–1937) and the Princesse de Polignac (1876–1962), as well as Fauré. Her own works, in an increasingly adventurous musical style, continued to be performed and published during these years. In the middle of the first decade of the twentieth century, Maddison moved to Berlin where, despite finding the musical community patronizing and unsupportive of women composers, she worked on larger scale compositions including her opera *Der Talisman* and her orchestral *Irish Ballad*. *Der Talisman* (libretto based on a play by Ludwig Fulda) was given eight highly successful performances at the Leipzig Opera House in the autumn of 1910. The critic for *The Times* was enthusiastic:

> There was a remarkable first performance here last night of a new opera by an English composer. . . . Mrs Adela Maddison, who after studying in Paris has worked in Berlin for four years, is not quite the first English composer to obtain acceptance of an opera by an important German theatre, but she is, I believe, the first who can claim a real success. *Der Talisman* was a success — qualified in some respects, but real — and the first impressions of German critics, who are held in peculiar awe, indicate that the composer has contributed to win esteem for English music, which is at present by no means high.[6]

By this time, Maddison's husband was dead and she was living with Martha Mundt, the woman who was, for the rest of her life, to be her companion and probably lover. The two women moved in lesbian circles in both Paris, where Mundt worked as a secretary to Maddison's friend, the notoriously lesbian Princesse de Polignac, and in England where the couple frequently visited Maddison's old friend, the amateur singer Mabel Batten and her lover, the novelist Radclyffe Hall, later renowned for her groundbreaking lesbian novel *The Well of Loneliness*.

During World War I Maddison and Mundt fled to London, where Mundt, a German, found it impossible to find work. Maddison, however, was able to re-establish herself as a composer with various performances and publications of her music. Toward the end of the war, Maddison moved to Glastonbury in Somerset. There she became involved with Rutland Boughton's radical Glastonbury Festivals, writing the music for a 1917 production of Miles Malleson's play *Paddy Pools* and a ballet, *The Children of Lir*, which was first performed in London in 1920 and repeated several times at Glastonbury later that year.

During the 1920s Maddison appears to have divided her time between London and Switzerland. While in London, despite suffering from increasingly bad health, she organized several concerts of her own music and continued to publish songs and chamber music. Further stage works, including the opera *Ippolita in the Hills* and the play *The Song* were also performed. She died on June 12, 1929, in a nursing home in Ealing.

Adela Maddison played no part in the mainstream world of the British musical establishment centered on men such as Hubert Parry (1848–1918), Charles Stanford (1852–1924), or Sir George Grove (1820–1900), on institutions such as the Royal Academy of Music, the Royal College of Music, Oxford and Cambridge Universities, or on the big provincial festivals and London concert halls. She moved instead in musical circles abroad and in British circles influenced by continental European developments. She was one of the many musicians who moved in the vibrant amateur upper-class musical circles, unfairly neglected by most histories of *fin-de-siècle* musical life, such as those of the Princesse de Polignac or Frank Schuster. She also found a place in professional worlds that stood outside the so-called British Musical Renaissance, such as Rutland Boughton's Glastonbury Festival movement.

Maddison was always remarkably secure in her belief in her own talent and abilities, as well as being totally absorbed in music. An undated letter she wrote to Delius (probably in 1909) vividly presents her understanding of the place that she held in the musical world of the early twentieth century:

> I quite agree with what you say about the French music but just now all music seems to me barren! I am conscious of having become childishly melodic in this work [*Der Talisman*]. Even Italian in places!!! & then feel the [Claude] Debussy (1862–1918) note that was born in us all at the same moment (& is no imitation — only he has had more opportunity of expressing it — in Pelléas surtout) & then again Wagner surges up in one! After all one can only express in languages one has heard and absorbed & assimilated the most: — hence I never admit — or rarely — that people are guilty of plagiarism because they give out what they've already taken in & digested — in another form. Just now I'm suffering from attacks of people who say my music is [Richard] Wagner [1813–1883], Debussy and Fauré and [Giacomo] Puccini [1858–1924] (!!!) served in a gravy of my own. I think it ought to make a quite nice dish anyhow![7]

Unfortunately, frustratingly little of Maddison's music has survived. Her manuscripts do not seem to have been preserved, although it is possible that Martha Mundt (the main beneficiary and executor of her will) may have deposited them in some as yet unknown location in Switzerland or Germany. Nevertheless many of her songs and a few chamber pieces were published and have therefore survived.

Maddison's earliest works are decidedly unadventurous. The songs, for example, display predictable harmonies and rhythms together with unexciting word setting. But by the 1890s she was developing an increasingly inventive musical language. By this stage in her career she was regarded by English critics as a thoroughly "modern" composer and her work was also described on at least two occasions as "Wagnerian" (the two terms were still inextricably linked for many commentators).[8] By the first decades of the twentieth century the French influence on her music is strikingly clear, especially in works such as *Trois Mélodies* (1915), to poems by Edmond Harancourt (1857–1914), in which color and texture have become more important than functional harmony.

The subject matter of Maddison's vocal and stage works often echoed the fashions of the circles in which she moved. One of her favorite poets appears to have been the still somewhat risqué Algernon Swinburne, whose lyrics she set several times (five of her *Twelve Songs*, for example, are to poems by Swinburne, including the erotic lyric *Stage Love*). She later turned to an exploration of her own Celtic roots, reflecting the artistic "Celtic Twilight" of the early twentieth century in works such as the orchestral *Irish Ballad*, her ballet *The Children of Lir*, and the songs *The Heart of the Wood* and *The Poet Complains*, both set to texts translated from the Irish by Isabella Augusta Gregory and published in 1924. Maddison also embraced the Edwardian obsession with the East in several of her songs. She undoubtedly knew K. N. Das Gupta since her setting of his *National Hymn for India* was published in 1917, the same year that he produced a play at Glastonbury.

Maddison's song *La bien-aimée . . .* , dedicated to Miss Jean Waterston, was one of her three settings of poems by the French poet Edmond Harancourt that were published by Augener in 1915. It is a through-composed and harmonically ambiguous work in which the declamatory vocal line often takes second place to the colors and rhythms of the piano part. *If You Would Have It So*, to a text by the Bengali poet Rabindranath Tagore (1861–1941), was published by Enoch in 1919. As with so many of her songs this haunting and deceptively simple setting features a duet between the piano right hand and the vocal line. *Tears* is a setting of a poem by the sixth-century Chinese poet Wang-Sen-Ju, in the translation by Launcelot Cranmer Byng from his collection of old Chinese texts, *A Lute of Jade* (1909). Cranmer Byng's translations were very popular with early twentieth-century British composers and this particular poem was also set by Frances Allitsen (see this volume) in her *Four Songs from "A Lute of Jade"* (1910) and by Granville Bantock (1868–1946) in his fifth set of *Songs from the Chinese Poets* (1934). Maddison based her song on the obviously "oriental" device of chords built from fourths.

Notes

1. "Notre Page Musicale," *Le Figaro* (October 1, 1898): 2. The newspaper had published Maddison's song *Rien qu'un moment,* a translation of her Dante Gabriel Rossetti setting *A Little While* from her collection of *Twelve Songs.*

2. Letter from Gabriel Fauré to Elsie Swinton, received July 11, 1898. Quoted in David Greer, *A Numerous and Fashionable Audience: The Story of Elsie Swinton* (London: Thames Publishing, 1997), 144-45.

3. See Robert Orledge, *Gabriel Fauré* (London: Eulenburg Books, 1979), 16-17, and Jean Michel Nectoux, *Gabriel Fauré: A Musical Life,* trans. Roger Nichols (Cambridge: Cambridge University Press), 282. The only evidence submitted by the biographers is a entry about Maddison from the diary of Marguerite de SaintMarceaux, which reads "The triumph of love. She's abandoned everything to follow the man she adores."

4. See an undated letter (probably written in 1909) from Maddison to Frederick Delius in which she refers to looking after her sick husband. Letter held by the Delius Trust, London.

5. Mona Caird, *The Daughters of Danaus* (London: Bliss, Sands, and Foster, 1894).

6. "New Opera at Leipzig," *The Times* (November 21, 1910), p.12.

7. Maddison to Frederick Delius, Delius Trust, n.d.

8. See for example, Anonymous, "Foreign Notes. Leipsic," *The Musical Times* (1910): 805; Anonymous review of David Bipsham concert in *The Atheneum* 3576 (May 9, 1896): 627; Christopher St. John, "Music," *Time and Tide* 1 (1920): 132.

List of Works

Songs and Other Vocal Works

Will You Forget? Text by Gerard Bendall. London: Metzler, 1882.

For a Day and a Night. Text by Algernon Swinburne. London: Metzler, 1888.

Rococo. Text by Algernon Swinburne. London: Metzler, 1888.

If You Were Life. Text by Algernon Swinburne. London: Metzler, 1889.

Deux Mélodies. London: Metzler, 1893.
1. *Ici-bas.* Text by Armand Sully Prudhomme
2. *Romance.* Text by François Coppée

Twelve Songs op. 9 & 10. London: Metzler, 1895.
Op. 9:
1. *Bleak Weather.* Text by Ella Wilcox Wheeler
2. *Before Sunset.* Text by Algernon Swinburne
3. *The Triumph of Time.* Text by Algernon Swinburne
4. *Stage Love.* Text by Algernon Swinburne
5. *An Interlude.* Text by Algernon Swinburne
6. *Rococo.* Text by Algernon Swinburne
7. *A Little While.* Text by Dante G. Rossetti
8. *Insomnia.* Text by Dante G. Rossetti
9. *O That 'Twere Possible.* Text by Alfred, Lord Tennyson
10. *A Lament.* Text by Percy Bysse Shelley

Op. 10 *Zwei Lieder*
1. *Liebe.* Text by Heinrich Heine
2. *An Den Mond.* Text Altes Volkslied

Give Me Your Hand. "The words from *The Pall Mall Gazette.*" London: Metzler, 1896.

Ob ich dich liebe. Unknown text. Unpublished. (Performed 1896.)

Im Traum. Unknown text. Unpublished. (Performed 1896.)

Soleils couchants. Text by Paul Verlaine. Choir (or soprano and mezzo-soprano duet) and piano. Paris: J. Hamelle, ca. 1896.

Six Mélodies. Paris: Choudens, 1897.

Deux Mélodies. Text by Albert Samain. Paris: J. Hamelle, 1900.
1. *Hiver*
2. *Silence*

Trois Mélodies sur des poésies de Goethe. Paris: A. Quinzard, 1901.
1. *Pourquoi je t'aime*
2. *Rêve*
3. *Fête de mai*

The Ballade of fair Agneta (*Die Ballade von der schonen Agnete*), op. 40. Text by Agnes Miegel, trans. Adela Maddison. London: Augener, 1915.

Little Fishes Silver (*Das madchen am Teiche singt*), op. 43. Text by Otto J. Bierbaum, trans. Adela Maddison. London: Augener, 1915.

Mary at Play (*Kleine Maria*), op. 42. Text by Margarete Bruch, trans. Adela Maddison. London: Augener, 1915.

Sail On, O Ship of State. Text by Henry Wadsworth Longfellow. London: Augener, 1915.

Trois Mélodies. Text by Edmond Harancourt. London: Augener, 1915.
1. *La Bien-aimée . . .*
2. *Soir en Mer . . .*
3. *Mon amour était mort . . .*

National Hymn for India. Text by K. N. Das Gupta. London: Union of the East and West, 1918.

If You Would Have It So. Text by Rabindranath Tagore. London: Enoch, 1919.

The Lum. A Wean's Nicht Thoughts. Text by John Fergus. London: Enoch, 1919.

Retrospect. Text by Rupert Brooke. London: Enoch, 1919.

The Heart of the Wood. Translated from the Irish by Isabella Augusta Gregory. London: J. Curwen, 1924.

Lament of the Caged Lark. Text by Lily Nightingale Duddington. London: J. Curwen, 1924.

The Poet Complains. Translated from the Irish by Isabella Augusta Gregory. London: J. Curwen, 1924.

Tears. Text by Wang-Sen-Ju. Adapted by Launcelot Cranmer Byng. London: J. Curwen, 1924.

Crocknaharna. Text and date unknown.

Operatic and Theatrical Works

Der Talisman. Text by Adela Maddison, based on play by Ludwig Fulda. Unpublished. (Performed 1910.)

Incidental music for *Paddy Pools*. Text by Miles Malleson. Unpublished. (Performed 1917.)

The Children of Lir. Ballet. Unpublished. (Performed 1920.)

Ippolita in the Hills. Text by Maurice Hewlett. Opera. Unpublished. (Performed 1920s.)

The Song. Text by Adela Maddison. Unpublished. (Performed 1926.)

Instrumental Works

Brer Rabbit. Piano. London: Metzler, 1882.

Diana. Piano. London: Metzler, 1888.

Berceuse. Violin and piano. Paris: J. Hamelle, 1898.

Romance. Violin and piano. Paris: J. Hamelle, 1898.

Irish Ballad. Orchestra ca. 1909.

Quintet. Two violins, viola, cello, and piano (1916). London: J. Curwen, 1925.

Bibliography

Fuller, Sophie. "Adela Maddison." *The Pandora Guide to Women Composers: Britian and the United States, 1629–Present*. London: Pandora, 1994.

Fuller, Sophie. "Women Composers during the British Musical Renaissance, 1880–1918." Ph.D. diss., London University 1998.

La bien-aimée . . .

Elle est venue, elle a souri la Bien-aimée.
Elle a dit: 'Que c'est mal!' Et m'a longtemps souri.
Son geste embaumait l'air comme un jardin fleuri,
Et la chambre s'en est lentement parfumée.
Et j'ai cru que la terre était montée aux cieux!
O Bien-aimée! Et puis elle a fermé les yeux
Comme d'autres, hélas! hélas! la Bien-aimée!

She has come, she has smiled, the Beloved.
She said: "How wrong is this!" And smiled at me for a long while.
Her friendly advance embalmed the air like a blossoming garden,
And the room is slowly perfumed by it.
And I thought that the earth had climbed to the heavens!
O Beloved! And then she closed her eyes
Like the others, alas! the Beloved.

Translation by Sophie Fuller

La bien-aimée......

Edmond Haraucourt

Adela Maddison (1915)
Sophie Fuller, editor

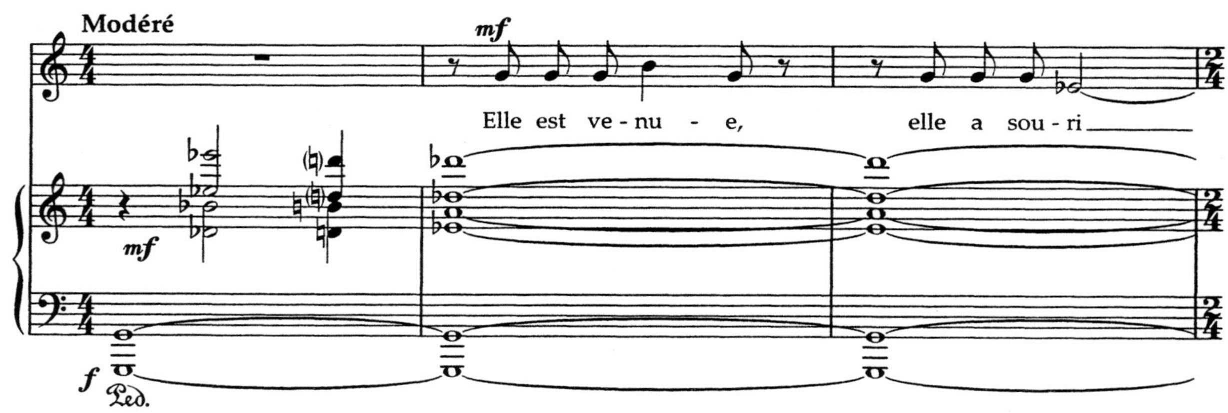

*This note is mistakenly a "C" in the original print.

11
Un peu plus animé
Et m'a long-temps sou-ri.
suivez
p
14
mf
Son ges - te em - bau - mait l'air comme un jar - din fleu -
poco cresc.
16
cresc.
En animant un peu
ri, Et la cham - bre
19
s'en est len - te - ment par - fu -
cresc.

22
Tranquillement
mé - - - - - e.
p
24
poco cresc.
stringendo
Et j'ai cru que la
26
cresc.
extasié
molto stringendo
ter - re é - tait mon - tée aux cieux!
f
cresc. molto
28
f
ff
3

30
retenez un peu
1er Mouvement
O Bien-ai-mé - e!
Et puis
dim.
33
elle a fer-mé les yeux,
dim.
36
poco string.
a tempo
cresc.
Com-me d'au - tres, hé-las! hé - las!
la Bien - ai -
40
Lentement
mé - e!
Con 8vb
8

If You Would Have It So

Rabindranath Tagore

Adela Maddison
Sophie Fuller, editor

Moderato
mf
3
3

4
mf
3
If you would have it so I will cease my sing - ing
mf
3

7
meno f
3
If it sets your
dim.
3

10
poco string.
cresc.
heart a - flut - ter
I will take my eyes a -
L.H.
12
a tempo
way from your face
15
mf
If it sud - den - ly start - les you in your walk
17
dim.
I will step a - side and take a - no - ther path
mf
dim.

20
p
If it con-fu - ses you in your
p
22
cresc.
flow - er weav - ing
I will shun your lone - ly
mf
24
gar - - - - - - - - - den
26
stringendo
p
If the wa-ters be wan-ton and wild
f

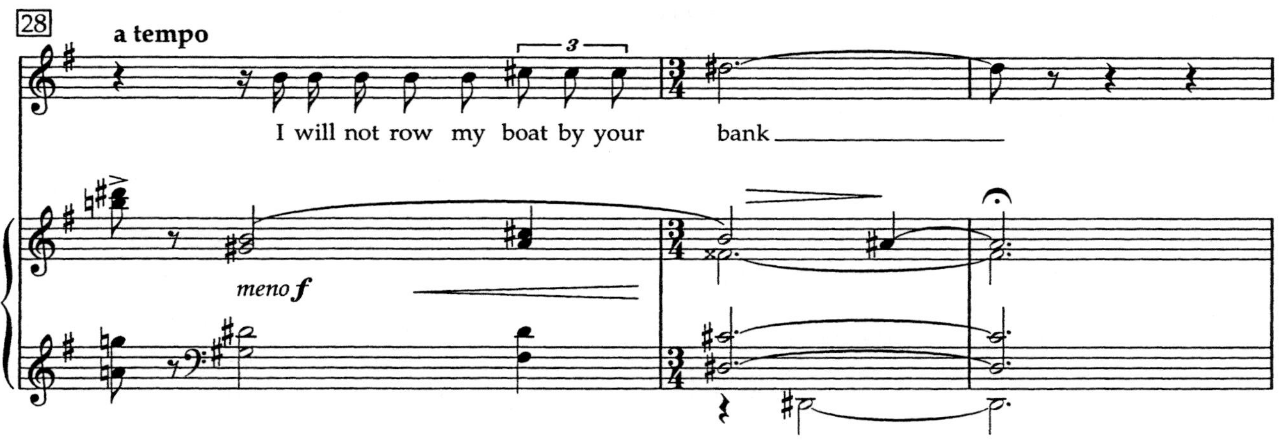
28
a tempo
I will not row my boat by your bank
meno f

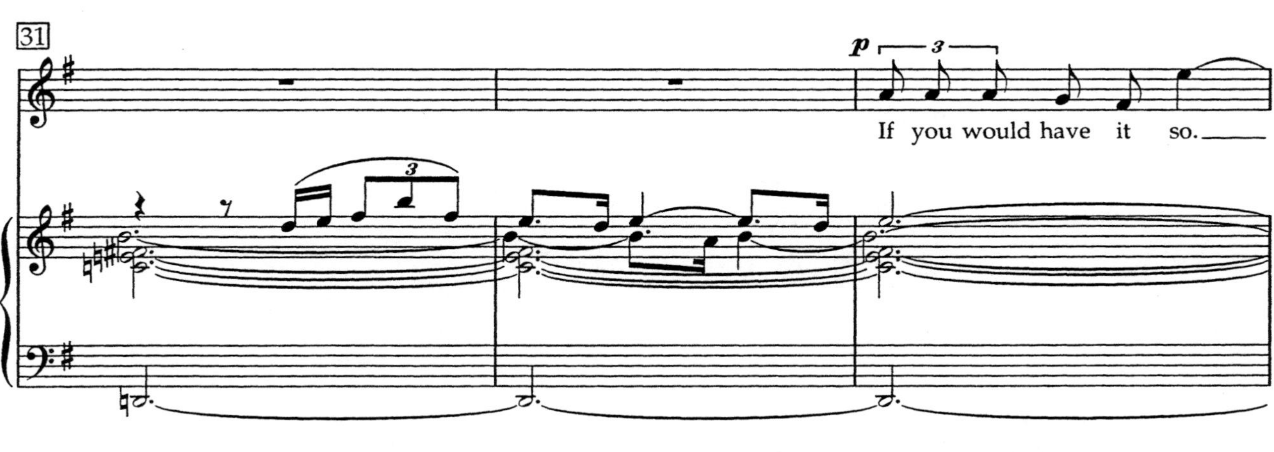
31
p
If you would have it so.

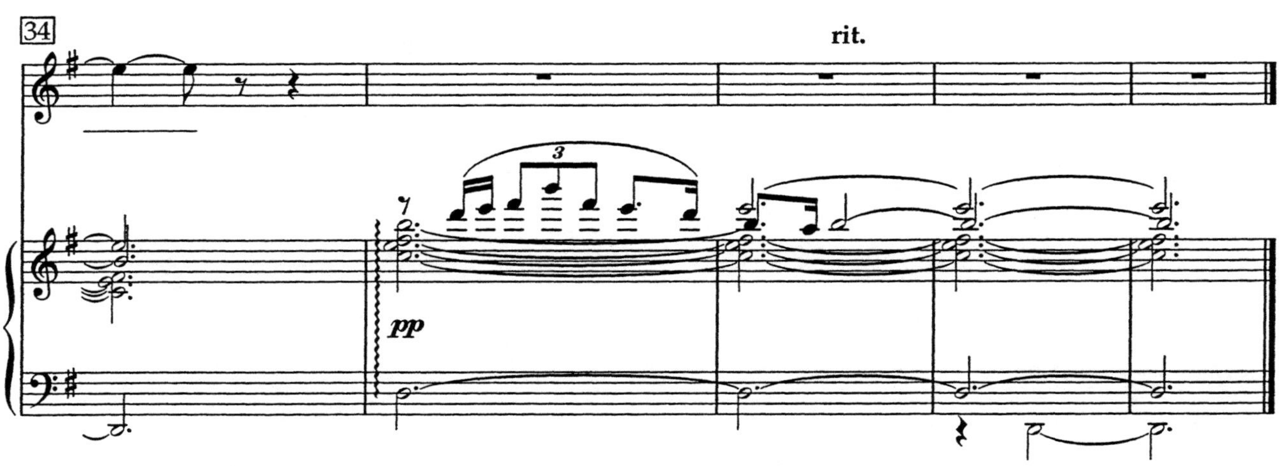
34
rit.
pp

Tears

Wang-Sen-Ju
translation by Launcelot Cranmer Byng

Adela Maddison
Sophie Fuller, editor

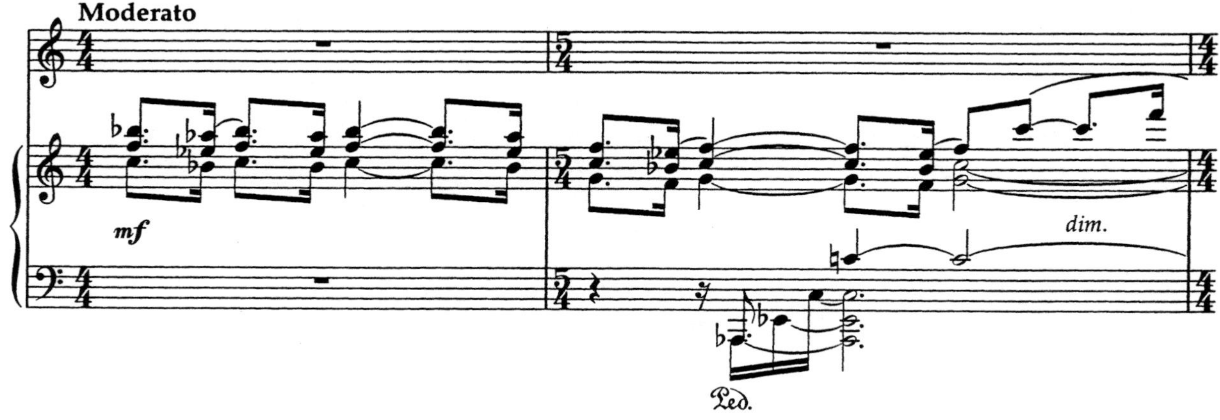

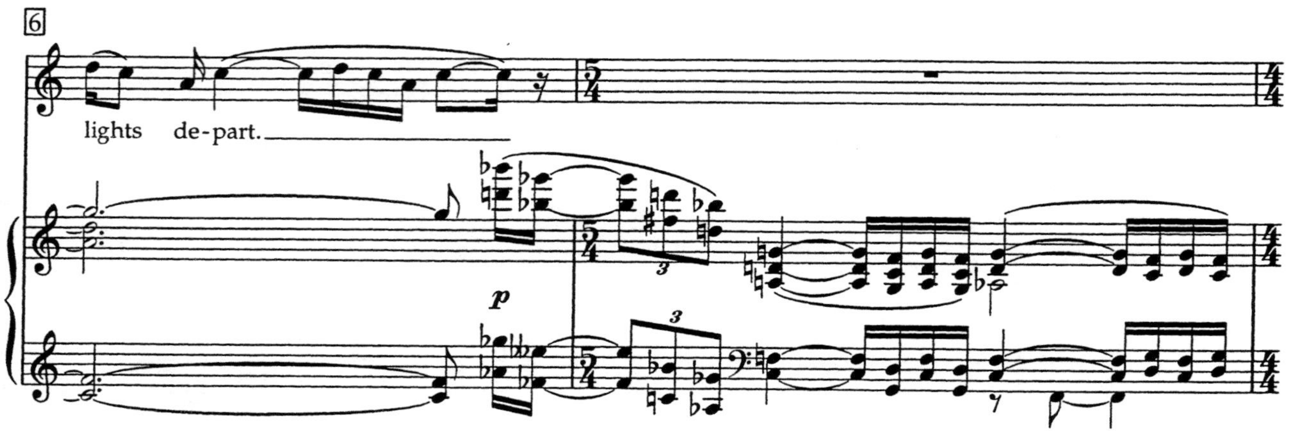

8
Poco più animato
mf
Dead springs are ris - - ing in my heart
mf
mf
cresc.
11
dim.
And there are tears....
dim.
cresc.
Ped.
14
mf
But that which makes my grief more deep Is that you know not.
mf
17
rit.
when I weep.
L.H.
p
ppp
Ped.

Amy Beach
(1867–1944)

ADRIENNE FRIED BLOCK

Amy Beach (born Amy Marcy Cheney in West Henniker, New Hampshire, September 5, 1867; died in New York, December 27, 1944) lived the first three years of her life in a provincial town in southern New Hampshire. She was the only child of Charles Abbott Cheney, a paper stock salesman, and Clara Imogene Marcy, a talented amateur pianist and singer. Amy's prodigious musical gifts for piano and composition were apparent almost from birth.

When she was four her family moved to Chelsea, a suburb of Boston, and in 1875 to Boston proper. She was schooled by her mother at home until she was ten, then attended a preparatory school for two years. Her mother was her first piano teacher; after two years, she studied with the first of two professional piano teachers, Ernst Perabo (n.d.) and Carl Baermann (n.d.). Formal training in composition was limited to one year of theory and harmony. Wilhelm Gericke, conductor of the Boston Symphony Orchestra, told her at age seventeen, to teach herself composition, which she did for the next ten years — and very well indeed.

Her piano debut, at age sixteen with an unnamed orchestra conducted by Adolph Neuendorff, was a triumph. She played recitals in and around Boston for a two-year period, which climaxed in 1885 with her Boston Symphony Orchestra debut, playing Chopin's *Concerto in F minor*. Thus launched, she was ready for the life of a concert artist, but her plans were changed when at eighteen she married Henry Harris Aubrey Beach, a man twenty-five years her elder, a physician and surgeon to Boston's elite. (The marriage ended phase one of her life, 1867–1885, and began phase two, 1885–1910.) Her husband decided that she was to stay at home and compose, and so she did, limiting her performances to one or two a year. During their twenty-five year marriage she composed nearly 200 works, almost all published and performed, earning an international reputation in the process. The death of Henry Beach in 1910, followed quickly by the death of her mother, left Beach quite alone and temporarily stopped her creative work.

The third phase of her life began in late 1911 with her first trip to Europe where she established herself as both composer and pianist. Returning home three years later at the outbreak of World War I, she continued her life as a composer-pianist until her late sixties when ill health required that she give up traveling. In 1940, a heart attack put an end to performing.

Beach composed over 300 works during her lifetime, was America's best-known woman composer — to some its most famous composer, a mentor and model for women in music. Beach died in New York at her residence, the Hotel Barclay, of heart disease on December 27, 1944.

Three themes stand out in Amy Beach's life: her commitment to music (she said there could be "no other life" for her),[1] her religious commitment (especially in later life), and her fascination with the natural world. Many titles of her instrumental compositions as well as the texts of her songs eloquently testify to these lifelong preoccupations. The three themes are important aspects of the poems she chose to set.

Songs were an important part of Amy Beach's oeuvre. No other genre had as direct an expression of feeling, or served as often as a storehouse of musical ideas for further development. Beach composed songs throughout her long creative life; the earliest improvised while still a toddler. There are well over 100 of them, beginning with the first to be published, *The Rainy Day* (composed 1880, published 1883), and ending with her last numbered work, *Though I Take the Wings of Morning*, op. 152 (published 1941). She set texts from five centuries, in three languages, creating a body of mainly art songs in a wide variety of styles. Although the strongest influence was that of the German lied, other influences included the French *mélodie,* the Elizabethan madrigal, the American parlor song, and national folk songs. Eleven have obbligati, either for violin or cello, and two more have obbligati for both violin and cello. All share the composer's lyrical gift and special sense of harmony regardless of the year in which, they were composed.

Of the four songs included here, *Juni* (*June*), op. 51, no. 3, and *Rendezvous,* op. 120 dedicated "To the Poet", celebrate the month of June. Both have violin obligattos. The first, set to a poem of Erich Jansen, was written in 1903, the second, to poetry by Leonore Speyer, in 1924. The difference between the two songs, apparent in their poetry and heard in their settings, suggests the extraordinary changes the twenty-one years brought in both the world and in

Beach's life. Both songs share the same theme, the poet's vision of the month of June when the apex of spring meets the lushness of summer. *Juni* describes a sun-lit and all but unshadowed landscape, rejoicing in the month's rich beauty and the sheer joy of living. "Hearts-ease and Roses," the thrice repeated and climactic phrase, refers to two flowers, the former a wild pansy, said to cure the pangs of love, the latter the rose, the symbol of love, an essentially romantic idea.

Arthur P. Schmidt published *Juni* in 1903 in German and English; in 1920, however, it appeared as *June*, in English only with the violin obbligato. It is likely, therefore, that the original text was German. The elimination of the German title and text in the 1920 edition reflects Americans' continuing anti-German sentiment in the aftermath of World War I.

The song opens with a scale-wise vocal line of successively rising phrases, animated by energetic upward leaps of an octave. Always alert to the dramatic possibilities of a text and the need for contrast, Beach introduces a harmonically dark passage at the lines "Yon leafy arbor, all tremulous there, Doth sigh as at night it reposes." The mood, however, dissipates as quickly as it comes, making the final exultant passage sound even brighter. Its melodic line and intensely forward-moving accompaniment depict the energy and passion of youth, while the mainly diatonic harmonies match the apparent stability of the years before World War I.

The first performance took place on February 14, 1904, at a Sunday evening concert at the Metropolitan Opera House in New York; the singer was Edith Walker. In 1906, Johanna Gadski sang *Juni* in a Symphony Hall program in Boston. In 1907 Beach prepared an orchestration, perhaps the one used when, in 1919, Grete Masson sang it in a Carnegie Hall concert conducted by Josef Stransky. Beach also arranged the song for women's and mixed-voice choruses, a sure sign of the work's popularity.

Although both *Juni* and *Rendezvous* share the same subject matter, their moods differ markedly. *Juni* looks eagerly forward; *Rendezvous* looks both forward and backward. The latter's urgent refrain, "Wait for me, June," anticipates the advent of June with impatience, yet not without anxiety: would June arrive without the speaker? Even June's landscape is darker than in the first song: rather than a sun-filled garden, the poet depicts the leafy shade of a woodland where bird songs bring not joy but solace and "solemn moods", and the stars of the night sky recall an "ancient grief still new." Time's passing is further marked by "the fern's unhurried rout" (to rhyme with "about"), and the refrain line, "One more month, so soon." The contrast between the two poems is powerful.

Beach sets *Rendezvous* with jaggedly falling chromatic vocal lines and sweeping piano arpeggios darkened by dissonance. Taking a cue from the words, Beach has the violin obbligato both foreshadow and shadow the voice. The song is in A major, but important phrases end a tritone away on D-sharp in anticipation of the *tranquillo* section in E-flat that begins, "Bring me your revelling fields and woods, your hills and lakes of solemn moods. . . ." Dissonances are completely resolved only at the final cadence, the postponed resolution an analog for the long winter before June's eagerly awaited arrival.

The first performance of *Rendezvous* was in New York in November 1926, at a concert of the Society of American Women Composers, a group organized by Beach, who was also its first president. With the soprano Ruth Shaffner, she presented *Rendezvous* and *Mirage* on a program at the White House in April 1934 for the first lady, Eleanor Roosevelt.

Oliver Ditson published the two songs of op. 100, *Mirage* (poetry by Bertha Ochsner, dedicated to Dr. and Mrs. A. J. Ochsner), and *Stella viatoris* (poetry by Jessie Hague Nettleton, dedicated to Mme Louise Llewellyn), in 1924. Both songs call for violin and cello obbligati. However, there is a note on the songs that the cello or even both strings may be omitted.

The poetry of *Mirage* suggests that nature is an illusion and its pallid mists hide a grievous reality. The scene is set by the ghostly chiming of bells high in the piano's treble, around which the strings (*con sordino*) weave in an anticipation of the vocal line. The high-floating harmonies lack forward motion; their ineffectual musical meandering ends with a slow descent of voice and instruments to the final cadence as the voice sings the lament of the one without hope. Resolution of dissonance is delayed until the ending in B-flat minor.

The second song of op. 100, *Stella viatoris* (The Traveller's Star), begins with an even more ominous text, with darkened sky and moaning wind. Slowly, the sky lightens, leading to an epiphany as the clouds part to reveal a single star, "like the kindness of God shining thro." The opening is dissonant and chromatic, portraying the threatening landscape. A series of unresolved harmonies follows, impressionistic in their effect. At the appearance of the star, the harmonies clarify and achieve a faith-affirming A-flat major, Beach's "blue" key. (Beach associated keys with colors.) A brief coda recalls the recitative section heard at the beginning before the vocal part resolves in A-flat to end the song.

The two songs of op. 100 are complementary, making a short cycle, suggested not only by the similarity of mood in the two poems, but also by the way the first song sets the stage for the dramatic conclusion of the second. The theme of lamentation stated in *Mirage* is echoed in the dark and barren landscape described in the opening lines of *Stella viatoris*. There are musical connections as well in the similarity of the opening phrase of *Mirage* and the closing phrase of *Stella viatoris*. An even more profound matter connects the poems: the belief that nature is an emanation of the Deity, a feeling shared by many including Beach, who probably agreed with music critic Henry Krehbiel that the "new trinity" consisted of God, nature, and music.[2]

Notes

1. Amy Beach to Mrs. Edward F. Wiggers, August 24, 1935; P. E. O. [Sorority] Archives, Chapter R, New York.

2. Henry Edward Krehbiel, *Music and Manners in the Classical Period,* 3rd ed. (New York: Charles Scribner's, 1899), 237.

Selected List of Works

Dates of composition are in parentheses, without parentheses are dates of publication.

Songs

(for voice and piano unless otherwise stated)

The Rainy Day (1880). Text by Henry W. Longfellow. Boston: Oliver Ditson, 1883.

Whither. Text by W. Müller. Accompaniment: Chopin, *Trois nouvelles études*, no. 3. Unpublished.

Four Songs, op. 1. Boston: Arthur P. Schmidt.
1. *With Violets*. Text by Kate Vannah. 1885
2. *Die vier Brüder* (The Four Brothers). Text by Friedrich von Schiller. 1887
3. *Jeune fille et jeune fleur* (Young Girl and Young Flower). Text by François A. R. Chateaubriand. 1887
4. *Ariette*. Text by Percy B. Shelley. 1887

Three Songs, op. 2. Text by Henry H. A. Beach. Boston: Arthur P. Schmidt.
1. *Twilight*. 1887
2. *When Far from Her*. 1889
3. *Empress of Night*. 1891

Songs of the Sea, op. 10. Boston: Arthur P. Schmidt, 1890.
1. *A Canadian Boat Song*.Text by Thomas Moore. For soprano, bass, piano
2. *The Night Sea*. Text by Harriet P. Spofford. For two sopranos, piano
3. *Sea Song*. Text by William E. Channing. For two sopranos, piano

Three Songs, op. 11. Texts by William E. Henley. Boston: Arthur P. Schmidt.
1. *Dark is the Night*. 1890
2. *The Western Wind*. 1889
3. *The Blackbird*. 1890

Three Songs, op. 12. Texts by Robert Burns. Boston: Arthur P. Schmidt, 1887.
1. *Wilt Thou Be My Dearie?*
2. *Ye Banks and Braes O' Bonnie Doon*
3. *My Luve is Like a Red, Red Rose*

Hymn of Trust, op. 13. Text by Oliver W. Holmes. Boston: Arthur P. Schmidt, 1891. Revised with violin obbligato, 1901.

Four Songs, op. 14. Boston: Arthur P. Schmidt, 1891; nos. 2-3 revised 1901.
1. *The Summer Wind*. Text by Walter Learned
2. *Le secret* (The Secret). Text by Jules de Resseguier
3. *Sweetheart, Sigh No More*. Text by Thomas B. Aldrich
4. *The Thrush*. Text by Edward R. Sill

Three Songs, op. 19. Boston: Arthur P. Schmidt, 1893.
1. *For Me the Jasmine Buds Unfold*. Text by Florence E. Coates
2. *Ecstasy*. Text by Amy M. Beach. Rev. with violin obbligato, 1895
3. *Golden Gates*

Villanelle: Across the World, op. 20. Text by Edith M. Thomas. Boston: Arthur P. Schmidt, 1894. Also with cello obbligato, 1894.

Three Songs, op. 21. Boston: Arthur P. Schmidt.
1. *Chanson d'amour* (A Song of Love). Text by Victor Hugo. With violoncello obbligato, 1899
2. *Extase (Exaltation)*. Text by Hugo, 1894
3. *Elle et moi* (My Sweetheart and I). Text by Félix Bovet, 1894

Four Songs, op. 26. Boston: Arthur P. Schmidt, 1894.
1. *My Star*. Text by Cora Fabbri
2. *Just for This*. Text by Fabbri
3. *Spring*. Text by Fabbri
4. "*Wouldn't That Be Queer?*" Text by Elsie J. Cooley

Four Songs, op. 29. Boston: Arthur P. Schmidt, 1894.
1. *Within Thy Heart*. Text by Amy M. Beach
2. *The Wandering Knight*. Text anonymous. Translation by J. G. Lockhart
3. *Sleep, Little Darling*. Text by Harriet B. Spofford
4. *Haste, O Beloved*. Text by William A. Sparrow

Four Songs, op. 35. Boston: Arthur P. Schmidt, 1896.
1. *Night* (Nachts). Text by C. F. Scherenberg
2. *Alone!* (Allein!). Text by Heinrich Heine
3. *With Thee* (Nähe des Geliebten). Text by Johann W. von Goethe
4. *Forget-me-not*. Text by Henry H. A. Beach

Three Shakespeare Songs, op. 37. Boston: Arthur P. Schmidt, 1897.
1. *O Mistress Mine*
2. *Take, O Take Those Lips Away*
3. *Fairy Lullaby*

Three Songs, op. 41. Boston: Arthur P. Schmidt, 1898.
1. *Anita*. Text by Cora Fabbri
2. *Thy Beauty*. Text by Harriet B. Spofford
3. *Forgotten*. Text by Cora Fabbri

Five Burns Songs, op. 43. Boston: Arthur P. Schmidt, 1898.
1. *Dearie*
2. *Scottish Cradle Song*
3. *Oh Were My Love Yon Lilac Fair*
4. *Far Awa'*
5. *My Lassie*

Three [Robert] Browning Songs, op. 44. Boston: Arthur P. Schmidt, 1900; nos. 1- 2 also with violin obbligato.
1. *The Year's at the Spring*
2. *Ah, Love, But a Day*
3. *I Send My Heart Up to Thee*

Four Songs, op. 48. Boston: Arthur P. Schmidt, 1902.
1. *Come, Ah Come.* Text by Henry H. A. Beach
2. *Good Morning.* Text by Agnes H. Lockhart
3. *Good Night.* Text by Lockhart
4. *Canzonetta.* Text by Armand Silvestre

A Song of Liberty, op. 49. Text by Frank L. Stanton. Boston: Arthur P. Schmidt, 1902, 1918.

Four Songs, op. 51. Boston: Arthur P. Schmidt, 1903. English translations by Isadora Martinez.
1. *Ich sagte nicht* (Silent Love). German text by Eduard Wissman
2. *Wir drei* (We Three). German text by Hans Eschelbach
3. *Juni* (June). German text by Erich Jansen
4. *Je demande à l'oiseau* (For my Love). French text by Armand Silvestre

Four Songs, op. 56. Boston: Arthur P. Schmidt, 1904.
1. *Autumn Song* (1903). Text by Henry H. A. Beach
2. *Go Not Too Far.* Text by Florence E. Coates
3. *I Know Not How to Find the Spring.* Text by Coates
4. *Shena Van.* Text by William Black, 1904. Also with violin obbligato, 1919

Give Me Not Love, op. 61. Text by Florence E. Coates. Boston: Arthur P. Schmidt, 1905.

When Soul is Joined to Soul, op. 62. Text by Elizabeth B. Browning. Boston: Arthur P. Schmidt, 1905.

After, op. 68. Text by Florence E. Coates. Boston: Arthur P. Schmidt, 1909; also with violin obbligato, n.d.

Two Mother Songs, op. 69. Boston: Arthur P. Schmidt, 1908.
1. *Baby.* Text by George Macdonald
2. *Hush, Baby Dear.* Text by Agnes L. Hughes

Three Songs, op. 71. Boston: Arthur P. Schmidt, 1910.
1. *A Prelude.* Text by Henry H. A. Beach
2. *O Sweet Content.* Text by Thomas Dekker
3. *An Old Love Story.* Text by Belle L. Stathem

Two Songs, op. 72. New York: G. Schirmer, 1914.
1. *Ein altes Gebet* (An Old Prayer). Text anonymous. English version anonymous
2. *Deine Blumen* (Flowers and Fate). Text by Louis Zacharias. English version by John Bernhoff

Two Songs, op. 73. German texts by Louis Zacharias. English texts by John Bernhoff. New York: G. Schirmer, 1914.
1. *Grossmütterchen* (With Granny)
2. *Der Totenkranz* (The Children's Thanks)

Four Songs, op. 75. New York: G. Schirmer, 1914.
1. *The Candy Lion.* Text by Abbie F. Brown
2. *A Thanksgiving Fable.* Text by Oliver Herford
3. *Dolladine.* Text by Brown
4. *Prayer of a Tired Child.* Text by Brown

Two Songs, op. 76. New York: G. Schirmer, 1916.
1. *Separation.* Text by John L. Stoddard
2. *The Lotos Isles.* Text by Alfred, Lord Tennyson

Two Songs, op. 77. New York: G. Schirmer, 1916.
1. *I.* Text by Cecil Fanning
2. *Wind O' the Westland.* Text by Dana Burnett

Three Songs, op. 78. New York: G. Schirmer, 1917.
1. *Meadowlarks.* Text by Ina D. Coolbrith
2. *Night Song at Amalfi.* Text by Sara Teasdale
3. *In Blossom Time.* Text by Coolbrith

In the Twilight, op. 85. Text by Henry W. Longfellow. Boston: Arthur P. Schmidt, 1922.

Spirit Divine, op. 88. Text by Andrew Read. Philadelphia: Theodore Presser, 1923.

Message, op. 93. Text by Sara Teasdale. Philadelphia: Presser, 1922.

Time Has Wings and Swiftly Flies (n.d.) Unpublished.

An Icicle Hung from the Eaves (n.d.) Unpublished.

If Women Will Not Be Inclined (n. d.) Unpublished.

Four Songs, op. 99. Philadelphia: Presser, 1923.
1. *When Mama Sings.* Text by Amy M. Beach
2. *Little Brown-Eyed Laddie.* Text by Alice D. O. Greenwood
3. *The Moonpath.* Text by Katharine Adams
4. *The Artless Maid.* Text by Louise Barili

Two Songs, op. 100. For soprano, violin, cello, piano. Boston: Arthur P. Schmidt, 1924.
1. *A Mirage*. Text by Bertha Ochsner
2. *Stella viatoris* (The Traveller's Star). Text by Jessie H. Nettleton

Jesus, My Saviour, op. 112. Text by Charlotte Elliott. For voice, piano or organ. Philadelphia: Theodore Presser, 1925.

Mine Be the Lips, op.113. Text by Leonora Speyer. Boston: Oliver Ditson, 1926.

Around the Manger, op. 115. Text by Katherine K. Davis. With violin obbligato. Philadelphia: Presser, 1925.

Three Songs, op. 117. Texts by Muna Lee. Cincinnati: John Church, 1925.
1. *The Singer*
2. *The Host*
3. *Song in the Hills*

Rendezvous, op. 120. Text by Leonora Speyer. With violin obbligato. Boston: Oliver Ditson. 1928.

On a Hill: Negro Lullaby. Arranged by Amy M. Beach. Boston: Arthur P. Schmidt, 1929.

Mignonnette. N. p., 1929.

Birth (1929). Text by Frederic L. Knowles. Unpublished.

Springtime, op. 124. Text by Susan M. Heywood. New York: G. Schirmer, 1929.

Two Sacred Songs, op. 125.
1. *Spirit of Mercy*. Text anonymous. Boston: Arthur P. Schmidt, 1930
2. *Evening Hymn: The Shadows of the Evening Hours*. Text by Adelaide A. Procter. Boston: Arthur P. Schmidt, 1934

Dark Garden, op. 131. Text by Leonora Speyer. Boston: Arthur P. Schmidt, 1932.

To One I Love, op. 135. Selma R. Quick (1932). Unpublished.

Fire and Flame, op. 136 (1932). Text by Anna A. Moody. Boston: Arthur P. Schmidt, 1933.

My Love Came Through the Fields (1932). Text by Robert Norwood. Unpublished.

A Light That Overflows (1932). Text by Robert Norwood. Unpublished.

May Flowers, op. 134 (1932). Text by Anna A. Moody. Boston: Arthur P. Schmidt, 1933.

Evening Song (1934). Unpublished.

The Deep-Sea Pearl (1935). Text by Edith M. Thomas. Unpublished.

I Sought the Lord, op. 142. Text anonymous. Voice, organ. Boston: Arthur P. Schmidt, 1935.

I Shall Be Brave, op. 143 (1931). Text by Katherine Adams. Boston: Arthur P. Schmidt, 1932.

April Dreams, op. 145 (1935). Katharine W. Harding. Unpublished.

Jesus, Tender Shepherd (1936). Unpublished.

Though I Take the Wings of Morning, op. 152 (1941). Text by Robert N. Spencer. Voice, organ or piano. New York: Composers Press, 1941.

Du sieh'st, das ist nicht so (You know this is untrue) (N. d.) For Bass and piano. Fragment. Unpublished.

Twelve Songs by Amy Marcy Cheney Beach (Mrs. H. H. A. Beach). Medium to High Voice. Edited by Deborah Cook. Bryn Mawr, PA: Hildegard Publishing Company, 1994.
1. *Wouldn't That Be Queer?* op. 26, no. 4. Text by Elsie J. Cooley
2. *Take, O Take Those Lips Away*, op. 37, no. 2. Text by William Shakespeare
3. *O Mistress Mine*, op. 37, no. 1. Text by William Shakespeare
4. *Fairy Lullaby*, op. 37, no. 3. Text by William Shakespeare
5. *Der Totenkranz* (Children's Thanks), op. 73, no. 2. Text by Louis Zacharias
6. *Juni* (June), op. 51 no. 3. Text by Erich Jansen
7. *Extase* (Exultation), op. 21, no. 2. Text by Victor Hugo
8. *Elle et moi* (My Sweetheart and I), op. 21, no. 3. Text by Félix Bovet
9. *Chanson d'amour* (A Song of Love) op. 21, no. 1. Text by Victor Hugo
10. *Prayer of a Tired Child* op. 75, no. 4. Text by Abbie Farwell Brown
11. *The Year's at the Spring*, op. 44, no. 3. Text by Robert Browning
12. *When Soul is Joined to Soul*, op. 62. Text by Elizabeth Barrett Browning

Choral Works

(for mixed chorus, SATB, unless otherwise stated)

Sacred

(for chorus and organ unless otherwise stated)

Four Chorales (1882). Unaccompanied. Unpublished.
1. *O Lord! How Happy Should We Be.* Text by J. Anstice
2. *Come, Ye Faithful.* Text by J. Hupton
3. *With Tearful Eyes I look Around*
4. *To Heav'n I Lift My Waiting Eyes*

Mass in E-flat, op. 5, for solo quartet, SATB, organ, and orchestra (1890). Organ-vocal score, Boston: Arthur P. Schmidt, 1890.

Graduale: Thou Glory of Jerusalem, insertion into Mass, op. 5. For tenor, orchestra; piano-vocal score, Boston: Arthur P. Schmidt, 1892.

O Praise the Lord, All Ye Nations, op. 7. Text Psalm 117. Boston: Arthur P. Schmidt, 1891.

Three Choral Responses, op. 8. Boston: Arthur P. Schmidt, 1891.
1. *Nunc dimittis.* Text from Luke 2:29
2. *With Prayer and Supplication.* Text from Phil. 4:6-7
3. *Peace I Leave With You.* Text from John 4:27

Festival Jubilate, op. 17. Text Psalm 100. For seven-voice chorus, orchestra (1891). Piano-vocal score. Boston: Arthur P. Schmidt, 1892; Bryn Mawr; PA: Hildegard Publishing Company; 1995.

Bethlehem, op. 24. Text by G. C. Hugg. Boston: Arthur P. Schmidt, 1893.

Alleluia, Christ is Risen, op. 27. Text after M. Weisse, C.F. Gellert, T. Scott, T. Gibbons. Boston: Arthur P. Schmidt, 1895. Arranged with violin *obbligato*, 1904.

Teach Me Thy Way, op. 33. Text from Psalm 86:11-12. Boston: Arthur P. Schmidt, 1895.

Peace on Earth, op. 38. Text by Edmund H. Sears. Boston: Arthur P. Schmidt, 1897.

Help Us, O God, op. 50. Text from Psalms 79:9, 5; 45:26. For five-voice chorus. Boston: Arthur P. Schmidt, 1903.

Service in A, op. 63. For solo quartet, SATB, organ.
1. *Te Deum,* Boston: Arthur P. Schmidt, 1905
2. *Benedictus,* Boston: Arthur P. Schmidt, 1905
3. *Jubilate*, Boston: Arthur P. Schmidt, 1906
4. *Magnificat*, Boston: Arthur P. Schmidt, 1906
5. *Nunc dimittis,* Boston: Arthur P. Schmidt, 1906

All Hail the Power of Jesus' Name, op. 74. Text by Edward Perronnet. Alternate text for *Panama Hymn:* see Secular Choral. New York: G. Schirmer, 1915.

Thou Knowest, Lord, op. 76. Text by Jane Borthwick. For tenor, bass, SATB, organ. New York: G. Schirmer, 1915.

Canticles, op. 78. New York: G. Schirmer, 1916.
1. *Bonum est, confiteri.* Text from Psalm 92:1-4. For soprano, SATB, organ
2. *Deus misereatur.* Text, Psalm 67
3. *Cantate Domino.* Text, Psalm 98
4. *Benedic anima mea.* Text, Psalm 103

Te Deum. For tenor, three-voice men's chorus, organ. Philadelphia: Theodore Presser, 1922.

Constant Christmas, op. 95. Text by Phillips Brooks. Philadelphia: Theodore Presser, 1922.

The Lord is My Shepherd, op. 96. Text, Psalm 23. For three-voice women's chorus. Philadelphia: Theodore Presser, 1923.

I Will Lift Up Mine Eyes, op. 98. Text, Psalm 121. Philadelphia: Theodore Presser, 1923.

Two Sacred Choruses, op. 103. For bass, SATB, organ. Boston: Oliver Ditson, 1924.
Benedictus es, Domine
Benedictus. Text from Luke 1:67-81

Let This Mind Be in You, op. 105. Text from Philippians 2:5-11. For soprano, bass, SATB, organ. Cincinnati: John Church, 1924.

Lord of the Worlds Above, op. 109. Text by Isaac Watts. For soprano, tenor, bass, SATB, organ. Boston: Oliver Ditson, 1925.

Around the Manger, op. 115. Text by Robert Davis. Boston: Oliver Ditson, 1925.

Benedicite omnia opera Domini, op. 121. Text from Daniel. 3:56-8. Boston: Arthur P. Schmidt, 1928.

Communion Responses, op. 122, supplement to *Service in A*. For solo quartet, SATB, organ. Boston: Arthur P. Schmidt, 1928. *Kyrie, Gloria tibi, Sursum corda, Sanctus, Agnus Dei, Gloria.*

The Canticle of the Sun, op. 123. Text by St. Francis of Assisi. Translation by Matthew Arnold. For solo quartet, SATB, orchestra. Organ- vocal score, Boston: Arthur P. Schmidt, 1928.

Evening Hymn: The Shadows of the Evening Hours, op. 125, no. 2. Text by Adelaide Proctor. Arrangement of song. For soprano, alto, SATB. Boston: Arthur P. Schmidt, 1934.

Christ in the Universe, op. 132. Text by Alice Meynell. For alto, tenor, SATB, orchestra. Organ-vocal score: New York: H. W. Gray, 1931.

God is our Stronghold, op. 134. Text by Elizabeth Wordsworth. For soprano, SATB, organ. Unpublished.

Hearken Unto Me, op. 139. Text from Isaish 51.1; 43.1-3; 40:28, 31. For solo quartet, SATB, orch. Organ-vocal score, Boston: Arthur P. Schmidt, 1934.

O Lord God of Israel, op. 141. Text from 1 Kings 8:23, 27-30, 34. For soprano, alto, bass, SATB. Boston: Arthur P. Schmidt, 1936.

Hymn: O God of Love, O King of Peace (1941). Text by Henry W. Baker. New York: Appleton-Century, 1941.

Lord of All Being, op. 146. Text by Oliver W. Holmes. New York: H. W. Gray, 1938.

I Will Give Thanks, op. 147. Text, Psalm 111. For soprano, SATB, organ. Boston: Arthur P. Schmidt, 1939.

Pax nobiscum. Text by Earl Marlatt. For three-voice women's chorus, organ; also for three- and four-voice men's chorus, organ. Boston: Arthur P. Schmidt, 1939.

Secular Choruses

The Little Brown Bee, op. 9. Text by Margaret Eytinge. For four-voice women's chorus. Boston: Arthur P. Schmidt, 1891.

The Minstrel and the King: Rudolph von Hapsburg, op. 16. Text by Friedrich von Schiller. For tenor, bass, four-voice men's chorus, orchestra. Piano-vocal score, Boston: Arthur P. Schmidt, 1890.

Singing Joyfully. Text by John W. Chadwick. For two-voice children's chorus, piano. Published in *Children's Souvenir Song Book*, ed. William L. Tomlins. London: Novello, Ewer, 1893.

An Indian Lullaby. Text anonymous. For four-voice women's chorus. N. p., 1895.

The Rose of Avon-town, op. 30. Text by Caroline Mischka. For soprano, alto, four-voice women's chorus, orchestra. Piano-vocal score, Boston: Arthur P. Schmidt, 1896.

Three Flower Songs, op. 31. Text by Margaret Deland. For four-voice women's chorus, piano. Boston: Arthur P. Schmidt, 1896.

1. *The Clover*
2. *The Yellow Daisy*
3. *The Bluebell*

Three Shakespeare Choruses, op. 39. For four-voice women's chorus, piano. Boston: Arthur P. Schmidt, 1897.

1. *Over Hill, Over Dale*
2. *Come unto These Yellow Sands*
3. *Through the House Give Glimmering Light*

Song of Welcome, op. 42. Text by Henry M. Blossom. For SATB, orchestra. Organ-vocal score, Boston: Arthur P. Schmidt, 1898.

Sylvania: A Wedding Cantata, op. 46. Text by Frederick W. Bancroft, after W. Bloem. For two sopranos, alto, tenor, bass, eight-voice chorus, orchestra. Piano-vocal score, Boston: Arthur P. Schmidt, 1898.

A Song of Liberty, op. 49. Text by Frank L. Stanton. For SATB, orchestra. Piano-vocal score, Boston: Arthur P. Schmidt, 1902. Arranged for four-voice men's chorus Boston: Arthur P. Schmidt, 1904.

Two Choruses, op. 57. Texts by Agnes L. Hughes. For four-voice women's voices. Boston: Arthur P. Schmidt, 1904.

1. *Only a Song*
2. *One Summer Day*

The Sea-Fairies, op. 59 (1904). Text by Alfred, Lord Tennyson. For soprano, alto, four-voice women's chorus, orchestra. Piano-vocal score. Boston: Arthur P. Schmidt, 1904; Bryn Mawr, PA: Hildegard Publishing Company, 1996.

The Chambered Nautilus, op. 66. Text by Oliver W. Holmes. For soprano, alto, four voice women's chorus, orchestra, organ *ad lib.* Piano-vocal score Boston: Arthur P. Schmidt, 1907; Bryn Mawr, PA: Hildegard Publishing Company, 1994.

Friends. Text by Abbie F. Brown. For two-voice children's chorus, piano. In *The Progressive Music Series,* Book 3, p. 83. Boston: Silver, Burdett, 1915, 1917.

Panama Hymn, op. 74. Text by William F. Stafford. For SATB, orchestra; arranged for SATB, organ/piano; with alternate text for *All Hail the Power of Jesus' Name*. New York: G. Schirmer, 1917.

Dusk in June, op. 82. Text by Sara Teasdale. For four-voice women's chorus. New York: G. Schirmer, 1917.

A Song of Liberty, [1918?].

May Eve, op. 86 (1921). Boston: Silver, Burdett, 1933.

Three School Songs, op. 94 (1922). N.p.: Hinds, Hayden and Eldridge, 1933.

1. *The Arrow and the Song.* Text by Henry W. Longfellow
2. *Clouds.* Text by E. H. Miller

3. *A Song for Little May.* Text by Frank D. Sherman

Peter Pan, op. 101. Text by Jessie Andrews. For three-voice women's chorus, piano. Philadelphia: Theodore Presser. 1923.

The Greenwood, op. 110. Text by William L. Bowles. N. p: C. C. Birchard, 1925.

Two Children's Choruses, op. 118. Boston: Silver, Burdett, 1938.
1. *The Moon Boat.* Text by Ella D. Watkins. For unison chorus.
2. *Who Has Seen the Wind.* Text by Christina G. Rossetti. For two-voice chorus.

Two John Masefield Choruses, op. 126. For four-voice men's chorus, piano. Boston: Arthur P. Schmidt, 1931.
1. *Sea Fever*
2. *The Last Prayer*

When the Last Sea is Sailed, op. 127. Text by John Masefield. For four-voice men's chorus. Boston: Arthur P. Schmidt, 1931.

Drowsy Dreamtown, op. 129. Text by Robert Norwood. For soprano, three-voice women's chorus, piano. Boston: Arthur P. Schmidt, 1932.

We Who Sing Have Walked in Glory, op. 140 (1940). Text by Amy S. Bridgman. Boston: Oliver Ditson, 1934.

A Bumblebee Passed by My Window (1935). For three-voice women's chorus. Unpublished.

O God of Love, O King of Peace. Text by Sir Henry W. Baker. Published in *Worship in Song* ed. By Caroline B. Parker. New York: D. Appleton-Century Co. Inc., 1942.

This Morning Very Early, op. 144. Text by P. L. Hills. For three-voice women's chorus, piano. Boston: Arthur P. Schmidt, 1937.

The Ballad of the P. E. O. New York: H. W. Gray, 1943.

Bibliography

Sources: An extensive collection of MSS, correspondence, printed music, scrapbooks, photographs, and memorabilia is in the University of New Hampshire, Durham, N. H.; additional MSS, printed editions, and correspondence are in the Library of Congress, especially in the Arthur P. Schmidt Collection; a smaller collection of Beachiana is at the University of Missouri in Kansas City. Orchestral scores are in the Fleisher Collection, Free Library of Philadelphia; scores of works for voices and orchestra at the New England Conservatory of Music, Boston.

Beach, Amy. Letter to Mrs. Edward F. Wiggers, August 24, 1935. P. E. O. Archives, Chapter R, New York.

____. "Why I Chose My Profession: The Autobiography of a Woman Composer," interviewed by Ednah Aiken. In *Mother's Magazine* 2 (February 1914): 7-8.

Beach, Mrs. H. H. A. "Emotion Versus Intellect in Music." In *Studies in Musical Education, History and Aesthetics.* Proceedings of the Music Teachers National Association, 1931, ed. Karl W. Gehrkens. Oberlin, Ohio: Music Teachers National Association, 1932.

____. "Music's Ten Commandments as Given for Young Composers," *Los Angeles Examiner,* June 28, 1915, 5.

Block, Adrienne Fried. *Amy Beach, Passionate Victorian: The Life and Work of An American Composer.* New York: Oxford University Press, 1998.

____. "Why Amy Beach Succeeded: The Early Years." *Current Musicology* 36 (1983), 41-59.

Cheney, Clara Imogene. [Biography of Amy M. Beach.] Holograph. Signed February 27, 1892. MacDowell Colony Papers. Manuscript Division, Library of Congress.

Eden, Myrna Garvey. *Energy and Individuality in the Art of Anna Huntington, Sculptor, and Amy Beach, Composer.* Metuchen, NJ: Scarecrow Press, 1987.

Elson, Louis C. *The History of American Music.* Rev. ed. New York: Macmillan, 1915, 1925. Reprint, New York: Burt Franklin, 1971.

Goetschius, Percy. "Mrs. H. H. A. Beach: Analytical Sketch." In *Mrs. H. H. A. Beach.* Boston: Arthur P. Schmidt, 1906.

Hughes, Agnes Lockhart. "Mrs. H. H. A. Beach; America's Foremost Woman Composer." *Simmons Magazine* 4 (October 1911): 476-78.

Jenkins, Walter S. *The Remarkable Mrs. Beach, American Composer,* ed. John Baron. Warren, Mich.: Harmonie Park Press, 1994.

Kelton, Mary Katherine. "The Songs of Mrs. H. H. A. Beach." D. M. A. diss., University of Texas, Austin, 1992.

Krehbiel, Henry Edward. *Music and Manners in the Classical Period,* 3d ed. New York: Charles Scribner's, 1899.

Merrill, E. Lindsey, "Mrs. H. H. A. Beach: Her Life and Music," Ph.D. diss., University of Rochester, 1963.

"Mrs. H. H. A. Beach." *Musikliterarische Blätter* (Vienna) 1 (March 21, 1904) 1-4.

Tick, Judith, "Passed Away is the Piano Girl." In *Women Making Music: The Western Art Tradition, 1150–1950*, ed. Jane Bowers and Judith Tick. Urbana: The University of Illinois, 1986.

Discography

Cabildo/Six Short Pieces. Lauren Flanigan, soprano; Charlotte Hellikant, mezzo-soprano; Anthony Dean Griffey, tenor: Paul Groves, tenor; Eugene Perry, baritone; Thomas Paul, bass; Christopher O'Riley, piano. *Give Me Not Love,* op, 61; *In the Twilight,* op. 85, *O Mistress Mine,* op. 37 no. 1; *Dark Is the Night,* op. 11, no. 1; *Jeune fille et jeune fleur,* op. 1, no. 3. Delos 3170 (1995).

Distant Playing Fields. Mary Ellen Callahan, soprano; Robert Guarino, tenor; Martin Hennessy, piano. *When Soul Is Joined to Soul,* op. 62; *Message,* op. 93; *Sea Song,* op. 10 no. 3; *Night Song at Amalfi,* op. 78 no. 2. Newport Classic 85629 (1998).

Canticle of the Sun. Guadelupe Kreysa, soprano; Richard Turner, tenor; Paul Hardy, organ/piano. *On a Hill* (arr. of traditional song); *Spirit of Mercy,* op. 125. Albany 295 (1998).

Songs by Clara Schumann, Poldowski, Amy Beach. Lauralyn Kolb, soprano; Don McMahon, piano. *Nachts,* op. 35, no. 1; *Fairy Lullaby* op. 37, no. 1; *Far Awa',* op. 43, no. 4; *Extase,* op. 21, no. 2; *Take, O Take Those Lips Away,* op. 37, no. 2; *Western Wind,* op. 11, no. 2; *Forgotten,* op. 41, no. 3; *Wir drei,* op. 551, no. 2. Albany 109 (1994).

Women at an Exposition. Sunny Joy Langton, soprano; Kimberly Schmidt, piano. *Sweetheart, Sigh No More,* op. 14, no. 3. Koch International Classics 7240 (1993).

Songs of an Innocent Age. Paul Sperry, tenor; Irma Vallecillo, piano. *Ariette,* op. 1, no. 4; *Take, O Take Those Lips Away,* op. 37, no. 2; *O Mistress Mine,* op. 37, no. 1. Albany 34 (1994).

Sure on this Shining Night. Robert White, tenor; Samuel Sanders, piano. *The Year's at the Spring,* op. 44, no. 1. Hyperion 66920 (1997).

The Art of Jussi Bjoerling. Jussi Bjoerling, tenor; accompanist not named. *Ah, Love, But a Day,* op. 44, no. 2. EMD/EMI Classics 66306 (1997).

Carolyn Heafner Sings American Songs. Browning Songs (3) for voice and piano, CRI 854 (2000).

Juni

O Junitage im Sonnenschein
Im flutenden, wolkenlosen!
Buntblumige Wiesen und blühender Wein!
Und in den Gärten, landaus, landein,
Herzkirschen und Rosen!

Herzkirschen und Rosen,
und Blühend am Hang
Resedaduftende Reben!
Die Nächte so weich und die Tage so lang!
So heiter die Stirnen, so hell der Gesang!
So wonig das Leben!

Die Geissblattlauben voll heimlichem Schall,
Voll leiseim flüsterndem Kosen.
Und jeder Lufthauch ein Duftesschwall,
Und überall Segen und überall
Herzkirschen und Rosen!

O sunny days of June divine,
Fresh beauty each hour discloses!
Of blossoming meadows, and zephyrs benign,
And in the gardens with fruit and vine,
Heartsease and Roses!

Heartsease and roses;
a perfume strong
The mellowing vineyards are giving!
The nights so lang'rous, the days so long!
So beaming the brow, and so ringing the song,
Such joy but in living!

Yon leafy arbor all tremulous there,
Doth sigh as at night it reposes.
Rich blessings fill all the scented air
With rapture surpassing; and ev'rywhere
Heartsease and roses!

June
[for Voice, Violin, and Piano]

Erich Jansen

Mrs. H. H. A. Beach
(Amy Beach)
Op. 51, No. 3

10
poco rit.
fruit and vine,
Hearts
ease and
mf
poco rit.
f
13
a tempo
rall.
Ro - - ses!
p
pp
dolce
a tempo
dolce
rall.
p
17
pp dolcissimo
a tempo
Heart's ease and Ro - ses; a per - fume strong The
pp dolcissimo
pp
a tempo
pp

20
cresc.
mel - low-ing vine-yards are giv - ing! The nights so lan - g'rous, the
pp
cresc.
23
days so long! So beam-ing the brow, and so ring-ing the song,
cresc.
26
f
poco rit.
Such joy but in liv - - - - -
f
dim.
poco rit.
f
Ped.
Ped.

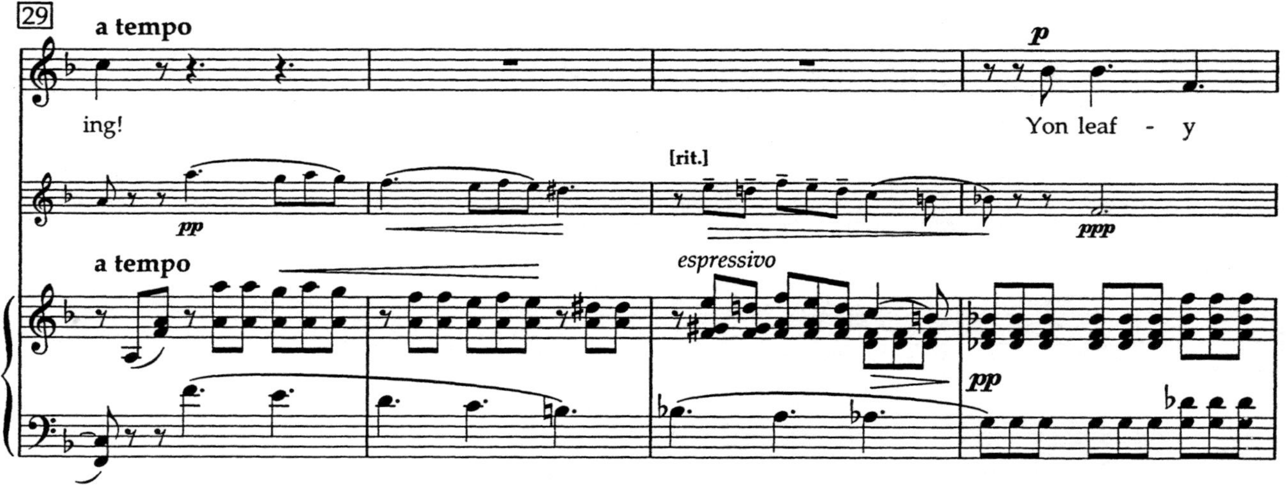
29
a tempo
p
ing!
Yon leaf - y
[rit.]
pp
ppp
a tempo
espressivo
pp

33
a tempo
cresc.
ar - bor all trem - u-lous there,
Doth sigh as at
dolcissimo

36
f
molto rit.
night it re-pos - es.
Rich bless - ings
cresc.
pp
molto rit.
f
colla voce
pp

39
a tempo
cresc.
fill all the scen - ted air With rap - ture sur-pass - ing; and
cresc.
a tempo
cresc.
42
rall.
ev - 'ry - where Heart's - - - ease and
f
rall.
ff
colla voce
45
a tempo
Ro - - ses!
ff
a tempo
ff

Rendezvous
[for Voice, Violin, and Piano]

Leonora Speyer

Mrs. H. H. A. Beach
(Amy Beach)
Op. 120

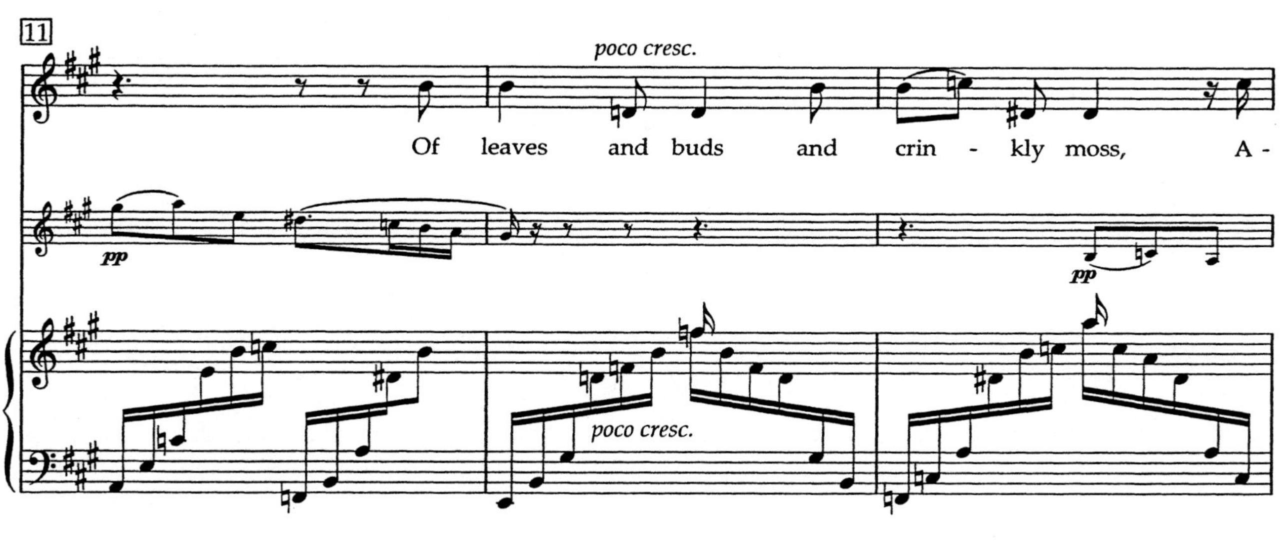
11
poco cresc.
Of leaves and buds and crin - kly moss, A -
pp
pp
poco cresc.

14
cresc.
bove me tan - gled boughs will toss,
cresc.
dolce marcato

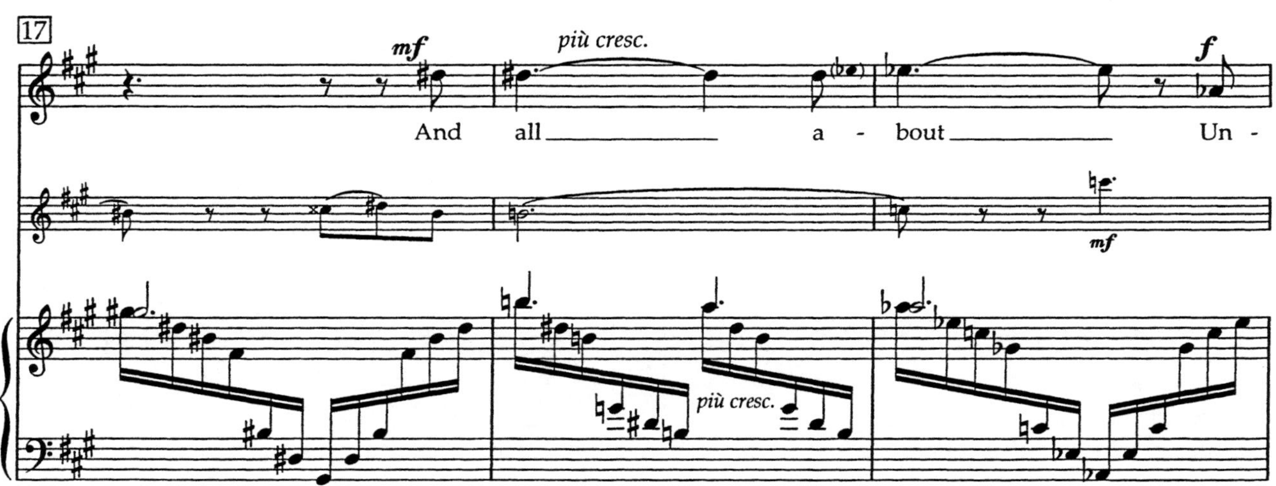
17
mf
più cresc.
f
And all a - bout Un -
mf
più cresc.

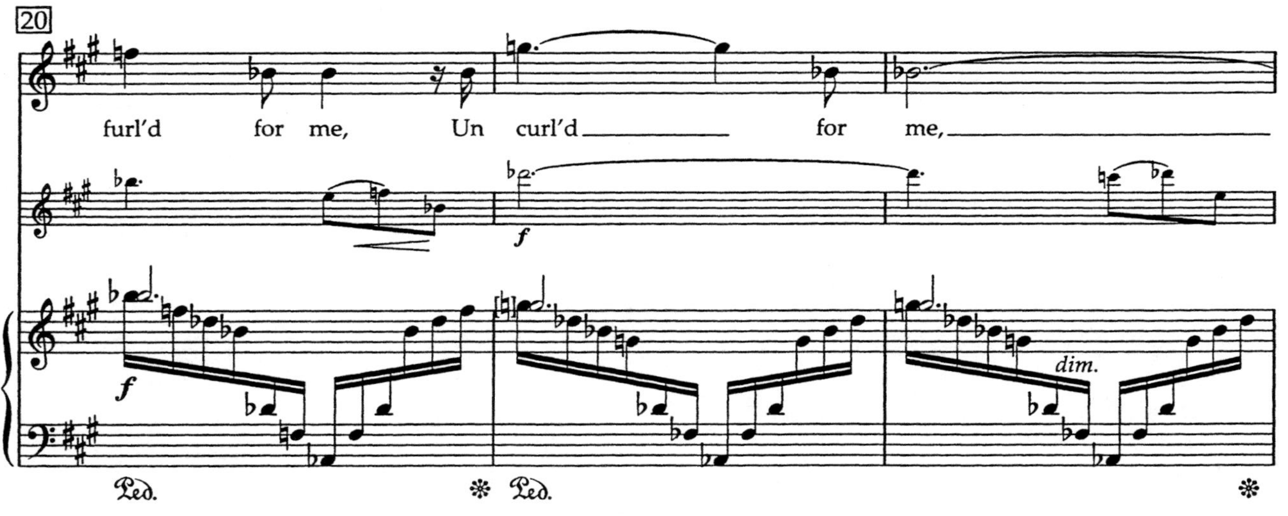
20
furl'd for me, Un curl'd for me,
f
f
dim.
Ped.
Ped.

23
dim.
The fern's un - hur - - ried
dim.
p
Ped.
Ped.

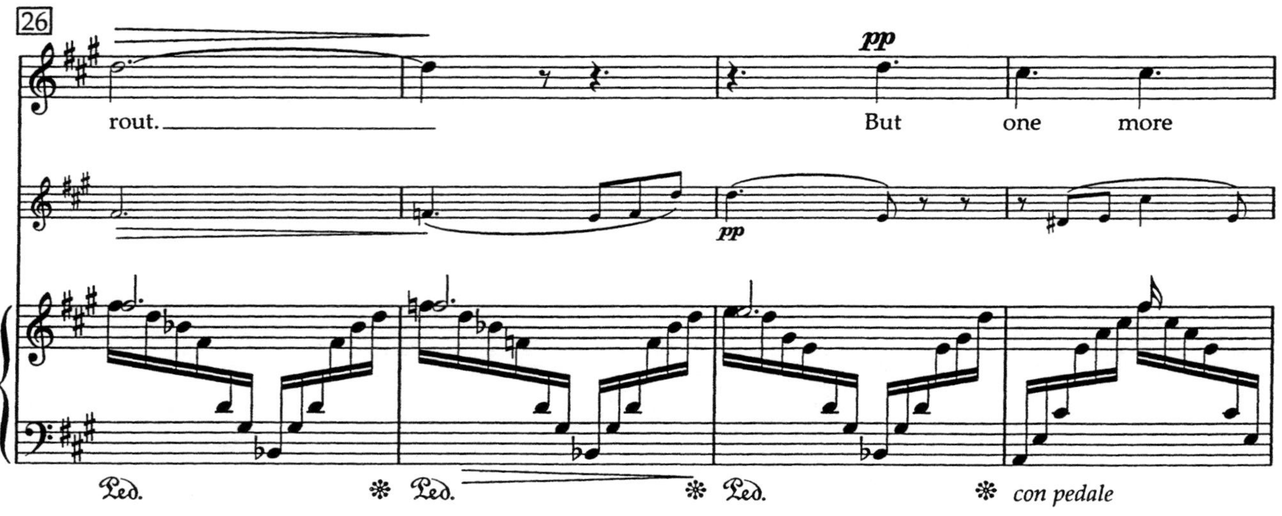
26
pp
rout. But one more
pp
Ped.
Ped.
Ped.
con pedale

30
mf
month so soon Wait for me, June,
cresc.
mf
34
f
my June.
ff
f
Ped.
38
rit.
p
pp
The birds, live
p
pp
rit.
p
pp
dim.
Ped.

42
a tempo
cups of sing - ing wine, On
dolciss.
a tempo
Ped.
Ped.
45
their tall stems of larch and pine Will
pp sempre
con pedale
48
cresc.
brim for me the glad day long The sol - ace of their
cresc.
cresc.

51
mf
bub - bling song.
The night - in -
mf
mf
Ped.
55
f
gale will trill for me, Will spill for
f
f
Ped.
Ped.
Ped.
58
dim.
me
Her shy, ex -
dim.
dim.

61
poco rit.
pp
ult - ant grail;
But
pp
poco rit.
pp
65
a tempo
cresc.
one more month so soon
mf
Wait for me,
a tempo
cresc.
mf
69
f
June, my June!
ff
f

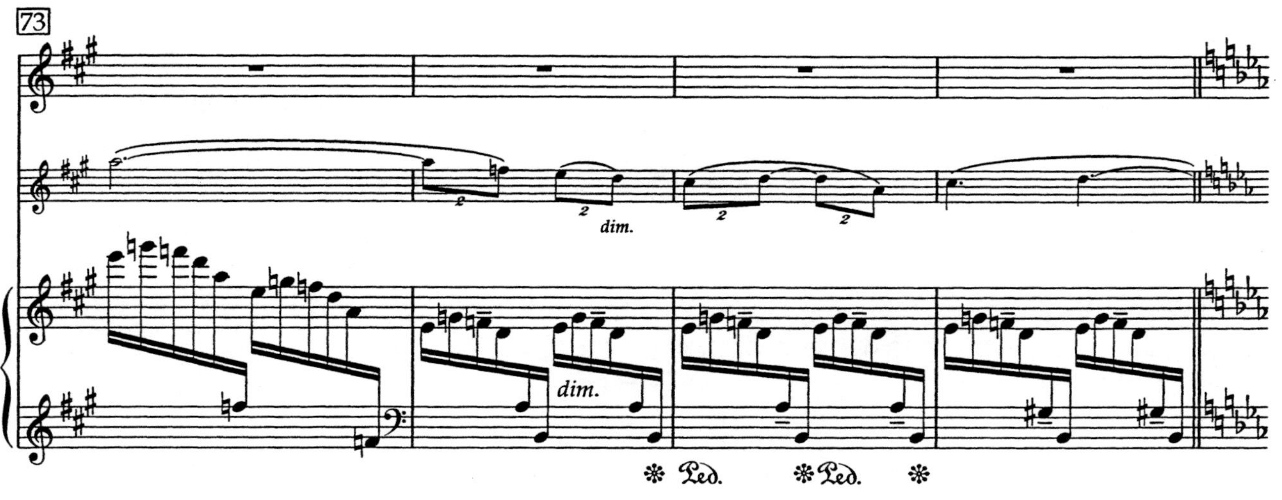
73
dim.
dim.
Ped.
Ped.

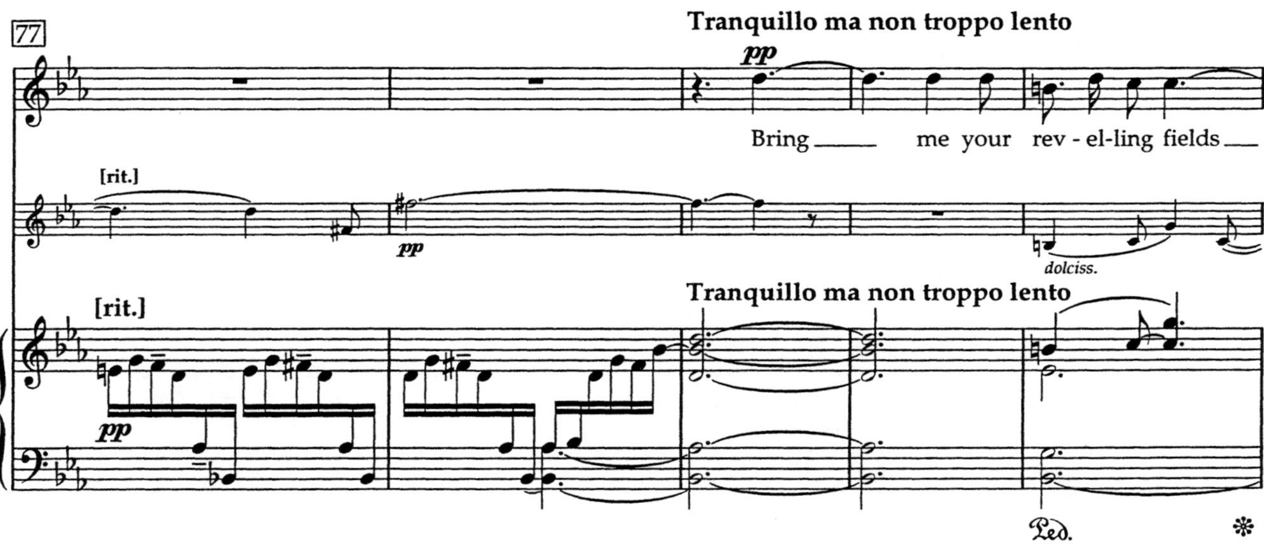
77
Tranquillo ma non troppo lento
pp
Bring ___ me your rev - el-ling fields ___
[rit.]
pp
dolciss.
Tranquillo ma non troppo lento
[rit.]
pp
Ped.

82
___ and woods, Your hills and lakes of sol - emn moods; ___
ppp
Ped.
Ped.
Ped.

87
dolcissimo
Gath - er the stars fresh pluck'd and
ppp
8va
91
sweet,
Scat - ter them there
(8va)
94
molto rit.
pp
where we two meet,
I
ppp
(8va)
molto rit.

97
Tempo I
bring to you still near to
dolciss.
Tempo I
ppp
101
me Still dear to me
dim.
105
p
My an - cient grief still
pp

109
rall.
ppp
new.
ppp
But
senza sordino
rall.
ppp
colla voce
una corda
113
a tempo
one more month so soon
ppp
cresc. poco a poco
cresc. poco a poco
tre corde
116
sempre cresc.
Wait for me, June, Wait for me,
f

119
ff
June,
my
f
f
123
rit.
June,
ff
rit.
Ped.
Ped.
126
Allegro molto
my
June!
ff
sfz
Allegro molto
8va
sfz

A Mirage
[for Voice, Violin, Cello, and Piano]

Bertha Ochsner

Mrs. H. H. A. Beach
(Amy Beach)
Op. 100, No. 1

*If the piano accompaniment is used alone, only the first two measures should be played as Prelude before the voice enters. The cello obbligato or both strings may be omitted.

10
sil - ver, While the moon, a disc of cob - webs, Shin - ing in the pal - lid

14
heav-ens, Ghost - like thro' the eve - ning shad-ows.
poco cresc.

18
poco cresc.
Now the loft - y eu - ca - lyp - tus Stretch - es forth its chalk - y

21
pp
branch-es Toward the love-ly, lus-tred heav - ens, While the drow-sy west-wind sigh - ing
pp
pp
pp

25
espr.
Sings the theme of lam-en - ta-tion, the
pp
dolcissimo
pp
dolcissimo
ppp

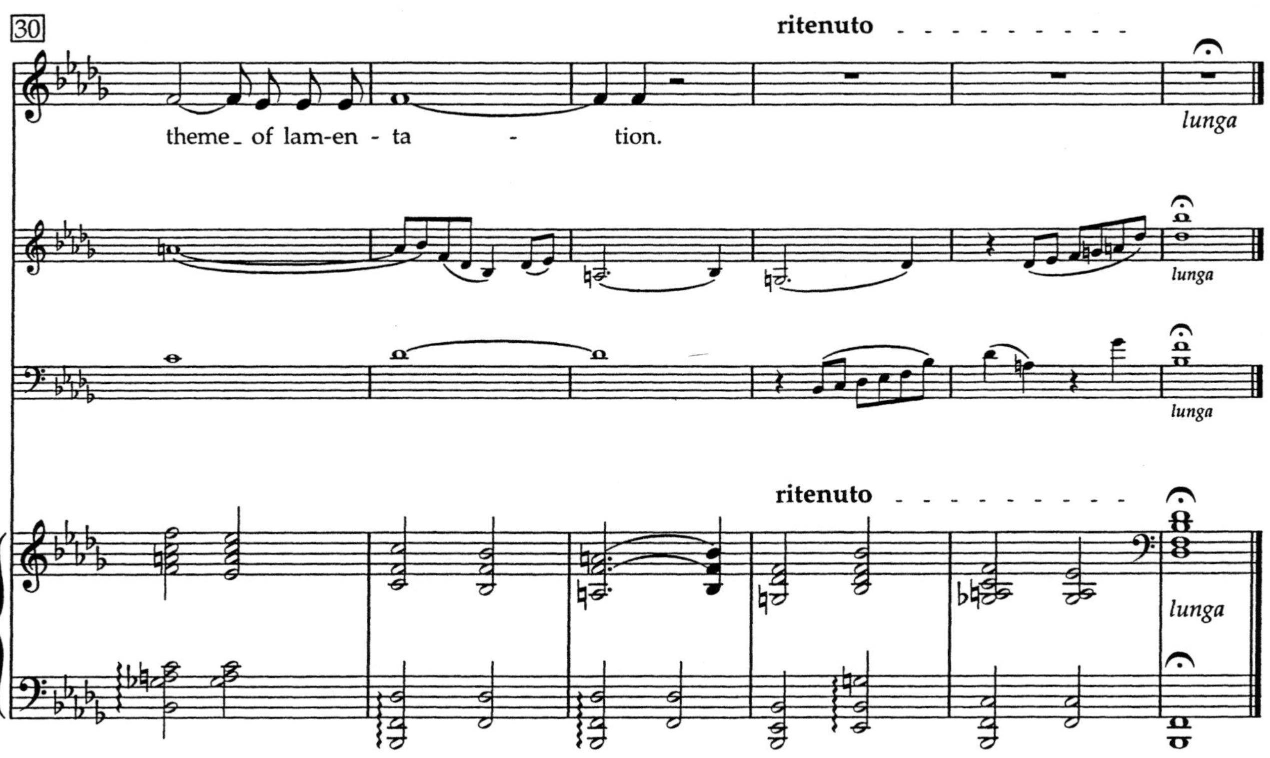
30
ritenuto
theme of lam-en - ta - tion.
lunga
lunga
lunga
ritenuto
lunga

Stella viatoris
[for Voice, Violin, Cello, and Piano]

Jesse Hague Nettleton **Mrs. H. H. A. Beach**
(Amy Beach)
Op. 100, No. 2

Adagio

Voice
Violin
Cello
Piano

pp
Dun grows the sky;

f p mf
*
L.H.
sfz ppp
L.H.
Ped.

6

p
The cloud-rack dark ___ In the west hangs
dim.

p
L.H.
p ppp
Ped.

*The cello obbligato, or both strings, may be omitted, and the piano accompaniment used alone. In the latter case, the choice notes (small print) should be played.

10
pp
p
low;
The wind moans by;
pp
p
pp
p
L.H.
L.H.
R.H.
pp
7
6
Ped.
Ped.

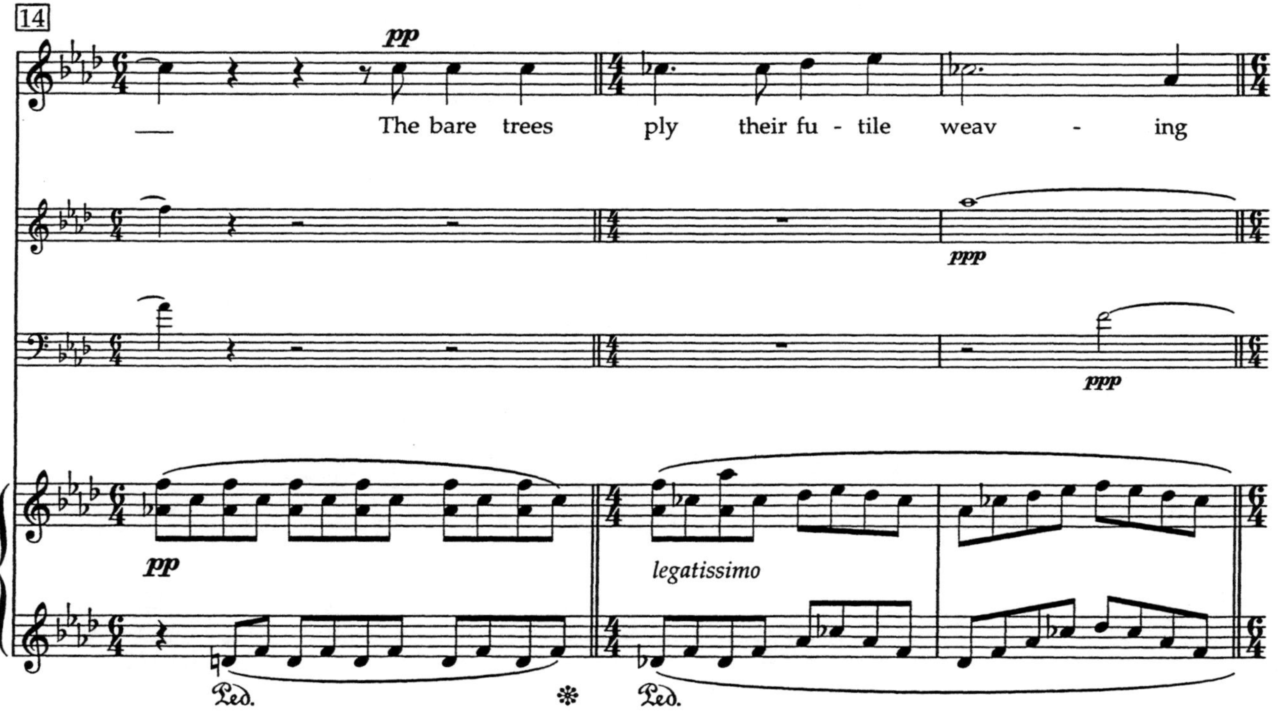
14
pp
The bare trees ply their fu - tile weav - ing
ppp
ppp
pp
legatissimo
Ped.
Ped.

17
dolcissimo
Sad and slow;
ppp
Ped.
Ped.
Ped.

20
pp
But o'er the east
The grim clouds
accel.
poco a poco cresc.
pp
pp
accel.
poco a poco cresc.
Ped.

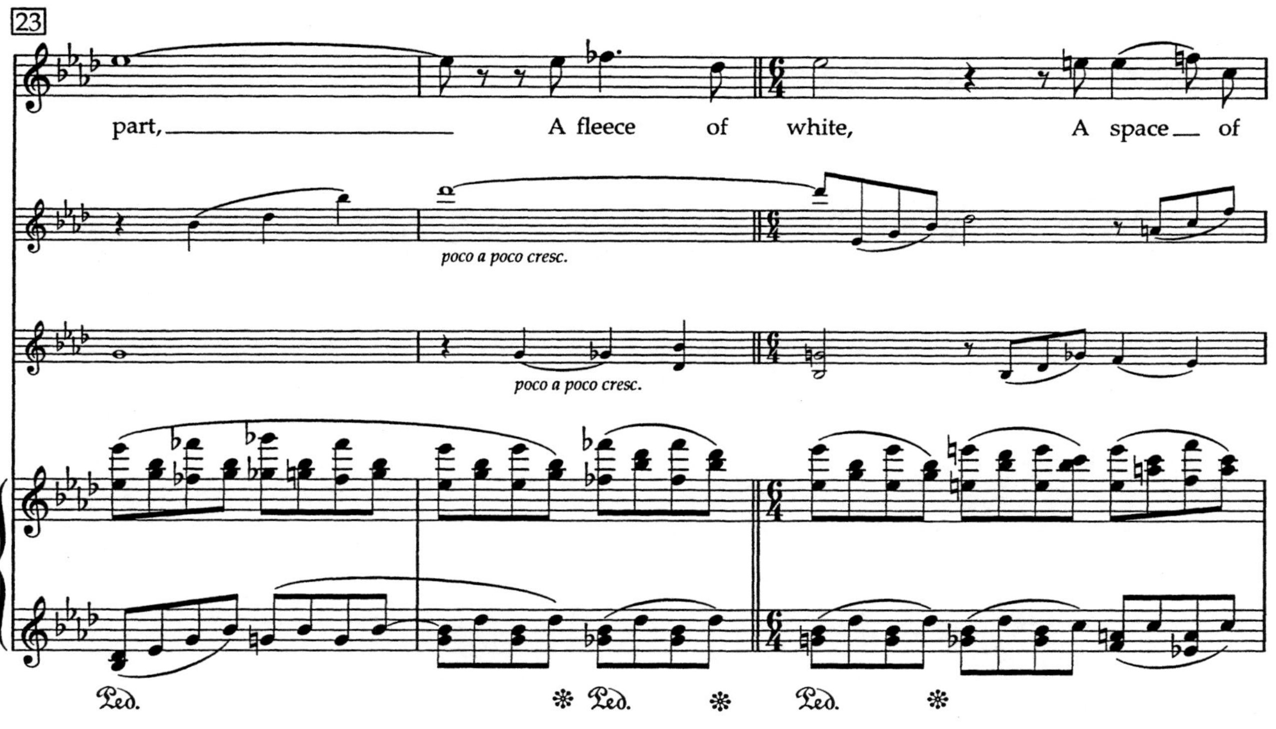
23
part,
A fleece of white,
A space of
poco a poco cresc.
poco a poco cresc.
Ped.
Ped.
Ped.

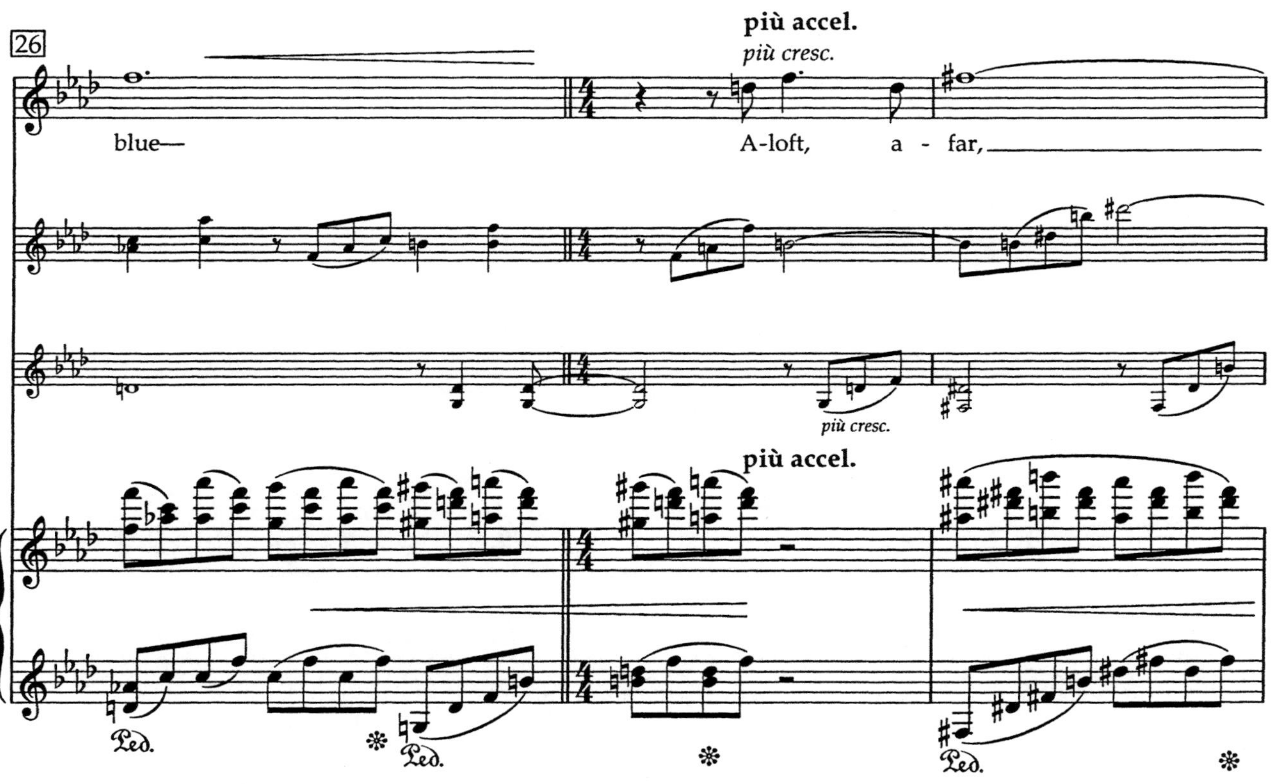
26
più accel.
più cresc.
blue—
A-loft, a - far,
più cresc.
più accel.
Ped.
Ped.
Ped.

29
cresc.
There's a sin - gle star,
Like the kind - ness of
Ped.
Ped.

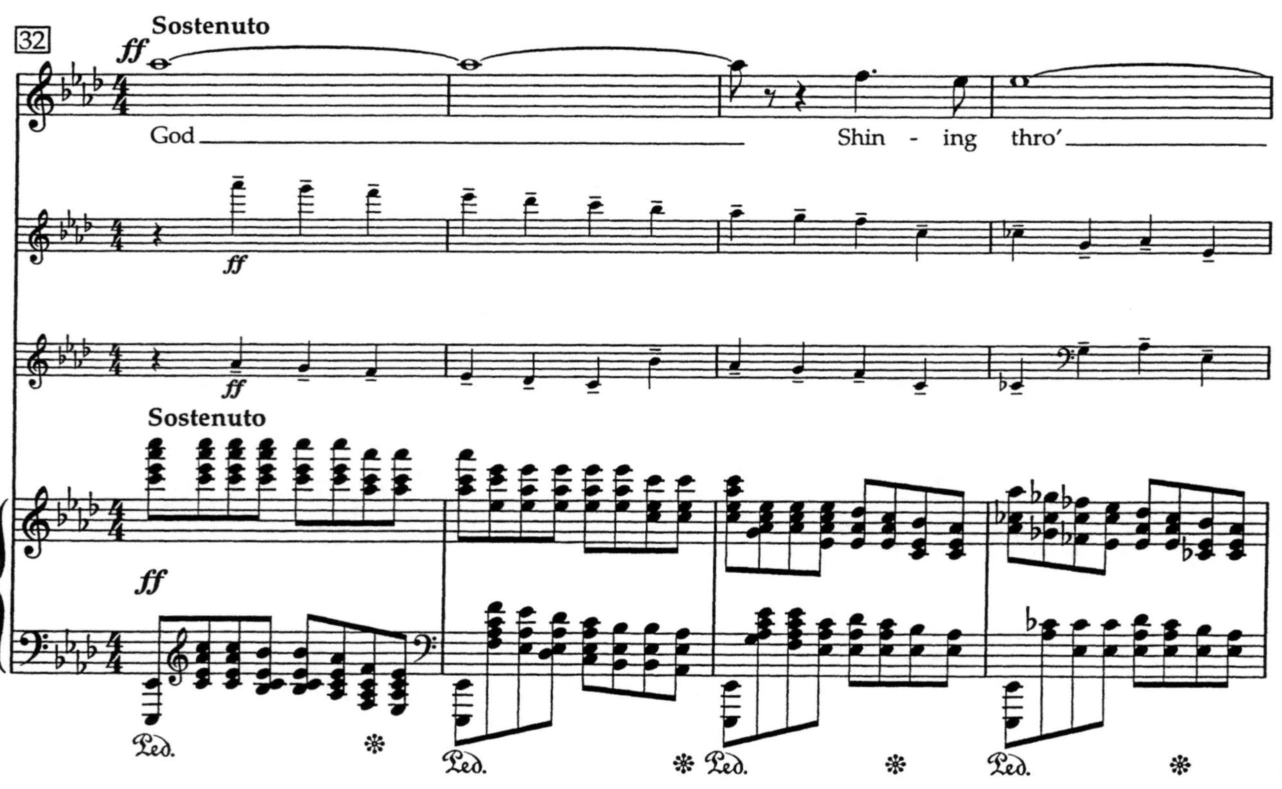
32
Sostenuto
God
Shin - ing thro'
Sostenuto
Ped.
Ped.
Ped.
Ped.

36
ff
Like the kind-ness of God

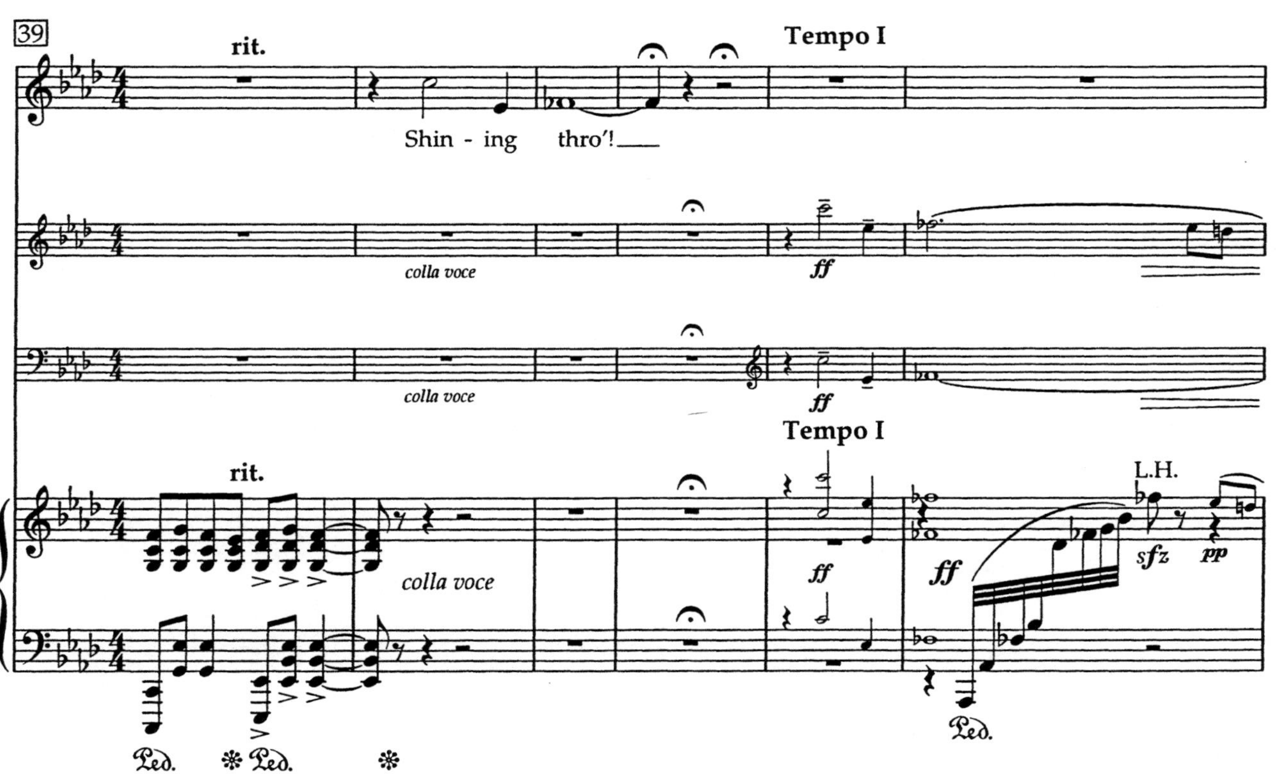
39
rit.
Tempo I
Shin - ing thro'!
colla voce
ff
colla voce
ff
Tempo I
rit.
colla voce
ff
ff
L.H.
sfz
pp

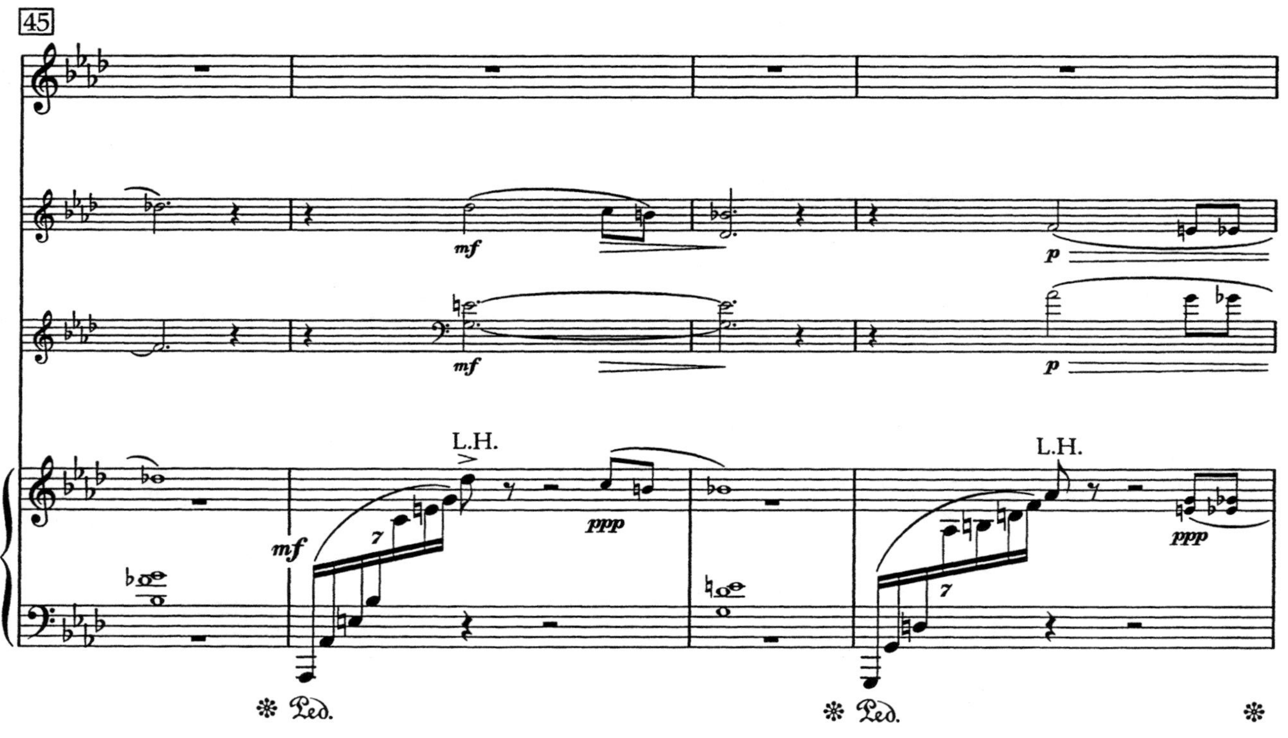
45
L.H.
L.H.

49
Like the kind - ness of God
Shin-ing thro'!

Margaret Ruthven Lang

(1867–1972)

Judith Cline

Margaret Ruthven Lang was born in Boston, Massachusetts, on November 27, 1867, to Francis Morse Burrage Lang and Benjamin Johnson (B. J.) Lang. She was the oldest of three children born into a musically rich household. Her mother was reportedly a gifted amateur singer and her father was an eminent composer, conductor, and teacher in the Boston community for more than fifty years. He was her principal teacher until his death in 1909, and had, perhaps, the greatest influence on his daughter's musical development, as well as her subsequent successful career as a composer. Margaret Ruthven Lang composed and published steadily for approximately thirty years during her long lifetime.

A better understanding of Lang's development as a composer may be gained by first explaining the illustrious career of her father. Benjamin Johnson Lang, a Bostonian, made his musical debut in 1849 at the age of twelve, playing Chopin's *Ballade*, op. 47, in A-flat. Six years later he left his positions as church organist and teacher to embark upon a three-year German sojourn to study and concertize. While on this trip he began lasting friendships with Franz Liszt (1811–1886) and Liszt's daughter, Cosima. In later years his friendship with Cosima would provide him with an entrée into the circle of luminaries surrounding Richard Wagner (1813–1883).

Upon his return to Boston in 1858, B. J. Lang began a thirty-nine year affiliation with the Handel and Haydn Society, serving as the organization's accompanist and director. He also founded two choral societies: the Apollo Club, a male chorus, and the Cecilia Society, a mixed chorus. His daughter was to premiere a number of her choral works with these two groups.[1]

B. J. Lang's importance as a performer and musical entrepreneur in Boston is indisputable, but perhaps his greatest influence on Boston's musical community came from the hundreds of pupils he taught, including Edward MacDowell (1860–1908), George Chadwick (1854–1931), and his own daughter.[2] B. J. Lang was a demanding, yet devoted teacher, and believed that technique was the basis for excellence in music.

Margaret Ruthven Lang was raised in a cosmopolitan household where visitors from overseas were welcome and frequently present. In addition, she was accustomed to traveling abroad with her parents, making her first trip to Europe at the age of two. As a child she visited the home of Richard Wagner and knew the Wagner children as playmates.[3]

Lang's studies in composition and piano with her father began at the age of twelve and continued for seven years. In 1886 she had the opportunity to study counterpoint with Ludwig Abel (n.d.) and violin with Franz Drechsler (n.d.) in Munich. Upon her return from a year abroad, she began composition and orchestration studies with George Chadwick, who was then a professor at the New England Conservatory and who would later become its president. Lang was a serious pupil, undertaking the composition of large instrumental forms as well as shorter solo piano works, art songs, and choral pieces. In addition to her orchestration studies with Chadwick, Lang interviewed each member of the Boston Symphony to discuss the possibilities of their instruments.[4] She was immensely critical of her own work and confessed to disposing of compositions that she did not deem to be of high quality.

Lang's public career began soon after her return from Europe in 1887. The first public performance of her songs was given on December 14, 1887, in Boston's Chickering Hall. Frequent performances followed over the next few years. European audiences heard her song, *Ojalà* ("Would to God" in Arabic, Spanish, and Hebrew), a stunning miniature work on a text by George Eliot, when it was premiered at the Paris Exhibition on July 12, 1889, with MacDowell as the accompanist. In a review of the concert, Lang's song was singled out as one of "the most interesting and original compositions in the program. . . ."[5]

Indeed, 1889 was an important year for her blossoming career. Not only were her songs being performed, they were also chosen for publication by Arthur P. Schmidt of Boston. A. P. Schmidt Co. was Lang's principal publisher, as well as a promoter and publisher of many other women composers of the time. The professional relationship she maintained with Schmidt and his company is chronicled in the Lang holdings of the A. P. Schmidt Collection in the Library of Congress in Washington, D.C. Manuscripts for most of Lang's published works are preserved there, as well as numerous pieces of correspondence revealing her shrewd business sense, her lack of vanity in regard to her work, and her careful attention to detail in every aspect of the publication of her works.

The event that places Lang most prominently in the history of American music took place in 1893. Lang's orchestral work, *Dramatic Overture*, op. 12, no. 2, was premiered by the Boston Symphony Orchestra under the baton of Arthur Nikisch. This performance marked the first time a major American symphony orchestra had programmed and performed an orchestral work by a woman composer. Lang was twenty-six years old at the time and looked back on the occasion in her later years with her characteristic humor and modesty, stating in a 1967 article that she "crept into the balcony and hid."[6] Reviews of the work were lukewarm, offering only modest encouragement and faint congratulations.

Lang wrote and published steadily until her early fifties. Her most prolific years were from 1893 through 1907, during which time seventy songs, seven solo piano works, and five choral compositions were published. After the death of her father in 1909, publishing became sporadic, with fallow periods of two to three years between compositions. Finally, in 1919, Theodore Presser published *Three Pianoforte Pieces for Young Players*, op. 60, her last work.

Lang's sudden silence in the midst of a successful composing career raises many questions. In an autobiographical note dated 1960, she wrote that she had had a calling from God to publish "messages" He was sending through her.[7] Six inspirational booklets, entitled *Messages from God, 1927–1939* are included in the Lang Family Papers found in the Boston Public Library. Lang wrote that she printed, at her own expense, over 6,000 copies of these booklets, and that she had spent all of her earnings from her music sales to do so.

In addition to her religious calling, another possible reason for Lang's decision to cease publishing music may have been her family obligations. Benjamin Johnson Lang died in 1909, leaving a large estate for the time, worth approximately $600,000. Margaret, who never married, was left to care for her aging mother. In an undated letter to her friend and colleague, composer Mabel Wheeler Daniels (1877–1971), Lang related part of the toll her mother's care was taking on her. "All dates and days have been alike since my mother's pneumonia; and it is only today that she is mending and I can look about me and pick up some of the threads."[8] For twenty-five years Lang was the companion and helper for her mother until Francis Lang's death in 1934.

One can imagine the sense of being "out-of-time" Lang must have had when, free from her responsibilities in the home, she began to look at the changes that had taken place in the world of music since 1919, the year her last work had been published. It may have seemed prudent to Lang, financially comfortable and sixty-seven years old at the time, to remain fully retired from the professional world.

She did remain intensely interested in the publication and sales of her music, although she indicated she thought it was out-of-date. In 1947, in response to a request for permission to arrange her song *Ghosts,* for three-part women's chorus, Lang responded positively, but added, " Why should anybody want to sing this song?"[9] Records of the A. P. Schmidt collection indicate the last correspondence to Lang was a notification of a broadcast fee and sales returns for *Day is Gone*, op. 40, no. 2 in December of 1951.[10]

In 1955, Lang, ever the critic and keen observer of the musical world, wrote to her longtime friend, Marian MacDowell,

> I have read your letter five times and have longed to be able to speak — instead of writing [,] for your reference to "modern music" opens a wide door. And I rejoice to learn of the welcome to MacDowell in Europe, as well as here. It is a most comforting and hopeful sign of hunger and welcome to the past.[11]

In the same letter, following a brief and critical discussion of Honegger's *Je suis Compositeur*, Lang continued, "I am glad, very glad not to be active in any musical way, but only a thankful listener."[12] The sentiments expressed in this letter show that Lang not only did not envision herself as a composer who had a place in the modern musical world, but that she did not wish to have a place in it either.

In fact, Lang was a "thankful" and devoted listener to many musical groups in Boston, most especially the Boston Symphony Orchestra. At the time of her death, she was the oldest subscriber in the Symphony's history. She had held season tickets for ninety-one consecutive years. In her honor, the Symphony placed a small plaque on the seat she customarily filled in Symphony Hall.[13] Lang was also honored by the Boston Symphony on November 24, 1967, in a celebration of her 100th birthday. Erich Leinsdorf led the orchestra in performances of the *Old One Hundredth* chorale and *Sheep May Safely Graze*. Also on that special day, Henry B. Cabot, then President of the Board of Trustees of the Boston Symphony Orchestra, persuaded Lang to accompany him to Symphony Hall by automobile. She declined a ride home after the concert, preferring to take her customary route on the subway.

Lang lived the rest of her very long life near her family home at 8 Brimmer Street in Boston's Beacon Hill area. She passed the time by attending concerts, reading, writing letters, and receiving visitors. According to family members, Lang was a voracious reader who developed passionate enthusiasms for new subjects. She thoroughly researched topics such as theology and philosophy but also enjoyed reading letters from her young nieces and nephews to whom she wrote amusing and informed responses. At the age of 103, Lang wrote to a great-nephew that she was corresponding with sixty to seventy people in three languages.

This remarkable woman remained in reasonably good health until shortly before her death on May 29, 1972, six months before her 105th birthday. Funeral services were held at the Church of the Advent in Boston, and in keeping with Lang's attention to detail in life, she had left directions to the clergy for her funeral and burial services. An interesting aspect of these directions is Lang's request for music, "the softest possible organ background of Hymnal Music." She also asked for the service to be "very simple, plain, holy and earnest."[14]

At the time of her death, she left few close relatives and only a handful of individuals who knew her beyond a passing acquaintance. As a composer, she had outlived her style of writing. In her mid-sixties she had looked back on her career and made a conscious decision to end her active musical life. From the carefully collected and edited scrapbooks she left for posterity to record her and her father's careers, one can see the pride she took in her accomplishments as a composer; positive reviews, articles and programs recall a prolific and moderately successful career. Her pride, however, was tempered by modesty. Lang seemed not to see her achievements as particularly unusual or groundbreaking. Describing them, as Ethel Syford wrote in *The New England Magazine*: "It is the more poetic truth and beauty which she strives for and attains and it is this unfailing quality which makes her songs of a higher order than those produced by any other American composer."[15]

Although the *Dramatic Overture*, op. 12, was never repeated after the 1893 performance, the disappointing reviews did not prevent Lang from continuing her pursuit of a career as an orchestral composer.[16] Lang submitted a score of another orchestral overture, *Witichis*, op. 10, to the Bureau of Music of the 1893 World's Fair (Columbian Exposition) in Chicago. From the total of twenty-one American composers who responded to the call for scores, only four works were chosen for performance, Lang's *Witichis* among them. Theodore Thomas and Max Bendix conducted the Chicago Orchestra in three performances of this work during the summer of 1893.

Lang's other orchestral works include another overture, *Totila*, op. 23, and three dramatic scenes for solo voice and orchestra: *Sappho's Prayer to Aphrodite*, for alto and orchestra, performed in 1896 in New York; *Phoebus's Denunciation of the Furies at His Delphian Shrine*, for baritone and orchestra; and *Armida*, op. 24, for soprano and orchestra. *Armida* was performed January 12, 1896, by the Boston Symphony Orchestra under the direction of Emil Paur.

Lang's last orchestral composition was the *Ballade in D*, op. 36, performed by the Baltimore Symphony in a "Women in Music Grand Concert" of 1901. All of her orchestral manuscripts have been lost or, more likely, destroyed by Lang herself. The only existing example of instrumental writing which might give a hint to her orchestral style is a chamber setting derived from the full orchestration for her 1916 choral work, *The Heavenly Noël*, op. 57.[17]

A. P. Schmidt published Lang's first piano works in 1894. In the same year, she published two piano compositions in *Half Hours with the Great Composers* (J. B. Millet), a collection of piano études, character pieces, and transcriptions. Other American composers represented in this collection were Edward MacDowell, George Chadwick, Horatio Parker (1863–1919), Arthur Foote (1853–1937), and Clara Kathleen Rogers (1844–1931) (see this volume and Volume 6).

Solo piano works interested Lang until the end of her composing career. Thick textures, depictive musical motifs, and adherence to traditional forms characterize the pieces. She published a total of twenty-one piano compositions, including three groups of pieces for young players. The last, *Three Pianoforte Pieces for Young Players*, op. 60, were study pieces published by Theodore Presser in 1919.[18]

Vocal compositions comprise the remainder of Lang's works. She composed seventeen choral works for standard SATB, women's chorus, men's chorus, and other chorus/soloist/instrumental accompaniment combinations. A. P. Schmidt published *The Jumblies*, op. 5, for baritone solo, male chorus, and two pianos in 1890. These humorous settings of five limericks by Edward Lear enjoyed a modest success after their premiere performance by the Apollo Club in 1890. The Handel and Haydn Society of Boston performed them as recently as 1975.

Lang published more than 132 songs between 1889 and 1916.[19] The record of sales receipts in the A. P. Schmidt Collection at the Library of Congress shows that her works were popular from coast to coast in the United States as well as in the United Kingdom. Lang experimented with various compositional styles throughout her career, trying to incorporate elements of impressionism and folk song into her fundamentally German Romantic technique. Her songs may be roughly divided into four categories: songs based solely on the German Romantic tradition, songs exhibiting the influences of impressionism, songs which have elements of folk song (usually from the British Isles, frequently in dialect), and a miscellaneous category including humorous songs and teaching songs for children.

One of Lang's earliest published songs to gain attention was the aforementioned *Ojalà*. The transparent texture of this song reflects the wistfulness of George Eliot's poetry asking the forces of nature to carry her away. The text setting is expert, the rhythmic values in the music being identical to the meter of the poem. The voice and piano parts are joined in a way that suggests a conversation between the poet and nature. In only thirty-three measures Lang created an elegant chorale with an effective musical interpretation of a simple poem.

In *Spinning Song*, op. 9, no. 2, published in 1892, Lang creates an ominous brooding atmosphere with the accompaniment. The text, by Lizette Woodworth Reese, tells the story of a young woman who is spinning while she awaits her lover's return from the sea. Given the title of the poem one might assume that Lang's use of a constant rhythmic motive, similar to that of Franz Schubert's (1797–1828) *Gretchen am Spinnrade*, is a depiction of the spinning wheel. However, Lang seems to be using this constant rhythmic motion to not only illustrate the spinning wheel, but also to depict the unsettled feelings of the woman. She appears to be working outdoors or at a window, enabling her to see white lilies and ships at sea. Her spinning is only referred to once, at the point in the poem when she displays her work, asking, "Was ever a whiter web than this that I spin today?" Here, Lang abruptly stops the rhythmic figure as if to draw attention to what the woman is saying. One can imagine the spinner stopping her frantic work to contemplate the results and the future of her labors. Will this thread be used for "a wedding gown or a winding sheet"? Throughout the song, Lang portrays a woman who is impatient and frustrated but seemingly resigned to her circumstances. This song provides the singer with varied melodic lines, effective ensemble passages with the piano, and well-written climactic moments. The most attractive aspect of the work is the dramatic development of the story and the character.

Lang is able to depict the changes in the woman by using strong unisons, sudden harmonic motions, turbulent rhythmic motives, and the abrupt absence of accompaniment.

In contrast to the forceful and tragic emotions of songs such as *Spinning-Song,* Lang also composed numerous children's songs. Included in her entire oeuvre of approximately 133 songs are many lullabies, songs depicting gardens, flowers, and babies, and two collections of songs (totaling twenty-six works) directed specifically to children. These contain skillfully written works, most notable in the collection entitled *Songs for Lovers of Children*, op. 39, published in 1903.

Lang also composed some unusual humorous songs, *Nonsense Rhymes and Pictures* and *More Nonsense Rhymes and Pictures*, settings of twenty-two limericks by Edward Lear. Although the texts are extremely silly, the songs themselves are sophisticated compositions. In a letter to Arthur P. Schmidt, Lang described these songs as "distinctly musical jokes for grown people, not children."[20]

Earlier in her career she had written settings of five Lear limericks for male chorus entitled *The Jumblies*. Throughout her life she retained a fondness for clever poems and word puzzles.[21] These solo vocal settings are ingenious and technically challenging. Lang overcame the metrical settings of the original limerick verses, setting many of them in $\frac{2}{4}$, $\frac{3}{4}$, or $\frac{4}{4}$. Perhaps the most amusing and difficult of the twenty-two limericks is *The Lady of Riga*, op. 42, no. 12, the text of which follows:

> There once was a Lady of Riga,
> Who smiled as she rode on a tiger.
> They returned from the ride
> With the Lady inside,
> And the smile on the face of the Tiger!

The song begins with an extended, rollicking piano introduction, affecting a jungle parade with, perhaps, drums and elephants. The imminent demise of "the Lady" is foretold with ominous *sforzando* chords. It seems all danger has passed once the singer enters. Lang uses rolled chords in the accompaniment, directions to sing slowly and gracefully, and a simple mid-range melody to lull the listener and "the Lady" into a false sense of security as she takes her ride on the tiger. All goes well until the singer reveals, with a sudden drop of a seventh, that "the Lady" is inside. The song is a technical and interpretive challenge for the singer, who must have solid command over an unusually wide range, as well as the ability to tell a joke set to music.

Many of Lang's songs are lighthearted, like the Lear settings, and some are quite sentimental. Certainly, Lang's biggest commercial success, *Irish Love Song*, op. 22, is an unabashedly sentimental song that was widely performed by many singers in America and the British Isles. *Irish Love Song* appears in the chronology of Lang's published vocal works between *Six Scotch Songs,* op. 20 (1895) and *Bonnie Ran the Burnie Down,* op. 25 (1897), a work for mixed chorus. At this time in American history, songs in various dialects and with obvious borrowed folk elements were very popular. The folk music of the British Isles was favored, along with texts that attempted to re-create the accents of Ireland and Scotland. Lang offered a body of compositions using these traits in eleven songs and three choral works published between 1895 and 1902.

Lang's later songs displayed an increasing musical maturity. One of the more interesting and satisfying works from this period is *Snowflakes*, op. 50, no. 3, set to a text by John Vance Cheney. Marked "quietly and delicately," *Snowflakes* is an effective musical depiction of falling snow. The initial piano introduction consists of cascading eighth note octaves, first in synchronization, then followed by a repetition of the same pitches in syncopation offset by a sixteenth rest. It is this pattern that produces the effect of parallelism that serves as an example of Lang's experiments with impressionism. The relationship between the voice and piano parts is skillfully explored by the weaving of melodic material from one part to the other. Lang preferred to evoke atmosphere in her songs, rather than to musically portray a specific text. We find in her songs instances in which she uses motives, such as in the falling pattern of *Snowflakes* or the spinning wheel motive in *Spinning-Song*, to suggest an overall mood or picture. Rarely does she isolate only a word or phrase to set in a pictorial manner. Because of this her songs allow interpretive freedom, dramatically supporting mood and text, but specific interpretation is rarely dictated in the music itself. Lang's published works represent the highest levels of song composition found in the latter half of the nineteenth century. Perhaps the prediction of the musicologist, Rupert Hughes, has yet to be realized when, in a description of Lang's compositional style, he said ". . . it is so sincere, so true to the underlying thought, that it seems to me to have an unusual chance of interesting attention and stirring emotions increasingly with the years."[22]

Notes

1. The two most successful works premiered by the Apollo Club were *The Maiden and the Butterfly* (1889) and *The Jumblies* (1890).

2. A cache of Lang Family Papers is located in the Boston Public Library Rare Books and Manuscripts Division. A folder of recollections by one of B. J. Lang's pupils, Mary P. Webster, gives insights into the teaching career of B. J. Lang.

3. Information from Francis Lang's diaries, Lang Family Papers, Boston Public Library.

4. Adams, Juliette A. Graves, "Musical Creative Work Among Women," *MUSIC* (Chicago) 9 (January 1896): 263-72.

5. Lang Family Papers, scrapbooks; Lang Family Papers, Boston Public Library.

6. Margo Miller, "Oldest B. S. O.Subscriber Recalls gentle World of the Past," *Boston Globe* (February 1967), Lang Family Papers Collection, Boston Public Library.

7. Lang Family Papers, Boston Public Library.

8. Lang and Daniels corresponded for many years. Their letters are in the Mabel Wheeler Daniels Collection at the Schlesinger Library, Radcliffe College.

9. A. P. Schmidt Collection, Library of Congress, letter dated April 11, 1947, from Hugh Gordon.

10. The broadcast fee was probably referring to a broadcast of Lang's only recorded work, *Irish Love Song*, op. 22, sung by Ernestine Schumann-Heinke on the Victor label and on the Pelican label, accompanied by orchestra. There is no documentation of Lang's having orchestrated this accompaniment.

11. Edward MacDowell's widow.

12. A. P. Schmidt Collection, Library of Congress, letter dated June 5, 1955.

13. 1st Balcony, Right, B1.

14. From a copy of the directions Lang left for the clergy at the Church of the Advent. Supplied by Betty Morris, librarian of the Church of the Advent.

15. Ethel Syford, "Margaret Ruthven Lang," *New England Magazine* 45/1 (March 1912).

16. George Chadwick, as well as Marian and Edward MacDowell, wrote notes of encouragement after this performance. Chadwick advised her to be philosophical about the newspaper critics who "do not respect themselves or one another, and they are absolutely no good to us." Lang Family Papers, Boston Public Library.

17. A manuscript found in the library of the New England Conservatory Boston, Massachusetts (Vault; ML 96; L29; op. 57). Arranged for three violins, cello, harp, women's chorus, solo voice, piano, and organ.

18. These pieces are listed in the holdings of the British Public Library and have not been cited in any other contemporary source. They are as follows: *One Summer Day*, op. 59 (Theodore Presser, 1919); and *Three Pianoforte Pieces for Young Players*, op. 60 (Theodore Presser, 1919). In a New York Manuscript Society list of works by Margaret Ruthven Lang, Lang added op. 59 under the heading of pianoforte solos, but then named it *Suite for Young Players*.

19. The number of songs Lang had published has been quoted in some sources as approximately 200. Given Lang's compulsion for detail, as evidenced by her rigorous record keeping and opus numbering, there is little possibility these additional seventy songs were published. With the addition of two songs which have not been located by this author, the entire oeuvre of Lang's songs numbers 133.

20. A. P. Schmidt Collection, Library of Congress.

21. *The Jumblies*, op. 5, 1890. Family members reported that Lang wrote anagrams and other word puzzles which she had printed and gave to veterans' hospitals in the 1940s and 1950s.

22. Hughes, Rupert, *Contemporary American Composers: The Women Composers* (Boston: L. C. Page, 1914).

List of Works

Songs

Lebewohl. (1889). Unpublished.

Der Sommer. (1889). Unpublished.

My Lady Jacqueminot. Text by Julie M. Lippincott. Boston: Arthur P. Schmidt and Co., 1889.

Lied der Nebenbuehlerin. (Song of the Rival Maid. Also referred to as *Roemerin*). Text by Joseph Victor von Scheffel. Boston: Arthur P. Schmidt and Co., 1889.

O What Comes Over the Sea. Text by Christina Rossetti. Boston: Arthur P. Schmidt and Co., 1889.

Eros. Text by Louise Chandler Moulton. Boston: Arthur P. Schmidt and Co., 1889.

Nameless Pain. Text by T. B. Aldrich. Boston: Arthur P. Schmidt and Co., 1889.

Song in the Twilight. Text by H. Bowman. Boston: Arthur P. Schmidt and Co., 1889. Huntsville, Tex.: Recital Publications, 1985.

Ghosts. Text by Richard Kendall Munkittrick. Boston: Arthur P. Schmidt and Co., 1889. Huntsville, Tex.: Recital Publications, 1985.

Ojalà. Text by George Eliot. Boston: Arthur P. Schmidt and Co., 1889. Bryn Mawr, PA: Hildegard Publishing Company, 2002.

In a Garden. Text by Algernon Charles Swinburne. Boston: Arthur P. Schmidt and Co., 1890. Huntsville, Tex.: Recital Publications, 1985.

A Spring Song. Text by Charlotte Pendleton. Boston: Arthur P. Schmidt and Co., 1890.

Deserted. Text by Richard Kendall Munkittrick. Boston: Arthur P. Schmidt and Co., 1890.

Meg Merriles. Text by John Keats. Boston: Arthur P. Schmidt and Co., 1890.

Beauty's Eyes. (1891) Unpublished.

Three Songs, op. 6. Boston: Arthur P. Schmidt and Co., 1891; Huntsville, Tex.: Recital Publications, 1985, nos. 2 and 3.
1. *Chinese Song.* Text by Judith Gautier
2. *A Bedtime Song.* Text by Eugene Field
3. *Lament.* Text by S. Galler

Three Songs of the Night, op. 7. Boston: Arthur P. Schmidt and Co., 1891. Huntsville, Tex.: Recital Publications, 1985, nos. 1 and 3.
1. *Night.* Text by Louise Chandler Moulton
2. *Slumber Song.* Anonymous
3. *The Harbor of Dreams.* Text by Frank Dempster Sherman

Boatman's Hymn. Boston: Arthur P. Schmidt and Co., 1892.

Three Songs of the East, op. 8. Boston: Arthur P. Schmidt and Co., 1892; Huntsville, Tex: Recital Publications, 1985, nos. 2 and 3.
1. *Oriental Serenade*
2. *Christmas Lullabye.* Text by John Addington Symonds
3. *A Poet Gazes on the Moon.* After Tang Yo-Su. Translated by Stuart Merrill

Four Songs, op. 9. Boston: Arthur P. Schmidt and Co., 1892; Huntsville, Tex.: Recital Publications, 1985, no. 4.
1. *Heliotrope.* Text by Frank Dempster Sherman
2. *The Sky Ship.* Text by Frank Dempster Sherman
3. *The Spinning Song.* Text by Lizette Woodworth Reese (Bryn Mawr, PA: Hildegard Publishing Company, 2002)
4. *Betrayed.* Text by Lizette Woodworth Reese

My True Love Lies Asleep. Text by Lizette Woodworth Reese. New York: G. Schirmer and Co., 1893.

Ay de Mi. Text by George Eliot. New York: G. Schirmer and Co., 1893.

Five Songs, op. 15. Boston: Arthur P. Schmidt and Co., 1893; Huntsville, Tex.: Recital Publications, 1983.
1. *King Olaf's Lilies.* Text by Lizette Woodworth Reese
2. *The Dead Ship.* Text by Lizette Woodworth Reese
3. *April Weather.* Text by Lizette Woodworth Reese
4. *The Garden of Roses.* From "Paul Palmer" by F. Marion Crawford
5. *Spinning Song.* Text by H. P. Kimball

Dear Land Of Mine (Mein theures land), op. 16. Text by Rudolf Baumbach. Translated by A. M. K. Boston: Arthur P. Schmidt and Co., 1893.

Hjarlis. (1894). Unpublished.

Five Norman Songs, op. 19. Text by John Addington Symonds. Boston: Arthur P. Schmidt and Co., 1894.
1. *My Turtle Dove*
2. *In the Greenwood*
3. *The Grief of Love*
4. *Before My Lady's Window*
5. *Desire*

Six Scotch Songs, op. 20. Boston: Arthur P. Schmidt and Co., 1895.
1. *Bonnie Bessie Lee.* Text by Robert Nicoll
2. *My Ain Dear Somebody.* Text by Robert Tanahill
3. *Maggie Away.* Text by James Hogg
4. *Love's Fear.* Text by Robert Tanahill
5. *Menie.* Text by Robert Nicoll
6. *Jock O'Hazeldean.* Text by Sir Walter Scott

Irish Love Song, op. 22. Boston: Arthur P. Schmidt and Co., 1895; Bryn Mawr, PA: Hildegard Publishing Company, 2002.

On An April Apple Bough. Text ed. Arthur Gray. New York: Bryan, Taylor and Co., 1896.

I Knew the Flowers Had Dreamed of You. Text by John B. Tabb. New York: Bryan, Taylor and Co., 1896.

The King is Dead, op. 27. Text by Madame Darmesteter. Boston: Arthur P. Schmidt and Co., 1898.

Three Songs, op. 28. Boston: Arthur P. Schmidt and Co., 1898.
1. *A Song for Candlemas.* Text by Lizette Wordworth Reese
2. *Arcadie.* Text by A. W. Coulton
3. *My Garden.* Text by P. B. Marston

Two Songs, op. 32. Text by Lizette Wordworth Reese. Boston: John Church, 1899.
1. *A Song of May*
2. *Lydia*

An Irish Mother's Lullaby, op. 34. Text by Mary Elizabeth Blake. Boston: Arthur P. Schmidt and Co., 1900. Also arranged for SSA, piano with violin obbligato.

Six Songs for Medium Voice, op. 37. Boston: Arthur P. Schmidt and Co., 1901.
1. *A Thought.* Text by John Vance Cheney
2. *Out of the Past*
3. *The Hills O'Skye.* Text by William McLennan
4. *Summer Noon.* Text by John Vance Cheney

5. *Tryste Noel.* Text by Louise Imogen Guiney
6. *Northward.* Text by Henry Copley Green

Four Songs, op. 38. Boston: Arthur P. Schmidt and Co., 1902.
1. *Orpheus.* Text by Mrs. Fields
2. *Sleepy-Man.* Text by Charles George Douglas Roberts
3. *The Span-O-Life.* Text by William McLennan
4. *Song in the Songless.* Text by George Meredith

Songs for Lovers of Children, op. 39. Text by Harriet Fairchild Blodgett. Boston: Arthur P. Schmidt and Co., 1903.
1. *Merry Christmas*
2. *Just Because*
3. *In the Night*
4. *Morning*
5. *Evening*
6. *The Sandman*
7. *To-Morrow*
8. *Three Ships*

The Sea Sobs Low. (1904). Unpublished.

Four Songs, op. 40. Boston: Arthur P. Schmidt and Co., 1904.
1. *Somewhere.* Text by John Vance Cheney
2. *Day is Gone.* Text by John Vance Cheney
3. *The Bird.* Text by Charles Kingsley
4. *Love is Everywhere.* Text by John Vance Cheney

Song of the Lilac, op. 41. Text by Louise Imogen Guiney. Boston: Arthur P. Schmidt and Co., 1904.

Nonsense Rhymes and Pictures, op. 42. Text by Edward Lear. Boston: Arthur P. Schmidt and Co., 1905; Huntsville, Tex.: Recital Publications, 1985; Bryn Mawr, PA: Hildegard Publishing Company, 1996.
1. *The Person of Filey*
2. *The Old Man of Cape Horn*
3. *The Person of Skye*
4. *The Old Man in the Kettle*
5. *The Old Man who said, "Hush!"*
6. *The Old Man who said, "Well!"*
7. *The Old Lady of France*
8. *The Young of Lady of Lucca*
9. *The Old Man with a Gong*
10. *The Old Person of Cassel*
11. *The Old Man in a Tree*
12. *The Lady of Riga*

More Nonsense Rhymes and Pictures, op. 43. Text by Edward Lear. Boston: Arthur P. Schmidt and Co., 1907.
1. *The Old Man of Dumbree*
2. *The Old Man with a Beard*
3. *The Young Lady in Blue*
4. *The Old Person of Ware*
5. *The Old Person of Rimini*
6. *The Young Lady Whose Eyes*
7. *The Old Person of Jodd*
8. *The Young Lady in White*
9. *The Young Lady of Parma*
10. *The Old Person of Ischia*

Grandmama's Songbook, op. 44. Words from "The Daisy and the Cowslip," poet unknown. Boston: Arthur P. Schmidt and Co., 1909.
1. *The Good Girl*
2. *The Worm*
3. *The Purloiner*
4. *The Truant*
5. *Come When You are Called*
6. *Dressed or Undressed*
7. *Faithful Pompey*
8. *The New Book*
9. *The Beautiful Doll*
10. *The Greedy Boy*
11. *The Bird-Catcher*
12. *Look at Your Copy*
13. *Miss Sophie*
14. *At Church*
15. *Going to School*
16. *Dangerous Sport*
17. *Politeness*
18. *The Hymn*

Three Songs, op. 46. Boston: Arthur P. Schmidt and Co., 1909.
1. *An Even Psalm.* Text by Marguerite Radcliffe-Hall
2. *Sometimes.* Text by Thomas S. Jones
3. *Out of the Night.* Anonymous

Spring, op. 47. Boston: Arthur P. Schmidt and Co., 1909.

Four Songs, op. 50. Boston: Arthur P. Schmidt and Co., 1912.
1. *A Garden is a Lovesome Thing.* Text by Thomas E. Brown
2. *A Song of the Spanish Gypsies (Solea).* Anonymous Translated by Alma Trettell
3. *Snowflakes.* Text by John Vance Cheney. Bryn Mawr, PA: Hildegard Publishing Company, 2002
4. *There Would I Be.* Text by John Vance Cheney

Two Songs, op. 54. Boston: Arthur P. Schmidt and Co., 1915.
1. *Into My Heart.* Text by A. E. Houseman
2. *Chimes.* Text by Alice Meynell

Cradle Song of the War, op. 55. Text by N. S. D. Boston: Oliver Ditson, 1916.

Choral

In a Meadow. (1889). Mixed chorus. Unpublished.

O Sweetheart Under the Gable Vine. (1889). Men's chorus. Unpublished.

The Maiden and the Butterfly, op. 4. (1889). Men's chorus. Unpublished.

The Jumblies, op. 5. Men's chorus. Text by Edward Lear. Boston: Arthur P. Schmidt and Co., 1890.

Love Plumes His Wings, op. 11. (1893). Mixed chorus. Unpublished.

Boatman's Hymn, op. 13. Mixed chorus. Boston: Arthur P. Schmidt and Co., 1892.

Bonnie Ran the Burnie Down, op. 25. Mixed chorus. Boston: Arthur P. Schmidt and Co., 1897.

Te Deum in E-flat, op. 35. Mixed chorus. Boston: Arthur P. Schmidt and Co., 1900.

Here's a Health to Ane I Love Dear. Men's or women's chorus. Boston: Arthur P. Schmidt and Co., 1901.

Alistair McAlistair. Men's chorus. Boston: Arthur P. Schmidt and Co., 1901.

White Butterflies. Mixed chorus. Boston: C. C. Birchard, 1904.

Praise the Lord, 0 My Soul. Mixed chorus. (1905) Unpublished.

The Lonely Rose, op. 43. Mixed chorus. Text by P. B. Marston. Boston: Arthur P. Schmidt and Co., 1906. (This work was mistakenly published under a previously assigned opus number.)

The Wild-brier. Women's chorus. Text by John Vance Cheney. Boston: Arthur P. Schmidt and Co., 1909.

Song of the Three Sisters. Women's chorus. Text by John Vance Cheney. Boston: Arthur P. Schmidt and Co., 1909.

Grant, We Beseech Thee, op. 51. Mixed chorus. Boston: Arthur P. Schmidt and Co., 1912.

Wind, op. 53. Women's double chorus. Boston: Arthur P. Schmidt and Co., 1913.

In Praesepio, op. 56. Mixed chorus. Text by R. L. Gales. Boston: Arthur P. Schmidt and Co., 1916.

Solo Piano Works

Petit Roman en Six Chapitres, A Suite for Pianoforte, op. 18. Boston: Arthur P. Schmidt and Co., 1894; [*Le Chevalier*]. Bryn Mawr, PA: Hildegard Publishing Company, 2002.

Starlight. Boston: J. B. Millet Co., 1894. (In *Half Hours with the Great Composers*).

Twilight. Boston: J. B. Millet Co., 1894. (In *Half Hours with the Great Composers*).

Rhapsody in E Minor for Piano, op. 21. Boston: Arthur P. Schmidt and Co., 1895.

Meditation, op. 26. Boston: Arthur P. Schmidt and Co., 1897; Bryn Mawr, PA: Hildegard Publishing Company, 1990.

Springtime, op. 30. Boston: John Church, 1899.

Revery, op. 31. Boston: John Church, 1899.

The Spirit of the Old House, op. 58. Boston: Arthur P. Schmidt and Co., 1917.

One Summer Day, op. 59. Bryn Mawr, PA: Theodore Presser, 1919.
1. *Hide and Seek in the Barn*
2. *Morning Lessons*
3. *Picnic in the Woods*
4. *Knitting for the Soldiers*
5. *Driving to the Blacksmith*

Three Pianoforte Pieces for Young Players, op. 60. Bryn Mawr, PA: Theodore Presser, 1919.
1. *Happy Days*
2. *Day Dreams*
3. *Rondoletto*

Voice and Orchestra

Armida, op. 24 (performed January 12, 1896). Soprano and orchestra. Unpublished.

Phoebus's Denunciation of the Furies at His Delphian Shrine. Baritone and orchestra. Lost.

Sappho's Prayer to Aphrodite (performed 1896). Alto and orchestra. Unpublished.

The Wild Huntsman. Solo, chorus and orchestra. Lost.

Orchestra

Witichis, op. 10 (performed June 30,1893). Unpublished.

Dramatic Overture, op. 12, no. 1 (performed April 8, 1893). Unpublished.

Totila, op. 23. Unpublished.

Ballade in D, op. 36 (performed March 14, 1901). Unpublished.

Estudiantina by P. Lacome. Lost

Other Works

Quintet for piano & strings (ca. 1879). One movement. Unpublished.

Evening Chimes, op. 29 (1898). Violin and piano. Unpublished.

Night of the Heavenly Star, A Cycle for Christmas, op. 52. Soli, mixed chorus, organ. Text by D. A. McCarthy. Boston: Oliver Ditson, 1913.

The Heavenly Noël, op. 57. Mixed chorus, mezzo soprano, orchestra. Text by R. L. Gales. Boston: Arthur P. Schmidt and Co., 1916.

Andante, Allegro moderato. Violin and piano. Lost.

Incidental music to Rostand's *"The Princess Far Away,"* including *Rudel's Song* and *Song to the Mariners*, 1906. Lost.

Bibliography

Adams, Juliette A. Graves. "Music Creative Work Among Women." *MUSIC* 9 (January 1896): 263-72.

Ammer, Christine. *Unsung: A History of Women in American Music*. Westport, Conn.: Greenwood Press, 1980.

Block, Adrienne Fried, and Carol Neuls-Bates. *Library of Congress Cataloging in Publication Data: Women in American Music*. Westport, Conn.: Greenwood Press, 1979.

Bowers, Jane, and Judith Tick. *Women Making Music*. Urbana, Ill.: Univ. of Illinois Press, 1986.

Commemorative Tributes to: Van der Stucken, Chadwick, Woodberrry, Cole, Hadley, Alderman, Matthews, and Channing. New York: American Academy of Arts and Letters, 1932.

Elkins-Marlow, Laurine. "American Women as Orchestral Composers, 1890–1960: An Unfamiliar Heritage," author's papers.

Elson, Louis Charles. *American Women in Music: The History of American Music*. New York: Macmillan, 1904.

Fox, Pamela. "The Benjamin Johnson Lang Family Papers: A Close Look at 75 Years of Musical Life in Boston." Paper presented at the annual meeting of the Sonneck Society, Boulder, Colorado, 1986.

Friedberg, Ruth C. *American Art Song and American Poetry*. Metuchen, N.J.: Scarecrow Press, 1981.

Hughes, Rupert. *Contemporary American Composers: The Women Composers*. Boston: L. C. Page, 1914.

Miller, Margo. "Oldest B. S. O. Subscriber Recalls Gentle World of the Past." *Boston Globe* (February 1967).

"M. R. Lang, Composer of Heavenly Noël." Obituary. *Boston Globe* (May 31, 1972).

Ryan, Thomas. *Recollections of an Old Musician*. New York: E. P. Dutton, 1899.

Syford, Ethel. "Margaret Ruthven Lang." *New England Magazine*, 45/1 (March 1912).

Tick, Judith. "Women as Professional Musicians in America 1870–1900." In *Yearbook for Inter-American Musical Research* 9 (February 1973).

Ojalà

Margaret Ruthven Lang

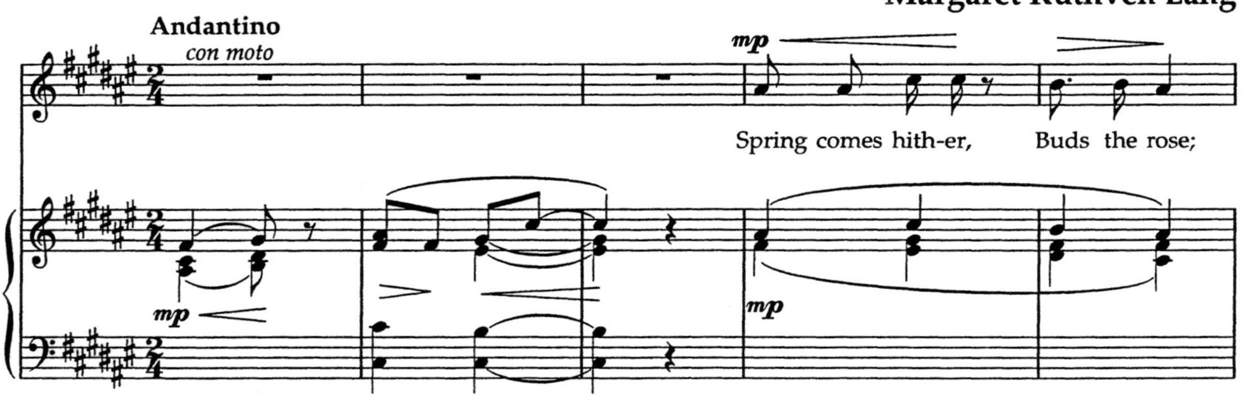
Andantino
con moto
mp
Spring comes hith-er, Buds the rose;
mp
mp

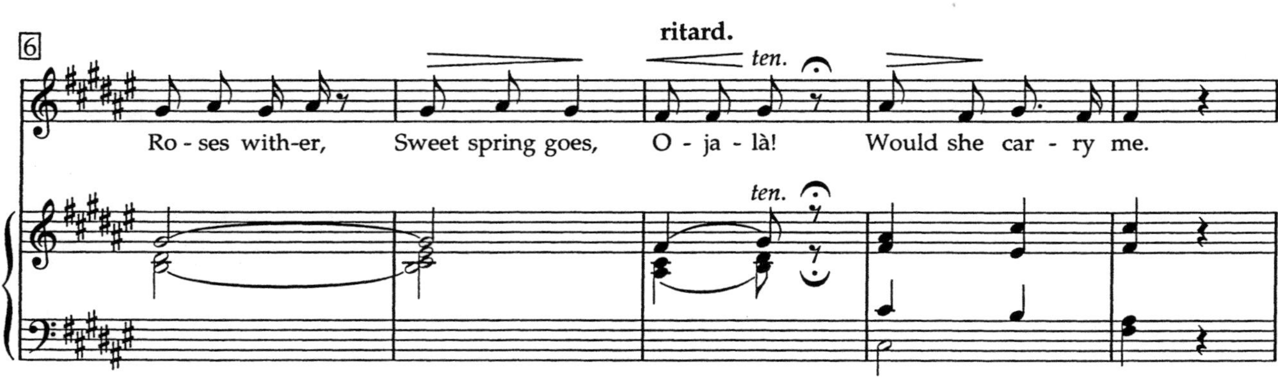
6
ritard.
ten.
Ro - ses with-er, Sweet spring goes, O - ja - là! Would she car - ry me.
ten.

11
mf
ten.
Sum-mer soars, Wide-winged day On-ward pours To the day; O - ja - là!
ten.
mf
ten.

16
Parlando
mp
Would he car - ry me.
Soft winds blow,
West-ward borne,
mp
20
accel.
f
On-ward go
Toward the morn;
O - ja - là,
Would they
f
24
ritard.
a tempo
mp
car - ry me.
Sweet birds sing
O'er the graves,
Then take wing
mp
29
p
ten.
Sostenuto
O'er the waves:
O - ja-là,
Would they car - ry me.
ten.
ten.
pp

Spinning-Song

Lizette Woodworth Reese

Margaret Ruthven Lang
Op. 9, no. 2

Con moto

mf

How ma-ny li - lies

mp

mf

4
be a-blow? Count them and see, Se - ven by the

8
wall, And se - ven by the door; 'Tis time he

12
f
came, 'tis time he came to me.
O
4
f
16
ritard.
4
Love's bit - ter
19
a tempo
mp
Was ev - er a whi-ter
dim.
mp
23
web than this that I spin to - day? A wed-ding gown or a wind-ing sheet, a

28
wed-ding gown or a wind-ing sheet, Love, which shall it be?
sf
34
un poco ritard.
a tempo
f
O Love's bit - ter!
4
39
mf
Two ships I see: one in the West
42
mf
Love, Love, is it
cresc.

45
f
decresc.
thine? One in the East in a win - dy
f
decresc.

49
mist; Oh, Love! Oh, Love, which is

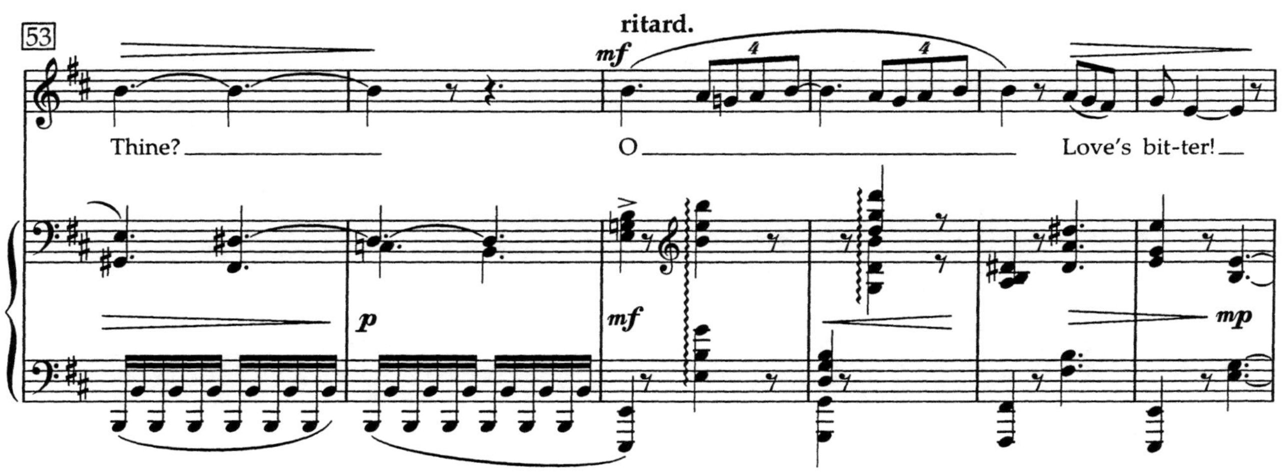
53
ritard.
mf
Thine? O Love's bit-ter!
p
mf
mp

59
mp
pp
Then speak the dames: "Her ship went down that night at
mp
pp

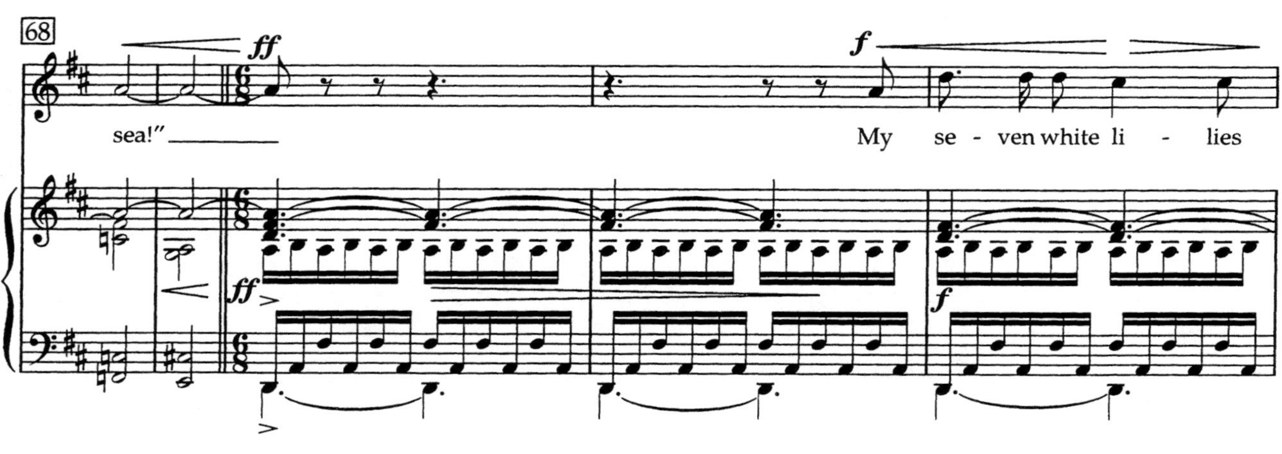
68
ff
f
sea!"
My se - ven white li - lies
ff
f

73
do ye hear? For this they speak of me!
"Her ship went down that

77
cresc.
night at sea, her ship went down that night;"
O
cresc.
f
f

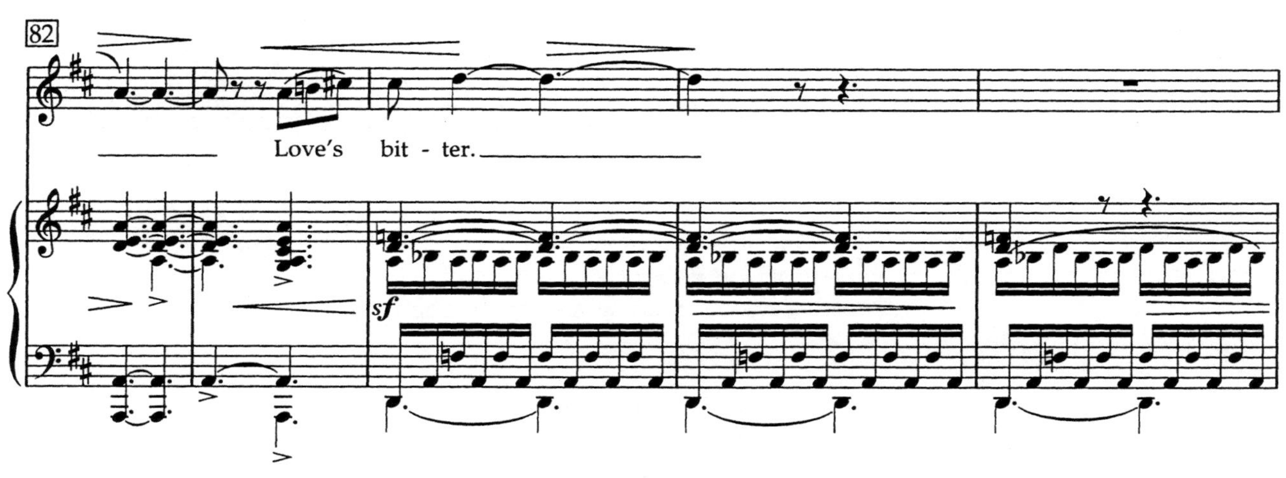
82
Love's bit - ter.
sf

87
sf
ff
Ped.

The Lady of Riga

Unknown*

Margaret Ruthven Lang
Op. 42, no. 12

Allegro moderato (♩. = 96)

p

Without Ped.

*Edward Lear

12
mf
mf
dimin.
Ped.

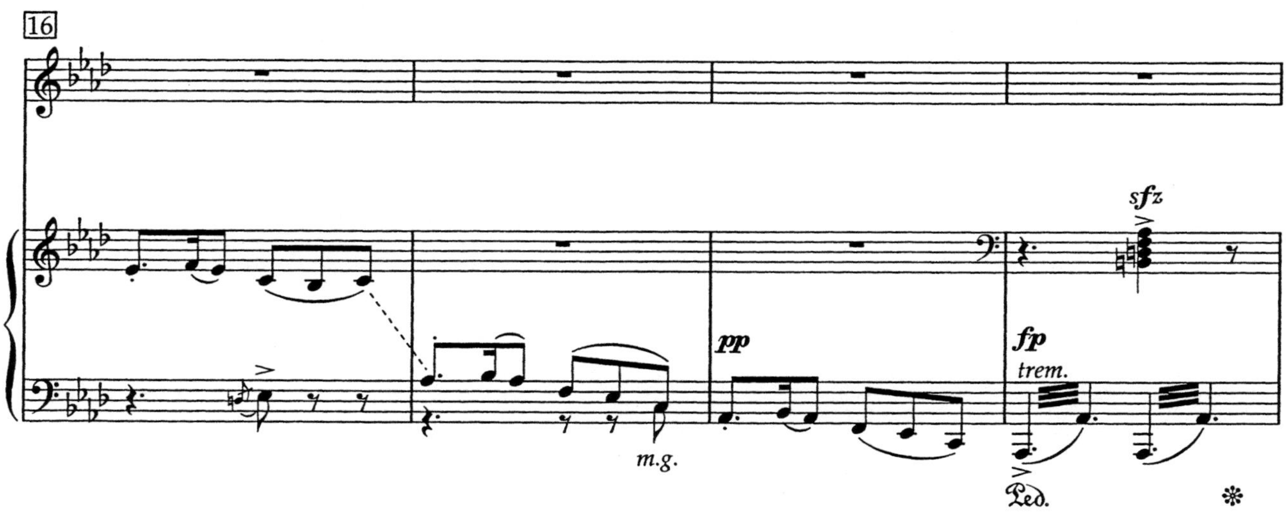
16
sfz
pp
fp
trem.
m.g.
Ped.

20
sfz
fp
trem.
f
mp
mf
Ped.
Ped.
Ped.

24
Gracefully, and very slowly
mf
There once was a La - dy of Ri - ga, Who
mp
mf
27
ten.
smiled, as she rode on a ti - ger; They re - turned from the ride, with the
ten.
ten.
30
ritard.
f
a tempo
La - dy in - side And the smile on the face of the ti - ger!!!
f
mf
ff

Irish Love Song

Margaret Ruthven Lang
Op. 22

Andantino
p

4
mp
O the time is long, Ma - vour - neen, Till I
mp

7
come a - gain, O Ma - vour - neen; An' the months are slow to pass, Ma -

10
ten.
vour - neen, Till I hold thee in my arms, O Ma - vour - neen!
ten.
13
ten.
Shall I see thine eyes, Ma -
ten.
mp
16
vour - neen, Like the ha - zel buds, O Ma - vour - neen; Shall I
19
ten.
touch thy dus - ky hair, Ma - vour - neen, With its shim'-rin glint o' gold, O Ma -
ten.

22
vour - neen?
ten. pp
O my
ten.
pp
25
love for thee, Ma - vour - neen Is a bit - ter pain, O Ma -
28
p
molto ritard.
vour - neen; Keep thy heart aye true to me, Ma - vour - neen, I should
pp
31
mf
ten.
f
ten.
die but for thy love, O Ma - vour - neen!
ten.
ten.
mf
ten.
f ten.
p

Snowflakes

John Vance Cheney

Margaret Ruthven Lang
Op. 50, no. 3

Quietly and delicately (♩ = about 72)

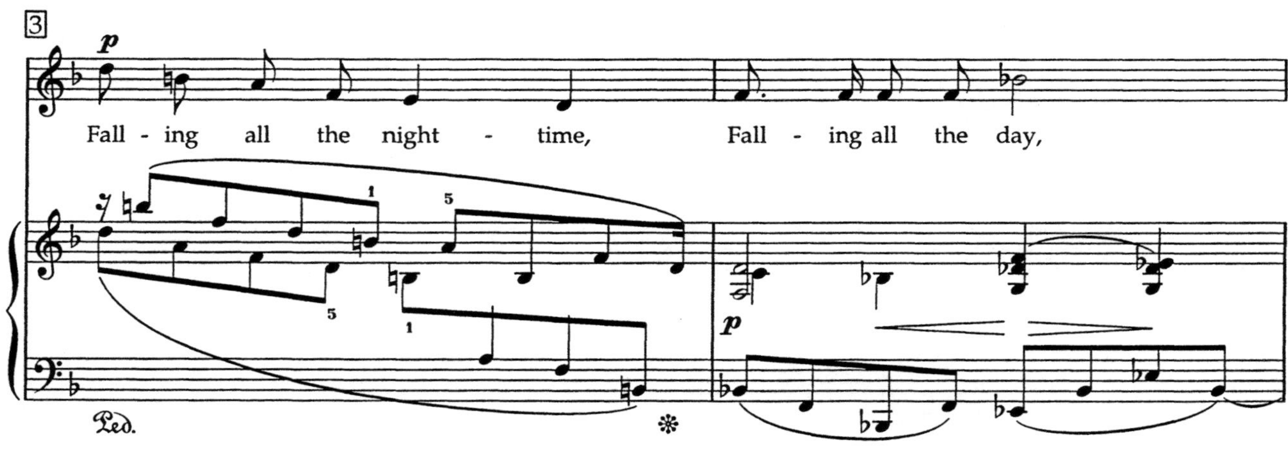

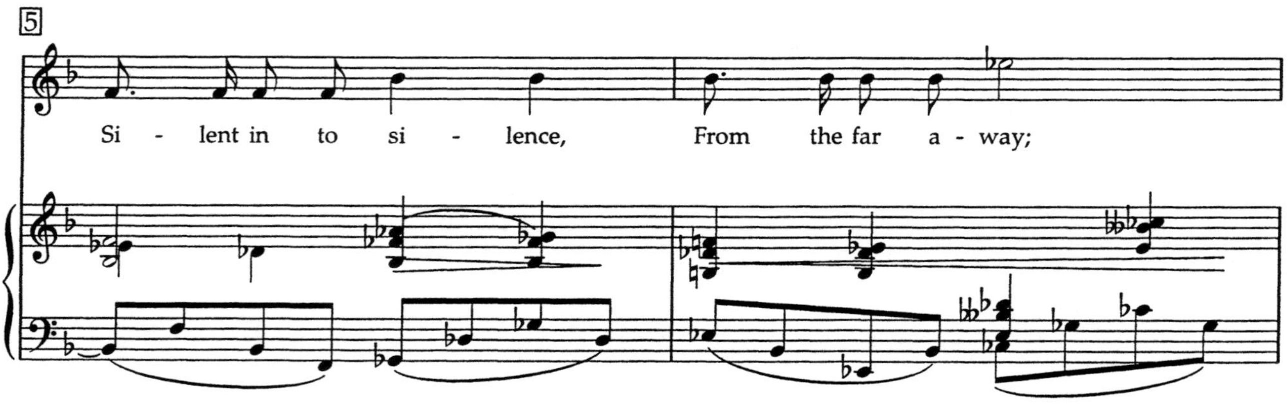

7
Stil - ly host un - num - bered, All the night and day
Ped. * Ped. * Ped. * Ped. *
9
Fall - - ing, Fall - - ing,
mf
Ped. * Ped. * Ped. *
11
Fall - - ing from the far a - way,
mf
Ped. * Ped. *
13
far a - way
mp
Ped. * Ped.

15
rit.
allargando
f espressivo
Nev - er came such
8va
mf
f espressivo
17
glo - ry To the fields and trees,
f
19
Nev - er sum - mer blos' - soms Thick and white as
21
these.
f

23
p
Fold - - ing,
subito p
mp
25
poco rit.
Fall - - - - - ing,
mf
f
27
Tempo primo
p ten.
Fold-ing, fold-ing, fold - ing,
Fold the world a-way,
ten.
mf
mp
ten.
29
Souls of flow-ers drift - ing
Down the win-ter day;
p

31
Fall-ing all the night-time, Fall-ing all the day, Fol - low,
34
Fol - low, Fol - low, fold it soft a - way;
mf
p
37
p
rit.
Soft a -
p
41
a tempo
way.
ten.
ten.
pp
mp
p
pp
pp

Jane Vieu
(1871–1955)

SONDRA WIELAND HOWE

Jane Vieu (Jeanne Elizabeth Marie) was born in Paris in 1871 and died there on April 8, 1955. Although there is very little information available about her life, over 100 works, vocal and instrumental, are extant.[1]

At the turn of the century, musical activities abounded in Paris. The Opéra Comique was active, operettas and vaudevilles were performed in many theaters, and chamber music societies and choral associations presented concerts. The Universal Exhibition of 1889 introduced Asian art and music to Europeans. There was a large market for songs and piano music to be played in the home.[2]

Vieu's songs, piano solos, chamber music, and dramatic works were published by Enoch (Paris), Giovanni Ricordi (Paris, Milan, London), the firm of Maurice and Jane Vieu (Paris), Max Eschig (who purchased the catalog of Jane Vieu's music in 1973),[3] Célestin Joubert, G. Gross, and Léon Grus of Paris, and Schott Frères of Brussels. Jane and Maurice Vieu (probably her husband) formed a publishing house located on the Rue de Rome in Paris that published works for piano and voice by Jane Vieu and other composers. Five of her songs have been published in modern editions,[4] her works are listed in Cohen, Pazdírek, and Schmidl,[5] and two songs have been recorded.[6]

Vieu composed several dramatic works. Performance scores now located in the Library of Congress indicate that she had contacts in the theater. *La belle au bois dormant*, a dramatic work with text and illustrations by Lucien Métivet, is dedicated to Madame Massenet. It tells the story of Sleeping Beauty (in nineteen scenes) with a modern twist. The beauty awakens and sees the prince on a bicycle. When she encounters the modern world with dirty factories, noisy cars and trains, and bustling cities, she decides to return to her palace and go back to sleep! The work was first performed in February 1902 at the Théâtre des Mathurins under the direction of J. Berny, and was published that year as a children's book.[7] *Aladin* [*sic*] is another fairy tale with text and illustrations by Métivet. Dedicated to a friend, Anne Delettrez, it tells the story of Aladdin and his magic lamp. First performed in February 1904 at the Théâtre des Mathurins, it was published as an illustrated children's book.[8]

Madame Tallien is a five-act historical work about the French political figure Thérésia Cabarrus (1773–1835) with text by Paul Berthelot and Claude Roland.[9] *Arlette* is an operetta in three acts with text by Claude Roland and L. Bouvet. Dedicated to Vieu's mother, it was first performed in Brussels, Belgium, on October 28, 1904, at the Théâtre Royal des Galeries St. Hubert.[10] *Au bal de Flore,* dedicated to Vieu's brother, is a ballet-pantomime in one act.[11] Set in a garden in 1797, the ballet tells the story of two couples. *Les fanfreluches de l'amour*, a ballet in one act by Vova Berky, was dedicated to the Viscountess Antoine de Contades. It was first performed in Paris on December 15, 1913, with costumes, scenery, and orchestra, and is available in a piano edition.[12] Other works include *L'amour en grève* with a text by Jacques Lemaire and Henry Houry; *Il était une fois,* with a text by Claude Roland; *Le bonhomme de neige; Les petites entravées,* with a text by A. Metzvil and R. Sydney; and *Salomette*, with a text by Jean Séry. These were published in piano scores with the story written above the music. Vocal selections were often published separately.

Forty-three songs by Vieu are located in the Women Composers Collection at the University of Michigan. Additional songs are in the Library of Congress. The songs were published between 1897 and 1913, most of them in the first few years of the twentieth century. The texts are by various French writers including Michel Carré, author of comedies and opera librettos, Robert de Montesquiou, and Benjamin Rabier, who wrote illustrated histories for young people. The songs have typical Romantic texts about love and nature. Vieu wrote three sacred songs: *Ave Maria*, *O salutaris*, and *Je vous salue*.

Vieu's piano music, composed between 1899 and 1911, includes minuets, waltzes, and instrumental arrangements of her songs. The *Nocturne* in A-flat major (1900), *Chanson du matin* (1899), and *Arabesque* (1908) are particularly appealing. *Caprice* (1903) is difficult with fast scales and arpeggios. *Les images en musique* is a set of ten easy piano pieces for young children, solos and duets, with delightful illustrations by Benjamin Rabier.[13]

Vieu also composed *Dix leçons de solfège*, a book of exercises for use in classes at the National Conservatory in Paris and dedicated to Gabriel Fauré, the director from 1905 to 1920.[14]

Historiettes chantées is a collection of twelve children's songs with texts by various authors, for singing, dancing, and pantomime. The book includes sketches by Berth Martinie and instructions for interpretive dances by Jeanne Ronsay.[15]

Chamber works by Vieu include music for violin, cello, guitar, and harp. The *Menuetto* for string quartet and piano (1901) has a melodic first violin part, and very easy parts for the second violin, viola, and cello. The piano is optional.[16] Seven of Vieu's piano solos were arranged for piano and orchestra.[17]

Lyrical vocal lines, arpeggios, and *ostinati* in the piano parts characterize Vieu's Romantic nineteenth-century style. Three of her songs are included in this volume. *Dernier baiser* (Last Kiss) is set to poetry by Robert Campion. Dedicated to Louise Planès it was published by G. Ricordi (1900?). The accompaniment portrays flying birds with ascending arpeggios. In E major, the music is largely limited to primary chords.

The first verse tells of the spring season and making nests. The stepwise melody includes grace notes. The interval of an ascending seventh is effectively used to ask questions (mm. 5-6, 13-14, 38-39). The second verse, about birds singing and finding shelter in the woods, repeats the music of the first verse. The third verse, portraying the last kiss, begins like the former verses, but is static with repeated notes as the "lips are closed" ("Car tes lèvres sont closes," mm. 25-26). It becomes more agitated with ascending scales and whole notes in a high range (mm. 27-30) as the "hearts are separated" ("Et nos coeurs désunis.") The accompaniment has a counter melody in measures. 28-34. The song closes with two lines of the opening music, then fades away with *pianissimo* ascending arpeggios.

Les étoiles is a setting of poetry by Robert Campion, dedicated to Madame Renée Richard, and published by G. Ricordi (1900). The four verses are in an ABAB rhyme scheme. The first verse, describing the magical stars hanging in an azure sky, is a recitative with a simple, chordal accompaniment in E major. The second verse repeats the harmony of measures 1 - 6, adding a repeated pattern in the right hand of the accompaniment; it then abruptly modulates to C major. The vocal line, describing poets looking at the ancient unchanging sky, differs from verse one, returning to the recitative style.

Verse three questions the origin of the stars — are they made of our souls and dreams? The music, moving from C major back to E major, grows more rhythmic as the melody becomes chromatic. The accompaniment is simple, with the left hand doubling the vocal line at the octave (mm. 21-26). The first verse and music are repeated, ending with the *ostinato* figure of verse two.

Puisque c'est l'été, a setting of a sonnet by Robert de la Villehervé, is dedicated to Georges Rey and was published by G. Ricordi (1900?). It is a lively piece describing the joys of summer. Utilizing a simple harmonic scheme in D major, the accompaniment often doubles the vocal line. Verse one, describing summer after a storm, has a lively melody. When the verse refers to crying and dreaming, the music is slow with an ascending triplet pattern (mm. 6-8). Each verse begins with the same music, which is then varied. Verse two calls "my charming" to the rose bush and ends dramatically, describing the name carved into the tree. The melody is in a high range, *forte*, with a repeated B minor chord over a dominant pedal (mm. 14-16). The left hand accompaniment has a counter melody. This verse ends softly and slowly, on the dominant, calling the lover's name, "Bradamante."

The climax of the piece occurs in verse three (mm. 18-35). The accented *forte* vocal line ascends to a whole note on G. The music fades away, as roses and beauty fade, with a slow descending line and a soft return of the original melody. The song then ends joyfully with a loud *fortissimo* accompaniment.

Vieu's style is harmonically simple; verses usually repeat without variation. The accompaniments often have *ostinati* and double the vocal line. This appealing music, with a variety of dynamics and tempo, frequently employs word painting.

Notes

1. Judy S. Tsou, "Vieu, Jane," in *The Norton/Grove Dictionary of Women Composers,* eds. Julie Anne Sadie and Rhian Samuel (New York and London: W. W. Norton, 1995), 478; Susan C. Cook and Judy S. Tsou, eds., *Anthology of Songs* (New York: Da Capo Press, 1988), x-xi.

2. "Paris, after 1870," in *The New Grove Dictionary of Music and Musicians*, ed. Stanley Sadie (London: Macmillan, 1980), 220-25.

3. Cook and Tsou, *Anthology of Songs,* x; *Music Printing and Publishing*, eds. D. W. Krummel and Stanley Sadie (New York: W. W. Norton, 1990), 231-32. This article states that some works were published under the pseudonym Pierre Valette. However, I have been unable to locate any of these works.

4. Cook and Tsou, *Anthology of Songs,* and *Jane Vieu: Five Songs* (New York: Classical Vocal Reprints, 1997).

5. "Vieu, Jane," in *International Encyclopedia of Women Composers*, vol. 2, ed. Aaron I. Cohen (New York: Books and Music, 1987), 725; Franz Pazdírek, *Universal-Handbuch der Musikliteratur aller Zeiten und Völker Vienna, 1904–10* (Vienna: Pazdírek, n.d.), 210-11; and "Vieu, Jane," in *Dizionario universale dei musicisti*, vol. 2, ed. Carlo Schmidl (Milan: Casa Editrice Sonzogno, 1938), 662.

6. *From a Women's Perspective Sound Recording: Art Songs by Women Composers* (Vienna: Vienna Modern Masters, 1993) has "Belle au bois dormant" and "Sérénade Japonaise."

7. *La belle au bois dormant: féerie chantée en 19 tableaux lumineux* (Sleeping Beauty of the Woods: Sung Fairy Tale in 19 Brilliant Scenes) (Paris: Enoch, 1902), 45 pp.

8. *Aladin* [*sic*], ombres Chinoises en quinze tableaux (Aladin,

[sic] Chinese Ghosts in Fifteen Scenes) (Paris: Enoch & Co., 1904), 47 pp.

9. *Madame Tallien, ou Thérésia Cabarrus* (Paris: G. Ricordi, 1901; New York: Boosey, 1901), 47 pp.

10. *Arlette: opérette en 3 actes* (Arlette: Operetta in 3 Acts) (Paris: C. Joubert, 1905).

11. *Au bal de Flore, ballet-pantomime en un acte* (Floral Dance, Ballet Pantomime in One Act) (Paris: G. Ricordi 1902; Milan: G. Ricordi, 1903).

12. *Les fanfreluches de l'amour* (The Trifles of Love) (Paris: Maurice & Jane Vieu, 1914), 77 pp.

13. *Les images en musique* (Pictures in Music) (Paris: Maurice & Jane Vieu, 1908), 35 pp.

14. *Dix leçons de solfège* (Ten Lessons of Solfège) (Paris: Maurice & Jane Vieu, 1913), 48 pp. Location: Harvard University.

15. *Historiettes chantées* (Short singing tales) (Paris: Maurice and Jane Vieu, 1910; Max Eschig & Cie., 1920), 32 pp. Location: Library of Congress.

16. *Menuetto* (Paris: G. Ricordi & Co., 1901). Location: Library of Congress.

17. "Vieu, Jane," *International Encyclopedia.*

Selected List of Works

Vocal works are located in Women Composers Collection, University of Michigan, unless indicated otherwise.

Solo Songs

Au bord du grand chemin. Text by Jacques d'Halmont. Paris: Maurice Vieu, 1907.

Au pays parfumé. Text by Michel Carré. Paris: Enoch, 1904.

Aubade. Text by Claude Roland. Paris: G. Ricordi, 1897.

Carillons blanc. Text by Louis Rocher. Paris: Enoch, 1901.

Chanson brève. Text by Pierre Reyniel. Paris: Enoch, 1905.

Chanson de l'hiver. Text by Benjamin Rabier. Paris: Maurice & Jane Vieu, 1910.

Chanson fleurie. Text by Louis Alotte. Paris: G. Ricordi, (1900?).

Chantons les roses. Text by René Louis. Brussels: Schott Frères, 1903.

Charité. Text by Jules Lafforgue. Paris: Enoch, 1903.

Credo. Text by Henri Lefebvre. Paris: Léon Grus, (1900?).

Dernier baiser. Text by Robert Campion. Paris: G. Ricordi, (1900?). Bryn Mawr, PA: Hildegard Publishing Company, 2002.

Dernier rendez-vous. Text by Robert de Montesquiou. Paris: Ricordi, (1900?).

Éperdûment. Text by Charles Fuster. Paris: G. Ricordi, 1899.

Je rêve d'une chanson douce. Text by Henri Lefebvre. Paris: Léon Grus, (1900?).

La belle au bois dormant. Text by Lucien Métivet. Paris: Enoch, 1902.

L'ange du rêve. Text by Ernest Simoni. London: Ricordi, 1900.

Le givre. Text by Ch. Grandmougin. Paris: Maurice Vieu, 1907.

Les bonnes fées. Text by Jean Meudrot. Paris: Maurice & Jane Vieu, 1913.

Les deux baisers. Paris: Enoch, 1904.

Les étoiles. Text by Robert Campion. Paris: G. Ricordi, 1900. Bryn Mawr, PA: Hildegard Publishing Company, 2002.

Les hirondelles. Text by Paul Villa. Paris: Maurice & Jane Vieu, 1907.

Madeleine. Text by Georges Boyer. Paris: G. Ricordi, 1900.

Mignonne, lève toi! Text by Eddy Lévis. Paris: G. Ricordi, (1900?).

Monsieur Noël. Text by J. Lafforgue. Paris: Enoch, 1902.

O salutaris. Paris: Enoch, 1903.

Pastorale Louis XVI. Text by L. Fortolis. Paris: Maurice Vieu, 1907.

Peine d'amour. Text by P. Padovani. Paris: Maurice Vieu, 1907.

Petits chemins. Text by Jean Rameau. Paris: G. Ricordi, 1899.

Pompadour. Text by Louis Rocher. Paris: Enoch, 1902.

Pour elle! Text by L. Hattais. Paris: G. Ricordi, (1900?).

Puisque c'est l'été. Text by Robert de la Villehervé. Paris: G. Ricordi, (1900?). Bryn Mawr, PA: Hildegard Publishing Company, 2002.

Roses blondes. Text by Francis Vielé-Griffi. Paris: G. Ricordi, (1900?).

Séduction. Text by Alf. Delilia. Paris: Enoch, 1902.

Sérénade d'Aladin. Text by Lucien Métivet. Paris: Enoch, 1904.

Sérénade rustique. Text by Marcel de Lihus. Paris: G. Gross, (1900?).

Si tu ne viens pas. Text by Lorenzi de Bradi. Paris: G. Ricordi, 1901.

Simplement. Text by Clovis Hugues. Paris: G. Ricordi, 1900.

Stances de Vénus. Text by G. de Dubor. Paris: G. Ricordi, 1900.

To the Land of Dreams. English text by Fred. de Faye Jozin. French text by René Louis. Paris: Enoch, 1905.

Trois mélodies sur des Tankas japonais. Text by Serge Rello. Paris: Enoch, 1902.

Vaines tendresses. Text by J. de la Vandère. Paris: G. Ricordi, (1900?).

Valse des rousses. Text by Alfred Delilia. Paris: Enoch, 1904.

Vers le rêve. Text by René Louis. Paris: Enoch, 1901.

Collections

Dix leçons de solfège. Paris: Maurice & Jane Vieu, 1913. Harvard University.

Historiettes chantées. Paris: Maurice & Jane Vieu, 1910. Library of Congress.

Modern Editions

Cook, Susan C., and Judy S. Tsou, eds. *Anthology of Songs*. New York: Da Capo Press, 1988.

Jane Vieu: Five Songs. New York: Classical Vocal Reprints, 1997.

Dramatic Works and Ballets
(located in the Library of Congress)

Aladin. Text by Lucien Métivet. Paris: Enoch, 1904.

L'amour en grève. Text by Jacques Lemaire & Henry Houry. Paris: Maurice & Jane Vieu, 1910.

Arlette. Text by Claude Roland & L. Bouvet. Paris: C. Joubert, 1905.

Au bal de Flore. Text by Georges de Dubor. Paris: G. Ricordi, 1902; Milan: G. Ricordi, 1903.

Il était une fois. Text by Claude Roland. Paris: G. Ricordi, 1906.

La belle au bois dormant. Text by Lucien Métivet. Paris: Enoch, 1902.

Le bonhomme de neige. Paris: Maurice & Jane Vieu, 1910.

Les fanfreluches de l'amour. Paris: Maurice & Jane Vieu, 1914.

Les petites entravées. Text by A. Metzvil and R. Sydney. Paris: Maurice & Jane Vieu, 1911.

Madame Tallien. Text by Paul Berthelot & Claude Roland. Paris: G. Ricordi, 1901.

Salomette. Text by Jean Séry. Paris: C. Joubert, 1911.

Chamber Music
(located in the Library of Congress)

Amoroso. Piano and violin. Paris: Enoch, 1904.

La Castillane. Mandolin. Paris: Enoch, 1901.

Le lever de l'aurore. Piano and violin. Paris: Maurice Vieu, 1907.

Marquis Bergers. Piano and orchestra. Paris: G. Ricordi, 1901.

Menuet de la Princesse. Violin and piano. Paris: Enoch, 1902.

Menuetto. String quartet with piano. Paris: G. Ricordi, 1901.

Tarentelle. Harp or piano and orchestra. Paris: G. Ricordi, 1901.

Valse lente. Harp or piano and orchestra. Paris: G. Ricordi, 1901.

Piano Music
(located in the Library of Congress and Women Composers Collection, University of Michigan)

Arabesque. Paris: Maurice & Jane Vieu, 1908.

Caprice. Paris: Enoch, 1903.

Chanson du matin. Paris: G. Ricordi, 1899.

Colombine. Paris: Enoch, 1904.

Griserie de Caresses. Paris: G. Ricordi, 1901.

La magicienne. Paris: Enoch, 1902.

La sieste. Paris: Enoch, 1904.

Le chevalier printemps. Paris: Maurice & Jane Vieu, 1911.

Les images en musique. Paris: Maurice & Jane Vieu, 1908.

Les libellules. Paris: Enoch, 1902.

Menuet de la princesse. Paris: Enoch, 1902.

Menuet de lys. Paris: Enoch, 1902.

Minuetto. Paris: Ricordi, 1900.

Nocturne. Paris: Ricordi, 1900.

Nymphes et papillons. Paris: Enoch, 1905.

Pompadour. Paris: Enoch, 1903.

Séduction. Paris: Enoch, 1902.

Sérénade d'Aladin [*sic*]. Paris: Enoch, 1904.

Suite espagnole. Paris: Enoch, 1904.

Tendrement. Paris: Hachette, 1902.

Valse des merveilleuses. Paris: G. Ricordi, 1900.

Valse des rousses. Paris: Enoch, 1904.

Bibliography

Cohen, Aaron I. *International Encyclopedia of Women Composers*, 2nd ed., 2 vols. New York, London: Books & Music (USA) Inc., 1987.

Cook, Susan C., and Judy S. Tsou, eds. *Anthology of Songs*. New York: Da Capo Press, 1988.

Music Printing and Publishing. Eds. D. W. Krummel and Stanley Sadie. New York: W. W. Norton, 1990.

The Norton/Grove Dictionary of Women Composers. Edited by Julie Ann Sadie and Rhian Samuel. New York and London: W. W. Norton, 1995.

Pazdírek, Franz. *Universal-Handbuch der Musikliteratur aller Zeiten und Völker Vienna, 1904–1910*. Vienna: Pazdírek and Co., n.d.

Schmidl, Carlo. *Dizionario universale dei musicisti*. Vol. 2. Milan: Casa Editrice Sonzogno, 1938.

Discography

From a Women's Perspective Sound Recording: Art Songs by Women Composers. Katherine Eberle, mezzo-soprano. Vienna: Vienna Modern Masters, 1993.

Dernier baiser

Poetry by Robert Campion

1. C'est la saison des nids:
   Si nous faisons le nôtre?
   Oui, les gels sont finis,
   Aimons-nous l'un et l'autre.
   C'est la saison des nids:
   Si nous faisions le nôtre?

2. Veux-tu l'abri des bois
   Où chantent les oiselles?
   C'est le nid d'autrefois,
   Mais avons-nous des ailes?
   Veux-tu l'abri des bois
   Où chantent les oiselles?

3. Pour ton dernier baiser
   Je tresserai des roses.
   Hélas! c'est malaisé!
   Car tes lèvres sont closes
   Et nos coeurs désunis
   A jamais ont perdu
   la science des nids!

   C'est la saison des nids:
   Referons nous le nôtre!

1. It is the season of nests:
   What if we make ours?
   Yes, the frosts are finished,
   Let us love one another.
   It is the season of nests:
   What if we make ours?

2. Do you want the shelter of the woods
   Where the birds are singing?
   It is the nest of old,
   But do we have wings?
   Do you want the shelter of the woods
   Where the birds are singing?

3. For your last kiss
   I will weave the roses.
   Alas! It is difficult!
   Because your lips are closed
   And our hearts are separated.
   Forever is lost
   The learning of the nests!

   It is the season of nests:
   Let us make ours again.

Les étoiles

Poetry by Robert Campion

1. Au fond des paradis lunaires,
   Suspendus dans l'azur changeant,
   Sont de magiques luminaires:
   Les étoiles aux yeux d'argent.

2. Depuis toujours qu'elles demeurent
   Et veillent immuablement,
   Pour Elles, les poëtes meurent
   A regarder le firmament.

3. Et qui sait si leurs blanches flammes
   Fascinant nos yeux éblouis
   Ne sont pas faites de nos âmes
   Et de nos rêves nos rêves infinis?

4. Au fond des paradis lunaires,
   Suspendus dans l'azur changeant,
   Sont de magiques luminaires:
   Les étoiles aux yeux d'argent.

1. At the heart of the lunar paradise,
   Suspended in a changeable blue,
   There are magical lights:
   The stars with eyes of silver.

2. They have remained forever
   And watch unchangeably.
   For them, poets are dying
   To look at the sky.

3. And who knows if their white flames
   Fascinating our dazzled eyes
   Are not made of our souls
   And of our dreams, our endless dreams?

4. At the heart of the lunar paradise,
   Suspended in a changeable blue,
   There are magical lights:
   The stars with eyes of silver.

Puisque c'est l'éte
Sonnet by Robert de la Villehervé

1. Puisque c'est l'été, puisque la tourmente
Ne chagrine plus le parc réservé,
C'est assez pleuré, c'est assez rêvé.
Voyez s'il fait bon sous l'ombre clémente!

2. Puisque c'est l'été, venez ma charmante
Au rosier d'amour que j'ai retrouvé.
Votre nom y reste à jamais gravé,
Gravé sur l'écorce, ô ma Bradamante,

3. Puisque c'est l'été, puisque les rosiers.
Au soleil d'Aôut sont extasiés,
Laissez, oh! laissez . . . . les siestes moroses.
La rose se fanne, aussi la beauté.

Cueillez le bonheur et cueillez les roses.
Puis l'hiver viendra, puisque c'est l'été.

1. Since it is summer, since the tempest
No longer troubles our secret park
It is enough crying, it is enough dreaming.
See if it is good under the merciful shade.

2. Since it is summer, come my charming
To the rose bush of love that I have found again
Your name stays there, forever engraved,
Engraved on the bark, oh my Bradamante,

3. Since it is summer, because the rose bushes
In the sunshine of August are ravishing,
Leave, oh! Leave the sullen siestas.
The rose fades, also beauty.

Gather happiness and gather the roses.
Then winter will come, since it is summer.

Translations by Sondra Wieland Howe

Dernier baiser

Robert Campion

Jane Vieu

Sondra Wieland Howe, editor

9
nis, Ai - mons - nous l'un et l'au - - tre.
fois, Mais a - vons - nous des ai - - les?
11
mf
C'est la sai - son des nids:
Veux - tu l'a - bri des bois
13
Si nous fai - sions le nô - - - - -
Où chant - ent les oi - sel - - - - -
15
p
tre?
les?
mf
3

17
19
p
3. Pour ton der - nier bai - ser
21
Je tres - se - rai des ro - - - - -
23
p
ses...
Hé - las! c'est ma - lai -

25
sé! Car tes lè - vres sont clo - - ses
27
mf
pressez - - - - - - - - - - - peu - -
Et nos coeurs dé - su - nis
mf
29
- - - - - - - - - - - à - - - - - - - - - - - - - -
A ja - mais ont per - du
mf
31
- - - - - - - - - - - peu - - - - - - - - - - - - - -
la sci - en - - - - - -
mf

33
rall.
Tempo I
p
- ce des nids!
suivez
p
36
p
C'est la sai - son des nids:
38
Re - fe - rons nous le nô - - - - -
40
pressez jusqu'á la fin
p
tre?
8va
mf
p
pp
ppp

Les étoiles

Robert Campion

Jane Vieu

Sondra Wieland Howe, editor

13
string.
jours qu'-elles de - meu - rent Et vei - llent im-mu - a - ble - ment, Pour
17
espr.
rit.
Lento
dolce
El - les, les po - ë - tes meu - rent A re-gar-der le fir-ma - ment.
p
21
p pressez un peu, avec angoisse
3. Et qui sait si leurs blan - ches flam - mes
p suivez
(en dehors)
25
rit.
rinf.
rall.
en pressant
con fuoco
f
Fa - sci-nant nos yeux é - blou - is Ne sont pas fai - tes de nos
suivez
f
(en dehors)

29
rit.
mf
dolce
rall.
â - mes Et de nos rê - ves nos rê - ves in - fi -
mf
p
33
Tempo primo
p mystérieusement
nis? 1. Au fond des pa - ra - dis lu - nai - res, Sus-pen -
37
p avec charme, en pressant un peu
Tempo I sans presser
mf
dus dans l'a - zur chan - geant, Sont de ma - gi-ques lu-mi-nai -
41
dolce
p
rit.
- res: Les é - toi - les aux yeux d'ar - gent.
3
p
pp

Puisque c'est l'été

Robert de la Villehervé

Jane Vieu

Sondra Wieland Howe, editor

Allegro

p *f* *p*

1. Puis - que c'est l'é - té, puis - que

3

la tour - men - te Ne cha - gri - ne plus le parc

5

p **rall.**

ré - ser - vé, C'est as - sez pleu - ré,

3 3 *suivez* 3 3 *p*

Ped. * Ped.

7

c'est as - sez rê - vé. Vo - yez s'il fait bon

3 3 3 3

* Ped. *

9
rall.
a tempo
mf
sous l'om - bre clé - men - te! 2. Puis - que c'est l'é - té, ve - nez
3
mf
11
ma char - man - te Au ro - sier d'a - mour
13
f
que j'ai re - trou - vé. Vo - tre nom y res - te
f
15
à ja - mais gra - vé, Gra - vé sur l'é - cor - ce,

17
rall.
a tempo
ô ma Bra - da - man - te, 3. Puis - que c'est l'é - té, puis - que
19
rall.
les ro - siers. Au so - leil d'a - oût sont ex - ta - si -
suivez
21
Lent
és, Lais-sez, oh! lais-sez.... les sies - tes mo-ro -
24
Toujours lent
ses. La ro - se se fa - ne,

26
pressez
aus - si la beau - té
28
Tempo I
mf
Cueil - lez le bon - heur et cueil - lez les ro - ses.
mf
30
f
Large
Puis l'hi - ver vien - dra, puis - que c'est l'é -
f
suivez
32
té.
f
ff

Anna Cramer

(1873–1968)

HELEN H. METZELAAR

Although Anna Cramer lived until 1968, information about this Dutch composer and pianist, born in Amsterdam on July 15, 1873, is extremely scanty. There was a nineteenth-century Amsterdam firm named "Cramer en Zelders"; Anna Cramer's mother, Merkje Helena Zelders, may have met her father, Jan Marinus Cramer, through business connections between these two families. Merkje Zelders was the daughter of a Dutch Reformed minister, Ds. Albertus Zelders,[1] while Jan Cramer, a merchant and oil producer, was Hersteld (Re-established) Lutheran. Merkje Cramer gave birth to four children, two of whom died in infancy.[2] The two surviving children, Anna and Albertina, continued this religious duality: Anna is registered as Dutch Reformed, while her younger sister is listed as Lutheran.

Nothing is known about Anna's childhood other than that her family moved frequently and her father died when she was fifteen. By the age of twenty she appears in Amsterdam municipal registers as a servant, but she later studied piano and composition at the Amsterdam Conservatory, graduating in 1897.[3] Her composition teacher was Bernard Zweers (1854–1924)[4]. There are no further extant facts other than the quote of the German philosopher and writer Johann Gottfried Herder (1744–1803) that she included in an album of verses belonging to a fellow pianist and composer, Elisabeth Kuyper (see vol. 6): "Music, even without words, has a sublimity of no other art, as if, like a language of geniuses, it only speaks directly to our innermost self as to an equal partner in creation."[5]

As many Dutch musicians did, Cramer went to Berlin after graduation, where she studied composition with Wilhelm Berger (1861–1911).[6] Her first composition was not published until 1903. That year the magazine *Die Woche* organized a song competition; hers was one of thirty songs chosen for publication from almost 9,000 entries.[7] This publication included her photograph with the caption that she was studying music in Meiningen, Germany. Although in 1903 Meiningen did not yet have a conservatory, she probably continued her studies there with Berger.[8]

The next trace we have of Cramer is in 1906, when the well-known German baritone Ludwig Wüllner (1858–1938) performed some of her songs in one of his three recitals in the Amsterdam Concertgebouw. According to his biographer, Wüllner's repertory included five Cramer songs: *Abendfrieden, Wa heet se doch, Bussemann, Bispill,* and *Ond's kommt au emôl e Zeit.*[9] The Dutch music periodical *Caecilia* reviewed Wüllner's recital enthusiastically:

> Some of the modern songs by a fellow countrywoman, Anna Cramer, struck us by something original in their quality as folksong, greatly arousing our desire to learn more about the works by this woman composer living in Berlin.[10]

In 1907, a good year for Cramer, Fürstner of Berlin published two collections of her songs, the humorous *Fünf Gedichte von Klaus Groth*, op. 1, and *Fünf Gedichte von O.J. Bierbaum*, op. 2. On April 11 four of her songs were performed in the huge Beethoven-Saal in Berlin, sung by the Dutch baritone, Gerard Zalsman. The program, devoted to Dutch music, combined songs accompanied by piano with orchestral works conducted by Jan Ingenhoven, a Dutch composer and conductor. However, other than an undated postcard to Ingenhoven's wife there is no evidence that Cramer maintained any contact with her Dutch colleagues. In 1907–1908 she studied in Munich, probably with Max von Schillings (1868–1933),[11] and her *14 Volkstümliche Lieder,* op. 3, was published. This collection indicates her continued interest in relatively simple songs with an appealing lyricism, a genre Herder had once staunchly promoted.

In 1908 *Die Musik* mentions that her songs were performed in Chemnitz, Germany.[12] The following year she appeared in Amsterdam, Rotterdam, and The Hague with a recital program compiled entirely of her own lieder, a common practice in Germany but unusual in Holland. She accompanied two singers in this program, the well-known Gerard Zalsman and the soprano Jeanne Broek-Landré. *Die Musik* mentions that she also appeared in Paris and Berlin with the same program.[13] Reviews were divided: some harshly negative, others highly enthusiastic. The Dutch periodical *Caecilia* commented on her dissonant accompaniments: "In the song 'Liebesbrief' the composer writes such a chromatic, often dissonant accompaniment, that one asks what will happen in a marriage if there's already so much dissonance during the engagement? Or will it all be resolved?" This critic remarked that the advertisements comparing her to Hugo Wolf had raised his expectations far too high, but that he nevertheless had been fascinated during the entire evening.[14] The critic for the *Weekblad voor Muziek*, although impressed with her sweeter songs, was also negative about the more dissonant lieder ("ugly parallel fifths"), finding the songs in low German "extremely contrived," with "saltless texts." He continued, "If all these mistakes are corrected and Miss Cr[amer] imitates less Strauss and other modernists, and if she acquires some melodic talent, she will please us much better."[15] Gustav Kanth in *Die Musik* reviewed her Berlin concert: this "evening of songs . . . was without pleasure."[16]

On the other hand, the *Algemeen Handelsblad* praised her choice of contemporary German poets, who inspired her to "subtle colors and textures." This critic was charmed by the delicious song *Flieder* (Lilac), whose piano accompaniment formed "an independent song," creating a duet "with warm intimacy and full of a dreamy spring-like mood." He reminded readers that the famed Ludwig Wüllner had already introduced Dutch audiences to her music.[17] A Rotterdam newspaper was also positive: "The first concert by Anna Cramer in her home country has been a success for the bright composer . . . , much personal and innerly felt work. . . . And what was especially striking is that Anna Cramer's music has character, its own character."[18]

Not much is known about her between 1910, when *Sechs lieder,* op. 4 was published in Berlin, and 1917, when she resurfaced in Munich.[19] Until she moved to Vienna in 1925 she traveled frequently, returning either to Berlin, or to Holland where she stayed with her mother.[20]

Once established in Vienna Cramer enjoyed a particularly productive five-year period, working closely with Walter Simlinger (1889–1976), a Viennese singer and composer, and author of the librettos of her two light-spirited operas, *Der letzte Tanz* and *Dr. Pipalumbo*. There she also wrote *Zigeunerlied* (Gypsy Song) for mixed chorus, violin and tenor soli, and orchestra. Her compositional style continued to develop: Kurt Weil-like elements appear in *Troubadour-Stänchen*, while *Episode* sounds like a cabaret song.

After Simlinger moved to Berlin at the end of the twenties, Cramer became mired in financial problems and could no longer pay her rent.[21] Sales of her songs did not provide a sufficient income, and there is a record of monthly allowances sent by her mother. In 1930 she was admitted to a psychiatric clinic in Vienna for a short period.[22] Shortly thereafter she returned to a reclusive life in Holland. Her 1939 registration card lists her as a composer,[23] showing that she still considered this to be her profession, although she avoided all contact with the Dutch musical world.

In 1958 Cramer deposited her music manuscripts, carefully ordered, in a bank safe. These manuscripts are striking because of the countless revisions made over a great number of years, on bits of music paper pasted over the original, sometimes many layers thick. The revisions rarely alter the basic harmonic development, but do condense the texture of the compositions. Cramer even revised her published music: in op. 4 she has crossed out the title of number 1, as if it no longer met her approval, adding to numbers 2, 3, and 4 "neu gearbeitet."

The manuscripts of Cramer's two operas (piano scores) were also revised, again using bits of music paper, glue, and clear adhesive tape. Here and there pages were cut out or added, making it necessary to renumber the pages. The revisions of *Der letzte Tanz*, a one-act opera, and *Dr. Pipalumbo*, an opera in three acts and an epilogue, have rendered the piano-vocal scores into enormous, stiff, cardboard-like compilations. This leads us to conclude that Cramer continued to revise both operas and various lieder long after World War II. Jeanine Landheer has discovered in correspondence with Walter Simlinger, that Cramer was still revising her Bierbaum songs in the 1950s.[24]

In 1960 Cramer was forcibly moved to a nursing home in Blaricum after being discovered in a neglected state in her Amsterdam apartment.[25] She remained there for the last eight years of her life, completely forgotten, dying just before her ninety-fifth birthday.

Cramer left some fifty-five songs for voice and piano, all in moderate vocal range. For two collections she specified the voice type: tenor for the Dauthendey songs, and baritone for the Liliencron songs. Her style may be characterized as romantic, ranging from light and unpretentious to dramatic and passionate. Her diatonic writing, exemplified in, but not limited to the collection *14 Volkstümliche Lieder,* is often in a minor key, has an appealing lyricism and is often strophic. Many songs have a folk-like quality, with easy to remember melodic phrases, such as the beautiful *Sah im Traum* and *Der Rautenkranz*.

In the more chromatic lieder, dissonance becomes the primary expressive vehicle. These songs are through-composed and dramatic, often with rich, seemingly orchestrally conceived piano accompaniments. Harmonic complexity dominates, with enharmonic alterations, altered chords and semitonal clashes. In songs such as *Fatinga* (poetry by Liliencron), contrasting tempi and meters abound.

Predominantly declamatory vocal lines are set against dramatic piano accompaniments. A good example is the beautiful Mahler-like *Souvenir de Malmaison*, in which the narrator recites on G-sharp before gradually yielding to a more lyrical line. Indeed, some of Cramer's songs include speech-like settings. For the phrase "Dein Sarg schloss zu" in *Souvenir* the vocalist is instructed: "fast gesprochen, tonlos" (almost spoken, without pitch).

A number of lieder refer to poignant grief in love. Her longest and most dramatic, *Erwachen in den grellen Tag*, ends in cold rage: "Der heisse Lavastrom der Liebe war zu Stein. . . . Kalt will deine Lüge ich einmeisseln ihm" (The hot lava of love turned into stone. . . . Coldly I want to chisel your lie into it).

Like Robert Schumann (1810–1856) and Hugo Wolf (1860–1903), Cramer compiled collections of songs devoted to a single poet. In the reed suitcase she brought to a bank safe in 1958, she had jotted down six names on a slip of paper used to bundle the manuscripts: Detlev von Liliencron, O. J. Bierbaum, Carl Busse,

Max Dauthendey, Walter Simlinger and Max Rosenfeld. By far the most interesting poetry Cramer set was by Detlev von Liliencron (1844–1909), followed by Bierbaum (1865–1910). Besides stylistic similarity to the music of Hugo Wolf, she adopted his use of the term *gedichte* instead of lieder for her song collections. This was a common practice in the late German romantic tradition.

Although Cramer's song collections are not cycles in the sense that they form coherent groups constructed upon internal musical schemes (like Schumann's *Dichterliebe* and *Frauenliebe und leben*), it is clear from a number of factors that Cramer took care in compiling them. In op. 2 the order, keys, and subject matter of the five songs are purposely structured to aid in large-scale unity. The seven unpublished Dauthendey lieder are united by the common theme of love. The ten Liliencron songs do not have a common subject matter, but Cramer's careful ordering, with its fitting alteration of moods and tempi, merits their performance as a whole.

The two songs included here, *Weisst du noch?* op. 2, no. 5 and *Girre graues Täubchen*, op. 3, no. 6 have been selected to indicate the range of her style, from complex chromaticism to a simpler diatonic lyricism.

The five songs of op. 2, based on poems by Otto Julius Bierbaum, form a love story, addressing the beloved with "just have faith" but ending with betrayal. After four relatively happy songs *Weisst du noch?,* no. 5 takes us by surprise. While the first four poems were laden with rich imagery and flowery metaphors, this is a wistful poem, each stanza opening with the same simple question. The essential answer to the repetitions of "do you remember?" is a feeling of betrayal. This may be the song of a betrayed woman, who, once filled with hope and told in the first song "have faith," now remembers the words, "Nun lass ich dich nimmermehr" (Now I'll never leave you again). Although little is known about Cramer's personal life, it is possible that she identified with this poem. Cramer is at her best in the depiction of personal emotion in this hauntingly beautiful song, one of her most evocative.

In strophic form, the song opens in E major, with the accompaniment forming a continuous lilting motion through syncopation. In the second bar Cramer begins the first wistful, slowly descending bass line, characteristic of a number of her songs. Expressiveness is often intensified by chromatic surprises, such as in measures 8-9, where the D-flat (m. 8) is an accented passing tone resolving to the A/C/E-flat/G-flat chord; followed by a D-natural (m. 9) leading to a C in the augmented sixth chord which follows (the bass and the voice forming the augmented sixth A-flat/F-sharp).

The first ten-measure stanza closes with the old oak tree standing guard outside the cottage. The German "hält Wacht" is linguistically more related to "waiting" than in English. This waiting is musically echoed by a fermata on the dominant of E major, effective in its simplicity.

In the third and last stanza (m. 22) the rocking motion of the accompaniment stops and two chords softly illustrate dusk: E/B/D/F-sharp followed by D/A/C/E-flat/G. The last nine measures slowly build up a sense of despair. Triplets depict sorrowful church bells in the distance; perfect fifths follow in half notes as the rising chromatic bass line gradually becomes louder, imitating a bell swinging heavily. The explosion of sorrow comes in measure 30 on the word "nimmermehr," sung on the highest, loudest and longest tone of this song: D-sharp, part of the mediant chord, G-sharp/B/D-sharp. As in Schumann's *Im wunderschönen Monat Mai* from *Dichterliebe*, the last chord of *Weisst du noch?*, C-sharp/E-sharp/G/B, an altered dominant seventh, is left unresolved, the song ending on the same question on which it began.

Girre, graue Täubchen, op. 3, no. 6, is another song about betrayal by a beloved. In keeping with the poem Cramer creates a wistful mood, opening and closing in F-sharp minor. This song is an example of her easier, diatonic style. Trills and parallel thirds in the accompaniment suggest the cooing of doves (mm. 1-2), while the darting about of little silver fishes is suggested by triplet sixteenths (mm. 11 and ff.). (Sequences of thirds used to portray birds are also found in Strauss's lieder, for example in *Die Drossel*, *Im Walde* and in the *Vier letzte Lieder*.)

Although diatonic and folk-like, this sad, lyrical song in strophic variation also employs meter changes. The opening lines with six syllables each are set as groups of three eighth notes in $\frac{9}{8}$ meter, in the following lines Cramer condenses these groups of threes into $\frac{6}{8}$ meter. She also increases the pace in the $\frac{6}{8}$ passages by setting many syllables to sixteenth notes.

Notes

1. I thank Niek Zelders for genealogical information on the Zelders family.

2. Birth certificates: Amsterdam Municipal Archive.

3. Samuel Dresden, comp., *Gedenkboek uitgegeven ter gelegenheid van het 50-jarig bestaan van het Amsterdamsch Conservatorium (1884–1934)*, 73.

4. Amsterdam Conservatory, *Bericht van het Dertiende Schooljaar, 1896–1897*, 10.

5. "Musik, auch in wortlosen Tönen, hat ein Erhabenes, das keine andere Kunst hat, als ob sie, eine Sprache der Genien, nur unmittelbar an unser Innerstes als einen Mitgeist der Schöpfung spräche." Album inherited by Elisabeth Kuyper's nephew, E. Kuyper of Amsterdam.

6. Jeanine Landheer, *Anna Cramer, mythe en werkelijkheid* (Utrecht: Koninklijke Vereniging voor Nederlandse Muziekgeschiedenis, 1999), 30.

7. *Wenn die Linde blüht* (Carl Busse) was published in *Im Volkston II, Moderne Preislieder komponiert für Die Woche*, 1903.

8. This was suggested to me by Herta Müller of the Max Reger

Archives in her letter dated March 3, 1992.

9. Franz Ludwig, *Ludwig Wüllner, sein Leben und seine Kunst* (Leipzig: Weibezahl, 1931), 233, 243.

10. *Caecilia* (1906), 506.

11. Landheer, *Anna Cramer*, 33.

12. *Die Musik* VII-10 (February 1908), 243.

13. *Die Musik* VIII-11 (March 1909), 61.

14. *Caecilia* (1909), 76.

15. *Weekblad voor Muziek* 16 (1909), 54.

16. *Die Musik* VIII-11 (March 1909), 311.

17. *Algemeen Handelsblad,* 28 January 1909, morning edition.

18. *Nieuw Rotterdamsche Courant,* 26 January 1909.

19. Landheer, *Anna Cramer*, 35.

20. Ibid., 36.

21. Ibid., 56.

22. Ibid., 47.

23. Personal registration cards: Central Bureau for Genealogy, The Hague.

24. Landheer, *Anna Cramer*, 77.

25. *Algemeen Handelsblad,* 2 March 1960.

List of Works

Manuscripts and published songs housed in the Nederlands Muziek Instituut, The Hague.

Opera

Der letzte Tanz [ca. 1926–1927]. Libretto by Walter Simlinger, based on the novella *Ihr letzter Tanz* by Marie Gieseltzenplitz. One act, voices, piano score. Two arias are orchestrated and intended for independent performance: *Serenata* and *Tanzlied.* Unpublished.

Dr. Pipalumbo [1926–1928]. Libretto by Walter Simlinger. Three acts and epilogue. Voices, pf score. Unpublished.

Choral

Zigeunerlied [ca. 1926–1930]. Text by Bogdan Zaleski. T, vn, SATB, orch. Unpublished.

Voice and Piano

Wenn die Linde blüht. Text by Carl Busse. Berlin: August Scherl, 1903.

Fünf Gedichte, op. 1. Text (in Low German) by Klaus Groth. Berlin: Adolph Fürstner, 1907.
1. *Bispill*
2. *Bussemann*
3. *Wa heet se doch?*
4. *De Jäger*
5. *Int Holt*

Fünf Gedichte, op. 2. Text by Otto Julius Bierbaum. Berlin: Adolph Fürstner, 1907.
1. *Glaube nur*
2. *Flieder*
3. *Gefunden*
4. *Glück im Traum*
5. *Weisst du noch?*

14 Volkstümliche Lieder, op. 3. Munich: Dr. Heinrich Lewy, [1908].
1. *Schenk' mir mal Bayrisch ein.* Anonymous
2. *Ond 's kommt au emôl e Zeit.* Text by Cäsar Flaischlen
3. *Sah im Traum.* Text by Julius Roger
4. *Der Rautenkranz.* Text by Julius Roger
5. *Samstag, jeden Samstag.* Text by Julius Roger
6. *Girre, graues Täubchen.* Text by Julius Roger
7. *Hirse sät' ich.* Text by Julius Roger
8. *Dore am Bühl.* Text by Johann Georg Fischer
9. *Es ist ein Brünnlein geflossen.* Text by Anton Naaff
10. *Volksweise.* Text by Anna Klie
11. *Der welke Kranz.* Text by Wilhelm Herz
12. *Lebewohl.* Text by Ludwig Uhland
13. *Polnisches Volkslied.* Text by Carl Busse
14. *Tanzliedchen.* Oberschwaben folk song

Sechs Lieder, op. 4. Berlin: Adolph Fürstner, 1910.
1. *Erwachen in den grellen Tag.* Text by Otto Julius Bierbaum
2. *Ave Rosa.* Text by Otto Julius Bierbaum
3. *Michel mit der Lanze.* Text by Otto Julius Bierbaum
4. *Vale carissima.* Text by Karl Stieler
5. *Auftrag.* Text by Ludwig Heinrich Christoph Hölty
6. *Waldhornklänge.* Text by Carl Busse

7 Gedichte aus "Die Ewige Hochzeit." Text by Max Dauthendey. Unpublished, n.d.
1. *Du blühst wie die Julirosen*

2. *Überall blüht nur die Liebe*
3. *Geliebte, mein Garten ladet Dich ein*
4. *Ich bin entbrannt für Deine lustigen Füsse*
5. *In meinem Ohr wohnt nur Dein Name*
6. *Seit ich Dich küsse*
7. *Jedem durchsichtig wird ein Verliebter bald*

10 Gedichte. Text by Detlev von Liliencron. Unpublished, n.d.

1. *Souvenir de Malmaison*
2. *In einer grossen Stadt*
3. *Blümekens*
4. *Briefwechsel*
5. *Spruch*
6. *Meiner Mutter*
7. *Auf einer grünen Wiese*
8. *Nach dem Ball*
9. *Siegesfest*
10. *Fatinga*

Zwei Notturnos. Text by Walter Simlinger. Unpublished, [ca. 1927].

1. *Im Pavillon*
2. *Am Meer*

Troubadour-Ständchen. Text by Walter Simlinger. Unpublished, n.d.

Episode, T, pf. Text by Max Rosenfeld. Unpublished, n.d.

Bibliography

Bierbaum, Otto Julius. *Erlebte Gedichte*. Berlin and Leipzig: Schuster & Löffler [1891].

____. *Gesammelte Werke*, vol I: *Gedichte*. Munich and Leipzig: Georg Müller [1912].

Dauthendey, Max. *Die ewige Hochzeit, Der brennende Kalender, Liebeslieder*. Stuttgart: Arel Juncker [1905].

Dresden, Samuel, comp. *Gedenkboek uitgegeven ter gelegenheid van het 50-jarig bestaan van het Amsterdamsch Conservatorium (1884–1934)*. Amsterdam: Amsterdamsch Conservatorium, 1934.

Landheer, Jeanine. *Anna Cramer, mythe en werkelijkheid*. Utrecht: Koninklijke Vereniging voor Nederlandse Muziekgeschiedenis, 1999. Includes English summary.

Liliencron, Detlev von. *Sämtliche Werke*, vols. 2-3: *Lyrik*, edited by R. von Dehmel. Berlin: Schuster & Löffler, 1911.

Ludwig, Franz. *Ludwig Wüllner, sein Leben und seine Kunst*. Leipzig: Weibezahl, 1931.

Metzelaar, Helen, "Anna Cramer, Nederlandse Muziekarchieven nr. 36." The Hague: Gemeentemuseum, 1993.

____. "Cramer, Anna." In *The New Grove Dictionary of Music and Musicians*. London: Macmillan, 2001.

Smeed, J.W., *German song and its poetry, 1740–1900*. London: Croom Helm, 1987.

Discography

Anna Cramer: Songs. Rachel Ann Morgan, mezzo-soprano, and Marjès Benoist, piano. 1994: Globe GLO 5128.

"Vrienden van het lied: Nederland 1850–1950." Includes four songs by Cramer: *Flieder*, *Weisst du noch*, *Glück im Traum*, and *Waldhornklänge*. Rachel Ann Morgan, mezzo soprano, and Tan Crone, piano. 1994: Sweetlove SLR 9401255.

Weisst du noch?

Poetry by Otto Julius Bierbaum

Weisst du noch das kleine Haus Zwischen Wald und See und Feld? Eine alte Eiche hält Wacht davor.	Do you still remember the little house Between forest and lake and field? An old oak is standing guard Before it.
Weisst du noch das Zimmerchen? Wie ein Käfig war es klein. Nur ein Tisch, ein Stuhl und ein Kanapee.	Do you still remember the little room? It was as small as a cage. Only a table, a chair and A sofa.
Weisst du noch die Dämmerung? Glockenklang vom Kloster her . . . ; "Nun lass ich dich nimmermehr!" Weisst du noch?	Do you still remember the dusk? The sounds of bells from the monastery . . . ; "Now I'll never leave you again!" Do you remember?

Girre, graues Täubchen

Poetry by Julius Roger

Girre, graues Täubchen, girr' im Neste nimmer, Ach, mein Heissgeliebter schmollt mit mir noch immer. Wie er mir auch zürne, wollt' er mich vergessen, Müsst' es ihm das Herze schier zusammen pressen.	Coo, little grey dove, coo never in the nest, Ah, my passionately beloved still always quarrels with me. However angry he was with me, if he wanted to forget me, Then it should almost shatter his heart.
Schwimme, Silberfischchen, schwimme durch die Wogen, Ach, mein Heissgeliebter wie hat mich betrogen Deine falsche Liebe: Möge sich des Armen Wie des Ungetreuen Gott der Herr erbarmen.	Swim, little silver fish, swim through the waves, Ah, my passionately beloved, how did Your false love deceive me: May God the Lord have mercy For the poor and for the unfaithful.

Translations by Helen H. Metzelaar

Weisst du noch?

O. J. Bierbaum

Anna Cramer
Op. 2 No. 5
Helen Metzelaar, editor

Andantino

p *cantabile*

Weisst du noch das klei - ne Haus

espr.

5

zwi-schen Wald und See und Feld? Ei-ne al - te

9

[a tempo]

Ei - che hält Wacht da - vor. Weisst du

dim. *cantabile* *p* *espr.*

13

noch: das Zim - mer - chen? Wie ein Kä - fig war es

17
klein. Nur ein Tisch, ein Stuhl und ein Ka-na-pee.
Ped.
21
poco riten.
a tempo
poco cresc.
Weisst du noch die Däm-me-rung? Glo-cken-klang vom
dim.
poco cresc.
25
cresc.
Klo-ster her; "Nun
29
ritard.
lass ich dich nim-mer-mehr!" Weisst du noch?
più rit.
dim.
espr.

Girre, graues Täubchen

Julius Roger

Anna Cramer
Op. 3 No. 6
Helen Metzelaar, editor

Andante

p

Gir - re, grau - es Täub - chen, girr' - im Ne - ste nim - mer ach, mein Heiss - ge-lieb - ter

4

schmollt mit mir noch im - mer. *mf* Wie er mir auch zür - ne, wollt' er mich ver-ges - sen,

7

müsst' es ihm das Her - ze schier zu-sam-men pres - sen, *dim.* schier zu-sam - men pres - sen.

11

a tempo

p

Schwim - me Sil - ber-fisch - chen schwim - me durch die Wo -

13
mf
gen, ach mein Heiss - ge - lieb - ter
mf
15
rit.
wie hat mich be - tro - gen dei - ne fal - sche Lie - be:
17
Più mosso
mp
Mö - ge sich des Ar - men wie des Un - ge-treu - en Gott der Herr er - bar - men,
mp
cresc.
cresc.
20
dim.
Gott der Herr er - bar - men.
dim.

Mary Carr Moore
(1873–1957)

CATHERINE PARSONS SMITH

Many women have sought careers as opera singers, but few have devoted their energy to composing operas. Mary Carr Moore (August 6, 1873–January 9, 1957, born Mary Louise Carr) did both. As a result of the confluence of many events in her life— attending theatrical events as a young child, her early career as an opera singer, inspiration by the American music movement, and a life lived principally in the Far West where "do-it-yourself" played a major role in all aspects of life—Moore completed eight stage works ranging in length from a vaudeville sketch to a four-act grand opera, using librettos variously in English, Italian, and French. The closing scenes of the last of these, *Legende Provençale*, are presented here.

Born in reconstruction-era Memphis (Tennessee) to Yankee parents, Moore demonstrated her musical talent from the age of five. She moved to the West Coast with her family in 1881 only a dozen years after her grandfather helped complete the first transcontinental railroad. Her training as a singer and composer took place in San Francisco under two highly respected, Leipzig-trained musicians, Henry Bickford Pasmore (1857–1944) for voice, and John Haraden Pratt (1848–1935) for composition.[1] Moore taught voice and coached amateur musical productions in nearby towns while still a student. At the age of nineteen she completed her first operetta, *The Oracle*, written for her musical friends and produced in San Francisco. Moore provided both the book and the music, gaining her first practical experience in orchestration in the process. She also sang the lead role. (The libretto is lost, but the songs survive, including several new ones composed for a revival in Seattle several years after the premiere.) Although she showed promise as a coloratura soprano, Moore's hopes for a singing career were ended in her early twenties by ill health while she was an apprentice with a local opera company. Conflicted about her artistic ambitions and her position in a close-knit Victorian family with aristocratic pretensions and a greatly diminished fortune, she joined her parents in tiny Lemoore, California in 1894; there and in neighboring towns she assumed a role as a musician and teacher, apparently with lowered horizons. Like her mother, Sarah Pratt Carr, who was ordained to the Unitarian ministry in middle age and preached to newly organized congregations in several nearby towns, Moore viewed her activity as a form of community betterment. Thus she became an early advocate of women's rights, practicing what is now seen as domestic feminism through her musical activities. In Lemoore, she married and bore her first child. A large number of songs were the major compositional achievement of these early years. (Her first, a lullaby, was published in 1889, when she was sixteen. The last of approximately 200 works appeared in 1952.)

Moore followed her husband and parents to the booming frontier town of Seattle in 1901. There she resumed teaching and bore two more children. Influenced by the American music movement and her growing personal unhappiness, she revived her aspirations as a composer, producing her first masterpiece, *Narcissa: Or, The Cost of Empire*, about the winning of the west. Divorced in 1914, she returned to San Francisco, where she resumed her teaching career. In 1926 she moved to Los Angeles, and pieced together a living teaching theory, composition, and music history at Chapman College and the Olga Steeb Piano School. For a time in the early 1930s she managed to support her mother, a daughter and two grandsons. Moore became an advocate of music by American composers, especially western Americans, in the early 1900s and remained an activist throughout her life. The Mary Carr Moore Manuscript Club, the California Society of Composers, and the Native American Composers, all organized in Los Angeles with her enthusiastic participation, touched the lives of such well-known composers as Charles Wakefield Cadman (1881–1946), Fannie Charles Dillon (1881–1947), William Grant Still (1895–1978), and, briefly, John Cage (1912–1992). In spite of all this activity, she remained a prolific composer of chamber music and songs as well as stage works. Her style evolved continuously over the decades.

Given Moore's geographical location and the absence of either a sojourn abroad or a period of study in an eastern United States city, it is not surprising that elements of late nineteenth-century popular and parlor song, as well as European opera and American theatrical music, appear in much of Moore's music, especially in her early works. She describes the style of *Narcissa: Or, The Cost of Empire* (1912) as "archaic."[2] The indigenous musical cultures of the west coast cities in which Moore worked provided her with a way to earn a modest living through her teaching, and with a limited amount of encouragement and opportunity. Though her opera scores make clear that her style and awareness of stage requirements continued to develop, they also betray the limitations imposed by her cultural position. The most striking of these are her lack of experience with a professional opera company and the virtually complete absence of serious critical give-and-take in the course of her career. From her background of home dramatics, community theatricals, and ad hoc productions, all virtually without the cosmopolitan intellectual and artistic exposure that the very concept of opera implies, Moore succeeded in writing viable opera. *Legende Provençale* represents the highest point in her aspirations as a serious creative artist and, as she herself knew, the peak of her achievement. That this ghost story, which could be staged so effectively in a modern opera studio, should almost have become a ghost itself, is perhaps the saddest irony of Moore's career.

Typically, Moore's music was politely received by critics who were bemused by her gender and could not or would not offer either descriptive or analytic commentary. James Sample, one of the conductors who examined the now-lost orchestral score of *Legende*, wrote Moore at some length about the opera. His letter turns out to be far and away the most incisive extant criticism of her music:

> I believe the *Legende* is the best work of yours that I have had the privilege to see. The story, and both librettos (Fr. & Engl) are excellent. . . . You have caught the atmosphere of the story, and of Provence. . . .
>
> I have only one adverse criticism of the work as a whole, and that is, I would like to see more dramatic sections, as a contrast to the many delicate sections. . . . The vocal lines of the work are really fine, and I mean that. I don't know of one American opera that even approaches it in this respect. . . . With a bit more dramatic punch here and there (which must come from the libretto) it is by far the best of the American operas I have come across. . . . *Manon* of Massenet, is so popular, but this is a better work in all ways — and if *Manon* is popular, how can this fail? . . . If the music is good, I am convinced that it can't be lost or buried long.[3]

The language of *Legende Provençale* is tonal, however it includes chains of non-resolving unstable chords, especially half-diminished sevenths, French sixths, and Neapolitan seconds. The religious texts are supported by conservative triadic harmony. The character Amiel's supernatural appearances are accompanied by a "ghostly" triplet figure featuring parallel fifths (heard early in the first excerpt). Leisurely plagal cadences outnumber authentic (dominant-to-tonic) ones; resolutions are widely spaced. Distinctions between recitative and aria are blurred, and the transitions between them are smoother than in Moore's earlier operas.

In retelling a French legend from the fifteenth century, *Legende Provençale* explores a question about truly romantic love. What happens when the characters really stick to their promises of single-minded fidelity? (The question had profound meaning for Moore, who had attempted suicide in response to her first husband's philandering.) In addition, it deals with themes of patriotism, honor, duty, religion, and mysticism, all essential to Moore's value system regardless of the conflicts they might have generated in practice.

After a prologue in which the Sacristan tells of the ghostly story to come, a chorus of women celebrates Rozanne's birthday. Amiel pledges eternal love to Rozanne promising, at her request, never to look at another woman. Enter Agnes Sorel, mistress to Charles VII, looking for recruits for an army to drive out the hated English. Amiel impulsively promises to support Sorel and her mission, technically violating his promise to Rozanne. The visiting sorcerer/entertainer Drascovie manipulates Rozanne to withhold forgiveness and persuades Amiel to wager his sacred honor that he will have the first dance with Rozanne at the evening's ball despite the (carefully cultivated) misunderstanding. In Act II, Rozanne throws his brief, imagined infidelity at him and refuses to dance with Amiel at the ball. Three times Amiel beseeches her, ever more passionately; three times she refuses him. After the third rejection, Amiel rushes out in despair, throwing himself off the battlements of the castle.

Act III takes place a year later. The ghost of Rozanne's suicidal lover appears nightly; she is unable to find comfort either from the priest who visits her or from Agnes Sorel, who apologizes for the tragedy she unwittingly caused. Rozanne sings *L'étoile du soir* (Star of Evening). Drascovie reappears to tell Rozanne that the lovers can be reunited under one condition, namely that Rozanne become a suicide like Amiel. In the first section included here, Amiel's ghost appears in the window, waking the sleeping Rozanne as he enters. They sing a duet of reconciliation, ending when Amiel leaves and Rozanne, clasping a crucifix to her breast, faints away as a storm rages outside.

The Epilogue, also reproduced here, is Rozanne's funeral, which takes place on All Souls' Night. An assortment of ghosts drifts about the churchyard as the monks are heard chanting a prayer for absolution from the Latin Requiem. As the procession emerges from the church, Amiel appears among the ghosts and summons Rozanne, who rises from her coffin and goes to join him on the hill above the churchyard. The lovers are ecstatically united for eternity as the procession completes its *Agnus Dei*.

Moore was very well aware that the harmonic language and dramatic demands of *Legende* were beyond the potential of the singers and volunteer groups upon whom she had relied for most of her creative career. Realizing the critical price she had paid for uneven productions and performances, she elected to hold out for a production worthy of this work's quality. (The presence of the Federal Music Project of the late 1930s, which in Los Angeles included an opera program, made this goal more realistic.) Although Moore circulated the orchestral score among several conductors in the early 1940s, there was little likelihood of a professional production in those wartime years. The only part of this opera then performed in public was Rozanne's Act III aria, *L'étoile du soir*, which was very well received when it was played by the WPA-sponsored Los Angeles Federal Symphony Orchestra in 1941 under conductor James Sample. Tragically, the score was lost. Probably it was accidentally destroyed by one of the conductors to whom she showed it. One copy of the 1935 piano-vocal score including a title page survives and lists the intrumentation: 2 flutes + 3rd flute (piccolo); 3 horns in F; 2 oboes + English horn; 2 trumpets in B-flat; 2 clarinets, 3 trombones + tuba; 2 bassoons; timpani; 2 tubular bells; usual percussion; celesta; harp; strings. Offstage effects: piano (Prologue); small organ (Epilogue).

After discovering the loss of the full score, Moore constructed a set of transparent master sheets of the piano-vocal score in her shaky, 1949 hand, but there was no longer any possibility of re-creating the orchestral score. In this second piano-vocal score there are no substantive changes. A few alterations in voicings, chord spellings, articulation marks, and indications concerning orchestration appear near the beginning. Enclosed numbers are original rehearsal numbers. In this edition, I have conflated the two manuscript versions. Moore copied out a full score and parts for the one aria that was performed with orchestra. She had also begun to extract the parts from the orchestral score, but completed only the first violin part.

Notes

1. Catherine Parsons Smith and Cynthia S. Richardson. *Mary Carr Moore, American Composer* (Ann Arbor: University of Michigan Press, 1987), 13, 23, 29-31.

2. Ibid.

3. Letter from James Sample to Mary Carr Moore, May 25, 1943. Mary Carr Moore Archive, Music Library, University of California Los Angeles.

Selected List of Works

There are songs, piano music, chamber music (a quintet for piano and string quartet entitled "Saul," the most important), a piano concerto, and some orchestral music. Except for those listed in modern editions all are in the Mary Carr Moore Archive, Music Library, University of California, Los Angeles. A complete catalog is found in Smith and Richardson.

Operas

The Oracle (1893–1942). Two-act operetta. Text by Mary Carr Moore. Unpublished.

Narcissa: Or, The Cost of Empire (1909–1911). Four acts. Text by Sarah Pratt Carr. Piano-vocal score. New York: Witmark, 1912.

The Leper (1912). One-act opera. Unpublished.

Memories (1914). One-act operatic idyll. Text by Charles Eugene Banks. Unpublished.

Harmony (1917). One-act musical farce. Text by Mary Carr Moore and Mission High School (San Francisco) students. Unpublished.

The Flaming Arrow (1919–1920). One-act Indian intermezzo. Text by Sarah Pratt Carr. Revised (1926?) as *The Shaft of Ku'pish-ta-ya*. Unpublished.

David Rizzio (1927–1928). Two-act Italian opera. Text by Emanuel M. Browne. Piano-vocal score. San Francisco: Wesley Webster, 1937; reprinted (with introduction by Catherine Parsons Smith) New York: Da Capo Press, 1981.

Legende Provençale (begun under the working titles *Drascovie*, *Macabre*, or simply "the French opera" in 1927–1928; acts 2 and 3 completed 1935; full score completed 1938; further work on the plainsong of the Epilogue as late as 1942). Three-act (French) opera. Text by Eleanore Flaig. Full score lost. Unpublished.

Los Rubios (1931). Three-act opera. Text by Neeta Marquis. Unpublished.

Flutes of Jade Happiness (1932–1934). Three-act operetta. Text by Laura Sweeney Moore. Unpublished.

Modern Editions

Sonata for Violin and Piano. Arranged for flute and piano. Charlotte, N.C.: ALRY, 1988.

Twelve Songs. Ed. Catherine Parsons Smith. Bryn Mawr, PA: Hildegard Publishing Company, 1995.

Bibliography

Rogers, Barbara Jean. "Mary Carr Moore's Chamber Music for Piano with Other Instruments," *ILWC Journal* (June 1994): 1-10.

____. "The Works for Piano Solo and Piano with Other Instruments of Mary Carr Moore (1873–1957)." DMA, University of Cincinnati, 1992.

Smith, Catherine Parsons. "Athena at the Manuscript Club: Reflections on John Cage and Mary Carr Moore," *Musical Quarterly* 79 (1995): 351-67.

Smith, Catherine Parsons, and Richardson, Cynthia S. *Mary Carr Moore, American Composer*. Ann Arbor; University of Michigan Press, 1987.

Editorial Comments

This edition represents a conflation of the two extant piano-vocal scores. The two scores are almost identical. There are occasional changes in chord spellings; I have used the simpler spelling, which is usually found in the second version. Articulations, particular slurs in the keyboard part, are taken from both versions since they supplement each other. Where the translation is improved in the second version, I have used that. Where there are note differences, very often the later version appears to be in error; I have selected what seems the more logical reading, usually from the earlier score. None of these choices are significant enough to indicate in the score.

Three languages are involved. The body of the text is given in both original scores in French and English, as specified on the title page. Both were supplied by Eleanore Flaig, the opera's librettist. Both languages are reproduced in the present piano-vocal score. Corrections of spelling and punctuation are not indicated. The parts of the Requiem that are sung in the Epilogue (and in part of Act III not included here) are sung in Latin. The Latin text excerpted from the Roman Catholic Requiem has been corrected to correspond more closely to the texts in the *Liber Usualis*. Since this text must be sung in Latin, unlike the main French text, which may also be sung in English, no translation was supplied by the composer or librettist. A translation drawn by the editor from several available English-language versions follows.

Act III, Scene 1

Amiel: Regardez! Comme la damoiselle dort en paix! Pendant que sa victime erre dans les ténèbres nocturnes.	Behold her, how the damozel sleeps in peace! The while her victim wanders thro' the midnight shadows.
	Rozanne (awakes in fright):
Amiel! Amiel!	'Tis thou! Amiel!
A. Aie! Je suis venu te réclamer!	Aye! I come at last to claim my own!
R. Ne me touches pas!	Do not touch me now!
A. Tu recules devant moi! Devant moi! Pour te plaire de toi ai sacrifié mon salut éternel	Dost recoil from my touch! From me! Who, because of thee, have sacrificed mine eternal peace
R. Que la ciel me rende temoignage, j'en ai payé le prix, mille fois Ma vie, n'a telle pas été un purgatoire.	Just heav'n above, be my witness, how I have paid the price in sorrow. My life, it has been naught but purgatory.
A. Je t'en ai prévenu ma promesse est non brisée.	I gave thee warning, my promise is still unbroken.
R. N'as tu point de pitié pour celle dont l'amour de toi dure malgré tout? Hélas	Hast thou no compassion for her whose love for thee endures despite all? Alas
A. Oui, je te plains de tout mon coeur, de tout mon coeur, mais les bornes de l'éternité, hélas! Sont entre nous et tu ne puis entrer dans ma vie Sauf par la Porte de la Mort.	Ah yes, with all my heart I grieve, I grieve for thee Yet the bonds of Eternity, alas! divide us still. Thou canst not joint with me in my life Save by the Portal of Death.
R. L'ange Noir, doux deliverateur.	Angel of Death, thou deliverer tender.
A. Deliverateur. A cause de péché auquel tu m'a forcé, on m'a condamné à la vallé de maudits. Pendant de longs mois, je suis resté esclave dans ce royaume de suicides.	Deliverer tender. Because of the sin I did for love of thee I have been condemn'd to the Valley of the Accurs'd. For lo these long months, have I been captive in the dark realms of the suicides.

R. Hélas, Gran' dieu, pas ça.	Alas, Ah Heav'n, alas.
A. Mais j'ai enfin regagné la liberté! Et si, ce n'était pas, que mon âme soupire constamment, après toi, Je serais déjà parmi les bénis.	Now at least, my liberty I have regain'd, And now, could I but still my soul's deep longing evermore for thee, I should long ago have been among the bless'd.
R. Qu'est que cela?	What do I hear?
A. Les éléments! Souhaitant la bienvenue à ma fiancée. Viens, donc! L'heure d'accomplissement est sonnée.	Thou hear'st the storm, the symphony of heav'n, to welcome my bride! Ah, come! The hour of fulfilment is at hand.
R. Laisse moi ou je deviendra folle! Arrière, va t'en! Va! Arrière.	Leave me now, I am terrified by death. Ah spare me, away! Ah, spare me.
A. Mais tu m'accompagneras, Allons, je marcherai à ton côté sur la route solennelle.	But thou shall accompany me. Ah, come, for I shall walk by thy side thro' the valley of death.
R. Arrière, gran' Dieu!	Ah spare me, Oh God!
A. Ah Rozanne, la vie est le songe, la mort est la portail d'Immortalité.	Ah, Rozanne, this life is the dream, and Death is but the portal of Immortality!
	(Amiel exits via the Tower window and vanishes.)
R. Amiel!	Amiel!
	(Rozanne looks toward the window, clasps a large bronze crucifix, and faints. End of scene.)

Act III, Scene 2: Epilogue

(All Souls' Night. Rozanne's funeral is going on inside the church; in the churchyard outside, spirits wander in the moonlight.) Latin text from *Liber usualis*

	(Priest, inside church. Absolution.)
Non intres in judicium cum servo tuo Domine, quia nullus apud te justificabitur homo, nisi per te omnium peccatorum, ei tribuatur, remissio. Non ergo eum, quaesumus tua judicialis, sententia premat,	Do not enter into judgment on thy servant, Lord, for no one becomes holy in Your sight unless You grant her forgiveness for all her sins. We beg you therefore, do not let the verdict of your judgment go against her
quem tibi vera suplicatio, fidei christianae, commendat, sed gratia tua illi succurrente, mereatur evadere judicium ultionis,	whom this loyal prayer of Christian faith commends to Your mercy. Rather, through Your grace, may she escape the sentence she serves,

qui dum viveret, insignitus est signaculo Sanctae Trinitatis.

for during her earthly life she was signed with the
seal of the Holy Trinity.

Qui vivis et regnas, in saecula saeculorum.

Thou who lives and reigns, world without end.

(Chorus of monks sings Responsory.)

Libera me, Domine de morte aeterna, in die illa tremenda;
Quando caeli movendi sunt et terra, dum veneris judicare,
Saeculum per ignem.
Tremens factus sum ego et timeo dum discussio
venerit atque ventura ira.
Quando caeli movendi sunt et terra.
Dies illa Dies irae calamitatis et miseriae,
dies magna et amara valde.
Dum veneris judicare saeculum per ignem.
Requiem aeternam dona eis Domine: et lux
perpetua luceat eis.
Requiem aeternum.

Deliver me, O Lord, from eternal death on that dreadful day when the heavens and the earth shall be moved, and Thou shalt come to judge the world by fire. I am seized with fear and trembling when I reflect upon the judgement and the wrath to come. When the heaven and the earth shall be moved. That day, a day of wrath, of wasting and of misery, a dreadful and exceedingly bitter day. When Thou shalt come to judge the world by fire. Give them eternal rest, O Lord, and let perpetual light shine upon them.

(Boy choristers)

Kyrie eleison.
Kyrie eleison.
Kyrie eleison.

Lord, have mercy.
Lord, have mercy.
Lord, have mercy.

Amiel (outside). Rozanne!

Rozanne!

(Boys, inside)

Christe eleison.

Christ, have mercy.

Amiel. Rozanne!

Rozanne!

Kyrie eleison.

Lord, have mercy.

(The procession emerges from the church.)

Amiel. Image de mon âme, Echo de mon soupir.
Amiel & Rozanne. Ah!
Amiel. Au delà se coule la riviere funèbre.
Et nous, nous trouvons enfin! Parmis les ombres bénies.

Belov'd of my soul, echo of my desire,
We have pass'd beyond the river of death,
united our souls, at peace,
mingling with shades of the bless'd.

Rozanne. Ah! "Puis je vis un nouveau ciel et une nouvelle terre,
car les premières choses ne sont plus.
Elles ne sont que des ombres trompeuses qui
s'étendent sur le sien de l'Infini."

And I see a new heav'n and a new earth,
for the former things are no more.
They are shadows that vanish like mist
in the light of Infinite Love.

Amiel & Rozanne. L'amour redemteur a vancu la Mort.
Tu et moi, un être unique,
un soupir mele, et notre amour une double prière,
un être unique,
un soupir mele, et notre amour une double prière,
Echo de mon soupir, image de mon âme, Ah.

Redeeming love has vanquish'd death.
Thou and I, our souls as one, in eternal love,
evermore a twofold pray'r.
Echo of my desire, belov'd of my soul.

In Paradisum deducant te,
Angeli in tuo adventu suscipiant te Martyres,
et perducant te in civitatem sanctum Jerusalem.
Chorus Angelorum te suscipiat
et cum Lazaro quondam paupere
aeternum habeas requiem.

(Monks: Antiphon, procession to cemetery, simultaneous with "Au delà" above.)
May the angels lead you into paradise;
May the Martyrs welcome you upon your arrival,
and lead you into the holy city of Jerusalem.
May a choir of angels welcome you,
and, with poor Lazarus of old,
may you have eternal rest.

Agnus Dei. Agnus Dei. Qui tollis peccata mundi,
Dona eis requiem.
Miserere, Miserere.
Agnus Dei. Qui tollis peccata mundi.
Agnus Dei. Dona eis requiem. Dona eis pacem,
Dona eis pacem sempiternam.

(Monks and choristers.)

Lamb of God. Lamb of God. Who takes away the sins of the world,
Give them eternal rest. Have mercy on them.
(End of opera)

Legende Provençale

from Act III, Scene 1

Eleanora Flaig

Mary Carr Moore
Catherine Parsons Smith, editor

(The tower chamber of Rozanne, one year later, [i.e. after the lovers' confrontation and Amiel's suicide. -ed.] Rozanne lies on her couch, sleeping. Outside the open casement window, the monks have been heard chanting the Lord's Prayer from the monastery, which is just across the churchyard from the tower.

*The double barline indicates different vocal entrances, not sectional divisions.

23
R.
A.
ff mp
cules ___ de - vant moi! ___ de-vant
coil ___ from my touch! ___ from
p
ff
mp
p
27 28 accel.
R.
A.
f mf mp
moi! pour te plaire ___ de toi ___ ai sac-ri-fié ___ mon sa -
me! Who, be-cause ___ of thee, ___ have sac-ri-ficed mine e -
28
f
30
R.
f mp
Que la ciel me rend - té maign-a - ge,
Just heav'n a - bove, be my wit - ness,
A.
lut e-ter-nel
ter - nal peace

Meno mosso
33
R.
A.
j'en ai pa - yé la prix, mille fois
How I have paid the price, in sor - row!
Ma vie, n'a t'elle pas é -
My life, it has been
36
té un pur-ga-toi - re
naught but pur-ga - to - ry
Je t'en ai préve - nu
I gave thee warn - ing
39
ma pro mes - se est non bri -
My prom - ise is still un -

42
R.
A.
N'as tu point de pi - tié pour celle
Hast thou no com - pas-sion for her
sée
bro - ken
45
riten.
dans l'a-mour de toi du - re mal - gré tout?
whose love for thee en-dures de - spite all?
48
29 Tempo, un poco più mosso
Oui je te pleins de tout mon
Ah, yes with all my heart I

52
R.
A.
pp
mf
coeur de tout mon coeur mais les bornes de l'e-
grieve, I grieve for thee Yet, the bonds of E-
pp
56
mp
mf
Hé-las
A-las
ter-ni-té hé-las! sont en-tre nous et
ter-ni-ty, a-las! di-vides us still thou
mp
60
mp
pp
tu ne puis en-trer dans ma vie Sauf par la Porte de la Mort
canst not join with me in my life Save by the por-tal of Death
mp

63
R.
L'an - ge Noir
An - gel of Death
doux de-liv - er - a - teur
thou de-liv - er - er ten-der -
A.
De-
De-
67
30
liv - er-a-teur
liv - er-er ten-der
A cause de pe-che
Be-cause of the sin
au-quel tu m'a for-cé
I did for love of thee
70
Hé-las!
A-las!
on m'a con-dam-né
I have been con-demn'd
à la val-lée de mau-dits
to the val-ley of the ac curs'd

73
R.
A.
Hé - las
A - las
Pen-dant de lon-gues mois, je suis re-ste es - clave
For lo, these long months, have I been cap - - tive
76
Gran
Ah
dans ce roy - aume de su - i - ci des
in the dark realms of the su - i - cides
79
Dieu Pas ça
Heav'n a - las
Mais j'ai en - fin re -
Now, now at last, my

83
31
R.
A.
f
mf
f
ga-gné la li-ber-té! Et si, ce n'é-tais pas, que mon
li-ber-ty I have re-gain'd And now, could I but still my
tr
8va
ff
86
âme sou-pire con-stam-ment, a-près
soul's deep long-ing e-ver-more for
(8va)
88
toi Je se-rais dé-jà
thee, I should long a-go

90
R.
A.
f
3
Qu'est que ce - la
What do I hear?
mf
par mi les bé - nis
have been a-mong the bless'd.
Thunder
6
7
tr
93
(storm arising)
Les é - lé-ments! Sou-hai-tant la bien-venu à ma fi - an - cée. Vien,
thou hear'st the storm, the sym-phon-y of heav'n, to wel-come my bride! Ah,
97
ff
(terrified)
Qu' est-ce que ce - la?
Ma - ry in heav'n
donc! L' - heure d'ac-com plisse-ment est son - née
come the hour of ful - fill - ment is at hand

101
R.
Lais - se moi ou je de-vien-dra fol - le! Ar-ri -
Leave me now, I am ter - ri - fied by death Ah,
A.
Ro - zan - na
Ro - zan - na
104
èrè va' t'en! Va!
spare me, A - way, Ah!
(tenderly)
Mais, tu m'ac -
But thou shalt ac -
32
108
(whispering in fright)
Ar-ri-ère
Ah, spare me
com-pag-ne-ras, Al - lons je mar-che-rais à ton co - té sur la
com-pan - y me. Ah, come for I shall walk by thy side thro' the

112
mf
f
(swoons)
R.
Ar-ri - ère gran' Dieu!
Ah, spare me Oh, God!
A.
rou-te so-le-nelle
val-ley of death
6
6
ff
pp
ppp
115 Agitato
rit.
33
Meno mosso
Amiel leans tenderly over Rozanne. He does not touch her.
p
Ah, Ro-zan -
Ah, Ro-zan -
f
f
118
mp
f
ne la vie, est le songe, La mort
ne this life is the dream and death
mp
f

*Any of these three measures may be repeated if more stage time is required.

Roz. takes large bronze crucifix from prie-dieux. She clasps it to her breast.
She comes down center.
131
R.
A.
mp
mf
ff
A-miel
A-miel
Ah
Ah
f
ff
135
As lightning floods the room, she sinks to the floor, crucifix still clasped to her breast.
sfz
[arp.]
ff
Thunder
fff
fff
Lights down. (Curtain) The scene is drawn aside, revealing the monastery as the next scene begins.
139
sfz
Thunder
ff
fff

Legende Provençale

Act III, Scene 2 (Epilogue)

Eleanora Flaig

Mary Carr Moore

Catherine Parsons Smith, editor

The monastery and churchyard, flooded by moonlight. Yews in the background. Upstage C, a half-recumbent tombstone is visible. Chapel R, through whose stained glass windows dim light is reflected.

The night of All Souls Day (Le Jour des Morts.) From either side appear, silently seeking, the spirits of the dead. A young nun passes by, counting her beads. A mother with a child in her arms. Lovers searching for one another meet, separate and seek again. From the start (1 to rehearsal 7), there is a continuous pageant of the spirits of the dead. At 7 , when Amiel calls Rozanne, the movement pauses. When the cortège emerges from the monastery between 8 and 9 , the spirits shrink nearer the wings, leaving Center clear.

The monks are heard from the chapel, chanting the Mass for the Dead at Rozanne's funeral. An organ sounds backstage, as from the chapel.

13
P.
mf
Non er - go e - um, qua es - u - mus tu - a ju - di - ci al - is, sen - ten - ti - a
2 (Two lovers meet)
(Many spirits searching in vein)
mf
16
pre - mat. quem ti - bi ve - ra sup - li - ca - ti - o, fi - de - i Chris - ti -
f
19
an - ae, com - men - det, sed gra - ti - a tu - a il - li suc - cu - ren - te,
22
me - re - a - tur e - vad - e - re ju - di - ci - um u - ti - on - nis
mf

25
P.
mf
qui dum vi - ver-et
in-sig-ni - tus est sig - na-cu-lo Sanc-tae Tri-ni -
f
28
ta - tis. Qui vi-vis et reg - nas, in sae-cu-la sae-cu - lo - rum.
31
ff
35
Chorus
A - men
3
Li-be-ra me, Do - mi-ne de
repeat if needed

Ch.
mor-te ae-ter - na, in die il-la tre-men - da, Quan - do cae - li mo -
ven-di sunt et ter - ra, dum ve-ne-ris ju-di-ca-re, Sae-cu-lum per ig - num
Tre-mens fac-tus sum e - go et ti - me-o dum dis-cus-si-o
4 2nd time cut to rehearsal 6
ven-e-rit at-que ven-tu - ra i - ra. Quan - do cae - li mo -

52
TTB
ven-di sunt et ter-ra Di-es il-la Di-es i-rae
5
56
ca-la-mi-ta-tis et mi-ser-i-ae, di-es mag-na et a-ma-ra val-de;
59
Dum ve-ne-ris ju-di-ca-re sae-cu-lum per ig-num
62 Priest
Re qui-em, ae-ter-nam, do-na e-is Do-mi-ne, et lux per-pe-tu-a lu-ce-at e-i.
Pageant of spirits gradually disappear. (a piacere)

The repeat is in accordance with the text of the Mass; it may be omitted here.

66 6 (2nd time)
Boy Choristers (SSA)
SSA
TTB
Kyrie eleison
Re-qui-em ae-ter-num.
Ky-ri-e e-le-i-
son
Ky-ri-e e-le-i-son
(Enter Amiel, Down R)
(calling softly)
(stands down R - on grassy mound - watches the monastery.)
A.
Ro-zan-ne
Ro-zanne
Ky-ri-e e-le-i-son

77
A.
SSA
mf
Chris - te e - le - i - son
mf
mf
mf
80
A.
SSA
mf
Chris - te e - le - i - son
f
Chris - te e - le - i - son
f
Funeral cortège emerges from chapel, carrying the coffin, monks preceded by choristers swinging censers; Rozanne, in her shroud, like a wraith slips behind the cortège toward Amiel, who lifts her beside him.
83
A.
mf
Ro - zan - na
Ro - zanne
8
SSA
mf
Ky - ri-e e - le - i -
mf
f
mf
8

86
A.
Ro - zan - -
Ro - zan
SSA
son
89
na
Ky - ri - e e - le - i - son
Ky - ri - e e - le - i -
92
Im - age de mon âme
Be - lov'd of my soul
son e - le - i - son

95
R.
E - cho de mon sou - pir,
E - cho of my de - sire
A.
opening his arms to Rozanne
mp
mf
98
rit. a tempo
Ah
Ah
pp
101
9
Ah
Ah
Au de - là se coule la ri-viere fu - nèbre Et
We have pass'd be - yond the ri - ver of death, U -
Monks (TTB)
TTB
[funeral cortège]
In Pa - ra - dis-um de-du - can -

104
R.
Ah
A.
nous, nous trou-vons en - fin! par - mis les om - bres bé - nies
ni - ted our souls at peace! ming-ling with shades of the bless'd
TTB
te, An - ge - li in tu - o ad-ven tu sus -

107
R.
"Puis je vis un Nou-veau ciel et un[e] nou - velle terre
And I see a new heav'n and a new earth
A.
Ro - zanne
Ro - zanne
TTB
cip - i - ant te Mar - ty - res et per-du - cant te

110
R.
A.
TTB
p
mf
car les pre - mières choses ne sont plus Elles ne sont que des om-bres trom-
for the for - mer things are no more, they are sha-dows that va-nish like
Ro-zanne
Ro-zanne
in ci-vi-ta-tem sanc-tum Je - ru - sa - lem.

113
R.
A.
TTB
mf
f
mp
peuses qui s'é - tendent sur le sien de l'In - fi - ni"
mist in the light of In - fi - nite love.
Ro-zanne
Ro-zanne
Cho-rus An - ge lo - rum, te sus-ci - pi - at

118
R.
Mort
Death
A.
pp
Mort Tu et moi
Death thou and I
SSA
pp 2
Ag-nus De - i
TTB
mf
Ae-ter - num ha-be-as re - qui - em.
mf
pp
mp

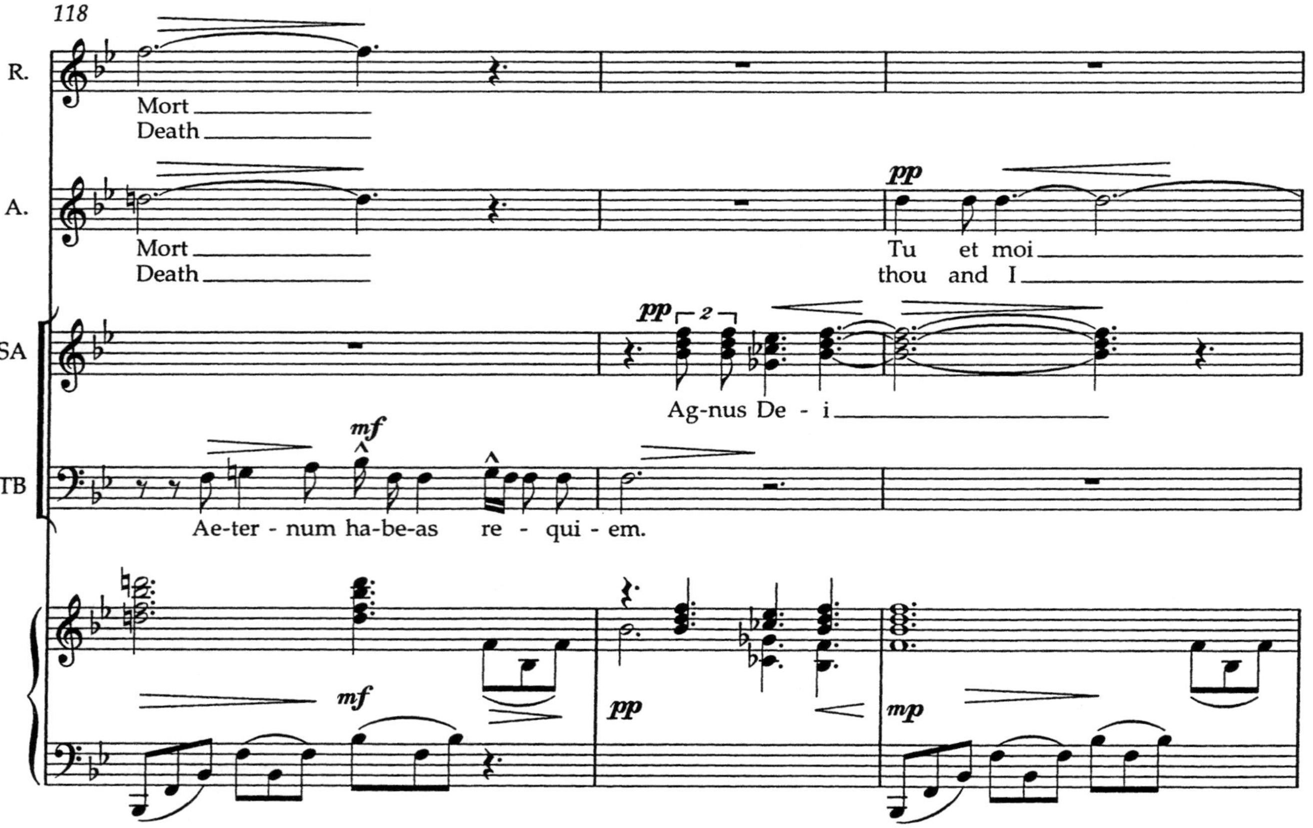

121
R.
Un être u-nique
Our souls as one
A.
Tu et moi
thou and I
un sou-pir me-
In e-ter-nal
SSA
Ag-nus De-i
Qui tol-lis pec-ca-ta mun-di
TTB
124
Et notre A-mour une dou-ble pri-ère
Our love e-ter-nal a two-fold pray'r
le
love
Notre a-mour une pri-ère
love e-ter-nal a pray'r
Do-na e-is re-qui-em.
Mi-se-re-re, Mis-se-re-re.

127
R.
mp
un être u - nique
our souls as one
A.
mp
un être u - nique
our souls as one
SSA
mf
Ag-nus De - i
Ag-nus De - i.
TTB
Qui tol-lis pec-ca - ta mun - di
mf
mp
130
R.
p
Un sou-pir me-le
in E - ter - nal love
11
mf
notre a - mour une pri - ère
E-ver more a pray'r
A.
p
Un sou-pir me-le
in E - ter - nal love
mf
notre a - mour une dou-ble pri - ère
E - ver more a two-fold pray'r
SSA
mf
Do - na e - is pa - cem
TTB
p
Do - na e-is re-qui-em.
11
p
mf

133
R.
E-cho de mon sou-pir. Im - age de mon âme
E-cho of my de-sire Be - lov'd of my soul
A.
Im-age de mon âme Im - age de mon âme
Be-lov'd of my soul Be - lov'd of my soul
SSA
Do-na e-is re - qui-em sem-pi-
TTB
Do - na e - is pa - cem sem-pi-
136
R.
Ah
A.
Ah
SSA
ter - nam.
TTB
ter - nam.
Curtain

Teresa Clotilde del Riego

(1876–1968)

JOSEPHINE R. B. WRIGHT

Teresa Clotilde del Riego was born in London, England, on April 7, 1876, of English-Spanish ancestry. She studied voice privately with Marie Withrow (n.d.)[1] and Francesco Paolo Tosti (1846–1916), and continued her vocal studies at London's West Central College of Music, where she also received instruction in piano, violin, and composition. She later earned certificates in these subjects at Trinity College. Her primary instructor in composition was Sewell Southgate (n.d.).[2]

Del Riego reportedly began writing music at the age of nine.[3] Best noted as a songwriter, she composed music for piano, chamber ensemble, chorus, and orchestra. She published over 300 songs for solo voice and piano from the late 1890s through the 1950s, including the cycles *Gloria* (1906), *Children's Pictures* (1909), and *Three Stuart Songs* (1955). Although only about one-third of this repertory has been located and cataloged to date, the wide dispersion of her songs throughout the United States, the United Kingdom, Canada, and Australia suggests that they were immensely popular during her lifetime. Several of them were sung by the leading singers of the day, including Nellie Melba and Leland Langley. He introduced her first major success, *O Dry Those Tears!* (1901), which reportedly sold 23,000 copies within six weeks of its publication.[4] The celebrated Irish tenor John McCormack recorded del Riego's *Thank God for a Garden*.

On October 31, 1937, del Riego wrote a letter to singer Marian Anderson in which she mentioned her song *Homing*. This letter is preserved in a collection entitled the *Marian Anderson Papers, ca. 1900–1993* held in the Rare Book and Manuscript Library at the University of Pennsylvania. It reads:

> Dear Miss Anderson
> I should be so pleased if you would look at these songs I am posting. Perhaps the Carol might appeal to you for the Xmas Season programmes. I am looking forward to hearing you again on the 5th & am a great admirer of your lovely art & voice.
>
> Do you by any chance sing my "Homing." A friend told me you did—that would be lovely indeed!
>
> It would be a great honour to have you sing some of my new work—& I shall be happy to meet you at any time, should you care to run through others here at my house.
> Yours with best wishes
> Teresa Del Riego[5]

Del Riego's choice of texts for her songs includes the poetry of the contemporary late nineteenth- and early twentieth-century male writers Robert Browning (1812–1889), Charles G. Mortimer (b. 1900), John Oxenham (1852–1941), and W. B. Yeats (1865–1939), as well as female authors Nora Chesson (1871–1906), Julie Allard Daudet (b. 1847),[6] Agnes Darmesteter (b. 1857),[7] Edith Nesbit (1858–1924),[8] and Ella Wheeler Wilcox (1850–1919). Del Riego also supplied her own texts for several of the songs she set, including *Happy Song* (ca. 1903), *Oh Loving Father* (1906), *Thank God for a Garden* (ca. 1915), *In Exile* (1916), *Rose-Marie of Normandy* (1922), *Life Is a Caravan* (ca. 1926), and *The Madonna's Lullaby* (1937).

O Dry Those Tears!, *Thank God for a Garden*, and *Homing* are representative samples of the style she adopted in the early twentieth century that was popular with contemporary audiences. They were published simultaneously in several keys to accommodate low, medium, or high voices. The melodies lie comfortably for the singer and rarely exceed the range of an octave and a half. The accompaniments contain chromaticism and modulatory schemes that require moderate to advanced keyboard skills from the pianist.

O Dry Those Tears! (author of text unknown) was published in multiple versions as well as in multiple keys. The edition included here is based on the 1901 publication by Chappell & Co. for voice and piano with organ and violin (or violoncello) accompaniment *ad lib*. Cast as a modified strophic form with two verses and a short, concluding coda (mm. 73-81), the instrumental introductions to stanzas one and two vary. Strophe one contains a twenty-four bar melody organized as an ABB^1 structure. Stanza two is slightly modified (mm. 63-72) by altering the ending of the melody in section B and manipulating both text and melody in section B^1.

Thank God for a Garden (text by Teresa del Riego) is dedicated to del Riego's father. It is a simple binary song in AA^1 structure. Arpeggiated chords in the piano frame its straightforward, lyrical melody.

Homing (text by Arthur Leslie Salmon) remained in the repertory of several singers of the late twentieth century, including Marian Anderson, Rosa Ponselle, Risë Stevens, Joan Sutherland, and, more recently, John Aler. Written in ABA song form and short in length, it is the most complex of these three songs because of its chromatic harmonies and the modulatory changes in section B (mm. 20-29), which move through the distant keys of F-sharp major, A major, and D-flat major within the span of nine measures.

Notes

1. Marie Withrow, an American singer, was born in Salem, Iowa. See Don L. Hixon and Don A. Hennessee, *Women in Music: An Encyclopedic Biobibliography*, 2d ed., vol. II (Metuchen, N. J.: Scarecrow Press, 1993), 1176. Withrow later published a book on voice culture, entitled *Some Staccato Notes for Singers* (Boston: Oliver Ditson Co.; New York: C. H. Ditson, ca. 1915).

2. *Étude* (November 1932): 762.

3. Aaron I. Cohen. *International Encyclopedia of Women Composers* (New York and London: Books and Music [USA], Inc., 1981), 189.

4. Sophie Fuller. "Riego, Teresa Clotilde del," in *The Norton/Grove Dictionary of Women Composers*, ed. Julie Anne Sadie and Rhian Samuel (New York: W. W. Norton, 1995).

5. Letter from Teresa del Riego to Marian Anderson dated October 31, 1937. *Marian Anderson Papers, ca. 1900–1993.* Folder 1419.

6. Julie Rosalie Céleste Allard (Madame Alphonse Daudet).

7. Mrs. James Darmesteter (later Mrs. Agnes Mary Frances Robinson Duclaux).

8. A popular Victorian author of children's stories.

9. Langley is identified as having sung *O Dry Those Tears!* on the title page of the song (London: Chappell and Co., ca. 1901).

List of Works

Songs

My Gentle Child. Text by Charles Kingsley. London: Chappell & Co., 1897.

Love Is a Bird. Text by Madame [James] Darmesteter. London: Chappell & Co., 1898.

Slave Song, op. 4. Text from *Father Christmas Annual* by E[dith] Nesbit. New York: Chappell & Co., 1899.

Bell, The. Text by Teresa del Riego. London: Chappell & Co. New York: Boosey, ca. 19—.

A Land of Roses. Text by Edward Teschemacher. London: Boosey & Hawkins, 1901.

O Dry Those Tears!. Sung by Mr. Leland Langley. London: Chappell & Co., 1901.

La vie est vaine (A Song of Life). Text by Leon de Montenaeken. English version by Teresa del Riego. London: Chappell & Co., 1902.

The Waking of Spring. New York: Chappell & Co., 1902.

Happy Song. Text by Teresa del Riego. Melbourne, London, and Sidney: Chappell; New York: Chappell-Harms, Inc., 1903.

Rest Thee, Sad Heart. Text by Edward Teschemacher. London: Chappell & Co.; New York: Boosey, 1903.

Where Love Has Been. Text by Edward Teschemacher. London: Chappell & Co.; New York: Boosey, 1903.

L'amour. Text by Madame Alphonse Daudet. London and New York: Chappell & Co., 1905.

Life's Recompense. Text by Edward Teschemacher. [New York]: Chappell & Co., 1905.

Album/ Teresa del Riego. London and New York: Chappell & Co., (1906?), 1899–1906.

1. *Red Clover.* Text from *Home Chat*
2. *Wishes.* Text by E[dward] Teschemacher
3. *All's Right with the World.* Text by Robert Browning
4. *The Butterfly.* Text by Austin Dobson
5. *Eglantine.* Text by [Robert?] Herrick
6. *An Olive Branch.* Text by [Robert?] Herrick
7. *A Moral Set to Music*
8. *Life's Recompense.* Text by Edward Teschemacker
9. *La vie est vaine.* Text by Leon de Montenaeken. English translation by del Riego

Gloria. Text by Stephen Coleridge. London: Chappell & Co., 1906.

1. *Callow Care*
2. *Up Through Love's Infinite Ascent*
3. *The Joys Laid Up Here-after*
4. *The Seaweed in the Dim-lit Cave*
5. *Sink, Sink, Red Sun into the West*

6. *Music in a Rhythmic Measure*
7. *I've a Cottage Down Out Devon Way*
8. *Fair Daughter of a Traitor Race*
9. *Dear, Is It Nothing, All the Years*

Oh Loving Father. Text by Teresa del Riego. New York: Chappell & Co., 1906.

To Phyllida. Text by Austin Dobson. London: Chappell & Co., 1906.

The Green Hills of Ireland. Text by Maud Shields. London and New York: Chappell & Co., 1907.

The Perfect Prayer. Text by James Whitcomb Riley. New York: Chappell & Co., 1908.

Children's Pictures. Text from Robert Louis Stevenson's *A Child's Garden of Verses*. London: Chappell & Co., 1913.

1. *Where's the Boat*? [Where Go the Boats?]
2. *Sleepsin-by* [A Good Boy]
3. *Time to Rise*
4. *Windy Nights*
5. *My Bed Is Like a Boat*
6. *Shadow March*

June, and My Lady. Text by Robert Browning. London: Chappell & Co., 1909.

I Lay My Laurels at Your Feet. Text by Ellen Collett. London, New York, and Melbourne: Chappell & Co., 1910.

Since I Must Love. Text by Edward Teschemacher. London, New York, and Melbourne: Chappell & Co., 1910.

Hayfields and Butterflies. Text by Teresa del Riego. Melbourne, London, and Sidney: Chappell & Co.; New York: Chappell-Harms, 1911.

The Red Rose Wooed the White Rose. Text by Philip Desborough. London, New York, and Melbourne: Chappell & Co., 1911.

Your Picture. Text by Teresa del Riego. London, New York, and Melbourne: Chappell & Co., 1911.

The Reason. Text by Ella Wheeler Wilcox. London and New York: Chappell & Co., 1912.

The Greatest Wish in the World. Text by Teresa del Riego. Cincinnati: John Church Co. [1913].

The Way of Life. New York: Ricordi, 1913.

Harvest. Text by P. J. O'Reilly. London: Chappell & Co., 1914.

How I Shall Miss You. Text by W. B. Yeats. London and New York: Chappell Co., 1914.

Mignonne! Here Is April. Text by François Coppée. English translation by Jessie Adelaide Middleton. London: Winthrop Rogers, 1914.

Thank God for a Garden. Text by Teresa del Riego. Melbourne, London, and Sidney: Chappell & Co.; New York: Chappell-Harms, 1915.

In Exile. Text by Teresa del Riego. New York: Chappell & Co., 1916.

Noel. Text by Théophile Gautier. London: Chappell & Co., 1916.

The Hills of Clare. Text by Edward Lockton. London and New York: Chappell & Co., 1917.

Homing. Text by Arthur Leslie Salmon. London and Melbourne: Chappell & Co., Ltd.; New York: Chappell-Harms, 1917.

The Resurrection. London: Winthrop Rogers; New York: G. Schirmer, 1917.

Blessing. Text by Nora Chesson. London: Chappell & Co., 1919.

Gladness after Sorrow. Text by Arthur L. Salmon. London: Keith, Prowse & Co., 1919.

Little Candles at the Altar. Text by Teresa del Riego. London: Chappell & Co., 1919.

All's well. Text by John Oxenham. London : Chappell & Co., 1921.

Art Thou Weary. Text by John M. Neale. Boston: Oliver Ditson, 1922.

Rose-Marie of Normandy. Text by Teresa del Riego. New York: Chappell-Harms, 1922.

A Song of Joy. Text by P. J. O'Reilly. London: Enoch & Son, 1923.

If Any Little Song of Mine. Text from *The Treasury of Consolation*. New York: Chappell-Harms [1925].

Life Is a Caravan. Text by Teresa del Riego. London: Chappell & Co., 1926.

My Ship. Text by Charles G. Mortimer. New York: Chappell-Harms, 1926.

The Legend of the Robin Redbreast. Text by Teresa del Riego. Boston: O. Ditson Co., 1929.

A Russian Lament. Text by Noel March. New York: Chappell-Harms, 1930.

Waking. Text by Arthur Leslie Salmon. New York: Chappell-Harms, 1931.

A Star Was His Cradle. Text by Florence Hoare. London: A. V. Broadhurst, 1934.

Cheer Up! Text by Helen Taylor. London: A. V. Broadhurst, 1935.

The Madonna's Lullaby. Text by Teresa del Riego. London and New York: Boosey, 1937.

Love Song at Sunset. Text by Noel March. New York: Galaxy Music, 1948.

Be Thou My Guide. Text by [William Stickles]. New York: Galaxy Music, 1949.

Three Stuart Songs. Text by Radclyffe Hall. London: J. Curwen & Sons [1955].

1. *The Queen Has Gone*
2. *Tell Me What Are You Looking For*
3. *Mary Queen*

Other Works

El Amor Waltz, for piano. London: Keith, Prowse & Co., 1919.

Air in E-flat, for violoncello (or violin) and piano. London: Chappell & Co., 1930.

Bibliography

Cohen, Aaron I. "Del Riego, Theresa (Teresa Clotilde) (Mrs. Leadbetter)." In *International Encyclopedia of Women Composers*. New York and London: Books and Music (USA), Inc., 1981.

Del Riego, Teresa. Correspondence with Marian Anderson. October 31, 1937.

Fuller, Sophie. "Riego, Teresa Clotilde del." In *The Norton/ Grove Dictionary of Women Composers*, eds. Julie Anne Sadie and Rhian Samuel. New York and London: W. W. Norton, 1995.

Laurence, Anya. *Women of Notes: 1,000 Women Composers Born Before 1900*. New York: Richards Rosen Press, 1978.

Discography

Homing. Alfred Piccaver, tenor, with piano. Decca 4286 (19—?).

Sink, Sink, Red Sun into the West. Marion Beeley, contralto, with piano and organ. His Master's Voice 3919 (19—?).

Thank God for a Garden. Alfred Piccaver, tenor, with piano. Decca GB 5885A (19—?).

Thank God for a Garden. John McCormack, tenor, with orchestra. Victrola K786A-1-2, matrix M786B-3-2 (19—).

Rosa Ponselle Sings Today. Rosa Ponselle, soprano, and Igor Chicagov, piano. Victor, LM 1889 (1955). *Homing*.

Homing. Risë Stevens, mezzo-soprano, with orchestra. Odyssey, Y 31738 (1972).

Songs My Mother Taught Me. Joan Sutherland, soprano, the New Philharmonia Orchestra, and Richard Bonynge, conductor. London OS 26367 (1973). *Homing*.

In Praise of Woman: 150 Years of English Women Composers. Anthony Rolfe Johnson, tenor, and Graham Johnson, piano. Hyperion CD A66709 (1994). *Slave Song*.

Bird Songs at Eventide. Robert White, tenor, and Stephen Hough, piano. Hyperion CD A66818 (1995). *O Dry Those Tears!*

Songs We Forget to Remember. John Aler, tenor, and Grant Gershon, piano. Delos DE 3181 (1996). *Homing*.

O Dry Those Tears!

for Voice and Piano

with optional Violin (or Cello) and optional Organ

unknown

Teresa del Riego

*G# in original print

16
poco ten.
Quicker
f
row; 'Twill come, a - las! But soon 'twill pass,
quasi arpeggi
f
Ped.
Ped.

21
dolce
cresc.
poco ten. poco rall.
With feeling largamente
ff
Clouds will be sun - shine to - mor - row. 'Twill come, a -
non arpeggi
p
cresc. colla voce
ff
Ped.

26
f
Quicker and hopefully
rit.
p con espress.
las! But soon 'twill pass, Clouds will be sun - shine to -
pp
f
p
col canto
Ped.
Ped.
Ped.
Ped.

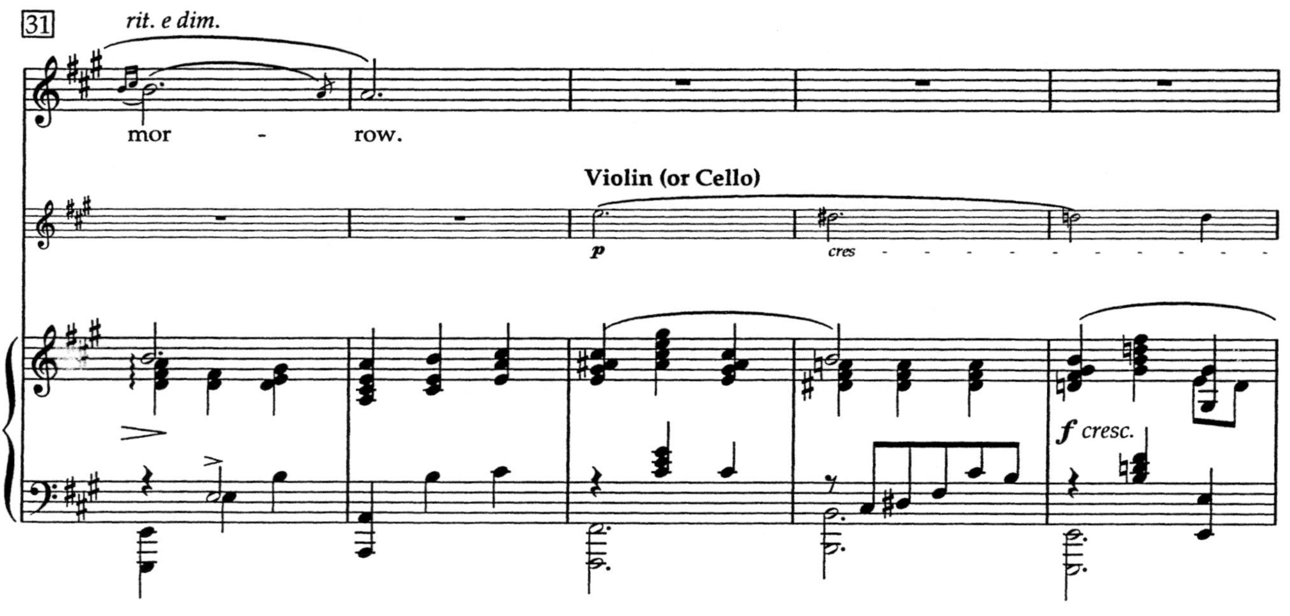
31
rit. e dim.
mor - row.
Violin (or Cello)
p
cres
f cresc.

36
Voice
cendo
f
p
rall.
Piano
f
fz p
Organ

*This tempo marking applies only to the instrumentalists, who accel. and rall. while the voice remains steady.

52
With feeling largamente
dolce
ff
sun; So is it ev - er with sor - row. 'Twill come, a -
(rall. in part here)
dolce
f
non arpeggi
cresc.
ff
dolce
f

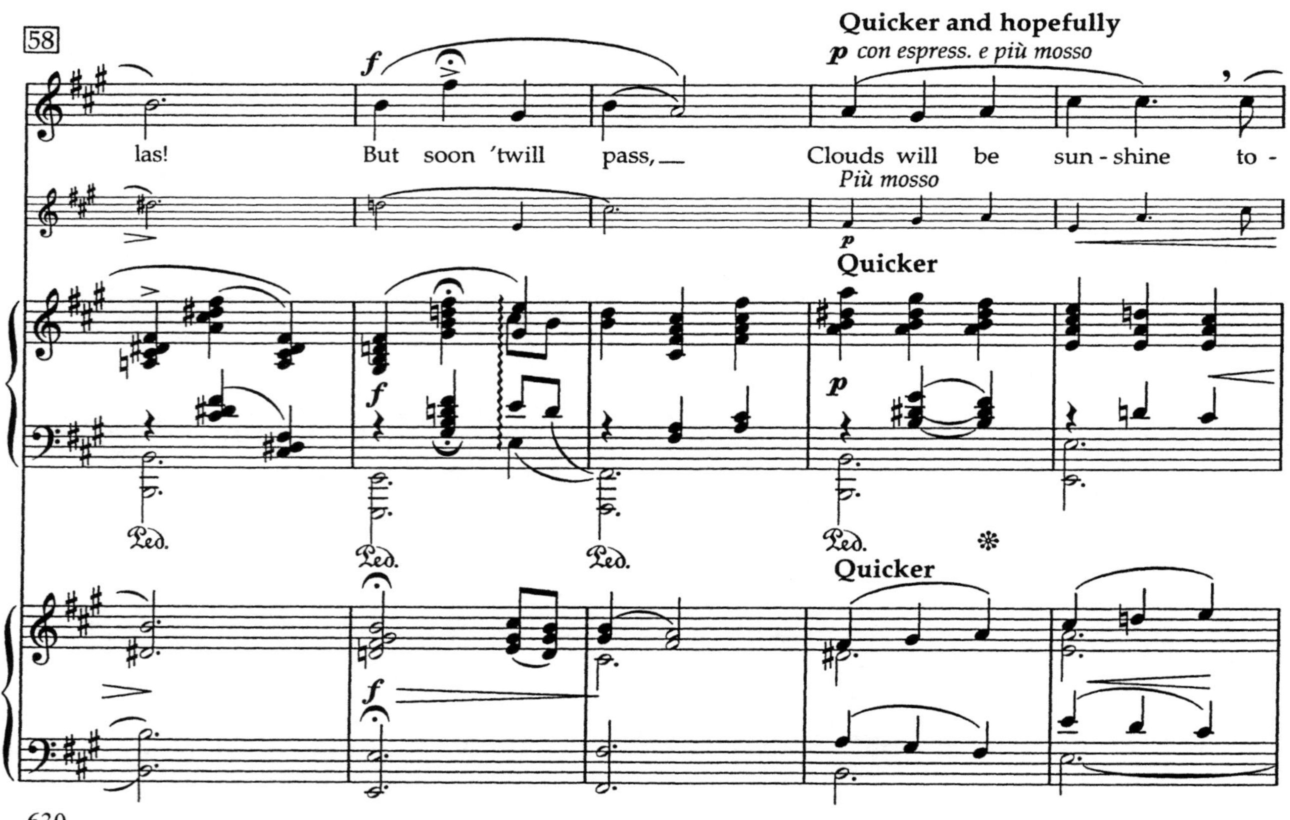
58
Quicker and hopefully
p con espress. e più mosso
f
las! But soon 'twill pass, Clouds will be sun - shine to -
Più mosso
p
Quicker
f
p
Quicker
f

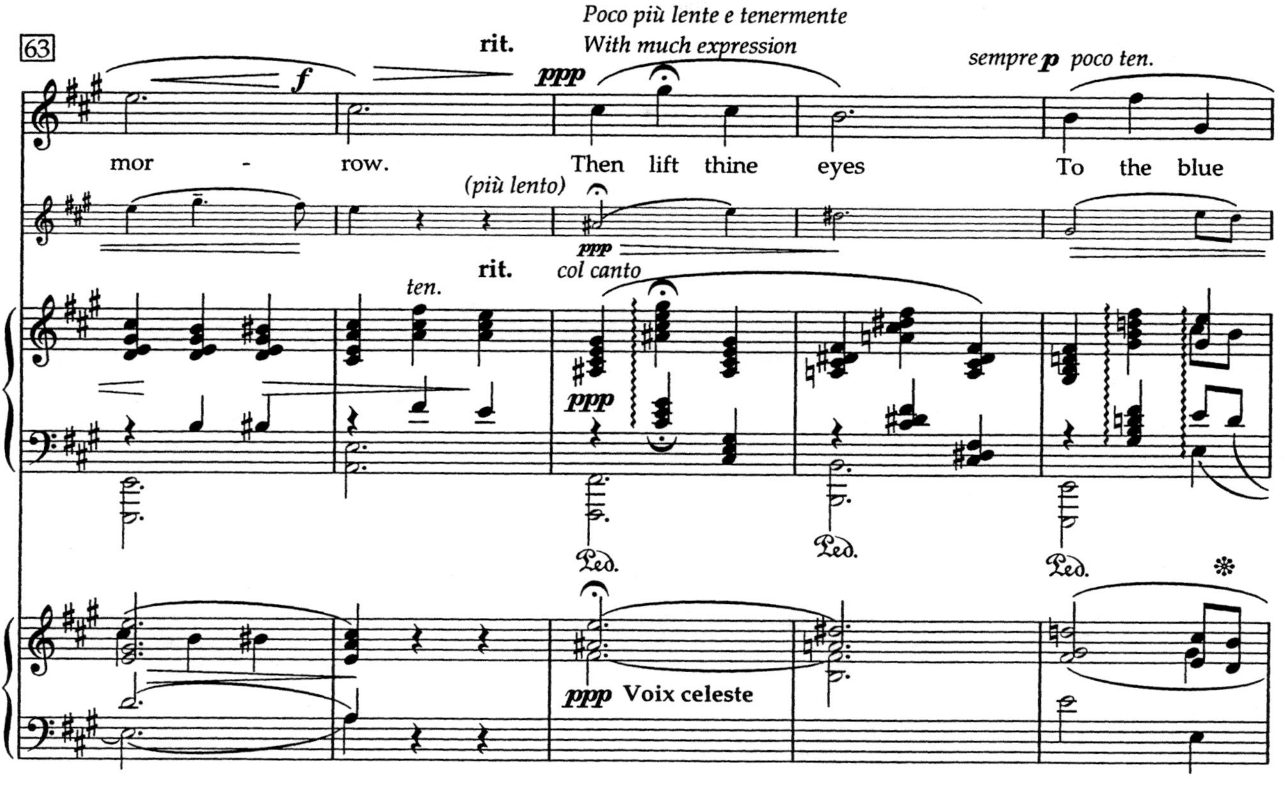
63
Poco più lente e tenermente
With much expression
rit.
sempre p poco ten.
mor - row. Then lift thine eyes To the blue
(più lento)
rit. col canto
ten.
ppp
Ped.
ppp Voix celeste

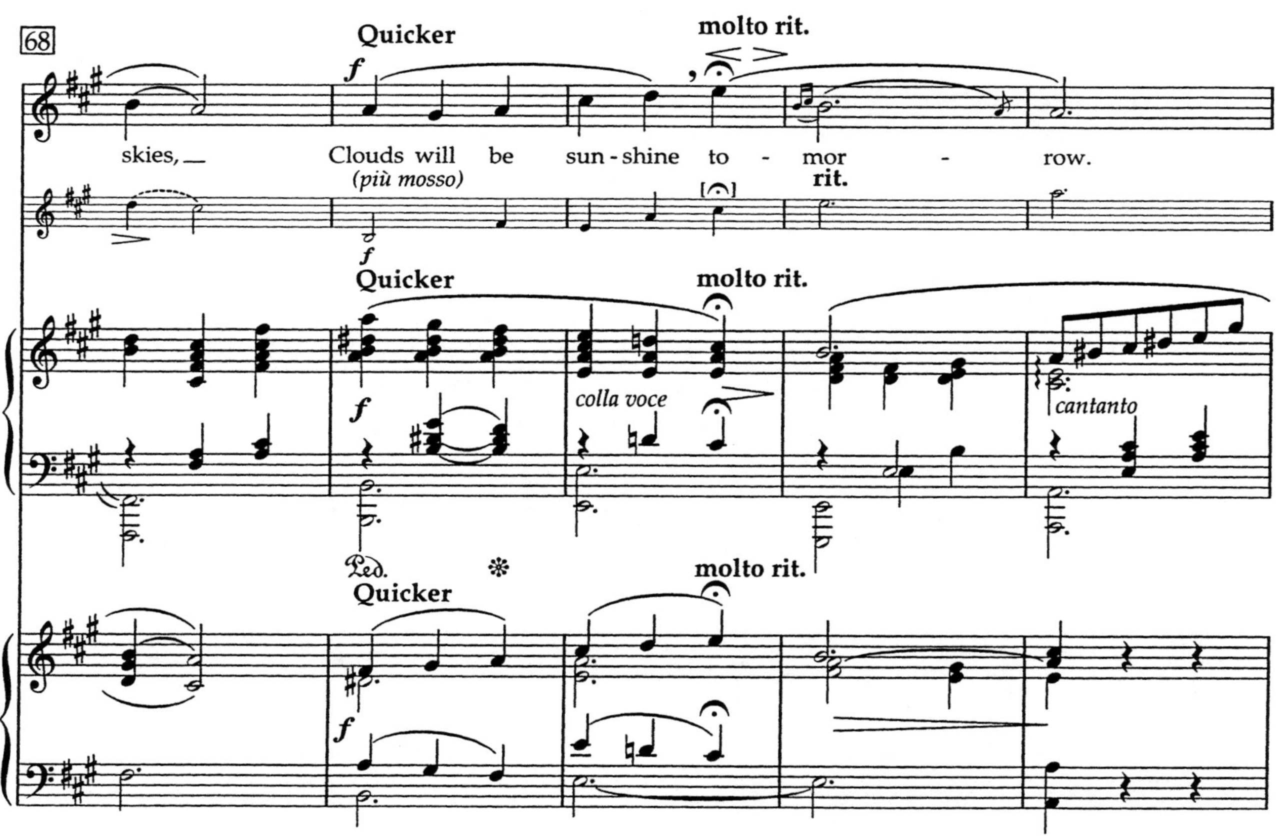
68
Quicker
molto rit.
skies, Clouds will be sun-shine to - mor - row.
(più mosso)
rit.
colla voce
cantanto
Ped.

73
a tempo
con espressione
f
mf
O dry those tears, Life is not
rall.
ff
a tempo
dolce e cresc.
ff
ppp
f
con espr.
pp
mf
a tempo
pp celeste
ff

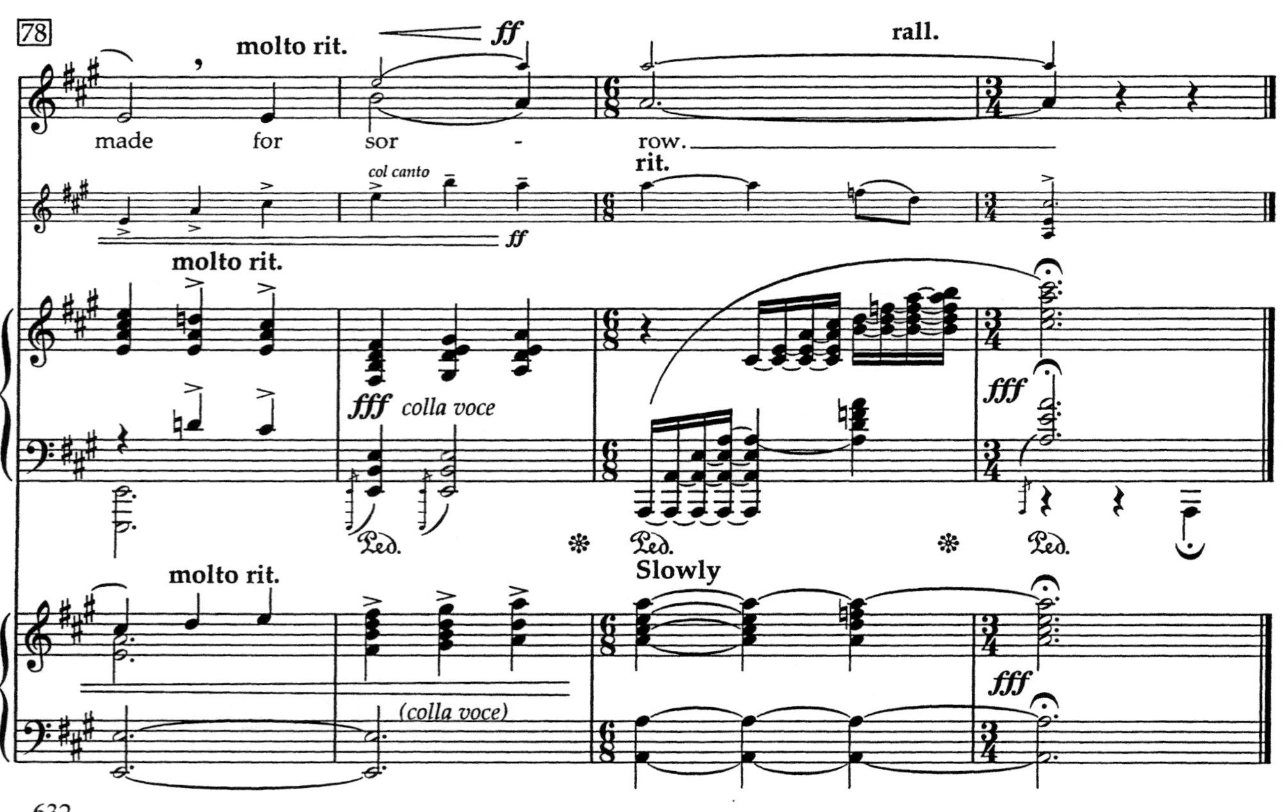
78
molto rit.
ff
rall.
made for sor - row.
col canto
rit.
ff
molto rit.
fff colla voce
fff
Slowly
fff
(colla voce)

Thank God for a Garden

Teresa del Riego **Teresa del Riego**

10
sun - shine, That comes flood-ing it all!
8
Ped.
13
Thank God for the flow - ers, For the rain and the
16
un poco rall.
dew, Thank God for sum - mer, That
19
a tempo
brings me you!
Ped.
Ped.
Ped.

21
rall.
f
R.H.
24
Slowly
riten.
p
Poco più lento
mp
Thank God for the
p molto legato
27
sun - rise, For the new morn - ing bright,
cantabile
dolce
30
Thank God for the sun - set, That is "Shep-herd's de -
ben cantabile

33
pp
light;" Thank God for the corn - fields,
pp
36
rall.
f
In the moon-light of blue, Thank God for
ff
8
39
ten.
rit.
sum - mer, Thank God for
L.H.
fz
fz
8
8
42
riten.
you!
ff
8

Homing

Arthur L. Salmon

Teresa del Riego

14
pp
rit.
a tempo
come back with the ev-'ning star
Hom - ing.
pp
18
Più mosso
f Broadly
3
Thou art my hun-ger and my need,
The
cresc.
f
f Maestoso
22
più f Con amore
3
goal and so-lace of my roam-ing.
Be thou my Ha-ven when I
più f
25
ff
speed
Hom - ing!
ben marcato
ff
legato
appassionato

29
riten.
Tempo I
pp dolce e tranquillo
All things come home at ev-en-tide, Like
pp
pp Ben sostenuto
33
birds that wear - y of their roam - ing, And I would
36
molto cresc.
f
hast - en to thy side, Hom - - - - ing!
molto cresc.
39
riten.
più cresc.
ff
ffz

Alma Maria Schindler-Mahler

(1879–1964)

NADINE SINE

The recent publication of Alma Mahler-Werfel's diaries for the years 1898–1902 illuminates the inner conflict between her desire to become a great composer and her need to be loved and admired by men. This tension continued throughout her marriage to Gustav Mahler (1860–1911), precipitating the events recounted in her memoir on life with him, and in her 1958 autobiography, *And the Bridge Is Love.* Though her compositional career was brief, it is nonetheless important because it reveals a great deal about how girls and women were educated and how their work was regarded at the beginning of the twentieth century. The complex story of her life is equally important as a reflection of the turbulent and brilliant Viennese culture she inhabited.

Alma Maria Schindler-Mahler (henceforth called Alma Mahler to avoid confusion with her husband, composer Gustav Mahler) was born August 31, 1879, the eldest daughter of Emil Jacob Schindler, a landscape painter whose stature was fully recognized only after his premature death, and Anna Bergen Schindler, a soprano who had given up a contract with the Leipzig Stadttheater to marry Schindler in 1878. Alma's formal education was haphazard, but she learned much about art from her father, whom she adored. His death in 1892 — Alma Mahler was just thirteen — affected her enormously: "All I did had been to please him. All my ambition and vanity had been satisfied by a twinkle of his understanding eyes."[1] She spent the next decade searching for a worthy replacement.

Just as frequently as Alma Mahler confessed her longing for her father in her diaries, she wrote of her antipathy for her mother, who had married one of Schindler's students, Carl Moll, in 1895. The family's social circle consisted of Vienna's artistic elite; Alma Mahler took part in dinner conversations with men such as Gustav Klimt, Max Burkhard, Josef Hoffmann and Hermann Bahr, and was knowledgeable enough to have strong opinions on art, literature and music. She regularly attended opera, theater and concerts, and she regarded Richard Wagner as a god, frequently playing and singing through entire acts of his operas. She also reported having great regard for the director of the Vienna Opera, Gustav Mahler; long before meeting him she wrote, "As for Mahler—I'm virtually in love with him."[2] During this period, Alma mentions her studies in French, sewing, piano, and especially composition. She had begun composition study with the blind organist Joseph Labor (1842–1924) in 1894, continuing in 1900 with Alexander Zemlinsky (1871–1942), who also taught Arnold Schoenberg (1874–1951).

Alma Mahler wrote often about composing, describing her lessons and struggles. While her teachers found her to be very talented, they each maintained that she had no real knowledge of harmony or counterpoint and worried that she lacked seriousness.[3] She accepted all of this as true. She also deferred to them in all judgments on the value of her compositions: "I composed a song . . . Whether it's good or bad will be decided on Tuesday [at Labor's]."[4] At times she lamented being a girl, noting the different education she would have had as a boy, and she longed to be the first woman to write a great opera or symphony. Yet she also regretted her lack of seriousness, agreeing with Labor that her life had been too easy.

At the same time, Alma Mahler knew that she was beautiful and that she could attract admirers and be the center of attention wherever she went. Her first great passion was Gustav Klimt, who was fifteen years older and a significant artist. Thwarted by her mother in developing that relationship, Alma engaged in a series of flirtations until she encountered Zemlinsky, only eight years her senior. His opera, *Es war einmal* (Once Upon a Time), had been produced under Mahler's direction. Although she initially found Zemlinsky to be ugly, she became enthralled with him when he finally consented to teach her. While he was very blunt about defects he perceived in her compositions, Alma Mahler found that "everything he said was so right."[5] Zemlinsky, initially questioning her sincerity and motives, eventually succumbed to her spell, and lessons became hours of passionate embraces.[6]

Then, on November 7, 1901, at a dinner party in the home of Bertha Zuckerkandl, she met her idol, Gustav Mahler. Nearly twenty years her senior, he was instantly intrigued with her and within a few weeks, after only a few private meetings, they became secretly engaged. She wrote a letter to Mahler in which she explained that she would be brief because she was working on a composition. Mahler responded in a long, heartfelt letter that he considered it impossible to have two composers in one family; he asked her to give up her composing and to consider his music as her music. He wanted her to decide before they met again.[7]

Upon receipt of this letter, she was stunned and considered giving up the relationship rather than composition. When her mother, perhaps recalling how she had cut short her own career, urged her to reject Mahler, she changed her mind.[8] Still clearly troubled at the prospect of relinquishing what she considered to be her profession, she wrote on December 20, "It might have come all of its own . . . quite gently . . . But like this it will leave an indelible scar." By the next morning she had fully capitulated and, in one of her characteristically abrupt reversals, wrote that "I must admit that scarcely any music now interests me except his."[9]

Alma Mahler's diaries reveal that she had been vacillating in her affections between Mahler and Zemlinsky for several weeks. On the one hand, Zemlinsky had inspired a physical passion in her, in part because of the sympathy he had for her music. Regarding Mahler, she wondered "whether I love the director of the Opera, the wonderful conductor—or the man . . . I felt nearer to him from a distance than from nearby . . . and what if Alex were to become famous?"[10] At the age of twenty-two, Alma Schindler chose Mahler, who held one of the most prestigious musical posts in Europe, over the poor, relatively unknown Zemlinsky, and thereby tacitly chose to stop composing.

Alma, who was pregnant, and Gustav Mahler married in March 1902, and they had two children: Maria Anna, who died at the age of five, and Anna Maria, who became a recognized sculptor, living until 1989. Alma also served as a copyist for Mahler as he wrote his symphonies. Her unpublished diaries of the next few years return repeatedly to her wish to compose again. In the summer of 1903 she wrote, "The role I impose on myself is only an illusion. I love MY art! . . . If only I had Zemlinsky to work with!"[11] With plenty of time on her hands, Alma could have composed, but she still obviously felt the need of a teacher's approval or correction.

During a stay at a spa in the summer of 1910, Alma Mahler began an affair with the promising young architect, Walter Gropius. When Mahler learned of this, she confessed her unhappiness, citing among other complaints her frustration at having to give up composition. In remorse, Mahler softened, and one day, returning from a walk, she heard him playing one of her hundred songs, which she carried in a trunk everywhere they went.[12] He now exclaimed how wrong he had been and how good the songs were. He insisted that she rework some of them for publication and begin to compose again. That winter he wrote to his mother-in-law, saying that "she is hard at work and has written a few delightful new songs that mark great progress."[13] Universal Edition published five of her songs, and *Laue Sommernacht* was performed in New York.[14] By that time, Mahler had fallen ill; they soon returned to Vienna, where he died on May 18, 1911.

In 1915, Alma Mahler was so taken by a poem by Franz Werfel, *Der Erkennende,* that she immediately set it to music. She never wrote about publishing the *Vier Lieder* in 1915, or the *Fünf Gesänge,* including *Der Erkennende,* in 1924. Rather, her autobiography tells the story of her love relationships highly edited to put herself in the best possible light: ". . . in a figurative sense I could now realize my childhood dream of filling my garden with geniuses."[15] A passionate three-year affair with Oskar Kokoschka began in 1912, during which the painter produced some of his greatest work.[16] When Alma Mahler grew restless and tired of Kokoschka's jealousy, she again reached out to Gropius, who was then making a name for himself. They married in August 1915 — he was already on active duty in the war — and their daughter, Manon, was born October 5, 1916.

Unable to sustain a long-distance marriage, Alma Mahler fell in love again in the fall of 1917, this time with the poet of *Der Erkennende,* Franz Werfel. Their affair led to another pregnancy. Gropius obtained a leave to attend the birth, learning shortly after that he was not the father of the child, Martin, who died within a year. Although some attempts were made to restore the marriage, she and Gropius divorced in 1920.

Though Alma Mahler and Werfel were nearly constant companions after 1918, she hesitated a long time before marrying again in 1929. In 1935 Manon, the daughter of Alma and Gropius contracted polio and died, inspiring Alban Berg (1885–1935) to dedicate his *Violin Concerto* "to the memory of an Angel."[17] When Hitler annexed Austria, she and Werfel, who was Jewish, fled to France, crossed a mountain into Spain on foot, and eventually moved to America. They settled in California, frequently hosting gatherings for their émigré friends, including Thomas Mann, Bruno Walter, and Arnold Schoenberg. In 1945, Werfel succumbed to a heart attack, and she eventually moved to New York, where she died in 1964.

Alma Mahler was extremely conscious of her position as Gustav Mahler's widow. She published his letters, a facsimile of his incomplete tenth symphony, and a memoir of their life together. She attended premieres and festivals of his music and had the Rodin bust of the composer installed in the Vienna Opera to mark the twentieth anniversary of his death. His pension and royalties allowed her to live in comfort. Alma Mahler also remained a significant force in the music world at large, hosting performances of new works and, through the Gustav Mahler Trust Fund, lending financial support to struggling composers, particularly Schoenberg.

When Walter Sorell asked her in the early 1960s if she had not always been the center of attention wherever she went, she replied:

> I could not help it . . . Also, perhaps I have always been ambitious. When I was young I saw myself as one of the first great women composers. But then I also began to realize the tremendous impression I could make on men, what an important role I could play in some of their lives, becoming literally the creator of creators. Would you want me to recall the works in music, literature, in painting and architecture which would never have been done without my having been there? No, let's not think back. I have had a wonderful life for which I sacrificed my becoming the first great woman composer. [She closed her blue-gray eyes for a moment.] At any rate it's nice to think I might have been that great artist I was not.[18]

By the time Alma Mahler began keeping diaries, Vienna was on the brink of one of the most exhilarating periods in its thousand-year history.[19] She was privy to the founding of the artists' society known as The Secession, viewed its exhibits repeatedly, and was well-acquainted with its members. She also remained very current in her reading of new poetry, plays, literature and criticism, all of which were undergoing significant transformations, and she encountered many of the writers and poets in her social circles. Even before she met Gustav Mahler, whose tenure at the Vienna State Opera has become known as its "Golden Age," she frequently attended performances there and at the city's other concert venues.

Beyond the multitude of public concert, theater and opera performances she was able to attend, Alma Mahler heard and participated in a number of private recitals and concerts. At the peak of popularity during the first two decades of the twentieth century, these salons often included dinner for a large invited gathering followed by performances by various guests.[20] It was here that Alma Mahler would play the piano, and on occasion her songs were sung, often by her mother. She also participated in private recitals sponsored by her piano teacher, and at one of these, "Fräulein Freystätt sang my lieder. She made a complete mess of one of them but the others were quite good. They were well received."[21] Alma Mahler never appeared in public as a professional pianist. She also reacted with despair to the music of the one woman composer of whom she was aware, Cécile Chaminade (1857–1944) (see vol. 6). "I'm only writing about her because I was so bitterly disappointed. . . . Now, after *this* concert, I know that a woman can achieve nothing, never ever."[22]

In addition to the brilliant artistic climate of Alma Mahler's youth, Vienna also witnessed the birth of modern psychology through the work of Sigmund Freud, as well as the 1903 publication of Otto Weininger's *Geschlect und Charakter* (*Sex and Character*), a book notorious for its attacks on "woman" and for its underlying anti-Semitism. It was widely read, and even Alban Berg cited it to explain to Schoenberg why Alma Mahler behaved in contradictory ways.[23] Indeed, the growing anti-Semitism in Viennese society is reflected in her diaries and memoirs. Throughout her life she was known for her offensive pronouncements about Jews; yet she married two Jews, shared Werfel's flight from Hitler's Europe, maintained friendships and supported the work of many prominent Jewish artists.[24] Like so many others, Alma Mahler-Werfel spent her last years transplanted to California where she tried to recreate the brilliant society of her youth among those now aging artists who were fortunate enough to have escaped with at least their lives.

Since only fourteen songs published during her lifetime, and two posthumously published are extant, most questions about the evolution of Alma Mahler's style and harmonic vocabulary will remain unresolved. When she fled Europe, she left her songs in the house on the Hohe Warte which, along with the opera house and the cathedral, was nearly destroyed in a bombing raid.[25] As a consequence, there are very few known autograph sources: the two songs published by Hildegard Publishing Company in 2000; a manuscript and microfilm of Gustav Mahler's copies of four songs which Alma eventually published in 1915; plus her own manuscript of *Ansturm*; the final versions prepared for the engravers.[26] Although we know the dates of composition for several of the songs from the diaries, we have no way of knowing how much revision they underwent before publication.

In the case of the *Fünf Lieder* published in 1910, we can neither know the role Gustav Mahler played in choosing the five songs from among 'the hundred' she described nor how much he assisted in making revisions to them; his contribution may have been substantial. It is surely significant that when Alma Mahler published the *Vier Lieder* in 1915, she chose songs which had been copied by Gustav Mahler, including the two Dehmel songs which must have been composed just before the onset of his final illness.[27] The *Fünf Gesänge* appeared in 1924, perhaps prompted by the fact that she was in the midst of writing the memoir of her life with Mahler, which produced considerable agitation as she recalled her frustrations.[28] The middle song, *Der Erkennende*, is the only one which can be firmly dated after Mahler's death. The second and fourth songs are from 1901 and 1900, while the first and last on poems by Novalis cannot be dated with any certainty.[29] With the exception of *Der Erkennende,* the final set of songs is the weakest of her published collections.

For her texts, Alma Mahler was drawn to very recent poems, particularly by Richard Dehmel, Rainer Maria Rilke, and Otto Julius Bierbaum, and to a few lyric poems of the German romantics.[30] The choice of evocative poems—they often express yearning and desire, with frequent symbolic reference to night and light—rather than narrative texts is hardly surprising for someone who held Wagner's *Tristan und Isolde* to be the greatest piece ever written.[31] Wagner's influence also appears very clearly in her syllabic text settings and constantly changing strophic structures in which exact repeats rarely continue beyond four or five measures. Although she makes occasional small changes to poems and at times repeats a word or phrase for emphasis, for the most part she makes the poetic structure clear, often by inserting a brief interlude between strophes. Most of the songs have a vocal range of about an octave and a half and the highest pitch encountered is an A. The music is highly chromatic, both in linear decoration and in harmonic function; indeed, the "Tristan" chord (the half-diminished seventh) seems to have been so ingrained that her hand went to it instinctively.[32] A number of the songs end without a tonic chord in root position: e.g., *Bei dir ist es traut* ends on a second inversion; *Laue Sommernacht* on a dominant-seventh chord.

As a pianist, Alma Mahler was able to create difficult and idiomatic accompaniments: large, frequently rolled, block chords, quick arpeggios, and rapid ornamental scale passages. The piano rarely doubles the vocal line, although there are fragmentary echoes with subtle alterations (e.g., in *Die stille Stadt*). Many of the songs exhibit a fine sense of balance and strong melodic contours. The extant lieder support the belief in her talent held by many, including Labor, Zemlinsky and, belatedly, Mahler.

The four songs published in 1915 have been chosen for inclusion here primarily because they are the only ones for which copies exist (prior to the engraver's copy), thereby shedding at least some light on the types of revisions that were probably made to the 1910 set.[33] The dating for all four songs is based on those given in the 1915 edition.

There are relatively few substantive changes between (Gustav) Mahler's copy of *Licht in der Nacht* (text by Otto Julius Bierbaum [1901]) and the printed version; it is impossible to know how much revision was made to this 1901 song before Mahler's copy was made. The opening two measures, which are recalled at the end of the song, create an *ostinato* of murky harmony surrounding D minor without ever stating it, veering off briefly to E-flat but never stabilizing in any key. Just as the little light of the poem goes out, the bass of the accompaniment descends by whole steps from E-flat to A. Although the voice outlines the D minor tonic at the end, there is no vertical statement of D minor, and the piano concludes with an unharmonized A below the bass staff. The song creates a genuinely mysterious mood at the opening, but the composer allows the climax of the song at the reference to "Jesu Christ" to overwhelm the atmosphere of the whole.

When Mahler urged her to begin composing again, Alma apparently had difficulty getting started after her nine-year hiatus. For the two new songs, she turned once more to the poems of Richard Dehmel, who had by this time become an acquaintance of the couple. Significantly, Zemlinksy had also appropriated both poems for works of his own. Kravitt has noted the similarity between the beginning of her *Waldseligkeit* (text by Richard Dehmel [1911]), and the piano fantasy of the same name by Zemlinsky.[34] The short song is atmospheric, very pianistic, and harmonically adventurous. Like the previous song, the key signature suggests D minor, but there is not a single D minor chord in the song. Rather, there are many "Tristan" chords, and the bass line is dominated by chromatic stepwise movement and whole-tone descents. Accompanied by a black-key glissando, the voice reaches its climactic and last note on G-flat, the seventh of the only chord which ever resolves, going to D-flat. The postlude varies the opening before cadencing on D-flat major with a major seventh. Such sounds were hardly shocking in 1911; they draw on the same vocabulary Alma was using in 1900 in *Kennst du meine Nächte*, though they are handled much better in this song. Mahler's copy of the song is again very close to the final printed version.

While *Waldseligkeit* reveals a similarity to Zemlinsky's piano fantasy, in the case of *Ansturm,* (text by Richard Dehmel [1911]), it seems that Alma Mahler must have had a copy of Zemlinsky's song setting available as a model.[35] Her song is quite different in many respects: its declamatory opening, its cascading arpeggios in the second half, its inconclusive cadence. Yet the formal layout and melodic contours of the vocal part, the placement and frequent use of the "Tristan" chord, and perhaps most tellingly, some small changes in Dehmel's poem, are all shared in the two settings. Mahler's copy breaks off in the middle of measure 14. This break may well have occurred when he contracted his final illness, just weeks after he reported to his mother-in-law that she had composed several new songs. The microfilm of his copies also contains a copy of the entire song in Alma Mahler's hand.

Of the *Vier Lieder, Erntelied* (text by Gustav Falke [1901]) displays the greatest number of changes from Mahler's copy to the published score. Indeed, the microfilm contains two versions in Mahler's hand, one breaking off at measure 58. The second version contains the full song, but with some significant differences from the published song, notably in the addition of several measures and the repetitions of the last line of text rather than the 'Ah' of the published version.[36] *Erntelied* is the longest of the *Vier Lieder* and, despite excursions into other keys, it is the only one with a clear-cut tonal center, D-flat major, with which it begins and ends in both voice and piano.

Notes

1. Alma Mahler-Werfel, *And the Bridge Is Love,* with E. B. Ashton (New York: Harcourt, Brace & Co., 1958), 14-15.

2. Alma Mahler-Werfel, *Diaries, 1898–1902,* ed., trans., and sel. by Antony Beaumont and Susanne Rode-Breymann, 76. Written after attending a Philharmonic Concert on December 4, 1898.

3. On March 4, 1901, she quotes Zemlinsky as saying: "Either you compose or you socialize—one or the other. If I were you, I'd stick to what you do best—socialize." Ibid., 380.

4. November 30, 1898. Ibid., 74.

5. October 18, 1900. She had played *Lobgesang* and *Engelgesang*, which had won Labor's approval, but Zemlinsky was "completely dissatisfied." Ibid., 332.

6. The diary entries from April through October 1901 contain several graphic descriptions of these encounters.

7. Mahler's letter is quoted in full in Henry-Louis de La Grange, *Gustav Mahler. Vienna: The Years of Challenge (1897–1904)* (Oxford: Oxford University Press, 1995), 448-52.

8. Mahler-Werfel, *And the Bridge Is Love*, 23. Alma wrote: "Had she taken his side, she might have stiffened my opposition; as it was, her unconditional loyalty to me brought me to my senses."

9. December 21, 1901. *Diaries*, 462.

10. December 3, 1901. The passage continues, "One question *plagues* me: whether Mahler will inspire me to compose—whether he will support my artistic striving—whether he will love me like Alex." Ibid., 448.

11. La Grange, *Gustav Mahler. Vienna*, 620.

12. Alma Mahler, *Memories and Letters,* 3rd ed., ed. Donald Mitchell, trans. Basil Creighton (Seattle: University of Washington Press, 1975), 76. Although some have questioned whether this quantity is an exaggeration, the numerous specific pieces she mentions in the diaries suggest that she was not inflating the number.

13. *Gustav Mahler: Letters* [February 1911], 371.

14. Frances Alda performed *Laue Sommernacht* on March 3, 1911, in a recital attended by Alma. The song was encored. Mahler-Werfel, *And the Bridge Is Love,* 58-60.

15. Ibid., 68. The publication of this book brought both private and public rebuttals from several of the players. See particularly Alfred Weidinger, *Kokoschka and Alma Mahler,* and Reginald Isaacs, *Gropius* (see Bibliography).

16. Originally the famous painting known as *The Tempest* (*Windsbraut*), depicting Kokoschka and Alma reclining, had as a working title, *Tristan und Isolde.* During this period, Alma became pregnant and had an abortion, an act Kokoschka never really forgave. See Weidinger, *Kokoschka.*

17. Willi Reich, *Alban Berg,* trans. Cornelius Cardew (London: Thames and Hudson, 1965), 100. See also Helene Berg's letter of condolence to Alma, which says of Manon, "sie war ein Engel" (she was an angel), in George Perle, "Mein geliebtes Almschi . . ." *Österreichische Musikzeitschrift* 35 (1980): 7.

18. Walter Sorell, "Alma Mahler-Werfel: Body and Mind," in *Three Women: Lives of Sex and Genius* (New York: Bobbs-Merrill, 1975), 5.

19. For an autobiography quite different from Alma's of the same period, see Stefan Zweig, *The World of Yesterday* (Lincoln, Neb.: University of Nebraska Press, 1964). Two of the most important studies of the era are Carl E. Schorske, *Fin-de-Siècle Vienna* (New York: Vintage, 1980) and Nicholas Powell, *The Sacred Spring: The Arts in Vienna 1898–1918* (New York: New York Graphic Society, 1974).

20. See Edward F. Kravitt, *The Lied: Mirror of Late Romanticism* (New Haven: Yale University Press, 1996).

21. February 2, 1900. Mahler-Werfel, *Diaries,* 240.

22. February 28, 1899. Ibid., 98-99.

23. Berg wrote: "She is, after all, only a woman! . . . It's nothing but capriciousness, born of the moodiness of a woman used to dispensing favor and disfavor according to momentary caprice and whim . . . Maybe *that* is what Weininger calls the *amorality of woman.*" See Alban Berg, *The Berg-Schoenberg Correspondence,* ed., sel., and trans. Juliane Brand, Christopher Hailey, and Donald Harris (New York: W. W. Norton, 1987), 242-43.

24. While finding Zemlinsky "beautiful," Alma worried about "marrying him, of bearing his children—little, degenerate Jew-kids," July 28, 1901. Mahler-Werfel, *Diaries,* 421. This concern was not expressed (at least in any surviving material) about having Mahler's or Werfel's children.

25. Mahler-Werfel, *And the Bridge Is Love,* 274. "Mahler's and Werfel's desks, with their priceless contents, had been burned to cinders . . . The manuscripts of my songs, the joy and grief of many years, had fed the flames that consumed the wretched house."

26. The existence of two manuscript songs with Alma Schindler's name suggests that these may have been copies made at the request of friends. For instance, the diaries mention that she made copies of songs (without specifying titles, unfortunately) for Josef Olbrich in 1899, and in 1900 for Alexander Zemlinsky. Since *Kennst du meine Nächte* was composed in March 1900, Zemlinsky's April request for copies of three songs might have included this one. Carl Moll also arranged to have a private edition made of three songs with a title page designed by Koloman Moser that summer; however, when Zemlinsky saw the "so-called brushplates" (sogenannten Bürstenabzug), he wrote to Alma saying the songs were full of mistakes. Mahler-Werfel, *Diaries,* 312. See p. 648 on sources for the 1915 edition.

27. Why she chose to issue the songs is a mystery. It may be that in her increasing unhappiness with Kokoschka and before reconnecting with Gropius she needed to think of herself as a composer again and chose those songs which had Mahler's imprimatur.

28. Susanne Keegan, *The Bride of the Wind: The Life and Times of Alma Mahler-Werfel* (New York: Viking, 1992), 240-41, quotes from the typescript of the later diaries: "The doctor forbade me work of any kind, but during the night I understood the true cause of my ailments, my writing about Mahler that has agitated me so much these past weeks. I have literally been writing day and night, from fear that I could lose the memories." That Alma characterized these pieces as *Gesänge* rather than *Lieder* probably reflects her feeling that they were more expansive than the songs of the earlier publications. See Kravitt, *The Lied*, 298, and "The Lieder of Alma Maria Schindler-Mahler," *Music Review* 43 (1988): 196.

29. In February 1918, Werfel wrote: "Alma, I think of your music, I think of your songs, of my song and above all of that of Novalis." Ibid., 227. She recalled after his death how much he had loved her songs. Mahler-Werfel, *And the Bridge Is Love,* 278. Since she never mentioned Novalis in the diaries, it is possible that these songs were written later, perhaps at around the same time as

Der Erkennende in 1915. The fourth song, *Lobgesang,* is mentioned several times in the diaries, including Zemlinsky's dissatisfaction with it.

30. Alma apparently regarded her instrumental works, primarily for solo piano, as student exercises; she never mentioned them outside of the diaries. Although she wanted to write symphonies and an opera, she made only brief attempts in those directions, abandoning a piano trio because she did not know enough about the instruments. Zemlinsky, who initially had insisted his pupil give up composing songs to concentrate on mastering formal structure by imitating Beethoven sonata movements, for example, cautioned Alma not to consider publishing anything for a long while. Mahler-Werfel, *Diaries,* 344, 347. He returned her draft of an operatic scene with some sharp criticism, including: "Above all, you must have a clear layout, i.e. a proper tonal plan." Keegan, *The Bride of the Wind,* 60.

31. One suspects that Mahler was attracted to *In meines Vaters Garten* precisely because it has a fairy-tale kind of narrative, complete with reference to military trumpets, and the setting has a clear tonal organization on the large level (pairing A-flat and E major, with inflections to C major) and relatively little chromaticism within strophes.

32. Arnold Schoenberg, *Theory of Harmony,* trans. Roy E. Carter (Berkeley: University of California Press, 1978), 255-58. In his chapter on "The frontiers of tonality," Schoenberg discusses 'vagrant' chords, a number of which Alma uses regularly. She composed by ear, and lacked formal training in theory — for years she got feedback based solely on her playing due to Labor's blindness — resulting in problems in notation and some awkward harmonic choices, as the two unpublished songs reveal. *Kennst du meine Nächte* begins each strophe with the "Tristan" chord and is very experimental throughout, but it also contains many problems. If the notation is truly what she intended, Alma concluded the piece with an added sixth.

33. See the critical notes for detailed comparisons; also, the discussion in Kravitt, "The Lieder of Alma Schindler Mahler."

34. Ibid., 199.

35. See above on her wish to "have Zemlinsky to work with" during her early married life. By 1905, Zemlinsky and Schoenberg were regular visitors to the Mahlers' home, and it seems quite likely that Alma would have had access to Zemlinsky's unpublished songs.

36. See Kravitt, "The Lieder of Alma Schindler Mahler," 197-99 for two facsimiles from the microfilm.

List of Works

Published Works

Schindler-Mahler, Alma. *Fünf Lieder.* Vienna: Universal Edition, 1910.
- *Die stille Stadt.* Text by Richard Dehmel
- *In meines Vaters Garten.* Text by Otto Erich Hartleben. Composed before November 2, 1901
- *Laue Sommernacht.* Text by Gustav Falke (actually *Gefunden* by Otto Julius Bierbaum)
- *Bei dir ist es traut.* Text by Rainer Maria Rilke
- *Ich wandle unter Blumen.* Text by Heinrich Heine. Composed January 7, 1899

Mahler, Alma. *Vier Lieder.* Vienna: Universal Edition, 1915.
- *Licht in der Nacht* (1901). Text by Otto Julius Bierbaum
- *Waldseligkeit* (1911). Text by Richard Dehmel
- *Ansturm* (1911). Text by Richard Dehmel
- *Erntelied* (1901). Text by Gustav Falke

Mahler, Alma. *Fünf Gesänge,* Vienna: Josef Weinberger, 1924.
- *Hymne.* Text by Novalis
- *Ekstase* (1901). Text by Otto Julius Bierbaum
- *Der Erkennende* (1915). Text by Franz Werfel
- *Lobgesang* (1900). Text by Richard Dehmel
- *Hymne an die Nacht.* Text by Novalis

Other Editions

Schindler-Mahler, Alma Maria. *Sämtliche Lieder.* Vienna: Universal Edition (Reprint of 1910, 1915, 1924 publications), 1984.

Mahler, Alma. *Der Erkennende.* Edited by Susan M. Filler. In *Historical Anthology of Music by Women,* edited by James Briscoe. Bloomington, Ind.: Indiana University Press, 1987.

Leise weht ein erstes Blühn von den Lindenbäumen (1900). Text by Rainer Maria Rilke. Edited by Susan Filler. Bryn Mawr, PA: Hildegard Publishing Company, 2000.

Kennst du meine Nächte? Author unknown. Manuscript (location unknown) with several extant copies. Edited by Susan Filler. Bryn Mawr, PA: Hildegard Publishing Company, 2000.

Unpublished Works

Schindler, Alma M. Manuscript (location unknown) with several extant copies.

Other Sources: Manuscripts, Facsimiles, Copies

Mahler, Alma. *Vier Lieder*. Gustav Mahler's copies of the four songs. *Ansturm* is incomplete in his hand, but it is copied again by Alma. In the midst of the manuscript, Gustav Mahler copied a Rückert translation of a Persian poem, *Mewlana Dschelaleddin Rumi*. Original in collection of Henry-Louis de La Grange (Paris). Microfilm made by New York Public Library from borrowed materials, 1956, Toscanini Archives, New York Public Library.

Mahler, Gustav. *Adagietto*. Edited by Gilbert Kaplan. New York: Kaplan Foundation, 1992. (Contains facsimiles of Alma Mahler's copy and Gustav Mahler's autograph fair copy of the fourth movement of his fifth symphony with documents and analysis.)

Works Cited in Tagebuch-Suiten (Diaries)

(dates are those of diary entry;
comments in parentheses are Alma Mahler's)

Lieder

(Some of the unidentified songs presumed lost may, in fact, be among those published.)

February 2, 1898.	*Wanderers Nachtlied*. Text by J. W. Von Goethe. Lost.
March 17, 1898.	*Lied*. Text by Goethe. Lost.
March 22, 1898.	*Ein Blumenglöckchen*. Author unknown. Lost.
June 19, 1898.	*Vom Küssen*. Text by Anna Ritter. Lost.
June 26, 1898.	*Lehnen im Abendgarten beide*. Text by Rainer Maria Rilke. Lost.
November 30, 1898.	*Wie es ging*. Text by Wohlgemuth. Lost.
December 20, 1898.	*Liederl*. Author unknown. Lost?
December 24, 1898.	*Die Frühlingsnacht*. Text by M. Weyrauther? Lost.
December 28, 1898.	*Gib dich darein*. Text by Gustav Falke. Lost.
January 5, 1899.	*Lied*. Text by Heinrich Heine. Lost.
January 7, 1899.	*Ich wandle unter Blumen*. Text by Heine. Published 1910.
January 24, 1899.	*Lied*. Text by Heine. Lost.
June 4, 1899.	*Hinaus*. Author unknown. Lost.
June 5, 1899.	*Lied* in slow tempo and strict form. Author unknown. Lost?
June 12, 1899.	*Nixe* (Still awaits elaboration). Author unknown. Lost.
August 27, 1899.	*Lied*. Author unknown. Lost?
September 15, 1899.	*Einsamer Gang*. Text by Leo Greiner. Lost.
September 20, 1899.	*Tränenkinder*. Author unknown. Lost.
September 20, 1899.	*Ich will den Sturm*. Author unknown. Lost.
October 3, 1899.	*Qual*. Author unknown. Lost.
October 3, 1899.	*Der Morgen*. Author unknown. Lost.
October 7, 1899.	*Lied*. Author unknown. Lost?
October 17, 1899.	*Ich trat in jene Hallen*. Text by Henrik Ibsen. Lost.
November 29, 1899.	*Gleich und gleich*. Author unknown. Lost.
December 2, 1899.	*Lied*. Text by Heine. Lost.
December 5, 1899.	*Aus meiner Erinnerung erblühen*. Author unknown. Lost.
January 9, 1900.	*Schilflieder*. A Cycle after Nikolaus Lenau. Lost.
January 21, 1900.	*Stumme Liebe*. Text by Lenau (one of the Lenau cycle). Lost.
March 19, 1900.	*Meine Nächte* (in progress). Author unknown.
March 30, 1900.	*Lied* (about pregnancy). Author unknown. One of projected cycle. Lost.
May 15, 1900.	*Lieder* (2). Authors unknown. Lost?
June 16, 1900.	*Lobgesang (?)*. Text by Richard Dehmel. Published 1924.
June 16, 1900.	*Engelgesang (?)* Text by Rilke. Lost.
August 5, 1900.	*Lieder* Cycle (3). Text by Rilke. Lost?
September 11, 1900.	*Erinnerung*. Author unknown (composed previous year—[December 5, 1899?])
October 21, 1900.	*Lied*. Author unknown. Lost?
November 16, 1900.	*Liedl*. Text by Eduard Möricke. Lost.
November 20, 1900.	*Unvermeidlich*. Author unknown. Lost.
November 20, 1900.	*Wanderers Nachtlied*. Text by Goethe [from 1898?] Lost.
November 20, 1900.	*Abend*. Author unknown. Lost.
November 20, 1900.	*Er ist*. Author unknown. Lost.
March 15, 1901.	*Lieder* (2). ('Downright bad'). Lost?
March 24, 1901.	*Ekstase*. Text by Otto Julius Bierbaum. Published 1924.
November 2, 1901.	*In meines Vaters Garten*. [Text by Otto Hartleben]. Published 1910.

Piano

(all lost)

June 7, 1898.	*Fünf Variationen*
December 15, 1898.	*Vom Küssen*
December 23, 1898.	*Adagio*
March 7,1899.	*Drei Clavierstücke*
May 20, 1899.	*Fantasia*
June 27,1899.	*Sonata* [First movement—inserts five bars in 4/4]
October 3, 1899.	*Etude*
May 19, 1900.	*Thema und Variationen*
October 7, 1900.	*Fuge*
November 20, 1900.	*Invention*
November 20, 1900.	"*Novelette*"
January 7, 1901.	*Variationen* [from 1900?]

March 6, 1901.	*Adagio*
April 19, 1901.	*Rondo*
September 16, 1901.	*Rondo*

Chamber Works

November 10, 1899.	*Violinsonate*. Lost.

Chorus

August 3, 1901.	*Chorus for mixed voices.* Text by Falke. Finished October 10, 1901. Lost.

Fragments
(all lost)

April 14, 1898.	*Movement* (for piano)
July 8, 1899.	*Italy.* A set of four or five piano pieces.
September 1, 1899.	*Trio mit Clavierbegleitung*
February 15, 1900.	*Rhapsody*
June 10, 1901.	[*Operatic scene*]. Fragment. Half an act. Text believed to be *Die Frau im Fenster* by Hugo von Hofmannsthal.
October 1901.	Unspecified medium. Longer poem by Goethe for the master, his apprentices, a chorus, a trio.

Bibliography

Colerus, Blanca. "Alma Mahler." In *Die schöne Wienerin.* Edited by György Sebestyén. Munich: Verlag Kurt Desch, 1971.

Filler, Susan M. "A Composer's Wife as Composer: The Songs of Alma Mahler." *Journal of Musicological Research* 4 (1983): 427-42.

____. "Alma Mahler: *Der Erkennende*." In *Historical Anthology of Music by Women,* edited by James R. Briscoe. Bloomington, Ind.: Indiana University Press, 1987.

____. *Gustav and Alma Mahler: a Guide to Research.* New York: Garland, 1989.

Fry, Varian. *Surrender on Demand.* New York: Random House, 1945.

Isaacs, Reginald. *Gropius: An Illustrated Biography of the Creator of the Bauhaus.* An abridged version of the original English text. (Complete text was published in German as *Walter Gropius: Der Mensch und sein Werk,* vol. I and II. Berlin: Gebr. Mann Verlag, 1983-84.) Boston: Little, Brown & Co., 1991.

Keegan, Susanne. *The Bride of the Wind: The Life and Times of Alma Mahler-Werfel.* New York: Viking, 1992.

Kravitt, Edward F. *The Lied, Mirror of Late Romanticism.* New Haven: Yale University Press, 1996.

____. "The Lieder of Alma Maria Schindler Mahler." *Music Review* 43(1988): 190-204.

La Grange, Henry-Louis de. *Gustav Mahler. Vienna: The Years of Challenge (1897–1904).* Oxford: Oxford University Press, 1995. Translated from *Gustav Mahler: Vers la Gloire (1860–1900)* and *Gustav Mahler: l'âge d'or de Vienne.* Paris: Librairie Arthème Fayard, 1983.

Mahler, Alma. *Gustav Mahler: Briefe 1879–1911.* Berlin: Paul Zsolnay, 1924. Edited and enlarged by Knud Martner, translated by Eithne Wilkins, Ernst Kaiser, and Bill Hopkins as *Selected Letters of Gustav Mahler.* London: Faber and Faber, 1979.

____. *Gustav Mahler: Erinnerungen und Briefe.* Amsterdam: Allert de Lange, 1940. Translated and enlarged as *Gustav Mahler: Memories and Letters.* 4th ed. Edited by Donald Mitchell and Knud Martner and translated by Basil Creighton. London: Cardinal, 1990.

Mahler-Werfel, Alma. *And the Bridge Is Love.* With E. B. Ashton. New York: Harcourt, Brace & Co., 1958. Published in German as *Mein Leben.* Frankfurt am Main: Fischer, 1960.

____. *Tagebuch-Suiten 1898–1902.* Edited by Antony Beaumont and Susanne Rode-Breymann. Frankfurt am Main: S. Fischer, 1997. Translated and abridged as *Diaries, 1898–1902.* Ithaca: Cornell University Press, 1999.

Mahler, Gustav. *Adagietto. Facsimile, Documentation, Recording.* Edited by Gilbert E. Kaplan. New York: The Kaplan Foundation, 1992.

____. *Ein Glück ohne Ruh': die Briefe Gustav Mahlers an Alma.* Edited by Henry-Louis de La Grange and Günther Weiss. Berlin: Siedler, 1995.

Oskar Kokoschka und Alma Mahler: Die Puppe. Epilog einer Passion. Frankfürt am Main: Städtische Galerie im Städel, 1992.

Perle, George. "Mein geliebtes Almschi . . ." *Österreichische Musikzeitschrift* 35 (1980): 2-15.

Rode-Breymann, Susanne. *Die Komponisten Alma Mahler-Werfel.* Hannover: Niedersächsische Staatstheater Hannover GmbH, Theater museum und-archiv, 1999.

Schollum, Robert. "Die Lieder von Alma Maria Schindler-Mahler." *Österreichische Musikzeitschrift* 34 (1979): 544-51.

Scholz-Michelitsch, Helga. "Eine Korrespondenz über eine Korrespondenz: Anna Bahr-Mildenburg und Alma Mahler zur

Edition von Briefen Gustav Mahlers." *Studien zur Musikwissenschaft* 43 (1994): 365-74.

Smith, Warren Storey. "The Songs of Alma Mahler." *Chord and Discord* 2 (1950): 74-78.

Sorell, Walter. "Alma Mahler-Werfel: Body and Mind." In *Three Women: Lives of Sex and Genius*. New York: Bobbs-Merrill, 1975.

Urban, Juliane. "Die Lieder von Alma Mahler-Werfel geb. Schindler (1879–1964)." Master's thesis, Freie Universität Berlin, 1994.

Weidinger, Alfred. *Kokoschka and Alma Mahler*. Edited by Jacqueline Guigui-Stollberg and translated by Fiona Elliott. New York: Prestel, 1996.

Werfel, Franz. *The Song of Bernadette: A Personal Preface*. Translated by Ludwig Lewisohn. New York: Viking Press, 1942.

Discography

Ausgewählte Lieder von Alexander Zemlinsky, Karl Weigl, Alma Mahler, Arnold Schönberg. Christopher Norton-Walsh, baritone; Charles Spencer, piano. Preiser 120 653 (LP). *Ich wandle unter Blumen; Laue Sommernacht; Die stille Stadt*.

Lieder of Alma Mahler and Juli Nunlist. Mary Sidoni, soprano; Patricia Cox, piano. AFKA-S4686. *Fünf Lieder*.

Songs of Lili Boulanger and Alma Mahler. Katherine Ciesinski, mezzo-soprano; Ted Taylor, piano. Leonarda LPI 118 (1983). *Vier Lieder*.

Alma Mahler-Werfel: Sämtliche Lieder. Isabel Lippitz, soprano; Barbara Heller, piano. CPO 999 018-2 (1987). *Fünf Lieder, Vier Lieder, Fünf Gesänge*.

Alma and Gustav Mahler: Lieder. Hanna Schaer, mezzo; Françoise Tillard, piano. Adda 581208 (1990). *Fünf Lieder*. (With Gustav Mahler, *Lieder und Gesänge aus der Jugendzeit*.)

Mahler, Mahler and friends: Songs by Alma Mahler, Gustav Mahler, Alexander Zemlinsky and Hans Pfitzner. Anne Gjevang, alto; Einar Steen-Nøkleberg, piano. Victoria VCD 19069 (1995). *Fünf Lieder*.

Alma Mahler-Werfel: Complete Songs. Ruth Ziesak, soprano; Iris Vermillion, mezzo; Christian Elsner, tenor; Cord Garben, piano. CPO 999 455-2 (1997). *Fünf Lieder, Vier Lieder, Fünf Gesänge*. (With Zemlinsky, op. 7.)

Alma Mahler-Werfel (1879–1964): The Complete Songs/Sämtliche Lieder. (Orchestrated by Julian Reynolds.) Members of the Brabant Orchestra; Charlotte Margiono, Soprano; Julian Reynolds, cond. *Fünf Lieder, Vier Lieder, Fünf Gesänge*, [2 Lieder] *Aus Dem Cyclus "Mütter"* von Rainer Maria Rilke. Globe GLO 5199.

Editorial Comments

Susan Filler

Several musicologists have discussed the compositional style of Alma Mahler's songs. Most crucial is the question of manuscript sources, which might give perspective to the creative process in comparison with the published editions. According to the composer herself, the manuscripts of her songs were destroyed in the bombing of Vienna during World War II. While we have no reason to doubt her statement, happily there are two exceptions to that information.

The first is the manuscript of two songs (*Leise Weht ein erstes Blühn* and *Kennst du meine Nächte*?) from *Aus dem Cyclus: "Mütter" von Rainer Maria Rilke*, apparently composed around the turn of the century when Alma Maria Schindler (not yet married) was studying counterpoint with Josef Labor and Robert Gound and composition with Alexander Zemlinsky. The second is the manuscript of the four songs which were ultimately published in 1915. The original manuscript is in the collection of Henry-Louis de La Grange (Paris) and a microfilm is in the Toscanini Memorial Archive at the New York Public Library. No comparable source for the songs published in 1910 and 1924 is known to exist. Therefore the existence of this manuscript offers a unique opportunity to make a critical edition by comparison of the manuscript and published sources. It is on that basis that we publish this edition.

There are several reasons to consider the manuscript significant. First, it combines the hands of Gustav and Alma Mahler, documenting her account of Gustav Mahler's assistance to her work during 1910–1911, the last year of his own life. Second, it includes not only the four songs in question but a poem in Gustav's handwriting between the first and second songs in the manuscript, which will be discussed below. Third, a careful comparison of the two versions of each song shows widespread alterations of the following types:

- addition and deletion of accidentals, time signatures, clefs, dynamic marks, and other performance signs
- redistribution of pitches between staves in the piano part
- addition, deletion and change of pitches, figures or rhythms
- other changes, including handling of verbal texts and enharmonic changes in the notation of pitches.

There are certain types of changes that should be taken for granted as part of the publication process. The redistribution of pitches between staves was probably undertaken by editorial staff, not by the composer, and is therefore not noted in the critical notes to this edition since it was surely done for purposes of clarification to the target audience, not as substantive alteration. The same considerations apply to the addition and deletion of accidentals, time signatures and clefs when they do not affect the composer's own pitches.

However, changes in individual pitches and melodic figures or in notated rhythms and addition or deletion of dynamic marks were presumably initiated by the composer—occurring frequently as they do in this instance—and are of great significance. In respect of the fact that the manuscript combines the hands of both Gustav and Alma Mahler, it is worth speculating about the reasons for the changes.

The order of the four songs is different in the manuscript from the order in the published score.

Manuscript version	Published version
Waldseligkeit	*Licht in der Nacht*
Licht in der Nacht	*Waldseligkeit*
Erntelied	*Ansturm*
Ansturm	*Erntelied*

The change in order of the songs may or may not be significant, in view of the fact that the songs are numbered in the published score but not in the manuscript. While none of the songs are dated in the manuscript, all four are dated in the published score. *Licht in der Nacht* and *Erntelied* are dated 1901, and *Waldseligkeit* and *Ansturm* are dated 1911. Thus, considering the change in order, the later songs were the first and last in the manuscript but the earlier songs occupied those positions in the published score. The dates themselves are significant, since the 1901 songs were written before her marriage whereas the songs written in 1911 were from near the end of the marriage. We cannot even mention the year 1911 without raising the question of whether Alma Mahler wrote the two later songs before or after Gustav's death on May 18 of that year. A partial answer may be found in the fact that *Waldseligkeit* is primarily in Gustav's hand whereas *Ansturm* is complete only in her's (Gustav began to copy it but covered only the first fourteen bars). It is relatively easy to differentiate their handwritings, not only because of characteristic differences in shape but because they used sharply different writing instruments. Gustav wrote in very distinguishable black ink, just as he did in most of his own manuscripts. Alma Mahler wrote in a lighter tint, which is obvious in the manuscript of *Ansturm* and may also show up in individual signs added to the other songs in Gustav's hand.

There is surprising coherence of style among the four songs, and this suggests that either (a) there was no advance in her compositional style in the ten-year hiatus, possibly because of Gustav's famous "ban" on his wife's compositions until the crisis in their marriage in the summer of 1910; or (b) the two earlier songs were revised in 1911, bringing them into line with the style of the two later songs.

The poem (not set to music) inserted between the first two songs in the manuscript is in Gustav's hand:

"Mewlana Dschelaleddin Rumi"
übersetzt aus dem Persischen von Rückert

Wo[h]l endet Tod des Lebens Noth,
Doch schauert Leben vor dem Tod,
Das Leben sieht die dunkle Hand,
Den hellen Kelch nicht, den sie bot.
So schauert vor der Lieb' ein Herz
Als wie vom Untergang bedroht.
Dann was die Lieb' erwachet, stirbt
Das *Ich, der dunkle Despot*.
Du lass ihn sterben in der Nacht
Und athme frei im Morgenroth.

The thirteenth-century Persian poet Rumi is identified as the author of this text. Friedrich Rückert, a poet whose own works exerted significant influence in Gustav's own oeuvre, was well known as a translator of poetry from Eastern languages, including Persian; but the appearance of this poem in the manuscript is a mystery, since neither Gustav nor Alma Mahler is known to have set it to music. Either he had copied the poem from an earlier page in her hand, or he himself found the poem, copied it and slipped it between the two songs in the manuscript as an offering or challenge to her musical skills.

Alma Mahler herself must have supplied the dates of the songs to the publisher. There is no other known informant who might have given such information to Universal Edition. But, with this certainty, there is also an unanswered question: on what basis did Gustav make copies in his own hand of his wife's songs? Presumably there were earlier unpublished sources in her hand from which he copied, with or without changes. The full manuscript of *Ansturm* survives as proof of that assumption, and the fourteen bars that Gustav did copy from her manuscript may have remained in their uncompleted state because of the multiplicity of his professional commitments, or (less likely) because of the onset of illness in February 1911.

By the same token, the many differences between the manuscript and published scores—sometimes startlingly radical—lead to the inescapable conclusion that, after her husband's death, Alma Mahler took a pen to these songs and made changes freely without interference from anyone. This shows a side of her character which she presumably suppressed from public view in her role as the Widow Mahler. The publication of the first book of songs in 1910 had been with her husband's active collaboration; but the publication of the second book in 1915 (not to mention that of the third book in 1924, and that by a different publisher) did not have such moral support. Could Alma's personal reputation have influenced the publishers? Or did others whose works were also published by Universal Edition and Josef Weinberger support her? Either way, she was clearly not finished as a composer until long after Gustav's death.

The following critical notes to each of the *Vier Lieder* spotlight the most significant changes between the manuscript and the published versions. Presumably there was at least one intermediary manuscript or proof source that is not known to us. In cases of changes too extreme to be summarized in words, transcriptions of the manuscript versions are included as Examples 1-13.

All changes are from the manuscript versions to the 1915 editions. (Abbreviations: pno = piano; RH = right hand; LH = left hand; vc = voice; bt/bts = beat or beats)

Licht in der Nacht

Bar 12: pno RH: bt 3, G-flat changed to F-sharp
Bar 13: pno RH: bt 1, A-flat changed to A-natural; bt 3 two chords deleted
Bar 14: pno LH: bts 1, 2 ms. has 4 eighth-notes (B-flat, C D, E-flat)
Bar 15: pno LH: bt 3, F-natural half-note
Bar 17: pno LH: bt 4, octaves added
Bar 19: roll added
Bar 20: vc: bts 1-4, changed from C-sharp A-sharp B-natural C-sharp
Bar 21: vc: bt 3, originally half-note
Bar 22: see Example 1
Bar 24: pno RH: bts 3-4, A-natural omitted
Bar 26: pno LH: bt 1, grace-note G and E-flat in ms.
Bar 31: pno: rolls added
Bar 35: vc: bt 1, originally dotted half-note
Bar 36: see Example 2
Bar 37: pno LH: lower E-flat added
Bar 38-39: ms. included E-flat with grace note in 3[d] staff
Bar 39 & 40: time signatures added
Bar 40: pno LH: bt 3, G-natural added
Bar 42: pno LH: bt 3, A added
Bar 43: vc: bt 2, grace-note G added; bt 3, alternate D added

Ex. 1 *Licht in der Nacht*
(M. 22)

Ex. 2 *Licht in der Nacht*
(M. 36)

Waldseligkeit

Bar 2: pno RH: bt 3, last note of triplet originally F-sharp; pno LH: bt 4, top note of chord originally B-natural
Bar 3: pno LH: bt 3, D-flat added
Bars 4-7: see Example 3
Bar 7: vc: "lauschen" originally "rauschen" in Gustav's hand (error corrected)
Bar 10: $\frac{3}{4}$ time signature added; "Innig" added
Bar 11: pno LH: bt 2, roll omitted; pno RH: bt 3, originally half-note
Bar 12: pno: bt 1, *ff* omitted; bt 2, crescendo added
Bar 13: time signature added; pno LH: bt 1, C-sharp changed to C-natural
Bar 16: pno LH: bt 2, rhythm changed from quarter-note to half-note; bt 4, rhythm changed to quarter-note
Bar 17: originally F-sharp in third chord of piano R.H.
Bar 21: piano LH originally included half-note E (continuation from Bar 20)
Bar 24: ms. included "acc."
Bar 25: ms. included f crescendo to ff
Bar 26: pno LH: bt 1, originally grace-note G-flat/A-flat; glissando added
Bar 27: pno RH: bt 4, last three notes from D-natural, E-natural, F-sharp changed to D-flat, E-flat, F-natural
Bar 28: pno LH: bt 3, roll added
Bars 29: "rit." moved to bar 30
Bar 30: Tempo I deleted; pno RH: bts 3-4, last four notes changed from literal repetition of first four notes to D-flat, E-flat, F-natural, G-natural
Bar 33: "sehr langsam" added

Ex. 3 *Waldseligkeit*
(Mm. 4-7)

Ansturm

Note: the first fourteen bars of this song are treated as three different versions (Gustav's ms., Alma's ms. and published edition); thereafter, with the cessation of Gustav's ms., comparison is made between Alma's ms. and the published edition.

Bar 1: time signature changed from common time to cut time

Bar 2: pno LH: Gustav's ms. and published edition omitted A. (He may have missed it or she may have added it.)

Bar 3: pno RH: octave C in ms.; Gustav wrote repeated A's as second and third notes

Bar 4: piano RH: Gustav's and Alma's mss.: fourth note in chord is A; pub. edition is B-sharp

Bar 7: $\frac{2}{4}$ time signatures added; pno LH: bt 2, half-rest in Gustav ms. after quarter rest

Bar 8: *Doppeltes* Tempo added

Bar 9: molto accel. originally in bar 10 in both mss versions

Bar 10: pno LH: bt 1, enharmonic B-flat to A-sharp

Bar 11: *schnell* added

Bar 12: time signature in both ms. versions originally is $\frac{4}{4}$

Bar 17: *acc.* in original omitted

Bars 18-20: accidentals added and deleted

Bar 19: *cresc.* added

Bar 20: pno RH: bt 2, E-flat enharmonic changed to D-sharp; bt. 3 changed to F-sharp, D-sharp, D-natural C

Bar 22: $\frac{3}{4}$ meter, *ten.*, mf and *accel.* added

Bar 23: meter and performance suggestions added

Bar 23: $\frac{2}{4}$ meter added; fermata over chord deleted; two bars of piano accompaniment follow this bar in ms. but were deleted from 1915 editions; see Example 4

Bar 25: bts 1-2 in pno RH one octave higher in ms

Bar 26: vc: notes 2-5 all eighth-notes in ms.; pno RH: bt 2 ½ one octave lower in ms.

Bar 27: vc: changed from whole-note (ms.) to half-note and half-rest; pno RH: eighth-rest added; pno LH: 32nd notes originally B, C-sharp, E G; *dolce* half-beat earlier in ms.; *espr.* added

Bar 29: pno LH: F originally quarter-note

Bar 31: pno LH: E added

Ex. 4 *Ansturm*
(after M. 23)

Erntelied

Bars 1-2: *Begleitung so undeutlich als möglich* added

Bar 10: pno RH: roll omitted; pno RH: last eighth note originally A-flat C

Bar 11: *sf* in ms. changed to *f*

Bar 12: pno LH: grace-notes added

Bar 13: fermatas added; pno RH: bt 2, D changed to E-double flat

Bar 14: see Example 5

Bar 15: vc: in ms. notes originally C-natural, E-flat, C-natural; pno RH: bt 3, A-natural changed to B-double flat; pno RH: bt 3, G added

Bar 16: pno LH: bts 3-4, quarter-notes added, E-natural added to last chord in pno RH

Bars 16-17: *ritard, a tempo* removed

Bars 17-21: see Example 6

Bar 21: A single bar of pno accompaniment follows this bar in ms.

Bar 24: pno RH: last note of second triplet originally G-natural

Bar 25: *accelerando* added

Bar 29: vc: changed to whole note (originally dotted half-note, quarter rest)

Bar 32: pno LH: bt 3, changed from G-natural to F double-sharp

Bar 33a: see bar 32; a single bar of piano accompaniment follows bar 33 in ms.; see Example 8

Bar 34: see Example 9

Bars 36-39: pno RH and LH: bts 3 and 4, alto and tenor originally half-note; G-natural eighth note added

Bar 37: pno LH: first four eighth-notes changed to eighth-rest followed by 3 eighth-notes

Bar 39: pno RH: 2nd eighth note G-flat in ms. changed to A-flat

Bar 46: vc: originally B-flat, A-flat, B-flat

Bar 47: *sf* originally in ms.; *klingen lassen* added

Bar 49: see Example 10

Bar 51: pno RH: bt 3, A-natural, B-natural, D in ms. changed to B-double flat, C-flat, E-double flat

Bar 52: see Example 11

Bar 53: roll in ms. preceding third beat deleted; A-naturals in ms. changed to B-double flats

Bars 54-61: see Example 12

Bars 62-66: vc: see Example 13

Bars 67-73: text originally "Auf, ja auf dem Wirken preise ihn, dem Wirken preise ihn" (ms.) completely deleted and replaced by "ah . . . ."

Bar 69: pno LH: bt 4, double flat added

Bar 70: naturals added

Bar 72: vc: originally B-flat, A-natural, A-flat, C-natural now G-flat, F, E-flat and rhythms changed from 4 quarter-notes to 2 quarter-notes and 1 half-note

Bar 74: vc: A-flat in ms. deleted

Bar 75: pno LH: originally half-note and two quarter-notes; pno RH: bts 3 & 4, originally four eighth-notes (F, E-natural, F, C)

Bar 76: pno LH: originally two half-notes

Bar 78: ppppp added

Ex. 5 Erntelied
(M. 14)
Ex. 6 Erntelied
(Mm. 17-21)
Ex. 7 Erntelied
(after M. 21)
Ex. 8 Erntelied
(after M. 33)
Ex. 9 Erntelied
(M. 34)
Ex. 10 Erntelied
(M. 49)
Ex. 11 Erntelied
(M. 52)

Ex. 12 *Erntelied* (from M. 54)

Ex. 12 cont.

Ex. 13 *Erntelied* (Mm. 62-66)

Acknowledgments

I am grateful for the collaboration of Nadine Sine, Juliane Urban, Sylvia Glickman and Martha Furman Schleifer, without whose support and advice this edition would not have been possible. Special thanks go to Henry-Louis de La Grange, the owner of the manuscript version, and Marina Mahler-Fistoulari, grand-daughter of Alma and Gustav.

Licht in der Nacht

Ringsum dunkle Nacht,
hüllt in Schwarz mich ein,
zage flimmert gelb fern her ein Stern!
Ist mir wie ein Trost,
eine Stimme still,
die dein Herz aufruft,
das verzagen will.

Kleines gelbes Licht,
bist mir wie ein Stern
überm Hause einst
Jesu Christ, des Herrn
und da löscht es aus!
Und die Nacht wird schwer!
Schlafe Herz!
Du hörst keine Stimme mehr!

Round about, dark night
shrouds me in blackness;
timidly flickers yellow a distant star!
Coming as a consolation,
a still voice,
summoning the heart
that verges on despair.

Tiny yellow light,
coming like a star
above the house
of Jesus Christ, the Lord
and then snuffed out!
And the night becomes heavy!
Sleep, my heart!
Thou hearest no voice anymore!

Waldseligkeit

Der Wald beginnt zu rauschen,
den Bäumen naht die Nacht,
als ob sie selig lauschen,
berühren sie sich sacht.

Und unter ihren Zweigen
da bin ich ganz allein,
da bin ich ganz mein eigen,
ganz nur dein!

The forest begins to murmur;
to the trees the night draws nigh
as though blissfully eavesdropping,
gently touching each other.

And under their branches
there I am quite alone
there I am quite my own,
quite wholly thine!

Ansturm

O zürne nicht, wenn mein Begehren
dunkel aus seinen Grenzen bricht,
soll es uns selber nicht verzehren,
muss es heraus ans Licht!

Fühlst ja, wie all mein Innres brandet,
und wenn herauf der Aufruhr bricht,
jäh über deinen Frieden strandet,
dann bebst du aber du zürnst mir nicht.

O be not angry when my desire
bursts darkly out of bounds,
lest we ourselves should be deformed,
it must see the light of day!

Then dost thou feel how all within me burns;
and when the tumult suddenly breaks forth,
devastating all your peace,
then dost thou tremble but dost not scold.

Erntelied

Der ganze Himmel glüht
in hellen Morgenrosen;
mit einem letzten losen
Traum noch im Gemüt
trinke meine Augen diesen Schein,
Wach und wacher wie Genesungswein.

Und nun kommt von jenen Rosenhügeln
Glanz des Tags und Wehn von seinen Flügeln,
kommt er selbst und alter Liebe voll,
dass ich ganz an ihm genesen soll
Gram der Nacht und was sich sonst verlor
ruft er mich an seine Brust empor!

Und die Wälder und die Felder klingen
und die Gärten heben an zu singen.
Fern und dumpf rauscht das erwachte Meer,
Segel seh' ich in die Sonnenweiten,
weisse Segel frischen Windes gleiten,
stille, goldne Wolken obenher
und im Blauen sind es Wanderflüge?
Schweig, o Seele, hast du kein Genüge?

Sieh, ein Königreich hat dir der Tag verliehn.
Auf! Dein Wirken preise ihn!
Ah!

The whole heaven glows
in bright pink of dawn;
with a final, random
dream in my brain
my eyes drink in this brightness,
awake and more awake, like a healing wine.

And now from that rosy mound arises
the day's first gleam and flutter of his wings;
now he himself appears all filled with ancient love,
that I by him alone should now be healed.
From gloom of night and all that one has lost
he calls me upward to his bosom!

And how the fields and forest ring
and the gardens start to sing.
Distant and muffled murmurs the awakened sea,
sails I spy on the sunny expanse;
white sails gliding on fresh winds,
quiet golden clouds above, clouds approaching
and in the blue—are those birds of passage?
Be still, my soul, have you no contentment?

See how the day has bestowed on thee a kingdom.
Arise! Glorify him with thy works!
Ah!

*Mewlana Dschelaleddin Rumi**

(translated from the Persian by [Friedrich] Rückert)

Wo[h]l endet Tod des Lebens Noth,
Doch schauert Leben vor dem Tod.
Das Leben sieht die dunkle Hand,
den hellen Kelch nicht, den sie bot.

So schauert vor der Lieb' ein Herz,
als wie vom Untergang bedroht.
Dann wo die Lieb' erwachet, stirbt
das *Ich, der dunkle Despot.*
Du lass ihn sterben in der Nacht
und athme frei im Morgenroth.

'Tis good that death ends life's trouble,
yet life trembles in the face of death.
The living see the dark hand,
but not the bright chalice it offers.

So the heart trembles in the face of love,
as though threatened with annihilation.
For where love is awakened,
the I, the dark despot, dies.
Surrender him to death at night
and breath free in the rosy light of dawn.

* The appearance of this poem in the manuscript is a mystery since neither Gustav nor Alma Mahler set it to music.

Translations by Nadine Sine

Licht in der Nacht

Otto Julius Bierbaum

Alma Maria Schindler-Mahler
Susan M. Filler, editor

15
ei - ne Stim-me still, die dein Herz auf-ruft, das ver-za - gen will.
19
Klei - nes gel - bes Licht,
22
bist mir wie ein Stern üb-erm Hau - se einst Je - su
steigernd
26
Christ, des Herrn und da löscht es
ausdrucksvoll
sf
sf

30
aus!
Und die Nacht wird schwer!
pp
34
rit.
Schla - fe Herz!
pp
dim.
38
Schla - fe Herz!
[𝄐]
3
41
ppp
Du hörst kei-ne Stim - me mehr!

Waldseligkeit

Richard Dehmel

Alma Maria Schindler-Mahler
Susan M. Filler, editor

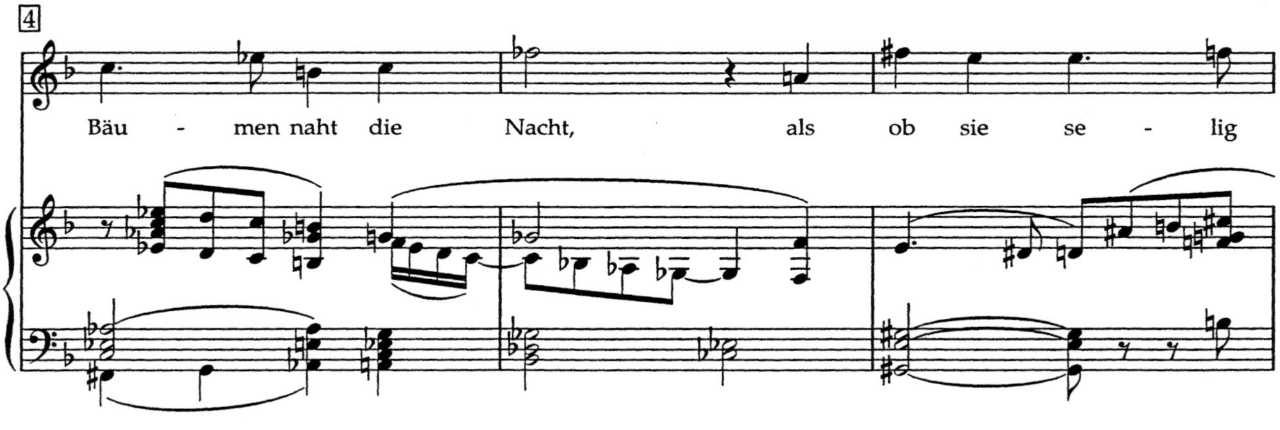

9
Innig
sacht.
L.H.
p dolce
12
steigernd
Und un-ter ih-ren Zwei - gen
16
da bin ich ganz al - lein, da bin ich ganz mein ei - gen,
20
ganz nur dein, ganz nur dein,

*glissando auf den schwarzen Tasten.
(on the black notes)

Ansturm

Richard Dehmel

Alma Maria Schindler-Mahler
Susan M. Filler, editor

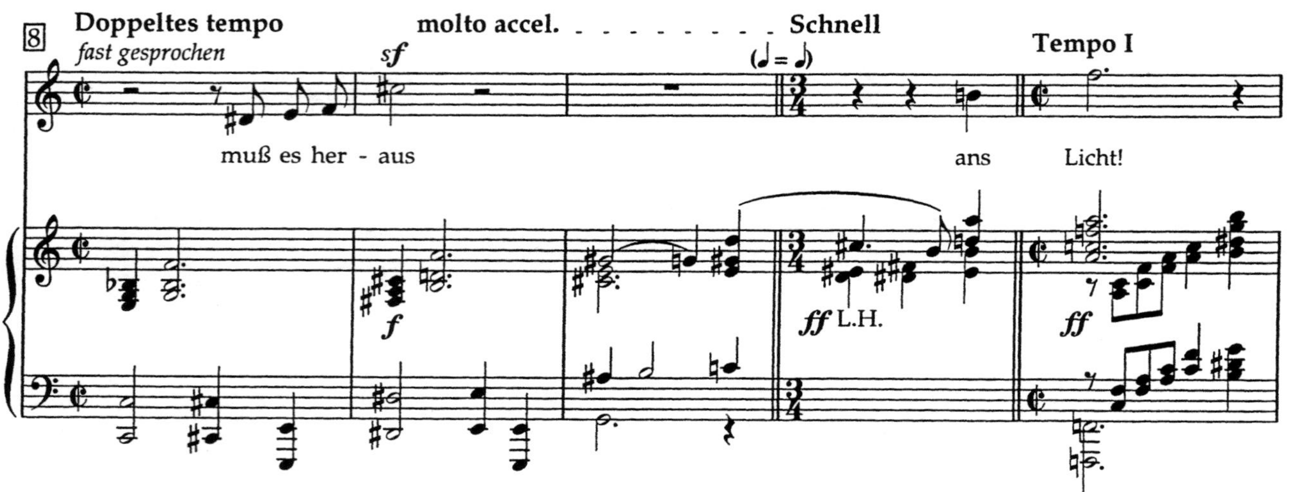

13
ans Licht!
Fühlst ja, wie all mein
p
17
Inn - res bran - det,
und wenn her - auf der
R.H.
L.H.
R.H.
ff
p
L.H.
Led.
19
Auf - - ruhr bricht,
L.H.
cresc.
20
jäh ü - ber dei - - - - - - - nen
molto
L.H.

*This note "B" in 1915 print.

Erntelied

Gustav Falke

Alma Maria Schindler-Mahler
Susan M. Filler, editor

Leicht bewegt
Begleitung so undeutlich als möglich
Der gan - ze Him - mel
glüht in hel - len Mor - gen - ro - sen;
mit ei-nem letz - ten lo - sen Traum noch im Ge - müt
trin-ken mei-ne Au-gen die-sen Schein,
trin-ken mei-ne Au - gen
p
f
4
7
10

13
die - sen Schein.
Wach und wa - cher wie Ge - ne - sungs -
17
wein.
mf
und non-kommt von je - nen
19
Ro - sen - hü - geln
Glanz-des Tags und Wehn von sei - nen
21
Flü - geln,
kommt er - selbst und
cresc.

23
al- ter Lie- be voll,
daß ich ganz an
25
accel.
a tempo
ihm ge- ne - sen soll
Gram der Nacht
ff
f
28
und was sich sonst ver - lor
30
f
ruft er mich an sei- ne Brust em- por,
espr.

34
ff
ruft er mich an sei - ne
ff
ff
36
p
Brust em - por!
p
40
pp
Und die Wäl-der und die Fel - der klin - gen und die
pp
43
Gär-ten he-ben an zu sin - gen. Fern und dumpf

46
rauscht das er-wach - te Meer,
Se-gel seh' ich in die Son-nen -
klingen lassen
49
wei - ten,
wei-ße Se-gel fri - schen Win - des glei - ten,
52
rit.
stil - le, gold - ne Wol - ken o - ben, Wol - ken o - ben -
55
her
und im Blau-en sind es Wan - der flü - ge?

58
p
Schweig, o See - - le,
cresc.
60
p
hast du kein Ge - nü - ge?
62
f
Sieh, ein Kö - nig reich hat dir - der Tag ver-liehn
f
64
ff
Auf! Dein Wir - ken prei - se ihn!
f cresc.
6
6

66
p
Ah,
dim.
p
dim.
69
ah,
ah,
dim. sempre
72
pp ppp
ah!
pppp morendo
75
ppppp

Marion Bauer
(1882–1955)

PEGGY A. HOLLOWAY

Marion Eugenie Bauer, the youngest of seven children, was born in 1882[1] in Walla Walla, Washington, into a musical and literary household. Her father, Jacques Bauer, a French-Jewish immigrant, was a tenor who also played "any of the instruments of the military band" during the Indian Wars.[2] Jacques was a respected, successful store-owner in Walla Walla, and Marion's mother, Julie Heyman Bauer, was a gifted linguist who taught at Whitman College.

After Jacques Bauer's death in 1890, the family moved to Portland, Oregon. Julie Bauer taught at Saint Helen's Hall while Marion's oldest sister Emilie Frances contributed to the family's support by giving piano lessons and writing music criticism for the *Portland Oregonion.* Marion attended Saint Helen's Hall and took piano lessons from her sister. She also tried composing, and displayed talent for drawing, writing, and teaching.[3]

Emilie Frances moved to New York City around 1900 and wrote for the *New York Evening Mail*, *Etude Magazine*, and the *Musical Leader*. Marion soon joined her there and began harmony studies with Henry Holden Huss. In 1905, the Bauer sisters met the French pianist Raoul Pugno. The next year Marion was invited to stay with the Pugno family in France where she gave English lessons to Pugno's daughter Renée and her friends, sisters Nadia (1887–1979) and Lili Boulanger (1893–1918) (see this volume). In return, Marion received lessons in harmony and composition, earning the distinction of becoming the first American student of the legendary Nadia Boulanger. While in France, Marion encountered the latest works of Debussy and Ravel, absorbing the elements of impressionism which later permeated her style.

On her return to the United States (1910), Bauer published her first song, *Light*, set to a popular poem by Francis Bourdillon. In 1913, another Bauer friend, conductor Walter Henry Rothwell, encouraged her to study in Germany with Paul Ertel. Bauer's German studies helped to strengthen her technical foundation and contributed to a linear approach to composition that remained a significant stylistic feature throughout her career. At the end of her stay, Bauer presented a recital of her works which were well received in spite of the German skepticism of American composers in general and female composers in particular! [4]

The years 1912–1921 represent Bauer's most prolific period of song composition and proved significant in the development of her style. During those years, her chief publisher was A. P. Schmidt of Boston. The eighteen songs published by Schmidt resemble the parlor song and other semi-popular styles of that era. Bauer's songs were favorites with a number of performers during these years, appearing on the programs of such well-known singers as Helen Stanley, Eva Gauthier, and Ernestine Schumann-Heink.[5]

For several years, Bauer relied considerably upon the advice and support of Arthur Schmidt. Around 1916, her correspondence with Schmidt indicates a developing artistic disagreement resulting from her increasing use of new compositional techniques largely influenced by impressionism. Her stylistic evolution, which ultimately resulted in a complete break with the publisher, took a major step in 1917 when she became acquainted with the music of Charles Griffes (1884–1920). Bauer and Griffes became close friends, forming what Bauer termed "a musical society of two" to exchange manuscripts and offer each other constructive criticism.[6] Griffes also introduced her to editor Oscar G. Sonneck of G. Schirmer, Inc. who encouraged Bauer to submit an article to the *Musical Quarterly*. Her resulting association with Sonneck was "most encouraging and stimulating to a young, unknown composer."[7] Bauer's first published article, "Natural Law: Its Influence on Modern Music," provides interesting insight into her developing philosophy of composition in which she considered modern rhythm to be a reflection of music as a means of expressing human emotions in an increasingly complex world.[8] Her friendship with Griffes was cut short by his untimely death in 1920, but Bauer continued to champion his works throughout her lifetime and his influence remained clearly evident in her own music.

Apparently, Bauer's new style was not perceived by Arthur Schmidt to be commercially viable; her music was not being purchased by the public in adequate quantities. In 1918, Bauer sought permission to submit her manuscripts to other publishers. Ultimately, her contract was not renewed, and her songs were issued by A. P. Schmidt for the last time in 1922, shortly after the death of Arthur Schmidt.

In 1921–1922, G. Schirmer published three of Bauer's songs that had been rejected by A. P. Schmidt. Sonneck was openly critical of what he saw as a lack of innovation among American song composers and was pleased to support the efforts of the more adventuresome "modernists" with whom Marion Bauer was becoming associated. Bauer had a residency at the MacDowell Artist's Colony in Peterborough, New Hampshire in July of 1921, the first of twelve visits scattered throughout her lifetime. While there she was able to devote herself to composing, an activity that she later came to see as an indulgence in her extraordinarily busy life, and she met artists of many disciplines. Some of Bauer's finest compositions were inspired by the Colony's nurturing atmosphere, including *From the New Hampshire Woods*, the *Symphony*, and several unpublished songs.

Bauer joined with a group of forward-looking young composers including Louis Gruenberg (1884–1964), Frederick Jacobi (1891–1952), Deems Taylor (1885–1966), and Albert Stoessel (1894–1943) to form the American Music Guild in 1921. During the three years of its existence the Guild featured Bauer's works, including several of her songs, on three concerts. Through her involvement with the Guild, she was given the opportunity to "assess her musical standards with regard to larger musical forms . . . which she had not yet attempted."[9] As a result she decided to continue her studies and in 1923 she went to France where she remained for several years.

She wrote the first *String Quartet* and second *Sonata for Violin and Piano* while in Paris. In 1924, G. Schirmer published Bauer's most significant contribution to American song literature, the *Four Poems*, op. 16, to texts of John Gould Fletcher. Bauer also published articles in a number of journals and the first of four books, *How Music Grew* (1925), written in collaboration with Ethel Peyser.

In December of 1926, Bauer's beloved sister Emilie Frances became seriously ill and Marion returned to New York. After Emilie's death in March 1927, Marion inherited her position as critic and correspondent for the *Musical Leader*.[10] In 1927, she was appointed to the music faculty of New York University; teaching soon became the primary focus of her career. She also taught at Mills College (Calif.), the Carnegie Institute in Pittsburgh (PA), Columbia University, and the Institute of Musical Art (later The Juilliard School of Music). From 1928 until 1952, Bauer served as a lecturer and critic for the New York Chautauqua Institution. Her weeklong lecture series each summer emphasized contemporary trends in music and offered her the opportunity to champion the works of such "radical" contemporary composers as Arnold Schoenberg (1874–1951), whom she met and interviewed in 1934.[11]

As a charter member of the League of Composers, Bauer became a regular contributor to the publication *Modern Music* and served as organizer of the Young Composers' Concert Series. She was also a founding member of the American Composers Alliance and the American Music Center.

In light of the extent of her activities as a teacher, lecturer, author, and organizational activist, it seems amazing that Bauer was able to eke out any time to compose. However, the 1930s and 1940s were productive years. Important works from those years include: *Four Piano Pieces*; *Suite for Oboe and Clarinet*; *Dance Sonata*; *Sonata for Viola*, op. 22; *Concertino for Oboe, Clarinet, and String Quartet*; *and Symphonic Suite for Strings*, op. 34. One of her greatest honors was the performance of the tone poem *Sun Splendor* by the New York Philharmonic under Leopold Stokowski in 1947.

Bauer's crowning compositional achievement was her *Symphony*, completed in July of 1950.[12] The *Prelude for Flute and String Orchestra* was premiered by the New Symphony Orchestra of New York in 1952. After her retirement from New York University in 1951, she collaborated with Ethel Peyser on another book, *How Opera Grew*, completed in July of 1955.

Bauer suffered a fatal coronary thrombosis on August 9, 1955, at the home of her friend and long-term collaborator on her Chautauqua lectures, pianist Harrison Potter. The year after her death, Potter and the Mu Sigma Music Honorary Society sponsored the first of what was to be an annual series of Marion Bauer Memorial Concerts. The inaugural concert included works by Bauer and new works by young composers. Sadly, the series was soon discontinued and Bauer's works received little attention until the recent burgeoning of women's music scholarship. Her memory is nevertheless preserved by the influence she exerted on other women composers, including Ruth Crawford Seeger (1901–1953), Beatrice Laufer (b. 1923), and Julia Smith (1911–1989).[13]

Marion Bauer is primarily remembered for her work as a musicologist, author, and promoter of contemporary music. Her composing style evolved as she came into contact with new ideas in her work as a musicologist and teacher of composition. Her art songs, which enjoyed some popularity during her lifetime, are virtually unknown. Bauer's early songs were written with commercial success in mind, but rose above the semi-popular genres cultivated by many of the song composers of her generation. Although her style was influenced by French impressionism Bauer chose primarily to set texts of American poets that create subtly romantic or dreamlike moods appropriate to her emerging impressionistic tendencies.[14] She composed over sixty works for solo voice, of which thirty-six were published;[15] the majority appeared before 1925.

Her vocal music may be divided into three periods: the early works, written between 1910 and 1918 published primarily by A. P. Schmidt; the mature songs of the middle period, 1919–1925; and the late vocal works, written after 1925. Her early works described as parlor songs, are notable for the emergence of modern and impressionistic elements, including mildly dissonant chromaticism, nonfunctional chord progressions, and the use of modal and altered scales. Ninth chords, half-diminished sevenths, and triads with added seconds or sixths are employed for coloristic effect. Bauer established musical moods to match her poetic texts, using repeated patterns and motives in the accompaniment and applying harmonic colors from the impressionists' palette.

It was during the early 1920s that Marion Bauer found her "true voice" and reached maturity as a composer, a development that culminated in the centerpiece of her composition for solo voice, the *Four Poems*, op. 16, to texts of John Gould Fletcher.

The publication of the *Four Poems* in 1924 marked the end of Bauer's concentration on song composition. She undertook her European studies (1923–1926) with the goal of expanding her efforts to the larger forms, although a number of songs remaining in manuscript indicate that she continued to compose songs with piano accompaniment. The unpublished songs display increased chromaticism and further departure from functional tonality. It is unfortunate that these songs were not published, as they represent Bauer's advanced stages of development as a composer and dispel the misconception of her as composer of "romantic songs with flowery titles."[16] Bauer's final published songs, issued in 1947, to texts by Edna Castleman Bailey, serve almost as a summary of her favorite mature compositional devices, including modality, polytonality, quartal and quintal harmonies, descending chromatic lines, pedal tones, and chord planing.

The six songs chosen for this publication represent Marion Bauer's evolution as a composer of art song. The manuscript for *Lad and Lass* is undated, but it is a setting of a poem by Cale Young Rice, a poet popular with Bauer ca. 1917. The song is harmonically conservative but exhibits the use of occasional impressionism that resulted in her rift with Arthur Schmidt, such as the whole tone scale in measure 42. *My Faun*, dated 1919, was composed at the MacDowell Colony. It is clearly indebted to Claude Debussy (1862–1918) in subject matter and in the use of an arpeggio motive reminiscent of the opening of *Prélude à l'après-midi d'un faune*. Bauer's association with Charles Griffes may have influenced her choice of a text by Oscar Wilde, a poet Griffes also used.

Bauer's experimentation with new ideas and techniques is evident in the songs from the early 1930s. *When the Shy Star Goes Forth* to a text by James Joyce is an interesting study in polytonality based perhaps on the theories of Henry Cowell (1897–1965), a composer featured by Bauer in her 1933 book *Twentieth-Century Music*. The highly dissonant *To Losers*, composed in 1932, is based on a chromatic four-note motive. Though not strictly serial in its construction, it is clearly influenced by Bauer's interest in Schoenberg's works during the early 1930s.

How Doth the Little Crocodile is one of a set of five songs to texts from Lewis Carroll's *Alice in Wonderland,* composed in 1928. The song is harmonically conservative and seems to represent Bauer's efforts in the late 1920s to produce more commercially viable music in response to her own assessment of the poor quality of solo song available to the public.[17]

The final song, *Here Alone Unknown*, was performed on a radio broadcast of Bauer's works on November 7, 1954. Although the manuscript is undated it serves as a fine example of Bauer's mature style in which she uses texture, ambiguous tonal centers and bitonality, and changing accompaniment patterns to capture the symbolism of Conrad Aiken's poetry.

Acknowledgment

The editor gratefully acknowledges the permission granted by the estate of Marion Bauer to use the manuscripts located in the Library of Congress and the Mount Holyoke College Library/Archives and for the publication of the songs included in this volume.

Notes

1. Susan Pickett, a professor at Whitman College in Walla Walla, Washington, determined from newspaper articles and birth records that Bauer was born in 1882 rather than 1887 as listed in contemporary biographies. The reason for this discrepancy is unclear, but may be related to her desire not to be older than her teacher Nadia Boulanger, who was born in 1887.

2. David Ewen, *American Composers Today* (New York: H. W. Wilson, 1949), 20.

3. Ibid.

4. Madeleine Goss, *Modern Music Makers: Contemporary American Composers* (New York: E. P. Dutton & Co., 1952), 132.

5. Letter from Marion Bauer to A. P. Schmidt, March 17, 1915.

6. Marion Bauer, "Charles T. Griffes as I Remember Him," *Musical Quarterly* 29 (1943): 366.

7. Ibid., 361.

8. Marion Bauer, "Natural Law: Its Influence on Modern Music," *Musical Quarterly* 6 (1920): 469-77.

9. Beatrice Laufer, "Marion Bauer: The musical life of an American Women Composer," unpublished manuscript (New York: American Music Center, Marion Bauer file), 5.

10. As Emilie Frances and Marion Bauer served as the New York correspondents for the *Musical Leader,* the publication included many articles about performances of Bauer's works and is an excellent documentation of her compositional activities during those years.

11. L. Jeannette Wells. *A History of the Music Festival at Chatauqua Institution from 1874 to 1957* (Washington, D. C.: The Catholic University of America Press, 1958), 158-223.

12. Irwin A. Bazelon. "Woman with a Symphony," *The Baton of Phi Beta Fraternity* 30: 3 (1951), 4-7.

13. Ethel Peyser, "Marion Bauer," *The Marion Bauer Memorial Concert*. Program notes.

14. The rights to all music by Marion Bauer published by A. P. Schmidt are held by Summy-Birchard, Inc. Master copies from microfilm are available upon request.

15. The original research on the songs for solo voice of Marion Bauer appeared in Peggy Holloway, "The solo vocal repertoire of Marion Bauer with selected stylistic analyses" (D.M.A. diss., University of Nebraska-Lincoln, 1994). The research was supported by a grant from Warren F. and Edith R. Day Student Aid Fund.

16. Norman Lebrecht, "Marion Bauer," in *Companion to Twentieth-Century Music* (New York: Simon & Schuster, 1992).

17. Letter from Marion Bauer to H. R. Austin, October 15, 1929.

Selected List of Works

Vocal

(Key for location of unpublished works: LC = Library of Congress; MHC = Mount Holyoke College Library/Archives. Treasure Room; PHC = Collection of Peggy A. Holloway.)

Light. Text by Francis W. Bourdillon. Cincinnati, Ohio: John Church Company, 1910.

Sieben Lieder, op. 4 (1910?). Leipzig: Ernst Eulenberg.
1. *Ich gehe hin*. Text by Otto Erich Hartleben
2. *Abends*. Text by Theodor Storm
3. *Fruhlingslied*. Text by Heinrich Heine
4. *Klage nicht*. Text by Klaus Groth
5. *Ich wandere einsam*. Text by Klaus Groth
6. *Dumpf und trube*. Text by Marion Bauer
7. *Duftet die Lindenblut*. Text by Klaus Groth

The Coyote Song. Text by John S. Reed. Boston: Arthur P. Schmidt Publications, 1912.

Star Trysts. Text by Thomas Walsh. Boston: Arthur P. Schmidt Publications, 1912.

Were I a Bird on Wing. German folk poem. Translated by Frederick W. Bancroft. Boston: Arthur P. Schmidt Publications, 1912.

The Red Man's Requiem. Text by Emilie Francis Bauer. Boston: Arthur P. Schmidt Publications, 1912.

Send Me a Dream. Text by Emilie Francis Bauer. Boston: Arthur P. Schmidt Publications, 1912.

Over the Hills. Text by Paul Lawrence Dunbar. Boston: Arthur P. Schmidt Publications, 1912.

The Mill-Wheel. German folk poem. Translated by Frederick W. Bancroft. Boston: Arthur P. Schmidt, 1912.

Das Erdenlied (1912–1916). Text by Sebastian Frank Wendland. Unpublished. LC.

Nocturne. Text by Emilie Francis Bauer. New York: G. Schirmer, 1912.

The Last Word. Text by S. William Brady. New York: G. Schirmer, 1912.

A Little Lane. Text by Ellen Glasgow. Boston: Arthur P. Schmidt Publications, 1914.

Melancolie (incomplete) (ca. 1914). Text by Camille Mauclair. Unpublished. LC.

Only of Thee and Me. Text by Louis Untermeyer. Boston: Arthur P. Schmidt Publications, 1914.

Phyllis. Text by Charles Riviere Defresny. Boston: Arthur P. Schmidt Publications, 1914.

Youth Comes Dancing. Text by Emilie Francis Bauer. Boston: Arthur P. Schmidt Publications, 1914.

The Linnet is Tuning his Flute. Text by Louis Untermeyer. Boston: Arthur P. Schmidt Publications, 1915.

Weavers, Weaving at Break of Day (ca. 1915?). Author unknown. Unpublished. LC.

By the Indus. Text by Cale Young Rice. Boston: Arthur P. Schmidt Publications, 1917.

The Minstrel of Romance. Text by John S. Reed. Boston: Arthur P. Schmidt Publications, 1917.

From Hills of Dreams. Text by Joyce Kilmer. Boston: Arthur P. Schmidt Publications, 1918.

With Liberty and Justice for All (ca. 1918?). Text by Marion Bauer. Unpublished. LC.

My Faun (1919). Text by Oscar Wilde. Unpublished. LC.

The Driftwood Fire. Text by Katherine Adams. Boston: Arthur P. Schmidt Publications, 1921.

Epitaph of a Butterfly. Text by Thomas Walsh. Philadelphia: Oliver Ditson, 1921.

Gold of the Day and Night. Text by Katherine Adams. Boston: Arthur P. Schmidt Publications, 1921.

Night in the Woods. Text by Edward Rowland Sill. New York: G. Schirmer, 1921.

Roses Breathe in the Night. Text by Margaret Widdemer. New York: G. Schirmer, 1921.

Thoughts. Text by Katherine Adams. Boston: Arthur P. Schmidt Publications, 1921.

A Parable. Text by Stephen Crane. New York: G. Schirmer, 1922.

Four Poems, op. 16. Texts by John Gould Fletcher. New York: G. Schirmer, 1924.
1. *Through the Upland Meadows*
2. *I Love the Night*
3. *Midsummer Dreams*
4. *In the Bosom of the Desert*

Songs from Alice in Wonderland and Through the Looking Glass (ca. 1928?). Text by Lewis Carroll. Unpublished. LC.
1. *Pig and Pepper*
2. *How Doth the Little Crocodile*
3. *You Are Old, Father William*
4. *The Lobster Quadrille*
5. *Jabberwocky*

Dusk (ca. 1930?). Text by Eunice Tietjens. Unpublished. LC.

When the Shy Star Goes Forth (1931). Text by James Joyce. Unpublished. LC.

To Losers (1932). Text by Frances Frost. Unpublished. LC.

Four Songs with String Quartet, op. 28 (1935). Text by Louis Untermeyer. Unpublished. LC.
1. *The Crocus — When Trees Have Lost Remembrance*
2. *Ragpicker Love*
3. *There's Something Silent Here*
4. *Credo — I Sing the Will to Love*

Songs in the Night. Text by Minny M. H. Ayers. New York: G. Schirmer, 1943.

The Harp. Text by Edna Castleman Bailey. New York: Broadcast Music, 1947.

Night Etchings (duet for soprano and tenor) (1947). Text by Edna Castleman Bailey. Unpublished. LC.

The Swan. Text by Edna Castleman Bailey. New York: Broadcast Music, 1947.

A Foreigner Comes to Earth on Boston Commons (cantata for mixed chorus, tenor, and soprano solos). New York: Composer's Facsimile Editions, 1953.

The Malay to his Master. Text by Cale Young Rice. New York: Composer's Facsimile Editions, 1959.

A Letter. Text by Chang Chi. Adapted by Marion Bauer. Fulton, Maryland: HERS Publishing, 1988.

Unpublished and Undated Works

Benediction (May the Lord Bless You and Keep You). Text-traditional. PHC.

Black-eyed Susan, Blue-eyed Grass. Duet. Text by Mabel Livingstone. PHC.

Here Alone Unknown. Text by Conrad Aiken.

If. Duet. Text by Mabel Livingstone. PHC.

Lad and Lass. Text by Cale Young Rice.

A Laugh is Just Like Sunshine. Trio. Text by Ripley D. Saunders. PHC.

Little Sleeper. Text by Richard Le Gallieuse. MHC.

The Moonlight is a Silver Sea (two versions). Text by Charles Buxton Young. MHC.

The Night Will Never Stay. Duet. Text by Eleanor Farjson. PHC.

The Shadows. Text by Charlotte Becker. MHC.

Untitled. Text by Margaret Widdemer. MHC.

Wood Song of Triboulet. Text by William Rose Benet. LC.

Bibliography

Ammer, Christine. *Unsung: A History of Women in American Music.* Westport, Conn.: Greenwood Press, 1980.

Bazelon, Irwin A. "Woman with a Symphony." *The Baton of Phi Beta Fraternity* 30:3 (1951): 4-7.

Bauer, Marion. "Charles T. Griffes: Griffes as I Remember Him." *Musical Quarterly* 28 (1942): 139-59.

____. "Impressionism in America." *Modern Music* 4 (1927): 15-20.

____. "Natural Law: Its Influence on Modern Music." *Musical Quarterly* 6 (1920): 469-77.

____. *Twentieth-Century Music: How it Developed, How to Listen to It.* New York: G. P. Putnam's Sons, 1933.

Bauer, Marion, and Ethel Peyser. *How Music Grew.* New York: G. P. Putnam's Sons, 1925.

____. *How Opera Grew.* New York: G. P. Putnam's Sons, 1955.

____. *Music Through the Ages.* New York: G. P. Putnam's Sons, 1932.

Block, Adrienne Fried, and Carol Neuls-Bates, eds. *Women in American Music: A Bibliography of Music and Literature.* Westport, Conn.: Greenwood Press, 1979.

Bowers, Jane, and Judith Tick, eds. *Women Making Music: The Western Art Tradition, 1150–1950.* Urbana, Ill.: University of Illinois Press, 1986.

Cohen, Aaron I. *International Encyclopedia of Women Composers.* New York: R. R. Bowker Company, 1981.

Downes, Olin. "Miss Bauer's Work Makes Up Concert." *The New York Times* 9 May 1951, L:41.

"Emilie Frances Bauer dies in New York." *Musical Digest* IX:22 (1926): 1.

Ewen, David. *American Composers Today.* New York: H. W. Wilson, 1949.

Goss, Madeleine. *Modern Music Makers; Contemporary American Composers.* New York: E. P. Dutton & Co., 1952.

Hinely, Mary Brown. "The Uphill Climb of Women in American Music: Conductors and Composers." *Music Educators Journal* (May 1984): 42-45.

Holloway, Peggy. "The solo vocal repertoire of Marion Bauer with selected stylistic analyses." D.M.A. diss., University of Nebraska-Lincoln, 1994.

Howes, Durward, ed. *American Women: The Standard Biographical Dictionary of Notable Women.* Los Angeles: American Publishers, Inc, 1939.

Hughes, Alan. "Marion Bauer Concert." *Musical America* 71 (1951): 18.

Laufer, Beatrice. "Marion Bauer: The musical life of an American Woman Composer." Unpublished manuscript. New York: American Music Center, Marion Bauer file.

Lieberson, Goddard. "More One-Man Shows." *Modern Music* 14 (1937): 9.

Lebrecht, Norman. "Marion Bauer." In *Companion to Twentieth-Century Music.* New York: Simon & Schuster, 1992.

Maisel, Edward. *Charles T. Griffes: The Life of an American Composer.* New York: Alfred A. Knopf, 1984.

"Marion Bauer." *Musical America* 71 (1951):18.

"Marion Bauer." *Panpipes* 44 (1952): 25.

"Marion E. Bauer, Composer, is Dead." *The New York Times* (11 August 1955): 21.

"Music Has Lost a Great Protagonist." *Musical Courier* 152 (1955): 33.

Pendle, Karin. *Women in Music.* Bloomington, Ind.: Indiana University Press, 1991.

Peyser, Ethel R. "In memory: Marion Bauer." *Baton of the Phi Beta Fraternity* 35 (1955): 5, 8.

____. "Marion Bauer." *The Marion Bauer Memorial Concert.* Program notes (May 11, 1956).

Pickett, Susan. "Why can't we listen to Marion Bauer's music?" *Providence Journal Bulletin* (August 23, 1994).

Reis, Claire. *Composers in America: Biographical Sketches of Living Composers with a Record of Their Works, 1912–1937.* First edition and revised edition. New York: Macmillan, 1938, 1947.

Renton, Barbara H. "Bauer, Marion (Eugenie)." In *The New Grove Dictionary of American Music*, ed. H. Wiley Hitchcock and Stanley Sadie. New York: Macmillan Press, Ltd., 1986.

Saleski, Gdal. *Musicians of Jewish Origin.* New York: Bloch Publishing Co., 1949.

Schonberg, Harold. "Champion of American Composer." *The New York Times* (14 August 1955): X7.

Stewart, Nancy Louise. *The Solo Piano Music of Marion Bauer.* Ph.D. Dissertation, University of Cincinnati, 1990.

"Two Individualists." *Musical America* 75 (1955): 4.

Upton, William Treat. *Art-Song in America.* Boston: Oliver Ditson Company, 1930.

____. "Aspects of the Modern Art-Song." *Musical Quarterly* 24 (1938): 11-30.

Villamel, Victoria Ethier. *A Singer's Guide to the American Art Song 1870–1980.* Metuchen, N. J.: Scarecrow Press, 1993.

Wells, L. Jeannette. *A History of the Music Festival at Chatauqua Institution from 1874 to 1957.* Washington, D. C.: The Catholic University of America Press, 1958.

"Worthwhile American Composers: Marion Bauer." *The Musician* (August 1929).

Discography

Women's Voices-Five Centuries of Song. Neva Pilgrim, soprano. Steven Heyman, piano. Leonarda 338 (1999). *I Love the Night,* op. 16, no. 2.

Lad and Lass

Cale Young Rice

Marion Bauer
Peggy Holloway, editor

13
3
flut - ter - ing crowd. The car - di-nal preached it
16
high and proud, Spring!
f
19
rit.
a tempo
And
p
marc.
pp
22
thro the warm earth their song went trill - ing, trill - ing,

25
mf
"Wake! a - rise!"
28
The king - cups quick - ly as -
p
pp
marc.
31
sem - bled, strong. The blu - ets stept from the moss in throng.
34
Like fai - ries too
L.H.
p
pp

*rhythm originally notated in eighth notes here.

50
[a tempo]
53
p
Your
56
eyes were kin - dled, your lips were warm, wild beau-ties broke from your
59
3
face and form. And all my

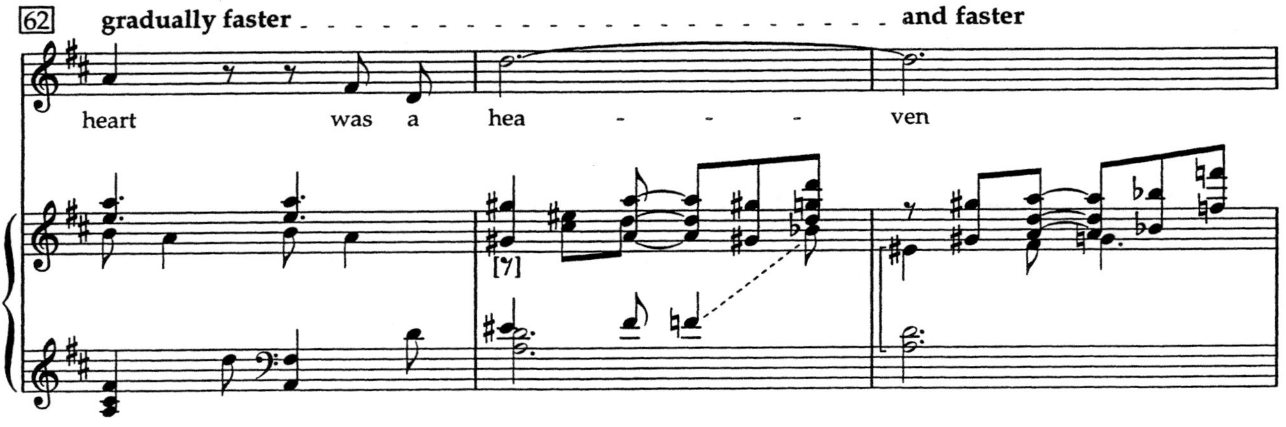
62
gradually faster
and faster
heart was a hea - - - ven

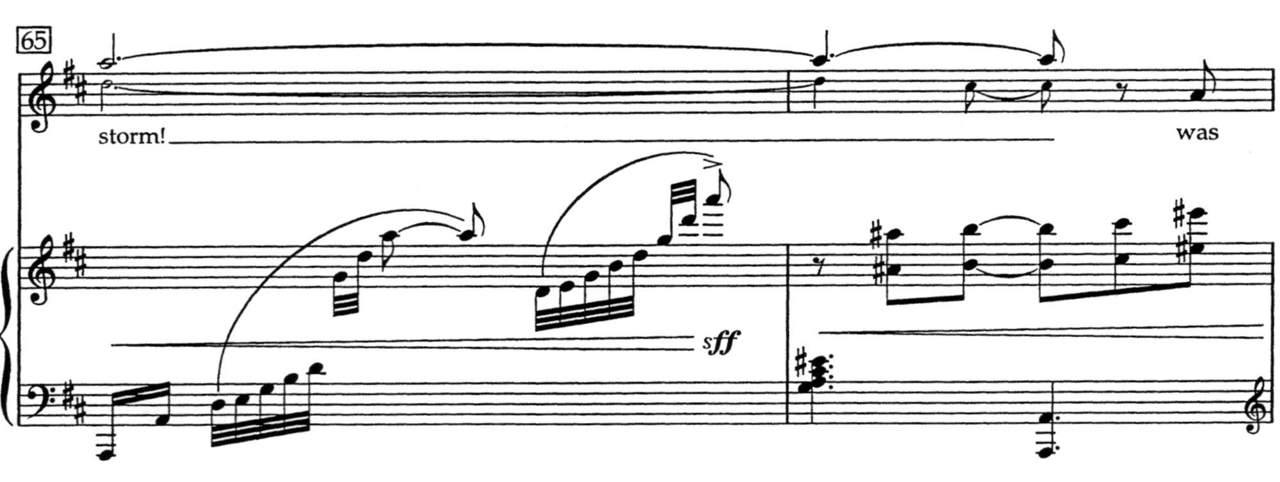
65
storm!
was
sff

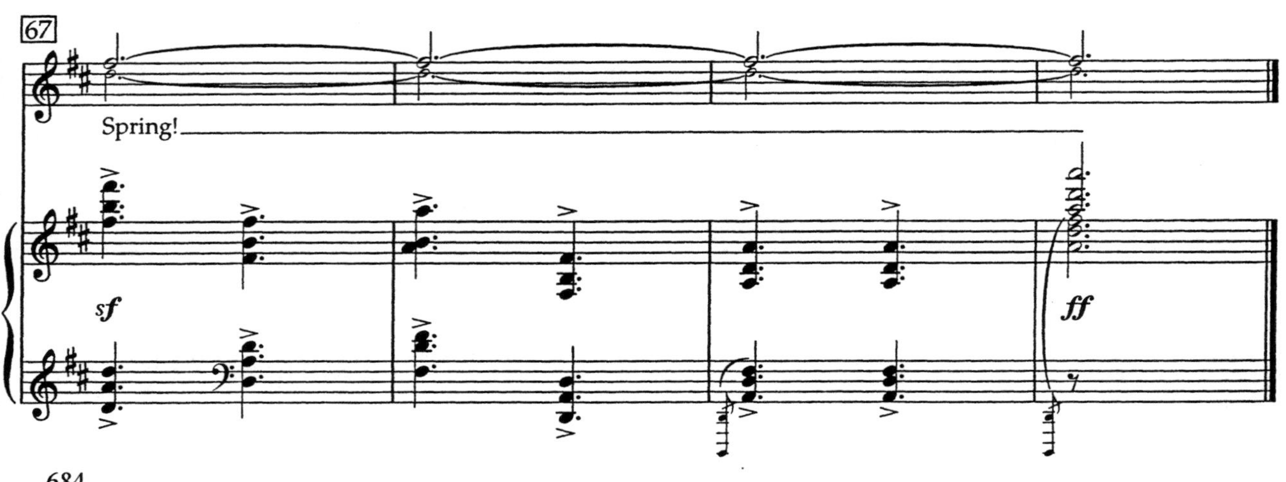
67
Spring!
sf
ff

My Faun

Oscar Wilde

Marion Bauer
Peggy Holloway, editor

13
f
accel.
Flash - es my Faun!
sf
ff
16
Moderately
He skips through the cop-ses
L.H.
pp sub.
p
19
sing - ing,
And his shad - ow danc-es a -
22
long,
f
And I know not which I should
f

25
accel.
Fol - - low, shad - ow or song!
p
28
lightly
pp
31
O
pp
34
poco a poco agitato
Hunt - er, snare me his shad - ow! O night - in-gale, catch me his

37
strain
Else
pp
pp
without Ped.
40
molto cresc.
moon - struck with mu - sic and mad - -
ff
molto cresc.
ff
43
pp
ness I track him in vain.
silence
46

When the Shy Star Goes Forth

James Joyce

Marion Bauer

Peggy Holloway, editor

p

When the shy star goes forth in heaven All

pp

pp

poco a poco cresc.

4

mf

maid-en-ly, dis-con-so-late, Hear you a-mid the drow-sy ev-en One who is

mf p

7

p

sing-ing by your gate. His song is soft-er

p

11

than the dew And he is come to vis-it you.

14
17
p
O bend no more in
pp
20
rev - er - y When He at ev - en - tide is call - ing.
f
23
p
Nor muse; Who may this strang - er be whose
mf
p
f
p

*rhythm in manuscript originally

To Losers

Frances Frost

Marion Bauer
Peggy Holloway, editor

15
hol - low Un-com-fort - ed by fern for the hours that are to
p
18
fol - low
mf
3
molto cresc.
21
[𝄐]
f
Ac - cuse the heart for what you lose The
ff
6
4
24
f
mf
heart- that wild dark bird of haste think-ing it heard What was not spok-en,
p

27
espressivo
Leav-ing the climb-ing emp-ti-ness of air And fall-ing to the
p
mp
p
30
voice that was not call - ing To the
33
breast that was not there.
3
36
ppp

How Doth the Little Crocodile

Lewis Carroll

Marion Bauer
Peggy Holloway, editor

mf

4

How doth the lit - tle croc - o - dile Im -

p

7

prove his shin - ing Tail, And pour the wa - ters

p

10

of the Nile On ev' - ry gold - en scale!

6

13
How cheer - ful - ly he seems to grin, How
fp
16
neat - ly spreads his claws
3
19
And wel - comes lit - tle fish - es in with
22
gent - ly smil - ing jaws!
f p f

Here Alone Unknown

Conrad Aiken

Marion Bauer
Peggy Holloway, editor

20
spot - light, as, you rise and fall on the wave of the mu -
24
sic. Nar - row-ing eyes at the light that daz - zles
28
Lan - guid-ly smil - ing.
32
3
Beau - ti - ful now are your cold white
4

36
shoulders... If I were Death my
40
hands might touch them If I were
44
Death, my mouth might kiss you,
48
3
Pas-sion-ate danc-er.

Rebecca Clarke

(1886–1979)

LIANE CURTIS

Rebecca Clarke was born in Harrow (near London) on August 27, 1886, to an American father and a German mother. Her father, Joseph Thacher Clarke, was an archeologist and inventor who worked for George Eastman; her mother, Agnes Helferich Clarke, was from a prominent Munich family and the grandniece of Leopold von Ranke. The oldest of four siblings, Rebecca was given violin lessons as a child, as her father wanted to have "chamber music on tap."

In 1903 Clarke enrolled as a violin student at the Royal Academy of Music in London. Her father withdrew her abruptly in 1905 when her harmony teacher, Percy Miles, proposed marriage. Evidently enamored with her the rest of his life, Miles' will left her his Stradivarius violin in 1921. After leaving the Academy, the following two years included travels with her father to Germany and France, and a trip alone to visit her father's friends and relatives in Boston, where she stayed with philosopher William James and his family. Clarke reported that it was during this trip she began composing; some early songs date from this time.

In 1907, Clarke enrolled at the Royal College of Music (London), where she was accepted as Charles Stanford's first female student of composition. Two violin sonatas and some songs remain from these years. Stanford also encouraged her to switch from violin to the viola, which soon became her main instrument. Clarke was unable to finish her course of study when her father suddenly banished her from the family home. Joseph Clarke's cruelty figures prominently in Rebecca's memoir about her late-Victorian childhood. As she wrote, "in hardly more than twenty-four hours, I had reached a watershed and the whole course of my life had begun to run in a different direction. I was living in London, a professional musician, preparing to earn my own living."[1]

Clarke embarked on a performing career as a violist. She was one of the first women to play professionally in an orchestra when Henry Wood admitted "six lady string players" to the Queen's Hall Orchestra in 1912.[2] In 1916 she took her first professional trip to the United States, touring and concertizing extensively with the cellist May Mukle, a lifelong close friend. Clarke also visited her brothers, both of whom had settled in the United States, one in Rochester and the other in Detroit. In 1918 and for several periods thereafter, she taught viola, violin and harmony privately, as documented in her diary and the advertisement she placed in the *Musical Courier*: "Rebecca Clarke, Viola Soloist. Lessons in Viola, Harmony and Ensemble."[3] She coached and played chamber music with amateurs, and performed as a professional soloist and ensemble player. More exotic travels included a stay in Hawaii in late 1918 and early 1919, and a trip around the world with Mukle in 1923 (concertizing in the British colonies, and ending with another Hawaiian sojourn).[4]

In 1918, Clarke attended the first Berkshire Festival of Chamber Music (held in western Massachusetts). Elizabeth Sprague Coolidge, who organized and sponsored the festival, encouraged her to enter the composition competition for the following year, which would feature a work for the viola. Seventy-two works were entered (anonymously) to be evaluated by a panel of six distinguished judges. Clarke's *Viola Sonata* tied for first place with Ernest Bloch's (1880–1959) *Suite for Viola*. Coolidge herself broke the tie and awarded the prize to Bloch. Clarke's involvement with the festival brought her a great deal of fame. She was again runner-up in the 1921 competition (for her *Piano Trio*); in 1923 Coolidge commissioned her to write a work, the *Rhapsody* for cello and piano. Coolidge is well known for her support of composers and performers, but this was her only instance of supporting a woman composer, and it was Clarke's only commission.[5]

Clarke's father died in 1920, which may have prompted her decision to return to London in 1924, where she and her sister assisted in caring for their mother. Neither sister married until after the mother's death in 1935. Clarke maintained a busy performing schedule, including string quartets with the D'Aranyi sisters (violinists Adila Fachiri and Jelly D'Aranyi, grandnieces of Joseph Joachim) and cellists May Mukle and Guilhemina Suggia (a protegé of Pablo Casals). Ensembles included the Euterpe Orchestra, the Aeolian Ensemble, and from 1927 the English Ensemble, a piano quartet consisting of Marjorie Hayward (violin), Kathleen Long (piano), and Mukle (cello). While later in life she maintained that she had been primarily an ensemble performer, in actuality she performed extensively as a soloist, including many BBC broadcasts, as on December 12, 1926, when she performed the Mozart *Symphonia Concertante* with violinist Antonio Brosa. She also performed in a number of recordings.

Clarke's own modesty, culturally encouraged as an acceptable feminine pose, contributed to her present obscurity; she talked little about her composing in her later years. Her diaries reveal a different perspective, however, emphasizing the importance of composing to her personal identity. By her own later admission, Clarke's illicit affair with baritone John Goss (Goss was married) contributed to the decreasing quantity of her output in the late 1920s and 1930s, but it also might be argued that the discouragement she faced as a composer (typified by her difficulties in finding a publisher for her *Piano Trio* and her song *Tiger, Tiger*) led to the diversion of her energies into romance.

The London period ended with the onset of World War II. Whether by accident or design (family members explain it in various ways) Clarke found herself in the United States living alternately with her two brothers and their families.[6] An awkward and uncomfortable period, it prompted her to return to composing; nine works survive from approximately two years. This productivity ended, not with her marriage, as has been reported,[7] but rather with her taking a live-in position as a nanny/mother's helper in 1942. A striking document of these years is her letter preserved in the scrapbook for the ISCM (International Society for Contemporary Music) Conference of 1942 (UC Berkeley). Clarke's modest, warm and charming note describes with embarrassment her current circumstance; its tone contrasts with letters from other composers in the scrapbook including Schoenberg and Bartók.

In 1944 Clarke became reacquainted with James Friskin, a piano faculty member at The Juilliard School (of Music), whom Clarke had first known when they were students together at the Royal College of Music, London. A touching series of letters survives from 1944 (leading up to their wedding on September 23, 1944). Clarke also wrote her next-to-last piece for him to honor his Scottish heritage, *I'll Bid My Heart Be Still*, an "arrangement of an old Scottish border melody" for viola and piano. While Friskin encouraged her to compose, she only completed two more pieces after her marriage, the songs *God Made a Tree* (1954) and *Binnorie: A Ballad* (late 1940s). She did, however, arrange her setting of *Down by the Salley Gardens* for violin and voice in the 1950s. Around the time of her ninetieth birthday, inspired by the renewal of interest in her music, she returned to revising some earlier scores, including that of *Cortège* (solo piano) and the song *Tiger, Tiger*. After her marriage Clarke lived in New York City until her death at age 93 on October 13, 1979.

The notion of separate spheres for women's activity in the nineteenth century offered a safe, approved space for creativity; the positive aspects of this social belief are worth considering. For some women composers, however, these cultural norms proved confining; discouraged from writing in large instrumental forms, they instead directed their attention to smaller genres, including songs, particularly light and accessible ones. Around the turn of the twentieth century, British publishers often played a role in perpetuating the ideology of the separate spheres.[8] Clarke's productivity in writing songs must be considered within this context. Although a violist by profession, and with no formal training in voice, she wrote more songs (a total of fifty-three) than works in other genres. While she was completely successful in her songs, one may speculate that she turned to the genre because it was deemed culturally appropriate for women. Writing songs allowed women to work in a well-established tradition even if the merit of their creations was often dismissed by the musical establishment.[9]

Clarke's songs are mostly for solo voice and piano, but there are several other combinations including vocal duets with piano, folk songs arranged for voice and violin, and one short work for string quartet and voice. Clarke's artistic vocabulary, as expressed in her songs, is one of power and sureness: each work is a distinct and self-sufficient statement. Her lifelong love of reading, literature, and theater is apparent in these compositions, as she chose her texts with great care. The settings convey her compelling understanding of them.

Fourteen songs were published in her lifetime. The rest remain unpublished. Some early works predate her formal study of composition. Several of these youthful songs represent treacly tunes of the parlor variety (that Clarke would so brilliantly parody in her 1929 song, *The Aspidistra*). *Shiv and the Grasshopper* and *Nach Einem Regen* stand apart as perfectly sculpted miniatures. *Du* and *Wandrers Nachtlied* are notable for their Brahmsian, thick, lush harmonies, *Das Ideal* for its dark chromaticism and dramatic effect.

Two early songs, *Shy One* and *The Cloths of Heaven*, were championed by the famous English tenor Gervase Elwes, which prompted Clarke to make them her first publications. The Danish soprano Povla Frijsh, who cited Clarke as an important American composer of song, recorded *Shy One* (ca. 1941). *Shy One* is a particularly charming, accessible song, but despite the lilting quality of its $\frac{5}{4}$ melody, a review in *The Musical Times* attacked its use of dissonance.

By far Clarke's longest song (at over 200 measures) is her setting of the traditional ballad *Binnorie*, which survives unpublished in two working copies. Along with *The Seal Man*, which sets John Masefield's prose, this song demonstrates her interest in Celtic myth, her skill at creating atmospheric effects in a large-scale structure, and her dramatic use of declamatory vocal writing. In later interviews she described *The Seal Man* as one of her favorite compositions.

Some of Clarke's most important works still remain unpublished. These include *Tiger, Tiger*; *Lethe*; and *The Donkey*. *Tiger, Tiger* is atonal in its foreboding, chromatic expressionism. Its rejection by publishers may have been a factor in slowing Clarke's output—after writing and publishing songs regularly throughout the 1920s she would apparently start no new ones in the entire decade of the 1930s. *Tiger, Tiger* was probably written with Goss in mind, as she relentlessly revised it during her romantic entanglement with him (ca. 1929–1933).

Clarke had extensive choral experience. She persuaded Ralph Vaughan Williams to lead students at the Royal College in singing music by Palestrina.[10] Her setting of Shelley's *Chorus from*

"Hellas" (SSSAA) is lushly and intensely chromatic, with long-spanned phrases of building intensity. Her setting of *Psalm 91* (SATB, with SATB soloists) is the weightiest of her choral works; with features such as melodic emphases of augmented seconds and choral unisons, it demonstrates both her admiration for Bloch and her exposure to Hebrew chanting through her contact with London's Jewish community.

Clarke's shorter instrumental pieces can be placed next to similar works by her British contemporaries. *Morpheus* (1917, for viola and piano), written under the pseudonym "Anthony Trent," for instance, develops a single melody with contemporary color devices such as pentatonic *glissades* on the piano and artificial harmonics on the viola. She wrote this and *Epilogue* (1921, cello and piano) for herself or for her friends (also professional musicians) to play. Much of Clarke's music was never published and is held by her estate today.

The *Viola Sonata* (1919) and *Piano Trio* (1921) are by far her best known works, as reprintings have made them the most accessible. They are powerful and expansive examples of post-romantic sonata form. Her use of cyclic structure refers to the Germanic tradition; her textures and impressionist vocabulary evoke comparisons with Franck, Debussy, and Ravel. One contemporary report hints that during the anonymous competition, some judges guessed Ravel as the author of Clarke's viola sonata, while *The Daily Telegraph* suggested the name "Rebecca Clarke" was a pseudonym. Dimensions of her musical personality not seen elsewhere are found in *Poem* (1926) and *Comodo e amabile* (1924), for string quartet. The intense *Poem* merges a single pervasive questioning motive with the harmony and texture of Debussy, again fusing French color with German depth in this profound and passionate work. *Comodo e amabile* contrasts completely with the *Poem*: sections with a buoyant lilting melody surround an interior that explores combinations of short motives, polymeter and polytonality, and the use of taut contrapuntal writing. It seems likely, however, that the two movements were conceived as part of a single work, since the parts to *Poem* are labeled "4th movement" and the score to *Comodo e amabile* is marked "1st movement." The neoclassical idiom of *Comodo e amabile* is further explored in her late work *Prelude, Allegro, and Pastorale* for clarinet and viola (1941), a work that Clarke valued highly, as she mentioned in a 1978 interview.[11] The only late work for which Clarke pursued publication was the *Passacaglia on an Old English Tune attributed to Tallis* (1940–1941) for viola and piano; she premiered this work herself in New York City and may have received direct encouragement that was lacking in the case of the *Prelude, Allegro, and Pastorale* whose premiere at 1942 Festival of the ISCM (Berkeley, Calif.) she was unable to attend.

The *Dumka*, scored for violin, viola, and piano, was probably written for Clarke and family members to play (as was the work for viola and clarinet). It employs not only the 3 + 3 + 2 rhythm employed by Dvőrák in his *Dumky Trio*, but also cross relations and other gestures that demonstrate a familiarity with eastern European folk influences in a work that is lively and modern.

While recent appraisals of Clarke have placed her among the most important of British composers of the interwar years,[12] a true understanding of her significance will only be reached when more of her music becomes accessible as part of the performing repertory.

The Cherry-Blossom Wand and *Cradle Song* have been selected for inclusion in this volume. Anna Wickham's poem *The Cherry-Blossom Wand* was widely read when it was first published in 1915. Although the poem is labeled "To be set to music" (Wickham herself trained as a singer), Clarke's is apparently its only setting (composed in 1927 and published in 1929). Clarke knew the poet through their mutual friend, cellist May Mukle. Mukle and Wickham had met in Wickham's native Australia, when Mukle was on one of her many concert tours. Wickham (like Mukle) was an acknowledged feminist; her husband's determination that she not publish her poetry became a central motivation for her in articulating her desire for freedom of expression. Clarke would go on to set three more works by women poets, the resulting songs a small but significant part of her output.[13] Clarke dedicated *The Cherry-Blossom Wand* to Anne Thursfield, a singer with whom she often worked.

With its imagery of flowers and romance, *The Cherry-Blossom Wand* might at first glance seem to be cheerful, but closer reading reveals a dark cynicism. Since the blossom-laden branch is being used to drive away the beloved, the poem provides a dark and fatalistic view of the fleetingness of all things of beauty; a relationship is ended in order that its participants will never grow disillusioned. Wickham's friend and editor, R. D. Smith, notes Wickham's "masochistic streak" and finds an "odd ambiguity" in *The Cherry-Blossom Wand.*[14]

Clarke approaches this text with sweeping melodic phrases and colorful bright accompaniment. She also captures the poem's enigmatic quality with asymmetrical and shifting phrases; Clarke treats meter pliably, and the harmonies resonate with expansive major seventh and ninth chords. She restates her striking melody, in varied treatments, in each of the four stanzas.

Clarke wrote several lullabies, including some instrumental works as well as this gentle and lilting *Cradle Song* (poetry by William Blake). This evocation of a traditional maternal posture can be interpreted as an attempt to create an identity as a composer that would be compatible with her perceived feminine role.[15] In this case she employs both a genre and a subject that are socially understood as feminine (another Blake setting, *Infant Joy*, also fits into this maternal category).

Cradle Song is formally conventional, with the four stanzas of the poem set to an A A^1B A^2 structure. Clarity of outline, the simplicity of the soothing rhythmic patterns of the accompaniment, and accessible poetic scansion are enriched by the chromatic direction of the melody. Employing the impressionist vocabulary of chordal parallelism, the accompaniment moves in descending gestures of first inversion triads, in the rocking rhythm of a *sicilienne*. The accompaniment is lush in its chromatic harmony, although each section ends with a recognizable cadence. The grace-note arpeggios that end section B and the final A^2 richly inflect the tonic G, both with the split third invoking major and minor (A-sharp [B-flat] and B-natural), and the diminished plus perfect fifth. The accompaniment is further nuanced by the tension of unresolved dominant sevenths and the instability of second inversion chords over a pedal note.

Cradle Song is an accessible and directly appealing work, yet crafted so skillfully that it bears repeated hearings; it has the potential to become popular with singers of all levels.

Acknowledgments

I would like to thank Mr. Christopher Johnson (of Brooklyn, New York), Clarke's musical and literary executor, for graciously allowing me to examine and quote from the materials of her estate.

Notes

1. "I had a Father Too (Or the Mustard Spoon)." Memoir primarily concerning Clarke's youth up to 1910. Clarke Estate, unpublished, 1969–1973.

2. Caption of photo from an unidentified British newspaper clipping. Clarke Estate.

3. *Musical Courier* 76, no. 6 (1918): 4.

4. This information is based in part on Clarke's extant diaries from 1919–1933.

5. Clarke's participation in the Coolidge festivals has been a focal point of interest. See, for instance, Cyrilla Barr's *Elizabeth Sprague Coolidge: American Patron of Music* (New York: Schirmer, 1998) and Ann Woodward, "Introduction", *Rebecca Clarke: Sonata for viola (or cello) and piano* (New York: Da Capo Press, 1986): v-vi.

6. In 1994 I interviewed Clarke's six nieces, her closest surviving relatives: Mrs. Ann Thacher Anderson, Mrs. Josephine Braden (who has since passed away), Mrs. Rebecca Clarke Evans, Mrs. Magdalen Madden, Mrs. Heidi Schultz, and Mrs. Mary Gray White. I am very grateful to them for their extensive and generous help.

7. Diane Peacock Jezic, *Women Composers* (New York: The Feminist Press, 1988), 159. Marcia Citron, presumably drawing on Jezic, makes the same statement, *Gender and the Musical Canon* (Cambridge: Cambridge University Press, 1993), 92. The reality is more complex, as Clarke herself pointed out in an interview with Ellen Lerner on September 14, 1978: "I didn't do any composing at all after I got married — I'm sure that's a shock to you. It wasn't because I got married that I didn't; I had been writing much less in the years before I got married."

8. Nancy B. Reich discusses the importance of the song genre to women in "European Composers and Musicians, circa 1800–1890," in *Women and Music: A History,* ed. Karen Pendle (Bloomington and Indianapolis: Indiana University Press, 1991), 102. Sophie Fuller documents the case of William Boosey (who worked first in the publishing company that bore his name, but from 1894 worked for Chappell), who encouraged women composers in the song genre only. "Women Composers during the British Musical Renaissance, 1880–1918" (Ph.D., Kings College, University of London, 1998), 91.

9. Fuller, "Women Composers," 106.

10. Letter from Vaughan Williams postmarked May 12, 1910, in Clarke Estate. I thank Mr. Daniel Braden, Clarke's grandnephew, for allowing me to examine this letter.

11. Interview with Ellen Lerner, 1978.

12. Malcom MacDonald, Review of *Rebecca Clarke: Music for Viola* (Patricia McCarty, et al.) *Gramophone* (February 1987): 1144, 1149; Richard Buell, concert review "Rediscovering Composer Rebecca Clarke," *Boston Globe,* September 28, 1999, B6.

13. *Greeting*, text by Ella Young; *Lethe*, text by Edna St. Vincent Millay; *God Made a Tree*, text by Katherine Kendall.

14. *The Writings of Anna Wickham, Free Woman and Poet* (London: Virago, 1984), 43-44.

15. I explore Clarke's feminine positioning further in my article "Rebecca Clarke: A Case of Identity," *The Musical Times* 137 (May 1996): 17.

List of Works

Based on the catalogue compiled in 1977 by Christopher Johnson in conjunction with the composer, with additions and corrections by Liane Curtis. Scores of the unpublished works are found in the Clarke estate, except where indicated.

Vocal

(solo voice and piano except where indicated)

Wandrers Nachtlied (1903?). Text by Goethe. Unpublished.

Chanson (1904?). Text by Mäterlinck. Unpublished.

Ah, for the Red Spring Rose (1904). Text author unknown. Unpublished.

Shiv and the Grasshopper (1904). Text by Kipling. Unpublished.

Aufblick (1904). Text by Richard Dehmel. Unpublished.

Klage (1904?). Text by Dehmel. Unpublished.

Stimme im Dunkeln (1904?). Text by Dehmel. Unpublished.

O Welt (1904?). Text author unknown. Unpublished.

Oh, Dreaming World (1905). Text author unknown. Unpublished.

Du (1905). Text by Richard Schaukal. Unpublished.

The Moving Finger Writes (1905?). Text by Khayyám, translated by Fitzgerald. Unpublished.

Wiegenlied, for voice, violin and piano (1905?). Text by Detlev von Liliencron. Unpublished.

Nach einem Regen (1906?). Text by Dehmel. Unpublished.

Durch die Nacht (1906). Text by Dehmel. Unpublished.

Vergissmeinnicht (1907). Text by Dehmel. Unpublished.

Manche Nacht (1907). Text by Dehmel. Unpublished.

Nacht für nacht, for soprano, contralto, and piano (1907). Text by Dehmel. Unpublished.

Magna est veritas (1907). Text by Coventry Patmore. Unpublished.

Das Ideal (1907?). Text by Dehmel. Unpublished.

Spirits, two voices and piano (1909?). Text by Robert Bridges. Unpublished.

The Color of Life (1910?). Text: "Old Chinese Words." Unpublished.

Return of Spring (1910?). Text: "Old Chinese Words." Unpublished.

Tears (1910). Text: "Chinese words." Unpublished. Clarke Estate and Sibley Music Library, Eastman School of Music, Rochester, New York.

The Folly of Being Comforted (1911?). Text by W. B. Yeats. Unpublished.

Shy One (1912?). Text by Yeats. London: Winthrop Rogers, 1920; Boosey & Hawkes, 1994.

The Cloths of Heaven (1912?). Text by Yeats. London: Winthrop Rogers, 1920; Boosey & Hawkes, 1994.

Weep You No More Sad Fountains (1912?). Text by John Dowland. Unpublished.

Away Delights, two voices and piano (1912–1913?). Text by John Fletcher. Unpublished.

Hymn to Pan, tenor, baritone, and piano (1912–1913?). Text by John Fletcher. Unpublished.

Infant Joy (1913?). Text by William Blake. London: Winthrop Rogers, 1924; Boosey & Hawkes, 1994.

Down by the Salley Gardens (1919). Text by Yeats. Winthrop Rogers, 1924; Boosey & Hawkes, 1994. Arranged for voice and violin in the 1950s, manuscript in Clarke Estate and another copy owned by Eileen Strempel.

Psalm 63, "O God, Thou art my God" (1920). Unpublished.

The Seal Man (1922). Text by John Masefield. London: Winthrop Rogers, 1926; Boosey & Hawkes, 1994.

Three Old English Songs arranged for voice and violin (1924). London: Winthrop Rogers 1925; Boosey & Hawkes 1994.
1. *It Was a Lover and His Lass*. Text by Shakespeare
2. *Phyllis on the New Mown Hay*. Traditional
3. *The Tailor and his Mouse*. Traditional

June Twilight (1925). Text by Masefield. London: Winthrop Rogers, 1926; Boosey & Hawkes, 1994.

Come, O Come, my Life's Delight (1926). Text by Thomas Campion. Based on Clarke's own earlier choral setting. Unpublished.

A Dream (1926). Text by Yeats. London: Winthrop Rogers, 1928; Boosey & Hawkes, 1994.

Sleep, tenor, baritone, and piano (1926?). Text by John Fletcher. Clarke Estate and Britten/Pears Library, Aldeburgh, Great Britain. Unpublished.

Sleep [version II] tenor, baritone, and piano (1926?). Text by John Fletcher. Britten/Pears Library, Aldeburgh. Unpublished.

Take, O Take Those Lips Away, tenor, baritone, and piano (1926?). Text by Shakespeare. Britten/Pears Library, Aldeburgh. Unpublished.

Three Irish Country Songs, arranged for voice and violin (1926). Texts: Traditional songs from an edition by Herbert Hughes. London: Oxford University Press, 1928.
1. *I Know My Love*
2. *I Know Where I'm Goin'*
3. *As I Was Goin' to Ballynure*

The Cherry-Blossom Wand (1927). Text by Anna Wickham. London: Oxford University Press, 1929.

Eight O'clock (1927). Text by A. E. Housman. London: Winthrop Rogers, 1928; Boosey & Hawkes, 1994.

Greeting (1928). Text by Ella Young. London: Winthrop Rogers, 1928; Boosey & Hawkes, 1994.

Cradle Song (1929). Text by William Blake. London: Oxford University Press, 1929.

The Aspidistra (1929). Text by Claude Flight. London: J. & W. Chester, 1930.

Tiger, Tiger (1929–1933, revised 1972). Text by William Blake. Unpublished.

Lethe (1941). Text by Edna St. Vincent Millay. Unpublished.

Daybreak, high voice and string quartet (early 1940s?). Text by John Donne. Unpublished.

The Donkey (1942). Text by G. K. Chesterton. Published in the *British Music Society Journal* vi, 1984.

Binnorie: A Ballad (1940s?). Text: traditional ballad, also known as *The Twa Sisters*, and *The Cruel Sister*. Unpublished.

Choral

Now Fie on Love, SATB (1906?). Unpublished.

Music, When Soft Voices Die, SATB (1907). Text by Percy Bysshe Shelley. Unpublished.

A Lover's Dirge, SATB (1908?). Text by Shakespeare. Unpublished.

The Owl, SATB (1909?). Text by Tennyson. Unpublished.

My Spirit Like a Charmed Bark Doth Float. SATB (1911–1912?). Text adapted from Shelley. Unpublished.

Come, Oh Come, My Life's Delight. SATB (1911–1912?) arranged for solo voice and piano in 1924. Text by Thomas Campion. Unpublished.

Philomela, SATB (1914?). Text by Sidney. Unpublished.

He That Dwelleth In The Secret Place (Psalm 91). SATB chorus plus SATB soloists (1921). Unpublished.

There Is No Rose Of Such Virtue (1928). Text and melody from anonymous English fifteenth-century carol. Solo baritone; ATBarB chorus. Unpublished.

Ave Maria. Text: traditional Christian, based on Luke 1:28 (1937?). SSA. New York: Oxford University Press, 1998.

Chorus from Shelley's "Hellas" (1943?). Text by Shelley. SSSAA. New York: Oxford University Press, 1999.

Instrumental

Sonata (single movement), violin and piano (1907–1909). Unpublished.

Sonata (three movements), violin and piano (1908–1909). Unpublished.

Lullaby, viola and piano (1909). Unpublished.

Lullaby on an Ancient Irish Tune, viola and piano (1913). Unpublished.

Lullaby, violin and piano (1918). Unpublished.

Lullaby and *Grotesque*, viola (or violin) and cello (1917?). London: Oxford University Press; 1930.

Untitled movement, viola and piano (1917–1918). Unpublished.

Morpheus, viola and piano (1917). Written under pseudonym Anthony Trent. New York: Oxford University Press, 2001.

Sonata, viola (or cello) and piano (1919). London: J. & W. Chester, 1921. Reprinted, Bryn Mawr, PA: Hildegard Publishing Company, 1999.

Chinese Puzzle, violin and piano (1921). London: Oxford University Press, 1925. Also arranged for strings and flute, unpublished.

Epilogue, cello and piano (1921?). Unpublished.

Trio for violin, violoncello, and piano (1921). London: Winthrop Rogers, 1928. Reprinted, New York: Da Capo 1981; London: Boosey and Hawkes, 1994.

Rhapsody, cello and piano (1923). Washington D. C., Library of Congress, Music Division. Unpublished.

Comodo et amabile, string quartet (1924). Unpublished.

Midsummer Moon, violin and piano (1924). London: Oxford University Press, 1926.

Poem, string quartet (1926). Unpublished, Clarke Estate (parts, and pencil draft, sketches), and University of California, Berkeley, Music Library (titled score).

Cortège, piano (1930, rev. in 1970s). Unpublished.

Untitled, two violins (1940?). Unpublished.

Dumka, violin, viola, and piano (1941?). Unpublished, Clarke Estate includes sketches, one of which is titled "Duo Concertante."

Prelude, Allegro, and Pastorale, viola and clarinet (1941). New York: Oxford University Press, 2000.

Passacaglia on an Old English Tune, attributed to Tallis, viola (or cello), and piano (1940–1941). New York: G. Schirmer; Chappell (U. K.): 1943. Draft of a violin arrangement of viola part in RC Estate. Bryn Mawr, PA: Hildegard Publishing Company, 2000.

Combined Carols, string quartet; also arranged for string orchestra (early 1940s). Clarke Estate and Rochester, New York, Eastman School of Music, Sibley Music Library.

I'll Bid My Heart Be Still (Old Scottish border melody), viola and piano (1944). Unpublished.

Bibliography

Banfield, Stephen. "Clarke [Friskin], Rebecca (Thacher)." *The New Grove Dictionary of Women Composers.* London: Macmillan, 1994; New York: Norton, 1995.

______. "'Too much of Albion'? Mrs. Coolidge and her British connections." *American Music* 4 (1986): 59-88.

Barr, Cyrilla. "A Style of Her Own: The Patronage of Elizabeth Sprague Coolidge." In *Cultivating Music in America: Women Patrons and Activists since 1860*, edited by Ralph P. Locke and Cyrilla Barr, Berkeley and Los Angeles: University of California Press, 1997.

______. *Elizabeth Sprague Coolidge: American Patron of Music.* New York: Schirmer, 1998.

Brian, Havergal. "Woman as a Composer." *Musical Opinion*, April 1936: 587-88; reprinted as "British Women Composers" in *Havergal Brian on Music*, edited by Malcom MacDonald, London: Toccata Press, 1986.

Clarke, Rebecca. Diaries, 1919–1933. Unpublished. (Held by Clarke estate.)

______. "I had a Father Too (Or the Mustard Spoon)." 1969–1973, memoir primarily concerning Clarke's youth up to 1910. Unpublished. (Held by Clarke estate.)

______. Letter to music critic Alfred Frankenstien, 1942; in scrapbook from 1942 International Society for Contemporary Music at University of California, Berkeley, Music Library. Unpublished.

______. Correspondence with Elizabeth Sprague Coolidge, 1918 though the 1950s; in The Library of Congress.

______. "Observations." Undated lists that Clarke wrote while working as a governess, 1942–ca. 1944. Unpublished. (Held by Clarke estate.)

______. Correspondence with James Friskin, 1944. Unpublished. (Held by Clarke estate.)

______. "RVW: A Remembrance." 1958, for radio broadcast. Unpublished. (Held by Clarke estate.)

______. Other miscellaneous correspondence, 1965–1979. Unpublished. (Held by Clarke estate.)

______. "Bloch, Ernest." *Cobbett's Cyclopedic Survey of Chamber Music*, I, edited by William Cobbett. London, Oxford University Press, 1929.

______. "Viola." *Cobbett's Cyclopedic Survey*, II, 536–38.

______. "The History of the Viola in Quartet Writing." *Music and Letters* 4 (1923): 6-17.

______. "The Beethoven Quartets as a Player Sees Them." *Music and Letters* 8 (1927): 178–90.

______. "La Semaine Anglaise at the Paris Colonial Exhibition." *The B.M.S. [British Music Society] Bulletin*, New Series 1 (Autumn 1931): 7-11.

Curtis, Liane. "Clarke [Friskin], Rebecca." *The New Grove Dictionary of Music and Musicians* (Revised edition, London: Macmillan, 2001).

______. "Rebecca Clarke: A Case of Identity." *The Musical Times* (London) 137 (May 1996): 15-21.

______. "Rebecca Clarke and Sonata Form: Questions of Gender and Genre." *The Musical Quarterly* 81/3 (1997): 393-428.

______. "Viola meets Clarinet: Rebecca Clarke's *Prelude, Allegro, and Pastorale* is finally Published." *The Strad* 110 (October 1999): 1078-83.

Evans, Edwin. "Clarke, Rebecca." *Cobbett's Cyclopedic Survey of Chamber Music*, I, ed. Cobbett. London: Oxford University Press, 1929.

Evans, Peter, and Stephen Banfield. *Music in Britain: The Twentieth Century,* edited by Stephen Banfield, *The Blackwell History of Music in Britain.* Vol. 6. Oxford: Blackwell, 1995.

Fuller, Sophie. *The Pandora Guide to Women Composers: Britain and the United States, 1629–Present*. London: Pandora, 1994.

Holbrooke, Joseph. "Women Composers." In *Contemporary British Composers*. London: C. Palmer, 1925.

Jacobs, Veronica. "Rebecca Clarke," *Viola Research Society Newsletter* 12 (April 1977): 4-5.

Johnson, Christopher. "Introduction." *Rebecca Clarke: Trio for Violin, Violoncello and Piano.* New York: Da Capo, 1980. [Reprint of 1928 publication of the Trio].

______. "Rebecca Clarke: A Thematic Catalogue of Her Works." 1977, Unpublished.

______. "Remembering the Glorious Rebecca Clarke," *American Women Composers News* 3 (1981): 3-6.

______. Sleeve note for recording *Rebecca Clarke: Music for Viola.* Northeastern Records, Boston, Mass.: LP 1985, CD 1989.

Kielian-Gilbert, Marianne. "On Rebecca Clarke's Sonata for Viola and Piano: Feminine Spaces and Metaphors of Reading." In *Audible Traces: Gender, Identity, and Music*, edited by Elaine Barkin and Lydia Hamessley. Zurich: Carciofoli Press, 1998.

Kohnen, Daniela. *Rebecca Clarke, Komponistin und Bratschistin* (Egelsbach: Verlag Hänsel-Hohenhausen, 1999).

Lerner, Ellen. "A Modern European Quintet c. 1900– c. 1960." Unpublished, typescript in The New York Public Library, Fine Arts Division, 1981; rev. 1985.

______. "Clarke, [Friskin], Rebecca (Thacher)." In *The New Grove Dictionary of American Music* I, ed. H. Wiley Hitchcock and Stanley Sadie. London: Macmillan Press Limited, 1986.

MacDonald, Calum. "Rebecca Clarke's Chamber Music (I)." *Tempo* 160 (1987): 15-26.

MacDonald, Malcom. Review of *Rebecca Clarke, Music for Viola (Patricia McCarty, et al.). Gramophone* (February 1987): 1144, 1149.

Ponder, Michael. "Double Talent." *The Strad* 97 (August 1987): 250-53.

______. "Rebecca Clarke," *British Music Society Journal* 5 (1983): 82-88 (includes list of works based on Johnson, 1977).

Reich, Nancy B. "Rebecca Clarke: An Uncommon Woman," *Sounds Australian: Journal of Australian Music* 40 (summer 1993–1994): 14-16.

Richards, Deborah. "'And you should have seen their faces when they saw it was by a woman': Gedanken zu Rebecca Clarkes Klaviertrio," *Neuland: Ansätze zur Musik der Gegenwart* [Cologne] 4 (1983–1984): 201-8.

Squire, W. H. "Rebecca Clarke sees Rhythm as Next Field of Development," *Christian Science Monitor* (December 12, 1922): 18.

Stanfield, M[illicent] B.: "Rebecca Clarke: violist and composer," *The Strad* 77 (1966): 297, 299.

Woodward, Ann M. "Introduction," *Rebecca Clarke: Sonata for viola (or cello) and piano.* Da Capo Press, New York, 1986. [Reprint of 1921 publication of Sonata].

Discography (Selected)

The Newstead Trio. Michael Jamanis, violin; Sara Male, cello; Xun Pan, piano. Princeton Productions 9801 P(1998). *Piano Trio* (1921).

Music by Rebecca Clarke, Jeanne Landry, Denis Gougon, Anton Rubinstein. Chantal Masson-Bourgue, viola; Mariko Sato, piano. SNE (Canada) 627 (1998). *Sonata for Viola and Piano* (1919).

The Cloths of Heaven: Songs & Music by Rebecca Clarke. Guild Music, GMCD 7208, 2000. Re-issue of 1992 CD on the Gamut label.

Sonatas '1919'-Hindemith, Clarke, Bloch. Thomas Riebl, viola; Cordella Hoefer, piano. Pan Classics 510098 (1997). *Sonata for Viola and Piano* (1919).

Music by Amy Beach and Rebecca Clarke. Members of the Endellion String Quartet with Martin Roscoe, piano. ASV, DCA 932 (1995). *Sonata for Viola and Piano* (1919), *Piano Trio* (1921).

Music by Clarke and Beach. Pamela Frame, cello; Barry Snyder, piano. Koch International Classics 3-7281-2H1 (1994). *Sonata for Viola and Piano* (1919) — cello version, *Epilogue for Cello and Piano* (1921).

In Praise of Woman: 150 Years of English Women Composers. Anthony Rolfe Johnson, tenor; Graham Johnson, piano. Hyperion CDA66709 (1994). *Shy One* (1912), *The Aspidistra* (1929).

English Music for Viola. Paul Colletti, viola; Leslie Howard, piano. Hyperion CDA 66687 (1994). *Lullaby* (1909), *Morpheus* (1917–1918), *Sonata for Viola and Piano* (1919).

Rebecca Clarke. Patricia Wright, soprano; Kathron Sturrock, piano; Jonathan Rees, violin. Gamut CD 534 (1992). *Midsummer Moon* (1924) and *Lullaby* for violin and piano; twenty-five songs, including: *Shy One* (1912), *The Seal Man* (1922), *June Twilight* (1925), *Three Old English Songs* (1924) for voice and violin, *Three Irish Country Songs* (1926) for voice and violin, *Eight O'clock* (1927), *The Cherry-Blossom Wand* (1927), *Tiger, Tiger* (1933), *Lethe* (1941), *The Donkey* (1941), *God Made a Tree* (1954).

Dreams and Fancies: Favourite Songs in English. J. Ireland, Delius, Vaughan Williams, Warlock, Howell, etc. Sarah Walker, mezzo-soprano; Roger Vignoles, piano. CRD 3473 (1992). *The Aspidistra, The Seal Man.*

British Piano Trios: Frank Bridge, Rebecca Clarke, John Ireland. The Hartley Trio. Gamut 518 (CD 1990). *Piano Trio* (1921).

Rebecca Clarke: Midsummer Moon. Rhapsody (1923) for cello and piano; *Morpheus* (1917–18) for viola and piano; *Cortege* (1930) for piano, *Lullaby* (1918) for violin and piano, and other works. Lorraine McAslan, violin; Michael Ponder, viola; Justin Pearson, cello; Ian Jones, piano. Dutton CD, 2000, CDLX 7105.

Rebecca Clarke: Music for Viola. Patricia McCarty, viola; Peter Hadcock, clarinet; Martha Babcock, cello; Virginia Eskin, piano. Northeastern Records NR 212. LP 1985; CD 1989. *Sonata for Viola and Piano* (1919). *Prelude, Allegro, and Pastorale* for viola and clarinet (1941), *Two Pieces (Grotesque and Lullaby)* for viola and cello (1918); *Passacaglia on an Old English Tune,* for viola and piano (1941).

Songs of America: on Home, Love, Nature, and Death. Jan DeGaetani, mezzo-soprano; Gilbert Kalish, piano. Elektra/Nonesuch 9 79178-2 (1988). *Lethe* (1941).

Piano Trios by Fanny Mendelssohn Hensel and Clarke. The Clementi Trio. Largo Records 5103 (CD 1986). *Piano Trio* (1921).

Songs of American Composers. Kristine Ciesinski, soprano; Shirley Seguin, piano. Leonarda LPI 120 (1984). *Down By the Salley Gardens, God Made a Tree, June Twilight, A Dream, The Seal Man, The Donkey.*

Piano Trios by Rebecca Clarke and Katherine Hoover. Virginia Eskin, piano, et al. Leonarda LPI 103 (1980). *Piano Trio* (1921).

Joy of Singing, Town Hall Series, released 1962. Povla Frijsch, Soprano. Recorded ca. 1941. *Shy One.*

The Cherry-Blossom Wand

Anna Wickham

Rebecca Clarke
Lianne Curtis, editor

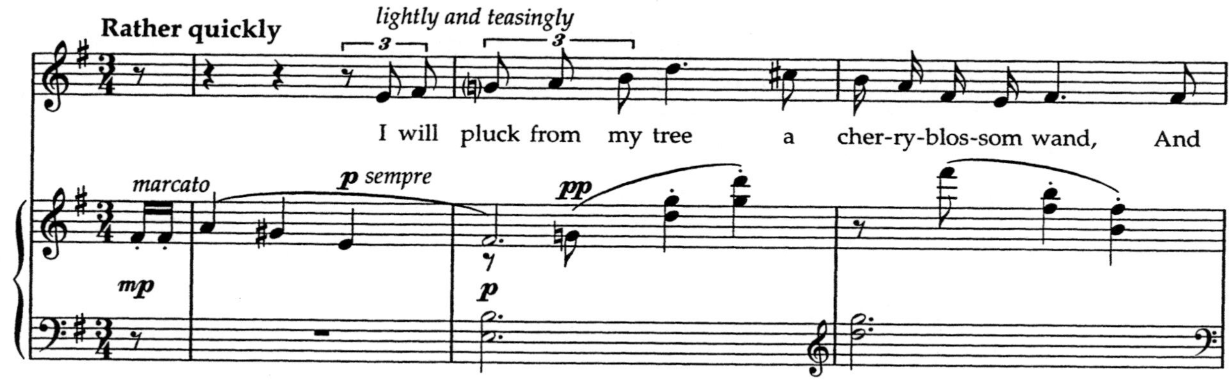

12
pp
wise.
Light are the pe - tals that fall from the bough,
p sempre
16
pp sempre
And light - er the love that I of - fer you now;
In a spring
p sempre
poco cresc.
20
day shall the tale be told of the beau - ti - ful
8va
pp
pp
24
poco a poco rit.
things that will nev - er grow old.
p
The
pp

28
A little slower
blos-soms shall fall in the night-wind,
And I will leave you so, to be
p
31
p
kind;
p
E - ter - - - nal
p espr.
34
in beau - ty are short - lived flowers,
poco cresc.
cresc.
38
f
allarg.
E ter - nal in beau - ty, these ex - quis - ite
dim.
f
Ped.

41
rit.
Tempo I
pp
hours. I will pluck from my tree a
p p
pp
45
pp sempre
cher-ry-blos-som wand, And car - ry it in my mer-ci - less hand, So
pp sempre
48
poco a poco rit.
pp
I will drive you, so be-witch your eyes, With a beau - ti - ful
pp
52
pp marc.
a tempo
thing that can nev - er grow wise.
pp
ppp
ppp
8va

Cradle Song

William Blake

Rebecca Clarke
Lianne Curtis, editor

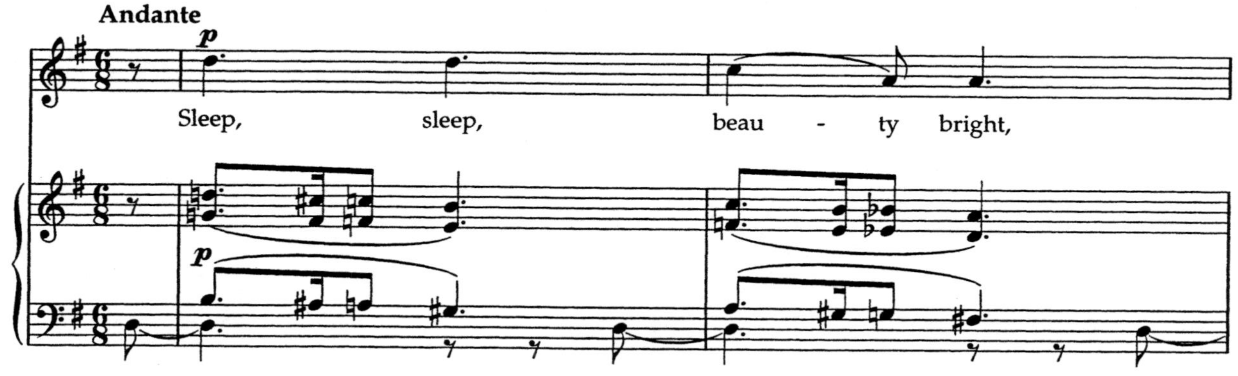

9
a tempo
mp
Sweet babe, in thy face
12
soft de - sires I can trace,
pp
Se - cret joys and
15
se - cret smiles, Lit - tle pret - ty in - fant wiles.
poco rit.
18
Slower
pp
As thy soft - est limbs I

20
feel
Smiles as of the
22
cresc.
morn - ing steal
dim.
O'er thy cheek,
cresc.
p
24
2
and o'er thy breast Where thy lit - tle heart doth
mp
dim.
27
rit.
pp
Tempo I
mp
O the cun - ning
pp
mp

29
wiles that creep
In thy lit - tle
heart a - sleep!
32
poco a poco rit.
p
When thy lit - tle heart doth wake,
molto rit.
pp
pp
34
a tempo
mp
Then the dread - ful night
dim.
mp
dim.
37
shall break.
p
pp

Lily Strickland

(1887–1958)

JOHN GRAZIANO

Lily Strickland was born on January 28, 1887 (1884 in some sources), at Echo Hall, the home of her maternal grandparents, Judge and Mrs. J. Pinckney Reed, in Anderson, South Carolina, where her father, Charles Hines Strickland, was employed by an insurance company. While she was still quite young, the family moved to New York City. After her father's sudden death, she and her mother returned to South Carolina, and joined her grandparents on the plantation, which she later referred to as a "beautiful old place in the midst of formal gardens."[1]

Strickland's first formal music education was at Converse College in Spartanburg, South Carolina. After three years of study there, from 1901 to 1904, she received a scholarship at the Institute of Musical Art in New York, now known as The Juilliard School (of Music). She studied piano, orchestration, theory, and composition with Frank Damrosch and Alfred Goodrich.

In 1912, Strickland married Joseph Courtenay Anderson, who was studying and teaching English at Columbia University. She continued to take courses at the Institute and studied orchestration privately with William Humiston. During this period, she began to write dialect songs, which brought her immediate fame. As America prepared to enter the first World War, Strickland volunteered to work with the YMCA at Camp MacArthur in Waco, Texas, where she entertained the troops and continued composing. Her travels through New Mexico, Kansas, and Oklahoma inspired compositions based on southwestern subjects. She transcribed native American melodies and incorporated them in some of her piano works, such as *Two Shawnee Indian Dances*.

In 1920, Strickland accompanied her husband to India. While they lived in Calcutta, they traveled through other areas of the country, as well as to Ceylon, Burma, the Philippines, China, Japan, and Europe. A trained musician, Strickland was quick to absorb the music of these varied cultures and she used them in her own compositions. Her interest in Indian music led her to study the music in great detail and to document the forms, legends, and history of Indian dance. During the ten years of their sojourn, Strickland published many articles on comparative musicology. In 1924, Converse College awarded her an honorary Doctor of Music.

On her return to the United States in 1930, Strickland first lived at Woodstock, New York, and later on Long Island in Great Neck, New York. Soon after her return, her oratorio *St. John the Beloved* was performed at the Spartanburg South Carolina Music Festival and later repeated in Atlanta, Georgia. During World War II, she and her husband spent some seven months in Charleston, South Carolina, where he organized a USO club for servicemen. Her stay there inspired her to write a six-movement work for orchestra, *Charleston Sketches*. In 1948, the Andersons retired to a twenty-six acre estate near Hendersonville, North Carolina. Lily Strickland died there on June 6, 1958.

Although she never sought an academic position, Strickland had strong opinions on American music and living musicians. She spoke often of the general lack of recognition and encouragement of American composers in their own country. She felt that Americans valued a European musical education too highly, which caused young musicians to go abroad too often for their musical training: "They can go to the continent for stimulation, for perspective, but they must live and feel American in order to compose American music."[2] She also spoke frequently about the need for developing creativity in children through musical training.

Although she probably viewed her music within the bounds of the cultivated tradition, many of Strickland's songs verge on the vernacular. They are breezy in style and exude an unaffected direct communication. While her songs are not performed frequently today, they are audience pleasers and deserving of rediscovery. In addition to her compositional endeavors, Strickland was also a poet and artist. She wrote under many pseudonyms and designed many of the covers that grace her publications.[3]

Bayou Songs, her set of four songs published in 1921, are set to poems by Michael De Longpré, one of Strickland's pseudonyms. The cover of *Bayou Songs* features a drawing, also by Strickland, of a Louisiana bayou. The poems are all written in a dialect that is meant to represent Louisiana cajun speech. Strickland demonstrates her mastery of early twentieth-century harmonic subtlety in each of the songs. Harmonic progressions are deceptively simple, but the chords contain unexpected nonharmonic tones that give the pieces a French tint that is reminiscent of the songs of her American contemporary Ethelbert Nevin (1862–1901). The first two songs are set in D major; the remaining two are set in A-flat major.

After a brief introduction, the first song, *Mornin' on ze Bayou*, begins with a call from the vocalist. While the listener is set to expect a D major chord underpinning the melody, Strickland playfully moves to a B minor chord before arriving on the dominant. As the first verse begins, Strickland avoids the tonic chord in root position. The tonic arrival does not occur until the beginning of the chorus in measure 24. Along with harmonic ambiguity, there is a fluidity of tempo in this song, with *accelerando*, *animato*, and *a poco ritard* occurring every few measures. At the end of the chorus, Strickland changes meter, from $\frac{6}{8}$ to $\frac{4}{4}$, indicating a slowing down with the marking *sostenuto*, and briefly modulates to E-flat major, the Neapolitan of D major. As the meter returns to $\frac{6}{8}$, the music once again moves to the dominant, which prepares the return to the tonic at the repetition of the chorus. The piano concludes with a postlude marked *brillante*. This would seem to indicate that the song has ended, but there is still a second verse to be sung. Strickland does not indicate the repeat clearly; it can return to the beginning of the introduction, or skip to measure 10. The question of how the song should be performed is not unique within this set; the remaining three songs are also unclear.

Ma Li'l Batteau, the second song in the set, also begins ambiguously. After a brief introduction the song begins on an E minor chord. The verse eventually moves to an A major chord, which serves as the dominant preparation for the tonic, D major. The chorus begins *a tempo grazioso* in the tonic, introducing the syncopated ragtime rhythm associated with vernacular music of the first decades of the twentieth century.

The third song, *Dreamin' Time*, continues with the ragtime rhythm as the narrator tells of the sights and sounds heard on the bayou. The vocalist, singing mostly descending major and minor thirds, mimics the call of an unspecified bird, probably the whippoorwill. This falling line is heard at the beginning of the verse and as a coda after the chorus.

The final song, *Li'l Jasmine-bud*, has an undulating accompaniment, which again makes reference to the syncopated rhythm heard in the previous songs. It is a lullaby set with two verses and a chorus. The gentle rhythms open in F minor, once again delaying the arrival of the tonic, A-flat major, which is heard only at the last measure of the verse. The chorus, marked "Not too slowly, sost. espress." is set as a double period, which moves through a circle of fifths progression. *Li'l Jasmine-bud* concludes, as the previous song did, with a tonic chord with a flatted seventh.

In all these songs, Strickland's detailed markings suggest that tempo is very flexible, with *accelerandos* and *rallentandos* that stretch the basic beat. Performers must use this *rubato,* while also avoiding exaggeration, to present these songs as charming examples of American parlor songs of the twentieth century.

Lily Strickland was a prolific composer with more than 400 compositions in her catalog. The vast majority are vocal works, including individual songs, song cycles, and several choral works, cantatas, and operettas. There are fewer instrumental pieces, including piano works, and miscellaneous pieces for violin, string quartet, and orchestra.

Notes

1. Ann Whitworth Howe, *Lily Strickland, South Carolina's Gift to American Music*. Published for the Tricentennial Commission by the R. L. Bryan Co., 1970.

2. Ibid., 19.

3. Ibid., 34.

Selected List of Works

This list is not complete; it does not include many of Strickland's larger vocal works nor most of her instrumental works.

Gathered Roses. Text by Lily Strickland. Cincinnati: John Church Co. Inc., 1904.

A Vain Wish. Text by Lily Strickland. Cincinnati: John Church Co. Inc., 1904.

When Twilight Dies. Text by Lily Strickland. Cincinnati: John Church Co. Inc., 1904.

His Voice. Text by Lily Strickland. Cincinnati: John Church Co. Inc., 1905.

I Plucked a Rose. Text by Lily Strickland. Cincinnati: John Church Co. Inc., 1905.

My Jeanie. Text by Lily Strickland. Cincinnati: John Church Co. Inc., 1905.

You Ask Why I Love Thee. Text by Lily Strickland. Cincinnati: John Church Co. Inc., 1905.

Hear Us O Father. Text by Lily Strickland. Cincinnati: John Church Co. Inc., 1906.

Home They Brought Her Warrior. Text by Alfred Lord Tennyson. Cincinnati: John Church Co. Inc., 1906.

Love Wakes and Weeps. Text by Sir Walter Scott. Cincinnati: John Church Co. Inc., 1906.

Night Song. Text by Lily Strickland. Cincinnati: John Church Co. Inc., 1906.

O Little Maiden. Text by Lily Strickland. Cincinnati: John Church Co. Inc., 1906.

Oh There's a Heart for Everyone. Text by Charles Swain. Cincinnati: John Church Co. Inc., 1906.

The Shepherd Boy. Text by Lily Strickland. Cincinnati: John Church Co. Inc., 1906.

The Wanderer. Text by Lily Strickland. Cincinnati: John Church Co. Inc., 1906.

A Complaint. Text by William Wordsworth. Cincinnati: John Church Co. Inc., 1907.

The Flower of Dumblame. Text by Lily Strickland. Cincinnati: John Church Co. Inc., 1907.

Love Is the Wind. Text by Lily Strickland; R. C. Noble. Cincinnati: John Church Co. Inc., 1907.

Peggie and Piggie. Text by Lily Strickland. Cincinnati: John Church Co. Inc., 1907.

Ye Who Are Oppressed. Text by Lily Strickland. Cincinnati: John Church Co. Inc., 1907.

As Through the Land at Eve. Text by Alfred Lord Tennyson. Cincinnati: John Church Co. Inc., 1909.

Esperanto. Text by Lily Strickland. New York: Arno Music Co., 1909.

Loneliness. Text by Lily Strickland. Boston: Oliver Ditson Publishing Co., 1909.

Midsummer Night. Text by Teresa Strickland. Cincinnati: John Church Co. Inc., 1909.

My Heart's Aye True. Text by Lily Strickland. Boston: Oliver Dison Publishing Co., 1909.

O Lord Hear My Voice. Text by Lily Strickland. New York: Arno Music Co., 1909.

Silver Moon. Text by Lily Strickland. New York: Arno Music Co., 1909.

Fate. Text by Teresa Strickland. Boston: Oliver Ditson Publishing Co., 1910.

A Pine Tree Stands Lonely. Text by Heinrich Heine. Translated by Wallace. New York: M. Witmark & Sons, 1910.

Spring Rapture. Text by Teresa Strickland. New York: Galaxy Music Corp., 1910.

There's Never an Hour. Text by Lily Strickland. New York: M. Witmark & Sons, 1910.

We Lift Our Hearts to Thee. Text by Teresa Strickland. Boston: Oliver Ditson Publishing Co., 1910.

When Thou Art Near Me. Text by Lady John Scott. New York: M. Witmark & Sons, 1910.

Flower o' the Moon. Text by Lily Strickland. New York: M. Witmark & Sons, 1911.

Heave Ho My Lads. Text by Van Zandt Wheeler. New York: M. Witmark & Sons, 1911.

In the Depth of the Woods. Text by Lily Strickland. New York: M. Witmark & Sons, 1911.

Mammy's Prayer. Text by Teresa Strickland. New York: M. Witmark & Sons, 1911.

My Heart's in Auld Scotland. Text by Lily Strickland. New York: M. Witmark & Sons, 1911.

Pickaninny Sleep Song. Text by Lily Strickland. New York: M. Witmark & Sons, 1911.

Thy Land of Lovely Ladies. Text by Van Zandt Wheeler. New York: M. Witmark & Sons, 1911.

At Dawn. Text by Amy Levy. Boston: Oliver Ditson Publishing Co., 1912.

The Cloud Ship. Text by Lily Strickland. New York: M. Witmark & Sons., 1912.

Compensation. Text by Lily Strickland. Boston: Oliver Ditson Publishing Co., 1912.

Since Laddie Went Awa'. Text by Lily Strickland. Boston: Oliver Ditson Publishing Co., 1912.

O Moon of My Desire. Text by Lily Strickland. New York: M. Witmark & Sons, 1913.

Sweet Dawn. Text by Teresa Strickland. New York: Galaxy Music Corp., 1913.

Because of You. Text by Lily Strickland. Boston: Oliver Ditson Publishing Co., 1914.

The King of Love My Shepherd Is. Text by H. W. Baker. New York: H. W. Gray Publishing Co., 1914.

My Lassie. Text by Lily Strickland. London: Chappell & Co., Ltd., 1914.

To Anthea. Text by Robert Herrick. Boston: Oliver Ditson Publishing Co., 1914.

'Bout Rabbits. Text by Teresa Strickland. London: Chappell & Co., Ltd., 1915.

Dere's Gwinter Be Er Lan'slide: A Negro Sermon. Text by Teresa Strickland. London: Chappell & Co., Ltd., 1915.

Little White Bird. Text by Teresa Strickland. Boston: Oliver Ditson Publishing Co., 1915.

Sweetheart. Text by Teresa Strickland. London: Boosey & Hawkes, 1915.

True Love's Eternal. Text by Lily Strickland. Cincinnati: John Church Co. Inc., 1915.

Kamasssa dvare bhikkhu: A Beggar at Love's Gate. Text by Aseret Dnommah (Lily Strickland).
New York: J. Fischer & Bro., 1917.
1. *Morning and Sunlight*
2. *Breath of Sandalwood*
3. *Temple Bells*
4. *Night and the Rain*
5. *Serenade*

Ballade of La Belle Dame Sans Merci. Text by John Keats. Cincinnati: John Church Co. Inc., 1917.

Colleen Aroon. Text by Lily Strickland. New York: G. Schirmer, Inc., 1917.

Dearest Eyes. Text by Lily Strickland. New York: Joseph W. Stern and Co., 1917.

If I Were the Wind. Text by Siegfried Swenson. Philadelphia: Theodore Presser Co., 1917.

Out from Rio. Text by Vivian H. Strickland. New York: Joseph W. Stern and Co., 1917.

Springtime for Love. Text by Lily Strickland. New York: Harold Flammer, Inc., 1917.

Today Is Fair. Text by Teresa Strickland. New York: J. Fischer & Bro., 1917.

Impromptu (for Piano). Text by T. H. Strickland. Philadelphia: Theodore Presser Co., 1918.

In Spring. Text by T. H. Strickland. Philadelphia: Theodore Presser Co., 1918.

To a Highlander. Text by Oscar Appleton Child. Boston: Oliver Ditson Publishing Co., 1918.

Aye but He's Bonnie. Text by Lily Strickland. London: Enoch & Sons, 1919.

Colleen o' Mine. Text by Terrence O'Shea. Boston: Oliver Ditson Pubvlishing Co., 1919.

Ireland My Home. Text by Terrence O'Shea. Philadelphia: Theodore Presser Co., 1919.

Laddie Mine. Text by Lily Strickland. Boston: Oliver Ditson Publishing Co., 1919.

Spring Is a Lady. Text by Lily Strickland. Philadelphia: Theodore Presser Co., 1919.

When Your Ship Comes In. Text by Lily Strickland. New York: Hinds, Hayden & Eldredge, Inc., 1919.

Wind o' the South. Text by Lily Strickland. Philadelphia: Theodore Presser Co., 1919.

Seven Songs from Way Down South. Text by Teresa Strickland. Philadelphia: Theodore Presser Co., 1920.
1. *Mammy's Sleepy Time*
2. *Mammy's Religion*
3. *Supplication: An African Jeremiad*
4. *Mistah Turkey*
5. *Hick'ry Tea*
6. *But I Prays*
7. *River Jurdan* [*sic*]

Come Join the Dance. Text by Lily Strickland. Boston: Arthur P. Schmitt and Co., 1920.

Legend of Jocassee. Text by Lily Strickland. Philadelphia: Theodore Presser Co., 1920.

Luck's Buccaneer. Text by Vivian Strickland. Philadelphia: Theodore Presser Co., 1920.

Mah Lindy Lou. Text by Lily Strickland. London: Chappell & Co., Ltd., 1920.

Run On Home. Text by Lily Strickland. New York: G. Schirmer, Inc., 1920.

Serenade. Text by Siegfried Swenson. Boston: Arthur P. Schmidt and Co., 1920.

Spring's Yesteryear. Text by Lily Strickland. New York: R. L. Huntzinger, Inc., 1920.

White Heather. Text by Lily Strickland. Philadelphia: Theodore Presser Co., 1920.

Bayou Songs. Text by Lily Strickland (Teresa Strickland, Michel deLongpre). New York: J. Fischer & Bro., 1921.
1. *Mornin' on ze Bayou*
2. *Ma L'il Batteau*
3. *Dreamin' Time*
4. *L'il Jasmine-bud*

Three Songs. Text by Lily Strickland. New York: G. Schirmer, Inc., 1921.
1. *The Bluebird's Return*
2. *Love's Symbol*
3. *Skeelan Dhul's Lament*

Lonesome Graveyard. Text by Lily Strickland. New York: Hinds, Hayden & Eldredge, Inc., 1921.

Ma Hame Folk. Text by Glen Cameron. Philadelphia: Theodore Presser Co., 1921.

Oh Lawdy. Text by Lily Strickland. New York: Hinds, Hayden & Eldredge, Inc., 1921.

Songs from the High Hills. Text by Lily Strickland. New York: G. Schirmer, Inc. 1922.
1. *By Jhelem's Stream*
2. *Here in the High Hills*
3. *Mir Jahan*
4. *O Little Drum*

Honey Chile. Text by Lily Strickland. New York: G. Schirmer, Inc., 1922.

Me an' Mah Pardner. Text by Lily Strickland. New York: G. Schirmer, Inc., 1922.

My Lover Is a Fisherman. Text by Lily Strickland. Boston: Oliver Ditson Publishing Co., 1922.

Sing High, Sing Low. Text by Lily Strickland. Philadelphia: Theodore Presser Co., 1922.

From a Sufi's Tent. Text by Ameen Rihani. New York: J. Fischer & Bro., 1923.
1. *Around the Well*
2. *But How the Funeral*
3. *Hark in the Minaret*
4. *Kiss the Rosy Cheeks*
5. *O Firmament*
6. *Oh My Companion*
7. *Or Sleep*
8. *The Sultan Too*
9. *Tread Lightly*
10. *The Way Unto the Sun*
11. *What Avails It*
12. *Whence Come*
13. *The Wilken Fiore*
14. *The Wine's Forbidden*

Negro Melodies of the Old South. Text by Lily Strickland. New York: M. Witmark & Sons, 1923.
1. *Convict's Song*
2. *Flood Song*
3. *Hymn*
4. *Plowing Song*
5. *Roll Jordan Roll*

Songs of Ind. [Sic] Text by Lily Strickland. New York: J. Fischer & Bro., 1923.
1. *Lal (Song of the Dancing Girl)*
2. *Jenandra (Song of the Rajput Love)*
3. *Lament (Song of the Burning Ghat)*
4. *Night Song (Song of the Waiting One)*
5. *Sweet the Music (Song of the Vine)*
6. *Tryst (Song of the Faithful Lover)*

At Eve I Heard a Flute. Text by Lily Strickland. Boston: Oliver Ditson Publishing Co., 1923.

Miss You So (A Southern Song). Text by Lily Strickland. New York: G. Schirmer, Inc., 1923.

My Arcady. Text by Lily Strickland. New York: J. Fischer & Bro., 1924.

Mo' Bayou Songs. Text by Lily Strickland. New York: J. Fischer & Bro., 1925.
1. *Lazy Days*
2. *Southern Moon*
3. *Ma Cherie*
4. *Belle Bayou*
5. *Nocturne*

Lonesome Moonlight. Text by Lily Strickland. Boston: Oliver Ditson Publishing Co., 1925.

Romance for violin and piano. New York: G. Schirmer, 1925.

Sweet Phyllis. Text by Lily Strickland. New York: G. Schirmer, Inc., 1925.

Dream Garden. Text by Lily Strickland. Philadelphia: Theodore Presser Co., 1926.

Driftin'. Text by Lily Strickland. Philadelphia: Theodore Presser Co., 1926.

Rose of Love. Text by Lily Strickland. Philadelphia: Theodore Presser Co., 1926.

Rose of Sevilla. Text by Lily Strickland. Philadelphia: Theodore Presser Co., 1926.

Oriental and Character Dances. Text by Helen Frost. New York: A. S. Barnes. 1927.

1. *The Carolinas.*
2. *Cole Black Daddy*
3. *I'se Trablin'*
4. *Sweet as Sugah*

Oubangi, Three Equatorial Songs. Text by Lily Strickland. New York: J. Fischer & Bro., 1927.

1. *Dioula's Song*
2. *Kalicongo*
3. *Oubangi*

Egyptian Scenes. Text by Lily Strickland. New York: G. Schirmer, Inc., 1927.

1. *Dusk in the Desert*
2. *Oasis of Love*
3. *Song of the Arab Shepherd*
4. *Twilight in the Desert*

Egyptian Scenes, three sketches for piano. New York: G. Schirmer, 1927.

1. *Dusk in the Desert*
2. *The Arab Shepherd's Song*
3. *Love's Oasis*

Ganza Drums. Text by Lily Strickland. New York: J. Fischer & Bro., 1927.

Home-Coming. Text by Lily Strickland. New York: Carl Fischer, Inc., 1927.

In Dreams. Text by Lily Strickland. New York: Carl Fischer, Inc., 1927.

Jes' Mah Song. Text by Lily Strickland. New York: G. Schirmer, Inc., 1927.

The Kama Dance. Text by Lily Strickland. Boston: Oliver Ditson Publishing Co., 1927.

Mah Rose. Text by Lily Strickland. New York: J. Fischer & Bro., 1927.

On Mah Way. Text by Lily Strickland. New York: G. Schirmer, Inc., 1927.

The Road to Home. Text by Lily Strickland. Boston: Oliver Ditson Publishing Co., 1927.

Twilight in the Desert. Text by Lily Strickland. New York: G. Schirmer, Inc., 1927.

Honey-Babee. Text by Frederick H. Martens. New York: DeSilva, Brown & Henderson, 1928.

Moon Dreams. Text by Lily Strickland. Boston: Oliver Ditson Publishing Co., 1928.

Moroccan Mosaics, four Eastern impressions for piano. New York: G. Schirmer, 1928.

Song of the African Exile. Text by Lily Strickland. Boston: Oliver Ditson Publishing Co., 1928.

Dream Ship. Text by Lily Strickland. New York: J. Fischer & Bro., 1929.

Robin's Advice. Text by Glen Carson. Philadelphia: Theodore Presser Co., 1929.

Four Aztec Love Songs. Text by Frederick H. Martens. Boston: Oliver Ditson Publishing Co., 1930.

1. *The Dancing Mask*
2. *The Ear-Drop*
3. *On the Lagoon*
4. *When You Are By*

Jus' Lovin' You. Text by Lily Strickland. New York: G. Schirmer, Inc., 1930.

Saharan Silhouettes for piano. Boston: Oliver Ditson Publishing Co., 1930.

St. John the Beloved, a sacred cantata for soli and a chorus of mixed voices. New York: J. Fischer & Bro., 1930.

Dance Moods, twelve compositions for piano solo. New York: J Fischer & Bro., 1931.

Give Me Today. Text by Lily Strickland. Philadelphia: Theodore Presser Co., 1931.

Meeting. Text by Lily Strickland. Philadelphia: Theodore Presser Co., 1931.

Question. Text by Lily Strickland. New York: Carl Fischer, Inc., 1931.

Down South. Text by Lily Strickland. Boston: Boston Music Co., 1933.

Hail to the Pioneers. Text by Lily Strickland. Cincinnati: Willis Music Co., 1933.

Indian Shepherd Song. Text by Lily Strickland. Cincinnati: Willis Music Co., 1933.

Jewel of the Desert, a musical comedy in two acts. Cincinnati: Willis Music Co., 1933.

Little Sing-Song Girl. Text by Lily Strickland. Boston: Boston Music Co., 1933.

Love's Benediction. Text by Lily Strickland. Philadelphia: Theodore Presser Co., 1933.

Snake Charmer's Song. Text by Lily Strickland. Cincinnati: Willis Music Co., 1933.

Soft the Music. Text by Lily Strickland. Cincinnati: Willis Music Co., 1933.

Somewhere. Text by Lily Strickland. Cincinnati: Willis Music Co., 1933.

Song of the Tropic Seas. Text by Lily Strickland. Cincinnati: Willis Music Co., 1933.

Troopin'. Text by Rudyard Kipling. New York: Carl Fischer, Inc., 1933.

Two East Indian Songs. Text by Lily Strickland. Boston: Boston Music Co., 1933.

Was There Ever a Day So Fair. Text by Lily Strickland. Philadelphia: Theodore Presser Co., 1933.

Hindu Slumber Song. Text by Lily Strickland. New York: J. Fischer & Bro., 1934.

Viking Song. Text by Lily Strickland. New York: Carl Fischer, Inc., 1934.

Chapel in the Mountains. Text by Edith Tillotson. Cincinnati: Willis Music Co., 1935.

A Little Song. Text by Lily Strickland. New York: Carl Fischer, Inc., 1935.

Sing a Song to Springtime. Text by Lily Strickland. Dayton, Ohio: Lorenz Music Publishing Co., 1935.

Song to Pan. Text by Lily Strickland. Dayton, Ohio: Lorenz Music Publishing Co., 1935.

Take What the Desert Offers. Text by Lily Strickland. New York: G. Schirmer, Inc., 1935.

To Phyllis. Text by Lily Strickland. Dayton, Ohio: Lorenz Music Publishing Co., 1935.

Make a Joyful Noise. Text by Lily Strickland. Dayton, Ohio: Lorenz Music Publishing Co., 1936.

On to the Desert. Text by Lily Strickland. London: Chappell & Co., Ltd., 1936.

Once on a Night in Bethlehem. Text by Lily Strickland. Philadelphia: Theodore Presser Co., 1936.

Sing O Song. Text by C. Wordsworth. Philadelphia: Theodore Presser Co., 1936.

Star Over Bethlehem, a Christmas cantata for solo voices, chorus and organ. London: Chappell & Co., Ltd., 1936.

By Killarney's Shore. Text by Lily Strickland. Philadelphia: Theodore Presser Co., 1937.

Jes' Lonesome. Text by Lily Strickland. Cincinnati: John Church Co., Inc., 1937.

My Shepherd Thou. Text by Lily Strickland. Philadelphia: Theodore Presser Co., 1937.

Old Prairie. Text by Lily Strickland. New York: J. Fischer & Bro., 1937.

Question and Answer. Text by Lily Strickland. Philadelphia: Theodore Presser Co., 1937.

Swingin' Along (Betty). Text be Lily Strickland. Cincinnati: Willis Music Co., 1937.

Who's for the Road. Text by Lily Strickland. New York: J. Fischer & Bro., 1937.

The Crusaders. Text by Lily Strickland. Cincinnati: Willis Music Co., 1938.

Dream Garden. Text by Lily Strickland. Chicago: Summy-Birchard Pub., 1938.

Jolly Sailor. Text by Lily Strickland. Cincinnati: Willis Music Co., 1938.

Keep On Singin' Ol' Bayou. Text by Lily Strickland. New York: G. Schirmer, 1938.

Send Me a Ship. Text by Lily Strickland. Cincinnati: Willis Music Co., 1938.

The Song of David, dramatic cantata for general use, Chappell & Co., Ltd., 1938.

Soudanesques. Text by Frederick H. Martens. New York: J. Fischer & Bro., 1939.
1. *Dawn*
2. *Nuba Girl Dance*
3. *Twala (Heaven)*

The Christ Child. Text by Lily Strickland. Chicago: Hall & McCreary Co., 1939.

Come to the Greenwood Fair. Text by Lily Strickland. Chicago: Hall & McCreary Co., 1939.

Mutiny of the Mary Anne, operetta in one act and one scene. Chicago: C. C. Birchard, 1939.

A Sailor's Way. Text by Lily Strickland. Chicago: Hall & McCreary Co., 1939.

Sing Your Song Today. Text by Lily Strickland. Chicago: Hall & McCreary Co., 1939.

Song of the Stream. Text by Lily Strickland. (New York?); Alice Remsen, 1939.

Come to the Ball. Text by Lily Strickland. New York: Galaxy Music Corp., 1940.

Praise Ye the Lord. Text by Lily Strickland. Dayton, Ohio: Lorenz Music Publishing Co., 1940.

Creole Boat Song. Text by Lily Strickland. Dayton, Ohio: Lorenz Music Publishing Co., 1941.

Frost Flowers. Text by Lily Strickland. New York: Jack Mills, 1941.

Hunting Song. Text by Lily Strickland. New York: Jack Mills, 1941.

If I Had My Wish. Text by Lily Strickland. New York: Jack Mills, 1941.

May Day. Text by Lily Strickland. Chicago: Schmitt, Hall & McCreary Co., 1941.

Night Flower. Text by Lily Strickland. Philadelphia: Theodore Presser Co., 1941.

Over the Hills. Text by Lily Strickland. Chicago: Schmitt, Hall & McCreary Co., 1941.

Prelude to Spring. Text by Lily Strickland. New York: Jack Mills, 1941.

Shepherd Lad. Text by Lily Strickland. New York: Jack Mills, 1941.

Sleepy Song. Text by Lily Strickland. New York: G. Schirmer, Inc., 1941.

Vagabond Call. Text by Lily Strickland. Boston: Oliver Ditson Publishing Co., 1941.

Winter Lullaby. Text by Lily Strickland. Chicago: Schmitt, Hall & McCreary Co., 1941.

I Remember. Text by Lily Strickland. New York: Jack Mills, 1942.

Birds in My Garden. Text by Lily Strickland. Boston: Oliver Ditson Publishing Co., 1943.

It's Always Good Morning. Text by Lily Strickland. Chicago: Hall & McCreary Co., 1943.

Little Fisherman. Text by Lily Strickland. Chicago: Hall & McCreary Co., 1943.

Treasure. Text by Lily Strickland. Chicago: Hall & McCreary Co., 1943.

Why Can't I? Text by Lily Strickland. Philadelphia: Theodore Presser Co., 1943.

Dat Moanin' Wind. Text by Lily Strickland. New York: Jack Mills, 1944.

Heralds of Spring. Text by Lily Strickland. Philadelphia: Theodore Presser Co., 1945.

My Heart Is Yours. Text by Lily Strickland. New York: Jack Mills, 1945.

On Holy Ground. Text by Lily Strickland. Dayton, Ohio: Lorenz Music Publishing Co., 1945.

Can't He Do de Same fo' Me? Text by Anonymous. New York: Galaxy Music Corp., 1946.

Summer Days. Text by Lily Strickland. Philadelphia: Theodore Presser Co., 1946.

Sweet Bells of Christmas. Text by Lily Strickland. Philadelphia: Theodore Presser Co., 1946.

Dreamin' Time Mah Honey. Text by John W. Bratton. New York: Bourne Co., Inc., 1947.

Fog in the Harbor. Text by Lily Strickland. Philadelphia: Elkan-Vogel Co., 1947.

Go Little Song. Text by Lily Strickland. Philadelphia: Theodore Presser Co., 1947.

Song of the Whippoorwill. Text by Theodosia Paynter. Boston: Oliver Ditson Publishing Co., 1947.

With My Heart I Follow You. Text by Theodosia Paynter. Boston: Oliver Ditson Publishing Co., 1947.

Life Triumphant, an Easter cantata for solo voices, mixed chorus and organ. Chappell & Co., Ltd., 1948.

O Take Me Back. Text by Harry R. Wilkins. Cincinnati: John Church Co., Inc., 1948.

White Moon. Text by W. Clark Harrington. New York: Galaxy Music Corp., 1948.

Joyful News We Bring. Text by Lily Strickland. Chicago: Hall & McCreary Co., 1949.

Surprise Christmas, an operetta for juniors in two acts. Wichita, Kan.: R. A. Hoffman, 1949.

Little Louise. Text by Anonymous Italian. Chicago: Hall & McCreary Co., 1951.

Love Will Find Out the Way. Text by Anonymous. Seventeenth century English. Chicago: Hall & McCreary Co., 1951.

When the Band Goes By. Text by Lily Strickland. Chicago: Hall & McCreary Co., 1951.

Woman Trouble Blues. Text by Lily Strickland. [n.p.]: Delta Music Co., 1952.

She Passed Along My Way. Text by Lily Strickland. New York: G. Schirmer, Inc., 1953.

As You Go Down the Road. Text by Lily Strickland. Chicago: Hall & McCreary Co., 1956.

I Follow My Star. Text by Lily Strickland. Chicago: Hall & McCreary Co., 1956.

If You Could Hear a Robin Sing. Text by Lily Strickland. Chicago: Hall & McCreary Co., 1957.

Spring Is In My Garden. Text by Lily Strickland. Minneapolis: Paul A. Schmitt Music, 1957.

Bibliography

Howe, Ann Whitworth. "Lily Strickland: her contribution to American music in the early twentieth century." Ph.D. diss., Catholic University of America, 1968.

______. *Lily Strickland, South Carolina's Gift to American Music.* Published for the South Carolina Tricentennial Commission by the R. L. Bryan Co. 1970.

Kinscella, Hazel Gertrude. "An American Composer at Home." *Better Home and Gardens* (September 1931).

Phifer, Mary. "Lily Strickland, Symphonist." *Holland Magazine* (April 1931).

Strickland, Lily. "The real nautch girl; an American composer, ten years resident in India, tells the truth about the exotic dancing maidens." *The Dance Magazine* (December 1929).

______. "The rhythmic prayers of Ceylon." *The Dance Magazine* (January 1930).

______. "Rhythms on the Bengal Border." *The Dance Magazine* (March 1930).

Wyeth, N. C. "Lily Strickland, Composer." *The Etude* (1931).

Mornin' on ze Bayou

Michael De Longpré
(Lily Strickland)

Lily Strickland
John Graziano, editor

16
accel.
a tempo
cresc.
Jean an' Pierre, an' laz - ee Jo' Come an' join me as I go, for a
Sun, he clim' - in' up ze sky How can you so sleep - y lie, w'en it's
20
ff
f
row, on ze ol' Ba - you!
morn, on ze ol' Ba - you!
24
animato
f
cresc.
Row, row, row, In ma li'l bat - teau, For it's
28
morn - - - in' For it's morn - - - - in' On ze

32
ol' Bay - ou!
ff
37
rall.
sostenuto
Mock - in' bird, sing so low, On ze
sostenuto
u.c.
40
dim.
ol' Bay - ou w'ere ze blos-soms bloom an' grow.
cresc.
dim.
cresc.
44
rall.
'Tis zere zat I mus' go! Ho-la! ho-la! ho - la!

48
animato
f
Row, row, row, In ma li'l bat - teau, For it's
f
[T.C.]
52
cresc.
ff
morn - - - - in', For it's morn - - - - in' on ze
cresc.
56
ol' Bay - ou!
ff col canto
brillante
60

Ma Li'l Batteau

Michael De Longpré
(Lily Strickland)

Lily Strickland
John Graziano, editor

17
f
rall.
a tempo
sost.
No one a-long to chide me, I drif' an' dream—
So hap-pi-ly I drif' a-long wiz Belle Ma - rie.
f
dim.
21
espr.
ad lib.
a tempo grazioso
La, la, la, la, la
Down on ze ol' Bay -
L.H.
R.H.
mp
lightly
R.H.
L.H.
u.c.
24
dolce
ou,
Me an ma li'l bat - teau;
27
cresc.
ten.
Down w'ere ze jas - mine's grow - in' An' sweet mag -
cresc.

30
poco accel.
no - lias blow; Down w'ere ze moon - path gleams,
33
cresc.
rit.
rall.
marc.
Night-ly I tak' ma dreams, Belle Ma-rie's not a
36
rall.
espr.
rall.
dim.
girl you know, But she's jus' ma_li'l bat - teau La
espr.
dim.
40
animato
la!
R.H.
lightly
R.H.
R.H.
R.H.
L.H.
L.H.
L.H.
L.H.

Dreamin' Time

Michael De Longpré
(Lily Strickland)

Lily Strickland
John Graziano, editor

Andante grazioso
mp dolce
dim.
5
mp espr.
sostenuto
1. Whip-o' - will,_ Sof' an' low;_ Cal - lin' on ze ol' Bay - ou,
2. Mock-in' - bird,_ Sweet' an' low;_ Cal - lin' on ze ol' Bay - ou,
mp
sostenuto
9
cresc.
f
rit.
poco rall.
dim.
ten.
'Ga-tors cal - lin' to ze moon_ W'ere ze breez - es croon:___
Jas-mine dream-in' in ze dew_ Stir ze heart of you.___
cresc.
f
dim.

13
p dolce espr.
mp
poco accel.
Dream-in' time on ze ol' Bay - ou;
p dreamily
mp

a tempo
17
poco cresc.
Dream-in' time w'ere ze sha-dows fall;
poco cresc.
lazily

21
poco accel.
cresc.
W'ere ze win' sing sof' and low; W'ere ze twi-light call I

a tempo
25
ten.
dim.
love ze dream-in' time bes' of all.
dim.
p
Ped.

28
pp
poco a poco dim.
Whip-o' - will, cal-lin' still,
Mock-in' bird, still am heard,
poco a poco dim.

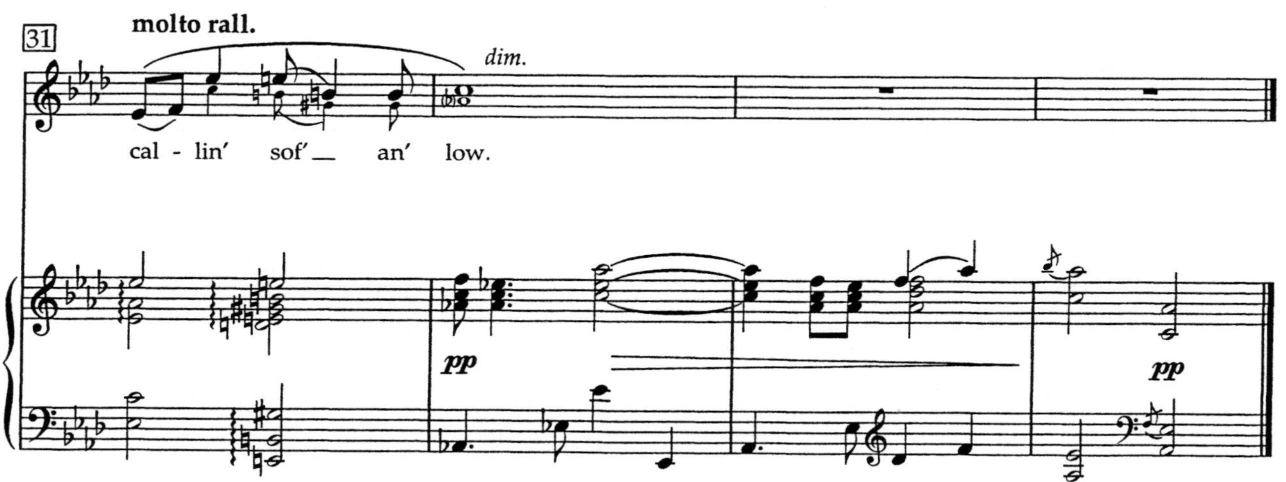
31
molto rall.
dim.
cal - lin' sof' an' low.
pp
pp

Li'l Jasmine-bud

Michael De Longpré
(Lily Strickland)

Lily Strickland
John Graziano, editor

15
poco accel.
An - gels de - fen' you, Li'l Jas - mine-bud, Close sleep - y eyes of
19
a tempo
blue Dream on 'til morn - in',
23
cresc.
rall.
ten.
a tempo
An wiz new dawn - in' Wiz a kiss I wak - en you, Lil'
ten.
27
rall.
a tempo
Jas - mine o' ma heart!
p dim.
pp

Florence Beatrice Price

(1887–1953)

RAE LINDA BROWN

Florence Price was the most widely known African-American woman composer from the 1930s until her death in 1953.[1] She was the first black woman composer to achieve wide recognition and one of the first African-American composers to write large-scale works that were premiered by major orchestras. Price wrote in all genres except opera, producing works for piano, organ, voice, chamber ensembles, orchestra, and chorus. She also arranged spirituals for voice and instrumental combinations. Her music was regularly performed by a professional coterie of friends and colleagues in Chicago as well as by some of the leading concert singers of the day, including Marian Anderson, Blanche Thebom, Roland Hayes, Abbie Mitchell, and Harry Burleigh. Price premiered many of her own works for piano and organ.

Born Florence Beatrice Smith in Little Rock, Arkansas, on April 9, 1887, she began piano study with her mother and gave her first public recital at the age of four. Price received encouragement and (possible) musical training from the public elementary school teacher Charlotte Andrews Stephens. She attended Capitol High School and graduated in 1903. During the 1880s, the Little Rock of Price's youth was known as "the Negro Paradise." It became a haven for educated blacks and skilled workers who were eager to move to Arkansas for its political and economic opportunities. The Negro middle class, to whom Price and her family belonged, constituted a small but significant population. Her father, Dr. James H. Smith, became the first black dentist in Little Rock when he moved there in 1876. For more than twenty years he was the city's leading dentist for both black and white patients; his lucrative practice even included one of the state's governors. Price's mother, Florence Irene Gulliver, taught elementary school in Indianapolis before she married and moved to Little Rock. She was a fine pianist and singer who later became an astute businesswoman. She worked as a secretary for the black-owned International Loan and Trust Company; she owned a restaurant, and she bought and sold real estate under her own name. Her endeavors enabled her to claim a measure of financial independence uncommon among women of her time. In the late 1880s, the process of disfranchisement slowly eroded all political gains by blacks, economic advances were lost, lynching was on the rise, and "Jim Crow" segregation laws were instituted. By 1900, Little Rock had become a shadow of its former self.

As a child, Price was exposed to a variety of stimulating social, political, and intellectual activities organized by the elite of the black community. Prominent Negro artists, both local and national, regularly performed in Little Rock, literary groups were organized, and lecture series were well attended.

After high school Price attended the New England Conservatory of Music in Boston, Massachusetts. There, she became seriously interested in composition; George Whitefield Chadwick (1854–1931), director of the Conservatory and an eminent composer accepted her as a private student. She also studied organ with Henry M. Dunham (1853–1929), and composition and counterpoint with Frederick Converse (1871–1940) from 1904 to 1906. Price received a Soloist Diploma in organ and a Teachers Diploma in piano in 1906. She found little time to pursue composing, however, until the late 1920s.

Price returned to the South, and taught at the Cotton Plant–Arkadelphia Academy in Arkansas (1906–1907), at Shorter College in Little Rock (1907–1910), and at Clark College in Atlanta (1910–1912), after which she returned to Little Rock to marry. She remained active as a teacher until her death. In 1926, although married and raising two daughters, she began to concentrate on writing music; she won several awards for her early piano works. In 1927 (or 1928) the family moved to Chicago to escape the oppressive proscriptions that relegated blacks to second-class citizenship in the South.

There, Price attended the American Conservatory and the Chicago Musical College, studying composition and orchestration with Carl Busch (1862–1943) and Wesley LaViolette (1894–1978). She received a post-graduate degree in 1934.

In the 1930s and 1940s, Chicago was a vital city that provided opportunities for black musicians to perform and composers to have their music heard. Price belonged to both Chicago branches of the National Association of Negro Musicians—the Chicago Music Association and the R. Nathaniel Dett Club—and was an active member of the national body. In addition, her music was regularly represented on the concert series of the local black churches, and much of her choral music was performed by her own Treble Clef Glee Club and the Florence B. Price A Capella Chorus that was directed by Grace W. Tompkins. Price's development as a composer was no doubt strengthened and accelerated by the many opportunities to hear her music in performance.

In the mid-1930s, Price separated from her husband and then earned her living from sales of her teaching pieces for the piano, writing popular songs (often under the pen name "Vee Jay"), and from orchestrating music for WGN radio, and accompanying silent films on the organ in the "Scroll" theater district of Chicago. Her music was promoted and performed by black and white organizations, including The Chicago Symphony Orchestra, the Women's Symphony Orchestra of Chicago, the U.S. Marine Band, the Michigan WPA Symphony, the Forum String Quartet (Illinois), the Detroit WPA concert band, The Chicago Club of Women Organists, Illinois Federation of Music Clubs, and the Musicians Club of Women. Price's arrangements of spirituals were sung by Marian Anderson and her other songs were performed by Roland Hayes, Leontyne Price, and Blanche Thebom.

As a composer, Price immersed herself in the black folk idiom. She evoked the Southern landscape in the titles of her early music, for example, *In the Land a' Cotton* (1926) and *At the Cotton Gin* (1927); and black dance (the "juba") rhythms provided the underlying impetus for much of her instrumental music. Although she rarely quoted folk melodies in her works notable exceptions are the *Fantasie nègre in E Minor*, for piano, based on *Sinner, Please Don't Let This Harvest Pass*, and the string quartet, *Five Folksongs in Counterpoint,* based on American folk themes. The essence of the Negro spiritual provided the melodic inspiration for many of the compositions she wrote in the 1930s. By no means, however, did Price feel compelled to write in the Negro idiom. Many of her works are free of such references. Those include *Adoration* and *In Quiet Mood* for organ, *Memory Mist* and *Placid Lake* for piano, and the art songs *An April Day*, *Dawn's Awakening*, and *The Moon Bridge*.

Price's early music, along with that of her contemporaries William Grant Still (1895–1978) and William Dawson (1898–1990), may be placed within the context of nationalism in American music. African-American folk music, both sacred and secular, provided the musical foundation for these composers. Her music may also be placed in the context of the Harlem Renaissance, or New Negro movement, of the 1920s and 1930s, in which race consciousness in art and literature was pervasive. Her *Symphony in E Minor* and two other compositions were entered in the 1932 Rodman Wanamaker Music Contest. All were prize winners, with the *Symphony* taking the five-hundred-dollar first place award. It was performed by the Chicago Symphony Orchestra on June 15, 1933. The *Concerto in One Movement* was performed by her student Margaret Bonds (1913–1972) at the Chicago World's Fair and by the Women's Symphony of Chicago in 1934. Price's large-scale works of the 1940s reveal a different attitude toward composition. With the ideals of the nationalist movement and of the Harlem Renaissance now passé, black artists looked for inspiration to realistic subject matter such as the Great Migration, the Depression, and adjustments to urban life. It is in the context of the second flowering of black artistic expression called the Chicago Renaissance (1935–1950) that Price's *Symphony No. 3* (1940) was conceived.

Price wrote over 100 songs during her career. They include art songs, popular songs, and arrangements of spirituals, which constitute a significant part of her oeuvre. For the most part, she chose poetry carefully, although there are a few banal texts taken from poems in magazines. Between 1932 and 1945, she set nine poems by Langston Hughes (1902–1967) and nineteen by Paul Laurence Dunbar (1872–1906).

One of Price's most provocative art songs is a setting of Georgia Douglas Johnson's poem from her collection *The Heart of a Woman.* In it, a woman's heart is metaphorically compared to a lone bird that "goes forth with the dawn" over "life's turrets and vales." Then it

> . . . falls back with the night
> And enters some alien cage in its plight
> And tries to forget it has dreamed of the stars
> While it breaks, breaks, breaks on the sheltering bars.

Published in 1918, Johnson's poem is strikingly feminist in its sensibility. Aware of how far women still had to travel before they were completely "emancipated," her poems speak of the "oppressiveness and pain of the traditional female lot."

Price set the two-verse poem in a modified strophic form. In the opening lines, as the heart/bird wings "restlessly on," so does the music. The harmony is not highly dissonant and the vocal line seems to wander aimlessly. In the entire twenty-five measure song, the E-flat tonic is alluded to only briefly, at the penultimate phrase of the poem. At the conclusion of the song — "while it breaks . . . " — the anticipated dominant chord is altered by a lowered third, resulting in a G minor seventh chord, after which the accompaniment slides chromatically into the final E-flat tonic arpeggio. The accompaniment and the several meter and tempo changes propel the music forward seamlessly in a setting that is one of the composer's most powerful. In this, her only setting of a poem by a black woman, the feelings of a "caged bird," pained in its trapped existence, are vividly portrayed, with the poet confessing broken, shattered dreams.

The Glory of the Day Was in Her Face, in E-flat major, is a short ABA form in $\frac{12}{8}$ meter notable for a remarkable modulation to distant E major in the middle section. In section A the repeated rippling accompaniment pattern beneath a vocal line of narrow range occurs six times on the tonic, moving to the subdominant in measure 7, and is followed by unresolved dominant chords for two measures before closing in measure 10. Section B, also ten measures long, moves to $\frac{6}{8}$ and features an accompaniment in repeated sixths in the right hand. In measure 13 an F-sharp chord sets up the dominant of E major (B) in measure 14, followed by an E-flat arpeggio heard as D-sharp. A series of seventh chords heralds the return to E-flat in measure 17, preparing for the reprise of section A in measure 21. A short coda (mm. 33-35) closes the song.

Notes

1. This article is an adaptation by Martha Furman Schleifer of *Price, Florence Beatrice* by Rae Linda Brown in the *International Dictionary of Black Composers*. Sections reprinted with permission, copyright 1999, Fitzroy Dearborn Publishers.

List of Works

Solo Voice

An April Day. New York: Handy Bros., 1949.

Ardella (1935). Unpublished manuscript.

Baby My Own (1928). Unpublished manuscript.

Because. Unpublished manuscript.

Beside the Sea. Unpublished manuscript.

Bewilderment. Unpublished manuscript.

The Bowl Is Cracked. Unpublished manuscript.

City Called Heaven. Unpublished manuscript.

Cobbler. Unpublished manuscript.

Crescent Moon (1934). Unpublished manuscript.

Dat's My Gal (1935). Unpublished manuscript.

Dawn's Awakening (1936). Unpublished manuscript.

Death's Gwinter Lay His Cold Icy Hand on Me. Unpublished manuscript.

Desire. Unpublished manuscript.

Dream Ships (1935). Unpublished manuscript.

Dreaming Town (1934). Unpublished manuscript.

The Envious Wren. Unpublished manuscript.

Every Dream Has a Scheme (1929). Unpublished manuscript.

Fantasy in Purple. Unpublished manuscript.

Feet o' Jesus. Unpublished manuscript.

Foggy Night (1946). Unpublished manuscript.

Forever. Unpublished manuscript.

Four Encore Songs. Unpublished manuscript.
Come, Come
Tobacco
A Flee and a Fly
Song of the Open Road

Four Songs for Bass-Baritone. Unpublished manuscript.
Easy Goin'
Goo-bye Jinks
The Photograph
Summah Night

The Glory of the Day Was in Her Face. Unpublished manuscript.

God Gives Me You (1946). Unpublished manuscript.

The Heart of a Woman. Unpublished manuscript.

Hitch Up Your Belts, Boys! (1942). Unpublished manuscript.

Hold Fast to Dreams (1945). Unpublished manuscript.

I Grew a Rose. Unpublished manuscript.

I Remember (1934). Unpublished manuscript.

I'm Goin' to Lay Down My Heavy Load. Unpublished manuscript.

In Back o' the Clouds (1930). Unpublished manuscript.

The Island of My Dreams (1928). Unpublished manuscript.

It's All on Account of the Sunshine. Unpublished manuscript.

Just a Dream That Never Came True (1929). Unpublished manuscript.

Just to Be Near You (1948). Unpublished manuscript.

Let's Build a Little Love Nest (1930). Unpublished manuscript.

Let's Give Love Another Try (1945). Unpublished manuscript.

Listen Baby (1928). Unpublished manuscript.

Little Things. Unpublished manuscript.

Looking for Someone to Love (1934). Unpublished manuscript.

Lord I Can't Stay Away. Unpublished manuscript.

Love Dreams (1930). Unpublished manuscript.

Love-in-a-Mist. Unpublished manuscript.

Lover's Lane. Unpublished manuscript.

Memories of You. Unpublished manuscript.

Morning. Unpublished manuscript.

My Dream. In *Art Songs and Spirituals by African-American Women Composers*. Bryn Mawr, PA: Hildegard Publishing Company, 1995.

My Little Soul's Goin' to Shine. Unpublished manuscript.

My Neighbor. Unpublished manuscript.

Night. New York. Edward B. Marks, 1946.

Nightfall. Unpublished manuscript.

O Lamb of God. Unpublished manuscript.

On the Other Shore. Unpublished manuscript.

Out of the South Blew a Wind. New York: Edward B. Marks, 1946.

Pittance. Unpublished manuscript.

The Poet and His Song. Unpublished manuscript.

The Retort. Unpublished manuscript.

Sentimental Moonlight (1947). Unpublished manuscript.

Ships That Pass in the Night. Unpublished manuscript.

A Smiling Face (1928). Unpublished manuscript.

Song Is So Old. Unpublished manuscript.

A Song of Living. Unpublished manuscript.

Song to the Dark Virgin (low voice). New York. G. Schirmer, 1941.

Sunset (1938). Unpublished manuscript.

Sympathy (1943). Unpublished manuscript.

Then I Found Heaven When I Found You (1938). Unpublished manuscript.

They Lie, They Lie. Unpublished manuscript.

To My Little Son. Unpublished manuscript.

Travel's End. Unpublished manuscript.

The Washerwoman. Unpublished manuscript.

We Have Tomorrow. Unpublished manuscript.

Weary Traveler. Unpublished manuscript.

What Is Love? Unpublished manuscript.

A White Rose. Unpublished manuscript.

Who Grope with Hands for Love. Unpublished manuscript.

Winter Idyll. Unpublished manuscript.

Winter Must Come. Unpublished manuscript.

Won't You Please Play Santa Claus? (1928). Unpublished manuscript.

Words for a Spiritual (1948). Unpublished manuscript.

You Didn't Know This Baby (1928). Unpublished manuscript.

You're in My Heart to Stay (1948). Unpublished manuscript.

Your Leafy Voice. Unpublished manuscript.

Choral Music

After the First and Sixth Commandments (SATB). Unpublished manuscript.

Alleluia (SATB). Unpublished manuscript.

Banjo Song (1933) (SSA). Unpublished manuscript.

Blue Bell. (SSA). Unpublished manuscript.

Communion Service (SATB). Unpublished manuscript.

Hold Out Yo' Light (SSA). Unpublished manuscript.

An Indian Summer on the Prairie (women's chorus unaccompanied). Unpublished manuscript.

It's Snowing. Unpublished manuscript.

The Moon Bridge (1930) (SSA). Chicago: Gamble Hinged Music, 1930. Also arranged for solo voice.

Natures Magic (SSA). Chicago: Clayton F. Summy, 1953.

The New Moon (SSAA). Chicago: Gamble Hinged Music, 1930.

Nod (TTBB unaccompanied). Unpublished manuscript.

Ode to Man (chorus, piano and organ). Unpublished manuscript.

Poem of Praise (SATB). Unpublished manuscript.

Resignation (1964) (SATB unaccompanied). Unpublished manuscript. Also arranged for solo voice.

Song for Snow (SATB). New York: Carl Fischer, 1957.

Summer Clouds (SAB). Unpublished manuscript.

Wander Thirst (SATB). Unpublished manuscript. Also arranged for solo voice.

The Waves of Breffney (SATB). Unpublished manuscript.

What's the Use? (1930). Unpublished manuscript. Also arranged for solo voice.

Witch of the Meadow (1947) (SSA). Chicago: Gamble Hinged Music, 1947.

As "Vee Jay"

If I Didn't Love You (1945) (voice and piano). Unpublished manuscript.

Soloists or Chorus with Orchestra *(chamber or full)*

Lincoln Walks at Midnight (chorus and orchestra). Unpublished manuscript.

Seagulls (SSA, flute, clarinet, violin, viola, cello, piano) (1951). Unpublished manuscript.

Song of Hope (voice and orchestra). Unpublished manuscript.

Spring Journey (SSA and orchestra). Unpublished manuscript.

The Wind and the Sea (mixed chorus, piano, string quartet) (1934). Unpublished manuscript.

Solo Instrumental Music

Violin

By Candlelight. Chicago: McKinley, 1929.

The Deserted Garden. Bryn Mawr: Theodore Presser, 1933.

Elfentanz. Unpublished manuscript.

Playful Rondo. Chicago: McKinley, 1928.

Cello

Sonatine. Unpublished manuscript.

Organ

Adoration. In *The Organ Portfolio*. Dayton, Ohio: Lorenz, 1951. Also in *Music of Florence Beatrice Price,* vol. 2, *Short Organ Works*. Fayetteville, Ark.: ClarNan Editions, 1995.

Allegretto. In *Music of Florence Beatrice Price,* vol. 2, *Short Organ Works*. Fayetteville, Ark.: ClarNan Editions, 1995.

Dainty Lass. Unpublished manuscript.

Evening Song. New York: Galaxy Music, 1951.

Festal March. In *Music of Florence Beatrice Price,* vol. 2, *Short Organ Works*. Fayetteville, Ark.: ClarNan Editions, 1995.

The Hour Glass. In *Music of Florence Beatrice Price,* vol. 2, *Short Organ Works*. Fayetteville, Ark.: ClarNan Editions, 1995. Note: originally titled *Sandman*.

In Quiet Mood. New York: Galaxy, 1951. In *Music of Florence Beatrice Price*, vol. 2, *Short Organ Works*. Fayetteville, Ark.: ClarNan Editions, 1995. Note: published version of *Impromptu*.

Little Melody. In Music of Florence Beatrice Price, vol. 2, *Short Organ Works*. Fayetteville, Ark.: ClarNan Editions, 1995.

Offertory. Dayton, Ohio: Lorenz, 1951. In *Music of Florence Beatrice Price,* vol. 2, *Short Organ Works*. Fayetteville, Ark.: ClarNan Editions, 1995.

Passacaglia and Fugue (1936). Unpublished manuscript.

A Pleasant Thought (1951). In *Music of Florence Beatrice Price,* vol. 2, *Short Organ Works*. Fayetteville, Ark.: ClarNan Editions, 1995.

Prelude and Fantasy (1942). Unpublished manuscript.

Retrospection. In *Music of Florence Beatrice Price,* vol. 2, *Short Organ Works*. Fayetteville, Ark.: ClarNan Editions, 1995. Note: originally titled *An Elf on a Moonbeam*.

Sonata no. 1 (1959). In *Music of Florence Beatrice Price,* vol. 4. Fayetteville, Ark.: ClarNan Editions, 1996.

Suite no. 1 (1942). In *Music of Florence Beatrice Price,* vol. 1. Fayetteville, Ark.: ClarNan Editions, 1993.

Variations on a Folksong: Peter Go Ring dem' Bells. In *Music of Florence Beatrice Price,* vol. 3. Fayetteville, Ark.: ClarNan Editions, 1995.

Piano

Annie Laurie (piano duet). Chicago: McKinley, 1929.

Arkansas Jitter (1938). Unpublished manuscript.

At the Cotton Gin (1927). New York: G. Schirmer, 1928.

Autumn Echoes. Unpublished manuscript.

Bayou Dance (1938). Unpublished manuscript.

Birds in the Forest. Chicago: McKinley, n.d.

Blue Skies. Chicago: McKinley, n.d.

The Bridle Path. Unpublished manuscript.

Brownies on the Seashore. Unpublished manuscript.

Bruno, the Bear (1948). Unpublished manuscript.

The Butterfly (1935). In *Pieces We Like to Play*. New York: Carl Fischer, 1936.

Climbing the Mountain. Unpublished manuscript.

Clover Blossom (1947). Chicago: McKinley, 1947.

Cotton Dance. In Oxford *Piano Course, Book Five*. New York: Oxford University Press, 1942.

Criss Cross (1947). Chicago: McKinley, 1947.

Dainty Feet. Unpublished manuscript.

Dance of the Cotton Blossoms (1938). Unpublished manuscript.

Dances in the Canebrakes (1953). Los Angeles: Affiliated Musicians, 1953. Also arranged for orchestra.

Dark Pool. Unpublished manuscript.

Echoes. Chicago: McKinley, n.d.

Evening. Chicago: McKinley, n.d.

Fantasie nègre (1929). In *Black Women Composers: A Century of Piano Music, 1893–1990*, ed. Helen Walker-Hill. Bryn Mawr, PA: Hildegard, Publishing Company, 1992.

Fantasie nègre no. 4 (1932). Unpublished manuscript.

Five Easy Compositions. Chicago: McKinley, 1928.
The Doll
Waltz
The Engine
The Waterfall
Anticipation
Waltzing Fairy

The Flame. Unpublished manuscript.

The Froggie and the Rabbit. Unpublished manuscript.

The Gnat and the Bee. In *Pieces We Like to Play*. New York: Carl Fischer, 1936.

The Goblin and the Mosquito (1951). Chicago: Clayton F. Summy, 1951.

Golden Corn Tassles. Unpublished manuscript.

Here and There (1947). Chicago: McKinley, 1947.

Hiking. Chicago: McKinley, n.d.

In the Land o' Cotton (1926). Unpublished manuscript.

Joy in June. Unpublished manuscript.

Lake Mirror. Unpublished manuscript.

Levee Dance (1937). Bryn Mawr, PA: Theodore Presser, 1937.

Little Pieces on Black Keys. Unpublished manuscript.

Little Pieces on White Keys. Unpublished manuscript.

A Lovely Winter Day. 1949. Unpublished manuscript.

March of the Beetles (1947). Chicago: McKinley, 1947.

Mellow Twilight: Tone poem. Chicago: McKinley, 1929. Also arranged for violin and piano.

Memories of Dixieland (1927). Unpublished manuscript.

Memory Mist. Unpublished manuscript.

The Moo-cow, Fido, and Kitty (1949). Unpublished manuscript.

Moon Behind a Cloud. Unpublished manuscript.

Nodding Poppies. Unpublished manuscript. Note: originally titled *A Field of Waving Grain.*

The Old Boatman. 1951. Chicago: Clayton F. Summy, 1951.

On Higher Ground. Unpublished manuscript.

On Parade. Chicago: McKinley, n.d.

On the Playground. Unpublished manuscript.

On Top of a Tree. Unpublished manuscript.

Pensive Mood. Unpublished manuscript.

A Photograph. New York: Carl Fischer, n.d.

Placid Lake. Unpublished manuscript.

Rock-a-Bye (1947). Chicago: McKinley, 1947.

Rocking Chair (1939). Unpublished manuscript.

The Rose. In *Pieces We Like to Play*. New York: Carl Fischer, 1936.

A Sachem's Pipe. In *Pieces We Like to Play*. New York: Carl Fischer, 1935.

The Sea Swallow (1951). Chicago: Clayton F. Summy, 1951.

Sonata in E Minor (1932). New York: G. Schirmer, 1997.

Strong Men, Forward! Unpublished manuscript.

Swaying Buttercups. Chicago: McKinley, n.d.

The Swing. Chicago: McKinley, n.d.

Tecumseh. In *Pieces We Like to Play*. New York: Carl Fischer, 1935.

Three Little Negro Dances. Bryn Mawr, PA: Theodore Presser, 1949.
Hoe Cake
Rabbit Foot
Ticklin' Tom (Note: published separately, 1933.)

Three Miniature Portraits of Uncle Joe, Written to Depict Various Stages of His Life at 17, 25, and 70 (ca. 1947). Unpublished manuscript.

Three Sketches for Little Pianists. 1937. Bryn Mawr, PA: Theodore Presser, 1937.
Bright Eyes
Cabin Song
A Morning Sunbeam

To a Little Girl. Unpublished manuscript.

Tree Boughs. Chicago: McKinley, n.d.

Two Fantasies on Folk Tunes. Unpublished manuscript.

Undecided. Unpublished manuscript.

Up and Down the Stairs (or Ladder). Unpublished manuscript.

A Wee Bit of Erin. Unpublished manuscript.

Who Will Dance with Me? Chicago: McKinley, n.d.

Winter Must Come. Unpublished manuscript.

Zephyr: Mexican Folk Song (1928). Chicago: McKinley, 1928.

Small Instrumental Ensembles

Five [Negro] Folksongs in Counterpoint (string quartet). Unpublished manuscript.
Calvary
Clementine
Drink to Me Only with Thine Eyes
Shortnin' Bread
Swing Low, Sweet Chariot

[Negro] Folksongs (string quartet). Unpublished manuscript.
Go Down, Moses
Lil' David Play on Your Harp
Somebodys Knockin' at Yo' Door
Joshua Fit de Battle of Jericho

Spring Journey (piano, two violins, two cellos, bass). Unpublished manuscript.

Suite for Brasses and Piano. Unpublished manuscript.

Two Moods (1953) (clarinet, violin, piano). Unpublished manuscript.

Quintet in E minor (1936) (piano and strings). Unpublished manuscript.

Soloists with Orchestra (chamber or full)

Concerto for Violin no. 2 in D minor (1952). Unpublished manuscript.

Concerto in One Movement (piano and orchestra) (1933). Unpublished manuscript.

Concerto no. 1 (violin and orchestra) (1952). Unpublished manuscript.

Rhapsody (piano and orchestra). Unpublished manuscript.

Full Orchestra

Chicago Suite. Unpublished manuscript.

Colonial Dance Symphony. Unpublished manuscript.

Concert Overture, no. 1. Unpublished manuscript.

Concert Overture, no. 2. Unpublished manuscript.

Ethiopia's Shadow in America (1932). Unpublished manuscript.

Mississippi River: The River and the Songs of Those Dwelling upon Its Banks (1934). Unpublished manuscript.

The Oak (tone poem). Unpublished manuscript.

Suite of Negro Dances. Unpublished manuscript.

Symphony in D Minor. Unpublished manuscript.

Symphony no. 1 in E Minor (1931–1932). Unpublished manuscript.

Symphony no. 2 in G Minor. Unpublished manuscript.

Symphony no. 3 in C Minor (1940). Unpublished manuscript.

Bibliography

Brown, Rae Linda. *The Life and Work of Florence B. Price*. Urbana, Ill.: University of Illinois Press, forthcoming.

_____. "Price, Florence Beatrice." In *International Dictionary of Black Composers*, ed. Samuel A. Floyd, Jr. Chicago: Fitzroy Dearborn, 1999.

_____. "William Grant Still, Florence Price, and William Dawson: Echoes of the Harlem Renaissance." In *Black Music in the Renaissance: A Collection of Essays* edited by Samuel A. Floyd, Jr., 1-86. Westport, Conn.: Greenwood Press, 1990.

_____. "The Women's Symphony Orchestra of Chicago and Florence B. Price's Piano Concerto in One Movement." *American Music* 11, no. 2 (June 1993): 185-205.

Holzer, Linda Ruth. "Selected Solo Piano Music of Florence B. Price (1887–1953)." D.M.A. thesis, Florida State University, 1995.

Hull, Gloria T. *Color, Sex, and Poetry*. Bloomington, Ind.: Indiana University Press, 1987.

Jackson, Barbara Garvey. "Florence Price, Composer." *Black Perspective in Music* 5, no. I (spring 1977): 30-43.

Locke, Alain. *The Negro and His Music*. Washington, D. C.: Associates in Negro Folk Education, 1936. Reprint, New York: Arno Press and the New York Times, 1969.

Price, Florence B. Letter to Frederick L. Schwass (Allen Park, Michigan), October 22, 1940. Price Materials, University of Arkansas.

Sawyer, Lisa Let. "Unpublished Songs of Florence B. Price." D.M.A. thesis, Conservatory of Music, University of Missouri, 1990.

Discography

Concerto in One Movement (piano and orchestra). Chromattica.

Cotton Dance, piano. Cambria CD-1097.

Dances in the Canebrakes, piano. Cambria CD-1097.

Fantasie nègre, piano. Leonarda CD-LE339.

My Dream, voice. Koch International Classics 3-247-2 H I.

Night, voice. Cambria CD-1037; Gasparo GSCD-287; Koch International Classics 3-247-2 HI; University of Michigan Records SM 00 15.

The Old Boatman, piano. Cambria CD-1097.

Sonata in E Minor, piano. Cambria CD-1097.

Song to the Dark Virgin (low voice). Cambria CD-1037; Gasparo GSCD-287; Koch International Classics 3-247-2 H1.

Suite no. 1, organ. Gambetta GAM CD.

Three Little Negro Dances, piano. *Hoe Cake, Rabbit Foot, Ticklin' Tom*. WCAL LP-592.

Ticklin' Tom. WCAL LP-592.

To My Little Son. Cambria CD-1037.

Travel's End. Cambria CD-1037.

The Heart of a Woman

Georgia Douglas Johnson

Florence B. Price
Rae Linda Brown, editor

Allegretto
mp
The heart of a wo-man goes forth with the dawn,
mp

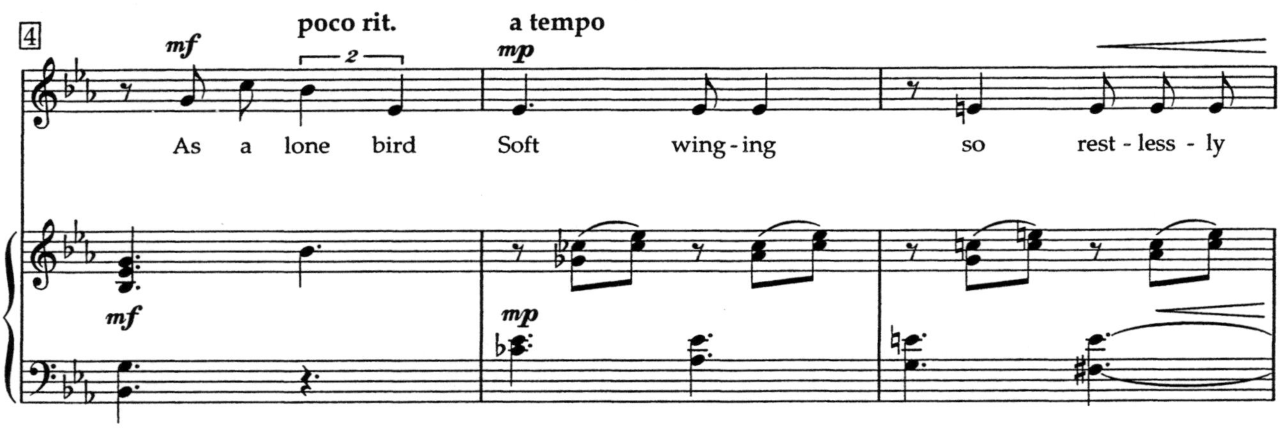
4
mf
poco rit.
2
a tempo
mp
As a lone bird Soft wing-ing so rest-less-ly
mf
mp

7
mf
on A - far on life's tur - rets and vales does it
mf

9
f
roam
In the
wake
of those e-choes the
heart
calls home.
[7]

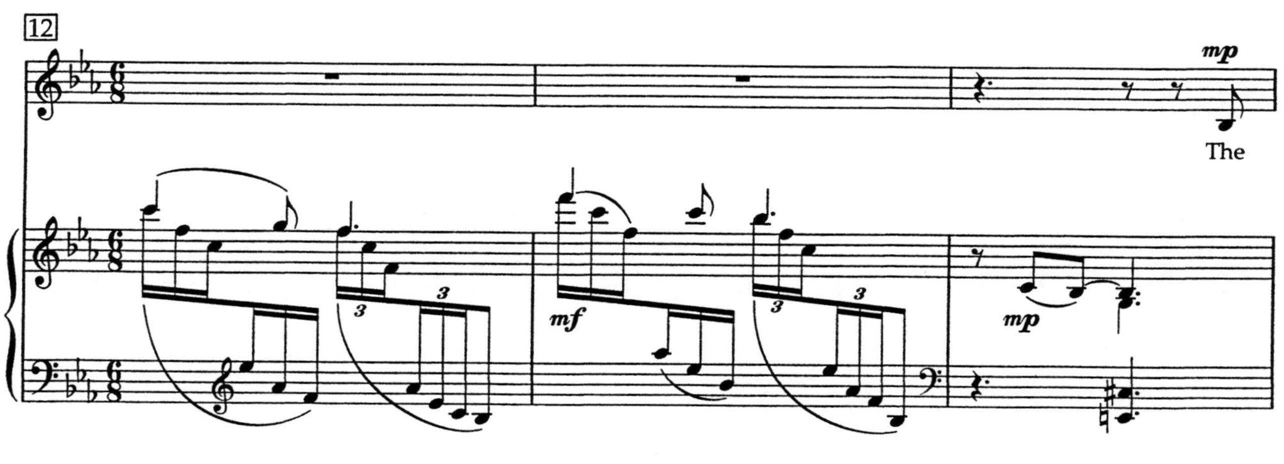
12
mp
The
mf
mp

15
poco rit.
heart of a wo-man falls
back with the night
And en-ters some

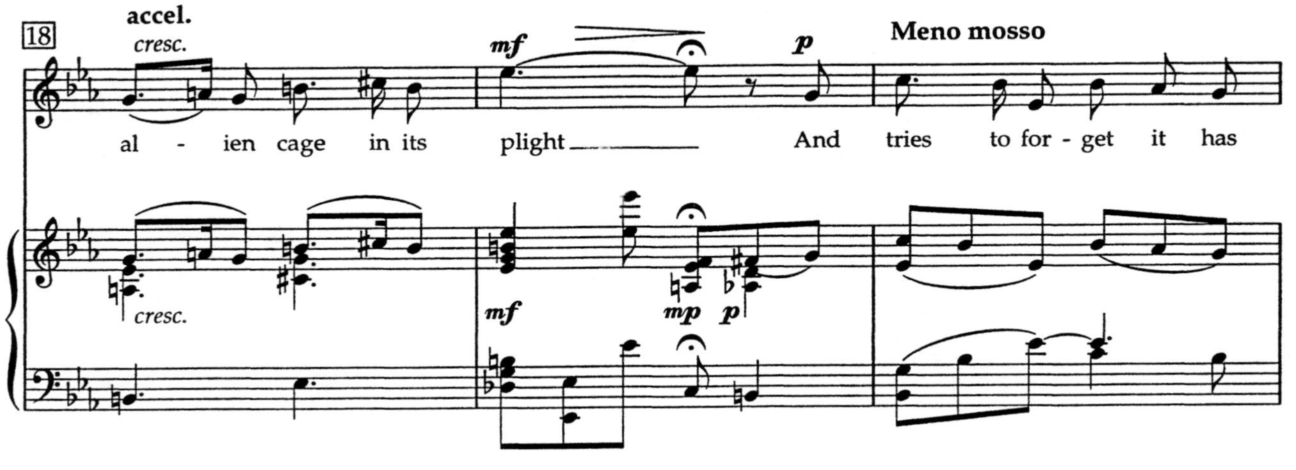
18
accel.
cresc.
mf
p
Meno mosso
al - ien cage in its plight
And tries to for - get it has
cresc.
mf
mp
p

21
A tempo
cresc.
dream'd of the stars
While it breaks,
breaks,
breaks,
cresc.

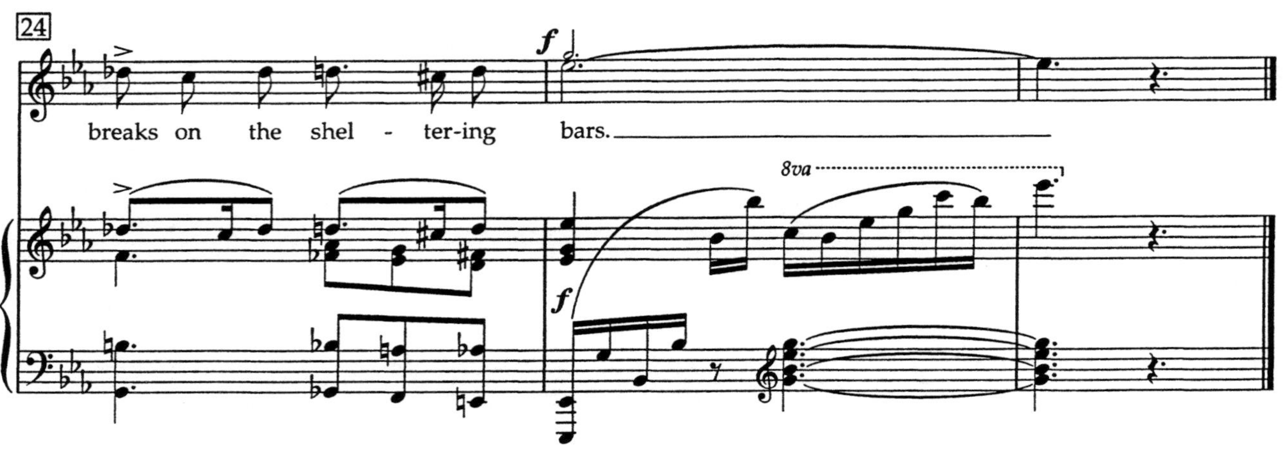
24
f
breaks on the shel - ter-ing bars.
8va
f

The Glory of the Day Was in Her Face

James Weldon Johnson

Florence B. Price
Rae Linda Brown, editor

7
poco rit.
a tempo
poco rit.
o - ver all her love - li - ness the grace Of
9
a tempo
poco rit.
a tempo
morn - ing blush - ing in the ear - ly skies.
p
11
mf
And in her voice the call - ing of the
mf
14
f
dove Like mu - sic of a
mf
f
mf

17
mp
sweet melo-di-ous part And
8va
21
in her smile the break-ing light of love; And
mp
23
all the gen-tle vir-tues in her heart; And
25
rit.
p
now the glo-ri-ous day the beau-te-ous night The
mf
p

27
Poco meno mosso
[Tempo primo]
cresc. molto
birds that sig - nal to their mates at dawn to my dull
p
cresc. molto
29
f
poco rit.
a tempo
mf
ears to my tear blind - ed sight Are
f
mf
31
rit.
a tempo
mp
one with all the dead since she is gone.
mf
mp
33
Meno mosso
rit.
Since she is gone!
p

Nadia Boulanger

(1887–1979)

ROGER O. DOYLE

(Juliette) Nadia Boulanger (hereafter referred to as Boulanger) was a composer, performer, conductor, and teacher of international reputation. With her direct influence on contemporary composers such as Aaron Copland (1900–1990), David Diamond (b. 1915), Elliot Carter (b. 1908), George Antheil (1900–1959), Gian Carlo Menotti (b. 1911), Thea Musgrave (b. 1928), Louise Talma (1906–1998), Virgil Thomson (1896–1989), and Ned Rorem (b. 1923), Boulanger was one of the most important musicians of the twentieth century. Through her prodigious study of music old and new, she was able to bring a remarkably analytical imagination to bear in her own compositions and to her teaching of others.

Boulanger was born in Paris on September 16, 1887, with a music heritage. Her paternal grandfather, Frederic, was a cellist in the court orchestra and his wife, Marie Julie, was a widely celebrated singer in the Opéra Comique. Ernest, Boulanger's father, entered the Paris Conservatoire at age sixteen where he studied piano, violin, and composition. Three years later (1835), foretelling the success of his daughters, Ernest won the coveted Prix de Rome for a one-act opera titled *Le Diable à l'École* (The Devil at School), to a libretto by Eugene Scribe. Ernest was performing in Russia in 1874 when he met a young Russian schoolteacher, Raissa Suvalov (née Myschetsky). Although she was already married, within two years Raissa immigrated to Paris to attend Ernest's singing class at the Conservatoire, and in 1877, at age twenty, married her sixty-two year old teacher. Ten years later, Juliette Nadia Boulanger was born.

Boulanger was not attracted to music as an infant. She was known to scream in response to the slightest sound of music and her father needed to put up heavy curtains while teaching students so as not to disturb the child.[1] The change came suddenly when, as a toddler, she attempted to recreate the sound of a passing fire brigade at the piano. "From that day on, it was music all day long! They couldn't make me leave the piano," she later recalled.[2]

Raissa Boulanger's personal and lifelong responsibility for the education of both her children was thorough and unrelenting. Reading and study at the parlor table were a part of the daily routine; even carriage rides presented opportunities for the mother to drill her daughter in grammar and spelling. The young girl's work was only rarely complimented and any sign of success was likely to be met with the mother's admonition against self-satisfaction.[3] By her sixth birthday, Boulanger was studying music when a second child, Lili (see this volume), was born. Ernest asked the older sister to pledge life-long care for the newborn girl.

In December 1896, just a few months short of her tenth birthday, Boulanger entered the Conservatoire. So insistent was Raissa in overseeing her daughter's education that she attended daily Conservatoire classes with the young student. As was the norm, Boulanger was first enrolled in solfège class, finishing in third place in the end-of-year competition. Her affinity for the keyboard had earlier been established by her private study with the blind organist Louis Vierne (1870–1937). She continued to matriculate at the Conservatoire, taking instruction in accompaniment with Paul Vidal (1863–1931) and composition with Charles Marie Widor (1844–1937) and Gabriel Fauré (1845–1924).

Despite being the youngest student in her classes, Boulanger excelled and became the first female to attract wide notice among the Conservatoire faculty. She had memorized the *Well-Tempered Clavier* by the age of twelve. In 1904, her last year at the Conservatoire, Boulanger took First Prizes in harmony, counterpoint, organ, fugue, and piano accompaniment.

Following her father's death in 1900, Boulanger became the sole financial and personal caretaker for her mother and her sickly sister until their deaths (Lili at age twenty-four in March, 1918 and Raissa at age seventy-seven in March 1935). The need for money in the household required that she begin accepting engagements as a keyboard soloist and/or accompanist. More importantly, she began teaching private students in the family's new residence on rue Ballu. For the next seventy-five years, amid furnishings belonging to her Russian grandmother, Boulanger welcomed students to this apartment. She would continue teaching there until her death.

In 1906, Boulanger was accepted as the assistant to Fauré at the great organ in the Madeleine Church. She became an ardent advocate of his music, particularly the *Requiem*, which she later premiered with several professional orchestras in the United States and Great

Britain. In that same year she won her greatest prize, the Deuxième Grand Prix de Rome.

While continuing to perform widely, Boulanger began an extended and somewhat fruitful association with the celebrated pianist/composer Raoul Pugno (1852–1914). Their most successful project was an opera titled *La Ville morte* (The Dead City) to a libretto by novelist Gabriele D'Annunzio.

Boulanger, who as a young girl had accepted her father's charge to see to the care of her younger sister Lili, showed both the ambivalence of a sibling rival and the pride of a parent when in 1913 Lili Boulanger became the first female to capture the coveted first prize in the Prix de Rome competition. Although Lili's success threatened to overwhelm her sister's considerable musical reputation, Boulanger's growing fame as a teacher provided a certain security that may have assuaged, to some degree, the negative comparisons which were made about the accomplishments of the two sisters.

Attendant to her ever-increasing reputation as a teacher of uncommon techniques, and unable to attain a guaranteed stipend allowing her time for creating new music, Boulanger found less opportunity for composition. By 1918, more than ten years after her only creative triumph, she was firmly established as a teacher and repeatedly gave voice to the strong conviction that her sister Lili was the premier composer in the family. But, in that same year, on March 15th, Lili succumbed to the Crohn's disease that had plagued her from infancy.

Although Boulanger was disappointed at not winning an appointment to the faculty at the Conservatoire, she received a most fortuitous teaching appointment in 1921 when she was invited to join the first faculty of the Conservatoire Américain at Fontainebleau. This summer school was a project largely financed by wealthy American donors anxious to contribute to the economic and social recovery of France from the devastation of the World War I. Boulanger taught harmony, counterpoint, and composition under the directorship of composer Paul Dukas (1865–1935). In that first summer she first met the twenty-year-old Aaron Copland.

Following Copland's lead, and for the next half-century, musicians from around the world, particularly from the United States, flocked to the Paris studio of this extraordinary teacher. Indeed, it may be argued that no other person, male or female, has exceeded Boulanger's impact on composers of the twentieth century. Ned Rorem has described her as "the most influential teacher since Socrates."[4] The weekly Wednesday tea and discussion of musical analysis at her apartment was an invitation sought by all musicians passing through Paris. The guest/student list reads like a biographical dictionary of twentieth-century concert music and includes: Antheil, Auric, Berkeley, Bernstein, Blitzstein, Carpenter, Carter, Casals, Chanler, Copland, Craft, Damrosch, Debussy, Dubois, Dukas, Dupré, Durand, Enesco, Estrella, Fauré, Franck, Harris, Honegger, d'Indy, Kabalevsky, Kirkpatrick, Kodaly, Koussevitsky, Kraus, Landowska, Lipatti, Lutosławski, Manziarly, Markevitch, Mengelberg, Menuhin, Messiaen, Milhaud, Monteux, Musgrave, Paderewski, Penderecki, Poulenc, Rachmaninoff, Ravel, Roussel, Rubenstein, Saint-Saëns, Satie, Skrowaczewski, Souzay, Stravinsky, Szering, Talma, Thomas, Thomson, Varèse, Vaughan Williams, Vierne, Widor, Wieniawski, and Ysaÿe.

In 1920 Boulanger accepted an appointment at the new École Normale de Musique directed by Paul Dukas. Upon his death in 1935 Boulanger was named professor of composition at the school, an appointment perhaps diminished by the announcement that her friend, Igor Stravinsky (1882–1971), would assist her. Her association with the École Normale de Musique ended shortly before she left France in 1939 for an extended stay in the United States. She continued to teach summer sessions at Fontainebleau and was named Director there in 1950, a position she retained until her death. In 1946, Boulanger was named to the faculty of the Conservatoire as professor of piano accompaniment; ironically she never attained a position there as professor of composition.

Following her first (and successful) United States tour in 1924 primarily as soloist in Aaron Copland's *Organ Symphony*, Boulanger came often to the United States as a teacher, lecturer, soloist, and conductor. At the end of her first visit she was offered, but declined a permanent professorship at the Curtis Institute of Music in Philadelphia. She became the first woman to conduct a major American orchestra when in 1938 she made her conducting debuts with the Boston Symphony Orchestra and the New York Philharmonic Orchestra. During World War II, she lived in the United States and lectured widely while fulfilling a three-year contract at the Longy School in Cambridge, Massachusetts. She was also a guest lecturer at Radcliffe College, Wellesley College, Harvard University, Yale University, Dartmouth College, Princeton University, Mills College, State University of New York at Potsdam, Oberlin College, and The Juilliard School (of Music).

Eagerly welcomed in Great Britain, Boulanger frequently conducted the London Philharmonic, the Halle Orchestra, and orchestras in Leeds and Bath. Her lectures, over a wide range of music topics, were heard in London at the Menuhin School, the Royal College of Music and the Royal Academy of Music, and were broadcast nationally on the BBC. She also served as a jurist of international piano competitions including, in 1966, the Tchaikowsky Competition in Moscow.

Boulanger was the recipient of many honorary degrees and was decorated by many societies and nations. In addition to the coveted Legion d'honneur, she seemed most pleased with the celebrations and honors bestowed on her by the citizens and Prince Rainier of Monaco.

Over the span of her lengthy career, Boulanger acquired hundreds of intensely devoted students, colleagues, and admirers. Stories of her keen insights and analytical powers are often coupled with anecdotes describing her intimidating, even insulting, manner. "She could be terribly withering in her critique of your work," one student recalls; "one rarely escaped the day unscathed."[5] Yet, her dedication to music and to teaching continued undiminished. Save for the physical frailties that limited her in old age, Boulanger remained an active teacher until she died in Paris on October 22, 1979, in her ninety-second year.

As a young woman, Boulanger was determined to make her name as a composer. She produced some two dozen works before she redirected her talent to conducting, performing, teaching, and lecturing. Despite wide interest in her compositions, by the early 1930s she announced that she had no interest in their performance.

Boulanger's considerable skill and significant potential as a composer are evident in the songs she wrote as a young woman and her penchant for evocative word setting is apparent. The song included here, *Élégie*, set to a poem by Albert Samain, was given its premier at the prestigious Salle Pleyel in March 1907, with the composer at the piano.

Élégie, like many of Boulanger's songs, follows the familiar *mélodie* style well-established by Hector Berlioz (1803–1869), Charles Gounod (1818–1893), Camille Saint-Saëns 1835–1921) and others in the French lineage leading to her own mentor Fauré. (Fauré has been called one of the "great masters of French song.")[6] The composition of songs was also Boulanger's primary genre, not surprising because of the greater likelihood of the works being publicly performed.

In a style not unlike that of many Fauré songs, Boulanger's *Élégie* shows her subtle yet delightful acquaintance with the nuances of the French language. She tends also to insert brief rhythmic complexities that establish a verse rhythm diverse from the accompaniment. The orderly structure of the song—two poetic stanzas equally divided into four parts by contrasting rhythmic, textural, and harmonic language— refers to a rather more simple structure than one finds in the songs of Fauré. The song's structure, its harmonic language, and the ambience created around the surrealistic poem, though not unusual for that time, indicates that Boulanger would have blossomed into a first-rate composer.

Acknowledgments

Special thanks to Glendower Jones of Classical Vocal Reprints for permission to use *Élégie* from *Nadia Boulanger: 10 Mélodies, Lieder, Songs* (CVR 2624), and to Professor Trudie M. Booth of the University of Portland (Ore.) for translating the poem.

Notes

1. Bruno Monsaingeon, *Mademoiselle, Conversations with Nadia Boulanger* (Manchester: Carcanet Press Limited, 1985), 20.

2. Ibid.

3. Leonie Rosenstiel, *Nadia Boulanger: A Life in Music* (New York: W. W. Norton and Company, 1982).

4. Ned Rorem, "Boulanger as a Teacher," in *Setting the Tone: Essays and a Diary.* (New York: Coward-McCann, Inc., 1983), 138.

5. Roger O. Doyle, "The Chronicles of Nadia," *Portland Magazine* (Portland, Ore.: University of Portland) 16, no.1 (1997) 24-25.

6. David Cox, *A History of Song*, ed. Denis Stevens (New York: W. W. Norton and Company, 1960), 208.

List of Works

Solo and Part Songs

Versailles (1906). Text by Albert Samain. Unpublished.

Soleils couchants (1906). Text by Paul Verlaine. Unpublished.

Les Heures claires (1908) with Raoul Pugno. Set of songs with texts by Emile Verhaeren. Unpublished.

Lux Eterna (ca. 1907). Text from Roman liturgy. Unpublished.

Chanson (1909). Text by Georges Delaquys. Unpublished.

Mélancolie (1909). Text by Heinrich Heine. Unpublished.

La Mer (1909). Text by Paul Verlaine. Unpublished.

Ne jure pas! (1909). Text by Heinrich Heine. Unpublished.

Prière (1910). Text by Henry Bataille. Unpublished.

Pour toi (1910). Text by Heinrich Heine. Unpublished.

Les Heures ternes. (1910). Set of songs with texts by Maurice Maeterlinck. Unpublished.

Le Beau navire (1910). Text by Georges Delaquys. Unpublished.

Nadia Boulanger: 10 Mélodies, Lieder, Songs. New York: Classical Vocal Reprints, 1995.

1. *Au bord de la route* (ca. 1910). Text by Camille Mauclair
2. *Cantique* (1910). Text by Maurice Maeterlinck
3. *Chanson, "Elle a vendu mon coeur"* (ca. 1911). Text by Camille Mauclair
4. *Doute* (ca. 1910). Text by Camille Mauclair
5. *Élégie* (1906). Text by Albert Samain
6. *J'ai frappé* (ca. 1912). Text by Jean-François Bourguignon
7. *L'Echange* (ca. 1912). Text by Camille Mauclair
8. *Le Couteau* (ca. 1912). Text by Camille Mauclair
9. *Soir d'Hiver,* (1915). Text by Nadia Boulanger
10. *Was will die einsame Thräne, "Larme solitaire"* (1909). Text by Heinrich Heine

Operas, Cantatas, and Dramatic Works

Dnégouchka (1913) a revision of *Roussalka*. Text by Georges Delaquys. Unpublished.

La Rédemption de Colin Muset (ca. 1913) with Raoul Pugno. Text by Maurice Leon and Henri Cain. Lost.

La Ville morte, (1913) with Raoul Pugno. Text by Gabriele D'Annuzio. Unpublished.

Roussalka (1908). Text by Georges Delaquys. Unpublished.

La Sirène (1908). Text author unknown. Unpublished.

Organ Works

Airs populaires flamands (1915). Unpublished.

Piano Works

Fantaisie pour Piano et Orchestre (1912). Solo piano with orchestra. Unpublished.

Rhapsodie variée (1912). Solo piano with orchestra. Unpublished.

Vers la vie nouvelle (1917). Solo piano. Unpublished.

Bibliography

Cox, David. *A History of Song*. Ed. Denis Stevens. New York: W. W. Norton and Company, 1960.

Doyle, Roger O. "The Chronicles of Nadia," *Portland Magazine*. Portland, Ore.: University of Portland, 16 (1997).

Monsaingeon, Bruno. *Mademoiselle, Conversations with Nadia Boulanger*. Translated by Robyn Marsack. Manchester: Carcanet Press Limited, 1985.

Rorem, Ned. "Boulanger as a Teacher," in *Setting the Tone: Essays and a Diary*. New York: Coward-McCann, Inc., 1983.

Rosenstiel, Leonie. *Nadia Boulanger: A Life in Music*. New York: W. W. Norton and Company, 1982.

Élégie

Une douceur splendide et sombre
Flotte sous le ciel étoilé
On dirait que là haut dans l'ombre
Un paradis s'est écroulé
Et c'est comme l'odeur ardente
L'odeur fièvreuse dans l'air noir
D'une chevelure d'amante
Dénouée à travers le soir.

Tout l'espace languit de fièvres
Du fond des coeurs mystérieux
S'en viennent mourir sur les lèvres
Des mots qui font fermer les yeux
Et de ma bouche où s'évapore le parfum
  des bonheurs derniers
Et de mon coeur vibrant encore
S'élèvent de vagues pitiés
Pour tous ceux là, qui, sur la terre
Par un tel soir tendant les bras
N'ont point dans leur coeur solitaire
Un nom à sangloter tout bas.

A splendid and somber sweetness
Floats under the starry sky
It seems that up there in the darkness
A paradise collapsed
And it is like the ardent fragrance,
The feverish odor in the black air
Of a lover's hair
Loosened during the night.

The entire space is languishing feverishly
From the bottom of mysterious hearts
Words that make the eyes close
Are fading away on the lips
And from my mouth where the scent
  of the last happiness is evaporating
And from my still vibrating heart
Rises a vague feeling of pity
For all those on earth who,
On such a night are reaching out
Without having in their lonely hearts
A name to sob about softly.

Translated by Professor Trudie M. Booth

Élegie

Albert Samain

Nadia Boulanger
Roger Doyle, editor

♩ = 60
rit.
a tempo
mystérieux
U-ne dou-ceur
pp
en dehors, mais ***p***

6
splen-dide et som - bre Flot - te sous le ciel é-toi-lé

11
sans hâte
On di-rait que là - haut dans l'om - bre Un pa-ra-dis

16
♩ = 76
s'est é - crou - lé
en dehors
Et c'est - com - me l'o -
21
animez
mf cresc.
deur ar-den - te L'o-deur fiè - vreu - se dans l'air noir D'u-ne che-ve-lu -
mf
26
animez encore
accel.
re d'a-man - te Dé-nou-ée à tra - vers le soir.
ff
31
rit.
Plus lent (♩ = 60)
Tout l'es - pa - ce lang-uit de fiè - vres Du

34
fond des coeurs mys-té-ri - eux
S'en vien-nent mou-rir sur les
37
rit.
a tempo
lè - vres
Des mots qui font fer-mer les yeux
40
Contenu (♩ = 76)
en animant
cresc.
Et de ma bouche où s'é-va - po - re le par -
mf animez
cresc.
43
ff
rit. molto (♩ = 60)
fum des bon-heurs der - niers
Et de mon coeur vi-brant en - co - re S'é -
ff

47
Très large
a l'aise
intense
lè - vent de va-gues pi - tiés Pour tous ceux - là, qui, sur la ter - re Par un tel
suivez
51
animez
rit.
a tempo
soir ten-dant les bras N'ont point dans leur coeur so - li tai - re Un
suivez
55
nom à sang-lo - ter tout bas
pp expressif
60
sans rit.

Ethel Glenn Hier

(1889–1971)

KARIN PENDLE

Ethel Glenn Hier was born in Madisonville, Ohio, a suburb of some 2,200 people located east of Cincinnati, in 1889.[1] Her father, a homeopathic physician, also served for a time as mayor. Ethel, the oldest of his three surviving children, graduated from Madisonville High School, then entered Ohio Wesleyan University. At the end of her freshman year she transferred to the Cincinnati Conservatory of Music, where she received a diploma in piano in 1908. Soon thereafter she opened a piano studio in the Madisonville building that housed her father's medical practice. The studio flourished but Hier craved a career with more challenges. How or when she discovered her talent for writing music is unknown, although it may have arisen as she found it necessary to write teaching pieces to help her students master particular techniques. In 1911 she returned to the conservatory, continuing her piano study and attending the composition classes of a new member of the faculty, Edgar Stillman Kelley (1857–1944), at that time a major figure on the American musical scene. Hier spent the summer of 1912 in Germany, studying with Hugo Kaun, then returned to continue her work with Kelley.

By 1912 Hier began publishing her works with the local firm of Willis Music—mostly teaching pieces for piano that bore fanciful titles: *The Fairies' Good-Morning*, *Night Song of the Pine Trees*, and *Dragonflies*. A curious feature of these pieces is that their composer is listed as E. Glenn Hier. Perhaps the publisher believed more sales would result if buyers thought the composer was male but some evidence suggests that Hier herself wanted to disguise her sex. By 1919, when her association with Willis was about to end, the firm brought out the song *Dreamin' Town*, the best of her compositions to date, under her full name, Ethel Glenn Hier.

Although study with Kelley was very beneficial, Hier realized that greater professional opportunities awaited her in New York. In 1917 she enrolled at the Institute of Musical Art (later, The Juilliard School of Music), where she studied theory and composition with Percy Goetschius while also working privately with Ernest Bloch. When Carl Friedberg joined the faculty in 1923 she resumed her piano study.[2] By this time she had opened piano studios in New York and in the New Jersey communities of Roselle and Roselle Park, and had begun to achieve success as a composer.

In 1918 Hier spent the first of many summers at the MacDowell Colony in Peterborough, New Hampshire. An important benefit of these residencies lay in the opportunity to meet not only other composers but poets, novelists, and visual artists as well. Composers Amy Beach (see this volume and vol. 6), Mabel Wheeler Daniels, Ruth Crawford, Helen Sears, and Mary Howe (see vol. 6) became her friends and associates, and poets Sara Teasdale and Leonora Speyer provided poems that Hier set to music. Two works inspired by Hier's experiences at the Colony are *A Day in the Peterborough Woods* (1924), a piano cycle; and *Boyhood and Youth of Edward MacDowell* (1926), a play with music that was widely performed by Junior MacDowell Clubs across the country.

By 1921 Hier's skill as a composer began to attract national attention; for example, a *Musical Courier* review of her *Theme and Variations* for piano, a serious and difficult work, opened with the words: "'Hats off, gentlemen, [a genius],' said Robert Schumann on discovering Chopin; so we say on discovering Ethel Glenn Hier. . ."[3] The reviewer went on to praise the work's "depth and sentiment," its bold theme, and the variety of treatments it received. The Cincinnati Conservatory awarded her an honorary Bachelor of Music degree in 1922. In 1925 she was invited to take part in a Festival of American Women Composers in Washington, DC, and in 1926 she became a founding member of the Society of American Women Composers, a group that included such prominent names as Amy Beach, Gena Branscombe, Mabel Wheeler Daniels, Marion Bauer (see this volume), and Mary Howe.

In the 1920s Hier had begun to explore the medium of chamber music, including pieces that combined instruments and voices, such as *Down in the Glen* and *If You Must Go, Go Quickly*. In the '30s she moved into the orchestral field, for which she was trained but not yet practiced.[4] *Choréographe*, an imaginative ballet, was premiered in 1930, and her best-known orchestral work, *Asolo Bells*, was finished by the mid-thirties.[5]

The 1930s also saw Hier beginning another phase of her career, that of lecture-recitalist. In 1933 she spent the summer in Austria, studying at the Austro-American Conservatory in Mondsee and learning more about modern musical techniques from Egon Wellesz

(1885–1974) and Alban Berg (1885–1935) in Vienna. In the summer of 1934 she went to Italy to work with Gian Francesco Malipiero (1824–1887). Thereafter, Hier spoke regularly on "Trends in Modern Music," illustrating her lectures by playing examples on the piano. Her repertoire of lecture–recitals grew to include "Music from the Middle Ages to Monteverdi," "Debussy, MacDowell, and the MacDowell Colony Composers," "Music in America," and "Women in Music," presented before college and university groups, music teachers' associations, and music clubs.

Another important development in the 1930s was Hier's association with Composers Press. Founded by Charles Haubiel for the purpose of publishing music of living Americans, Composers Press also sponsored regular concerts of works in its catalogue and offered annual prizes for the best works submitted in particular categories. Hier's works were frequently performed at Haubiel's concerts, and in 1953 her *Three Orchestral Pieces* (including *Asolo Bells*) won a Composers Press publication award.

By 1939 Ethel Glenn Hier, now fifty years old, was sufficiently well known that Marion Bauer could include her in her history of music, *How Music Grew*, in a list of America's best women composers of songs.[6] About this time another new medium, choral music, attracted Hier's attention. Most noteworthy is the cycle *Mountain Preacher* (1940) for baritone solo, chorus, and orchestra, using poems by James Still.

In 1948, assisted by a few other New York music teachers and composers, Hier founded Composers Concerts, a series designed to promote both the music of American composers and the talents of American students. Students of the member–teachers performed new works by member-composers on the series, and the concerts were often broadcast as part of radio station WNYC's continuing series of American Music Festivals. Composers Concerts continued until at least 1955 and received enough national attention to inspire similar projects in other cities.

Although a conservative composer, Hier was neither old-fashioned nor out of step with major trends in American music. Much of her harmonic vocabulary recalled impressionism and the works of such modern eclectics as her teachers Bloch and Malipiero. Streams of parallel chords, delicate shades of instrumental color, and an overall lyricism pervade her music. Although she did explore bitonality in her *Swiss Music Box* for piano, she was most comfortable with the kind of expanded tonality characteristic of most serious American music of her time.

The range of Hier's work was large, from the simplest of teaching pieces to songs and piano works requiring performers of professional caliber. She took little interest in absolute music, preferring instead to write pieces with text or works that had semi-programmatic, picturesque titles. Like many American composers of the first half of the twentieth century, Hier at times incorporated specifically national idioms in her music: the minstrel-show style in *Dreamin' Town*, jazz in *Badinage* (also called *Study in Blue*), and hymn tunes in *Then Shall I Know*. If she avoided the most avant-garde techniques it was not because she was unaware of them but because she chose deliberately to chart her own course.

By 1946 Hier had acquired a home near Lakeside, Connecticut where she spent many summers. At the end of 1953 she closed her New York studio and moved with her sister Florence to Lakeside. She still visited New York frequently and published more than a dozen works in manuscript facsimile through Composers Facsimile Editions. Sometime in the late 1960s Hier and her sister moved to Winter Park, Florida. Hier's health began to fail during 1970 and she died in Florida on January 14, 1971.

Ethel Glenn Hier chose poetry for her songs that was written by some of the finest poets of her day: Elinor Wylie, Nancy Byrd Turner, James Still, Sara Teasdale, Leonora Speyer, Louis Untermeyer, and Paul Laurence Dunbar. Though lesser known, Katharine Adams and Eloise Robinson also created verses of quality, integrity, and musical appeal.

The poems of Paul Laurence Dunbar (1872–1906) are among the most significant monuments of African-American literature. Born in Dayton, Ohio, the son of former slaves, Dunbar discovered early in life that even an educated black man could hope to find no better than menial jobs in his hometown. He began to write poetry, however, and published two collections in Dayton before leaving to explore further options on the East coast. *Lyrics of Sunshine and Shadow* (1905), his last collection of verse, contains the dialect poem "Dreamin' Town" that Hier chose to set in a minstrel-show style. Indeed, Dunbar himself was involved in minstrel shows and musical revues, and he often used a folk dialect as a mask to disguise his true feelings as a black man in white America.[7] In this poem, for example, the good life is only a dream, with a somewhat ironic, expressive climax when the speaker imagines a place where "our hands an' our hea'ts are free." The musical "call-and-response" technique, thought to have originated in Africa is basic to the poem's structure.

The pervasive dotted rhythms of Hier's *Dreamin' Town*, which could be "jazzed" into triplets in performance, suggest the composer's awareness of the minstrel-show tradition. Though many such shows were strongly racist, presenting all the negative stereotypes of American blacks, Hier's choice of a dialect text by a respected African-American poet suggests that at least on an artistic level she did not share this racism. She sets the words clearly in a modified strophic form that highlights significant ideas of the poem. In stanza two (mm. 16-17) the poet's hope of finding a place where his heart "hol's everything" prepares the way for the first high note (F-sharp) of the song, drawing attention to "An' my soul can allus sing," an idea so passionate that the singer needs a fermata and most of measure 18 before he can return his attention to his beloved Mandy Lou. The third stanza describes a dream of freedom (mm. 21-23) that Hier underscores with parallel ascending triads that momentarily do away with dotted rhythms. Then, behind the mask once more, the singer returns to his jaunty camouflage.

Katharine Adams, author of "Down in the Glen," was born in Elmira, New York, probably in the mid-1890s, and lived at least until the late 1940s.[8] Her family was probably wealthy, for she was educated at Mme Yeatman's School in Neuilly, France and later enrolled in courses at Columbia University. She married Percy Alexander Walker, and the dedication of her novel *Scarlet Sheath*

(1936) to "my beloved Sally Caroline Patricia" suggests that she had a daughter.[9] Though her fame rests on some thirteen novels and a collection of short stories for teenagers, Adams did publish one volume of verse, and single poems appeared in periodicals.[10] Most of her books were published in the years between the World Wars, and several were reprinted more than once.[11] According to *Who's Who in America*, Ethel Glenn Hier was not the only composer to set Adams' poetry.[12] "Down in the Glen," with its parallel strophes and musical allusions, is surely a poem that would have attracted a composer. Its magical *Midsummer Night's Dream* atmosphere and its invitations to "Listen," "Harken," and "Follow" draw the reader into the silvery, moonlit scene.

Eloise Robinson was more active as a scholar than a poet. The most substantial evidence of her work is her edition, *The Minor Poems of Joseph Beaumont*, "issued under the auspices of the department of English Literature, Wellesley College" in 1914.[13] Its date of publication and its link to a series sponsored by an exclusive college suggest that Robinson may have been an advanced, or even a graduate student there around 1910. This would place her birth date in the 1880s and suggest that her family was well-to-do. Robinson's "If You Must Go, Go Quickly" arranges its dignified, formal language into a sonnet form. Emotions, though strong, are held in check, inviting the composer to create a subtext that allows the poem's underlying passion to emerge.[14]

Down in the Glen and *If You Must Go, Go Quickly*, set for voice and piano trio, were published in 1925. Both works reveal Hier's clear grasp of the chamber idiom as one involving individual performers in collaboration as equals. In both songs, harmony and tonality are freely and flexibly treated. Hier's formal sense is subtle and text-based in these songs. Some basic ideas, announced at the beginning of each piece, are varied, transposed, reharmonized, extended, inverted, and placed in different textural contexts that are seldom conventional, although generally related in a clear structural plan. In *Down in the Glen* the opening bars present two ideas in differing versions: the interval of a fifth (mm. 1-2, violin; mm. 1-3 piano LH) and a descending scale (mm. 1-4, cello; mm. 1-3, piano RH; mm. 3-5, voice). As the text strophes have parallel construction, the return of these musical ideas, always varied, provides a strong but fluid musical logic.

Similarly, in *If You Must Go, Go Quickly*, a more passionate song, the descending parallel triads of the introduction are basic to the structure but never return in the same way (compare mm. 1-2, 11-14, 34-36, 40-42, 54-56, 59-64), reflecting the speaker's changing emotions as the poem progresses. The song's highest note, a high A in measure 57, occurs at the text's dramatic climax; the vocal line then dissolves into a hurried, broken conclusion.

The career of Ethel Glenn Hier, though perhaps modest by today's standards, was exceptional for her time. Her works reveal a combination of imagination, skill, and technique that make them worthy of notice and revival.

Notes

1. Madisonville was annexed to Cincinnati in 1911.

2. Various sources date Friedberg's tenure at the Institute from either 1914 or 1916. The *Musical Courier* of 1923, however, carried four notices to the effect that Friedberg was just then joining the Institute's faculty, and that he had not been in the United States since 1914. See issues of February 8, 1923, 41; March 12, 1923, 10; May 17, 1923, 53; and November 8, 1923, 42.

3. *The Musical Courier* 83 (August 4, 1921): 42.

4. A manuscript of her first orchestral piece, the unpublished *Scherzo for Small Orchestra*, written while she was still a student at the Conservatory, contains notes on the ranges and tone qualities of the various orchestral instruments and comments in Kelley's hand.

5. The first version of *Asolo Bells* to be published, however, was that for solo piano, which appeared in 1938. The piece is also arranged for piano duet.

6. Marion Bauer and Ethel Peyser, *How Music Grew* (New York: G. P. Putnam's Sons, 1939), 481.

7. See Dunbar's "We Wear the Mask" (1896), a poem in standard English telling how black Americans hide their true thoughts and feelings from white society behind a perpetual mask. *The Collected Poetry of Paul Laurence Dunbar* (New York: Dodd, Mead and Co., 1913), 71.

8. None of the few sources of information about Adams cites birth or death dates. My speculations are based on her publication record: her first book (poetry) appeared in 1917 and a final collection of short stories came out in 1947. See *National Union Catalog Pre-1956 Imprints* (Chicago: Mansell Information/Publication Limited, 1968), 3:518.

9. Katharine Adams, *Scarlet Sheath* (New York: Macmillan, 1936).

10. An example is "New Hampshire House," reprinted in Margery Mansfield, ed., *American Women Poets 1937* (New York: Henry Harrison, 1937), 136.

11. The most popular novel, *Red Caps and Lilies* (New York: Macmillan, 1924), was reprinted in 1925, 1926, 1928, 1932, and 1936.

12. *Who's Who in America* (Chicago: A. N. Marquis, 1928), 15:145.

13. Joseph Beaumont, *The Minor Poems*, ed. Eloise Robinson (Boston and New York: Houghton Mifflin, 1914).

14. Robinson also provided poems for Hier's *Three Memorial Sonnets* (1927) for voice and piano trio.

Selected List of Works

This list includes only published works. Some pieces exist in more than one arrangement. For example, the songs with chamber ensemble accompaniment also appear in versions for voice and piano.

Piano Solos

Easy Piano Compositions in the Earliest Grades, op. 10. Cincinnati: Willis Music, 1912.

Night Song of the Pine Trees, op. 15. Cincinnati: Willis Music, 1912.

[Piano Pieces] of Medium Difficulty, op. 13. Cincinnati: Willis Music, 1913.

Theme and Variations, op. 17. New York: Carl Fischer, 1921.

Fairy Folk: Three Melodious Piano Solos. New York: Carl Fischer, 1926.

A Day in the Peterborough Woods, op. 19. Chicago: Gilbert Music, 1924.

Asolo Bells, op. 21. New York: Composers Press, 1938.

Badinage, op. 22. New York: Composers Press, 1949.

Swiss Music Box, op. 23, no. 3. New York: Composers Facsimile Edition, 1952.

Songs with Piano or Chamber Ensemble

Dreamin' Town. Text by Paul Laurence Dunbar. Cincinnati: Willis Music, 1919.

Japanese Lullaby (1917). Text by Eugene Field. Chicago: Gilbert Music, 1925.

The Fairy Ring (1918). Text by Abbie Farwell Brown. Chicago: Gilbert Music, 1925.

Down in the Glen (1919). Text by Katharine Adams. For voice and piano trio. Chicago: Gilbert Music, 1925.

If You Must Go, Go Quickly (1923). Text by Eloise Robinson. For voice and piano trio. Chicago: Gilbert Music, 1925.

Avalon. Text by Nancy Byrd Turner. New York: Composers Press, 1938.

Click o' the Latch (1932). Text by Nancy Byrd Turner. New York: Composers Press, 1938.

The Lonely Cabin (1923). Text by Herbert Gorman. For voice and string quartet. New York: Composers Press, 1940.

The Bird in the Rain (1923). Text by Elinor Wylie. New York: Composers Facsimile Edition, 1955.

In the Carpenter's Shop (1917). Text by Sara Teasdale. New York: Composers Facsimile Edition, 195– .

Three Memorial Sonnets (1927). Texts by Eloise Robinson. For voice and piano trio. New York: Composers Fascimile Edition, 195– .

Quintet for Voice and Four Instruments [flute or violin, viola, cello, harp]. "Approach" (1934): text by Frances Frost; "Swans" (193–): text by Leonora Speyer; "To Gulls Wading" (1932): text by Leonora Speyer. New York: Composers Facsimile Edition, 1965.

Music for Orchestra

Carolina Christmas for chamber orchestra (1926–1929). New York: Composers Facsimile Edition, 1955. Also available for string quartet.

Choréographe (1928). New York: Composers Facsimile Edition, 1952.

Three Orchestral Pieces (*Foreboding, Asolo Bells, Badinage*). New York: Composers Press, 1954.

Chamber Music

Joy of Spring for violin and piano (1923). Chicago: C. F. Summy, 1926.

Rhapsody for violin and piano (1927). New York: Composers Facsimile Edition, 1957.

Choral Works

Then Shall I Know for SATB chorus, baritone or alto solo, organ (1945). Text from I Corinthians 13:12 and John 14:1-4. New York: Composers Facsimile Edition, 1952.

Mountain Preacher for SATB chorus, baritone solo, orchestra (1938–1940). Text by James Still. New York: Composers Facsimile Edition, 1966.

Play with Music

The Boyhood and Youth of Edward MacDowell. Peterborough, N. H.: Nubanusit Press, 1926.

Bibliography

"American Women Composers." *Musical America* 48, no. 3 (May 5, 1928): 28.

Ammer, Christine. *Unsung: A History of Women in American Music*. Westport, Conn.: Greenwood Press, 1980.

"Artists Everywhere." *Musical Courier* 97 (February 28, 1929): 38.

Barnes, Edwin N. *American Women in Creative Music*. Washington, D.C.: Music Education Publications, 1936.

Block, Adrienne Fried. "Hier, Ethel Glenn," in *The Norton/Grove Dictionary of Women Composers*, eds. Julie Ann Sadie and Rhian Samuel. New York: W. W. Norton, 1994.

______, and Carol Neuls-Bates. *Women in American Music*. Westport, Conn.: Greenwood Press, 1979.

Cohen, Aaron I. *International Encyclopedia of Women Composers*. 2nd ed. New York and London: Books and Music, 1987.

"Composer on Platform." *Musical Courier* 120 (July 1, 1939): 21.

"Composers Concerts in Fifth Season." *Musical America* 73 (April 15, 1953): 21.

"Composers Press Songs of Imaginative Quality." *Musical America* 60, no. 16 (October 25, 1940): 36.

"Contemporary American Musicians, no. 168: Ethel Glenn Hier." *Musical America* 34, no. 2 (1921): 29.

"Ethel Glenn Hier Active in Recital and Teaching Fields." *Musical Courier* 116 (December 15, 1937): 26.

"Ethel Glenn Hier Appears in Lectures and Recitals." *Musical Courier* 117 (June 1, 1938): 13.

"Ethel Glenn Hier, Composer [,] Combines Musical Activites." *Musical Courier* 145 (May 1, 1952): 20.

"Ethel Glenn Hier Conducts Symphonic and Opera Classes." *Musical America* 55, no. 19 (December 10, 1935): 33.

"Ethel Glenn Hier Honored." *Musical America* 50, no. 6 (March 25, 1930): 34.

"Ethel Glenn Hier Pupil Wins New Jersey State Prize." *Musical America* 50, no. 9 (May 10, 1930): 43.

"Ethel Glenn Hier Returns from Study in Austria." *Musical America* 53, no.16 (October 25, 1933): 25.

"Ethel Glenn Hier's Recent Engagements." *Musical Courier* 115 (May 29, 1937): 12.

"Ethel Glenn Hier's Works Heard in Lecture-Recitals." *Musical Courier* 125 (April 5, 1942): 43.

"Ethel Glenn Hier's Works Have Performances." *Musical America* 68 (September 1948): 38.

"Ethel Glenn Hier's Works Presented." *Musical Courier* 134 (September 1946): 38.

"Ethel Hier's *Asolo Bells* an Asset to Duo Pianists." *Musical America* 67 (May 1947): 38.

Osburn, Mary Hubbell. *Ohio Composers and Musical Authors*. Privately printed, 1942.

Pendle, Karin. "The Web of Friendship: Amy Beach and Ethel Glenn Hier." Paper delivered at the conference "Amy Beach and Her Times," University of New Hampshire, October 28, 1998.

_____. "Cincinnati's Musical Heritage: Three Women Who Succeeded." *Queen City Heritage* 41 (1983): 41-55.

"The Pick of the Publications" [Hier's piano works]. *Musical Courier* 95 (September 29, 1927): 32, 36.

"Reviews of New Music" [Hier's *Theme and Variations*]. *Musical Courier* 83 (August 4, 1921): 42.

"Studio Notes." *Musical Courier* 103 (October 31, 1931): 39.

"Women Composers in Third Concert." *Musical America* 47, no. 26 (April 14, 1928): 21.

"Works by Ethel Glenn Hier Presented by Barrère Little Symphony." *Musical America* 50, no. 8 (April 25, 1930): 40.

"Works of Pianist and Composer Receive Performances at Various Centers." *Musical America* 46, no. 6 (May 28, 1927): 36.

Collections of Hier's music, printed or in manuscript, may be found at the American Music Center, New York; the library of the College-Conservatory of Music, University of Cincinnati; Delta Omicron Collection in the Public Library of Cincinnati and Hamilton County; the Ohioana Library in Columbus, Ohio; and the Library of Congress.

Dreamin' Town

Paul Laurence Dunbar

Ethel Glenn Hier
Karin Pendle, editor

7
rit.
a tempo
days is nev - ah col', An' no sheep strays f'om de fol', Man - dy Lou.
p
10
rit.
a tempo
Ain't you tiahed of eve - ry day,
mf
13
Man - dy Lou, Man - dy Lou, Tek my han' an' come a - way,
cresc.
15
Man - dy Lou; To de place whaih dreams is King,

17
rit.
Whaih my heart hol's eve - ry-thing, An' my soul can al - lus sing,
19
rit.
[𝄐]
a tempo
rit.
Man - dy Lou.
pp
22
pp misterioso
Come a - way to dream wid me, Man - dy Lou, Man - dy Lou,
pp misterioso
24
rit.
Whaih our han's and hea'ts are free, Man - dy Lou;

26
a tempo
Whaih de sands is shin - in' white, Whaih de riv - ahs glist - ens bright,
28
rit.
In dat dream - land
rit.
[molto rit.]
of de - light,
pp
30
[accel.]
a tempo
Man - dy Lou,
rit.
[a tempo]
Come a -
p
33
way to dream - land town, Man - dy Lou, Man - dy Lou, Whaih de
p

35
rit.
a tempo
fruit is bend - in' down,
Des fu' you, Smooth your
mf
37
brow of lov - in' brown An' my love will be its crown, Come a -
39
rit.
a tempo
rit.
way to dream - in' town, Come a - way to dream - in'
41
a tempo
rit.
a tempo
town, Man - dy Lou.
pp

Down in the Glen
[for Voice, Violin, Cello, and Piano]

Katharine Adams

Ethel Glenn Hier
Karin Pendle, editor

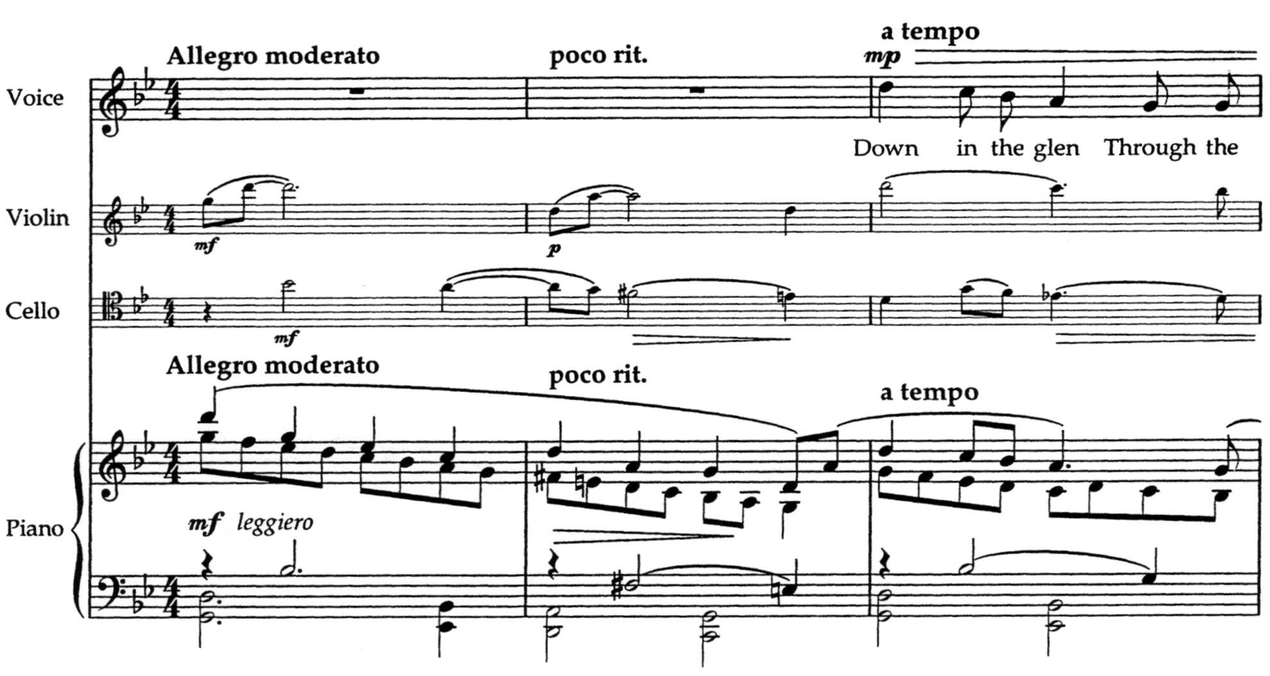

7
rit.
a tempo
soft - ly clear,
Mus - ic,
and see glist-en
cresc.
cresc.
8va
rit.
a tempo
cresc.
10
Sil - ver wings,
Some-thing sings,
Down in the
p
p sub.
8va
tremolo
p sub.
13
rit. poco a poco
molto rit.
Meno mosso
pp
glen.
Down in the glen In the
pp
p
rit. poco a poco
molto rit.
Meno mosso
p

16
express.
won - der, the won-der of the night,
Hark - en! By the
marcato
express.
pp
express.
19
rit.
p
rit.
p
a tempo poco a poco accel.
cool si-lent pool,
Shad-ows, as they dark - en,
See the gleam Of a
express.
pp
p
p
rit.
rit.
L.H.
a tempo poco a poco accel.
22
a tempo
dream
Down in the glen.
decresc.
decresc.
a tempo
decresc.

25
mf
Down in the glen Where the
pp
pp
mf
mf
[pp]
[mf]
28
poco a poco accel.
moon - light weaves a path
Fol - low You will see, In
poco a poco accel.
8va
31
3
ec - sta - cy,
poco rit.
Fair - ies
p
Scherzando a tempo
Fair - ies danc-ing in the
pp
p
(8va)
poco rit.
Scherzando a tempo
p

34
poco a poco rit.
decresc.
hol-low Of a tree,
Mer - ri - ly,
Down in the
decresc.
poco a poco rit.
8va
trem.
37
glen, Down in the glen,
decresc.
40
rit.
a tempo
rit.
Down in the glen
Fol - low
rit.
a tempo
rit.

If You Must Go, Go Quickly

[for Voice, Violin, Cello, and Piano]

Eloise Robinson

Ethel Glenn Hier
Karin Pendle, editor

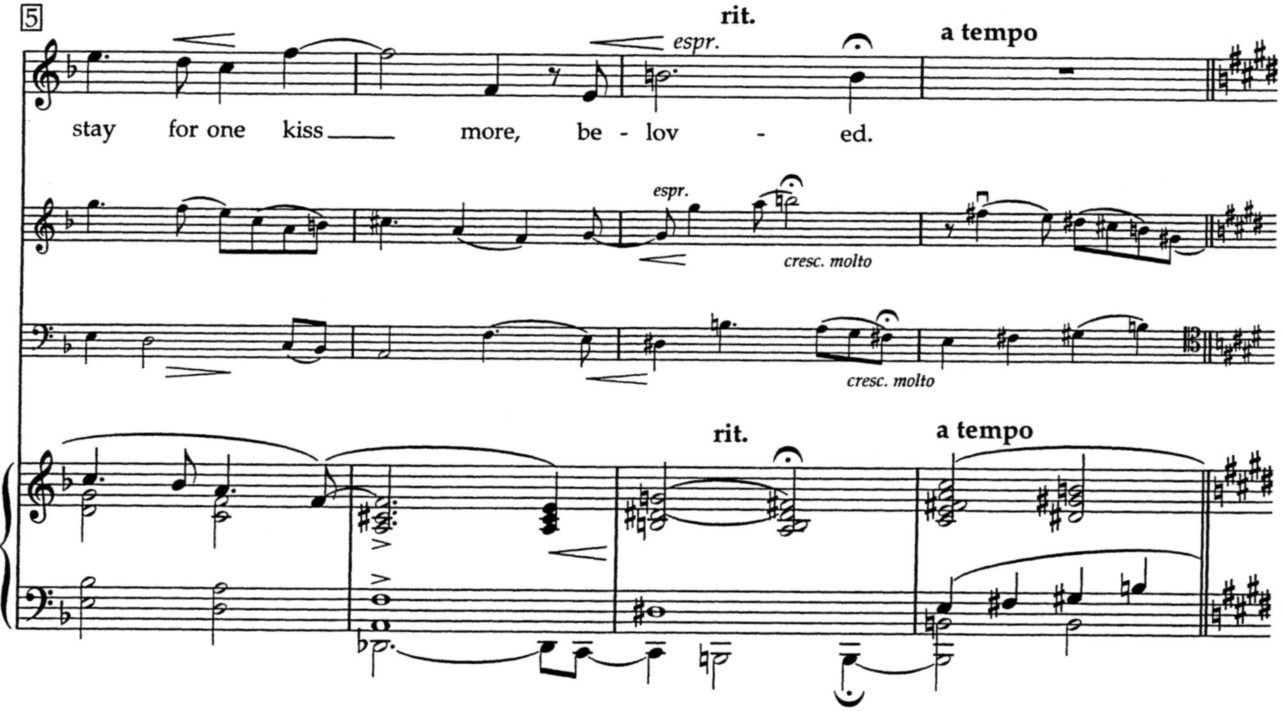

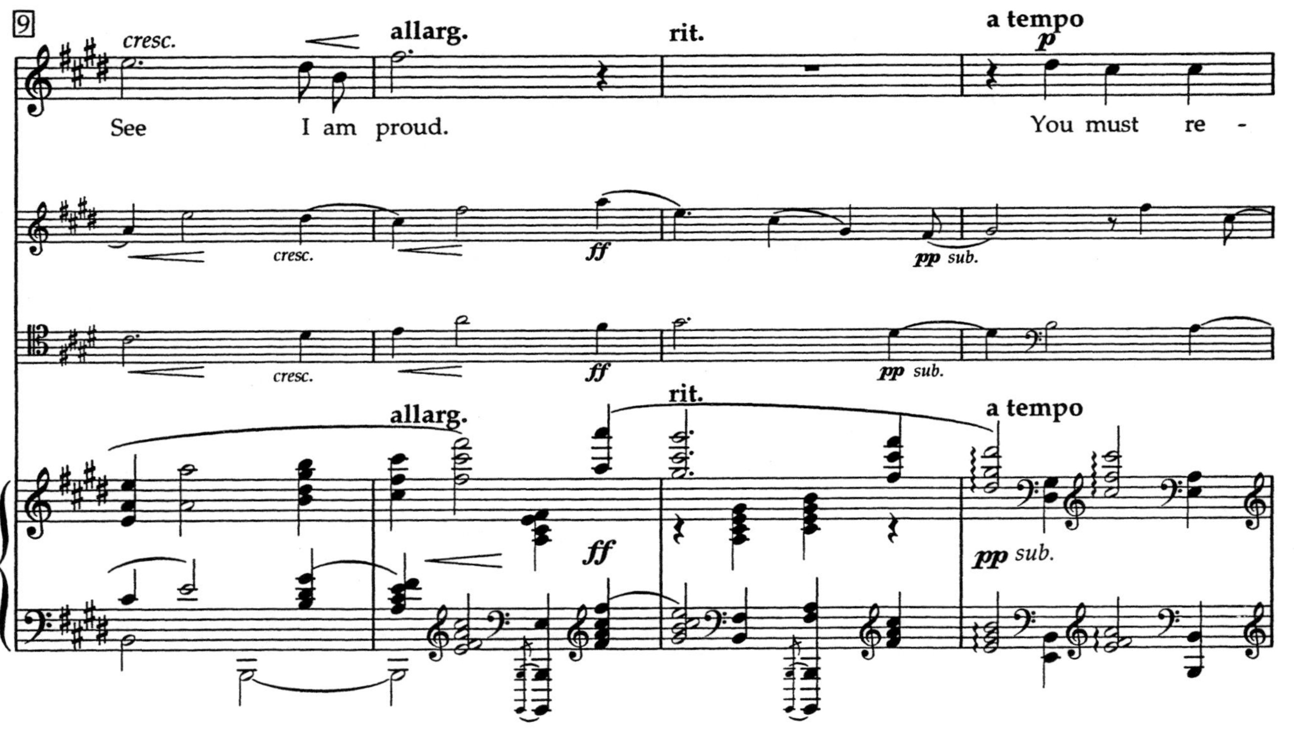
9
cresc.
allarg.
rit.
a tempo
p
See I am proud.
You must re -
cresc.
ff
pp sub.
cresc.
ff
pp sub.
allarg.
rit.
a tempo
ff
pp sub.

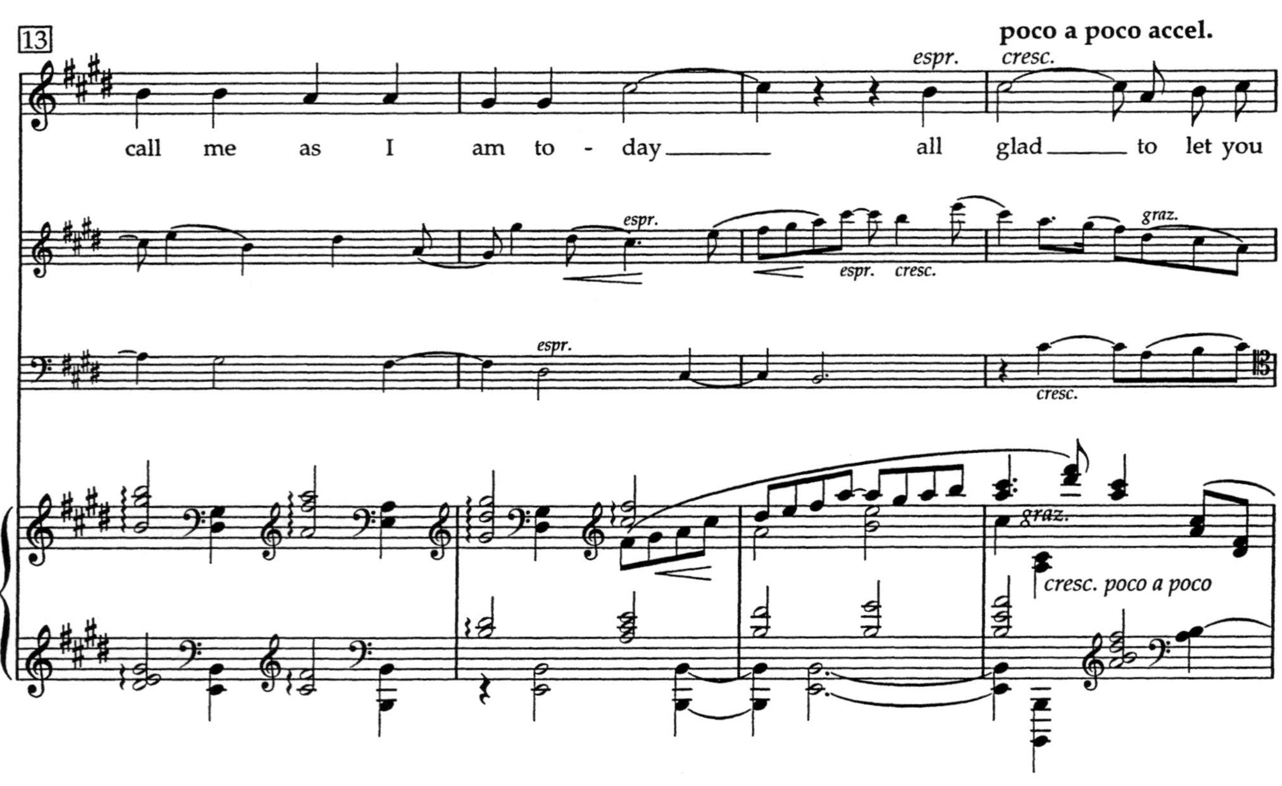
13
poco a poco accel.
espr.
cresc.
call me as I am to - day all glad to let you
espr.
espr. cresc.
graz.
espr.
cresc.
graz.
cresc. poco a poco

17
molto rit.
Poco lento
pp
go and ra - diant browed.
Think of me still in this blue
graz.
cresc.
pp
cresc.
pp
molto rit.
Poco lento
cresc.
pp

22
dress you love.
Its col - or
not more qui - et than my
pp
p
pp

27
molto cresc.
rit.
f
ff espr.
eyes; Plumb them and see you have not line e-nough to
cresc.
f
appass.
molto cresc.
rit.
molto cresc.
ff

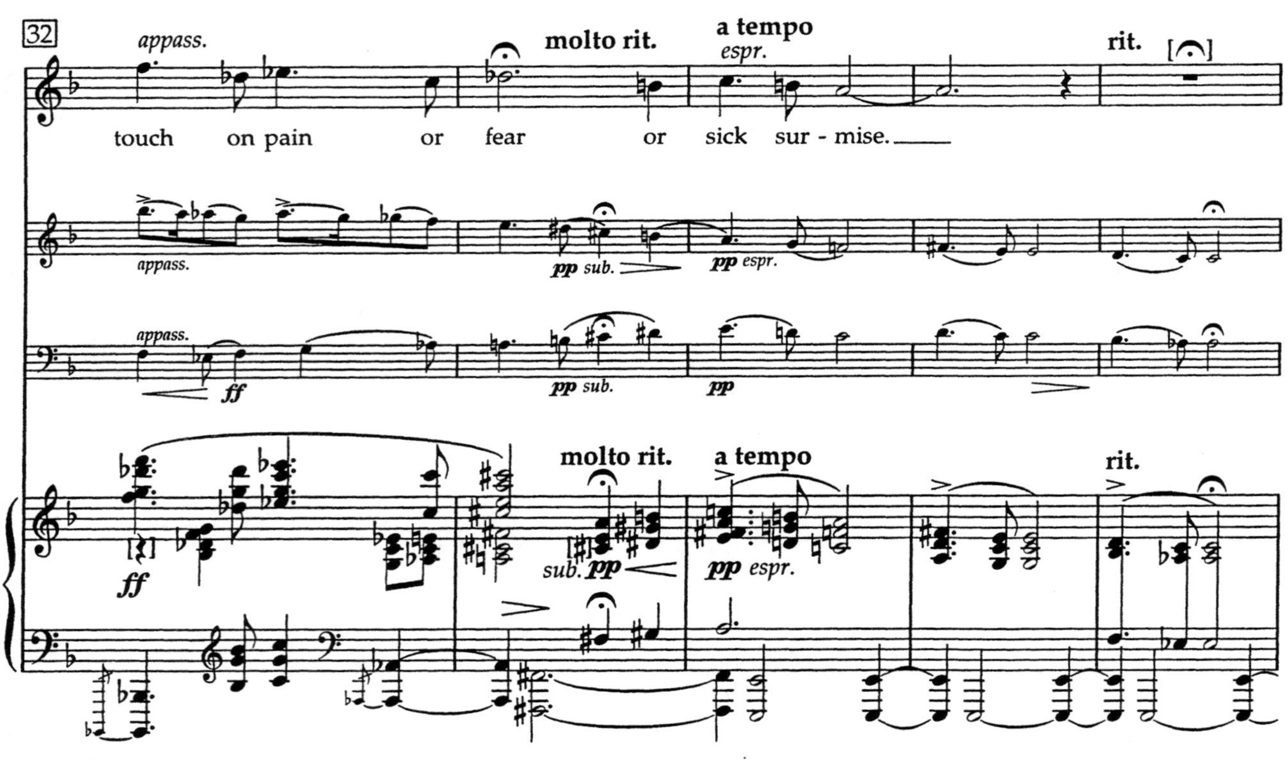
32
appass.
molto rit.
a tempo
espr.
rit.
touch on pain or fear or sick sur - mise.
appass.
pp sub.
pp espr.
appass.
ff
pp sub.
pp
molto rit.
a tempo
rit.
ff
sub. pp
pp espr.

37

a tempo
p
I have re - mem-bered to make
a tempo
p
p

42

glad for you all of my thoughts, put laugh - ter on my
graz.
graz.
grazioso

46
p espr.
mouth, With kis - ses that shall seem as cool as
espr.
p espr.
espr.
espr.
p

49
rit.
rit. espr.
dew When you re - mem - ber them in time of drouth.
8va
espr.
espr.
rit.
rit.
decresc.

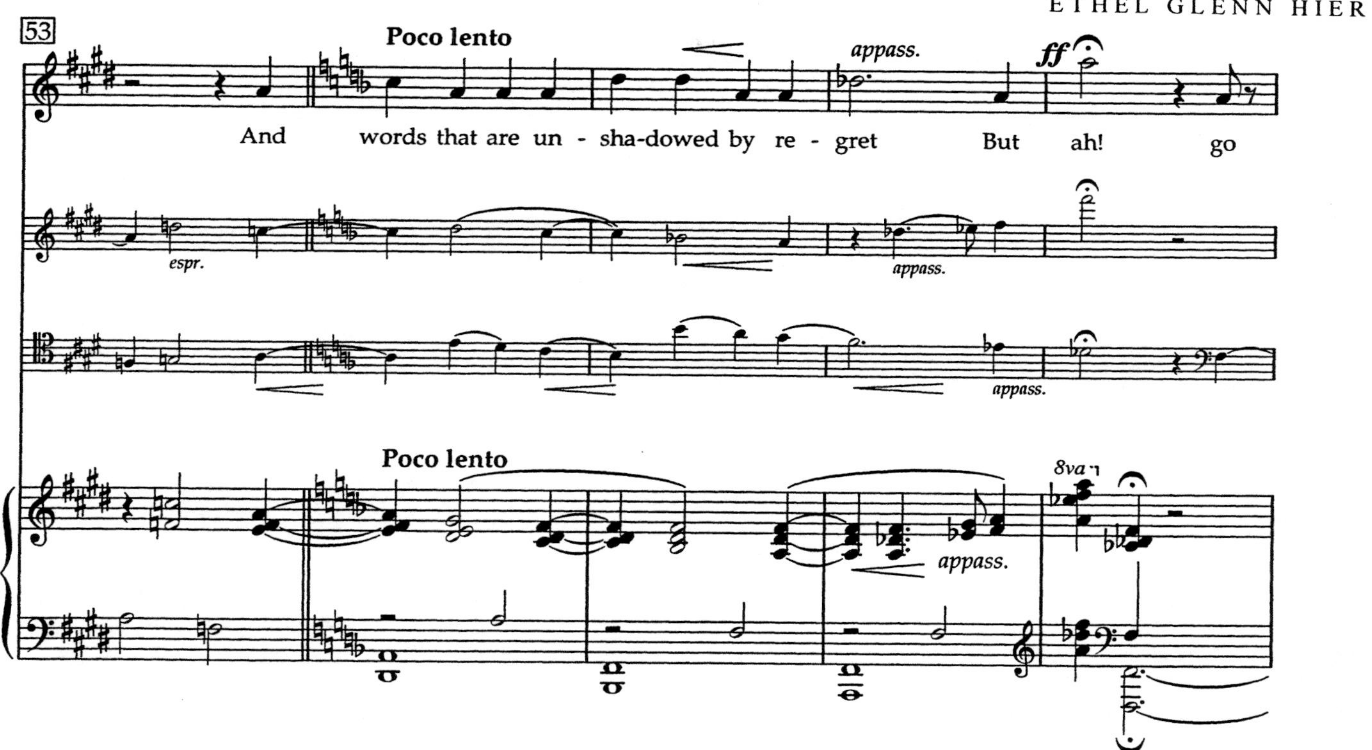
53
Poco lento
appass.
ff
And words that are un - sha-dowed by re - gret But ah! go
espr.
appass.
appass.
Poco lento
8va
appass.

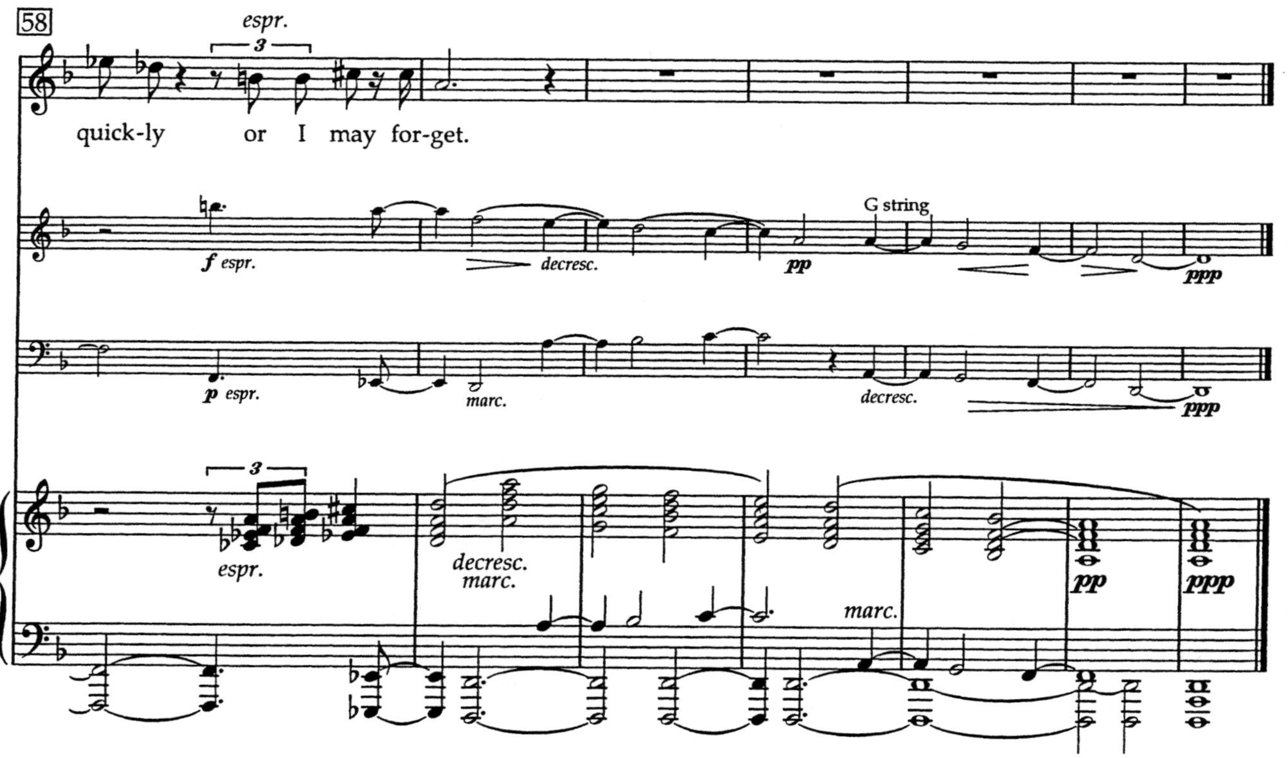
58
espr.
3
quick-ly or I may for-get.
f espr.
decresc.
G string
pp
ppp
p espr.
marc.
decresc.
ppp
espr.
decresc.
marc.
marc.
pp
ppp

Catherine Urner
(1891–1942)

DAVID ZEA

During the last decade of the nineteenth century and the first few years of the twentieth, the voice of a singular American composer emerged from the heartland: the voice of Catherine Murphy Urner, born March 23, 1891, in Mitchell, Indiana. Opting early for a musical career, her undergraduate training, with concentrations in piano, voice, and composition, was undertaken at Goucher College, The Peabody Conservatory, and Ohio's Miami University, from where she graduated with a B.A. in 1912.

In 1914, Urner enrolled at the University of California, Berkeley, to do postgraduate work in music. Before leaving the university on September 26, 1916, she had composed the music for the spring 1916 production of the university women, *The Partheneia*, a masque presented in the Faculty Glade. This presentation, based on a series of scenes written by classmate Maude Meagher, was entitled *Aranyani of the Jasmine Vine*. Urner's contribution was hailed in the following excerpt from a review in the 1917 *Blue and Gold* (the UC Berkeley yearbook): "The music, composed by Catherine Urner [class of] '15 . . . was of unusual beauty." [1] Her efforts won her the first esteemed *George Ladd Prix de Paris* for 1920–1921.[2]

With the $1,900 prize in hand, Urner embarked on the first of five sojourns in France. She studied voice with Andrée Otemar and began what were to become her decade-long studies in advanced composition and orchestration with her new mentor, Charles Koechlin (1867–1950), an interaction which was to radically alter her compositional style.

Upon her return to the United States in 1921, she was appointed Director of Vocal Music at Mills College (Oakland, California), a position she held until 1924. From this time on, Urner worked as a composer and concert singer, chiefly in the United States, France, and Italy. Significant premières of her works took place under the auspices of the Société Musicale Indépendante (of which Koechlin was one of the founders) and the Salle Pleyel. In the latter, for example, her *Quartet for Strings* was given its first performance by the Krettly Quartet (Robert Krettly, René Costard, Georges Taine, Pierre Fournier) on March 31, 1925.

Urner became acknowledged as an accomplished singer of ancient and classic songs, French-impressionist *mélodies* and American-Indian tribal chants. Many of these were harmonized and arranged for voice and piano by her close associate Jeanne Herscher-Clément (who was subsequently to instruct and lecture at the Urner-Van Löben Sels Studio in Oakland, California). Some two years before her final journey back to the United States, where she returned to teaching, she began to arrange lecture tours for Koechlin at leading universities. Her recitals continued to draw attention:

> In that which concerns more especially her vocal interpretation, one will have the joy of confirming that her musical gifts and her comprehension of the works are doubled by a singing technique altogether superior, by a full voice, colored with a pure and velvety timbre.[3]

Back in America again by the mid-thirties, Urner received her certificate in music education from UCLA in 1935 and taught for the University Extension division of the university. On October 10, 1937, Urner married Charles Rollin Shatto, composer, pianist, and organist, in a ceremony at picturesque Bird Rock, La Jolla, California. They collaborated on many projects and, until Urner's untimely passing in a tragic car accident on April 30, 1942, in San Diego, she devoted herself to composition, singing, teaching and choir-directing, not to mention homemaking — at which (according to her late husband) she was expert.

Koechlin learned of Urner's death from Darius Milhaud, one of his closest friends and a faculty member at Mills College.[4] As a memorial to his revered pupil, Koechlin set about orchestrating her *Esquisses Normandes* (Norman Sketches), a four-movement suite inspired by the Normandy countryside and seacoast. This haunting, melodious work was premiered by the Bay Area Women's Philharmonic, JoAnn Falletta conducting, on April 20, 1990, in Berkeley, California. The performance received critical acclaim as Timothy Pfaff, the *San Francisco Examiner* staff critic, wrote the next day:

. . . Falletta led with an absorbing traversal of "Esquisses Normandes," a four-movement tone poem by Catherine Urner . . . A coloristic composition that works in deep pigments, it ran its ecstatic course from the muted strings of "Chant d'Automne" to the bright turbulence of "La Mer Joyeuse."[5]

This moving premiere can be seen as a final tribute to Urner and her full creative life, cut short by tragedy.

With the following intensely worded excerpt from a letter to Koechlin dated February 6, 1935, the typically outspoken, unusually perceptive Catherine Urner conveyed some of her most unequivocal views on *la vie artistique* (the artistic life) to her lifelong mentor and friend:

> Society is always grateful to those who make material life more attractive — the plumber, the inventor of the telephone and other comforts. But those who are concerned with the needs of *l'âme* (the soul), with the true beauty of music, of poetry, suffer indignities, even cruelties. Such a society does not even deserve the designation "civilisée (civilized)." These are the same things you have told me many times.[6]

Though Urner was very gifted and enterprising, it was a struggle for her to maintain a meaningful, dedicated musical career.

Elise Kuhl Kirk, in a splendid and very informative paper, "A Parisian in America: The Lectures and Legacies of Charles Koechlin," discusses the close relationship between Koechlin and Urner in the following passage, referring to Urner's position among Koechlin's pupils—a class including composers as diverse as Cole Porter, Alexander Lang Steinert and Charles Shatto in America, and Francis Poulenc, Germaine Tailleferre and Henri Sauguet in France:

> One student in particular, however, occupied a very special place in the life of the composer; the name Catherine Urner permeates Koechlin's writings throughout the greater part of his life. He found the comely woman to be a true artist with special gifts in melodic composition and he speaks of her frequently as having an intelligence more profound, more European, than any other American musician he had known. This truly gifted American was responsible for bringing Koechlin to the California coast for his last three teaching visits and, indirectly, for his receipt of the Hollywood Bowl prize in 1929.[7] But, more significantly, through the strong bonds of friendship, affection, and respect which they maintained for each other throughout the years, the musical styles of Charles Koechlin and Catherine Urner became inextricably intertwined.[8]

Urner was a professional singer who composed voluminously for the voice.[9] The two songs here include the darkly philosophical *Nichts ist dauernd* (Nothing is Lasting) from the well-known *Denkrede auf Jean Paul* (Memorial of Jean Paul) by famed nineteenth-century German journalist and critic Ludwig Börne, and the impassioned *After Parting*, a setting of the love poem by American Sara Teasdale. Both stand as quintessentially Urneresque, clearly revealing her broad range of interests and concerns.

Her settings reflect the moods and thoughts of the texts vividly: *Nichts ist dauernd* with the quiet depth of a Wolf lied, the Teasdale burnished with a Gallic-American lyricism and subtle grace. Touches of the style so characteristic of Koechlin are present in both works. These miniatures exemplify a number of the more salient aspects of Urner's mature style: a compelling sense of the melodic; terse, gem-like form; adventurous harmonies; and use of counterpoint. Although, according to Charles Shatto, there is a certain "elusive" quality to this music, perseverance will reveal each work's essence. Together, these factors proclaim Catherine Urner a conservative though uniquely individual member of earlier twentieth-century composers.[10]

Notes

1. *Blue and Gold* (University of California, Berkeley yearbook) (Berkeley: 1917).

2. Previously, Urner had been introduced to the renowned French master, Charles Koechlin, by her UC Berkeley harmony professor, William J. McCoy, at a Christmas dinner in San Francisco on December 19, 1918, during Koechlin's first American tour. He was a member of a prestigious seven-member commission of French scholars and artists, headed by Theodore Reinach, whose mission was to reveal the intellectual and physical viability of the French people to other nations, thus contravening Prussian propaganda to the contrary. It was at this time Koechlin observed that Urner "was extremely good at writing melodies, though less good at harmonizing them." Koechlin, quoted in Robert Orledge, *Charles Koechlin (1867–1950) His Life and Works* (Chur, Switzerland: Harwood academic publishers, 1989), 144.

3. Sempol [no first name], excerpt from a preview of an Urner recital (Nice: *L'Éclaireur de Nice et du Sud-Est*, January 19, 1932). "En ce qui concerne plus spécialement son interprétation vocale, on aura la joie de constater que ses dons musicaux et sa compréhension des oeuvres sont doublés d'une technique de chant tout à fait supérieure, d'une voix ample, colorée, au timbre pur et velouté."

4. In a letter dated March 21, 1945.

5. Timothy Pfaff, excerpt from a review of The Bay Area Women's Philharmonic concert of April 20, 1990, when the world premiere of Urner's *Esquisses Normandes* was presented (*San Francisco Examiner*, April 21, 1990).

6. Elise Kuhl Kirk, "A Parisian in America: The Lectures and

Legacies of Charles Koechlin," *Current Musicology*, no. 25 (1978): 59-60.

7. The winning work referred to here was the finale of Koechlin's *Études antiques* (Ancient Studies), *La joie païenne* (Pagan Joy); Urner suggested Koechlin submit it. The prize ($1,000 plus performance) was awarded by a three-judge panel whose members were Leopold Stokowski, Eugene Goossens, and Henry Eicheim. The world premiere took place at the Bowl on August 13, 1929, Eugene Goossens conducting.

8. Kirk, "A Parisian in America," 57.

9. With the exception of *Aranyani of the Jasmine Vine*, in the Bancroft Library of the University of California, Berkeley, the entire Urner Archive is housed in the university's Music Library. Reproductions of the manuscripts can be supplied by contacting The Music Library, 240 Morrison Hall, University of California, Berkeley, Berkeley, CA 94720, USA; (510) 643-6197; FAX (510) 642-8237.

10. A catalog of Urner's entire oeuvre and "manuscript facsimile" editions of the following works are available through The F. Eugene Miller Foundation by contacting Judy Green Music, 1616 Cahuenga Boulevard, Hollywood, CA 90028, USA; (323) 466-2491; e-mail: judyjgm@aol.com

Barcarolle (Organ)
Madonna's Lullaby (Organ)
Two Traditional American Indian Songs (Organ)
Suite for Children (Piano)
Comme une berceuse (Flute and Organ) (Score and Part)
After Parting (Voice and Piano)
Nichts ist dauernd (Voice and Piano)
Esquisses Normandes (Chamber Orchestra) (Score and Parts)

List of Works

All works in manuscript unless otherwise noted.

Vocal Solo

After Parting. Text by Sara Teasdale.

As Comets Flash. Text by Mary Ledingham. Cycle of sixteen very brief songs without titles.

Ave Maria (1932).

Bright Star, Would I Were Steadfast as Thou Art. Text by John Keats. (String quartet accompaniment.)

Broken Promise. Text by Archibald MacLeish.

Brumes et pluies (Mists and Rains) (1934). Text by Charles Baudelaire.

Chanson (II) (Song). Text by Maurice Maeterlinck.

Chant de nuit (*Nacht-Gesang*) (Night Song). Text by Stephen George. French translation by Albert Dreyfus.

Chloë et Caelia (from "Songs from 'The Unknown Lover'") (1930). Text by Edmund William Gosse.

Conifers. Text by Mary Ledingham.

El camino real (The Royal Highway). Text by May Stanley.

Five Songs (from *Les Nouvelles Nourritures* [The New Fruits of the Earth]) (1937). Text by André Gide. (Flute and piano accompaniment.)

1. *La brise vagabonde* (The Wayward Breeze)
2. *Printemps plein d'indolence* (Spring Full of Indolence)
3. *Adam neuf* (New Adam)
4. *Ne plus attendre!* (Wait no More!)
5. *La sagesse n'est pas dans la raison* (Wisdom Is Not in Reason)

Floating on the Pool of Jo-Ya. Spring. Text by Chi Wu-ch'ien. (Flute and viola [or clarinet in B-flat or A] accompaniment.)

Four Songs (from *Fir Flower Tablets*). Poems translated from the Chinese by Florence Ayscough and Amy Lowell. Scored for soprano, flute, clarinet in A, violin, viola, violoncello, and piano.

1. *Dancing*. Text by Yang Kuei-fei
2. *Songs of the Courtesans*. Text by Ting Liu Niang
3. *Ai Ai Thinks of the Man She Loves*. Text by Ting Liu Niang
4. *Song of Grief*. Text by Pan Chieh-yü

Four Songs (from *L'âme d'une Gopi* [The Heart of a Gopi]) (1941–1942). Text by Raihana Tyabji.

1. *Étrange est le coeur d'une femme* (Strange Is the Heart of a Woman)
2. *À l'aube* (To Dawn)
3. *Sur Vrîndavan* (Overlooking Vrîndavan)
4. *Chanson de Sharmilah* (Song of Sharmilah)

Hymn to Ishtar. Text by V. C. C. Collum.

Impression of Night. Text by Mary Ledingham.

Indra. Text by Mary Ledingham.

Invitation. Text by Richard Le Galliene.

Invocation. Text by Mary Ledingham. Violin, or flute, and piano accompaniment. Score; flute part.

La haute falaise domine la mer (The High Cliff Looks Down upon the Sea). Text by Suzanne Koechlin.

Larghetto to Be Played on a Summer Evening. Text by Edward Doro.

Le récif de corail (The Coral Reef) (from *Les trophées* [The Trophies]) (1926). Text by José-María de Heredia.

Le rêve et la vie (The Dream and Life).Text by Jean de la Ville de Mirmont.

L'été noir (Black Summer). Text by Edward Doro.

L'étranger (The Stranger) (from *Petits poèmes en prose* [Little Poems in Prose]). Text by Charles Baudelaire. (Also a version with String Quartet accompaniment).

L'ibis mort (The Dead Ibis) (1928). Text by Tristan Klingsor.

L'infidèle (The Infidel) (1928). Text by Tristan Klingsor.

Mein Schmerz ist das Meer (My Sorrow Is the Sea). German translation from the Irish by Käte Müller-Lisowski. Also scored for mezzo-soprano, two flutes, two oboes, English horn, two clarinets in B-flat (A), two bassoons, two horns in F, two trumpets in C, two trombones, triangle, cymbals, piano (or harp) and strings.

Moth Flowers. Text by Jeanne Robert Foster.

Nichts ist dauernd (Nothing Is Lasting) (from "Denkrede auf Jean Paul" [Memorial of Jean Paul]). Text by Ludwig Börne.

Nocturn (1930). Text by Francis Thompson. Scored for soprano, flute, and piano; also scored for soprano, flute, violin, viola, violoncello, and piano (or harp).

O mer (O Sea). Text by Suzanne Sarazin.

¡O mi pasión dolorosa! (O My Sad Passion!) (1933). Text by Gil Vicente. Original language, Portuguese.

O vie (O Life) (1931). Text by Suzanne Koechlin. Scored for soprano (or tenor) solo, soprano, mezzo-soprano, contralto, two violins, two violas, and two violoncellos.

Prophecy. Text by Rupert Brooke.

Quatre mélodies (Four Melodies) (English translations included). Paris: Éditions Maurice Senart (Salabert), 1928.

1. *La lune se lève* (The Moon Rises). Text by Jacque Madeleine
2. *Ici-bas* (Here, on Earth). Text by Sully Prudhomme
3. *Le papillon* (The Butterfly). Text by Alphonse de Lamartine
4. *Colloque sentimentale* (Sentimental Colloquy). Text by Paul Verlaine

Return. Text by Archibald MacLeish. (Written in collaboration with Charles Shatto.)

Romance (from *Underwoods*). Text by Robert Louis Stevenson.

Ro, ro, ro. Text by Gil Vicente. Original language, Portuguese.

Sails of Faith. Text by Elsa Barker.

Seafarer. Text by Archibald MacLeish.

Sea-Woman. Text by May Stanley.

Shadow of a Cloud. Text by V. C. C. Collum.

Silence (from "Sagesse" [Wisdom]). Text by Paul Verlaine.

Six Songs. Paris: Éditions Maurice Senart (Salabert), 1928.

1. *Sonnet*. Text by Maude Meagher
2. *Song* (from "April"). Text by Irene Rutherford McLeod
3. *Come Away, Death* (from *Twelfth Night*). Text by William Shakespeare
4. *Music I Heard with You*. Text by Conrad Aiken
5. *Dusk at Sea*. Text by Thomas Jones Jr.
6. *The Lake Isle of Innesfree*. Text by William Butler Yeats

Songs from the Cypress (1936). Text by H. D.

1. *Where Is the Nightingale?*
2. *What Are the Islands to Me?*

Starlight in the Music. Text by May Stanley.

The Carrion Spring. Text by Archibald MacLeish.

The Heart of the Woman (from *The Wind Among the Reeds*) (1930). Text by William Butler Yeats.

The Hills of Iris (*The Iris Hills* [from *Rosamunde*]). Text by George Sterling.

The Lilac Tree. Text by Fannie Stearns Davis.

The Mushroom Meadows. Text by Thomas Walsh.

The 'Wakening. Text anonymous (1622). Flute and piano accompaniment.

To Grief (1929). Text by Dina Moore Bowden.

Two Poems from the Chinese.
1. *Separation.* Text anonymous
2. *Looking South on the River.* Text by Wen Ting-yün. Flute and viola accompaniment

Verses (1928). Text by Maude Meagher.

Vocalises for Solo Voice (1929–1932).

Where Poppies Blow. Text by Helen Moriarty. (Lost?).

Choral

Unaccompanied

Annabel Lee (SATB). Text by Edgar Allen Poe.

Ave verum (SATB).

Five Canons for Two Voices (no. 5 specifically SA).

The Great God Pan (SATB). Text by Elizabeth Barrett Browning.

Laudemus te (SATB/SATB) (Also a version with organ accompaniment).

Political Prayer (SATB). Text by Upton Sinclair.

Salute (SATB) (1939). Text by Archibald MacLeish.

Sanctus (from *Mass*) (SSA).

Accompanied

Alleluja (SSA) (Piano accompaniment [optional]).

Babylonian Dirge (Anonymous). Scored for soprano solo, SSA, two flutes, oboe, and English horn.

Mass (Soli/SATB) (Organ accompaniment).
1. *Kyrie eleison*
2. *Gloria in excelsis Deo*
3. *Sanctus*
4. *Benedictus*
5. *Agnus Dei*

O Earth, Return! (SCTBar Soli /SATB). Various texts by William Blake. (Urner-Shatto: Introductory Fugue by Urner.) (Organ accompaniment).

O salutaris (1932) (SSA). (Organ accompaniment).

Out of the Depths (Psalm 130) (SC Soli/SATB). (Organ accompaniment).

Psalm 15 (SCT Soli/SATB). (Organ accompaniment).

Ten Vocalises for two Soprani and contralto. (Piano accompaniment).

The Mystic Trumpeter (Excerpts from "From Noon to Starry Night" from *Leaves of Grass*) (SATB, trumpet Solo). Text by Walt Whitman. (Score and Parts [New, computer-engraved edition]).

Operatic

Anoemone (Libretto by Isabelle S. Churchman). Operetta in two acts for children soli and children's chorus with piano accompaniment.

Piano Solo

Carcassone.

Choral pour Noël (1932). (Chorale for Christmas).

Chorals for C.R.S. (*Charles Rollin Shatto*) (1938).

Crossing Arizona Sands (1929).

Fantaisie-études (Fantasy-Studies).

Four Sketches (La Jolla).
1. *Mañana (Tomorrow)*
2. *The Duchess*
3. *The Three Old Ladies*
4. *White Cliffs*

From a Car Window in France — Six Sketches.
1. *Cathedral at Dusk*
2. *Summer on the Oise (Valmondois)*
3. *Tea on the Sidewalk*
4. *Apple Blossoms in Normandy*
5. *A Sentimental Walk (In Boileau Street — Paris)*
6. *White Sails (At Le Canadel)*

Fughetta.

Hymn for Mother's Birthday (1933) (Also an arrangement for organ by Urner).

Images — Six Short Sketches after the Poetry of Richard Aldington (1926).

Jubilee Suite — Five Short Preludes to the Fisk Jubilee Singers (1931).

L'attente (The Awaiting).

Soir (Evening).

Suite for Children.
1. *Hunting Song*
2. *Valentine*
3. *Fairies in the Dew*
4. *Choral* (Chorale)
5. *Sans souci* (Carefree)

Tendrement à un ami (Chant à la Tagore) (Tenderly to a Friend [Song in the Manner of Tagore]) (1930).

Two Nocturnes.
1. Andantino (With suggested corrections by Charles Koechlin)
2. Lento molto (Last composition [?])

Western Suite.
1. *Desert Wild Flowers*
2. *Stalking the Buffalo*
3. *Cradle in a Sod House*
4. *Rodeo*

Woodland Reveries (Three untitled pieces) (No. 3, 1928).

Yaltah — Danseuse orientale (Yaltah — Oriental Dancer).

Two Pianos

Sonata Noël (Christmas Sonata).

Piano and Organ

Choral and Fugue.

Organ Solo

Barcarolle (1932–1933).

Chant pour la Toussaint (Song for All Saints' Day) (1929).

Deux fugues (Two Fugues) (1931).

Fugue in D minor (1937).

Fugue in E-flat minor (Introductory Fugue to *O Earth, Return!*).

Fugue in G.

Fugue in G minor (On a subject inspired by César Franck) (1937).

Grave.

Impromptu in E-flat (1941).

Litany (1939).

Nocturne.

Pastorale.

Three Holiday Chorals (Chorales) (1932).
1. *Choral pour Noël* (Chorale for Christmas)
2. *Choral pour l'autre année* (Chorale for the Old Year)
3. *Choral pour une nouvelle année* (Chorale for a New Year)

Chamber

Adagio for clarinet in A and piano.

Allegretto for flute and piano (1929).

Chant (Song) for violoncello and piano (1926).

Chant funèbre (Funeral Song) for string sextet (With optional Bass) (1920) (Score and parts).

Étude chromatique (Chromatic Study) for clarinet in B-flat (or A) and piano.

Lamento (Lament) for viola and piano (1930).

Petite suite (Little Suite) for flute and viola (1929) (Score and parts).

Petite suite for flute, violin, viola and violoncello (or string quartet) (1930) (Score and parts).

Petite suite for harpsichord (or harp) and flute (1932) (Score; flute part [First Movement only]).

Quartet for Strings (No. 1) (Lost).

Quartet in A minor for Strings (1931).

Quartet in C-sharp minor for Strings (Score and parts).

Quartet in E minor for Strings (1932).

Quartet in G-sharp minor for Strings (1926).

Sonata for two violins and piano (Score and parts).

Sonata in C for violin and piano (1941–1942) (Score and part).

Sonata in C-sharp minor for violin and piano (1938–1939).

Sonata in E minor for violin and piano (Score and part).

Sonatine for flute, viola, violoncello and harp (or piano) (1932).

(Score; parts [first three movements only]).

Sonatine for violoncello and piano (Score and part).

Suite for string quartet and flute (Score and parts).

Three Nocturnes for viola and piano (1929).

Trio for flute and two clarinets in B-flat (or A) (1932–1935).

Trio for Flute (or Clarinet in B-flat or A), Clarinet in B-flat (or A) and violoncello (may also be performed as a String Trio) (1933).

Trio in B minor for piano, violin and violoncello (Score and parts).

Trio in D minor for strings (1929).

Trio in D minor for strings (1931).

Valse Sentimentale (Sentimental Waltz) for piano with flute obbligato (1932).

Orchestral

Concerto for Flute and Orchestra (1940).

Elegy (1920–1921) (Score and parts).

Esquisses Normandes (Norman Sketches) (1929) Orchestrated by Charles Koechlin (1945) (Score and parts).

1. *Chant d'automne* (*Dans un cimetière à la campagne*) (Song of Autumn [In a country cemetery])
2. *Solitude sur les falaises* (Solitude on the Cliffs)
3. *Aux champs* (In the Fields)
4. *La mer joyeuse* (The Joyous Sea)

Rhapsody of Amairgin of the Golden Knee (1934–1938) (After a Celtic poem of the eleventh century [English version by V. C. C. Collum]) (Score and parts).

The Bride of a God. Symphonic poem after an old Hindu legend. (Written in collaboration with Charles Koechlin).

The Partheneia 1916 — Aranyani of the Jasmine Vine (A masque based on a series of scenes by Maude Meagher) (Score and parts).

Three Movements for Chamber Orchestra (1939–1940) (Score and parts [New, computer-engraved edition]).

Arrangements

Chant d'automne (Song of Autumn) from *Esquisses Normandes* (Norman Sketches) (Arranged for organ, C. Shatto).

Comme une berceuse (Like a Berceuse) (Melody, C. Urner; Harmonization, C. Shatto) (Arranged for flute and organ [also, flute and piano], C. Shatto) (Score and part).

Concerto for Flute and Orchestra — First Movement (Arranged for organ, C. Shatto).

Jubilee Suite (Arranged for flute and piano, C. Shatto) (Score and part).

Nocturne (Arranged for violin and organ, C. Shatto) (Score and part).

Two Sketches from From a Car Window in France (Arranged for organ, C. Shatto).

1. (3.) *Tea on the Sidewalk*
2. (5.) *A Sentimental Walk (In Boileau Street — Paris)*

Two Traditional American Indian Songs (Arranged for organ, C. Urner).

1. *Corn Grinding Song*
2. *Sun Dance*

Bibliography

Kirk, Elise Kuhl. "A Parisian in America: The Lectures and Legacies of Charles Koechlin," *Current Musicology* 25. New York: Columbia University, 1978.

Orledge, Robert. *Charles Koechlin (1867–1950) His Life and His Works*. Chur, Switzerland: Harwood Academic Publishers, 1989.

Sempol. Nice: *L'Éclaireur de Nice et du Sud-Est* (Nice, France), January 19, 1932.

Discography

Esquisses Normandes. The Bay Area Women's Philharmonic (now The Women's Philharmonic), JoAnn Falletta, conductor. Berkeley: Archival Tape (world premiere), 1990.

Three Movements for Chamber Orchestra. The Women's Philharmonic, Apo Hsu, conductor. San Francisco: Archival Tape (world premiere), 1998.

Sur les flots lointains, poème symphonique sur un chant de C. Urner (On the Distant Waves, Symphonic Poem on a Theme of C. Urner) op. 130 by Charles Koechlin; selections 2 and 4 on this CD are full orchestra and string orchestra versions respectively. Rheinland-Pfalz Philharmonic, Leif Segerstam, conductor. Sheffield (Yorkshire, UK): Marco Polo, 8.223704, 1994.

Several recent archival recordings — including the *Mystic Trumpeter* (Scott Farthing, conductor; James Elswick, trumpet; Chorus of Members of the Vocal Studies Department, University of Missouri — Kansas City Conservatory of Music) and two songs, *Music I Heard With You* and *Colloque Sentimental* (Sentimental Colloquy) (Christine Tremonti, soprano; Alfredo Oyagüez, piano), as well as a few primitive early discs (Urner herself recorded on one) may be heard at The Music Library, 240 Morrison Hall, University of California, Berkeley.

Editorial Comments

The overriding editorial principle here has been to produce clear and simple scores, avoiding, wherever possible, ambiguous or "fussy" notation. In the piano accompaniments, for instance, in accordance with idiomatic piano style where the damper pedal is to be employed, if one voice acts for two (as in the left hand of the piano part in measures 6 and 16 of *After Parting*), this notation has been adopted. Since several autographs exist for each song, questions involving dynamics, articulation, hand divisions, etc. have posed somewhat more of a conundrum, considerable consultation with Charles Shatto notwithstanding. Despite these hurdles, a conscientious effort has been expended to resolve all issues and to come up with practical yet musically appropriate versions of these exquisite compositions.

Nichts ist dauernd

Nichts ist dauernd als der Wechsel,
nichts beständig als der Tod.
Jeder Schlag des Herzens schlägt uns eine Wunde,
und das Leben wäre ein ewiges
Verbluten, wenn nicht die Dichtkunst wäre.

Nothing is lasting but change,
nothing certain but death.
Every heartbeat brings but wounds,
and bated breath!
All of life were but pain, eternal bleeding, if poetry were not.

Translated by Catherine Urner

Nichts ist dauernd

Ludwig Börne

Catherine Urner
David Zea, editor

After Parting

Sarah Teasdale

Catherine Urner
David Zea, editor

Allegretto moderato [♩ = 63–72]

Voice

Piano

mp L.H. *(sotto)* R.H. *legato [con Ped.]* *p*

3

mf Oh I have sown my love so wide That

mf

5

poco rit. [a tempo] poco rit.

he will find it eve - ry - where;

[sopra]

8

a tempo *mp* poco rit.

It will a-wake him in the night, It will en-fold him

[mp] L.H. [L.H. *sopra*]

10
molto rit.
a tempo
poco rit.
in the air.
L.H.
[p leggiero]
[mp cantabile]
[senza Ped.]
[sotto]
[mf]
13
a tempo
mf
I set my shad-ow in his sight And I have winged it
mf
con Ped.
16
poco rit.
a tempo
p
[molto cresc.]
ff
[mf]
with de - sire, That it may be a cloud by day And
[p]
molto cresc.
ff
[p]
19
f
poco rit.
a tempo
poco rit.
in the night a shaft of fire.
f
mf
p

Lili Boulanger
(1893–1918)

NICOLE LABELLE

Lili Boulanger was born in Paris, on August 21, 1893. (See vol. 6 for a more complete biography, list of works, bibliography, and discography.) Frail since childhood, she died from Crohn's disease at the age of twenty-four. She received her first music lessons from her mother and her older sister, Nadia (1887–1979) (see this volume), learning to play the piano, violin, cello, and harp. Her first composition, a song, *La lettre de mort*, dates from 1906, and is probably a farewell to her father who died in 1900. She had sketched many compositions between 1906 and 1909 which she destroyed after she completed her musical training. At sixteen, Boulanger decided to dedicate herself to music, taking lessons in harmony, counterpoint, and fugue with Georges Caussade (1873–1936). Two years later she entered the composition class of Paul-Antoine Vidal (1863–1931) at the Conservatoire de Musique de Paris, where she studied from 1909 to 1913. Her notebooks contain a great number of composition exercises that she undertook in preparation for the tests of the Prix de Rome; she was the first woman recipient of this prize in 1913. She was also the first woman invited to reside at the Villa Médicis in Rome (part of the prize) where she went in March 1914 for the first time, staying for several months. The advent of World War I in September kept her from returning until March 1916. However, due to illness, she did not return to Paris until the end of June. Although her health continued to deteriorate, she completed some of her best works in the last two years of her life. She died on March 15, 1918.

The musical production of Boulanger, not voluminous but dense, contains a considerable amount of choral music, sacred as well as secular. Three periods of creativity can be distinguished during her life: the early years (1906–1909), the years of apprenticeship (1910–1913), and the years of mastery (1914–1918). Her choral output may be divided into two very distinct parts: secular and sacred. She composed eight secular works before World War I and five sacred works during the war, although she did try her hand at setting religious texts for chorus and piano as early as 1906–1907.

The secular choral works, written during her second creative period (1910–1913), includes *Sous bois* for chorus and orchestra and *Les Sirènes* for mezzo-soprano, chorus, and piano (both 1911). She also set *Renouveau*, a poem by Armand Sylvestre, as an accompanied vocal quartet. This won the Prix Lepaulle in 1912.

In that same year, Boulanger wrote some of her most important choral works including *Soir sur la plaine*, for soprano, tenor, chorus, and orchestra; the choruses *La Source*, and *Pendant la tempête*, and *Hymne au soleil*. She also composed *Pour les funérailles d'un soldat* (1912–1913), for solo baritone, mixed chorus, and orchestra, inspired by verses originating from "La coupe et les lèvres" by Alfred de Musset. (This work earned her the Prix Lepaulle in 1913.)

Almost all the choruses mentioned above were composed as preparatory exercises for the Prix de Rome competition. The candidates had to submit to elimination rounds: in five days, in isolation at the Château de Compiègne, they each wrote a fugue on a given subject and set a chorus with orchestra on an assigned text. Those who qualified had the right to participate in the final round. Again in isolation at the Château for a month, they composed cantatas for soloists and orchestra on a given text. Boulanger passed the first examination for which she produced the choral work *Soir sur la plaine*, and was admitted to the second test. Her cantata *Faust et Hélène* received the coveted prize, which she shared with Claude Delvincourt.

Boulanger's masterworks were written between 1914 and 1918. She sketched *Psalms 129* and *130* in 1910, and completed the former during her sojourn in Rome in 1916 and the latter in 1917. *Psalm 24*, the shortest of her three extant psalms, was started in September 1915 and completed in March 1916. Through these three works Boulanger demonstrated her mastery of large choral and instrumental ensembles. *Psalm 24* (V. 23), *La terre appartient à l'éternel*, scored for tenor, mixed chorus, organ, brass instruments, timpani, and harp, is an optimistic work, quite unusual among her compositions. Archaic and aggressive sonority opens this compact, concise work that attests to unexpected strength and power from a young woman ravaged by illness. The wide homophonic style of *L'Hymne au soleil* and *Funérailles pour un soldat* prepared her to conceive this granite block, harsh and glittering.

Psalm 129 (V. 128), *Ils m'ont assez opprimé*, is a dramatic work for baritone, male chorus and orchestra. The roughness of the opening measures and later harsh pungency of the music contrast strikingly with a final song of comfort expressed softly by the baritone over women's voices humming pianissimo—soft soothing lightness after painful supplications.

Psalm 130 (V. 129), *Du fond de l'abîme*, the well-known *De Profundis*, was begun in 1914 at the Villa Médicis, and completed in February 1917 at the Boulanger summer home in Gargenville. For contralto, tenor, chorus, organ and orchestra, it is her masterpiece. In this, her longest and most complex composition, the text expresses not only pain and anguish, but also hope for relief. A powerful and heartbreaking work, its harrowing distress never finds consolation, even in the final epilogue that plunges back into the darkness of the abyss.

The *Vieille prière bouddhique*, based on an old Buddhist text translated by her friend Suzanne Karpelès, is a meditation on universal love. She began it in Rome in 1914, and completed it in Arcachon, in the Gironde, in 1917. Composed for tenor, chorus and orchestra, this work on an eastern theme employs a chant that by its incessant repetitions acts as an obsessive ritual.

Boulanger sketched the sonorous, contrapuntal *Pie Jesu* in 1909, and resumed work on it in 1913. The last notes were dictated to her sister Nadia, a few days before she died. The work is spare and discrete, from the unique child's voice to the organ accompaniment, to the string quartet and the harp heard only at the very end. The last verse brings back the chromaticisms of the organ while the harp overlaps the quartet and the voice rises in a soft "Amen" over a discreetly polytonal atmosphere.

Three unpublished choruses from the preparatory exercises for the tests for the Prix de Rome are presented here: *Sous bois*, *Pendant la tempête*, and *La Source*. The manuscripts are held at the Département de la Musique at the Bibliothèque Nationale de France.

Sous bois, for mixed chorus and piano, is dated August 25-30, 1911. The text, an excerpt of *L'Herbier, Fleurs et feuilles* (1890), is by Philippe Gille (1831–1901); the manuscript, 310 x 245 mm., is numbered Ms. 19491, 9 folios. It is marked at the end "Copied September 23, 1911, at Gargenville," and signed Lili Boulanger. (According to Léonie Rosenstiel, *Sous bois* existed in an orchestral version. She saw it in November 1973 at Nadia Boulanger's residence; but never saw the version with piano.[1]) We now know that Nadia Boulanger gave the piano/choral manuscript to the Bibliothèque Nationale de Paris, and not the orchestral one that seems to have been lost or destroyed.

Boulanger set the text to music in six hours and forty-five minutes as indicated on the first page of the manuscript. Marked *Moderato très à l'aise*, the piece is written in D-flat major, in $\frac{4}{4}$ meter. The short, eight-measure introduction contains syncopated parallel fourths based on the dominant, played in the high register of the keyboard. The voices enter successively, first the basses, then altos and sopranos, with the tenors joining in measure 12 as the piano adds a brief evocative bird song motif (mm. 10, 12). The second phrase opens with the tenors who initiate a small canonic passage on the words "Le rossignol chante" (The nightingale is singing) (m. 16). After a brief silence the voices come together to declare that "Nos coeurs sont d'accord" (Our hearts are in agreement) (m. 24). The first *forte* climax is reached at "Écoutons sa voix" (Let us listen to its voice) (m. 28), resolving in E-flat minor (m. 29). A brief piano interlude based on the rhythm of the introduction leads to a soprano solo marked *avec mélancolie, presque triste* (m. 33), which asks "Pourquoi faut-il que tout s'efface?" (Why must everything be erased — ?). The basses announce "Ces bois verront une autre aurore" (These woods will see another dawn) (m. 46), increasing the tempo until the tenors join in double *forte*, "Pour y chanter de nouvelles amours" (Singing of new loves) (m. 51). During this section, the piano accompanies with elaborated patterns of the introduction. A rapid *diminuendo* (mm. 54-55) from *fortissimo* to *piano* leads back to the *pianissimo* of the opening, now based on the tonic D-flat, marked *Lent Plus calme encore qu'au commencement* (m. 56). The female voices, in unison, are joined by the male voices in octaves (m. 57), dividing the chorus into two duets. The sopranos sing long notes on "ah!" (m. 70) while the other voices conclude the last verses of the text "comme un murmure" (like a murmur); after ascending scales in fourths at the keyboard (mm. 70-71) the voices are divided into seven parts (mm. 72-73) at the final cadence. The stylistic features inherent in the choral music of Boulanger are found in this work. Elegiac in tone, this chorus distinguishes itself by the delicacy of the writing.

Pendant la tempête, for tenors, baritones, basses, and piano, dated April 17 and 23, 1912, the text is excerpted from *Poésies nouvelles, España* (1844) by Théophile Gautier (1811–1872). The manuscript is 345 x 260 mm., numbered Ms. 19492, 8 folios. The original title of the poem, "Pendant la tempête," is found in the second introductory folio. Léonie Rosenstiel asserts that the chorus *Pendant la tempête*, seems to have been lost or destroyed. It is most likely the same chorus she discusses that bears the title *La tempête*.[2]

The work, clearly more dramatic than *Sous bois*, is in F-sharp minor, in $\frac{4}{4}$. Although not indicated, a *tempo agitato* is suggested. In a short introduction of seven measures, *fortissimo* triplets of descending and ascending broken chords in the high register of the keyboard overlay a bass made up of chords and octaves that enters at measure 3 in a rhythm of two against three. At measure 8 the voices join in softly, starting with the tenors, followed by the baritones and then the basses. The fairly tight contrapuntal texture continues above an undulating accompaniment that becomes more and more agitated through a rhythmic *ostinato* that seems to reflect the verse at measure 12, "La vague nous jette au ciel en courroux" (The wave thrusts us against the angry sky). The voices reach a climax at the verse "Près du mât rompu" (By the broken mast) (m. 19), and then are *piano* in measure 22, "Prions à genoux" (Let us fall to our knees).

The second stanza, although written in $\frac{3}{2}$, maintains the same accompaniment figuration, moving to E-flat minor in measure 28. The meter returns to $\frac{4}{4}$ in the third verse (m. 34), and the music modulates chromatically and unwinds in a long crescendo reaching a dazzling *fortissimo* on the last word "l'éclair" (lightning) (m. 47). Boulanger paints the meaning of the text through both dynamics and key changes. After a short pause (m. 48), the voices return *moins vite* in a syllabic setting over an accompaniment made up of octaves and tremolos in the low register of the piano. The last verse (m. 62) is a complete recapitulation of the first stanza. A piano postlude of nine measures (m. 79), containing the features of the introduction, ends the work softly.

La Source, for mixed chorus and piano, text from *Poèmes antiques* (1852) by Leconte de Lisle (1818–1894), dated 1912, was recopied by an unknown copyist on April 1, 1915. The manuscript, 350 x 270 mm., is numbered Ms. 19489, 8 folios. *La Source*, for mixed chorus and orchestra is undated. It is also 350 x 270 cm., numbered Vma. ms 1151, and is 27 pages long. The version for mixed chorus and piano was composed for the elimination round for the Prix de Rome in 1912. Rosenstiel assumes that this was lost or destroyed, and that the version for orchestra was adapted from the piano version. Both manuscripts do exist, however, but there are some discrepancies between the two.[3] Written for piccolo, two flutes, two oboes, English horn, two clarinets in A, two bassoons, four horns in F, two timpani, triangle and cymbals, two harps, strings and four-voice mixed chorus, the orchestration explores the impressionist effects suggested by a bucolic and evocative text. While the vocal parts are written in $\frac{3}{4}$, the orchestra begins in $\frac{9}{8}$, ensuring a free rhythmic flow between the two groups while illustrating the cradling movement of the water. (Boulanger is a master of word painting.) Written in B major, the work begins *pianissimo* and translates the atmosphere of the text into delicate *glissandi* played by the harps, suggesting waterfalls against very discreet trills of timpani executed with sponge sticks in measures 13-17 and later. Through the morning haze, several notes pierce the air at the start, sustained by the woodwinds on F-sharp while the low strings play *arco* and *pizzicato*. In the fourth measure, the sopranos initiate the first stanza, imitated by the tenors, while the violins embellish with descending and ascending pentatonic motives answering one another. As the music unfolds, the strings create a warbling effect but always with ethereal delicacy and restraint, never leaving the initial key except for a brief passage in the tonic minor key (m. 12). At measure 17 the orchestra adapts the $\frac{3}{4}$ meter of the chorus. The horns indicate the transition to the second very pastoral stanza (m. 19), begun by the tenors in ornamented counter-point with the violins (m. 20).

A very sparse orchestration of strings and woodwinds accompanies the tenors. In an orchestral interlude (m. 32) the cellos introduce a brief ascending chromatic motive repeated by the English horn while the violins sing a more florid melody. The flutes (mm. 36-50) in turn enable us to hear the bird song against a sonorous background of divided strings that accompanies the alto solo (m. 39) while the harps create a floating texture (m. 38 ff), joined by clarinets and horns with their *glissandi* in measure 50 ff.

In the transition leading to the fourth stanza (m. 56) the meter returns to $\frac{9}{8}$. Three upper voices (m. 57) are accompanied by material similar to that in the first stanza. The basses join the chorus for the two final verses (m. 69). The violins play tremolos against the flutes' bird songs and the tinkling of the harps and timpani, while in a last burst the violins reprise their small *grupetti* from the end of the first stanza. Although the work never goes beyond *mezzo forte,* it sustains the listener's interest with charming subtleties, impressionistic effects, and the sharpness of its detail.

These three choruses, composed in less than one year by an eighteen year old, reveal her ability to translate into music poetic texts inspired by nature, nature that brought her comfort and balance in the turmoil of her severe illness. She also succeeded in synthesizing homophonic and contrapuntal styles while creating beautiful lyrical melodic lines.

Acknowledgments

We express our gratitude to M. Bernard Brossollet, general director of Durand Editions and Cliché Bibliotèque Nationale de France, Paris.

Notes

1. Léonie Rosenstiel, *The Life and Works of Lili Boulanger* (Rutherford, N. J.: Farleigh Dickenson University Press, Inc., 1978), 55-56.

2. Ibid., 146.

3. Ibid., 279, note 106.

List of Works

Lili Boulanger or her sister destroyed most early compositions after she began to study music seriously. The designations "unpublished" and "incomplete" are taken from source files at the Bibliothèque Nationale in Paris.

Songs

Les pauvres (undated). Text by Verhaeren. Incomplete.

La lettre de mort (voice, piano) (1906). Text by E. Manuel. Destroyed.

Ave Maria (1908). Destroyed.

Reflets (1911). Text by Maurice Maeterlinck. Paris: Ricordi, 1919.

Attente (1912). Text by Maurice Maeterlinck. Paris: Ricordi, 1918.

Le retour (1912). Text by Georges Delaquys. Paris: Ricordi, 1919.

Clairières dans le ciel (1913–1914). Text by Francis Jammes. Paris: Ricordi, 1919. Paris: Durand, 1970 (revised by Nadia Boulanger). Songs 1, 5-7, 10-13 orchestrated.

Dans l'immense tristesse (1916). Text by B. Galeron de Calone. Paris: Ricordi, 1919.

Pie Jesu, soprano, harp, organ, string quartet (1918). Paris: Durand, 1922.

Stage

La Princesse Maleine (opera) (1912–1918). Text by Maurice Maeterlink. Incomplete.

Choral

Psalm 126 (chorus, orchestra) (undated). Incomplete. Lost.

Apocalypse (1909). Incomplete. Destroyed.

Psalms 131, 137 (1907). Destroyed.

I Corinthians 13 (1909). Destroyed.

Psalms 1, 119 (1909). Destroyed.

Psalm 129, Ils m'ont assez opprimé (1909–1916). Paris: Durand, 1924.

Psalm 130, Du fond de l'abîme (1910–1917). Paris: Durand, 1925.

Maïa, cantata (1911). Text by Fernand Beisser. Unpublished.

Les sirènes (1911). Text by Charles Grandmougin. Paris: Ricordi, 1918.

Soleils de septembre (1911). Destroyed.

Sous bois (1911). Text by Phillipe Gille. Manuscript.

Frédégonde (1911–1912). Text by Charles Morel. Incomplete. Unpublished.

Renouveau (1911–1912). Text by Armand Silvestre. Paris: Ricordi, 1918.

Hymne au soleil (1912). Text by Casimir Delavigne. Paris: Ricordi, 1918.

Pendant la tempête (1912). Text by Théophile Gautier. Manuscript.

Le soir (1912). Destroyed.

Soir d'été (1912). Lost.

La source (1912). Text by Leconte de Lisle. Unpublished.

Pour les funérailles d'un soldat (1912–1913). Text by Alfred de Musset. Paris: Ricordi, 1918.

Two fugues, four voices (1912, 1913). Unpublished.

Alyssa (1913). Lost.

Faust et Hélène, piano and voices (1913); orchestra and voices (1920). Text by Eugène Adenis, after J. W. von Goethe. Paris: Ricordi, 1913; Paris: Durand, 1970.

Soir sur la plaine (1913). Text by Alfred Samain. Paris: Ricordi, 1918.

Vieille prière bouddhique (1914–1917). Paris: Durand, 1921–1925.

Psalm 24, La terre appartient à l'éternel (1916). Paris: Durand, 1926.

Bibliography

Chailley, Jacques. "L'Oeuvre de Lili Boulanger." *La Revue Musicale* 353-354 (1982): 17-44.

Citron, Marcia J. "European Composers and Musicians, 1880–1918. Lili Boulanger." In *Women Composers and Music. A History*, ed. Karin Pendle. Bloomington and Indianapolis: Indiana University Press, 1991.

Croguennoc, Sylvie. "Les mélodies de Lili Boulanger." In *Actes du Colloque autour de la mélodie française*. Rouen: 1987.

Debussy, Claude. "La musique espagnole. *Faust et Hélène* par Lili Boulanger." *S.I.M.* (December 1, 1913): 43-44. Reprinted in *Claude Debussy. Monsieur Croche et autres écrits*, ed. François Lesure. Paris: Gallimard, 1971.

Dumesnil, René. "Lili Boulanger." In *Portraits de musiciens français*. Paris: Librairie Plon, 1938.

Fauser, Annegret. "Die Musik hinterer Legende: Lili Boulangers Liederzyklus *Clairières dans le ciel." Neue Zeitschrift für Musik*, Jg. 151, no. 11 (1990): 9-14.

______. "Eine verlorene Prinzessin der Avantgarde? Zum Schaffen von Lili Boulanger." *Neue Züricher Zeitung*. 193 (August 21/22, 1993): 55-57.

_______. "Lili Boulanger." In *The New Grove Dictionary of Music*. London: Macmillan, 2001 (work list with R. Orledge)

Honegger, Marc. "Lili Boulanger." In *Dictionnaire de la musique*, vol. I, ed. Marc Honegger. Paris: Bordas, 1986.

Jameux, Dominique. "Lili Boulanger." In *The New Grove Dictionary of Music and Musicians*, ed. Stanley Sadie. London: Macmillan, 1980.

Jezic, Diane Peacock. In *Women Composers: The Lost Tradition Found*. New York: The Feminist Press, 2nd ed., 1994.

Charles Koechlin. "Evolution de l'harmonie." In *Encyclopédie de la musique et Dictionnaire du Conservatoire*. Paris: Delagrave, 1925.

Landormy, Paul. "Lili Boulanger." *Musical Quarterly* 16 (1930): 510-15.

Lebeau, E. *Lili Boulanger*. Preface by Antoine Terrasse. Paris: Bibliothèque Nationale, exhibition catalogue, 1968.

Mattis, Olivia. "Lili Boulanger: polytoniste." *Lili Boulanger-Tage Bremen 1993. Zum 100. Geburtstag der Komponistin*, ed. K. Mosler. Bremen: Zeichen und spuren frauenliteraturverlag, 1993.

Mauclair, Camille. "La vie et l'oeuvre de Lili Boulanger." *La Revue Musicale*. 2/10 (1921): 147-55.

Méry, Jules. "Lili Boulanger." *Rives d'Azur* 167 (1924): 891-93.

Nies, C., and R. Aulenkamp-Moeller, eds. *Lili Boulanger 1893–1918*. Kassel: Catalogue for 3rd International Festival on Women Composers, 1993.

Orledge, Robert. "Lili Boulanger." In *The Norton/Grove Dictionary of Women Composers*, eds. Julie Anne Sadie and Rhian Samuel. London: Macmillan, 1994.

Palmer, Christopher. "Lili Boulanger." *The Musical Times* 109 (1968): 227-28.

______. "The Boulanger Phenomenon." *Gramophone* 71 (July 1993): 30-31.

Reeser, H. Eduard. "Lili Boulanger." *De Muziek* 7 (1933): 210-21, 264-79.

Rosenstiel, Léonie. *The Life and Works of Lili Boulanger*. Rutherford, N. J.: Fairleigh Dickinson University Press, 1978.

______. "Lili Boulanger." In *Historical Anthology of Music by Women*, ed. James Briscoe. Bloomington, Ind.: Indiana University Press, 1987.

Discography

Chamber Works by Women Composers. Joseph Roche, violin; Paul Freed, piano. Vox SVBX 5112, 3 records (1979). *Nocturne, Cortège*.

For the Flute. Katherine Hoover, flute; Barbara Weintraub, piano. Leonarda LP1 104. *Nocturne, D'un matin de printemps*.

In memoriam Lili Boulanger. Emile Naoumoff, Isabelle Sabrié, Sylvie Robert, Doris Reinhardt, Catherine Marchese, Olivier Charlier, Roland Pidoux. Patrimoine Naxos 8.550982 (1993). *Thème et variations, D'un matin de printemps, Nocturne, Cortège, Clairières dans le ciel* (excerpts), *D'un vieux jardin, D'un jardin clair, Dans l'immense tristessse, Le retour, Pie Jesu*.

Lili Boulanger. Martin Hill, Andrew Ball, The New London Chamber Choir, James Wood, conductor. Hyperion CDA 66726 (1994). *Clairières dans le ciel, Les sirènes, Renouveau, Hymne au soleil, Soir sur la plaine, Pour les funérailles d'un soldat*.

Lili Boulanger. James Wood, conductor. Recorded at a public concert March 1, 1975, in the Chapel of Trinity College, Cambridge, by Jonathan Halliday; booklet by Christopher Palmer. *Du Fond de l'abîme, Three pieces for violin and piano: Cortège, Nocturne, D'un matin de printemps, Pie Jesu*.

Lili Boulanger. Chorale Elisabeth Brasseur, Orchestre Lamoureux, Igor Markevitch, conductor. Everest Stereo SDBR 3059 (1960). Everest EVC 9034 (1995). *Psaume 130, Psaume 24, Psaume 129, Vieille prière bouddhique, Pie Jesu*.

Premiere: Recorded Performances of Keyboard Works by Women. Sister Nancy Fierro, piano. Avant Records (1974). *Cortège, D'un vieux jardin*.

Songs by Lili Boulanger. Kristine Ciesinski, soprano; Ted Taylor, piano. Leonarda LP 1 118 (1983). *Clairières dans le ciel*.

Editorial Comments

Comparison between Durand and Labelle editions:

Sous bois

Measure	Durand edition	Labelle edition
5	piano rh, 2nd sixteenth note moves down; crescendo in ms. missing	piano rh, 2nd sixteenth note moves up
70	alto part D-natural	D-flat as in ms.

Pendant la tempête

Measure	Durand edition	Labelle edition
	Title page: "Chorus for four voices with piano"	Work is written for three male voices and piano, see p. 816 following
36		piano LH flat added to E in chord

La Source

The Durand edition is for chorus and piano. This edition is with full orchestra. Lili Boulanger made some corrections to the orchestral setting three years after she composed the piano version. Observations are based on the Durand edition for piano and Labelle edition for orchestra.

Measure	Durand edition	Labelle edition
7	on "fo" alto C	B (follows soprano line)
8	on "mu" alto G-sharp quarter note on "Dé-ro" tenor E-D on "te" bass D	E eighth note B-C G-sharp
23	on "tes" D	C-sharp (as bar 21)
31	piano rh beat 3 C-sharp	flute C-natural (agrees with clarinet)
35	piano rh, beat 2 A-sharp	violin 1, A-natural (continues harmony from previous measure)
58	on "grands" tenor G-sharp	F-sharp
59	on "cerfs" tenor F-sharp on "in" tenor F-sharp	G-sharp G-sharp
60	on "grands" alto quarter rest, two quarter notes B	half note B, quarter note A-sharp
61	on "in" alto D-natural	D-sharp
62	on "ro" soprano C-sharp	B
65	alto rest	tied quarter note F-sharp
67	on "Dor" soprano B, piano B-sharp on "po" tenor B on "sées" tenor B-sharp	B-naturals A-natural C-sharp
68	on "dorment" tenor A-sharp, B-sharp	A-natural, B-natural
72	on "dais" alto F-natural	A-natural
75	on "Reposées" bass E's on two eighth notes, dotted quarter, eighth rest	E, F-sharp, E, two eighth notes half note
76	on "syl" bass E-sharp	E-natural
78	on "seux" tenor D-sharp and F-sharp	D-sharp
80	notes are held through the first beat	voices end on the first beat of m. 79

Sous bois

Marchons devant nous
Bien douce est la pente.
Le rossignol chante
Dans l'ombre des bois.
Nos coeurs sont d'accord
Et la nuit est belle.
Elle nous appelle
Écoutons sa voix.

Let us step forward
Smooth is the slope.
The nightingale is singing
In the shade of the woods.
Our hearts are in accord
And the night is beautiful.
It is calling us
Let us listen to its voice.

Pourquoi faut-il
Que tout s'efface
Que ces rameaux
Sur nous penchés
Á d'autres demain
Aient fait place
Par le temps flétris
Et séchés?

Why must all
be erased
Why must these branches
bent over us

Be replaced by time-wilted and dried up tomorrows?

Ces bois verront
Une autre aurore
Et d'autres nuits
Et d'autres jours.
Des oiseaux y viendront encore
Pour y chanter de nouvelles amours.

These woods will see
another dawn
And other nights
And other days
The birds will come here again
Singing of new loves.

Et ce doux sentier qui nous charme
En l'absence d'un coeur glacé
Recevra peut-être une larme
Où tant de bonheur a passé.

And this sweet path that is charming us
In the absence of a cold heart
Will perhaps receive a tear
Where so much bliss has passed.

Pendant la tempête

La barque est petite et la mer immense
La vague nous jette au ciel en courroux
Le ciel nous renvoie au flot en démence
Près du mât rompu, prions à genoux!

Small is the boat, immense is the sea.
The waves thrust us against the angry sky
The sky returns us to the insane waters,
By the broken mast, let us pray on bended knees!

De nous à la tombe, il n'est qu'une planche
Peut-être ce soir dans un lit amer
Sous un froid linceul fait d'écume blanche
Irons-nous dormir, veillés par l'éclair!

Between us and our tomb, there is but the width of a board
Perhaps tonight in a bitter bed
Under a cold shroud made of white foam
We will sleep, watched over by lightning,

Fleur du Paradis. Sainte Notre-Dame
Si bonne aux marins en péril de mort,

Flower of paradise, Blessed our Lady
So kind to sailors threatened by death,

Apaise le vent, fait taire la lame
Et pousse du doigt notre esquif au port.

Appease the wind, silence the wave
And with the push of a finger, bring our fragile huff into the port.

La barque est petite et la mer immense
La vague nous jette au ciel en courroux
Le ciel nous renvoie au flot en démence
Près du mât rompu, prions à genoux!

Small is the boat, immense is the sea.
The waves thrust us against the angry sky
The sky returns us to the insane waters
By the broken mast, let us pray on bended knees!

La Source

Une eau vive étincelle en la forêt nue et muette
Dérobée aux ardeurs du jour,
Et le roseau s'y ploie et fleurissent autour
L'hyacinthe et la violette.

Si les chèvres paissant les cytères amers
Aux pentes des proches collines,
Ni les pasteurs chantant sur les flûtes divines
N'ont troublé la source aux flots clairs.

Les noirs chênès aimés des abeilles fidèles
En ce beau lieu versent la paix,
Et les ramiers blottis dans le feuillage épais
Ont ployé leur col sous leurs ailes.

Les grands cerfs indolents par les Balliers mousseux,
Yument les tardives rosées,
Sous le dais lumineux des feuilles reposées.
Dorment les sylvains paresseux.

Quick waters sparkle in the barren and silent forest
Hidden from the heat of the day,
And the reeds bend and bloom around
The hyacyinth and violet.

If the goats grazing the bitter herbs
On the slopes of the nearby hills,
Neither shepherds singing on their divine flutes
Have disturbed the limpidity of the clear springs.

Dark oaks beloved by loyal bees
Bring forth peace in this beautiful place,
And the wood pigeons huddled in the dense foliage
Have bent their necks under their wings,

Indolent stags inhale the belated dew,
Under the luminous cover of the fallen leaves
Sleep the lazy sylvas.

Translations by Colette and Michel Guggenheim

Sous bois

Philippe Gille

Lili Boulanger
Nicole Labelle, editor

Moderato très à l'aise

Soprano
Alto
Ténor
Basse

Moderato très à l'aise

8va
pppp
8va
8va
pp
Piano
pppp

4

presser
presser

(8va)
presser
pp
*
presser
mf
**

*Durand edition: second sixteenth note chord moves down a step; mss. moves up.
**Crescendo missing in Durand edition.

7
rall.
Très simple
pp
Mar-chons de-vant
en dehors mais pp
Mar-chons de-vant
pp
p
Mar - chons de - vant
(8va)
f
rall.
Très simple
pp
p
10
p
nous, bien douce est la pen - te.
nous, bien douce est la pen - te
p
Mar-chons de - vant
pp
nous, bien douce est la pen - te.
8va
8va

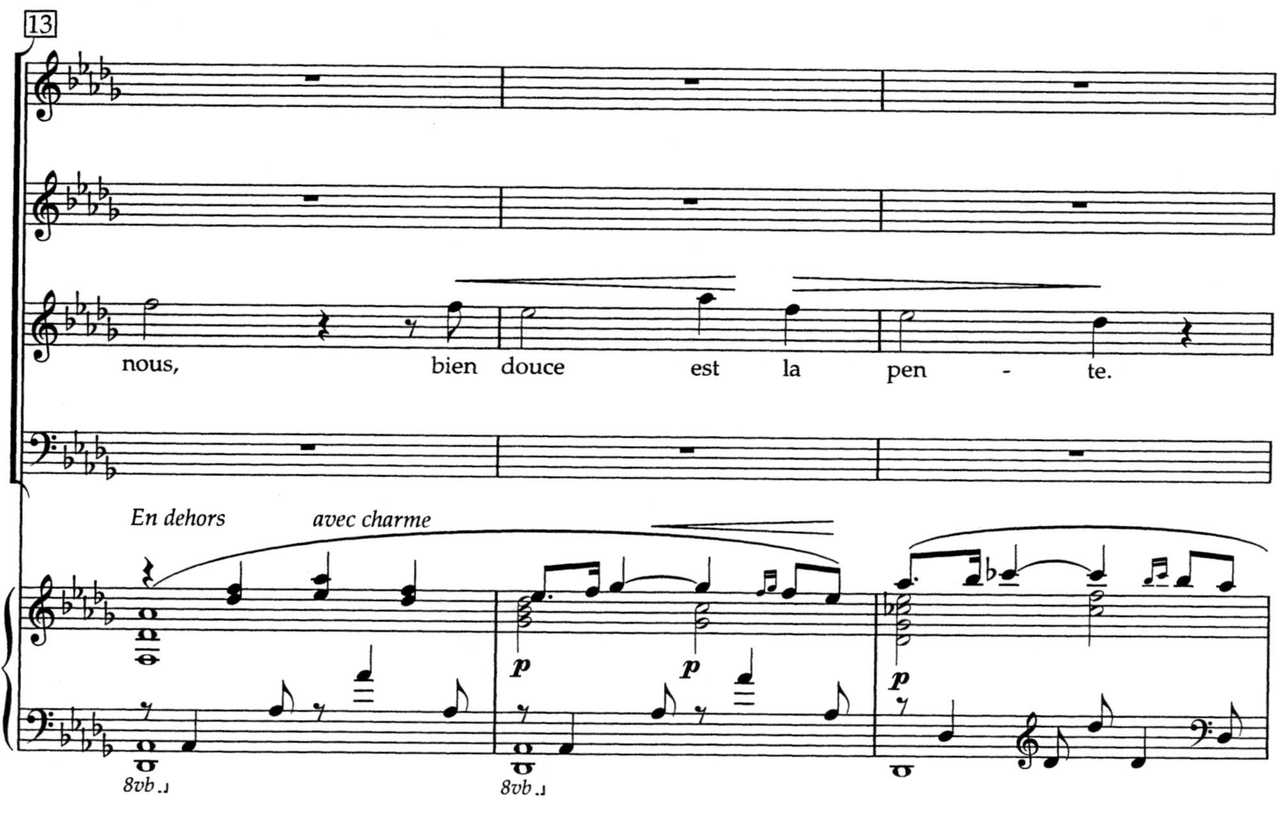
13
nous, bien douce est la pen - te.
En dehors
avec charme
p
p
p
8vb

16
pp
Le ros-si-gnol chan - te dans l'om - bre des bois.
3
8va

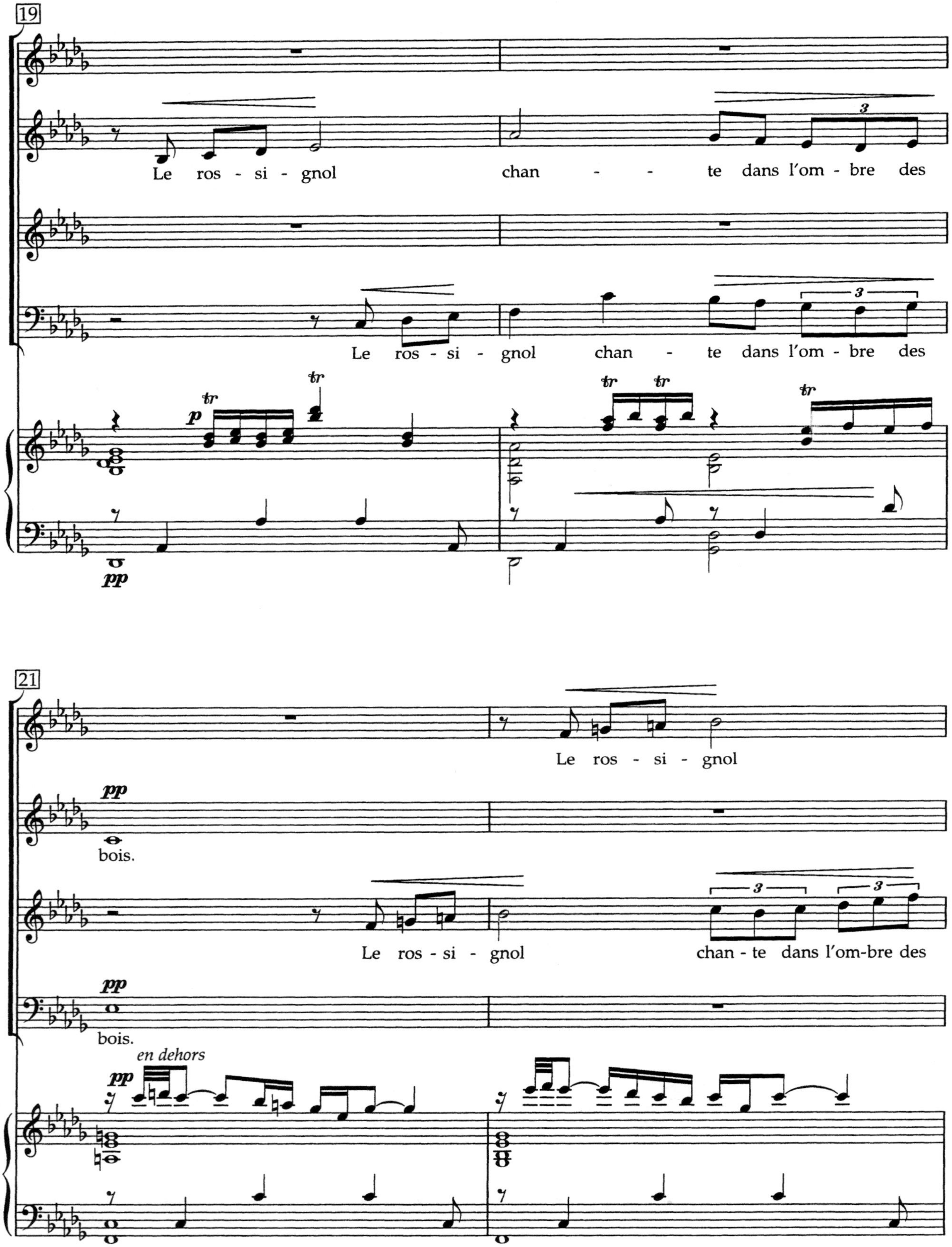

19

Le ros - si - gnol chan - - te dans l'om - bre des

Le ros - si - gnol chan - te dans l'om - bre des

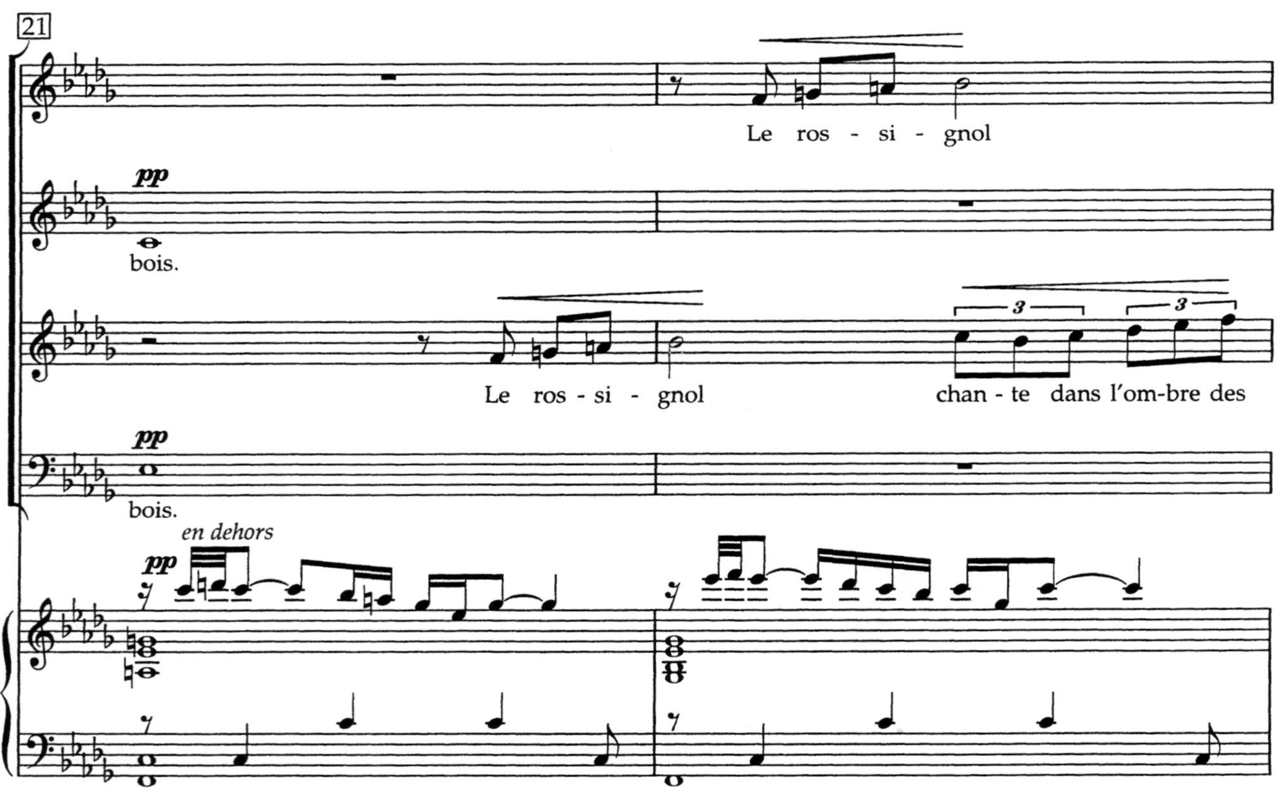

*This rall., in the manuscript, is missing in the Durand edition.

*faire attendre le temps suivant

32
avec mélancolie, presque triste
p
Pour-quoi faut - il que tout s'ef - fa - ce Que
p
détaché

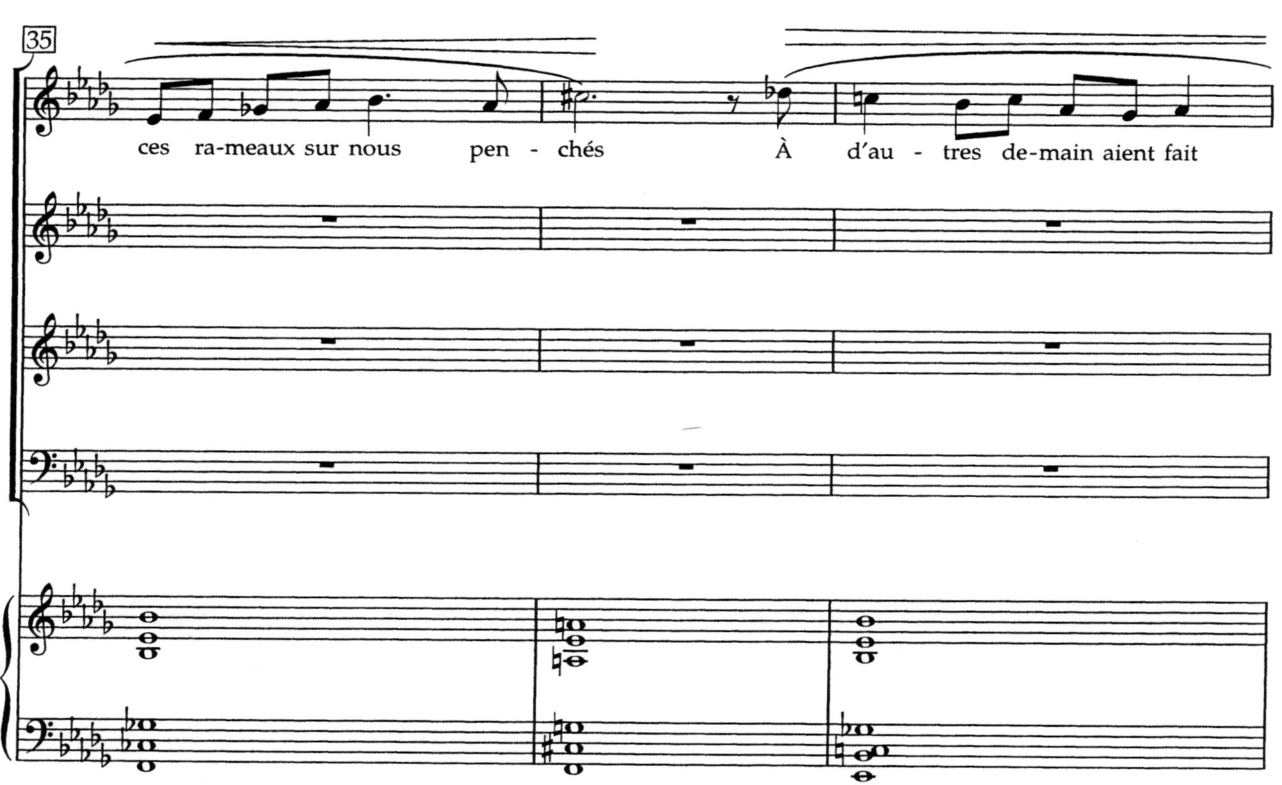
35
ces ra-meaux sur nous pen - chés À d'au - tres de-main aient fait

38
pla - ce Par le temps flé-tris et sé - chés?
f

42
Un peu plus lent
Un peu plus lent
8va
pp
p

45
presser à partir de cette mesure de plus en plus en
p
Ces bois ver-ront une autre au-ro - re Et
(8va)
48
augmentant beaucoup
f
mf
d'au - tres nuits et d'au - tres jours. Des oi -
(8va)
f

50
ff
Pour y chan -
ff
ff
seaux y vien dront en - co - - re Pour y chan -
f
52
rall.
fff
ter de nou - vel - les a - mours.
fff
ter de nou - vel - les a - mours.
rall.
8va
ff
fff

54
Lent Plus calme encore
qu'au commencement
ppp
Et ce
ppp
Et ce
(8va)
3
3
ff
p
Lent Plus calme encore
qu'au commencement
ppp

57
doux sen-tier qui nous char - me En l'ab - sen - ce d'un coeur gla -
doux sen-tier qui nous char - me En l'ab - sen - ce d'un coeur gla -
Et ce doux sen-tier qui nous char - me En l'ab-sen -
Et ce doux sen-tier qui nous char - me En l'ab-sen -
p
p
p

*Durand has D-natural here; ms. has D-flat

*Durand has D-natural here; ms. has D-flat

Pendant la tempête*

Théophile Gauthier

Lili Boulanger
Nicole Labelle, editor

*In the Durand edition the title page reads: "Chorus for four mixed voices with piano." The work is scored for three male voices and piano.

10
mer im - men - - se La va - gue nous
ti - te et la mer im - men - se
barque est pe - ti - te et la mer im -
3
13
jette au ciel en cour - roux Le
La va - gue nous jette au ciel en cour -
men - se La va - gue nous jette au
3

15
ciel nous ren - voie au flot en dé -
roux Le ciel nous ren - voie au flot en dé -
ciel en cour - roux Le ciel

17
men - ce Près du mât rom -
men - ce
nous ren - voie au flot en dé - men -

19

pu — oui, près du mât rom -

Près du mât rom - pu —

- - ce

23
rall.
a tempo
pri - ons à ge - noux!
pri - ons à ge - noux!
pri - ons à ge - noux!
rall.
a tempo
f
25

27
Piano
mf
29
Baryton
mf
De nous à la tom - - be
31
il n'est qu'u - ne plan - - - -
f
33
che
p
Peut - ê - tre ce
p

*Durand edition has C#'s in this measure.

47
Ténor
[moins vite]
Fleur du Pa-ra - dis, Sain - te No-tre-Da - me
Baryton
clair!
Fleur du Pa-ra - dis, Sain - te No-tre-Da - me
Basse
Fleur du Pa-ra - dis, Sain - te No-tre-Da - me
[moins vite]
51
Si bonne aux ma - rins en pé - ril de mort, A-pai - se le vent,
Si bonne aux ma - rins en pé - ril de mort, A-pai - se le vent,
Si bonne aux ma - rins en pé - ril de mort, A-pai - se le vent,

56
p
rall.
fais tai - re la la - me
p
fais tai - re la la - me Et pous-se du doigt notre es -
p
fais tai - re la la - me
rall.
61
Tempo primo
p
La barque est pe - ti - te et la
quif au port
p
La barque est pe -
p
La
Tempo primo
f
p

64
mer im - men - - se La va - gue nous
ti - te et la mer im - men - se
barque est pe - ti - te et la mer im -
67
jette au ciel en cour - roux Le
La va - gue nous jette au ciel en cour -
men - se La va - gue nous jette au

69
ciel nous ren - voie au flot en dé -
roux Le ciel nous ren - voie au flot en dé -
ciel en cour - roux Le ciel
3

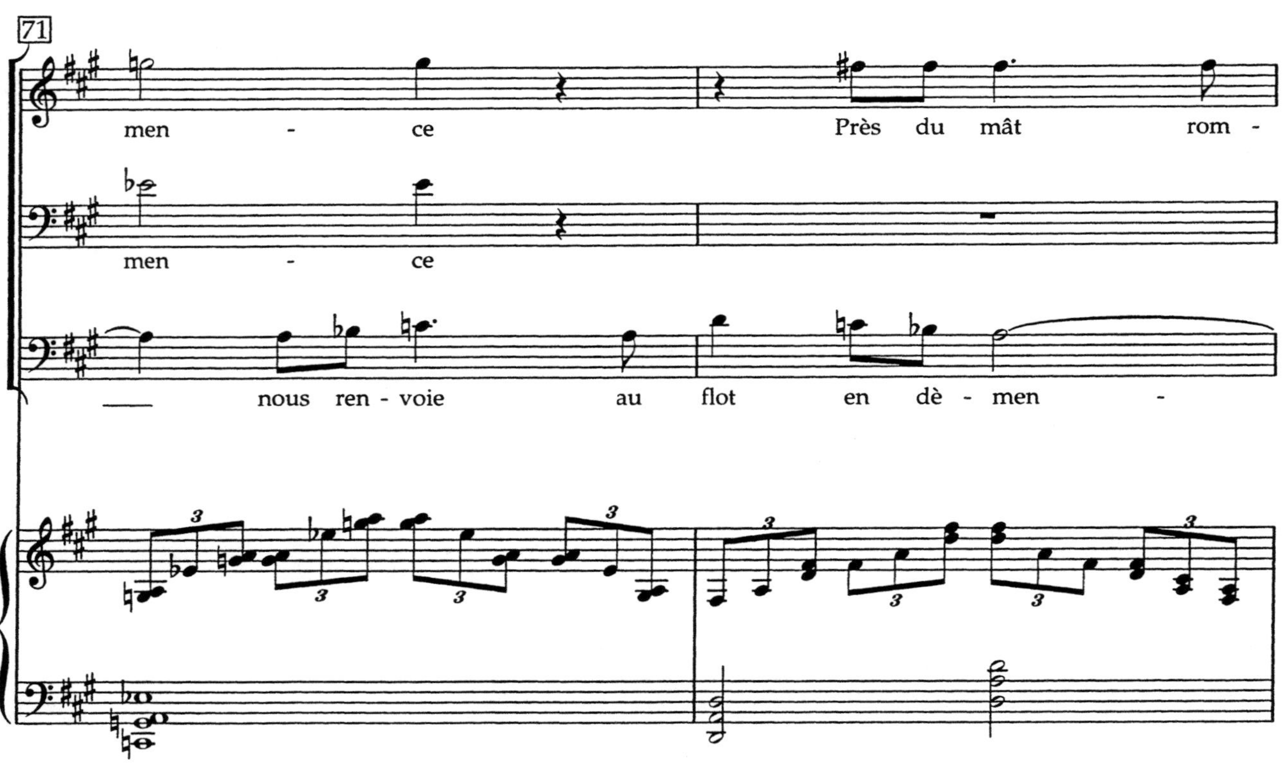
71
men - ce Près du mât rom -
men - ce
nous ren - voie au flot en dè - men -
3

73
pu,
oui, près du mât rom -
Près du mât rom - pu,
- - ce

75
pu,
pri - ons,
pri - ons,
Près du mât rom - pu,
pri - ons,

77
— pri - ons à ge - noux!
— pri - ons à ge - noux!
— pri - ons à ge - noux!

79

81

83
Piano

85

La source

Leconte de Lisle

Lili Boulanger
Nicole Labelle, editor

4
Picc.
Fl. 1,2
Ob. 1,2
E.H.
Cl. 1,2 in A
Bn. 1,2
Hn. in F
Timp.
Tri. Cym.
Hp. 1
Hp. 2
S.
A.
T.
B.
Vn. 1
Vn. 2
Va.
Vc.
Cb.
p en dehors
Une eau vive é - tin - celle en la fo - rêt mu - et -
Une eau vive é - tin -
Une eau vive é - tin - celle en
Une eau vive é - tin - celle en
unis. pizz.

7
Picc.
Fl. 1,2
a2
Ob. 1,2
E.H.
Cl. 1,2 in A
Bn. 1,2
Hn. in F
1 2
3 4
Timp.
Tri. Cym.
Hp. 1
Hp. 2
S.
- te Dé - ro - bée aux ar - deurs du jour
A.
celle en la fo - rêt mu - et - - te
T.
la fo - rêt mu - et - - - te Dé - ro - bée aux ar -
B.
la fo - rêt mu - et - te Dé - ro - bée aux ar -
Vn. 1
Vn. 2
Va.
Vc.
Cb.

10
Picc.
Fl. 1,2
Ob. 1,2
E.H.
Cl. 1,2 in A
Bn. 1,2
Hn. in F
Timp.
Tri. Cym.
Cym.
Hp. 1
Hp. 2
S.
Et le ro - seau s'y ploie et fleu -
A.
Dé - ro - bée aux ar - deurs du jour Et le ro -
T.
deurs du jour Et le ro - seau s'y ploie et fleu - ris -
B.
deurs du jour Et le ro - seau s'y ploie et fleu -
Vn. 1
très chanté
Vn. 2
Va.
Vc.
div. arco
Cb.
pizz.

*Grace note notated F sharp in manuscript.

**Bassoons have dotted half notes only in mm. 14-15 in manuscript.

16
Picc.
Fl. 1,2
a2
Ob. 1,2
E.H.
Cl. 1,2 in A
Bn. 1,2
Hn. in F
Timp.
Tri. Cym.
Hp. 1
Hp. 2
S.
et la vi - o - let - - - - te.
A.
et la vi - o - let - - - - te.
T.
et la vi - o - let - - - - te.
B.
et la vi - o - let - - - - te.
Vn. 1
8va
Vn. 2
div.
unis.
Va.
Vc.
Cb.
[unis. pizz.]

19
Picc.
Fl. 1,2
Ob. 1,2
pp
E.H.
pp
Cl. 1,2 in A
Bn. 1,2
[1.]
p
p
Hn. in F
Timp.
Tri. Cym.
Hp. 1
Hp. 2
S.
A.
T.
p
Si les chè - vres pais - sant les cy -
B.
très chanté
(8va)
Vn. 1
p
Vn. 2
tr
p
Va.
p
unis.
div.
Vc.
p
Cb.

22
Picc.
Fl. 1,2
1.
3
p
Ob. 1,2
E.H.
Cl. 1,2 in A
Bn. 1,2
Hn. in F
1 2
3 4
Timp.
Tri. Cym.
Hp. 1
Hp. 2
S.
A.
T.
tè-res a-mers
aux pen - tes des pro-ches col-li - nes,
B.
Vn. 1
Vn. 2
Va.
Vc.
Cb.

25
Picc.
Fl. 1,2
Ob. 1,2
E.H.
Cl. 1,2 in A
Bn. 1,2
Hn. in F
Timp.
Tri. Cym.
Hp. 1
Hp. 2
S.
A.
T.
B.
Ni les pas - teurs chan - tant sur les flû - tes di -
Vn. 1
Vn. 2
Va.
Vc.
Cb.
[arco]

28
Picc.
Fl. 1,2
(1.)
p mais en dehors
a2
Ob. 1,2
pp
E.H.
Cl. 1,2 in A
pp
Bn. 1,2
pp
Hn. in F
1
2
3
4
1.
p
p
Timp.
change F♯ to A and B to E
Tri. Cym.
Hp. 1
Hp. 2
S.
A.
T.
p
vi - - - - - - - nes N'ont trou - blé la
B.
Vn. 1
Vn. 2
Va.
Vc.
Cb.

31
Picc.
Fl. 1,2
Ob. 1,2
E.H.
très chanté
Cl. 1,2 in A
Bn. 1,2
1.
Hn. in F
Timp.
Tri. Cym.
Tri.
Hp. 1
Hp. 2
S.
A.
T.
source aux flots clairs.
B.
très chanté
Vn. 1
Vn. 2
Va.
Vc.
Cb.

34
Picc.
Fl. 1,2
1.
2.
Ob. 1,2
E.H.
Cl. 1,2
in A
Bn. 1,2
1
2
Hn.
in F
3
4
Timp.
Tri.
Cym.
(Tri.)
Hp. 1
Hp. 2
S.
A.
T.
B.
Vn. 1
Vn. 2
Va.
Vc.
Cb.

37
Picc.
Fl. 1,2
Ob. 1,2
E.H.
Cl. 1,2 in A
Bn. 1,2
Hn. in F
Timp.
Tri. Cym.
(Tri.)
Hp. 1
Hp. 2
S.
A.
Solo
Les noirs chê -
T.
B.
Vn. 1
Vn. 2
Va.
Vc.
Cb.
div.

40
Picc.
Fl. 1,2
Ob. 1,2
E.H.
Cl. 1,2
in A
Bn. 1,2
Hn.
in F
Timp.
Tri.
Cym.
Hp. 1
pp
Hp. 2
pp
S.
A.
- vres ai - més des a - beil - les fi - dè - - - - -
T.
B.
Vn. 1
Vn. 2
pp
Va.
Vc.
Cb.

43
Picc.
Fl. 1,2
Ob. 1,2
E.H.
Cl. 1,2 in A
Bn. 1,2
Hn. in F
1
2
3
4
Timp.
Tri. Cym.
Hp. 1
Hp. 2
pp
S.
A.
les En ce beau lieu ver - sent la paix,
T.
B.
Vn. 1
Vn. 2
Va.
Vc.
Cb.

46
Picc.
Fl. 1,2
Ob. 1,2
p
E.H.
Cl. 1,2 in A
Bn. 1,2
Hn. in F
1 2
3 4
Timp.
change E to D
Tri. Cym.
Hp. 1
pp
Hp. 2
S.
A.
Et les ramiers, blot - tis dans le feuil -
T.
B.
Vn. 1
Vn. 2
Va.
Vc.
Cb.
unis.

49
Picc.
Fl. 1,2
Ob. 1,2
E.H.
Cl. 1,2 in A
Bn. 1,2
Hn. in F
Timp.
Tri. Cym.
Hp. 1
Hp. 2
S.
A.
T.
B.
Vn. 1
Vn. 2
Va.
Vc.
Cb.
pp
ppp
lage é - pais
Ont plo - yé leur
bien chanté unis.
mf

52
Picc.
Fl. 1,2
Ob. 1,2
E.H.
Cl. 1,2 in A
Bn. 1,2
Hn. in F
1 2
3 4
1.
pp
pp
pp
Timp.
change A to F♯ and D to B
Tri. Cym.
Hp. 1
Hp. 2
S.
A.
col
sous
leurs
ai
T.
B.
Vn. 1
3
Vn. 2
Va.
Vc.
Cb.

*English Horn and Clarinets have dotted half notes only in m. 53 in manuscript.

58
Picc.
Fl. 1,2
1.
p
Ob. 1,2
E.H.
Cl. 1,2 in A
Bn. 1,2
Hn. in F
1
2
3
4
Timp.
Tri. Cym.
Hp. 1
p
Hp. 2
p
S.
cerfs in - do - lents par les Bal - liers mous -
A.
[tutti] pp
Les grands
T.
Les grands cerfs in - do - lents par les Bal -
B.
Vn. 1
pp
Vn. 2
Va.
Vc.
Cb.

61
Picc.
Fl. 1,2
Ob. 1,2
E.H.
Cl. 1,2 in A
Bn. 1,2
Hn. in F
Timp.
Tri. Cym.
Hp. 1
Hp. 2
S.
seux, Hu - ment les tar - di - ves ro - sées,
A.
cerfs in - do - lents par les Bal - liers mous -
T.
liers mous - seux Hu - ment les tar - di - ves ro - sé - es
B.
Vn. 1
Vn. 2
Va.
Vc.
Cb.

*Grace note notated E double-sharp in manuscript.

67
Picc.
Fl. 1,2
Ob. 1,2
E.H.
Cl. 1,2 in A
Bn. 1,2
Hn. in F
Timp.
Tri. Cym.
Hp. 1
Hp. 2
S.
A.
T.
B.
Vn. 1
Vn. 2
Va.
Vc.
Cb.
Dor - ment les syl - vains pa - res - seux
les tar - di - ves ro - sées,
feuil - les re - po - sées Dor - ment les syl - vains pa - res -

70
Picc.
Fl. 1,2
Ob. 1,2
E.H.
Cl. 1,2 in A
Bn. 1,2
Hn. in F
Timp.
Tri. Cym.
Hp. 1
Hp. 2
S.
Sous le dais lu - mi - neux des
A.
Sous le dais lu - mi -
T.
seux
Sous le dais lu - mi -
B.
Sous le dais lu - mi -
Vn. 1
Vn. 2
Va.
Vc.
Cb.

73
Picc.
Fl. 1,2
Ob. 1,2
E.H.
Cl. 1,2 in A
Bn. 1,2
Hn. in F 1 2 3 4
Timp.
Tri. Cym.
Hp. 1
Hp. 2
S.
feuil - les re - po - sées Dor - -
A.
neux des feuil - les re - po - sées
T.
neux des feuil - les re - po - sées
B.
neux des feuil - - - les re - po - sées
Vn. 1
Vn. 2
Va.
Vc.
Cb.

76
Picc.
Fl. 1,2
[a2]
tr
pp
Ob. 1,2
E.H.
Cl. 1,2 in A
Bn. 1,2
Hn. in F
Timp.
ppp
Tri. Cym.
Hp. 1
Hp. 2
S.
ment les syl - vains pa - res - seux.
A.
Dor - - ment les syl - vains pa - res - seux.
T.
Dor - - ment les syl - vains pa - res - seux.
B.
Dor - ment les syl - vains pa - res - seux.
Vn. 1
8va
Vn. 2
div.
Va.
Vc.
[unis.]
Cb.

79
Picc.
Fl. 1,2
Ob. 1,2
E.H.
Cl. 1,2 in A
Bn. 1,2
Hn. in F
Timp.
Tri. Cym.
Hp. 1
Hp. 2
S.
A.
T.
B.
Vn. 1
Vn. 2
Va.
Vc.
Cb.
unis.
[div.]
(8va)
ppp
pppp
pp

Eva Alberta Jessye

(1895–1992)

JOSEPHINE R. B. WRIGHT

Eva Jessye was a pioneering female conductor of choral music, and the first woman of African-American descent to achieve international recognition professionally in this field.[1] She composed and arranged music, wrote poetry, and acted on the stage and in films. Born in Coffeyville, Kansas, on January 20, 1895, to Albert and Julia Jesey,[2] she acquired her earliest musical training there. The family was musical and she studied piano during grade school.[3] In 1908 Jessye gained early admission to the Quindaro State School for the Colored,[4] in a suburb of Kansas City, Kansas, where she completed high school in 1914. She majored in poetry and oratory and studied music theory, harmony, composition, music history, piano, and organ. Jessye then enrolled at Langston University in Oklahoma, graduating in 1919 with a B.A. degree and a permanent teaching certificate for the state of Oklahoma.[5] Following short stints teaching in the public schools of Haskell, Muskogee, and Tulahassee, in Oklahoma, and at Morgan State and Clafin College, she left the field of education in 1922 and moved to New York City. There she studied privately with Will Marion Cook (1869–1944), the African-American composer,[6] and from 1926–1928 she corresponded with the music theorist Percy Goetschius who critiqued her work.[7] Both encouraged her professional aspirations.

Jessye's early years in New York overlapped the period of the Harlem Renaissance, the intellectual movement among African-American writers, musicians, artists, and dancers who sought to celebrate their cultural heritage through the creative and performing arts. Influenced by composers Cook, Harry T. Burleigh (1866–1949), R. Nathaniel Dett (1882–1943), and J. Rosamond Johnson (1873–1954), Jessye decided she would devote much of her time to preserving the Negro spiritual and black folk song traditions.[8] Around 1925 she organized a choral group, first called the Original Dixie Jubilee Singers and later renamed the Eva Jessye Choir.[9] She regularly directed the choir in performances on such shows as the "Major Bowles Family Radio Hour" and "The General Motors Hour." By 1926 the choir had established a solid reputation as a major professional choral ensemble in the United States, earning commissions for performances and touring widely throughout the country.[10]

Jessye also organized and conducted other choirs. In 1929 King Vidor hired her to provide choral music for his epic film *Hallelujah*, one of the earliest black musicals.[11] In 1934 Virgil Thomson recruited Jessye's choir for performances of his opera *Four Saints in Three Acts*, libretto by Gertrude Stein.[12] Jessye is listed as choral director for the New York production. However, her name is not listed for the première in Hartford, Connecticut, although she was the choral director and her choir functioned as the nucleus of the chorus.[13] The following year (1935) Jessye directed the choir in the first performance of George Gershwin's opera *Porgy and Bess*. Program credits included the Eva Jessye Choir and Eva Jessye as choral director.[14] She would later conduct numerous revivals of that opera during the 1940s, '50s, and '60s throughout the United States and in Europe. The Eva Jessye Choir continued successful appearances through 1970. However, at the peak of its acclaim Jessye said "The time came for me to redirect my energies and to conquer new fields."[15]

Jessye often composed and arranged the music she conducted. Among her works are three oratorios, *The Life of Christ in Negro Spirituals* (1931), *Paradise Lost and Regained* (1934), and *The Chronicle of Job* (1936), which combine Negro spirituals with narrative.[16]

In 1927 Jessye published *My Spirituals,* perhaps her best known work, an anthology of sixteen Negro spirituals arranged for solo voice and piano from which the selections included here — *Stan' Steady, Ain't Got Long to Stay Heah,* and *March Down to Jerdon* — are drawn. This volume belongs to the solo concert spiritual movement that began in 1917 with Harry T. Burleigh's publication of his arrangement of the spiritual *Deep River* as an art song for solo voice and piano accompaniment. Prior to the Burleigh arrangement, audiences around the world had known the Negro spiritual primarily through the concert choral arrangements popularized after the Civil War by the Fisk Jubilee Singers and similar student concert groups. In the preface to *My Spirituals* Jessye explains that the collection is "simply a recording of some songs I grew up with"[17] in Coffeyville, a small town near the

Kansas-Oklahoma border settled largely after the Civil War by ex-slaves from Alabama, Arkansas, Georgia, Kentucky, Tennessee, and Texas. According to Jessye, "They are the songs of my childhood and my own people. I have sung them all my life."[18]

The three songs retain the traditional chorus-verse structure of the traditional slave spiritual. *Stan' Steady*, a spirited song learned by Jessye from childhood playmates,[19] is syncopated throughout and resembles a shout spiritual — i.e., an upbeat, improvised sacred song sung by slaves and free blacks in the nineteenth century to accompany the "shout" or "holy dance."[20] The song contains a lively eight-bar chorus which shares a short refrain ("Doan mind what Satan says") with the verse. The chorus and verse are linked melodically as well as textually, in conformity with a common formulaic pattern for the Negro spiritual.

At first glance the title of Jessye's *Ain't Got Long to Stay Heah* suggests that it might bear some relationship to the familiar spiritual *Steal Away,* first published in 1872 by Biglow and Main for the Fisk Jubilee Singers.[21] The Jubilee song, *Steal Away*, and *Ain't Got Long to Stay Heah* both use the identical one-line text refrain that Jessye uses as the title. Jessye's spiritual bears no other relationship, however, to the spiritual *Steal Away,* either in its overall text or melody. Though short, fragmentary phrases of texts, such as "I'm heab'm bound," "Religion's like a bloomin' rose," or "Jordon's Stream is deep and cold," can certainly be found in refrains of choruses and verses within the traditional repertory of slave spirituals, no text or melodic concordances are known for Jessye's version.

Jessye advises her readers that she obtained this song from black migrant workers who went from Kansas each fall to work in the cotton fields of the Indian Territories in order to earn enough money to tide them over during the winter months:

> The pickers prided themselves on the amount of cotton they could weigh off daily, and there was keen interest in the tally at noon-day. Competition was strongest between the native Territorians and the visiting Kansans, with large wagers being laid as to the ability of both sides.
>
> Each group had its own song leader, whose business it was to keep a tune going to lighten the toil and thus speed up the cotton picking. The native leader, a strapping boy of nineteen summers, inspired his contingents with "Goin' To Pick Dis Cotton 'Tell De Sun Go Down," while the visitors, led by a short fat woman . . . replied with the pointed plaint: "Ain't Got Long To Stay Heah."[22]

The opening chorus of the spiritual is based upon a pentatonic mode and revolves around a three-note motif (A-F-G), creating the effect of a dirge or moan. Only in the contrasting verse does the range of the melody expand to the octave, and this occurs abruptly on the anacrusis of measure 15, punctuating the words "An' only them that has it [i.e., religion] knows" (verse one) and "It [Jordon's stream] chills the fame but not the soul" (verse two).

March Down to Jerdon, the final selection, is one of the few spirituals actually identified in the literature as a baptismal song.[23] Jessye wrote: "'On Jerdon's Stormy Bank I Stand' is . . . common to all sections of the country but in this particular locality [the banks of the Verdigris River], 'March Down To Jerdon,' was just as often used."[24] Martial and lively in character, Jessye captures inflections of blue notes within both the melody and the accompaniment of the song.

Jessye remains faithful to the folk-song heritage of the Negro spiritual by striking a delicate balance in her arranged spirituals between the solo voice and piano accompaniment, carefully avoiding pianistic virtuosity that would overshadow the melody. Similarly, she employs a conservative, post-romantic harmonic language in her accompaniment that preserves the integrity of the straightforward melodies.

Prior to her death, Jessye established archival collections at the University of Michigan, Ann Arbor (1974), and at Pittsburg [*sic*] State University in Kansas (1977). The collection in Michigan contains materials from her professional life and career and the other personal effects.

Acknowledgments

Permission to use Eva Alberta Jessye's *Stan' Steady*, *Ain't Got Long to Stay Heah*, and *March Down to Jerdon*, from *My Spirituals*, eds. Gordon Whyte and Hugo Frey (New York: Robbins-Engel, Inc., 1927) has been granted by Belwin Music for Warner Brothers.

Notes

1. Eileen Southern, *The Music of Black Americans: A History*, 3d ed. (New York: W. W. Norton, 1997), 422.

2. Eva Jessye changed the spelling of her last name in the late 1920s so that it would not be mistaken for a first name. Donald Fisher Black, "The Life and Work of Eva Jessye and Her Contributions to American Music" (Ph.D. diss., Music Education, University of Michigan, Ann Arbor, 1986), 18.

3. Ibid., 19-20.

4. The school, also known as Western University, a normal school, granted teaching certificates for the state of Kansas. It was run by the African Methodist Episcopal Church and the state of Kansas. Elementary schools in Coffeyville were integrated, but the high school was for whites only, requiring black students who wanted further schooling to continue their educations elsewhere. Ibid., 21.

5. Ibid., 21-24.

6. Jessye met Cook in 1908 while he was preparing scores at Western University. He asked her to assist him as a copyist and suggested that she pursue music as her career. Ibid., 22.

7. Ibid., 72.

8. Ibid.

9. Southern, *The Music of Black Americans*, 422.

10. Eileen Southern, *A Biographical Dictionary of African and African American Musicians* (Westport, Conn.: Greenwood Press, 1982).

11. Black, "Life and Work of Eva Jessye," 30.

12. Ibid., 36.

13. Ibid.

14. Ibid., 39.

15. Ibid., 61.

16. Ibid., 72-73.

17. Eva Jessye, *My Spirituals,* ed. Gordon Whyte and Hugo Frey (New York: Robbins-Engel, Inc., 1927), [Preface] n.p.

18. Ibid.

19. Ibid., 29. Jessye identifies her source as the Switzler children, whose parents came from either the Carolinas or Louisiana.

20. Southern slaves called the "holy dance" the "shout." For references to contemporary nineteenth- and early twentieth-century writings describing the shout, consult Eileen Southern and Josephine Wright, compilers, *African-American Traditions in Song, Sermon, Tale, and Dance, 1600s–1920: An Annotated Bibliography of Literature, Collections, and Artworks* (Westport, Conn.: Greenwood Press, 1990); for contemporaneous illustrations of the shout and further discussion, see Eileen Southern and Josephine Wright, *Images: Iconography of Music in African-American Culture (1770s–1920s)*, Music in African-American Culture series (New York: Garland Publishing, 2000).

21. See Theodore F. Seward, ed. *Jubilee Songs: Complete, as Sung by the Jubilee Singers of Fisk University* (New York: L. Biglow and Main, 1872), 28.

22. Jessye, *My Spirituals,* 33. That some black field hands after the War should choose to sing spirituals rather than secular songs while they worked suggests a continuity between their cultural traditions and those of their slave ancestors, who were Christians and refused to sing field hollers or "Devil" ditties.

23. See Southern and Wright, comps., *African–American Traditions in Song, Sermon, Tale, and Dance.*

24. Jessye, *My Spirituals*, 38.

List of Works

Songs

My Spirituals, eds. Gordon Whyte and Hugo Frey. New York: Robbins-Engel, Inc., 1927.

1. *Who Is Dat Yonder?*
2. *Spirit o' the Lord Done Fell on Me*
3. *An' I Cry*
4. *Bles' My Soul an' Gone*
5. *I Been 'Buked an' I Been Scorned*
6. *Stan' Steady*
7. *Ain't Got Long to Stay Heah*
8. *March Down to Jerdon*
9. *John Saw de Holy Numbah*
10. *I'm a Po' Li'l Orphan*
11. *When Moses Smote de Water*
12. *So I Can Write My Name*
13. *I Can't Stay Away*
14. *Tall Angel at the Bar*
15. *Got a Place at Las'*
16. *I'se Mighty Tired*

Oratorios

The Life of Christ in Negro Spirituals (1931).

Paradise Lost and Regained (1934). Text by John Milton. SATB, solo parts for soprano, alto, tenor, and two narrators. Source: University of Michigan, Ann Arbor (Eva Jessye Collection), fragment score.

The Chronicle of Job (1936). Text adapted from the Bible by Eva Jessye. SATB, solo parts for soprano, alto, tenor, and bass, and dancers. Source: University of Michigan, Ann Arbor (Eva Jessye Collection).

Bibliography

Black, Donald Fisher. "The Life and Work of Eva Jessye and Her Contributions to American Music." Ph.D. diss. University of Michigan, Ann Arbor, 1986.

[n.a.] "Going Backstage with the Scribe: Eva Jessye Choir Goes on the Air." *Chicago Defender*, December 24, 1932, 7.

Seward, Theodore F., ed. *Jubilee Songs: Complete, as Sung by the Jubilee Singers of Fisk University*. New York: L. Biglow and Main, 1872.

Southern, Eileen. *The Music of Black Americans: A History*. 3d ed. New York: W. W. Norton, 1997.

______, and Josephine Wright, compilers. *African-American Traditions in Song, Sermon, Tale, and Dance, 1600s–1920: An Annotated Bibliography of Literature, Collections, and Artworks*. Westport, Conn.: Greenwood Press, 1990.

______. *Images: Iconography of Music in African-American Culture (1770s–1920s)*. Music in African-American Culture series. New York: Garland Publishing, 2000.

Wilson, Doris Louise Jones. "Eva Jessye: Afro-American Choral Director." Ed.D. diss., Washington University, 1989.

Discography

Paradise Lost. Voice of American videocassette tape, featuring chorus, soloists, orchestra, and Eva Jessye, conductor (October 1979). Source: Pittsburg [*sic*] Kansas State University (Eva Jessye Collection).

Stan' Steady

Traditional

Eva A. Jessye
Josephine Wright, editor

Lively
Stan' stead-y, Stan' stead-y bre - ther-en
mf

4
Stan' stead-y, Doan mind what Sat - an says: Stan' stead-y,

7
Stan' stead-y bre - ther-en Stan' stead-y, Doan mind what Sat - an says:

10
Sat-ans' de man wid de i - ron shoe,
Sat - an thought he had me down,
Doan mind what Sat - an says:
12
If you doan mind gwine to clamp it on you,
I thank God I'm a heav - en boun',
Doan mind what Sat - an says:
14
Stan' stead-y,
Stan' stead-y bre - ther-en
16
ritard.
Stan' stead-y,
Doan mind what Sat - an says:

Ain't Got Long To Stay Heah

Traditional

Eva A. Jessye
Josephine Wright, editor

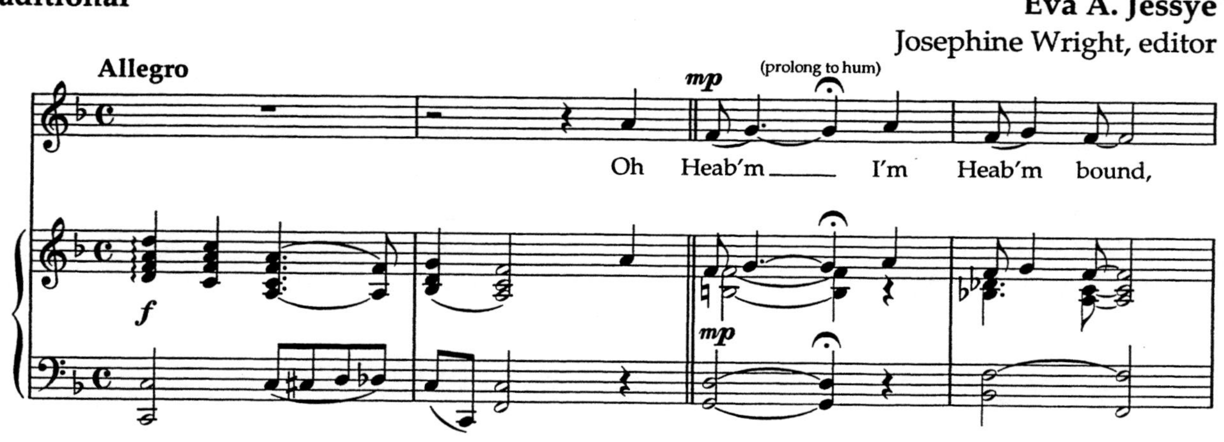

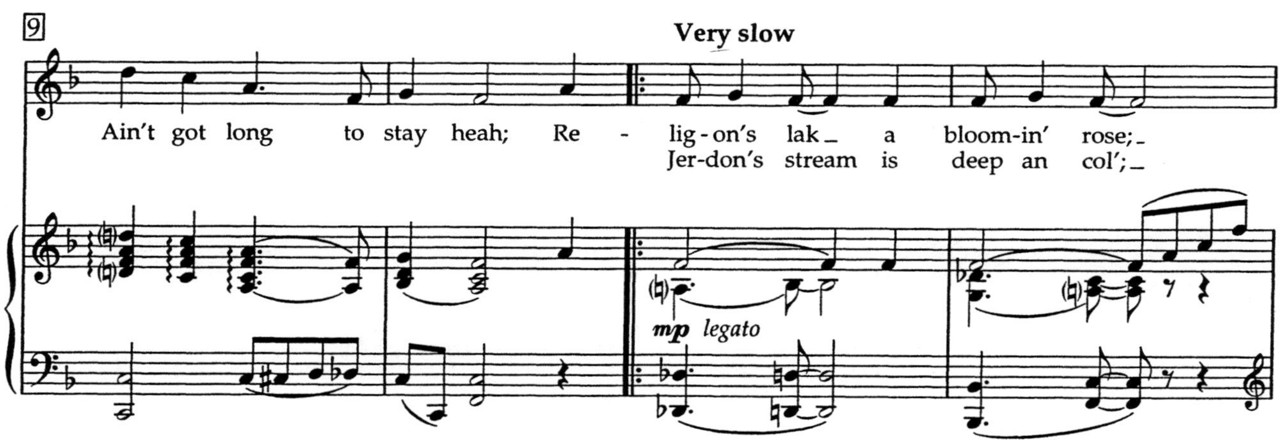

13
fervently
Ain't got long to stay heah; An' on - ly them_ that_
Ain't got long to stay heah; It chills the fame,_ but_
p
f
16
has it knows;_ Ain't_ got long to stay heah. Oh
not the soul;_ Ain't_ got long to stay heah. Oh
19
Heab'm_ I'm Heab'm bound, Ain't got long to stay heah; Oh
23
rall.
1.
2.
Heab'm_ I'm Heab'm bound, Ain't got long to stay heah. Ah stay heah.
L.H.
R.H.

March Down To Jerdon

Traditional

Eva A. Jessye
Josephine Wright, editor

Measurely fashion **Lively**

Yes; I'm gwine tu march___

mf *p* *mf*

13
whar yo' gwine mour - nah, Oh whar yo' gwine I say? Gwine
mf
17
down to de rib - ber of Jer - don, For to wash my sins a -
20
way. Yes, I'm gwine tu march down! March
mf
24
down yes, I'm gwine tu march down to Jer - don, Hal - le - lu - jah!

Barbara Giuranna

(1899–1998)

PAOLA DAMIANI

Barbara Giuranna (stage name Elena Barbàra Giuranna) was born in Palermo, Sicily, on November 18, 1899. Her mother, Elena Sensales Proto, was a gynecologist at one of the best clinics in Sicily and her father, Giuseppe Barbara, was a bank official at the Banco di Sicilia. He was also an amateur musician, a philosopher, and a sketch artist. At the age of six, Elena Barbàra, accompanied by one of her sisters, was sent to Naples to study music at the Instituto Mater Dei. She returned to Palermo in 1910 where she attended the Collegio Reale Maria Adelaide, graduating in 1917. She also studied piano privately with Guido Alberto Fano and began to write short compositions while giving piano lessons to support herself. When she was twenty she returned to Naples to study composition with Camillo DeNardis and Antonio Savasta. For her entrance exam she submitted a lyric composition on a French text (*Avec l'âme*), perhaps an homage to Claude Debussy. After graduating in 1923, she moved to Milan where she continued private composition studies with Giorgio Federico Ghedini. The following year she married conductor Mario Giuranna, with whom she moved to the United States. In 1929 Frederick Stock, conductor of the Chicago Symphony Orchestra, introduced two of Giuranna's symphonic works to the American public: *Apina rapita dai nani della montagna* (1924) (Apina Kidnapped by the Mountain Dwarfs), and *Marionette* (1925) (Puppets). The compositions were successfully received and performed again in New York under the direction of conductor Louis Pelletier at the Metropolitan Opera House in 1930.

Returning to Italy in 1933, Giuranna won a contest organized by the Sindacato Musicisti Italiani (Musicians Union) with her *Sonatina* for piano. Her first son, Bruno, was born the same year, followed two years later by her second son Paolo. In 1936 she became the first Italian woman composer invited to participate in the Festival di Musica Internazionale di Venezia (International Musical Festival in Venice) where her chamber work, *Adagio and Allegro for Nine Instruments*, was performed. Giuranna moved to Rome in August 1936, and on November 30 of that year was awarded first prize by the Sindacato Musicisti Italiani for her heroic symphonic poem *X Legio*. On that same day, tragically, her husband died in an accident in Naples where he was serving as superintendent of the San Carlo Theater. Alone and with two small children to raise, Giuranna continued to compose as she began a long teaching career at the Saint Cecilia Conservatory in Rome (1937–1976). In 1938 her *Toccata for Orchestra* was chosen to represent Italy at the Brussels International Festival.

Giuranna completed her lyric opera *Jamanto* in 1941. It was successfully staged at the Donizetti Theater in Bergamo and revived in Padua in 1942. However, as most theatrical activity in Italy ceased during World War II, there were no subsequent performances. Shortly after the end of the war Giuranna became a typist for RAI (Radiotelevisione Italiana) and in the 1950s worked as a musical consultant, realizing, transcribing and revising eighteenth-century Neapolitan operas, including *Le astuzie femminile* and *I due baroni di Roccazzurra* by Domenico Cimarosa (1749–1801) and *Il re Teodoro in Venezia* and *La Molinara* by Giovanni Paisiello (1740–1816); as well as a *Sonate for viola* by Antonio Vivaldi (1678–1741).

With the encouragement of the composer Alberto Bruni Tedeschi (1915–1996), Giuranna returned to writing opera and completed *Mayerling* (spelled *Majerling* in the score) in 1956. It was submitted to a competition sponsored by the Opera Theater in Rome, a competition later canceled because of presumed irregularities. However, this author discovered unofficially that she would have been the winner. Mario Labroca, a judge for the competition, organized a radio performance of the opera in 1958. It was performed again at the San Carlo in Naples 1960, and again in Palermo. *Mayerling* was presented for the first time in Rome at the Opera Theater in 1993.

In 1967 Giuranna won the International Prize of the City of Trieste for her second *Concerto per Orchestra*. In the late seventies she returned to the musical theater with *Hosanna*, a work based on current events to a libretto by Carlo Pinelli. This opera was performed in Palermo in 1978 at the Massimo Theater with *Cordovano*, an opera by Goffredo Petrassi (b. 1904).

In 1980 Giuranna wrote *Solo per viola* for her son Bruno. In 1983 she was the first woman elected to the Accademia di S. Cecilia, and in 1985 she was awarded the Domina Prize for Arts and Sciences. Her last work, the mass *Sinite parvulos*, was performed in Rome in 1990 during a concert in her honor. The event was organized by the Leonard Bernstein International Academy of the Arts (Accademia Internazionale delle Arti "Leonard Bernstein").

In August 1998, at the age of ninety-eight, Giuranna died in Rome. Her children and grandchildren carry on the family musical tradition. Bruno is a violist and teacher at the Hochschule in Berlin; Paolo, Giuranna's second son, is a theater director and dramatic composer. His two sons Damiano (b. 1964) and Riccardo (b. 1965) play the violin and piano.

Barbara Giuranna forged her career during the 1930s and 1940s, a period in Italian musical life rife with contradictions. The first signs of change appeared at the beginning of the twentieth century with the arrival of the avant garde movement. World War I marked an irreparable fracture with the past. The debate between tradition and innovation centered on opera. The *antiveristica* (against the *verismo* movement) attacks on new opera increased after the death of Giacomo Puccini (1858–1924). Poet Gabriele d'Annunzio, the fiercest critic, had a great influence on Italian musical taste of the time. Lively debates among artists and critics influenced many composers and resulted in a series of interesting works but they did not change the old, strongly conservative mood of a country naturally predisposed to nationalism. Italian culture suffocated under the new organization imposed by fascism beginning in 1922, and audiences turned to less problematic personalities including composers Umberto Giordano (1867–1948), Riccardo Zandonai (1883–1944), and Ottorino Respighi (1879–1936). The more complex and sensitive artists such as Alfredo Casella (1883–1947), Gian Francesco Malipiero (1882–1973) and Luigi Dallapiccola (1904–1975), were marginalized.

Aside from the conservative public, which favored the works of the great artists of the past, there was in Italian society an elitist group in search of something new. Their wishes were encouraged and supported by the fascist regime. Festivals of contemporary music were founded, composition competitions were held, and prestigious new works were supported. Mario Labroca (1896–1973), composer and artistic director of the May Florentine Musicals during the 1930s, joined painters De Chirico and Sironi with music, creating interdisciplinary shows of extraordinary quality. Fedele D'Amico wrote that music, because of its abstract nature, enjoyed the favor of the dictatorship and very rarely incurred censorship.[1] Many young composers, even those of different political thought, heard their works performed. During the war works of foreign artists were also performed in concert.

The limited popularity of contemporary music during fascism is proven by the data about which works were most often performed.[2] It also shows that there were a great number of new works which did not become part of the standard repertoire. The composers with the greatest number of performances were those from the *verista* tradition such as Pietro Mascagni (1863–1945), Umberto Giordano, Francesco Cilea (1866–1950) and Riccardo Zandonai. During the war years—the time of Giuranna's operatic debut with *Jamanto*—the dictatorship, in more and more difficulty, allowed the revival of older works to satisfy the public taste.[3] After the war, the panorama changed drastically; a cultural revival took place in all the arts, including literature, theater and cinema. The public was no longer interested in melodrama but in songs and variety shows broadcast over radio and later by television. Composers were finally free to experiment, negating the belief that ". . . the opera, as world, is a thing of the past."[4]

In the fifties the Italian musical avant-garde represented by Bruno Maderna (1920–1973), Luciano Berio (b. 1925), Luigi Nono (1924–1990), and others, was busy recovering lost time in assimilating the achievements of the Vienna School and electronic experimentation. The first theatrical works of this generation of Italian musicians burst into the sleepy Italian panorama only in the following decade, as in the case of the stormy theatrical debut of Luigi Nono's *Intolleranza 1960* at the Teatro alla Scala in Milan in 1961.

The Giuranna work reproduced in this anthology is excerpted from the opera *Mayerling*, her most important work. This tragic story of Rudolph of Hapsburg, heir to the Austro-Hungarian Empire, and the young baroness Maria Vetzera reaches its climax when the young couple commits suicide the night of January 29, 1889. The event marks the end of the Hapsburg dynasty and political equilibrium in Europe. Today, the work still retains a halo of romantic mystery that keeps it alive in the imagination and makes the events extremely fascinating as a melodrama plot. Vittorio Viviani, son of the Neapolitan poet and playwright, Raffaele, wrote the libretto. The declaration of love made by the young ethereal heroine to the surprised Rudolph is the unconventional beginning of this story. The relationship with Vetzera becomes liberation for the restless and tormented prince. Death with his lover is the only way of redemption.

Solidly tonal music accompanies the drama. The composer creates powerful scenes in which reality seems suspended. In the first scene we hear an obstinately frivolous and carefree Vienna represented by a waltz and a trio while disquieting, ominous notes creep into the violin part. In the more intimate scenes a dreamy atmosphere prevails as, for example, in the ecstatic rapture of the protagonists in the duet included here or in the *finale* where a visionary delirium characterizes Rudolph's monologue. This monologue changes into an unreal calm when Maria arrives and the lovers decide to take the final step together. Love, death, and denied freedom are themes prevalent throughout the entire score. Early musical themes reappear in the *finale* as mementos of the leading characters' tragic fates. A nostalgic reference to the past, even more evident in the second act at the vivacious and captivating grand ball in the German Embassy, is intensified after Maria's entrance with a highly dramatic musical citation from Schubert's *Death and the Maiden*.

The duet included here (Act I, Scene 2) takes place on the Prater boulevard during a fall night. Rudolph walks with his cousin John who is trying to convince him to become the leader of a demonstration against the emperor, his father. The Hapsburg heir is instead absorbed in distant thoughts, in imaginary and romantic fantasies. They seem to materialize when the moonlight shines on

Maria Vetzera, a young noblewoman in love with the melancholic prince whom she wishes to meet. John moves away and Rudolph approaches the woman. When she reveals her name, the rarefied atmosphere becomes sweeter and the orchestral sonorities richer and more captivating (Reh. #18, m. 2). The protagonists give voice to their emotions at first together followed by Maria's aria, *Sento in me una fragranza di fiori* (I feel in me the perfume of the flowers) (Reh. #24, m. 3). After fading away to a *pianissimo*, Rudolph's aria, *Oh Carezza di mani fresche sulla fronte* (Oh caress of cool hands on my forehead) (Reh. #28) echoes her music. Shortly afterward, the theme previously heard in the instrumental prelude, reappears in the bass on the words "afraid of the world" (Reh. #30, m. 1). This symbolizes the night and gives the episode a suspended air of mystery. The main musical idea of the opera is based on Rudolph's last words. It symbolizes the lovers' destiny of love and death so much that Maria shudders on these strange *pianissimo* chords (Reh. #32) as if the night, until then the protector of the lovers, becomes for a moment hostile and threatening. The promise of happiness with which Maria takes her leave from Rudolph is proven wrong by the return of the "fatal love" theme (Reh. #34) played this time by the woodwinds.

Acknowledgments

A heartfelt thanks to Bruno and Paolo Giuranna for granting authorization to publish a passage from *Mayerling*, and to Riccardo Giuranna for providing bibliographical material.

Notes

1. Fedele D'Amico, "La musica sotto il fascismo," in *Un ragazzino all Augusteo* (Torino: Einaudi, 1991), 226-33.

2. Fiamma Nicolodi, *Musica e Musicisti nel ventennio fascista* (Fiesole: Discanto, 1984), 22-24.

3. Guido Salvetti, "L'opera nel primo novecento," in *Musica in scena,* ed. Alberto Basso, (Torino: UTET, 1996), 451 ff.

4. Antonio Cirignano, "Il teatro nel secondo dopo guerra," in *Musica in scena*, ed. Alberto Basso, (Torino: UTET, 1996).

List of Works

Theater

La trappola d'oro (1929). Ballet. Unpublished.

Jamanto (1941). Lyric opera in three acts. Libretto by Giuranna. Unpublished.

Mayerling (1960). Lyric opera in three acts. Libretto by V. Viviani. Unpublished.

Hosanna (1978). Lyric opera in one act. Libretto by C. Pinelli. Unpublished.

Vocal Music

La Guerriera. Voice and orchestra. Milan: Ricordi, 1934.

Canto arabo. Voice and orchestra. Milan: Ricordi, 1934.

Tre cori per voci maschili (1940). Male voices. Unpublished.

Tre coretti per voci femminili e cinque strumenti (1940). Female voices and five instruments. Unpublished.

Quattro canzoni per voci infantili (1940). Childrens voices. Unpublished.

Tre canti alla Vergine (1949). Soprano, female chorus, and small orchestra. Unpublished.

Messa sinite parvulos (1990). Unpublished.

Instrumental Music

Nocturnal (1923). Orchestra.

Apina rapita dai nani della montagna. Orchestra. Milan: Ricordi, 1924.

Adagio e Allegro da Concerto. Nine instruments Milan: Ricordi, 1935.

Sonatina per pianoforte. Milan: Ricordi, 1935.

Toccata per pianoforte. Milan: Ricordi, 1937.

X Legio (*Poema eroico*). Orchestra. Milan: Ricordi, 1936.

Toccata. Orchestra. Milan: Ricordi, 1938.

Patria. Symphonic poem. Milan: Ricordi, 1939.

Sonatina. Harp. Milan: Ricordi, 1941.

Episodi. Woodwinds, brass, timpani, and piano. Milan: Ricordi, 1942.

Concerto for Orchestra (1942). Unpublished.

Concerto for Orchestra, no. 2 (1966). Unpublished.

Musica per Olivia (1970). Small orchestra. Unpublished.

Solo per viola (1982). Unpublished.

Bibliography

Adkins Chiti, Patricia. *Almanacco delle virtuose, priemedonne, compositrici e musiciste d'Italia*. Novara: De Agostini, 1991.

______. *Donne in musica*. Roma: Armando, 1996.

Artan, Sandra, and Anna R. Calabro. *Sorelle d'Italia*. Milano: Rizzoli, 1989.

Basso, Alberto, ed. "Barbara Giuranna." In *Dizionario Enciclopedico della Musica e dei Musicisti*. Torino: UTET, 1986.

Bruni, Daniela Alessandra. *Una vita per la musica. Incontro con Barbara Giuranna,* in *Il Mondo della musica*. IV. Roma 1992.

______. *Barbara Giuranna, una vita, una musica, an secolo,* program for *Mayerling*. Roma, Teatro dell'Opera, March 1993.

Cirignano, Antonio. "Il teatro nel secondo dopo guerra." In *Musica in scena*, ed. Alberto Basso, II. Torino, UTET, 1996.

Damiani, Paola, "Barbara Giuranna." In *The New Grove Dictionary of Women Composers*, ed. Julie Anne Sadie and Rhian Samuel. London: Macmillan Press, 1994.

D'Amico, Fedele. "La musica sotto il fascismo." In *Un ragazzino all Augusteo*. Torino: Einaudi, 1991.

Nicolodi, Fiamma. *Musica e musicisti nel ventennio fascista*. Fiesole: Discanto, 1984.

Pironti, Alberto. "Barbara Giuranna." In *The New Grove of Music and Musicians,* ed. Stanley Sadie. London: Macmillan Press, 1980.

Salvetti, Guido. "L'opera nel primo novecento." In *Musica in scena* ed. Alberto Basso, Torino UTET, 1996.

Discography

X Legio, Orchestra Sinfonica dell' EIAR, dir. Femdando Previtali, Microsolco: CETRA CB-20305.

Stornello, soprano Maria Caniglia, Compact disc: CLUB 99 CL-508.

Majerling
Act I , Scene II

Maria:	Altezza Signore!	Maria:	Your Highness!
Rodolfo:	Oh! Siete giunta!	Rodolfo:	You have arrived!
Maria:	M'attendavate? Vostra cugina dunque vi aveva parlato di me? Sono Maria Vetzera. E vi chiedo perdono, se sono stata audace. Ma non potevo fre nare in me quest'ansia di conoscervi. Di parlare con voi ed ora non riesco.	Maria:	Were you waiting for me? Has your cousin spoken to you about me? I am Maria Vetzera. And I ask your forgiveness, I am daring. But I could not control my anxiety in getting to know you . . . of speaking with you and now not being able to.
Rodolfo:	Perché tacete? Perché? Nel silenzio le vostre parole hanno una strana risonanza. È un incanto dolce il suono della vostra voce lascia un eco profonda.	Rodolfo:	Why are you silent? Why? In the silence your words have a strange resonance. The sound of your voice is sweet enchantment, leaving a deep echo.
Maria:	Voglio dirvi che v'ho recato in dono la mia piccola vita. Dono modesto ma purissimo.	Maria:	I want to tell you that I have brought you, as a gift, my small life. I give it modestly but purely.
Rodolfo:	O soavitâ perseguita da sempre è mai raggiunta, il vostro dono e nell' anima mia disceso dai cieli dell'ideale.	Rodolfo:	Either sweetly pursuing for a time or again rejoined, your gift is in my soul as if fallen from the heavens.
Maria:	Oh! Sento in me una fragranza di fiori che si schiudono come fontane candide. E il profumo mi porta con sè verso frescure ignote nelle zone supreme della felicità. S'irradiano sentieri di luce su cui corro leggera come ala. Sento in me una fragranza di fiori che si schiudono come fontane candide.	Maria:	Oh! I sense a fragrance of flowers that opens like a white fountain. And the perfume carries me towards an unknown assurance of happiness. It radiates paths of light that race lightly as wings. I sense a fragrance of flowers that opens like a white fountain.
Rodolfo:	Oh, carezza di mani fresche sulla fronte scomposta di pensieri. Cullato amor dell'onda di pura infanzia inseguirò sorrisi fra penombre di trine. E sull'alba, al primo sole m'aprirò come fiore di campo senza offesa di vento. Impaurito di mondo respirerò l'azzurro nell'infinito cielo dell'anima tua ah ! Accordi di tenerezza.	Rodolfo:	Oh, caressing one's forehead with cool hands softens unseemly thoughts. Pure waves of cradled love chase smiles about the faint light of dusk. And at the first light of dawn, the sun blossoms as a flower in the calm field. Afraid of the world, I breathe the blue in the infinite sky of your soul, ah! You grant tenderness.
Maria:	Abbrivi dire mi sento come le foglie di queste piante antiche al fruscio del vento autunnale.	Maria:	In a word, I feel like the blades of ancient plants in the rustle of the autumn wind.
Rodolfo:	Sorridi.	Rodolfo:	Smile.
Maria:	E domani?	Maria:	And tomorrow?
Rodolfo:	Così, sempre.	Rodolfo:	As always.
Rodolfo e Maria:	Sempre!	Rodolfo and Maria:	Always.

Translation by Randi Marrazzo

Majerling
Act I, Scene 2

Vittorio Viviani

Barbara Giuranna
Paola Damiani, editor

movendo con fantasia
Picc.
Fl. 1,2
1.
p espr.
Hp.
movendo con fantasia
Vn.
1
2
div.
Va.
pp
Cb.
p
Fl. 1,2
Ob. 1,2
1.
p espr.
p
pp
Hp.
p
Ella come folgorata dall 'emozione di cosi
improvvisa realà gli si prostra davanti
Maria
via sordina
Vn.
1
2
Va.
Vc.
pp
Cb.

17
p espr.
pp
poco ritenuto
Fl. 1,2
B♭ Cl. 1,2
Hp.
Maria
p (timidamente)
Al - tez - za... Si - gno - re!
Rod.
(aiutandola a sollevarsi)
Oh! Sie-te
1º Solo
Vn.
Moderato (𝅗𝅥 = 72)
Ob. 1,2
espr.
M'at-ten-da-va - te?
(un po' liberamente)
Vo - stra cu -
giun - ta!
Va.

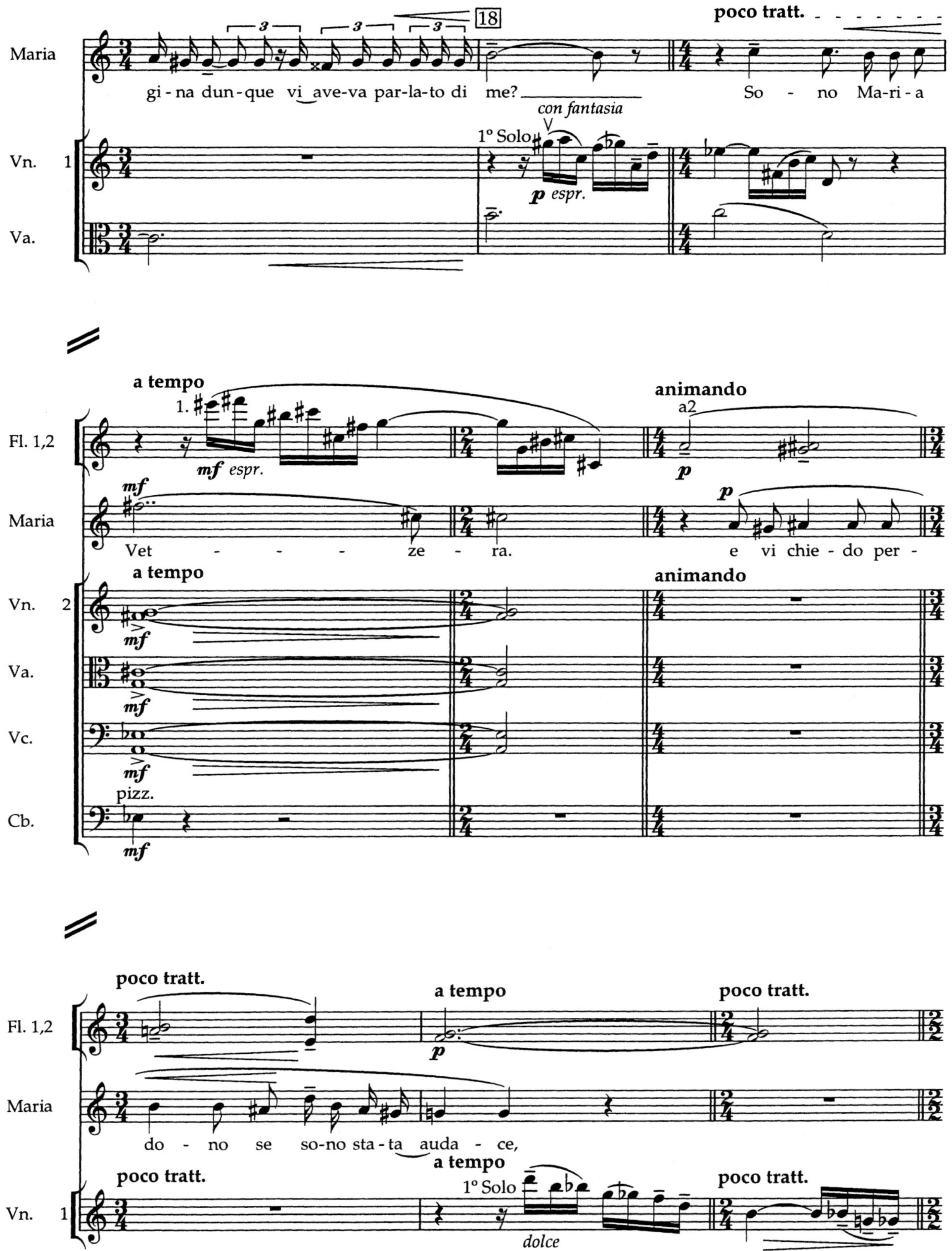

18
poco tratt.
Maria
gi - na dun - que vi ave - va par - la - to di me?
So - no Ma - ri - a
con fantasia
1º Solo
p espr.
Vn. 1
Va.
a tempo
animando
1.
a2
Fl. 1,2
mf espr.
Vet - - - ze - ra.
e vi chie - do per -
Vn. 2
Vc.
pizz.
Cb.
mf
p
poco tratt.
a tempo
do - no se so - no sta - ta auda - ce,
dolce

19 a tempo (♩ = 80-84) rubato con fantasia)
poco rall.
Fl. 1,2
Ob. 1,2
B♭ Cl. 1,2
Bn. 1,2
p espr.
p dolce
p dolce, amoroso
Maria
Ma non po-te - vo fre na-re in me que - st'an-sia di co-no - scer-vi,
Vn. 1
pochiss. rall.
Di par-la - re con voi ed or-a non ri-es - co,
Vn. 2
Va.
Vc.
Cb.

20 a tempo
(1.)
B♭ Cl. 1,2
pp
Hp.
p
Rod.
p
Per - chè ta - ce - te?
Per - chè?
20 a tempo
tutti
Vn.
1
2
pp espr.
div.
pp
Va.
pp
pizz.
Vc.
pp
1.
Fl. 1,2
p
B♭ Cl. 1,2
Hp.
p
la!
Rod.
Nel si - len - zio le vo - stre pa - ro - le
Vn.
1
2
Va.
Vc.

*Passaggio dubbio: invece della pausa si suggeriscono due accordi, mi-natural, sol-natural, si-natural, do# fa#

21 allarg. assai
Ob. 1,2
1º
B♭ Cl. 1,2
Hn. 1,2
Hp.
Maria
Vog -lio dir - vi...
Rod.
vos - tra vo - ce l'a-scia un'e co pro - fon - da.
21 allarg. assai
Vn.
unis.
Va.
Vc.
arco, div.
Cb.

riprendendo (♩ = c. 88)
pochiss. tratt.
Ob. 1,2
1.
p dolce espr.
Hn. 1,2
1.
pp
Maria
che v'ho re-ca - to in do - no la mia pic - co-la vi - ta,
riprendendo (♩ = c. 88)
pochiss. tratt.
div.
Vn. 2
Va.
p
pizz.
Vc.
pp

a tempo (più disteso)
22
1°
Fl. 1,2
mp
1°
Ob. 1,2
mp
B♭ Cl. 1,2
mp
Hp.
mf
Maria
mf
Do - - - no mo - de - - - - - sto
22
a tempo (più disteso)
Cb.

allarg. assai
Hn. 1,2
1°
Hp.
Maria
ma pu - ris - - si - mo.
allarg. assai
Vn.
div.
Va.
div. a3
Vc.
div. a3 [arco]
Cb.
div. arco
Lento
Fl. 1,2
Hn. 1,2
1.
p dolcissimo
Rod.
pp dolce
O soa vi - tā per-se - gui - ta da sem - pre e mai rag-giun - ta
Lento
[unis.]
Vn.
Va.
[unis.]

animando
allarg. sub.
23
Fl. 1,2
Ob. 1,2
B♭ Cl. 1,2
Hn.
1,2
3,4
Hp.
Rod.
Va.
Vc.
Cb.
mf
cresc.
f
a2
il vos - tro do - no é nel - la - ni - ma mi - a di - sce

a tempo
Fl. 1,2
Ob. 1,2
B♭ Cl. 1,2
1°
mp dolce
Hn.
1,2
3,4
Hp.
Rod.
p
so dai cie - li del - l'i - de - a - le
a tempo
Vn.
1
2
Va.
Vc.
Cb.
p

allarg.
B♭ Cl. 1,2
Hp.
Maria
pp
Oh!
Oh!
Oh!
allarg.
Vn.
1
2
Va.
Vc.
Cb.
24
rit.
Hp.
p espr.
1 Solo
6
6
Vn.
1
2
Va.
Vc.
Cb.

Dolcemente animato (♩ = 88)
1. Solo
Hn. 1,2
p
Hp.
p
Maria
p dolcissimo
Sen - to in me un - a fra-gran - za di
Dolcemente animato (♩ = 88)
Vn. 2
pp
div.
1.
Fl. 1,2
p leggiero
Ob. 1,2
1º
p espr.
Hn.
1,2
3,4
pp
3. pp
Hp.
Maria
fio - ri che si schiu - do-no co - me fon - ta - ne
Vn. 2

Fl. 1,2
1.
Ob. 1,2
Hn.
1,2
3,4
Hp.
Maria
can - di - de,
Vn.
1
2
Va.
Vc.
Cb.

25
Hp.
Maria
E il pro - fu - mo mi por - ta con sè
Vn. 1 2
div.
Va.
p
Fl. 1,2
1.
p dolce
Ob. 1,2
1.
mf espr.
Hp.
Maria
ver - so fre - scu - re i - gno - te nel - le zo - ne su - pre - me
Vn. 1 2
Va.
Vc.
Cb.

Fl. 1,2
1.
mf
Ob. 1,2
Hn. 1,2
1.
mp (fuori)
Hp.
mf
Maria
del-la fe-li - ci - tà
Vn.
1
2
sfp
Va.
sfp
Vc.
sfp
Cb.
sfp

26
Fl. 1,2
Ob. 1,2
(1.)
mf fuori
B♭ Cl. 1,2
1.
p dolce
Hn.
1,2
2.
3,4
3.
Maria
mf
S'ir - ra - dia-no sen - ti - eri di lu - -
26
Vn.
1
2
pp
Va.
pp

(1.)
Fl. 1,2
mf
pp
Ob. 1,2
B♭ Cl. 1,2
(2.)
1,2
Hn.
3,4
4.
Hp.
Maria
ce su cu - i cor - ro leg - ge - ra co - me a -
1
Vn.
2
Va.
Vc.
Cb.

Fl. 1,2
B♭ Cl. 1,2
Piatto
Hp.
Maria
Vn. Solo
Vn.
Va.
Vc.
Cb.
27
a2
pp
p
- - - - - la
Sen - to in me u-na fra -
div.
unis.
arco

ritenendo
1.
Fl. 1,2
p
1.
Ob. 1,2
mf espr.
f
B♭ Cl. 1,2
f
2.
1,2
Hn.
pp
mf
4.
3,4
pp
mf
Tbn.
1, 2, 3
pp
mf
cresc. poco alla volta
e sub. dim.
Piatto
f
ossia:
-ta ne can - di - de
Maria
gran-za di fio - ri che si schiu-do - no co - me_ fon - ta - - ne
cresc. poco alla volta
e sub. dim.
ritenendo
unis.
1
Vn.
2
Va.
Vc.
Cb.

assai
a tempo (più calmo) (♩ = 69-72)
28
Fl. 1,2
pp
Hn.
1,2
3,4
2.
4.
p
Cel.
Hp.
ppp
Maria
ah!
can - - di - de
Rod.
(con rapimento)
Oh, ca-rez-za di ma-ni
assai
a tempo (più calmo) (♩ = 69-72)
via sordina
28 div.
Vn.
1
2
Va.
Vc.
Cb.
pizz.

1.
Bn. 1,2
p
1,2
Hn.
3,4
Hp.
Rod.
fres - che sul - la fron - te scom-pos-ta-di pen - sie - ri. Cul - la - to a - mor -
1
Vn.
2
div.
Va.
p
Vc.
p

Bn. 1,2
Hn. 1,2
3,4
Hp.
Rod.
del - l'onda di pu-ra in-fan - zia in - se - gui - rò sor -
Vn. 2
Va.
Vc.
Hp.
Rod.
ri - si fra pen - om - bre di tri - ne.
Vn. 1
2
Va.
Vc.

29
Animando leggermente
Fl. 1,2
B♭ Cl. 1,2
Bn. 1,2
p espr.
Cel.
Rod.
poco più f
E sul - l'al - ba, al pri - mo so - le m'a - pri -
Hn.
1,2
3,4
rò co - me fio - re di cam - po sen - za offe - sa di
Vn. 2
Va.
Vc.

30 Più animato
Fl. 1,2
p
B♭ Cl. 1,2
p
Bn. 1,2
a2
p
1,2
Hn.
3,4
Rod.
mf
ven - - to
Im - pa-u-ri - to di
30 Più animato
1
Vn.
p
2
p
Va.
p
Vc.

poco tratt.
(segue)
Fl. 1,2
cresc.
mf
p sub.
(segue)
B♭ Cl. 1,2
cresc.
mf
p sub.
Bn. 1,2
cresc.
Rod.
f
mp
mon-do res-pir-er-ò l'az - zur - ro nel-l'in-fi-ni-to ciel-o del-
poco tratt.
1
Vn.
2
p
p
Va.
p
Vc.
p
Cb.

rall.
Fl. 1,2
Ob. 1,2
mp
cresc.
B♭ Cl. 1,2
cresc.
(a2)
Bn. 1,2
mp
Hn.
1,2
3,4
Rod.
cresc.
l'a - ni - ma tu - a
ah!
rall.
Vn.
1
2
cresc.
Va.
cresc.
Vc.
cresc.
Cb.
mf
f

31 Andante (♩ = c. 54)
Hn.
1,2
3,4
sfp
Rod.
p
Ac - cor - di di te - ne -
Va.
mf espr.
sfp
Fl. 1,2
1°
p
B♭ Cl. 1,2
p
pp
Bn. 1,2
1.
pp
Hn. 3,4
[3.] p
4.
pp
Rod.
rez - za
Vn.
1
2
p
pizz.
arco
p dim.
Va.
pizz.
p
Vc.
pizz.
p
Cb.
pizz.
p

32 Calmo (♩ = c. 80)
B♭ Cl. 1,2
Bn. 1,2
Hn. 3,4
Piatto
Hp.
Pno.
p l.v.
Maria
pp ma intenso
Ab-bri-vi di - re mi sen - to co-me le
Calmo (♩ = c. 80)
32
Vn.
Va.
arco
Vc.
arco
espr.
Cb.

cedendo
Piatto
Hp.
8vb
8va
Pno.
Maria
fog - lie di que-ste pian-te an-ti - che
al - fru - scio del ven - to a-u-tun-
cedendo
8va
Vn.
1
2
Va.
Vc.
Cb.

Fl. 1,2
Ob. 1,2
Bn. 1,2
Piatto
Hp.
Maria
Rod.
Vn.
Va.
Vc.
Cb.
ritenendo
33
quasi a tempo
espr.
mp espr.
na - le
Sor - ri - di

ritenendo
a tempo
tratt. assai
Fl. 1,2
pp
Ob. 1,2
Bn. 1,2
Maria
E do-ma - ni?
Sem - pre!
Rod.
mp
co-sì, sem - pre. Sem - pre!
Vn.
1
2
div.
sfp
Va.
Vc.

Andante appassionato (♩ = c. 66)
34
ritenendo - - - - - - - - assai - - - - - - - -
Fl. 1,2
a2
ff
fp
Ob. 1,2
Bb Cl. 1,2
Hn.
1,2
3,4
1.
2.
3.
4.
f
(E con lo sguardo teso a Rodolfo si allontana indietreggiando verso il fondo)
Maria
Vn.
1
2
Va.
Vc.
Cb.
sfp

Più lento
Fl. 1,2
pp
Ob. 1,2
pp
a2
Tpt. 1,2
pp
Timp.
pp
strisciata
Piatto
pp
Hp.
p
Più lento
1
Vn.
2
pp
pp
div.
Va.
pp
div.
Cb.
p

Biographies of Editors

Sylvia Glickman, New York born musician, holds bachelor's and master's degrees in Performance from The Juilliard School and an L.R.A.M. in Performance from the Royal Academy of Music in London. A Fulbright Scholar, she received the Hecht Prize in Composition from the Royal Academy and the Loeb Prize from Juilliard. She was among the first group awarded a Solo Recitalist Grant from the National Endowment for the Arts and has performed to critical acclaim throughout the United States, and in Europe, Israel and Africa. She was honored by Women's Way of Philadelphia in 1986 and received the New York Women Composers annual award in 1995 for "distinguished service in support of concert music composed by women." Glickman's anthology *Amy Beach: Virtuoso Piano Music* was published 1982 by Da Capo Press and her *Anthology of American Piano Music from 1865–1909* is Volume IV in *Three Centuries of American Music* (G. K. Hall, 1990). With Martha Furman Schleifer she co-edited *From Convent to Concert Hall: A Guide to Women Composers* (Greenwood Press, 2003). Her own compositions, for large and small instrumental and vocal groups, have had many performances in the United States and abroad and a CD of her music entitled "The Walls Are Quiet Now: A Holocaust Trilogy," was released in 2001. She is a reviewer for *Choice: Books for College Libraries* and served on the Music Panel of the Pennsylvania Council on the Arts from 1989–91. Glickman is founding President of the Hildegard Publishing Company, a press devoted to furthering the music of women composers, past and present. She is the President of the Hildegard Institute, devoted to research on music by women, and Artistic Director of the Hildegard Chamber Players, a group devoted to playing this repertoire. She has served as a board member and Coordinating Editor for the *Journal* of the International Alliance for Women in Music, and was elected to the Board of Directors of the Musical Fund Society of Philadelphia in 1998.

Martha Furman Schleifer, a graduate of Temple University, received a doctorate in musicology from Bryn Mawr College. She is a member of the Music History faculty at Temple University and is Senior Editor of Hildegard Publishing Company. Schleifer is the author of *American Opera and Music for the Stage - Eighteenth and Nineteenth Centuries,* and *American Opera and Music for the Stage - Early Twentieth Century*, volumes 5 and 6 of *Three Centuries of American Music*, and co-author of the *Cumulative Index for Three Centuries of American Music* included in Volume 12. Author of numerous articles and papers on music and musicians in Philadelphia and introductions for Hildegard Publishing Company publications, she has also made contributions to *The New Grove Dictionary of Women Composers*, London: The Macmillan Press Limited, 1995; the *New Grove Dictionary of American Music*, London: Macmillan Press Limited, 1986; and to *The New Grove Dictionary of Music and Musicians* (London, 2001). She co-edited *From Convent to Concert Hall: A Guide to Women Composers* (Greenwood Press, 2003) with Sylvia Glickman, is co-editor of *Latin American Classical Composers: A Biographical Dictionary* (Scarecrow Press, 1996; second edition, 2002) and co-edited *Three Centuries of American Music* (Boston: G.K. Hall & Co, 1986–1992), a twelve-volume anthology of music by American composers. Schleifer is a Series Editor for *Composers of North America,* a series in continuous publication by Scarecrow Press in Lanham, MD, and was the author of *William Wallace Gilchrist (1846–1916),* the first book in the series. She was the review editor for the *Journal* of the International Alliance for Women in Music, Fall 1995–Spring 1998.

Biographies of Contributors

Jamée Ard is currently the director of National Outreach and Alumni Affairs at The Juilliard School and has worked in arts management at IMG Artists and Young Concert Artists. In addition, she has been both educator (at Smith College) and performer, appearing in opera and concerts nationally and internationally. Ard holds degrees from St. Olaf College (B.M.), the University of Southern California (M.M.), and The Juilliard School (D.M.A.). She currently resides in New York City.

Tamara Beldom holds a bachelor of music degree from Trinity College, London. A clarinetist, she also plays the piano, teaches and plays chamber music, and performs in a professional gypsy orchestra.

Adrienne Fried Block is a musicologist (Ph.D. City University of New York, 1979) who specializes in the history of American music with an emphasis on women. Her biography, *Amy Beach, Passionate Victorian*, won the Deems-Taylor ASCAP Award and the Society for American Music's Lowens Award. *Women in American Music: A Bibliography of Music and Literature*, co-edited and compiled by Block, remains a standard reference. Currently she is co-director (with John Graziano) of Music in Gotham, a project chronicling musical life in New York City from 1862 to 1875. Supported by a Fellowship from the National Endowment for the Humanities, 2001–02, it now benefits from a three-year collaborative grant from NEH plus matching money from the Baisley Elebash Powell Endowment.

Rae Linda Brown is associate professor of Music at the University of California, Irvine. She holds an M.A. in African American Studies and a Ph.D. in musicology from Yale University. She has completed a biography of composer Florence B. Price, *The Heart of a Woman: The Life and Music of Florence B. Price*, (forthcoming University of Illinois Press) and has edited many Price scores for performance by ensembles including the American Symphony Orchestra and the Women's Philharmonic (San Francisco). Brown's editions have been recorded on the Cambria and Koch labels. Her publications of Price's music include the *Sonata in E Minor for Piano* (G. Schirmer, 1997), the *Symphony in E Minor* and the *Symphony No. 3 in C Minor* (A-R Editions). Her articles have appeared in *American Music*, *Black Music Research Journal*, *Black Music in the Harlem Renaissance: A Collection of Essays* (1990), and the *New Grove Dictionary of Music*. Brown was the music editor of the five-volume *Encyclopedia of American History and Culture* (Macmillan, 1996).

Liane Curtis, musicologist, music critic and cultural activist, is a scholar at the Women's Studies Research Center of Brandeis University. Recent publications include "The Sexual Politics of Teaching Mozart's *Don Giovanni*" in the *National Women's Studies Association Journal* (2000), and "Western Classical Music" in *The Routledge Encyclopedia of Women's Studies* (2001). As part of her advocacy for women composers, Curtis forged an initiative to add Amy Beach's name to the 87 names of male composers that adorn the Hatch Shell in Boston. Through the support of the Boston Women's Heritage Trail, Beach's name was added to the Shell in July 2000. Dr. Curtis is writing a biography of Rebecca Clarke. A conference on Clarke that she organized at Brandeis University, Sept. 1999 included the première of music for string quartet and led to the founding of The Rebecca Clarke Society, Inc. (www.rebeccaclarke.org). The RCS organized the premières of Clarke's two early violin sonatas (ca. 1909) in 2000 and of Clarke's monumental song, *Binnorie: A Ballad*, in 2001.

Paola Damiani born in Rome, studied piano and composition privately. She graduated from the University La Sapienza in Rome with a dissertation on: "Il canto dell'Exultet in the liturgy of Benevento." She collaborated with Channel 3 RAI Italian Radiotelevision in the production of musical programs including a series dedicated to Italian women composers and edited the entries on Italian musicians in the *New Grove Dictionary of Women Composers* and in the *Dictionnaire de L'Art Vocal Bordas*. She edits chamber music and has written for the journal *Reset*.

James Deaville is associate professor and former director of the School of the Arts at McMaster University, Hamilton, Ontario. He has published widely on 19th- and 20th-century topics in journals incluing the *Journal of Musicological Research*, *Notes*, *Journal of the American Liszt Society*, *Hamburger Jahrbuch fuer Musikwissenschaft*, *Canadian University Music Review*, and in books published by Oxford University Press, Cambridge University Press, Indiana University Press, and Garland Press. His research interests include Franz Liszt, the New German School, the women around Liszt, the Allgemeiner Deutscher Musikverein, television news music, and the music of African-Americans in continental Europe around 1900.

Roger O. Doyle has been a professor of music at the University of Portland (OR) since 1973. From 1989 to 1998, he served as chair of the department of Performing and Fine Arts during which time the University's music program won national accreditation. Appearances as guest conductor have taken place in Rome, Vienna, Amsterdam, and London and he is the founder and music/artistic director of Mock's Crest Productions, a professional music theater company. He has served the American Choral Directors Association as state president and as a member of the national board of directors. He has written articles on Handel, Mozart, and Nadia Boulanger, and is a regular pre-concert commentator and lecturer for The Oregon Symphony Orchestra. During a 1998 sabbatical leave in Ireland, Doyle was a guest lecturer at Trinity College, Dublin on the subject "American Choral Styles and Traditions."

Susan M. Filler was born in Indiana and educated at the University of Illinois-Chicago (B.A. 1969) and Northwestern University (M. M. 1970, Ph.D. 1977). Her research has encompassed the works of Gustav and Alma Mahler and, recently, Jewish music. She has lectured at meetings in the United States, Canada, France, Italy, the Netherlands and China. She has published in periodicals including *College Music Symposium*, *Journal of Musicological Research*, *Shofar*, *Music & Letters* and *MLA Notes*, Her book *Gustav and Alma Mahler: A Guide to Research* was published by Garland in 1989 and is in the process of revision and updating for a new edition (forthcoming: Routledge, 2004). She was co-editor and contributor to *Essays in Honor of John F. Ohl: A Compendium of American Musicology* (Northwestern University Press, 2001). Filler's current research includes work on a source book of musicological literature from the Nazi period (Indiana University Press), a performing version of Gustav Mahler's unfinished *Scherzo in C minor* and *Presto in F major*, and an essay for *Perspectives* on Gustav Mahler (Ashgate Press). She has edited *Two Lieder of Alma Mahler* (Hildegard Publishing, 2000) and written liner notes for the CD *Alma Mahler: The Songs* (recorded by Charlotte Margiono with the Brabant Orchestra conducted by Julian Reynolds, 1999).

Sophie Fuller is a lecturer in music at the University of Reading and author of *The Pandora Guide to Women Composers - Britain and the United States* (Pandora, 1994). She studied Russian at SSEES (London University) and then worked as a flute teacher and busker before embarking on various music degrees at King's College (London University). She spent several years working for the national organization Women in Music, developing a touring audio-visual exhibition and establishing the WiM Archive and Information Service. With Nicola LeFanu, she organized Britain's first Music and Gender conference, held at King's College in 1991. Fuller researches many different aspects of music, gender and sexuality. She focuses in particular on the role that gender played in the musical life of late 19th- and early 20th-century Britain as well as the lives and work of Victorian and Edwardian women composers. Publications include *Queer Episodes in Music and Modern Identity*, a collection of essays co-edited with Chip Whitesell, published by Illinois University Press in 2002 and the forthcoming *The Idea of Music in Victorian Literature*, a collection of essays co-edited with Nicky Losseff, to be published by Ashgate in 2003.

John R. Gardner was elected the first Honorary Life Member of the Sir Arthur Sullivan Society (founded in 1977). He worked in Fleet Street for over twenty years while pursuing his interests in music.

John Graziano, Ph. D., Yale University, received several NEH and NEA Fellowships. Graziano researches and writes principally on American music and music in America; he has been a Rockefeller Scholar-in-Residence at the Schomburg Center for Black Culture, New York Public Library. His books include an English version (with introduction) of Rossini's *La cenerentola*, and an anthology of eighteenth-, nineteenth-, and early twentieth-century American chamber music. He has co-edited *Vistas of American Music: Essays and Compositions in Honor of William K. Kearns*, and *Music for Strings* by the little-known American composer Charles Hommann (1803–1872). With Adrienne Fried Block he is co-director of Music in Gotham, a constituent program of the Barry S. Brook Center for Research and Documentation at the Graduate Center of City University, whose current project is investigating professional and amateur music making in New York City from 1863 to 1875.

Peggy A. Holloway teaches voice at Wayne State College in Wayne, Nebraska. She earned a bachelor's degree from Nebraska Wesleyan University, the bachelor's and master's degrees from the University of Nebraska at Omaha, and a doctorate from the University of Nebraska-Lincoln. She developed a seminar on women in music at the University of Nebraska-Lincoln. Holloway performs in musical theatre, opera, oratorio, and solo recitals. A strong proponent of new music, she has presented the World Premiere of several song cycles by Nebraska composers. She regularly presents lecture/recitals at regional, national and international conferences, specializing in the art songs of Marion Bauer and other women composers.

Sondra Wieland Howe is an independent scholar and piano teacher in Wayzata, Minnesota. She received an A.B. from Wellesley College, an A.M.T. from Radcliffe College, and an M.A. and Ph.D. from the University of Minnesota. She has taught college courses on women composers and writes the materials for the Minnesota High School Music Listening Contest. Howe has published *Luther Whiting Mason: International Music Educator* (Harmonie Park Press, 1997) and numerous articles on the history of music education in the *Journal for Research in Music Education*, *The Bulletin of Historical Research in Music Education*, and the *Bulletin of the Council for Research in Music Education*.

Elaine Keillor is a professor at Carleton University, Ottawa, Canada, where she teaches Canadian music, ethnomusicology, performance practice, and Baroque and Classical music courses at the undergraduate and graduate levels. Keillor is Chair of the Canadian Musical Heritage Society (www.cmhs.carleton.ca) which has published twenty-five volumes of Canadian music written before 1950. Among her publications are a monograph on John

Weinzweig (1994), and essays in the *Encyclopedia of Music In Canada* (1992), *Profiles of Canada* (1998), *New Grove Dictionary of Music and Musicians* (2001), and the *Garland Encyclopedia of World Music: North America* (2001). As a pianist and chamber musician, she has made nine CDs that have received wide air-play throughout North America and Europe.

Harald Krebs is professor of music theory in the School of Music at the University of Victoria, Canada. He has published numerous articles on the tonal and rhythmic structure of nineteenth- and early twentieth-century music, and has lectured and performed widely in North America and Europe. His book *Fantasy Pieces: Metrical Dissonance in the Music of Robert Schumann* was published in 1999 (Oxford University Press). His current research on the life and songs of Josephine Lang is supported by the Social Sciences and Humanities Research Council of Canada and by the German Academic Exchange Program. He performs frequently as a vocal accompanist and in chamber ensembles.

Nicole Labelle is a professor of musicology at the University of Ottawa's Department of Music. Pianist and organist, she received her bachelor and master degrees from the University of Montreal, her Premier Prix in history of music from the Conservatoire de Musique of Montreal and her Ph.D. from the Sorbonne-Paris, France. Recipient of many grants, she is the author of books, monographs and articles. Her annotated edition of the *Lettres et Écrits d 'Albert Roussel* (1987) was awarded the Rene Dumesnil prize from Institut de France for the best book on music published in 1987. Other publications include *Catalog raisonné de l'oeuvre d' Albert Roussel* (1992); the *Répertoire des oeuvres des compositrices du Québec au XXe siècle* (1997) and *l 'Oratorio*. She is currently completing a monograph on Albert Roussel.

Lydia Ledeen, founder and director of the Drew Chamber Players is a graduate of The Juilliard School, has an M.A., Ph.D., and Ed.D. from Columbia University and worked with Nadia Boulanger at Fontainbleau. She is a recipient of a French government grant, a Prix d'Excellence for the performance of French music, and an NEH grant. She has performed as a soloist and with chamber groups both in the US, Europe, and China. Her editions of music by Maria Grandval, and Leopoldine Blahetka are published by Hildegard Publishing Company. Her chapter on Cecile Chaminade appears in *Women Composers Through the Ages*, vol. 6. Ledeen has recorded all the Mozart piano concerti which will be released in the near future. She is a professor of Music at Drew University.

Delight Malitsky was professor emerita at Indiana University of Pennsylvania where she taught violin and piano. Before coming to I.U.P., she taught in California and was assistant concertmaster of the San Francisco Little Symphony. While concertmaster of the Honolulu Symphony, she received a bachelor of arts degree at the University of Hawaii. Later she completed an M.M. degree with a double major in violin and piano from the Manhattan School of Music in New York. Malitsky appeared as soloist with many orchestras including the Honolulu Symphony, the Houston Symphony and the Stüttgart Philharmonic. She gave numerous recitals in the U.S. and Europe as a violinist or pianist throughout her teaching career. She edited Clara Kathleen Rogers's *Sonata Dramatico*, op. 25, for Hildegard Publishing Company.

Helen Metzelaar, born in Cambridge, Mass., received her Ph.D. in musicology from the Utrecht University (Netherlands). Her research chiefly focuses on lesser known historical contributions to Dutch music history. The essay "Spiritual Singing Brings in the Money: the Fisk Jubilee Singers Tour Holland" is forthcoming in Karen Ahlquist (ed.), *Chorus and Community* (Chicago: University of Illinois Press). Her most recent publication is a biography on the Dutch composer/pianist Henriëtte Bosmans (1895–1952). She has contributed essays to *Een Muziekgeschiedenis der Nederlanden* (Amsterdam University Press, 2001), and her Dutch translation of a travel diary written in French in 1790–1791 by Nina d'Aubigny was published in 2000. Her revised dissertation, *From Private to Public Spheres: Exploring Women's Role in Dutch Musical Life from c. 1700 to c. 1880 and Three Case Studies*, appeared in 1999 (Koninklijke Vereniging voor Nederlandse Muzekgeschiedenis). Metzelaar has also contributed articles to *The Essential Guide to Dutch Music* (Amsterdam University Press, 2000) and to the new editions of *The New Grove Dictionary of Music and Musicians* and *Die Musik in Geschichte und Gegenwart*. She is currently a staff member at the Dutch Women and Music Foundation and teaches at the Amsterdam Music School.

Ruth Ochs received a bachelor's degree in music from Harvard University and a master's degree in orchestral conducting from the University of Texas at Austin. In 1997–98 she pursued research on Fanny Mendelssohn Hensel in Berlin, Germany with a fellowship from the Germanistic Society of America and a Fulbright Traveling Grant.

Karin Pendle has published chapters and essays on French opera of the years 1760–1860 and on women in music, and has edited *Women and Music: A History*, now in its second edition. She is professor of musicology at the College-Conservatory of Music, University of Cincinnati.

Judith Radell is assistant professor of Music at Indiana University of Pennsylvania, where she teaches piano and piano pedagogy. She holds the doctor of musical arts degree in piano from the University of Illinois, and was the 1991 recipient of a Performance Fellowship from the Pennsylvania Council on the Arts. As soloist and chamber musician, Radell has performed music by women composers in such venues as the Frick Museum in Pittsburgh, the Philadelphia Free Library, and on college campuses throughout the United States. Recently, she recorded the piano music of Katherine Hoover for Parnassus Records. She has edited Fanny Mendelssohn Hensel's *Two Piano Sonatas* and *Six Piano Pieces from the 1820s* for Hildegard Publishing Company.

Nancy B. Reich wrote her doctoral dissertation (New York University) on Johann Friedrich Reichardt. The discovery of the songs of Louise, talented daughter of Reichardt, initially sparked her interest in music by women composers. Her subsequent discovery of the unpublished correspondence between Clara Schumann and a descendant of Reichardt led to the research on and writing of her award winning book, *Clara Schumann: the Artist and the Woman*, Cornell University Press, 1985, a work that has been translated into Japanese, German and Chinese. A revised edition of the book appeared in 2001. Dr. Reich has taught at a number of universities and colleges and has been a Visiting Professor at Bard College and Williams College. She has lectured on women in music in Australia, Austria, Germany, and at universities throughout the United States and Canada. She was the recipient of the Robert Schumann Prize of the City of Zwickau, awarded in 1996.

Nadine Sine is currently professor and chair of the music department at Lehigh University (PA). In papers and published articles, she has presented studies of Schoenberg's *Gurrelieder* and various cultural and musical treatments of the Salome figure at the turn of the century. In 1999, she directed an NEH Summer Seminar entitled, *The World of Yesterday: Viennese Perspectives on the Arts, Culture and Ideas, 1890–1940*, which centers on a comparison of Alma Mahler's autobiography with that of Stefan Zweig's *The World of Yesterday*.

Catherine Parsons Smith is professor of music emerita at the University of Nevada Reno. She is a co-author of a biography of Mary Carr Moore (University of Michigan Press, 1987) and the author of a volume on the African American composer William Grant Still (University of California Press, 2000.) She is currently at work on a book about music making in Progressive-Era Los Angeles. In addition she has written some landmark feminist essays (for example, in Cook and Tsou, *Cecelia Reclaimed*). She is the former principal flute of the Reno Philharmonic, with which she performed for more than three decades.

Suzanne Summerville, mezzo-soprano, completed her doctoral studies in historical musicology at Berlin's Freie Universität. She recently retired as professor of music and Women's Studies at the University of Alaska Fairbanks. Her research interests in 19th- and early 20th-century German and American poets and composers has led to the making of three CDs: *There Be None of Beauty's Daughters*, produced by MDR Radio Leipzig, featuring previously unrecorded vocal works by Fanny Hensel (Querstand, 1999), *Auf der Wanderung: The Poetry of Adelbert von Chamisso in Song* (*ArtsVenture*, 2002) and *From an Old Garden: Songs of Edward McDowell* (*ArtsVenture*) 2002.

Sean M. Wallace is currently the Director of Choral Activities and Director of Vocal Studies at the University of New Orleans, where he conducts the choral ensembles and teaches classes in conducting, music education, and women in music. He holds an undergraduate degree in music education from John Brown University, a master's degree in choral conducting from the Eastman School of Music, and a master's degree in musicology and a doctoral degree in choral conducting from Michigan State University. The choral music of Fanny Mendelssohn Hensel is the subject of both his master's and doctoral research.

David Zea, is Editor and Archivist for The F. Eugene Miller Foundation. He studied piano, theory and composition with Charles Shatto, coming in contact with the Koechlin/Urner legacy at an early age. Zea has concertized extensively, often performing his own works, as well as those of other twentieth-century composers including Catherine Urner.

Index